"No other guide has as much to offer . . . these books are a pleasure to read."   Gene Shalit on the *Today Show*

". . . Excellently organized for the casual traveler who is looking for a mix of recreation and cultural insight."
Washington Post

★ ★ ★ ★ ★ (5-star rating) "Crisply written and remarkably personable. Cleverly organized so you can pluck out the minutest fact in a moment. Satisfyingly thorough."
Réalités

"The information they offer is up-to-date, crisply presented but far from exhaustive, the judgments knowledgeable but not opinionated."   *New York Times*

"The individual volumes are compact, the prose succinct, and the coverage up-to-date and knowledgeable . . . The format is portable and the index admirably detailed."
John Barkham Syndicate

". . . An abundance of excellent directions, diversions, and facts, including perspectives and getting-ready-to-go advice — succinct, detailed, and well organized in an easy-to-follow style."   *Los Angeles Times*

"They contain an amount of information that is truly staggering, besides being surprisingly current."
Detroit News

"These guides address themselves to the needs of the modern traveler demanding precise, qualitative information . . . Upbeat, slick, and well put together."
Dallas Morning News

". . . Attractive to look at, refreshingly easy to read, and generously packed with information."   *Miami Herald*

"These guides are as good as any published, and much better than most."   *Louisville* (Kentucky) *Times*

Stephen Birnbaum Travel Guides

Canada
Caribbean, Bermuda, and the Bahamas
Disneyland
Europe
Europe for Business Travelers
Florida for Free
France
Great Britain
Hawaii
Ireland
Italy
Mexico
South America
United States
USA for Business Travelers
Walt Disney World

ADVISORY EDITORS

Claire Hardiman
Marcia Wallace

CONTRIBUTING EDITORS

Cathy Beason	Rob McGregor
Janet Bennett	Erica Meltzer
Barbara Currie	Anne Millman
Michael Finn	Mike Morgan
Lou Garcia	Robin Nelson
Alice Garrard	Tamara Newell
Martha Gilkes	Susan Pierres
Joel Glass	Ann Pleshette
Jack Gold	Maria Polvay
Ben Harte	Linda Post
David Jacobs	Virginia Puzo
Mark Kalish	Allen Rokach
Peter Kramer	Alexandra Roll
Jane Kronholtz	Jaryn Schneider
Richard Lee	David P. Schulz
Mary Dell Lucas	Steve Wasserstein
Karen Matusic	Karen Weiner
Alexandra Mayes	Leslie Westbrook

COVER Robert Anthony

MAPS Etta Jacobs

SYMBOLS Gloria McKeown

A Stephen Birnbaum Travel Guide

Birnbaum's
CARIBBEAN,
BERMUDA,
and the
BAHAMAS 1989

Stephen Birnbaum
EDITOR

Brenda Goldberg
EXECUTIVE EDITOR

Kristin Moehlmann
Barbara Benton
Senior Editors

Brian Hotchkiss
Diana Perez
Associate Editors

Stephen Coleman
Editorial Assistant

HOUGHTON MIFFLIN COMPANY BOSTON 1988

For Perry Wachtel, who helped more than he knows.

This book is published by special arrangement
with Eric Lasher and Maureen Lasher.

Copyright © 1988 by Houghton Mifflin Company

All rights reserved. For information about permission to reproduce selections
from this book, write to Permissions,
Houghton Mifflin Company, 2 Park Street,
Boston, Massachusetts 02108.

ISBN: 0–395–48163–5
ISSN: 0749–2561 (Stephen Birnbaum Travel Guides)
ISSN: 0883–248X (Caribbean, Bermuda,
and the Bahamas)

Printed in the United States of America

WP 10 9 8 7 6 5 4 3 2 1

Contents

PERSPECTIVES

A cultural and historical survey of the islands, their history, people, food, music, religions, folk life, and environment.

ISLAND-BY-ISLAND HOPPING

Thorough, qualitative guides to all the islands — including the Bahamas and Bermuda — and the most popular Caribbean coastal destinations. Each section offers a comprehensive report on the island or area's most compelling attractions and amenities, designed to be used on the spot. Directions and recommendations are immediately accessible because each report is presented in consistent form.

DIVERSIONS

A selective guide to more than a dozen active and/or cerebral vacation themes, including the best places to pursue them.

A Word from the Editor

I'm afraid I'm one of those people who occasionally goes clucking around the Caribbean, pointing at new hotels and resort developments, sorrowfully describing them with paragraphs that begin, "You should have seen how it used to be . . ." The truth of the matter is that although I do, in fact, treasure memories of beaches without high-rises on their periphery, and remember inland trails before they became four lanes of macadam, I've got to confess that the good old Caribbean days weren't all that wonderful for visitors.

My own personal remembrance of ancient history has to do with what it was like to be a young boy in Puerto Rico. I spent a fair amount of my early years in and around the islands of the Caribbean, and a careful reader of my published works may have noticed that I don't write many stories about those early days in San Juan. It's nothing personal, just that when I was about ten years old we lived in a small hotel on the site of what is now the Caribe Hilton, and to most outward appearances it was a pretty idyllic existence. The problem was that my mother was something of a fanatic on the subject of milk for young people — something about bones and teeth, as I recall — but cow's milk was not a commodity in great supply in Puerto Rico in those days. So my brother and sister and I were virtually force-fed goat's milk, and my mother's only concession to its rather strong taste was to permit us to dilute it with locally made chocolate syrup.

The resultant mixture was not in any way a pleasant potable, and from its taste stems my writer's block when it comes to San Juan. My problem is that I can't sit down at a typewriter to write anything about that island without tasting a thick coating of that chocolate-flavored goat's stuff on my tongue, and that taste is not exactly conducive to getting one's creative juices flowing. So much for the halcyon days of Caribbean travel.

I've tried to take a substantially less prejudicial view during the creation and revision of this Caribbean guide and to put such tawdry personal bias aside. The extensive development of the Caribbean area during the past several decades — and its increasing appeal to US travelers — has made it one of the most important travel magnets on this planet. Although often referred to as a single destination, the Caribbean encompasses countless cultures, and the marvelous blending of all these influences has spawned an environment that is both unique and compelling. It has been our aim to produce a guide that accurately reflects the diversity and allure of this vast canvas, complete with all bouquets and blemishes.

The broadening sophistication of island travelers and the (often wrenching) maturation of the islands themselves have made it essential that Caribbean guidebooks also evolve, if only to keep pace with their readers. So we've tried to create a guide that's specifically organized, written, and edited for this newly knowledgeable traveler, for whom qualitative information is infinitely more desirable than huge quantities of unappraised data. We think that our series represents a new generation of travel guides, ones that are uniquely responsive to the needs and interests of contemporary travelers.

For years, dating back as far as Herr Baedeker, travel guides have tended to be encyclopedic, seemingly much more concerned with demonstrating expertise in geography and history than in any real analysis of the sorts of things that preoccupy a typical tourist. But today, when it is hardly necessary to tell a traveler where the Virgin Islands are located, it's hard to justify devoting endless pages to historical perspectives. In many cases, the traveler has been to a given island nearly as often as the guidebook editor, so it becomes the responsibility of that editor to provide new perceptions and to suggest new directions to make his guide genuinely valuable.

That's exactly what we've tried to do in our travel guide series. I think you'll notice a more contemporary tone to the text, as well as an organization and focus that are distinctive and different. And even a random examination of what follows will demonstrate a substantial departure from previous guidebook orientation, for we've not only attempted to provide information of a different sort, but we've also tried to present it in an environment that makes it especially accessible.

Needless to say, it's difficult to decide what goes into a guidebook of this size — and what to omit. Early on, we realized that giving up the encyclopedic approach precluded the inclusion of every route and restaurant, and this fact helped define our overall editorial focus. Similarly, when we discussed the possibility of presenting certain information in other than strict geographic order, we discovered that the new format enabled us to arrange data in a way that we feel best answers the questions travelers typically ask.

Large numbers of specific questions have provided the real editorial skeleton for this book. The volume of mail I regularly receive continually seems to emphasize that modern travelers want very precise information, and so we've tried to address ourselves to these needs and have organized our material in the most responsive way possible. Readers who want to know the best restaurant in Bermuda or the best beach on Jamaica's north coast will have no trouble whatever extracting that data from this guide.

Travel guides are, above all, reflections of personal taste, and putting one's name on a title page obviously puts one's preferences on the line. But I think I ought to amplify just exactly what "personal" means. I am not at all a believer in the sort of personal guidebook that's a palpable misrepresentation on its face. It is, for example, hardly possible for any single travel writer to physically visit a thousand restaurants (and nearly that number of hotels) in any given year and provide accurate appraisals of each. And even if it were physically possible for one human to survive such an itinerary, it would of necessity have to be done at a dead sprint, and the perceptions derived therefrom would probably be even less valid than those of any leisurely layman visiting the same establishments. It is, therefore, impossible (especially in a large, annually revised and updated guidebook *series* such as we offer) to have only one person prepare all the data on the entire world.

I also happen to think that such individual orientation is of substantially less value to readers. Visiting a single hotel for just one night, or eating just one hasty meal in a given restaurant, hardly equips anyone to provide appraisals that are of more than passing interest. No amount of doggedly alliterative or oppressively onomatopoeic text can camouflage a technique that is specious on its face. We have, therefore, chosen what I like to describe as the "thee and me" approach to restaurant and hotel appraisal and, to a somewhat more limited degree, to the sites and sights we have included in the other sections of our text. What this really reflects is personal sampling by myself and knowledgeable associates, tempered by intelligent counsel from informed local sources; these additional friends-of-the-editors are usually residents of, or frequent visitors to, the island and/or area about which they are consulted.

But despite this considerable number of researchers and numerous insightful local correspondents, very precise editing and tailoring keeps our text fiercely subjective. So what follows is the gospel according to Birnbaum, and it represents as much of my own tastes and insights as is humanly possible. It is probable, therefore, that if you like your beaches clean and uncrowded, prefer hotels with personality to high-rise anonymities, and can't tolerate fresh fish that's been relentlessly overcooked, then we're likely to have a long and meaningful relationship. Readers with dissimilar tastes may be less enraptured.

I also think I ought to point out something about the person to whom this guidebook is directed. Above all, he or she is a "visitor." This means that such elements as restaurant choices have been specifically picked to provide that visitor with a representative, enlightening, hopefully exciting, and above all pleasant experience. Since so many extraneous considerations can affect the reception and service accorded a regular restaurant patron, our choices can in no way be construed as a definitive guide to resident dining. We think we've got all the best places listed, in various price ranges, but they were chosen with a visitor's viewpoint in mind.

Other evidence of how we've tried to tailor our text to reflect changing travel habits is most apparent in the section we call DIVERSIONS. Where once it was common for travelers to spend an island visit nailed to some single beach, the emphasis today is on pursuing some active enterprise while basking in the tropical rays. Such is the amount of perspiration regularly engendered by today's "leisurely" vacationer that the by-product of a typical modern holiday is often the need to take another vacation immediately after the first one is over. So we've selected every activity we could reasonably evaluate and organized the material in a way that is especially accessible to activists of either an athletic or cerebral bent. It is no longer necessary, therefore, to wade through a pound or two of extraneous prose just to find the best golf course within a reasonable radius of where you'll be vacationing.

If there is one single thing that best characterizes the revolution and evolution of current holiday habits, it is that Americans now consider travel a right rather than a privilege. No longer is a trip to the far corners of the world necessarily a once-in-a-lifetime thing; nor is the idea of visiting exotic, faraway places in the least worrisome. Travel today translates as the enthusiastic desire to sample all of the world's opportunities and to find that elusive quality of experience that is not only enriching but comfortable. For that reason, we've tried to make what follows not only helpful and enlightening, but the sort of welcome companion of which every traveler dreams.

Last, any contemporary guide to the Caribbean must include some comment on the existing concern among a number of prospective Caribbean visitors about matters of safety. I think it's fair to say that this concern is the by-product of events, now spanning several years, that have received a far higher level of media coverage than an objective observer might otherwise feel they deserve. That's not to say that prospective island visitors should not be made aware of the political and social conditions at their chosen holiday site, but rather that the amount and intensity of the coverage generated by even the least untoward incident seems to bear little relationship to coverage of similar events when they occur elsewhere in the world.

I suspect that part of the problem has to do with the nearly endless stream of island advertisements that enthusiastically promise "paradise," and whose Edenesque images are easily destroyed by even the slightest intrusion of reality. My theory gains some weight when one considers that a political demonstration, or even a far more threatening event, hardly ever affects tourism to London, Paris, or Rome, yet can easily lay waste a tourist-dependent island economy for years.

I suppose I'm suggesting that you consider these reports in the light of simple reason; that is, assess any disquieting reports from prospective Caribbean destinations just as you would those from any other part of the world. Many island nations fall into the broad category of "emerging" countries and are thus subject to certain swings of the social pendulum that reflect the newness of self-determination and the legitimate effort to stabilize an island infrastructure that better represents the desires of its citizens. But almost without exception, a tourist is usually very well insulated from the vagaries of island politics, and there are few instances in which even the most acrimonious island dispute spills over to affect a visitor's beachside reverie.

I would also like to point out that every good travel guide is a living enterprise; that is, no part of this text is in any way cast in bronze. In our annual revisions, we are constantly refining and expanding our material to serve your travel needs better. To this end, no contribution is of greater value to us than your personal reaction to what we have written, as well as information about your own experiences while trying our suggestions. We earnestly and enthusiastically solicit your comments on this book *and* your opinions and perceptions about places you have recently visited. In this way, we are able to provide the best information — including the actual experiences of the travel public — to make that experience more readily available to others. Please write to us at 60 E 42nd St., New York, NY 10165.

We sincerely hope to hear from you.

STEPHEN BIRNBAUM

How to Use This Guide

A great deal of care has gone into the organization of this guidebook, and we believe it represents a real breakthrough in the presentation of travel material. Our aim has been to create a new, more modern generation of travel books and to make this guide the most useful and practical travel tool available today.

Our text is divided into four basic sections in order to present information on every possible aspect of a Caribbean vacation. This organization itself should alert you to the vast and varied opportunities available in and on these unusual islands and countries — as well as indicating all the specific data necessary to plan a Caribbean trip. You won't find much of the conventional "swaying palms and shimmering sands" text here; we've chosen instead to provide more useful and purposeful information. Prospective Caribbean itineraries tend to speak for themselves, and with so many diverse travel opportunities, we feel our main job is to explain them and to provide the basic information — how, when, where, how much, and what's best — to let you make the most intelligent choices possible.

Here is a brief summary of our four basic sections — what you can expect to find in each one. We believe that you will find both your travel planning and on-island enjoyment enhanced by having this book at your elbow.

GETTING READY TO GO

This small encyclopedia of practical travel facts is meant to be a sort of know-it-all companion that can provide all the precise information needed to create a Caribbean holiday. There are nearly three dozen separate sections, including how to travel, what preparations to make before you leave, how to deal with possible emergencies while traveling, what to expect in the different regions of the Caribbean, what your trip is likely to cost, and how to avoid prospective problems. The individual entries are specific, realistic, and, where appropriate, cost-oriented.

We expect that you will use this section most in the course of planning your trip, for its ideas and suggestions are intended to make this often confusing period easier. Entries are intentionally concise in an effort to get to the meat of the matter with the least extraneous prose. This information is augmented by extensive lists of specific sources from which to obtain even more detailed information and some suggestions for obtaining travel information on your own.

PERSPECTIVES

Any visit to an unfamiliar destination is enhanced and enriched by a basic understanding of the cultural and historical heritage of that area. We have, therefore, provided just such a background section on the Caribbean — its history, people, food, music, religion, folk life, and similar subjects. We feel that this is a necessary touchstone to this vast area of diverse peoples, lands, and cultures.

ISLAND-BY-ISLAND HOPPING

Here are the individual reports on every island and Caribbean country, including the Bahamas and Bermuda. Though the specific data are of substantial value while planning a trip — especially our evaluations of the best hotels and restaurants — this section is really designed to travel with you and to be used continually on the spot.

Each opening essay introduces its subject island or country within both historical and contemporary contexts, providing not only a cultural overview but an interpretation of current island life as well. The *At-a-Glance* material is actually a site-by-site survey of the most important, interesting, and sometimes most eclectic sights to see and things to do. *Sources and Resources* is a concise listing of pertinent tourist information, meant to answer a range of potentially pressing questions as they arise — from something simple like the address of the local tourist office to something more difficult like the best nightlife guide, the best place to rent scuba equipment, or the best beach. We even discuss such minutiae as where to hail a taxi. The *Best on the Island* section is just that: our choice of the very best places to eat and sleep on each island. You will note that we have included choices for every budget, and these considerations are clearly marked.

DIVERSIONS

This section is designed to help travelers find the very best locations in which to satisfy their fondest vacation desires — without having to wade through endless unrelated text. This selective guide describes the broadest possible range of vacation activities, including all the best places to pursue them.

We start with a list of possibilities that will require some perspiration — sports preferences and other rigorous pursuits — and go on to a number of more cerebral and spiritual vacation possibilities. In every case, our suggestion of a particular location — and often our recommendation of a specific resort — is intended to guide you to that special place where the quality of experience is likely to be highest. So whether you opt for golf or tennis, scuba or snorkeling, tours of spectacular resorts or epic shopping areas — we've even got a guide to gorgeous beaches, including a few where in-the-buff bathing's okay (they call them "free" beaches nowadays) — each entry is the equivalent of getting a comprehensive checklist to the absolute best of the islands.

Although each section of this guidebook has a distinct format and a special function, all have been designed to be used together to provide the most complete package of travel information possible. Sections have been carefully cross-referenced, and you will often find that as you finish an entry in one section you will be directed to another entry in another section for some additional data. To use this book to full advantage, take a few minutes to scan the table of contents and a few random entries in each section. This will give you a good idea of how all the material fits together.

We think of the sections of this book as building blocks, to be put together according to your special preferences to help you create the best possible trip. Use them selectively as travel tools — a source of ideas, a reference for specific facts, and/or a guide to the best buys, the most compelling sights, the most pleasant accommodations, and the most memorable food and drink. We want to help make your next Caribbean visit absolutely the best travel experience you have ever had.

GETTING READY TO GO

When and How to Go

Finding the Islands

 In the waters between the tip of Florida and the northern coast of South America there lies an immense chain of islands, beginning with Cuba and curving south to Trinidad. They are called the West Indies, and the group creates the border between the turbulent, chilly Atlantic Ocean and the calm, warm Caribbean Sea. The four largest of these islands — Cuba, Jamaica, Hispaniola, and Puerto Rico — are the Greater Antilles; they stretch east from the mouth of the Gulf of Mexico. Beyond Puerto Rico this chain of great islands fragments into a crescent of smaller ones that form the northeastern border of the Caribbean: the Virgin Islands and the Windward and Leeward Islands. Off the coast of Venezuela (known to earlier travelers as the Spanish Main) runs another group of islands: the Netherlands Antilles. And farther west the circle of Caribbean destinations comes almost to a close at the Belize coast and the Yucatán peninsula of southern Mexico.

North of the West Indies lie two groups of islands that share the warm-weather fortunes of the Caribbean. Just 50 miles northeast of the Greater Antilles, running parallel to Cuba and Hispaniola, are the Bahamas, a maze of 700 low coral islands and islets. And 800 miles north of the Bahamas, 570 miles east of the Carolinas, are the Bermudas, planted firmly in the Atlantic Ocean but warmed by the Gulf Stream. Though neither the Bahamas nor the Bermudas can correctly be called Caribbean, they are part of the Caribbean world in climate, culture, and popularity as vacation spots.

BERMUDA

Geographically, Bermuda is an entity unto itself, situated in the Atlantic 570 miles east of the Carolinas. Actually, the Bermudas consist of some 150 islets and islands, but the four major ones — Bermuda, Ireland, St. George, and Somerset — make up the destination that's commonly referred to as Bermuda. The Gulf Stream provides Bermuda with warm waters and a temperate climate. Because of its mid-ocean locale, the shore waters are salty and buoyant, while the offshore areas contain intricate reefs and coral heads that serve as buffers against stormy seas. This combination has helped make beaches one of Bermuda's most appealing features. What is more, the very compact land area of 21 square miles is easily traveled by bicycle or motorized transportation.

Bermuda is a British Commonwealth Colony that was granted self-government in 1968. Today it enjoys a sophisticated lifestyle that combines three centuries of British rule with a sometimes formal but highly receptive response to tourism, its major industry.

THE BAHAMAS

Starting just 50 miles east of central Florida, the Bahamas spread in a gentle arc for 700 miles to the southeast. They comprise a maze of 700 islands, innumerable cays (pronounced keys), and myriad coral reefs.

The most popular tourist centers are Nassau, the capital, on the island of New

Providence, and Freeport, on Grand Bahama, which is barely 30 minutes by plane from Palm Beach. A number of less well known destinations, equally popular with yachtsmen, fishermen, and escapists, are in the outlying islands. These include Bimini, about 50 miles east of Miami, famous for its deep-sea fishing; the Berry Islands, once frequented by private vessels cruising between Florida and Nassau; Andros, the largest island in the Bahamas, a few miles northeast of the Great Bahama Bank, the world's third largest barrier reef; Eleuthera, the most developed of the outlying islands; Harbour Island, noted for its beach; the Exuma chain, the site of the annual Family Island Regatta; and San Salvador, the first island — according to Bahamian tradition — claimed by Columbus in 1492. Others with facilities for visitors are the Abacos, Cat Island, Long Island, and Spanish Wells.

Since 1973, the Bahamas have been an independent nation affiliated with the British Commonwealth. Their chief natural attributes are an appealing subtropical climate, with temperatures averaging between 70° and 90° the year round, and an extensive range of islands and well-charted sailing waters scattered over almost 100,000 square miles.

THE CARIBBEAN REGION

What is popularly referred to as "the Caribbean" is actually the Caribbean Sea and all the islands (West Indies) and continental coastal areas (South America, Central America, and the Yucatán peninsula of Mexico and Belize) that encompass it. The Caribbean Sea covers an area of 750,000 square miles and is geographically a tiny arm of the Atlantic Ocean. In contrast to the Atlantic, however, the Caribbean is characterized by calm waters — thanks to the protection offered by the arc of Lesser Antilles islands that separates the two bodies of water — and a warm climate due to its latitude. The midpoint of the Caribbean Sea is roughly midway between Florida and the equator.

The West Indies have the subdesignations of Greater and Lesser Antilles, which make a literal distinction between the larger island-nations of the north and the arc of smaller ones that form the Caribbean's eastern border. Aruba, Bonaire, and Curaçao — which, with three smaller Dutch islands farther north constitute the Netherlands Antilles — are off the northwestern coast of Venezuela.

The continental countries covered in this volume with coastal areas fronting the Caribbean are Venezuela, Colombia, Belize, and the islands off Mexico's Yucatán. The following descriptions begin with Cuba and continue in a roughly clockwise direction.

Cuba – Ninety miles south of Key West, Florida, Cuba is a long and linear island (745 miles from east to west), the largest in the West Indies. With a semitropical climate, it has long been known for fine beaches and some of the hemisphere's most challenging deep-sea fishing waters. Cuba's topography ranges from flat plains, where its economically vital sugar crop is cultivated, to fertile valleys and mountain jungles. Cuba covers an area of 44,000 square miles and has a population of 10 million. (Havana, its capital, has about 2.5 million residents.)

Cuba was discovered by Columbus on his first Atlantic voyage, and despite an often turbulent history during the intervening centuries, the Spanish heritage prevails. For several decades during the middle of this century, Havana was a playground and popular gambling center for Americans, but the Revolution ended this in 1959, when the country was closed to US visitors. For a brief period between 1977 and 1982, the barriers were lifted and US citizens were again permitted to visit Cuba, though in somewhat limited numbers. However, the US government has again banned travel to Cuba by all citizens, except those with family on the island and reporters or scholars on assignment. Canadians arranging trips through recognized operators can still visit freely.

Cayman Islands – Grand Cayman (22 miles long), Little Cayman (10 miles long, 2 miles wide), and Cayman Brac (12 miles long, 1 mile wide) make up this island group perched in the northwestern waters of the Caribbean roughly 100 miles south of Cuba.

West Beach, also known as Seven Mile Beach, on Grand Cayman is the most developed tourist area, although beaches throughout the islands are good. The offshore waters are considered exceptional; they are clear and spotted with numerous colorful reefs that attract deep-sea divers and professional big-game fishermen. The island group has a population of 21,000 people, 9,500 of whom live in the capital, George Town.

Jamaica – Some 90 miles south of Cuba's southeastern coast, Jamaica is a lush, mountainous island with a tropical climate tempered by trade winds. It covers a total area of just under 4,500 square miles. Dotted around the coast are clusters of fine beaches and good harbors, and several major resort communities have established tourism as a principal industry. Columbus discovered Jamaica in 1494 during his second Atlantic voyage, and the island was a Spanish trading outpost for more than 150 years, until the British seized it in 1655. Today it is an independent nation affiliated with the British Commonwealth. Its capital, Kingston, has a population of about a million.

Haiti – The Republic of Haiti covers the western third (almost 11,000 square miles) of the island called Hispaniola, the second largest single landmass in the Caribbean. Like Jamaica, Haiti is mountainous and lush, but little of the land is agriculturally productive. Discovered (and named) by Columbus on his first voyage, Hispaniola was divided in 1697, when the Spanish ceded the portion that is now Haiti to the French, who imported the African slaves (from whom 90% of Haiti's population of more than 6 million is descended today). Haiti is the world's oldest black republic. Its official language is French, although most of the natives speak a Créole dialect derived from the Normans, the French, and the Spanish, as well as the Arawak Indians.

Dominican Republic – Covering the other two thirds of Hispaniola (19,000 square miles), the Dominican Republic has many of the small coastal, climatic, and physical characteristics of its neighbor, Haiti. A notable feature is the exceptionally high western mountain system dominated by Pico Duarte, at 10,417 feet the highest peak in the West Indies. Spanish is the dominant influence, reinforced by the heritage of the capital, Santo Domingo, the oldest city established by Europeans in the Western Hemisphere (1496). The country has about 6.2 million residents, 2 million of whom live in the capital.

Turks and Caicos Islands – Geographically these tiny islands (total population, about 8,000) fit within the orbit of the Bahamas and are at the southern tip of that island group, 90 miles north of the island of Hispaniola. A British Crown Colony, Turks (the plural is always used) and Caicos Islands consist of eight major islands and a number of cays surrounded by warm currents. Average temperatures range from 70° to 90° throughout the year. The islands of most interest are Grand Turk (the site of Cockburn Town, the capital), Salt Cay, South Caicos, Middle Caicos, North Caicos, Providenciales ("Provo"), and Pine Cay. A new jetport on Provo — to say nothing of the opening of the *Club Med Turkoise* — has pushed that island to the forefront of tourist interest.

Puerto Rico – The easternmost member of the Greater Antilles, Puerto Rico is approximately 1,000 miles southeast of Miami. The island is surrounded by generally placid seas; the coastal area has a number of wide natural beaches; and the interior is a mixture of rain forest, mountains, and agricultural plains. Puerto Rico is a US commonwealth with an autonomous government, but its Spanish tradition is strong. Tourism is a major industry, notably in San Juan, the capital, where the Condado Beach and Isla Verde sections are centers for modern hotels, restaurants, shops, and resort recreations. The island has a total of 3,500 square miles and a population of 3.2 million, 500,00 of whom are in San Juan.

US Virgin Islands – St. Thomas, St. John, and St. Croix, each with its own distinct characteristics, are the major islands of this group, which includes 50 formations that make up a territory of 136 square miles, bought by the US from Denmark for $25 million in 1917. Fifty miles east of Puerto Rico, the US Virgin Islands have a salubrious climate that is tempered by trade winds even during the hot summer months. The major islands are mountainous, with coastal areas lined with coves, bays, and beaches. St. Thomas, the most commercially developed of the islands, is the site of the administrative capital, Charlotte Amalie, one of the most heavily trafficked cruise ports and shopping communities in the Caribbean. It is also one of the Caribbean's most active ports for yacht charters and sailing expeditions. St. John is the least developed as a tourist center, but it is probably the most appealing in that much of it is part of the Virgin Islands National Park, with underwater coastlines popular for snorkeling and scuba and skin diving. St. Croix's coastal waters have equally attractive features, but the island is better known for its resorts and well-preserved historical landmarks.

British Virgin Islands – All of the characteristics of the US Virgin Islands apply to the British group, immediately northeast of the American. Tortola and Virgin Gorda are the major islands; Jost Van Dyke, less than 5 miles west of Tortola, is a popular destination for sailing vessels.

Anguilla – Divorced from St. Kitts and Nevis since l981, 35-square-mile Anguilla lies 3½ miles north of St. Maarten/St. Martin. Its chief attributes are peace, simplicity, stunning beaches, smallish resort properties, and few (approximately 7,500) but friendly people. Recent additions to the island's inventory of accommodations suggest that it has been "discovered" by visitors.

St. Maarten/St. Martin – The two designations apply to the same island, half Dutch, half French, with each sector ruled as a dependency of, respectively, the Netherlands Antilles and the French Department of Guadeloupe. About 150 miles due east of Puerto Rico, the island marks the point at which the Lesser Antilles begin their southern curve to the coast of South America. The island is noted for its natural swimming beaches and is emerging as one of the more popular tour destinations of the Caribbean. Its climate is good, it's easily accessible (3½ hours nonstop flying time from New York), and it offers quite a few sophisticated hotels, as well as many more modest ones. Duty-free shopping facilities and the combined Dutch and French living sectors are also attractions. The island has a population of 27,000 and covers about 37 square miles.

St. Barthélemy – About ten minutes by inter-island plane southeast of St. Martin, "St. Barts" is a small, quiet island of some 3,050 people and has a pastoral atmosphere. Like French St. Martin, it is a dependency of Guadeloupe. Gustavia, its capital, faces a harbor that is a stillwater mooring place for sailing vessels.

Saba – Physically, this is one of the most unusual islands of the Caribbean: a jagged volcanic cone rising out of the sea, with community life starting halfway up. The lowest town, appropriately named The Bottom, is Saba's capital. There are two villages higher up. Saba is Dutch, although much of its population is of Scottish descent. This is a true island retreat, and tourist accommodations are somewhat limited.

St. Eustatius – Another Dutch dependency, "Statia" (as it's more conveniently called) is one of the most unspoiled islands of the Caribbean. It is dominated by the Quill, a 2,000-foot truncated volcanic cone with a crater 1,000 feet deep.

St. Kitts/Nevis – The nation of St. Kitts/Nevis consists of two islands just a few miles south of St. Eustatius that claim an exceptionally even climate and low humidity; the highest and lowest temperatures recorded are 92° and 62° respectively. St. Kitts is the site of the first successful colony established by the English in the West Indies (1623). Nevis, separated from St. Kitts by a 2-mile strait, is topped occasionally by a halo of clouds ringing 3,232-foot Nevis Peak.

Antigua – Another of the self-governing states of the British West Indies, Antigua is a volcanic and coral island about 40 miles east of Nevis with a total area of about 100 square miles and a population of 79,000 people. Its climate is relatively dry and sunny; its beaches are white sand protected by reefs. A number of hotels are concentrated along the northwest coast on either side of St. John's, the capital, but several others are considerably farther out along the coast. Landlocked English Harbour on the north coast, the site of the impressively reconstructed dockyard that was Nelson's headquarters in the Caribbean, is a major yacht charter center and port of call. Water sports are the chief recreational activity. Some 32 miles to the north is Barbuda, a low-lying island with long stretches of unspoiled beaches and a heavily wooded interior. Minimally developed for tourism, it is part of Antigua.

Montserrat – This tiny island is mountainous and highly cultivated. Soufrière, its highest peak and a dormant volcano, is a major sightseeing attraction. The island traded British and French flags several times before finally being ceded to Britain in 1783. It is a British Crown Colony, with an area of 39 square miles and 12,000 residents.

Guadeloupe – This island, midway down the eastern archipelago of the Lesser Antilles, possesses some of the finest beaches in the eastern Caribbean. Several are preserved for nude sunbathing, which makes this one of the few islands where the activity is sanctioned. Shaped like a butterfly, Guadeloupe is actually two islands divided by a narrow river. On the western, or Caribbean, side is the island of Basse-Terre, covered with mountainous rain forests and topped by a sulfurous volcano. Grande-Terre, the eastern part, is relatively flat, with good beaches and sailing waters. Three island destinations — Îles des Saintes, Marie Galante, and La Désirade, east and south of Guadeloupe — are accessible by plane or boat. These small islands, along with French St. Martin and St. Barthélemy, are governed as dependencies of Guadeloupe, which in turn is an overseas department of France. It covers 530 square miles and has about 332,000 residents.

Dominica – In 1979, Hurricane David devastated this relatively undeveloped 300-square-mile island between Martinique and Guadeloupe. Thousands were homeless; agriculture and tourism were destroyed. But experts who said it would take years to repair the damage underestimated nature's healing powers, help from neighbors and friends, and 83,000 Dominicans' own buoyant determination. Today, British-associated but independent Dominica — the site of the world's only Carib Indian reservation — is wildly beautiful again. Its 365 rivers course down lush jungled mountainsides; its modest tourist plant — except for the planned rebuilding of the historic *Fort Young* hotel — is not only restored, but in some cases better than before.

Martinique – The southernmost island of the French West Indies is an intertropical zone with warm average temperatures and a yearly mean of 79°. But it is also in the path of two trade-wind currents that cool its atmosphere. The irregular coastline has five major bays and dozens of coves; the major interior geographic features are three mountain formations, the largest and most famous of which — Mont Pelée — was the site of an annihilating eruption in 1902. Flowering vegetation is a major natural attraction. French is the official language, although many people speak English and a Créole patois is common. Smaller than Guadeloupe, with 425 square miles of land, Martinique offers a fully developed tourist industry with a range of hotels and visitor facilities. Some 330,000 people live on the island.

St. Lucia – Dozens of inlets line the coast of this nugget-shaped island, 25 miles below the southern tip of Martinique. This is a volcanic island with forest mountains rising to a 3,117-foot peak. It is an independent nation within the British Commonwealth and has an area of 238 square miles, with a population of over 134,000.

St. Vincent and the Grenadines – Another independent nation of the British Commonwealth, St. Vincent's governing sphere is a scattering of small islands known as the northern Grenadines, the major ones being Bequia, Mustique, Young Island, Palm Island, Petit St. Vincent, Canouan, Mayreau, Union, and the Tobago Cays. The island constellation covers a total area of about 150 square miles. St. Vincent is another major center for yachting; boating and water sports are the primary recreations.

Grenada – Formerly an Associated State of Great Britain, Grenada became an independent nation within the Commonwealth in 1974. Just 90 miles off the Venezuelan coast, Grenada's sailing waters are exceptional, and it serves as the southern terminus for the increasing number of yachts and vessels that cruise the Grenadines. With the two Grenadine islands it administers — Carriacou and Petit Martinique — it covers an area of 133 square miles and has a population of about 98,000.

Barbados – This easternmost island of the West Indies sits by itself about 100 miles east of St. Vincent. The west coast is lined with good swimming beaches, along with most of the hotels and resorts, which benefit from the calmer winds and waters of the Caribbean. The east coast is rocky and subject to Atlantic trade winds. Barbados has been British (now independent but a Commonwealth state) for more than three centuries. A strong English tradition prevails, as do pronounced English accents. The island has good roads, modern hotels and resorts, and is a popular cruise port. It has 258,000 people and an area of 166 square miles.

Trinidad and Tobago – These are the southernmost of the eastern group of the West Indies islands; Trinidad sits astride Venezuela's Gulf of Paria. Essentially British, Trinidad and Tobago (the latter, smaller island is about 25 miles northeast) joined to become an independent nation in 1962 and in 1976 established their country as an independent republic associated only economically with Great Britain. The official language is English, although some islanders speak a French patois and a few speak Spanish. Together, they have an area of almost 2,000 square miles and more than 1 million residents.

Aruba, Bonaire, and Curaçao – Situated from 15 to 50 miles off the northwestern coast of Venezuela, these three islands, along with St. Maarten, Saba, and St. Eustatius, make up the Dutch presence in the Caribbean and, with the exception of Aruba, are known as the Netherlands Antilles. Aruba, Bonaire, and Curaçao together form the trio colloquially known as the ABC islands. Curaçao in particular has a Dutch atmosphere, with a number of 18th-century Dutch homes and a pontoon bridge at the entrance to the harbor of its capital, Willemstad. Curaçao and Aruba are well-developed tourist centers, whereas Bonaire is a growing center for scuba diving and training. Aruba withdrew from the Netherlands Antilles on January 1, 1986, and maintains a separate political status, although not total independence, from the Netherlands. All of the islands promote duty-free shopping and gambling. However, they cover only 363 square miles, with a total population of about 238,000.

Venezuela – The Caribbean coast of this major South American country is a relative newcomer to volume tourism from the north, although the city of La Guaira has long been a port of call for cruise ships, from which passengers make day tours to Venezuela's nearby capital, Caracas. Resort alternatives are Macuto, just east of La Guaira, the newer Dorado del Mar farther east, and the free-port island of Margarita. Coastal temperatures are warm; Caracas, in the hills, averages about 75°.

Colombia – Like Venezuela, Colombia is often associated with cruise ship stopovers. Cartagena (pronounced cart-a-*hay*-na) and Santa Marta are occasional ports of call for ships traveling through the nearby Panama Canal. The most likely site for new resort development is the tip of the Guajira Peninsula on the Gulf of Venezuela.

Belize – Cramped beneath Mexico's Yucatán peninsula, with its entire coastal area facing the Caribbean, Belize declared its independence from Britain in 1981 and is beginning to promote the undeveloped islands of its offshore deep-sea reef areas to tourists. The coastal terrain is mostly swampland, with Belize City on the coast as its major population center (the country's total population is 166,000). Belize has remains of stone cities built by the Maya. Its climate is largely subtropical.

Yucatán Peninsula – Two resorts near the tip of this Mexican peninsula are major destinations for tourists. Cozumel Island is a 12-mile ferry ride off the coast and essentially a low-key vacation retreat. The waters and climate are temperate; scuba diving, deep-sea fishing, and other water recreations are the principal activities, notably around Palancar Reef, toward the southern tip of the island. It is a port of call for ships from Miami and New Orleans. Cancún is a modern resort on its own seahorse-shaped peninsula near the tip of the Yucatán. It has more than two dozen hotels and condominiums, a broad spectrum of restaurants, a convention and entertainment center, and very good swimming beaches. A third small island, Isla Mujeres, long a well-kept secret of peace-seeking beach and diving buffs, is in the process of being "discovered." On the peninsula, the well-known Maya ruins at Chichén Itzá and Uxmal and the slightly less famous ones at Tulum are among Mexico's most noteworthy attractions. Peninsula weather is warm and can be uncomfortably humid during summer months, although the coastal regions benefit from sea breezes. The Yucatán is readily accessible by regularly scheduled flights from Mexico City and several southern US cities into Mérida, the capital, Cozumel's airstrip, and Cancún's modern jetport.

When to Go

 CLIMATE: The lures of Bermuda, the Bahamas, and the Caribbean are essentially natural: sun, sand, and sea in a climate that virtually begs you to relax. But the elements do vary; logically, the best weather is to be enjoyed for the highest prices during the peak seasons. Bermuda is a midyear retreat, where the best weather is from April through October. The Bahamas, in a semitropical zone, offer warmer temperatures throughout much of the year, although the midsummer months can be enervating; December through April are the peak months. Most of the Caribbean and the Yucatán peninsula share the Bahamas' peak season, whereas the "southern Caribbean" of the Netherlands Antilles and the coastal waters of Venezuela and Colombia peak from November to April.

Some islands — even allowing for the heat and humidity of summer — are noted for exceptionally healthy climates throughout the year. These islands include the Havana region of Cuba, Puerto Rico, both the US and British Virgin Islands, Antigua, St. Kitts and Nevis, St. Martin, St. Eustatius, Montserrat, and Aruba. Even Bermuda's winter months, despite bracing weather, can be invigorating. Island tourist offices, airlines, cruise lines, and travel agents can offer more specific information for particular times of the year. However, take their advice with some caution: Their main objective is to sell tickets. A friend or friend of a friend who's actually been there is probably a more disinterested and reliable source.

SEASONAL PRICE VARIATIONS: If money is a major consideration, plan your trip during the off-season. The best savings during these periods are in accommodations, since hotel prices are routinely cut from 30% to 65%. In addition, many island properties offer special promotions that include such things as house-hotel cocktail parties, a free bottle of rum, discount coupons for meals or shopping, and cut-rate fees for golf, tennis, diving classes, and other recreation. An exceptionally good buy is an off-season package that combines air fare, accommodations, sightseeing, special features, and an optional (added cost) meal plan (see *Package Tours*).

Traditionally, the so-called off-season is almost exactly twice as long as the peak season and usually stretches from April 16 to December 15. The specific dates may vary a few days from resort to resort, but virtually every major tropical hotel observes the seasonal delineation. Exceptions occasionally offer a "shoulder" season (generally the periods of late April/May and November/early December), but even in these few instances, appreciable savings are available.

Hotel rates are not the only prices to decrease in the off-season. Many airline fares have a seasonal bias, and the dawning of April 16 often brings a diminution of resort-directed fares that averages about 15%. What's more, the passing of the high season usually spawns a host of new promotional packages that can include accommodations, autos, and a host of other money-saving extras. Look for the packages with numbers preceded by the letters IT or ITX; booking them may entitle you to tour-basing air fare savings, too.

But financial considerations are only part of the allure of off-season travel. The destinations themselves actually take on a different, more friendly cast with the passing of the high-season hordes, and even the most basic services are performed more efficiently. In theory, off-season service is identical to that offered during high season, but the fact is that the absence of demanding crowds inevitably begets much more thoughtful and personal attention. The very same staff that can barely manage to get fresh towels onto the racks during January and February has the time to chat pleasantly during April and May. And the very same activities and amenities — from water-ski tows to the use of snorkel gear, windsurfers, sailboats, chaises, and such — that can add a not so small fortune in extra charges to your bill at the height of winter are often included in daily rates the rest of the year.

It is not only the hotels that benefit from the absence of the high-season mobs. Fine restaurants, absolutely unbreachable when the professional high rollers are passing out tips large enough to pay off the maître d's mortgage, pay rapt attention to mere mortals during the off-season. And the food preparation and service are also likely to be best when the chef is required to create only a reasonable number of meals.

The most common concern about off-season travel has to do with weather. The misguided reasoning seems to be that if tropical temperatures are suitable for swimming in the dead of winter, they must be absolutely skin-scorching come spring. Absolutely wrong! Not only do temperatures remain in a fairly narrow range throughout the year, but the almost constant presence of trade winds provides a cooling effect. And what about the rainy season? Well, the usual line is that September is the only month that is more than normally risky as far as rain is concerned, but there is not even unanimity on that. Certainly the periods of late April, May, June, and then late October, November, and early December qualify as prime tropical times, since the weather during these months is generally superb. Only in summer are you likely to encounter any uncomfortably warm weather, and then not everywhere. And uncomfortable weather is highly relative — most islands are cooled by trade winds, and there is always the sea nearby. What would be unbearable in New York City or Chicago can be a delightful day on the beach, with plenty of suntan oil, shade, an occasional cool drink, and, of course, the sea. Be aware of these off-season weather patterns:

1. Bermuda temperatures drop in November and a sporadic rainy season sets in, accompanied by winds, well into February.
2. Rainy months in the Bahamas are usually May and June (sporadic) and September and October (sometimes squallish).
3. In the Caribbean, July through September is the hot and/or humid period, noticeably so in the Turks and Caicos, Jamaica, the Cayman Islands, Haiti, and the Dominican Republic in the north, in Guadeloupe and Martinique in the middle of the eastern archipelago, and in the Netherlands Antilles and the coast of Venezuela in the south. Belize can be very sticky from April to August.
4. Hurricane paths occasionally begin through the southern and central islands (St. Vincent to Antigua), leaving little more than wind debris, but they're sometimes damaging to Jamaica, Cuba, and other more northerly islands during the late summer and early fall.

Traveling by Plane

 Air travel is the choice of vacationers who are going to stay on one island (or group of islands) for their entire visit; cruise ships may dock at one port for several days, but generally they function mostly as hotels for passengers rather than as efficient transportation. Air travel is far faster and more direct; it is rare to have to spend more than a day getting to even the most inaccessible part of the Caribbean from the US by air. The less time spent in transit, the more time spent on the islands. And that is even truer as direct flights to an increasing number of Caribbean destinations become available from major US cities.

SCHEDULED FLIGHTS: Below is a list of carriers flying from North America on a regularly scheduled basis to the destinations covered in this volume. Also included are inter-island carriers. The list was up to date as we went to press, but it is subject to frequent service and scheduling changes by the individual carriers. What's more, frequency of service varies dramatically with the season.

Anguilla: Air Anguilla, Air BVI, American, Coastal Air Transport, Winair, LIAT

Antigua: Air Canada, American, BWIA, Eastern, LIAT

Aruba: American, ALM, Delta, Eastern, Suncoast, Viasa

Bahamas: Air Canada, Bahamasair, Delta, Midway, Pan Am, TWA, United, Eastern; plus Caribbean Express, Chalk's International, and other small carriers from Florida cities

Barbados: Air Canada, American, BWIA, Eastern, Pan Am, LIAT

Belize: TACA, TAN-SASHA

Bermuda: Air Canada, American, British Airways, Delta, Eastern, Pan Am, United

Bonaire: ALM

British Virgin Islands: Air BVI, American, Crown Air, Eastern, LIAT

Cancún and Cozumel: Aeroméxico, American, Continental, Eastern, Lacsa, Mexicana, Northwest, United; inter-island service on Aero Caribe between Cancún and Cozumel

Cayman Islands: Eastern, Cayman Airways

Colombia: Avianca, Eastern

Cuba: Cubana Aviación (from Montréal), various charters

Curaçao: ALM, American, Eastern

Dominica: Air Caribe, Air Guadeloupe, Air Martinique, LIAT

Dominican Republic: Air Canada, American, Dominicana, Eastern, Pan Am, Wardair

Grenada: BWIA, LIAT (connections via Barbados or Trinidad)

Guadeloupe: Air Canada, Air France, Air Guadeloupe, American, Eastern, LIAT

Haiti: Air Canada, Air France, ALM, American, Eastern, Haiti Trans Air

Jamaica: Air Canada, Air Jamaica, ALM, American, BWIA, Eastern, Northwest

Martinique: Air Canada, Air France, Air Martinique, American, Eastern, LIAT

Montserrat: LIAT

Puerto Rico: Air BVI, ALM, American, BWIA, Delta, Dominicana, Eastern, LIAT, TWA, Wardair

Saba: Winair

St. Barthélemy: Air Guadeloupe, Air St. Barthélemy, Coastal Air Transport, Virgin Air, Winair

St. Eustatius: LIAT, Winair

St. Kitts/Nevis: American, BWIA, LIAT, Winair

St. Lucia: Air Canada, Air Martinique, American, BWIA, Eastern, LIAT

St. Maarten/St. Martin: Air Guadeloupe, Air St. Barthélemy, ALM, American, BWIA, Eastern, LIAT, Pan Am, Winair

St. Vincent: Air Martinique, LIAT

Trinidad and Tobago: Air Canada, ALM, American, BWIA, Eastern, LIAT, Pan Am

Turks and Caicos: Pan Am, Trans-Jamaican Airlines, Turks and Caicos National Airlines

US Virgin Islands: Aero Virgin Islands, Air Caribe, American, Eastern, LIAT, Midway, Pan Am, Sunaire

Venezuela: Dominicana, Pan Am, Varig, Viasa

The major inter-island carriers for the Caribbean are LIAT, Winair, and ALM. LIAT (Leeward Island Air Transport) is based in Antigua and flies on a regularly scheduled daily basis to most of the islands of the eastern archipelago from the Virgin Islands to Trinidad. Winair (Windward Island Airways) is based in St. Maarten and serves Anguilla, St. Barthélemy, Saba, St. Kitts/Nevis, and St. Eustatius; it offers charter flights to other islands as well. ALM (Antillean Airlines), based in Curaçao, flies there from Miami via Haiti, Aruba, or Bonaire; its inter-island flights serve Jamaica, Puerto Rico, and Trinidad as well as the Dutch Caribbean.

A number of other small carriers providing flights out of individual islands include Air BVI, Air Guadeloupe, Air Martinique, BWIA (British West Indian Airways), and Turks and Caicos National Airways (TAC National), all of which have small planes for charter.

Fares – Air fares change so rapidly that even experts find it difficult to keep current. In general, however, the great variety of fares to the islands can be reduced to three basic categories: first class, coach (sometimes called economy or tourist class), and excursion or other discount and promotional fares. A first-class ticket is your admission to the section of the aircraft with larger seats, more leg room, better food than in coach, free drinks, and above all, the presence of flight attendants who make you the object of special attention. This service normally costs at least half again as much (usually more) as a ticket in coach.

Coach passengers sit more snugly, behind the first-class section, and receive far less lavish meal service. Like full-fare first-class passengers, passengers paying the full coach fare are subject to none of the restrictions attached to less expensive discount fares. There are no advance booking requirements, no minimum stay requirements, and no cancellation penalties. Tickets are sold on an open reservation system: They can be bought for a flight up to the minute of takeoff if seats are available, and if the ticket is round-trip, the return reservation can be made anytime you wish — months before you leave or the day before you return. Both first-class and coach tickets are generally good for a year, after which they can be renewed if not used; if you ultimately decide not to fly at all, your money will be refunded.

Excursion and other discount or promotional fares are the airlines' equivalent of a sale. They may masquerade under a variety of names and may vary from destination to destination, but they invariably have strings attached. A common requirement is that the ticket be purchased a certain period of time — sometimes as much as 30 days — before departure, though it can be booked weeks or months in advance. Another common condition is a minimum and maximum stay requirement; i.e., 3 to 30 days, 6 to 21 days. There are usually cancellation penalties, meaning that if you want to change the date or time of your flight or to cancel your plans entirely once you've been ticketed, it will cost a significant sum to do so. Even when none of the above conditions apply, prospective passengers can be fairly sure that the number of seats available per flight at the lowest price is strictly limited or that the discount fare will be offered for only a set period, which means that prospective travelers will have to move fast to be among the fortunate few traveling least expensively. Passengers flying on discount fares sit with and receive the same service as full-fare coach passengers, although on a few Caribbean routes advance purchase excursion fares are sold for first-class travel as well.

Still lower "tour-basing" fares (GIT, ITX) are frequently available. These require prepaid booking of a minimum level of ground arrangements (accommodations, car rental, etc.) at the destination, purchased at the same time you buy your plane ticket. Ask your travel agent or the airline directly whether such fares exist to the island of your choice and what it takes to qualify for them.

No matter what kind of ticket you buy, it is essential that you confirm your round-trip reservations — *especially the return leg from your island idyll.* Most airlines recommend that you confirm your return flight 48 hours in advance; others, 72 hours. Be aware that failure to reconfirm frequently results in the automatic cancellation of your reservation — even if you have a confirmed, fully paid ticket in hand — and this can be a particular problem on islands with only a very limited number of flights each day.

Seats – Airline seats are assigned in advance or on a first come, first served basis at the time of check-in. You must decide if you want a smoking or nonsmoking section, a movie section, or one of the few nonreclining seats.

Some airlines furnish seating charts, which make choosing a spot much easier, but in general, there are a few basics to consider. Airline representatives claim that most craft are more stable toward the front and midsections, while seating farthest away from the engines is quietest. Passengers with long legs should request an aisle seat or a seat directly behind the emergency doors. Bear in mind, too, that watching a movie from the first row is difficult and uncomfortable. A window seat protects you from aisle traffic and provides a view; an aisle seat enables you to get up and stretch your legs; middle seats in a group of three or more are the least desirable.

Meals – Just as seating can be arranged in advance, special meals can be ordered before flight time. Most, if not all, of the major airlines offer kosher, salt-free, low cholesterol, vegetarian, dietetic, and other special meals at no extra charge. You should order what you want at least 8, preferably 24, hours before your flight.

Baggage – Free baggage allowances between the US and island points vary according to the airline and the destination, and size limits for carry-on bags have become quite strict. This can be a special problem for souvenir-toting travelers who may have carry-on bags arbitrarily checked when they don't fit under the seat in front of them or in the overhead racks. Bags that are checked late often miss the flight and, in general, cause considerable inconvenience. Between the US, Puerto Rico, and other Caribbean points, each passenger is allowed to check two 70-pound bags — one with combined dimensions (height, width, length) totaling 62 inches, one totaling 55 inches, and one 40-pound, 45-inch bag. Passengers may carry on up to two bags, the combined size of which should not exceed 45 inches. Charges for excess baggage also vary. If you plan to take part of your trip by inter-island carrier, note that baggage allowances tend to be less generous than those on the flight to and from the US; a total of 44 pounds per person is common.

Getting Bumped – A special air travel problem is the possibility that an airline will accept more reservations (and sell more tickets) than there are seats on a given flight. This is entirely legal and is done to make up for passengers who don't show up for a flight for which they have reservations. If the airline has oversold the flight and everyone does show up, the airline is subject to stringent rules laid down to protect travelers.

The airline first seeks ticketholders willing to give up their seats voluntarily in return for a negotiable sum of money or some other inducement, such as upgraded seating on the next flight or a voucher for a free trip at some other time. If there are not enough volunteers, the airline may bump passengers against their wishes. Anyone inconvenienced in this way, however, is entitled to an explanation of the criteria used to determine who does and does not get on the flight, as well as to compensation if the resulting delay exceeds certain limits. If the airline can put the bumped passengers on an alternate flight that gets them to their planned destination within one hour of their originally scheduled arrival time, no compensation is owed. If the delay is more than an hour, they must be paid denied-boarding compensation equivalent to the one-way fare to their destination (but not more than $200). If the delay is more than two hours beyond the original arrival time on a domestic flight or more than four hours on an international flight, the compensation must be doubled. (These rules may vary depending on the carrier and do *not* apply to inbound flights from abroad, even on US carriers.) The airline may also offer bumped travelers a voucher for a free flight instead of the denied-boarding compensation. The passenger can choose either the money or the voucher (the dollar value of which may be no less than the monetary compensation to which the passenger would be entitled). The voucher is not a substitute for the bumped passenger's original ticket; the airline continues to honor that as well.

The rules do not apply if the flight is canceled or delayed, or if a smaller aircraft is substituted due to mechanical problems. In such cases, some airlines provide amenities to stranded passengers, but these are strictly at the individual airline's discretion. Deregulation of the airlines has meant that travelers must find out for themselves what they are entitled to receive. A useful booklet, *Air Travelers' Fly Rights,* is available for $1 from the Superintendent of Documents, US Government Printing Office, Washington, DC 20402; stock number 050-000-00-513-5.

CHARTER FLIGHTS: The days when joining a charter "affinity group" was more complicated than getting into the world's most exclusive country club are gone. Nowadays, charters can be organized by anybody (any club, group, or individual — with or without a professional travel background — as well as by experienced tour operators, travel agents, and the airlines themselves) and can be bought by anybody at any time — up to and including the day of departure. No more membership or advance purchase rules; no more complicated itinerary or ground arrangement requirements.

The basic economics remain the same: The charter operator buys as much as a planeload of seats from an airline — which is sometimes a recognizable name, sometimes strictly a chartering outfit — at a low bulk rate and resells them at a relatively low price based on the assumption that close to 100% of the offered space will be sold. The bottom line for the traveler is usually a savings of 30% to 40% off the regular airline ticket price under normal peak conditions. The big change brought about by the lack of rules has been the number and variety of charter flights offered. In the Caribbean specifically, it has meant an increase in flights — especially from the Midwest and to islands where gambling is a favorite indoor sport.

This new charter freedom — to sell any seat at any price and then to "discount" space that remains unsold close to flight time — carries with it a new consumer caution: if not "Buyer, beware," then "Buyer, be wary." When the price of a given flight or tour seems fire-sale low, ask yourself where the fire was. Is yours actually one of *a few* seats priced to move just before flight time? Or is it one of many — because the destination, or the hotel, or the package features included aren't all they should be? Try to get answers from a well-informed, professional travel agent who knows the territory, or contact someone (ask the charter tour operator for a few names) who has been on a trip with this operator. Meanwhile, bear in mind that:

1. Generally, though not required by law, advanced booking and payment — on confirmation — are part of the contract. You must commit yourself and your money early.
2. If you are forced to cancel your flight on short notice, you will lose some or possibly all of your money unless you have cancellation insurance (this is a must; see *Insurance,* in this section).
3. You must leave and return on the specified dates, and if you miss your plane, you lose your money. There are no refunds.
4. By virtue of the economics of charter flights, your plane will almost always be full; you'll fly crowded, though not necessarily uncomfortably.

When you do decide on a charter, read the contract's fine print carefully, noting:

1. When you are to pay the deposit and balance and to whom the check is to be made out. Ordinarily, checks are made out not to the charter company but to a bank escrow account. This means that the bank pays the charter airline and any providers of ground arrangements before the flight, but doesn't release the balance of the

account to the charter company until after the flight is completed. The charter company should be bonded, and the name of the bonding agent (against whom any future claims should be made) and the time limit within which claims must be filed should be specified.

2. Stipulations regarding cancellation by the consumer. Frequently, if you cancel well in advance (often 6 weeks or more), you may forfeit only a small amount. If you cancel only 2 or 3 weeks ahead, there may be no refund at all unless you or the operator can supply a substitute passenger.

3. Stipulations regarding cancellations and major changes made by the charterer. Charters may be canceled by the operator up to 10 days before departure for any reason, usually underbooking. Your money will be returned in 2 weeks in this event, but that may leave you too little time to make new arrangements. (The charter may not be canceled within 10 days of departure except for circumstances such as natural disasters or political upheavals.) Charterers may make "major changes," such as in the date or place of departure or return, but if you don't accept these changes, you are entitled to cancel and receive a full refund. They are also permitted to assess a surcharge (for fuel or other rising costs) of up to 10% of the fare up to 10 days before departure. If the increase is more than 10%, that, too, is a major change, giving you the right to a refund. Prices may not be increased within 10 days of departure.

DISCOUNT TRAVEL SOURCES: An excellent source of information on economical travel opportunities is the *Consumer Reports Travel Letter,* published monthly by Consumers Union. It keeps abreast of the scene on a variety of fronts, including package tours, rental cars, insurance, and more, but it is especially helpful for its coverage of air fares, offering guidance on all the options from scheduled flights on major or low-fare airlines to charters and discount sources. For a year's subscription, send $37 to Consumer Reports Travel Letter, Subscription Dept., Box 5248, Boulder, CO 80322.

Still another way to take advantage of bargain air fares is open to those who have a flexible travel schedule. A number of organizations, usually set up as travel clubs and functioning on a membership basis, routinely keep in touch with travel suppliers to help them dispose of unsold inventory at the last minute at discounts of between 15% and 60%. A great deal of the inventory consists of complete tour packages and cruises, but some clubs offer air-only charter seats and, occasionally, seats on scheduled flights. Members pay an annual fee and receive the toll-free number of a telephone hot line to call for information on imminent trips. In some cases, they also receive periodic mailings with information on trips for which there is more advance notice. Despite the suggestive names of the clubs providing these services, last-minute travel does not necessarily mean that you cannot make plans until literally the last minute. Trips can be announced with as little as a few days or as much as two months' notice, but the average is from one to four weeks before departure. It does mean that your choice at any given time is limited to what is offered and, if your heart is set on a particular destination, you might not find what you want, no matter how attractive the bargains. Among these organizations are:

Discount Travel International, The Ives Bldg., Suite 205, 114 Forrest Ave., Narberth, PA 19072 (phone: 215-668-2182). Annual fee, $45 per household.

Encore Short Notice, 4501 Forbes Blvd., Lanham, MD 20706 (phone: 301-459-8020). Annual fee, $48 per household.

Last-Minute Travel Club, 132 Brookline Ave., Boston, MA 02215 (phone: 617-267-9800 or 800-LASTMIN). Annual fee, $30 per person, $35 per couple or family.

Moment's Notice, 40 E 49th St., New York, NY 10017 (phone: 212-486-0503). Annual fee, $45 per family.

On Call to Travel, 14335 SW Allen Blvd. Suite 209, Beaverton, OR 97005 (phone: 503-643-7212; members may call collect). Annual fee, $45 per family.

Spur-of-the-Moment Tours and Cruises, 10780 Jefferson Blvd., Culver City, CA 90230 (phone: in California, 213-839-2418; elsewhere, 800-343-1991). No fee.

Stand Buys Ltd., 311 W Superior, Suite 404, Chicago, IL 60610 (phone: in Illinois, 312-943-5737 or 800-972-5858; elsewhere, 800-367-4443). Annual fee, $45 per family.

Worldwide Discount Travel Club, 1674 Meridian Ave., Miami Beach, FL 33139 (phone: 305-534-2082). Annual fee, $50 family; $35 individual.

NET FARE SOURCES: The newest notion for supplying inexpensive travel services comes from travel agents who offer individual travelers "net" fares. Defined simply, a net fare is the bare minimum amount at which an airline or tour operator will carry a prospective traveler. It doesn't include the amount that would normally be paid to the travel agent as commission. Traditionally, such commissions can run from 8% to 20% on international tickets and 10% on domestic fares — not counting significant additions that are payable retroactively when agents sell more than a specific volume of tickets or trips for a single supplier. Instead of making their income from conventional commissions, some agencies assess a fixed fee that may or may not be a bargain for travelers; it requires a little arithmetic to determine whether you're better off with a net travel agent or one who accepts conventional commissions.

McTravel Travel Services (130 S Jefferson, Chicago, IL 60606-3691; phone: 312-876-1116 in Illinois; 800-333-3335 elsewhere) is a formula-fee based agency that rebates its ordinary agency commission to the customer. For domestic flights, their agents will find the lowest retail ticket price, then rebate 10% of that price minus a $10 ticket-writing charge. The rebate percentage for international flights varies from 8% to 20%, depending on the airline selected, and the ticket-writing fee is $20. McTravel will rebate on all tickets including max-savers, super savers, and senior citizen passes. Available seven days a week, reservations should be made far enough in advance to allow the tickets to be sent by first-class mail as extra charges accrue for special handling, and there may also be charges for reservations that require a considerable amount of research. It's possible to economize further by making your own airline reservation, then asking *McTravel* only to write/issue your ticket. For travelers who live outside the Chicago area, business may be transacted by phone, and purchases may be charged to a credit card.

CONSUMER PROTECTION: Consumers who feel that they have not been dealt with fairly by an airline should make their complaints known. Begin with the customer service representative at the airport where the problem occurs. If he or she cannot resolve your complaint to your satisfaction, write to the airline's consumer office. In a businesslike, typed letter, explain what reservations you held, what happened, the names of the employees who were involved, and what you expect the airline to do to remedy the situation. Send copies (never the original) of the tickets, receipts, and other documents that back your claims.

Until December 31, 1984, travelers with problems could also contact the Civil Aeronautics Board, which was responsible for overseeing the airline industry in a number of areas crucial to passengers. The Airline Deregulation Act of 1978, however, mandated the gradual phasing out of the CAB, though the law that put it out of business did not cancel the consumer protection regulations established by the CAB, nor its consumer assistance responsibilities. These responsibilities, along with many former CAB employees, were transferred intact to the Department of Transportation. Passengers with consumer complaints — lost baggage, compensation for getting bumped, smoking rules, charter regulations, deceptive practices by an airline — should now write to the Consumer Affairs Division, Room 10405, Office of Intergovernmental and Consumer Affairs, US Department of Transportation, 400 Seventh St., SW, Washington, DC 20590, or call the office at 202 366-2220. DOT personnel stress that consumers still should initially direct their complaints to the airline that provoked them.

To avoid more serious problems, charter flights and tour packages should *always* be chosen with care. When you consider a charter, ask your travel agent who runs it and carefully check out the company. The Better Business Bureau in the company's home city can tell you the number of complaints, if any, lodged against it in the past. As stressed above, protect yourself with trip cancellation and interruption insurance, which can help safeguard your investment if you or a traveling companion is unable to make the trip and must cancel too late to receive a full refund from the company providing your travel services (this is advisable whether you're buying a charter flight alone or a tour package for which the airfare is provided by charter flight or scheduled flight). Some travel insurance policies have an additional feature to cover the possibility of default or bankruptcy on the part of the tour operator or airline, charter or scheduled — no longer a remote one, given estimates that some 50 commercial passenger airlines of all sorts have ceased operations since the advent of airline deregulation in 1978.

Should this type of coverage be unavailable to you (state insurance regulations vary, there is a wide difference in price, and so on), your best bet is to pay for airline tickets and tour packages with a credit card. The federal Fair Credit Billing Act permits purchasers to refuse payment for credit card charges where services have not been delivered, so the onus of dealing with the receiver for a bankrupt airline falls on the credit card company. Do not rely on another airline to honor the ticket you're holding, since the days when virtually all major carriers subscribed to a default protection program that bound them to do so are long gone. Some airlines may voluntarily accommodate the stranded passengers of a fellow carrier, but this is now an entirely altruistic act.

Traveling by Cruise Ship

There was a time when travel by ship was expensive, time-consuming, and utterly elegant. Cruise travel today is still the most leisurely way to get to, and through, the Caribbean islands, but it is no longer the province of the leisured classes only. To be sure, cruises and cruise liners are luxurious, but the majority of Caribbean sailings today are designed for people of moderate income — prices are reasonable and cruises last no more than 1 or 2 weeks.

Some of these cruises still sail from New York, but many more sail from such places as Port Everglades (Fort Lauderdale), Miami, San Juan, New Orleans, Los Angeles, and San Francisco. Moreover, to make them more accessible to people living anywhere on the continent, the cruise lines offer fly/cruise, rail/sail, and other plans that cut the cost of travel between your home and the port of departure considerably.

More important, cruise lines promote a "total vacation" concept for individual sailings. They seek to convey the idea that a cruise ship is a self-contained resort offering transportation, accommodations, meals (practically around the clock), entertainment, a full range of social activities, sports and recreation, sea travel, sightseeing (at the ports of call), and a "get away from it all" vacation in the sun.

And it is; a cruise offers all of these facilities. But the variety of cruises is tremendous, and the quality, while generally high, varies depending on shipboard services, the tone of shipboard life, the cost of the cruise, and itineraries. Herewith, a rundown on what to expect from a cruise, a few suggestions on what to look for and arrange when purchasing one, and some representative prices to different destinations.

CRUISE LINES: Most of the ships offering regular cruises to Bermuda and to ports in the Bahamas and the Caribbean are now structured for 1- and 2-week sailings. On an average, they accommodate from 500 to 750 passengers and provide a range of facilities, food, and entertainment that will keep shipboard life sufficiently varied from day to day so that the passengers won't feel they're confined to a ritual. Passengers who don't want to participate in what may be an overwhelming variety of activities can always find privacy on a less active deck or in a lounge, bar, or their own cabins.

Below is a list of cruise lines and ships that offer 3- and 4-night trips to the Bahamas and 1- to 2-week sailings to Bermuda, the Bahamas, and the Caribbean from US or island ports.

Admiral Cruise Line (from Florida): *Emerald Seas* (from Los Angeles)

Bermuda Star Line (from Florida, New Orleans, New York, and San Diego): *Bermuda Queen, Bermuda Star, Canada Star, Veracruz*

Carnival (from Florida): *Carnivale, Celebration, Festivale, Holiday, Jubilee, Mardi Gras, Tropicale*

Chandris (from Miami, New York, and San Juan): *Amerikanis, Galileo, Victoria*

Commodore (from Florida): *Caribe I*

Costa (from Florida and San Juan): *Carla C., Costa Riviera, Daphne*

Cunard (from New York, Florida, the West Coast, St. Thomas, and San Juan): *Cunard Countess, Cunard Princess, Queen Elizabeth 2, Sagafjord, Sea Goddess, Vistafjord*

Dolphin (from Florida): *Dolphin*

Exploration Cruise Lines (from San Juan): *Explorer Starship*

Holland America Line (from Florida): *Nieuw Amsterdam, Noordam, Rotterdam*

Home (from Florida): *Atlantic, Homeric*

Norwegian Caribbean (from Florida and San Juan): *Norway, Skyward, Southward, Starward, Sunward II*

Paquet French Cruises (from Miami and San Juan): *Mermoz*

Premier Cruise Lines (from Florida): *Star/Ship Oceanic, Star/Ship Royale*

Princess (from Florida and San Juan): *Pacific Princess, Royal Princess, Sea Princess, Sun Princess*

Regency Cruises (from Tampa): *Regent Sea*

Royal Caribbean (from Florida, New York, and San Juan): *Nordic Prince, Song of Norway, Song of America, Sovereign of the Seas, Sun Viking*

Royal Cruise Line (from Los Angeles and San Juan): *Crown Odyssey, Royal Odyssey*

Royal Viking Line (from New York, Florida, and the West Coast): *Royal Viking Sea, Royal Viking Sky*

Sitmar (from Florida, San Juan, and the West Coast): *Fairsea, Fairsky, Fairwind*

Sun Line (from Florida and San Juan): *Stella Solaris*

CABINS: The single determinant of the price of the cruise is the price of the cabin, which depends on its size and location. Cabin size can vary considerably on the older ships, less so on the newer or more recently modernized ones.

Basically, shipboard accommodations follow the same pricing pattern as that used in hotels. The highest-priced units are the suites — a sitting room–bedroom combination and sometimes a small private deck that might be likened to a patio. Prices for other cabins (interchangeably called staterooms) usually follow the formula of the most expensive on the upper passenger decks, the least expensive on the lower ones. In addition, the outside cabins with portholes facing the water are more desirable (hence, costlier) than inside cabins. Single accommodations are more expensive on a per-person basis than double. If you're traveling alone but want to reduce the cost by sharing a double cabin, be prepared to wait for a confirmed booking until the ship line finds another person of the same sex willing to share quarters. (The cabin price also increases if the cabin has a bathtub, as distinct from a shower. A bathtub will add $50 or more per week to the cruise fare per person.)

All cruise lines provide brochures for each ship in their fleet, as well as a brochure that includes a deck plan showing the location of each cabin and a scale of rates on any scheduled cruise. In order to get a specific cabin (and cruise fare), make your reservation as soon as possible after the cruise is announced. You may select your cabin at the time of the booking; but if it's not available you'll have to wait until the cruise line gives you a list of alternate spaces that they consider closest in price, room size, and location to your original request.

FACILITIES AND ACTIVITIES: You may not use your cabin very much. Organized shipboard activities are geared to keep you busy, particularly on the shorter cruises. A standard schedule might consist of daytime visits to cruise ports or (when at sea) swimming, sunbathing, and numerous other outdoor recreations. Evenings are devoted to leisurely dining, lounge shows or movies, bingo and other organized games, gambling, dancing, bar-hopping, and a midnight buffet. Your cruise fare includes all of these activities — except the cost of drinks.

All cruise ships have at least one major social lounge, a main dining room, several bars, an entertainment room that may double as a discotheque for late dancing, an exercise room, indoor games facilities, at least one pool, and shopping facilities that can range from a single boutique to an arcade. Still others have gambling casinos and/or slot machines, card rooms, libraries, children's recreation centers, indoor pools (as well as one or more on open decks), separate movie theaters, and private meeting rooms. Open deck space should be ample, because this is where most passengers spend their days at sea.

Usually there is a social director and staff to organize and coordinate activities. Evening entertainment is provided by professionals. Movies are mostly first-run and drinks are moderate in price (or should be) because a ship is exempt from local taxes when at sea.

Shore excursions at the various ports of call generally are not included in the cruise price, although some lines now list them in their brochures so that passengers may book them when making a cruise reservation. Most shore excursions are half-day trips and range between $15 and $30. Those including lunch or dinner ashore or the use of special equipment will be more. Most excursions can be purchased aboard ship until the day before docking at the port where the trips take place. If you haven't visited a particular port before, the basic sightseeing tour is a good way to get oriented.

To prepare for possible illness, travelers should get a prescription from their doctors for pills or stomach pacifiers to counteract motion sickness. All ships with more than 12 passengers have a doctor on board and facilities for handling sickness or medical emergencies.

MEALS: Evening meals are taken in the main dining room, where tables are assigned according to the passengers' preferences. Tables usually accommodate from two to ten; specify your preference when you book your cruise. If there are two sittings, you can also specify which one you want at the time you book or, at the latest, when you board the ship. Later sittings are usually more leisurely. Breakfast is frequently available in your cabin as well as in the main dining room. For lunch, many passengers prefer the buffet offered on deck, usually at or near the pool, but again, the main dining room is available. If you're in port and having a meal ashore, you pay your own tab.

DRESS: Most people pack too much for a cruise on the assumption that daytime wear should be chic and every night is a big event. Comfort is a more realistic criterion.

Daytime wear on most ships is decidedly casual. For women, a coverup worn over a bathing suit will serve properly through breakfast, swimming, sunbathing and deck activities, lunch, and early cocktails without any change. For men, shorts (with swim trunks underneath) and a casual shirt will be appropriate on deck or in any public room. Bare feet and swimsuits are usually proscribed in the dining room.

Evening wear for most cruises is dressy-casual. Formal wear is not necessary for 1-week cruises, optional for longer ones. There aren't many nights when it's expected. Most ships have a Captain's cocktail party the first or second night out and a farewell dinner near the end of the cruise. Women should feel comfortable in summery hostess gowns, cocktail dresses, or stylish slacks. (To feel completely secure, you may want to pack one very dressy item.) Jackets and ties are always preferred for men in the evening, but a long-sleeved, open-necked shirt with ascot or scarf is usually an acceptable substitute.

TIPS: Tips are a strictly personal expense, and you *are* expected to tip — in particular your cabin and dining room stewards. Allow $2.50 a day for each steward (more if you wish), and additional sums for very good service. (*Note:* Tips should be paid by each individual in a cabin, whether there are one, two, or more.) Others who may merit tips are the deck steward who sets up your chair at the pool or elsewhere, the wine steward in the dining room, porters who handle your luggage (tip them individually at the time they assist you), and any others who provide you with personal service. On some ships you can charge your bar tab to your cabin; throw in the tip when you pay it at the end of the cruise. Smart travelers tip twice during the trip: about midway through the cruise (to put a little extra pocket money in the hands of the crew, who are going ashore just like the passengers and like to shop as well) and at the end. In all, expect to distribute about 15% of your total fare in tips. Holland America Line, for example, has a no-tipping-required policy. You are not penalized by the crew for not tipping, though, naturally, you aren't penalized for tipping either. If you can restrain yourself, it is better not to tip on those few ships that discourage it. However, never make the mistake of not tipping on the majority of ships, where it is a common, expected practice.

SELECTING A CRUISE: Your basic criteria should be where you want to go, the time you have available, how much you want to spend, and the kind of environment that suits your style and taste (in which case price is an important determinant). Rely on the suggestions of a travel agent, but be honest with the agent (and with yourself) in describing the type of social structure to which you're accustomed. Ask suggestions from friends who have been on cruises; if you trust their judgment, they should be able to suggest a ship on which you'll feel comfortable.

Absolutely the best way to obtain objective information about the cruise ships sailing into Caribbean waters is to deal with a travel agent who specializes in cruise bookings. Fortunately, this is as easily done as said. Contact the National Association of Cruise Only Agents (NACOA), PO Box 7209, Freeport, NY (phone: 516-378-8934). They will provide the name of a member agency near your home.

Don't overlook the fly/cruise arrangements. If you're not in the general vicinity of the port from which a particular cruise departs, be aware that almost all 1- and 2-week cruises have some kind of fly/cruise arrangement for getting you there. This simply involves a scheduled round-trip plane connection from your city to the city or port of departure, along with transfers between plane and ship. Most cruise brochures spell out these arrangements in detail, giving the additional price (often considerably less than regular air fare) from various cities. These brochures and additional information are available directly from the cruise lines or from travel agents.

The "Live Aboard" cruise, such as the kind offered from New York to Bermuda, is so called because the passenger uses the ship for accommodations, meals, etc., even when the vessel is docked at port for several days. Similar cruises are available to the Bahamas from both New York and Florida.

Caribbean cruises range anywhere from 6 to 16 days, and a major attraction, aside from warm weather, is the variety of ports a ship will visit. These can include the

English-, Dutch-, French-, and Spanish-accented islands as well as the US possessions. The 1-week cruises stop at an average of four different ports. Those sailing out of Florida route their itineraries through the upper Caribbean, usually stopping at St. Thomas and/or San Juan and two other ports or islands, the most popular being Nassau, Haiti, the Dominican Republic, St. Martin, and Jamaica. The 2-week cruises out of Florida will average eight or nine port calls. The additional time permits a ship to span the entire Caribbean, which means additional port cities in either Colombia or Venezuela, one of the Netherlands Antilles islands, and a half-dozen more along the eastern archipelago. Ships sailing out of San Juan on a regular basis are able to stop at four or five southern ports during a week's sailing.

Caribbean cruises usually travel at night and arrive in the morning at the day's port of call. Passengers are free to do what they please on shore provided they return in time for the ship's departure in the evening. This can entail having lunch in town, sightseeing, shopping, or perhaps going to a beach on the island.

Trans–Panama Canal cruises are offered by several lines with ships sailing between San Francisco/Los Angeles and San Juan/Port Everglades. One-way routings through the Canal are mostly timed for 14 days and may include two port calls on the Pacific coast of Mexico and another four in the Caribbean. Return is by air, a fly/cruise arrangement that is usually part of the cruise price.

Traveling by Chartered Boat

 Once you are in the islands, few travel experiences are more exhilarating than sailing on your own, or with a crew, among the islands of the Caribbean. An immense variety of private vessels may be chartered (rented) by anyone seeking an authentic sea experience. Vessels are available for couples, groups (usually up to a maximum of 6 or 8), and sometimes for individuals willing to book on a single basis and share with whomever books the same way.

CREWED BOATS: Don't shy away because you're a neophyte. It's estimated that more than 80% of travelers booking sailing holidays are inexperienced or have never before been on yachts. Most vessels can be rented with full crews as well as with sleeping accommodations, water sports and fishing equipment, meal provisions, a fully equipped bar, and other features.

There are numerous advantages to chartering a vessel with a crew. The most important is that professional sailors run the ship while the chartering group decides the itinerary (where to stop, etc.). In addition, a crewed vessel can pick up and drop off the chartering group at any island with air service — but the group must allow for the cost of the ship's getting from and to its home port.

BAREBOAT CHARTERS: Experienced seahands for whom the operation and sail of a vessel are the important objectives go by bareboat (without crew) charters, which are readily available, again in all sizes and types.

Bareboating is for experts. Parties chartering without crews should check in advance with the rental agents to learn what specific experience and qualifications are required.

PRICES: The costs vary depending upon size and accommodations as well as upon season. Most charter parties average from 4 to 6 persons at a per-person cost of from $120 to $180 per day for a vessel with a crew; $50 to $100 per person per day for a 42-foot bareboat (without food or crew). Charters are rarely available for less than a week.

Vessels accepting individual bookings are referred to as head boats because they take passengers on a head (one-by-one) basis. The number on board can range from a half dozen to 100 or more, and the cost is usually reasonable. Itineraries will usually include islands within a week's sailing distance from the home port. Again, the vessels are well stocked with living and water sports equipment.

The Bahamas and the Caribbean, by virtue of having excellent sailing waters, also have the most plentiful collections of charter craft. Among the best-known locations for rentals are Marsh Harbour in the Abacos and Nassau in the Bahamas as well as St. Thomas in the US Virgins and Road Town in the British Virgins, Antigua, Guadeloupe, St. Vincent, and Grenada.

A number of yachting specialists, in addition to their bases in these ports, maintain agents or offices in the US. Among the best known are:

Anchor Travel, PO Box 432160, S Miami, FL 33242, or 10300 Sunset Dr., Suite 411, Miami, FL 33173 (phone: 800-243-9936; in Florida, 305-598-2812)

Caribbean Sailing Yachts, Box 491, Tenafly, NJ 07670 (phone: 201-568-0390 or 800-631-1593)

The Moorings, 1305 US 19 S, Suite 402, Clearwater, FL 34624 (phone: 800-535-7289; in Florida, 813-535-1446)

Nicholson Yacht Charters, 9 Chauncy St., Cambridge, MA 02138 (phone: 800-662-6066; in Massachusetts, 617-661-8174)

West Indies Yacht Charters, 2190 SE 17th St., Suite 203, Fort Lauderdale, FL 33316 (phone: 800-327-2290; in Florida, 305-525-4123)

World Wide Yacht Charters, 145 King St. W, Toronto, Ont. M5H 1J8 (phone: 416-365-1950)

World Yacht Enterprises, Pier 62, W 23rd St. and Hudson River, New York, NY 10011 (phone: 212-929-7090)

See also the charters listed in the individual island reports.

Package Tours

A package tour is an economical and convenient arrangement that combines several travel services — transportation, accommodations, sightseeing, meals, etc. — into a one price–one booking package. The cost of the entire package is usually well below the combined price of the same services if bought independently, and the passenger is freed from the bother of making separate arrangements.

There are dozens and dozens of package tours available to the Caribbean today. They are offered by airlines, travel agencies, tour operators, and special interest groups. A typical package tour might include transportation to and from an island, accommodations for the duration of a stay, a sightseeing tour of the area, and several meals. The total price (particularly if transportation is on a charter flight) may be less than a standard round-trip economy airline ticket to the destination on a regularly scheduled flight. Travel agents are your best resource and guide for information on current package tours.

Lower prices are made possible because tour packages are designed for high-volume participation. In pricing the packages, the organizer can take advantage of lower air fares and blocks of hotel space made available at lower rates because of volume purchases. Most of these packages, however, are subject to restrictions governing the duration of a trip and require total payment by a given time before departure.

Tour packages are available in many variations, depending on who is offering the package — a travel wholesaler, airline, hotel, special interest organization — and what's included. The most common type is put together by a tour wholesaler and sold by a retail travel agency. It may or may not include air fare (but by buying a package trip, you may qualify for a lowered, "tour-basing" fare); it will include accommodations and, usually, transfers between airport and hotel plus one special feature. There may also be optional features (available at additional cost) such as meal arrangements, upgraded rooms, or car rental. Air transportation and car rental are the basic components of what are popularly advertised as fly/drive packages; these are rarer in the Caribbean than elsewhere because of the limited number of cars available. However, "a car for a day" may be a package feature on the larger islands.

Other packages may offer more extensive arrangements and may be built around activities such as golf, tennis, or scuba diving or may provide special features such as a day of sailing, a sightseeing tour, a book of discount coupons for shopping, or a free cocktail party. Still others may just cover arrangements at a specific hotel. Honeymoon packages are essentially organized by hotels, although they usually include some service features that might be termed extras.

To select the right tour package, read the brochure or descriptive literature and determine specifically what is included in the price. Brochures almost always highlight, in eye-catching type, the lowest price at which a tour is offered. However, this price may be available off-season only, during midweek, at the lowest-priced hotel in the program (which nonetheless may be quite satisfactory), or in such limited numbers that this price classification is available only on a waiting list.

Examine the price list in the brochure to find out the range of prices so as to get a generally accurate reading of the cost of the trip. And remember that prices quoted in brochures are always based upon double-occupancy accommodations. The price listed is for *each* of two people. If you travel alone, the single surcharge can be up to 55% more (see *Hints for Single Travelers,* in this section). Also note that when the price listed includes round-trip transportation, departure is from a specific city; add the cost of round-trip transportation from your home to the departure city to get the total cost of the package. Finally, read the responsibility clause (in fine print) to find out what the tour operator is — and is not — liable for. In reading the brochure, ask yourself the following questions:

1. Does the tour include air fare or other transportation, sightseeing, meals, transfers, taxes, baggage handling, tips, or any other services? Do you want all these services?
2. If the brochure indicates that "some meals" are included, does this mean a welcoming and farewell dinner, two breakfasts, or every evening meal? It makes a difference.
3. What classes of hotels are offered?
4. Do you get a refund if you cancel? (If not, be sure to obtain cancellation insurance.)
5. Can the operator cancel if too few people join?

Read the responsibility clause on the back page. Here the tour operator usually reserves the right to change services or schedules as long as you are offered equivalent service; this clause also absolves the operator of responsibility for circumstances beyond human control such as floods, famines, or injury to you or your property.

Because of the many different types of tour packages and their almost unlimited availability from cities throughout North America, the best guide for finding a suitable package is a good travel agent. The agent should be able to tell you what's available for the island you want to visit at the time you want to go and at a price that fits your budget.

The following examples of tour packages to or at island destinations are indicative of the variety of programs available, the range of prices, and the different special interest arrangements that can be included. All prices are subject to revision by the package organizer. All can be booked through any travel agent. Note that most — not all — are for off-season periods.

Bahamas–Freeport, Grand Bahama – Three-night honeymoon package, *Bahamas*

Princess Resort and Casino. Includes *Tower* or *Country Club* accommodations with champagne, souvenir photo, welcoming rum punch, $50 discount booklet, cable TV, sightseeing tour of Princess estate, transportation to Princess Beach, taxes and tips. $148 per person for the first 3 nights; each additional night, $46.

Bermuda – A golf package, the Southampton Princess Royal Tee Special, includes 3 nights' accommodations with 4 days' unlimited golf on the 18-hole, par-3 Executive Course, with golf cart; 2 rounds of golf on your choice of *Port Royal* or *Belmont* hotel courses; breakfast and dinner daily, rum swizzle, 10% discount at pro shop, admission to the evening show plus 2 drinks, glass-bottom-boat cruise, round-trip transfers, and all taxes and gratuities. Rate is about $605 per person. The *Sonesta Beach* hotel's honeymoon package, for $1,453 and up per couple, includes 6 nights' accommodations, dining in the Port Royal dining room, bottle of wine at dinner, one breakfast in bed, souvenir photo, rum swizzle, champagne party, moped for one day, dinner (including gratuities) at either of the hotel's other 2 fine restaurants, and one free admission to the health spa for each person. Both packages are in effect April to November.

Bonaire – One-week divers' package at the *Flamingo Beach* hotel. Includes 7 nights' air-conditioned accommodations, daily breakfast and dinner, transfers, welcome drink, use of basic scuba gear (bring or rent regulator, mask, fins), six dive trips, taxes, and porterage. Priced from about $859 (April to December).

Club Med – Most week-long package prices do not include air fare but cover all sports activities, land features (except bar drinks and sundries), and meals with wine. The club location list includes Martinique (Buccaneer's Creek), Guadeloupe (Caravelle), the Bahamas (Paradise Island, Eleuthera), Mexico (Cancún, Playa Blanca, Sonora Bay, Ixtapa), the Dominican Republic, plus the island of Providenciales (Provo) in the Turks and Caicos (Turkoise) and in Bermuda (St. George's Cove); the club in Haiti is currently closed. Accommodations are in simple, colorful, air-conditioned rooms with private baths. Most Caribbean "villages" have space for about 500 to 700 guests. Club Meds are erroneously considered exclusively swinging singles places; in fact, they're also geared to couples, families, and easygoing singles looking for an extremely friendly, casual holiday atmosphere. Prices vary with the place and season. From mid-April to mid-December, for example, you may pay about $500 to $900, excluding air fare, for a week at most Caribbean villages. Check with your travel agent or the Club's information number: 800-CLUBMED.

Cayman Islands – A dive package at the *Hyatt Regency Grand Cayman* at Britannia utilizes the resort's own full-service dive operation. The 4-day/3-night package includes 2 morning 2-tank dives, 1 1-tank afternoon dive, unlimited airfills, pac weights, belts, tanks, and air. In addition, there is a welcome cocktail, complimentary T-shirt, and 1 hour of tennis daily. Cost per person, double occupancy is about $470 in winter, $335 in summer. Nondiver rates are $130 lower.

Dominican Republic – Six hotels in Puerto Plata offer four-day packages to be taken as long weekends or linked for week-long vacations. For example, welcome drink, air-conditioned room, breakfast and dinner daily, free daytime tennis, and other sports features are included at *Puerto Plata Beach Resort;* all meals, water sports, horseback riding, and tennis are included at *Heavens.* Both of these packages include round-trip air fare. Priced from about $489 to $629 (winter season); week-long resort stays also available.

Jamaica – One-week vacation package at an all-inclusive club-type resort in a choice of three different locales — Ocho Rios (couples), Negril (singles or couples), and Montego Bay (couples). Includes 7 nights' air-conditioned room, transfers, unlimited bar drinks, unlimited use of sports equipment and facilities (windsurfing, snorkeling, scuba diving, tennis), nightly entertainment, taxes, and service charges. From about $670 for a single to about $1,600 per couple for a room during summer season.

Martinique, Guadeloupe, St. Martin, and St. Barthélemy – One-week vacation package. Includes 7 nights' air-conditioned room with private bath, welcome drink, full American breakfast, a bottle of rum or wine, 10% tax and service charge, plus one buffet dinner with show (Martinique), one dinner with champagne (Guadeloupe), airport transfers (St. Barts); discounts on car rental, taxes, service charges, and special feature according to island. "Fête Française" prices from about $263 to $893 per person (double occupancy) on all islands, summer season.

Puerto Rico – One-week golf package at the *Hyatt Dorado Beach* hotel. Includes transfers, 7 nights' air-conditioned accommodations, 3 full meals daily with exchange dining at the *Hyatt Cerromar Beach* hotel with gratuities, greens fees for four 18-hole Robert Trent Jones courses, unlimited tennis, bicycles for an hour daily, and a full guest-activities program ranging from water aerobics to casino lessons; cocktail party, too. Priced from about $387 per person, double occupancy, from June to October; slightly higher April through May and November to mid-December.

St. Kitts – One-week vacation package at the *Jack Tar* hotel includes 7 nights' accommodations, 3 meals daily, round-trip transfers, unlimited drinks, sports, tennis, greens fees, sailing, windsurfing, waterskiing, taxes and gratuities. Winter season rate from about $1,015 per person; summer $910.

Preparing

Calculating Costs

Accurately estimating what a trip will cost is always difficult. Aside from the basic costs (transportation, hotels, meals), there are important variables such as price changes by season, the comfort and level of luxury you prefer, and the duration of the trip. However, most travelers will find that a vacation to Bermuda, the Bahamas, or the Caribbean will cost less than the equivalent time spent in Europe — the most common region for comparison — since the islands and areas described in this book are essentially low-key, low-activity destinations, rather than centers for sightseeing, side trips, and entertainment.

To offer some idea of costs in advance, sample fares and prices are listed below for the major components of your trip — air transportation, hotel accommodations, and car rentals are also included. Entries in the individual island reports in ISLAND-BY-ISLAND HOPPING also give specific price information on activities, facilities, hotels, and restaurants. Literature available from tourist offices and travel agencies will help you estimate some of the other expenses you're likely to incur after you arrive, particularly recreation fees, such as the cost for using golf courses, renting scuba equipment, etc. Also, you should allow sums for local transportation (if you don't rent a car), personal shopping, and tips. The total of all these elements should approximate the cost of your vacation, or at least give you a starting point for determining how you want to allocate your vacation funds.

TRANSPORTATION COSTS: "Flux" is too mild a term to describe the state of air fares since deregulation. However, air travel is still generally the least flexible major element in a vacation budget. Fares for regularly scheduled flights do drop (but not much) in the off-season: mid-April to mid-December in the Bahamas and the Caribbean, November through February in Bermuda. Charter fares, most often built into a total package plan, are usually the lowest available. Weekend travel costs more than midweek travel by about $20 to $50 per person per flight. Excursion fares mean savings if you can fit a given time frame; these and reduced tour-basing fares (for which you qualify by booking a package or ground arrangements of a set value) mean savings on travel to the most popular island destinations. But since the CAB virtually threw out the rule book, special promotional fares can be offered almost anytime. So check each airline serving your destination (ask specifically about excursion and tour-basing prices), and, to guard against human and computer error, *triple* check the price quoted by the airline you pick before making a final booking.

ACCOMMODATION COSTS: There is usually a wide spread in the types and prices of hotels on the islands throughout the year. Moreover, costs for accommodations can be substantially lower (about 10% in Bermuda, 25% to 50% in the Bahamas and the Caribbean) during the off-season (see *When to Go,* in this section).

The most economical arrangements are charter packages that combine low-cost air fares with accommodations (usually without meals, although meal plans are available). Such packages have a number of qualifications governing their availability and should be investigated carefully before purchase.

DETERMINING A BUDGET: You can simplify the entire cost-computing procedure if you make reservations through a travel agent. An experienced and conscientious agent will give you an accurate appraisal of what you'll probably spend in addition to providing information or literature on less specific expenses, such as recreational activities, taxi fares, and shopping bargains at island stores.

The following prices are approximate, but they have been computed to give you a reasonable and realistic range of what you can expect to spend for the services and facilities described. In the case of air fares, all rates quoted are round-trip; midweek rates mean that you must travel to and from the destination between Monday and Friday. Hotel prices quoted, unless otherwise specified, are per person for two in a room.

Bahamas – Round-trip plane fares from New York are from $365 weekdays and from about $411 weekends during the high season. Lodging prices vary according to the island, with hotel packages representing the most convenient booking arrangements. The following are typical double-room prices for 1 week (7 nights' accommodations) without meals: in the Nassau/Paradise/Cable Beach area, about $350 to $1,400; in Freeport/Lucaya, about $360 to $735; in the Family Islands, from about $300 including breakfasts at a moderately priced beach resort to about $2,000 including breakfasts and dinners at an exclusive country-club–like establishment.

Car rentals in Nassau and Freeport range from $48 to $125 per day and from $288 to $720 weekly with unlimited mileage.

Bermuda – Round-trip 21-day excursion air fare from New York is about $314 up midweek and about $340 up weekends during peak season (May through October). Rates the rest of the year are 5% to 7% less, with special round-trip tour-basing fares also available. (A tour-basing fare is offered only in conjunction with accommodation packages.)

Peak season hotel rates may start as early as March 1, but in most hotels it begins on April 1. Typical per-person daily rates during peak season run from $49 EP (European Plan, without meals) at a small Hamilton hotel to $135 up MAP (Modified American Plan, which includes breakfast and one other meal, usually dinner) at the *Southampton Princess*.

A few of the hotel dining rooms are considered among the best eating establishments on the islands. There are also a number of restaurants and snack bars. If you plan on taking lunches and dinners out, estimate roughly $40 to $75 per day per person.

Martinique – Peak-season round-trip excursion air fares from New York are about $604 midweek, $674 weekends; lower tour-basing fares apply if you book a package. The range of hotels is extensive, with some in or around the capital at Fort-de-France, more across the bay at Pointe du Bout. Rates on a room for two range from about $80 to $200 in the winter season, from $60 to $110 mid-April to mid-December. Most prices include Continental breakfasts, with most of the larger hotels including full American buffet breakfasts in their rates. If you take meals on your own, estimate $35 to $40 per person per day as a minimum.

Netherlands Antilles – Round-trip air fares start at about $555 from New York and from about $354 from Miami during peak season, with numerous promotional and tour-basing fares, usually lower during most of the rest of the year.

Aruba has a number of good hotels, most of them along the western beach-lined coast. During the peak winter months, daily rates per room range from about $85 to $280. Other months, the range is $60 to $190. The above rates are without meals, although the hotels all have flexible meal plans. For MAP add about $36 per person per day during peak season, a few dollars less during the rest of the year.

US Virgin Islands – Typical round-trip fares during the peak winter months range from approximately $472 up from northeastern US cities, $730 up from the Midwest, $769 up from the West Coast, and $541 up from Texas; tour-basing fares run about 25% less.

Hotel rates for two persons sharing accommodations without meals during peak season range from about $45 at a small hotel in Charlotte Amalie or Christiansted to about $395 for a deluxe beachside double at a luxury resort. For MAP plans, add $30 to $40 per person. All these rates are per day. During the off-season, hotel rates are as much as 40% less.

Restaurants are numerous in St. Thomas and St. Croix but are on the expensive side. If you take all your meals out, allow at least $40 a day.

Car rental facilities are also numerous. Peak-season rates are $40 and up a day in St. Thomas and $220 up weekly with unlimited mileage; $36 up daily and $205 up weekly in St. Croix.

Planning a Trip

123 There are those of us who make lists and those who don't. Even if you include yourself in the latter category, preferring free-form, unstructured, "let anything happen" vacations to those with itineraries and schedules, you should nonetheless consider the advantages of at least a certain degree of planning. It is generally agreed that the more attention you pay to travel arrangements before you leave, the less likelihood there is of being confronted with unexpected expenses, delays, or the need to seek out alternate plans because of unforeseen developments. Even if you resolutely oppose list-making in any form, you should take the time to consider what you want to do during your vacation, where you want to go, how you would like to get there, and how much you want to spend. In addition, you should reflect on the following:

1. How much time will you have for the complete vacation, and how much of that time are you willing to spend actually traveling?
2. What kinds of activities (sports, hobbies, or other interests) do you want to participate in during your vacation? Ask yourself what will provide an enjoyable change from your normal routine.
3. What time of year are you going?
4. How much money do you want to spend?

At the same time, consider the following: How much comfort do you need? Do you want to be completely independent or would you prefer the scheduled reliability of a tour? How much responsibility do you want? Will you consider a package trip?

There is plenty of travel information on the Caribbean available in the United States. You can pick up literature from travel agencies, tourist offices, airlines, and cruise ship offices. Make certain any hotel literature includes a list of room rates and meal plans. For a list of places where you can get information on particular countries, see *Island Tourist Offices,* in this section, and the *Sources and Resources* section of the individual island reports in ISLAND-BY-ISLAND HOPPING.

Plan ahead. If it applies to your schedule, pay particular attention to the dates when off-season rates go into effect. For instance, if you can travel anytime during April, a trip after the 15th may reduce the cost of your hotel accommodations in the Caribbean by 30% to 50%, compared to the rates at the beginning of the month. Weather, facilities, and service don't change much in those few short weeks. Off-season rates are frequently lower for car rentals and other facilities, too, although the reduction is not as radical. In general, it is a good idea to beware of holiday weeks or weekends, unless you make plans well in advance. Very often, rates at hotels are higher during these periods and rooms are heavily booked. Service is apt to be under par unless more staff people are employed for the holidays, since the regular bellmen, maids, dining room personnel, and others are catering to a full house instead of being able to provide personal attention to individual guests. If you are traveling by plane and want to benefit from savings offered through charter flights to certain destinations (see *Traveling by Plane*), it is advisable to make reservations in advance. Even during low season it is a good idea to book ahead.

If you make your own arrangements, you can book your hotel room by corresponding directly with the establishment. However, this is the most inefficient method because of the time needed for the mail to travel back and forth. Until you receive a reply, you will not know if your reservation has been confirmed. You can also contact many island hotels through their US representatives, listed under Hotels — Out of Town in the yellow pages; many firms and major reservation services — to which a number of chains and large hotels subscribe — have toll-free (800) telephone numbers. Or you may dial direct to islands with 809 area codes or place operator-assisted calls for more costly, but more immediate, results. Airlines have toll-free telephone numbers, too; if an airline is not listed in the phone book, call toll-free information: 800-555-1212. If you use a car rental firm's toll-free number, request written confirmation of your reservations. The car rental firm should be able to mail it to you before you leave the States. Be sure you get a receipt for any deposit.

It saves a lot of time and energy if you let a travel agent make all reservations and arrangements for you. Except when cables or long-distance phone calls are necessary or when you pick a hotel that pays no commission, it won't cost you any extra money and may even save you some. There is no charge for these services, and often a travel agent can advise you of package programs that incorporate your basic requirements and cost less than individual arrangements.

Before leaving, make a special effort to find out what the weather is like at your destination during the time of year you'll be visiting. It may help you to decide what to buy as well as what to include in your wardrobe. It is also a good idea to read about the island's history, culture, people, food specialties, and major places of interest — especially if you are visiting for the first time.

In addition to taking care of services such as telephone, gas, electricity, that may need to be temporarily disconnected during your absence, it is a good idea to attend to the following household details:

1. Arrange for mail to be forwarded, held at the post office until your return, or picked up daily at your home. It is a good idea to ask someone to check your door from time to time to pick up unexpected deliveries. Thieves are quick to notice telltale piles of brochures, leaflets, packages, etc., which are, in themselves, announcements that no one is home.
2. Cancel all deliveries (newspapers, milk, etc.).
3. Arrange for the lawn to be mowed at the same time as if you were home.
4. Arrange for pets to be taken care of.
5. Etch your social security number on all appliances; it reduces their attractiveness to thieves and aids the police in identification in case of theft.
6. Leave your itinerary and house key with a friend or relative, and notify the police that you are leaving. Let them know with whom you have left the itinerary and key.
7. Empty the refrigerator and lower the thermostat.
8. Be sure that all doors, windows, and garage doors are securely locked.

It is also advisable to install variable timers that switch lights and the television on and off several times in different rooms. This helps discourage thieves, too.

For your own protection, it is a good idea to make copies of a list of your valuables, including the serial numbers of traveler's checks and credit card numbers. Leave one copy at home and take the others in your pocket, purse, and luggage. When you label your luggage, put your name and address both inside and outside your suitcases. Airlines will not accept unlabeled luggage, but you may use a tag that keeps your address covered as long as it is accessible.

Last but not least: Check to make sure you have your tickets and travel documents. If you are traveling by air, check to see that your ticket has been filled in correctly. The left side of the ticket should have a list of each stop you will make (even if you are only stopping to change planes), beginning with your departure point. Be sure that the list is correct, and count the number of carbons to see that you have one for each plane you will take. If you have confirmed reservations, be sure that the column marked Status says "OK" beside each flight. Have in hand vouchers or proofs of payment for any reservations paid in advance. This includes hotels, transfers to and from the airport, sightseeing, car rentals, special events, etc.

Finally, if you are traveling by plane, call to confirm your flight. While this is not required on domestic flights (as it is on international flights), it is always advisable.

How to Pack

The best thing about packing for a warm climate is that you don't have to pack much. Just how much, however, depends more on what you plan to do than where you plan to go. As a first step, find out about the general weather conditions — temperature, rainfall, seasonal variations — at your destination. This information is included in the individual island reports in ISLAND-BY-ISLAND HOPPING; other sources of information are airlines, travel agents, and government tourist offices (see *Island Tourist Offices,* in this section).

If you are going to Bermuda between April and October, you'll want to take summer-weight clothes, plus light wraps for occasional cool evenings; during the rest of the year, pack clothing that would be suitable for the spring and fall months in the northern part of the US. Evenings are often cool enough to require sweaters, even during the summer. Topcoat temperatures prevail from mid-November to mid-March.

For the Bahamas and other islands, take spring or summer clothing during the peak season (late October through early April). Women should add a shawl and men a sweater or light jacket as protection for the evenings during December and January, even in the southernmost areas. During the warmer, off-season months (mid-April to October) it will be hot and sticky. Pack lightweight, loose-weave fabrics. Despite the obvious advantages of wash-and-wear synthetics, natural fiber clothing is usually more comfortable. For all island destinations, jeans, shorts, at least two swimsuits, and sandals and/or espadrilles are appropriate. You can take hose or socks, but you probably won't need them. For the evenings, a colorful, casual, hostess gown will make a woman feel she's appropriately dressed anywhere, while white or light-color slacks and an open sport shirt usually suffice for a man. If you expect to spend a number of formal social evenings during your vacation, add two or three changes of clothes for those dressy occasions. At night, nicely cut pants are also quite acceptable for women; bear in mind that coordinates are a good way of altering the wardrobe without adding to the luggage content. Bring styles and colors of clothes that can be matched to give you as much variety with as few articles of clothing as possible. Drip-dry fabrics travel best, and prints look fresher longer than solids. If you will be on the move — in a plane, ship, car, or bus — give priority to loose-fitting clothes that do not wrinkle.

The idea is to get everything into the suitcase and out again with as few wrinkles as possible. Put heavy items on the bottom toward the hinges of the suitcase, so that they do not wrinkle other clothes. Candidates for the bottom layer include shoes (stuff them with small items to save space), toiletry kit, handbags (stuff them to help keep their shape), and alarm clock. Fill out this layer with things that will not wrinkle or will not matter if they do, such as socks, bathing suit, and underwear.

If you get this first, heavy layer as smooth as possible with the fill-ins, you will have a shelf for the next layer of the more easily wrinkled items, like slacks, jackets, shirts, dresses, and skirts. These should be buttoned and zipped and laid along the whole width of the suitcase, with as little folding as possible. When you do need to make a fold, do it on a crease (as with pants), along a seam in the fabric, or in a place where it will not show, such as shirttails. Alternate each piece of clothing, using one side, then the other, to make the layers as flat as possible.

On the top layer, put the things you will want at once: nightclothes, an umbrella or raincoat, or a sweater. With men's two-suiter suitcases, follow the same procedure. Then place jackets on hangers, straighten them out, and leave them unbuttoned. If they are too wide for the suitcase, fold them lengthwise down the middle, straighten the shoulders, and fold the sleeves in along the seam.

SOME PACKING HINTS: Cosmetics and any liquids should be packed in plastic bottles or at least wrapped in plastic bags and tied. Prepare for changes in the weather or for atypical temperatures; on abnormally hot or cold days, dress in layers so that as the weather changes, you can add or remove clothes as required.

Some travelers like to have at hand a small bag with the basics for an overnight stay, particularly if they are traveling by plane. Always keep necessary medicine, valuable jewelry, travel documents, and business documents in your handbag, briefcase, or hand luggage. Never check these things with your luggage. Tuck a bathing suit into your carry-on bag too; in case of interisland delays or lost luggage, it's frustrating to be without one.

Golf clubs may be checked through as luggage (most airlines are accustomed to handling them), but tennis rackets should be carried onto the plane. Scuba tanks, appropriately packed with padding and depressurized, may also go as baggage. Snorkeling gear should be packed in a suitcase, duffel, or tote bag. Check with the airline before departure to see if there is a specific regulation regarding any special equipment or sporting gear you plan to take.

It is always a good idea to add an empty, flattened airline bag or similar piece of luggage to your suitcase. It is indispensable for carrying items to the beach. Keep in mind, too, that you're likely to do some shopping, and save room for those items.

For more information on packing clothes, send a stamped, self-addressed business envelope to American Society of Travel Agents, PO Box 23992, Washington, DC 20026, for its free *Packing Tips* pamphlet.

How to Use a Travel Agent

Despite a long campaign conducted by travel agencies, some of their cleverer friends in the airline industry, and ASTA (the American Society of Travel Agents) and ARTA (American Retail Travel Agents), many people still do not recognize that most travel agents make no charge for reservation and ticket issuing services.

The reason for this, very simply, is that the agent derives most of his or her working income from commissions built into the charges for hotels, resorts, cruises, flights, auto rentals, and tours. These commissions are paid by the suppliers of these services (i.e., hotels, ship lines, airlines, etc.). Commissions are usually 7% to 12% — sometimes significantly more on greater volume — of the total cost of the service. A traveler pays only for the cost of tickets and accommodations, and not using an agent does not cut cost. There is no extra charge for the agent's services except when the communications involved (phone calls, telexes) require actual cash outlay on the agent's part. This is unlikely with packaged trips, but it may be part of the legitimate cost of setting up a more complicated independent itinerary. Ask the agent in advance so there'll be no surprises.

If you are still skeptical, it should be pointed out that you will not get a different price if you book directly with the hotel, airline, or car rental establishment. The cost will be exactly the same, whether you make your purchase from the source or the agent. There are two things to keep in mind when you approach a travel agent:

1. You'll get better service at the agent's desk if you arrive with your basic itinerary already planned — at least in your mind. The vaguer your ideas, the more difficult it is for the agent to help you resolve them. At least submit an idea of where you'd like to go and the nature of what you want to do. The agent can tell you about facilities, activities, special flights, cruises, and available packages to your destination or alternatives within the basic framework of your proposed itinerary. Then the agent can book reservations. Note that all the advance efforts are services a good agent will perform without charge to encourage your confidence and — not incidentally — establish you as a steady client. Remember that the commission system serves as an incentive for the agent. If you go in asking for suggestions on places to camp with the family car, the agent is likely to be less enthusiastic and may be reluctant to give you very much time.
2. There is always the danger that an incompetent or unethical agent will send you to the place offering the best commission rather than to the place that's best for you. It is important to deal with a travel agent you can trust.

You should choose a travel agent with the same care with which you would choose a doctor or lawyer. You will be spending a good deal of money on the basis of the agent's judgment, so you have a right to expect him or her to be informed and interested. At the moment, unfortunately, there aren't many standards within the industry to help you gauge competence or expertise. The quality of individual agents varies enormously. Only one state (Rhode Island) currently licenses agents, although others have considered such a move. While state licensing of agents cannot guarantee competence, it can at least ensure that an agent has met some minimum requirements.

Perhaps the best-prepared agents are those who have completed the 18-month course at the Institute of Certified Travel Agents and carry the initials CTC (Certified Travel Counselor) after their names. This indicates a relatively high level of expertise, but only a very small percentage of US travel agents have this certificate. An agent's membership in the American Society of Travel Agents (ASTA) can also be a useful guideline in selecting a travel agent. But keep in mind that ASTA is an *industry* organization, and it requires only that its members be licensed in those states where required, be certified to sell airline tickets, and be ready to comply with professional principles set down by the group. It does not guarantee the competence, ethics, or financial soundness of its members.

At the moment, the best way to find a travel agent is by word of mouth. If the agent (or agency) has done a good job for friends over a period of time, it probably indicates a certain level of commitment and concern. Always ask for the name of the specific agent, for it is that individual who will serve you, and quality can vary widely within a single agency.

Once you've chosen an agent, be entirely candid. Budget considerations rank at the top of the candor list, and there's no sense in wasting the agent's (or your) time poring over itineraries you know you can't afford. Similarly, if you like a fair degree of comfort, that fact should not be kept secret from your travel agent, who may assume that you wish to travel on a tight budget when that's not the case.

Hints for Handicapped Travelers

 From 35 to 50 million people in the US alone suffer from some sort of disability, and at least half this number are physically handicapped. Like everyone else today, they — and the uncounted disabled millions around the world — are on the move. More than ever before, they are demanding facilities they can use comfortably, and they are being heard. The travel industry has dramatically improved services to the handicapped in the past few years, and though accessibility is far from universal, it is being brought up to more acceptable standards.

PLANNING A TRIP: Good planning is essential: Collect as much information as you can about your specific disability and about facilities for the disabled in the Caribbean; make your travel arrangements well in advance; and specify to all services involved the exact nature of your condition or restricted mobility. The local chapter or national office of the organization that deals with your particular disability — for example, the American Foundation for the Blind or the American Heart Association — will provide the best, most up-to-date information on the subject. In addition, there are some excellent travel-oriented organizations for the disabled to help plan your trip.

Mobility International/USA (MIUSA), the US branch of *Mobility International,* a nonprofit British-based organization with affiliates in some 35 countries, offers advice and assistance to disabled travelers — including information on accommodations, access guides, and study tours. Among its publications are a quarterly newsletter and a comprehensive sourcebook, *World of Options: A Guide to International Educational Exchange, Community Service, and Travel for Persons with Disabilities.* Individual membership is $20 a year; newsletter subscription only is $10 annually. For more information, contact MIUSA, PO Box 3551, Eugene, OR 97403 (phone: 503-343-1284, voice and TTY).

Moss Rehabilitation Hospital's Travel Information Service is a service designed to help disabled travelers plan trips. It cannot make travel arrangements but, for a fee of $5 per package, it will supply information from its files on as many as three cities, countries, or special interests. Write to the Travel Information Service, Moss Rehabilitation Hospital, 12th St. and Tabor Rd., Philadelphia, PA 19141 (phone: 215-329-5715).

The *Paralyzed Veterans of America (PVA)* is a national organization that operates as an information and advocacy organization for veterans with spinal cord injuries. PVA also sponsors *Access to the Skies,* a program that coordinates the efforts of the national and international air travel industry in providing airport and airplane access for the handicapped. Membership includes several helpful publications as well as regular notification of conferences on subjects of interest to the handicapped traveler. For membership information, contact PVA/ATTS Program, 801 18th St., NW, Washington, DC 20006 (phone: 202-USA-1300).

The Society for the Advancement of Travel for the Handicapped (SATH) helps members keep abreast of developments in travel for the handicapped. Membership in SATH, a nonprofit organization whose members include travel agents, tour operators, travel suppliers, and consumers, costs $40 ($25 for students and people 65 and over), and the fee is tax deductible. SATH publishes a quarterly newsletter and can provide information on travel agents or tour operators in the US and overseas who have experience or an interest in travel for the handicapped. Send a stamped, self-addressed envelope to SATH, 26 Court St., Penthouse, Brooklyn, NY 11242 (phone: 718-858-5483).

Louise Weiss's *Access to the World: A Travel Guide for the Handicapped* (Facts on File; $16.95) provides extensive information on transportation and hotels and offers sound tips for the disabled traveler abroad. *The Wheelchair Traveler,* issued annually by Douglass R. Annand (Ball Hill Rd., Milford, NH 03055; phone: 603-673-4539), is particularly useful, with ratings of hotels and restaurants, sightseeing attractions, and airlines. It covers some Caribbean destinations and offers hints on cruising. *The Itinerary,* a travel magazine for people with disabilities, is published every other month with information on accessibility, listings of tours, news of adaptive devices, travel aids, and special services, as well as numerous general travel hints. To subscribe ($9 a year), write *The Itinerary,* PO Box 1084, Bayonne, NJ 07002-1084 (phone: 201-858-3400).

It should be noted that almost all of the material published with disabled travelers in mind deals with the wheelchair-bound traveler for whom architectural barriers are a prime concern. For travelers with diabetes, a pamphlet entitled *Your Turn to Fly* is available for 25¢ from the New York Diabetes Association, 505 8th Ave., 21st Floor, New York, NY 10018 (phone: 212-947-9707). Another, *Travel for the Patient with Chronic Obstructive Pulmonary Disease,* is available for $2 from Dr. Harold Silver, 1601 18th St., NW, Washington, DC 20009.

AIR TRAVEL: Disabled passengers should always make reservations well in advance and should provide the airline with all relevant details of their condition when doing so. These details include information on mobility, toileting, and whether airline-supplied equipment such as a wheelchair or portable oxygen will be necessary. Be sure that the person you speak with understands fully the degree of your disability — the more details provided, the more effective the help that can be given. The day before the flight, call back to make sure that all arrangements have been taken care of, and on the day of the flight, arrive early so that you can be boarded before the rest of the passengers. Carry a medical certificate with you, stating your specific disability or the need to carry particular medicine. (Some airlines require the certificate, so be sure to check the regulations of your airline well beforehand.) In most cases, you can be wheeled as far as the plane, and sometimes right onto it, in your own wheelchair; if not, a boarding chair may be used. Your own wheelchair will be folded and put in the baggage compartment and should be tagged as escort luggage to ensure that it's available at the plane immediately on landing rather than in the baggage claim area.

Passengers who use oxygen may not use their personal supply in the cabin, though it may be carried on the plane as cargo when properly packed and labeled. If you will need oxygen during the flight, the airline will supply it (there is a charge) provided you have given advance notice — 24 hours to a few days, depending on the carrier.

Several booklets describe procedures for accommodating the handicapped in flight: *Air Transportation of Handicapped Persons* explains the general guidelines that govern air carrier policies (free when requested in writing from the Distribution Unit, US Department of Transportation, Publications Section, M-443.2, Washington, DC 20590; request Free Advisory Circular #120-32); *Seeing Eye Dogs as Air Travelers* can be obtained free from the Seeing Eye, Box 375, Washington Valley Rd., Morristown, NJ 07960 (phone: 201-539-4425).

The Airport Operators Council International publishes *Access Travel: Airports,* a complete list of facilities for the handicapped at 519 airports in 62 countries, including a number of island destinations. For a free copy, write to Consumer Information Center, Access America, Dept. 571T, Pueblo, CO 81009. To help travel agents planning trips for the handicapped, this material is reprinted with additional information on tourist boards, city information offices, and tour operators specializing in travel for the handicapped (see "Tours," below) in the North American edition of the *Official Airline Guides Travel Planner,* issued quarterly by Official Airline Guides, 2000 Clearwater Dr., Oak Brook, IL 60521.

GROUND TRANSPORTATION: Perhaps the simplest solution to getting around is to travel with an able-bodied companion who can drive. Competition is fierce among rental car companies, and prices are relatively reasonable. Hand-controlled cars are virtually nonexistent in the Caribbean. If you plan far ahead, you may be able to bring your own hand controls and have them installed, but for a short vacation it is probably not worth the trouble. The manager of your hotel is generally your best source of advice on the possibility of making such arrangements. On the whole, you'd be better advised to ask him to line up a reliable car and driver for you if you are traveling alone.

TOURS: The following travel agencies or tour operators specialize in making group or individual arrangements for the handicapped traveler. Programs designed for the physically impaired are run by specialists who have traveled in advance or have thoroughly researched hotels, restaurants, and places of interest to be sure they present no insurmountable obstacles.

Evergreen Travel Service/Wings on Wheels Tours, 19505 L, 44th Ave. W, Lynnwood, WA 98036 (phone: 206-776-1184, 800-435-2288 nationwide, or 800-562-9298 in Washington State). Handles cruises, group tours, and individual arrangements for the physically disabled and the blind.

Flying Wheels Travel, 143 W Bridge St., Box 382, Owatonna, MN 55060 (phone: 507-451-5005 or 800-533-0363). Handles tours and individual arrangements for the physically disabled and the elderly.

The Guided Tour, 555 Ashbourne Rd., Elkins Park, PA 19117 (phone: 215-782-1370). Offers tours for persons with developmental and learning disabilites, and sponsors separate tours for members of the same population who are physically disabled or who simply need a slower pace.

Handi-Travel, First National Travel Corp., 300 John St., Thorn Hill, Ontario L3T 5W4, Canada (416-731-4714). Arranges tours and individual trips.

Interpretours, Ask Mr. Foster, 16660 Ventura Blvd., Encino, CA 91436 (phone: 818-788-4118 or 818-788-4515, voice and TTY). Arranges independent travel, cruises, and tours for the deaf, with an interpreter as tour guide.

Mobility Tours, 84 E 10th St., 2d Fl., New York, NY 10003 (212-353-0240). Arranges tours for both physically and developmentally disabled persons.

Travel Horizons Unlimited, 11 E 44th St., New York, NY 10017 (phone: 212-687-5121). Arranges cruises, tours, and independent travel for those who require hemodialysis.

Whole Person Tours, PO Box 1084, Bayonne, NJ 07002-1084 (phone: 201-858-3400). Publishers of *The Itinerary,* this agency's catalogue of foreign and domestic programs designed for travelers with disabilities, is available for $2.

Hints for Traveling with Children

 What better way to see the Caribbean than with the young, wide-eyed members of your family? Your children's company does not have to be a burden or their presence an excessive expense. Whether the trip is a delight or a disaster depends a great deal on how well the trip is planned for their pace and the things they enjoy.

PLANNING: Take some extra time beforehand to prepare children for travel. Here are several hints for making a trip to the Caribbean with children easy and fun.

1. Children, like everyone else, will derive more pleasure from a trip if they have knowledge of a place before they arrive. Begin their education about a month before departure, using maps, atlases, travel magazines, and travel books to make clear exactly where they will be going and how far away it is. Part of the excitement of the journey will be associating the tiny dots on the map with the very real places the children will visit a few weeks later. Keep lessons age-appropriate, light, and anecdotal.

2. Children should be in on the planning of the itinerary, and schedules should reflect some of their ideas. If they know enough about architecture and geography before they go, they will have the excitement of recognition when they arrive, and the illumination of seeing how something is or is not the way they expected it to be.

3. Familiarize the children with the currency they will be using (see *Credit and Currency*). Give them an allowance for the trip and be sure they understand just how far it will or won't go.

4. Give children specific responsibilities. When traveling, the job of carrying their own flight bags and looking after their personal things, along with other light tasks, will give them a stake in the journey. Tell them how they can be helpful checking in or out of hotels.

5. Give each child a travel diary or scrapbook to take along. Filling these with impressions, observations, and mementos will pass the time on trains and planes and help children assimilate their experiences.

PACKING: Choose your children's clothes much as you would your own. Select a basic color (perhaps different for each child) and coordinate everything with it. Plan their wardrobes with layering in mind — shirts and sweaters that can be taken off and put back on as the temperature varies. Take only drip-dry, wrinkle-resistant items that they can manage themselves and comfortable shoes — sneakers and sandals. Younger children will need more changes, but keep packing to a minimum. No one likes to carry added luggage (remember that *you* will have to manage most of it!).

Take along as many handy snacks as can be squeezed into the corners of your suitcases — things like dried fruit and nut mixes, hard candies, peanut butter, and crackers — and moist towelettes for cleaning. Don't worry if your supply of nibbles is quickly depleted. Airports and train stations are well stocked with such items, and it's fun to try foreign-made snacks.

Pack a special medical kit (see *Staying Healthy in the Islands*), including children's-strength aspirin or acetaminophen, an antihistamine or decongestant, Dramamine, and diarrhea medication. Do not feel you must pack a vacation's worth of diapers. Disposable diapers are available in almost any Caribbean drugstore. A wide selection of excellent baby foods is available in local shops and supermarkets, but you might prefer to bring the infant formula to which your baby is accustomed — in the "ready-to-feed" cans. Disposable nursers are expensive but handy. If you breast-feed your baby, there is no reason you can't continue abroad; be sure you get enough rest and liquids.

Good traveling toys for infants are the same things they like at home — high-quality, brightly colored huggables and chewables; for small children, a favorite doll or stuffed animal for comfort, spelling and counting games, and tying, braiding, and lacing activities; for older children, playing cards, travel board games with magnetic pieces, and hand-held electronic games. Softcover books and art materials (crayons, markers, paper, scissors, glue sticks, stickers) ward off boredom for children of most ages, as do radio-cassette players with headphones. Take along a variety of musical and storytelling cassettes, maybe even an extra set of headphones so two children can listen, and extra batteries. *Advice:* Avoid toys that are noisy, breakable, or spillable, those that require a large play area, and those that have lots of little pieces that can be scattered and lost.

When traveling, coordinate activities with attention spans; dole out playthings one at a time so you don't run out of diversions before you get where you're going.

BY PLANE: Begin early to investigate all available discount and charter flights, as well as any package deals and special rates offered by the major airlines. Booking up to two months in advance is sometimes required. You may find that charter plans offer no reductions for children — or at least not enough to offset the risk of last-minute delays or other inconveniences to which charters are subject. The major scheduled airlines, however, almost invariably provide hefty discounts for children. (For specific information on fares and in-flight accommodations for children, see *Traveling by Plane.*)

Request seats on the aisle if you have a toddler or if you think you will need the bathroom frequently. (Try to discourage children from being in the aisle when meals are served.) Carry onto the plane all you will need to care for and occupy your children during the flight — diapers, formula, favorite toys, books, sweaters, and so on. (Never check as baggage any item essential for a child's well-being, such as prescription medicine.) Dress your baby simply, with a minimum of buttons and snaps, because the only place you may have to change a diaper is at your seat. Your flight attendant will warm a bottle for you. For takeoffs and landings, have a bottle or pacifier on hand for an infant and some gum or hard candy for older children. This will keep everyone swallowing properly and ensure against earaches caused by rapid changes in air pressure. (Don't shush a baby who cries during takeoff or landing; he or she may *need* to yowl a bit to alleviate ear pain.) Newborn babies, whose lungs may not be able to adjust to the altitude, should not be taken on an airplane. (*Note:* Some airlines refuse to carry pregnant women in their eighth or ninth month for fear that something could go wrong with an in-flight birth. Check with the airline ahead of time. You should also consult your obstetrician about any travel plans.)

BY SHIP: Some shipping lines offer cruises that feature special activities for children, particularly during periods that coincide with major school holidays like Christmas, Easter, and the summer months. On such cruises, children usually are charged special cut-rate fares, and there are youth counselors to organize activities. Occasionally, a shipping line even offers free passage during the summer months for children under the age of 16 occupying a stateroom with two (full-fare) adult passengers. In this case, again, there are special activities for children. Your travel agent should know which cruise lines offer such programs.

ACCOMMODATIONS AND MEALS: Cabins or bungalows offer families privacy, flexibility, some kitchen facilities, and often lower costs. In many hotels large discounts are available for families who all stay in the same room. Some families find that the privacy of a separate room for the kids is well worth the extra money and prefer adjoining rooms with an inside door. In the Caribbean, many hotel chains such as the *Holiday Inn, Hilton,* and *Marriott* do not charge for children under 12 who occupy the same room as their parents; *Sherton*'s policy allows children 17 and under to stay at no charge as long as the hotel does not have to provide extra beds. In addition, a few hotels offer special youth activities programs, particularly during summer months. Detailed information can be obtained from a travel agent. A few hotels offer day-camp programs during school holiday periods. The *Hyatt Cerromar Beach* and *Hyatt Dorado Beach* hotels in Puerto Rico provide such a service, as do *Grotto Bay Beach, Elbow Beach,* and *Sonesta Beach* in Bermuda. For those nights when grownups wish to go out on the town or do something special alone during the day, most hotels can arrange for babysitters.

For more information on how to arrange alternative accommodations such as villas, apartments, and cottages, see *Rental Villas and Vacation Homes.*

THINGS TO DO: Most children have a limit of about half a day of sightseeing. They usually enjoy more of what they see if they have read or been told something about the places they are visiting.

Devote some of each day to less structured activities like swimming at a beach or pool or going to a playground or park.

Try to spend at least two nights at each stop on your tour, and find out what festivals, like pre-Lenten Carnival, will be taking place during your trip because these are especially rewarding and colorful experiences for kids. (For information on these events, see the *Special Events* section of each island in ISLAND-BY-ISLAND HOPPING.)

The greatest advantage of taking children on a Caribbean trip is that they are loved and welcomed almost everywhere. Children love the Caribbean, too. Virtually all their time may be spent outside. Beaches and water sports abound. Activities include boating, sailing, water skiing, scuba diving, snorkeling, deep-sea and offshore fishing, or just plain swimming; kids can also experience new and exciting spectator sports like soccer, rugby, or cricket.

In addition, many islands have special attractions that appeal to the young. Below is a partial list:

Anguilla – August carnival features sailboat races. Other attractions include softball and cricket matches.

Antigua – A 10-day celebration begins in late July and continues into August with steel-band contests, parades; regular cricket, soccer, netball matches on St. John's Recreation Grounds; good shallow-water snorkeling, scuba instruction. Nelson's Dockyard spellbinds young sailors.

Bahamas – Nassau surrey rides; Fort Charlotte tours; cricket, soccer, field hockey matches at Hanes Oval; Sea Floor Aquarium show; flamingos at Ardastra Gardens; Freeport's Underwater Explorers Society museum; Nassau's Coral World; Hartley's Underwater Wonderland; scuba lessons.

Barbados – Picture-taking at Careenage (island workboats, Harbour Police); *Jolly Roger* sails; ghost stories at the parish church in Christ Church (the *Moving Coffin Mystery*); pirate tales at Sam Lord's Castle; sugar history at Morgan Lewis Mill; monkey-watching at Cherry Tree Hill; meeting the flying fish fleet at Bathsheba or Oistins; beach riding in St. Michael; the Hilton bike hike.

Bermuda – Biking (pedal-powered); sightseeing (Gibbs' Hill light, St. George's, Fort St. Catherine, the ship *Deliverance,* King's Square's stocks and pillory, Bermuda Perfumery, candle factory); hookless fishing at Devil's Hole; Hamilton buggy rides; spelunking at Crystal and Leamington caves; ferry and glass-bottom boat trips; horse and carriage rides; the Blue Grotto Dolphin Show; fish-watching at the aquarium; Maritime Museum treasures; nature walks along the Bermuda Railway Trail. Pipers parade at Fort Hamilton (off-season).

British Virgin Islands – Carnival with parades, fairground festivities in early August; snorkeling at Smugglers Cove; Peter Island Yacht Club and Bitter End Yacht Club for a wide range of water sports. Little Dix Bay has holiday, summer programs.

Cayman Islands – Turtle-watching at the Cayman Turtle Farm; mailing postcards to pals from Hell; glassbottom-boat excursions; for swimmers, excellent scuba instruction, trips. Snorkeling is available at most resorts. *Atlantis* or *RLS* submarine excursions.

Grenada – Glass-bottom boat rides; snorkeling; fort-exploring; swimming and picnicking at Annandale Falls; visits to the zoo, spice factories, plantations; hiking into the rain forest; Bay Gardens.

Guadeloupe – Fort Fleur d'Epée visit; Parc Naturel exploring (nature trails, waterfalls, picnic places, Soufrière's smoking fumeroles); morning call at the market and wharves where the Îles des Saintes fishermen land; the grottoes; the pre-Columbian rock carvings in the archaeological park at Trois-Rivieres; pony excursion at Le Criolo (riding school at St. Felix); coffee plantation at La Griveliere on the Caribbean side of Bas-Terre.

Jamaica – Rafting on the Rio Grande and Martha Brae River; the Governor's Coach picnic train ride; plantation tours at Brimmer Hall, Prospect; swimming and climbing at Dunn's River Falls; Rose Hall and Annie Palmer ghost stories; bird-feeding at Rockland Station; Shaw Park Gardens and Carinosa Gardens; Good Hope Plantation (a coconut and coffee farm with marked trails for horseback riding).

Martinique – Visit to St. Pierre's Volcanic Museum, Doll Museum at Leyritz Plantation, Josephine's birthplace; horseback riding; picnic at Diamant Beach across from HMS *Diamond Rock*.

Puerto Rico – Exploration at El Morro fortress and Fort San Cristóbal; Arecibo Observatory; Río Camuy Cave Park; combined trip to El Yunque, Luquillo Beach; Icacos Island snorkel trip; ferry ride across San Juan Harbor; LeLoLai festivities.

St. Martin/St. Maarten – Live eagle show with falconer, near Pointe Pirouett.

US Virgin Islands – Each island has its festive season (April Carnival on St. Thomas, Christmas on St. Croix, July Carnival on St. John), with parades, music, and fun for all ages. St. Thomas also has the fascinating Coral World, with an underwater observation tower and aquarium, glass-bottom boat rides, catamaran picnic sails. Resorts and local companies offer fine sailing, scuba instruction. On St. John: underwater trail snorkeling at Trunk Bay; family camping at Cinnamon and Maho bays. On St. Croix: Buck Island Reef trip; Whim Greathouse.

Hints for Single Travelers

Just about the last trip in human history in which the participants were neatly paired was the voyage of Noah's Ark. Ever since, passenger lists and tour groups have reflected the same kind of asymmetry that occurs in real life, as countless individuals set forth to see the world unaccompanied (or unencumbered, depending on your outlook) by spouse, lover, friend, or relative.

There are some things to be said for traveling alone. It forces you to see more; it requires that you be self-reliant, independent, and responsible. It also necessitates that you be more outgoing, and, therefore, you tend to meet more people than you would traveling in a pair. Unfortunately, it also turns you into a second-class citizen.

For the truth is that the travel industry is not yet prepared to deal economically with people who vacation by themselves. Most travel bargains, including package tours, hotel accommodations, resort packages, and cruises, are based on *double-occupancy* rates. This means that the per-person price is offered on the basis of two people traveling together and sharing a double room. For exactly the same package, the single traveler will have to pay a surcharge, called the "single supplement," which can add 30% to 55% to the basic per-person rate.

There is obviously some method to this madness, as hotels and other tourist facilities clearly make more money from two people than one. But, understandable or not, the situation is galling for people who prefer to travel alone or simply have no choice.

Traditionally, the way to beat the system was to find a traveling companion. Recently, however, a number of alternatives have emerged. A few ship lines have begun to offer occasional special cruises for singles. Enterprising travel agents have created travel clubs and tours for single travelers 20 to 60 years old and up. Some charge minimal membership fees, others offer the service for free. But in all cases the goal is to cater to the needs of the unattached traveler or to match people for the purpose of traveling together.

Club Med, 3 E 54th St., New York, NY 10022 (phone: 800-CLUBMED, or call one of the Club Med Boutiques: in New York at 212-750-1687, or San Francisco at 415-982-4200). Operates scores of resorts in more than 25 countries and caters to the single traveler as well as couples and families. Though the clientele is often under 30, there is a considerable age mix: the average age is 37. *Club Med* has 14 resorts scattered among Bermuda, the Bahamas, and the islands of the Caribbean: one each in Bermuda, the Dominican Republic, Guadeloupe, Haiti, Martinique, St. Lucia, the Turks and Caicos; Paradise Island and Eleuthera in the Bahamas; and five in Mexico — Cancún, Ixtapa, Playa Blanca, Sonora Bay, plus the new Huatulco in the state of Oaxaca. In Cancún, along with the regular features of resort living, excursions are arranged to the major Maya ruins of the Yucatán peninsula. In a departure from its usual recipe, *Club Med* also manages several "archaeological" villas on the Yucatán — at Chichén Itzá, Uxmal, and Cobá — and on the outskirts of Mexico City — at Teotihuacán and Cholulua — that were specifically designed for people who wish to leisurely and comfortably explore the magnificent ancient ruins of the Toltec, Maya, and Aztec cultures. The Paradise Island facilities offer the special feature of 20 tennis courts on a $13 million, 21-acre resort. *Club Med* offers the single traveler a package-rate vacation with air fare, food, wine, lodging, entertainment, and athletic facilities included. The atmosphere is relaxed, the dress informal, and the price reasonable.

Singleworld, 444 Madison Ave., New York, NY 10022 (phone: 212-758-2433; 800-223-6490 in the continental US and Canada). This is more nearly a young singles agency than any of the others. Roughly half its departures are designated "under 35"; others are for "all ages." Besides organizing singles tours and placing sharers on existing packages, it also puts groups of single travelers on the 3-, 4-, and 7-day cruises of major cruise lines. Annual fee, $18.

Travel Companion Exchange, PO Box 833, Amityville, NY 11701 (516-454-0880). Publishes a bimonthly directory of singles looking for traveling companions and provides members with full-page profiles of likely partners. Membership ranges from $3 to $11 per month, depending on age category, length of membership, and level of service; a 6-month minimum enrollment applies.

Travel Mates, 49 W 44th St., New York, NY 10036 (phone: 212-221-6565). This organization for men and women of any age arranges shares on existing package tours as well as organizing group tours for its members. Annual fee, $15.

Jamaica has its own equivalent of *Club Med,* the *Hedonism II* in Negril. But the entire Negril area enthusiastically caters to fun-loving singles and outdoor enthusiasts. The atmosphere is sybaritic, and far from being a quiet island retreat, Negril is a place for active vacationers. And all along Jamaica's northern coast, hotels have begun to ease up on the singles price penalty in an attempt to lure this lucrative market.

Not all single travelers are looking for a swinging scene. Some take vacations to rest and relax, and they prefer being by themselves. Generally, people who want this quieter mode of travel have to accept that their accommodations will cost more than if they were part of a couple.

For single women traveling alone, the Caribbean is a comfortable, relatively safe choice. In picking a vacation locale, decide what you want to do, be it golfing, tennis, sunning, seashell gathering, or whatever. Then select a place where this pastime is available. Not only will you be assured of doing what you enjoy, but the people you meet are likely to be interested in the same pursuits. This helps to eliminate awkward or pressured social situations.

Hints for Older Travelers

Free to take long, leisurely vacations without the limitations of work schedules, older travelers can benefit from off-season, off-peak travel, which is usually less expensive and more pleasant than traveling in high season. Cruises in particular offer excellent service and a perfect opportunity to socialize. This form of travel is good for older people who can't or don't enjoy too much walking. Older travelers who do like to sightsee, shop, and take part in an active urban environment while vacationing will find many organized tours available. It is important that older travelers remain selective and careful in choosing both their destination and tour program — travel agents or touring agencies can easily underestimate or misjudge an older person's preferences and energy level.

DISCOUNTS: The traveler over 55 is entitled to a variety of discounts. Since rules change from place to place, inquire about discounts for transportation, hotels, concerts, movies, museums, and other activities. The *Sheraton* offers a 25% senior citizens' discount at all its properties, while *Holiday Inn*'s discounts to the elderly are at the discretion of the management of each individual hotel. Transportation savings may also be substantial through the use of off-season, midweek, and standby rates. Off-season hotel rooms are often offered at reduced rates.

In order to take advantage of these discounts, you should carry proof of your age (or eligibility). A driver's license, membership card in a recognized senior citizens' organization, or a Medicare card should be adequate.

PACKAGE PROGRAMS/GROUP TRAVEL: There are two ways of approaching group travel — through a travel agent or tour operator who specializes in this field or through membership in a senior citizens' group.

Nearly every American community of any size has a choice of senior citizens' clubs. Some are purely social; others are organized within a larger church, fraternal, or ethnic structure. Membership dues are usually low, and, while bound by group decisions, you can take an active role in planning vacations. Membership in two or more groups increases the field of choice, and membership in a larger national organization often provides a selection of prepackaged tours. Among the most active national organizations are:

American Association of Retired Persons (AARP), 1909 K St., NW, Washington, DC 20049 (phone: 202-872-4700). Travel programs in the Caribbean are almost exclusively discounted cruises. Membership is open to anyone age 50 and above, whether retired or not; dues are $5 per year or $12.50 for 3 years.

Mature Outlook, 3701 W Lake Ave., Glenview, IL 60025 (phone: 312-291-7800). Annual dues, $7.50 (individuals or couples).

National Council of Senior Citizens, 925 15th St., NW, Washington, DC 20005 (phone: for membership, 202-347-8800). Asks for an annual fee of $12 for single persons, $16 for married couples; runs tour programs for its members; and sends out a newsletter with details concerning travel and other activities.

Some travel agencies and tour operators specialize in organizing tours for older travelers. Two such agencies are *Gadabout Tours,* 700 E Tahquitz Way, Palm Springs, CA 92262 (phone: 619-325-5556; 800-521-7309 in California; 800-952-5068 elsewhere); and *Grand Circle Travel,* 347 Congress St., Suite 3A, Boston, MA 02210 (phone: 617-350-7500 or 800-221-2610). *Grand Circle* publishes a helpful free booklet entitled *101 Tips for the Mature Traveler Abroad.*

Many travel agencies, particularly the larger ones, are delighted to make presentations to help a group select destinations. A local chamber of commerce should be able to provide the names of such agencies. Once a time and place are determined, an organization member or travel agent can obtain group quotations for transportation, accommodations, meal plans, and sightseeing. Groups of 40 or more usually get the best breaks.

HEALTH: Puerto Rico and St. Thomas and St. Croix in the US Virgin Islands are the only places in the Caribbean whose doctors and hospitals will routinely honor Medicare coverage. If you have specific medical problems, bring an adequate number of prescriptions on your trip and a "medical file" carrying the following items:

1. Summary of medical history, current diagnosis
2. List of drugs to which you are allergic
3. Most recent electrocardiogram, if you have heart problems
4. Your doctor's name, address, and phone number

If you have heart disease:

1. Get a low-fat, low-cholesterol diet (which you can request from an airline in advance if you are flying).
2. Avoid altitudes above 5,000 feet (airplane cabins, of course, are pressurized).
3. If using anticoagulant drugs, carry your chart with you and have a hospital checkup every two weeks.
4. If you have a pacemaker, have it tested a month before leaving and carry basic information on the machine — serial number, manufacturer, date of implantation.

An excellent book to read before embarking on any trip, domestic or foreign, is Rosalind Massow's *Travel Easy: The Practical Guide for People Over 50,* available for $8.95 (plus $1.75 for postage and handling) from AARP Books, c/o Scott, Foresman, 1865 Miner St., Des Plaines, IL 60016 (phone: 202-728-4313 or 800-238-2300). It discusses a host of travel-related subjects, from choosing a destination to getting set for departure, with chapters on transportation options, tours, cruises (including a rundown on who's who aboard a cruise ship and whom to tip), avoiding health problems, and handling dental emergencies en route. Another excellent guide for the budget-conscious older traveler is *The Discount Guide for Travelers Over 55* by Caroline and Walter Weintz (E.P. Dutton; $7.95).

Insurance

The amount and kind of insurance you carry when you go to the islands depends in large part on your own feelings about traveling, the insurance policies you have already, and your method of transport. There are four basic types of insurance any traveler should consider in the Caribbean, though by no means are all — or any — a necessity:

1. Baggage and personal effects insurance
2. Personal accident and sickness insurance
3. Trip cancellation and interruption insurance
4. Flight insurance

If you are renting a car in the islands, automobile insurance *is* a necessity, but the required coverage will be included as part of the rental contract.

BAGGAGE AND PERSONAL EFFECTS INSURANCE: Ask your agent if baggage and personal effects are covered by your current homeowner's policy regardless of where you lose them. If not, find out about the cost and coverage of a floater to protect you on vacation. The object is to protect your bags and their contents in case of damage or theft anytime during your travels, not just while you're in flight and covered by the airline's policy. Furthermore, only limited protection is provided by the airline. For most international flights, including domestic portions, the airline's liability limit is approximately $20 per kilo ($9.07 per pound) for checked baggage and $400 per passenger for unchecked baggage. On domestic flights, the limit of liability on most airlines is $1,250 per passenger. But these limits, which should be specified in the fine print of your ticket, represent maximums and payments are not automatic; the amount paid is based on the value of your baggage and its contents.

If you are carrying goods worth more than the maximum protection provided, you should consider excess value insurance, available from the airlines for about $1 per $100 of protection provided (which can be bought at the ticket counter at time of check-in). You will need to have receipts to prove that what you are claiming exceeds the airline insurance allowance. Excess value insurance is also included in certain of the combination travel insurance policies discussed below.

One note of warning: Be sure to read the fine print of any excess value or baggage insurance policy; there are often specific exclusions such as money, tickets, furs, gold and silver objects, art, and antiquities. (Remember that ordinarily insurance companies will pay the depreciated value of the goods rather than replacement value.) To protect goods traveling in your luggage, photograph your valuables, and keep a record of the serial numbers of such items as cameras, typewriters, radios, etc. (Original purchase receipts can also be useful in later litigation with the airlines.) This will establish that you do, indeed, own the objects. If your luggage disappears en route or is damaged, deal with the situation immediately, at the airport. If an airline loses your luggage, you will be asked to fill out a Property Irregularity Report before you leave the airport. If your property disappears elsewhere, report it to the police at once.

PERSONAL ACCIDENT AND SICKNESS INSURANCE: This insures you in case of illness on the road (hospital and doctor's expenses, etc.) or death in an accident. In most cases this is a standard part of life and health insurance policies, though you should check with your broker to be sure that your policy will pay for medical expenses incurred out of the country.

TRIP CANCELLATION INSURANCE: Most package tours, cruises, and charter flights require full payment a substantial period of time in advance of departure. Although cancellation penalties vary, rarely will you get more than 50% of this money back if you are forced to cancel within a few weeks of leaving. Any refund of money paid for a charter flight canceled even well in advance may depend on your being able to supply a substitute passenger. Therefore, if you take a package tour or a charter, you should have cancellation insurance to guarantee the full refund of your money should you, a traveling companion, or a member of your immediate family get sick and force you to cancel your trip or *return home early.* The key is not to buy just enough insurance to guarantee full reimbursement in case of cancellation. The amount should be sufficient to cover the cost of having to catch up with a tour after its normal departure date or having to return home at the full economy fare if you have to forgo the return portion of a discounted or charter flight.

Cancellation insurance designed to cover a specific package is frequently offered by tour operators (and sold by the travel agent who sells you the tour). Otherwise, it can be bought through travel agents or from insurance agents as part of a combination travel insurance policy. Read any policy carefully before you buy it. Be sure it provides enough money to get you home from the farthest point on your itinerary.

And check the fine-print definition of "family members" and "pre-existing medical condition." Some policies will not pay if you become ill from a condition for which you have received treatment in the past.

DEFAULT AND/OR BANKRUPTCY INSURANCE: Note that trip cancellation insurance usually protects you in the event that you the traveler are unable to take — or complete — your trip. A recent innovation is coverage in the event of default and/or bankruptcy on the part of the tour operator, airline, or other supplier. In some travel insurance packages, this contingency is included in the trip cancellation portion of the coverage; in others, it is a separate feature. Either way, it is becoming increasingly pertinent. Whereas most travelers have long known to beware of the possibility of default or bankruptcy when buying a charter flight or tour, in recent years more than a few respected scheduled airlines have unexpectedly revealed their shaky financial condition, sometimes leaving stranded ticketholders in their wake. Moreover, the value of escrow protection of a charter passenger's funds has lately come into question. While default/bankruptcy insurance will not ordinarily result in reimbursement in time for you to pay for new arrangements, it can assure that you will eventually get your money back, and even independent travelers buying no more than an airplane ticket may want to consider it.

FLIGHT INSURANCE: Before you hastily buy last-minute flight insurance from an airport vending machine (as many, many travelers do), consider the question in light of your total existing insurance coverage. Do you really need more coverage? A review of your current policy may show that it is adequate and that it pays double, or even triple, the amount provided for by the insurance you'd buy at the airport. And know that airport insurance, bought from a counter or a vending machine, is among the most expensive forms of life insurance coverage available anywhere.

Airlines have carefully established limits of liability for the death or injury of passengers. On tickets for international flights, these are printed on the ticket: a maximum of $75,000 in case of death or injury. *But remember, these limits of liability are not the same as insurance policies; they merely state the maximum an airline will pay in the case of death or injury,* and every penny of that is usually the subject of a legal wrangle.

If you buy your ticket with an American Express, Diners Club, or Carte Blanche credit card, you are automatically issued life and accident insurance at no extra cost. American Express provides $100,000 coverage; Carte Blanche, $150,000; and Diners Club, $650,000. American Express offers additional coverage at extremely reasonable prices if you sign up in advance for it: $3 per ticket buys $250,000 worth of insurance; $5.50 buys $500,000 worth; and $11 gets $1 million worth of coverage.

COMBINATION POLICIES: A number of insurance companies offer all-purpose travel insurance packages that include baggage, personal accident and sickness, trip cancellation insurance, and, sometimes, default and bankruptcy protection. They cover you for a single trip and are sold by travel agents, insurance agencies, and others. One such policy, called Travel Guard International (underwritten by Insurance Company of North America), is the only policy endorsed by the American Society of Travel Agents (ASTA). It is available through authorized travel agents.

Staying Healthy in the Islands

With a little care, you need have no worries about your health during a visit to the Caribbean. Typically, tourists suffer two kinds of health problems in the islands, but neither is inevitable. The first is the stomach upset known the world over as the scourge of travelers: Cairo crud, Delhi belly, *la turista,* and, in Mexico, Montezuma's Revenge. The second is more familiar: simple sunburn.

DIARRHEA AND STOMACH UPSETS: Montezuma's Revenge is really nothing more than a violently upset stomach. It has several causes. The first is the change of routine represented by traveling. Anytime the body is subjected to a radical change of routine, the stomach — as well as most other physical processes — is disturbed and upset. Dr. Kevin M. Cahill, an expert in tropical diseases, has commented, "Changes in atmospheric pressure for the airborne traveler, exposure to new diets, and the almost universal tendency to overindulge in rich foods and alcohol on a plane or boat, the reaction to new virus strains in water, disruption of one's 24-hour cycle, the normal tension associated with travel or separation from the security of one's home, and many, many, relatively minor causes may all lead to an alteration in bowel movements."

It is very important to take the first few days easy. Drink and eat lightly. Most intestinal disorders contracted while traveling come from unsanitary food preparations, so the best way to guard against them is to prepare your own meals or make sure you eat in decent restaurants. Impure water is another common source of stomach problems. Avoid drinking tap water. With the exception of tinned brands, milk is often unpasteurized, so it may be best to avoid it. Stay clear of uncooked dairy products, uncooked vegetables, fruit peels, and old grease. Use water purifying tablets, and iodine wash on fruits and vegetables.

Fortunately, the vast majority of intestinal disorders encountered during travel represent only a temporary inconvenience, which will go away with rest and time. However, serious intestinal trouble is almost invariably the product of drinking water contaminated by a particular strain of *E. coli* bacteria. These bacteria inhabit the human intestinal tract and are transmitted through fecal matter, and from there into plumbing and any unpurified water system. They are as common in Western or Eastern Europe as in Mexico, parts of the Caribbean, and South America. When they are ingested through tainted water, or by eating fruit washed in tainted water, they multiply in the victim's system until they release a strong toxin that causes the cells affected to produce more salts and water than the intestinal tract can tolerate. The result is Montezuma's revenge.

There is one very simple way to avoid it: Don't drink the water; brush your teeth with bottled carbonated water (be sure you're not getting a used bottle refilled with tap water); and wash fruit with purified water. As a matter of course, it is wise to stick to bottled carbonated water or substitute wine or beer at meals. You might also carry standard GI water purification tablets (halazone). Just drop one of these tablets in a carafe of water and let it stand for half an hour. Or substitute a bottle of tincture of iodine. (Don't worry about what other people think of your precautions.)

If you are struck by the bug, there are several remedies you can carry for some relief. For mild cases, Kaomycin or its sister drug (without the antibiotic action), Kaopectate, if used according to directions, should have you back on your feet within 12 to 14 hours. But both come in bulky bottles. Many find equally effective Pepto-Bismol, which comes in a handier tablet form.

There has been some experimentation using Sulfathaladine and other sulfa drugs as a preventive measure. They are effective in reducing the incidence of Montezuma's revenge, but the body tends to build an immunity or tolerance to any drug taken regularly, and this may render any sulfa preparation ineffective when it's really needed. Doxycycline has been successfully used as a prophylactic drug in the treatment of *E. coli* infection; however, because it is a tetracycline drug, it is not effective against all viral infections, and it may, in some cases, act to photosensitize the skin — an important consideration in the tropics. The two drugs of choice at this time are paregoric, an opiate, and Lomotil. Dr. Cahill prefers paregoric as treatment, since its opiate action tends to dull the accompanying cramps, and it can be taken orally at the onset of stomach upset, before things get out of hand. Lomotil is slightly controversial since it can have long-range side effects; still, for emergency use it can be very effective. But since neither paregoric nor Lomotil are prophylactic, if other symptoms persist or get worse although the diarrhea is corrected, seek medical help at once. And check with your family doctor before leaving on your trip.

Most pharmacies throughout the Caribbean stock a range of over-the-counter drugs that astonishes most first-time visitors from the US. There is really no need to take along a trunk full of remedies. However, it is still advisable to bring a small medical kit with you. Start by getting some water purification tablets (halazone or similar) from your pharmacy or army-navy store and one of the medications for diarrhea mentioned above. Also bring something to settle a slight stomach upset, like Milk of Magnesia or Pepto-Bismol tablets. It would be a good idea, especially if you plan on traveling to some out-of-the-way places, to bring disposable syringes (they are illegal in some US states, even with a prescription). In many countries, especially in sections off the main tourist routes, reusable needles are the norm, and these can be less than perfectly sanitary. Improperly disinfected needles can be a source of AIDS (acquired immunodeficiency syndrome) and hepatitis, so insist that the doctor or pharmacist use disposable syringes whenever necessary.

INFECTIOUS HEPATITIS OR JAUNDICE: The most serious potential threat to a good vacation. The unwary traveler can contract it from improperly prepared food, contaminated drinking water, or unsanitary toilet conditions. Care in all these matters is the best prevention, but an additional measure of protection can also be secured with a gamma globulin shot from your family doctor before your departure.

SUNBURN: The burning power of the sun in the tropics is phenomenal and can quickly cause severe sunburn. Its glare can produce conjunctivitis. Sunstroke is another serious disorder to guard against. If the symptoms of chills, fever, nausea, headaches, and vertigo appear, a doctor should be consulted at once. Protection against the ill effects of too much sun are the obvious ones: a wide-brimmed hat, sunscreen lotion, sunglasses, and plenty of shade.

Many people use a suntan lotion to get a smooth tan and to protect themselves from burning. However, to provide real protection, any sunning agent must block 85% to 90% of the sun's ultraviolet rays, the rays that are actually harmful to the skin. To do this, use a sunscreen that has a PABA base (PABA stands for the drug para-amino-benzoic acid). Most of the numerous PABA sunscreens now on the market are labeled with a PF (Protection Factor) rating of 1 (minimal) to 15 (up to 90%); there's also a 25 rating — as close as the industry has come so far to an absolute block-out product.

Some notes on sunning:

1. When judging if you've had enough sun, remember that time in the water (in terms of exposure to ultraviolet rays) is the same as time lying on the beach.
2. A beach umbrella or other cover doesn't keep all the rays of the sun from reaching you. If you are light-sensitive, be especially careful.
3. As many ultraviolet rays reach you on cloudy days as on sunny days. Even if you are not warm, you are still exposed to rays.

Where heat is concerned, it is well to remember that full acclimatization to high temperatures takes about two weeks. Until this occurs, it is normal to feel listless and apathetic. The best way to deal with this problem is to drink plenty of liquids, use extra salt on food or take salt tablets, and avoid extreme exertion, especially in the hotter hours of the day. The main remedy, however, is time.

INSECTS AND SNAKES: Insects in parts of the Caribbean can be not only a nuisance but also a real threat. Some are carriers of serious diseases, such as malaria. To avoid contact, do not sleep on the ground. When necessary, sleep under mosquito netting. Burning mosquito coils containing pyrethrin and using an effective insect repellent on the skin are both effective precautions, too. If you do get bitten, the itching can be relieved with baking soda or antihistamine tablets. Antihistamines should not be combined with alcohol, driving, or cortisone cream. Should a bite become infected, which is common in the tropics, treat it with a disinfectant or antibiotic cream.

Though rarer than insect bites, bites from venomous snakes, spiders, scorpions, or sea creatures such as jellyfish can be serious. If possible, always try to catch the villain for identification purposes. In most cases, particularly when spasms, numbness, convulsions, or hemorrhaging occurs, consult a doctor at once. The best course of action may be to head directly to the nearest emergency ward or outpatient clinic of a hospital.

Fortunately, you can almost always find well-trained, English-speaking doctors in the major cities of the Caribbean. However, medical standards vary greatly from place to place. In Jamaica, for instance, there are about 30 hospitals, 7 of which are specialty oriented. There are also more than 150 clinics, health centers, and dispensaries throughout the island. Puerto Rico has the greatest number of physicians of any of the Caribbean islands, with medical standards comparable to those in most other US communities. San Juan alone has 14 hospitals. On the other hand, the smaller Grenadines offer almost no medical facilities whatever. Travelers taken ill here must take the ferry to St. Vincent where there are two general hospitals and one private hospital.

PREVENTION AND IMMUNIZATION: Specific information on the state of medicine in any particular country can be secured from its consular services in the US or from the Caribbean Tourism Association. If you live in or near New York City, you can take advantage of the International Health Care Service set up by New York Hospital–Cornell Medical Center "to encourage and facilitate proper preventive health measures." In addition to individual pre-trip counseling and post-trip checkups based on your specific itinerary, it offers a complete range of immunizations at moderate per-shot rates. By appointment only, from 4 to 8 PM Mondays through Thursdays (24-hour coverage for urgent travel-related problems) at 440 E 69th St., New York, NY 10021 (phone: 212-472-4284). In addition, sending $4.50 (with a self-addressed envelope) to this address will procure the Service's publication, *International Health Care Travelers Guide.*

Be sure to find out which vaccinations or immunizations are required or advisable, especially those that guard against smallpox, yellow fever, typhoid, and poliomyelitis. Although most of the Caribbean is free from at least the first three of these scourges, a tetanus shot or up-to-date booster is always a good idea, especially if one plans to spend a lot of time going barefoot. Also, children should be inoculated against diphtheria, whooping cough, and measles, especially since the latter two exist in a more virulent form in the Caribbean than at home.

A nonprofit organization called the International Association for Medical Assistance to Travelers (IAMAT) publishes a booklet listing its participating English-speaking doctors, clinics, and hospitals around the world. Also included is a sample climate chart and inoculation information for the part of the world in which you intend to travel. Contributions are appreciated. Delivery can take 6 to 8 weeks, so plan ahead. To join, write to IAMAT, 417 Center St., Lewiston, NY 14092 (phone: 716-754-4883).

It is also a good idea to carry an identification card at all times, with your name, address, the name of someone to contact in case of an emergency, your social security number, date of birth, any chronic health problems, and your health insurance number.

You might want to pack any or all of the following: sunglasses, ear plugs to prevent outer-ear infections from swimming water, insect repellent, water sterilizing tablets, salt tablets, antimalarial drugs, an antibiotic ointment, travel sickness pills, and antacids, as well as the sunscreen and antidiarrheals mentioned earlier.

If you do buy drugs in the Caribbean, remember the shelf life of some items, particularly vaccines and antibiotics, is greatly reduced under tropical conditions. Check the expiration date carefully.

Older travelers or anyone suffering from a chronic medical condition, like diabetes, high blood pressure, cardiopulmonary disease, or ear, eye, or sinus trouble, should consult a physician before leaving home. A checkup is advisable. Take an adequate supply of necessary medication and appropriate prescriptions. Ask for advice on how to take care of oneself and what to avoid on the road, and bring a letter describing the specifics of any health problem in the languages of the countries to be visited. An extra pair of eyeglasses and a prescription for lenses is also a worthwhile precaution for people who are lost without their glasses. And a pretrip dental checkup is not a bad idea, either.

Following all these precautions will not guarantee an illness-free trip, but it should minimize the risk. As a final hedge against economic if not physical problems, make sure your health insurance will cover all eventualities while you are away. If not, there are policies designed specifically for travel. Many are worth investigating. As with all insurance, they seem like a waste of money until you need them.

Obviously, your state of health is crucial to the success of a vacation. There's nothing like an injury or illness, whether serious or relatively minor, to dampen or destroy a holiday. And health problems always seem more debilitating when you are away. Any US citizen traveling to the tropical Caribbean will be exposed to different health risks from those encountered at home. However, most problems can be prevented or greatly alleviated with intelligent foresight and attention to precautionary details.

On the Islands

Credit and Currency

 FOREIGN CURRENCY: US currency is accepted almost everywhere in the Caribbean. The advantages of dealing in local currency are that you save money by not negotiating exchange rates for every small purchase and that you have no difficulty in remote spots where US currency is not readily or happily accepted. Several Caribbean states actually use the dollar as the official currency of exchange; in most, there is a local currency that is bought and sold at various rates in relation to the dollar. *Throughout this book, unless specifically stated otherwise, prices are given in US dollars.*

The official currencies for the various islands and countries covered in this guide are listed below, as are the operative exchange rates in effect as we went to press.

Bahamian dollar (1.02 to $1 US)
Bermudian dollar (1 to $1 US)
Eastern Caribbean dollar (3.03 ECD to $1 US) — Anguilla, Antigua, Dominica, Grenada, Montserrat, St. Kitts/Nevis, St. Lucia, St. Vincent
Barbadian dollar (2.17 Barbados to $1 US)
Belize dollar (2.22 to $1 US)
Cayman dollar (0.88 Cayman to $1 US)
Colombian peso (203 pesos to $1 US)
Cuban gold peso (1 peso equals 100 centavos; about 80 centavos to $1 US)
Dominican Republic gold peso (5.74 pesos to $1 US)
Haitian gourde (about 14.71 gourdes to $1 US)
French franc (about 5.76 FF to $1 US) — Martinique, Guadeloupe, St. Martin, St. Barts
Jamaican dollar (about 6.55 J to $1 US)
Mexican peso (2,300 pesos to $1 US)
Netherlands Antilles Dutch florin, now the guilder (about 2 to $1 US) — Aruba, Bonaire, Curaçao, St. Maarten (Dutch side), Saba, St. Eustatius
Trinidad and Tobago dollar (5.71 TT to $1 US)
Venezuelan bolívar (approximately 31 bolívars to $1 US)

The US dollar is the official currency of Puerto Rico and the US Virgin Islands and for all practical purposes the prevailing medium of exchange in the British Virgin Islands and the Turks and Caicos.

Exchange rates for some of these currencies are listed daily in most metropolitan newspapers. Information may also be available from currency exchange firms and banks, particularly those engaged in international transactions. You can exchange money in hotels, restaurants, and shops, but you will get better rates at banks. If you do spend US dollars at local shops, be sure to get your change in US currency, not local currency.

TRAVELER'S CHECKS: Traveler's checks are the safest substitute for cash and are readily recognized and convertible at any of the destinations covered in this guide.

However, don't assume that smaller shops or establishments in remote locations are going to have change for checks in large denominations. If you want change in US dollars, ask if it's available *before* you countersign your check. You might otherwise end up with a pocketful of island coins, and few travelers want to go through the procedure of exchanging coins at the airport.

With adequate proof of identification (birth certificate, passport), traveler's checks are as good as cash in most hotels, restaurants, stores, and banks. And they are refundable. For safety's sake, keep your purchaser's receipt and an accurate listing of your checks by serial number in a separate place from the checks themselves.

Traveler's checks can be purchased at most banks. The decision of which company's checks to buy should be based on how widely they are accepted in the Caribbean (most are accepted throughout the islands) and how easily refunds are available in case of loss or theft (see below). Several companies charge a 1% fee for purchase of checks while others don't, but the issuing institution (i.e., the particular bank at which you purchase them) may itself charge a fee.

> *American Express:* To report lost or stolen checks in the continental US, call 800-221-7282; in Alaska or Hawaii, 800-221-4950.
>
> *BankAmerica:* To report lost or stolen checks in the US except California, call 800-227-3460. Outside the US, call 415-622-3800 or 415-624-5400, collect.
>
> *Citicorp:* To report lost or stolen checks in the US, including Alaska and Hawaii, call 800-645-6556. Elsewhere, call 813-623-1709, collect.
>
> *MasterCard:* To report lost or stolen checks in the US except New York State, Alaska, and Hawaii, call 800-223-9920; from those states or outside the US, call 212-974-5696, collect.
>
> *Thomas Cook MasterCard:* To report lost or stolen checks in New York State, Alaska, Hawaii, Bermuda, the Bahamas, and the Caribbean, call 212 974-5696, collect, 24 hours a day. Elsewhere in the US, call 800-223-9920.
>
> *Visa:* To report lost or stolen checks in the US except California, Alaska, and Hawaii, call 800-227-6811; in California, 800-632-0520; in Alaska and Hawaii, 800-227-6830; outside the US, 415-574-7111, collect.

CREDIT CARDS: There are two different kinds of credit cards: so-called travel and entertainment cards and bank cards. Travel and entertainment cards — American Express, Diners Club, and Carte Blanche are the most widely accepted — cost the cardholder a basic membership fee (between $40 and $55), but put no fixed limit on the amount that the cardholder may charge on the card in any month. However, the entire balance must be paid, in full, at the end of each billing period (usually a month), which means that the cardholder is not really extended any meaningful long-term credit. Bank cards, with the exception of Sears' Discover Card, are also rarely issued free these days, and are true credit cards in the sense that the holder is allowed to pay a minimum amount of the total balance in each billing period. For this privilege the cardholder is charged an interest rate — currently three to four times the going bank passbook rate — on the balance owed. In addition, the holder may charge only up to a fixed maximum amount — the limit of credit the company is willing to extend — which is set when the card is issued. The major bank cards are Visa and MasterCard, though American Express has recently introduced its own extended-payment Optima card.

Getting any credit card involves a fairly rigorous credit appraisal. To pass you'll need a job (at which you've worked for at least a year), a minimum salary of $10,000 a year, and a good credit rating. Application for any credit card will involve a detailed check of prior credit history and financial references.

In any case, all types of credit cards are a handy additional means of avoiding having to carry a lot of cash. However, establishments on the islands may not accept *all* the major cards. So make certain you have several different credit cards if you plan to rely on them to cover the cost of shopping, outside meals, or other expenses. Following is a list of cards with international usage:

American Express: Emergency personal check cashing at American Express or representatives' offices (up to $200 cash in local currency, $800 in traveler's checks); emergency personal check cashing for guests at participating hotels (up to $250 in US or Canada; $100 elsewhere), and, for holders of airline tickets, at participating airlines in the US (up to $50). Extended payment plan for cruises, tours, and airlines tickets. $100,000 free automatic travel accident insurance on plane, train, bus, and ship if ticket was charged to card; up to $1 million additional flight insurance available at low cost. Contact: American Express Card, PO Box 39, Church St. Station, New York, NY 10008 (phone: 800-528-4800, nationwide except New York; 212-477-5700 in New York).

Carte Blanche: Emergency personal check cashing at participating Hilton hotels in the US (up to $1,000) and for guests at other participating hotels and motels (up to $250 per stay). Extended payment plan for airline and cruise tickets. $150,000 free travel accident insurance on plane, train, and ship if ticket was charged to card; up to $500,000 additional low-cost travel accident insurance available. Contact: Carte Blanche, PO Box 17326, Denver, CO 80217 (phone: 800-525-9135).

Diners Club: Emergency personal check cashing at participating Citibank branches, and other designated banks, worldwide (up to $1,000, with a minimum per check of $50 in the US and $250 overseas); emergency personal check cashing for guests at participating hotels and motels (up to $250 per stay). Extended payment plan for all charges can be arranged. $350,000 free air travel accident insurance if ticket was charged to card; collision-damage reimbursement coverage when rental car was charged to card; checked-baggage coverage when airline ticket was charged to card. Medical, legal, and travel assistance available worldwide (phone: 800-356-3448, or collect from outside the US, 214-680-6480). Contact: Diners Club, PO Box 17193, Denver, CO 80217 (phone: 800-525-9135).

Discover Card: Launched in early 1986 by Sears, Roebuck and Co., it provides the holder with cash advance at more than 500 locations nationwide and offers a revolving credit line for purchases at a wide range of service establishments. Other deposit, lending, and investment services are also available. At this time, its acceptance in the Caribbean is limited. For information, phone 800-858-5588.

MasterCard: Cash advance at participating banks worldwide. Interest charge on unpaid balance and other details are set by issuing bank. Check with your bank for information.

Visa: Cash advance at participating banks worldwide. Interest charge on unpaid balance and other details are set by issuing bank. Check with your bank for information.

One of the operative lunacies of trying to manage money while you are traveling has to do with the way credit card companies determine exchange rates. It is a cold fact that the amount of money you think you are spending when you purchase an item in foreign currency using a major credit card does not necessarily bear any relation to the amount you will ultimately be billed when the charge finally appears on your monthly statement. The explanation for this bizarre phenomenon varies from company to company. As far as American Express is concerned, charges bear no relation to the exchange rate on the day a purchase is made. Instead, charges are calculated at the rate prevailing on the date a particular charge slip is received at the local American Express service center. When asked whether there was any time limit on how long a vending establishment could hold a charge before sending it to the service center, the company said that the only requirement was that charges be submitted within one year of the transaction date.

Diners Club reports that charges are determined by the prevailing rate on the day a charge slip is received in Denver. The rate Visa uses to process an item is a function of the rate the shop's bank used to process it. Thus, though up to 60 days may pass between the date of your purchase and the date Visa converts it, the conversion rate most commonly used is the one prevailing about 2 weeks after your purchase was made, assuming the foreign merchant makes deposits weekly and that his bank processes them in 3 to 5 days. Remember, too, that virtually all international credit card transactions include a fee of approximately 1% for currency conversion — a fact the credit card companies conveniently fail to publicize.

The impact on the traveler is clear. Using your credit card abroad subjects you to capricious charges over which you have absolutely no control — that is, if you don't like to brawl. In some instances, you might actually do better than if the exchange rate in effect on the day you made the purchase were used. At other times you will lose money. But what is most interesting is that customer service persons at the companies are apparently empowered to negotiate even after they explain how absolute such charges are. They are prepared to back down when pressed, and apparently if you yell loud enough you may be able to exact some adjustment.

So you play a kind of exchange roulette in the sense that you take the chance that exchange rates will break to your advantage, with the hidden kicker that if things go against you, you can always raise a little hell and probably enjoy some redress. The bottom line is to charge ahead and be prepared to negotiate.

Dining in the Islands

 Island dining is casual and usually quite leisurely. Also, it's usually more expensive than equivalent meals in hotels or restaurants in the US or Canada, since most islands have to import most of their food, including (bottled) table water.

Many hotels offer meal arrangements on a basis popularly known as MAP (Modified American Plan), which includes breakfast and one other meal daily, usually dinner. In peak season, a number of hotels permit room reservations *only* MAP, which can add from $18 to $35 (or even more) per day per person to the daily room tab, exclusive of personal tips; many hotels now include a 10% service charge. Most hotel guests choose dinner as their extra meal and use lunchtime to visit island restaurants or the buffets at other hotels. At some hotels you can also opt for an occasional MAP lunch in order to sample the island's restaurants in the evening.

Quality often depends on price. The dining rooms of modern and luxury hotels are invariably expensive because you supposedly pay for the service and ambience that go with their class of establishment. Usually, so are the restaurants that require reservations and jackets for men.

In some locales (for example, Aruba and Nassau), dine-around plans are available to guests staying at certain hotels. These permit MAP guests to get a change of scene — and menu — by having dinner at other hotels at no extra charge.

You should sample at least one local restaurant during any stay, but since the quality of even the most reputable eating establishment can change (usually when there's a change of chef), seek out recommendations. Ask for suggestions from people who have been to the island recently or others who are visiting when you are. Or ask your hotel manager for recommendations; most are very accommodating. And be aware of certain realities regarding Caribbean food.

There's a widely held perception among Caribbean hoteliers that American guests — by far the largest segment of any island's visitors — will eat nothing but meat and potatoes, so you will find menus redolent with red meat offerings. Almost always, these will be inferior to similar dishes served on the mainland, though through no fault of the chef. The problem is that there are virtually no island facilities for the raising, slaughtering, or aging of top-quality meat, so the steak you see sitting on your plate in a Caribbean dining room likely flew (or floated) in from Chicago not long before you did. Almost all meat in the Caribbean has been frozen and portion-controlled and then imported into the islands — often under circumstances involving erratic refrigeration. Close your eyes and imagine the trip your steak took from packing house to *pension* and you can find at least a half-dozen stops along the way at which it was subject to a variety of climatic vagaries.

Hence the word "gourmet" — a word that should be forcibly excised from any menu vocabulary — has even less meaning on a Caribbean island than elsewhere in the world. A chef, no matter how talented, is only as good as his ingredients, and your own common sense tells you that fresh is best.

So by all means try the local food. The Caribbean as a whole hasn't developed a great reputation for haute cuisine, but some islands have delicious specialties. The Dutch islands feature rice dishes and curries (the influence of Mother Holland's early Far East holdings). Créole concoctions are favored in Jamaica, Cuba, Haiti, and in the French West Indies. Try fresh deep-sea fish whenever it's offered, prepared to your taste, in Bermuda, the Bahamas, Belize, or in South American ports, and whatever fresh fish and seafood is caught off other island shores. The Caribbean equivalent of lobster is called langouste (guinea chicks in Bermuda). It's a bit smaller and not quite as sweet as its Maine cousin, but an imaginative chef can make it absolutely irresistible.

The best source of information on what to eat and where to eat it is usually an island's (or country's) tourist office in the US or Canada. Most are staffed by former island residents who frequently are delighted to tell you about their favorite foods back home. For more specific suggestions, see the individual *Eating Out* listings for each island in ISLAND-BY-ISLAND HOPPING.

Hotels, Inns, and Guesthouses

In most of these islands and countries, accommodations range from large, modern, luxury hotels to small, simply furnished, but quite comfortable guesthouses. What you get, therefore, should not be just a question of what you're paying for but, more important, what you're looking for.

Most of the newer and larger hotels, for instance, offer a wide range of sports, recreation, and entertainment facilities in addition to a larger staff for service. Invariably they have swimming pools, but this shouldn't be a major criterion; most islands have excellent sand beaches and swimming waters. If tennis or golf is a major consideration, you'll find several hotels with their own courts and courses on the grounds. But don't overlook others that provide transportation to nearby facilities.

Most of the new hotels fit into a category now commonly known as "international standard." Rooms are large and frequently have two oversize beds, ocean-view balconies, conventional modern facilities, and full room service. They feature a variety of restaurants, poolside bars, and discotheques. A number also have their own casinos (making gambling the primary activity), and some even have a small convention center, or at least meeting facilities. *Hilton, Holiday Inn, Sheraton, Marriott,* and *Loews* are among the major US hotel groups represented in the islands, as are France's *Azur, Club Med, Méridien, PLM,* and *Novotel* chains — primarily in Martinique, Guadeloupe, St. Martin, and St. Barts in the French West Indies.

Independent modern establishments in the islands are often even more elegant than the chains. Word of mouth among the social set is a mainstay of their reputations, and how good — and well patronized — they are is usually reflected in their prices. To find out, stop by for a look or ask for a brochure with a tariff sheet.

. Medium-size hotels can be equally modern, or at least modernized, but are more likely to offer local ambience and charm. In general, they're also more reasonably priced. They won't have the trappings of luxury, the superb facilities, or the famous guests of the super-resorts, however. What you gain in cash you give up in cachet.

Don't overlook inns, guesthouses, and other small establishments. What they lack in range of facilities is usually compensated for in personal service. Some are even historic, like the former plantation homes of St. Kitts and Nevis, which once belonged to wealthy landowners. Frequently these small establishments will have original furnishings in a public sitting room where tea or drinks are served.

Anguilla, Dominica, Montserrat, Saba, St. Eustatius, and the Turks and Caicos are probably the islands most limited in tourist facilities, but their owners make a concerted effort to provide guests with simple comfort in depth as well as very personal attention from both the resident management and staff.

Rental Villas and Vacation Homes

 The range of possible accommodations in the islands is not limited to hotels, inns, and guesthouses. These days, several other alternatives offer various levels of luxury and convenience at the price you want to pay — whether it's $10,000 a week for Princess Margaret's villa on Mustique or $75 a night for a studio apartment in the Bahamas.

One of the charms of staying in a villa, apartment, or cottage rather than a hotel is that you will feel much more like a traveler than a tourist. You find out what it's like to haggle in the markets and experiment with local foods. You may hear of small, out-of-the-way beaches and restaurants that only natives know about. Most important, you live in the environment you choose to visit, not in a mini-US that's been decorated with palm trees and blue seas.

The main charms are probably economic: For a family of four, or two or more couples, the price per night can work out up to 60% less than the cost of comparable hotel accommodations. (For one or two people the *economic* advantages do not amount to quite as much.) Then, too, there is the added bonus of space, usually far more than is offered in any but the most extravagant hotel suite.

Don't expect these savings to extend to food, however. On many islands in Caribbean, groceries are notoriously expensive. A recent US Virgin Islands Labor Department study compared food prices on St. Thomas, St. Croix, and St. John with those for the same items in Washington, DC. Depending on the specific purchase, the Caribbean prices proved to be from 19% to 49% higher than those in our nation's capital.

Housekeeping accommodations fall into four main categories: villas, condominiums, apartments, and cottages. All provide cooking utensils, flatware, and linens, but some important differences are noted below:

VILLAS: These are the Brahmins of island real estate rentals. Some are fully staffed, most have maid service 3 or 4 hours a day, a cook, and a gardener; some even have a private swimming pool and a car. The more luxurious places arrange pickup service at the airport and supply provisions for the first day — eggs, milk, bread, butter, fruit, and a chicken, as well as soap, toothpaste, other toilet essentials, and in some cases a bottle of rum.

CONDOMINIUMS: These usually have a front desk and almost always daily maid service. It's like having a first-class hotel room with a living room, dining area, and kitchen or kitchenette. Almost all have swimming pools. Transportation may be necessary for sightseeing, but not for purchasing provisions.

APARTMENTS: These can be rented through US representatives or local real estate agents. Maid service is usually optional. They are generally close to shopping, but a car may be necessary if the property is not close to town.

COTTAGES: Beachcombing, romance, roughing it . . . well, not necessarily. Many so-called cottages resemble cabanas on wealthy US estates. They snuggle around a swimming pool and the means of preparing a daiquiri are more evident than the utensils for a five-course meal. Equally often they are what they say: simple cottages with a kitchen and bath and the ocean for swimming and fishing. Open-air fruit and vegetable stands and supermarkets may be a taxi or car ride away.

To inquire about villa/condominium/apartment rentals, write to the island's nearest US tourist office (see *Island Tourist Offices,* in this section), to the US representatives listed below, or to the island offices. When you write to the two latter, it is useful to ask the following questions:

1. How do you get from the airport to the accommodation?
2. Is a rental car advisable?
3. Will there be food in the refrigerator upon arrival?
4. Are babysitters, cribs, bicycles, available?
5. Who is in charge locally if there are any problems?
6. Is the accommodation near what is important to you, such as good beaches, tennis, golf, nightlife?
7. Does a housekeeping staff come with the place and what will they do for you?

Below are some US agencies operating in two or more areas of the Caribbean:

At Home Abroad, 405 E 56th St., Apt. 6H, New York, NY 10022 (phone: 212-421-9165), operates private homes and some apartments in Barbados, Jamaica, Montserrat, Mustique, the Dominican Republic, St. Lucia, Tortola, St. Martin, St. Croix, and Nevis. Minimum stay is 1 week, except at Christmas. Prices range from $750 to $18,000 a week. All have been individually inspected. All have maid service. $50 registration fee procures a selection of listings and photographs.

Caribbean Connection Plus, PO Box 261, Trumbull, CT 00611 (phone: 203-261-8603) has villas and apartments on Anguilla, Antigua, the British Virgin Islands, Dominica, Montserrat, St. Kitts/Nevis, St. Lucia, St. Maarten (French and Dutch sides), Tobago, and the US Virgin Islands.

Caribbean Home Rentals, PO Box 710, Palm Beach, FL 33480 (phone: 305-833-4454), has villas, apartments, and cottages in Anguilla, Antigua, the Bahamas, Barbados, Bequia, the British Virgin Islands, Cancún, the Caymans, Dominican Republic, Nevis, Tobago, the USVI, Grenada, Jamaica, Montserrat, Palm Island in the Grenadines, Puerto Rico, St. Lucia, St. Martin/St. Maarten, and Mustique. Weekly prices range from $700 for a one-bedroom cottage to around $17,000 for a six-bedroom villa. The staff of CHR personally inspect all properties; they also arrange airfare and transfers and can provide car rentals and prestock villas. The minimum stay is 1 week, 2 weeks at Christmas.

Condo World, 26645 W Twelve Mile Rd., Southfield, MI 48034 (phone: 313-352-6262; 800-521-2980), has condominiums and villas in the Bahamas, Cancún,

Cozumel, Puerto Rico, Jamaica, Montserrat, Antigua, St. Lucia, St. Thomas, St. Croix, Barbados, and St. Maarten. A typical condo would have maid service; most villas have a staff including a cook. Rates begin at $60 per night in summer; top winter rate is $600 per night for four-bedroom villa.

Hideaways International, PO Box 1270, Littleton, MA 01460 (phone: 617-486-8955; 800-843-4433), provides comprehensive illustrated listings of accommodations in Aruba, the Bahamas, Cayman Islands, the Dominican Republic, Jamaica, Puerto Rico, Turks and Caicos, the US Virgin Islands, the British Virgin Islands, the Windwards, and the Leewards. Villas average from $800 to $3,000 a week for four to ten people. Many come with maid service, although in more affluent areas such as the US Virgin Islands and Puerto Rico this may be optional. A yearly subscription for two issues of *Hideaways Guide* is $65; this price also includes a quarterly newsletter, discounts on airfares and rental cars as well as at condos and small resorts.

Travel Resources, PO Box 1043, Coconut Grove, FL 33133 (phone: 305-444-8583; 800-327-5039) lists both villas and condominiums in Antigua, the Bahamas, Barbados, Bermuda, Cancún, Grand Cayman, Jamaica, St. Barts, St. Lucia, St. Maarten/St. Martin, Tortola, and the USVI. Some villas come with a maid, cook, and gardener; condos have maid service. Daily as well as weekly rates can be arranged.

Villas and Apartments Abroad, 444 Madison Ave., Suite 211, New York, NY 10022 (phone: 212-759-1025 or 800-433-3020), specializes in luxury villa rentals on Jamaica, Barbados, St. Lucia, Montserrat, Mustique, Antigua, and St. Martin. Rentals run from $750 to $9,500.

Villas International Ltd., 71 W 23rd St., New York, NY 10010 (phone: 800-221-2260), rents villas in the Bahamas, Barbados, the British Virgin Islands, Cayman Islands, the Dominican Republic, Guadeloupe, Jamaica, Montserrat, Mustique, St. Barts, St. Lucia, St. Maarten, and the US Virgin Islands. Villas and condos on Barbados, Jamaica, and St. Lucia include staff; on other islands, the staffing varies. All include maid service. Minimum 1 week stay.

Villa Leisure, PO Box 1096, Fairfield, CT 06430 (phone: 203-222-9611), is the agent for accommodations in Jamaica, Anguilla, Antigua, St. Maarten, the US Virgin Islands, the British Virgin Islands, Montserrat, Barbados, Mustique, St. Lucia, and Cancún. Minimum stay is 1 week; for condos only, that drops to 4 nights in the summer. Weekly rates average $4,400 for a three-bedroom villa in high season; $2,100 for a two-bedroom condo. Villa rates include car, transfers, staff, and private pool or beach; condo rates include maid service.

Information on other properties can be obtained by contacting the following (approximate rates given are for summer rentals):

Anguilla – Anguilla Tourist Information Office, c/o Medhurst & Associates, 1208 Washington Dr., Centerport, NY 11721 (phone: 516-673-0150), has data on villas, apartments, and cottages. All have maid service. Car required for shopping. They range from about $450 to $4,025 a week for a two-bedroom accommodation. Other island sources: the Anguilla Hotel and Tourist Association, PO Box 104, The Valley, Anguilla, WI (phone: 809-497-2944); Anguilla Hotel and Reservation Clearinghouse, c/o ITR, 25 W 39th St., New York, NY 10018 (phone: 212-840-6636); Property Real Estate Management Services, PO Box 256, George Hill, Anguilla, WI (phone: 809-497-2596); and Sunshine Villas, PO Box 142, Anguilla, WI (phone: 809-497-2149).

Antigua – Antigua Department of Tourism and Trade, 610 Fifth Ave, New York, NY 10010 (phone: 212-541-4117). Ask for *Cottage and Apartment Rental Information.* It lists a half-dozen hotels with housekeeping facilities and several real estate agents. Car advisable. Caribbean Home Rentals is also represented in Antigua.

Aruba – Aruba Tourist Bureau, 1270 Sixth Ave., Suite 2212, New York, NY 10020 (phone: 212-246-3030). Ask for *Information on Accommodations Other Than Hotels*. Apartments can be rented usually on a nightly basis, houses on a weekly or monthly basis. Maid service is not always included but can be arranged.

Bahamas – Self-catering accommodations are available throughout much of the Bahamas. They range from about $480 a week for a one-bedroom cottage to around $1,225 per day for a five-bedroom, air-conditioned villa. Take your pick. Caribbean Home Rentals and Travel Resources represent properties in the Bahamas.

Barbados – Write to the Barbados Board of Tourism, 800 Second Ave., New York, NY 10017 (phone: 212-986-6516), requesting apartment and cottage rate and villa rental information. Daily rates range from $120 off-season, to $1,690 during peak season. Most villas come with a staff, and a car is usually essential. At Home Abroad, Condo World, Caribbean Home Rentals, and Villa Leisure are well represented in Barbados.

Bermuda – Contact any of the Bermuda tourist offices listed in *Island Tourist Offices* in this section. Ask for *Where to Stay in Bermuda* and *Accommodation Through Real Estate Agents in Bermuda.* Some cottage colonies have kitchenettes for snacks but do not permit the preparation of full meals. Public transport is very good. It has to be; visitors are not permitted to drive a car. "Seasonal" rentals in Bermuda — from a week to 3 months — range from $900 to $2,000 per month for a one-bedroom apartment to $4,000 up per month for a four- or five-bedroom house. Maid service is usually extra ($6.50 to $8 per hour), and babysitting is easily arranged.

Bonaire – Carib Vacations, Ltd., PO Box 110325, 1133 Royal Palm Beach Blvd., Royal Palm Beach, FL 33411 (phone: 212-819-9890 or 407-793-8016), handles Bonaire rentals. Outside Kralendijk you need a car; there are no public buses.

British Virgin Islands – From the BVI Tourist Board, 370 Lexington Ave., New York, NY 10017 (phone: 212-696-0400), you can request information on apartments and hotels with housekeeping facilities. Also contact Caribbean Home Rentals or Persia Stoutt, Rockview Holiday Homes, PO Box 263, Road Town, Tortola, BVI. Taxis are usually available on Tortola, Anegada, and Virgin Gorda. If you are used to driving blind curves on the left-hand side, rent a Jeep or a mini-moke. Otherwise walk.

Cayman Islands – Cayman Rent-a-Villas, PO Box 681, Grand Cayman, British West Indies (phone: 809-947-4144), and Caribbean Home Rentals are well represented. Maid service usually included. Honda motorcycles are the most practical means of transport for one or two people. If it takes four to shop, rent a car. The rate sheet and fact folder are available from any of the Cayman Island tourist offices listed in *Island Tourist Offices.*

Colombia – According to the Colombian Tourist Office in New York, these types of accommodations can be arranged through local real estate agents in Colombia.

Cuba – Self-catering accommodations are not currently available for US citizens.

Curaçao – The *Las Palmas Hotel and Vacation Village,* Piscadera Bay, Curaçao, has 94 villas with kitchenette, dining area, and terrace for outdoor dining. There is a small market adjacent. Rates are from about $130 per day for up to six people. There is a free shuttle bus to town.

Dominican Republic – Contact the Dominican Tourist Information Center (see *Island Tourist Offices*). At *Casa de Campo,* a best-in-class resort with a strong appeal for golf and tennis nuts, one-, two-, and three-bedroom villas (mostly twos) are priced from about $115 a day in summer, about $495 for a three-bedroom villa in winter. Villa and cottage rentals at Puerto Plata are not so steep: summer rates start at about $50 a day, or $600 for 2 weeks. Contact Costambar Beach Resort, 9050 55th Ave., Elmhurst, NY 11373 (phone: 718-507-6770), or AOT Tours, 212-55 26th Ave., Bayside, NY 11360 (phone: 718-423-6900).

Guadeloupe – Contact the French West Indies Tourist Board (see *Island Tourist*

Offices). The Guadeloupe Tourist Office, BP 1099, Angle des rues Schoelcher et Delgres 97110, 97181 Pointe-à-Pitre Cedex, Guadeloupe, FWI, has a complete list of villas for rent. *PLM Azur Callanago Village* has 93 studios and 22 duplexes, with maid service, from about $80 for a single studio to $102 up for a double studio in winter. US representatives: Pullman International Hotels, 200 W 57th St., Suite 1310, New York, NY 10019 (phone: 212-757-6500 or 800-223-9862). *Trois Mats* marina apartments, at St. François, has doubles that cost between $110 and $150 during winter; contact Jacques de Larsay, 622 Broadway, New York, NY 10012 (phone: in New York, 212-477-1600; elsewhere, 800-223-1510).

Jamaica – *Jamaica Association of Villas and Apartments* (JAVA), 1320 S Dixie Hwy., Suite 845, Coral Gables, FL 33146 (phone: 305-667-0179). JAVA represents 80% of all the villas available in Jamaica. Most have private swimming pools and all have access to private or public beaches. Most villas have a staff (maid and cook), whose wages are included in the rent. An initial supply of food and liquor is provided at the guest's expense. Car rental is recommended. The few apartments available start at about $540 a week, double occupancy; a three-bedroom villa starts at about $1,345 a week in summer. There is a wide range of accommodations and prices. For information about short- and long-term rentals, contact Carib Vacations, Ltd., PO Box 110325, 1133 Royal Palm Blvd., Royal Palm Beach, FL 33411 (phone: 212 819-9890 or 407-793-8016). Villas and Apartments Abroad, Caribbean Home Rentals, At Home Abroad, Villa Leisure, Travel Resources, and Hideaways are all represented in Jamaica.

Martinique – Contact the French West Indies Tourist Board (see *Island Tourist Offices*) or the Office Départemental du Tourisme, Service Location de Villas, BP 520, 97206, Fort-de-France, Cedex, Martinique, FWI, for villa rentals. All are close to the beach and food markets. Maid service available, sometimes included in the price. Studios with kitchenettes start at about $166 per week in winter.

Mexico – The luxurious 327-apartment complex at Cancún called *Casa Maya* has its own beach, pool, restaurants, shops; the public bus to the best food stores, about 10 minutes away, stops at the front door. Apartments accommodate three to four people and cost from about $190 to $240 a night during the winter season.

Montserrat – Montserrat Villas, PO Box 58, Plymouth, Montserrat, and Neville Bradshaw Agencies, PO Box 270, Plymouth are licensed Realtors. Villas available from $300 (2 bedrooms and a pool) a week in summer, $1,400 in winter. Most include half-day maid service. Caribbean Home Rentals, At Home Abroad, and Villa Leisure also represent properties on Montserrat.

Puerto Rico – Contact the government tourist office (see *Island Tourist Offices*). *ESJ Towers,* PO Box S-3445, San Juan, PR 00905, has efficiencies and one-bedroom apartments with full kitchens, dishwashers, washer-dryers, cable TV, and maid service. *Palmas del Mar* consists of four villages with one-, two-, three-, and four-bedroom villas. Food stores are close by and maid service is included. Their Villa Value program includes 7 nights in a completely furnished villa, with access to all facilities (casino, tennis courts, golf, swimming pools, fitness center, etc.). Rates begin at $600 for a one-bedroom; a surcharge is added during peak season. Contact Palmas del Mar, PO Box 2020, Humacao, PR 00661. Caribbean Home Rentals is also represented. The government tourist office can also provide a list of *paradors* (country inns), which have some of the features of villas (phone: 800-443-0266).

St. Barts – Brook Lacour, Manager, Sibarth Rental, BP 55, Gustavia, 97133 St. Barthélemy, has an extensive listing of villas for rent by the week or month. The *PLM Azur Jean Bart* has 50 rooms, 35 with kitchenettes and all with balconies, at $139 up per double (including continental breakfast in winter). There is a food market just across the road. Contact Pullman International Hotels, 200 W 57th St., New York, NY 10019 (phone: 212-757-6500 or 800-223-9862). *Emeraude Plage, St. Jean Gardens,*

Térrasses de St. Barts, Kerjan, Hibiscus, and *Village St. Jean* are representative proper-ties that offer studios and apartments with kitchen facilities in hotel/resort–like set-tings; *Le P'tit Morne* is a chalet-style property with 12 apartments with kitchenettes and a pool.

St. Lucia – Contact the St. Lucia Tourist Board (see *Island Tourist Offices*). At Home Abroad handles villas that come with maid service; Caribbean Home Rentals is also represented. A car is essential. Villas range from $145 to $290 a night in summer.

St. Martin/St. Maarten/Saba/St. Eustatius – Contact the tourist boards (see *Island Tourist Offices*). On the French side, *Grand Case Beach Club* and *Le Pirate* (in Marigot) offer housekeeping suites and apartments, of varying degrees of luxury, right on the beach. *Le Pirate*'s rates run from about $126 to $180 a night in winter for a one-bedroom unit with kitchenette; *Grand Case*'s, from about $170 up. Judy Shepherd, Manager, St. Maarten Rentals, Pelican House; Beacon Hill, St. Maarten, represents about 30 villas in both St. Martin and St. Maarten. Minimum stay is 1 week, and half-day maid service is included in the tariff, which is available on request. You'll be met at the airport by a company representative who will help you with car-rental documents and escort you to your villa. A first day's breakfast and liquor supply are also provided. Also try Caribbean Connection Plus, Caribbean Home Rentals, Condo World, and Villa Leisure. Summer rates for these start at around $750 a week for a small one-bedroom unit and rise to about $2,000 for a multibedroom luxury retreat off-season; winter rates run from about $1,500 to $4,000 a week. There are no self-catering facilities on Statia, but Saba has a few small homes for rent.

Trinidad and Tobago – Contact the Trinidad and Tobago Tourist Board (see *Island Tourist Offices*) for brochures. Several hotels have condominium units. On Tobago try Tobago Villas Agency for listings.

US Virgin Islands – Contact any US Virgin Islands tourist office (see *Island Tourist Offices*). Ask for the comprehensive accommodations brochure, whose maps indicate where the respective accommodations are and whether or not you will need a car. Taxis are plentiful. Villas on St. John range from about $400 to $800 (in winter) a week. On St. Thomas and St. Croix there are numerous condominiums, housekeeping cottages, apartments, and villas.

Venezuela – According to the Venezuelan Tourist Office in New York, there are no self-catering properties in the Venezuelan Caribbean.

Couples' Resorts and Club Med

While the Caribbean has always been a special magnet for honeymooners and other lovers, it's only recently that resorts catering exclusively to couples — both married and unmarried — have emerged in depth. Some quite ex-plicitly bar singles and children; at others, the atmosphere alone is probably enough to make the unattached feel uncomfortable — if not expressly unwelcome. As the director of *Couples* resort in St. Mary's, Jamaica, puts it, "We are not anti-single; but we are now going to celebrate the couple." There are now at least eight Caribbean resorts that enthusiastically celebrate the couple, six of them on Jamaica alone. Despite the common bond, their tone varies considerably, from frantically active to get-away-from-it-all peaceful.

COUPLES' RESORTS

COUPLES, St. Mary, Jamaica: In a small village near Ocho Rios, this property was once the *Tower Isle* hotel, now completely refurbished and quietly elegant in both appearance and mood. Besides accommodations, the price includes airport transfers, food, drinks, tips, entertainment, golf, squash, scuba, cigarettes, a shopping tour in Ocho Rios, and an excursion to nearby Dunn's River Falls. No singles, triples, or children. Information: Couples, PO Box 330, Ocho Rios, Jamaica (phone: 809-974-4271) or International Life Styles Ltd., 416 Atlantic Ave., Freeport, NY 11520 (phone: 516-868-6924 or 800-858-8009).

COUPLES, Malabar Beach, near Castries, St. Lucia: Including in its price the same options as the *Couples* resort in Jamaica, this offers the added advantage of splendid semi-isolation on an island that has still managed to mostly resist "improvements" by developers. Sports options include tennis, water sports, and horseback riding, and the price includes a boat trip plus all service charges and taxes. No singles, triples, or children. Information: Couples, Malabar Beach, Castries, St. Lucia (phone: 809-452-4211).

EDEN II, Ocho Rios, Jamaica: Golf, tennis, all water sports, horseback trail riding 2,000 feet above sea level, Nautilus gym, massage, and hot tub are included in the single price, as are airport transfers, 3 meals a day for two at either of two restaurants or the snack bar, drinks, tips, entertainment, cigarettes and cigars, shopping tour, and a Dunn's River Falls cruise. There's also a private nude beach as well as the conventional kind. No singles, triples, or children. Information: Eden II, Ocho Rios, Jamaica (phone: 800-223-1588 except Canada and New York; 800-531-6767 in Canada; 212-661-4540 in New York).

HEDONISM II, Negril, Jamaica: Set on an almost perfect crescent of white beachfront, this resort lives up to its name. Besides a half-dozen tennis courts, all manner of water sports, and competitive diversions from basketball to backgammon, it is big on toga nights and pajama parties, and loud rock and reggae provide an almost constant background. The one-price-covers-everything policy — accommodations, transfers to and from the airport, food, drinks, tips, entertainment, sports, even cigarettes — make pocket money entirely superfluous during a stay here. Information: Hedonism II, Negril PO, Jamaica; or International Life Styles, Ltd., 416 Atlantic Ave., Freeport, NY 11520 (phone: 516-868-6924 or 800-858-8009).

JACK TAR VILLAGE II, Montego Bay, Jamaica: Its 1- and 2-week packages include airport transfers, food, drinks, sports, games (volleyball, table tennis), whirlpool, sauna, and massage. For those who can tear themselves away, its Montego Bay location is perfect for sightseeing. Information: Jack Tar Village II, Montego Bay, Jamaica (phone: 809-952-4340).

JAMAICA, JAMAICA, Runaway Bay, Jamaica: Farther down the north shore, this resort offers cricket and soccer as well as the usual assortment of water sports, and meals include such native dishes as pepper pot, curried goat, and johnnycakes. One price covers airport transfers, drinks, food, sports, entertainment, a horse and buggy ride, shopping shuttles to Ocho Rios (with a stop at Dunn's River Falls), a sailing cruise, and something called the Essentials Kit & Caboodle, which includes clothing to put guests in the island spirit. Information: Jamaica, Jamaica, PO Box 58, Runaway Bay, Jamaica (phone: 809-973-2436).

PARADISE, PARADISE, Paradise Island, Bahamas: Not quite as isolated as most of its Jamaican counterparts, this resort on Paradise Beach offers access to the large local casino and a host of restaurants and related diversions. Nearby Nassau adds the option of sightseeing. The price includes all water sports; drinks are not included. Information: Paradise, Paradise, c/o Resorts International (Bahamas) Ltd., 915 NE 125th St., N Miami, FL 33161 (phone: 800-321-3000).

SANDALS, Montego Bay, Jamaica: Unlike most of the other one-price-covers-everything couples' resorts, this very adult resort doesn't serve meals family style; couples may eat alone or join others in a group of up to 20. In addition to the breakfast and lunch buffets and à la carte dinners, soup, hamburgers, and fresh tropical fruit are served all day on a terrace beside the white sand beach. The resort's proximity to the airport is only a minor drawback. The first-rate health club is a decided asset. The price includes airport transfers, food, drinks, and sports. Information: Sandals, PO Box 100, Montego Bay, Jamaica (phone: 809-952-5510). Unique Vacations handles reservations (phone: 305-284-1300 or 800-327-1991).

CLUB MED

A special breed of destination which has been described as "summer camp for adults," *Club Med,* founded in 1950, now has nearly 100 locations worldwide. The self-contained resorts, or "villages," all share the one-price-covers-everything policy (accommodations, meals, wine, sports), and each has its own distinct personality, now seldom consistent with the old swinging-singles image that gave the clubs their flying start. This also applies to the clubs off the southeastern coast of the US, stretching down into the Caribbean, and especially to the "archaeological" villas on the Yucatán and just outside Mexico City. There are currently 19 in operation, including the archaeological villas. For general information and reservations, contact Club Med, 3 E 54th St., New York, NY 10022 (phone: 800-CLUBMED).

BUCCANEER'S CREEK, Martinique: At the farthest southeastern corner of this French-flavored island, it almost single-handedly maintains Club Med's image as a magnet for action-seeking singles. The beaches here are the best, and the spirit is mostly nonstop partying.

CARAVELLE, Guadeloupe: One of its draws is the south shore town of Ste. Anne — among the prettiest places on the southeastern coast. Singles and couples seem to inhabit the beach chaises in almost equal numbers.

CLUB MED CANCÚN, Cancún, Mexico: The most modern Club Med campus in the western Caribbean, with spectacular scuba and snorkeling. The beach is world class, and access to the Mayan ruins on the mainland is a significant plus.

CLUB MED ST. LUCIA, St. Lucia: The new member of the Club Med Caribbean family, this village encompasses 90 acres on the southeast coast of the island. Sports are emphasized; a sailing center organizes all-day and overnight trips. Horseback riding, golf practice, and a driving range are available.

CLUB MED TURKOISE, Turks and Caicos: Among the newest of the operations, it's on the lonely island of Providenciales, or "Provo." Facilities — including an abundance of fitness equipment — cater to the "pressured executive." Jacuzzi and bicycles are available; deep-sea fishing excursions are extra.

ELEUTHERA, Bahamas: On the Bahamian island of the same name, it offers a Mini-Club with special facilities for children aged 2 to 12. Scuba programs for divers of all levels of ability are a special lure. Deep-sea fishing excursions are extra. Not a very swinging scene.

PARADISE ISLAND, Bahamas: Atypically close to civilization, it offers easy access to the Paradise Island casinos and Nassau shopping. Tennis is king here, with 20 courts. This club has perhaps the greatest variety of activity in all the Caribbean "villages." Offers a Mini-Club and a Baby Club for infants 4 months to 1 year old.

PUNTA CANA, Dominican Republic: A very popular computer workshop is the surprise hit at this resort on the easternmost end of Hispaniola. The appeal of the property itself greatly increased with the opening of an airport only minutes away. Offers a Mini-Club.

ST. GEORGE'S COVE, Bermuda: Atop a hill at the eastern end of the island, it offers a computer workshop and includes an 18-hole golf course — a Club Med first. Of all the Caribbean "villages," it's by far the most conservative. Bicycle rental and deep-sea fishing excursions are available for an extra charge.

Language and Religion in the Islands

The languages spoken and the varieties of Christianity practiced in the Atlantic and Caribbean islands and in the Central American area reflect the region's turbulent history and current social and political makeup. This was the original New World discovered by Columbus. Explorers and settlers in the 16th and 17th centuries claimed these lands for Spain, France, England, and the Netherlands, and more recently the US engaged in its share of imperialism, too. But, unlike those in Mexico and Peru, the lures were not gold and silver. The West Indies offered profits in sugar and rum, in salt and Sea Island cotton. Strategic advantage played a key role and competition was keen, and some of the islands changed hands many times. Today's various cultures document this vast struggle for empire (see PERSPECTIVES).

The extermination of the native Indian population on most of the islands led to heavy trafficking in slaves. First the Portuguese, then the Dutch, brought in thousands of blacks from the west coast of Africa. Privateering deflected many boatloads of blacks from their original destinations; hence, even those islands that did not engage directly in the sale took slaves as booty, and blacks came to outnumber Europeans in the islands.

This pervasive African influence has added some odd twists to the practice of Christianity, particularly to the celebration of Church holidays. Purely non-Christian rites are not unknown, and the rhythms and words of African languages have helped shape island speech. In some cases this has produced only a lilting cadence to European language; in others, full-fledged dialects.

The effects of colonization were somewhat different on the mainland. There the pervasive European influence was Spanish and the Indian populations were too large to be totally exterminated. Despite some coastal settlement from the West Indies, the civilization of Venezuela and most of Central America was the product of various blends of Indian and Spanish culture; Belize, essentially Mayan and British, was a notable exception.

Trinidad and the Netherlands Antilles deserve special mention. When Trinidad emancipated its slaves in 1834, after slavery was abolished in the British Empire, most of the black population took to farming small holdings. In the 1860s and 1870s new labor was imported, and a great wave of Hindus, Muslims, and Parsees arrived on the island, bringing with them their different cultures. The Dutch, with characteristic religious tolerance, were quick to welcome the Jews, and Jewish settlements spread, especially during the Second World War. Finally, the production of crude oil in Venezuela and Trinidad and its refining on Aruba and Curaçao have attracted settlers from all nations. Aruba, Bonaire, and Curaçao even have their own language, Papiamento — a mixture of French, Dutch, Spanish, Portuguese, English, and Arawak.

Antigua and Barbuda – Crown Colonists until 1967, when they became members of the Commonwealth, these islanders speak English and may be Anglican, Roman Catholic, Lutheran, Baptist, Moravian, Methodist, or any of several other fundamentalist Protestant faiths.

Bahamas – Bahamian English has a pleasant island quality, and the Bahamas' churches, though not numerous, represent the standard Christian sects.

Barbados – The most British of the Commonwealth islands, Barbados is English-speaking. Its religious services are Anglican; Catholic; Baptist, Methodist, and those of other Protestant sects; and Jewish.

Bermuda – St. Peter's Church in St. George's is the oldest Anglican church in continuous use in the hemisphere, and Hamilton's cathedral establishes the Church of England's importance. But a number of other Protestant sects and Catholicism are also represented in the colony.

Belize – Until 1973 Belize was British Honduras. English is the official language and, of course, the language of tourism; but natives speak a local dialect which is an English-based Créole. Spanish is widely spoken, too. Churches are Anglican, Methodist, and Roman Catholic.

British Virgin Islands – English is almost British Standard. Churches are Anglican, Roman Catholic, Lutheran, and Quaker.

Cayman Islands – The Caymans, ceded to the British Crown under Charles II in 1670, speak an English that relies heavily on nautical terms and combines the sounds of a Scottish burr, a British slur, and an American Southern drawl. Their churches are Anglican, Roman Catholic, Seventh-Day Adventist, Pilgrim Holiness, the United Church of Jamaica, Presbyterian (on Grand Cayman), and Baptist (on Cayman Brac).

Colombia – This is a Spanish-speaking country (Colombians are reputed to speak some of the best Spanish in the Americas), and not much English is spoken outside the tourist areas. Services are Catholic, although Barranquilla offers an Evangelist church and a synagogue.

Cuba – A Spanish colony until the War of 1898, the island is Spanish-speaking. English is widely spoken and government tour guides speak all major languages.

Dominica, St. Lucia, St. Vincent, the Grenadines, Grenada – Throughout their long history, these islands were often exchanged between the French and English. The results are evident: English is the official tongue on all these islands, but most of the people also speak a French patois. Catholicism and Anglicanism predominate, but the Methodists, Presbyterians, Baptists, and Seventh-Day Adventists also have churches.

Dominican Republic – Despite early colonization by a number of nations, the language and religion of the original Spanish settlers have prevailed. Santo Domingo is the oldest Spanish city in the New World and the Spanish influence is strongly felt. English is, however, widely spoken. Catholicism is dominant.

Haiti – The first black republic combines French culture with the folkways of the Sudan, the Gold Coast, Senegal, and Dahomey. The official language is French and the lingua franca a Créole patois. English is compulsory in secondary schools. Religion is mostly Roman Catholic, but there is a notable Anglican mission influence, and voodooism flourishes too.

Jamaica – This island dominated the 18th-century slave trade and also received large influxes of Portuguese, Jews, East Indians, Chinese, and Lebanese. Its official language is English. The native patois is based on Welsh dialect and African words. Island faiths include Anglicanism, Catholicism, Hinduism, Judaism, Quakerism, Rastafarianism, Pocomania, and several Protestant sects.

Martinique and Guadeloupe – Islanders speak a Créole patois and, except for a few Methodists, Evangelists, Seventh-Day Adventists, and Jehovah's Witnesses, are Roman Catholic. People in the hotels and on tourist routes speak English.

Mexican Caribbean – Spanish is the official language and the natives converse in Mayan, but tourists will have no trouble finding English-speaking guides and service personnel. Churches are Roman Catholic.

Montserrat – A brogue is still heard in the English on this island, which was originally settled by Irishmen who fled the strict English Protestantism on St. Kitts. While Catholicism still predominates, it coexists with Anglicanism as well as with Methodist, Baptist, Seventh-Day Adventist, and Pentecostal churches.

Netherlands Antilles – While the official language of Aruba, Bonaire, and Curaçao is Dutch, the people converse in their own polyglot Papiamento. Arubans and the people of Curaçao also usually speak Spanish and English. St. Maarten/St. Martin is split between the Dutch and French cultures; Statians and the natives of Saba — most of whom are of Scotch-English descent — speak English, though the language of the government is Dutch, and many of those who speak English also speak Dutch. St. Martin is mostly Roman Catholic, whereas St. Maarten, Saba, and St. Eustatius are largely Protestant. Aruba, Bonaire, and Curaçao offer Catholic and Protestant services, and Aruba and Curaçao also have their Muslim and Jewish congregations. The Jewish presence in Curaçao dates from the 17th century, and Willemstad, the capital, claims the oldest synagogue extant in the New World. The language of specific services should be checked.

Puerto Rico – Spanish is the official language but English is prevalent — especially on tourist routes. Roman Catholicism predominates, but there are services for Episcopalians, Lutherans, Baptists, and Jews. Many are held in English.

St. Kitts, Nevis, and Anguilla – The English settled these islands and, despite having to split St. Kitts with the French for more than 150 years, held on to them until 1967. Consequently the language is English and religious affiliations are split between several Protestant sects and Roman Catholicism.

Trinidad and Tobago – Thanks to its British-Spanish-French background and its 18th-century importation of workers from the East, Trinidad boasts the Caribbean's most intriguing racial and religious mix. Its people are Catholics, Anglicans, Protestants, Hindus, Parsees, Muslims, Buddhists, Jews, and Zoroastrians — all with active churches and temples. Tobago is largely Protestant.

Turks and Caicos – These islands, like the Bahamas, were settled from Bermuda, and the inhabitants speak English. Churches are Catholic, Anglican, Baptist, Methodist, Seventh-Day Adventist, God of Prophecy, and New Testament of God.

Venezuela – Spanish is the dominant tongue, but English is spoken in the larger tourist areas, notably Caracas. Most churches are Roman Catholic, but Protestant and Jewish congregations can be found.

US Virgin Islands – The language is English with a West Indian lilt. Catholic, Jewish, and several Protestant sects offer services.

Functioning in a Foreign Land

All of the islands and countries described in this guide require visitors to produce some legal documentation. The documents necessary to visit the countries on the Caribbean coast are similar to those needed in European countries, except with regard to vaccination certificates. The islands generally require less formal documentation, but the rules vary from one to another.

PROOF OF CITIZENSHIP, PASSPORTS, VISAS: The only universal requirement is proof of citizenship, but officials at most destinations may also ask to see a return or ongoing ticket and/or proof of substantial funds. Proof of citizenship generally means a birth certificate, affidavit of birth, voter's registration card, or passport. Although a current passport is preferable, an expired passport is often acceptable as proof of citizenship. *A driver's license will not suffice.* While few of these governments demand visas, several require tourist cards, and many impose limits on length of stay. Visas are issued by consulates. Most tourist cards should be obtained ahead of departure time from a consulate, government tourist office, airline, or travel agent. Some tourist cards are available on the spot. A few governments impose a small departure tax.

The following documents are required to enter the countries and islands listed below:

Anguilla – For a day's snorkeling trip you need an official photo ID, such as a driver's license; overnight visitors will need a valid passport or birth certificate with raised seal and an onward or return ticket (otherwise you must post a bond equal to the cost of same). For stays of more than 6 months, you'll need a permit. Vaccination certificates are required only of arrivals from an infected area.

Antigua, Barbuda, St. Kitts, Nevis, Dominica, Montserrat, St. Vincent, the Grenadines, Grenada – These eastern Caribbean islands require only that visitors carry with them proof of citizenship (a valid passport or birth certificate accompanied by an official photo ID such as a driver's license) and a valid return ticket. Vaccination certificates are required only of persons coming from an infected area. For stays of more than 30 days, check individual island requirements.

Aruba, Bonaire, Curaçao – Officials of the ABC islands demand outward-bound tickets and proof of citizenship. Note that even on short inter-island visits, customs must be cleared; so carry your proof of citizenship with you.

Bahamas – Bahamian officials demand proof of citizenship, in the form of a passport or stamped birth certificate, and return tickets for stays of up to 6 months for Americans, 3 weeks for Canadians. Those arriving from infected areas need smallpox and/or cholera immunizations.

Barbados – US citizens and Canadians must present citizenship documents (a passport or original birth certificate plus photo ID) and ongoing or return tickets.

Belize – US citizens and Canadians need a valid passport and a return ticket for stays of up to 3 weeks. The government may also require proof that travelers have sufficient funds.

Bermuda – US and Canadian citizens need only proof of citizenship and return or ongoing tickets for stays of up to 3 weeks.

British Virgin Islands – A valid passport is rated "strongly desirable," but an outdated passport, birth certificate, or voter's registration card (plus ongoing ticket) may be accepted.

Cayman Islands – US and Canadian citizens need only show outward-bound tickets and proof of citizenship (in the form of a passport, birth certificate, or voter's registration card).

Colombia – US and Canadian citizens staying for less than 90 days need valid passports and tourist cards. The cards are available free and immediately when you present a valid passport and a round-trip ticket (or a letter from your travel agent outlining your itinerary and stating that reservations for your trip have been made) at the Colombia Government Tourist Office or at the airline on which you'll travel. Instead of getting a tourist card, travelers may contact local Colombian consulates in the US and Canada for a visa. Vaccination certificates are not required.

Cuba – A government ban has effectively halted travel to Cuba by all US citizens except those with family on the island and reporters or academic researchers on assignment. US and Canadian citizens must have valid passports and visas or tourist cards. For Canadian citizens, visas are available from Cuban consulates in Canada. For Canadians traveling with a group or arranging travel through a recognized operator, the tour company will usually handle arrangements, and visas are distributed on landing in Cuba.

Dominican Republic – A $10 tourist card, valid for approximately 90 days, can be obtained by presenting a citizenship document to a consulate, carrier, or — on arrival — an immigration official. An ongoing or return ticket will be needed.

Haiti – The requirements are a return ticket and a valid passport or an original birth certificate.

Jamaica – US and Canadian citizens are allowed to visit for up to 6 months, provided they can show citizenship proof, ongoing or return tickets, and, possibly, proof that they can support themselves during their visit.

Martinique, Guadeloupe, St. Barthélemy – In addition to a return or ongoing ticket, travelers need proof of citizenship (a valid passport or one that's expired within the past 5 years or a birth certificate with raised seal or voter's registration card plus some form of government-authorized photo ID).

Mexican Caribbean – Mexico does not require any vaccination certificates for US citizens or Canadians arriving directly from home. US and Canadian citizens need proof of citizenship. A valid passport is preferred. Also acceptable is a birth certificate used in conjunction with a photo ID.

Puerto Rico – People from the United States need only prove their citizenship. Canadians follow the rules for entering the US mainland.

St. Lucia – Proof of citizenship (authorities require a valid passport or a birth certificate or notarized copy with a photo ID) plus a return ticket are asked for from both US and Canadian citizens staying for up to 3 months.

St. Maarten/St. Martin, St. Eustatius, Saba – US and Canadian visitors need proof of citizenship (a valid passport, or an expired one not more than 5 years old, a voter's registration card, or a birth certificate with raised seal) plus a return ticket; only if you land on the French side of St. Martin will you also be asked for a government-authorized ID card or other official document with photo.

Trinidad and Tobago – All visitors need valid passports (good for 6 months beyond proposed visit) and ongoing tickets. US or Canadian citizens will not need vaccination certificates unless arriving from an infected area (unlikely).

Turks and Caicos – An ongoing or return ticket and some proof of citizenship are required. US and Canadian citizens need only a voter's registration card, birth certificate, or passport. Other nationalities need passports and, in some cases, visas.

US Virgin Islands: St. Thomas, St. Croix, St. John – For US visitors, officials of the US Virgins ask only for proof of citizenship. Canadians must have a valid passport.

Venezuela – All visitors need valid passports and return tickets. For stays of up to 30 days, tourists need tourist cards, which should be obtained free from airline desks at the last stop before landing in Venezuela and validated by an immigration officer on arrival. For longer stays or for business trips, travelers need a tourist visa issued by the nearest Venezuelan consulate.

IMMUNIZATION: While the immunization requirements for the Caribbean coastal countries vary, people traveling in the Central American area are well advised to get vaccinations for smallpox, cholera, and yellow fever. This is especially recommended for multiple-destination travelers, as the entrance requirements and areas of infection are changeable. Where certificates are required, authorities may demand both the origin and batch number of the serum used. The US Public Health Service advises typhus and tetanus shots for people traveling in many of these areas. Anyone who expects to spend much time barefoot should get a tetanus shot. Inquire at the government tourist office or at your travel agency about the immunization requirements for your destination. Be sure to ask about any local epidemics (some diseases — like polio — that have been virtually eliminated in the States persist in the islands) so that you can obtain the proper immunization before departure. Gamma globulin injections help guard against hepatitis. (For more information on immunization, see *Staying Healthy in the Islands*, in this section.)

LEGAL AID AND CONSULAR SERVICES: Except for minor infractions of the local traffic codes, there is no reason for any law-abiding traveler to run afoul of immigration, customs, or any other law enforcement agency. Occasionally, however, tourists get involved in situations that require legal aid. These can be anything from traffic incidents to drug busts.

If, however, you are involved in a serious accident, where an injury or a fatality results, arrange for a lawyer to assist you. If you have a traveling companion, request him or her to call the US consulate unless either of you has a local contact who can help you quickly. Competent English-speaking lawyers reside in most parts of the Caribbean. Even in Spanish-speaking Mexico, Colombia, and Venezuela, it is possible to obtain good legal counsel on short notice. The first step, in any of these places, is to contact the American consulate and ask the consul to locate a lawyer for you.

Do not labor under the illusion that in a scrape with foreign officialdom, the consulate can act as arbitrator or ombudsman to intervene on an American citizen's behalf. Nothing could be farther from the truth. Consuls have no power, authorized or otherwise, to subvert, alter, or contravene the legal processes of the country in which they serve. They cannot oil the machinery of a foreign bureaucracy. Nor can they provide legal advice, although the "welfare duties" that are the consul's responsibility include providing a list of English-speaking lawyers and information on local sources of legal aid, assigning of an interpreter if the police have none, informing relatives in the US, and organizing and administering any defense moneys sent from home. If a case is tried unfairly or the punishment seems unusually severe, the consul can make a formal complaint to the authorities.

Other welfare duties, not involving legal hassles, cover cases of both illness and destitution. If you should get sick, the US consul can provide names of English-speaking doctors and dentists as well as the names of all local hospitals and clinics; the consul will also contact any family members in the US and help arrange special ambulance service for a flight home. In a situation involving "legitimate and proven poverty," the consul will contact sources of money (such as friends or family in the US), apply for aid to agencies in foreign countries, and in the last resort — which is *rarely* — arrange for repatriation at government expense.

The consulate is not solely occupied with emergencies and is certainly not there to aid in trivial situations, such as lost baggage or canceled reservations, no matter how important these matters may seem to the victimized tourist. The main duties of any consulate are the daily administration of statutory services, such as the issuance of passports and visas, the providing of notarial services, the distribution of VA, social security, and civil service benefits, depositions and extradition cases, and reports to Washington of births, deaths, and marriages of US citizens living within the consulate's domain.

Time Zones, Business Hours, and Holidays

 TIME ZONES: There are three time zones in the Caribbean region, each an hour apart. Taking Bogotá, it is also noon in the Bahamas, the Turks and Caicos Islands, Cuba, the Cayman Islands, Jamaica, and Haiti. It is an hour earlier (11 AM), however, for all the countries of Caribbean Central America — except Panamá — and for the Mexican Caribbean. It is an hour later (1 PM) in Bermuda, the Dominican Republic, Puerto Rico, the US and British Virgin Islands, the Windward and Leeward Islands, Barbados, Trinidad and Tobago, the Netherlands Antilles, and Venezuela. A glance at a map helps clarify these differences.

Only Bermuda, the Bahamas, the Turks and Caicos, Cuba, and Jamaica have Daylight Saving Time. In each case, daylight time starts in May and ends in late October for all participating islands except Cuba, where it concludes in the third week of September.

BUSINESS HOURS: Business and shopping hours in this region vary widely. For the sake of simplicity they can be divided into two broad categories.

First, there are the nations of Central and South America bordering the Caribbean and such islands as the Turks and Caicos, the British Leewards and Windwards, the French islands, and Aruba, Bonaire, and Curaçao. All follow what might be termed "the siesta system" of split hours. Stores and businesses open at 8 or 9 AM, close for between one and two hours in the middle of the day, then reopen in the afternoon, remaining open until from 4 to 7 PM. Throughout the rest of the Caribbean, business hours are similar to those in the United States. Establishments open at 8 AM or (in most cases) 9 AM and stay open until 4 or (more often) 5 or 6 PM. The one exception to both these cases is Cuba, where business hours are from 12:30 to 7:30 PM. In addition, most stores are open Saturdays, at least in the morning.

Banking hours are equally varied. The vast majority of countries employ a split banking day, which sometimes runs from as early as 8 AM (in Antigua, Aruba, Grenada, Guadeloupe, Montserrat, St. Barts, St. Kitts, St. Lucia, St. Vincent) to noon or 1 PM, then from 2 or 2:30 to 4 or 5 PM. There are exceptions: the banks of the British Leewards, Belize, and Panamá, which are open from 8 AM to noon; those of Haiti and the Mexican Caribbean, which are open from 9 AM to 1 or 1:30 PM; and those of Bermuda, the Bahamas and Jamaica, which function from 9 or 9:30 AM to 2:30 or 3 PM. Most banks are also open from 3 to 5 PM on Fridays (pay day). In a few instances (Puerto Rico, for one), there are Saturday banking hours as well.

HOLIDAYS AND FESTIVALS: Caribbean holidays are too numerous to mention individually here, but they are listed in detail under *Special Events* in each of the ISLAND-BY-ISLAND HOPPING chapters. There are countless festivals of purely local significance, celebrations of national heroes and battles, and endless saint's days.

Nevertheless, some holidays are widely celebrated throughout the islands, though not always on the same date in each country. The nations of the Latin American Caribbean as well as Haiti, Jamaica, Barbados, and Trinidad and Tobago observe an Independence Day (sometimes called Liberty Day), which falls on different days in different countries. Labor Day, generally in early May, is widely celebrated. So is Columbus Day, October 12 — at least in former Spanish territories. For those countries which were once under the control of Britain and the Netherlands or remain so, the queen's birthday is a big event. Commonwealth (formerly Empire) Day is observed in former British colonies.

Naturally, it goes without saying that the major Christian holidays — Christmas and Easter — are celebrated in grand style — except in Cuba. So is New Year's Day.

The grandest of all Caribbean holidays is Carnival. In most cases, this is a pre-Lenten festival of parades, balls, parties, elaborate costumes, and dancing in the streets. Carnival usually occurs in February and is particularly joyous in Venezuela, Trinidad and Tobago, Haiti, the Dominican Republic, and the French West Indies. But Carnival can also take place in the spring, as in the Dutch Antilles and St. Thomas. In the British Leeward Islands, Carnival is generally celebrated in August.

Mail, Telephone, and Electricity

MAIL: Delivery in this part of the world is slow. Always use airmail, and unless advised otherwise locally, allow ten days for delivery to and from the United States. Hotels will hold mail for guests, and clients of American Express can use its offices in the Caribbean as a mail drop.

TELEPHONE: All of the islands covered in this guide have phone service. However, in many out islands and in backcountry areas of coastal countries, service may be spotty. Occasionally restaurants have no phones or the ones they have are unlisted; in such cases you sometimes can get in touch by calling the local operator and asking to be connected. In larger cities, on main islands, in capitals, and throughout the developed islands, there is direct and relatively efficient phone service. Note that the number of digits in phone numbers is not standardized throughout the Caribbean or even, in some cases, within a country or island. A capital may have seven-digit numbers while the dialing code for outlying areas varies from three to five digits.

Using area code 809, you can now dial direct to many Caribbean islands. This can come in handy when making (especially spur-of-the-moment) arrangements or leaving an itinerary behind. Check your travel agent, your hotel's literature, or dial 809 555-1212 for information.

A note on hotel surcharges: Some hotels add exorbitant surcharges on long-distance calls made through their switchboards. These can be avoided by calling collect or using a telephone company credit card.

ELECTRICITY: Most islands have the same electrical current system as the US — 110 volts, 60 cycles, alternating current (AC). This means, in general, that American appliances can be used without an adapter. However, 110 volts is not universal, and where European current is standard — 220 volts, 50 cycles, direct current (DC) — American appliances will require adapters. Though some larger hotels keep several on hand, it is best to bring your own. For information on specific islands, see *Sources and Resources* in individual island reports, ISLAND-BY-ISLAND HOPPING.

Also remember that different appliances need different adapters. Appliances that draw small amounts of electricity, such as shavers and irons, use a different adapter from those that use a great deal of juice, like hair dryers. Shops that specialize in gadgets sell kits containing both.

The norm throughout the islands is 110 to 120 volts. Exceptions are as follows:

Antigua and Barbuda: 110 or 220 volts, 60 cycles AC
Bonaire: 127 volts, 50 cycles AC
Curaçao: 110 to 127 volts, 50 cycles AC
French West Indies, Grenada, St. Lucia: 220 volts, 50 cycles AC
Montserrat: 110 or 220 volts, 60 cycles AC
St. Kitts/Nevis: 220 volts, 60 cycles AC
Dominica, St. Vincent, the Grenadines: 220240 volts, 50 cycles AC

Voltage in the coastal countries varies, but the current is always alternating. In Venezuela, various locations may use 110, 115, 120, 208, 220, or 230 volts, and in Colombia, 110, 220, and 260 volts. Voltage in the Central American countries of Belize and Mexico is 110 in some places, 220 in others.

In most places the current alternates at 60 cycles per second. Exceptions are in parts of Venezuela and Mexico, Jamaica, Grenada, the French West Indies, Barbados, and Curaçao and Bonaire, where the alternation is at 50 cycles per second.

The French West Indies also use European-style plugs.

Drink and Drugs

In general, the laws concerning alcohol throughout the Caribbean are lenient, while those concerning drugs, even "soft" drugs, are quite strict.

DRINKING: Regulations vary from island to island. On some, the legal drinking age is as young as 15. Often there are no legal closing hours, though a lack of demand leads most local Caribbean bars to close between 11 PM and midnight. Nightclubs and hotel bars are likely to remain open somewhat later. But again, be prepared for variations. In the Bahamas' outlying islands everything may be buttoned up tight by 10 PM, while in Venezuela, things run until dawn.

DRUGS: Marijuana, opiates, barbiturates, and hallucinogens are almost always illegal throughout the Caribbean — though that hardly means that they are in short supply. Penalties for possession range from deportation to fines (with deportation) and lengthy jail sentences. And smuggling is dealt with even more severely. The important things to bear in mind are: (1) the quantity of drugs involved is of very minor importance, and (2) US representatives, either from an embassy or consulate, can't get American citizens out of jail. Persons arrested are subject to the laws of the countries they are visiting, and these laws and their procedures are often very stringent. The strictest governments, and ones most likely to search and jail tourists, are those of Mexico, all Central America, Colombia, Venezuela, the Cayman Islands, the Dominican Republic, Jamaica, Haiti, Barbados, and, for those who must clear customs, Puerto Rico. Jamaica poses the most tempting problems for prospective users since the local Rastafarian sects use marijuana as part of their religious practice. Tourists do not, however, enjoy the same police tolerance of *ganja* use shown the Rastas.

It may also be worth mentioning that Central and Latin American governments often have irrational, almost violent reactions to people they suspect are part of the so-called counterculture, folks who used to be called "hippies." So if you have long hair or wear funky clothes, expect to be hassled about drugs. Better to travel clean.

Tipping

It is common practice for Atlantic and Caribbean island hotels to add 10% to 15% to their bills for "service." Though not universal, it is wise to ask ahead to avoid paying twice or rushing around trying to find "your" waiter or chambermaid at the end of a visit. If the charge is included, there is no reason to leave anything except the small change returned when paying a bar bill or other checks paid in cash. If service is not included, it is usual to leave 12% to 15% in restaurants, nightclubs, and bars. If the hotel bill includes meals, the waiter gets $15 to $20 a week, depending on the number of meals. Taxi drivers, bartenders, and wine stewards expect 15%. Porters and bellmen get 40¢ to 50¢ per bag, and maids, $1 per day. The notable exception to this is the island of Cuba, where there is no tipping at all.

In Mexico, waiters should receive 15% of the bill, and skycaps and bellmen at least 1,000 pesos per bag, and chambermaids, 2,000 to 2,300 pesos per night. Taxi drivers are usually not tipped.

In the coastline countries, service people expect a little less, and charges are often included in restaurant bills. If not, 10% to 15% is customary. It is peculiar, but porters and maids get one half of the local monetary unit per bag or per day, regardless of the exchange rate for the particular currency. And cab drivers expect very little, unless they have provided guide service as well.

Tipping on Caribbean cruises is another consideration. Luckily, most shiplines provide their passengers with fairly clear directions on whom and how much to tip. When in doubt, you can ask the purser, but remember, he is an officer and as such should not be tipped. General guidelines based on two to a cabin are: $3 per day to the cabin steward or stewardess and to the dining room steward; $2 per day to the night steward if you use his services; $5 to $10, for the full length of the cruise, to the deck steward if you use his services; $10 to $15, for the full cruise, to the head dining room steward and the wine steward; and 15% to 20% of the total bar tab to the bar steward. Standard procedure is to put your gratuities in separate envelopes and distribute them to the appropriate people on the last night of the trip. Some cruise lines suggest that a lump sum be handed over to the designated representative of the crew, but this is optional. You may still prefer to do it all in person.

One thing to remember is that tips are payments for service and are, at the very least, semivoluntary. Give the minimum when you feel it's appropriate. Give extra and a word of thanks when someone has gone out of his or her way for you. Either way, the more personal the act of tipping, the more appropriate it seems.

Radio, TV, and Local Publications

 The English-speaking traveler will find little published or broadcast in English in the coastal countries except in Panamá and Belize. Some publications in English are available in tourist centers and serve largely as advertising for the restaurants and shops in the immediate areas. American newspapers and magazines are fairly widely distributed in Venezuela.

The islands, however, have a good deal of American and European imports — both publications and broadcast programming. Some nearby islands also receive Miami and New York newspapers or the *International Herald Tribune* (now printed in Miami).

Below is a quick survey of some of the English-language information services in the islands. These are rapidly being supplemented by satellite TV reception that is pulling in signals from all over the world. For information on specific islands, see the *Sources and Resources* section of individual island reports, ISLAND-BY-ISLAND HOPPING.

Anguilla – Two radio stations — Air Anguilla and the Caribbean Beacon — broadcast daily. Twenty-four-hour TV programming arrives via satellite from the US and locally.

Antigua – The ABS (Antigua Broadcasting Service) handles TV and radio for both Antigua and Barbuda. Other radio stations are ADK and Radio Lighthouse; for TV, station CTB. Newspapers are the *Outlet* and the *Workers' Voice.* TV is available in major hotels.

Aruba, Bonaire, and Curaçao – Aruba and Curaçao have some locally produced television and radio in Dutch, some in English, and some in Papiamento. On Bonaire, Trans-World Radio does English newscasts five times a day Mondays through Fridays. Aruba has an English-language paper called the *News;* otherwise, except for tourist publications like *Aruba Holiday, Bonaire Holiday,* and *Curaçao Holiday,* publications are in Dutch and Papiamento.

Bahamas – Three major newspapers, Nassau's *Guardian* and *Tribune,* and the *Freeport News,* are published daily and Sundays; *Best Buys* is a tourist publication with both Nassau and Freeport editions. The *New York Times, Daily News,* and *Wall Street Journal* reach Nassau and Freeport newsstands the day after publication. The *Miami Herald* reaches Nassau and Freeport the day of publication. ZNS-TV and ZNS Radio broadcast throughout the Bahamas, and major resorts also have satellite TV pickup from the US.

Barbados – A daily paper, the *Barbados Advocate,* has a Sunday supplement; the *Nation,* a tabloid, is published six times a week and as the *Sun* on Sundays. A general monthly magazine is the *Bajan. Barbados News* and the *Visitor* are tabloids designed for tourists. Rediffusion BBS-FM and the Voice of Barbados broadcast radio programming in English, and the Caribbean Broadcasting Corporation (CBC Radio and CBC-TV) offers local programming plus a combination of British, Canadian, and American productions.

Bermuda – Has ZBM radio and television and ZFB radio. Visitors Service Broadcasting (daily, 7 AM to 12 noon) is directed to tourists. It focuses on what is going on each day. There is also a service for tourists on cable TV, the Bermuda Channel, available through all major hotels. DeFontes pay television and ZBM are expanding their cable offerings. CNN, ESPN, and TBS are the major cable stations. The *Royal Gazette* is the daily paper; the *Mid-Ocean News* and the *Bermuda Sun* are both weeklies; the *Bermudian* is a monthly magazine. Two tourist publications are *This Week in Bermuda,* published weekly, and *Preview of Bermuda,* a biweekly.

British Virgin Islands – Has two weekly papers: the *BVI Beacon* and the *Island Sun;* an AM radio station, ZBVI; Channel 10 picks up programming from the CBS affiliate in St. Thomas. The *Welcome Tourist Guide* is published bimonthly.

Cayman Islands – The *Caymanian Compass* is published five times a week. *Tourist Weekly* covers local news and events of interest to visitors. Radio Cayman is the government-run AM/FM radio station.

Dominica – DBS Radio broadcasts 17 hours a day, mostly in English, but with some programs in French patois. Voice of Life Radio and Voice of the Island are religious stations. Marpin Television Co., Ltd. and Video One are the TV stations. The *New Chronicle* is the weekly paper.

Dominican Republic – Although local radio and TV stations broadcast only in Spanish, cable TV is received from the US. *Listin Diario, El Caribe,* and *Última Hora* are daily Spanish-language newspapers. The weekly *Santo Domingo News* reports tourist happenings and special events in English. Most hotel newsstands usually carry both the *Miami Herald* and the *New York Times.*

French West Indies – Are departments of France and receive the French daily papers *Figaro* and *Le Monde* in addition to the local daily, *France-Antilles.* The *International Herald Tribune* is also available. Television is in French, but radio, which is locally produced or picked up from neighboring islands, broadcasts in several languages, including an English nightly news program on Martinique-Inter. (Most hotels have satellite-dish facilities.)

Grenada – The *Grenadian Voice,* the principal newspaper, is published weekly, as is the *Informer.* There is also one TV station and Grenada Radio-Station.

Haiti – Most of the media broadcast and publish in French and Creole. Tele-Haiti (Channel 4) has occasional English television programming. A cable TV station, subscribed to by a number of hotels, also broadcasts movies in English. *The News of Haiti,* in English, is a tourist news tabloid. Of the French papers, *Le Matin, Haiti Libérée, Panorama, Le Nouveau Monde,* and *Nouvelliste* are the major dailies. Metropole and Haiti Inter are the major French radio stations.

Jamaica – The two daily papers are the *Daily Gleaner* and the tabloid *Star.* The *Sunday Gleaner* and *Montego Bay Beacon* are weeklies. Jamaica Broadcasting Corporation (JBC) produces radio and television programs; Radio Jamaica (RJR) broadcasts music, news, and features.

Montserrat – Has two weekly English-language newspapers — the *Reporter* and the *Montserrat Times* — and radio programming in English, French, German, and Spanish.

Puerto Rico – The English-language daily is the *San Juan Star.* The government's monthly tourist publication, *Que Pasa,* is excellent. WHOA broadcasts in English, and Puerto Rico Cable TV carries local English programming. Two TV stations broadcast in English: WPIR, public television, and WSJU, an NBC affiliate.

St. Kitts/Nevis – The two newspapers are the weekly *Democrat* and the biweekly *Labour Spokesman.* ZIZ radio broadcasts a little over 17 hours a day; ZIZ-TV, from 3 to 11:30 PM daily; both carry local programs plus US and BBC pickups.

St. Lucia – Has a weekly paper, the *Crusader,* and the biweekly *Voice of St. Lucia.* Radio St. Lucia and Radio Caribbean broadcast local programming, and TV station HITZ carries local as well as some US programs.

St. Maarten, Saba, St. Eustatius – The *Chronicle, Newsday, Clarion,* and *New Age,* all published on St. Maarten, are distributed on all three islands. The *Saba Herald* is published monthly. The *New York Times, New York Daily News, New York Post,* and

San Juan Star get to St. Maarten on the afternoon of publication. There is broadcasting in English on all the islands, TV on St. Maarten. *St. Maarten Holiday, St. Maarten Events, St. Maarten This Month,* and *What To Do* are guides for island visitors.

St. Vincent and the Grenadines – Have five weekly papers (the *Star, Vincentian, New Times, Justice,* and *Unity*), radio station 705, television programming from Barbados, and their own TV station.

Trinidad and Tobago – Have several daily papers, the *Guardian* and the *Express,* the *Sun* and the *Evening News* on weeknights, and on Fridays, a sensationalist paper called *The Blast. TNT Mirror* is a biweekly paper, and the *Sunday Punch* and *Heat* come out on weekends. Trinidad and Tobago Television and Radio Trinidad have local shows as well as a broader range of programming.

Turks and Caicos – The *Turks and Caicos News* and the *Conch News* are weekly newspapers. The radio stations are RTC and the Beacon, and there is TV via satellite pickup from the US.

US Virgin Islands – In addition to CBS television programming on WBNB, ABC News-feed on St. Croix's WSVI, and PBS on WTJX, many hotels on St. Thomas and St. Croix now have cable reception, which brings in movies and wider TV programming. There are two FM radio stations on St. Croix — WIVI and WVIS — and one on St. Thomas — WGOD (religious). There are two AM stations on St. Croix — WRRA and WSTX — and two on St. Thomas — WSTA and WVWI. St. Croix has a daily paper, the *Avis;* the *Virgin Islands Daily News* is circulated on all three islands. There are a host of tourist publications on the islands: several weeklies, including *This Week in St. Croix* and *St. Thomas This Week;* a monthly magazine, *Pride; Caribbean Boating,* a biweekly for the yachting community; and the annual *Playground* magazine.

Sources and Resources

Notes on Sports

Principally the islands mean water — the sea, the shore, the reefs — and any kind of sport that can be practiced on, under, or around water has its place in the Caribbean. But the sea and its attendant diversions are not the exclusive interest of the area. Golf and tennis facilities abound on many of the islands, and are as good as those offered in any other major resort area in the world. And, happily, there are adequate equipment rental facilities throughout the islands for all major sports.

For a complete report on an island's sports facilities, see the *Sources and Resources* section of individual island reports in ISLAND-BY-ISLAND HOPPING. For a list of the very best spots for various sports and activities throughout the islands, see DIVERSIONS. Below is a quick survey of the sports possibilities in the islands as detailed elsewhere in the book.

BASEBALL: It's a big sport in the Dominican Republic, but Puerto Rico has the most extensive and professionally developed program, with six teams making up La Liga Profesional de Beisbol Puertorriquena. Each of the cities in the league has its own stadium; the San Juan–Santurce stadium seats close to 25,000. Tickets are about $1 for bleachers and $4 for *palcos* (box seats). Competitive play begins in late November, following the US World Series, and extends into early February, when Puerto Rico holds its own series playoffs. The winner continues to the Serie del Caribe, which includes the best teams from the Dominican Republic, Mexico, and Venezuela. Each team in the Puerto Rican league may enroll up to eight "imported" players (that is, from US major leagues) for the season.

CRICKET: On any island with a British heritage, this cousin of US baseball is being played on pitches (fields) ranging from exquisitely manicured greens to vacant lots. On Antigua, Barbados, Bermuda, and Jamaica, in particular, it's followed with a passion. Cricket is a spectator sport that is also a social event, much like Carnival. Most islands have amateur leagues as well as an island team that competes against others from the West Indies. The best players, though, end up on the West Indies All-Star squad, which regularly bashes the English, Australian, and Indian teams in the tension-filled World Series matches. The height of the cricket season in Bermuda is the two-day public holiday in July when St. Georges from the eastern end meets Somerset from the western side. This is the only time Bermudians can legally gamble, and they enjoy a game called Crown & Anchor. For upcoming matches, check with the tourist board of the island you plan to visit or consult the sports section of the island newspaper.

DEEP-SEA FISHING: Among the best locales are the waters off Bermuda; Cuba; Bimini, Cat Cay, and Walker's Cay in the Bahamas; the north coast of Jamaica; the west and south coasts of Barbados; the US Virgin Islands; the Puerto Rico Trench; the east coast of the Dominican Republic; the Caymans, and Cozumel.

GOLF: All the major islands of the Caribbean have courses, many of them designed by professionals and worthy of the designation "18-hole championship course." La

Romana in the Dominican Republic is rated as one of the top 50 courses in the world, for example. The best concentration of very good ones is in Bermuda, however, where a number of the hotels have their own or at least adjacent courses. Puerto Rico and Jamaica are other notable golf isles. Typical costs: greens fees, $7.50 to $25 for an 18-hole course per person per day; golf cart, $13 to $16; caddy, $10 for one bag, $14 for two; club rentals, about $5 up per round; and lessons, about $10 up per half hour.

SAILING: There's considerable small-boat sailing and racing around Bermuda, but the most popular yacht cruising waters surround the Bahamas, the Virgin Islands (both US and British), and the Grenadines, between St. Vincent and Grenada. There are good yacht harbors in all of these places as well as in Antigua and St. Lucia. Vessels are usually rented on a weekly basis, with berths for from two to ten. Rates vary according to the number of persons aboard, size of vessel, and crew.

SCUBA DIVING: The Bahamas have the most comfortable waters, along with a number of certified operators for instructing the venturesome vacationer in how to make dives. The barrier reef off Bahamian Andros Island is the world's third largest; that off Central American Belize is second (Australia's is first). And the sea bottom all around — especially off Mexico's Cozumel, the Caymans, the US Virgins, and the British Virgins' Anegada Reef — is dotted with the coral-crusted wrecks of ships of all ages, from Spanish galleons to modern liners. There's even a submerged train (off North Eleuthera in the Bahamas) and an airplane (off Jamaica's Negril) to poke around. If you're a certified expert and have your own equipment and a buddy, you can dive anywhere — including primitive Belize. If you're a relative or actual beginner, zero in on islands with certified, fully equipped dive shops and instructors. Antigua, the Bahamas, Barbados, Bermuda, Bonaire, the Caymans, Jamaica, the Turks and Caicos, and the US Virgin Islands are especially good. For a 3-hour lesson and dive, allow $35 to $60, depending on the instructor and whether equipment and a dive trip are included; a certification course will run anywhere from $70 to $225.

SNORKELING: It wouldn't be far wrong to say that anyplace is a good place. Beginners can put on a mask and flippers and paddle around any of the clear waters of the islands. Certainly the underwater trail of Virgin Islands National Park provides one of the most beautiful snorkeling experiences. Others: Buccoo Reef off Tobago, Buck Island off St. Croix, and the Abacos and Exumas in the Bahamas. Snorkeling trips of 1½ to 2 hours will cost about $15 to $25. Many hotels offer snorkeling equipment at little or no charge. For better gear, allow $3 to $10 a day during peak season. Goggles, flippers, and 10 to 15 feet of water are all that's necessary.

SURFING: The Caribbean isn't traditionally considered a top spot for this sport, but there are some game coastal waters here. Try Rockley Beach on the southwest coast of Barbados and Puerto Rico's Punta Higuero, between Aguadilla and Rincon on the island's west coast, the site of the 1968 world surfing championship.

TENNIS: Courts are available everywhere. All the new hotels have their own courts and many older ones have added them. If a hotel has courts, it will usually say so prominently in the hotel literature. Serious players should check number of courts, surface, and the availability of lights for cooler night play. Rates could be gratis for hotel guests up to $5 to $7.50 per hour.

Weights and Measures

One interesting sign of Great Britain's influence in the Caribbean is that the vast majority of islands, despite their various European heritages, follow the British system of weights and measurements (ounces, pounds, feet, miles). Notable exceptions are Aruba, Bonaire, Curaçao, and the French West

Indies, which employ the metric system. However, most of the other islands are in the process of converting to the metric system.

Almost all of the Central and South American countries that border on the Caribbean (Mexico, Colombia, and Venezuela, for example) adhere to the metric system. The exception is Belize, which still clings to the British system.

There are some specific things to keep in mind during your trip. Fruits and vegetables at a market are measured in kilos (kilograms), as is your luggage at the airport and your body weight. A kilo is 2.2 pounds and 1 pound is .45 kilo. Body temperature is measured in centigrade or Celsius rather than Fahrenheit, so that a normal body temperature reading is 37°, not 98.6°, and freezing is 0° rather than 32°.

CONVERSION TABLES: METRIC TO US MEASUREMENTS

Multiply	by	to convert to
LENGTH		
millimeters	.04	inches
meters	3.3	feet
meters	1.1	yards
kilometers	.6	miles
CAPACITY		
liters	2.11	pints (liquid)
liters	1.06	quarts (liquid)
liters	.26	gallons (liquid)
WEIGHT		
grams	.04	ounces (avoir)
kilograms	2.2	pounds (avoir)

US TO METRIC MEASUREMENTS

Multiply	by	to convert to
LENGTH		
inches	25.	millimeters
feet	.3	meters
yards	9	meters
miles	1.6	kilometers
CAPACITY		
pints	.47	liters
quarts	.95	liters
gallons	3.8	liters
WEIGHT		
ounces	28.	grams
pounds	.45	kilograms

TEMPERATURE

$$°F = (°C \times 9/5) + 32 \qquad °C = (°F - 32) \times 5/9$$

APPROXIMATE EQUIVALENTS

Metric Unit	Abbreviation	US Equivalent
LENGTH		
millimeter	mm	.04 inch
meter	m	39.37 inches
kilometer	km	.62 mile
AREA		
square centimeter	sq cm	.155 square inch
square meter	sq m	10.7 square feet
hectare	ha	2.47 acres
square kilometer	sq km	.3861 square mile
CAPACITY		
liter	l	1.057 quarts
WEIGHT		
gram	g	.035 ounce
kilogram	kg	2.2 pounds
metric ton	MT	1.1 tons
ENERGY		
kilowatt	kw	1.34 horsepower

Gas is sold by the liter (3.8 to a gallon), but machines measuring air for tires are in pounds, just as in the United States. Highway signs are written in kilometers rather than miles (1 mile equals 1.6 kilometers; 1 kilometer equals .62 mile). And speed limits are in kilometers per hour, so think twice before hitting the gas when you see a speed limit of 100. That means 62 miles per hour.

The accompanying conversion tables should provide you with the information you will need on your travels in the Caribbean.

Camera and Equipment

Vacations are everybody's favorite time for taking pictures. After all, most of us want to remember the places we visit — and show them off to others — through spectacular photographs. Here are a few suggestions to help you get the best results from your travel picture-taking.

BEFORE THE TRIP: If you're taking your camera out after a long period in mothballs or have just bought a new one, check it thoroughly before you leave to prevent unexpected breakdowns and disappointing pictures.

1. Shoot at least one test roll, using the kind of film you plan to take along with you. Use all the shutter speeds and f/stops on the camera, and vary the focus to make sure everything is in order. Do this well in advance of your departure so there will be time to have the film developed and to make repairs, if necessary. If you're in a rush, most large cities have custom labs that can process film in as little as an hour. Repairs, unfortunately, take longer.

2. Clean your camera thoroughly, inside and out. Dust and dirt can jam mechanisms, scratch film, and mar photographs. Remove surface dust from lenses and camera body with a soft camel's-hair brush. Next, use at least two layers of crumpled lens tissue and your breath to clean lenses and filters. Don't rub hard and don't use water, saliva, or compressed air on lenses or filters because they are so easily damaged. Persistent stains can be removed by using a Q-Tip moistened with liquid lens cleaner. Anything that doesn't come off easily needs professional attention. Once your lenses are clean, protect them from dirt and damage with inexpensive skylight or ultraviolet filters.

3. Check the batteries for the light meter, and take along extras just in case yours wear out during the trip. They may be impossible to find on the smaller Caribbean islands.

EQUIPMENT TO TAKE ALONG: Keep your gear light and compact. Items that are too heavy or bulky to be carried comfortably on a full-day excursion will likely stay in your hotel room.

1. Most single lens reflex (SLR) cameras come with a 50mm, or "normal," lens — a general-purpose lens that frames subjects within an approximately average angle of view. This is good for street scenes taken at a distance of 25 feet or more and for full-length portraits shot at 8 to 12 feet. You can expand your photographic options with a wide-angle lens such as a 35mm, 28mm, or 24mm. These give a broader than normal angle of view and greater than normal "depth of field," that is, sharp focus from foreground to background. They are especially handy for panoramas, cityscapes, and for large buildings or statuary from which you can't step back. For extreme close-ups, a macro lens is best, but a screw-on magnifying lens is an inexpensive alternative. Telephoto lenses, 65mm to 1000mm, are good for shooting details from a distance (as in animal photography), but since they tend to be heavy and bulky, omit them from vacation photography equipment unless you anticipate a frequent need for them. A zoom, which is a big but relatively light lens, has a variable angle of view and so affords a range of options. Try a 35mm to 80mm; beware of inexpensive models that give poor quality photographs. Protect all lenses with skylight or ultraviolet filters, which should be removed for cleaning only. A polarizing filter helps to eliminate glare and reflection and to achieve fully saturated colors in very bright sunlight. Take along a couple of extra lens caps (they're the first things to get lost) or buy an inexpensive lens cap "leash."

2. Travel photographs work best in color. Good slide films are Kodachrome 64 and Fujichrome 50, both moderate- to slow-speed films that provide saturated colors and work well in most outdoor lighting situations. For very bright conditions, try slower film like Kodachrome 25. If the weather is cloudy, or you're indoors with only natural light, use a faster film, such as Kodachrome or Ektachrome 200 or 400. These can be "pushed" to higher speeds. There are now even faster films on the market for low-light situations. The result may be pictures with whiter, colder tones and a grainier image, but high-speed films open up picture possibilities that slower films can not.

Films tend to render color in slightly different ways. Kodachrome brings out reds and oranges. Fujichrome is noted for its yellows, greens, and whites. Anticipate what you are likely to see, and take along whichever types of film will enhance your results. You might test films as you test your camera (see above).

If you prefer film that develops into prints rather than slides, try Kodacolor 100 or 400 for most lighting situations. Vericolor is a professional film that gives excellent results, especially in skin tones, but suffers shifts in color when subjected to temperature extremes; take it along for people photography *if* you're sure you can protect it from heat and cold. All lens and filter information applies equally to print and slide films.

How much film should you take? If you are serious about photography, pack one roll of film (36 exposures) for each day of your trip. Film is especially expensive abroad, and any extra can be bartered away or brought home and safely stored in your refrigerator. Processing is also more expensive abroad and not as safe as at home. If you are concerned about airport security X-rays damaging your undeveloped film (X-rays do not affect processed film), store it in lead-lined bags, sold in camera shops. This possibility is not as much of a threat as it used to be, however. In the US, incidents of X-ray damage to unprocessed film (exposed or unexposed) are few because low-dosage X-ray equipment is used virtually everywhere. As a rule of thumb, photo industry sources say that film with speeds up to ASA 400 can go through security machinery in the US five times without any noticeable effect. Overseas, the situation varies from country to country, but at least in Western Europe the trend is also toward equipment that delivers less and less radiation. While it is doubtful that one exposure would ruin your pictures, if you're traveling without a protective bag, you may want to ask to have your photo equipment inspected by hand, especially on a long trip with repeated security checks. (Naturally, this is possible only if you're carrying your film and camera on board with you — a good idea, because it helps to preclude loss or theft or the possibility at some airports that checked baggage will be X-rayed more heavily than hand baggage.) In the US, FAA regulations require that if you request a hand inspection, you get it, but overseas the response may depend on the humor of the inspector. One type of film that should never be subjected to X-rays, even in the US, is the new very high speed film with an ASA rating of 1,000. If you are taking some of this overseas, note that there are lead-lined bags made especially for it. Finally, the walk-through metal detector devices at airports do not affect film, though the film cartridges will set them off.

3. A small battery-powered electronic flash unit, or "strobe," is handy for very dim light or night use, but only if the subject is at a distance of 15 feet or less. Flash units cannot illuminate an entire scene, and many museums do not permit flash photography, so take such a unit only if you know you will need it. If your camera does not have a hot-shoe, you will need a PC cord to synchronize the flash with your shutter. Be sure to take along extra batteries.

4. Invest in a broad camera strap if you now have a thin one. It will make carrying the camera much more comfortable.

5. A sturdy canvas or leather camera bag, preferably with padded pockets (not an airline bag), will keep equipment organized and easy to find.

6. For cleaning, bring along a camel's-hair brush that retracts into a rubber squeeze bulb. Also take plenty of lens tissue and plastic bags to protect equipment from dust.

SOME TIPS: For better pictures, remember the following pointers:

1. *Get close.* Move in to get your subject to fill the frame.
2. *Vary your angle.* Shoot from above or below — look for unusual perspectives.
3. *Pay attention to backgrounds.* Keep it simple or blur it out.
4. *Look for details.* Not just a whole building, but a decorative element; not an entire street scene, but a single remarkable face.
5. *Don't be lazy.* Always carry your camera gear with you, loaded and ready for those unexpected moments.

Island Tourist Offices

 Below is a list of island tourist offices in the US and Canada. Tourist offices on the islands themselves are listed in the ISLAND-BY-ISLAND HOPPING section of this guide. These offices provide a wide variety of useful travel information, most of it free for the asking. For best results, request specific information on hotels, tourist attractions, maps, etc., as well as information about your interests: facilities for specific sports, tours and itineraries of special interest, accommodations in certain areas. Because most of the material you receive will be oversized brochures, there is little point in sending self-addressed and stamped envelopes with your request.

Some small islands and less heavily visited destinations — for example, Belize and Montserrat — don't have their own offices; they rely on a central bureau: the Caribbean Tourism Association, 20 E 46th St., New York, NY 10017 (phone: 212-682-0435).

Anguilla – Anguilla Tourist Office, c/o Medhurst & Associates, 1201 Washington Dr., Centerport, NY 11721 (phone: 516-673-0150), or the Caribbean Tourism Association, 20 E 46th St., New York, NY 10017 (phone: 212-682-0435)

Antigua – Antigua Department of Tourism, 610 Fifth Ave., Suite 311, New York, NY 10020 (phone: 212-541-4117); also 60 St. Clair Ave. E, Suite 205, Toronto, Ont. M4T 1N5 (phone: 416-961-3085)

Aruba – Aruba Tourist Bureau, 1270 Ave. of the Americas, Suite 2212, New York, NY 10020 (phone: 212-246-3030)

Bahama Islands – Bahamas Tourist Office: Headquarters — 150 E 52nd St., New York, NY 10022 (phone: 212-758-2777). Other offices — 85 Richmond St. W, Toronto, Ont. M5H 2C9 (phone: 416-363-4441); 1255 Phillips Sq., Montréal, Qué. H3B 3G1 (phone: 514-861-6797); 2957 Clairmont Rd., Suite 150, Atlanta, GA 30345 (phone: 404-633-1793); 1027 Statler Office Bldg., Boston, MA 02116 (phone: 617-426-3144); 875 N Michigan Ave., Chicago, IL 60611 (phone: 312-787-8203); Suite 186, World Trade Center, Dallas, TX 75258-1408 or PO Box 581408 (phone: 214-742-1886); 5177 Richmond Ave., Suite 755, Houston, TX 77056 (phone: 713-626-1566); 26400 Lahser Rd., Suite 112A, Southfield, MI 48034 (phone: 313-357-2940); 255 Alhambra Circle, Suite 425, Coral Gables, FL 33134 (phone: 305-442-4860); 3450 Wilshire Blvd., Los Angeles, CA 90010 (phone: 213-385-0033); 44 Montgomery St., San Francisco, CA 94101 (phone: 415-398-5502); 1730 Rhode Island Ave. NW, Washington, DC 20036 (phone: 202-659-9135); Lafayette Bldg., 437 Chestnut St., Room 212, Philadelphia, PA 19106 (phone: 215-925-0871); 470 Granville St., Suite 129, Vancouver, BC V6C 1V5 (phone: 604-688-8334)

Barbados – Barbados Board of Tourism, 800 Second Ave., New York, NY 10017 (phone: 212-986-6516); 3440 Wilshire Blvd., Suite 1215, Los Angeles, CA 90010 (phone: 213-380-2198); 20 Queen St. W, Suite 1508, Box 11, Toronto, Ont. M5H 3R3 (phone: 416-979-2137); 615 Dorchester Blvd. W, Suite 960, Montréal, Qué. H3B 1P5 (phone: 514-861-0085 or 800-268-9122)

Bermuda – Bermuda Department of Tourism, 310 Madison Ave., New York, NY 10017 (phone: 212-818-9800); 44 School St., Suite 1010, Boston, MA 02108 (phone: 617-742-0405); 150 N Wacker Dr., Suite 1070, Chicago, IL 60606 (phone: 312-782-5486); 235 Peachtree St. NE, Suite 2008, Atlanta, GA 30303 (phone: 404-524-1541); 1200 Bay St., Toronto, Ont. M5R 2A5 (phone: 416-923-9600)

Belize – Caribbean Tourism Association, 20 E 46th St., New York, NY 10017 (phone: 212-682-0435)

Bonaire – Bonaire Tourist Information Office, 275 Seventh Ave., New York, NY

10001-6788 (phone: 212-242-7707); 815A Queen St. E, Toronto, Ont. M4M 1H8 (phone: 416-465-2958)

British Virgin Islands – British Virgin Islands Tourist Board, 370 Lexington Ave., New York, NY 10017 (phone: 212-696-0400); 1686 Union St., San Francisco, CA 94123 (phone: 415-775-0344)

Cayman Islands – Cayman Islands Department of Tourism, 420 Lexington Ave., Suite 2312, New York, NY 10170 (phone: 212-682-5582). Other offices: 250 Catalonia Ave., Suite 604, Coral Gables, FL 33134 (phone: 305-444-6551); 820 Gessner, Suite 170, Houston, TX 77024 (phone: 713-461-1317); 980 N Michigan Ave., Suite 1260, Chicago, IL 60611 (phone: 312-944-5602); 3440 Wilshire Blvd,. Suite 1202, Los Angeles, CA 90010 (phone: 213-738-1968); 234 Eglinton Ave. E, Suite 306, Toronto, Ont. M4P 1K5 (phone: 416-485-1550)

Colombia – Colombian Government Tourist Office, 140 E 57th St., New York, NY 10022 (phone: 212-688-0151)

Cuba – Cuban Interests Section, 2639 16th St. NW, Washington, DC 20009 (phone: 202-797-8609, between 10 AM and 1 PM weekdays); and, for Canadian citizens, the Consulate of Cuba, 372 Bay St., Suite 406, Toronto, Ont. M5H 2W9 (phone: 416-362-3622); 1415 Ave. de Pine W, Montréal, Qué. H3J 1B2 (office open only from 10 AM to 1 PM weekdays; phone: 514-843-8892)

Curaçao – Curaçao Tourist Board, 400 Madison Ave., Suite 311, New York, NY 10017 (phone: 212-751-8266) or c/o Chandra Smouse, 812 N 46th Ave., Hollywood, FL (phone: 305-374-5811).

Dominica – Caribbean Tourism Association, 20 E 46th St., New York, NY 10017 (phone: 212-682-0435)

Dominican Republic – Dominican Tourist Information Center, 485 Madison Ave., New York, NY 10022 (phone: 212-826-0750); and the Dominican Republic Tourist Office, 2355 Sanzedo St., Coral Gables, FL 23134 (phone: 305-444-4592)

Grenada – Caribbean Tourism Association, 20 E 46th St., New York, NY 10017 (phone: 212-682-0435); Grenada Tourist Office, 141 E 44th St., New York, NY 10017 (phone: 212-687-9554), or 439 University Ave., Suite 820, Toronto, Ont. M5G 1Y8 (phone: 416-595-1339)

Guadeloupe/Martinique/St. Barthélemy/St. Martin – French West Indies Tourist Board, 610 Fifth Ave., New York, NY 10020 (phone: 212-757-1125), or French Government Tourist Office, 9401 Wilshire Blvd., Beverly Hills, CA 90212 (phone: 213-271-6665), for written inquiries. Others to these or French Government Tourist Offices at 645 N Michigan Ave., Suite 630, Chicago, IL 60611 (phone: 312-337-6301); 103 World Trade Center, Dallas, TX 75258 (phone: 214-742-7011); 1 Hallidie Plaza, Suite 250, San Francisco, CA 94102 (phone: 415-986-4161); 1981 Av. McGill College, Suite 490, Montréal, Qué. H3A 2W9 (phone: 514-288-4264); 1 Dundas St. W, Suite 2405, Toronto, Ont. M5G 1Z3 (phone: 416-593-4717)

Haiti – Haiti National Office of Tourism, 630 Fifth Ave., Suite 2109, New York, NY 10020 (phone: 212-757-3517); Consulate General of Haiti, 60 E 42nd St., 13th Fl., New York, NY 10165 (phone: 212-697-9767); 330 Biscayne Blvd., Suite 808, Miami, FL 33132 (phone: 305-377-3547); 919 N Michigan Ave., Chicago, IL 60611 (phone: 312-337-1603); 2311 Massachusetts Ave. NW, Washington, DC 20008 (phone: 202-332-4090). Also represented by consulates at: 71 Dunmurray Blvd., Toronto, Scarborough, Ont. M1T 2K2 (phone: 416-886-3398); 44 Fundy, Etage F, Pl. Bonaventure, Montréal, Qué. H5A 1A9 (phone: 514-871-8993)

Jamaica – Jamaica Tourist Board, 866 Second Ave., 10th Floor, New York, NY 10017 (phone: 212-688-7650). Other offices: 1320 S Dixie Hwy., Coral Gables, FL 33146 (phone: 305-665-0557); 36 S Wabash Ave., Suite 1210, Chicago, IL 60603 (phone: 312-346-1546); 8411 Preston Rd., Suite 605, L.B. 31, Dallas, TX 75225 (phone: 214-361-8778); 3440 Wilshire Blvd., Suite 1207, Los Angeles, CA 90010 (phone: 213-

384-1123); Mezzanine Level, 1110 Sherbrooke St. W, Montréal, Qué. H3A AG9 (phone: 514-849-6387); 1 Eglinton Ave., E, Suite 616, Toronto, Ont. M4P 3A1 (phone: 416-482-7850)

Mexico (Cancún, Cozumel) – Mexican National Tourist Council, 405 Park Ave., Suite 1002, New York, NY 10022 (phone: 212-755-7261). Other offices: 1615 L St., NW, Suite 430, Washington, DC 20036 (phone: 202-659-8730); 70 E Lake St., Chicago, IL 60601 (phone: 312-565-2778); 2707 N Loop W, Suite 450, Houston, TX 77008 (phone: 713-880-5153); 10100 Santa Monica Blvd., Suite 224, Los Angeles, CA 90067 (phone: 213-203-8191); 1 Pl. Ville Marie, Suite 2409, Montréal, Qué. H3B 3M9 (phone: 514-871-1052); 181 University Ave., Suite 1112, Toronto, Ont. M5H 3M7 (phone: 416-364-2455)

Montserrat – Caribbean Tourism Association, 20 E 46th St., New York, NY 10017 (phone: 212-682-0435)

Puerto Rico – Government of Puerto Rico Tourism Company, 1290 Ave. of the Americas, New York, NY 10104 (phone: 212-541-6630); PO Box 8053, Falls Church, VA 22041-8053 (phone: 703-671-0930); 11 E Adams St., Chicago, IL 60603 (phone: 312-922-9701); 3386 Van Horn, #106, Trenton, MI 48183 (phone: 313-676-2190); 3228-I Quails Lake Village Lane, Norcross (Atlanta), GA 30093 (phone: 404-564-9362); 200 SE First St., Suite 903, Miami, FL 33131 (phone: 305-381-8915); PO Box 2662, St. Louis 63116 (phone: 314-481-8216); 3637 Rialto Way, Grand Prairie (Dallas), TX 75051 (phone: 214-660-8343); 2504 Maryland Circle, Petaluma, CA 94952 (phone: 707-762-3468); 3575 W Cahuenga Blvd., Suite 248, Los Angeles, CA 90068 (phone: 213-874-5991); 10 King St. E, Suite 501, Toronto, Ont. M5C 1C3 (phone: 416-367-0190)

St. Kitts/Nevis – St. Kitts/Nevis Tourism Office, 412 E 75th St., New York, NY 10021 (phone: 212-535-1234); and the Caribbean Tourism Association, 20 E 46th St., New York, NY 10017 (phone: 212-682-0435)

St. Lucia – St. Lucia Tourist Board, 41 E 42nd St., Room 315, New York, NY 10017 (phone: 212-867-2950)

St. Maarten, Saba, and St. Eustatius – St. Maarten, Saba, and St. Eustatius Tourist Office, 275 Seventh Ave., New York, NY 10001-6788 (phone: 212-989-0000), or 243 Ellerslie Ave., Willowdale, Toronto, Ont. M2N 1Y5 (phone: 416-223-3501)

St. Vincent and the Grenadines – St. Vincent and the Grenadines Tourist Board, 801 Second Ave., New York, NY 10017 (phone: 212-687-4981); and Caribbean Tourism Association, 20 E 46th St., New York, NY 10017 (phone: 212-682-0435)

Trinidad and Tobago – Trinidad and Tobago Tourist Board, 118-35 Queens Blvd., Forest Hills, NY 11375 (phone: 718-575-3909). Other offices: 330 Biscayne Blvd., Suite 310, Miami, FL 33132 (phone: 305-374-2056); 40 Holly St., Suite 102, Toronto, Ont. M4S 3C3 (phone: 416-486-4470)

Turks and Caicos – Caribbean Tourism Association, 20 E 46th St., New York, NY 10017 (phone: 212-682-0435); Turks and Caicos Tourist Board, 121 SE First St., Suite 510, Miami, FL 33131 (phone: 305-871-4207); 90 Burlington St., Unit 2, Toronto, Ont. M8V 2L2 (phone: 416-259-8042)

US Virgin Islands – US Virgin Islands Division of Tourism, 1270 Ave. of the Americas, New York, NY 10020 (phone: 212-582-4520). Other offices: 7270 NW 12th St., Suite 620, Miami, FL 33126 (phone: 305-591-2070); 1667 K St. NW, Suite 270, Washington, DC 20006 (phone: 202-293-3707); 343 S Dearborn St., Suite 1003, Chicago, IL 60604 (phone: 312-461-0180); 3450 Wilshire Blvd., Suite 915, Los Angeles, CA 90010 (phone: 213-739-0138); 1300 Ashford Ave., Condado, Santurce, Puerto Rico 00907 (phone: 809 724-3816)

Venezuela – Venezuelan Government Tourist & Information Center, 7 E 51st St., New York, NY 10022 (phone: 212-826-1660)

PERSPECTIVES

History

The history of the Caribbean region is in most respects the direct reflection of external, primarily European, forces. The peoples who inhabit the Caribbean, with few exceptions, migrated or were forcibly transported from Europe and Africa. Since its discovery, the Caribbean has been a theater of competition among foreign powers and foreign investors, who have found various commodities worth exploiting.

In the 1500s and into the 1600s, the Caribbean was chiefly a strategic key to the invaluable treasures that Spain plundered from the lands of Central and South America. Later, in the 1700s and 1800s, the islands themselves became extremely valuable sources of sugar, and to some extent coffee, for insatiable European and North American appetites.

Only in the early nineteenth century did the concept of island nationhood begin to emerge, and it had barely been born when the twentieth century plunged the Caribbean into the wake of another huge foreign power — the United States. The overwhelming fact of US-Caribbean diplomacy was the strategic position of the Caribbean to the maintenance of the Panamá Canal. Equally significant, the area witnessed the growth of a commodity as valuable as anything it had ever known: the attractions of sand and sun and the advent of a steady and steadily growing industry — tourism. The development of rapid air travel brought more waves of foreigners than ever before.

ARAWAKS AND CARIBS: THE PRE-COLUMBIAN PERIOD

Prior to the arrival of the Europeans, the islands were inhabited by peaceful tribes of Indians called Arawaks. Today there is barely a trace of them. They had no written language and their only records were in the form of wood and stone carvings. What we know of them comes from the records of sixteenth-century Spanish writers and from the examination of burial caves.

There is no question that the Arawaks were a peaceful, primitive race and that they enjoyed the natural advantages of their fertile region. They were expert fishermen. They fashioned dugout boats of rather large dimensions out of the trunks of silk-cotton trees. They engaged in some agriculture, raising maize, cassava (their principal starch), and tobacco. The Arawaks made baskets as well. They produced polished stone implements — knives, axes, scrapers — that compare with the artifacts of the Neolithic period in Europe. They had no knowledge of hard metals, but in some of the islands they panned gold from streams, which they molded into personal jewelry and trinkets; they fashioned ornaments out of coral as well. They had no wheeled vehicles, no beasts of burden. They slept sometimes in caves, more often in thatched huts, where they used hammocks instead of beds, a habit that impressed the Spanish seamen, who quickly adopted the practice. Little is known of Arawak religion and government. Some chiefs did reign over rather large dominions and seem to have been powerful.

The real warriors of the pre-Columbian period were the Caribs, bands of belligerent Indians who pushed their way up across the northern parts of South America to the Caribbean. These invasions probably began less than a century before the arrival of the Europeans. The Caribs settled only on the easternmost islands of the West Indies and made periodic raids on the Lesser Antilles, where they enslaved and annihilated the passive inhabitants. The Caribs were canoe-borne marauders who engaged in cannibalism (Carib means cannibal in Spanish) for ritualistic purposes as well as for food. They practiced the sacred rite of castration on young Arawak captives. In the course of several months they would feed their captives a diet of maize and eggs and fruit and would prevent them from engaging in active labor so as to cultivate tender flesh, then they would eat them. Though a handful of Caribs survive today in Dominica, even less is known of their early culture than that of the Arawaks. They were menacing enemies, and after a few encounters, the Spanish left them to their own islands — only to discover that other Europeans would seize the islands they had passed over.

DISCOVERY AND CONQUEST

The recorded history of the Caribbean region (and of the New World) begins at dawn on the twelfth of October, 1492, when Christopher Columbus landed on a fertile, wooded isle in the chain of islands now known as the Bahamas. He called it San Salvador — now it's also Watling Island — and he claimed it for Christendom and for the king and queen of Spain. Within two weeks his expedition was cruising the northern coast of Cuba — which Columbus deduced was either the coast of Japan or northern China — where his search for the gilded cities of Cathay continued; but he found no gold, no civilization, only various clusters of naked Indians. Columbus did discover another island on his first expedition and called it Española, where he shipwrecked the largest of his tiny fleet, the *Santa María.* He left half his crew there and with his two remaining craft returned to Spain in 1493.

King Ferdinand and Queen Isabella of Spain, who had sent Columbus, were favorably impressed and believed that an easy trade route to the riches of the East Indies was now within their grasp; they were unaware that they had stumbled upon a vast empire in the New World. Columbus returned to the Caribbean three times. On his second voyage (1493–1496) he brought with him animals, supplies, more men, horses, seeds, and (quite significantly) shoots of sugar cane. His party landed on Hispaniola, which became Europe's first permanent settlement in the Americas. On his third voyage (1498–1500) Columbus sailed along the coast of Venezuela; he deduced from the magnificent waters of the estuary of the Orinoco River that the mainland was a great continent. In his last voyage (1502–1504) he searched for gold along the shores of Central America but was unable to show any real profit. He never realized what he had discovered. It took the Italian cartographer Amerigo Vespucci to do that: "I have found, in these southern lands, a continent," he wrote. "One can, with good reason, name it the New World." He was rewarded for his splendid reasoning when Europe named it America.

Still, Columbus was responsible for naming many of the Caribbean Islands. Before his arrival the Arawaks and Caribs had given their islands exotic names: Madinina (Island of Flowers) later became Martinique; Caira (Land of the Hummingbird) became Trinidad; Liamuiga (the Fertile Island) became St. Kitts.

With the Spanish came the Catholic culture. Columbus named the large landmass Española (now Haiti and the Dominican Republic) for mother Spain (España), then honored saints, churches, feast days, and even himself. St. Martin, St. Lucia, St. Vincent, and St. John the Baptist were charted, along with Antigua (for the magnificent Santa Maria la Antigua Church in Seville) and Guadeloupe (for Our Lady of Guadeloupe). The navigator's telescope also spied an abundance of turtles and called what are now the Cayman Islands Las Tortugas to signify their presence. A trio of peaks, divined to represent the moon, became Trinidad. Another island seemed to display a ring around a mountain resembling a snowcap; it became Las Nieves (Nevis), which is Spanish for snow. A large chain of islands was christened Las Virgenes to commemorate the 11,000 martyred Ursuline maidens. Marie Galante was named for Columbus's ship, and what is now shortened to St. Kitts was formerly St. Christopher, for the explorer himself. One of his lieutenants, Alonso de Ojeda, set out on his own expedition, and when he reached the coast of northern South America, he named it for his captain, who was never to land there; he called it Columbia, now spelled Colombia.

Even before Columbus's death in Spain in 1506, other Spanish explorers were moving along the coasts of Central and South America, and Spanish settlements spread from Hispaniola to other Caribbean islands. In 1509 Juan de Esquivel began the settlement of Jamaica near what is now St. Ann's Bay, where Columbus had been stranded in 1502. Jamaica yielded no precious metals. It supported a small population of cattle ranchers and never achieved importance in Spanish times. The more significant enterprise of settling Cuba was undertaken shortly afterward. Sebastian de Ocampo sailed around Cuba to prove, contrary to Columbus's assertion, that it was an island. With a small force of followers, Diego de Velásquez quelled native resistance and occupied the island in 1511. He chose excellent locations for settlements.

The Spanish were natural urbanites. Accustomed to cluttered cities in the Old World, they came to the New World with the impulse to establish towns, and they founded Santiago and Havana, along with five other towns, in the first five years of settlement. In fact, most of the major Spanish-speaking centers in the Caribbean, Central America, and South America were established in the first years of the Spanish conquest.

A fourth major island settlement was on Puerto Rico (1521). It was less immediately fruitful because of the intrusive groups of Caribs from the Lesser Antilles who had already ensconced themselves there; they offered more formidable resistance than the natives of the other islands. As a result, the settlement of Puerto Rico was slower and less complete and failed to attract many Spanish settlers in the sixteenth century.

Hispaniola was the base for the conquest of Cuba and for all the settlements until 1519, when Cuba became new base for conquest. That year marks two major events in the history of the Americas. It was then that Hernán Cortés, a well-educated Spanish gentleman, was lured by reports of cities of gold and legends of El Dorado and launched his conquest of the Mexican mainland from Cuba. In the same year Ferdinand Magellan left Spain on a voyage that was to illustrate graphically the gigantic size of the globe and the true western route to the East Indies. The Spanish had failed to discover a convenient passage to the East, but they had stumbled into an enormous empire, an empire that was to make Spain the great European power of the sixteenth century. The conquest of Incan Bolivia and Perú in the 1530s, and the subsequent exploitation of the silver mines at Potosí, served only to make this more evident. As a result of these discoveries, the Caribbean became the strategic gateway between Europe and the Spanish empire in the Americas.

THE SPANISH INDIES

The mainland provinces very quickly overshadowed the islands in population, wealth, and royal esteem, especially when the small reserves of gold discovered in Hispaniola and Cuba began to play out. The islands were not abandoned, however, and Spain's dominion was firmly established. Santo Domingo was already a town of some significance and remained for a number of years the administrative center of Spain's Caribbean operations. Outside the towns, undeveloped estates and huge ranges of wild lands were bought up by businessmen, who did not participate in the mad, frenzied rush for booty in Mexico and Perú.

The Spanish communities in the West Indies, then, lived by a chiefly agrarian economy. Cultivation of bananas from the Canary Islands was introduced and there was some cattle raised, but the chief crop was sugar. Cattle ranching and sugar culture both required seasonal efforts, and leading landowners refused to live permanently in the countryside, preferring the towns. The corporate town, rather than the great landed estate, was the focal point of the Spanish ruling class. The business of founding and administering an urban center was the primary responsibility and concern of the Spanish elite. The contrast with later English settlers, whose leaders became essentially a class of country gentry, is striking.

Spanish shipping to and from America was both precious and vulnerable. It offered great temptation to interlopers during peacetime and to all of Spain's enemies during wartime. Concentrated in narrow but predominantly undefended channels, the ships were easy to intercept. The West Indies, relatively insignificant economically in themselves, soon began to attract the interest of foreigners, either as a source for smugglers or as a vantage point for raids on the flow of riches between the New World and Spain.

THE CHALLENGE TO SPAIN

The French, the Dutch, and the English refused to accept the sharing of the whole New World between the monarchs of Spain and Portugal, which the papacy's Treaty of Tordesillas made law in 1494. As early as 1523, the French privateer Jean Fleury seized a portion of the booty that Cortés sent to Charles V from Mexico. The value of the capture thrilled Europe with the prospect of riches and whetted the appetites of Spain's competitors.

Foreign interference took two forms: illicit but peaceful trade in European products and slaves, and armed raids on harbors and ships during wartime. To the Spanish government these distinctions were relatively unimportant, but to the settlers of the Indies they were extremely significant. Spain held a monopoly on all trade in the islands, and generally the West Indians welcomed smugglers, who provided goods at considerably lower prices than those of the Spanish monopolists. Until the late 1500s, the chief smugglers were the Portuguese, who dealt heavily in African slaves. Isabela, Columbus's early settlement on the north coast of Hispaniola, was a favorite spot for smugglers. There, slaves could be safely deposited — in return for hides, sugar, or silver — whence they were taken to work on the big plantations.

The middle of the sixteenth century witnessed the extension of Europe's wars to the Caribbean theater. Spain's major rivals on the European continent — France, and later England and the Netherlands — became its major competitors in the Indies.

In 1553, the French pirate François Le Clerc, whom the Spanish called Pie de Palo (Timberleg), crossed the Atlantic with a squadron of ten French warships and systematically looted and burned port towns in the West Indies. In 1554 he took Santiago, and the following summer his lieutenant, Jacques Sores, seized Havana and burned it to the ground. Such events are characteristic of hundreds of similar episodes through a century and a half of West Indian history. Spain's response was to commission first-rate naval commanders capable of protecting the Caribbean ports and flotas — the carriers of the really valuable goods from South America. Pedro Menendez de Aviles served the king of Spain for nearly twenty years and in 1561 was appointed captain-general of the Armada de la Carrera de Indias, the most significant fleet Spain possessed. But his (and Spain's) concern was not the economy of the islands; rather, he sought to establish West Indian ports, Havana in particular, purely as bastions of defense for Spanish goods.

Spain had Menendez; England had Sir Francis Drake. This was the period of England's emergence as a European power, and the Caribbean provided England with a testing ground on which to challenge Spain's hegemony. Generally, though, the French and English attempts failed to break up Spain's monopoly in the sixteenth century. Spain did not decline until perhaps a generation and a half after the death of Philip II in 1598.

THE OTHER EUROPEANS

The seventeenth century was the golden age of the Dutch. With a fleet of more than 1,000 ships in 1600, the Dutch were merchants to the world; at home they were building a remarkably creative bourgeois society and Amsterdam was becoming a major center of finance and trade. This was also the era of Hals, of Rembrandt, of Vermeer.

It was the Dutch who, by example, taught the French and English that Europeans could survive in the Caribbean by means other than plundering and piracy. When the Dutch were expelled from Brazil in 1654, they traveled to Guiana and to some of the smaller islands off the coast of South America: Curaçao, Aruba, Bonaire. Their search for sources of salt led them to the deposits at Araya, near Cumana, in Venezuela. They established a West India Company, which, like their East India Company, was designed to promote trade. Most significant, they brought more slave labor and the knowledge of cultivating and processing sugar. They passed on their sugar technology to the scattered colonies of French and English settlers in the Indies, and it is this technology that firmly established an economy and a new kind of society in the islands.

It was inevitable, however, that England, as a rising maritime power, should be Spain's greatest challenger. Its settlements in the Caribbean, which parallel its North American settlements, began approximately a century after those of the Spanish. The Mayflower Compact was drawn up in 1620, three years before the founding of the first English settlement in the West Indies at St. Kitts. Winthrop and his settlers arrived at Salem four years after John Powell and his group of tobacco planters, backed by Sir William Courteen (a London merchant with Dutch connections), set up homes at Hole Town on the gentle east coast of Barbados. Between 1630 and 1642, the great migration from England to the Massachusetts Bay Colony amounted to 16,000 people. But Massachusetts (and Virginia and Maryland) were not the only destinations of English, Irish, and Scots settlers; they also landed in Antigua, Montserrat, and Nevis. Connecticut and Maine were settled in the same decade in which the English took Jamaica from the Spanish.

If the French lagged behind the English in settling the Caribbean, it was because they were more dependent upon governmental approval of such schemes. Not until 1635 was Cardinal Richelieu adequately free to intervene effectively in the West Indies. The establishment of the Compagnie des Iles d'Amérique and the settlement of Martinique and Guadeloupe date from that year. But these islands, inhabited by savage Caribs, developed at a slower pace than the settlements in St. Kitts and Barbados.

THE BUCCANEERS

The seventeenth century was the great age of the buccaneers, who must not be confused with the earlier privateers of the sixteenth century — Drake, for example — nor with the outlawed pirates of the eighteenth century.

By the early seventeenth century the oppressive colonial policy of Spain had almost depopulated Hispaniola, and it became the haven of huge herds of wild cattle and pigs, descendants of escapees from Spanish farms. The natives perfected a technique for curing the meat of these animals by smoking it over an open fire, a process called boucanning. The adventurers, smugglers, convicts, indentured servants, seafarers, and generally unsavory types who found their way to the island learned it for survival and became known as buccaneers. Gradually Hispaniola became the scene of an illicit meat and hides trade.

Buccaneering developed into a profitable enterprise in the 1630s. Tortuga was seized and converted into a magazine for smuggled goods; Santo Domingo remained the hunting ground. In 1641 the Spanish attacked Tortuga and massacred every settler they could seize. The few who escaped, returned, and the buccaneers, now in open hostility to Spain, began to gain recruits from every European trading nation. For three-quarters of a century they became the scourge of the Spanish-American dominions and trade. Had they tried to fight Spain at the height of its power, in the sixteenth century, they would unquestionably have been defeated, but Spain was now a decadent power. By the middle of the century the buccaneers had formed dangerous outlaw bands, accustomed to hardship, well armed, and (for so long as they chose to obey) extremely well led. Like most wild and lawless communities, they had their conventions and rigidly adhered to the "custom of the coast."

The most prominent leaders of the buccaneers were Edward Mansfield and Henry Morgan, whose exploits are legendary. Mansfield, in 1664, conceived the idea of a permanent settlement on a small Bahamian island — New Providence — and Morgan, a fearless and ruthless Welshman, joined him. Mansfield's untimely death destroyed any possibility of rational settlement for those "masterless men," and Morgan set them on a course of plunder and profit. He led the expedition that surprised and besieged Porto Bello, one of the best fortified ports in the New World. Backed by Jamaica's governor, Morgan routed the coast of the Spanish Main. His most famous attack was on Panamá in 1671, when his men besieged the city, killed the inhabitants who had not fled into the jungle, and burned the town to the ground. The period between 1671 and 1686, then, was one of the buccaneers' ascendancy, essentially because they had the backing of European finance against the decaying Spanish empire. The English and French buccaneer unity was finally broken when William and Mary ascended the throne of England in 1689 and England and France went to war. By the eighteenth century, wars were fought in the Caribbean by disciplined forces under responsible leadership, not by gangs of marauders for private profit. The Royal Navy and the British Crown outlawed the buccaneer and made him obsolete; the age of the buccaneer was followed by the age of the admiral.

THE SUGAR REVOLUTION: ECONOMIC TRANSFORMATION OF THE ISLANDS

Whereas the Spanish had used the Indies primarily as bases for their more valuable property on the mainland, the English and French found in the islands a commodity that made them valuable in their own right: sugar. Tobacco and indentured labor were unsound bases for an island economy; the islands could never hope to compete with Virginia. Ginger could be raised easily but was in little demand. Cotton, on the other hand, required too much land. Sugar was the obvious choice, and unlike tobacco it could only be grown in the tropics. The demand for sugar in Europe was growing by leaps and bounds and seemed insatiable. In the Spanish West Indies sugar was one product among many; in the French and English islands it became the single product of importance.

This totally transformed the society of the islands. Growing sugar required considerable capital. A factory for processing sugar had to be built, and a plantation, in order to run economically, had to be large enough to provide constant supplies for the factory. But once established, the whole enterprise became enormously lucrative. It needed large estates, and this resulted in the buying out of many small farmers and the establishment of a few, powerful landowners. It needed cheap labor as well, and for this a poor class of white laborers from Ireland and England, often men condemned to the gallows, was shipped in; but the cheapest souce was from Africa: The slave trade was the indispensable handmaid of the sugar industry.

The Africans imported for this labor were of various origins: Senegalese, Coromantees, Nagoes, Pawpaws, Ibos, Mocoes, Congolese, Angolans, and Mandingoes. But beneath differences of language and origin the newcomers exhibited similar characteristics and reacted with courageous violence against their brutal enslavement. The entire period of the great sugar plantations was punctuated by mutiny — and the threat of mutiny.

The white planters believed, with good reason, that their safety depended on maintaining strict discipline among the slaves. Severe penalties were imposed and often carried out. Typical punishments were flogging, for threatening a white person; the loss of a hand, for striking a white person; the loss of an ear, for theft; or for repeated thefts, hanging. The punishments for mutiny were savage and included, in some extreme instances, burning alive.

The profits of sugar were responsible for this new society, a society founded on slavery and directed by a small plantocracy.

THE TRANSITION TO MODERN TIMES

The eighteenth century witnessed a prolonged Anglo-French rivalry in Europe and around the world that is often referred to as the Second Hundred Years' War. England and France went to war four times in the century, and indirectly the French fought the English in America during the War of Independence. The Caribbean was, naturally, a scene of combat, but it was only one military theater among many.

Toward the middle of the century, the ideal economic existence the rich planters had enjoyed with the phenomenal success of sugar began to wane. The British West Indies, as always, relied on the government in London for assistance: They wanted lower duties on their sugar, cheaper slaves, the prohibition of North American trade with the French West Indies (to maintain their monopoly), and easier facilities for borrowing upon West Indian securities; but they encountered a government that was less willing than before to legislate on their behalf. The Seven Years' War (1756-1763), which resulted in the French loss of Canada, had drawn the attention of English mercantilists to wider economic options.

Other groups were beginning to voice their opinions. Grocers, refiners, and distillers in England wanted sugar and molasses and did not greatly care whether or not these products were native. Slavers wanted a plantation market, British or foreign, for their slaves so long as the price was high. Manufacturers of textiles and hardware — the vanguard of the great Industrial Revolution in England — wanted large, populous, wealthy provinces as markets for their wares, not small islands that produced nothing but sugar and bought nothing but large quantities of slaves. Economic imperatives were beginning to shift from the West Indies to North and South America and from the Caribbean to the Atlantic as a whole. Even after England lost its North American colonies, it continued to find them a prime source of investment and exports.

The age of the French Revolution in Europe and America was one of transformation for the West Indies. Like most countries in the Western world, the radical ideology of the Enlightenment, which the French Revolution spread, had its impact on the Caribbean in the 1790s. Haiti experienced a revolution under the remarkable leadership of Toussaint L'Ouverture, a former slave, and became the first black republic. But most of the islands remained governed by their mother countries. What transformed society was the gradual decline of slavery. Enlightenment thinkers in France — Voltaire, Rousseau, Diderot — condemned slavery as barbaric and antidemocratic. Eventually slavery was abolished: in France with the Revolution, in England in 1807, and throughout the British Empire in 1833.

No longer could the slave system of the large plantation oligarchs continue, and the nineteenth century witnessed a period of gradual economic decline. The West Indies encouraged the immigration of workers — many from India — to work the land, and systems of "apprenticeship" for workers were adopted in all Crown colonies in the 1830s. Production costs increased with the end of slavery; profits declined. And the patterns of colonial government in most of the islands — especially Spain's — were not particularly inspired.

But the period from 1860 to 1920 in the British and French West Indies was a watershed. The labor shortage in Trinidad and British Guiana was being alleviated; through a new and satisfactory scheme of immigration, a rising tide of East Indian labor flowed in. By 1870 there were 28,500 Indians in Trinidad, 48,000 by 1883. Simultaneously, conditions encouraged peasants to settle on the land, which led to an increase in the number of small holders and an increase in their economic importance. By World War I, cheap land and profitable crops produced a gainfully occupied population on these islands. In the French islands the general economy was bolstered by the development of other crops and the discovery of minerals. The First World War also had positive effects: Shortages of primary products increased the price of sugar by five times.

A combination of nascent nationalism, constitutional and administrative reform, and renewed economic initiative was to work wonders in the islands in the first half of the twentieth century.

THE TWENTIETH CENTURY

The international life of the Caribbean in the twentieth century has been governed chiefly by two factors: the rise of the US as a world power and the advent of an industry as valuable to the region as any commodity it has ever produced — tourism.

In the War of 1898 against Spain, the US set out on a course of imperialism and annexation. It claimed Puerto Rico permanently from the Spanish and briefly occupied Cuba but did not annex it; since 1898 the American presence in the Caribbean has worked to replace the older European powers as the chief military and commercial force. Teddy Roosevelt's "corollary" to the Monroe Doctrine in 1904 was the legal expression of American interests in Latin America. When they felt the need, American presidents since that time have intervened in the political life of the Caribbean.

Cuba is a unique case historically. The largest Caribbean island, it remained under the control of the decadent imperial power of Spain for too long.

During most of the nineteenth century, the Cuban independence movement consisted mainly of conspiratorial discussions by committees of exiles in the US and a few ineffectual armed expeditions from nearby points on the American continent — precursors of the Bay of Pigs. Cuba (and Puerto Rico) experienced Spanish rule for many more years than did the other Spanish American colonies, which were liberated in the first quarter of the nineteenth century in a wave of nationalism that followed the American and French revolutions. It was only logical that an indigenous, nationalist, revolutionary movement should crystallize first as a reaction against Spanish and then American domination of the island's economy.

During the 1920s, Cuba was ruled with an iron fist by a self-styled fascist, a kind of small-time Mussolini named Gerardo Machado; his government was overthrown by a revolution in 1933. This was a major turning point in Cuba's history and, in a sense, the ideological and tactical model for Castro's revolt in the 1950s. Castro appealed to disparate groups of opponents of the Batista regime, which for many represented the corrupt presence of powerful American investors in control of much of the island's sugar and tobacco industries. When the revolution finally was achieved in 1958-1959, all those who had united against a common foe suddenly found themselves divided. To consolidate his power, Castro purged those forces that threatened his authority; thousands went into exile.

For Cuba, for the Dominican Republic, for Haiti, for all the major island nations of the Caribbean, nationalism was a major feature of twentieth-century political life. By contrast, many of the smaller islands opted to remain under the rule or influence of their mother countries. Guadeloupe and Martinique, for example, chose departmental status and representation in Paris over independence. Others, like Trinidad, Tobago, and Jamaica, achieved total independence from Britain in the 1960s but continued to embrace British cultural influence.

The problems that beset many West Indian colonies as they developed into self-governing, autonomous communities were not essentially political; more often they were administrative. And administration was only achievable through education: the education of public servants, doctors, teachers, engineers, chemists, and so on. The foundation of institutions of higher education was the response to this need for skilled citizens.

But the major factor that altered the economies and the importance of many of the islands was the advent of modern tourism. The development of rapid air travel made possible the brief holiday vacation to the Caribbean from points in North America. Pan Am commenced carrier service to Havana in 1929 and was by the 1940s flying daily to a network of points in the Caribbean and South America. Air France began flying to Guadeloupe from New York in 1950; the development of the jet made possible direct flights from Paris in the 1960s. The Caribe Hilton, the first overseas resort hotel of the Hilton chain, was opened on December 7, 1949, in San Juan. Club Méditerranée opened its first Caribbean village at Fort Royal, Guadeloupe, in 1968. The generation after World War II saw the rise of tourism as a major industry; with modernization, the Caribbean was finally able to take advantage of its most natural asset — its climate. But whether or not this newfound industry will serve the interests of the island communities themselves remains a very real political problem.

The face of the Caribbean has changed enormously during the past few decades. The colonial pendulum swung sharply in the opposite direction with the coming of widespread independence, and the new governments reacted with understandable distaste toward anything that smacked of the old regimes and strictures. This did not always mean a warm welcome for visitors, though in more recent years island residents have come to understand how much their own economic well-being is tied to a continuous flow of tourists' currency.

The pendulum now seems to be swinging back to a more moderate middle ground. Formerly radical regimes have put a far friendlier face on their welcome toward tourists, and it appears that a new chapter in island history is rapidly being written. This chapter includes benefits for both visited and visitors alike, and the modern era seems on its way toward establishing a more realistic, more pleasant relationship between varying interests.

Music and Dance

 The pulsating rhythms of Caribbean music permeate the air. Both islanders and travelers feel the incredible energy and are beguiled by the intricate harmonies of the steel band, the rapid renderings of calypso singers, and the seductive twists and turns and sensuous drumbeats of native dances.

The Caribbean is a blending of many world cultures. Its music, singing, and dancing reflect all the traditions and rituals that have influenced West Indian life over nearly five centuries, especially on those islands of Spanish and/or French heritage. Based on soulful Spanish songs, French ballads, tribal war and fire dances from Africa, and whatever could be retained from indigenous Indian rites, the West Indians created their own dances, folk songs, and regional music. They extended the African drumbeat, blended African and Spanish dances, and borrowed from the French to produce their own popular culture. As a result, Cuba gave the world the rumba, the conga, the guaracha, the mambo, and the bolero; Puerto Rico, the bomba and plena; Santo Domingo, the merengue; the French islands, the beguine; and Trinidad, calypso.

The origins of calypso are many and without documentation, but the most frequently told story is that calypso began with West Indian slaves who were allowed to sing but were forbidden to talk with one another. These workers in the field communicated through their unique songs and made it even more difficult for their masters to understand by creating a very personal slang and speech pattern. We are told that this evolutionary process has gone on for hundreds of years, expanding even into the early 1940s, when the style (if not the spirit) was co-opted into American musical idiom.

While all calypso songs have a special lilt to them — the melodic beat is in 2/4 and 4/4 time — most of them function as running commentaries on politics, love and lovers, and controversial current events. The lyrics are highly personalized, often humorous, sometimes insulting, and frequently sexy. And the very special idea behind it all is improvisation, to a quick and intricate tempo and in rhyme. Not only do the calypso singers write their own songs and tunes, they also create distinctive nicknames for themselves, such as Attila the Hun, Mighty Chalkdust, and Lord Confusier. And the songs they sing range from simple "All Day, All Night, Mary Ann" to descriptions of Queen Mary and Princess Margaret and the Bahamas' "Love and Love Alone," which tells the story of Edward VIII's abdication.

What makes calypso unique is its superb delivery by a calypsonian — and what makes it fun for the tourist is that when asked a few facts about himself, his life can suddenly be turned into a song and sung in finger-snapping, foot-tapping style, as though it had always been part of the standard calypso repertoire. Sometimes the lyrics are embarrassing — especially to the uninitiated — but most of them are so good-humored that soon even new-comers are caught up in the fun. Good calypso music is always a delight.

Calypso bands, at their most sophisticated, use electric guitars, accordions, string basses, and maracas. The primitive variety, known as scratch bands, are backed by rhythm sections playing gourds carved so that when scratched, they produce a sort of banjo-plunking beat. These combine with flutes and long, simple pieces of bamboo pipe to form a trio.

The vitality of calypso is said to express the essence of the people in Trinidad, and it is often called the King of the Caribbean Sea as its contagious rhythms spread from island to island. Although it began in Trinidad, calypso became popular throughout the Caribbean due mainly to the reaction of tourists, who were entranced by everything about it, particularly the risqué lyrics and the good-natured performance of the singer-composer. Few tourists come away from the Bahamas or Jamaica without knowing at least one chorus of such calypso-based favorites as "Peas and Rice," "Yellow Bird," and "Day-O."

The excitement of the pre-Lent Carnival begins in Trinidad right after the New Year. Rehearsals are held for the competition that will ultimately determine (by popular vote) which calypso song will win the coveted honor of being named the road march. The bands rehearse nightly in preparation in huge tents before large audiences, and the winning calypsonian is given the honored title of king.

At Carnival time — now celebrated in virtually all the islands — calypso dancing is at its most spirited, uninhibited high. Resembling traditional bop or bebop (dances that originated in Harlem), it is danced in gay abandon in Trinidad, along with the limbo, bongo, beguine, jump-up, calinda, and road march. The response to the basic African beat in calypso music is evident everywhere during Carnival festivities.

Steel drum music, similar to calypso, also had its beginnings in Trinidad. Sawed-off oil drums, with their tops hammered to produce scale notes and different voices — from bass to "ping pong" — replaced bongo drums as the accompaniment to calypso lyrics. Bamboo music predated even the steel band. Musical sounds were created simply by knocking bamboo sticks together or ramming or beating them with other sticks. Today, Trinidadians beat any two random objects together to accompany calypso and steel band repertoires that range from "Belly to Belly" to Bach and Brahms. Nearly everyone joins in with his knife against his glass or spoon against cup. The ability to create music — wherever and whenever the desire takes hold — is basic to all Trinidadian life.

Although most people think that Cole Porter began the beguine, he simply based his song on it. The beguine's true origins were on the French islands, where this sensuous, provocative dance is enjoyed by islanders and visitors seduced by its rhythms, whether at the traditional Carnival spectacle, La Fête de la Diablesse, or at a Pointe du Bout disco.

On the other hand, the merengue, which originated in Santo Domingo, has all the Spanish overtones that blend softly into the Dominican Republic's sunny skies.

The African population that is the foundation of most of the West Indian islands adapted such European dances as the Polish mazurka, the Austrian waltz, the French quadrille, and the Spanish danza into its own style. The minuet, the contradanza, and the rigadoon of the plantation aristocracy were also mimicked for the pleasure of their slaves.

The French influence blends nicely with the Créole, especially when performed by the Grand Ballet de la Martinique. Clad in colorful traditional costumes, the performers portray the story of the harvest in the country dance "Les Négriers" and lost love in the melancholy "Adieu Foulard, Adieu Madras." Other parts of Europe also influenced West Indian dancing and folklore. Irish jigs and fiddles are still popular with country people on Barbados; digging songs (similar to sea chanties) are heard on Jamaica; the tumba is the dance of Curaçao's countryside; the bomba, Puerto Rico's traditional African-style dance; and the decimas' tunes resemble Spanish ballads.

Haitians are considered the most dramatically visible heirs to the African dance legacy. The merengue is very popular there and in the Dominican Republic (where a Merengue Festival is held each July). Shango and voodoo, pagan religions, are practiced secretly all over Haiti, with all the attendant rituals and ceremonial dances regularly taking place. And the Créole elite of Haiti adapted many of the European dances — waltzes, quadrilles, minuets — to their own style. On Saturday nights, Haitians have Bambouches, peasant celebrations, similar to voodoo in style but without religious significance, performed in an open-air theater. You'll also find performance of lively war dances, tribal fire dances, and contortions rituals of every other sort, combining calypso and Indian styles with African rhythms.

Another West African tribal dance, with various interpretations throughout the Caribbean, is the limbo, an acrobatic dance said to imitate the movements of an imprisoned slave wriggling toward freedom. The acrobatics involved have made this dance a feature of floor shows in many of the nightclubs and hotels scattered throughout the islands. There are usually five performers — two drummers, two to move the long bar lower each time the lone dancer has to arch his way underneath, and the principal dancer. The drum sounds grow louder as the bar is lowered, and, when the show is over, visitors are invited to compete. To the chagrin of most beginners, more unused muscles than prowess are usually discovered on the dance floor.

On Jamaica, the ska, a hip-swiveling combination of rock and calypso, and a movement called rock steady are especially popular with young Jamaicans. And, early in the 1960s, reggae, a rhythmic soul- and cult-oriented music, began to take hold, and today it's heard, not only at Jamaica's June Reggae Sunsplash, but in discotheques all over the world.

Last, but certainly not least, there's flamenco, performed in authentic Spanish style in Puerto Rico, transplanted from the Old World without visible tropical change.

The various combinations of music and dance inspire a number of festivals throughout the islands. Many are based on religious beliefs, others are extensions of folkloric rituals and customs. Barbados's summer Crop Over festival celebrates the cutting of cane with music, song, parades, and sporting events. Curaçao calls it Sehoe and holds its harvest festival in March, while Bonaire does the same with folk dancing in the streets to celebrate Simadan.

On Puerto Rico, brilliant bonfires light up the countryside to herald the beginning of the harvest with a celebration called La Virgen de la Candelaria. Bastille Day (July 14) means colorful parades and firework displays on Martinique, Guadeloupe, and St. Lucia; there is a special carnival to mark Independence Day (February 27) in the Dominican Republic; and on now and former British islands' Emancipation Days (August 1 and 2).

Celebrating the abolition of slavery brings all British Virgin Islanders to their feet in August to dance in the streets to the music of *fungi* bands — musical combos peculiar to the British Virgins — consisting of a guitar, sax, drum or bass, flute, and "musical" instruments fashioned of cut or carved bamboo and plumbing pipe remnants. The next-door US Virgin Islanders do their festival dancing — complete with Moko Jumbis on towering stilts — at their own Carnival in April. There is a week-long summer festival with spontaneous "jump-up" dances, parades, and a wow of a steel band competition in Antigua in August.

Saints' days mean music and dancing all over the Caribbean. On St. John's Day (June 24), Arubans line up to perform the Derramento di Gai, a unique folk dance that dates back to the Arawaks; Puerto Ricans light bonfires on the beach, and groups of "tuna" singers in ribbons and capes serenade in honor of San Juan Bautista. And each Puerto Rican town has its own patron saint's day, the most spectacular being the Feast of Santiago Apostal in the former slave village of Loiza Aldea, where the bomba dancing starts on July 25 and goes on for three days. On August 30, St. Lucia puts on a flower festival dedicated to St. Rose of Lima. Guadeloupe's parades and beguines commemorate St. Cecilia on November 22; and on St. Barts the islanders set aside two August weekends for a party that has all the color and excitement of a French country fair.

Christmas is Jamaica's Junkanoo season, when troops of weirdly costumed, stilt-wearing dancers whirl to fife and drumbeats in a pantomime parade that's Afro-Christian in origin, with English and East Indian overtones. In a more solemn spirit, nightly candlelight processions mark Holy Week in Colombia.

Among the many musical and dance festivals in Puerto Rico, the most distinguished of them all is the annual Casals Festival, begun in the late 1950s by the master cellist Pablo Casals. This festival runs for two weeks in the beginning of June and attracts some of the greatest musical performers in the world. Puerto Rico also has its own symphony, an opera company, a classical ballet troupe (the Ballet de San Juan), and the more folk oriented Areyto Ballet.

It is, however, the pre-Lenten carnivals, or Mardi Gras, that are the most festive and joyous time throughout the Caribbean islands. Merrymaking is rife everywhere, with steel band music, masked "devils" and beautiful queens, minstrels, decorated floats, singers, dancers, and musicians on every street corner. Carnival time is shared by islanders and tourists alike, and it provides a special insight into the heritage and culture of these islands.

Religion and Religious Heritages

 Religion has played an important part in the lives of the people of the Caribbean since the days of the Arawaks. It has taken many forms, from the animistic practices of the Indians in the fifteenth century to Rastafari, a politically oriented movement that began when the twentieth century was well under way.

In between came Christianity, Judaism, Islam, Hinduism, and all manner of cults and sects. Oddly enough, many West Indians worship God and the African gods at the same time. Superstition, voodoo, and witchcraft are pervasive beliefs, even among those who are members of Christian churches.

The masked devils who appear in colorful costume during the pre-Lenten carnivals each year make "devil-making" fun. But during the rest of the year, the devils are spirits that can be attacked, even admired, but never ignored.

The early Spanish settlers brought both Catholicism and African slaves with them. What resulted was a combination of African and Christian practices that exists to this day. It is not at all strange to see someone at Sunday mass who has spent the evening before ridding himself of evil spirits to the sound of the drums. The same odd combination holds true in medicine — the taking of a druggist's prescription is often accompanied by plant leaves tied around the forehead to break a fever.

As immigrant groups settled on the Caribbean islands, new languages, cultures, and religions were added to the population's ethnic composition.

Of the many races and nationalities represented in this part of the American world, the African is the dominant. Most of the islands' inhabitants are black or of mixed Negro ancestry, although there are substantial numbers of Chinese, Dutch, English, Danish, French, East Indian, Spanish, Portuguese, and Carib Indians. Most of these people speak English, Spanish, or French, some in various dialects or patois.

The variety of religious beliefs and practices is a result of the complex cultural and racial composition of the islands. In 1975, the approximately 27 million people of the West Indies were more than 60% black, African, or of mixed African and European descent; 35% European; and 5% Asian.

On the individual islands, the racial composition is markedly different. Most of the whites are of Spanish descent and live in the Dominican Republic, Puerto Rico, or Cuba. Most of the Asians live on Trinidad. Other islands, including Haiti (the world's first black republic), are occupied by blacks. Jamaica is reminiscent of the older plantation islands, with a black population of almost 80%, approximately 17% mulatto, about 1% white, and the remainder a mixture of East Indians, Chinese, and others.

Most Caribbean people belong to at least one Christian sect; Catholicism is strongest in the Spanish- and French-speaking areas. The various forms of Protestantism — Anglican, Moravian, Methodist, Baptist — gained a solid position with the arrival of the British settlers. French immigration strengthened Roman Catholicism, while the East Indian Hindus and Muslims maintained their own languages and religions. Even further diversification came with the arrival of the Syrians and Lebanese. And the Dutch islands welcomed the Jews persecuted in Europe.

On many islands West African cults such as Shango, from Nigeria, and Rada, from Dahomey, exist alongside major Christian sects; and Haitian voodoo represents a marriage of Christian and African practices. What is most significant about all these rituals and beliefs, mixed and jumbled as they are among so many ostensibly competing religious ethics, is that at the center of consciousness most Caribbean peoples hold a distinctly religious sense of life, and no matter how it is celebrated, religious spirit and belief in magic are pervasive.

In part, this ragtag mixture of religious practice and belief was inevitable as the islands filled with colonizers from various countries and with slaves and indigenous Indian populations, each of which had firmly established views. In part, the intention of the European colonizers was to establish missions. The Spanish, especially, were filled with a zeal to convert — which has made Catholicism the most widespread Western religion in the islands — but the English and the French (also Catholic) were not far behind. And it did not take long for slaveowners to learn that converted slaves were more manageable workers, so spreading the Word became sound economic policy.

The combination of Christian religious worship and pagan ritual performance is evident in the Trinidadian Shango sect, so named by its members after the Yoruba god of thunder and lightning. Here, too, something is distilled from both Christian and non-Christian mythology, as Shango gods are identified with Catholic saints. Ajaja is St. John, Ogun is St. Michael, Zeno is "the Lord God," and Eshu is Satan. During Shango ceremonies and dances, the evil gods are exorcised in a frenzy of drumbeating and dancing around enormous fires; it is believed that should a Shango throw himself into such a fire, he will emerge unscathed.

Ceremonial dance as a form of religious expression is even stronger on Haiti than it is on Trinidad. Although Haiti's official religion is Catholicism, belief in the powers of voodoo is widespread, despite censure by the Church. Named for the god Vodun, voodoo has a formal liturgy, conducted by a voodoo doctor, priest, or priestess, who is always held in great veneration by the worshippers. Songs, chants, dances — set forth in a series of symbolic drawings — are performed to the accelerating rhythm of percussion instruments. The relentless, stimulating beat of the drummers and the singing during the voodoo ceremony rise to a pitch of such intensity that the dancers work themselves into trances. It is believed that when this climactic point is reached, the dancer is possessed by one of the gods, called the loa, from whom guidance is sought. The god has responded directly to the special songs, chants, and dances.

Voodoo ceremonies are held in local temples adorned with symbolic charms, decorated bottles, colored paper, and other items suspended from the ceiling, signifying the loas. The dancers move fast and furiously around a colorful central pole until they are possessed. Throughout the ritual, baffling, esoteric designs are drawn on the floor. Their meanings are not explained, and to the uninitiated spectator, they remain as mysterious as voodooism itself.

A similar but not identical island religion is obeah, based on the Ashanti obi (priest) practice of removing or placing curses on people, a malevolent witchcraft that inspires its believers with terror. When a victim is chosen, certain objects or things are endowed with supernatural powers to be used against him by an enemy. The spell is cast by an obeahman or obeahwoman, also called bush doctors because of their knowledge and use of poisonous and medicinal herbs. The belief is so strong that the victim will go to any lengths to find his own obeahman to counteract or transfer the curse that has been put upon him. The chief effects of obeah are said to be severe illness or sudden insanity.

The current belief in the power of obeah and jumbies — the spirits of the recent dead, occasionally visible and always frightening — is not as prevalent as it once was. And nowadays a talisman is considered helpful to ward off duppies, ghosts that provoke every kind of illness and disaster.

As Catholicism was introduced to the Caribbean islands by the Spanish and French immigrants, Episcopalianism arrived with the British. St. Peter's Church in St. George's, Bermuda, is the oldest continually used Anglican place of worship in the Western Hemisphere. Rooted early on Barbados, the Church of England exerted such influence that the white islanders seldom married Africans, a frequent occurrence on other islands.

Barbados is still the site of a theological seminary, and among its earliest churches is the imposing St. John's, built in the seventeenth century south of Bathsheba, in a magnificent location along the rugged eastern coast. The majority of white Bajans — including almost all of the planters — belonged to the High Church. The Catholic Church and the smaller Protestant sects addressed themselves to the slave population. The missionaries of these smaller churches, working to better black people's lives, stood in direct opposition to the planters.

The Church of England became strong on Jamaica with the influx of British settlers. They ousted the Spanish, thereby greatly diminishing the power of the Catholic Church, but they were unable to wrench many of the islanders from witchcraft, already in practice for 150 years.

Although the majority of Jamaicans belong to the Church of England, there are also large numbers of Baptists and Catholics, and almost every Christian denomination is represented on the island. There were also great numbers of Portuguese Jews, and a large Jewish population exists today, along with sizable Hindu, Muslim, and Ethiopian communities.

Jamaica is also the home for many popular and revivalist sects that base their beliefs on Christianity but whose forms of worship differ widely from those usually accepted by traditional churches. The Pocomania sect, for example, emphasizes spirit possession; the Cumina cult offers rituals characterized by heavy drumming and dancing and spirit possession in memory of the dead. The most prominent of these sects, however, is the Rastafari movement, which began on Jamaica in 1930. About 70,000 black Jamaicans belong to this group, which worships the late Emperor Haile Selassie I of Ethiopia as the messiah. (Ras Tafari was his name before he became emperor.) Members of this group have adopted many of the beliefs of Marcus Garvey, a Jamaican and a black leader in America who died in 1940. He urged all blacks to consider Africa their real home and to aspire to live there. Rastafarians consider themselves Africans, not Jamaicans, and along with their feelings of black superiority, they were among the first to enunciate the themes of black dignity and black pride.

In the Bahamas, the Baptists are the largest religious group (with a membership of close to 50,000). The Episcopal (Anglican) and Catholic churches follow, with about 40,000 members each. And the Methodist and Evangelical churches claim 10,000 to 12,000 members each.

Twenty-one religious faiths are represented on Bermuda, with about half the population belonging to the Church of England. More than 5,000 residents belong to the African Methodist Church and a smaller number to the Catholic Church.

On the other hand, the population on Martinique is generally Catholic, with the exception of a few groups within the jurisdiction of the Methodist Missionary Society and several Seventh-Day Adventist communities.

Superstition, in one form or another, exists everywhere on the islands. Clearly, it originated in many other areas besides Africa and was so deeply imbedded that the immigrants brought these beliefs as part of their heritage. As religion and education and a higher standard of living took hold of the new settlers' lives, the fear of duppies, zombies, and obeah lessened, but the hold of superstition remains, in good part because tales of obeahmen, vampires, and other such horrifying creatures are the ghost stories of the area, and West Indians delight in hearing them.

In addition to the advent of Christianity on the islands, Jews from Spain and Portugal sought religious freedom there during the Spanish Inquisition. Although they dared not reveal themselves in the Spanish-speaking Caribbean, they found homes among the French, Dutch, and Danish islanders, who welcomed them openly. An important stronghold was on St. Thomas, in the Virgin Islands, where a synagogue was built and rebuilt many times before the present building was constructed in 1833.

The Mikve Israel-Emanuel congregation was founded on Curaçao, and the synagogue built there in 1732 is the oldest still in use in the Americas. Soon after it was built, Curaçao became the most important Jewish community in the Caribbean and its synagogue the most impressive.

East Indians brought to the islands to replace slave labor were either Hindu or Muslim. Small mosques were built on the estates to which the Muslims were commissioned, and the Feast of Ramadan, when Muslims fast during daylight hours for 30 days, is still observed today.

Island Food and Drink

Fungi, Gundy, Callaloo,
Plantains, Seagrapes, Boiled Foo-Foo;
Paw Paw, Soursop, thick Goat Stew,
Johnny cakes and Jug Jug too!

 This bit of island rhyme would most likely horrify the cuisinières of the French West Indies, who pride themselves on Parisian specialties and elaborate Continental dishes. However, it is an accurate listing of the most popular fruits, vegetables, and island dishes found throughout the Caribbean.

The food may sound more familiar in standard English — curried goat stew, boiled codfish with hot peppers, fried cornmeal with okra — but it is no less delicious and no less exotic on the tongue. Most island resort hotels produce acceptable Continental cuisine (though little that's exceptional, as we explain in *Dining in the Islands,* GETTING READY TO GO), but more and more are adding local dishes, and the menus come alive when they turn native.

Basically, all these recipes go back to the enterprising Arawak and Carib Indians, who were forced to live off the land in the pre-Columbian era. Over the years, African, Spanish, French, Hindu, and Indonesian influences have crept in, adding subtle flavors to the island's seafood, fruits, and vegetables.

At the beginning, the Indians found proper nutrition in all of these, while their tribesmen with medical and magical inclinations were able to heal with indigenous herbs and spices. The leaves of the lime bush were boiled to make tea to cure upset stomachs; mango leaves were distilled to soothe rheumatism; the stems of the genip tree were boiled to ease fevers; and wild okra was used for washing out inflamed eyes.

Today, resident island chefs use basic Caribbean recipes jazzed up with variations inspired by any one of the ethnic influences in the islands, while native West Indian cooks continue with their own hand-me-down recipes to create the fish and vegetable dishes that are not only nutritious but inexpensive. And, no matter what variations the ethnic cultures have added, island specialties prevail. The island's bountiful fruit trees are used in dozens of different ways. The coconut, especially when the top is expertly sliced off with a quick machete chop, is a favorite for its milk and its meat, which can be a meal in itself. Or, as the visitor soon discovers, coconuts turn up in various ways: in coconut bread; in *sopito* (a coconut soup made on Curaçao); in *tembleque* (a custard in Puerto Rico); in *tourment d'amour* (a dessert tart on Îles des Saintes or filled with spicy chunks of chicken in the Virgin Islands); and in homemade ice cream.

Another fruit used for ice cream is the soursop. Its juices are also found in refreshing tropical drinks, enhanced by "a dash of rum."

The guava, rich in vitamin C, appears in the form of juices, syrups, and butter and in one of the most popular products, guava cheese, really a candy, for which the pulp of the fruit is boiled and sugar added. When the mixture solidifies, it is cut into squares and sold in small packets.

Try papaya, or paw paw, as your breakfast melon; you will find this fruit in eggnog, cake, custard, jams, jellies, and even in deep-fried fritters.

Without the mango, there would be no chutney. Similar to the guava and the papaya, it has many different uses in the Caribbean. Especially popular in the Grenadines and Puerto Rico, it is eaten as is or with its juices as the base of a cool drink. Elsewhere it can be found in desserts such as brown Betty.

Avocados (or simply "pears," as they are called locally) are always a treat no matter how they are prepared. Try them mashed with cream cheese, chives, and onions as an appetizer; in a fruit or seafood salad; filled with saltfish gundy; stuffed with crabmeat; or as *féroce d'avocats* in the French West Indies, where chefs have admittedly added ferocious seasonings — a mixture something like guacamole.

Though the delicately flavored Bermuda onion is often taken for granted, islanders use its subtle flavor in a vast array of dishes. Also in Bermuda, the cassava, a heavy whitish root something like a potato, is used to make a crust for chicken or meat pie. It is also the source of tapioca, and after the juice is pressed out and the meal dried, it makes breads, such as cassava pone in the Cayman Islands and the Grenadines.

Plantains, similar to bananas in appearance, cannot be eaten raw and are served as a cooked vegetable. Thickly sliced, dried, and deep fried, they are served as an hors d'oeuvre. Puerto Ricans call these "plantanutres" and package them as if they were peanuts or potato chips. Boiled and mashed plantains are used in meat pies, such as *pasteles* in Puerto Rico; when fried, they become the base for blaff, a spicy Martinique fish stew; when boiled, mashed, and rolled into balls, they're called "foo-foo" and float in soups; when mashed, wrapped in banana leaves, and boiled with cinnamon, they're known as conkie; or when mixed with coconut and pineapple, they become a sweet dessert, quite popular in Santo Domingo.

Pigeon peas and rice, two favorite staples in any West Indian diet, serve as the basis for several dishes and make an inexpensive and spicy side dish. Yams, quite different from our sweet potatoes, are baked in cream, used in croquettes, deep fried, and even serve as the base of a rich hollandaise-like sauce.

Among the most important daily staples are balls of cornmeal, known as fungi, sometimes served with *mauffay,* a salt pork dish. On some of the islands, such as Antigua and Barbados, these fritters are called "coo coo."

Gundy is a stew variation in which codfish, herring, or salmon is mixed with potatoes, beets, or peppers and garnished with hard-boiled eggs.

Carne de cerdo, pork served many ways, is a Dominican favorite, as is roast suckling pig. Another taste treat made from pig is souse, well liked throughout the islands. Basically, it is made from a boiled pig's head, tail, and feet — on Barbados, the tongue is also included — stewed in an onion and pepper sauce. Cucumbers and limes are sometimes added.

The pig turns up roasted, along with goat, on picnics in the Virgin Islands, while goat stew, especially in such places as Captain Weekes' *Ten Grand* restaurant on St. Croix, is the *pièce de résistance.* A favorite Jamaican dish is curried goat and rice; in Haiti goat is marinated Créole style and called "cabrito"; the people of Montserrat and Antigua call their stew goat "water."

Perhaps the most famous Caribbean dish is *callaloo.* Spellings differ, as do the ingredients, but essentially it is a potpourri of fat pork, crab, salt meat, and fresh fish stewed with okra and spinach-like callaloo greens. On some islands, such as Dominica, conch is used instead of (or in addition to) crab, and in many parts of the Caribbean it is always served garnished with floating fungi (balls of cornmeal), which lend it a distinctly Caribbean flavor.

Other island favorites are: Santo Domingo coffee, the standard drink in the Dominican Republic and the anticipated conclusion to any meal; *tassot,* the Haitian version of a highly spiced Indian creation of meat or fowl; *jug jug,* the cornmeal and meat dish traditional with the Bajans; *lappe,* a wild hare stew, loved in Trinidad; *crapaud* (mountain chicken), the large frogs that provide frog's legs on Dominica; and *quenk,* wild hog cooked Créole style, a specialty on Tobago. *Sancocho,* often considered the Dominican Republic's national dish, is a soup stew made with two dozen ingredients, including up to seven different meats!

Freshwater rivers and streams supply Jamaicans with different types of mullet, many of which are superb. Sample *accra,* pounded saltfish mixed with yeast and seasonings and then deep fried, or have some boiled whelks in a lemon and butter sauce. Try land crabs fricasséed on St. Barts and *crabes farcis* on Guadeloupe, or as a St. Lucian specialty in which the meat is served in its own shell. Bahama crabs are especially good and usually plentiful.

On Nevis, eggs are often prepared with sea urchin, and on most of the French islands, octopus stew is served as *chatron.* In Nassau, turtle pie is a favorite.

The true king of the Caribbean Sea is lobster, whether it's langosta, crayfish, or langouste. In addition, you'll find wonderful conch stews and chowders in the Bahamas; pickled conch on Bonaire; grilled conch (called lambi) on Martinique; raw conch cocktails on the Cayman Islands; and conch boiled and served with butter sauce or in deep-fried fritters.

The French cuisine on Martinique is not without its own West Indian flavor. Remember that here, as elsewhere in the islands, almost all foods except fresh fish and fruit must be imported. And if that turns your mind from Chateaubriand to the sea, try codfish balls, called "accra mori."

Centuries ago, the Indians discovered the way to quench thirst. Caribbean potions, medicinal or otherwise, were created when they discovered that the bark of the maubi tree and the juices of the seagrape could be distilled. Maubi bark is boiled with nutmeg and cinnamon; seagrape juices are nurtured with cloves and ginger; and the Caribbean's basic ingredient, rum, is distilled to everyone's satisfaction. Whether it's Cruzan, Bajan, Jamaican, or Puerto Rican — light or dark — it invariably appears with a twist of lime. Piña coladas, Cuba libres, swizzles, and rum and Coca-Colas cool the tourist easily. Native wine sangrias also help travelers enjoy themselves. Besides producing inexpensive rum in substantial volume, Trinidad originated angostura bitters, which are still manufactured there. And don't leave the islands without a glass or two of Curaçao, the famous liqueur from the island of the same name.

Flora, Fauna, and Fertile Lands

 No wonder so many visitors to the Caribbean consider their second and third trips returns to paradise. The lush greens and exotic, tropical flora that cover the island landscapes with blankets of color combine with the brilliant blue of the sky and the rich blue-green of the sea in dazzling scenes that indeed seem out of this world.

The earliest descriptions of vegetation in the Caribbean were found in petroglyphs on the rocky promontories of the islands. But it wasn't until Christopher Columbus recorded his impressions that written documentation existed. On his first voyage to the New World, Columbus wrote of his arrival at Hispaniola: "Its lands are high, and there are in it very many sierras and very lofty mountains . . . all are most beautiful, of a thousand shapes . . . and filled with trees of a thousand kinds, some so tall they seem to touch the sky. And I am told that they never lose their foliage, as I can understand, for I saw them as green and as lovely as they are in Spain in May . . . some of them were flowering, some bearing fruit, and some in another stage, according to their nature. And the nightingale was singing, and there were other birds of a thousand kinds."

In the last several centuries, however, so many new plants and trees have been introduced and have thrived in the Caribbean that Columbus's observations would likely be even more amazed today. On most of the islands, you will find the banyan tree from Ceylon; the tall and stately breadfruit tree, first introduced by Captain Bligh, who brought a shipload of seedlings to Jamaica from Tahiti in 1794; the exquisite red-flowered tulip tree from Africa, with blooms big enough to serve as birdbaths; and the dozens of varieties of plantains that grow throughout the West Indies on shaggy-leafed plants called "fig trees" on some islands. And there is the century plant, with its tall, spindly stem and flowers that make it resemble a 20-foot candelabrum. Some Virgin Islanders use it as a Christmas tree, and you will see it growing on island hillsides, where it may take as long as ten years to bring forth its bouquets of blooms.

The flamboyant, or royal poinciana, has the same fire-red blossoms as the African tulip, only on a smaller scale. And, although hibiscus grows in many varieties, its ruby-red incarnation is the most familiar in the West Indies.

Bougainvillea blooms in deep orange, lavender, white, and bright red. The fragrant frangipani tree sprouts star-shaped blossoms in pink, red, and yellow; the natives often use the milky substance inside the limbs for a poultice.

Among the edibles are the cassava, a squat shrub about six feet high, whose roots are grated, boiled, and made into a coarse bread. There is also the mammee, or marmalade tree, whose fruits are used to make jelly. Perhaps the most decorative is the calabash, which produces oddly shaped fruits that resemble gourds and are used in several interesting ways. Cut in half, they serve as drinking cups, as baking dishes, or even as boat bailers. Whole, they are carved into musical instruments for scratch bands.

Two of the largest trees in the islands are the mahogany and the manchineel. The mahogany resembles an oak but has smaller leaves and bears orange blossoms. The manchineel is poisonous; its sap, apples, and leaves are deadly. *Warning:* During a rainstorm, *do not* seek shelter under this full tree. When the rains hit its leaves, the resultant drippings can cause severe burns.

The rest of the foliage in the Caribbean is nothing but sheer beauty. Even a cursory explorer will find tangled mangroves and low-lying seagrapes all along the shores, great feather-shaped ferns, and orchids growing wild. Lime, sugar apple, and mangoes are there for the picking, and sunsets evoke heady scents of frangipani and night-blooming jasmine. And, in this world of fabulous blooms and Edenic landscapes, one of the prettiest sights of all is a tiny flower with a whimsical name — "jump-up-and-kiss-me" — which opens in a burst of color early in the morning and closes for the night when the sun goes down.

ALL AT SEA

The silent world beneath the Caribbean Sea is just as spectacular along its coral reefs, and your own splash down into the warm waters is the last sound you'll hear before resurfacing. As you snorkel along the reef trails, you'll find a dazzling variety of shapes and colors. Each coral formation is different, with the staghorn the most delicate, and the stunning pillar coral growing in cathedral-like spires.

The sea fans, with their lacy leaves, add the blues, pale greens, and lavenders, while the fuzzy skeletal formations called corky sea fingers are brown and resemble cactus.

What is perhaps most striking is the harmony; everything blends together in effortless beauty. Sea fans wave with the motion of the water, while schools of fish, seemingly suspended in the sea, glide by as gracefully as a corps de ballet.

There are thousands of fish in dozens of colors and species — angels, trumpets, cardinals, and jewfish. The angelfish are friendly little seafarers in all shades of blue, yellow, and green, and one variety is called the queen because of the crown on its forehead; another, the gray angelfish because of its silver tones; and another, the French angelfish, is black with a sprinkling of yellow spots. No matter what their coloration, they all appear to be pouting.

This is not so with the long, thin trumpetfish. Nor with the jewfish or sea bass, one of the giants of the reef, with many individual finny examples stretching to eight feet and weighing 700 pounds. And it should come as no surprise that the small cardinalfish are clothed in bright red and have what appears to be a regal bearing.

Search for the coral reef's so-called corps of professionals — surgeons, doctors, schoolmasters, and sergeant majors — each doing his job with easy precision. The schoolmaster, related to the larger snapper family, is about two feet long and has a severe and dour countenance, while the sergeant major, sporting military-like chevrons on its flanks, is the most cheerful and approachable.

Several brown stripes on a beige body mark the doctorfish, while the ocean surgeon, which varies in color, has a circle of small blue lines around its eyes, giving the impression that it's wearing mascara.

Farther along the coral reef are butterflies, peacocks, parrots, and squirrels. The butterfly fish are delicate and small, as their name implies, and they have black stripes across their eyes, almost as if they were wearing eyepatches. The peacock, a flatfish of the flounder family, is beige with blue starlike spots and a colorful tail resembling the prancing peacock on shore.

The same is true of the parrot fish, whose bright green, red, and yellow colors blend together as naturally as those of its feathered counterparts. The squirrel fish, however, with its spiny dorsal fins, looks like prickly cactus as it swims.

Watch out, too, for the spades, jacks, kings, and queens. The spadefish, silver with black stripes, look like miniature zebras; the queens wear the crowns in many species. Amberjacks, yellow jacks, and kingfish swim by occasionally; they are more often in deeper waters and are considered among the prize catches of sport fishermen.

Finally, no matter which reef you travel in the Caribbean, you may very well be met by a grunt (their name comes from the sound they seem to make), or by schools of sunshine, small, golden members of the damselfish family.

There are many fine reef trails in the Caribbean, but the best known are off Buck Island, 5 miles from Christiansted Harbor on St. Croix; off Anegada in the British Virgin Islands; and the underwater trail at Trunk Bay in Virgin Islands National Park, on the US Virgin Island of St. John.

ON THE HOOK AND IN THE SKY

While the snorkeler on the reef sees it all, the sport fisherman takes his lot one at a time, and a hefty and varied lot it can be. The Bahamas, immortalized by Ernest Hemingway in his stories about Bimini, boast endless varieties of fish — tuna, barracuda, mackerel, sailfish, amberjack, marlin, dolphin, bonefish, and wahoo.

You'll likely see the blue marlin in the US Virgin Islands; blackfish (and even whales) off St. Vincent; marlin, kingfish, dolphin, wahoo, bonita, barracuda, tuna, mackerel, and snapper in Jamaican waters; wahoo, marlin, and many more off Trinidad.

The islands are also a special delight for bird-watchers. There must be more than 1,000 bird species in the Caribbean, ranging from parrot and trogon to many varieties of waterfowl. Some nest high in the mountains, others leave their tracks in the sand near the edge of the sea, and others are simply seen "on the wing." They can be found (and heard) everywhere on the islands and are surely an additional source of enjoyment for the visitor.

Some hard-bitten ornithologists had maintained that Columbus first heard a mockingbird, not a nightingale as he claimed, but recent studies have shown that the nightingale does in fact live in high mountainous areas and is one of the few Caribbean birds that continue to sing during the October-November rainy season. Columbus landed on the islands in the fall, and his notes about hearing a bird in the high and lofty mountains point to the nightingale. And although the nightingale is a difficult bird to see face-to-beak, its song is indeed often heard.

Different notes (on a smaller scale) come from the varied Caribbean hummingbirds, all of them tiny, but some with bright emerald breasts (on Trinidad and Tobago), and others with flaming red breasts (on Aruba and Curaçao). On Little Tobago, birds of paradise are certainly the most famous, but hardly the only interesting birds to be seen. Others include a rare hummingbird, the blue-throated saberwing, the magnificent frigate bird, and a variety of thrushes and woodpeckers, among many other species.

For great color, the St. Vincent parrot is a handsome bird that spans the artist's color wheel from pale yellow to deep violet. And for pastel shades, the West Indian flamingo, an oversized wading bird with spindly legs and pink and salmon-colored feathers, can be seen on the breeding grounds of Bonaire and Great Inagua in the Bahamas. Of special interest to tourists visiting Nassau is Ardastra Gardens, where the highly trained flamingos take commands and march in precision, offering the only show of its kind in the world.

Blue herons, lovely little birds of cobalt blue, often hide in the mangroves on Jamaica, Trinidad, and Tobago. And the egret, similar to the heron in shape but snow-white and with a yellow bill, is often seen in the open fields, circling or lighting on or near the cattle in the Dominican Republic, in Jamaica, or on St. Croix.

One of the most visible birds on St. John is the pearly-eyed thrasher, or thrushee, considered more of a pest than a pleasure because he nibbles away at anything — tree, shrub, or table — he can find. The bananaquit, or yellow-breasted sugar bird, comparable in size to the thrushee but far sweeter and not at all destructive, is the official bird of the Virgin Islands. Sometimes found nesting in cactus, it is more often observed on sunny mornings nipping into the sugar bowl on tourists' tables. Although it has many different names throughout the islands — black see-see on St. Vincent, the chibichibi on Bonaire, and the honeycreeper on Haiti — the bird's constant quest for something sweet and his amusing antics are always the same.

Bird-watching is such a natural activity throughout the Caribbean that you don't even need binoculars. The birds are simply everywhere to be seen and heard. So you often find yourself standing in awe as you watch the pelicans glide and plummet into the sea around Trinidad. Or you listen to laughing gulls giggle on St. Martin, hear owls screech on Carriacou, mourning doves coo-coo in the Netherlands Antilles, follow the lilting notes of the yellow warbler everywhere, and revel in the glorious song of the nightingale.

FRUITS OF THE SOIL

Citrus fruits are grown on many of the islands of the Bahamas along with small amounts of pigeon peas, okra, sweet and hot peppers, and tomatoes. Sisal is also grown, but today is used mainly for the straw work sold at the tourist markets. Cucumbers from Abaco and Andros and pineapples from Eleuthera are still exported to Nassau and to the United States. And sun-dried salt is produced by the Morton Company on Great Inagua in one of the largest salt complexes in the world.

Solar salt is also produced on Bonaire, while its sister islands are definitely in the oil business. On Aruba, where there once was gold, there is now a subsidiary of Standard Oil of New Jersey, and Shell Oil has its Netherlands Antilles headquarters on Curaçao.

On the French islands, sugar cane is still the principal product. In addition, Guadeloupians raise cattle and grow coffee, bananas, cocoa, and pineapples. Martinique has pineapples, too, along with vanilla and bananas; its showiest specialty is the patent red anthurium flowers it raises for export.

There is a small cattle industry in the Cayman Islands, but the emphasis and money there are on turtle farming. Every part of the turtle, except its head, has a commercial value: The skin is cured for leather, the flesh cooked for soups and stews, the meat grilled for steaks, and the shell crafted for jewelry and other decorative uses.

Timber is a flourishing business on the island of St. Lucia, where mahogany and pine trees abound; citrus fruits, bananas, cocoa, and a small amount of sugar cane are also grown there.

Sugar cane plantations have hardly died out completely. There are still a few hundred, each one at least ten acres, which have been in continual use on Barbados since the seventeenth century. On this richly verdant island, mangoes, avocados, bananas, melons, and breadfruit grow in abundance. Bajans also raise livestock, operate more than two dozen dairies, mine limestone, and are now in the process of drilling for crude oil.

Jamaica is another of the more productive Caribbean islands, with sugar and tobacco plantations and coffee fields all along the slopes of its Blue Mountains. Among the island's even more lucrative exports are bauxite ore (which is converted into alumina), gypsum, some copper and iron, and an abundance of marble.

Bauxite and marble are also mined in the Dominican Republic, as well as copper, cobalt, amber, and crude oil. Sugar is still its biggest crop. Rice cultivation is on the upswing, and its rich and delicious coffee continues to be appreciated worldwide.

On Antigua, an island that was once a plantation owner's dream, there is little left of the sugar cane, but the introduction of Sea Island cotton has helped make up for the loss. Sea Island cotton is also abundant on the island of Nevis, which has little else, and on Montserrat, which also grows enough peppers, onions, and carrots for export.

Grenada has always been called the Spice Island because of its nutmeg, mace, cinnamon, cloves, and ginger, while Anguilla maintains itself with its lobsters. Sought after from St. Vincent is its arrowroot, which is plentiful enough to be exported to Canada, Great Britain, and the US. St. Croix has a new money crop called sorghum, which is supposed to solve the cattle-feeding problem.

But agricultural output and resources aside, the greatest commodity produced by the Caribbean is sunshine, plus azure waters, cooling trade winds, and powder-sand beaches, a habitat ideal for flora, fauna — and tourism.

Folk Legends and Lore, Literature, Art, and Crafts

 The Caribbean's African, Indian, and European inheritance is apparent throughout its legends, literature, and folk arts. Each of these is a fascinating and curious merger of cultural heritages, a variety of languages, and the effects of successive waves of conquest and submission.

FOLK TALES

Because the African influence in the West Indies was a product of European colonization (European whites initiated the slave trade, bringing some West African slaves to the islands to work and holding others for eventual sale in the US), African and European stories, aphorisms, folk tales, and superstitions entered the islands at about the same time. Some of the earliest West Indian stories are derivations of West African folk tales and beliefs; others are distinctly European.

An example of a Caribbean proverb, borrowed and idiomized from Europe, indicates the influence: "Not everything wha' got sugar is sweet." (The European equivalent is "All that glitters is not gold.") "Who got out starch clothes mus' look out fo' rain" is the island form of "People in glass houses shouldn't throw stones." Often only the vocabulary in which a sentiment is couched is changed. A proverb describing God's omnipotence says, "God-a-mighty nebber shut He eye," and to describe a hypocrite, "He got two faces under one cap." Flattery is to "sweet-mout" and to wink flirtatiously is to give "the sweet-eye."

Many of the proverbs used on the islands are short and to the point: "New broom sweep clean, but old broom know the corners" and "If yo' bundle a dirty clothes too heavy, try pickin' up yo' neighbor own"; others mix philosophy with wry humor: "If crab don't walk, he get gat, but if he walk too far he end up in the pot!"

Folklore perpetuates old legends and myths simply by passing them on from one generation to the next. Caribbean children are enthralled by traditional tales, and it is not surprising that they are recast in contemporary forms. The process that has been going on for centuries. The African story "Buh Jack and His Ancestors" became "Jack the Giant Killer," and "Buh Rabby" turned into "Br'er Rabbit" by the time it reached the US Southland.

Animals — big cats from the jungles of Africa, rabbits, dogs, and cats from the tropics — are the powerful figures in much of African–West Indian folklore. Animals have magical powers giving them the ability to assume human shapes and to frighten and outwit enemies with greater physical strength. Ananse (a legendary African figure known as Nanzi, Anansi, or Anancy, depending on the island on which the story is told), is a famous example of this. Translated from the African, *ananse* means spider. His adventures, as he achieves his goals, are an endless source of wonder and education to the young. The stories serve as learning vehicles and explain such mysteries as how spiders weave webs and why wasps sting.

Ananse's tales are told throughout the islands; on Curaçao the folk hero has become the protagonist of a theatrical presentation that acquaints visitors with the islanders' most revered traditions. A musical stage show, *Nanzi and the Shon King,* is often presented in Willemstad during special festivals. Performed in English during festivals, it is also performed in Dutch and Papiamento in the Curaçao schools.

Ananse stories are also very popular on Jamaica, and as a human character in one of the all-time favorite tales, he confronts an owl and their characteristics are exchanged. But, no matter how animalistic Ananse becomes, or how human the owl seems, Ananse outwits any and all odds, and the story ends with the usual West Indian conclusion, "Jack Mandora, me no choose none," which, when literally translated, means "any similarity to characters living or dead is purely coincidental!"

West Indian legends are so intertwined with superstitions that it is difficult to tell where one begins and the other leaves off. Many of these have to do with witches, devils, and ghosts.

A legend important to all the islands is that of the Spanish Jar. It claimed that treasures were buried in earthenware jars by the Spaniards, whose ghosts surrounded them as protection. Should anyone be told where they were hidden — and, as the story goes, this could only happen in a dream — they would face the insurmountable problem of convincing the ancient caretakers to give them up.

ISLAND LITERATURE

Although traditional legends and folklore are interwoven in the daily texture of Caribbean lives, most writers draw from this aspect of their heritage indirectly. They are more concerned with writing about the history and current events of life on the islands or, through the use of fiction, about their personal problems of identity and rootlessness.

Nowhere is the personal dilemma of the West Indians more clearly expressed than in their contemporary literature. The transplanted Africans' conflict — the desire to leave and the desire to stay — is the heart and soul of Caribbean writing. The terrible tension of a strong inheritance from Africa and a rootless existence on the islands, the feelings of suspension and of belonging nowhere, recur as themes of all black writers in the Caribbean.

Their dilemma is further compounded by the isolation of the islands, particularly from the world of writers, critics, publishers, and readers. No matter what their origins, creative artists need to expand their experience and acquire more worldly knowledge. After living in the small, insular society of the West Indies, the desire for outside contact is almost obsessive. The island writers realize they must venture forth, not only to get their works published, but to enjoy the company of their peers, mingle with a reading public, and have access to the judgment of critics.

The tumultuous history of the islands and the personal predicament of transplanted Africans make social protest a natural and frequent theme. The West Indian writer has been an astute observer of the alienation of his people and a severe critic of his own society and Western values.

The problems articulated by contemporary writers are by no means new. The Caribbean islands have a long and complex history. Each island is unique and has its own background of conquests, races, and languages. Many underwent a series of invasions, starting with the Carib Indians and ending with the Europeans; all have undergone the changes wrought by centuries of slavery and colonialism. The extremes of wealth, the concern about unemployment, the number of languages, and the mixture of cultures on these crowded little islands continue to stir the sensibility and spark the indignation of the black writers throughout the Caribbean.

During the last century, French West Indian writers were content with the literary nourishment received from France. Their work was easily influenced by trends in Paris. It was not until the 1920s and 1930s that island writers began to deal with the harsh realities of Caribbean life and the complexities of the people.

A dominating figure on the Guadeloupe-Martinique literary landscape is Aimé Césaire, born on Martinique in 1913, author of poems, plays, and essays concerned with the effects of colonial exploitation. He brought the concept of negritude to the West Indies, a theme central to all the black literature that followed, and wrote about the cultural alienation of the West Indian people, the dehumanized, oversophisticated white civilization, and the deeply human values of Africa before colonialization. An immensely powerful writer with a surrealistic style, Césaire's best-known works are *Les Armes Miraculeuses* (1946), *Discours sur le Colonialisme* (1950), and *Une Saison au Congo* (1966). He is universally recognized as a poet, politician (he served as mayor of Fort-de-France), and political philosopher.

Guy Tirolien, born on Guadeloupe in 1918, is a nationalist famous for *Balles d'Or,* which he wrote in 1958. His work acknowledges the beauty of nature on the islands, but its deepest interests are political.

Edouard Glissant, born on Martinique in 1930, writes obscure, poetical novels about heroes engaged in revolution. His *La Lézarde* won the 1959 Prix Goncourt.

Dr. Frantz Fanon, born in 1925 on Martinique, earned a distinctive position in French Caribbean literature for his revolutionary writings. He died of cancer in Washington, DC, in 1961. Among his works, *The Wretched of the Earth* (1961) is a classic study of the reactions of colonized man and the dangers following independence in a new society.

Until the late 1920s, Haitian writers were content to emulate the style and subjects of their French ideals. The essays of Dr. Jean Price-Mars, particularly *Ainsi Parle à l'Oncle* (1928), revived nationalistic motifs in Haitian works. His work encouraged the study of African heritage and its civilizations. Jacques Roumain (1907–1944) was the first renowned Haitian novelist, followed by Jacques-Stephen Alexis, born in 1929, and the poet René Depestre, born in 1930. Other important poets include Luc Grimard, Roussan Camille, and René Belance.

The combination of French and African influences on Haitian writers resulted in a distinctive Créole literary output. Emile Roumer pioneered with Créole poetry, and more recently, such classics as *Antigone* have been translated into this relatively new language.

In the English-speaking islands of Jamaica, Barbados, and Trinidad, very few writers were known to the general public until the early 1950s. One of the exceptions was Frank Collymore, born on Barbados in 1893. Considered the "grand old man of Caribbean literature," he was a schoolteacher and a novelist as well as a distinctive poet and an editor of *Bim*, the Barbados literary magazine. His poignant poetry fills five volumes, as he describes his love of the sea and his island and his feelings about transplanted Africans living "in exile, living apart but yet mingling in haphazard and experimental union to produce the unpredictable mixture" (from his poem "This Land").

During the early 1930s, a group of young intellectual Trinidadians formed the Beacon Group, a step forward in the literary development of the island. Under the editorial guidance of Alfred Mendes, the group published the *Beacon Magazine*, the first literary publication in the Caribbean to cover music, literature, art, and, most significant, politics.

Much of the written work in the 1930s and 1940s was decidedly nationalistic. Roger Mais, a Jamaican, was a leading figure in the nationalist movement, and he was jailed for six months for "Now We Know," an essay judged subversive. He published three novels, *The Hills Were Joyful* (1953), *Brother Man* (1954), and *Black Lightning* (1955), as well as numerous short stories and plays.

In the period just after World War II, the outside world knew only C. L. R. James, the distinguished Trinidadian novelist and historian; Adolphe Roberts of Jamaica, a novelist and political writer; and Edgar Mittelholzer, the British Guianan and author of twenty-three novels. Among his books, *A Morning at the Office* (1950) was the first West Indian novel to bear the imprint of the esteemed British publisher Penguin Books. His Kaywana Trilogy later earned him an even greater worldwide reputation.

Victor Reid, born in Jamaica in 1914, broke new ground with the publication of his first novel, *New Day*, in 1949. This historical novel traced Jamaica's volatile history from the 1865 rebellion to independence in 1962. His second novel, *The Leopard*, was set in Africa.

The islands began to get serious attention from poetry readers and critics when young Derek Walcott — then nineteen — published *25 Poems* in 1949. Born on St. Lucia, Walcott is a playwright as well as a poet and has written more than a dozen plays, one of which was performed at the New York City Shakespeare Festival. He founded the Trinidad Theatre Workshop and won acclaim for *A Far Cry from Africa*, which traces the West Indians' ties with

Africa. His work, and that of Bajan poet Edward Braithwate, have received high praise from critics throughout the literary world.

George Lamming, born in Barbados in 1927, gained wide public acclaim with the publication of his first novel, in 1953, *In the Castle of My Skin. The Emigrants,* a sociological documentary, and *Of Age and Innocence,* a symbolic work about a West Indian community at home and in exile, followed.

The writer from the English-speaking islands who has gained the widest international reputation is V. S. Naipaul. Born and raised in Trinidad, the descendant of immigrants from India, Naipaul is now a British citizen. His first novel, *The Mystic Masseur,* appeared in 1957. His best-known novels are *A House for Mr. Biswas* (1961) and *Guerrillas* (1975), a tale of Caribbean politics and revolution. In addition, *The Loss of El Dorado* (1969) is a nonfiction account of Caribbean history and society.

In addition, there are many established writers from this area who have been prolific, such as Michael Anthony and Earle Lovelace of Trinidad, Geoffrey Drayton of Barbados, and Andrew Salkey and H. Orlando Patterson of Jamaica.

The writers of the English-speaking islands use humor, unlike their French-speaking counterparts, even when describing existing social conditions and class and color stratifications. The scope of their writings has gone beyond their own territory to include the West Indians in Great Britain, Canada, and the United States, and they have not dwelled on antislavery or on Aimé Césaire's concept of negritude.

The current Spanish-speaking writers of Puerto Rico and the Dominican Republic are part of an existing literary tradition. These islands are large enough to establish the identities of their writers, with resulting prestige, but it is nonetheless impossible for them to make a living from writing alone. However, the existing classic social and economic problems serve to stimulate the writers' imagination as they describe city life. Social problems — the migration of rural people into the cities, the population explosion, and the need for mass-produced goods and services, including education — provide rich material for the islands' writers.

Some of the distinguished Spanish-speaking island authors are Juan Bosch, born in 1910, the author of several volumes of short stories; Alejo Carpentier, born in Cuba in 1904, whose many novels include *The Lost Steps,* winner of the Prix du Meilleur Livre Étranger in 1956; Eliseo Diego, also Cuban, born in 1920, well known for his prose and poetry; Nicolás Guillén, born in Cuba in 1904, a political prose writer and poet who integrated Cuban folk songs into literature and popularized African folklore as artistic material; and Pedro Juan Soto, born in Puerto Rico in 1928, a short story writer, novelist, playwright, and editor of the *San Juan Review.*

ART IN THE ISLANDS

Primitive paintings as works of art are a prominent form of expression in Haiti. These wonderfully colorful paintings trace early African tales and Christian religious themes in a simple but powerful way. Many biblical stories are imaginatively transferred to typical Haitian settings in an effort to relate them directly to the Haitian people.

A painting of St. John, for example, depicts his baptism in a well-known Haitian waterfall while Haitian women wash their clothes nearby. In another work, Jesus is portrayed in his symbolic flowing robes and is protected by soldiers wearing Haitian military uniforms. The painting also shows two women, dressed in contemporary Haitian style, observing the ritual.

Another beautiful example of this style is *Garden of Eden,* by André Normil, in which the artist has surrounded Adam and Eve with brilliantly colored animals against a background of a familiar Haitian waterfall.

The murals of the Anglican Cathedral of Ste. Trinité in Port-au-Prince represent the best of Haiti's contemporary religious art. There, visitors can see a whole spectrum of religious art by some of Haiti's outstanding artists.

In Puerto Rico, both religious and Spanish influences can be seen in their santos, hand-carved, painted religious figurines. Carvings of the Three Kings, madonnas, and special saints display a beauty and a skill in a unique craft whose techniques have been shared with generations of Puerto Ricans. The Casa de los Contrafuertes in Old San Juan houses a fascinating collection of this special art form.

ISLAND CRAFTS

Other craftwork throughout the Caribbean shows African influences as well as improvisations on earlier, traditional Spanish and French motifs. Also of interest are the pottery methods and styles of the Arawak Indians carried into modern times, along with straw weaving and boatbuilding.

The Indians were the islands' earliest weavers, and evidence of their innovative craftsmanship and ingenious methods can be seen in contemporary styles. The Caribbean people weave together thick sheets of palm, for example, add four bamboo sticks, turn the product upside down, and use the table they have just made.

Through the years, French weaving techniques added delicacy and more refined forms to the art of basket weaving on the islands. Hats and handbags, woven from grass imported from the island of St. Barts, were turned into fashionable wearing apparel.

Shopping in the Caribbean yields a great deal of satisfaction for gifts and personal souvenirs as well as bargain hunting.

On St. Lucia, khus khus grass is dried and braided and used for making fans, placemats, and small purses. And in Martinique, beautiful wicker baskets and covers for clay pottery are crafted, while braided grass rugs and women's hats with butterfly embroidery are made by the skilled Dominicans.

Before departing, be sure to enjoy the art of boatbuilding on the Bahamas, Carriacou, and the Virgin Islands, where native sloops are still built according to plans sketched out and used centuries ago.

ISLAND-BY-ISLAND HOPPING

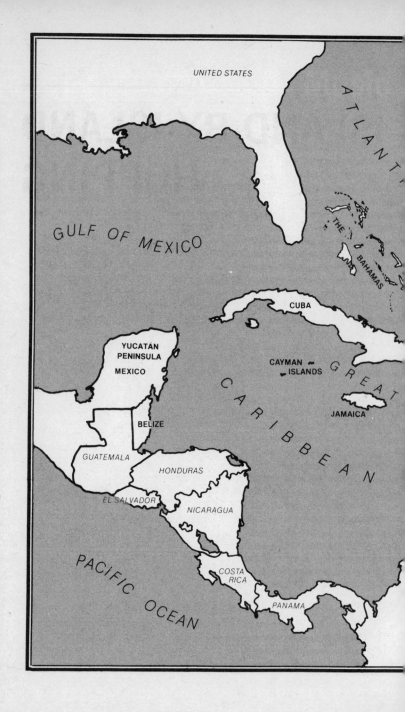

BERMUDA ❧

BERMUDA,
THE BAHAMAS,
AND
THE CARIBBEAN

N

OCEAN

TURKS AND CAICOS

LEEWARD ISLANDS

HAITI DOMINICAN
REPUBLIC

VIRGIN • ANGUILLA
ST. MARTIN/ST. MAARTEN
ISLANDS ST. BARTHELEMY
PUERTO SABA • ST. EUSTATIUS
RICO ST. KITTS ◇ANTIGUA
NEVIS
MONTSERRAT GUADELOUPE

ANTILLES

DOMINICA WINDWARD

LESSER MARTINIQUE

SEA ANTILLES ST. LUCIA ISLANDS

ST. VINCENT
NETHERLANDS THE GRENADINES BARBADOS
ARUBA ANTILLES
BONAIRE GRENADA
CURAÇAO

TOBAGO
TRINIDAD

VENEZUELA

GUYANA

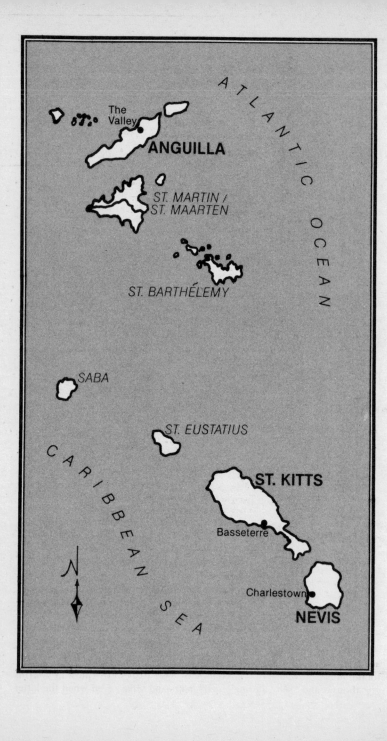

ANGUILLA

Through much of its known history, Anguilla has been a sleeper. For its first four and a half centuries, it managed to laze away its days in what seemed — to the outside world, at least — a content, if comatose, state. In fact, it is doubtful that any islander noticed when Columbus, sailing by in 1493, gave the island its name, the Italian word for "eel," because of its long, narrow shape and serpentine shoreline. No Spanish foot ever imprinted its sands, so its Indian residents went on dozing until 1650, when the first British settlers arrived. These adoptive Anguillians remained alert for a period and contributed to Caribbean history by helping to colonize the Virgin Islands in 1680, when Governor John Richardson bequeathed to his heirs a small sloop, the *Sea Flower,* to "go forward with the settlement to St. Croix." In the years that followed, Anguillians were stung to attention twice by French attacks: in 1745 at Crocus Bay and in 1796 at Rendezvous Bay; on both occasions, the invaders were forced to retreat — so much for "interaction."

For the next century and a half, no one — except Anguillians — thought much about the island. And even they failed to react with any force in 1825, when the British government made a single Crown Colony of St. Kitts, Nevis, and Anguilla. In the 1950s the Anguillians began to mutter — quietly at first. But in 1966, when Britain saw fit to make an associated state of the three-island colony without giving Anguilla a say in its own government, the islanders objected loudly. Pushed beyond forbearance by what they perceived as subjugation to a "foreign" power — the legislature in distant St. Kitts — Anguillians noisily seceded from their former partnership, and the voice of the Eel was heard in the lands to the north, south, east, and west. Newspapers and networks sent international correspondents. Neighboring islands talked of sending expeditionary forces. To forestall any precipitous local action, the Crown dispatched precipitants of its own — a "peacekeeping force" of paratroopers who dropped from the sky on Anguilla in 1969. To their surprise, they were greeted warmly by the Anguillians, who were waving Union Jacks instead of submachine guns. When the dust had settled, no lives had been lost (or, as it turned out, risked — the one barrage reported turned out to be photographers' flashbulbs rather than militants' gunfire). And in response to its subjects' wishes, in 1971 the Mother Country once more took Anguilla under its colonial wing. In February 1976, a new and separate constitution providing a ministerial system of government, with elected representatives handling most island affairs, went into effect. Soon after that Anguilla, now wide awake, took its first look at tourism as a source of potential income, even prosperity.

There were two major drawbacks to start with: obscurity and a dearth of accommodations for comfort-craving, let alone luxury-seeking, guests. The total number of rooms for transients was fewer than 150 — most in no-frills guesthouses and "self-catering" apartments and villas; even when the latter were attractive, they suffered from lack of service, especially in the restaurant department. On the other hand, Anguilla's bone-dry climate and isolation — however burdensome to permanent residents — also blessed the island with spectacular natural attractions: truly glorious beaches, incredibly clear water, and undisturbed reefs alive with fantastic fish.

Aware of others' mistakes, the government early on declared itself "committed to development of a *controlled* tourist industry" and began exploring possibilities. Entrepreneurs projected grand, albeit low-rise, dreams. At one point, five new resort developments with 300 new rooms (an increase of about 200%) were promised for a single year. It not only sounded too good to be true, it was — thanks to predictably unpredictable construction delays. But now, at last, several new low-rise, first-class, and luxury hotels, villas, and condominiums are actually habitable reality. Others are quietly and quickly popping up around the island. Signs of growth abound. Fortunately, the government's sincere determination "to preserve the peace and tranquillity that current visitors to Anguilla enjoy" has put it squarely on the right — and realistic — path. However, the skinny eel is beginning to bulge and is no longer "the Caribbean's best-kept secret.

Anguilla's hotels — small, serene, and select — are among the most talked-about in the Caribbean, and more of them will be open by 1989 — some 400 new luxury rooms in all, including additions to existing structures. In every sense, tourism is becoming big business on this small island.

This mini-boom notwithstanding, by no stretch of the most elastic imagination could Anguilla be described as exciting, which is a large part of its appeal. Besides sunning, some lazy snorkeling, a sail, or a picnic, there really isn't much to do. More comforts and diversions are on the way, but for now, if you really mean it about those books and a beach and the sun being enough, do we have an island for you.

ANGUILLA AT-A-GLANCE

FROM THE AIR: Anguilla, northernmost of the British Leeward Islands, stretches for 16 miles from southwest to northeast at 18°15' N latitude, 63° W longitude, with small Scrub Island floating off its northeastern end and minuscule Anguillita Island off its southwestern tip. It is actually much closer to the neighboring French/Dutch island of St. Martin/St. Maarten, 7 miles south, than to any bit of British land. St. Kitts, with which Anguilla was formerly associated, is 70 miles south and slightly east; Puerto Rico is 150 miles due west. It is believed that Columbus called the island Anguilla — Italian for "eel" — because it is skinny (only 3 miles across at its widest point) and the shining white coral beaches that notch its coasts make its shoreline seem to wiggle in and out. Its main road leads from West End, a village in the southwest, to The Quarter, a small settlement at the island's midpoint; the road then loops up to Island Harbour and back again. At a number of places, auxiliary roads branch off north and south toward beaches and fishing villages. The island's central area, and, besides The Quarter, the closest thing to what we would consider a town, is called The Valley.

The 35-square-mile island that rises only 213 feet above sea level has no cities, no rivers, no streams or rushing waterfalls; the land is dry, with a few palm trees but mostly short, sparse vegetation. The 7,500 inhabitants pay no income tax on the money they earn working for the government, in the tourism industry, building hotels and the famed Anguillian boats, lobstering and fishing, and harvesting salt at the Salt Pond. Some live in the settlement called Sandy Ground at Road Bay, the island's principal port of entry, on the north coast. Ferries to Marigot on St. Martin leave from Blowing Point on the south coast. Small Wallblake Airport is in the middle of the island near The Quarter and The Valley, the administrative center for Anguilla's elected ministerial government. The British government is represented by His Excellency the Governor.

 SPECIAL PLACES: On Anguilla, beaches definitely get top billing: with over 30 to choose from, you probably won't even have time to see them all. Many vacationers visit several of them before settling on one or two favorites — you'll need a car to do this, although hitchhiking is perfectly acceptable. On the south shore, sweeping Rendezvous Bay is among the most beautiful and is currently experiencing some development; it is also where the French landed in 1796 to try to take the island from the British (they failed). During the summer of 1986, some 3,000 pieces of ancient pottery, as well as some human remains from a large AmerIndian settlement (possibly dating back to 100 BC), were found during excavations for a hotel on the beach at Rendezvous Bay. Carbon dating is under way. Following the south coast west, facing the rolling hills of St. Martin, are the white shores of Cove and Maundays Bay, the latter very good for shelling and the site of *Cap Juluca,* a sparkling new, super-luxury resort sprawling over 179 acres of land and water. At the northeastern edge of Anguilla is Captain's Bay, one of the most secluded beaches on the island, with coral outcrops bracketing a romantic stretch of white sand. You're unlikely to find another soul here. Heading west past the fishing village of Island Harbour along the north coast, you'll find a turnoff for Shoal Bay (not to be confused with Shoal Bay "West" on the southwest coast), an ideal spot for lazy snorkelers with its coral reef coming right up to the shore (most snorkeling elsewhere around the island must be done from boats farther offshore). There is also good snorkeling at Little Bay, on the northern end of Crocus Bay, which is accessible by boat or via steep cliffs from the road's edge. Framed by the island's largest hill, vast Crocus Bay is the departure point of many Anguillian boat races but otherwise is very peaceful. The calm, clear waters of Road Bay are studded with peacefully anchored yachts and the occasional small cruise ship, as well as a reminder of less tranquil days — the rusting hulls of several freighters wrecked in a November 1984 hurricane. Sandy Ground, on Road Bay, between the Salt Pond and the sea, is a small harborside village that is one of the island's prettiest. While Sandy Ground and Shoal Bay are the most commercial of Anguilla's many beaches, they are, by any standards, clean, uncrowded, and picturesque.

Currently under way above Shoal Bay is the excavation of a cave known as The Fountain, which contains a large stalagmite and a number of interesting petroglyphs (ancient rock carvings). Few are aware that Anguilla has so many archaeological sites, some dating from as early as the second millennium BC. Anguilla is establishing its first National Park around The Fountain and plans to protect the area as well as to develop its potential as a tourist attraction. The Fountain is currently closed to visitors, but there is a weekly walking tour of historic buildings, departing from the old Wall Blake House on Tuesdays at 10 AM.

SOURCES AND RESOURCES

TOURIST INFORMATION: Information about Anguilla can be obtained from the Anguilla Tourist Office, 1208 Washington Drive, Centerport, NY 11721 (phone: 516-673-0150 or 212-869-0402; in Anguilla, 809-497-2944), or by writing directly to the Director of Tourism, The Valley, Anguilla, WI (phone: 809-497-2759 or 2451). The office will reply immediately, but allow at least two weeks for mailed correspondence. Further information may be obtained and hotel and other reservations made through Steven Hicks, ITR Inc., 25 W 39th St., New York, NY 10018 (phone: 212-840-6636 or 800-223-9815).

Local Coverage – *The Chronicle,* published in St. Maarten, arrives daily except Sundays and is presently the best source of summarized world and local news. Two new Anguilla publications, *What to Do in Anguilla* and *Anguilla Life,* are useful sources of local news and events.. There are several other locally produced tourist publications, including a sketchy map of the island (tourist maps may be purchased at the drugstore and other shops, and also at the Department of Tourism; a very detailed one is available at the Department of Lands and Survey); *Anguilla, The Basic Facts,* a neat, fact-filled booklet that is quite outdated but has some very interesting background information; and hotel and villa rate brochures that are updated seasonally. These are available at the the Department of Tourism at the Secretariat Building in The Valley as well as by mail from the Anguilla Tourist Office in New York. There are two AM radio stations on Anguilla — Radio Anguilla (1,000 watts), owned by the government, and the Caribbean Beacon, which is privately owned and broadcasts 20 hours a day — and one FM station. Caribbean Television International is available island-wide; cable TV, beamed in via US satellite, reaches most of Anguilla, but not the West End.

Telephone – Dial direct to Anguilla by adding the area code 809 and the prefix 497 to the numbers given below.

ENTRY REQUIREMENTS: All visitors are required to show some sort of identification with a photo. If you're staying overnight, you'll be asked for proof of citizenship (a valid passport is preferred) and a return or ongoing ticket. For stays of more than a month, check with the Immigration Office.

CLIMATE AND CLOTHES: Anguilla is in the path of the easterly trade winds, which means cooling breezes and low humidity throughout the year. The average temperature, year-round, is 80°F (27°C). Rainfall is light but erratic, given Anguilla's topography, and may fall at any time of year. However, the wettest months are usually September through December and sometimes April and May. You'll need only light, casual sports clothes (lots of beachwear), unless you feel like dressing up for dinner at the *Malliouhana* hotel (but it's not necessary).

MONEY: Anguilla's official currency is the Eastern Caribbean Dollar (EC), pegged to the US dollar and valued at about $2.68 to $1 US. Prices in shops are usually quoted in $ EC, but hotels and restaurants more often use $ US, and most have $ US change to give. To avoid misunderstandings, be sure to ask which "dollars" are meant. Traveler's checks, and often personal checks, are more readily accepted than credit cards, although this is changing. Barclays Bank International has a branch in The Valley, and there are two other commercial banks, Anguilla National and Caribbean Commercial. Several offshore banks are registered for business. Hours are 8 AM to 1 PM on weekdays and 3 to 5 PM on Fridays; closed Saturdays, Sundays, and holidays.

LANGUAGE: English.

TIME: Atlantic Standard Time all year — one hour ahead of Eastern Standard in winter (when it's noon on the East Coast, it's 1 PM on Anguilla), the same as Eastern Daylight Saving Time in summer.

CURRENT: In most places, 110 AC. Check your hotel to be sure, and if a converter is required for your American travel appliances, bring one along.

GETTING THERE: There are no direct flights from the US mainland or Canada. But American Eagle now runs two flights daily from San Juan, PR, direct to Anguilla. From Dutch St. Maarten's Juliana Airport, Windward Island Airways (Winair) schedules three daily flights (flying time: 7 minutes; fare, about $15 one way). From both Antigua and St. Kitts, LIAT offers regular service. From Tortola and St. Thomas, there is Air BVI three times a week. Tyden Air provides charter service to most Caribbean islands, aero-photographic excursions, and special day trips to St. Barthélemy for $80. Air Anguilla runs scheduled service to St. Thomas and charters to other islands. Anguilla's spanking new air terminal attests to the growing popularity of this newly discovered vacation destination. Regular ferry service links Marigot, French St. Martin, and Blowing Point, Anguilla, from about 7 AM till 10:30 PM or so; fare is $6 one way, $10 round-trip. Night fare (one boat leaves Anguilla at 6:15 PM and another, the last, at 10:15 PM) costs $10, one way. These power boats, most built by Anguilla's famed craftsmen, make the trip in about 15 minutes. There is a $1.50 departure tax at Blowing Point and a $5 departure tax at the airport. However you travel, it's a good idea to check for last-minute schedule changes.

CALCULATING COSTS: At present, the island's medium-priced small hotels charge about $150 to $180 for two without meals in winter; summer rates are 30% to 50% lower. But the price range for double rooms goes from a rock-bottom $30 at a guesthouse to $350 at the *Malliouhana*. In addition, pretty, very comfortable villas on or near the beach cost $450 and up per week year-round. There's an 8% accommodation tax and normally a 10% service charge.

GETTING AROUND: Taxi – A sociable way to meet the island is to learn something of its lore. Drivers will show you every nook and cranny in a couple of hours. The current going rate for an around-the-island tour is $40 US. This includes about 2½ hours of sightseeing, after which the driver will drop you at a lunch spot or beach of your choice and pick you up at an appointed time to meet your boat or plane. Other more or less established rates for trips between the following points are: Blowing Point (where the ferry from Marigot on St. Martin comes in) and Shoal Bay, $12.50 one way; Sandy Ground, $6; Meads Bay, $8; and Island Harbour, $13. These rates are for 2 passengers with not more than 2 suitcases each. There is an extra charge of $1 for each extra person or bag.

Car Rental – Varying vintages are available; newer models go for about $30 up per day, $35 with air conditioning (unlimited mileage; you pay for gas, plus an additional $5 US per day for collision-damage waiver at some places). A $35-a-day car goes for $215 a week, and special summer rates are available. *Connors Car Rental* is the largest source (phone: 6433, 6541). Others include *Bennie's,* now representing *Avis* (phone: 2221), both a short taxi ride from Blowing Point; *Budget* (phone: 2217); *Apex* (phone: 2642); *National* (phone: 2433); *Jedell's* (phone: 2747); and *Island Car Rentals* on the Airport Road (phone: 2723, 2804). The only full-service gas station is in The Valley; there is a small pump on the way to Blowing Point. Driving is on the left, and note that you must obtain an Anguillian driver's license by showing your home license and paying a fee of about $6 US. Mopeds, scooters, and motorbikes may also be rented but are fairly expensive. Call *Boo's* (phone: 2323) or *R & M* (phone: 2430).

Travel Service – Local tour operators include *Bennie's Tours* (phone: 2788, 6221, 2360), *Paradise Ventures* (phone: 2107), *Bertram's* (phone: 2256), and *Mellow Tones Tours* (phone: 2680). For airline reservations and travel arrangements, contact *J. N.*

Gumbs Travel Agency (phone: day, 2238; night, 2838), *Malliouhana Travel & Tours* (phone: 2431), or *Bennie's* (phone: 2221). *Bennie's* offers a "transfer" service for visitors arriving and departing via St. Martin, including all taxis and boat, for $50 round-trip per person by day, $65 at night.

 SHOPPING: Fashionably speaking, the island's top shop is the *Malliouhana* hotel's *La Romana,* cloned from the chic boutique of the same name on St. Martin and St. Barthélemy. Boutiques at *Cap Juluca, Cul de Sac, Cinnamon Reef, The Mariners,* and the *Riviera* restaurant feature chic women's beachwear, shell jewelry, some island artwork, and crafts. *Sunshine Boutique* at South Hill has colorful resortwear for women, and *Janvel's* at Blowing Point also features some sun clothes. You'll find local crafts, as well as some books on local history, flora, and fauna, on sale at the *Anguilla Arts and Crafts Center* in The Valley and also at shops scattered about the island, in a number of restaurants, and at the airport. *Hallmark,* on the Airport Rd. (near the National Bank of Anguilla), has small stocks of brand-name English bone china, porcelains, perfumes, and linens, as well as Caribbean souvenirs; British goods sell at below-US prices. The Valley Post Office's stamps appeal to collectors. If you're in the market for a traditional hand-built Anguillian racing boat, contact Egbert Connor; or, for a super-strong wooden craft made with the WEST System, contact David Carty. Small models and other souvenirs and local crafts are on sale at *Bertram's Shop* at Sandy Ground. Otherwise, splendid shells are Anguilla's top souvenirs — yours for the finding on all island beaches, especially the north side of Rendezvous Bay and Maunday's Bay.

 TIPPING: A 10% service charge is added to inn bills and that takes care of everyone, although waiters/waitresses and barpersons do not object to a little something more; if you are pleased with the service, show it. The same holds true for taxi drivers, especially if they have given you a good tour. Young boys help arriving visitors with baggage (in their wheelbarrows) at Blowing Point, and $1 will usually make them very happy. There are no official porters at Wallblake Airport, but you probably won't need one. If someone should help with your bag, a smile and a heartfelt thank you is all he probably expects.

 SPECIAL EVENTS: *Carnival,* climaxing on the first Monday in August, is a weeklong holiday incorporating boat races, sports events, costume parades, music competitions, and nonstop partying. Anguillians living abroad head for home for these colorful festivities. The island's three national holidays are *Constitution Day* (August 5), *Anguilla Day* (May 30), "marking the commencement of the Anguilla Revolution and secession from the Associated State of St. Christopher-Nevis-Anguilla in 1967," and *Separation Day* (December 19). Other public holidays include *New Year's Day, Good Friday, Easter Monday, Whitmonday,* the *Queen's Official Birthday* (June 13), *Christmas,* and *Boxing Day* (December 26).

SPORTS: Boating – Sailboat racing ranks as the island's "national" sport, not only during August Carnival, but year-round, when ad hoc races setting sail from Sandy Ground, Shoal Bay, or Crocus Bay are often accompanied by beachside barbecues, jump-up partying, and betting. If you want a closer look at the Anguillian boats made by the island's famed master builders, don't miss the fishing village of Island Harbour. Those who prefer to sail rather than observe can make arrangements for a day cruise to Prickly Pear Cays or to any of the other lovely secluded coves on David Darling's *Darling I,* a 35-foot British-built yacht that leaves *Johnno's Jetty* at Sandy Ground at 9:30 AM, returning at 4:30 PM. Maria prepares fresh lobster salad, and the bar is open all day. Cost is $69 per person (children under 16,

$40), including use of snorkeling gear (phone: 2502, and ask for Amanda). *Tropical Watersports,* at *Cap Juluca,* does day trips on a 25-foot cabin cruiser (phone: 6779, 6666). Also available for day or longer charters is the 60-foot schooner *Rackham Le Rouge* out of Island Harbour (phone: 4488). If you choose to be your own skipper, you shouldn't be without William Eiman's *St. Maarten/St. Martin Area, St. Kitts & Nevis Cruising Guide,* which includes Anguilla and is available at the *Shipwreck Shop* in Philipsburg, St. Maarten.

Sea Excursions – Pretty, palm-tufted Sandy Island and the even more remote Prickly Pear Cays used to be ideal escape sites but have recently become crowded with day-trippers from St. Martin. Both still offer good snorkeling and beach bars that grill lobster, chicken, and ribs for lunch. A boat will take you there from Sandy Ground at 10 AM and bring you back later. Ask at the small jetty by *Johnno's* or contact Neville Connors at *Sandy Island Enterprises* (phone: 6395 or 6845). There is also an attractive snack bar on Scilly Cay, an acre or so of coral, sand, and exotic plants opposite Island Harbour Jetty, where a boat collects people (if it's not there, ask any of the fishermen or inquire at *Le Fish Trap*).

Snorkeling and Scuba – *Tamariain Water Sports* (phone: 2020, 2798, 2900) offers PADI-certified basic, open-water, advanced open-water, and divemaster courses as well as PADI specialty ratings (Night Diver, Deep Diver, Wreck Diver, and Search & Recovery Diver) by instructors Iain Grummitt and Tom Peabody, who also offer a Medic First Aid course; prices do not include regulators or BCDs; also available are resort scuba courses plus dive and/or snorkel trips around Anguilla and to nearby cays. Iain and Tom offer very personal service, with a maximum of 12 divers to a boat. A one-tank dive costs $30; a two-tank dive, $50; and resort courses, $70. *Tamariain Retail Shop* carries snorkeling and diving equipment for sale and rental. There are branches at both the *Malliouhana* and at Sandy Ground next to *Johnno's* or write Tamariain, PO Box 247, The Valley, Anguilla, WI. Snorkeling, sailboat rentals, and other watersports equipment are available from *Sandy Island Enterprises* (phone: 6395, 6433, 6845) and from *Tropical Watersports* at *Cap Juluca* (phone: 6666, 6779). *Shoal Bay Watersports,* next to *Happy Jacks,* also has snorkeling equipment and Sunfish. Guides from these establishments and various island fishermen will take you to nearby cays and along the secret coves of Anguilla's splendid coast. Although there are no wall dives here, there are deep dives (130 feet on coral) and at least a dozen excellent dive sites. There is also good diving off Prickly Pear Cays and 2½ miles northwest at Dog Island, where the southeast shore drops off from 20 to about 80 feet. The reefs surrounding West and Mid cays, off Anguillita Island, and between Scrub Island and Anguilla's eastern end are also worthwhile. Prickly Pear Cays, Scrub Island, Sandy Island, and Little Bay are best for snorkeling, but you won't even need a boat to get to the offshore reefs at Shoal Bay.

Sport Fishing – *Tropical Watersports* (phone: 6666, 6779) has a 25-foot cabin cruiser and 46-foot Bertram ($900 a day) available. Trips with local skippers and fishermen can be arranged through hotels at about $25 per person a day. Bring your own tackle.

Swimming and Sunning – Available off absolutely superb beaches (see *Special Places*). Note that topless and nude bathing are not allowed on Anguilla. Since there is no organized lifeguard system, you should be careful about observing common-sense safety rules: Don't swim out too far alone and beware of currents, especially near the reefs (coral scratches take an annoyingly long time to heal in tropical climates). Generally, waters off most beaches here are calm, clear, and safe even for children.

Tennis – There are 4 courts at *Malliouhana,* 2 at *Cinnamon Reef* and *Coccoloba Plantation* (which has a Peter Burwash International Tennis Program), others at *The Mariners, Carimar, Covecastles, Rendezvous Bay,* and *Cap Juluca.* Check the new hotels, too.

Windsurfing and Water Skiing – *Tropical Watersports* at *Cap Juluca* (phone: 6666,

6779) charges $12 per hour for a windsurf board, $35 for instruction, and $15 for 15 minutes of water skiing. Check out *Sandy Island Enterprises* (phone: 6395, 6433, 6845), *Tamariain* (phone: 2020, 2798, 2900), and major hotels.

 NIGHTLIFE: Although this is a quiet island, there is normally something going on somewhere every night of the week. The traditional Thursday night performance of the Mayoumba Folklore Troupe at the *Cul de Sac* is not to be missed. Popular with visitors and residents alike, the show is usually followed by dancing. There is live music most nights at *Cap Juluca*'s *Pimms* restaurant, twice a week at *Lucy's Harbour View* and *Coccoloba Plantation,* and Saturdays at the *Mariners. Cinnamon Reef* usually has music nightly, often just a singer with nonamplified guitar, except on Fridays, when a steel band plays for the manager's poolside cocktail party and outdoor barbecue. Friday and Saturday nights *Johnno's Beach Bar* at Sandy Ground is *the* place to be; the music is good and loud, and the flavor decidedly local. In addition, several of the beach bars and small restaurants set up local string and scratch bands some afternoons and evenings, especially if there is an occasion, such as a small cruise ship anchored offshore; most hotels offer nightly entertainment in season. There are two discos in town: the *Dragon* in South Hill and *Keg's Palace* in George Hill. Check with your hotel or, better yet, with your taxi driver, who might just be Keith Gumbs, owner of *Keg's* and a popular island entertainer. Bankie Banx, Anguilla's own reggae superstar, has returned after several years in Europe and has been performing here, often on Scilly Cay and St. Maarten. If it's still too quiet for you and you want a real "night on the town," *Mystic Boat* (phone: 6289) leaves Blowing Point at 7 PM for a night run to St. Martin and returns at 1 AM. For $69 to $74 per person, depending on where you're picked up on Anguilla, you get transfers to Blowing Point, the boat trip to Marigot, transfers to the *Great Bay* hotel, dinner, nightclub, and a $5 casino certificate plus a return trip to your Anguilla hotel. Or simply take a late afternoon boat to Marigot for drinks and dinner, then return to Anguilla on the 10:45 PM boat (*Big Bird Too* or *Tee-Zech*).

BEST ON THE ISLAND

 CHECKING IN: Little Anguilla's big building boom has finally made headlines. Early in 1988, super-luxury *Cap Juluca* hit the *Hideaway Report* just as soon as it quietly opened its first six rooms. The *Anguilla Great House* followed suit with an elegant champagne party launching the island's first entirely Anguillian-owned world-class resort. In deference to both government wish and owner preference, new properties are low-rise and high-quality. They will add to the island's stock of full-service hotel rooms, rather than the once preponderant "self-catering" housekeeping facilities. Cottage and villa architecture — shaped to fit the land as well as the island's beach-oriented outdoor-indoor vacation style — remains appealingly dominant. Some places are too new to judge; some are still getting their finishing touches; and several now under construction are due to open for the first time for the 1988–89 winter season. Among those to watch are *Sea Grape Beach Club* on Meads Bay (2-bedroom villas, 12 rooms in all), the *Fountain Beach and Tennis Club* on Shoal Bay North (30 rooms), the *Pelican* hotel on Cove Bay (30 rooms), *KaruKera Beach* hotel (7 rooms), and a 25-room project at Sandy Hill, as yet unnamed. Rates can run as high as $1,540 per day for a 4-bedroom villa at *Cap Juluca,* $1,200 for a 3-bedroom villa at the *Malliouhana,* or $750 for 3 bedrooms at *Covecastles.* We classify $250 and up for a double room without meals in winter as expensive, $150 to $250 as moderate, and below that as inexpensive. There are some bed-and-breakfast accommodations that cost less than $50, a list of which may be obtained from the tourist offices in New York and Anguilla. An 8% government tax is added to all rates, as is, normally, a 10% service charge. Summer rates are reduced from 20% to 50%. Many vacationers who stay at a hotel one season will arrange to rent an apartment or cottage for the following year. A rate list for apartments, villas, and cottages is also available from the Department of Tourism. Because they are so popular here, and the total number of hotel rooms is still so limited (only half as many as St. Maarten's single largest hotel), we have included choice villa properties in our list of available accommodations.

Cap Juluca – The Caribbean's newest and most appealing luxury resort, on Anguilla's magnificent Maundays Bay beach, has created a style of its own, an exotic North African oasis on this desert island of turquoise sea and brilliant white sand. There's nothing West Indian here except the name — that of the Arawak rainbow god of Anguilla. Spread over 179 acres of southwestern coast and overlooking the smoky mountains of St. Martin, *Cap Juluca* is just a few miles — but several worlds — away from the glittery gambling establishments dotting the opposite shores. The latest and most elaborate endeavor of Robin and Sue Ricketts (co-creators of *Malliouhana*), *Juluca*'s style is exquisitely Moroccan — with Moorish arches, domes, flowered courtyards, and colorful rugs and antiques from Casablanca and Marrakesh. Luxury doubles and 1- and 2-bedroom suites, with covered or roof terraces, and 3- and 4-bedroom villas with built-in patio barbecues are spacious and splendidly appointed. Sensuous double bathtubs with leather headrests next to private sunning areas may well keep some guests off the spectacular, mile-long crescent beach, where every imaginable water sport is offered. Other amenities include an intricately designed free-form pool. A tennis court and an excellent restaurant, *Pimms,* complete the picture for now. Maundays Bay (phone: 6779, 6666). Very expensive.

Coccoloba Plantation – Following a $4-million renovation, the former *La Santé* has reopened as a super-luxury resort straddling the point between the beautiful white sand beaches of Meads and Barnes bays. At the main house, there's a handsome swimming pool with swim-up bar and an excellent restaurant featuring French cuisine with a tropical touch. Strung along the quiet beach are 50 large gingerbread villas trimmed in yellow and white, each having a raised bedroom with two double beds; makeup and dressing area; sitting area with refrigerator; and oversize bathroom with fluffy terry robes, built-in hair dryer, and toiletries. All villas also have seaview patios and air conditioning, plus ceiling fans. There's stunning new landscaping, full water sports, and 2 tennis courts with pro Peter Burwash. Luxury touches abound under manager E. David Brewer, formerly of *Jumby Bay* and Rockresorts. Barnes Bay (phone: 6871). Very expensive.

Covecastles – This fully staffed, ultramodern complex of four 3-bedroom, 2-bath luxury private villas and eight new 2-bedroom, 2-bath beach houses was designed by New York architect Myron Goldfinger. The elegant appointments include terra cotta tile floors, raw silk–upholstered custom rattan furniture, and hand-embroidered cotton sheets. Other amenities include a tennis court with night lighting, satellite cable TV, a café lounge (for guests only), a lovely beach, windsurfing, and a charter yacht for day sails. On Shoal Bay West (phone: 6801). Very expensive.

Malliouhana – Definitely the name to drop (if you can pronounce it; *Malliouhana* is the Arawak word for "Anguilla"), though we suspect *Cap Juluca* will give it a run for its money — and money is what guests need most at each of these sleek resorts. A soaring, white arched structure, perched on a cliff overlooking Meads Bay at the northwestern reaches of the island, the *Malliouhana* has quickly established itself as one of the Caribbean's most elegant and distinguished resort complexes. Owned and managed by the British magnate Leon Roydon and his wife, Annette, the luxury property has 49 units in all: 40 doubles, 7 one-bedroom suites, and 2 two-bedroom suites, all stunningly furnished and decorated. Haitian tapestries adorn the public areas, and bedrooms come with four-poster bamboo beds, Indonesian rattan chairs, latticed French doors opening onto spacious balconies, and huge bathrooms of Italian marble. Amenities include an exercise center, 3-tiered freshwater pool, 4 Laykold tennis courts, a water-sports center with diving facilities, *La Romana* boutique, a hairdresser, stylish bar, and a restaurant created by Jo Rostang, chef-owner of the two-star *Bonne Auberge* in Antibes. Meads Bay (phone: 6111, 6741). Very expensive.

Cinnamon Reef – New Yorker Richard Hauser and his son Scott designed and built this attractive property as if it were a large vacation home for their friends. A lot of attention has been paid to details — big beds, lots of fluffy towels, soft classical music in the breezy restaurant by day, and a soothing guitar at dinner. The Moorish-arched main building is surrounded by 16 cottages, including 2 double-unit beach villas good for family or friends. Each cottage has an unobstructed sea view, oversize bedroom, sunken living room, dressing room, spacious bath, and breezy patio. With a 60-by-40-foot swimming pool and 2 Deco Turf tennis courts, snorkeling on its own offshore reef, sailing, windsurfing, paddleboat, and fishing rods, all at no extra charge to guests. New management from Haiti's grand old *Oloffson* hotel has added Haitian naifs to the walls, batiks to the boutique, and sparkle to the menu. This place just keeps getting better. Little Harbour (phone: 2727, 2781). Expensive.

Anguilla Great House – A new West Indian gingerbread-style hotel in traditional cheery pastels on lovely Rendezvous Bay, facing St. Martin and distant Saba. This Anguillian-owned property has all the makings of a world-class resort, though the decor is somewhat modest by comparison to the spectacular beach site. Five-unit buildings include 2 studios (with kitchenettes) that may be combined with adjacent double rooms or rented on their own. There's also a lovely restaurant/bar; an additional dining room was not yet open at press time. (phone: 6061). Moderate.

Carimar Beach Club – These tastefully furnished and thoughtfully outfitted 2- and 3-bedroom units, with full kitchen facilities and patios or balconies, share Meads Bay with the posh *Malliouhana* hotel. Tennis and water sports are available nearby (at you-know-where). Meads Bay (phone: 6881). Moderate.

Cul de Sac – On a very tiny and private manmade beach at the road's end stands this lovely inn, with 6 sunny, spacious suites (bedroom/sitting room, bath, dining room with kitchen, porches like outdoor living rooms). Formerly owned by the *Malliouhana* ménage and recently refurbished under new European management. Don't miss the popular Thursday-night performances of the *Mayoumba Folklore Troupe* in the pretty *Pappagallo* bar/restaurant. Shaddick Point (phone: 6461 or 6462). Moderate.

The Mariners – A charming West Indian–style resort with world-class amenities on one of Anguilla's most picturesque beaches, *The Mariners* draws yachtspeople, local dignitaries, and expatriates to its friendly bar and breezy gazebo, where a strolling guitarist sings island songs, and to its terraced restaurant, which overlooks the perfect cliché of a white sand beach. There are 16 gingerbread cottages, each with a wide verandah with handsome deck furniture and 2 double rooms connected by a "studio," which has kitchen facilities and a foldaway bed. You can rent one, two, or all three rooms (all have private baths). There is also a 3-bedroom apartment in the reception building which is a very good value. Live entertainment several times weekly, tennis court, water sports, and video. Sandy Ground (phone: 2671, 2815). Moderate.

Shoal Bay Resort – Fifteen well-appointed 1- and 2-bedroom units, with full kitchen facilities, living area, patio or terrace, and a foldaway bed for extra guests. Next to *Shoal Bay Villas* on a spectacular beach. Shoal Bay (phone: 2011). Moderate.

Shoal Bay Villas – A small condominum resort on the shores of spectacular Shoal Bay, with 2 miles of beach that is the stuff of which island dreams are made. There are 9 very attractive units, ranging from studios to duplex suites (for 4 people), each with patio or terrace, plus a new villa with 2 doubles and 2 singles; also a good, reasonably priced restaurant, called *Happy Jack's,* and small water-sports concession. Shoal Bay (phone: 2051). Moderate.

Skiffles – Five attractively furnished 2-bedroom villas surround a freshwater pool high above the sea. Lower South Hill (phone: 6619). Moderate.

La Sirena – Nine handsomely furnished 2- and 3-bedroom villas, each with 2 and 3 baths, respectively, verandah or patio, kitchen facilities, and lounge or living/dining room. Only 300 feet from Meads Bay Beach (phone: 6827). Moderate to inexpensive.

Easy Corner Villas – Twelve comfortable, attractive, 1-, 2-, and 3-bedroom units, with full kitchen, color TV, and balconies overlooking the salt pond and Road Bay. Convenient to island amenities and only a 5-minute drive from the beach at Sandy Ground. Owned by Maurice Connor of the island's largest car rental, so cottage/car packages are available. South Hill (phone: 6433, 6541). Inexpensive.

Inter-Island – Fourteen simple but clean rooms with bath, family-style restaurant, and gracious West Indian hospitality. Lower South Hill (phone: 6259). Inexpensive.

Lloyd's Guest House – A pretty West Indian house on Crocus Hill, opposite the hospital. It offers 14 no-frills, budget rooms. The Valley (phone: 2351). Inexpensive.

Rainbow Reef Villas – Four 2-bedroom villas, all with verandahs overlooking the sea and furnished with good-looking Haitian rattan. A gazebo on the beach, which is better for snorkeling than lazy swimming, is outfitted with barbecue facilities. Perfectly private, isolated, and quiet. Six days' housekeeping service included in weekly rate. Sea Feathers (phone: 2817). Inexpensive.

Rendezvous Bay – Guests will enjoy the casual atmosphere and warm hospitality of the Gumbs family, who make everyone feel right at home. Recently refurbished, the 20 rooms are simple and clean, each with private bath. Its dining room, where meals are served family style, has a reputation for good Anguillian cooking. Flanked by lovely dunes, its vast crescent of white sand beach is one of the best on the island. Snorkeling and fishing equipment and tennis are available. Rendezvous Bay (phone: 6549). Inexpensive.

Sea Horse – A pair of cottages comprising, in all, 4 very pleasant apartments with full housekeeping facilities. Blowing Point (phone: 6751). Inexpensive.

Other handsome rental villas and villa-apartments to ask about are *Masara, Palm Grove, Chinchary, Sea Feathers, Spindrift, Blowing Point Beach Apartments,* and *Harbour Villas,* starting at about $400 a week for two and ranging up to $200 a day (including utilities and maid service) in winter. A reliable on-island rental agency is *Sunshine Villas* run by Judy and Jim Henderson (phone: 2149).

Reservations for all hotels, guesthouses, and villas can be made by writing to Anguilla Hotels Reservations Clearing House, 25 W 39th St., New York, NY 10018 (phone: 212-840-6636 or 800-223-9815).

 EATING OUT: Fresh fish and spiny lobster, caught by the fishing boats that sail out of Island Harbour, Crocus Bay, and Sandy Ground, are staples. Meals are prepared and presented in a range of styles from elaborate to delightfully informal. Expect to pay $80 or more for a meal for two, not including wine, tip, or drinks, in those restaurants listed below as expensive, $50 to $80 in those listed as moderate, and under $50 inexpensive.

Cinnamon Reef – On a pretty and spacious terrace of the hotel of the same name, this restaurant has a fixed dinner menu of standard favorites as well as several daily specials. An Anguillian chef turns out admirable West Indian fare as well as some Continental dishes. Lunches can be light, with an interesting selection of salads. Friday night is jump-up, with a manager's cocktail party, poolside barbecue, and steel band. Little Harbour (phone: 2727 or 2781). Expensive.

Coccoloba Plantation – Luxury-hotel food consultant Jean-Yves Loizance designed a new food-and-beverage concept combining his own French and Créole backgrounds, and executive chef Eric Sciuller (from Brittany) masterminds the excellent results. The luscious lobster Coccoloba is special, but so is everything else. Lunches feature exotic salads, fresh local fish. Barnes Bay (phone: 6871). Expensive.

Cul de Sac – Most nights the pretty waterfront terrace is prime territory, except Thursdays, when guests might want a better view of the traditional Mayoumba Folklore Show in the candlelit dining room–bar. Specialties include Italian dishes such as Genoese pasta al pesto, as well as light conch fritters, red snapper *en papillote* Anguillan-style. Try the fluffy banana mousse for dessert. Shaddick Point (phone: 6461/2). Expensive.

Le Fish Trap – Certainly among the island's top two or three restaurants, *Le Fish Trap* overlooks the beach at Island Harbour, where fishermen bring their daily catch. Belgians Patricia and Thierry Van Dyck combine the classics with Créole cooking to produce truly original and gratifying dishes such as lobster terrine, stuffed crab, scallops flambéed with gin, seafood pasta, *boudin Créole* ("black" pudding), crayfish grilled with garlic butter or steamed on a bed of leeks, duck in raspberry vinegar sauce, and a remarkable tomato pie. If you can manage dessert, try the fresh raspberry *bavarois*. Island Harbour (phone: 4488). Expensive.

Malliouhana – The ambience of this sleek hotel's restaurant is as you would expect — soft lights and sea breezes, elegant tableware, and fresh flowers during high season. However, because of limited seating, hotel guests are given priority and it is often difficult to get reservations in high season. The imaginative menu was created by Jo Rostang, chef-owner of the two-star *La Bonne Auberge* in Antibes, which, at least during the winter season, loans the *Malliouhana* several chefs and a maître d'hôtel. Among the excellent offerings are fresh salmon in croissant pastry with a compote of onions, terrine of *foie gras,* lobster ravioli, *farcis de crayfish aux cèpes et aux épinards,* and the prized *volaille de Bresse* (duck or chicken roasted on the spit). There is also a vast wine cellar, reported to hold some 35,000 bottles — at the *start* of last season. Early wrinkles seem to have been ironed out, and the kitchen is now worthy of its 2-star family. Meads Bay (phone: 6111 or 6741). Expensive.

Pimms – Perched on a point overlooking Maunday's Bay, *Cap Juluca*'s breezy Moorish-style oasis features delectably light lunches of fresh fish and lobster, a special fish pie, pasta of the day (which might be seafood ravioli in Noilly Prat), superb salads, cold soups, and grilled meats. Dinners give full reign to the French chefs' many talents, which include a vegetable terrine, rockfish salad, and house specials of local grouper and diced conch with crayfish sauce or a hardy bouillabaisse with a piquant rouille and croutons. The *crème brûlée* and *Devil Made Me Do It Mousse* are sinfully good conclusions. Maundays Bay (phone: 6914). Expensive.

Warden's Place – In a lovingly restored 18th-century stone and wood residence, this new steakhouse also serves grilled lamb, fresh lobster, and crayfish. It also does occasional theme nights — West Indian, South American, Mexican — not to be missed for good value and fun with live music. Local art and archaeological finds are displayed in the gallery downstairs. Book early for one of two small terrace tables. The Valley (phone: 2930). Expensive.

Barrel Stay – This thatch-roofed beachside bar and restaurant with barrel stays for
tables features a good fish soup, fresh red snapper in "Portuguese" sauce
(tomatoes, onions, green peppers), barbecued lobster, Hawaiian ham steak, and a
creamy chocolate mousse. Open for lunch and dinner. Sandy Ground (phone:
2831). Expensive to moderate.

The Mariners – Lunch or dinner on this breezy West Indian porch overlooking the
very white sand beach at Sandy Ground is a lovely experience. The menus are
unpretentious: Lunches feature salads, soups, and hamburgers as well as fresh
grilled fish of the day and lobster. Poached snapper or grouper in lemon butter
sauce, seafood salads, and chicken baked with coconut and ginger are regular
dinner offerings, but don't miss the lobster (kept live offshore until you order it)
grilled with fresh basil butter. Thursday is barbecue night, and on Saturday there
is a traditional West Indian dinner, both with live music. Sandy Ground (phone:
2671 or 2815). Expensive to moderate.

Ferryboat Inn – Pretty, breezy terrace with simple seafood, steaks, snacks, and a
friendly bar. Blowing Point (phone: 6613). Moderate.

Lucy's Harbour View – Perched on a hill overlooking Road Bay and the lagoon,
Lucy's is best at dusk, when you can watch the glorious Anguilla sunset. The
conch soup, curried goat or chicken, and whole red snapper, all Créole style, are
famous on the island. Service is not speedy, so come before your normal mealtime
and enjoy a rum punch with the spectacular view. Open for lunch and from 6:30
PM for dinner. South Hill (phone: 6253). Moderate.

The Old House – This popular restaurant, set in a charming West Indian–style
house on George Hill, dispenses fine local fare. The catch of the day here might
include "old wife" or "hind" (yellowtail or grouper, respectively), prepared Anguillian style (with tomatoes, onions, lemon, butter, fresh thyme, and chibble).
Barbecued chicken, pork, and beef are also featured. Open for breakfast, lunch,
and dinner. George Hill (phone: 2228). Moderate.

Riviera – Another pretty beachside bistro, featuring seafood with a Japanese touch:
sushi, sashimi, and oysters (when available) sautéed in soy sauce and sake, and the
island's best fish soup, thick and chunky with a properly piquant *rouille*. The
friendly bar attracts visiting yachts people and coin collectors, and well-traveled
French host Didier Van tells some tall tales worth hearing — good fun. Happy
Hour is 6 to 7 PM. Sandy Ground (phone: 2833). Moderate.

Happy Jack's – A friendly bar and invitingly informal dining area on the magnificent beach next to *Shoal Bay Villas*. The menu is modest, but the crayfish, lobster,
conch, and burgers are all good, and the lobster pie is superb. Open 8 AM to 10
PM. Shoal Bay (phone: 2051). Moderate to inexpensive.

Hybernia – A new French treat in a charming guesthouse courtyard at Sandy
Ground (phone: 2297). Moderate to inexpensive.

Roy's – For a taste of English heaven and everything you ever wanted to know about
Anguilla's goings-on, visit Roy and Mandy Bossons' eatery, the only one on quiet
Crocus Bay and the only tropical pub on the island. The fish and chips are fresh
and cooked to perfection, the Sunday roast beef is rare and delectable, and the
Yorkshire pudding is coveted by British expatriates. There's a lovely terrace, and
you'll never be lonely at the bar. Crocus Bay (phone: 2470). Moderate to inexpensive.

Trader Vic's – What was originally a thatch-roofed beach bar and grill has now
expanded into a vast restaurant across the road, which dispenses proper meals and
occasionally a good buffet with a live band. The à la carte menu features fish or
conch soup, grilled lobster, crayfish, grouper, snapper, and barbecued chicken or
ribs. Lunches are still served at the very pleasant beach bar. Shoal Bay (phone:
2091). Moderate to inexpensive.

Johnno's – Everyone on the island, Anguillians and visitors alike, seems to turn up here for al fresco dancing or to "hang out" with friends and have a beer on the beach. *Johnno's Beach Stop* features barbecued chicken, fish, and ribs daily from 10 AM to 6 PM, but is especially popular on Friday and Saturday nights and Sunday afternoons, when a local band brings in the crowds. Sandy Ground (phone: 2728). Inexpensive.

Oasis – Snack bar on the beach near *Covecastle* on Shoal Bay West. Open daily from 11 AM (no phone). Inexpensive.

Uncle Ernie's Shoal Bay Beach Bar – With one tiny table on its tiny terrace and another two in the sand, this tiny shack on the beach next to *Trader Vic's* is one of the most popular places on booming Shoal Bay. You can get a beer and a delicious barbecued chicken leg, rib, or fish (if anyone has caught some), all served with a smile for very little. Shoal Bay (no phone). Very inexpensive.

Other restaurants/snack bars serving "local" food include *The Aquarium* (mostly Créole-style seafood), *Cora's Pepper Pot* (for *rôti,* a full West Indian meal wrapped into a hamburger-size pastry), *Millie's Cross Roads* near the government buildings in The Valley (try her stewed conch), the *Round Rock Café* on Shoal Bay (for Eunice's famous "goat water" — the best hangover cure), *The Palm* (for stewed lobster), and *Amy's Bakery* (for chicken and chips as well as cakes, pies, and pizzas). If you crave Chinese, the *Oriental* restaurant in The Quarter is open later than most. For picnics on the beach or fancy take-out fare (especially if you're staying in a villa), *Fat Cat Gourmet* does escargot, quiche, chile, pasta salads, chicken or conch stew, and pastries (phone: 2752).

ANTIGUA

Don't be surprised if on the way in from Antigua's airport your driver suggests a short stop at the cricket field; and if you agree, don't be surprised when the short stop turns into an afternoon's diversion as that slow and stately English game progresses to its appointed climax. And don't be surprised if your driver doesn't understand your impatience as the afternoon wears on, not so much with the game, which Americans find genetically incomprehensible, but with the long, unplanned delay.

Life is simply like that on Antigua (pronounced an-*tee*-gaa). Cricket might be the metaphor for island life — not just because so much about the island is unquestionably British, but because, like that game, it is devoted to doing things in the fullness of time, with great enthusiasm but little rush.

In short, Antigua is tranquil. Even its history reflects that mood. The island was inhabited for 3,000 years by Indians: first the Siboney, or "stone people;" then the Arawaks, a pastoral South American tribe; and finally the warlike Caribs, who harassed European settlers here as late as the 1700s. It was discovered by Columbus in 1493 during his second voyage into the Caribbean. While he never came ashore, he did stop long enough to name it after Santa María la Antigua of Seville.

About 130 years passed before a group of Englishmen sailed over from nearby St. Kitts and settled the island on behalf of England. Antigua has been British ever since, except for one brief year (1666) when the French took possession. No one was killed or wounded during the invasion, and Antigua was returned to the British in 1667.

During the next 200 years the British built forts on the shoreline and a major naval installation at English Harbour (the site of Nelson's Dockyard) while waiting for the French to come back. They never did. But in 1784 a dashing young naval captain named Horatio Nelson arrived and took command of the yard. Under his command was the captain of the HMS *Pegasus,* Prince William Henry, Duke of Clarence (he later became King William IV). Clarence House, which sits on a hill opposite the yard, was built for the young prince while he was serving there.

As naval vessels grew larger and as skirmishes between Britain and France diminished, Antigua's importance as a naval base receded and the yard was officially abandoned in the early nineteenth century.

The dockyard, after 150 years of neglect, has been faithfully restored and is now a museum and active yacht marina. And work has begun to restore the fortifications atop Shirley Heights, which overlooks English Harbour.

But while Antigua's history and way of life is one of tranquillity, there is still lots to do besides watch the gulls soar on the trade breezes. Virtually all the first-class hotels have tennis courts, and several sponsor annual tournaments. The island has one 18-hole and two 9-hole golf courses. And the water sports are unexcelled: miles of reefs for snorkeling and diving and numerous

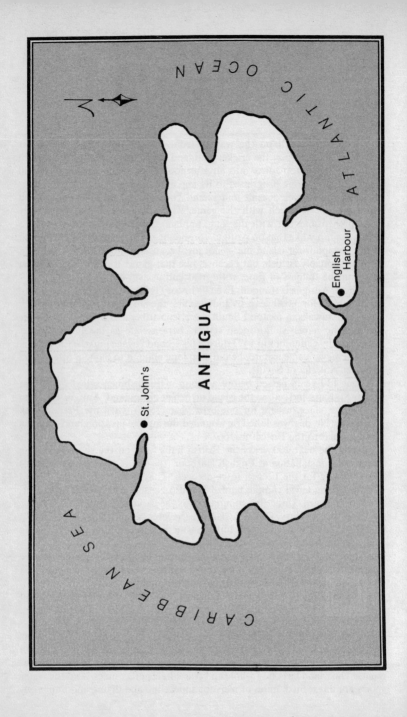

coves for sailing Sunfish. For serious deep-water sailors there is Race Week, held each spring in late April or early May, which features a series of regattas interrupted only by a generous number of land parties. And, at day's end, the peripatetic nightbird may while away the evenings at Antigua's clubs and casinos.

ANTIGUA AT-A-GLANCE

FROM THE AIR: Antigua is the true chameleon of the Caribbean. During the dry season (February through April), it gradually turns dusty and brown. But when the rains come, Antigua turns as green and lush as the Vermont countryside in May. The island lies between 61°40′ and 61°54′ W longitude and 17°00′ and 17°10′ N latitude. Antiguans like to think of the island as being in the heart of the Caribbean, the keystone of the arc of islands known as the Lesser Antilles. From its shores you can see Guadeloupe, Montserrat, Nevis, and St. Kitts. Antigua is small — a scant 108 square miles — as are the other two islands that make up the state — Barbuda, 32 miles due north and covering 68 square miles, and Redonda, a half-mile square of rock pinnacle that juts from the sea 20 miles to the southwest. There are about 75,000 people on Antigua, 1,500 on Barbuda, and only seagulls on Redonda.

SPECIAL PLACES: Though the focal point of sightseeing on the island is Nelson's Dockyard, the completely restored 18th-century naval yard on the southern side of the island, most visitors will begin their tour of the island in St. John's, the island's capital and major city.

St. John's – There are three things to see here: the farmers' market at the southern edge of town, the Antigua Museum, and St. John's Cathedral. The bustling outdoor market is best seen on a Saturday morning, when the colorful fruit and vegetable stands have been set up early in the morning and everyone turns out to shop. From the market, it is just a short taxi ride to Newgate Street for the museum and the cathedral. The Museum of Antigua and Barbuda (Long St.; phone: 463-1060) is a collection of eary Indian artifacts from some 120 prehistoric and historic sites on the island. A pet project of Desmond Nicholson of the well-known yacht chartering family, it is not elaborate or extensive but does have some interesting archaeological artifacts on exhibit, plus displays that ably convey significant historical facts and relationships. Originally built in 1683, St. John's has been rebuilt twice, in 1745 and again in 1845. The exterior is stone, but the interior is cased in pitch pine (which helped it survive subsequent earthquakes). The gates were constructed by the vestry in 1789.

ELSEWHERE ON THE ISLAND

At the village of Falmouth, just north of Nelson's Dockyard, is an area that used to be heavily devoted to producing sugar. Several antique stone sugar mill towers have been converted into homes; none, unfortunately, is open to the public, but most are visible along the road. From Falmouth, the route to the dockyard is well marked.

Nelson's Dockyard – The British navy used the dockyard continuously from 1707 until 1899, by which time ships had become too large to negotiate the relatively tortuous entrance to the harbor. The impressive installation saw its finest moments during the four-year command of Captain Horatio Nelson, from 1784 to 1787. During his stay, Nelson established a fast friendship with Prince William Henry, Duke of Clarence. The house visible across the harbor from the dockyard was built for the duke and still bears his name. It is sometimes open to the public and is well worth a visit.

The main buildings of the yard are *Admiral's Inn* (now a hotel and restaurant), constructed of bricks that came to Antigua as ships' ballast; the Admiral's House, now a museum; the Officers' Quarters, which are being rebuilt; and the *Prince William Careenage* — once the Capstan House and the Copper & Lumber Store, now a charming and unusual inn.

Shirley Heights – Just north of Nelson's Dockyard is the town of English Harbour; the ridge of hills above the town was fortified in 1787 by General William Henry Shirley and came to be known as Shirley Heights. Leaving the yard, return to the crossroads at English Harbour and bear right for the road to the summit of Shirley Heights. Along the way you will see the extensive fortifications, barracks, and powder magazines for the troops that guarded the dockyard from potential invaders. (They did their job well, for Antigua never was attacked.) The Antigua Historical Society has now identified all the ruins and has published a complete map of the facilities along the route. A small museum contains artifacts from the British era as well as some Arawak relics. The restaurant on the bluff provides light refreshment and a stunning view of the English Harbour.

Fig Tree Drive – The best drive in Antigua is along the beautiful but hard-to-find Fig Tree Drive. It has no fig trees, first of all; fig is the Antiguan name for banana. Second, it is difficult to find because it is unmarked — there are almost no road signs on the whole island. Typical directions (which are perfectly clear once you're following them): "Fig Tree Drive is the major road opposite the pink coral Catholic church just outside the town of Liberta, north of Falmouth. You can't miss it." Bearing southwest at the church, it winds through Antigua's rain forest and the hilliest section of the island, rising and falling steeply around Fig Tree Hill — farmland verdant with banana, mango, and coconut groves — before descending to Old Road and the Curtain Bluff area. No major sights, but a pleasant drive.

SOURCES AND RESOURCES

TOURIST INFORMATION: The Antigua Department of Tourism, 610 Fifth Ave., New York, NY 10020 (phone: 212-541-4117), supplies information on Antigua's attractions. The address in Canada is 60 St. Clair Ave. E, Suite 205, Toronto, Ont. M4T 1N5 (phone: 416-961-3085).

The tourist office in Antigua is on Long Street in St. John's. There are also information centers at V. C. Bird International Airport and at the passenger ship terminal in St. John's (central phone for all: 2-0029).

Local Coverage – The *Visitors Guide* and a helpful island map, free at the tourist office and hotel desks, carry information on entertainment, restaurants, sightseeing, and special events. Other locally produced guides and booklets are available at the tourist office at little cost. An excellent guide to Antigua is *Antigua and Barbuda: The Heart of the Caribbean* by Brian Dyder, who lives on the island.

The *Worker's Voice* is the island's newspaper, printed three times a week. The Sunday *New York Times* (and, occasionally, the weekday edition) arrives several days late.

Telephone – Dial direct to Antigua by adding the area code 809 and the prefix 46 to the numbers given. Barbuda now has telephone service as well.

ENTRY REQUIREMENTS: US and Canadian citizens need only proof of citizenship (passport, birth certificate, or voter's registration card) plus an onward ticket for entry. A smallpox vaccination is not required unless you are coming from a contaminated area.

CLIMATE AND CLOTHES: Temperatures range from an average low of 73°F (23°C) in the winter to a high of 85°F (30°C) in the summer and fall. And with the exception of September, there's a constant trade wind of 19 to 30 miles per hour, making for cool, pleasant evenings. There are few days without sun, and the annual rainfall averages only 45 inches. September, October, and November are the wettest months, when there are daily showers that usually last 10 minutes or less.

While many islands have gone completely casual, Antigua has not. Swimwear is for the beach, not hotel dining rooms or the streets of St. John's. Sightseeing or shopping requires casual street clothes (not shorts). After a morning on the beach, hotels prefer guests to slip into a shirt or coverup and a pair of sandals before sitting down to lunch. The British tradition of men dressing for dinner (jackets and ties or just jackets) still survives during the winter season in a few deluxe hotels like *Curtain Bluff* and *Half Moon Bay*. Restaurants are a different story; they are all casual and the "shirtjack" usually rules the day (or evening).

 MONEY: The official currency of the island, the Eastern Caribbean dollar (called Bee Wee or EC) is valued at about $2.70 to the US dollar. Banks exchange at exactly the day's exchange rate; hotels and shops will change at a bit less. US and Canadian dollars are accepted everywhere. Credit cards (principally American Express and Visa-Barclays) and traveler's checks are now accepted at all major hotels and at many shops and restaurants.

Banking hours are 8 AM to 1 PM on weekdays and 3 to 5:30 PM on Fridays only. Banks are closed Saturdays, Sundays, and holidays.

 LANGUAGE: English is spoken here and has been since the island was settled in the 1630s. However, you may well wonder what you are hearing when you listen to two Antiguans passing the time of day in their lilting accent liberally sprinkled with Antiguan colloquialisms.

 TIME: Antigua is on Atlantic Time, one hour ahead of New York in winter; in summer, when Daylight Saving Time is in effect, noon in New York is also noon in Antigua.

 CURRENT: Another of Antigua's little quirks. Most hotels operate on 110 volts, 60 cycles — the same as in the US and Canada. However, some have 220 volts (and to confuse matters a bit more, many of these have 110-volt shave outlets). However, most 220-volt hotels maintain an inventory of transformers for guests.

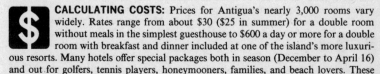 **GETTING THERE:** American Airlines and BWIA fly direct to Antigua from New York; Air Canada and BWIA fly nonstop from Toronto; BWIA flies nonstop from Miami, and Eastern flies both nonstop and via connecting flights in San Juan from Miami. LIAT provides air links to most other Caribbean islands.

 CALCULATING COSTS: Prices for Antigua's nearly 3,000 rooms vary widely. Rates range from about $30 ($25 in summer) for a double room without meals in the simplest guesthouse to $600 a day or more for a double room with breakfast and dinner included at one of the island's more luxurious resorts. Many hotels offer special packages both in season (December to April 16) and out for golfers, tennis players, honeymooners, families, and beach lovers. These usually include room, meals, sightseeing, and airport transfers, but not airfare. The Department of Tourism (New York and Toronto) has complete details.

Antigua has a number self-contained housekeeping units. A complete listing — not always including rates, however — is available from the Department of Tourism.

A 10% service charge is tacked on to all hotel rates (which frees guests from having to tip for individual services) and a 6% tax on all hotel sales. Some hotels quote only MAP rates (including breakfast and dinner); others quote EP rates (room only) but offer an optional MAP add-on (for breakfast and dinner) of $25 to $35 per person a day.

 GETTING AROUND: Taxi – Always available at the airport, in St. John's, at the deepwater harbor, and at the hotels. The rates are fixed by law (no meters). Fares are about the same as New York City prices. From the airport to St. John's, expect to pay about $5 US; to the most distant hotel, about $20 US; St. John's to Nelson's Dockyard, about $18.

Touring by taxi is one of the best ways to see the island, especially if the idea of left-hand driving intimidates you (which it needn't). Antiguan drivers on the whole are friendly and informative, particularly since the government has provided them with an information booklet — available to tourists upon request — detailing much of the island's history, natural resources and general facts, figures, tidbits, and trivia. If you get a quiet driver, chances are he's shy (something many Antiguans suffer from), not sullen. Given a friendly attitude on your part and a bit of time, he'll warm to his task. A full tour of Nelson's Dockyard, Shirley Heights, Fig Tree Drive, and shopping in St. John's will cost about $50 US; shorter variations on the same theme are less.

If you want an especially knowledgeable driver who can impart more local lore, agricultural and meteorological facts, tourist tips, droppable names, and rumor-mill oddments per mile than any we've encountered in the islands, contact Irving Mason at *Capital Rental* on High St., St. John's (phone: 2-0863).

Bus – Public transport does exist, but on a strictly informal basis. Schedules are generally "sometime in the morning" and "sometime in the afternoon." Tourists seldom use buses, but the tourist office can help with schedules if you want to try one.

Car Rental – The best way to get around if you plan on staying for any length of time and want to travel around the island. Driving is on the left, and you'll need an Antiguan driver's license, which can be obtained at the airport or the police station in St. John's for $10 US and a valid US license. Rates for rental cars are about $40 to $45 a day, and about $225 a week. There are no mileage fees with rental cars; gasoline runs about $2 US per gallon.

All rental firms on the island are locally owned but represent major international chains as well as independent operations. Among the best: *Antigua Car Rental,* an Avis affiliate (phone: 2-1815), *Budget* (phone: 2-2544), *Carib Car Rental* (phone: 2-2062), *Sunshine* (phone: 1-2426), *Hertz* (phone: 2-3397), and *National* (phone: 2-2113). During certain holiday peaks — Christmas, Easter, and Race Week — reserve ahead.

Sea Excursions – Lunch, all-day, and evening cocktail cruises are rapidly becoming very popular in Antigua. A number of yachts and the pirate-ship-shaped *Jolly Roger* are offering such trips. Buffet or barbecue cruises, with lunch, rum punches, swimming, and lots of music, cost about $30 per person; dinner cruises with dancing run about the same. Reservations can be made through the hotel.

Caribbean Link Ltd. offers high-speed ferry service between Antigua and Montserrat, Guadeloupe, Dominica, St. Kitts, Nevis, St. Maarten, and Barbuda. Its new 320-passenger *Carib Jet* travels an expanded route that includes Martinique, St. Lucia, St. Kitts, Nevis, St. Maarten, and St. Eustatius. Round-trip rates range from $44 (to Montserrat) to $160 (St. Lucia). Day trips to Barbuda — including round-trip fare, tour, and beach party — are offered on Sundays for $75. For information, contact Carib Link (2-4225).

SHOPPING: Liquor prices are among the best in the Caribbean, except for French wines and certain French cognacs. Cavalier, the local rum, is about $2.50 US for 26 ounces, an outstanding bargain in anyone's book. (Local liquor stores generally carry cards showing cost, including extra duty, for those people wishing to bring back more than a single liter. Check them.) Prices on English bone china, gold jewelry, lead crystal, Swiss watches, and cameras are no better than those found elsewhere in the Caribbean (and usually no less than in mainland discount outlets), but Sea Island cotton products (all made in Japan) are excellent buys. Shops in St. John's to know: for liquor, *Friday's* at the Warehouse, *Manuel Dias',* and *Quin Farara;* jewelry, crystal, and watches, *The Gift Centre, Specialty Shop, Norma's Scent Shop;* for clothes and perfume, *Coco Shop* (terrific fabrics, also pottery), *The Studio,* and *Nubia Shop;* for batiks, print fabrics, island T-shirts, and *Kel-Print.* The Redcliffe Quay Shopping Center at the end of Redcliffe Street has several interesting boutiques (the *Spice Island Perfume Shop* has delicious potpourris, herbs and spices, scents). For unusual pottery, take a run out to Seaview Farms (a small village about 15 minutes east of St. John's) and ask for Cedric. Don't expect to find a fancy shop — it's his workshed — but it's worth the trip.

Island-made bead necklaces are available on the beaches, at the dockyard, wherever a "bead lady" can set up. A favorite souvenir is a warri board (an Antiguan game that you are guaranteed to learn at some point during your stay).

Shopping hours are from 8 AM to noon and 1 to 4 PM Mondays through Saturdays, except Thursdays, when some shops close for the afternoon.

TIPPING: The 10% service charge added to your hotel bill in virtually all Antiguan hotels and restaurants covers all but very special service. When a service charge is not included (if in doubt, ask), tip waiters 10% to 15%, hotel maids $1 US per day, bellboys and airport porters 50¢ EC per bag. Taxi drivers get about 10% of the fare.

SPECIAL EVENTS: Antigua has three special celebrations: *Tennis Weeks, Race Week,* and *Summer Carnival. Tennis Week,* held at several top-flight hotels in early January, features a week-long series of amateur men's and women's tournaments, pro-ams, and professional men's singles and doubles tourneys. Previous winners include Vitas Gerulaitis. There's also a *Women's Tennis Week* in early April.

In late April, Antigua's festive spirit turns to the sea for *Race Week,* seven days of ocean racing and shoreside parties. It's a delightful mixture of breathtaking scenes and breathtaking rum, and the evening parties shift from hotel to hotel. The last day and evening, called Dockyard Day, is a landlubber's delight. It features tugs-of-war between sailing crews, a greased pole race, and spinnaker flying. When the sun sets, Lord Nelson's Ball begins. Amid drinking and dancing, the week's awards are presented.

At the end of July and in early August is *Summer Carnival,* a week to ten days of fetes, steel bands, Carnival Queen and calypso competitions, parades, and more fetes.

More sedate and official holidays observed by bank and state include *New Year's Day, Good Friday, Easter, Whitmonday, Independence Day* (November 1), *Christmas,* and *Boxing Day* (December 26).

SPORTS: Since beaches are Antigua's main draw, it's only natural that most of the island's visitors can be found on or near one of the 365 stretches of sand that dot the island's perimeter. There is, however, a continued commitment to cricket and soccer and a rapidly growing interest in tennis.

Boating – Most hotels have Sunfish or Sailfish available (often without cost to guests). The *Anchorage* and the *Curtain Bluff* have their own yachts for day and cocktail cruises. Individual day charters are not readily available; the few that serve the island are especially busy in the peak season. However, a quick check with *Nicholson Yacht Charters* (phone: 3-1059; 800-662-6066) will determine what is available at Nelson's Dockyard. Nicholson handles over 80 charter yachts, and more often than not, at least one or two are in for provisioning. Prices vary according to the boat's size and the length of the trip.

Cricket – Antigua's main sporting passion is played on pitches (fields) ranging from exquisitely manicured greens to vacant lots. Cricket is a spectator sport that is also a social event, much like Carnival. Antiguans are proud that two native sons — Vivi Richards and Andy Roberts — rank among the world's best (a stamp has been issued in their honor). Matches are played Thursday afternoons, Saturdays, and Sundays.

Golf – There may be no championship courses in Antigua, but there are two layouts that offer diversion for the average amateur. Cedar Valley is a 6,077-yard, 18-hole, par-70 course, while the layout at the *Half Moon Bay* is 2,140 yards for a 9-hole, par-34 course. Rentals, in US dollars: clubs $5; carts $20; greens fees $16 for 18 holes; caddies $3.50. Hourly lessons are available at $25 US. Weekly greens fees are available at both courses. In the high season, it is a good idea to check course availability at the *Half Moon Bay* (guests are guaranteed a place).

Hiking – There are no organized trails or routes. And because of the limited public transportation, it is best to plan *round-trip* walking tours. For the stout of heart, a hike (more like a trek) up the face of Monk's Hill (opposite the *Catamaran* hotel) offers a rewarding view of the fortifications atop the hill and a spectacular view of the island. *Warning:* Start early, take your time, and bring a snack.

Horseback Riding – The government is trying to discourage horseback riding on the beaches. However, the *St. James's Club* keeps a stable of Texas quarter horses for guests, and the *Galley Bay* still offers riding.

Horseracing – None of the "thoroughbreds" that parade to the post at the flat-racing course (look for a field with a rail around it) would qualify for US races, but that doesn't keep the betting action from being fast and furious, or the local improvers of the breed from putting on the ritz and acting as if this patch of grass out by the west end of the runway at Bird Airport (and hard by the local winery) is every bit as authentic as Epsom Downs. There's more news to be gotten from the inside track here in one afternoon than you'll hear in a week at a resort hotel.

Snorkeling and Scuba – Most hotels offer fins and masks free or for a nominal fee. For serious diving, the reefs and wrecks off Antigua's northeast, south, and west coasts provide good diving and make excellent day-trip destinations. There are underwater parks at Boons Point: Saltfish Tail Reef and Cades Reef. Several hotels maintain their own equipment and offer instruction, including *The Anchorage, Halcyon Cove, Blue Waters Beach, Curtain Bluff, Jolly Beach, Long Bay, Runaway Bay, Royal Antiguan,* and the *St. James Club.* Dive operators include *Dive Antigua* (phone: 2-0256), *Dive Runaway* (phone: 2-1318), and *Long Bay* (phone: 3-2005). Single tank dives cost around $35 US; instruction begins at about $50 US. Look also to Barbuda for excellent scuba grounds. The waters off the island are strewn with wrecks that provide an outstanding day's dive.

Sport Fishing – Among the hotels operating sportfishing boats are *Runaway, Blue Waters Beach,* and *Long Bay;* half-day deep-sea trips cost about $125, inshore trips about $25 per person. The 31-foot *Octo Pussy* (phone: 3-1036) is available for half days ($240) or all day ($340), while the 35-foot *Nightwing* (phone: 2-1281) is available for $280 for four hours. All prices are in US dollars.

Swimming and Sunning – Still the supreme interest of vacationers. And with good reason. The beaches are many and excellent. Because three quarters of the island rests comfortably inside the Caribbean Sea and that which does not is well protected by reefs, there are rarely heavy breakers or dangerous undertows. All beaches in Antigua are public. Antigua's neighbor island Barbuda is all beach (the best place for shelling, by the way). Unfortunately, Barbuda can be reached only by plane and, at the moment, has limited accommodations. However, time permitting, visitors to Antigua should consider a day trip.

Tennis – *St. James' Club* (5 lighted courts), *Half Moon Bay* (5 courts), *Curtain Bluff* (4 Har-Tru courts and 1 grass), and the *Anchorage* (3 courts) are the island's tennis leaders. All have resident pros and complete shops. *Blue Waters, Hawksbill, Galleon Beach, Galley Bay, Halcyon Cove,* and *Jolly Beach* also offer tennis, though with fewer facilities. *Half Moon Bay,* the *Anchorage,* and *Halcyon Cove* host the annual Tennis Week's professional tournaments each January. *Curtain Bluff*'s annual informal tournament is a spring event. Most hotels don't charge guests for court time.

Water Skiing – Offered by many of the hotels and listed in the tourist office's activities chart. Cost is about $15 per person for a half-hour.

 NIGHTLIFE: In season, most hotels offer something every night: steel bands, limbo, dance bands, or fire eating. There are several casinos: one with adjacent lounge entertainment at the *Royal Antiguan* hotel; a small, European-style casino at the glitzy *St. James' Club* next to the disco; and one with a lounge and nightclub at the *Halcyon Cove.* They operate every night and feature blackjack, craps, roulette, and one-armed bandits. Clubs and discos seem to sprout during the height of the winter season and then disappear, sometimes permanently. Among the perennial favorites is live late-night music at *The Victory* restaurant at Redcliffe Quay in St. John's, where jazz is featured one night, steel bands another. Another resident club is *18 Carrot* on lower Church St., a salad and sandwich bar by day, a swinging disco by night. *The Solid Gold Disco* and *Tropix* nightclub both swing on weekends. Outside town, the *Bel-Aire* offers nightly entertainment on Old Parham Rd., just off Airport Rd., hard by the renamed V. C. Bird Airport.

BEST ON THE ISLAND

 CHECKING IN: From the 472-room complex at *Jolly Beach* resort to the 6 compact, airy suites at *Siboney Beach Club,* Antigua offers a staggering diversity of resort facilities and accommodations — and the range covers size, shape, ambience, and price. The island's tourism minions can look you right in the eye and boast that there is something for everybody — because there is. In general, it is safe to assume that the smaller the hotel, the more personal the treatment accorded the guest; there are no huge, tour group hotels. Summer rates (in effect from April 16 to December 15) drop by 30% to 45%, meaning that a room for two at the island's most luxurious haven, *Jumby Bay,* which costs $600 US including all meals in mid-January, will cost only $300 or so in July. Expect to pay $220 plus for a room for two (MAP, including breakfast and dinner) in high season at hotels listed as expensive; $150 to $210 in places noted as moderate.

Curtain Bluff – Like a vintage wine, the *Bluff* improves with age. Owner Howard Hulford demands the best from the staff and gets it. Result: true value. With only 60 rooms, the atmosphere is clubby. Four tennis courts, a practice court, and a resident pro (Howard likes tennis). A yacht for day sails (Howard likes sailing), two beaches, all water sports (included in the room rate), and excellent food. Owner Hulford occasionally gets twitted by rival hoteliers because of his unbendable rule that men wear ties after 7 PM; he believes his guests want it that way. Chef Ruedi Portman is well known for his imaginative island cuisine. The wine cellar is perhaps the best in the Caribbean. There are 6 new hillside suites that are as close to the ultimate in combined luxury, comfort, and setting as any Caribbean accommodation currently offers. Old Road (phone: 3-1115). Expensive.

Half Moon Bay – Antigua's answer to the country club. Its rather pleasant 100 rooms are part of a complex that includes a 9-hole golf course, 5 tennis courts (2 lighted), all water sports, dancing nightly in season, and a pool. The restaurant is greatly improved from years back, as is the management. Half Moon Bay (phone: 3-2101). Expensive.

Hawksbill Beach – An impressive 37-acre beachfront site and astute management have made *Hawksbill* one of the island's up-and-coming resorts. Features include deluxe, superior, and standard accommodations for up to eight guests in a separate great house (reserve 6 months to a year in advance), with its own beach and coral reef for offshore snorkeling, most other water sports, a pool, and tennis. On the south coast, a half-hour's drive from the airport (phone: 2-0301). Expensive.

Jumby Bay – A cool $5 million has been spent to make this private-island resort more comfortable for its maximum 76 guests, who have the entire 300-acre islet — one mile north of Antigua — to themselves. Guests make their way around the resort by van, bicycle, or on foot. Two beautiful beaches (the more secluded one has an honor bar), use of Sunfish, windsurfers, snorkel gear, water skiing, tennis, and all food and drink are part of the package. Charter sailing, fishing, and scuba excursions can be arranged. No clocks, telephones, or radios; just a sociable, utterly relaxed atmosphere. *Jumby Bay*'s real luxury lies in its very pretty, thoughtfully appointed, private cottage suites which have delightful cross ventilation (no air conditioning necessary). Open November through August (phone: 2-6000). Expensive.

Royal Antiguan – Antigua's newest hotel, on Deep Bay, has 270 rooms in the main buildings plus 12 one-bedroom and 18 two-bedroom suites in adjacent cottages. All are air-conditioned, have radio/TV and VCR, minibar, and refrigerator. There are four restaurants on the premises, two lounges, and a European-style casino. All water sports, 8 tennis courts (4 lighted), swimming pool, and yacht marina (phone: 2-2826). Expensive.

St. James's Club – This overdone glitter-dome-by-the-sea features an activity-rich environment and is certainly comfortable, but part of the premium price is returned only in the intangibles of seeing and being seen. Dress accordingly. There are 90 suites and studios, plus a private yacht club on a 100-acre point at Mamora Bay. Rates cover use of two big pools, sun decks, beaches, snorkel gear, windsurfers, sailboats, gym, and 5 tennis courts; scuba, jet skiing, water skiing, sport fishing, and riding (from the club's own stable of quarter horses) cost extra. Other amenities include a beauty salon, 24-hour room service, 4 restaurants, nightclub/disco, and a small European-style casino (phone: 3-1430 or 3-1113). Expensive.

Copper and Lumber Store – Unique setting and authentic 18th-century decor (Oriental rugs, antique four-posters, nautical memorabilia, period furniture, etc.) for 14 opulent suites in meticulously reconstructed Nelson's Dockyard warehouse. All have admirably modern kitchens. No sports facilities, but transport to the beach across the harbor is provided. The restaurant offers English specialties and some island dishes (phone: 3-1058). Expensive to moderate.

Halcyon Cove Beach Resort and Casino – On Dickenson Bay, this 154-room hotel offers lots of activities, a pool, tennis, all water sports, the *Warri Pier* for lunch and drinks (but be prepared for slow service), nightly entertainment and/or dancing, and a casino (phone: 2-0256). Expensive to moderate.

Hodges Bay Club – Gleaming Mediterranean villas shelter 26 smartly comfortable 1- and 2-bedroom condominium apartments (with cathedral ceilings, Italian tile floors, balconies or terraces, deluxe kitchens) overlooking a pretty if narrow white sand beach; double bedroom rentals are also available. Nearby Prickley Pear Island offers first-rate snorkeling, picnicking. Secluded, yet handy to golf course, airport, and the town of St. John's (phone: 2-2300). Expensive to moderate.

Barrymore Beach – Brian and Linda Gordon are the amiable hosts offering luxury 1- and 2-bedroom apartment units with kitchenettes. Only minutes from the activity and nightlife of Dickenson Bay's bigger hotels, it's easy to relax in quiet solitude here. And if you're too relaxed to cook, there are several beachfront restaurants on the bay (phone: 2-4101 or 4-4140). Moderate.

Blue Heron Beach – A friendly enclave on a sandy, reef-protected beach fine for swimming and snorkeling. There are 40 rooms, all with balcony or verandah, plus a tennis court, beach bar, breezy cocktail lounge, and restaurant particularly strong on authentic West Indian dishes. Johnson's Point Beach (phone: 3-1421). Moderate.

Blue Waters Beach – One of the few hotels with air-conditioned rooms, it's pleasant in an old English sort of way, and the new British owners are enlarging and upgrading it. Dancing or entertainment nightly during the winter. The cuisine is consistently good. Amenities include all water sports, a tennis court, and a pool. Soldiers Bay (phone: 2-0290). Moderate.

Galley Bay Surf Club – Here are 28 double rooms in what seems to be a very remote setting. Actually, it is only 5 miles from St. John's and is a favorite of several celebrities, including Greta Garbo, who was once caught on the beach by a national magazine photographer sans attire. Excellent beach and water sports, also a tennis court and horseback riding. At Galley Bay (phone: 2-0302). Moderate.

Long Bay – Small, pleasant, somewhat isolated on the northeastern coast of the island, right at the water's edge; balconied rooms face a lagoon. All water sports, including scuba diving. Interesting packages available, including year-round honeymoon plans. Long Bay (phone: 3-2005). Moderate.

Siboney Beach Club – Almost hidden by palms and bougainvillea, this property features 12 suites (light housekeeping, bedroom plus sofa beds) in a greenery-laden 3-story building with a pool and small restaurant-lounge. An informal, congenial setting where the service can be as relaxed as the atmosphere and the food surprisingly good. If it's intimacy you crave, this is it. Try for top-floor balcony suites (phone 2-3356). Moderate.

Jolly Beach – If you love company and have been searching for a reasonably priced Caribbean vacation, this 472-room resort has your number. A highly organized activities schedule takes hold of the tour-package client from arrival to departure (presumably tanned and exhausted); there are 7 bars to dispense the appropriate potables to those who don't swim, frolic, or play other games. Larger rooms are comfortable, if rather institutional, in layout and decor; smaller size units are downright tight. Off-season tour packages, including airfare, are some of the bargains of all time (phone 2-0061). Moderate to inexpensive.

Admiral's Inn – This delightful 200-year-old inn is the heart of Nelson's Dockyard, and most of the yard's social life is centered there. When the ships are in, you'll find millionaires and boat bums drinking and eating side by side at the bar or in the courtyard. The rooms are small but well appointed. Great restaurant for just about everything. No beach, but the management will run you across the harbor to one nearby. The manager, Ethelyn Philip, makes the pieces fit together quite well. English Harbour (phone: 3-1027). Inexpensive.

 EATING OUT: Like most Caribbean food, native Antiguan dishes tend to be spicy, using sauces that are highly influenced by East Indian foods. A wide variety of curries is found on most island menus. Prices are extremely reasonable. Expect to pay around $50 for two at the restaurants we list as expensive, about $25 at moderate, and less at inexpensive.

ST. JOHN'S

Cockleshell Inn – An indoor-outdoor spot strictly for dinner and seafood. The treat is clamlike local "cockles" done with island spices Winston's way. On Fort Rd. outside St. John's (phone: 2-0471). Expensive.

DuBarry's – West Indian warmth, Continental flavor, on a pretty terrace. Beautiful soups (red bean, curried pumpkin, seafood bisque), entrées (lobster fra diavolo, red snapper and lobster mornay, tournedos au château), desserts (hot fudge pie, home-made ice cream). Lunch is tasty (try the lobster smile), less costly. In the *Barrymore* hotel on Fort Rd. (phone: 2-1055). Expensive.

Spanish Main – Businessmen's luncheon spot, in a large old home. Very comfortable. Continental menu (phone: 2-0660). Expensive.

The Yard – Delicious garden atmosphere, excellent pumpkin soup, coconut-breaded shrimp, lobster, seafood, steaks at both lunch and dinner. In St. John's at the corner of Upper Long and East sts. (phone: 2-1856). Expensive.

Darcy's – Outdoor restaurant well known to cruise passengers. Sometimes a steel band plays at lunch hour. Everything from hamburgers to West Indian specialties. Kensington Court (phone: 2-1323). Moderate.

Golden Peanut – Luncheon spot in the center of St. John's, with everything from hamburgers to West Indian dishes. Entertainment cover charges at night (phone: 2-1415). Moderate.

Brother B's – Has rapidly become *the* place for lunch. Features a West Indian menu with a special each day, outdoor tables. It will be crowded, so expect to take some time eating; try the pepperpot. Lunch for one will run slightly more than $5 Bee Wee ($2 US) (phone: 2-0616). Inexpensive.

Chalet Suisse – Surprise! It's an island deli dispensing rotis, spicy crab backs, and overstuffed sandwiches. Redcliffe Quay (phone: 2-4221). Inexpensive.

ELSEWHERE ON THE ISLAND

Clouds – Attempts to create and consistently present *haute cuisine* in the Caribbean have generally ranged from the disappointing to the ludicrous. Yet so determined was *Halcyon Cove* corporate management to pull it off at this spectacularly situated hilltop restaurant that an executive vice president was seen toiling in the role of *maître d'hôtel*. Their efforts have won accolades — even from rival hoteliers — that run as high as "world class." The experience provided is unique enough, given the splendid view and the novelty of formal French service, sauces, pastries, and vintage wines, to warrant its stiff prices. Reservations via *Halcyon Cove* front desk. Expensive.

Le Bistro – One of Antigua's most elegant, with a distinctly French-toned menu: lobster bisque or onion soup to start; lobster in the shell, Dover sole in a cream and spinach sauce, red snapper with fennel, as well as veal and beef entrées; crème caramel, pêche melba, and chocolate mousse pie to finish. Hodges Bay near the *Antigua Beach* hotel (phone: 2-3881). Expensive.

Colombo's – Every sort of seductively shaped pasta imaginable (the Italian Flag appetizer starts you off with three; *tagliatelle al pesto* is ambrosial) — all home-made. Entrées of veal, tournedos Rossini, suckling pig (different choices each evening), are followed by fruit ices or ice creams, if you've a cranny left. At the *Galleon Beach Club* (phone: 3-1024). Expensive.

L'Aventure – Elegant dining at Indian Town Point, on Long Bay. Diners travel from resorts on the eastern end of the island just to sample the fine Continental fare, with Antiguan accents. You will also find one of the better wine lists on the island here (phone: 3-2003). Expensive.

Admiral's Inn – The ground floor of the 200-year-old inn. Delightfully decorated, with an open courtyard. The Continental island menu usually features fish dishes (try the lobster). The rum punch is excellent. Reservations suggested for dinner in season. Nelson's Dockyard (phone: 3-1027). Expensive to moderate.

Shirley Heights Lookout – Housed in a restored 18th-century fortification with a spectacular view of Nelson's Dockyard and English Harbour. Specialties include lobster and fresh fish dishes, as well as familiar standbys such as burgers and fries. Open daily for lunch and dinner; steel band and barbecue every Sunday afternoon. Shirley Heights (phone: 3-1274). Moderate.

The Yacht Club – Nautical crowd (visiting captains, crews, et al.), clubby but casually congenial air. The food is inventive, delicious (sample shrimp with breadfruit, linguine with cockles). Nelson's Dockyard (phone: 3-1444). Moderate.

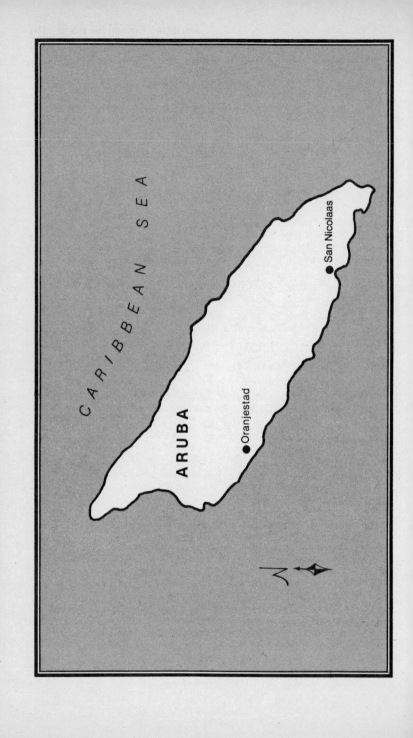

ARUBA

Aruba is sunny, small, and very much an island on the move. This 74-square-mile bit of land has fine beaches, several high-rise casino resort hotels, and a wide variety of smaller hotels. It has a good shopping district, but it is less formal than Curaçao. Tremendous investments in Aruba's tourism sector during the past year have turned this island into one of the Caribbean's fastest-growing destinations.

The island is Dutch and an integral part of the kingdom of the Netherlands. But as of January 1986, it ceased, of its own volition and with the agreement of the rest of the kingdom, to be just one of the islands of the Netherlands Antilles, administered through Curaçao. Aruba remains a part of the Dutch kingdom, but now has direct ties with Holland and control over its own aviation, immigration, customs, communications, and other internal and external matters.

For several decades, potential visitors tended to think of Aruba as a less developed and smaller version of its sister "ABC" island, Curaçao. There are similarities: Both are dry (cacti far outnumber palms), Dutch, and autonomous (citizens of Willemstad and Oranjestad enjoy the same rights and privileges as their fellow Netherlanders in Amsterdam); both islands offer duty-free shopping (though the stocks in Curaçao's shops are larger) and casino gambling; and both have economies that were substantially shored up by oil refineries until 1985, when Exxon closed its local refineries for good.

But Aruba no longer lives in Curaçao's shadow. Aruba boasts more than 1,900 thoroughly modern hotel rooms on its Palm Beach, a five-mile stretch of pure white sand that outstrips any strand Curaçao has to offer. These, plus just over 700 first-class rooms on smaller Eagle Beach and Druif Bay (both south of Palm, nearer Oranjestad), raise Aruba's luxury and first-class room count to nearly 2,600. A new 210-room *Ramada Renaissance* hotel and casino on Eagle Beach, scheduled to open in the winter of 1989–90, and a 360-room *Hyatt* scheduled for completion on Palm Beach in April 1990, are the latest tourism developments. Aruba now has as many casinos as Curaçao (six each), and in season, more shows playing in its hotel nightclubs. In sum, Aruba caters to vacationers in a big way.

Historically, it was discovered in 1499 by Alonzo de Ojeda, who claimed the island for Spain. There is still some question about whether he christened it Oro Uba — Spanish for "gold was there" — or whether the name came from *ora,* the Carib word for shell, or from *oubao,* island. The Spanish considered the island valueless (not worth colonizing) and therefore allowed its Arawak Indian population to live. Today, even though 2,000 Indians were rounded up and shipped off to labor in the mines of Hispaniola — where the Indians had been exterminated — Arawak features survive on the faces of many natives.

In 1636, nearing victory and the end of their 80-year war with Spain, the Dutch turned their attention to the Caribbean. They arrived to assess the area, then unceremoniously took over this neglected territory with little opposition from the Spanish. In 1643, Peter Stuyvesant was appointed governor of Aruba and the rest of the Netherlands Antilles, a post he held for four years before moving north to New Amsterdam. And, with the exception of a brief period in the early 19th century when the British flag flew over these islands, the Dutch have been in peaceful residence ever since.

For a time it looked as though Aruba's fortune lay in gold, discovered in 1825 and mined successfully near Balashi. But in 1916 the cost of gold mining reached a point where the meager yield became unprofitable. In 1929, with the opening of the Lago Oil and Transport Company's refinery — then the world's largest — the island began to prosper as never before.

Of the 65,000 people who live on Aruba today, 75% were born on the island; the rest are European Dutch, British, North American, and Venezuelan. New hotels and more visitors mean new jobs to replace those lost with the death of the oil-refining industry in 1985 — one reason that Arubans are eager to have their tourist industry flourish.

It seems to be doing just that — not strictly because of the sleek hotels and casinos, the extraordinary beaches, and bright, warm sea, but because Arubans make their island an especially pleasant place to be. They bridge the gap between their red-roofed cottages and tall hotels. They are friendly people, and they want visitors not only to see their island but to understand it — which is why taxi touring here is worth the extra investment. In the course of a half-day's drive, you learn a little Papiamento (*bon dia* for good morning, *masha danki,* thank you), hear about Aruban courtship (before a young man may call on a girl seriously, he must build himself a house), find out who Lloyd G. Smith was (and why the waterfront drive was named for him), and make at least one Aruban friend — your driver.

You also learn that Aruban smiles aren't asking for anything. Quite simply and genuinely, they mean *bon bini* — welcome. It feels so good that people often come back for more.

ARUBA AT-A-GLANCE

FROM THE AIR: Aruba, shaped like a dolphin swimming northwest to southeast toward South America, is the smallest and westernmost of the Dutch "ABC" islands that lie just off the Venezuelan coast. At 12°30′ N latitude, 70° W longitude, Aruba is 15 miles north of Venezuela and 42 miles west of Curaçao. It is just 19.6 miles long and 6 miles at its widest point — a total of only 70 square miles.

The mouth of the dolphin is Rodgers Bay, near the Seroe Colorado residential area at the island's southern point; its right fin is the capital city of Oranjestad, on the west coast, and the end of its tail is a lighthouse on the island's northern tip. Princess Beatrix Airport lies 1 mile southeast of the capital. Jets make the 2,090-mile flight from New York in 4 hours; from Miami, in 2½ hours.

The best way to see Aruba from the air is aboard one of the small ALM commuter planes that make several flights a day between Aruba and its sister islands, Bonaire and Curaçao. These low-flying craft show you the dolphin in all its diversity, with divi-divi trees bent by the wind along the southern shore, the wild surf crashing along the east coast, the desolate dunes on the island's northern tip, and all manner of sailing craft at anchor at the island's southern corner.

 SPECIAL PLACES: Oranjestad – Tempting shopping opportunities and quaint Dutch architecture are the chief attractions of the island's capital, one of the busiest towns in the Caribbean. Its bustling main avenue, Nassaustraat, the most fashionable shopping street, is lined on either side with banks, offices, boutiques, and stores that offer good duty-free buys from all over the world. Allow at least half a day to explore it — and travel on foot. Head for the harbor and walk along the wharf where the local fishing boats and island schooners are moored. Every morning, fresh fish and produce are sold directly from these boats. In the center of them all, the exotic Indonesian houseboat restaurant *Bali* lies at permanent anchor. Stroll along Lloyd G. Smith Boulevard (named for an early Lago oil refinery general manager) to Wilhelmina Park, a brilliant showcase of tropical gardening on the waterfront. You can lunch at one of any number of interesting restaurants in the area — a tropical Italian *Papagayo* upstairs overlooking the schooner market or the *Dragon Phoenix Bar & Restaurant* a block away (Chinese food). Or buy some Dutch cheese and fresh fruit and head north to the picnic grove at Manchebo — or a half mile farther to Eagle Beach, which has palm-thatched picnic shelters. Should you choose to see Oranjestad in the afternoon, remember: Many shops are closed for siesta between noon and 2 PM. Follow your shopping with cocktails on the *Bali* wharf and dinner on the floating houseboat beside it or at the breezy *Surfside, Talk of the Town,* or stylish *Papiamento.*

ELSEWHERE ON THE ISLAND

For touring the island, the recommended route heads north out of Oranjestad along Eagle Beach and Palm Beach to the northernmost tip of the island and continues clockwise. On this route you will see:

De Olde Molen – An authentic old windmill brought from Holland, piece by piece, and set up as a restaurant.

California Dunes – At the northernmost tip of the island, the desolate site of the California Lighthouse.

Cunucu – The interior countryside, where flat landscapes are marked by cactus, huge boulders, aloe, and divi-divi trees (the latter, permanently bent by the wind, look as though their branches were blowing away), and pastel houses enclosed by cactus fences.

Hooiberg (Mt. Haystack) – Aruba's most prominent mountain, at the center of the island. Several hundred carved steps climb up to its peak, a 541-foot height from which Venezuela is visible on clear days. Mt. Yamanota (617 feet) and Mt. Arikok (577 feet) are taller, but not as accessible.

Casa Bari and Ayo – Here, to the northeast of Hooiberg, are building-sized stacks of diorite boulders that look as though they've been dumped on the landscape just to puzzle geologists and impress travelers.

Bushiribana – On the northeast coast, you can visit abandoned gold mines and the ruins of a pirate's castle that legend (unsubstantiated) dates back to 1499.

Andicouri – Along the east coast, the pounding surf has carved out a natural bridge and an old plantation on the cove is a beautiful spot for a picnic.

Arikok National Park – Site of the island's best-preserved Indian drawings, it's near the mountain of the same name.

Boca Prins – Another coastal attraction, where it's traditional to slide down the dunes (wear tough jeans and sneakers).

Fontein and Guadiriki Caves – Inland caves decorated with still undeciphered ancient Indian drawings.

San Nicholas – In the southeast, Aruba's "second city," near Seroe Colorado, is a modern community designed and built for North Americans who came to work for Exxon's Lago Oil Refinery, now closed. Visitors are welcome at the *Aruba Golf Club,* just north of San Nicholas.

Sauaneta – Aruba's oldest town, slightly more than midway between San Nicholas and Balashi.

Balashi – Here are the 19th-century ruins of gold smelting work and the settlement, now abandoned. Built during Aruba's "gold rush," it is northwest of Spaans Lagoen, a bit southeast of the center of the island.

SOURCES AND RESOURCES

TOURIST INFORMATION: The Aruba Tourism Authority, 1270 Ave. of the Americas, Suite 2212, New York, NY 10020 (phone: 212-246-3030 or 800-TO-ARUBA), and PO Box 012348, Miami, FL 33101 (phone: 305-358-6360), can provide free literature and information on hotels, attractions, and the like.

The Aruba Tourism Authority's office, with a very helpful staff and an excellent collection of maps, guides, and brochures, is in the heart of Oranjestad, at A. Schuttestraat 2, on the corner of Arnold Schuttestraat and Lloyd Smith Boulevard, opposite the wharf (phone: 23777).

Local Coverage – *Aruba Holiday,* a green tabloid-size monthly guide to vacation activities, shopping, restaurants, and nightlife, is distributed free at the Tourist Bureau, airport, hotels.

Aruba in Full Color, a book by photographer Hans Hannau, is available in gift shops.

The *San Juan Star,* the *Miami Herald,* and *The New York Times* normally reach Aruban newsstands on the day of publication.

Telephone – Dial direct to Aruba by adding 011-2978, the international access code to the numbers given below.

ENTRY REQUIREMENTS: For US and Canadian citizens, the only documents required are some proof of citizenship (passport, birth certificate, or voter's registration card; a driver's license is *not* acceptable) and an ongoing or return ticket. There is a $9.50 departure tax at the airport. In 1987, Aruba introduced preclearance facilities for US Immigration at the airport; preclearance for Customs may be introduced this year.

CLIMATE AND CLOTHES: Aruba is one of the few islands where newspapers don't publish weather reports. Since only about 20 inches of rain fall annually, the island guarantees one of the most stable all-year climates in all of the Caribbean. Temperatures rarely fall below 75°F (24°C) or rise above 85°F (24°C). But the wind never stops blowing in Aruba. Incessant trade winds keep the divi-divi trees in constant motion, although permanently slanted at a 45° angle to the ground. The winds also keep the humidity down and blow mosquitoes and other insects away from the island. Casual, lightweight resortwear is right for daytime in all seasons. Leave your raincoat at home and use the space for extra swimsuits and scarves. Islanders do not wear shorts or slacks in town, but it's okay for visitors. Bathing suits, however, are strictly for beach or poolside. In the evenings, especially in the casinos in season, women like to dress up a bit and men usually wear jackets.

MONEY: Although US dollars are accepted everywhere, the official currency is the Netherlands Antilles florin or guilder ($1 US equals 1.77 NAfl, approximately). There's really no advantage to changing your dollars, but banks are open from 8 AM to noon and 1:30 to 4 PM on weekdays. Shops give no discount for payment in US dollars and, like most restaurants and hotels, honor major credit cards.

LANGUAGE: There probably isn't a more linguistically versatile island in the Caribbean. Arubans speak Dutch (the official language), Spanish, English, Portuguese, and, as if that isn't enough, Papiamento, a mixture of all the above and a few words left over from the days of the Arawaks. But you'll have no trouble getting along in English.

TIME: Aruba is on Atlantic Standard Time all year round. When it's noon in New York it's 1 PM in Aruba; when the eastern US is on Daylight Saving Time, the hour is the same in both places.

CURRENT: At 120 volts, 60 cycles, converters and adapters are not necessary.

GETTING THERE: Air service to Aruba has improved dramatically in the past year. Regularly scheduled flights depart daily from New York (American Airlines) and Miami (Eastern, ALM, and VIASA). Both American and Eastern have connecting flights from several US cities via San Juan, and there's direct service from Europe on KLM. In addition to scheduled flights, Aruba has charter service out of New York; Rochester; Boston; Philadelphia; Baltimore; Washington, DC; Detroit; Chicago; Houston; and other US cities.

There are no regularly scheduled direct flights from Canada. However, a considerable number of charters fly from Toronto and various other North American gateways. It is possible to include visits to Curaçao and/or Bonaire for the same fare; ask your travel agent for details. There are also frequent casino-oriented charter packages.

Many cruise ships sail out of New York, Miami/Port Everglades, and other US ports and stop at Aruba for sightseeing and shopping.

CALCULATING COSTS: Rates at deluxe and first-class hotels on the Palm Beach strip range from $120 a day for two to $300 during the winter season (that's European Plan, without meals). There's a 5% tax and 11% service charge on all hotel rooms except the Golden Tulip Aruba Caribbean, which charges 15%. You can also stay at one of the commercial hotels in town for about $55 up, double, EP, or at one of the guesthouses near the beach for about $75. Come mid-April, rates drop dramatically — 35% to 45% — and stay down until mid-December. Modified American Plan (breakfast and dinner included) is offered by resort hotels at an additional $40 to $45 a day per person in the winter season, a few dollars less in summer. Dinner, including a drink and tip, costs $30 to $35 up per person at the top restaurants. There is also a 10% or 15% service charge on food and beverages at major hotels. The Bushiri Beach Hotel offers all-inclusive packages for winter and summer, which are an excellent value.

GETTING AROUND: Taxi – Taxis aren't metered, so it's a good idea to establish the rate to your destination with the driver before getting into the cab. The fare from the airport to most resort hotels is about $12 for up to four people. There is no need to tip taxi drivers except for special services, such as helping with an unusually heavy load of luggage.

Bus – Airport buses serve all hotels but require prepaid travel coupons issued by travel agents. Public buses make 10 runs daily (except on Sundays and holidays) between town and the hotels on Eagle Beach and Palm Beach. One-way fare is 65¢, and the bus leaves from the parking lot on Lloyd Smith Blvd. across from the Tourist Bureau. Going into town, buses pick you up on the boulevard in front of your hotel.

Car Rental – Plenty of cars are available, and renting one is the most pleasant way to stay flexible, see the most of the island, and shop and dine whenever you want. Roads are good and clearly marked, and your US or Canadian driver's license is valid. Rates range from about $28 to $65 a day, depending on the type of car you choose. Your hotel can make the arrangements for you if you haven't reserved a car ahead of time. Rental companies in Oranjestad include *Avis* (phone: 28787), *Budget* (phone: 28600), *Hertz* (phone: 24545), *National* (phone: 21967 or 24641), and a number of local agencies, including *Marco's* (phone: 25295). Motorcycles are also available at *Dollar Rent a Car* (phone: 22783 or 25651).

Motorcycles and Mopeds – *Trimon Cycle Rental* (phone: 32059) and *Nelson Motorcycle Rental* (phone: 26801) rent mopeds and motorcycles at an average price of $20 to $45 per day.

Sightseeing Taxi Tours – Aruba cab drivers are genial and informative and can serve as superb guides. Ask your hotel to recommend one and arrange it. A 1-hour tour is about $20 for up to four passengers. *De Palm Tours* (phone: 24400) is Aruba's largest operator, offering both island excursions and shopping tours. *Pelican Tours* (phone: 23888) also offers excellent tours and can book most water sports.

Sightseeing Bus Tours – Cheaper, but not as personal as a taxi tour; operated by *Bruno Tours* (phone: 22423). A 3½-hour tour costs about $15 per person. If oil interests you, the Lago Oil Refinery offers free guided tours of its plant (at the southeastern tip of the island) on Tuesdays and Thursdays; make reservations with *Bruno Tours* for the $4 bus round trip.

Sea Excursions – Offered by *De Palm Tours,* whose glass-bottom boat cruise takes you out to see coral reefs, tropical fish, and shipwrecks for about $15 per person. A 2-hour round-the-island cruise on the trimaran *Aquaventure* or *Seaventure* is about $15 per person with snacks on board. *De Palm* also offers sunset cruises with beach barbecues, day sailing on a 75-foot ketch, scuba diving, deep-sea fishing, and horseback riding. *Pelican Tours* (phone: 23888) offers scuba-diving courses, dive trips, glass-bottom-boat trips, and cruises.

Island-Hopping Tours – Both *Lee Air* (phone: 26363, 24071, and 23881; after business hours, 21365, 26897, or 22723) and *Oduber Aviation* (phone: 23080; after business hours, 25333) run charter flights with guided day tours to Bonaire and Curaçao. Longer trips can be organized for Venezuela. Both offer charter flights anytime almost anywhere and can make arrangements for emergency flights from Miami in a matter of minutes. Local buses run daily between Oranjestad and hotels on Palm Beach and Eagle Beach. Check hotels for schedules.

SHOPPING: Technically, Aruba is not a free port, but the duty on most items is so low (3.3%) that Nassaustraat, the shopping hub, is a center for bargains from all over the world. But not all items are bargains, so be sure to check basic Stateside prices on things in which you're especially interested before you leave home. With that in mind, shop for: Royal Copenhagen porcelain; Delft Blue pottery; Dutch, Swedish, and Danish silver and pewter; Swiss watches; liquor and liqueurs; Madeira embroidery; German and Japanese cameras and optical goods; Italian wood carvings; French perfumes; British woolens; Indonesian spices; Hummel figurines; and much, much more. *Spritzer & Führmann,* one of the best-known firms in the Caribbean, has four stores in a cluster downtown, offering the most comprehensive selection of jewelry, china, crystal, and other luxury items. Other well-known emporia are *J. L. Penha, Palais Oriental,* the *Aruba Trading Company* (especially for perfumes, liquor), *DeWit's* (for Dutch pewter, Delftware), *Kan Jewelers,* the *Artistic Boutique* (Indonesian imports, ivories, earrings), *Fanny* (perfumes, imported cosmetics, gifts). For disco clothes, *Aquarius* is biggest, trendiest, often offering substantial discounts on the latest, largest names. For last-minute, no-hassle shopping, most hotels house branches of one or two downtown stores with smaller selections, same prices. Most downtown stores are open Monday through Saturday, 8:00 AM to 6:30 PM.

TIPPING: Hotels add an 11% to 15% service charge to the bills, which takes care of bellboys, maids, waiters, and bartenders, so you tip hotel personnel only for extra service. Restaurants usually add 10% to 15%; check your tab, and if service is not included, a 10% to 15% tip is the norm. Airport porters get 50¢ for each bag carried. Taxi drivers do not expect tips.

SPECIAL EVENTS: *Carnival* celebrations are the biggest event of the year and begin in the middle of January with the *Tumba Contest* for musicians; then there are children's parades and other festivities on various days; the climax is the *Grand Parade* and *Jump-Up* (check the exact date of the latter with the Tourist Authority office, for hotel space gets tight). Holidays, when banks and stores are closed (although when cruise ships are in port, some stores open for a few hours) are: *New Year's, Carnival Monday* (the day after the *Grand Carnival Parade*), *National Flag and Anthem Day* (March 18), *Good Friday, Easter Monday, Queen's Birthday* (April 30), *Labor Day* (May 1), *Ascension Day* (May), *St. John's Day* (June 24), *St. Nicholas Day* (December 5), *Christmas,* and *Boxing Day* (December 26). Special annual sporting events now include the *Aruba Annual Marathon* (third week of June), the *Pan American Race of Champs, International Drag Racing* (second week of November).

SPORTS: Boating – Most hotels have Sunfish for loan or rent (about $17 an hour); and larger craft can be chartered from boat owners (ask at your hotel or the Tourist Board). *Aruba Nautical Club* marina, at the mouth of Spanish Lagoon between Oranjestad and St. Nicholas, offers reef-protected, all-weather mooring for yachts; members of other yacht clubs are welcome for a modest fee, charged according to size of craft; for information write to the club (Box 161; phone: 23022). Farther down the shore, docking facilities are also available for $6 per day at *Bucuti Yacht Club* (Box 743; phone: 23793).

Cycling – Bikes can be rented at hotels and from *Aru Rentals* for about $9 per day (phone: 22498).

Dune Sliding – A sport unique to Aruba at Boca Prins on the north coast; wear sneakers and your strongest pair of jeans.

Pedalboats and sea jeeps are popular craft at Aruba resorts. The *pedalos* rent for $7 per half hour, $9 an hour. Sea jeeps — two- or four-person small motorboats — are fun to buzz around in for about $18 for the two-seater, $20 for the larger model per half hour. Check your hotel's water sports center.

Fitness – *Body Language* is a complete health and fitness center, including Nautilus machines, at the Eagle Club, 12 Engelandstraat (phone: 22808). The spa at the *Holiday Inn Aruba* also offers a complete fitness program (phone: 23600).

Golf – The *Aruba Golf Club,* a 9-hole course near St. Nicholas, on the eastern end of the island, is described by *Aruba-Holiday* as a "new experience in golfing, what with the wind and the goats, and oiled sand greens!" There are also 20 sand traps and 5 water traps. Greens fees are $6 for a day's play of as many rounds as you can stand; caddy fees, $4 for 9 holes; club rental, $5 a day. Complete clubhouse and bar (phone: 9-3485).

Horseback Riding – Usually available at Rancho El Paso (phone: 23310); for further information, inquire at your hotel or *De Palm Tours.*

Snorkeling and Scuba – Major activities in clear, warm, Aruban waters, where the visibility is up to 100 feet deep and there is a great variety of coral, lacy sea fans, reefs, and multicolored tropical fish for divers to see and photograph. A favorite dive is the one down to the 400-foot sunken German freighter *Antilla,* which was scuttled off the northwestern tip of the island during World War II, or the wreck of the *Pedenales,* an oil tanker lying in only 25 feet of water. Arrangements for equipment rental, diving trips, and instruction can be made through the activities desk at your hotel. *De Palm Water Sports* (phone: 24400 or 24545) and *Pelican Watersports* (phone: 23888) operate hotel concessions. Prices run about $48 for a beginner's course (lecture, pool instruction, and dive); guided trips for the experienced diver with a "C card" are about $40 per dive, equipment included. One-hour snorkel trips with boat, equipment, and guide are $14 per person (minimum, three). For snorkeling on your own, equipment can be rented for $4 per hour, $8 a day. A 10% service charge is added. The new $4-million *De Palm Island Beach Club* offers fine swimming and snorkeling on Palm Reef Island, reached by five-minute ferry ride (contact *De Palm Tours*). The island has a water-sports activity center, restaurants, and boutiques.

Spectator Sports – Soccer, baseball, and volleyball (strictly amateur teams) at Wilhelmina Stadium.

Sport Fishing – Aruba's waters are best for sailfish, wahoo, blue and white marlin, tuna, and bonito. Fishing charters can be arranged through your hotel's water sports desk or *De Palm Watersports* (phone: 24400). Rates, which include bait, tackle, soft drinks, and beer, are about $250 for a half-day's fishing for a boat that takes up to six passengers, of whom four can fish at the same time. There is an international White Marlin Tournament at the end of October each year, which lures anglers from the US and South America.

Surfing – The rugged, windswept northern shore attracts some intrepid surfers to such beaches as Dos Playa and Andicouri, but only at their own risk; visitors are warned that the sea can get pretty rough.

Swimming and Sunning – Sea and sand are what Aruba is all about, and the gleaming white beaches stretch along the island's Turquoise Coast — its western and southwestern shores. The best are two strands above Oranjestad: Palm Beach, shared by a number of hotels (nonguests can use facilities for a small fee), with a gentle slope that makes it especially good for kids and less adventurous swimmers; and Eagle Beach, closer to town, a free public park with thatch-roofed shelters for picnicking. Palm Reef Island is another excellent location for these activities.

Tennis – A different game at times because of the relentless trade winds, but it's popular, and there are courts at most of the principal hotels on the beach strip: the *Golden Tulip Aruba Caribbean, Americana Aruba, Aruba Beach Club, Aruba Palm Beach, Divi-Divi, Holiday Inn, Tamarijn Beach,* and *Concorde;* the *Holiday Inn* seems to have the best wind shields. Several hotels have tennis pros, and a number of the courts are lighted for night play. Games can be arranged by nonguests when courts are not in use; tennis at the hotels is free to guests during the day; some hotels charge about $2 per hour for night lights.

Water Skiing – Available at most oceanfront hotels. Charge is about $12.50 for 20 minutes; lessons are about $28.

 NIGHTLIFE: Aruba's lively nightlife is centered around its casinos. Five are in hotels along Palm Beach. The *Golden Tulip Aruba Caribbean, Americana Aruba, Aruba Palm Beach, Concorde,* and *Holiday Inn* all have plush gaming parlors where those who feel lucky try their hands at blackjack, craps, roulette, or the slot machines; the *Aruba Palm Beach* also has a special room set aside for baccarat. The most unusual, the *Alhambra Casino* and the *Alladan Theater* are parts of an entertainment complex that also includes 10 shops, restaurants, and night spots near the *Divi-Divi* and *Manchebo* hotels and a short ride from the *Talk of the Town.* Low betting limits and the obvious absence of high rollers and junket players give it a pleasantly relaxed atmosphere. Casinos open for action after lunch and keep going until the small hours. Those who don't gamble can dance, drink, and watch a show in any of the hotel cocktail lounges or supper clubs. *Note:* No one under 18 is admitted to Aruba's casinos. The *Americana*'s *Le Club* lounge has two bands and a show that goes on at midnight; its *Stellaris* (phone: 24500) is a large theater-like nightclub. The *Aruba Palm Beach*'s *Galactica* is a lively lounge for drinks, dancing, and occasional entertainment; in its elegant red and gold *Rembrandt Room* (phone: 23900) there's dining and dancing till midnight. The *Golden Tulip Aruba Caribbean*'s *Fandango* (phone: 22250) features imported talent on a cabaret stage. The *Holiday Inn* has its *Palm Beach Room* and *L'Esprit* nightclub (phone: 23600) for dining, dancing, and a show (best on folkloric Sundays). The sleekest hotel spot, featuring Continental acts and disco dancing, is the *Concorde*'s *Arubesque* (phone: 24466), with more pizzazz than New Orleans jazz about it. If you're headed for a hotel supper club, check in advance to make sure it's not closed for a guests' buffet or beach barbecue; and you will need reservations. Other night places: *Talk of the Town*'s *Contempo,* doing its disco thing till 3 AM; the *Scaramouche,* Oranjestad's other disco (piano bar, too). The *Divi-Divi*'s *Pelican Terrace* has a local band for nightly dancing; *Tamarijn Beach*'s outdoor bar also spotlights local music. And the *Manchebo Beach* celebrates "Tropical Night" with a buffet, fashion show, and music on Wednesdays. Most hotels have theme nights, featuring lavish buffets and entertainment as regular weekly events, from "Pirate Night" on Wednesday at the *Talk of the Town* to "Little Mexico Night" Mondays at the *Bushiri Beach.*

BEST ON THE ISLAND

CHECKING IN: For a double room in the hotels listed below as expensive you can expect to pay $115 and up per day without meals in winter; and from $80 to $100 in moderate. There are no truly inexpensive tourist hotels. There's a 5% hotel tax, and most hotels add a 10% to 15% service charge.

PALM BEACH

Americana Aruba – Stylish, active kind of atmosphere, with handsome public areas, 206 moderate-size guestrooms, 2 tennis courts, swimming pool, spacious beach, water sports, beauty salon, and shopping arcade. There are also 3 restaurants, an ice-cream parlor, theater-style nightclub and casino (phone: 24500). Expensive.

Aruba Concorde – Biggest of the big (500 rooms), towering 14 stories above expansive beach and pool layout. Good-size, attractive rooms with balconies, air conditioning, fridges, color TV, and truly elegant shopping plaza, weirdly mishmashed lobby decor. An $8-million renovation has polished this resort so that the rooms and all public facilities sparkle. Currently a favorite group-package target, with tennis, nightclub, and casino, of course. Nonsmoking rooms are available, but room service is seriously limited. (phone: 24466). Expensive.

Golden Tulip Aruba Caribbean – Set in exotic tropical gardens, this 400-room, 23-suite property underwent a $40 million refurbishment in 1986, transforming the island's oldest high-rise resort into one of its premier vacation showplaces. There are 120 rooms in the original Barbizon wing, 10 poolside lanai suites, a Garden wing with 80 rooms, and the 176-room Caribbean wing. Facilities include a shopping arcade, 4 restaurants, a beautiful lounge featuring afternoon tea, *Fandango* nightclub, casino, 24-hour room service, health and fitness center, 4 tennis courts with floodlights, complete water sports center, and golf practicing facilities (phone: 33555; in New York, 212-247-7950; elsewhere, 800-344-1212). Expensive.

Holiday Inn Aruba – On Palm Beach, this 7-story hotel has been totally revamped by a $6-million effort completed in 1987; now its 388 rooms, lobby areas, and 4 restaurants sport new faces. The casino and nightclub are well patronized after dark while during the day, the beach — with its gamut of water sports — is the main attraction. The hotel also has a generously stocked shopping arcade, complete spa/health club, and extensive water-sports program that includes scuba diving, jet-ski instruction, windsurfing, and sailing (phone: 23600). Expensive.

Playa Linda – A stylish time-share resort with a clublike atmosphere and full hotel-style services, it has 60 spacious suites and 185 rooms. Low-rise with peaceful atmosphere (no charter groups, no casino), but within strolling distance of brighter lights when you're in the mood. With a small market, a restaurant, drugstore, beach, and water sports; tennis arranged. The second and third phases, under way at press time, will have added more rooms by 1989 (phone: 31000). Expensive.

Aruba Palm Beach – Striking high-rise with Moorish lines, Delft blue and white color scheme, gardens, completely renovated by a $3-million project in 1987. Its 200 king-size rooms have private balconies. The ideal choice for vacationers who crave water sports and nightlife on the same property. A 1,200-foot beach, tennis, freshwater pool, water sports; shopping arcade. Stylish *Rembrandt Room* supper club and casino (phone: 23900). Expensive to moderate.

MANCHEBO AND DRUIF BAY BEACHES

Aruba Beach Club – Relaxed compound of 133 suites, nicely refurbished in 1987, each with TV, kitchenette, and telephone. There's also a pool, tennis, indoor-outdoor restaurant, entertainment area, and specialty-foods minimarket. The children's activity program makes it a favorite with families. Interchangeable facilities with sister hotel, *Talk of the Town* (phone: 24595). Expensive.

Dutch Village – Sleek townhouse complex with all comforts, inside and out, including satellite TV, Jacuzzis in every one of its 52 studio, 1- and 2-bedroom apartments, plus swimming pool, tennis, shops, restaurant, and bar. Exchange privileges with *Divi-Divi* and *Tamarijn Beach* hotels (phone: 24150). Expensive.

Divi-Divi Beach – Pleasantly rambling low-rise with Spanish architectural accents; lanais and casitas with patios right on the white, white beach. It has 6 superlative suites and 202 air-conditioned rooms — all with balconies or patios. Features include 2 freshwater pools, tennis courts, lots of lounging space, outdoor bar and dining in a relaxed, informal atmosphere. Try *The Red Parrot* for excellent French cuisine; the *Alhambra Casino,* Aruba's most unusual, and only free-standing, casino for some excitement; or the boutiques in the Alhambra Bazaar for interesting shopping (phone: 23300). Expensive to moderate.

Best Western Manchebo Beach – Friendly, informal, with great wide beach, considered by many, including its large European clientele, to be the best and least crowded on the coast. It has 74 neatly modern, air-conditioned rooms and a genuinely welcoming atmosphere. The new 60-room *Bucuti Beach Resort* was added in 1987, with its own pool, bar, and snack bar, and integrated services with Manchebo Beach. At press time, another 90 rooms were under construction for 1989. Pool, water sports; nearby tennis. Guests have full exchange privileges at *Talk of the Town* hotel. First-rate restaurant (see *Eating Out*); outdoor dancing at night (phone: 23444). Expensive to moderate.

Bushiri Beach – In 1987, a $10-million refurbishment spruced up this property. It now has 154 extra-large rooms and a staff that's eager to please (it is part of the

Aruba Hospitality Trades Training Center). There's also a pool, a pleasant indoor-outdoor restaurant, and local entertainment every evening. Offers excellent vacation packages year-round, and all-inclusive 3- or 7-day vacations are available (phone: 25216). Moderate.

Casa del Mar – Offered 32 deluxe suites at press time, with 75 more due for completion by early 1989. Each will have two bedrooms, two baths, kitchen, dining room, large patio, TV, and phone. There's also a restaurant, beach, pool, health center, two tennis courts, and a shopping arcade. Punto Bravo Beach (phone: 27000). Moderate.

Divi Tamarijn Beach – All 236 rooms, including those in the 50-room addition, are within only a few barefoot steps of its 2,000-foot beach; appealing Andalusian style (red tile roofs, white walls) inside and out. Pool, 2 Jacuzzis, intimate *Bunker Bar* directly on the ocean and nightly music by local groups. Exchange arrangement with *Divi-Divi Beach* hotel just up the shore (phone: 24150). Moderate.

ELSEWHERE ON THE ISLAND

Best Western Talk of the Town, Oranjestad – Best known for its restaurant (see *Eating Out*), its handiness to downtown, and its appeal to a European clientele. With 62 nicely done rooms overlooking the Caribbean and surrounding an attractive pool patio. The atmosphere is so inviting (thanks to award-winning hotelier Ike Cohen and his wife, Grete, who own and run it) that it deserves mention. Full exchange privileges at *Manchebo Beach;* tennis at *Eagle Tennis Club*. Not on the beach, but with pool, outdoor whirlpool, bar; 62 rooms, some with kitchenettes; 1- and 2-bedroom suites with kitchenettes and TV. Caribbean entertainment most nights, *Surfside* snack bar and restaurant (super bar for sunset watching on calm nights) across road (phone: 23380). Moderate.

Vistalmar – Spacious 1-bedroom apartments surrounded by gardens, just 100 yards from the Caribbean. Units have full kitchens and TV. Guests will find their refrigerators stocked with complimentary breakfast foods on arrival, and water sports are also complimentary. Very reasonable weekly rates both seasons (phone: 47737). Inexpensive.

EATING OUT: Perhaps because it grows so little of its own food, Aruba is short on native cuisine. Its tastiest native dishes are *stobà* (a lamb or goat stew) and *sopito* (a fish chowder that owes its special flavor to coconut milk — in addition to fish, salt pork or corned beef, onions, tomatoes, garlic, peppers, fresh cream, and a bouquet of spices). It requires such expertise and patience that on their sopito chef's day off, most restaurants and hotels simply remove it from the menu. If you like fish and it's on the menu, try it — preferably with *funchi,* a sort of cornmeal pudding–bread, as a companion dish. Favorite Aruban snacks include *cala* (bean fritters), *pastechi* (a meat-stuffed turnover), and *ayacas* (a leaf-wrapped meat roll). The most exotic eating around is Indonesian (from other onetime Dutch islands), and its most spectacular form is the *rijsttafel* (rice table), which may be loaded with 25 or more different herbed and spiced shrimp, meat, vegetable, pickle, and fruit dishes — some very hot — to be piled around and eaten with your basic mountain of rice. A number of Aruban restaurants do a scaled-down version; they also offer other Indonesian specialties like *nasi goreng* (a one-plate rijsttafel of meat, shrimp, chicken, and vegetables crowned with a fried egg), *Java honde portie* (rice, steak, vegetables, fried eggs, all seasoned with curry — literally, a hound's portion), and *bami goreng* (with a base of Chinese noodles instead of rice). Also of Dutch island origin: *keshi yena* (an Edam cheese stuffed with a savory mixture of shrimp or meat or chicken, with tomato, onion, olives, pickles, and raisins) and *capucijners* (mixed beans, meat, marrow, bacon, onions, and pickle). Portions tend to be enormous — or larger.

At most of the big hotels there's a terrace restaurant that's casual at lunch, dressier (both patrons and menu) at night, plus a more expensive specialty restaurant and/or supper club. In town there are also a number of good Aruban and Oriental places with both Chinese and Indonesian choices. You'll also find Argentinian, Mexican, German, Italian, French — even New York deli-style fare if you look. With just a few exceptions, reservations aren't necessary. And major credit cards are generally accepted. In the listings that follow, dinner — without wine, drinks, or service charge — at a restaurant described as inexpensive runs about $15 or less per person; about $15 to $30 is moderate; more than that is expensive.

PALM BEACH

Adriana – Just what you didn't expect: a truly tasty Italian *ristorante* tucked away in the lower lobby of the *Aruba Concorde*. À la carte choices from antipasto to al dente pasta to Italian ices (phone: 24466). Expensive.

Buccaneer – Very popular with the citizenry, it specializes in fish and seafood served in an attractive seaquarium-like atmosphere. On big nights, there may be a line, but they won't take reservations. Gasparito St. (phone: 26172). Moderate.

De Olde Molen – It really is an old windmill, built in Holland in 1804, knocked down, shipped, and reassembled in Aruba in 1960. Obviously a tourist-oriented number, but loaded with cozy atmosphere. Continental menu (steaks, lobster, veal cordon bleu) — not surprising, but good. Reserve for 6:30 or 9 PM sitting. Off Palm Beach Dr. (phone: 22060). Moderate.

Salon International – Candlelit setting, Mediterranean atmosphere, a rather imaginative Continental menu, and accommodating service make dinner here a relaxing pleasure. At the *Holiday Inn* (phone: 23600). Moderate.

ORANJESTAD

La Dolce Vita – Considered one of Aruba's best Italian dining spots and definitely among the most popular, it features excellent veal and seafood dishes. Dinner only. Reservations recommended. Nassaustraat (phone: 25675). Expensive.

Bali Floating Restaurant – Lunches, drinks, and snacks served at tables on the pier; inside the Oriental houseboat, more exotic atmosphere and fare including a 20-dish rijsttafel. Good food, super atmosphere; obviously tourist-focused, but fun. Reserve a day ahead for rijsttafel. Off Lloyd Smith Blvd. (phone: 22131). Moderate.

Dragon-Phoenix – Gilded Chinese setting (with dragons, but no discernible phoenix), lengthy menu that's mostly Cantonese, with curries and a couple of Indonesian additions. You can't go wrong with Dragon Phoenix (boned chicken, fresh lobster, vegetables) or Foo Dip Har (pan-broiled shrimp with water chestnuts). Havenstraat (phone: 21928). Moderate.

Papagayo – Lush green setting for steaks and Italian specialties. Handy for lunch with a harbor view; romantic at dinner (phone: 24140). Moderate.

Papiamento – *The* place to try in town; an antique house with a suave and surprisingly compatible contemporary interior. Continental menu well handled (savory quiches, Chateaubriand, seductive pastries). A bit much for lunch (though popular with local businesspeople), but elegant for dinner, with music. Jackets and reservations requested. Wilhelminastraat (phone: 24544). Moderate.

Surfside – Breezy shoreline spot, great for sunset drinks, steaks, seafood, and Aruban specialties. Just across from *Talk of the Town* (phone: 23380). Moderate.

Talk of the Town – At lunch, its salad bar (about $6 per person when you make a whole meal of it) is a cool treat. At dinner, they turn on the candle glow, present a bill of fare that includes escargots à la Bourguignonne, crabmeat crêpes, veal cordon bleu, broiled lobster, and excellent Caribbean frogs' legs. If a high decibel count disturbs you, plan on finishing before 10 PM, when they start discoing at

Contempo Disco and at *Surfside*'s *Scorpio's*. *Talk of the Town* hotel, Airport Rd. (phone: 23380). Moderate.

Trocadéro – Not fancy looking, but serving some of the town's best food. Aruban and Dutch treats (including *uitsmijters* — open-face meat sandwiches with a fried egg topping), plus super special seafood — lobster, shrimp diablo, fresh clams, and snapper, plus such exotica as baby shark steak, broiled conch, green turtle steaks, and marinated squid. The service is slow, but the food's worth it. Nassaustraat (phone: 33839). Moderate to inexpensive.

Wine Cellar – Cozy wine and cheese spot patterned after those in Amsterdam. Fine light lunch idea. Klipstraat (phone: 24543). Inexpensive.

ELSEWHERE ON THE ISLAND

French Steak House – Simply and straightforwardly French, with emphasis on quality rather than show-off cuisine. Escargots, filet mignon, Chateaubriand, are specialties. Romantically candlelit dining room, but no jackets or ties required. *Manchebo Beach* hotel (phone: 23444). Moderate.

Nueva Marina Pirata, Spanish Lagoon – Surveying the water from a private pier where fresh fish is landed daily, this open-air café specializes in seafood Aruba style — a Créole tomato sauce spiked with peppers, onions, herbs, and spices. Good down-home fungi (cornmeal pudding) comes along as a matter of course. Affable service; good prices, too (phone: 27372). Moderate.

Brisas del Mar, Savaneta – Very casual, friendly place that Arubans recommend for its fresh fish, seafood, island dishes (fried plantains and *pan bati* — corn-millet pancake — go well with whatever is ordered). By the sea just west of San Nicolaas (phone: 47718). Inexpensive.

La Paloma – Aruban and northern Italian specialties are served up here; try *cari cari,* stewed conch, or the combination fish platter. There's steak, too. A 5-minute drive from Palm Beach (phone: 24611). Inexpensive.

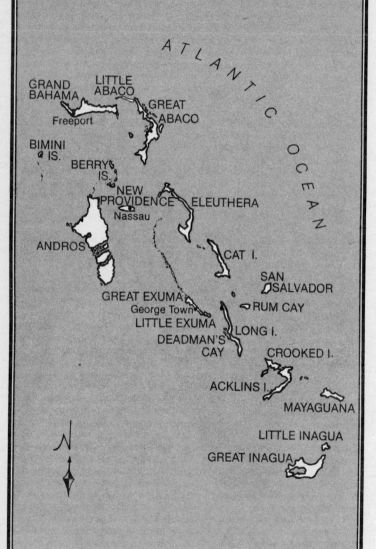

THE BAHAMAS

ATLANTIC OCEAN

GRAND BAHAMA

Freeport

LITTLE ABACO

GREAT ABACO

BIMINI IS.

BERRY IS.

NEW PROVIDENCE

Nassau

ELEUTHERA

ANDROS

CAT I.

SAN SALVADOR

GREAT EXUMA

George Town

LITTLE EXUMA

RUM CAY

LONG I.

DEADMAN'S CAY

CROOKED I.

ACKLINS I.

MAYAGUANA

LITTLE INAGUA

GREAT INAGUA

N

BAHAMAS

The islands of the Bahamas group have always been close to the United States. Not just physically — though lying only 50 miles off the Florida coast, they are that — but in a number of other ways as well. Thought by many, especially many Bahamians, to be the point at which Columbus first landed in the New World, the islands got a somewhat earlier start than the US historically. But unlike some islands of the West Indies, the Bahamas have felt Spain's influence only minimally. The native Lucayan Arawak Indian population, however, which greeted Columbus with gentleness, awe, shyness, and great respect, was brutally exterminated within 25 years by Spanish raiders, who forced them onto ships and took them to Hispaniola to work and die in their mines. Then Ponce de León, thirsting for the Fountain of Youth, thought for a fleeting moment he had found it on South Bimini. But otherwise the Spaniards, distracted by gold lust, left these islands alone.

So the British influence became dominant in the Bahamas, as it did in the colonies on the American mainland. In 1620, pilgrims from England in search of religious freedom landed in what was to become Plymouth, Massachusetts. In 1647, for similar reasons, the first British, fleeing Bermuda, landed in the Bahamas and settled permanently on the island they christened Eleuthera, meaning "freedom." In 1656, another Bermudian group settled on a nearby island they named New Providence, following the example of the Rhode Islanders, who had founded their "old" Providence 20 years earlier. And, in 1660, all these British colonists were finally (and formally) linked when King Charles II gave the Lords Proprietors of the Carolinas dominion over their Bahamian neighbors.

For more than a century, this connection made little difference on either side, for each was preoccupied with its own problems. The Carolinians became absorbed in pre-Revolutionary matters, and the Bahamians, with an invasion of pirates who found the islands, with their hundreds of coves, harbors, and remote anchorages, ideal ambush and hideout territory. For 35 years, the likes of Edward Teach (a/k/a Blackbeard), Henry Morgan, Anne Bonney, and Mary Read had their way in these islands, and wrecking, raiding, and pillaging became the islands' principal industries. Ships of all countries fell prey, and Spain became so infuriated that it attacked and destroyed the New Providence island city of Charles Town. A year later it was rebuilt and — in the best new king, new name tradition — it was rechristened Nassau in honor of King William III, formerly William of Orange-Nassau.

It was not until 1718 that order was really established, thanks to the king's man, Captain Woodes Rogers (a South Seas privateer so scarred from battle that he had only half a face), whose statue today stands guard outside the *British Colonial* hotel and after whom the waterfront walk was named. The choice he offered his piratical constituency was simple: Cease and desist or die. After eight hangings, reform took hold, and Rogers was appointed royal governor of what was now, officially, a British colony. The motto on its crest — *Expulsis Piratis, Restitua Commercia* (Piracy Expelled, Commerce Restored) — survived until independence almost two and a half centuries later, when it was replaced by "Forward, Upward, Onward, Together" by the new government under reformist Prime Minister Lynden O. Pindling (whose bank account was discovered in 1984 to hold nearly half a million dollars that was traced to Paradise Island Resort and Casino's operator, Resorts International). The parliamentary government that Rogers established lasted even longer; it is the basis for Bahamian government even today.

During the American Revolution, the Bahamas became such an important British supply base that the US Navy-to-be attacked and took Nassau for a day in 1776, then withdrew. Subsequently, Tory refugees from the mainland began arriving in considerable numbers, and Spain, for obscure reasons, came back to conquer the Bahamas one more time. When the Treaty of Versailles returned the islands to Britain in 1783, it was one such ex-Carolinian loyalist, Colonel Andrew Deveaux, who drove the last Spanish rascals out and established Bahamian peace for some time to come.

Twice more the Bahamas played an offshore part in US history: during the Civil War, when they helped ships to run the North's blockade in aid of the South, and during Prohibition, when Nassau, Bimini, and the town of West End on Grand Bahama Island were all major rumrunning depots. Both were very profitable businesses. But it was not until the 1940s that the industry that is currently the islands' number one source of revenue emerged.

Tourism was a quite different animal then. "Catnipped" by the presence of HRH the Duke of Windsor, appointed royal governor by his brother, and the superchic duchess (their romance is immortalized in the still-sung Bahamian calypso "Love Alone"), precursors of the modern jet set ritually met and mingled in Nassau from Christmas to Easter. The DC-3 flight from New York took over six hours; from Miami, over two. And when the rich folk flew home again in April, the capital's three hotels — the dowager British Colonial, the Royal Victoria, and the Fort Montagu (only the first one survives) — were shuttered through spring, summer, and fall.

In the late 1950s, when neighboring Florida discovered summer and began promoting year-round vacations, the pattern in the Bahamas changed too. Tourism today is a 12-month operation, with arrivals topping 3 million last year. Some tourists are still rich and chic, but most are more average types, for whom both summer and winter vacations are apt to be the rule. Nassau is no longer the Bahamas' only destination. Paradise Island alone attracted 321,000 visitors in 1987, after all major resorts underwent major refurbishment and expansion to polish the tiny island's image. Grand Bahama's Freeport — the 1953 commercial-industrial brainchild of developer Wallace Groves — has added its Lucaya resort area. And the outlying islands — now called the "Family Islands" by government decree but still affectionately known as the "Out Islands" to those who have visited and come to love them — havens once known to Juan Trippe, Henry Luce, and God alone, are being explored by divers and other earthly escapists who want to get away completely. The Bahamas are among the world's most popular destinations for sportfishing, cruising, and scuba diving, and each island boasts a growing number of water-sports activities every year.

The question is whether you will like any or all of the above. And the answer is "That depends." For dedicated divers, yachtsmen, serious fishermen, and genuine beach addicts who visit the outlying islands, the response is 99% yes. Most gamblers and many golfers can find happiness in Freeport/ Lucaya, Nassau, and Paradise Island, where casinos and some of the world's finest 18-hole championship courses make up for the lack of island-born atmosphere. And talk of cruise ship crowds and diminishing chic notwithstanding, some of Nassau — pretty old buildings, fringe-topped surreys, straw-market hustle — and Paradise Island still have very viable charms, including hotels that can be great fun when you're in a resort mood. And if you haven't returned recently, you're in for a pleasant surprise: Older hotels have been newly spiffed up, and the government also recently announced plans for a $40-million harbor expansion of the Port of Nassau..

But it has not been all mangoes and cream. In the early days of self-government — ages ago in 1964 — considerable resentment toward tourism was reported by visitors to Nassau and Freeport (blessedly, the outer islands mostly remained immune). But time and consistent effort by both government and local hoteliers has had some positive effect. Despite a government that seems mired in self-interest, scandal, and indifference, islanders seem to understand more clearly now the economic importance of tourism and the legitimate pride that's part of doing any job well. That doesn't mean that there still aren't difficulties between islanders and visitors, but things seem to be getting a bit better.

BAHAMAS AT-A-GLANCE

FROM THE AIR: Counting every reef, rock, and bump, there are some 700 landmasses in the Bahamas scattered over 90,000 square miles of the Atlantic Ocean, beginning only 50 miles off the coast of Florida and extending 760 miles southeast to a point just above the Windward Passage that separates Cuba and Haiti.

The city of Nassau, the Bahamas' capital and chief port of entry, is at 25°05′ N latitude, 77°25′ W longitude on the island of New Providence, near the middle of the group. The Bahamas' other major resort center — also with an international jetport — is Freeport/Lucaya on Grand Bahama Island, less than 60 miles east of Florida. The flight from Miami to Nassau or Freeport takes less than 45 minutes; New York is 1,100 miles and 2½ hours by air; Toronto, 1,500 miles and 3 hours.

SPECIAL PLACES: Nassau, New Providence Island – The best way to get acquainted is through a morning or afternoon walking tour (preferably with camera), starting from Rawson Square. Across Bay Street, impressive pink and white government buildings, the Court House and Parliament, are the backdrop for a statue of Victoria as a very young queen. Make your way across Rawson Square (which, if you can make it out in the jostle, is actually oval) toward Prince George Wharf, where the big cruise ships are berthed, and turn left along the waterfront on Woodes Rogers Walk. Follow the walk to the end (about two blocks) and turn left (south). To your right is the great pink bulk of One Bay Street, better known as the *Sheraton British Colonial,* dowager queen of Nassau's hotels. Carrying on straight ahead up George Street, you pass Christ Church Cathedral (Anglican), an imposing island-Gothic structure built on the site of the earlier (1840) parish church. George Street ends at Duke Street, halfway up the hill. Above the intersection, a long flight of white steps leads up to a twice-life-size (12-foot) statue of Columbus standing guard in front of Government House, the gracefully dignified 1801 mansion that is now the official residence of the queen's personal representative to the Bahamas; on alternate Saturdays, the grounds are open for the spit-and-polish changing of the guard cere-mony, performed at 10 AM sharp.

At Government House turn left (east) and stroll the three blocks past the dogleg where Duke becomes Shirley Street, lined with pretty old pastel houses; pause just beyond Parliament Street. The octagonal yellow building down the garden path to the left is the Public Library, built in 1797 as a jail. Up the hill to the right, the *Royal Victoria* hotel sits in an impressive tangle of junglelike gardens. Built in 1861 and opened during the Civil War, it operated as a hotel until 1971. The government now maintains the gardens, where there are occasional concerts.

Two blocks farther east, at Elizabeth Avenue, is the Queen's Staircase, 65 steps hewn out of solid limestone by slaves in the late 18th century, which leads up to Fort Fincastle. Its shape and decklike ramparts remind some people of a Mississippi stern-wheeler, and the view from the ramparts is fine. But the vantage point from the adjacent 126-foot water tower is even better and particularly beautiful just before twilight, when the town lights begin to wink on.

Other sights east of Rawson Square include Fort Montagu on East Bay Street, Nassau's oldest fort (1742), and out the Eastern Road, Blackbeard's Tower, a mossy ruin said to have been erected by the pirate Edward Teach.

Across the Mackey Street bridge (for a $2 toll) is Paradise Island, known four or five decades back as Hog Island, when it served as farm country for Nassau. In its present, more elegant incarnation it boasts several luxury hotels, picture-perfect Paradise Beach (from which the island took its new name), and the terraced Versailles Gardens, behind the Ocean Club, with a 14th-century French cloister, imported stone by stone by Huntington Hartford when Paradise was his fiefdom. In January 1987, Coral World, an underwater observatory with a natural coral reef, shark tanks, marine garden aquarium, and many undersea exhibits, opened on Silver Cay, a short water-taxi ride from Nassau. It's the only facility in the Northern Hemisphere to show live sponges, coral, and other marine life in natural light. The unique construction of the exhibits allows visitors to descend below sea level to the ocean floor without getting wet. Open daily. Admission is $10 for adults and $7 for children 3 to 12; children under 3 are admitted free.

West of town, where Bay Street heads out toward the Cable Beach hotels, you come to Hanes Oval, where the best of British football (soccer), cricket, and field hockey are played on weekends (no charge; just park and go watch the action); Fort Charlotte, the islands' largest fort (1788), complete with moat, battlements, and dungeons; Ardas-tra Gardens, where trained flamingos parade (don't ask why) at 11 AM and 4 PM. More fauna (dolphins, this time) perform at the Seafloor Aquarium next door. Nearby are the blessedly peaceful Botanic Gardens, 18 green acres of lovingly landscaped lawns, shrubs, walks, lily ponds, and waterfalls.

Freeport/Lucaya, Grand Bahama Island – Historic sightseeing on Grand Bahama Island is an oxymoron, since the resort opened in 1953. Modern manmade interest points include the International Bazaar, a 10-acre enclave of shops and restaurants that reproduce 11 different European, Asian, and Near Eastern settings adjoining that Moorish-style marvel, the Princess Casino; the Straw Market, stacked with everything from handbags and hats to placemats and potholders; the Rand Memorial Nature Centre, 100 lush acres of tropical plants, flowers, and birds; the new, 40-acre Lucayan National Park, with a mile of footpaths and elevated walkways, 1,000 feet of beach strand with high dunes, a wild mangrove area with air plants, stands of Ming trees, wild tamarind and gumbo limbo, an observation platform, and two caves reached by stairs; and the Garden of the Groves, picturesquely contrived floral displays with a lake, waterfalls, a grotto, a children's playground, and a museum tracing the area's development, dedicated to Freeport's founder and his wife. The opening of Port Lucaya, a $10-million shopping complex and marketplace (near *Lucayan Beach Resort and Casino*) will add more shops, restaurants, a 50-slip marina, and daily entertainment to Freeport's list of attractions.

For a look at a mellower side of Bahamian life, head out across Pinder Point causeway toward Grand Bahama's West End. The drive through the fishing villages of Eight Mile Rock, Sea Grape, Holmes Rock, and Bootle Bay makes a pleasant day trip. En route you can visit West End's Bird Sanctuary. Pack a picnic or stop for a Bahamian lunch at *New Peace & Plenty* in Eight Mile Rock or *Harry's American Bar* at Deadman's Reef farther out.

■**EXTRA SPECIAL:** The 23-year-old Underwater Explorers Society (UNEXSO) is one of the most successful dive operations in the world. Located across from the *Lucayan Beach* hotel, its complex includes such fascinating marine attractions as the Museum of Underwater Exploration, featuring displays, movies, and multimedia presentations depicting Bahamian dives and deep-sea discoveries. Their new "Dolphin Experience" lets visitors swim with 6 dolphins ($40 per person). "Shark Shot Reef" allows divers to hold and be photographed with sharks (fiber glass sharks, that is). And nondivers can take resort or full-certification courses here, taught by highly qualified staff. Videotapes of your experiences are also available (phone: 373-1244).

THE OUTLYING ISLANDS

The Abacos – This 130-mile-long, boomerang-shaped group is the northernmost Bahamas. Consisting of Great Abaco, Little Abaco, and a sprinkling of cays (pronounced *keys*) along their north central coast, they were first settled in the 1650s by Englishmen, followed by American Tories fleeing the Revolution. Not surprisingly, their most picturesque settlements look like Cape Cod with palm trees. New Plymouth, on Green Turtle Cay, is a tiny town of neat lanes and pastel clapboard houses, one of which is the Albert Lowe Museum, with exhibitions related to early Bahamian life. Man-O-War Cay is a small salty settlement where you can still watch dedicated craftsmen building the islands' best workboats by hand. Hope Town, on Elbow Cay, is the Bahamas' most-photographed village, thanks to its candy-striped lighthouse, recently repainted for the bicentennial celebration of the Loyalists' arrival. Both it and Man-O-War Cay are reached by a small ferry from Marsh Harbour, the Abacos' "commercial hub" and growing yacht charter center. The Abacos are also famous for scuba diving and sport fishing: Walker's Cay and Treasure Cay host major billfish tournaments each year, and the marina and resort operations are considered among the world's finest.

Andros – The biggest Bahama (2,300 square miles – 108 miles long and about 46 miles wide) has a forested interior (pine, mahogany, hardwoods), a marshy west coast (straightforwardly called "the Mud"), and is best known as a scuba diver's paradise, with good facilities on North Andros at the *Andors Beach* hotel and on the south coast at *Small Hope Bay* resort. In fact, the island's chief sight is underwater: the 120-mile reef, said to be the third longest in the world, that parallels its eastern edge. Among its most picturesque settlements: Staniard Creek, with its 2 miles of white sand beach, and Nicholl's Town, near the island's northern tip, outside of which — at Morgan's Bluff — there's said to be buried treasure.

Bimini – Fifty miles east of Miami, it is famous for its game fishing (more than fifty record blue marlin have been caught off the nearby Great Bahama Bank) and as the haunt of such salty celebrities as Ernest Hemingway, Michael Lerner, and the late

Congressman Adam Clayton Powell, whose favorite *End of the World Bar* still stands in greater metropolitan Alice Town on the North Island. Another Bimini landmark includes the *Compleat Angler* hotel and bar, Hemingway's beloved watering hole. Local legend places the Fountain of Youth on South Bimini Island, but nobody is sure quite where.

Cat Island – One of the Bimini group (not to be confused with Cat Cay in the Berry group), Cat Island boasts the islands' highest point, Mt. Alvernia (a towering 206 feet), capped by the Hermitage, a chapel, religious retreat, and home designed and built by hand by the Bahamas' beloved Father Jerome. Near Port Howe, in the south, stand the remains of the Deveaux Mansion, built by Andrew Deveaux, USN, who recaptured Nassau from the Spanish in 1783; there's also an Arawak cave. Up north, Arthur's Town was the boyhood home of actor Sidney Poitier.

Eleuthera – This skinny ribbon of land over 100 miles long lying due east of Nassau (with a few bit-sized Exumas in between) was settled by the Company of Eleutherian Adventurers, who sailed south from Bermuda in 1647. Their direct descendants still live on and fish off the curiously all-white island of Spanish Wells, off the main island's north end. Across the sound, east of North Eleuthera Airport, pretty, New England–like Dunmore Town on Harbour Island dates back to the 17th century. The main island of Eleuthera (Greek for "freedom") is the most explorable of the island group because of the variety of its terrain and the good (albeit occasionally potholed) road that runs from one end to the other. From north to south, its chief features are: the Current and the Bluff, two early settlements, and nearby Preachers Cave, where the Adventurers are said to have taken refuge after their ship wrecked; Gregory Town, heart of the Bahamas' pineapple country, where the Thompson family concocts its super-smooth pineapple rum; Hatchet Bay, famous as a yacht haven (have a drink at its mite-sized Yacht Club) and as the home of the islands' largest dairy farm; the Cliffs and Glass Window Bridge, curious limestone formations carved by the sea; Governor's Harbour, the island's earliest settlement with its oldest houses in the process of restoration on Cupid's Cay (that heavenly smell is wafting from *Mamie's Bakery;* don't miss her cinnamon buns); Tarpum Bay, a small town full of picture possibilities (boat-lined beach, pastel houses, tiny church, graveyard, and a kooky "castle" on the hill); and Rock Sound, with its airport and resorts. Just off the east coast of Eleuthera is Windermere Island, home to the exclusive *Windermere Island Club,* favorite haunt of royalty and celebrities. Back on the main island, the *Cotton Bay Club* has a first-rate 18-hole championship golf course designed by Robert Trent Jones, Sr., and *Club Med* is a longtime favorite.

San Salvador – The Atlantic-edged eastern island, where Bahamian tradition says Columbus landed, has been rediscovered by scuba buffs who stay at the island's only resort, *Riding Rock Inn,* and, in their moments on land, visit the small New World Museum (relics from Indian times on) in Cockburn Town, the ruins of Watling's Castle (built in the 1680s by the infamous pirate-turned-Christian farmer), and the four (count them, four) monuments that mark the exact spots where Christopher is said to have come ashore.

The Exumas – A long sandy spine of steppingstone islands that start east of New Providence and stretch 100 miles south and east to a point just off Long Island, they are favorites with bluewater sailors because they offer so many secluded anchorages and such incredible diving. Exuma National Land and Sea Park near Sampson Cay has super snorkeling reefs only three to ten feet below the surface of the water. Most colorful for land exploring: the old villages of Rolle Town, Rolleville, Steventon, and Williams Town, Great Salt Pond, and the plantation ruins on Little Exuma Island.

■ **EXTRA SPECIAL:** *George Town,* capital of all the Exumas, is one winsome, living example of how pretty, pink, and friendly an outlying island place can be. Its 800 residents and resort guests share all major excitements (e.g., the weekly arrival of the mail boat, Saturday market), including, of course, the yearly April "Regretta," when refreshment stands line the town pier, boats crowd the roadstead, and nobody goes to bed for a week. There are three hostelries to choose from: the mellow *Peace and Plenty* hotel in town, *Pieces of Eight* just outside, and the sportier *Out Island Inn* on the beach about ten minutes' stroll away. Whatever the night's entertainment (school Christmas pageant or Saturday dance), the group that gathers in the *Peace and Plenty*'s bar will know where it is.

■ **ANOTHER EXTRA SPECIAL:** The Bahamas' *People-to-People at Home Program,* with more than 500 islanders lined up to entertain interested visitors with a "truly Bahamian experience." Hosts and guests are matched according to mutual interests and hobbies. To participate, contact your hotel's social hostess or a Tourist Office Information Bureau. It's free.

SOURCES AND RESOURCES

TOURIST INFORMATION: Bahamas tourist offices, which will supply descriptive brochures and information on island accommodations, sightseeing, sports, nightlife, and transportation, can be found in 14 North American cities:

Atlanta: 1950 Century Blvd., NE, Atlanta, GA 30345 (phone: 404-633-1793)

Boston: 1027 Statler Office Bldg., Boston, MA 02116 (phone: 617-426-3144)

Chicago: 875 N Michigan Ave., Chicago, IL 60611 (phone: 312-787-8203)

Dallas: 2050 Stemmons Fwy., Suite 186, World Trade Center, Dallas, TX 75258-1408 (phone: 214-742-1886)

Detroit: 26400 Lahser Rd., Suite 112A, Southfield, MI 48034 (phone: 313-357-2940)

Houston: 5177 Richmond Ave., Suite 755, Houston, TX 77056 (phone: 713-626-1566)

Los Angeles: 3450 Wilshire Blvd., Los Angeles, CA 90010 (phone: 213-385-0033)

Miami: 255 Alhambra Circle, Coral Gables, FL 33134 (phone: 305-442-4860)

Montréal: 1255 Phillips Sq., Montréal, PQ H3B 3G1 (phone: 514-861-6797)

New York: 10 Columbus Circle, Suite 1660, New York, NY 10019 (phone: 212-758-2777)

Philadelphia: Lafayette Bldg., 437 Chestnut St., Room 216, Philadelphia, PA 19106 (phone: 215-925-0871)

Toronto: 85 Richmond St. W, Toronto, Ont. M5H 2C9 (phone: 416-363-4441)

Vancouver: 470 Granville St., Vancouver, BC V6C 1V5 (phone: 604-688-8334).

Washington, DC: 1730 Rhode Island Ave., NW, Washington, DC 20036 (phone: 202-659-9135)

In Nassau, the tourist offices offer information on special events, sightseeing advice, people-to-people arrangements, and answers to any questions. They are open daily at four locations: two at the airport, one in the arrivals area (8:15 AM to 10:30 PM) and the other in the departure area (9 AM to 5 PM); and two downtown, in Parliament Square (8:30 AM to 5:30 PM) and at Prince George Dock (8:30 AM to 4:30 PM). On Grand Bahama, there's a Visitors Information Centre at the International Bazaar (9 AM to 5 PM weekdays; 10 AM to 2 PM Saturdays; closed Sundays and holidays).

Local Coverage – Several digest-size guides, free to visitors and available locally, provide current information on shopping, sightseeing, restaurants, night spots, island recipes, and lore. These include: *What to Do in Nassau, Pocket Guide to the Bahamas,* and *Best Buys in the Bahamas. The Bahamas Handbook* ($13.95) goes into Bahamian life in depth for the benefit of potential (business) investors and those considering buying property or moving to the islands. The quarterly *Bahamas* magazine carries full-color features on island destinations and tourism industry news.

Two daily newspapers are published in Nassau: the *Tribune* and the *Nassau Guardian*. The *Freeport News* is published in Freeport. The *New York Times, Wall Street Journal,* and *Miami Herald* are available on newsstands on the day of publication; other major North American newspapers are also flown in daily.

Telephone – Telephone systems vary from island to island, but the seven-digit numbers given in this chapter can be dialed direct by using the area code prefix 809. To phone a place that does not have a standard number, ask the operator to connect your call.

ENTRY REQUIREMENTS: US and Canadian citizens need only proof of citizenship (passport, birth certificate, or *certified* copy of birth certificate with an additional positive photo identification) and an ongoing or return ticket.

CLIMATE AND CLOTHES: In winter months, the Gulf Stream warms the Bahamas to a balmy average of 70°F (22°C). April through October, the average thermometer reading is 80°F (27°C), and in November it's about 75°F (24°C). Casual, lightweight resortwear is the rule, with some dressing up in the evenings (long dresses, skirts, or evening tops and pants for women; jackets or long-sleeved "shirtjacks" for men), particularly for dining, dancing, and the casinos in Nassau, Paradise Island, or Freeport. Women should bring a scarf, stole, or evening sweater for occasional cool nights. The farther from Nassau and Freeport you get, the more casual it is; at resorts like *Cotton Bay* or *Treasure Cay,* there's still a tendency to spruce up at night. Bathing suits are *never* worn in town, on any island.

MONEY: The Bahamian dollar is on a par with the US dollar. US and Canadian dollars are accepted throughout the islands, as are traveler's checks. Credit cards are more widely honored in Nassau and Freeport than on the outlying islands. Banks are open Mondays through Thursdays from 9:30 AM to 3 PM, and on Fridays from 9:30 AM to 5 PM.

LANGUAGE: English with a decidedly Bahamian accent.

TIME: Same as Eastern Standard and Eastern Daylight. When it's noon in New York, it's noon in Nassau, whatever the season.

CURRENT: At 120 volts, 60 cycles; traveling appliances will work without adapters.

GETTING THERE: Airlines that schedule direct (one-plane or nonstop) flights from North American cities to Nassau and/or Freeport include Eastern from New York, Atlanta, Baltimore, Chicago, Dallas, Houston, Philadelphia, Phoenix, Tucson, Washington, DC, Miami; Eastern Express also flies from Miami to Abaco and Eleuthera on a regular schedule; Pan American from New York and Miami; TWA from New York; Air Canada from Toronto and

Montréal; United from Chicago; Delta from New York, Detroit, Cleveland, Boston, Dallas, Atlanta, and Fort Lauderdale. From Atlanta, Tampa, Orlando, Fort Lauderdale, and Miami, Bahamasair serves Treasure Cay, Governor's Harbour, Inagua, Mayaguana, North Eleuthera, Marsh Harbour, Freeport, Nassau, and connects via Nassau with other Family Island destinations. From West Palm Beach, Fort Lauderdale, and Miami, Chalk's International offers seaplane service to Paradise Island, Bimini, and Cat Cay. Caribbean Express serves Nassau from Ft. Lauderdale and West Palm Beach (phone: 800-423-0535); Florida Express flies from Orlando and Ft. Lauderdale to Nassau (phone: 800-FASTJET). A number of smaller commuter airlines fly direct to a variety of Family Island airports from Florida gateways; there are also a number of air taxi services. Ask your travel agent about these and frequent charter departures from major North American cities.

Getting to the outlying Family Islands used to be iffy, but the arrival of two new air carriers has taken the hassle out of flying to most of the larger ones. Aero Coach, based in Fort Lauderdale, offers complete reservation service from point of departure to final island destination. They operate from West Palm, Fort Lauderdale, and Miami to Bimini, George Town (Exuma), Governor's Harbour, Marsh Harbour, North Eleuthera, Rock Sound (Eleuthera), and Treasure Cay (phone: 800-327-0010; in Florida, 800-432-5034). Piedmont serves North Eleuthera, Rock Sound, Treasure Cay, and Marsh Harbour from Ft. Lauderdale (phone: 800-251-5720).

Many cruise lines include Freeport and Nassau as regular stops, including overnight stays that allow passengers to disembark and enjoy the casinos, cabarets, golf courses, and shops. Visitors to Ft. Lauderdale or Miami, Florida, can take day trips to Freeport (or 3-day packages) aboard the *Sea Escape* or *Viking Express* for shopping and sightseeing. Check with a travel agent for current cruise schedules.

CALCULATING COSTS: Rates for a double room at the best Nassau, Cable Beach, and Paradise Island hotels run from about $135 up a day European Plan (without meals) from mid-December to May, but breakfasts and dinners add $35 to $50 per person a day. There are many more moderately priced places — especially on the outlying islands, where much of the Bahamas' charm lies these days. There you'll find all the creature comforts, but no show-off chic, at rates that run from about $130 up a day for two — including two, and sometimes three, meals. From May to mid-December, prices drop 30% to 50% across the board. Package tours, offered year-round, are especially popular in summer to Nassau/Paradise and Freeport/Lucaya. Prices for 8-day/7-night packaged stays on the outlying islands run from about $310 (per person) up in winter, about $190 up in summer; a number of water sport features are usually included, but air fare is extra. An 8-day/7-night stay in a best-rated Nassau hotel, including sightseeing tour, aquarium admission, and transfers, is priced at about $375 up per person in winter, about $225 up per person in summer, with air fare extra. Individual hotels and resorts also offer specialized tennis, golf, diving, and honeymoon packages that include special extras at considerable savings. Several operators offer weekend and week-long packages combined with charter flights, designed to attract high rollers at very low prices.

A room tax of 6% of the EP (room only) rate is added to hotel bills. There is also an airport departure tax of about $5 per adult, $2.50 per child (2 to 12 years).

Lunch at one of the better Nassau restaurants runs about $30 for two; dinner, about $50 and up, with drinks and tip extra. Even breakfasts of $7 to $10 are not unusual in the better hotels.

GETTING AROUND: Taxi – Readily available at airports and hotels in Nassau and Freeport. Cabs are metered, and their rates are fixed by law: $1.20 for the first ¼ mile and 20¢ for each additional ¼ mile for one or two passengers; $1.50 for each additional passenger (children under three, no charge). Approximate fares for one or two passengers from Nassau International Airport: to downtown Nassau, about $12; to Cable Beach hotels, about $10; to South Ocean Beach Club, $6; to East Bay Street hotels, $14; to Paradise Island (including $2 bridge toll), $18. From Freeport International Airport to hotels in Freeport area, about $4; to hotels in Lucaya area, about $7. On the outlying islands, the unmetered taxi rates may run slightly higher but are negotiable. The usual tip is 15% of the fare. Many taxi drivers are good, knowledgeable, and/or amusing guides to their particular islands. Ask your hotel to recommend one; rates in Nassau and Freeport are about $12 to $15 per hour for a five-passenger cab.

Jitney – Minibuses run from outlying sections of the island to downtown Nassau for 50¢ to 75¢, and in Freeport for 50¢. They're fast, cheap, and comfortable; just wave and they'll stop for you. Many Cable Beach and Paradise Island hotels provide free shopping bus service to Rawson Square for their guests several times a day.

Car Rental – Daily rates with unlimited mileage range from about $47 to $70, depending on make of car and season; weekly rates range from $170 to $385. Gas, which currently costs the same to about 10¢ per gallon more than in the US, is extra. International agencies in Nassau include *Avis* (phone: 322-2889; airport, 327-7121), *Budget* (phone: 327-7405), and *National* (phone: 327-8300 and 325-3716); and in Freeport, *Avis* (phone: 353-1102; 352-7666).

You can also rent a car on some outlying islands, but it won't be a late model, and chances are it will have traveled some pretty rough roads before it gets to you. So be sure to check its tires (including the spare) and general condition and listen to the motor before accepting delivery. There isn't always a phone handy in case of a breakdown. On Abaco, try *H & L Car Rentals* (phone: 367-2854) in Marsh Harbour; on Eleuthera, *Dingle Motors Service* (phone: 334-2031) in Rock Sound; on Great Exuma, *R. & M. Rentals* (phone: 336-2112) and *Exuma Transport* (phone: 336-2101), both in George Town.

US and Canadian driver's licenses are valid, but remember: *Drive on the left.*

Motor scooter rentals are increasingly popular in Nassau, on Paradise Island, and in Freeport/Lucaya and are also available on Eleuthera and in George Town, Great Exuma. Hotels have their own stands or will direct you to the nearest outlet. Rates run about $23 (plus a $20 deposit) per bike for a 8 or 9 AM to 5 PM day; most have an extra seat behind the driver. Standard two-wheeled bikes rent for about $10 a day.

Sightseeing Bus Tours – Local operators offer a wide variety of sightseeing tours on both New Providence and Grand Bahama islands — though it's more fun to explore Nassau on your own (walking, in a buggy, on a motor scooter, or with a taxi driver). And there isn't that much to a Freeport tour. Your hotel travel desk is the best place to find out what's offered and for how much. *Majestic Tours* (phone: 322-2602) runs, among other things, a nightclub tour of Nassau and Paradise Island that has garnered rave reviews. If you're hesitant about roaming on your own, ask your hotel travel desk to book a table for the dinner show at the *Peanuts Taylor's Drumbeat Club* (Bahamian sounds) or *Valentine's* in Nassau, *Le Cabaret* (Vegas-style glitter) on Paradise Island, or the *Kasbah* in Freeport — and a good driver to take you and bring you home.

At least once — maybe for part of a Nassau tour — take your pick of the fringe-topped surreys lined up at Rawson Square or on Frederick Street, just off Bay Street, and clip-clop around town for a while. Often a horse with a hat you admire has a driver you'll like too. His commentary will be worth the $8 per hour for up to three persons. The Freeport alternative: sociable buses that do a 2-hour all-around tour for about $12.50 per person.

Sea Excursions – Small glass-bottom boats at the Prince George Wharf charge about $10 per person for an hour's Sea Garden tour; on the ultimate glass-bottom trip, the 97-foot "surface submarine" *Nautilus* charges $15 for a 2-hour daytime harbor/Sea Gardens cruise, $25 per person (including dinner at *Capt. Nemo's*) for the night ride from Mermaid Marina at Bay and Deveaux sts. The Nassau-based catamaran *Tropic Bird* sails from Prince George Wharf for a sea tour with music by a goombay band and a swim on a remote beach at 10:15 AM and returns at 1:15 PM (Mondays through Saturdays, $15 per person). The sailing schooner *Wild Harp* leaves the Yacht Haven's dock for a lunch cruise with calypso music and a swim on a secluded Rose Island beach; about $30 per person includes wine and an island picnic (10 AM daily, returning 2 PM; sunset supper cruises too); check your hotel's tour desk for information on other picnic and cocktail sails. In Freeport/Lucaya, the "World's Biggest Glass Bottom Boat" leaves the *Lucayan Beach Resort* dock at 10 AM, noon, and 2 PM daily for tours of the reefs off the coast. Excursions to tiny, uninhabited Treasure Island on the 43-foot *Sandy Cay* for snorkeling, swimming, and beach picnicking cost $35 (phone: 322-8184 in Nassau).

Mail-boat trips that connect the islands with Nassau and Freeport and with each other can provide off-beat travel on the cheap. Example: from Potter's Cay Dock, Nassau, to South Andros, a 4- to 6-hour trip, usually on Tuesdays (schedules are haphazard), costs about $20 per person one way; but book an island bed before you leave.

Local Air Services – There are no packaged air tours, but Nassau's Trans Island Airways (phone: 327-8329), Fort Lauderdale's Trans Air (phone: 800-327-7605; in Florida, 305-763-5220), Red Aircraft (phone: 305-523-9624), and Safe Air International (phone: 305-765-8430), and Freeport's Lucaya Air Service (phone: 352-8885, 352-8886) are available for charter island-hopping trips; rates are based on mileage and size of aircraft. More than 45,000 private planes fly into the Bahamas each year. They're required to land first at an official port of entry (West End on Grand Bahama and South Bimini are the two closest to the US) and to file a Declaration of Private Aircraft (forms available at most US airports) and the usual immigration cards distributed on arrival. An air navigation chart is free from any tourist office branch. There are small-plane landing strips in the Abacos, on Andros, the Berry Islands, Bimini, Cat Island, Eleuthera, the Exumas, Long Island, and San Salvador — among others. Most of the Bahamas' 52 airports and strips have 100-octane fuel. Pilots can get up-to-date information by calling the Bahamas Pilot Briefing Center (phone: in the US, 800-327-7678).

SHOPPING: Except for the occasional straw market under a sheltering island tree (as in George Town on Great Exuma) or special finds like the Thompson Bros. pineapple rum (ask at their store in Gregory Town, Eleuthera), the splendid straw hats Spanish Wells lobstermen wear (ask the man wearing one where they're for sale), or the great canvas sail bags and totes Norman Albury makes (look for *Uncle Norman's Sail Loft* on Man-O-War Cay), bargain hunting is a New Providence/Grand Bahama sport. But before you head for Nassau's Bay Street or Freeport's exotic International Bazaar — where most of the shops are — you should know that the Bahamas are *not* duty-free territory; nor do they have shops where you can order and pay duty-free prices for in-bond merchandise to be delivered to your plane or ship. However, there *are* bargains on imported merchandise — especially because of the '78 round of tariff reductions on china, crystal, porcelain, watches, cameras, sweaters, and woolens from Europe and Japan, most of which are now 30% to 45% less expensive (not counting at-home sales taxes) in the Bahamas than in the States. There are also good buys in French perfumes, some jewelry, and liquor (chiefly liqueurs). But all imported merchandise does not necessarily cost less in the islands. So it's important to research comparative US prices before you leave home — particularly if you're going to be faced with the bazaar's profusion/confusion of foreign-accented shops. A department store catalogue brought along for quick reference is the best kind of help; otherwise, do some pretrip browsing and take notes. Check discount outlets for "real" prices on cameras and electronic equipment (Bahamian savings on these items are usually quoted as X percent below a "manufacturer's suggested list price" — which is higher than you'd have to pay at home). And don't buy an unfamiliar brand of watch, camera, radio, tape recorder, or anything else that might need repairs without making sure there's a Stateside service shop that will honor its warranty. Finally, you can save steps by checking a local source like *Best Buys in the Bahamas, What-to-Do*, or the *Pocket Guide* to find out which stores specialize in the things you're looking for. And get an early morning start so you can shop when crowds are smallest and salespeople most cheerful.

Most shops are open Mondays through Saturdays from 9 AM to 5 PM, and, in Freeport, sometimes until 6 PM. A few close one afternoon a week (usually on Thursdays, Fridays, or Saturdays).

NASSAU

Imported bargains are a specialty in their own right at *Barry's*, corner Bay and George sts. (big on everything British — wool sweaters, woolen suitings, men's furnishings; also guayabera shirts, dashikis, gold, silver, and jade jewelry); *Bernard's*, Bay St. between Charlotte and Parliament (substantial savings on Wedgwood and Royal Copenhagen china, Baccarat and Lalique crystal, Ernest Borel Swiss watches, gold jewelry); *Carib Shops*, Bay St. between Market and Frederick (Girard-Perregaux Swiss watches, English bone china, Swedish crystal, 18-karat gold jewelry, crystal paperweights, are best buys; also Spanish wood and ironware, Portuguese copper, Hong Kong furniture); *John Bull*, Bay St. between East St. and Elizabeth Ave. (town's biggest selection of cameras and accessories plus Rolex and Seiko watches; also extensive jewelry collection, Limoges porcelain, English bone china, crystal, and calypso records); *Nassau Shop*, Bay St. between Frederick and Charlotte (town's largest department store, with good buys in French perfumes, watches, jewelry, British knitwear for men and women); *Treasure Traders*, West and Marlborough sts. (imported china, crystal, cutlery); *Solomon's Mines*, Bay St. and *Holiday Inn* on Paradise Island (suitably dazzling collection of bone china, Waterford and Swedish crystal, figurines, jewelry).

Women's fashions aren't much less expensive than back home, but if you like shopping anyway, you'll find the best selections at *Amanda's*, Marlborough St. opposite the Bank of Nova Scotia (tops in imported sweaters — Pringle, Viennese; blouses, scarves, accessories); *Ambrosine*, Marlborough St. between West and Nassau (toniest boutique in town, featuring Pucci, Mirsa, Bleyle, et al.); *Mademoiselle* on Bay St. — especially for its corner of Androsia batik sportswear; *Francesca's*, in the new Paradise Island shopping mall (resort fashions by name designers from London, Paris, Milan, and New York; shoes and accessories too). In the jewelry department: *Greenfire*, at the *Paradise Towers Hotel* (for Colombian emeralds "direct to you, at substantial savings"); *Colombian Emeralds*, in the *Britannia Towers* hotel, open until 12:30 AM, in case you win at the casino next door; and *Treasure Box*, Bay St. near Market (nicely done conch and coral jewelry, also large gold chain collection). *Galaxy*, Bay St. in the Beaumont Building, near the *British Colonial* (Nassau's most complete shoe shop for women and men, with Bally of Switzerland, Dunlop and Adidas sport and tennis shoes; big selection of imported sandals).

Miscellaneous finds include the *Linen Shop*, Parliament St. south of Bay St. (all sorts of lavish table and bed things up to and including hibiscus-embroidered tea cozies, printed linen tea towels attractive enough for wall hanging); the *Brass & Leather Shop*, Charlotte St. just off Bay St. (imported English and European horse brasses, teapots, bookends, lots of gift ideas, plus good-looking belts, wallets, luggage from Gucci and Bottega Veneta); *Bahamas Divers*, in the *Pilot House* hotel on East Bay St. (the best dive gear, of course, but also bikinis and Speedo swimsuits, dive watches, camera housings, books, black coral and shell jewelry); *Scottish Shop*, Charlotte St. off Bay (tams, clan jewelry, tartan ties, scarves, kilts, etc.); *Pipe of Peace*, Bay St. between

Charlotte and Parliament (pipes, cigars, cigarettes, lighters, plus cameras and English candies); *Francis Peek,* George St. south of Bay (English antiques, artworks, hand-painted Herend china at about half the US price); *Lightbourn's Pharmacy,* Bay and George sts. (biggest perfume selection in town, worthwhile savings); and *K. F. Butler,* Marlborough and West sts. (large stock of whiskeys, rums, liqueurs — overall good prices); *Pyfrom's,* Bay St. between Frederick and Charlotte (town's biggest stock of out-and-out souvenirs — dolls, steel drums, Nassau T- and sweat shirts, you name it).

Local crafts — mostly straw things from hats to handbags, totes, baskets, and the like — are the raison d'être for the *Straw Market,* in its own big building opposite Market St., on Bay, where bargaining before you buy is accepted and expected.

FREEPORT

The big *International Bazaar* is so full of a number of things that it can get quite confusing. Don't try to sort it out without a map (pick one up at the Tourist Information Centre near the Scandinavian Section) and your list of comparative prices. Basically there are two sorts of merchandise for sale: imports that are bargains because Bahamian duty is low, and imports that may be good buys because you like them, but for which you'd pay about the same price back home. Two Nassau shops — *Pipe of Peace* and *Colombian Emeralds International* (see listings above) — have bazaar branches selling similar merchandise. The big *Ginza* import store is the Freeport version of Nassau's *John Bull,* with similar buys in cameras, watches, jewelry, etc. *Solomon's Mines* is good for china, crystal, and pottery. *Midnight Sun* stocks all the best Scandinavian names — crystal by Iittala, Kosta, Orrefors, Holmegard; Bing & Grøndahl, Royal Copenhagen porcelain — plus Daum, Lalique, Baccarat, most at 25% or more below US prices. *Thai Crystallery* and the *Discount Bazaar* are also centers for import bargain shopping. And don't overlook *Port Lucaya,* Freeport's new multimillion-dollar marketplace with 85 boutiques, 6 restaurants, and daily Bahamian entertainment, near the *Lucayan Beach Resort.*

Women's fashions from all over the world are featured in a dozen boutiques. Among the best: the *London Pacesetter* (British imports, sports clothes); *Evelyn of Lucaya* (bright separates, accessories), *CariBah* (great island batiks and clothes made from them, straw things, handicrafts), *Fol-O-Fashion* (the place for the Bahamas' favorite Androsia batiks, fashions), *Penny Lane, Bahamian Tings,* and *UNEXCO. Dynasty* (pretty, exotic things from all over the Orient); *Azteca de Oro* (bright Mexican shirts, caftans, jewelry). For perfumes at lower-than-stateside prices: *Parfum de Paris* and *Casablanca Perfumes. Freeport Jewelers* has 18-karat gold chains among other valuables. *Island Galleria* offers handsome jewelry (especially coral), crystal, china, as well as artworks. At *Far East Traders* (lace tablecloths, linens), don't miss the shell shop upstairs. For liquor: *La Bodega* and *The Wine Cellar.* The *London Bookshop* has lots of paperbacks. *Pat Paul's Raspini* is the place for menswear; *Bata* has lots of shoes for men and women. And for crafts, a wood carver and a steel drum maker (Little Sparrow) keep stands at the east side of the bazaar across from the *Straw Market.*

 TIPPING: Most hotels and restaurants add a service charge of 15%, which covers all service. If you're not sure whether it has been added, ask; if it wasn't, tip waiters 15% of the check (providing the service has been pleasant); hotel room maids, $1 per day; bellhops, 50¢ per bag, but not less than $1. For airport porters: 50¢ per bag; taxi drivers: 15% of the fare.

 SPECIAL EVENTS: Holidays, when shops and businesses are closed, are: *New Year's Day, Good Friday, Easter Monday, Whitmonday* (seventh Monday after Easter), *Labour Day* (first Friday in June), *Independence Day* (July 10), *Emancipation Day* (first Monday in August), *Discovery* — or *Columbus — Day* (October 12), *Christmas* and *Boxing Day* (December 26). Both Boxing Day and

New Year's Day are occasions for Junkanoo Parades, with celebrants in fantastic crepe-paper costumes and masks bounding along to the rhythm of cowbells, goatskin drums, and whistles. *Goombay,* the ongoing summer celebration, offers visitors a variety of folklore and cultural events. Special events on the sporting calendar are too numerous to list, but among the most famous are more than 20 annual sportfishing tournaments, including the prestigious 6-tournament *Bahamas Championship* competition, which ends in June.

Popular regattas include *Regatta Time* each June in Abaco; the *Family Island Regatta* in Exuma in April; and the *Green Turtle Cay Regatta* in July.

Golf and tennis tournaments, windsurfing competitions, powerboat racing — it's all here each year (phone: 800-32-SPORT).

SPORTS: To first-rate golf, tennis, and every kind of water sport, the Bahamas have added something new — a toll-free hot line to handle queries on sporting events and facilities throughout the islands: dial 800 32-SPORT (more prosaically, 800 327-7678.) Meanwhile, you'll find:

Boating – Lots of possibilities on both a large and small scale. Most island hotels have Sailfish, Sunfish, and sometimes Hobie Cats to rent (about $10 to $22 for the first hour, $5 an hour after that) for small-craft sailing. Island resorts often have Boston Whalers or other outboards available — sometimes free to their guests, sometimes for rent at rates that vary widely from a few dollars an hour up.

For yachtsmen, the Bahamas' calm open waters, safe bays, and vast number of anchorages (not to mention the swimming and diving waters found in and near them) make this an exceptionally fine cruising area. All sizes and types of boats are available for charter to experienced skippers. Arrangements can be made through a travel agent, your hotel, and specialists like *Nassau Yacht Haven* (phone: 322-8173); *Abaco Bahamas Charters,* Hope Town (phone: 367-2277); and *Marsh Harbour Marina* (phone: 367-2700). Bareboat charters are a specialty of *Bahamas Yachting Services* at Marsh Harbour in the Abacos (phone: 367-2080).

Well-equipped marinas on a number of islands provide water, fuel, food, ice, showers, sometimes a bed for the night. *In Nassau/Paradise Island,* they include: *Bayshore Marina* (phone: 322-8232); *Hurricane Hole Marina* (phone: 325-5441); *Nassau Yacht Haven* (phone: 322-8173); *East Bay Yacht Basin* (phone: 322-3754); *Nassau Harbour Club* (phone: 323-1771). *On Grand Bahama: Lucayan Harbour Inn Marina* (phone: 373-1666); *Running Mon Marina* (phone: 352-6834); *Xanadu Marina* (phone: 352-8720). *In the Abacos: Treasure Cay* (phone: 367-2570) and *Green Turtle Marina* (phone: 367-2572); *in Marsh Harbour: Marsh Harbour Marina* (phone: 367-2700) and *Conch Inn Marina* (phone: 367-2800). *On Andros: Andros Beach Hotel Marina* (phone: 329-2012). *In the Berry Islands: Great Harbour Cay Marina* (radio phone only); *Chub Cay Marina* (phone: 325-1490). *In the Biminis: Bimini Blue Water* (phone: 347-2166), *Brown's Marina* (phone: 347-2227), and *Weech's Docks* (phone: 347-2028) — all on North Bimini. *On Harbour Island: Romora Bay Club* (phone: 333-2325); *Valentine's Yacht Club* (phone: 333-2142). *On Spanish Wells: Spanish Wells Beach Resort* (phone: 332-2645) and *Sawyer's Marina* (phone: Spanish Wells 255). *The Exumas: Happy People Marina* (phone: Staniel Cay 4-2217); *Staniel Cay Yacht Club* (phone: in Florida, 305-334-2217). *Long Island: Stella Maris Marina & Yacht Club* (phone: 336-2106).

For complete detailed cruising information — including small charts, landfall sketches, anchorage and approach descriptions — *The Yachtsman's Guide to the Bahamas* is invaluable; it's $9.95 plus $2 postage stateside, $4 overseas, from Tropic Isle Publishers, PO Box 611141, N Miami, FL 33161.

Cricket – This cousin of US baseball is played on pitches (fields) ranging from exquisitely manicured greens to vacant lots. Cricket is a spectator sport that is also a social event, much like Carnival. For upcoming matches, check with the tourist board of the island you plan to visit or consult the sports section of the island newspaper.

Golf – In a very, very flat country, the experts have managed to devise an amazing number of challenging courses — 14 full-scale 18s and several 9s. Grand Bahama is the champ with six: in Freeport/Lucaya, the *Bahamas Princess Country Club* (phone: 352-6721), *Bahama Reef Golf and Country Club* (phone: 373-1055), *Fortune Hills Golf and Country Club* (phone: 373-4500), *Lucayan Golf and Country Club* (phone: 373-1066), and — in West End — the *Grand Bahama Hotel and Country Club* (phone: 348-2030). Nassau and Paradise Island have four 18-hole championship golf courses between them: the *Cable Beach Golf Club* (phone: 327-7070), *Divi Bahamas Beach Resort and Casino* (phone: 326-4391), *Paradise Island Golf Club* (phone: 325-7431), and *Lyførd Cay Club* (private membership). There are also 18-hole courses on the outlying islands at *Treasure Cay Golf Club,* Abaco (phone: 367-2570), on Great Harbour Cay in the Berry Islands (9 holes restored at press time; phone: 329-2026 to check 18-hole status), and *Cotton Bay* (334-2101) on Eleuthera. All 18s have complete facilities: rental carts and clubs and resident pros. Greens fees average $12 to $20 a round in winter, somewhat less in summer.

Horseback Riding – Along lanes of casuarinas and seagrape-lined beaches, it's a beautiful way to go — especially in the early morning. There are stables at Coral Harbour on New Providence (*Happy Trails;* phone: 323-5613) and on Paradise Island (*Harbourside Riding Stables;* phone: 326-3733); in Freeport (*Pinetree Stables;* phone: 373-3600). It's about $20 for a 1½-hour ride.

Regattas – All year long, for both sail and power boats. Among the major annual races: the Miami-Nassau Yacht Race and Nassau Cup Yacht Race in February; Long Island Sailing Regatta in May; Hope Town Cup Series Regatta in June; Bahamas "500" (ocean powerboat race) in June; Abaco Regatta in July; Cat Island Regatta in August; Discovery Day Regatta in October; and the Miami-Nassau Powerboat Race in December. Most fun: the Out Island Regatta (sometimes pronounced "regretta"), a fierce competition for island workboats held every April in George Town in the Exumas. There are only two rules: Don't bump, and throw no man overboard. Every vessel that can goes to George Town to race or watch, making this one of the all-time great parties afloat and ashore.

Snorkeling and Scuba – Incredible visibility, scores of reefs and drop-offs close to shore, and the rich variety of Bahamian marine life make a number of these islands great sites for underwater exploration. Masks and flippers can be borrowed or rented for a small fee (usually $2 to $3 a day) at almost every hotel beach, and snorkeling is casual fun at all of them. First-rate guides and instruction are available at many island sites. These are some of the best:

In Nassau/Cable Beach/Paradise: All hotels can arrange for certified instruction; many, at their own pools and off their own beaches through qualified concessionaires. *Peter Hughes' Dive South Ocean* at the *Divi Bahamas Beach Resort and Country Club* (phone: 326-4391);*Bahama Divers* at the *Pilot House* (phone: 326-5644) and *Underwater Tours* at Divers Haven (phone: 322-3285) rent scuba and snorkeling equipment, arrange diving trips. Among the best sites are Rose Island Reefs close to Nassau harbor (good place for novices to try their fins); the wreck of the *Mahoney* (a steel-hulled ship sunk in 30 feet of water just outside the harbor); Goulding Cay Reefs at the far western end of the island (favorite "set" for underwater movies); Gambier Deep Reef off Gambier Village (80 to 90 feet down); Green Cay heads and elkhorn coral stands (off Green Cay, 40-foot depth); Booby Rock Channel (large fish population, strong current; boat needed); South Side reefs (tiny, isolated reefs; good snorkeling, bad boating due to shallowness); Clifton Pier Drop-off, off the south shore of New Providence (sheer drop starting at 110 feet; for experienced divers only).

In Freeport/Lucaya: The *Underwater Explorers Society* (phone: 373-1244) has what is certainly the most complete setup for instruction and dive trips in the islands, and probably one of the best anywhere in the world — including an instruction tank 18 feet deep where beginners can really master fundamentals to a degree impossible in shallower hotel pools. They're tops in all departments. Interesting dive sites include Treasure Reef, where the $1.2 million Lucayan Treasure was discovered in 1964; the Wall and Black Forest Ledge (a one-mile drop-off starting 125 feet down off the south shore); Zoo Hole, five miles west of Lucaya (fantastic fish variety); the Caves (heavy reef coral formations, very tame fish); and *Theo's Wreck* (a 230-foot steel freighter on its side in 100 feet of water, perched on a ledge), with a weekly scheduled dive (Wednesdays). In addition, UNEXSO has a new dive operation at West End and at *Jack Tar Village.*

On the islands: In the Abacos, rentals and dive trips can be arranged at the *Dive Abaco,* Marsh Harbour (phone: 367-2014); *David Gale's Island Marine,* Hope Town (actually offshore on Parrot Cay; phone: 367-2822); *Elbow Cay Beach Inn,* Hope Town (phone: 367-2748); *Walker's Cay Dive Shop,* Walker's Cay (phone: 305-522-1469 in Fort Lauderdale; 800-432-2092 in Florida, 800-327-3714 elsewhere in the continental US); and *Treasure Cay Beach* hotel, Treasure Cay (phone: 367-2520); the best diving spots are coral-lined Devil's Hole, 8 miles north of Treasure Cay, 2,000-acre Pelican Cay National Park, between Lynyard and Tilloo cays south of Marsh Harbour; also Scotland, Spanish, and Deep Water cays, and the wreck of the Union warship USS *Adirondack,* 20 feet down. On Andros, *Small Hope Bay Lodge* near Fresh Creek (Nassau phone: 328-2014) has complete dive facilities and offers resort course, rentals, trips; so does *Undersea Adventures* at the *Andros Beach* hotel at Nicholls Town (phone: 305-763-2188 in Florida; 800-327-8150 elsewhere). (The Andros Barrier Reef, 12 to 20 feet down, with its deep outside drop-off and plunging Blue Holes, is a truly spectacular site.) On Bimini, *Bimini Undersea Adventures* (phone: 800-327-8150; in Florida, 305-763-2188) on North Bimini provides boat and equipment rentals, guided dive trips; most intriguing sites are the submarine stone formations off North Bimini, believed by some to be the remains of the Lost Continent of Atlantis, and more than a dozen sunken ships off North Rock Light and South Bimini. In the Exumas, the *Exuma Dive Company* in George Town (phone: 336-2030) and *Exuma Aquatics* at the *Pieces of Eight* hotel outside George Town (phone: 336-2600) have dive boats and equipment; the Exuma National Land and Sea Park sea gardens three to ten feet below the water's surface are beautiful for snorkeling; Thunderball Grotto at Staniel Cay, the Mysterious Cave off Stocking Island near George Town, and the wreck of a 1560 privateer off Highborne Cay are the best dive sites. On the main island of Eleuthera, equipment, boats, and information are available at *Winding Bay Beach Resort* near Rock Sound (344-2020); dive sites include the maze of coral reefs in Six Shilling Channel between Eleuthera and Nassau, a steamship wreck off the northern coast, Egg Island reef northwest of Current, and — are you ready? — a wrecked *train* that went down with a Cuba-bound barge off North Eleuthera. On Harbour Island, the *Romora Bay Club* south of Dunmore Town (phone: 333-2325) is fully equipped for instruction and trips; Valentine's Yacht Club (phone: 333-2142) also boasts a first-rate scuba/snorkeling/fishing setup. In Spanish Wells, *Spanish Wells Beach Resort Club* (phone: 332-2645) provides facilities for its own guests and others. In the Berry Islands, the *Chub Cay Club* (phone: 325-1490) has diving equipment, boats; sites include Mamma Rhoda Rock, Whale Cay reefs, Hoffman Cay, and a mystery wreck with cannon between Little Stirrup and Great Stirrup Cays. On Long Island, *Stella Maris Inn* (phone: 336-2106) features snorkel trips, has a diving center. On Rum Cay, east of Long Island, the *Rum Cay Club* (Fort Lauderdale phone: 305-467-8355) concentrates on undersea sports, particularly scuba, and has complete resort facilities.

Spectator Sports – Cricket, soccer, and rugby are played in season on Haynes Oval near Fort Charlotte in Nassau and on fields in Freeport and throughout the islands. Weekends are the big game times; consult local newspapers for specific schedules and details. At this writing there is no horse racing in the Bahamas.

Sport Fishing – Bahamian waters are great grounds for tuna (Allison, bluefin), barracuda, amberjack, bonefish, marlin (blue and white), dolphin, grouper, kingfish, sailfish, tarpon, wahoo. More than 20 tournaments, including the annual 6-tournament *Bahamas Billfish Championship,* are open to residents and visitors, are scheduled every year. Fishermen out of Bimini alone hold 50 world's records. Hotels and marinas can arrange fishing trips. Rates for parties of two to six — including boat, crew, fuel, bait, and tackle — run from about $200 to $300 for a half day and $350 to $450 for a full day's sport.

Swimming and Sunning – There are hundreds of miles of sandy beach on these 700 islands: from dusty pink to gleaming white; long, shining expanses and small crescent coves — all washed by a sea that is truly, incredibly clear. If you're staying in Nassau, on Cable Beach, on Paradise Island, or in Freeport/Lucaya, chances are your hotel will be built on its own stretch of sand; if not, it will have made arrangements for its guests to use a beach close at hand. On the islands, the beach is either right there or a short stroll away. And many hotels have pools. But that's only the beginning. Whatever your hotel's facilities, there's lots more shore out there waiting when you feel the need for a change of beach scene. Among the most beautiful: Saunders Beach and Love Beach on the north shore, Adelaide and South Beach on the south shore of New Providence (Nassau's island); Paradise Beach on Paradise Island and the *Holiday Inn's* perfect semicircular cove; Taino Beach on Grand Bahama. Treasure Cay's crescent beach on Great Abaco offers good shelling, as does Great Harbour Cay, one of the handsomest beaches in the Bahamas. There's also 2 miles of fine white sand lining the shore at Staniard Creek on Andros; Stocking Island off George Town on Great Exuma (ideal destination for day sailing trips, private picnics); the fantastic length of pink beach on Harbour Island; the miles-long coral sand shore east of Governor's Harbour, Eleuthera; and the whole sandy rim of unspoiled Mayaguana, a virtually undiscovered island south of the Acklins, with no accommodations but the best shelling in the Bahamas.

Tennis – Biggest court layout is at Paradise Island's *Club Med,* with 20 composition courts (8 lighted) plus a full staff of instructors, instant replay TV, ball machines, and all the latest teaching paraphernalia. But tennis is big all over the Bahamas. At last count there were 76 courts (36 lighted) in the Nassau/Paradise area; 58 courts (31 lighted) on Grand Bahama; and a total of 55 courts on the outlying islands (16 with lights). On Cable Beach, the *Nassau Beach* hotel now has 6 lighted courts. The *Holiday Inn, Paradise Towers, Ocean Club,* and *Loew's Harbour Cove* hotel on Paradise Island; the *Divi Bahamas Beach Resort and Country Club* has 4 courts on New Providence; Freeport/Lucaya's *Holiday Inn, Bahamas Princess, Jack Tar Village,* and *Xanadu Beach* hotel also have tennis facilities (*Jack Tar Village* has 16 courts); on the outlying islands, *Treasure Cay* and *Cotton Bay* also have top layouts. Court time is usually free to guests and available to nonguests at a fee of about $2 to $6 an hour, more for night play.

Water Skiing – The best sea sites for it are off Nassau's Cable Beach, Paradise Island, and on the protected waters around Freeport/Lucaya; some of the larger outlying island resorts (*Treasure Cay* and *Club Med,* for example) also have boats and equipment, though most prefer to concentrate on diving; rates run from about $10 up for a 20-minute tow. Nassau/Paradise and Freeport/Lucaya also offer parasailing on a parachute towed behind a speedboat (about $15 to $25 a ride) and spinnaker-flying (riding a trapeze suspended from a wind-filled sail).

Windsurfing – This is becoming popular, especially on Nassau's Cable Beach (site of the Annual Bahamas International Windsurfing Regatta) and on Paradise Island; at Grand Bahama's *Atlantik Beach* hotel and *Jack Tar Village* at West End; in the Abacos at Hope Town, Walker's Cay, Green Turtle Cay, and Treasure Cay; on Harbour Island; Eleuthera; Andros; Pittstown Point on Crooked Island; and *Stella Maris* on Long Island. More and more water-sport centers offer sailboard rentals — 23 at last count.

NIGHTLIFE: Though the islands tend to be quiet after dinner — with maybe a little bar talk or terrace sitting — there's plenty happening on the Nassau/ Paradise Island scene and in Freeport/Lucaya. Nassau/Paradise offers the greatest variety, starting with two casinos — the enormous, late-playing one on Paradise Island and the 20,000-square-foot casino in the *Cable Beach* hotel. In its 1,000-seat theater, a Lido-esque French-format show (lots of sequins, feathers, and flesh) called *Les Fantastiques* takes the stage nightly (admission: about $17 per person). Next door to the Paradise Island Casino, *Le Cabaret* stages big, girly, Vegas-gone-island-type shows (charge: for the show and two drinks, about $23 plus 15% service charge; for the dinner show, about $38 plus service; phone: 326-3000). Also on Paradise, the *Paradise Island Casino*'s *Club Pastiche* and *Le Paon* at the *Sheraton Grand* hotel are the discos to know; the *Trade Winds Lounge* at the *Paradise Towers* has live music for dancing. Out Cable Beach way, one of the liveliest hotel spots is apt to be the *Nassau Beach*'s *Rum Keg* — both loud and crowded with dancers. There are jumping "island" shows (flaming limbos, drums, frenetic dancers) at the *Nassau Beach* hotel on Thursday Junkanoo nights. But wonder-drummer Peanuts Taylor's *Drumbeat Club* on West Bay St. (phone: 322-4233) is more fun and lots more genuinely Bahamian; and run, don't walk, to see a singer called Eloise wherever she's playing — she's a one-woman special event. The *British Colonial*'s *Bayside* and the *Holiday Inn*'s *Pirates Cove* deal in disco; the *Palace* on Elizabeth Street in town rates highly with both international visitors and residents. Later: *Nemo's Harbour Watch* nightclub and bar (overlooking the harbor at Deveaux and Bay sts.), with live band, is open until 4 AM; and the *Pink Pussycat* at Delancy and Augusta streets (don't call, just go right on over) swings like anything.

In Freeport/Lucaya, most night things happen near the *Princess Casino*, where you can play for keeps until 4 AM; a second casino has now opened at the *Lucayan Beach* hotel. The *Casino Soiree* is the big showplace (8 PM dinner show; phone: 352-7811). The *Sultan's Tent* of the *Princess Tower* and *Xanadu Beach* hotel's *Ports of Call* are worth checking out, as is the *Skipper's Lounge* at the *Princess Country Club* for live jazz (no cover charge); the *Holiday Inn*'s *Panache, Studio 69* on Midshipman Rd. in Lucaya, and the *Capricorn Lounge* on Sunrise Highway are also big sound scenes. Island shows play the *Holiday Inn, Castaways,* and *Yellow Bird.*

BEST ON THE ISLANDS

CHECKING IN: After a shakedown and realignment period that yielded substantial improvements in the government properties, the hotel situation in Nassau/Paradise Island and Freeport/Lucaya has improved significantly of late, with many major resorts spending millions of dollars on much-needed renovations and room refurbishment. Meanwhile, established inns on the outlying islands — with their stunning beaches, relaxed sports, genuinely personal service — continue to delight repeat guests.

Most Nassau/Paradise and Freeport/Lucaya hotels quote European Plan (EP) rates (without meals); more resorts on the islands beyond — where there aren't that many places to eat out — include breakfasts and dinners (Modified American Plan, MAP), sometimes all meals (American Plan, AP), in their rates, and most add a 15% service charge, 6% government tax, even an "energy surcharge." Expect to pay $135 and up in winter for a double without meals in a hotel listed here as expensive; between $90 and $120 in moderate; and between $45 and $60 in inexpensive. Some hotels offer MAP add-ons (covering breakfast and dinner) for about $20 to $45 per person a day. Between late April and mid-December, prices in all categories drop by about 30% to 50%.

NASSAU–CABLE BEACH

Royal Bahamian – The former Balmoral Beach Club, this property was recently restored to its old quiet elegance with the feel of a private club, which it once was. With 145 good-size rooms in its 6-story Manor House tower and 25 more in 10 garden-surrounded villas (2 with private pools, sunrooms, wet bars, whirlpools in master suites) that offer both special concierge and butler service. With health spa, big pool terrace, beach with extensive water sports, outdoor café and handsome dining room, cocktail and evening entertainment in season. Like the *Ambassador Beach* and *Cable Beach,* it is operated by Wyndham Hotels (but with a more dignified touch), and guests of all three may use the par-72 *Cable Beach* golf course (phone: 327-7481). Expensive.

Ambassador Beach – Another Wyndham property (along with *Cable Beach* and *Royal Bahamian*), the *Ambassador* has undergone a major refurbishing. The U-shaped 400-room structure has 1,800 feet of white sand beach, pool, 8 tennis courts, and several bars and restaurants. Water sports, including scuba diving and fishing, are available. Across the road from the *Cable Beach* golf course. On Cable Beach (phone: 327-8231). Expensive.

Crystal Palace Hotel – Carnival Cruise Lines' new $100-million, 740-room resort, on the site of the former *Emerald Beach Hotel.* Phase one — 225 suites in an 11-story tower — will accept guests for the first time during the winter of 1988/89; phase two, 4 additional towers, should be ready by the fall of 1989 (phone: 800-222-7466). Expensive.

Graycliff – The very small (10 rooms, one pool cottage, and one deluxe apartment), quietly elegant former home of Lord and Lady Dudley, across from Government House. No sports, but grassy gardens, a small pool, and the atmosphere of a genteel private house. Perfect for the discriminating clientele it attracts; far from the casino and glitter mobs. With one of the island's best restaurants (see *Eating Out*). West Hill St. (phone: 322-2796). Expensive.

Nassau Beach – A newly renovated 425-room fixture in the heart of Cable Beach, the liveliest, most jovial on this shore, with lots of land and water sports, planned activities; happenings day and night, and a deluxe *Palm Club* wing offering all-inclusive vacations. Good choice if you're up for convivial but not overpowering action. A Trusthouse Forte hotel. On Cable Beach (phone: 327-7711). Expensive.

Wyndham Cable Beach Hotel & Casino – The new entrant — in scale and decor (lots of glass, greenery, gilding). A $100-million playground offering 693 air-conditioned, balconied rooms and suites, special concierge floors, 5 restaurants, innumerable bars, plenty of court space (10 for tennis — 5 clay, 5 lighted, 1 stadium — plus 3 squash, 3 racquetball), a recently refurbished championship 18-hole golf course, extensive sands, big freshwater pool, 2 lagoons, and a world of water sports with sails (including para-), skis (towed and jet-powered), snorkeling, scuba, excursions headquartered at the beach pier. Umbilically linked — by a shopping arcade — to an immense late-playing casino-nightclub-theater complex. On Cable Beach (phone: 800-822-4200). Expensive.

Casuarinas – This attractive 76-apartment hotel offers a choice of 1- or 2-bedroom, efficiency, and studio setups right on Cable Beach. Rec room, pools, on site; other sports, activities, arranged by staff. Pool bar; restaurant specializing in Bahamian food. Owner Nettie Symonette was voted one of the top 100 International Businesswomen of 1987 and has trained her staff in the art of personalized service as one of this resort's attractions (phone: 327-7921). Moderate.

Lighthouse Beach – New owners, new management, and new face for the 100-room former *Mayfair* hotel. Downtown, overlooking Nassau Harbor, the beach, and Nassau Lighthouse, with unique rooftop pool. Bay St. (phone: 322-4474). Moderate.

Pilot House – Across from the marina, a great favorite with sailors, people who like informality, but pleasant, personal service. New lobby, small pool, two commendable restaurants (see *Eating Out*); you can also be served in the garden. With 125 comfortable, unremarkable rooms, studios. Off East Bay St. (phone: 322-8431). Moderate.

Sheraton British Colonial – Once the social queen of them all (with the late, lamented Royal Victoria), the pink palace has been refurbished and is back with 350 guestrooms, fresh-faced public rooms, a new disco, *Howard Johnson's* and . . . *McDonald's*. Needless to say, the grand dame has lost much of her charm, but the location — in the heart of Nassau at Number 1 Bay Street — is still prime. Bay St. (phone: 322-3301 or 800-334-8484). Moderate.

Corona – A new, small addition to the Nassau scene, this family-run inn has 21 air-conditioned rooms with balconies and a restaurant with nightly entertainment. TV available. Bay St. (phone: 326-6815). Moderate to inexpensive.

Towne – Simple, in town, personably managed. Friendly, but no frills; favorite for short stays, business travelers. Small swimming pool; restaurant serves island specialties. 46 rooms. George St. (phone: 322-8450). Moderate to inexpensive.

PARADISE ISLAND

Ocean Club – Built in the 1930s as a private home (2 colonnaded stories around a pink patio), bought by millionaire Huntington Hartford in the 1950s, who converted it to an exclusive club, and owned since the 1960s by Resorts International, the *Ocean Club* is certainly the handsomest place in Paradise — or Nassau, for that matter. Secluded, with a backdrop of the Versailles Gardens that Hartford built, it has 71 balconied rooms, all (except for the 12 simple tennis cabanas) with fans, air conditioning, color TV, and fridge; the 5 private villas have Jacuzzis and enclosed patios. Beautiful big pool, 9 tennis courts, beach, golf nearby. Total, quiet luxury with a recent upgrading. Lovely galleried dining courtyard with pond and fountain (phone: 326-2501). Expensive.

Paradise Island Resort and Casino – *Brittannia Towers, Paradise Towers,* and the *Paradise Island Casino* comprise the most extensive resort in the Bahamas, with a total of 1,100 guestrooms and suites. Facilities include 2 health clubs, shopping arcade, 2 pools, 12 tennis courts, and 3 miles on Cabbage Beach. Guests have their choice of 14 restaurants and lounges. The *Paradise Club* (not to be confused with the *Club Paradise*) offers VIP concierge floors that have separate check-in, concierge services, separate elevators with passkeys, and a hospitality lounge. The casino was expanded by 30,000 feet in early 1987 and is now the largest gaming facility in the world. The *Club Paradise,* a new, all-inclusive luxury wing on the beach, has 150 rooms: All facilities, including sports and meals, are included in the price (phone: 800-321-3000; in Miami, 305-895-2922; in Fort Lauderdale, 305-462-1370). Expensive.

Sheraton Grand – A multimillion-dollar renovation program begun in 1986 has resulted in a truly luxurious hotel deserving of the name *Grand.* The 360 rooms of the former *Grand* hotel have been refurbished, each with a refrigerator, satellite TV, and direct-dial phone. Two VIP Grand Tier floors offer use of a special lounge which serves complimentary continental breakfast, wine and cheese in the afternoon, and evening cocktails. There are 12 oceanfront suites and a spectacular array of beach and water sports activities. *Julie's,* a four-star country French specialty restaurant, and *Le Paon* disco both require chic dress. Other features include tennis, pool with waterfall, and a shopping arcade (phone: 800-325-3535). Expensive.

Club Land'Or – Set in a quiet cove on a lagoon opposite *Brittania Towers,* this small and charming resort has 71 one-bedroom villas with fully equipped kitchens and private patios or balconies. Facilities include a swimming pool, lovely courtyard, excellent *Blue Lagoon* restaurant (some of the best seafood on the island), and the *Oasis Bar* with piano entertainment. The emphasis is on attentive and personalized service, with an extensive daily activities program. Another 50 units are to be added sometime in 1988 (phone: 809-326-2400). Expensive to moderate.

Loews Harbour Cove – Breezy 250-room high-rise overlooking the channel with smallish manmade beach, pool, first-rate tennis courts. Altogether pleasant, nicely decorated. It's too bad that the place isn't on a natural beach, but guests can sunbathe on a small manmade beach. Continental breakfast included for all guests; attractively priced MAP add-on includes Tuesday show and Bahamas buffet, Saturday steak night (phone: 326-2561). Expensive to moderate.

Bay View Village – A beautiful, lushly landscaped resort with privacy its primary attraction, it offers 43 rental units in either villa, townhouse, apartment, or penthouse configurations, all with complete kitchens, private balconies, and patios or garden terraces. Other features include 3 swimming pools, tennis court, daily maid service, and an extremely charming staff. Five minutes' walk to beaches, casino, and other attractions (phone: 809-326-2555 or 326-2336). Moderate.

Club Med – Recently refurbished, this *Club Med* has the familiar theme and camaraderie, but with emphasis on tennis (20 courts, teaching staff, TV playback). Plus all the usual *Club Med* pursuits — from morning yoga to late-night disco. Families are welcome; a Mini Club for children, with supervised activities, gives parents a rest. All double accommodations (300 rooms) with unusual number of double beds available. Some singles at extra charge. Weekly rates cover all activities, including tennis instruction, all meals, house wine to match (phone: 322-7641). Moderate.

Holiday Inn – Don't even think of associating this resort with most of its roadside American counterparts. With 535 refurbished rooms and a multi-million-dollar renovation, this high-rise rates a luxury label. Features include a setting on Pirate's Cove, a beautiful lagoon with a fine beach, huge free-form swiming pool, theme poolside buffets, tennis courts, a shopping arcade, and a host of water sports and guest activities (phone: 809-326-2100 or 800-HOLIDAY). Moderate.

Paradise/Paradise – This informal, 100-room, low-rise hotel is on the beach for which the island was named. Totally renovated and refurnished from lobby to balconied rooms, it has a pavilion restaurant, cocktail lounge. Very inclusive rates (covering Continental breakfast, sailing, snorkeling, windsurfing, water skiing, day and night tennis, aerobics, volleyball, activity program, and casino transport) make it a noteworthy Paradise buy (phone: 326-2541). Moderate.

Villas in Paradise – Luxury resort accommodations in 25 one- and two-bedroom apartments and one- to four-bedroom villas, 15 of which feature private swimming pools in enclosed patios. All units have fully equipped kitchens and two full baths. Complimentary rental car for three days is included with a seven-night stay (phone: 809-326-2998). Moderate.

WESTERN NEW PROVIDENCE ISLAND

Divi Bahamas Beach Resort & Country Club – Formerly the *South Ocean Beach Hotel*. Facilities include 120 refurbished rooms, the elegant *Papagayo* restaurant, the *Peter Hughes* dive shop and water-sports center, and an 18-hole Joe Lee golf course with resident pro and complete pro shop (phone: 800-367-3484 or 607-277-3484). Moderate.

GRAND BAHAMA

Eastern Grand Bahama, Deep Water Cay – This small (16-guest), exclusive lodge attracted celebrities and keen sportfishermen before fire destroyed it. Now rebuilt, it offers 2 luxury cottages, a private airstrip, and superb bonefishing (phone: 305-684-3958). Expensive.

Xanadu Beach & Marina – The newly reopened hotel that once served as the residence of the late billionaire Howard Hughes. After a multimillion-dollar renovation, this smaller, more exclusive resort now has 175 luxury rooms, 3 two-story villas, suites, adjoining mile-long beach, pool, 3 lighted tennis courts, a dock for large yachts, 3 restaurants, a disco, and good service (phone: 352-6782). Expensive.

Bahamas Princess – Two *big* hotels (565 and 400 rooms) on 2,500 acres with grand public spaces, essentially group-oriented approach to resort life, now partnered with a casino that's been given a $9-million facelift. Within strolling distance of the Bazaar, the Towers adjoins the *Princess Casino* and is more gambling-oriented; the *Bahamas Princess Country Club,* across the road, is for the sporting set, with two 18-hole PGA championship golf courses, 6 tennis courts, a pool, jogging trail, and transportation to the *Princess Beach Club.* Guests at both have access to water sports and the seaside restaurant at the *Beach Club,* on the ocean. Intimate island atmosphere is not their strong suit; but they do share extensive sport facilities, 9 restaurants, 6 bars, 2 nightclubs, and casino showroom. Low-priced packages — especially off-season — are available (phone: 352-6721, 352-9661). Expensive to moderate.

Holiday Inn – Now undergoing a $16-million top-to-bottom renovation, this expansive (614-room) hotel on the beach has lots going on, lots of group movement, something happening most nights. It's a good family resort, with playground and activities for children. Full complement of land and water sports, including tennis and scuba (phone: 800-HOLIDAY). Expensive to moderate.

Lucayan Beach – This 247-room resort rests on 1½ miles of white sand beach, with a huge casino on the beach, 5 restaurants, and the *Flamingo Showcase Theatre,* a spectacular Las Vegas–style cabaret. The Underwater Explorers Society dive shop and water-sports center offers guests a full range of aquatic activities. Two styles of accommodation: regular hotel rooms in the main *Lucayan Beach Resort;* or more elegant (and more pricey) rooms at the *Club Lucaya* wing, each with private access to the beach from a waterfront balcony (phone: 800-331-2538 or 800-772-1227). Expensive to moderate.

New Atlantik Beach – A $5-million renovation did wonders for this Swiss International property, next door to the *Lucayan Beach.* With the *Lucaya Golf and Country Club,* this beachfront resort has a new shopping arcade, two additional floors of its exclusive *Corona Classic Club,* 175 upgraded guestrooms, and new beach club and cabanas. Its 42 suites, all with a fresh look, have kitchens, TVs, phones, and mini-bars. Facilities include a PGA-rated 18-hole golf course, 8 tennis courts, a new beach club on a fine beach, and most water sports, including boardsailing school (phone: 809-373-1444; in US, 800-622-6770). Expensive to moderate.

Jack Tar Village, West End – A sprawling, 2000-acre playground with the largest swimming pool in the Bahamas, 27-hole golf course, 10 tennis courts, 100-slip yacht marina, and all water sports, including full scuba program through UNEXSO. This all-inclusive resort has 424 air-conditioned rooms, and week-long or weekend packages include everything from drinks and meals to tips. No casino. 32 miles from Freeport (809 346-6211 or 800 527-9299). Moderate.

Lucayan Marina – The official Bahamas port of entry and the other half of the *Lucayan Beach* complex, on Lucayan Bay. It offers 148 rooms; a 150-slip, full-service marina; commissary and restaurant; pool; and free ferry service to the *Lucayan Beach* hotel (phone: 800-772-1227). Inexpensive.

THE ABACOS

Treasure Cay Beach, Great Abaco – The casual life with a touch of country-club class and a plethora of oceangoing activities, from extravagant sightseeing boats to scuba and sportfishing. The main clubhouse serves as a focal point for resort, land development operation. An 18-hole championship golf course, 6 tennis courts, 4 pools, superb 3-mile beach with beautiful swimming, picnicking, shelling, when tide's right. Full-service marina with excursions, deep-sea and bonefishing, and scuba diving. Total of 190 resort rooms, garden villas, housekeeping apartments. New Treasure Islands Club all-inclusive vacations feature bargain packages ideal for those addicted to water sports and the outdoors (phone: 800-327-1584; in Florida, 800-432-8257). Expensive.

Walker's Cay Club, Walker's Cay – All the comforts (smartly done rooms, restaurant, bar) in palm-fringed setting with two pools, fine shelling, swimming beach, 75-slip marina. All kinds of fishing possibilities — deep-sea, reef, bone, with native guides — plus scuba (certified instruction, choice dive sites). Populated year-round by an eclectic cast of serious sportfishing pros and those chasing world-record billfish. The hotel offers 34 double rooms, 5 cottages. Packages include airfare from Fort Lauderdale. (Fort Lauderdale phone: 305-522-1469). Expensive to moderate.

Abaco Inn, Elbow Cay – A small gem, ensconced between the Atlantic on one side and the calm blue sound on the other — which means lazy swimming and al fresco dining on either of two terraces, no matter which way the wind is blowing. With 10 rooms, a unique swimming pool shaped into the shore by the ocean; first-rate diving, fishing, surfing, and windsurfing. The restaurant is one of the best in the Bahamas. This inn is special (phone: 367-2666). Moderate.

Bluff House, Green Turtle Cay – Perched on a hilltop with a picture-postcard view of New Plymouth. There's a marina, beach, tennis, saltwater pool; sailing, snorkeling, fishing, exploring, loafing, are favorite sports. Under new ownership in 1988, with 26 rooms and villas (phone: Green Turtle Cay 5211). Moderate.

Conch Inn, Great Abaco – A favorite with scuba divers and yachtsmen, this inn-marina enclave is full of cheerful charm and affable boating people. Rooms that don't look like much from the land side are fresh and pretty inside, each with harbor-viewing balcony and air conditioning. Minuscule pool is scene of large water polo action; fishing, boating, beaching, easily arranged. Coffee shop does breakfasts, fine chowder, fritters, fish, burgers. Small, handsome restaurant has been slipping lately (phone: 367-2800). Moderate.

Green Turtle Club, Green Turtle Cay – One of Abaco's most charming island enclaves, with its own marina, is a center for all sorts of waterborne activity (power- and sailboating, fishing, skiing); scuba equipment too. Choice of three beaches, pool. With 31 rooms, some in cottages with own boat slips. Sociable evenings created by the friendly management (phone: 367-2572). Moderate.

Hope Town Harbour Lodge, Elbow Cay – Former island commissioner's home is the nucleus of this relaxed resort, with its own dock on one side and beach on the other, right in the heart of Hope Town. Sailing, scuba, snorkeling, water skiing, deep-sea fishing, are daily possibilities. Next to the swimming pool is a friendly bar that does informal lunches, a traditional meeting spot for locals in this friendly little town. With 21 rooms, some cottages (phone: 367-2277). Moderate.

New Plymouth Inn, Green Turtle Cay – This charming in-town choice is in New Plymouth's most elegant old residence, beautifully maintained, with high-ceilinged, cozy rooms out of another century. Friendly American management (phone: 367-5211). Moderate.

Elbow Cay Club, Elbow Cay – Appealing to families, boaters, and fishermen, this informal, Danish-operated property of only 27 units is spread over a large expanse. Don't try to move the furniture — it's a continuation of the wall or floor. It's the only place on the island that does a regular jump-up a couple of nights a week, and the whole island turns up. Sailing, windsurfing, fishing, snorkeling, scuba diving (phone: 367-2748). Moderate to inexpensive.

Guana Beach, Great Guana Cay – A suitably unpretentious island inn for those who *really* want to get away from it all; with a small marina at the front and a superb beach at the back of the property. Guana is bound to be discovered by developers soon: the small island is completely ringed with gorgeous, deserted beaches. Friendly bar and extremely informal restaurant. PO Box 474, Marsh Harbour, Abaco, Bahamas (phone: 367-2546). Moderate to inexpensive.

Great Abaco Beach and Boat Harbour Marina, Marsh Harbour – One of Abaco's charming spots, now under new ownership, completely renovated and refurbished. There are now 10 standard and 10 deluxe rooms, and 5 luxury villas, all overlooking the water. The hotel adjoins the *Sand Bar,* a new 140-slip marina and pool complex. Complete marina services and pleasant staff have already won enthusiastic regulars. An excellent scuba program is offered through the legendary Captain Skeet LaChance's *Dive Abaco.* There are also good restaurants and lots of camaraderie (phone: 809-367-2736). Inexpensive to moderate.

ANDROS ISLAND

Andros Beach – Recently upgraded by new management, this 20-room inn attracts divers with its *Andros Undersea Adventures Dive Shop.* There's also a lovely beach, a pool, beachside bar, and lush gardens for strolling. Nicholl's Town (phone: 329-2011). Moderate.

Las Palmas – Small sporty resort with 20 air-conditioned rooms and a private beach and pool. Masks, snorkels, fins, free to guests; divers need own gear, but there's a compressor on the premises. Free putting green, driving range; sailboats, outboard rentals; new disco. Congo Town (phone: 329-4661). Moderate.

Small Hope Bay Lodge – Dedicated divers' and discriminating travelers' resort with 20 rooms on palm-lined beach. Daily diving trips to the reef one mile offshore; underwater photography, seminars. Snorkeling, fishing, beach-based hot tub, too. Very informal; management has been known to scissor off neckties on sight. Great relaxed fun, nice people, extended-family atmosphere. The origins of that fabulous, colorful line of Androsia batik fashions are here; ask about the factory. Fresh Creek (Nassau phone: 328-2014). Moderate.

THE BERRY ISLANDS

Chub Cay Club – Condominiums clustered around complete marina; life focuses on deep-sea and bone fishing, diving, boating. Only 12 rooms are open for public rental; restaurant, tennis courts, and villas are limited to members. Small commissary on premises. Excellent diving facilities. On Chub Cay (Nassau phone: 325-1490). Expensive to moderate.

THE BIMINIS

Bimini Big Game Fishing Club – Exactly what its name says. Simple, friendly, with marina admirably set up to arrange deep-sea and bone fishing charters. There's a pool, tennis court, and a pair of bars that tend to liven up when the boats come in. With 50 rooms, owned and comfortably run by the Bacardi rum people. Alice Town, North Bimini (phone: 347-2391). Moderate.

Blue Water Marina/Anchorage, North Bimini – Small, simple 12-room inn overlooking the sea, up the hill from the marina. Home of several fishing tournaments each season, but open to non-anglers, too. Good restaurant and friendly bar (phone: 809-347-2291). Moderate.

Compleat Angler, Alice Town, North Bimini – Ossie Brown's decades-old hotel is one of the funkiest places in all of the Bahamas. Hemingway used to hang out here, and it still attracts an extraordinary cast of characters. Great people-watching at the bar and in the lobby. Bar walls are lined with hundreds of photos, forming a chronology of Bimini's fishing tournament history. The *Compleat An-*

gler is not for everyone — there are only 12 plain, noisy rooms — but it's worth seeing (phone: 809-347-2122). Inexpensive.

CAT ISLAND

Cutlass Bay Yacht Club – Small resort (14 rooms) with lots of sports possibilities: superfine beaching, diving, snorkeling, bonefishing, sailing, biking, spelunking in Indian caves, mountain (well, sort of) climbing to visit the ruins of Father Jerome's Hermitage atop Mt. Alvernia (206 feet). Pleasant lobby lounge with sloop-hull bar; good food. Near New Bight (phone: Cutlass Bay). Moderate.

Fernandez Bay Village – A lovely, lazy group of 6 cottages, sized to sleep two to eight people, each individually and appealingly decorated and endowed with all the housekeeping essentials, including maid and laundry service; small grocery on property. Right on a beauty of a beach ideal for swimming, sunning, beachcombing, snorkeling; fishing, small-boat sailing, windsurfing too. (Fort Lauderdale phone: 305-764-6945.) Moderate.

ELEUTHERA

Cotton Bay – One of this island's most luxurious resorts, once the private playground of Juan Trippe, Henry Luce, and their friends (some of whom still turn up from time to time). The new owners plan to expand to 100 rooms and refurbish existing ones to recapture its former reputation. There's great golf (an 18-hole Robert Trent Jones course), terrific tennis (6 courts), water sports, fine fishing from nearby marina, 2 miles of gleaming white sand beach, and an air of deep-seated well-being. Good-looking clubhouse with small pool, inviting dining room. There are now 77 rooms in clubhouse and beachside cottages. Near Rock Sound (phone: 800-225-4255 or 212-696-4566). Expensive.

Windermere Island Club – Discreetly luxurious, beautifully cared for islet reached by bridge, where the seclusion-seeking rich and famous (Prince Charles and Princess Di, for example) find a lifestyle to their liking, spending their days playing tennis, boating, water skiing, snorkeling, or sunning on the private beach or beside the pool. With 21 handsome rooms, 10 suites, 7 cottages, 10 apartments; clubhouse with lounge, bar, dining room (ties and jackets at night), occasional entertainment. It's 18 miles from Rock Sound Airport (phone: 332-2566). Expensive.

Winding Bay Beach – Lining a strip of pink sand beside what was once Arthur Vining Davis's beach house, with fishing, diving facilities; small sailboats, snorkel gear for rent. Two lighted tennis courts, *Cotton Bay* golf privileges. Presently has 36 rooms in good-looking natural stone cottages, all with patios, but recently began construction of 250 additional rooms. Near Rock Sound (phone: 334-2020). Expensive.

Oleander Gardens – A cluster of breezy vacation villas sheltering 16 good-looking, good-sized guestrooms and apartments with kitchenettes overlooking the water and a private beach. With terraced central clubhouse for drinks, meals, gathering. Choice of water sports, some informal nighttime entertainment. Near Gregory Town (phone: 333-2058). Moderate.

HARBOUR ISLAND, OFF NORTH ELEUTHERA

Romora Bay Club – This lovely inn has a total of 32 rooms in the cottages and main house. Once a private home, it overlooks terraced flower gardens and a small cove. Main-house dinners are an occasion (book a table early, even if you're a hotel guest). Diving and other water sports are very popular. There are scuba (including instruction) and snorkel trips daily, tennis courts, a hot tub, a big beach a few minutes' stroll away, and a coveside pavilion for lunch buffets, sunset gatherings, and informal nighttime entertainment (phone: 333-2325). Expensive.

Coral Sands – Congenial 33-room complex overlooking the beach, where most guests spend their days. Water sports, free snorkeling, sailing, tennis (charge only for lighting). Known for its good home-style food, good wine, its inviting atmosphere, and informal and entertaining evenings, especially Fridays (phone: 333-2320, 333-2350). Expensive to moderate.

Pink Sands – Family resort at the edge of the island's incredibly beautiful pink (honest) sand beach. Nice sense of privacy in 49 cottage rooms; maids cook breakfast in individual kitchenettes. Three tennis courts, boating; fishing arranged with local skippers. Dining room, bar (phone: 333-2030). Expensive to moderate.

Runaway Hill Club – An intimate Bahamian-style inn overlooking a hillside pool and lovely wide beach. Only 8 rooms (the 5 in the main house are best), tastefully (if simply) decorated, with terra cotta floors, white wicker, and *Casablanca*-style ceiling fans. Good restaurant (reserve), and a Calypso group on Tuesdays (phone: 333-2150). Expensive to moderate.

Valentine's Yacht Club – A small 21-room inn on the sound with its own pool, with a following of fishing, diving, and yachting folk. Sailing, snorkeling, diving; bone, bottom, or reef fishing arrangements. New small spa, gym, exercise programs (including yoga), hot tub. Informal, but a thoughtful management and staff always ready to help. Dunmore Town (phone: 333-2142). Moderate.

THE EXUMAS

Out Island Inn Village – Handsome native stone main building and cottages along a seagrape-lined beach. The 80 air-conditioned rooms all have a patio or balcony. With water sport equipment at the ready: sailboats, outboards, water-ski boats; snorkeling, deep-sea and guided bone fishing trips arranged. Two tennis courts; free transport to Stocking Island. Great inclusive packages available. Seaside dining room, entertainment some evenings. About 5 minutes' walk from George Town (phone: 336-2171). Expensive to moderate.

Peace and Plenty – Classic island hostelry with 32 air-conditioned rooms and an informal guesthouse atmosphere, agreeable staff. Virtually in town, with small swimming pool overlooking the harbor. Ferry service to beach club with bar and snack service on beautiful Stocking Island, just across the water. Fishing, sailing, snorkeling arranged. Some evening entertainment. Bar is local meeting and greeting place. George Town (phone: 336-2551). Moderate.

Sand Dollar – Small island inn overlooking a pair of beautiful, white sand, crescent beaches. With cheery rooms, bar, restaurant. On Little Exuma not far from George Town (phone: 336-2192). Moderate.

SAN SALVADOR

Riding Rock Inn – Finally renovated and reopened, this long-time favorite haunt of scuba buffs has 24 rooms, a pool, tennis, and 4 villas available for rent. Excellent dive facility, complete with photo lab and instruction. Good vacation packages with airfare included from Fort Lauderdale (phone: 800-272-1492; in Florida, 305-761-1492). Moderate.

LONG ISLAND

Stella Maris Inn – Rambling cottage resort with 50 air-conditioned rooms in apartments, cottages, villas. Extensive diving facilities, program, including instruction, day and night dives, island day and overnight cruises. Compressors and training tank on premises. Also sailing, fishing, snorkeling, windsurfing, water skiing. Three swimming pools, 2 tennis courts. Informal night patio, pool, beach, and cave parties. Stella Maris (phone: 336-2106). Moderate.

RUM CAY

Rum Cay Club – The island's only resort is designed for dedicated divers and snorkelers but hopes to extend its appeal to yachtspeople, private plane flyers, anglers, and hideaway seekers in general. Besides authorized PADI instruction and certification, the club now offers deep-sea and sandy-flat fishing programs, hiking, underwater photography, and private charter service from Fort Lauderdale. There are 17 rooms in a modern clubhouse on a limestone bluff above the sea. Onshore options include a sun deck, hot tub, choice of beaches to comb, bar/lounge with a view, restaurant, night movies, and slide shows. Week-long packages are available. (Fort Lauderdale phone: 305-467-8355.) Expensive.

EATING OUT: Meals in the larger Nassau/Paradise and Freeport/Lucaya hotels tend to be expensive and unimaginative, with too many "turf and surf" specials that never do justice to either the filet mignon or the lobster tail involved. When it comes to good restaurants, the Freeport/Lucaya choice is limited. Nassau does somewhat better, with several places where first-rate chefs use their Continental skills to make the most of fresh local fish and seafood (except for chicken, most meat is imported frozen). There are also some tasty Bahamian places where prices — while not cheap — tend to be somewhat gentler, and the food, home-cooked and good. Favorite island dishes include lots of conch (pronounced "konk") served as "salad" (*ceviche*), fritters, chowder, and "cracked" (that is, pounded thin and deep-fried); baked Bahamian crab; broiled or boiled grouper (the latter a favorite Bahamian breakfast, really a nicely spiced fish stew); and — of course — peas (really beans) and rice. On the outlying islands especially, most bread is locally baked — fresh, crusty, and delicious. Sweet, fresh Eleutheran pineapple turns up lots as a breakfast starter or a dessert. And rum, in just about any form, is the favorite local drink. Expect to pay $60 or more for a meal for two at the restaurants we have listed in the expensive category; $30 to $60 in moderate restaurants; and under $30 in those restaurants considered inexpensive. A three-night Dine-Around Plan, with a choice of restaurants, is about $85 per person at Cable Beach hotels, about $100 at Paradise Island restaurants; it's very good if you want to eat around, as you usually enjoy unrestricted choices from any menu. Prices do not include wine, drinks, or tip.

NASSAU

Beef Cellar – Small, cozy, with a limited menu: appetizer, soups, dessert, and filet mignon — which you broil just the way you like it on a brazier at your table. In the *Nassau Beach* hotel (phone: 327-7711). Expensive.

Buena Vista – In a rambling house built in the early 1800s, one of the pleasantest all-around eating experiences in Nassau. Soothing atmosphere, deft service, excellent food. A number of great grouper recipes (en coquille, au gratin, or Bonne Femme, baked in white wine sauce, or Bahamian style), delicate veal Buena Vista; incredible cold soufflé desserts. Prettiest in warm weather, when tables are set in the garden. Dinner only; reservations essential. Delancy St. (phone: 322-2811). Expensive.

Graycliff – Leisurely Continental and Bahamian lunches and dinners served with true English elegance in the house that was once the home of the earl of Dudley. Menu includes perfectly steamed fresh lobster, elegant grilled grouper with white truffles, tender nodino vitello (a special cut of veal rarely found outside Italy), luscious chocolate mousse, lots more. Cocktails are served in the antique-filled drawing room; service is perfect, the wine list is notable, and the ambience unforgettable. Reservations required. West Hill St. opposite Government House (phone: 322-2796). Expensive.

Sun And . . . – Indoor-outdoor dining around a fountain-centered patio or in a wood-paneled main dining room, depending on the weather — glinting crystal, silver, candlelight. The romantic atmosphere is a big draw — book well in advance. The conch chowder is memorable, and you might follow it with a poached grouper soufflé, veal piccata, or roast rack of lamb. Dinner only; closed Mondays. Reservations requested. Lakeview Ave. — take a taxi so you won't miss the turn (phone: 323-1205). Expensive.

Pilot House – Two very pleasant restaurants have come from recent renovations: the toney *La Regatta* (lobster thermidor, rack of lamb, Chateaubriand, seafood Regatta — a melding of grouper and shrimp), and the *Three Ladies,* featuring island specialties (conch curry, steamed turtle, baked, stuffed grouper poached in white wine). Or, if you can't make up your mind, take a table Under the Dilly Tree in the garden, and order from there. Bahamian buffet with live music Thursday nights and Sundays at noon (phone: 322-8431). Expensive to moderate.

Bridge Inn – Thanks to great Bahamian fish dishes, what started as a small friendly island restaurant is now a big friendly one. Good chowder, conch, and grouper plus other Bahamian, American, and European choices. A 4 to 6 PM happy hour (two drinks for the price of one) and Early Bird Special (complete dinner, about $13). Music for dancing later. Cordial atmosphere all the time. Lunch and dinner reservations advised. East Bay St. at the foot of the Paradise Island Bridge (phone: 323-2077). Moderate.

Charley Charley's – A sort of Bahamian brauhaus, with Bahamian as well as German cuisine: everything from conch to wienerschnitzel. Try the apple schnapps for an unusual after-dinner drink. Dinner only, from 5 PM till 3 AM. Closed Sundays. Augusta and Delancy sts. (phone: 322-2425). Moderate.

Casuarinas' Round House – Part of a small apartment complex out Cable Beach way, where Nettie Symonette does delicious things with old Bahamian recipes — naturally, and especially, fresh fish and seafood. Reasonably priced *table d'hôte* dinners. West Bay St. (phone: 327-7921/2). Moderate to inexpensive.

Green Shutters – Longtime Nassau favorite — especially at lunchtime and especially with Her Majesty's subjects. Friendly English pub feeling, some traditional British food (bangers and mash, steak and kidney pie, shepherd's pie, roast beef and Yorkshire pudding), Bahamian fish and seafood, lots of imported beer on tap. More crowded for cocktails than for dinner. Wednesdays you'll catch "Wide World of Darts," but any day is good game. 48 Parliament St. (phone: 325-5702). Moderate to inexpensive.

Parliament Terrace Café – Continental and Bahamian specialties served in an indoor/outdoor garden complete with tropical birds (wear a jacket during the winter). Calypso singer most evenings. Conch chowder, turtle pie, and various curry dishes are specialties. Free salad bar; oversized exotic drinks. Lunch from 11:30 AM to 4 PM; dinner from 6 to 10:30 PM. 18 Parliament St. (phone: 322-2836). Moderate to inexpensive.

Mai Tai – For Chinese/Polynesian fare in pleasant surroundings overlooking gardens bordering a lake. Lunch to 3 PM, dinner till midnight. Waterloo Lodge, East Bay St. (phone: 326-5088, 323-3106). Moderate to inexpensive.

Roselawn Café – Italian specialties with live entertainment evenings from 6:30 till late. Open for lunch from 11:30 AM to 2:30 PM. On Bank Lane just off Bay St. (phone: 325-1018). Moderate to inexpensive.

Tony Roma's – Tender, meaty baby back ribs, crispy loaves of onion rings, and barbecued chicken are the standard fare at this island outpost of the famous chain. West Bay St. (phone: 325-6502). Moderate to inexpensive.

Traveller's Rest – Fine Bahamian dishes, great drinks, good Sunday jump-up with music. On Western Road 10 miles from Nassau. Closed Wednesdays (phone: 327-7633). Moderate to inexpensive.

Bayside Buffet – At the *Sheraton British Colonial,* on the water, it's the best dining value in Nassau for lunch or dinner if you crave buffet-style extravaganzas — and this one is quality (phone: 322-7479). Inexpensive.

Poop Deck – Bahamian favorites like cracked conch and grouper share the menu with steak and spaghetti. Sandwiches served at lunch. Informal, with a fine marina view, a popular hangout for boating people. Nassau Yacht Haven on East Bay St. (phone: 322-8175). Inexpensive.

PARADISE ISLAND

Boathouse – Overlooking Paradise Lagoon, features steaks sizzled to your taste on tableside grills; seafood too (phone: 326-3000). Expensive.

Café Martinique – Gilded dining in an intimate setting rare on Paradise, a former home surrounded by greenery and water views. Continental menu is usually skillfully done. Service can vary from excellent to exasperating. But if you're lucky, dinner here can be elegantly rewarding (phone: 326-3000). Expensive.

Julie's – Nicely nostalgic, intimate (85 seats), with an elegant, if not dazzlingly different, menu. Choices: pâté of duckling, fettuccine al pesto, caviar and vodka appetizers; main course medallions of veal and scampi, raspberry duckling, Bahamian lobster with herb butter; flaming desserts. Reservations essential. In the *Grand Hotel* (phone: 323-8011). Expensive.

Ocean Club – One of the prettiest restaurants in the Nassau area, the *Courtyard Terrace* features al fresco dining framed by swaying palms in a galleried courtyard with a fountain. Chefs are Swiss and Irish; service is sometimes slow, but the setting is worth the often only average cuisine (phone: 326-2501). Expensive.

Villa d'Este – Another of the luxe restaurants appended to the *Britannia Beach* complex. Decor is unconvincing mock Mediterranean, but menu is Italian with some tasty pasta dishes and plenty of veal — a good place to get away from grouper if you've been here awhile (phone: 326-3000). Expensive.

Coyaba – Best of the casino restaurants, with Trader Vic look-alike setting and excellent Polynesian food. Reservations are a good idea. In Bird Cage Walk between the casino and *Britannia Beach* hotel (phone: 326-3000). Expensive to moderate.

FREEPORT/LUCAYA

Crown Room – Best bet for pre-casino show at the *Princess.* Standard fare, while well prepared and efficiently served, offers no surprises or spices. Princess Casino (phone: 352-9661). Expensive.

Lucayan Country Club – Away from the hotel bustle, popular with residents for its country club ambience. Menu, in the international Freeport tradition, offers standard fare at top prices. Albacore St. off Sgt. Major Dr. (phone: 373-1066). Expensive.

Rib Room – Snug but unsurprising hideaway that goes the escargots, prime rib, surf 'n' turf, cherries Jubilee route — all well done and well served. In the *Princess Country Club* (phone: 352-6721). Expensive.

Troubadour Room – Residents rate its food, service, and ambience well above average. Specialties: escalope de veau with chanterelles, grilled breast of chicken with white grapes and bacon. In the *Holiday Inn* (phone: 373-1333). Expensive.

Captain's Charthouse – All kinds of steaks (sirloin, teriyaki, New York strip), prime ribs, lobster and shrimp in season. Polynesian-rustic decor, music for dancing. Closed Sundays. Sunrise Hwy. at Beachway (phone: 373-3900). Expensive to moderate.

Guanahani's – Garden and waterfall view, soothing music for a welcome change, if not very exciting fare. Start with deep-fried grouper fingers; then try Bahamian lobster and fish pot or ribs and chicken; chocolate-fruit fondue for dessert. In the *Princess Country Club* (phone: 352-6721). Expensive to moderate.

Stoned Crab – Breezy beachside restaurant on the ocean. With the freshest fish and seafood, steaks broiled over hickory charcoal. Very good drinks. Reservations suggested. On Taino Beach (phone: 373-1442). Expensive to moderate.

Buccaneer Club – Swiss-run restaurant beloved by the crême of Freeport, serving European versions of Bahamian dishes: okra soup, lobster bisque, conch fritters, broiled lobster, wienerschnitzel. Lovely beachside setting well worth the drive to Deadman's Reef. Open from 5 PM for dinner only, although frequent beach parties are arranged. Closed Mondays (no phone). Moderate.

Harry's American Bar – Island drinks, lingering lunches on the seaside terrace (conch chowder, fritters, fish 'n' chips, burgers); seafood, ribs, and chicken dinners by Nassau-born hosts (the only real Harry is in Venice). Setting and happy atmosphere are worth the trip to Deadman's Reef, about half an hour from Freeport. Closed Tuesdays (no phone). Moderate.

Marcella's – Pasta, pizzas, the works, at reasonable prices. The Mall at Kipling Lane (phone: 352-5085). Moderate.

Black Beard's – Cheerful, rustic spot serving seafood, fresh fish, chicken, ribs; burgers and sandwiches for lunch. On Fortune Beach (phone: 373-2960). Inexpensive.

Fat Man's – Large proprietor, small restaurant, where tourists and locals dine out Bahamian style on conch specialties, chicken and pork dishes, local lobster. At Pinder's Point (phone: 352-2931). Inexpensive.

Freddy's Place – Highly commended by savvy Bahamians. All kinds of conch (salad, chowder, cracked, or steamed), grouper, local lobster (the seafood platter samples all three); plus steak, daily island specials (pea soup and dumplings, short ribs, souse). At Hunters Village (phone: 352-3250). Inexpensive.

New Peace & Plenty – Homey, family-run spot is worth the pilgrimage for lunch or dinner. Helda Williams's conch fritters may be the best and lightest in this or any world; more conch in salad, chowder, or cracked; lobster tails, grouper, tangy ribs too. Eight Mile Rock (phone: 348-2206). Inexpensive.

Pub on the Mall – As much for fun as for food. British fare includes fish and chips, steak and kidney pie, Bass ale on tap. Low-priced lunch and dinner specials. Mall at Ranfurly Circus (phone: 352-5110). Inexpensive.

Scorpio's – Authentic Bahamian food — cracked conch, spicy conch salad, turtle steaks, daily specials. Normally only lunch, but call if you're interested in dinner. Explorer's Way, downtown (phone: 352-6969). Inexpensive.

Other inexpensive eateries include *Basil's* and *The Village Gate* on Queen's Highway for Bahamian food and several somewhat successful places among the narrow passageways of the International Bazaar. The *Japanese Steak House* and *China Palace* are truly ethnic, while *Le Rendezvous* serves French specialties such as le hamburger and (alas) French fries and ice cream cones; *Café Valencia* does full Spanish deli service (prime ribs and apple pie, too); and *Michael's* does a French-style pizza.

BARBADOS

If you were going to design a pleasure island, chances are it would look a good deal like Barbados. Barbados has all the postcard beauties: A west coast lined with white beaches and a sea so clear and gentle it looks like polished tourmaline; an east coast pounded by the Atlantic Ocean; southern cane fields that ripple as breezes comb across them; and craggy northern highlands where cool, morning mists burn off to reveal sweeps of valley and sea framed by majestic mahogany trees. It has seaside villages and English country churches that date from the seventeenth century.

Its prettiest hotels, built of pink coral stone, have rambling gardens and lush landscaping, and since the trade winds are steady and the climate reliably kind, their leeward sides are often terraced and open to fresh air and the view. While some are very, very luxurious, others are quite simple. And there are seaside apartments where guests can be entirely self-sufficient and casual, hotels that provide superb service 24 hours a day, and vacation houses for rent — they're called villas here — completely staffed.

The beach life is superlative; golf is good; and there are several superior setups for teaching and playing tennis. Exhibition tennis is played at *Sandy Lane* and at the *Cunard Paradise Beach,* and the government maintains public grass courts at the Garrison Savannah. You can also hike, bike, or ride horseback through the hills of St. Michael or rolling St. Philip Parish. There are plenty of land sites — historic, botanic, and scenic — to explore when you're tired of seeing sea. And spectator sports (cricket, soccer, horse racing, polo) to watch when you've done enough playing for a while. And it's all pleasantly accessible thanks to the island's handily compact size (22 miles long by 14 miles at its widest).

Two things are special about Barbados' atmosphere. The first is its lingering trace of British customs — in spite of the fact that the island has been an independent nation since 1966. It's more than Nelson's statue on Bridgetown's Trafalgar Square or the middies and wide-brimmed boaters worn by the Harbour Police; or afternoon tea laid out as a matter of course in the lounge of a number of St. James coast hotels. It is also the Police Band, resplendent in their white caps and tunics, offering a concert from the gingerbread-frilled Victorian bandstand on the Esplanade, and a white-wigged magistrate hurrying by on his way to court, and kids in uniforms trooping home from school — all symbolic of a system of government, justice, and education built on the British model.

It's not surprising when you think that for over 350 years — from the time the first Englishmen settled permanently at Holetown (then called Jamestown) until Independence Day, 1966 — Barbados was ruled continuously by the British. Pedro a Campos, the Portuguese said to have discovered the island in 1536, named it Los Barbados — "the bearded ones" — for the ban-

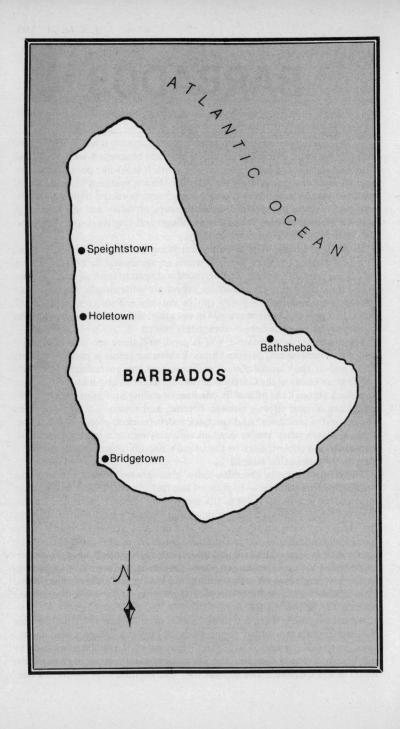

yan trees with their shaggy, exposed roots he sighted on the shore. But, presumably because it lay on the Spanish rather than the Portuguese side of the line of demarcation established by a papal bull in 1493, he failed to claim the island for Portugal. As a result, in all its modern history, Barbados has lived under only two flags: England's and its own.

As a matter of fact, compared to its neighbor islands, Barbados' history has been fairly free of strife. Its extreme easterly position, upwind of all the other Lesser Antilles, made it relatively difficult to approach from the west and undoubtedly served as protection from attack by buccaneers. Later, possibly because so many of the planters were either criminals shipped out as indentured servants or dissenters forced to emigrate from England for religious or political reasons, they treated the African slaves imported to help cultivate their cane fields in a relatively humane manner, although there were brief slave uprisings in 1672, 1696, and 1702. One of the legends about early Bajan days concerns a man named Sam Lord, who earned the wherewithal to build the magnificent house known as *Sam Lord's Castle* — now the centerpiece of Marriott's Barbados resort — by engaging in the unscrupulous practice of wrecking, i.e., luring ships onto shoals by hanging lanterns in palms along the shore to simulate port lights, and relieving them of their cargoes when they wrecked.

Today's Bajans are much more hospitable. Their openness and lack of hostility toward tourists makes the island's atmosphere especially appealing. In no time you feel at ease. But then Barbados has known tourism for several hundred years. As early as the seventeenth century, visitors came to Barbados for their health. In 1751, George Washington accompanied his tubercular half brother, Lawrence, on a visit to Bridgetown, where, it is generally conceded, they did not stay in the house at the corner of Bay Street and Chelsea Road now called the George Washington House. For the future first president, the island did not turn out to be a salubrious choice — there he contracted the smallpox that marked him for life. Still, he declared the place "a delight" and himself "enraptured with the beautiful prospects."

Most of today's visitors, enjoying the island in health, are delighted, too. And that pleases their hosts, whose love of and pride in their island is deep and genuine. The fact is that Bajans are sure — in the nicest possible way — that "Bim" (as they call their homeland) and the life on it is the best in the Caribbean. Or in the world for that matter. Feeling as they do, they may leave home to study or travel or get job experience, but almost without exception they plan to come home again. A friend who'd returned to Bridgetown after three years in the States put it this way: "I loved New York and the fun of it, the excitement. But Barbados is where life feels right to me. That's why I came back home." Even though a visitor's time on the island is limited, it is hard to miss seeing that Bajans want you to feel at least a little that way.

Is Barbados the perfect island? Not quite. And not for everyone. Downtown Bridgetown is worthwhile for shopping, but it's certainly not sugar-coated pretty. Glitter addicts won't find Vegas shows or gambling; but history buffs will find greathouses and antique churches and lots more to explore. Winter prices will seem astronomical to some; for others the peace and the place will be worth every penny; and still others will wait for summer, when prices drop by at least a third, for the best of both worlds. For some people, jackets for dinner are stuffy; for others, it's just a nice touch of class.

It all depends. But Barbados could be where "life feels right" to you, too.

BARBADOS AT-A-GLANCE

FROM THE AIR: Barbados' bright green cane and cotton fields, neatly framed by hedgerows, look like a tropical translation of rural England, an echo of the country's longtime British ties. The easternmost island of the West Indies, it lies outside the main arc of the Caribbean's Windward Islands chain, about 100 miles due east of St. Vincent and about 340 miles north of Guyana on the north coast of South America, at 13°4′ N latitude, 50°37′ W longitude. It is small — 166 square miles, 22 miles long by 14 miles at its widest point — and relatively densely populated, with about 260,000 inhabitants.

The island is shaped like a pear, stem end pointing north, with its capital, Bridgetown (pop. 65,000), on the curve of the southwestern coast. Just inland from the southern coast, 11 miles east and slightly south of the city's center, near Seawell, is Grantley Adams International Airport. The 2,100-mile jet flight from New York takes just over 4 hours; from Toronto (about 2,916 miles), it's 5 hours; the flight from Miami (about 1,610 miles) takes about 3¼ hours.

The island is rimmed by beaches. Its eastern edge, above a coast surf-combed by a dark blue Atlantic Ocean, is hilly and rugged; Bathsheba, a small fishing village, sits at the midpoint of its shoreline. The land along the western coast — on which Bridgetown and the centuries-old settlements of Holetown and Speightstown, as well as most resort hotels are located — is gentle and rolling, washed by a calmer leeward sea.

SPECIAL PLACES: Except for traffic-tangled Bridgetown, Barbados is ideal to explore by car, provided you don't try shortcutting from one main route to another without *very explicit* directions or a good map. In Barbados all numbered routes — laid out in a fanlike pattern — lead to or from Bridgetown. Though sometimes narrow, they are reasonably well marked with crossroad signs, and people are pleasant when you stop to ask directions. With this in mind, we suggest a two-part plan consisting of a sightseeing/shopping morning in Bridgetown, using hotel bus and/or taxi transport, and a day's drive around the island, including lunch and a swim on the east coast — preferably on your own, but otherwise in a taxi with a congenial driver.

Bridgetown – Barbados' capital is an architectural hodgepodge with an inscrutable network of one-way streets that — in rush hours — seem to epitomize the triumph of car over man. So it's lucky that its few points of interest are within strolling distance of each other and of Broad Street's in-bond shopping. Aim to arrive at Trafalgar Square, the heart of town, at about 10 AM, when the worst of the morning rush hour is over. Like its London namesake, the square (really the area between the edge of the inner harbor and the Public Buildings across Trafalgar Street) honors Nelson's 1805 naval victory; like London's, it is endowed with a statue of the great admiral. This Horatio was sculpted and installed in 1813, some 30 years before its British counterpart; but in the years since, widening streams of traffic have cut the ground from around him so that his iron-fenced pedestal now stands alone in a sea of cars. Considerably more popular with Bajans is the huge statue of the Freed Slave Bussa, which stands at a crossroads on St. Barnabas Highway just outside Bridgetown. Other landmarks: Fountain Garden, with its three-dolphin fountain, commemorating the advent of piped water in 1865, plus a memorial cenotaph to the dead of World Wars I and II, and an arch erected in 1987 at the Bay Street entrance to Bridgetown to commemorate the twenty-first anniversary of independence.

Facing the north side of the square, the great, gray, Victorian-Gothic Public Buildings (1874) house the Assembly (on the right) and the Legislative Council (in the left-hand towered building). The jarringly modern Financial Building dominates the square's east end.

The square's southern boundary is the edge of the old harbor, better known as the Careenage, because from the earliest days, ships were brought in here and careened (tipped on their sides) to have their bottoms scraped, caulked, and painted. Nowadays, island workboats berth beside trim, elegant sailing yachts. Congratulate yourself if you sight a Bajan Harbour Policeman in his Nelsonian sailor suit with its blue-collared middy and wide-brimmed straw hat.

St. Michael's Cathedral (Anglican) is around the corner and to the right behind the Financial Building. Completed in 1665 and rebuilt after hurricanes in 1780 and 1831, it is said to be the place where George Washington worshiped when he visited Barbados with his brother, Lawrence, in 1751. Today it offers cool moments on a hot day and a chance to inspect a collection of antique memorial tablets.

That's about it for urban sightseeing (elapsed time: about three quarters of an hour). At this point you can proceed to Broad Street for an hour of heavy shopping. Or hail a cab and ask the driver to take you out to the Garrison Savannah, where the Barbados Museum, once the Old Military Barracks, built by the Royal Engineers in 1820, features Arawak Indian relics, antique furniture, old maps, prints, coins, assorted artifacts, flora, and fauna (small admission fee).

On the way out Bay Street, Carlisle Bay and the Esplanade Pavilion (where the Barbados Police Band holds its concerts) will be on your right. A little farther along, across from the entrance to the *Barbados Yacht Club,* Chelsea Street turns off to the left; on its near corner stands the structure apocryphally called "the Washington House," where — historians agree — it is highly unlikely that either George or his brother ever slept.

Have your driver wait at the museum, then take you back into Bridgetown, to the *Deep Water Harbour* for a browse through *Pelican Village* (see *Shopping*). In case of cruise crowds, substitute lunch at *Brown Sugar, Peter's Patio* at the *Island Inn* on Hilton Drive, or the *Pelican* restaurant. Then home for a swim and siesta.

ELSEWHERE ON THE ISLAND

Most organized tours travel counterclockwise through Oistins Town, then out to *Sam Lord's,* up the east coast, west across the island, and head back through Speightstown and Holetown. On your own tour, do just the opposite: get an early start, drive north along the island's western edge, and continue clockwise, visiting:

Holetown – The little old St. James coast settlement where an obelisk marks the spot where the British ship *Orange Blossom* landed in 1627.

St. James Church – One of the Caribbean's oldest (dating to 1660), it might have been transported — bell tower and all — from England, except for its tropical poinsettia hedge, which blooms bright red at Christmas.

Platinum Coast – Nickname for the shore of St. James and St. Peter parishes along which you're driving; lined with the island's plushest hotels and winter homes (including those of international personalities such as Claudette Colbert).

Speightstown – Once a major sugar port, still a fishing town, with old houses, a picturesque restored church (St. Peter's), and a bustling waterfront. Its shiny new shopping mall leaves its main-street market ladies with their piles of produce and crafts undaunted. Turn east on Highway 1 to cross the island and visit:

St. Nicholas Abbey – Jacobean greathouse, built between 1650 and 1660, notable for its architecture and antiques, including a stunning 1810 Coalport dinner service and an extensive collection of Wedgwood medallions. The home movie of the voyage from Britain and 1920s plantation life taken by the owner's father is worth the $5 BDS price of admission; open 10 AM to 3:30 PM Mondays through Fridays.

Farley Hill – A national park with gardens, rich green lawns, and enormous trees surrounding the shell of a once splendid greathouse, partially rebuilt during the filming of *Island in the Sun*, later destroyed by fire again. Monument commemorates dedication by Queen Elizabeth II; also picnic tables, lookout points, stunning views.

Barbados Wildlife Reserve – Across from the entrance to Farley Hill, operated under the auspices of the Barbados Primate Research Center, and the home of throngs of rare green monkeys (said to have been brought from West Africa three centuries ago), deer, hares, tortoises, and various birdlife in a mahogany forest setting. Open daily from 10 AM to 5 PM. Admission $3 US.

Morgan Lewis Mill – Turn left (north) below Farley Hill and follow the signs to the only remaining windmill in Barbados with its working parts intact.

East Coast Highway – A wide, scenic road that follows the ocean shore south; about halfway down there's a snack bar and picnic place at Barclay's Park.

Andromeda Gardens – Famous for terraced collection of exotic tropical plants and view of the Bathsheba coast. Small admission fee.

Bathsheba – Small fishing village that gives this coast its name. Favorite Sunday beach area for Bajans. Nearby Tent Bay is home port for a flying-fish fleet.

St. John's Church – Built in the mid-1600s in the parish of the same name; known for its English look and the tomb of Ferdinand Paleologus, the Emperor Constantine's last descendant.

Codrington College – This stately, gray stone Georgian seminary of the Anglican Community of the Resurrection opened in 1745; it has an avenue of palms, stunning ocean vista.

Sam Lord's Castle – Elegant home of the celebrated 19th-century rogue, now the centerpiece of Marriott's Barbados resort hotel complex.

Other sites include:

Turner's Hall Wood – The last remaining 45 acres of the natural forest that once covered the island. Also part of the Barbados National Trust. It's inhabited by birds and monkeys, and features a boiling spring. Open daily.

Welchman Hall Gully – St. Thomas parish site of the National Trust's developing Botanical Garden with many marked, tropical specimens. Occasionally you'll sight wild monkeys. Worthwhile — if you're a flower person.

Harrison's Cave – Next to Welchman Hall. Spectacular caverns endowed with great cream and crystal rooms, subterranean streams, pools, and waterfalls; and wonderfully easy to explore thanks to an electric tram that carries you down and out again (small admission fee).

Flower Forest – Designed as a living legacy for coming generations, a serene 50-acre garden spot with exotic flowers, specimen fruit and spice trees; glorious view. Light snacks, fruit for sale. Admission fee.

Gun Hill – Lookout point as famous for its 17th-century carved lion as for one of the best views of the island.

Barbados Zoological Park – Located in St. Philip at Oughtenson Plantation, it contains a collection of Caribbean wildlife, including endangered species of parrots. The Great House at the center of the park is full of antiques and interesting curios. Admission $3 US.

■**EXTRA SPECIAL:** On Wednesday afternoons from mid-January through the first week of April, a different greathouse is open each week for public touring, affording a close look at today's elegant lifestyle as well as island antiques. Tickets (about

$4 US) benefit the National Trust. Watch the Sunday papers, call the National Trust (phone: 426-2421), or ask at the Board of Tourism for specifics. Villa Nova in St. John Parish, once owned by Anthony Eden, earl of Avon and a former British prime minister, is open from 10 AM to 4 PM Mondays through Fridays. Admission $3 US.

SOURCES AND RESOURCES

 TOURIST INFORMATION: The Barbados Board of Tourism supplies information on attractions and accommodations. It also publishes a season-by-season list of rates and facilities at island hotels and guesthouses along with details on summer and winter package plans. The Board of Tourism has offices in the following North American cities:

Los Angeles: 3440 Wilshire Blvd., Suite 1215, Los Angeles, CA 90010 (phone: 213-380-2198; 800-221-9831)
Montréal: 615 Dorchester Blvd. W, Suite 960, Montréal, Que. H3B 1P5 (phone: 514-861-0085)
New York: 800 Second Ave., New York, NY 10017 (phone: 212-986-6516)
Toronto: 20 Queen St. W, Suite 1508, Box 11, Toronto, Ont. M5H 3R3 (phone: 416-979-2137 or 979-2138)

In Barbados, the Board of Tourism office (phone: 427-2623/4) is in the Harbour Industrial Park near the Deep Water Harbour in Bridgetown. There are also tourist information centers at Grantley Adams International Airport and on the cruise ship pier at the Deep Water Harbour.

Local Coverage – The *Barbados Advocate* is the island's daily paper. Given a two- or three-day time lag, Miami papers are also generally available; *The Nation* is published six times a week and appears as *The Sun* on Sundays. *The New Bajan,* a monthly magazine, focuses on local happenings, history, and people.

Barbados Rediffusion radio, the Voice of Barbados, BBS-FM, and the Caribbean Broadcasting Corporation (daily radio, morning CNN news from the US, and evening TV) are the island's broadcast media.

The solid *Official Guide to Barbados* (sightseeing tips, sports, and entertainment information) is distributed free at the Board of Tourism office. The board's compact *Things You Should Know* brochure covers a good deal of useful information (transport companies and costs, shopping, restaurants, nightspots, etc.); the *Visitor,* a tourist-oriented tabloid published by the *Nation,* highlights current nightlife, restaurants, and sightseeing, as does the weekly *Sun Seeker,* published by the *Advocate;* all are distributed free at hotels, the Board of Tourism, and other tourist areas.

Telephone – Dial direct by adding the area code 809 to the phone numbers given below.

 ENTRY REQUIREMENTS: US and Canadian citizens need only proof of citizenship such as a birth certificate or driver's license with photo, although passports ensure easy reentry home, plus a ticket for onward or return transportation.

 CLIMATE AND CLOTHES: Constant sea breezes temper the heat of the sun, which, according to official Barbadian records, shines more than 3,000 hours per (8,760-hour) year. Winter temperatures range from 68°F (20°C) to 85°F (31°C); summer's, from 76°F (25°C) to 87°F (31°C). Showers are frequent but brief, and thanks to the trade winds, the air seldom stays muggy for long. Wettest months are September, October, and November; February and March are driest. Rooms at most hotels and guesthouses are at least partially air conditioned.

As for clothes, only Bermuda is trimmer — a circumstance that, on both islands, can probably be traced to the lingering British influence. The effect is well groomed rather than stuffy: Bajans aren't all that keen on knee socks and walking shorts, but they do appreciate guests neatly turned out. Bare is beautiful on beaches only. Customarily, you slip into a shirt or coverup for lunch on a hotel terrace; a shirt and pants or a skirt or sport dress for daytime sightseeing; something roughly equivalent to what you'd wear on a warm evening at a country club at night. Only a few of the posher hotels (*Sandy Lane* and *Coral Reef Club*, for example) suggest men wear summer dinner jackets on Saturday evenings during the winter holiday season; otherwise, most hotels and restaurants request jackets but not necessarily ties after dark. In summer, it's less formal.

 MONEY: The Barbados dollar is valued at approximately 50¢ US — a constant ratio since it is *officially* pegged to the US dollar. Shops accept both US and Canadian dollars as well as traveler's checks. Some of the larger stores and a number of hotels and restaurants also honor American Express, Diners Club, Visa, and MasterCard. But stores do not offer tourist discounts for payment in US cash or traveler's checks. There is little difference between the exchange rate offered by banks and that given in hotels, shops, and restaurants.

Banking hours at Barclays are 9 AM to 3 PM; at most others, 8 AM to 1 PM on weekdays, 3 to 5:30 PM on Fridays only; closed weekends and holidays.

 LANGUAGE: Bajans speak English with their own special island lilt. It has been the official language for more than 350 years — since 1627 when the British landed.

 TIME: Barbados time is one hour ahead of Eastern Standard (when it's noon in New York, it's 1 PM in Bridgetown), or the same as Eastern Daylight Time.

 CURRENT: 110 volts, 50 cycles; compatible with American and Canadian appliances.

 GETTING THERE: American Airlines and BWIA fly to Barbados nonstop from New York; Pan Am flies direct (same plane) from Boston and Washington, nonstop from Miami and New York; Air Canada flies direct, sometimes nonstop, from Montréal and Toronto; BWIA also provides nonstop service from Toronto, Miami, and San Juan; Eastern Airlines has nonstop flights from Miami. San Juan and Miami are connecting points for flights from the US South, Midwest, and West. Air Martinique, Cubana Airways, and LIAT provide air links to other Caribbean islands.

 CALCULATING COSTS: With more than 14,500 rooms, the price range is wide: from under $35 US ($20 US in summer) per night for a double room without meals in a simple guesthouse to a rather splendid $355 US and up in season for a hotel room for two with breakfasts and dinners. A great number of moderately priced apartment-style accommodations equipped with kitch-enettes are available also. Between mid-April and mid-December, rates for these facilities run 30% to 50% lower than comparable conventional hotel rooms. In summer, weekly summer rates run from under $125 per person in a self-catering apartment to about $500 per person in the poshest hotel. Special summer packages (for golfers, tennis players, honeymooners, and just vacationers) often include room plus sightseeing, airport transfers, and other special features for as little as $150 US per person, double occupancy (air fare is extra). Twice a year, the Board of Tourism issues *Hotel and Guest House* rates plus *Apartments and Cottages,* a semiannual roster of properties with housekeeping units that rent for from less than $300 US a week (for a studio apartment for two) in the spring, summer, and fall to $950 or so for a two-person suite in winter; most include daily maid service, as well as linens and kitchen and dining equipment, and represent worthwhile savings whatever the season. All hotel and rental rates are subject to a 5% government tax and 10% service charge.

The difference between EP (European Plan, without meals) and MAP (Modified American Plan, breakfast or lunch and dinner) is about $30 to $40 US per person. Restaurant prices vary widely, too: from under $15 US for two for a lunch of dolphin or flying fish at a small island place to about $50 US and up per couple for a dinner with cocktails, wine, and service at one of the more Continental spots.

 GETTING AROUND: Taxi – Readily available at the airport, at stands in downtown Bridgetown, at the Deep Water Harbour, and outside hotels. They are not metered; but rates are fixed, and drivers carry lists of standard fares to which you can refer. From the airport, it costs between $6 and $8 US to taxi to a south coast hotel in Oistins; about $10 US to *Sam Lord's Castle;* about $11 US to the *Barbados Hilton* or *Grand Barbados;* about $11 US to the Bridgetown City Centre; and between $15 and $22 US to a hotel on the St. James coast.

Bus – Not hand-painted or given exotic names like those on some other islands, buses make up for what they lack in color with springs, comfort, and reliability. Islanders use them a lot, and more tourists should, too, since they reach many major interest points. No. 1 travels the west coast road from Bridgetown to Speightstown and beyond; Nos. 6 and 7 run between Bridgetown and Bathsheba and Bridgetown and Codrington College, respectively. Fare is 75¢ BDS no matter how long the ride, and exact change is required. Ask at Board of Tourism centers for current schedule information.

Jitney buses, owned and operated by a number of hotels, shuttle guests to and from Bridgetown for sightseeing and shopping several times a day. In some cases, the service is free; in others, there's a small charge.

Car Rental – A great way to get around once you get the hang of keeping left (a bit of practice in a parking lot generally does the trick). Rates range from about $40 US a day for a Mini Moke to about $50 US per day for an automatic-shift four-passenger car, with unlimited mileage, basic insurance. Gas, at $1.15 BDS per liter, is extra. If you don't have a credit card, you'll be asked for a substantial deposit. Also, cars can be difficult to obtain, so advance booking is advised.

Local firms: *National of Barbados* (phone: 426-0603), *H. E. Williams* (phone: 427-1043), *Courtesy* (phone: 426-5871), *Johnson's* (phone: 426-5186), *Dear's* (phone: 429-9277), *Sunny Isle* (phone: 428-8009), and *Barbados Rent a Car* (phone: 425-1388).

If you plan to drive *at any time* during your stay, while still at the airport after arrival, and even before you pass the immigration officer, change about $5 US for $10 BDS at the Bank of Barbados window and take it to the police window to obtain your Barbados visitor's driving permit. Otherwise, some car rental companies now issue permits, while others will arrange for you to take a taxi to a station house to get one.

Jumbo Rentals of Bridgetown (phone: 426-5689) rents motor scooters. Rates, including pickup at your hotel, are about $20 US a day with a two-day minimum, $100 US a week; a deposit is required. You must have a Barbados visitor's driving permit ($5 US) to operate a motor bike.

Bicycles – *M. A. William Bicycle Rentals* (phone: 427-1043, 427-3955) in Hastings can accommodate a cyclist for about $8 per day.

Sightseeing Taxi Tours – If you don't like driving yourself, this is a good way to still get a closeup of the island. Bajan drivers are friendly, dignified, and proud of their country. A day's trip with one of them gives you a closer, more personalized feel for the country than a more routine bus tour. A 6- to 7-hour tour costs about $80 to $90 US for a party of two, three, or four. Optional asides: a stop for a soda or a rum and Coke at Barclay's Park scenic overlook; for lunch and a swim at *Marriott's Sam Lord's Castle* or the *Crane Beach Hotel.*

Sightseeing Bus Tours – *L. E. Williams,* one of the main tour companies, offers a day tour that covers the island (80 miles) and includes lunch, at a cost of about $40 US (phone: 427-1043). Other island firms, such as *Dear's Garage* and *Johnson's,* also organize tour groups, but require minimum numbers.

Sea Excursions – Lunch and cocktail cruises mainly, scheduled by a number of sailing ships. The *Jolly Roger* for about $35 US per person provides a snorkeling stop and steak barbecue, open bar, entertainment by the crew and you, and transportation from your hotel. For about the same price, *Capt. Patch* and the *Bajan Queen* do similar trips; the catamaran *Irish Mist* offers slightly more serene day and evening trips.

Island-Hopping Trips – One-day flying and longer sailing expeditions to nearby Dominica, Martinique, St. Lucia, St. Vincent, the Grenadines, Grenada, and Tobago cost about $200 per person, including transfers, air fare, lunch, and sightseeing, and are operated by *Caribbean Safari Tours* (phone: 427-5100) in Bridgetown.

SHOPPING: For best buys (20% to 50% below stateside prices) on classic imports — English bone china, crystal, perfumes, liquor, watches, jewelry, and clothes (especially British sweaters, tweeds, sportswear), in-bond sections of major department stores and specialty shops on and around Bridgetown's Broad Street are where it's at. In these designated areas, merchandise is tagged with two prices: in-bond and take-away. The in-bond one is always lowest, but the take-away tag may still represent a saving over what you'd pay back home. For in-bond (duty-free) savings on liquor and tobacco products, a visitor must shop at least 24 hours before scheduled departure time and select from display merchandise; purchases will be delivered directly to your plane or ship. However, all other duty-free items can be taken as they are paid for, provided you show proof of being a visitor (airline ticket and passport or ID). Big store names to know are *Cave Shepherd, Y. De Lima,* and *C. F. Harrison. India House* majors in imported fashion. *Baldini, Bayley's,* and *Correia's* are jewelry specialists.

If you're staying at a west coast hotel, you can save time and feet by shopping in-bond departments of *Bayley's, Cave Shepherd, India House,* and others at the *Sunset Crest* shopping center; *Cave Shephard* also has a Speightstown branch. Stocks aren't quite as large as those downtown, but neither are crowds. And prices are the same. The smaller, double-decked *Skyway Shopping Plaza* at Hastings, handy to South Shore hotels, is stronger on crafts and souvenirs than in-bond buys. There are also coveys of shops (branches and independent boutiques) at the *Hilton, Sandy Lane, Sam Lord's,* and *Paradise Beach.*

A dozen boutiques — many in hotel gardens or lobby niches — offer sleek sport and resort clothes at prices that range from okay to outrageous. No need to go into town; just start in the Speightstown neighborhood, or at the south edge of the city, and browse your way down the coast road. Worth a stop: *Gatsby* at *Sandy Lane, Hibiscus* at Payne's Bay. *Petticoat Lane,* next to the *Waterfront Café* on the Careenage, spotlights imaginative clothes by owner Carol Cadogan, as does Simon's shop at *Giggles* in St. Peter.

For top-quality island crafts, see the *Best of Barbados* (at the *Sandpiper Inn, Sam Lord's, Mall 34, Skyway Plaza* in Christ Church, and the *Flower Forest*) select stocks of winsome children's clothes, toys, ceramics, woven things, baskets, and Jill Walker's works (fresh-looking fabrics as well as prints of her appealingly good-humored island watercolors). Down near the Deep Water Harbour, *Pelican Village*'s stalls are a mixed bag in terms of quality, but fun to wander through for the sake of watching artisans at work or special finds like the pottery and sculpture at the *Devonish Gallery*, much of it the creation of Courtney Devonish, a bright-eyed, bearded Bajan artist of international reputation, who may be in the shop or polishing one of his favorite "root sculptures" in the studio across the road. The government *Handicraft Emporium*, just down Harbour Drive, is stacked to its warehouse rafters with fair-priced woven work, khuskhus and pandannus mats, hats, rugs, baskets, and such; the *Barbados Handicraft Center* on Bridge St., and *West Indies Handcrafts* and *Articrafts* in Norman Centre are noteworthy downtown sources. On the artistic side: *Antiquaria*, St. Michael's Row, Bridgetown, and the *London Gallery* in Holetown, St. James (period furniture, art); *Talma Mill Gallery*, Christ Church (modern paintings, fabrics, stained glass, drawings).

Shopping hours are from 8 AM to 4 PM, weekdays; 8 AM to 1 PM on Saturdays.

Fly Fish Inc. offers visitors a unique souvenir. Flying fish, the island's national dish, is available flash frozen and vacuum-packed, with a reusable freezer gel pack (approved by the major airlines for carry-on), from the counter in the departure lounge at the airport. Fresh tropical floral bouquets are also sold.

 TIPPING: The extra 10% added to your bill in most hotels and restaurants covers all but special extra service. When a service charge is not included, tip waiters 10% to 15%, hotel maids $1 US per room per day, bellboys 25¢ US per bag (but not less than $1 US per trip for one or two people), and about $1 US for a special errand. Airport porters should also be tipped 50¢ US per bag; and taxi drivers, 10% of the fare.

 SPECIAL EVENTS: Barbados' big annual bash is *Crop Over*, a two-week succession of parties, parades, craft displays, plantation fairs, and open-air concerts shared and genuinely enjoyed by both Bajans and island visitors. Its high point is the historically rooted *Cane Cutters Spree* — a night of jump-up partying, singing, and dancing held in a central plantation yard. Overall dates are mid-July to early August.

The official national holidays list observed by banks and most businesses includes *New Year's Day, Good Friday, Easter Sunday* and *Whitmonday, May Day* (May 1), *Kadooment* (climax of the *Crop Over* festival, first Monday in August), *UN Day* (first Monday in October), *Independence Day* (November 30, commemorating the day in 1966 when Barbados became a self-governing nation within the British Commonwealth), *Christmas*, and *Boxing Day* (December 26).

SPORTS: Since sun, sand, and sea constitute 90% of what lures visitors to the island, the beach is where you'll find most of the people, most of the time, mostly doing nothing and loving it. When the untoward urge to activity strikes, Barbados offers a number of worthwhile alternatives:

Beaches – While not very wide (exceptions: the *Hilton*'s broad expanse shored up by stone jetties and the surf-pounded Crane Beach, considered by many to be one of the world's best), beaches are pink-tinged coral sand. The majority of hotels command their own stretches of sand (though, technically, all island beach is public); guests of those that don't are usually just across the road from a beach they can think of as theirs. Most are endowed with chaises, snack and drink bars — all the life-sustaining essentials — so there's not much beach-hopping. But if you're west-based, you ought to try to make it to the east coast at least once — if only to view the pounding drama of the surf. There's swimming on the broad-beached eastern shoreline northwest from Bathsheba, but no regular lifeguard service; don't try it alone. *Marriott's Sam Lord's Castle* and the *Crane Beach* hotel offer wave-bathing that's more organized.

Boating – Most hotels have Sunfish, Sailfish, and/or Hobie Cats to loan or rent right on the beach, and most can book sailing yachts for day and party cruising. Individual charters, skippered or bareboat, aren't easy to arrange on the spur of the moment; but ask your hotel travel desk, or call the commodore at the *Barbados Cruising Club* (phone: 426-4434) or the *Barbados Yacht Club* (phone: 427-1125). From January through May, both clubs sponsor frequent regattas.

For a truly unique boating experience and a breathtaking underwater view of the coral reefs, make reservations on the submarine *Atlantis*. A one-hour dive costs about $48 US (phone: 436-8929).

Cricket – Inscrutable to most US spectators, it ranks as the number one sport and national passion, with Barbados fielding championship teams at both West Indian and World Test Match levels: the *Advocate* carries match schedules in season (June to January).

Golf – A round on the championship 18 at *Sandy Lane* (phone: 432-1405 or 432-1145) will cost $25 US for greens fees, about $12 US for club rental, about $20 US for a cart, and $12 US and up per a caddy. There is also a 9-hole course at *Rockley Resort* and an 18-hole course at *Heywoods*.

Hiking – The Barbados National Trust (phone: 426-2421) organizes hikes during the winter season, and the Outdoors Club of Barbados (phone: 436-5328 or 426-0024) offers half- and full-day hikes (including meals) from $30 to $50 BDS. If you're keen on walking on your own, you might take the public bus to Codrington College, follow the abandoned railway right-of-way from there along the east coast to the *Atlantis* hotel at Tent Bay (nice place for an island lunch); bus back from nearby Bathsheba.

Horseback Riding – On hill trails and along beaches in St. Michael parish and in the countryside around *Sam Lord's* in St. Philip, it's as scenic as it is athletic. English saddles predominate. Contact *Ye Olde Congo Road Stables* in St. Philip (phone: 423-6180), *Brighton Riding Stable,* St. Michael (phone: 425-9381), or *Valley Hill Stables,* Christ Church (phone: 423-0033). Rates, with guide, run about $25 US per hour, including transportation to and from hotel.

Snorkeling and Scuba – The recently formed *Eastern Caribbean Diving Association* is having a big impact on the development of diving on the island. In addition to assisting with the operation of a new decompression chamber, the association is also involved in marine conservation.Borrow or rent masks and flippers for a small fee at most west coast hotels. For diving, reefs off the west and south coasts make intriguing day-trip destinations. Visit the coral reef of the three-zoned (for scientific research; snorkeling, scuba, and glass-bottom boat trips; swimming, skiing, sailing, and water sports) *Folkestone National Marine Reserve, Park, and Marine Museum* at Holetown. For experienced, guided divers, the deliberately sunk freighter *Stavronikita* beyond the reef is an added attraction, offering not just a breathtaking dive but also an opportunity for some fabulous underwater photography. Several hotels have fully equipped watersports centers on their own premises: Check *Dive Boat Safari,* at the *Hilton,* for scuba diving (phone: 427-4350 or 426-0220, ext. 395); *Scuba Safari,* on the Hilton Drive, for snorkeling (phone: 426-0621); and *Underwater Barbados,* a Peter Hughes/Divi Hotel operation associated with the *South Winds* hotel (phone: 428-7181). If your hotel doesn't have a scuba place of its own, contact *The Dive Shop* (phone: 426-9947 or 426-2031 at night) in St. Michael, or *Willie's Water Sports* and *Heywoods* and Black Rock (phone: 425-1060). Other dive operations include *Dive Barbados, Sandy Beach Watersports, Blue Reef Watersports,* and *Les Wotton* at Coral Reef. Lessons run about $20 US; dives are about $30 US each.

Spectator Sports – There is also a good deal of soccer and polo (July to February on the Garrison Savannah, St. Michael, and Holder's, St. James), and horse racing — also on the Savannah — on occasional Saturdays from January to May and from July to November, complete with snack booths (fried flying fish is the big seller), steel bands — all the trappings of a small carnival. From time to time, there are motor rallies too.

Sport Fishing – Not one of Barbados' best sporting attractions, but blue marlin, barracuda, dolphin, wahoo, tuna, and occasional cobia are caught in waters north and south of Barbados. Contact — or have your hotel get in touch with — *Jolly Roger* (phone: 432-7090) or Paula Manning at *Blue Jay Charters* (phone: 422-2098 or 436-8648). The rate is about $250 US for a half day, $500 US for a full day for up to six people.

Squash – *Heywoods* and *Rockley Resort* have 2 air-conditioned squash courts each; the *Sea Breeze Apartment* hotel has 1. Use is free to guests; others pay about $6 US per hour. The *Barbados Squash Club* (phone: 427-7913) in Christ Church charges about $7 US per 45 minutes; while the *Casuarina Beach Club* (phone: 428-3600) charges about $5 US for the same amount of time.

Surfing – Bajans do their surfing at Rockley Beach on the southwest coast between Worthing and St. Lawrence and at Enterprise Beach near Oistins as well as at Bathsheba.

Swimming and Sunning – Barbados has two kinds of coast: the surf-pounded east; and the serene west, where most hotels are. Western waters are so clear and buoyant that even real swimming seems to cause unnecessary splashing; so you tend to float a lot and/or paddle about on float boards provided by hotels.

Tennis – The *Casuarina Beach Club, Marriott's Sam Lord's Castle, Hilton, Rockley Resort, Heywoods,* and *Cunard Paradise Beach* all have courts. *Sandy Lane* and *Paradise Beach* not only have courts and pros in attendance, but setups suitable for exhibition matches. The *Sunset Crest Club* near Holetown also has 4 courts, lighted, as are those at the *Marriott, Heywoods, Paradise Beach, Rockley Resort,* and *Southwinds.* Most hotels charge about $5 US per hour of court time. The charge is $3 US per hour to play on the government's grass court at the Garrison Savannah and $8 US per hour at the *Paragon Tennis Club.*

Water Skiing – Best on calm western waters. If your hotel doesn't have its own setup, they'll make arrangements with the nearest facility — possibly *Sandy Lane* in St. James, *Willie's Water Sports* at *Heywoods,* or *Scuba Safari* at the *Hilton.* Cost is about $15 US per person per quarter-hour.

Windsurfing – Growing ever more popular at south shore beach hotels — especially *Barbados Windsurfing Club* hotel's *Club Mistral* (phone: 428-9095 or 428-7277) at Maxwell, Christ Church. *Willie's Water Sports* (phone: 425-1060) and other St. James coast shops offer board rentals, instruction too.

 NIGHTLIFE: When the sun goes down, even the most laid-back visitor may give in to the temptation to "jump-up" (dance) into the beckoning Barbadian night. Although there are no big Las Vegas–style revues or casinos, there's always something going on. During the winter season, the larger hotels (particularly *Marriott's Sam Lord's* and the *Hilton*) feature elaborate entertainment. Steel bands and calypso singers are showcased at various nightspots and hotels around the island. The *Bel Air Jazz Club* in Bridgetown is renowned for some of the smokiest music this side of New Orleans. Among the most popular island bands, the Merrymen, Spice, Jade, Ivory, Hot Gossip, Split Ends, KGB, and Private Eye rank highest; watch the local papers for when and where they'll be.

Throughout the year, there are must-see historical performances such as *1627 and All That Sort of Thing,* staged by the talented Barbados Dance Theatre every Thursday and Sunday night at the Barbados museum, and accompanied by a delicious Bajan buffet and more. *Barbados, Barbados,* a musical based on the successful life of the island's most notorious madam, takes place Tuesday nights at Balls Plantation in Christ Church. The *Plantation* restaurant, outside Bridgetown, and the *Island Inn* offer Caribbean-flavored dining and entertainment. The new *Xanadu Nightclub* (at the *Ocean View* hotel) offers dining, dancing, and occasional dinner theater.

Those with stout hearts and cast-iron stomachs can dance at sea aboard the *Jolly Roger*'s *Sundowner Calypso Cruise* or the slightly more sedate *Bajan Queen.* On land, clubs for the energetic include *Rockley Resort*'s *Rendezvous Room* and the *Club Miliki* at *Heywoods* — as well as the *Warehouse* (above the *Waterfront Café*), *Mr. Bojangles* (on lower Bay Street), and *Harbor Lights* (formerly *Rachel's*) all in Bridgetown. In St. Lawrence Gap, try the popular *After Dark, Shooters,* or the less frenetic *Winelight,* next to *Pisces* restaurant.

The assortment of British-style pubs on the island includes the *Ships Inn* (St. Lawrence Gap); the *Boatyard* (on Carlisle Bay), a nautical hang-out; or the *Bamboo Beach Bar* (St. James), which closes too early (1 AM). Baxter's Road (Bridgetown), on the other hand, never seems to close — traditional Saturday night strolls up and down its food stall–lined length provide everyone with a real taste of Barbadian nightlife.

Clubs in Barbados generally charge an admission fee of about $5 US, while drinks run about $2 to $4 US (more at hotels).

BEST ON THE ISLAND

CHECKING IN: Barbados hotels are among the most pleasant, prettiest, and best run in the Caribbean. Lots of sea views, gardens, beaches, relaxed atmosphere — like being the house guest of rather well-off friends. In summer, when rates drop 30% to 50% from winter highs, a number are genuine bargains in elegant, in-depth comfort. Double-room rates at first-class places run from about $65 US and up a day without meals (EP), about $120 US and up including breakfasts and dinners (MAP), and mid-April to mid-December package plans that sweeten the deal with special-feature options are excellent buys. In winter, deluxe hotel rates run from about $250 US a day for two, including two or three meals, but few, if any, extras. More moderately priced south coast apartment hotels that ask $80 to $110 US EP, for two between December 15 and Easter, tend to be either older places that have seen better days or newer hotels with small rooms designed to handle — efficiently — a continuous stream of charter groups. A few special places noted below offer big value for relatively little money whatever the season if you like their style. And in a sincere effort to hold the price line, a number of seaside places now include free water sports (except deep-sea fishing and scuba trips) in their rates. Suites and apartments with kitchenettes — especially on the southern shores of Christ Church — often make up in the reasonableness of their cost what they lack in comfort and/or style, but the tasteful-though-barefoot alternative doesn't really exist. Villa suites, apartments (quite a few in hotels), and rental cottages with their own cooking facilities (from $275 US a week in summer, about $400 and *way* up in winter) do offer some savings potential. The Board of Tourism issues seasonal lists of apartment and cottage rentals; *Caribbean Home Rentals,* PO Box 710, Palm Beach, FL 33480, maintains constantly updated listings and is especially good at villa and family-sized bookings.

Given this, the places below are recommended. Those listed as inexpensive ask about $50 US and up for two without meals in summer, $70 to $80 US and up in winter; moderate, $70 US and up for two without meals in summer, about $110 US and up in winter; expensive, $100 to $110 US and up without meals in summer, $190 and up,

MAP, in winter. A number of hotels offer only MAP (including breakfast and dinner) rates during the winter season, but several offer dine-around plans that allow some variety.

ST. JAMES

Colony Club – Rambling, coral stone main house, villa rooms near beach and in garden. Attractive public rooms open to blue, seascape views. Super waterside terrace for breakfast, lunch, stay-all-day beach life; pleasant service. Good summer packages (phone: 422-2335). Expensive.

Coral Reef Club – This classic resort, on 12 beautifully landscaped acres, offers 75 cottages and suites. The reception lobby and lounge are open-air and very tropical, and there's a lovely restaurant overlooking sea and gardens; also good tennis and water sports. Family-owned and run with a special touch (phone: 422-2372). Expensive.

Discovery Bay – A Swiss-run resort with an international flavor. It has 95 rooms (including some junior suites), all with radios, phones, balconies, and air conditioning; also two restaurants, bars, entertainment, barbecues, game room, and library. It's located on a beautiful beach, with water sports available, golf nearby, and conference facilities for 70 (phone: 432-1301). Expensive.

Glitter Bay – A Pemberton resort ensconced on what was once the Cunard estate, this quietly splendid condominium complex exudes luxury and sheikly chic in its Moorish modern design, flowered landscaping, palms, and sweep of blue sea. With free water sports, boating, and tennis; golf and riding arranged. There's a patio-surrounded freshwater pool and an excellent restaurant, *Piperade.* Each suite has fully equipped kitchen, air-conditioned bedroom(s), fan-cooled living room, terrace or balcony (phone: 422-4111). Expensive.

Royal Pavilion – A luxury Pemberton resort, Barbados's newest, on a beautiful 1,200-foot stretch of beach. The sister hotel of *Glitter Bay,* it offers complimentary water sports and tennis on lighted courts, beachfront coffeeshop and restaurant (phone: 422-4444). Expensive.

Sandpiper Inn – Island-style enclave with indoor-outdoor South Seas sort of look; 20 air-conditioned suites and apartments, pleasant decor. Freshwater pool, beach; lots of nearby sports, shopping, supermarket. Exchange dining (phone: 422-2251). Expensive.

Sandy Lane – A 112-room hotel and resort complex on 380 acres, designed for Beautiful People, with first-rate tennis layouts, beach, and golf. Its formerly first-rate reputation is being regained thanks to a $4-million renovation and an emphasis on personal touches: Each guest is met at the airport; guestroom amenities include personal bathrobes; special summer packages are offered for honeymooners. A Trusthouse Forte hotel (phone: 432-1311). Expensive.

Settlers Beach – Coolly luxurious villa apartments circling a swimming pool set in neat, green lawns and gardens by the sea. Each of the 22 villas has 2 bedrooms, baths, living room/dining area, fully equipped kitchen; come-in cooks available, too. All sports, shopping nearby. Pleasant beach restaurant serves excellent lunches and dinners. Exchange dining, too (phone: 422-3052). Expensive.

Barbados Beach Village – A comfortable and popular informal beachfront resort, now even better since the first of three major renovation phases was completed in 1987. The pool is twice its old size; the reception lobby and poolside deck–bar area are new; and the general facelift has not resulted in a price increase. There are 88 rooms (60 double, 28 suites with kitchenettes), a restaurant, 2 bars, and entertainment most nights. Management warns that the layout of units is not conducive to handicapped access (phone: 425-1440). Expensive to moderate.

Divi St. James – Recently renovated resort with 131 rooms and suites with fully equipped kitchenettes. New rates range from EP to all-inclusive packages that cover transfers, rooms, all meals, drinks, water sports, day tennis, golf (greens fees, clubs, transport), squash, use of saunas and fitness center, tour and cruise, night entertainment, taxes, and service. The wonderful, intimate *Piano Bar,* open late each evening, is a special plus. Divi Hotels owns six other resorts in the Caribbean, including *Southwinds* (see below) (phone: 432-7842). Expensive to moderate.

Coconut Creek Club – Offers 50 air-conditioned rooms, bedroom–sitting room combinations, and apartments — all with balconies or patios — in an attractive garden setting. Pretty beach; golf and riding nearby. Congenial pub, good food, relaxed international clientele. There's a newly installed conference facility for 120 people, with fully equipped sound system (phone: 432-0803). Expensive to moderate.

Tamarind Cove – Terraced or patioed rooms encircle a palm-shaded garden with small freshwater pool at edge of white sand beach. Free water sports on site, others nearby. Attractive outdoor dining room, evening entertainment in season (phone: 432-1332). Expensive to moderate.

Treasure Beach – A family-owned and -run hotel featuring a lovely arrangement of 24 modern beachfront suites, identical except for their relation to the nicely tended garden and beach. The management is especially caring, the atmosphere pleasing. With pool, popular restaurant noted for pleasant atmosphere, and entertainment. Children accepted only on request (phone: 432-1346). Expensive to moderate.

Inn on the Beach – Garden-edged pool, patio, and beach are the focus for compact set of 20 smallish but bright efficiency studios — each with kitchenette, ocean view. Two good-looking 2- and 3-bedroom villas, too. With outdoor dining room and bar that attract a lively afternoon and nighttime clientele (phone: 432-0385). Moderate.

ST. PETER

Cobblers Cove – A gracious, small (38 lovely suites) resort made special and charming by little touches and attention to detail. Luxurious atmosphere, villa rooms with balconies or patios surrounding pretty, pink main house, once a private home. Beach (one of the best coves on Barbados), pool, and bar within steps of each other. All rooms have kitchenettes, but most guests prefer to dine on the terrace, where they can enjoy excellent Continental cuisine as well as Bajan specialties while basking in tropical breezes. Good summer packages (phone: 422-2291). Expensive.

Heywoods – First full-scale luxury resort at the island's superbly scenic northern end. Seven handsome buildings each with an individual theme (306 air-conditioned rooms and suites) set among palms and gardens on an old sugar plantation site. With 3 freshwater pools, a mile-long white beach with all water sports, 5 lighted tennis courts, 2 air-conditioned squash courts, and an 18-hole golf course. Plus crafts market, boutiques, choice of bars, restaurants from informal to elegant, appealing disco. Caring staff and Caledonian management (phone: 422-4900). Expensive.

Sandridge – Small set of balconied, air-conditioned hotel rooms, studios, suites (some duplexes) with kitchenettes, made attractive by surrounding gardens, pool, appealing beach bar, restaurant, helpful staff (phone: 422-2361). Inexpensive.

ST. PHILIP

Marriott's Sam Lord's Castle – The old rascal's elegant mansion — beautifully kept and thoughtfully screened from the resort's modern 259-room resort complex — is its centerpiece. The rooms, open-air dining room, sports, and beach are just through the trees beyond. Surf swimming, lighted tennis, nearby riding, and evening entertainment are big features. To our mind, choicest of the resort's rooms are in the castle (furnished with antiques and four-poster beds) and the sleek buildings closest to the sea. Pleasant. Lots of entertainment (phone: 423-7350). Expensive.

Crane Beach – What once seemed an impossibly rundown, turn-of-the-century hotel is now one of the island's most appealing. Somewhat remote, but undeniably romantic, its site is spectacular, overlooking the Atlantic, with pillared pool and surf beach. The air-conditioned rooms and antique-decorated apartments (all with four-posters, new kitchenettes, tiled baths, vistas) may be the island's handsomest. More rooms at adjoining Boxill Great House. The *Pavilion* dining room features fresh seafood, fine wines; EP only (phone: 423-6220). Expensive to moderate.

ST. MICHAEL

Barbados Hilton International – On Needham's Point at the south edge of Bridgetown. Built around a central court full of tropical gardens, its medium-size rooms and standard services are Hilton International; but it's also amazingly personal and Bajan. Major renovations in 1986 and 1987 have greatly enhanced the property. Unique activities: bike touring, yacht cruises, Bajan nights. Enormous beach, complete water sports, tennis. Good restaurant, disco nightclub (phone: 426-0200). Expensive.

Cunard Paradise Beach – Beachside reception/entertainment/dining area recently and handsomely redone with string of new hillside rooms to match (those at either end of lengthy beach offer most peace and privacy). All water sports, top tennis ready when you are; accommodating tour desk sets up golf, riding, sightseeing, car rentals, etc. Where-it's-at reputation vis-à-vis nightly entertainment. Also has an impressive new conference center (phone: 429-7151). Expensive.

Grand Barbados – A stunning, Barbadian-owned deluxe 133-room beachfront resort. A range of menus is offered at 3 restaurants, from an informal seaside café to the elegant *Golden Shell* (already receiving very good reviews from both residents and visitors). Wonderful service and attention to detail, 24-hour room service, valet service; 2 executive floors with hospitality suite, 24-hour receptionist, and secretarial services available. All rooms have satellite TV, phone, hair dryer, and mini-bar. Complimentary water sports for guests, *Mistral* windsurfing school on the beach (phone: 800-223-9815; on Barbados, 426-0890). Expensive.

Island Inn – Just around the corner from the *Hilton,* but worlds away in size, style, cost. Simple, friendly, casual; great favorite with neighboring islanders. No sports of its own, but steps from Carlisle Bay beach. Good island food, ditto rum drinks (phone: 436-6393). Inexpensive.

CHRIST CHURCH

Southwinds – Smart, 20-acre hotel-condominium complex with tennis and racquetball courts, good-looking central pool and raised restaurant, plus two additional pools, own beach club (with bar, restaurant) on St. Lawrence Beach just across the road. Pleasantly stylish air-conditioned studios and double rooms; 1- and 2-bedroom duplex suites, with living rooms, kitchens, balconies, baths. Nice atmosphere. *Underwater Barbados* dive and water sports center is one of its best attractions. Good dive packages year-round. Exchange program with *Divi St. James Beach* for dining and recreation facilities. Run by Divi (phone: 428-7181). Expensive to moderate.

Best Western Sandy Beach – Uniformly good-looking 1- and 2-bedroom suites facing garden and/or wide Worthing beach. Affable staff, accent on things Bajan (food, drink, entertainment, activities), very good packages and free day and night sightseeing features. Special attention to business travelers; cheerfully innovative management. This is one of the few Barbados hotels with US cable TV programming. EP rates include all water sports; high MAP add-on (about $38.50 per person) covers caviar-to-crêpes choice from à la carte menu (phone: 428-0933). Moderate.

Casuarina Beach Club – Immensely popular casual resort, with 64 rooms, a good-sized pool, and a choice of water sports as well as tennis and squash (phone: 428-3600). Moderate.

Sichris Apartments – Across from (rather than right on) Dover Beach, and not much to look at from the road, but most attractive inside. With a market, small pretty pool, good restaurant, cheerful service. All 24 inviting air-conditioned apartments have phones, balconies, kitchenettes (phone: 427-5930). Moderate.

Welcome Inn – High-rise buildings around a landscaped pool patio on Maxwell Beach; 110 trim air-conditioned studios, all with kitchenettes, balconies, radios, telephones. Good restaurant, bar, minimart, boutique; some night entertainment. All sports, excursions arranged. Popular with Canadians (phone: 428-9900). Moderate.

Asta – Sixty apartments, each with fully equipped kitchen. With 2 big blue pools, small market, boutique, game room, restaurant. Set in a 2½-acre garden on Palm Beach (phone: 427-2541). Moderate to inexpensive.

Rockley Resort & Beach Club – Clusters of smart studios and townhouse apartments scattered around a 9-hole guests-only golf course in the hills. Country club atmosphere with pools, tennis courts (lighted, with a pro), squash courts, supermarket, boutique, bar, restaurant, disco. Water sports at beach club with restaurant, bar, shuttle service (phone: 427-5890). Moderate to inexpensive.

Half Moon Beach – Older place with large double rooms, studios, apartments (some with room-size porches). On wide white beach, with pool, water sports (especially windsurfing), indoor-outdoor restaurant, bar, some night entertainment. Sporty, value-conscious clientele (phone: 428-7131). Inexpensive.

Maresol Beach Apartments – Attractive, managed and served by nice people, and right on the sea; 1- and 2-bedroom units, some air conditioned, with commissary. Fine buy for families, long stays. St. Lawrence (phone: 428-9300). Inexpensive.

Ocean View – Venerable but very appealing hotel on the sea in Hastings. Big pluses: Old World charm, agreeable service, pin-neat housekeeping, popular Bajan dining room overlooking the sea. Reef-rimmed beach; rooms (some air conditioned) take all sorts of shapes (phone: 427-7821). Inexpensive.

 EATING OUT: Native Barbados cookery is interesting rather than exotic. The Board of Tourism's emblem is also the national dish: flying fish — served broiled, baked, deep-fried, stuffed, and in stew. Delicate and moist, it's the perfect visitor food: it sounds rather exotic and tastes delicious. Other favorite seafoods: crab-in-the-back (deviled, and served in a crab shell!), langouste (lobster), dolphin, and kingfish. Most meat (except goat and some poultry) is imported and only so-so. Bajans also fancy pudding (sausage stuffed with mashed sweet potato and spices, with or without blood added), souse (a melange of pig parts pickled with onion, cucumber, and pepper), and more generally appealing side dishes like coo coo (cornmeal and okra), jug jug (green peas and guinea corn flour), and casava pone are Christmas specialties. Among island-grown fruits: pawpaw (papaya), soursop (luscious in ice cream), avocado, banana, and coconut (super in milk sherbet). Guava is another — stewed, made into preserves, or cooked down and cooled into "cheese."

Mauby, a nonalcoholic liquor brewed from bark, sugar, and spices, is sold down by the Careenage, in neighborhood bars, and often made and served in Bajan homes; it is spicy and pleasant to sip (if you like liqueurs, you'll probably like it). Falernum, brewed from sugar, is another specialty liqueur. But Barbados rum — the world's smoothest, richest, and best — has no rivals. It turns up in punches, mixed with soda or tonic, and in daiquiris. The "rum snap" and rum cocktail are traditional drinks. *Mount Gay* brand has fueled generations of yachtsmen and is sold in a variety of grades from everyday Eclipse to superior, oldest, darkest Sugar Cane Brandy. *Cockspur* is another excellent brand. Generally, prices on bottles to take home are half what they are in the US.

Most of the island's best restaurants fall under one of two headings: Continental and expensive, or Bajan and not so. Some combine the two. It's easy to run up a check for $75 or more US for two at *Reid's,* or feast on a pair of flying fish at the *Ocean View* or the *Pelican* in Bridgetown for around $15 US per couple. Lunches are even less. For the best at any price:

ST. MICHAEL

Golden Shell – At the *Grand Barbados.* Elegant, epicurean dining for lunch or dinner. Continental and seafood specialties. Smart dress anytime; jackets for men at night (phone: 426-0890). Expensive.

Brown Sugar – Behind the *Island Inn.* Smart setting, an ideal place to sample Bajan specialties like pumpkin soup, pepperpot, soursop ice cream. Very popular noon buffet. Off Hilton Rd. (phone: 426-7684). Expensive to moderate.

Peter's Patio – The *Island Inn's* latticed porch is a handy, pleasantly breezy alternative to *Brown Sugar's* noontime busy-ness (phone: 436-6393). Inexpensive.

CHRIST CHURCH

Josef's – Pleasant style; its Continental menu rates high marks for unusually good meat dishes (veal Cordon Bleu and Viennoise, filet béarnaise) as well as kingfish St. Lawrence, dolphin meunière, flying fish Créole. In the St. Lawrence Apartments (phone: 428-3379). Expensive.

Pisces – Delicious fish and seafood in a small, pretty house on the shore at St. Lawrence Gap. Recommended: sea eggs, callaloo soup, flying fish in wine sauce, nutmeg ice cream. Off Highway 7 (phone: 428-6558). Expensive.

da Luciano – Italian cuisine in a handsomely restored antique mansion. Try the *misto mare* (mixed marinated seafood), *caciucco alla livornese* (an Italianate bouillabaisse). "Staten," Hastings (phone: 427-5518). Expensive to moderate.

Flamboyant – Appealing little house on the South Coast road run by a husband and wife, with unique menu mix (he's Bajan, she's German) of European and island dishes. Friendly; good rum punches, too (phone: 427-5588). Moderate.

Spinniker's – Seaside, candlelit dining, featuring fresh seafood, including the ever-popular garlic shrimp. There is live entertainment on Tuesdays and Fridays. Open for dinner only (phone: 428-7308). Moderate.

Virginian – The menu is a mix of fresh seafood, Continental, Bajan dishes — each prepared to order. Lobster and flying fish (several ways), shrimp, prime rib, are specialties; don't miss the yam croquettes, Virginian crêpe finale. In the *Seaview* hotel (phone: 427-7963). Moderate.

Witch Doctor – Quaint setting, tasty island cookery. Favorites: split pea and pumpkin soup, fish fritters, chicken piri-piri (authoritatively marinated in lime, garlic, chili peppers, then baked), ice cream with homemade rum-raisin topping. St. Lawrence Gap (phone: 87856). Moderate.

Ocean View – Pretty green and white dining room with palms on the porch by the sea. Limited but very good Bajan and Continental menu (savory soups, crisp flying fish); old school service, reasonable prices. Thoroughly enjoyable (phone: 427-7821). Moderate to inexpensive.

Captain's Carvery at the Ship's Inn – A restaurant nestled next to a cozy pub, with the best features of both. Friendly service. St. Lawrence Gap (phone: 428-9605). Inexpensive.

Melting Pot – Unpretentious little place (dinner only) that's popular with residents. Curried chicken, lamb chops, other Continental specialties. St. Lawrence Main Rd. (phone: 428-3555). Inexpensive.

T.G.I. Boomers – The only American-Barbadian restaurant on the island; a cool, tropical hideaway. St. Lawrence Gap (phone: 428-8439). Inexpensive.

ST. JAMES

La Cage aux Folles – A tiny (22 diners) place where the small menu changes frequently. Reserve *way* ahead. Paynes Bay (phone: 432-1203). Expensive.

Piperade – Elegant European cuisine in a romantic island setting. Chef's pâté, shrimps in ginger, lobster bisque, fillets of beef topped with shrimp and demiglace sauce are all commendable. And there's dinner music. In the garden of the *Glitter Bay* hotel (phone: 422-4111). Expensive.

Reid's – In a covered garden setting, with a highly polished mahogany bar. Caters to a social, chic crowd. The menu includes lobster, shrimp Créole, roast duckling, and a variety of veal and beef dishes. In Derrick, across from the *Coconut Creek* hotel. Reservations recommended (phone: 432-7623). Expensive.

Château Créole – In a house that was once a home off the West Coast Road. Basically international menu with Créole, Bajan additions. Emphasis on seafood, fish; homemade ice cream, pies for dessert (phone: 422-4116). Expensive to moderate.

Koko's – A real find offering adventurous "nu-Bajan" cuisine. Try the *koq-ka-doo* (chicken stuffed with banana and rum sauce) or the shrimp christo (sailing in little christophene boats). Overlooking the sea at Prospect. Reservations recommended (phone: 424-4557). Expensive to moderate.

Noelle's – A pristine white room with hanging plants and bright prints provides an appropriate backdrop for sophisticated nightly specials. On Holetown main road. Reservations recommended (phone: 432-6159). Expensive to moderate.

Treasure Beach – A popular family-run restaurant offering island specialties in a charming, intimate setting. Reservations are a must (phone: 432-1346). Expensive to moderate.

Raffles – Easily the West Coast's coziest, most relaxed restaurant, *Raffles* does not stop at creating the best in island atmosphere but also delivers some of the best food, including specialties such as Bajan blackened fish and Bajan lime pie. Given such attributes, it's not difficult to imagine its popularity, so reservations are a must. Holetown (phone: 4321280). Moderate.

Coach House – Attractive gathering place, popular for its informal atmosphere and simple, excellent food at reasonable prices. Live entertainment heats things up at night, and those so inclined can dance. Check the local listings (phone: 432-1163). Moderate.

ST. PETER

Giggles Beach Bar – Enjoy cool sea breezes and a tasty steak lunch on the spacious outdoor patio overlooking a quiet stretch of sand, or quench your thirst at the indoor bar, graced by Lisa the monkey, who lives in a big cage surrounded by palm fronds and a crumbling carved fish fountain. But beware: Lisa eats *anything,* including the eyeglasses of unwary guests and occasional camera straps. Open daily for breakfast, lunch, and dinner; beach barbecue on Sundays (no phone). Moderate.

Mullin's Beach Bar – Also known as Mama Leone's, a lively seaside spot with

Italian and Bajan specialties. Very informal. At Mullin's Bay (phone: 422-2484). Inexpensive.

OTHERS ON THE ISLAND

Pavilion, Crane Hotel, St. Philip – A really fine dining room. Specialties: fresh fish, seafood, langouste done with just the right light Continental touch. Well-thought-out wine list. Large Sunday brunch. On the sea (phone: 423-6220). Expensive to moderate.

Ginger's, Ginger Bay Beach Hotel, St. Philip – An outdoor dining patio with an interesting prix fixe menu (smoked meats and fish are the specialties), friendly staff, and attractive setting. Reservations recommended (phone: 423-5810). Moderate.

Waterfront Café, Bridgetown – Overlooking the yachts moored in the Careenage, this hot spot attracts an eclectic crowd of sailors, yachters, tourists, and well-heeled residents. Informal lunches. Menu includes sandwiches and Indonesian-style sate. Dinners are often accompanied by romantic piano music (phone: 427-0093). Moderate to inexpensive.

Atlantis, St. Joseph – Enid Maxwell sets out one of the island's best Sunday dinners, overlooking Tent Bay near Bathsheba, a noon buffet laden with Bajan treats such as divine dolphin, flying fish, turtle steak; spinach cakes, pumpkin fritters, pickled breadfruit, and incredible pies — all made from scratch in her family-staffed kitchen. Daily lunches, dinners too. Call ahead for reservations on Sundays (phone: 433-9445). Inexpensive.

Kingsley Club, Cattlewash-on-Sea – Once a plantation owners' private club, now a charming little inn offering splendid prix fixe lunches; split pea and pumpkin soup, baked yam casserole, sinfully good coconut meringue pie. Reservations recommended. Near Bathsheba (phone: 433-9422). Inexpensive.

GULF OF MEXICO

MEXICO

YUCATÁN PENINSULA

Ambergris
Cay

Belize City

BELIZE

GUATEMALA

CARIBBEAN SEA

HONDURAS

BELIZE

South of Mexico's Yucatán Peninsula and east of Guatemala is the small, sparsely populated, relatively underdeveloped nation of Belize. Formerly known as British Honduras, Belize is a country of dense jungle, coastal mangrove swamps, majestic karstic mountains, and lovely untouched offshore cays (pronounced *keys*). Sheltered by the world's second longest barrier reef, it has been a melting pot for immigrants from Africa, the Caribbean, Mexico, Central America, Europe, and Asia for 300 years. But it can trace its native culture and ancestry well beyond that — to the mysterious and ancient Maya, whose immense cities still stand throughout the region. Even while European settlements were being established on Belize's coast, just a few miles inland late Maya towns existed undetected, protected by the dense jungle that only the Indians knew how to penetrate with ease. And while many of the early settlements have long since washed away, the mammoth religious structures of the Maya abide.

The Mayan civilization in this region did not completely "collapse" in the eighth century, as did other famous city-states in Guatemala and Honduras. At Santa Rita Corozol, in northern Belize, gold earrings from the Aztecs were found at the burial site of an important fourteenth-century ruler, suggesting that Belize was still part of a major Maya trading route at this late date.

Spain had claimed *all* of the New World (except for those areas assigned to Portugal by papal decree) but found no gold in the impenetrable swamps of coastal Belize. Its attempts to eradicate native culture resulted in pitched battles with the Maya. These, together with the navigational hazards of the Barrier Reef, kept Spanish interest in the area at a minimum. In 1604, Great Britain and Spain signed the Treaty of London, which specified that any area not effectively occupied by Spain was open to colonization by England.

It was not until Peter Wallace, a Scottish privateer, landed here with his crew that the Spanish became possessive about Belize. Wallace originally left England as a lieutenant in Sir Walter Raleigh's 1603 pirate-hunting expedition. With six ships, Wallace put into the Caribbean pirate stronghold of Tortuga, only to emerge sometime later with a new allegiance and a new flag — the skull and crossbones. Soon after, however, Wallace and his crew were shipwrecked off Belize and became the first white men to colonize it.

The swamps and jungles of their new home proved to be rich in timber, and almost every type of fish in the Caribbean could be found feeding off the reef. The jungles were full of game, and the rivers provided fresh water. First logwood, which produces a dye, and then the lumber trade proved almost as profitable as pirating and, with slaves to supply the labor, was easier and safer. These early arrivals became known as "Baymen" (after the Bay of Honduras), and with them the lumber trade began. English soldiers and sailors did establish villages here in the 1690s, but these were logging camps, not permanent settlements.

Britain soon challenged Spain's claim to the area, and the English government encouraged immigration, providing some limited financial and military support. By 1745, the slaves who had been imported from the very beginning of European colonization accounted for 71% of the population, and by 1800 the number had risen to 86%. With the shift in economic activity from logwood to mahogany, more slaves, land, and capital were needed, and in 1787, the settlers began to pass a series of laws which soon resulted in a dozen settlers owning four-fifths of all the land. This monopoly of land ownership was a fundamental aspect of the new colony.

The country abolished slavery in 1838, but because the majority of the land was controlled by "mahogany lords," the freed men were forced to seek employment with their former masters, who passed a system of labor laws designed to keep workers under firm control. In addition, the practice of "advancing" wages bound workers to their employers by keeping them in debt. This system of land and labor control lasted into the middle of the twentieth century.

Belize became the colony of British Honduras in 1862, after years of pleading by local British residents who were fearful of attacks by mestizos and Spaniards from the "War of the Castes" on the Yucatán Peninsula and in northern Belize. The designation as a colony followed by just three years a treaty between Great Britain and Guatemala fixing the borders of those two countries. However, problems exist to this day, and both Mexico and Guatemala continue to claim that, as inheritors of the Spanish lands in the area, they are entitled to Belizean territory.

Along with British immigration came the beginnings of a Caribbean influence, readily apparent in the singsong speech that the traveler hears so often on the Caribbean islands. The earliest Caribbean immigration was involuntary — slave labor brought from Africa and Jamaica in the early 1700s to work in the lumber industry. At the start of the nineteenth century, the ethnic mix in Belize was basically black slaves, white British settlers, Créoles (a mixture of black and white), and a few Maya. By the mid-nineteenth century, the ethnic mix had become further broadened by Honduran garifunas (the progeny of escaped African slaves and Carib Indians), mestizos escaping from the "War of the Castes" in the Yucatán Peninsula, Asian immigrants, and southerners from the post–Civil War US. Between 1870 and 1890, they were followed by East Indians who were brought to Belize by the British as indentured servants originally to work the new sugar plantations of the Toledo district in the south.

Through the nineteenth and the early twentieth centuries, immigrants from all over the world joined the Belizean mix, further broadening the country's incredible melange of ideas, cultures, and customs. While the population of Belize in 1840 was just 6,000, it had jumped to over 25,000 by 1861; to 60,000 by 1942; and today stands at about 150,000. Some 65% of Belize's population is composed of three different groups of inhabitants, all with African origins: Créoles, who speak "Créole"; Garifuna, whose language is a mixture of African and Carib; and, on the offshore islands, Africans mixed with Maya, whose primary language is Spanish. The most recent group of immigrants are the refugees from the civil wars in El Salvador and Guatemala.

During the twentieth century, the Belizean government slowly evolved into a more representative form and, in 1963, a new constitution was written providing self-government for the first time in the nation's history. As early as 1961, the British government made it plain that Belize (the name was changed from British Honduras in 1973) could become totally independent whenever it wished. However, because of a well-founded fear that without Britain's protection their country would soon be run over by neighboring Guatemala, Belizeans chose to retain their British ties. After Britain agreed to retain a small protective military presence in the country, Belize declared itself an independent nation on September 21, 1981.

Belizeans like to refer to their nation as an "undiscovered paradise," and, in fact, it is. But it won't remain so, as more and more Americans and Canadians discover one of the last remaining outposts of almost virgin territory in the world.

BELIZE AT-A-GLANCE

FROM THE AIR: Belize is a patchwork of subtropical lowlands, marshes, and swamps, with mountains and forests to the west and beaches, the Great Barrier Reef, and some 175 offshore cayes and islands to the east. It is on the Caribbean coast of the Yucatán Peninsula, separated from Mexico on the north by the Río Hondo and from Guatemala to the south by the Sarstoon River. This tiny nation, once known as British Honduras, is only 174 miles north to south and 69 miles east to west at its widest point — 8,600 square miles of landmass, of which about half is used for farming. The rest is rugged jungle terrain, mountains, and swamps; 266 square miles of offshore cayes; and about 300 miles of rivers.

The first view of Belize from the air is of the 200-mile-long barrier reef — largest in the Western Hemisphere, and second in the world only to Australia's Great Barrier Reef. Interspersed are cayes and islands of all sizes stretched like a chain set in the blue-green Caribbean Sea. The desolate swamps and deep jungles in the north, dotted with small towns and villages, gradually give rise to the vast Maya Mountains in the southwest. These are topped by Victoria Peak, at 3,680 feet, the highest in the entire Cockscomb range, of which it is a part. The country is traversed by a number of rivers: The New River runs parallel to the Río Hondo in the north; and there are several small rivers in the south. The Belize River originates in Guatemala and crosses the country's central region from west to east.

The entire country sits on a vast, continental block of limestone that extends 800 miles north to south, and about 400 miles across. This ledge slopes at a downward angle, so that Belize City on the Caribbean coast is only 18 inches above sea level, and high water easily flows inland, causing bad flooding.

Most visitors will arrive at Belize International Airport, 9 miles north of Belize City. Belize has some 150,000 inhabitants, of whom 45,000 live in Belize City. About 5,000 have moved to the modern capital of Belmopan, which was built after Hurricane Hattie tore through coastal Belize City in 1961, killing 200 people and destroying much property. Several thousand refugees set up a village outside Belize City and named it Hattieville; about 3,000 people still live there. The new capital is about 50 miles inland.

In total there are two cities in Belize, seven towns, and 160 villages and settlements of varying size. There is more jungle and mountain than there is rural or urban life, even including the resorts on the coast and the cays.

SPECIAL PLACES: Belize City – Hot, humid, and an interesting mixture of British colonial architecture and small-town friendliness, Belize City, with a population of 45,000, is the only real city in the country. It is filled with old, mostly wooden buildings and ramshackle houses, the line broken only occasionally by Victorian government buildings.

The most colorful thing about the city is the street names: the Queen's Square uses animal names such as Antelope, Armadillo, and Sea-Gull streets; the Mesopotamia area has Middle Eastern names like Euphrates, Cairo, and Tigris; and the Caribbean Shores area relies on church figures for names. Visitors may find disconcerting the sort of vague and habitual surliness — but not quite genuine antagonism — projected by many Belizeans. However, the city is really more unpleasant than dangerous, unless you're foolish or reckless enough to get involved with one of the gentlemen cruising the streets in the evenings, offering to sell "ganja" (marijuana). If you do get the urge to buy, a walk past the Belize Penitentiary on Gaol Street should cool you out.

The city's small business and shopping area is centered around the few blocks on either side of Belize Swing Bridge. Here are Albert and Queen streets, which make up the commercial district, and Regent Street, which houses the government buildings. At the northeast end of the bridge is the Paslow Building, an interesting bit of architecture which contains the post office. Across the street from this building, at 91 Front Street, is the Belize Philatelic Bureau, where collector stamps may be purchased. Covered with drawings of Belizean wildlife, shells, historical events, and the British royal family, these lovely stamps are unusual and inexpensive mementos. The Baron Bliss Institute, on Southern Foreshore, near the Swing Bridge, was dedicated to the multimillionaire who left several million dollars to Belize City in the 1920s; it contains carved stone monuments from the ancient Maya ceremonial center of Caracol in the Maya Mountains.

Also located on the southern side of the Swing Bridge is Old Fort George, with its Memorial Park, and standing along Regent Street are some of the old slave quarters. Also on Regent, across from the *Mopan* hotel, is a bookstore which has a small selection of Belizean historical publications. St. John's Cathedral is one of the oldest Anglican cathedrals in Central America, built in 1826.

You can also drop in on the studio of George Gabb, reputedly Belize's best carver, at 74 Albert Street. The small, cluttered workshop is open every day from 8 AM to 6:30 PM. The genial Gabb, widely known as a pork-barrel philosopher, will show you how he carves the native zirocote hardwood, which, when cut across the grain, reveals a brown and black "rose" on a white background. Most of his work is exported, and the 12-foot statue *To Be Born Again*, which he donated to the US for its Bicentennial, is now at Lansing (Michigan) Community College.

Belmopan – This new capital of Belize was carved out of the jungle in the late 1960s after Hurricane Hattie seriously damaged Belize City, and was occupied by the government in July 1970. Its Assembly Building, which dominates the government complex, was designed to represent a Maya temple. At first, many of the Belizeans who worked in Belmopan commuted from Belize City, but the population has grown to almost 5,000, and the town is developing a personality of its own. On Monday, Wednesday, and Friday afternoons the Archaeology Commission conducts guided tours through its vault, which houses a collection of artifacts from the country's archaeological sites. (There is no museum within the country.) Call ahead to make arrangements (phone: 08-2106). Belmopan is also home to the *Bullfrog*, one of the best restaurants in the country as well as a nursery with orchids, bromeliads, and other local flora. It also has some rooms for rent and is next door to the *Circle A* hotel.

Some 15 miles past Belmopan, 81 miles from Belize City, is Mountain Pine Ridge, a national forest reserve encompassing hundreds of miles of natural pine, bald hills, orchids, wildlife, and rivulets. Its most famous attraction is the 1,000-foot Hidden

Valley Falls, which actually tumbles 1,300 feet into the valley below. There are 15 miles of roads to cover here, and a picnic should be the order of the day. All necessary facilities are available for travelers, campers, and day-trippers.

Dangriga (Stann Creek) – On a lovely stretch of white sand, Dangriga is 105 miles south of Belize City and can be reached by car, bus, or air (*Maya Air* has daily service). The majority of its population of 2,500 are Garifuna (black Caribs) who first settled here in 1823, an event commemorated annually on November 19, with dancing, public ceremonies, and a re-enactment of the first landing. The barrier reef is only a short boat ride from Dangriga, and fishing, swimming, snorkeling, or diving excursions can be arranged through the *Pelican Beach* resort (phone: 05-2044), which can also help visitors find the two famous Belizean oil painters, Benjamin and Pen, who live and work here.

Just a few miles south of Dangriga, on the beach, is the garifuna village of Hopkins, and the world's first and only jaguar preserve is in Cockscomb Basin, 30 miles south. Ask at the *Pelican Beach* for information on getting into the park.

Punta Gorda – Flanked by hills on the west and northwest, Punta Gorda lies at the southern end of Belize. It is the capital of the Toledo district, whose population of almost 12,000 is a mixture of garifunas, Créoles, Maya, East Indians, Chinese, and other ethnic groups. The town overlooks the Bay of Honduras, with Guatemala and Honduras only a few miles across the sea. Boats can be hired to take the adventurous to Livingston, Guatemala. Unfortunately, there are no decent hotels here, and only one restaurant, the *MiraMar,* which serves Chinese food. The town can be reached by road, air, or water.

A few miles away from the huge promontory at the southern end of Punta Gorda is the site of the former Toledo settlement, home of the US Civil War refugees, and nearby are several picturesque Maya villages. There is a simple, clean hotel, *Bowles Hilltop,* in the village of San Antonio. A mile north of San Pedro Colombia is the trail to the ancient Maya ceremonial center of Lubaantun. The mile-long trail to the site is not too great, except in the dry season. The site itself, however, which is made up of temples built from stone blocks, is well worth the effort. Several miles north of the Punta Gorda–San Antonio turnoff and a few miles south of Big Falls is the trail into Nim Li Punit, a Maya ceremonial center noted for its carved stone monuments, or *stelae,* which show ancient rulers "letting blood" into braziers to appease the gods.

Placencia – This tiny fishing village is strung along the beach of a thin peninsula, reached by boat from either Mango Creek or Big Creek, or by a four-wheel-drive vehicle. The beaches here are the loveliest in Belize and are seldom reached by tourists. There are several good hotels here, and nearby Seine Bight, north of Placencia, is an interesting Garifuna village.

San Ignacio – This town sits on the bank of the Macal River, a branch of the Belize River, 72 miles west of Belize City, in the foothills of the Maya Mountains. The Maya, mestizos, Mennonites, and, most recently, Americans and Europeans who make up its population are mainly farmers and cattle ranchers. The wealthiest district in Belize, it has several good hotels and guest ranches. *Explore Belize* owner Bart Mickler (phone: 092-2164) offers tours of many of the attractions of the area, including Tikal, Guatemala. The *San Ignacio* hotel (phone: 092-2034), *Chaa Creek Cottages* (phone: 092-2037), and *El Indio Suizo* guest ranch also offer tours into the Maya Mountains and Tikal.

Orange Walk Town – On the left bank of the New River, about 66 miles north of Belize City — the heart of the country's sugar-producing area — is the the second largest town. Three miles south, at Tower Hill, stands Belize's only sugar-processing factory. The area was originally settled by mestizos during the middle of the last century, at the time of the "War of the Castes," and Spanish is still commonly spoken here.

Behind the Cuello Brothers Rum Distillery, 3 miles west of Orange Walk Town on the Yo Creek Road, is Cuello, the oldest Maya site yet found, dating from 2500 BC. While here, visitors may also want to stop in at Central America's second largest distillery.

Hidden in the jungle, 30 miles upriver from Orange Walk Town, is the fascinating ancient trading center of Lamanai, with spectacular temples and masks still intact. The only way to reach the site is by boat, a trip that is half the day's enjoyment. To make arrangements, contact Bader Hasan (phone: 03-2115) or *Explore Belize* (phone: 092-2164), and be sure to bring along a picnic lunch.

Corozol – A Maya stronghold known as Chetumal until the middle of the 19th century, Corozol is the northernmost town in Belize. In addition to its location on Corozol Bay, a beautiful expanse of blue-green water ideal for swimming and fishing, it offers visitors Santa Rita Corozol, a Maya ruin, and, nearby, Cerros Maya, another archaeological site accessible only by boat (make arrangements at *Tony's* motel).

Crooked Tree Wildlife Sanctuary – Located 33 miles northwest of Belize City and 2 miles off the Northern Highway, this wildlife refuge consists of a network of lagoons, swamps, and waterways that provide a variety of habitats for Belize's flora and fauna, including thousands of birds. There are several species of herons, snowy and great egrets, all five species of kingfishers, plus ducks, kites, storks, and many others. Visitors will also see crocodiles, black howler monkeys, coatimundi, turtles, and iguanas. Further information can be obtained from the Belize Audubon Society (PO Box 1001, Belize City).

Altun-Ha – Only 30 miles north of Belize City is the ancient Maya ceremonial center of Altun Ha. It was here that a carved jade head of the sun god, Kinich Ahau, was unearthed during the 1960s by a Royal Ontario Museum team. The head is six inches long and weighs ten pounds, but there have been many other discoveries in these three square miles of ruins. It was the other items — bowls, tools, and jade objects — that helped to pinpoint the degree of advancement of Maya civilization represented here. To reach the site, drive toward Orange Walk on the Northern Highway. Turn right at Maskall Road (also the old highway to Orange Walk) and continue on for about 15 minutes. There is a sign on the left marking the site.

Xunantunich – This Maya ruin, about 80 miles southwest (inland) of Belize City, is almost at the Guatemalan border. The site is filled with stone buildings 1,400 years old. Towering over the site is El Castillo, a magnificent 127-foot pyramid and a monument to the wisdom of the past. To reach the site, drive southwest on the Western Highway from San Ignacio for 5 miles and take the ferry, which operates daily from 9 AM to noon and 1 to 5 PM.

Maya artifacts are not to be removed from either site, and the authorities are very strict about enforcing this. Even the Ontario Museum could not keep their findings. This ruling also includes items which local individuals may attempt to sell you, illegally. Government permits are required for any artifact taken from the country.

■**EXTRA SPECIAL:** More than 75% of the visitors to Belize spend their vacations on one of the offshore islands such as Caye Caulker, Turneffe Island, English Caye, or St. George's Caye. But *Ambergris Caye* is the most popular with visitors from the US. The 30-mile-long island sits 36 miles northeast of Belize City, just 15 minutes away by small plane. (Both *Maya* and *Tropic Air* have daily regularly scheduled flights from Belize City.) Arrivals land on the 2,500-foot gravel strip that is just a few steps from the heart of the island's only village, San Pedro. Despite a population of 1,800, everything about it is simple, primitive. There is little TV or radio and only a few telephones; the streets of San Pedro are pure white sand, and almost everything is just a short, easy stroll away. The island has a few Land Rovers, one policeman (who's also the fire chief, postman, and immigration and customs officer), and about 1,800 residents (many of them fishermen involved with the village's cooperative venture).Most of the places to stay, the largest of which has only 18 rooms, are within a quarter mile of the landing strip. The farthest is 3 miles away and is reached by boat.

What's most exciting about Ambergris Caye is the Great Barrier Reef about 300 yards offshore. Nearly 200 miles long, it is the longest reef in the Western Hemisphere, and worldwide, second in size only to Australia's. It's also a paradise for divers. Underwater visibility is over 100 feet at Ambergris Caye, and what a spectacle: crimson parrotfish and yellowtail damselfish, their black bodies dotted with bright blue; zebra-striped sergeant majors; green moray eels (peaceful, unless you provoke them); and many more, gliding and darting amid a staggering variety of corals and sea plants. Off the southern tip of the island, an underwater national park was recently created to protect the natural beauty of the area. Snorkeling equipment, glass-bottom boats, and diving trips can be arranged through most of the hotels in San Pedro.

At night stroll over to the *Navigator Bar,* at the *Barrier Reef* hotel. There you will find a mix of locals, Americans, and visiting British troops who have come for rest and recuperation from their mainland bases. With its white sand floor, bamboo decor, formica tables, and hi-fi tapes, this is *the* nighttime gathering place of Ambergris Caye. If you're lucky, a member of a Scottish Highland Regiment will be there, playing his bagpipes, and triggering a Highland Fling. Other favorite watering holes are the *Tackle Box* and the bar at the *Ambergris Lodge.*

SOURCES AND RESOURCES

TOURIST INFORMATION: The Caribbean Tourism Association, 20 E 46th St., New York, NY 10017 (phone: 212-682-0435), will be glad to supply whatever information possible. The staff does not have a lot of handouts but is friendly and very helpful. The Embassy of Belize, 1575 Eye St., NW, Suite 695, Washington, DC 20005 (phone: 202-363-4505), can also answer travel questions.

The Belize Tourist Board, 53 Regent St., Belize City (phone: 7213), can provide literature, maps, advice, and help. Newspapers are in English, and there is a tourist guide of sorts, but it's not very helpful.

Radio Belize broadcasts in English and Spanish.

Telephone – Dial direct by prefacing the desired local number with 011-501.

ENTRY REQUIREMENTS: Passports are not necessary, but proof of citizenship — passport, birth certificate, voter's registration card — will be needed for US and Canadian citizens. For stays of more than 30 days, and for visits by other nationalities, passports will be required. Be aware that customs and immigration officials have absolute power of discrimination; they will not allow anyone to enter whose appearance they do not approve of, even with the appropriate papers. The border crossings from Mexico and Guatemala may be time-consuming, but they are simple. If planning to drive into Belize from Mexico and then return to Mexico, a visitor must have a Mexican tourist card, which is not available at the border. They can, however, be obtained at the Mexican consulate in Belize City.

CLIMATE AND CLOTHES: Belize is a subtropical area with temperatures ranging from the mid-70s in January to the upper 90s in August. At midday, shade temperatures of 95° to 100° are not uncommon. Rainfall in the northern part of the country averages 50 inches per year, but in the south 170

inches per year is normal. The rainy season generally runs from June through August, and the driest period is from February through May. During the rains, Belize is susceptible to hurricanes, and the humidity hovers around 80%.

Extremely light, informal clothing is the norm, and with good reason. Although some businesspeople do wear coats and ties, it is unnecessary. Women tend to wear summery dresses to dinner, although tropical safari gear might be more appropriate the rest of the time. Shorts are fine on the offshore islands, but not in town.

MONEY: The official currency is the Belize dollar (BH or Bz.), which has been stabilized at $1 US to $2 BH. Banks are generally open from 8 AM to 1 PM, weekdays. Hotels will usually exchange currency with little or no commission; however, there are no exchange facilities at the airport. Do not exchange Mexican pesos if possible, as the rate is very poor in Belize.

LANGUAGE: English is the official language, but it comes with a variety of accents, British, Caribbean, and Spanish. Many Belizeans speak Spanish, Chinese, Créole, or a Maya tongue, and there are several German-speaking Mennonite settlements.

TIME: The country is on Central Standard Time, which makes it even with Chicago except in summer: When the US switches to Daylight Saving Time, Belize does not.

CURRENT: Most of Belize uses the same 110-volt, 60-cycle current as the US.

GETTING THERE: Daily flights are available from TACA (the airline of El Salvador) and TAN-SAHSA (the airline of Honduras).The flights originate from New Orleans, Miami, and Houston. There is no regular sea service, although cargo craft have been known to pick up and drop off passengers. The road from Mexico is good, but the road from Guatemala City is unpaved for most of the way and in terrible condition. Buses are available from Guatemala City, at a cost of about $12 US, and from Chetumal, Mexico, at roughly $3.50 US, but crossing the border by bus can be difficult and time-consuming.

CALCULATING COSTS: Rates at the best hotels in Belize City run about $40 US to $60, double, but in some areas the rates are up to an exceptional $170 US per day including all meals, guide, etc., at a mainland fishing resort, and $50 to $100 US (including meals) on the cayes. Inland the rates drop to about $35 to $40 US. All Belize hotels will add a 5% room tax, and some will add a 10% service charge. There are few eating places outside the hotels that attract visitors, but those that do are inexpensive, usually in the $5 to $10 US range. The national diet of Belize seems to be beans and rice, corn tortillas, and sometimes a little meat. Budget about $90 US per day.

GETTING AROUND: Within the cities, transportation is easy, but once in the countryside, roads are extremely variable. The main highway in northern Belize is very good. The western highway is now finished. The Hummingbird Highway south from Belmopan may be the worst road in the country, but it passes through some of the most magnificent scenery. The southern highway, south of Dangriga, is dirt but, except in the rainy season, is usually well maintained.

Taxi – There are no meters, but the rates are set by the government. However, if you are leaving from a hotel, check what the fare should be beforehand, as taxi drivers have been known to overcharge. From Belize International Airport to Belize City is $12.50 US, and there are always drivers. Watch out for drivers who will compute the fare in Belize dollars and try to collect in US dollars.

Bus – Long-haul buses between towns and villages aren't very comfortable, but they do try to maintain some type of schedule. Fares range from $1 US to $4, according to destination. Local Belize City buses are about 50¢ US.

Car Rental – Land Rovers used to be the only practical way to tour Belize's difficult roads. However, the roads in Belize have been improved, and all major roads in the north are paved. If you decide to drive, expect to pay $50 to $70 US a day (less if you rent for several days) with unlimited mileage. Gas will cost about $1.70 US a gallon. In Belize City, try *Smith's Auto Rental,* 125C Cemetery Rd. (phone: 3779), *Elijah Sutherland,* 127 Neal Pen Rd. (phone: 3582), and *Pancho's* (phone: 2813); they all offer a variety of vehicles, from Land Rovers to buses.

Ferry – The *Miss Belize* runs mornings and afternoons from Belize City to Caye Caulker and Ambergris Caye. It costs $17 BH and can be boarded behind the National Bank building.

Local Air Service – *Tropic Air* has several regularly scheduled flights each day from Belize City to San Pedro on Ambergris Caye and can arrange charters to anywhere in the country (San Pedro, Ambergris Caye; phone: 026-2117, 024-5671). *Maya* has daily scheduled flights to most destinations within the country (PO Box 458, Belize City; phone: 02-7215).

SHOPPING: Belize is not exactly a shopper's dream. The in-bond stores do, however, carry watches, perfumes, and other imports at duty-free prices, but it is hardly comparable to other free ports in the Caribbean. There are nice rosewood carvings, and woodwork formed from zirocote, the two-toned wood native to the area. The government operates *Cottage Craft Industries,* 26 Albert St., Belize City. Good buys include straw goods made from jipijapa straw in the Punta Gorda area, and jewelry made from Belizean black coral. It's illegal to bring turtleshell items into the US.

TIPPING: Very few places add a service charge, so plan to add 10% if you're satisfied. Taxi drivers are not normally tipped, but airport porters get about 50¢ per bag.

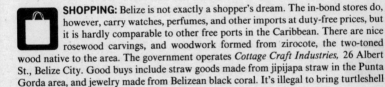

SPECIAL EVENTS: *National Day* is the big holiday in Belize. It kicks off on September 10 with parades, floats, sports activities, patriotic rallies, and beauty contests. There used to be a nationwide *pre-Lent Carnival,* but now that is pretty much restricted to San Pedro on Ambergris Caye. The *Fiesta del Virgen del Carmen,* at Benque Viejo del Carmen, in July, features costumes and much dancing in the streets. The *Fiesta de San José* (March-April) at San José Succotz climaxes with a re-enactment of a battle between the Moors and the Spaniards. The second week in November is devoted to tourism, with booths, displays, and food. The arrival of the Garifuna from Honduras is celebrated on November 19 in Dangriga and nearby villages with costumed dancers, booths, and displays. And a *regatta* is held on the Belize River to honor Baron Bliss, the country's major benefactor, on March 9.

SPORTS: Fishing in the nation's rivers and off the coast is the main attraction, closely followed by scuba diving and snorkeling in and around the Barrier Reef.

Climbing – The Maya Mountains, in the southwest, present a challenge to even experienced climbers. Victoria's Peak, at 3,680 feet, crowns the Cockscomb Range. The chief forest officer, Ministry of Natural Resources, Belmopan, Belize, will put you in touch with a qualified guide.

Hunting – A license is required, and you must be accompanied by a guide holding a government concession. Jaguars and ocelots are protected by law, but the Belize jungles abound with other game animals, such as wild pig, deer, game birds, and waterfowl. Contact the Chief Forest Officer, Ministry of Natural Resources, Belmopan, Belize, CA, for details and recommendations. Also contact the commissioner of police, police headquarters, Belmopan, if you plan to bring firearms into the country. Ask the forest officer to put you in touch with them.

Snorkeling and Scuba – Divers are advised to bring their own gear. The average cost for a boat, with guide, is a minimum of $75 a day with two dives. The *Coral Beach Dive Shop* (phone: 7036) and *Ramon's* (phone: 2071; in the US, 504-443-2100 in San Pedro on Ambergris Caye have a full-time internationally certified dive master/guide. But some resorts do hire certified personnel on a somewhat irregular basis. Several one- and two-boat operators are also certified. Check before you make reservations; ask about a working compressor too. When air is rare, try snorkeling; it is readily available, and like scuba here, truly spectacular.

Sport Fishing – Name the fish. If it's in the Caribbean, it can be caught off the coast of Belize. Average cost for a boat, guide, and equipment is about $85 US per day, plus gas ($15 to $20 extra), for up to four. Most of the hotels and resort areas have these facilities available, and private individuals can be hired at times.

Swimming and Sunning – Swimming is good off the sandy beaches of the cayes and on the southeast coast. Sunbathing on your very own caye is tops.

Tennis – The three nicest courts are at the *Pickwick Club* in Belize City, but it is open only to members and their guests.

NIGHTLIFE: Belize City is not a night town. There's live dancing late in the evenings at the *Château Caribbean* and *Bellevue* hotel, and quiet music and conversation at the bar of the *Fort George* hotel or *Villa* hotel, overlooking the harbor. If you meet a local who's a member of the *Pickwick Club,* ask him to bring you along to see how the upper-crust Belizeans spend evenings. The *Big Apple* and *The Pub* are currently favorite after-dark gathering places.

BEST IN THE COUNTRY

CHECKING IN: No one has yet accused Belize of being a center of deluxe hotels, and US travelers may find that none of the accommodations available suit sophisticated tastes. For the broad-minded traveler, however, Belize does offer acceptable living quarters. They range from little four- or five-unit converted homes to the more formal and, by Belizean standards, large 41-room *Fort George.* On the offshore islands such as Ambergris Caye, there is no air conditioning anywhere. Offshore accommodations range from quite spartan fishing lodges and thatch-roofed and bamboo cabins to tiny rooms in formerly private houses.

In winter, with the exception of the new *Belizean,* which costs a whopping $320 for a double (MAP), expect to pay more than $75 US for a double room, including meals, in a hotel listed below in the expensive range; some fishing resorts also charge much more. Hotels in the moderate range cost between $55 and $75; less than that is inexpensive. Prices are reduced somewhat in the summer, but the strict Caribbean winter/summer seasonal rate changes don't affect Belize as much as the island nations.

Belizean – Opened in January 1986, Belize's first and only deluxe hotel lolls on 18 acres of unspoiled, palm-fringed beach at Ambergris Caye. Its 6 rooms feature tile baths, wet bars, refrigerators, satellite TV with VCR, telephones, air conditioning, and ceiling fans — and all steps away from the ocean. Activities include excellent snorkeling, scuba diving, and deep-sea fishing. Breakfast and dinner are included in the rates. Managed by Chris and Maria Tilling, formerly of the deluxe Caribbean hideaway Marina Cay, in the British Virgin Islands (phone: 800-235-3505 or collect, from New York State and Canada, 212-689-3048). Very expensive.

Belize River Lodge – A unique, 12-room lodge for the fisherman. This hotel sits on the fish-packed Belize River, onto which guests are taken, overnight if desired. It is partially air conditioned, with a pleasant restaurant featuring native cuisine. Package rates include guides, boats, all meals. Five-day minimum stay (phone: 02-5-2002). Expensive.

Fort George – One of Belize's largest properties, with 41 air-conditioned rooms, all with private bath. The hotel is run in a proper British manner, quite efficient and very dull. It is the most popular hotel among businesspeople and older tourists, and makes a good home base for touring the country. There is a gift shop, spacious starched-white-tablecloth restaurant with picture-window view of the harbor, a lounge with music on weekends, and a pool. A 10% service charge is added to bills (phone: 7242). Expensive.

El Pescador – This remote hotel has 10 double rooms, 3 miles north of San Pedro, on Ambergris Caye. It is accessible only by boat, which the hotel uses to pick up arrivals in San Pedro. Life at El Pescador is devoted to the fisherman. All the rooms have twin beds and private facilities, plus verandahs offering striking views of the sea. Ambergris Caye (phone: 7215). Expensive.

Pyramid Island Resort – This hotel, with 30 rooms, is devoted to the intrepid offshore diver. All rooms have private facilities. In addition to sea sports, sail boards, and 2 tennis courts, there is a cocktail lounge, laundry service, patio bar and restaurant overlooking the Great Barrier Reef. Caye Chapel, 16 miles from Belize City. PO Box 192, Belize City (phone: 4190). Expensive.

Rum Point Inn – Very charming, comfortable cottages in a garden setting on the beach on the northern part of Placencia Bay (phone: 06-2017; in the US, 415-752-8008). Expensive.

Turneffe Island Lodge – This remote resort is 30 miles off the coast on Caye Bokel. All 8 rooms have private facilities. Majors in fishing. There is a restaurant, bar, and beach. Week-long packages only, including guides, boats, accommodations, meals (no phone). Expensive.

Adventure Inn – A new property with pleasant thatch-roofed bungalows overlooking beautiful Corozal Bay. Box 35, Corozol Town (phone: 04-2187; in the US, 813-377-5036). Moderate.

Ambergris Lodge – Offers 13 rooms directly on the beach in San Pedro. Mayan decor abounds, and all the rooms have two double beds and private facilities. Ambergris Caye (phone: 026-2057). Moderate.

Bellevue – One of Belize City's few alternatives to the *Fort George* is this converted, modern private home with air conditioning and one of the city's best restaurants (phone: 7051). Moderate.

Chaa Creek Cottages – A guest ranch 3 miles outside of San Ignacio, in some of the prettiest countryside Belize has to offer (phone: 092-2037). Moderate.

Château Caribbean – A converted mansion overlooking the sea, with clean rooms, air conditioning, and private baths. Off-street parking is also provided, a nice extra since it's said that an untended car on the street is quite likely to be ransacked or stolen before sun-up. Belize City (phone: 2813). Moderate.

Glover's Reef – Small, simple cottages strung along the beach of an island within Glover's Reef, one of the four newly forming atolls in the Western Hemisphere. For weekly packages, including boat transport to the island, contact Lomont Enterprises, Box 563, Belize City (phone: 02-2548). Moderate.

El Indio Suizo – A guest ranch on the banks of the Belize River in San Ignacio, it offers swimming, boating, and horseback riding. Write to Colette Gross, Benque Viejo, Belize. Moderate.

Maya Mountain Lodge – A guest ranch with garden cottages and delicious food. PO Box 46, San Ignacio (phone: 092-2164). Moderate.

Paradise – This is a Tahiti-like resort on Ambergris Caye, offering 18 units in thatched-roof and bamboo huts, all with private facilities. There is a pleasant, family-style dining room, and a bar in a separate building. Fishing and diving facilities available. PO Box 888, Belize City (phone: 026-2083). Moderate.

Pelican Beach – A very pleasant, family-run hotel on the beach just north of Dangriga. The owners are hospitable and helpful (phone: 05-2044). Moderate.

Placencia Cove – The oldest resort in Placencia, it has several pleasant bungalows and caters to fishermen (phone: 06-2024). Moderate.

Ramón's Reef – Cozy, thatch-roofed bungalows on the beach; the only property in San Pedro with a swimming pool (phone: 026-2071). Moderate.

San Ignacio – A very well run establishment, with a swimming pool, overlooking the Macal River. 18 Buena Vista St., San Ignacio (phone: 092-2125). Moderate.

San Pedro Holiday – This hotel caters primarily to deep-sea fishermen, though divers come too, and more than 90% of its business is repeat, a very good sign. Cooking is done by the owner, and served in a homey, unpretentious dining room. On the beach (phone: 02-44632 or 026-2014). Moderate.

Turtle Inn – Small but very nice, with 6 thatch-roofed bungalows on the beach in Placencia. Meals are included in the price (phone: 06-2046, Ext. 111). Moderate.

Villa – New and well maintained, it has 12 air-conditioned rooms with private baths and one of the best restaurants in town. 13 Cork St. (phone: 4-5743). Moderate.

Baron – On the main highway just south of the center of Orange Walk Town, this new hotel offers basic accommodations and a swimming pool (phone: 03-2518). Inexpensive.

Coral Beach – Family-run hotel with comfortable accommodations and the best food on the island. Caters to divers. San Pedro, Ambergris Caye (phone: 026-2001). Inexpensive.

Mom's – Basic, clean accommodations in a converted colonial building. 11 Handyside St., Belize City (phone: 45523). Inexpensive.

Mopan – Simple, family-run establishment that takes pride in dispensing personal service. This is the place where visiting archaeologists and scientists stay. 55 Regent St. (phone: 7351). Inexpensive.

EATING OUT: Aside from the restaurants in the hotels, Belize offers painfully little in the way of good food. All the hotels prepare meals for their guests, and most, especially those on the offshore cayes, will accommodate visitors from other establishments, if notified in advance. In Belize City, hardly any non-hotel restaurants are recommended. If you feel adventurous, try one of the city's Chinese restaurants, which serve passable food but are not very pleasing to the eye. Our advice is to stick to the hotel dining rooms. The basic fare in this country is beans and rice cooked with coconut milk, which is delicious.

Meal prices in Belize City are low, usually between $5 to $10 US in the restaurants that are acceptable, and range up to $10 to $15 per person at the major hotels.

Belizean beer, which is consumed in great amounts by the populace, is brewed by a German brewmaster and is delicious. Imported US beer costs $2.50 or more. Belizean cigarettes cost only 75¢ US per pack but are not easy to smoke. US cigarettes, however, are hard to find and cost around $1.70 US. These prices do not represent profiteering by the establishments, but a "protective import tariff" imposed by the government to help support native products.

BERMUDA

Bermuda is, plain and simple, the quintessential tourist island — a fact inspired as much by necessity as inclination. For the truth is that tourism is Bermuda's only authentic industry, and an instinct for self-preservation and the recognition of economic reality have manifested themselves in an island population that recognizes how much their island depends on tourist traffic. So while Bermuda surely has its share of political disagreement and social acrimony, a visitor is very unlikely ever to be aware of any sort of disharmony.

Every Bermudian depends — to a greater or lesser degree — on tourism for his or her livelihood, and each member of the population seems to be willing to stretch himself a bit to keep the tourists coming. That Bermuda has probably the highest incidence of return visitors of any island in this book testifies most dramatically to how well Bermudians do their job. From the taxi driver who describes his island with obvious pride to the shop clerk who sets an all too seldom seen standard of service and helpfulness, Bermudians cater to visitors as they would treasure a natural resource. And the almost omnipresent smiles set a tone of friendliness that is hard to resist.

Physically, Bermuda is as pretty as its postcards — maybe prettier. The green hills, the white roofs, the pastel houses, flowers, pink sand beaches, and bright blue and turquoise seas are all waiting as your plane lands at the airport or your ship glides past Spanish Point into Hamilton Harbour. You can count on it, as visitors have since 1779 when the first known American tourist went to Bermuda for his health.

Bermuda's earliest visitors didn't stay long. The Spaniard Juan de Bermúdez, for whom the islands (Bermuda is really a chain of isles) are named, discovered them in passing on his way to the Caribbean in 1503. Forty years later, the next recorded drop-in — full identity unknown — carved the initials T.F. and the date 1543 on Spanish Rock and disappeared. Fifty years later, an English sea captain, Henry May, who was wrecked on Bermuda in 1593, made his way back to England to tell the tale.

Early reports like his, though they're said to have inspired Shakespeare to set *The Tempest* in "the still-vex'd Bermoothes," weren't calculated to attract tourists or settlers. They told of a place that was haunted by devils, of reefs and wrecks and a sea that "swelled above clouds, and gave battell unto Heaven." This last is a description of the weather that forced Admiral Sir George Somers, who was headed for Virginia, to ground his ship *Sea Venture* off St. George's Island in 1609, the date now given for Bermuda's first settlement. Sir George had no intention of remaining. Starting with the *Sea Venture*'s remnants and adding Bermuda cedar, he and his crew built two ships — the *Patience* and the *Deliverance* — and carried on to Jamestown. When they found the Virginia colony starving, Sir George decided to return to Bermuda for food. The expedition succeeded but lost its leader; Sir George Somers died in Bermuda in November 1610.

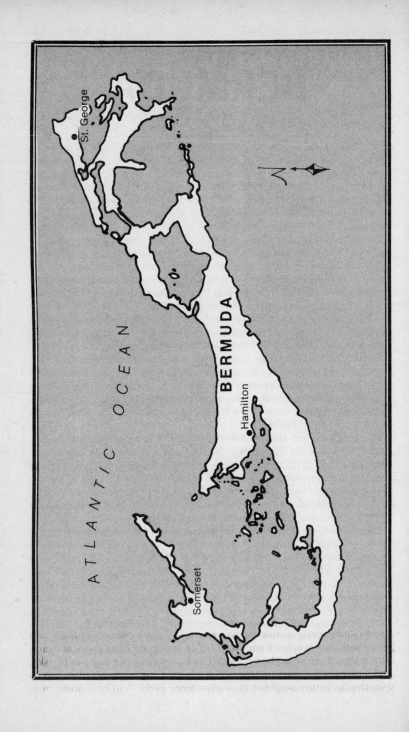

St. George

ATLANTIC OCEAN

BERMUDA

Hamilton

Somerset

The first English settlers to come to Bermuda on purpose arrived in 1612, and by 1620 (when the Pilgrims landed at Plymouth Rock), the new islanders had built themselves bridges, a fort, a church, and the State House in St. George that still stands, the colony's oldest building. Once established, Bermudians tried to do some colonizing on their own. In 1649, Bermudian Puritans, discomfited when fellow islanders defied Cromwell to remain Royalist, formed the Company of Eleutherian Adventurers and settled the Bahamian island of Eleuthera. In 1668, more Bermudians set out to found their own colony on Turks Island, south of the Bahamas.

At its own request, Bermuda became a British Colony with the right to self-government in 1684, but from the earliest Jamestown days its American ties were strong. Bermudians smuggled gunpowder to George Washington, and, in gratitude, the Continental Congress authorized the shipment of a year's provisions to Bermuda, where food was then in short supply. And during the Civil War — influenced by their long association with the originally English settlements in North and South Carolina as well as Virginia — the islanders sent fast Bermudian ships to run the North's blockade and deliver supplies to the Confederacy.

In the peaceful years that followed, Mark Twain discovered Bermuda, and he is traditionally thought of as the colony's first modern American tourist. Mr. Clemens, who liked islands better than sea travel, found it "paradise . . . but one has to go through hell to get there." He visited many times and became the first of this island's special breed: the return visitor. In recent years, fully 36% of the colony's visitors were coming back for a second, third, even sixth or seventh time — a very impressive statistic.

People come back because they like to relax and enjoy. And they know they can count on Bermuda to be all they knew and loved last time. They can count on first-rate places to stay, good service, and fine sports facilities. But other resorts offer good hotels, service, and sports. What makes the difference is the something extra Bermuda adds: the gentle beauty and peace of the place. Bermudians work hard to preserve them both — not only because it sells but because for them it is home. People live in those storybook cottages, and the postcard images are more than just isolated façades.

In 21 square miles of island, there isn't room for two worlds — one for tourists and one for real people, so Bermudians and visitors share a lot. They buy their Shetland sweaters and tennis rackets at the same shops, play on the same golf courses, have Sunday brunch and Thursday dinner at the same restaurants. They sail the same waters and watch the same soccer matches. They enjoy the same sense of un-rush and love the same scenery. For visitors, these are vacation pluses. For Bermudians, they're essentials for everyday life — and worth protecting.

For that reason, Bermuda doesn't change much. Cars still drive on the left, slowly (not over 20 mph), and there aren't too many of them. So the coral-walled lanes stay narrow and twist when they want to. Hotel building is carefully monitored because the island fathers feel it's essential to keep their hills, roads, and beaches from becoming crowded. Building codes are carefully enforced. So no high-rise hotels block views or poke holes in the sky. And a twentieth-century cottage is likely to bear a strong resemblance to its seventeenth-century neighbor or — even more likely — to be a house built between then and now and restored. Neon signs are still strictly forbidden; in fact, even additional traffic lights in Hamilton are likely to cause enough furor to merit the attention of the Bermuda National Trust. And gambling is "most unlikely," says one official, "in this century or the next." Even the 1985 arrival of *Club Med* (on St. George's) and the onslaught of hurricane Emily, which inflicted $30 million worth of damage in 1987, have failed to fluster the local calm.

There will, however, continue to be all manner of first-class places to stay. And service that's friendly and good. And fine golf courses and tennis courts you don't have to book days in advance (except perhaps for weekends). And pink beaches that — magically — never seem to get crowded. There will still be green hills and white roofs and pink cottages with herb-bordered gardens and palm trees. And clear nights when the smell of jasmine and cedar smoke fills the air. And a way of life that sends you home restored.

In Bermuda, thanks mostly to the Bermudians, you can count on it.

BERMUDA AT-A-GLANCE

FROM THE AIR: The self-governing British Colony of Bermuda is a fish-hook-shaped chain of nearly 150 islands — at some points linked by bridges you don't even notice as you cross over them — anchored in the Atlantic Ocean (not the Caribbean) 600 miles due east of Cape Hatteras, North Carolina. Geographically centered at 32°20'N latitude, it curves from 64°38' to 64°54' W longitude, which makes it about 23 miles long and, for most of its length, barely ½ mile wide. Composed of lava, coral, and limestone (of which most Bermudian cottages are built), it is based on the summit of a long-extinct volcano.

At the islands' western end, the bight of the "fishhook" curves protectively around Little Sound and Great Sound, at the eastern end of which is the city of Hamilton, capital of the colony and its chief cruise port. The airport at Kindley Field is about 14 miles northeast at the western edge of the much larger US Naval Air Station.

The colony's most famous and photographed beaches lie along the islands' southern edge, and their fine, soft coral sand is actually tinged with pink. Many visitors are surprised that Bermuda has very few indigenous palm trees; that's because its climate is subtropical rather than tropical. And although much of it is green and rolling, it has no rivers or streams. It depends entirely on rainfall for its fresh water supply; water is caught on the white roofs of its houses and stored in tanks belowground. (To a Bermudian home owner, the size of his cistern is often a greater source of pride than the size of the house itself.)

The Olde Towne of St. George — Bermuda's first capital and second city — sits at the far eastern tip of the islands. Colonized in 1612 by members of the Virginia Company after the islands' discovery in 1609 by Sir George Somers, it is the site of considerable ongoing restoration, exemplified by its Somers Wharf shopping mall. Cruise ships call here as well as in Hamilton and Dockyard, which is rapidly developing at the western end of the islands.

SPECIAL PLACES: Hamilton – The colony's capital city is a pretty pink and white town on the inner shore of the island fishhook, at the eastern end of Bermuda's Great Sound. It's the very exceptional visitor who doesn't come here at least once to shop, have a pint in one of its pubs, maybe even take a carriage ride. Many never make it farther than Front Street, the main street that runs along the water's edge from Albuoy's Point (site of the Ferry Dock and the august Royal Bermuda Yacht Club) at its west end to King Street in the east. And it's fair to say that you won't be culturally disadvantaged if you don't either. Still, a walking tour of the town's landmarks takes little more than an hour and provides some interesting background on local history and government.

If you haven't already picked up a *Handy Reference Map, Welcome to Hamilton, Welcome to the West End–Somerset, Welcome to St. George's,* and the *Bermuda Railway Trail,* along with the latest issue of *Preview of Bermuda* and *This Week in Bermuda,* begin with a stop at the Visitors' Service Bureau at Albuoy's Point. Then cross at the foot of Queen Street (where the policeman directs traffic from his "birdcage") and walk east along Front Street. On your left you'll be passing the colony's most prestigious shops; on your right, the carriage stand, the flagpole (at the foot of Burnaby Street), where reviewing stands are set up for colonial parades and the Bermuda Regiment stages its twilight tattoos, and, from May through mid-November, cruise ships tied up at the piers. (Part of Bermuda's tourist traffic control regulations specify a limit of three cruise ships tied up in Hamilton at any one time.)

The Cenotaph between Parliament and Court streets honors Bermuda's World War I and II dead. In the park behind sits the Cabinet Building, where the Senate (the upper house of Bermuda's Parliament, third oldest in the world; only England's and Iceland's are older) meets and where you'll find a number of government offices. Walk into the park for a closer look, then turn north (away from the harbor) on Parliament Street. One block up, at Reid Street, you'll come to another park block on your right. The imposing building in the middle is Sessions House, the home of the House of Assembly (lower chamber of Parliament) and the Supreme Court (house leaders and court judges still wear white wigs, British style); the clock tower on the building's southwest corner was added to celebrate Queen Victoria's Jubilees in 1887 and 1897.

At the intersection of Parliament and Church streets, the post office will be on your left (southwest corner) and the Wesley Methodist Church, across the street (northeast corner). Turning left (west) on Church Street, you come to the Gothic Bermuda Cathedral (Anglican), built in 1885; walk inside to admire the architecture and the needlepoint prayer cushions. A short block and a half farther, the City Hall of Hamilton, with its modern wind-clock tower, was completed in 1960; inside there's a small theater, an elegant Mayor's Parlour (for receptions), the offices of the Corporation of Hamilton, and, upstairs, the headquarters of the Bermuda Society of Arts, with rotating exhibits by local and foreign artists and sculptors; open from 10 AM to 4 PM, it is often the scene of special events, particularly during Rendezvous Time (see *Special Events*).

Turn left on Queen Street and walk downhill on the right-hand side until you pass a patch of green (in it stands Bermuda's oldest rubber tree) and just past it, the old-fashioned Perot Post Office (named after the colony's first postmaster, who made his appointed rounds with the mail stashed inside his top hat); it shares Par-La-Ville Gardens with the Public Library (its collection of island newspapers dates back to 1787) and the Bermuda Historical Society, with more exhibits of Bermudiana. Following the circular garden path brings you back to Queen Street in five minutes, unless you stop to enjoy the carefully labeled flora. There are public restrooms at the park entrance.

In addition, given time and the inclination (plus a bike or a cab), you can head up King Street (at the east end of Front Street) to visit Fort Hamilton (turn right on Happy Valley Road just beyond the Seventh-Day Adventist church), a restored Victorian stronghold, for its city and harbor views and the Rendezvous Time "Skirling Ceremony" performed by marching bagpipers. Following King Street, you come to the Government Tennis Stadium. Going past it and right on Marsh Folly Road, continue to the fork and bear left on Langton Road through the Black Watch Pass, a deep limestone-walled cut engineered by the famous British regiment in 1847. On your right on Mt. Langton Hill above North Shore Road is Government House, another Victorian monument in semitropical gardens, the residence of Bermuda's governors since 1892.

ELSEWHERE ON THE ISLAND

Outside the capital, principal sightseeing routes head east and west from one of two traffic rotaries (called roundabouts here) south and southeast of the city. You reach the first by bearing right on Crow Lane at the end of Front Street. At the circle, you can go three-quarters of the way around, peel off at The Lane, then go right on Harbour Road for a purely scenic bike ride along the water (detour at snapshot-worthy Salt Kettle Cove) past the Belmont Wharf, then on to Burnt House Hill past Riddell's Bay Golf Club to Middle Road.

Or leave the first rotary halfway around and take the second turn up Trimingham Hill and to a second traffic circle, off which you can go east or west on the South Shore Road.

Going west toward Somerset:

South Shore Road West – On the road to Somerset you pass the island's most beautiful beaches (at Warwick Long, Stonehole, Chaplin, and Horseshoe bays). Just beyond the *Southampton Princess* golf course (on your right), turn right up Gibbs Hill to the world's oldest cast-iron lighthouse ($1 pays your way to the top for a 360° view, but even from its base, the view is grand); the climb takes five minutes, with convenient rest areas along the way. Back on South Shore Road, turn right past Church Bay to join the Middle Road, which passes the Port Royal Golf Course, crosses Somerset Bridge (the world's narrowest drawbridge, with a "flap" just wide enough to let a sailboat mast through), and becomes Somerset Road. At this point, Ely's Harbour and Cathedral Rocks are on your left. The Middle Road continues past Fort Scaur (a fine, grassy picnic spot) and into Somerset Village with its pretty, restored Library. Pick a lunch spot (the *Somerset Country Squire* or *Village Inn* — see *Eating Out*) and/or press on to Ireland Island and the Dockyard, where you can get a bite at *Freeport Gardens* and explore Bermuda's newest and noteworthy attractions.

Start with the outstanding *Bermude Maritime Museum,* housed in the keep of the former Royal Navy Dockyard inside a protective wall 30 feet high and 20 feet thick. Be sure to see Queen Elizabeth Hall, built in 1850, with an original vaulted ceiling 4 feet thick; the Treasure House, containing artifacts from the wreck of the *Sea Venture,* including pieces of eight, a 19-ounce gold ingot, and a gold bar weighing over 2 pounds; and the Forster Cooper Building, celebrating 175 years of the Royal Navy here. The two towers of the Dockyard storehouse are Bermuda landmarks; the large stone building west of them is not an attraction but a prison. Admission to the museum is $4 for adults, 50¢ for children; try to go on Thursday or Saturday, when the knowledgeable Ivor Grant is on duty.

Right across the road from the museum, visit the *Crafts Market* for handmade gifts (open daily) and the *Bermuda Arts Centre,* which displays and sells artwork depicting Bermude scenes, plus locally designed clothing and jewelry (closed Mondays, holidays, and weekend mornings). Also take a half hour to see the well-written and well-presented multimedia show *The Attack on Washington,* the story of Bermuda's part in the War of 1812. The dock in this area is being extended to accommodate large ships, and the surrounding warehouses will be converted to shops in the next couple of years, creating a hub of activity similar to that in St. George and keeping cruise-ship visitors from overrunning Front Street. When you're ready to leave, take the ferry from Ireland Island or Watford Bridge back to Hamilton.

Going east toward the Olde Towne of St. George:

South Shore Road East – Back at the Trimingham Hill roundabout, go east along the South Shore Road past the Botanical Gardens (special: its exotic-plants house; pick up a map in the main house at the entrance) and Camden, a restored home that now serves as Bermuda's official "White House." About two miles down the road, Collectors Hill Road forks off to the left. If you're not in a hurry, follow it up to Verdmont, an

18th-century Bermuda Trust home with gardens and antiques. Then coast down Flatt's Hill Road into tiny Flatt's Village to the Aquarium. (It's a fine one, with a zoo and birds, too.) Leave via Harrington Sound Road, which goes by Devil's Hole (hookless fishing — fun for kids, dull for grownups), Leamington and (some say prettier) Crystal Caves, and the *Swizzle Inn* or *Bailey's Ice Cream Parlor* for a rest stop nearby. The Perfume Factory and Gardens are free; from April through July, perfume is made here, and it's fun to see the passion flowers growing like grapes on vines outside. We'd skip the Bermuda Pottery and the Blue Grotto Dolphin Show (unless you've never seen one) and go along the causeway past the airport to St. George's Island. Possible detour (especially if you're hungry for fish): a right on St. David's Road to visit century-old St. David's Lighthouse, from which Bermudians keep watch for Ocean Race winners, and funky *Dennis' Hideaway,* where Dennis Lamb spins Bermudian yarns as he cooks up a seafood banquet ($25 per person) in his shanty café; call him ahead of time (phone: 297-0044). If you pass up the detour, it's on to the Olde Towne.

■**EXTRA SPECIAL:** *St. George,* Bermuda's first capital, founded in 1612, is the focus of considerable thoughtful and continuing restoration. It offers intriguing old sites to see: great, gray Fort St. Catherine, with historic dioramas and replicas of the crown jewels; St. Peter's Church, the oldest Anglican place of worship in the Western Hemisphere; the handsome 1620 State House, for which a one-pepper-corn rent is handed over with great ceremony every April; museums full of carriages and Confederate memorabilia. Explore its narrow alleys (Featherbed, Shinbone, and One Gun); finish with a walk around King's Square (there's a pillory for stock snapshots, a life-size bronze statue of Bermuda's founder, Sir George Somers, and a replica of the antique ship *Deliverance* to inspect for $1.50 per adult, 50¢ per child) and a cool drink at the *White Horse, Fisherman's Wharf,* or the *Carriage House.*

SOURCES AND RESOURCES

TOURIST INFORMATION: The Bermuda Department of Tourism has excellent and constantly updated supplies of literature — maps, sports and accommodation brochures, planning tips — all free. Its offices in North America are at 310 Madison Ave., Suite 201, New York, NY 10017 (phone: 212-818-9800); 150 N Wacker Dr., Suite 1070, Chicago, IL 60606 (phone: 312-782-5486); 44 School St., Suite 1010, Boston, MA 02108 (phone: 617-742-0405); 235 Peachtree St., NE, Suite 2008, Atlanta, GA 30303 (phone: 404-524-1541); 1200 Bay St., Suite 1004, Toronto, Ont. M5R 2A5 (phone: 416-923-9600).

In Bermuda, the main office of the Bermuda Department of Tourism is in Global House at 43 Church Street in Hamilton (phone: 292-0023). There are Visitors' Service Bureaus at Albuoy's Point (where the ferry docks in Hamilton), at the airport, on King's Square opposite the Town Hall in St. George, and at the crossroads in Somerset (summers only, limited hours).

Local Coverage – Bermuda has two tourist publications: *This Week in Bermuda* and the biweekly *Preview of Bermuda;* both concentrate on sightseeing, sports, and general information and carry updated schedules of entertainment at various hotels and restaurant listings. The *Bermuda Book Store,* on Queen Street near Front Street, stocks the latest books about Bermuda. Dial 974 for the day's happenings, 977 for the weather, and 909 for time and temperature. Tune to radio station VSB — 1235 AM — for nonstop tourism broadcasting.

The *Royal Gazette* is the daily paper; the *Bermuda Sun* and the *Mid-Ocean News* are published on weekends. *The Great Bermuda Catalogue* ($4.95) provides an in-depth look at select shops, spas, restaurants, and attractions. *Dining Out in Bermuda* ($2) is invaluable with more than 50 reproduced menus from the islands' top dining spots. Both magazine-format books are available in local shops.

At St. George, see *The Bermuda Journey,* an audiovisual show depicting 375 years of the islands' history and heritage. At the Dockyard, the multimedia *Attack on Washington* tells of Bermuda's role in the War of 1812.

The Tempest is said to have been set in Shakespeare's fantasy version of Bermuda. For background reading, try *Sea Venture* by Willoughby Patton (Longmans Green, New York).

Telephone – You can dial direct to Bermuda by adding the area code 809 and to the phone numbers given below.

ENTRY REQUIREMENTS: For stays deemed reasonable by Bermuda Immigration, US and Canadian citizens need no passports or visas. However, immigration officers will request that you show a return or ongoing ticket, plus some proof of citizenship (passport — valid or expired, birth certificate, or US voter's registration card). You may also be asked for proof that you have a place to stay. For long stays, apply to the Chief Immigration Officer. A departure tax of $10 per person is collected at the airport. Ship lines collect a tax of $20 per passenger.

CLIMATE AND CLOTHES: Bermuda is a subtropical island in the Gulf Stream with a moderate year-round climate and no particularly rainy months. It sits in the Atlantic a full thousand miles north of Caribbean latitudes, so it does have two seasons: a May-to-November "summer," when daytime temperatures reach 85°F (30°C) and evenings are in the 70s (about 22°C); and a springlike "winter" that lasts from mid-November to late March, with daytimes in the 60s and the low 70s (about 22°C) and evenings in the 50s and low 60s (about 16°C). December and January days are seldom warm enough for swimming. "In-between" seasons — from mid-November to mid-December and from late March through April — are usually quite springlike.

The Department of Tourism describes Bermuda's style of dressing as "one of British reserve and dignified informality." American translation: wear the kind of clothes, day or evening, you'd wear at a rather toney suburban country club — golf clothes for golf, tennis clothes (preferably whites) for tennis. Short shorts, cut-off jeans, and dirty sneakers are tolerated but not appreciated. Casually tailored clothes, Bermuda shorts, and slacks are right for daytime downtown. Bermudian men often wear Bermuda shorts, jackets, and ties to business functions and out in the evening (especially in summer). The secret of their neat look is that their socks stay up. For visitors wearing shorts, the best rule is knee socks or none. Bathing suits, including bikinis, are seen on the beach or at the pool, but nowhere else. Be cautious about the sun; take coverups to the beach. On your first day of cycling, use a sunscreen or wear long-sleeved shirts and slacks to prevent burn on the back of your neck, arms, and knee tops. Evening dressing is on the slightly formal side. Almost all hotels require jackets and ties for men after 6 PM; slacks, tie, and blazer look fine. Formal dinner clothes are only necessary if you've been invited to a private party. For summer: lightweight classic sports and after-dark clothes in cottons and no-iron blends. In winter, cottons and lightweight woolens, sweaters, and slacks are most comfortable for daytime. In the evening, a shawl or a light sweater is good insurance against too-cool air conditioning or brisk breezes.

MONEY: Official currency is the Bermuda dollar (BD$) divided into 100 cents. It is pegged to the US dollar (one BD$ = one US$). US and Canadian currencies are accepted at par in most shops, restaurants, and hotels. Banks are open from 9:30 AM to 3 PM on weekdays, with a special opening from

4:30 to 5:30 PM on Fridays; closed Saturdays, Sundays, and holidays. Most restaurants, shops, and large hotels accept credit cards, although a number of small hotels and cottage colonies do not. Check your hotel's status before you leave home. Traveler's checks are accepted everywhere.

LANGUAGE: The Queen's English spiced with a bit of Bermuda slang. Examples: To sweet someone is to please him or her; to be gribbled is to be annoyed. He or she who is hot may not be amorous but has certainly had too much to drink.

TIME: Bermuda runs on Atlantic Standard Time from the last Sunday in October to the last Sunday in April, on Atlantic Daylight Time the rest of the year. This puts it one hour ahead of eastern US cities; when it's noon in Boston, New York, or Philadelphia, it's 1 PM in Bermuda.

CURRENT: At 110 volts, 60 cycles AC, there's no problem with North American travel appliances.

GETTING THERE: American Airlines jets to Bermuda directly from New York and Boston; Pan American, from New York and Boston; Delta, from Atlanta, Hartford, and Boston; Eastern, from New York, Newark, Philadelphia, and Baltimore/Washington; British Airways, from Baltimore/Washington and Tampa. Air Canada flies direct from Toronto, with connections from the rest of the Dominion. Bermuda is 774 miles from New York, 2 miles farther from Boston, and 822 miles from Washington, DC. The jet flight from any of the three takes approximately 2 hours; flying time from Toronto (1,120 miles) is about 2½ hours and from Montréal (1,027 miles) about 3½ hours via Toronto.

The newest ship on the New York–Bermuda run is Royal Caribbean Cruise Line's *Nordic Prince,* making Wednesday afternoon departures from May to September. It docks in St. George till 3 PM on Fridays, then goes on to Hamilton for the weekend (the first and only ship to weekend in Bermuda). From May to October, the SS *Bermuda Star* schedules 7-day cruises form New York every Saturday with Monday calls at St. George, Tuesday and Wednesday stops in Hamilton. Chandris's *Amerikanis* and *Galileo* make weekly sailings from May to October as do Home Lines' *Atlantic* and *Homeric* from April to October. A number of other cruise lines — Norwegian American, Costa, Carnival, and Cunard, among them — schedule special voyages to Bermuda from East Coast ports. In all cases, the ship serves as its passengers' hotel in Bermuda.

CALCULATING COSTS: Bermuda really has no "off" season, though from mid-November through March (Rendezvous season) rates at some hotels drop as much as 20% to 40% per day per person. Throughout most of the year, the larger hotels ask about $195 to $200 per person per day double occupancy (that includes breakfasts and dinners); small hotels ask about $120 to $175 per person per day double occupancy MAP; cottage colonies, about $180 to $225 per person per day double occupancy MAP; with BP (that's Bermuda Plan, including full breakfast only) set at about $30 per person less a day. It's about $90 to $150 per person a day EP (without meals) for an apartment with a kitchenette; about $90 per person a day BP at guesthouses. Many places offer special package deals for families, honeymooners, golfers, and tennis players. Prices for a typical 7-day/6-night package run about $700 and up plus airfare per person, double occupancy, including room, breakfast, dinner, and special features (many are golf, tennis, or honeymoon oriented);

increasingly, hotels list 4-day/3-night long weekend packages as well. Packages usually offer a substantial saving on conventional costs, and knowledgeable returnees regularly espouse some package plan or other. Golfers especially save on greens fees and cart rentals. A 6% tax is added to all hotel bills.

 GETTING AROUND: Taxi – They meet every flight and cruise ship. All are metered and carry a maximum of four people. Drivers are cheerful and courteous and very well informed. Approximate fares from the airport: to Tucker's Town, including 10% to 15% tip, about $9; to Hamilton, about $15; to South Shore hotels, about $20; to Somerset, about $28. There's no charge for baggage carried inside the car, but there's a 25¢-per-item fee (maximum $2 per trip) for luggage carried "in the boot" (that's British/Bermudian for trunk) or on the roof; drivers sometimes waive it, however. There's also a 25% surcharge on trips between midnight and 6 AM. For the South Shore and points west, it costs about half as much to share a limousine from the airport. Contact *Airport Services of Bermuda* (phone: 293-2500); after 5 PM, 293-8436). If you arrive in Bermude with no transportation, check to see if a waiting limo has room for you.

Bus – Painted pink with a dark blue stripe, buses cover all major routes on the island. Service is efficient and follows regular daytime schedules. The islands are divided into 14 zones. Fare is $1 per person within up to three zones, $2 for any longer trip. (Fares are less if you purchase tokens in advance.) Exact change is required; 3-day and 7-day passes are available. All buses leave from the Central Bus Terminal on Washington Street, just off Church Street and a few steps east of Hamilton's City Hall. Route 1 goes from Hamilton to Castle Harbour and, less frequently, St. George via John Smith's Bay; Route 3, Hamilton to Grotto Bay via Devil's Hole and the Caves; Route 6, from St. George to St. David's; Route 7, from Hamilton to Sonesta Beach via South Shore beaches and from Hamilton to Somerset via South Shore; Route 8, Hamilton to the Dockyard and Maritime Museum; and Routes 10 and 11, from Hamilton to St. George via the Aquarium, Perfume Factory, and Dolphin Show. Route 1 to St. George is more scenic, passing the splendid homes of Tucker's Town; it takes about 10 minutes longer than Routes 10 and 11. If you leave for St. George from the West End, ask for a free transfer; you'll change buses at Hamilton. For further information on routes and schedules, phone: 2-3854.

Bermuda Buggy Ride – The traditional Bermuda buggy ride, in a patent leather– bright carriage, is sentimental, a shade corny — and fun (every honeymoon should have one). If you've no place special in mind, the driver will probably tour Hamilton and its suburbs (including the one they call Fairylands). Rates run about $7.50 per half hour for a single carriage for two, $10 per half hour for a double carriage for four. Arrange- ments for night rides should be made in advance. Drivers congregate on Front Street near the flagpole and cruise ship docks.

Car Rental – You cannot rent (or drive) a car in Bermuda. Because of the islands' small size, officials strictly limit the number of cars to only one per resident family.

Bicycle Rental – If you're feeling energetic, you can rent pedal bikes, as they're called in Bermuda (mopeds are called bikes here). Pedal bikes are best suited to touring around Hamilton or Dockyard or the western part of the old Railway Trail. For a 3-speed bike, at $5 a day, contact *Ray's Cycles Ltd.,* Middle Rd., Southampton West (phone: 234-0629) or at the *Lantana Colony Club;* for a 5-speed, at $10 the first day and $5 thereafter, check with *Wheels Limited,* Trott Rd. off Church St., Hamilton (phone: 295-0112) and Devil's Hole (phone: 293-1280). Bicycles conveniently ride for free on the ferries.

Moped Rental – On the other hand, this couldn't be easier. Years before the US discovered the moped, this motor-assisted bicycle became Bermudian tourists' favorite means of transport. Bike liveries are handy at most hotels, and once or twice around the parking lot is generally enough to give you the hang of maneuvering one. Though you can rent bikes with pillions (that's the extra seat behind) if there are two of you, two bikes are better than one for safety and maneuverability. Doubles are $26 a day plus an $8 repair waiver; singles run $18 a day.Rates include third-party insurance, lock, basket, helmet, delivery and collection, breakdown service, and your first tank of gas. If your hotel doesn't have its own bike rental setup, somebody at the desk will be happy to make arrangements; delivery is usually possible within an hour. Or contact *Ray's Cycles Ltd.,* Middle Rd., Southampton West (phone: 234-0629); or *Oleander Cycle,* Valley Rd., Paget (phone: 236-5235) and Gorham Rd. Hamilton (phone: 295-0919). *Honda Cycles,* Front St., Hamilton (phone: 292-3775), now has rental scooters ($33 a day; rental to two passengers only) as well as motor-assisted bikes available.

Bermuda is just the right size for mopeding. You can get from Hamilton to St. George in the east or Somerset in the west in 30 to 45 minutes; but hardly anyone moves that far or that fast in one day. Of all the trails cyclists can follow (equestrians and pedestrians, too, for that matter), most fun is the now-paved Bermuda Railway Trail, which follows the route the railroad took before cars were introduced in 1946; the best stretch for scooters is from Somerset bus terminal to Frank's Bay in Southampton. The most important element in any moped or bike rental on Bermuda — after the warning to beware of the sun's rays — is to keep mumbling to yourself (especially at the roundabouts), "Keep left and don't look back." And remember, it's illegal to bike without a helmet, and most gas stations are closed Sundays. Mopeds may be taken on ferries for $2.

Taxi Touring – This is fun because you can plan it yourself, see what you like, leave out the rest. Drivers with small blue flags on their cabs have passed special exams to qualify as tour guides; they're almost always most informative and a pleasure to have as guides. When you discuss the route, let the driver know if you're interested in taking pictures; he knows the best vantage points. The rate is $16 an hour, with a 3-hour minimum. A 5-hour daytime tour of Harrington Sound and St. George is $30 per person (including admission fees). *Penboss Associates* (phone: 295-3927) offers several, including a 3-hour trip to Harrington Sound, a 4-hour Somerset tour, and a 5-hour St. George's Island tour; prices start at $15 per person for a half-day trip.

Sightseeing Bus Trips – Taxi touring is much more fun and more flexible; *Penboss* (phone: 295-3927) also runs bus tours from March through November, as does *St. George's Transportation and Scenic Tours* (phone: 237-8492).

Ferry Services – The best seagoing buy on the island is a ride on one of the Bermudian government ferries that crisscross the Great Sound, with stops at Hamilton, Paget, Warwick, and Somerset. This means that you can use the ferry dock for much more than just point-to-point transportation, since this waterborne perspective (easily acquired on a once-around-the-harbor ride) provides real insight into Bermuda's ocean-going lifestyle. Sample one-way fares: Hamilton to Paget and Warwick, $1; Hamilton to Somerset, $2. Pedal bikes ride at no charge; mopeds may be carried on (at the captain's discretion) for $2. For information, call 295-4506.

Sea Excursions – All sorts of craft — cruisers, glass-bottom boats, catamarans, and yachts — take off from Hamilton Harbour in all directions. Rates run from about $15 per person for a 2-hour Sea Gardens cruise to about $40 per person for full-day trips, including lunch, rum swizzles, and calypso entertainment. Among the best: a 3-hour small-boat cruise that explores not only the Sea Gardens but the nooks and crannies of Great Sound (where large craft can't go for fear of reefs) for about $20 per person (by *Bermuda Water Tours;* phone: 295-3727); the all-day classic that includes a swim and picnic on Hawkins Island, a shopping stop at Somerset, swizzles, and sing-along entertainment priced at $37 per person (*Bermuda Island Cruise;* phone: 2-8652); and a late afternoon/early evening cruise to Somerset that includes a glass-bottom boat trip to the Sea Gardens and a real Bermudian dinner at the *Village Inn* in Somerset for about $44 per person (*Looking Glass Cruises;* phone: 236-4065).

SHOPPING: It's a quality operation all the way; even standard souvenirs look less tacky here than they do in other parts of the world. And there are substantial bargains, especially on imported British goods like woolens (men's sportswear, blazers, kilts, bolts of tartan, tweeds) and Shetland sweaters (about $20 for the crew-necked model you'd pay $60 or more for in the States). The absence of a sales tax in Bermuda means added savings. Fine china and crystal are also good buys; a place setting of Aynsley china priced at about $60 on Front Street costs about $93 plus tax in New York City; and the Waterford champagne glass that's about $38 in New York is under $29 in Hamilton. Other worthwhile buys: Harris tweed jackets, at about half the going US price, French perfumes and some cosmetics at 30% below stateside prices.

Liquor is up to 50% less expensive than back home. So you save even when you buy more than your one-liter-per-person duty-free allowance. The average duty paid by one person bringing back one gallon of liquor is $8.75; the average paid by two people bringing back one gallon is $5.50. So on a five-bottle (one-gallon) pack worth $40 in New York, for which you pay $20 in Bermuda, savings are still substantial. Remember to shop early — at least 24 hours before you leave — to allow time for delivery to your plane or ship. Also remember that US duty on wines is nominal — only 4¢ per bottle is due on table wines, 14¢ on sherry and Dubonnet, and 68¢ on champagne and sparkling wines — so if you know your wines and your prices, you can make good buys here, too.

Though you won't find many authentic Bermuda antiques for sale (Bermudians are extremely reluctant to let them leave the colony), you can find excellent buys in British antiques even when you add in the cost of shipping and insurance. There is no US duty on any piece over 100 years old. *Trimingham's, Smith's, Bluck's, Heritage House, Timeless Antiques,* and *The Thistle Gallery* in Hamilton, and the *Old Market* in Somerset are specialists.

Among Bermuda's products, Outerbridge's Sherry Peppers Sauce (to spice up your own chowders, soups, and Bloody Marys) and the Royall line of men's aftershave lotions and soaps are standouts. Bermuda-made perfumes aren't that exciting.

For general shopping, start with Front Street's Big Three:

A. S. Cooper & Sons – Top-quality British-cut sportswear (Jaeger woolens and sweaters) for men, women, and children, plus fine collections of crystal and china (Wedgwood, Waterford, Belleek, Bing & Grøndahl, and more). They also have a branch on Somers Wharf in St. George and shops in several hotels.

H. A. & E. Smith – For big names in British sportswear (including large sizes), Liberty prints and tartans by the yard, and a rather large selection of classy gifts for less than $20 (porcelain placecard holders, pomander balls, Bermuda scarves, china flower pins, earrings, and paperweights). It has a branch in St. George and others in a couple of the larger hotels.

Trimingham's – For classic tweeds, sweaters, woolens; Daks sportswear for men, Donald Davies of Dublin for women, Liberty print dresses for little girls; plus perfumes and miscellaneous knickknacks. In addition to its Front Street location, it has branches in several of the larger hotels; on Somers Wharf in St. George; in Somerset (two shops); near Crystal Cave in Bailey's Bay; and on the South Shore Road in Paget.

In addition, these other Hamilton stores are worth looking into (all are on Front Street unless otherwise noted):

E. R. Aubrey – Gold and precious-stone jewelry at up to 35% below US prices.

Bananas – Colorful boutique featuring resortwear and beach gear. Two branches on Front St., also at the *Sonesta Beach* and *Bermudiana* in St. George.

Bluck's – Lots of china, silver, and some very nice antiques. There are branches in St. George as well as in the *Southampton Princess* and the *Sonesta Beach.*

Archie Brown & Son – British sportswear for both men and women, Braemar sweaters, Pringle cashmeres, and a large selection of tartan items. If you're up to it, they also have Fair Isle sweater kits so you can knit your own. A large children's department also offers toys and books.

Calypso – Polly Hornburg's place, Bermuda's best-known women's specialty shop for patio and beach clothes. (Note that her Polly Pants seem to cover most hip and thigh situations without strain or bagging.) Also carries some imported perfumes, cosmetics, and original Haitian paintings. Branches in the *Hamilton* and *Southampton Princess,* and at *Coral Beach Club.*

Vera P. Card – Porcelain, figurines, china, crystal, pearls and other precious jewelry, and high-quality Bermuda souvenirs. Branch stores at the *Sonesta Beach,* the *Bermudiana, Castle Harbour,* and in St. George.

Cécile – Knitwear from all over the world, T-shirts, sweaters, dresses; lots of famous names at up to a third off US prices. Branches at the *Southampton Princess,* the *Sonesta Beach,* and *Castle Harbour.*

Chameleon – Bermuda's exclusive agent for Alafoss knitwear from Iceland. The garments are wonderfully warm and woolly. Lopi yarn is available for do-it-yourselfers. On Bermuda House Lane, off Front Street; branches in the *Hamilton Princess, Southampton Princess, Bermudiana, Elbow Beach,* and *Sonesta Beach* hotels.

Crisson – More real jewelry, a good selection of imported watches. On Queen St., Reid St., and Front St.; two branches in St. George, at *Castle Harbour* and *Elbow Beach* hotels.

Heritage House – Truly beautiful and unusual, but not necessarily costly, gifts from all over the world. Crystalware, pottery, fruit and flower prints, are especially lovely. Fine antiques upstairs.

Irish Linen Shop – Predictably stocked with good-looking placemats, tablecloths, napkins, and the like; unpredictably, with French bikinis (very teeny) in Souleiado provincial prints, with totes, tops, and more to match. Also antique laces; French and Italian fabrics by the yard at half what you'd pay in New York. Branches on Somers Wharf in St. George and on Cambridge Rd. in Somerset.

Pegasus Print and Map Shop – Old and new prints, maps, framed and unframed; also hand-colored miniatures framed in Bermuda cedar, an Andrew Wyeth print of Ely's Harbour, and a selection of greeting cards and ceramic house signs. In an old Bermuda home on Pitt's Bay Rd. across from the *Hamilton Princess.*

Peniston-Brown – The colony's largest collection of fine French perfumes at substantially discounted prices. The main store is on Queen St. (the sign reads "Guerlain"); branches are on Front St. and King's Square, St. George (also called "Guerlain").

St. Michael – Everything from resortwear to sleepwear to sweaters bearing the brand name of British retailers Marks & Spencer. Good quality at modest prices. On Reid St. in Hamilton.

Triangles – Small and exclusive, with the best prices anywhere on splashy Diane Freis dresses. There are also Oscar de la Renta silk designs, striking evening wear, bags, and other accessories. On Reid St. in Hamilton.

Windjammer Gallery – Bermudian arts — paintings, sculpture, ceramics, wall hangings, photographs. Also limited-edition prints and a gallery cat named Toulouse Lautrec. No US duty on art. In a traditional Bermuda cottage with a sculpture garden, on the corner of Reid and Kings Sts.

Otto Wurz – Lots of small treasures: charms, decanter labels, silver thimbles, coffee spoons, bangles, imported watches. Near the *Bermudiana.*

And two specialists:

Bermuda Book Store – The place for paperbacks and books about Bermuda. In a wonderful old building on Queen St.

Bermuda Coin & Stamp Company – Sets of Bermudian and British coins from antique gold doubloons to new decimal coins, plus lots of collectable stamps. Check US regulations on importing gold. Up Old Cellar Lane off Front St.

Worth visiting elsewhere: *Art House,* on the South Shore Road, for Bermuda-scenic prints, original paintings, lithographs (autographed by artist Joan Forbes, if you like); *Cow Polly East,* on Somers Wharf in St. George, the place to find needlepoint kits in original Bermudian designs, selected handicrafts, appealing gifts; and the *Craft Market* at Dockyard.

Most stores in Hamilton, St. George, and Somerset are open Monday through Saturday from 9 AM to 5:30 PM, but several open at 9:15 AM and close as early as 5 PM. Many stores are open evenings and Sundays when cruise ships are in port. For last-minute purchases, it's worth noting that hotel branches of these stores are often open later or on Sundays when their Hamilton headquarters are not. When the ships are in Hamilton, try less crowded Somerset and St. George stores for shopping. Prices are the same, though the shops and selections are smaller.

TIPPING: Most Bermudian hotels, cottage colonies, and guesthouses add a 10% to 15% service charge in lieu of tips; many restaurants do, too. When no service charge is added, leave waiters 10% to 15% of the check; taxi drivers should be tipped 10% to 15% of the fare. Leave $2 per room per day for your hotel maid; give bellboys and airport porters about $1 for two to three suitcases — more if they're huge.

SPECIAL EVENTS: In addition to the sports competitions for which Bermuda is famous (sailing race weeks, tennis weeks, international game fishing and golf tournaments), Bermuda has two special seasons of major interest to tourists. They are the *College Weeks,* timed for the student vacation period in the spring and crammed with all manner of parties and undergrad happenings (and a time when any member of the over-21 crowd would be wise to consider staying at home); and *Rendezvous Time,* from mid-November to the end of March, with daily special events to warm up the winter season — the mayor's welcome in St. George, a "pub crawl," a skirling pipers' band parade at Fort Hamilton, and more. Its stellar *Bermuda Festival of the Performing Arts* (most of January and February) attracts top names in theater, music, and dance. In addition, from March till May, private houses and gardens are open to the public one afternoon a week; about $5 per person pays for a day's tour under the auspices of the Garden Club of Bermuda.

Public holidays (when banks, stores, and government offices are usually closed) include: *New Year's Day, Good Friday, Bermuda Day* (third Monday in May, after which it's considered socially okay for Bermudians to go swimming; now part of the annual *Heritage Week* celebration), the *Queen's Official Birthday* (third Monday in June), *Cup Match* (cricket) and *Somers Day* (usually the Thursday and Friday before the last weekend in July), *Labour Day* (first Monday in September), *Remembrance Day* (November 11), *Christmas,* and *Boxing Day* (December 26).

SPORTS: On both land and sea, Bermuda's sports are of championship caliber all year long. Though most winter days are unsuitable for swimming, they're usually temperate and great for golf and tennis. In spring, summer, and fall, everyone plays everything.

Aerobics – Get a good workout for $6 at the *Sonesta Beach Spa,* rated one of the world's ten best by *Lifestyles of the Rich and Famous.* For $15, you can enjoy the sauna, whirlpool, and the gym, whether you're a hotel guest or not. At the *Sonesta Beach* hotel (phone: 238-1226).

Boating – Great Sound and Harrington Sound are the places, whether you skipper yourself or leave the pull-hauling to someone else and sign on for a sail on one of the several schooners that take groups out. Bermuda is one of the world's sailing capitals, and the facilities are extensive. Sunfish rent for about $45 for a half day; roomier day-sailers, about $75 a day. Outboard motorboats rent for about $45 for a minimum 2 hours, $70 for 4 hours. If you're in the mood for something bigger, the 33-foot cruiser *Magic Carpet* charters, skippered, for about $210 for 4 hours, $350 for 8. She'll carry up to 16 people. Contact *Salt Kettle Boat Rentals* (phone: 236-3612 days), which has boats of all sizes for hire. Other good boat names: *Bermuda Water Tours* in Hamilton (phone: 295-3727); *John Shirley Boat Rentals* in Somerset (phone: 234-0914).

Cricket – This cousin of US baseball is played on pitches (fields) ranging from exquisitely manicured greens to vacant lots. Cricket is a spectator sport that is also a social event. The height of the cricket season in Bermuda is the two-day public holiday in July when St. George from the eastern end of the island meets Somerset from the western side. This is the only time Bermudians can legally gamble, and they enjoy a game called Crown & Anchor. For upcoming matches, consult the sports section of the newspaper.

Golf – The latest addition to the championship roster is the hilltop St. George course, redesigned by Robert Trent Jones, Jr., and opened in 1985. Three more first-class championship 18-hole courses are open to the public: Port Royal in Southampton, designed by Robert Trent Jones, and the courses at the *Belmont* and *Castle Harbour* hotels. The Port Royal course is by far the most challenging of this trio, with greens fees that run $18 a day; golf carts, $18 per round. The *Southampton Princess* has a short, 18-hole "executive" (par 3) go-round; and there is a good public 9-hole course at Queen's Park in Paget. The islands' most famous course is at the *Mid Ocean Club*, where guests must be introduced by a member. As the number of available caddies has declined, *Mid-Ocean* has added a few carts for players. Greens fees are $50, plus $25 for a motorized cart for two, or $17 per bag and a tip to the caddy); *Riddell's Bay* is a private club, too. If you're interested in either one, consult your home pro before taking off; or ask at your hotel (some have staff members who belong). *Mid Ocean* requires that guests play only on Tuesdays, Wednesdays, or Fridays.

Horseback Riding – *Spiceland Riding Centre* in Warwick (phone: 238-8212) offers breakfast rides (about $30 per person for 2 hours) and trail riding ($15 an hour). *Lee Bow Riding Centre* in Devonshire (phone: 292-4181) specializes in lessons for children.

Jogging – Every day on every roadway (almost), but especially along the Railway Trail and on Tuesdays, when you can join the Bermudians for a 2-mile run that takes off at 6 PM from Camden House in the Botanical Gardens, early April to late October. There's also a 10-kilometer and a marathon (26 miles) for international contestants every January.

Snorkeling and Scuba – The beaches mentioned below, plus East and West Whale bays on the South Shore, are best for snorkeling. The North Shore off Devonshire can be interesting, too. If your hostelry is on the beach, it probably will have fins, mask, and snorkel to loan or rent for a small fee; or you can buy gear in town (*Masters,* on Front St. carries a complete line). If you scuba or want to learn, *South Side Scuba* at the *Sonesta Beach* (phone: 238-1833; after 5 PM, 236-0394), *Skin Diving Adventures* at Somerset Bridge (phone: 234-1034), and *Nautilus Diving* at the *Southampton Princess* (phone: 238-2332) are all set up both to teach and to take you reef or wreck diving. Rates run about $60 per person for a half day's diving trip. But even if you can't dog-paddle, you can explore the Bermudian depths with *Hartley's Under Sea Adventures* (phone: 234-2861) or *Hartley Helmet Diving Cruise* (phone: 292-4434), who will provide you with a helmet straight out of Jules Verne and, after a few minutes' briefing, take you walking on the seafloor. The 3½-hour trip costs $28 per person.

Spectator Sports – Always on Sundays, on fields all over the island, when Bermudians aren't playing, they're watching cricket from May to September, rugby from September to April, soccer from September to April. Sunday also means Sunfish racing on Harrington Sound, motorboat racing from May to November on Ferry Reach in St. George, and go-kart racing all year except July and August at the Naval Annex in Southampton. Check local newspapers for times and places.

Sport Fishing – Allison tuna, false albacore, wahoo, dolphin (the fish, not the mammal), oceanic bonito, blackfin tuna, rainbow runners, barracuda, and blue and white marlin are waiting in the deep. Horse-eye bonito, rockfish, yellowtail snapper, amberjack, and grey snapper are found in the reefs offshore. Bonefish and pompano are caught by shore anglers. Full-day deep-sea trips run about $480, including bait and tackle, for six persons. (Ask about the skipper's policy on caught fish in advance; unless otherwise determined, the catch is legally assumed to be his.) Contact Captain Russell Young in Somerset (phone: 234-1832). Marinas rent rods and reels for shore fishing for about $10 a day, $35 a week; or contact *Four Winds* fishing- tackle company on Par-la-Ville Rd. in Hamilton (phone: 292-7466).

Swimming and Sunning – The South Shore's expansive pink beaches are the ones you see in the promotional pictures. Amazingly, even when there's not a room to be had in the colony, the beaches never seem crowded. The biggest and most beautiful (Warwick Long Bay, Horseshoe Bay, and Church Bay) are all open to the public at no charge. Many have restrooms; must-see Horseshoe Bay has dressing rooms, lockers, refreshments, and beach-equipment rentals. Tobacco Bay, in St. George, is also a pleasant beach. Most inland and town hotels have beach club affiliations or provide beach transport for their guests, but more adventurous visitors bike out, taking picnics from their hotels. Officially, Bermudians swim from Bermuda Day till Labour Day only. Visitors aren't that limited — any warm day any time of year will do. Though you can't count on specific dates, there are almost always a couple of good beach days even in December, January, and February. In addition to the beaches, most hotels and guesthouses have pools — some indoors.

Tennis – The court game made its Atlantic crossing from England to the US via Bermuda. The island's first court was laid out at Clermont in Paget Parish in 1873. A year later a Bermudian, Mary Gray Outerbridge, showed the members of the Staten Island Cricket and Baseball Club how to lay out the first US court. Now there are over 100 courts in the colony, including those at the ultra-exclusive *Coral Beach.* Most of the larger hotels have courts; the ones at the Government Tennis Stadium north of Hamilton (about $4 per hour; tennis whites required) and 4 Plexi-paved courts at the Port Royal golf complex are also open to the public ($5 a court per hour in daylight; $7 per hour extra at night). Hotels usually make court time available free to their guests, charge others $4 to $8 per hour when time is available. A dozen court sites (including the Government Tennis Stadium) have pros and offer lessons; a number of hotels — the *Belmont, Bermudiana, Elbow Beach, Sonesta, Southampton Princess, and Grotto Bay* — have 2 or more lighted courts. Since the game is so popular, it's a good idea to reserve a day ahead whenever possible. Many hotels offer tennis packages with guaranteed court time built in, which make great sense if you're keen on the game. Check with your travel agent. Incidentally, squash addicts can set up playing time with a call to the Bermuda Squash Racquets Club in Devonshire (phone: 292-6881). There are also paddle tennis courts at the *White Heron Inn* (phone: 238-1655).

Water Skiing – The protected waters of Great and Harrington sounds are best for water skiing. *Bermuda Waterski Centre* (phone: 234-3354) and *Bermuda Water Sports/ Ski Bermuda* (phone: 293-2640) rent boats at about $35 for a half hour, $65 for a full hour, and lessons are also available.

Windsurfing – *Watlington's Windsurfing Bermuda,* based at *Glencoe* (phone: 236-6218), charges $35 for a 1½-hour lesson, $95 for a three-lesson course for up to four people.

NIGHTLIFE: For a place that has never claimed to have much, Bermuda actually has a good deal. No Las Vegas–style nudie shows or chorus lines, and early golf tomorrow may mean a 10 o'clock bedtime tonight. But there's considerable action when you're in the mood. Far and away the prettiest places for cocktails and sunset watching are the *Gazebo Lounge* of the *Hamilton Princess,* from which you can watch the lights blink on all around Great Sound; the terrace of the *Inverurie,* with its view of Hamilton bathed in an incredible peach-colored light (you really have to be there); and the dramatically situated terrace or poolside of *The Reefs,* overlooking its own South Shore beach. After dinner, the big hotels schedule different shows each night; the Talbot Brothers, Gene Steede, and Hubert Smith and the Coral Islanders are the current long-run favorites, and there are the usual limbo, calypso, and combos to fill in. A big *Follies* show has been installed in the *Empire Room* of the *Southampton Princess* (phone 238-2555) for the April to November season; its *Neptune Lounge* has live entertainment and dancing. Smaller hotels and guesthouses do more intimate numbers — often with a calypso singer or a solo piano supplying dinner music. The *Clay House Inn* on North Shore Road in Devonshire puts on the liveliest island show around — lots of limbo, calypso, steel band music, and dancing. There's a $12.50 cover charge; best call ahead for reservations (phone: 292-3193). *Clay House* also plays host to occasional traveling musicals from the States. Liveliest stops on the pub circuit are the *Rum Runners* on Front Street; *Robin Hood* on Richmond Road; the *Golden Hind* on South Shore Road west of *Elbow Beach,* which itself draws a regular crowd to its nightclub and pub; and *Henry VIII* on the South Shore Road just across from the *Sonesta Beach.* A low-key alternative is the friendly, intimate bar at *Show Bizz* restaurant, on King Street at Reid. But the really big move is in the disco direction. The under-30 crowd heads for *Oasis* in the Emporium Building on Front Street. *The Club* above *Little Venice* on the Bermudiana Rd. in Hamilton is the current favorite of the over-30, tie-and-jacket smart set. Cover charge is $7 per person; drinks run about $3.50 each; live jazz on Sundays. *Grotto Bay Beach*'s cave-ensconced *Cheek to Cheek* nightclub, *Castle Harbour*'s *Bayview Lounge* with piano music, and the *Touch Club* at the *Southampton Princess* hark back to a gentler touch-dancing era.

BEST ON THE ISLAND

CHECKING IN: Bermuda probably has more attractive guestrooms per square mile than any other resort island in the world. Basically, its accommodations fall into four different categories: hotels, cottage colonies, housekeeping apartments, and guesthouses. Large resort hotels usually have their own beaches or beach clubs and pools; several have golf courses. Most offer the usual luxury resort services and activities, including a social desk and/or director, cycle livery, sports, bars, restaurants, nightclubs, and entertainment. Small hotels offer much the same on a less opulent scale. Cottage colonies are uniquely Bermudian — a main clubhouse with a dining room, lounge, and bar, plus beach and/or pool, in the midst of a group of cottage units with kitchenettes. The third category, housekeeping apartments and cottages — most with a beach or pool nearby — look like cottage colonies minus the clubhouses; each unit has a full kitchen and usually some maid service. Guesthouses are frequently old homes that have been modernized to include comfortable rooms or apartments, dining rooms (some do breakfast only), and informal facilities; they are not only agreeably priced but frequently offer a chance to get acquainted with a Bermudian family as a vacation bonus.

Bermuda's hoteliers and innkeepers offer many package plans, which can mean substantial savings to tennis players, golfers, families, and honeymooners. They are most numerous in fall and winter and include room, breakfast, dinner, court or course time, or sightseeing and other features. Check out the possibilities with your travel agent.

For the purposes of this guide, $195 to $220 and up a day for two people (in season) with breakfasts and dinners (MAP) is considered expensive; $125 to $175 a day for two (MAP) is considered moderate; $100 and below for two (MAP) is considered inexpensive. Some hotels also offer EP rates (without meals); others offer CP (with Continental breakfast) or BP (with full Bermudian breakfast). Rates without meals run approximately $35 per person per day below MAP rates. Many large and small hotels now honor credit cards. The cottage colonies often do not, but they will honor personal checks with advance notice. It's a good idea to double-check the payment policy in advance. Rendezvous (mid-November through March) prices can mean savings of up to 40% on airfare and accommodations packages. If you're planning a winter holiday, note that a number of hotels close for periods as short as two weeks or as long as two months sometime between December 1 and March 1.

RESORT HOTELS

Elbow Beach – This venerable and friendly place is fresh and handsome after a $4-million renovation of its grounds, rooms, restaurants, and public spaces. Overlooking their own long pink beach in Paget are 300 air-conditioned rooms, all kinds of accommodations: balconied bedrooms, duplex cottages, lanai rooms overlooking pool and ocean, and new surfside lanais. Pool on hillside; beach with terraces, snack bar, games facilities below. Small health club with exercise machines. Good tennis, too, plus dancing and shows nightly (phone: 6-3535). Expensive.

Hamilton Princess – At the edge of Hamilton Harbour, classy, classic, and handsome as can be thanks to its recent $15 million restoration. With 450 air-conditioned rooms, many with balconies. Two oceanside pools, luncheon terrace, shopping arcades, beauty salon, barbershop. Complimentary transportation to the Southampton Princess Beach Club and 18-hole executive golf course shared with its sister *Southampton Princess* — with which it has complete exchange privileges. Nightly show in season. Extremely pleasant service. Right in the heart of Hamilton, if that's where you want to be (phone: 5-3000). Expensive.

Sonesta Beach – On its own South Shore beach in Southampton. In splendid shape, with 100 rooms (including 29 split-level suites) in its new Bay Wing to bring its total to 400. All are air conditioned, with balconies overlooking the sea or the adjacent sheltered bays. With 2 heated pools (1 bubble-roofed), garden patio, smart shopping arcade, and marina. Handsome, expertly run European/American spa and health club is a big plus; nightly music and dinner-and-dancing at *Lillian's* restaurant (phone: 8-8122). Expensive.

Southampton Princess – On a hilltop overlooking the sea, with its own beach and tennis club across the road. This luxury spot is atypically large for Bermuda — with 598 air-conditioned rooms, all with balconies, superb views, and cable TV — and it is completing a $20-million renovation that includes the addition of a new 50-room deluxe Newport Club wing with special luxury amenities. Despite its size, it is certainly one of the best of the colony's large hotels. Private par 3, 18-hole golf course, pro shop, clubhouse on premises, plus shopping arcade, beauty salon, health club, indoor and outdoor pools, and free ferry to Hamilton. Surprisingly efficient service. Lots of entertainment and disco. Beach club has dive shop and snorkeling; 11 first-rate tennis courts. There are 7 restaurants (the *Newport Room* and *Waterlot* are best), plus a dinner show in the nightclub. The only drawback is a dark, cavernous lobby (phone: 8-8000). Expensive.

Marriott Castle Harbour – This historic 250-acre property, overlooking Harrington Sound in Tuckers Town, reopened in June 1986 after a beach-to-ramparts $45-million refurbishing. In addition to 415 rooms and attractive, airy common areas, the resort now includes 3 pools, 3 restaurants, a shopping arcade, full convention facilities, tennis courts, beaches on the property with full water sports, and beautifully manicured grounds. The revitalized championship golf course remains one of Bermuda's best (phone: 293-2040). Expensive.

Belmont – This sports-minded member of Trusthouse Forte's island trio sits on a 110-acre estate overlooking Hamilton Harbour in Warwick. Shares facilities, exchange privileges, with the *Bermudiana* in Hamilton, *Harmony Hall* in Paget. With a sporty 18-hole golf course, pool, tennis courts; free transport to Bermudiana Beach Club; dancing and entertainment; several restaurants and an inviting bar. All three properties were extensively spruced up in the course of a multimillion-dollar refurbishing in 1985 (phone: 6-1301). Expensive to moderate.

Grotto Bay Beach – On the ocean, near the airport, but 12 miles from Hamilton town. Recently spruced up, with a good-looking expansion of its inviting *Moongate Terrace* restaurant, it has 201 air-conditioned rooms with private balconies and wide sea views. Two beaches plus pool, bar, and boating; full scuba program; tennis courts. Unique caves on property, site of daily grotto swims, nightclub. Super-luxury ELE (for Every Little Extra) Club rates (about $9 daily surcharge per person double occupancy in specified bank of suites) bring fruit, flowers, turn-down service, lots of special treatment. Excellent children's program (phone: 3-8333). Expensive to moderate.

Club Med, St. George's Cove – On the eastern end of the island, across from Fort St. Catherine and a half hour's walk from downtown St. George. It offers water sports, 9 tennis courts, 2 pools (one atop Fort Victoria), a disco, and 6 restaurants, including Moroccan, Chinese, and Italian. There's also special access to a redesigned 18-hole golf course — a *Club Med* first. Reopened in 1988 after extensive damage from hurricane Emily in 1987 (phone: 7-8222). Moderate.

SMALL HOTELS

Stonington Beach – Good-looking Bermuda-modern main building plus several 2-story 8-room units built into the hills above a small, idyllic South Shore beach. Special because its very professional top management heads a staff made up almost entirely of students in Bermuda College's Hotel Technology department; resulting student-supervisor teamwork means double service for guests. Attractive public spaces, especially cozy library with fireplace, game tables; 64 less attractive double rooms, all with ocean views, terraces. Pool, all beach and ocean sports, 2 tennis courts, afternoon tea, weekly wine-tasting parties (phone: 236-5416). Expensive to moderate.

Waterloo House – An elegant, small-scale harborside hotel where staying is a lot like being at the house party of a well-to-do British/Bermudian family. Bright decor warmed with antiques; wonderful views. There are 31 rooms and 5 cottages, a pleasant dining room, bar, luncheon terrace, pool (phone: 295-4480). Expensive to moderate.

Glencoe – On Salt Kettle Bay in Paget. This appealing place, 250 years old in 1988, grew up around a sea captain's home and now has 41 air-conditioned rooms, garden pools, cove swimming, sailing, and water skiing. A favorite of the nautical set. Casual, fun. Ask about the Campanile rooms. One minute to the ferry (phone: 236-5274). Moderate.

Newstead – At the edge of Hamilton Harbour in Paget, a Bermudian mansion with 50 air-conditioned rooms. Handsomely redone without losing a bit of its classy, classic charm. Genteel, friendly house party atmosphere. Heated pool, sauna, deepwater swimming. Near tennis, golf, beach, dancing. Short walk to Hamilton ferry (phone: 236-6060). Moderate.

Palmetto – A pleasant place in Flatts Village on Harrington Sound and handy to all the water sports thereon. Recently redone in white-roofed Bermudian tradition; 42 rooms, lovely parlor, pretty gardens, pool, free transportation to beaches, chummy *Ha'Penny Pub* that's a favored drop-in spot at lunchtime and after dinner. *Inlet* restaurant is pleasing and popular (phone: 293-2323). Moderate.

Pompano – Small, inviting central clubhouse surrounded by a pretty colony of 56 studio cottages, suites, and cabanas overlooking the South Shore sea. Hillside pool, beach, water sports; scuba easily arranged. With cozy bar, lounge, dining room with a view; entertainment. Adjacent to the Port Royal golf course. Cordial young owners and staff (phone: 4-0222). Moderate.

The Reefs – Dramatically set above its own South Shore beach, with a small central building and 64 lanai and cabana rooms stair-stepped along a bluff overlooking the sea. Terrace, heated pool, private beach, and an open-air restaurant great for sunset dinners. Near Port Royal golf. Popular summer evening entertainment spot, with friendly young owners (phone: 238-0222). Moderate.

Rosedon – In gardens near Hamilton, with 43 air-conditioned rooms (one an inexpensive single) in and around an old manor house surrounded by lawns and flowers. There's a large, heated pool, and everything is nicely maintained. Within walking distance of shops, ferry, and restaurants (phone: 295-1640). Moderate.

COTTAGE COLONIES

Cambridge Beaches – On a private point in Somerset, at the westernmost tip of the island. A 78-room cottage colony (and at 60 years of age, probably the island's oldest) that's got just about everything idyllically escapist going for it. Pretty setting in 25 acres of garden, long private beaches, sailing, water sports, fishing, tennis courts, heated pool. Live entertainment nightly, dancing. Remote and private, but very close to the ferry to Hamilton and offering shuttle service to the ferry three times a week (phone: 24-0331). Expensive.

Fourways – No longer just a fine restaurant, it has expanded to include a small number of deluxe accommodations with private balconies, patios, and kitchenettes, a pool, pretty gardens, and access to a private beach. Bathrooms have hair dryers and bathrobes. Ten minutes from Hamilton, on Middle Rd. (phone: 236-6517 or 800-962-7654). Expensive.

Horizons – High on a hilltop in Paget. This resort contains 50 rooms in the main house and cottages (some with fireplaces) and has a heated pool, sun terrace, 9-hole mashie golf course, 18-hole putting green, and tennis courts. Dancing and ocean swimming at Coral Beach Club nearby. Some cocktail-hour entertainment (phone: 236-0048). Expensive.

Lantana Colony Club – Overlooking Great Sound in Sandys Parish. These 61 rooms in cottage units are set around landscaped grounds, with private beach, pool, sun patio, 2 good tennis courts, ocean swimming, sailing, water skiing from own dock, and bike rental on premises. It's also close to the Port Royal Golf Course, and a five-minute walk from the ferry to Hamilton. Honeymooners prefer the Pool House. Extremely fashionable, with an excellent dining room in an arbor-lined solarium (phone: 234-0141). Expensive.

Pink Beaches – On a private South Shore beach in Smith's Parish. Quiet luxury exemplified by 82 air-conditioned rooms in cottages rambling over a seaside estate. Elegant international clientele (many celebrities) and superb service. This was the site of the romantic honeymoon scenes in the film *Chapter Two*. Large pool, sun terrace, fine tennis, friendly service. The toaster in your room is used by the room service waiter/waitress each morning (God forbid the toast should be cold) after breakfast has been set on the patio (phone: 293-1666). Expensive.

St. George's Club – It's sometimes difficult to get one of the 61 rental units in this faultlessly maintained time-share property perched on a hill overlooking St. George. There are fully equipped, pretty cottages, a dining room, pub, lounge, 3 pools (one heated in cooler months), tennis, and reduced fees at the St. George Golf Course next door. Off Old Maid's Lane, with an entrance off the main road into St. George (phone: 297-1200 or 800-843-7810). Expensive.

Ariel Sands – On the South Shore in Devonshire: 45 air-conditioned rooms in cottages by the ocean, with a private beach, heated pool, 3 tennis courts, patio, attractive restaurant, and inviting bar. Tennis, too. Relaxed atmosphere (phone: 236-1010). Moderate.

HOUSEKEEPING COTTAGES AND APARTMENTS

Cottages at Marley Beach – Spectacularly perched above their own South Shore beach, with stunning views from the pool. There are 14 apartments, some with fireplaces, secluded but handy to restaurants and nightlife. Very pretty indeed. Just east of Astwood Park (phone: 236-1143). Moderate.

Munro Beach – Overlooks the sea beside Port Royal's scenic sixteenth hole, perfect for golf and tennis buffs. Families like it, too. A friendly, family-run place with 16 cottage apartments, no restaurant or pool, but pleasant, secluded beach (phone: 234-1175). Moderate.

Somerset Bridge – Has 24 attractive, self-contained apartments with kitchenettes, some with balconies. Picturesque location on an inlet, with the commendable *Blue Foam* restaurant, a pool, and very pleasant family management (phone: 4-1042 or 800-221-2335). Moderate.

Surf Side Beach Club – Secluded, and overlooking its own very nice South Shore beach. Varied group of 35 apartments and cottage units in good-looking Bermuda-contemporary style, well-maintained buildings and grounds. Coffee shop. Extremely pleasant atmosphere (phone: 236-7100). Moderate.

Angel's Grotto – Seven apartments on Harrington Sound (ask for a water view). Nice sense of privacy, yet within easy reach of Flatts Village, water sports, beaches, restaurants, sites to see. Thoughtful resident owner, Mrs. Hart (phone: 293-1987). Moderate to inexpensive.

Astwood Cove – Small, shining white complex of 6 suites and 12 studio apartments, each with neat kitchenette and patio or balcony overlooking both pool and South Shore ocean vista through the trees across the way. On-site amenities include a sauna, small pool, laundry facilities, barbecues; also a citrus orchard and banana patch from which guests may pick. Congenial management and clientele (phone: 236-0984). Inexpensive.

GUESTHOUSES

Royal Heights – Small, modern guesthouse with a stunning view of Riddell's Bay Golf Course and the sounds (Great and Little) from a Southampton hillside. Small pool, lovely common rooms. Pleasantly managed. On Light House Hill, near the *Southampton Princess* (phone: 238-0043). Inexpensive.

Pleasant View – In Princess Estate, a family home with a sweeping North Shore view. Four double bedrooms plus one studio, one apartment. Pin neat, nicely cared for by a pleasant couple (phone: 2-4520). Inexpensive.

Pretty Penny – This little guesthouse on a hilly lane in Paget is large on old-fashioned charm. It offers 9 studio apartments, a small garden pool, and privacy (phone: 236-1194 or 800-525-2266). Inexpensive.

Royal Palms – In an old Victorian home, it has 12 rooms, a terrace, tiled porch, dining room, and bar. On Rosemont Ave. off Pitts Bay Rd., opposite the *Princess* (phone: 292-1854). Inexpensive.

 EATING OUT: Bermudian food is surprisingly good these days, although most meat still has to be imported. Knowledgeable diners stick to the wide (and excellent) variety of seafood; specialties include tangy mussel pie, Bermuda fish chowder liberally laced with sherry peppers and black rum, sweet Bermuda lobster (in season, September 1 through March 31), large tiger shrimp that look a lot like rock lobsters (called guinea chicks), and traditional Hoppin' John (black-eyed peas and rice). At Christmastime, visitors will also be treated to cassava pie — no Bermudian Yule would be complete without it. An item called Bermuda Fish is found on most menus without additional reference. It will be whatever's been caught that day, and is served either pan-fried or broiled. Try it. And if you're invited to a "Bermuda Breakfast," expect to find codfish and chopped eggs.

At the tonier restaurants, expect to pay $40 to $60 and up per person for dinner, including a drink and tip, but chances are you will feel you've gotten your money's worth in food and atmosphere. There are also a number of British-accented pubs that are fun for lunch, an informal supper, and/or a sociable pint or two before or after dinner. At one of these establishments, dinner for two can cost as little as $20 to $30, plus drinks and tip. During Rendezvous season (mid-November through March), many fine restaurants participate in a "dine-around" program, serving full-course meals at slightly reduced prices. The Bermuda Collection hotels offer carousel dining year-round. Most restaurants request that men wear jackets for dinner; a number require both jacket and tie. When in doubt, check. Neat but casual dress is okay for Bermuda's favorite meal, Sunday brunch, which is more apt to feature a big buffet than crêpes and eggs Benedict; it's especially good at the *Waterlot* (our favorite because of the good Dixieland jazz), *Fourways, Henry VIII,* and the *Hamilton Princess. Fourways* has developed such a following that it now serves Sunday brunch on Thursdays, too. Reservations are always a good idea. (A word of advice: Steer clear of Chinese restaurants in Bermuda.)

ST. GEORGE'S

Carriage House – Pleasant service at lunch or dinner. Lantern-lit, romantic at night. Sample the shrimp dishes, prime beef, extensive salad bar. Children's dishes also available. Water Street at Somers Wharf (phone: 297-1730). Expensive to moderate.

Black Horse Tavern – Friendly, informal outpost purveying such home-cooked local fare as fine Bermuda chowder, conch stew, pan-fried fish steaks, stuffed rock lobster, other fresh seafood. Hobnob with locals, gaze out at Smith's and Paget islands. On St. David's Island (phone: 293-9742). Moderate to inexpensive.

Fisherman's Wharf – Breezy Somers Wharf pub with sandwiches, burgers, soups, and chowders at lunch, more substantial fare at dinner. Limited menu, but attractive and fun. Closed Sundays (phone: 297-1515). Moderate to inexpensive.

White Horse Tavern – Guests enjoy the atmosphere more than the food or service in St. George's oldest tavern. On the harbor in King's Square (phone: 7-1838). Moderate to inexpensive.

Clyde's – What locals know and tourists never suspect is that this unassuming corner café has the best home-cooked food in St. George. Order the fish chowder or fish and chips. Closed Tuesdays. On Duke of York Street across from Somers Garden, a couple of blocks from King's Square (phone: 297-0158). Inexpensive.

HAMILTON PARISH

Plantation Club – A congenial countryside setting for sampling Bermudian specialties, especially rich fish chowder, lobster in season. Plantation Salad, sweets from
the trolley, Irish coffee are tasty, too. Next to Leamington Caves in Bailey's Bay
(phone: 293-1188). Expensive.

Tom Moore's Tavern – Elegant setting in a historic 17th-century house. There are
several dining rooms, with stone walls, wood beams, fireplaces, and an upstairs
bar. Impeccable service complements a surprisingly full Continental menu —
duck is a specialty, as is lobster in season. Jackets are required. Adjacent to
Walsingham Bay (phone: 293-8020): Expensive.

Bailey's Ice Cream Parlour – The place for all-natural treats, including fruit sorbets
(in summer), sandwiches, and other light fare. The original is across from the
Swizzle Inn at Blue Hole Hill. There are also branches on Front Street in Hamilton
and in Smith's Parish on the South Road (phone: 293-9333). Inexpensive.

THE CITY OF HAMILTON

Little Venice – Veal is the specialty, featured in no fewer than 10 dishes at dinner,
from Parmigiana to Milanese. Popular with Bermudian business folks for lunch.
Dinner guests receive complimentary admission to *The Club* upstairs. Uphill from
Front St. on Bermudiana Rd. (phone: 295-3503). Expensive.

Once Upon a Table – This old Bermudian home, all prettied up with lace curtains,
is the best place to dine in town. The menu tries for (and succeeds at) deliciously
different touches without getting too tricky. Recommended: poached Bermuda fish
in sorrel sauce, wahoo Doris with capers and white wine sauce, rack of lamb. It's
worth ordering a bottle of wine just to see the Victorian opener in action. Serpentine Rd. (phone: 295-8585). Expensive.

Penthouse – A pretty place with a large à la carte menu that includes game in
season. Serves lunches and stylish dinners. Try the chilled avocado soup for an
appetizer, then on to the lobster tails or Scottish pheasant carved at the table. It's
worth the two-flight climb. Overlooking Front St. (phone: 232-3414). Expensive.

Romanoff – Notable for its Russo-European elegance, beginning with borscht,
carrying on to chicken Kiev and a formidable tournedos flambé Alexandra. In the
Imperial Building on Church St. (phone: 295-0333). Expensive.

Show Bizz – If you lived in Bermuda, this would be your local place. On the menu
are chicken wings, chowder, burgers, sweet and sour fish, short ribs. Several small
dining nooks, ceiling fans; videos of top black performers, including Whitney
Houston, Lionel Richie, and Anita Baker (not too loud, either); jazz guitarists on
Friday and Saturday nights, when reservations are a good idea. On King St. at
Reid (phone: 292-0676). Moderate.

Tavern on the Green – Enjoy Continental and Italian cuisine on the terrace of this
delightful restaurant nestled in the Botanical Gardens. The red ravioli stuffed with
lobster and the salmon or shrimp in champagne sauce are as good as they sound.
Inside the Botanical Gardens in Paget. Tour the gardens, then stop in for a drink
or luncheon special. In summer, Thursday is Bermuda Night (phone: 236-7731).
Moderate.

Lobster Pot – Bermudians choose it for spicy fish chowder, mussels, lobster (native
September till April, from Maine other times); the ubiquitous Bermuda fish does
very nicely indeed. The atmosphere's informal, the value excellent. Best for lunch
during a Hamilton shopping excursion. Up the hill on Bermudiana Rd. (phone:
292-6898). Moderate.

Loquats – A creative menu and cozy setting, with wood beams, shutters, and
semicircular booths. Offers fish specialties, such as chargrilled amberfish with herb

sauce. Piano music nightly. Across from terminal No. 6 on Front Street, with the entrance on Bermuda House Lane (phone: 292-4507). Moderate.

Fourways Pastry Shop – This popular coffee shop is owned by the well-known *Fourways* restaurant in Paget, which delivers its freshly baked breads, pastries, and croissants to the shop each day. Large windows facing the busy street make people-watching a favorite pastime for customers having breakfast, lunch, or an afternoon snack. Stop in for coffee, tea, and sandwiches or sweets 8 AM to 5 PM daily. Reid St. (phone: 295-3263). Moderate to inexpensive.

Hog Penny – Inside the paneled rooms of this cozy local tavern, draft beer and ale and informal lunches and dinners are served. Try bangers and mash (sausage and potatoes), other English specialties, or curry. Burnaby Street, half a block from Front Street (phone: 232-2534). Moderate to inexpensive.

Rum Runners – There's the pub with a balcony overlooking the harbor for lunch and the Lord Halifax Room for more substantial lunching, dinners. Both have Watney's on tap and loyal local followings. Live band in the evenings. Across from ship terminal No. 6 on Front St. (phone: 292-4737). Moderate to inexpensive.

Porto Fino – For a quick, informal lunch, this small Italian café has pizza and pasta. Just down the street from the fancier *Little Venice,* on Bermudiana Rd. (phone: 292-2375). Inexpensive.

PAGET PARISH

Fourways – We rate it the island's best restaurant (with the best service), in one of its oldest buildings, built in 1727. Excellent seafood and French dishes. Super lobster bisque with cognac, lamb, and veal. Snug bar and both indoor and outdoor dining. Very popular; reserve one or two days ahead. The piano music alone is a reason to visit. Sunday and Thursday morning brunches. Lunch served other days. Where Cobbs Hill Rd. crosses the Middle Rd. (phone: 236-6517). Expensive.

SOUTHAMPTON PARISH

Waterlot Inn – In a restored inn near the water (run by the *Southampton Princess* hotel), with its own dock for lunchers arriving by boat or hotel ferry. The food, the site, the atmosphere, are all elegantly evocative. Order anything (especially Bermuda fish or filet Stephanie) with wine to match. Make the most of the mood, the candlelight. They serve a generous brunch buffet on Sundays (including first-class Dixieland jazz). Reserve well ahead, and ask for the second seating (around 1 PM) so you can linger. On the Middle Rd. near Riddell's Bay (phone: 238-0510). Expensive.

Henry VIII Pub & Restaurant – Features English and Bermudian fare (mussel pie, steak and kidney pie, roast sirloin, Yorkshire pudding) in its informal lunches and popular Sunday brunches. The bar is always busy and draws convivial crowds for after-dinner piano entertainment. Wear smart casual attire. On the South Shore Rd. across from the *Sonesta* (phone: 238-1977). Expensive to moderate.

WARWICK

Golden Hind – What used to be the *Bermudiana Beach Club* is now under the same ownership as *Henry VIII* and working hard to develop a similar clientele. Lunch and dinner, Sunday brunch, clifftop location, pretty decor, terrace dining, nightly entertainment. The fixed price dinner includes a hot or cold appetizer, soup, salad, rack of lamb or Bermuda fish, dessert, and coffee. On South Shore Rd. near *Elbow Beach* (phone: 236-5555). Expensive.

Herman's – Stop by for a bite on the way to the beach, or order to go. On South Shore Rd. just west of the *Golden Hind* (phone: 238-9635). Inexpensive.

SANDYS PARISH

Lantana Colony Club – A fine dining room in a flowery solarium (part of the elegant cottage colony), known for its fine service, style, and wine cellar. Worth the trip from the middle island. Well-executed Continental menu, and a lovely tradition of serving after-dinner coffee in the stylish main lounge or on the terrace. Between Somerset Bridge and Fort Scaur (phone: 234-0141). Expensive.

Il Palio – A local favorite that occupies a 2-story building just across from the Somerset Cricket Club. Italian specialties, including passable pizza and first-rate pasta. Closed Tuesdays. Reservations suggested; ask for an upstairs table by a window. Main Rd. on the southern outskirts of Somerset (phone: 234-1049). Expensive to moderate.

Village Inn – Pleasant, quiet dining spot on the Great Sound, featuring good local cuisine, from barbecue to Bermuda fish. Closed off-season. At Watford Bridge (phone: 238-9401). Moderate.

Freeport Gardens – The equivalent of a Bermuda diner, it's a relaxed spot to enjoy Bermuda fare with Bermudians. Try the homemade soups and fish sandwiches. Open for lunch and dinner, breakfast from 9 AM weekdays. Just inside the gate at Dockyard (phone: 234-1692). Inexpensive.

Somerset Country Squire – A cheerful pub-restaurant that's especially jolly for lunch or Sunday brunch on the waterside terrace. Draft beer that's a treat. Downtown Somerset, on Mangrove Bay (phone: 234-0105). Inexpensive.

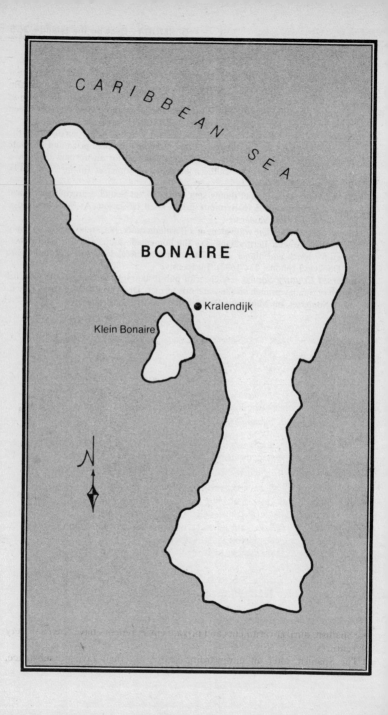

BONAIRE

Bonaire — the sleepy little land dot between Aruba and Curaçao — has been quietly blooming as a tourist destination for a couple of decades now. In 1960, a mere 1,555 visitors found their way to its sun-warmed shores. By 1987, that number had multiplied more than twentyfold: Over 28,000 arrived by ship and plane, many of them return visitors. And these days, even with a relatively small number of hotel rooms, the island rates a place on the savviest list of about-to-be-discovered Caribbean destinations — for good, if not immediately obvious, reasons.

Bonaire is scarcely a stereotypical tropic isle. The top of a 24-mile-long volcanic ridge poking out of the sea, it is anchored off the South American coast about 1,200 miles south of Florida — actually quite reachable in spite of its distance from New York, Chicago, and even Miami. At last count, it boasted 500 hotel and condo rooms, a smattering of duty-free shops, and a small, sincerely hospitable population of about 9,900. But the sudden surge of serious investment interest in Bonaire could double the number of hotel/condo rooms by 1989, according to government officials. At least four new projects have been approved.

Salty, sandy, and dry, Bonaire's south end is desert, covered with countless species of cactus, century plants, and intriguingly contorted prickly-pear trees. Its hilly northern end, though occasionally greener, is still desertlike and very dry. Ashore, Bonaire is as intriguing to photographers and naturalists as it is offshore to the hundreds of divers who come to explore its watery depths.

Over the ages, live coral has grafted itself onto the dead volcanic limestone base that slopes so steeply into the sea all around the island. The result is that Bonaire is surrounded with formations and sea gardens almost beyond belief, living, glowing, growing, moving languidly with the tide. What distinguishes this from other such places, where dive sites can be reached only after several hours of cruising out to sea, is that the 50 regularly visited dive sites lie immediately off the Bonaire shore. Moreover, Bonaire offers waters with visibility of more than 100 feet, four first-rate diving operations, and a government dedicated to protecting its environment, on land and under the sea.

The discovery of these submarine attractions and tourism's arrival represent the end of a five-century search by the island's various owners to establish a viable economic base. Ever since 1499, when Columbus didn't discover it (Amerigo Vespucci, the inventor of longitude and latitude, who also sailed for the Spanish, did), governments and private entrepreneurs have tried a variety of ventures.

The Spanish, after an unrewarding search for their favorite substance, gold, relied on the island as a source of wood, salt, and meat. They stripped it of its hardwoods and dyewoods, "panned" and dried salt from the sea around it, and produced meat from its goats and sheep, which had multiplied into wild herds after they were introduced early in the sixteenth century.

The Dutch, who arrived in 1623, were no more successful. Nor were the British, who took over briefly in the early nineteenth century and ended by leasing the entire island and its 300 slaves in 1810 to a US merchant, Joseph Foulke. He also failed to make good. When the Dutch returned in 1815, they tried building ships, growing tobacco and flax, making brick and tile, raising stock (donkeys, horses, and cattle), and weaving hats. Nothing worked. In recent years, Bonaire's men, unable to sustain themselves on the proceeds of the salt lake and the wild goat population, were forced to find work elsewhere, mostly in the oil refineries of Curaçao, Aruba, and Venezuela.

Neighbors on the sister islands and South America, probably learning about Bonaire from the migrants, began to come to Bonaire to get away from it all. They fished and lazed and took home tales of the stunning flocks of migratory flamingos at Goto Meer and Pekel Meer. And thus the island began to emerge as a tourist destination.

Birders followed in ever growing numbers. Enraptured at the sight of the big, pink birds balanced on their mudpie nests and taking off in clouds for their twilight flights, the watchers catalogued 170 species — warblers, doves, hummingbirds, sea swallows, gulls, green parrots, white and blue heron, native Bonairean "lorikeets" or parakeets, and dozens more — which also homed in on Bonaire.

The island's first hotel, the Zeebad — an internment camp for German prisoners during World War II, since completely rebuilt and renamed the *Divi Flamingo Beach Resort and Casino* — was opened in 1952. The second, the *Bonaire Beach* hotel, opened in 1962, about the time the full tourist potential began to be realized. The first scuba divers arrived and with them the realization that Bonaire's future lay less on its dry land than in the fabulous world below the surface of the sea around it.

Not only an irresistible diver's drawing card, Bonaire has other attractions as well: its natural park; its eerie, sea-carved grottoes; and the petroglyphs left behind by the Caiquetios Indians, the island's original Arawak inhabitants. The sun shines all year, and its capital, Kralendijk, with its colorful, tidy, toylike houses, is appealing — as are its several white sand beaches. The population, almost 100% literate, is courteous, friendly, and glad to see visitors. Their bon bini — Papiamento for "welcome" — is real. This, plus a sense of unspoiled atmosphere, is attracting not only bird watchers and divers, but those who just want to be serene and, perhaps, snorkel a bit, too.

Queen Juliana, on her state visit in 1955, may have touched on the secret of Bonaire's attraction. After extending her glass-bottom boat ride 25 minutes beyond its scheduled time, Her Majesty landed, obviously refreshed. Turning to the member of the legislature for Bonaire who had accompanied her, she said, "Thank you, I've been myself for half an hour."

BONAIRE AT-A-GLANCE

FROM THE AIR: Bonaire is shaped like a rough crescent, with its back to the trade winds blowing from the northeast. Its windward coast is surf-pounded and wild, but on the leeward side the crescent encloses a natural, protected harbor, with the uninhabited island of Klein Bonaire in the center of the huge bay. In its calm, clear waters a startling variety of marine life flourishes in depths easily enjoyed by snorkelers and novice scuba divers. Beaches stretch to the south and north, but inland, the two halves of the island are quite different. The south is flat and desertlike, with many varieties of cactus growing in volcanic soil, as well as wind-flung divi divi and a few dyewood trees. The southern tip is marked by ponds of contrasting colors, where salt is manufactured by solar evaporation. The northern half of the island is hilly with much more greenery, especially within 13,5000-acre Washington/Slagbaai Park on the north coast.

Bonaire (12°09′N, 68°17′W) is 40 miles east of Curaçao and 80 miles east of Aruba, its sister islands in the Netherlands Antilles just north of the coast of Venezuela. With an area of 112 square miles and only 9,900 inhabitants, Bonaire is one of the most sparsely populated Caribbean islands and consequently one of the most unspoiled. Its capital of Kralendijk, its four hotels, and its Flamingo Airport are on the leeward side near the center of the crescent.

The trip from New York — including flight connecting time — takes about 7 hours; from Miami, nonstop flights now make it in about 2½.

SPECIAL PLACES: Kralendijk – A clean, well-kept town whose name means coral dike or reef, with many of its brightly painted buildings notable as examples of Dutch colonial architecture. A half-hour walk can take it all in: the fish market that looks like a pink Greek temple; the duty-free shops of Breedestraat; the waterfront with its promenade and a lighthouse; the pier lined with fishing boats and island sloops; the old fort with three ancient cannon.

Bonaire Marine Park – This so-called park actually comprises the entire coastline of the island, down to 200 feet. "Park" means that the area is protected by law, and visitors, whether boating, snorkeling, or diving, may not take *anything,* alive or dead, from its reefs. Established in 1978, it is one of the few successful efforts in marine conservation in the Caribbean.

ELSEWHERE ON THE ISLAND

An island tour falls naturally into two circuits, northern and southern.

Northern Route – Driving northward from Kralendijk, you take a macadam road that follows the shoreline along low coral cliffs. It's a striking ride along ocean so transparent you can see patches of elkhorn and other coral forms below the surface of the blue-green water. Every half mile or so there's a place to park and look, or get out of your car and walk along cactus-lined cliffside paths with views of curving beaches. One of these paths, carved from the coral rock, is known as Thousand Steps. It leads down to one of Bonaire's finest sites for scuba or snorkeling. (There aren't actually that many steps; it just seems that way when you're carrying tanks and other scuba gear.)

The main road continues north along an extraordinary section where a sort of continuous grotto in the hillside forms a natural arch along the roadway. Long, long ago, it appears, the ocean surface, now 30 or 40 feet lower, was at the level of the roadbed. Over the centuries, waves and tides ate into soft coral rock and created this series of caves that in some places extend deeply inland.

The road turns inland at a point where you see a group of huge tanks. This is the Bonaire Petroleum Corporation's storage depot for oil from Africa and the Middle East, brought here by supertankers. Here this oil is transferred to smaller tankers for shipment to the US.

The road winds uphill, then dips again to one of Bonaire's most beautiful sites — an inland lake, Goto Meer, which might have been lifted intact from the Scottish moors, except that this one is salt water, with an island in its center. Along its irregular shoreline you see flocks of long-necked flamingos, their pink plumage brilliant against the blue of the lake.

If you want to make a day of it, turn toward Washington/Slagbaai Park, which lies at the northern tip of the island. The park is nature untouched; no point in going if you're in a hurry, for you'll want to leave your car to picnic and explore. This 13,500-acre tract is a preserve interlaced by 22 miles of dirt road. Though no overnight camping is permitted, Slagbaai (Slaughter Bay) is a great favorite with picnickers. From two special observation points for bird watching, it is possible to spot most of Bonaire's 135 species. Along the park's shores there are hidden bathing beaches and rocky caves where surf pounds against the coral rock. You can fish there, too. Incidentally, the name Washington originated in the days when this area was all one plantation to which the owners had given the name "America." The most important place in "America" was where the workers got their pay, and they called that "Washington." The park is open to the public from 8 AM to 5 PM daily, except Mondays. Admission is $2; children under 15 are free. Near the entrance is a small museum whose featured exhibit, in addition to cooking utensils, pottery, etc., is an antique hearse.

If you skip Washington/Slagbaai Park or leave it for another day, head along the inland road to Rincón, oldest town on the island, with pastel buildings. Schoolchildren wave to you from the street. Stop at the bar near the center for a beer or soft drink, and jukebox music. Local men, sitting at the half-dozen tables, will stare at you just as appraisingly as you'll study them; but simply say hello and tell where you're from, and the curtain of aloofness disappears. Bonairians are friendly and courteous, but not likely to start a conversation unless you invite it.

The next spot to visit is Onima, on the eastern coast, to see the grottoes. Continue on the paved road for 2 or 3 miles east from Rincón, and then, at the roadside sign, turn left along a dirt road toward Boca Onima. Stepping from your car, you'll find yourself staring at a cliff face, perhaps 50 feet high, honeycombed with odd formations. It's well worth walking a quarter-mile or so along the cliff base to look at the patterns and indentations carved in the volcanic rock by centuries of wind and water. Returning to the parking area, you'll see shallow, open caves with ceilings inscribed with pink-red petroglyph designs painted by the Caiquetios Indians at least 500 years ago. The same patterns, which have never been deciphered by archaeologists, are repeated in various caves on Bonaire. On the return ride to Kralendijk, take a short bypass via Seroe Largo for a special view of Kralendijk and many miles of the western shoreline. This observation point is one to remember. Some night when there's bright moonlight, drive out again. It takes only a few minutes, and the reward is a splendid visual nocturne: the lights of Kralendijk and the boats in the bay; the lovely coastline; the moon reflected on the water; and a glow on the horizon from the lights of Curaçao, 40 miles away.

Southern Route – The tour south from Kralendijk is totally unlike the northern trip. Driving down the highway past the airport and the shore homes for five miles or so, you'll pass a nest of radio towers belonging to one of the world's most powerful transmitters: the 810,000-watt Trans-World Radio, a Protestant missionary station that broadcasts in 16 languages to all of the Caribbean and to South America.

After a shoreline drive where you can see hundreds of sea birds, large and small, you come to the Antilles International Salt Company's salt mountains, great pyramids of dazzling white sea salt. They are produced by a distillation process that starts with ocean water flowing into a rectangular pond, where the sunshine and trade winds evaporate some of the water; then the residue is pumped to a second pond, where more water is evaporated. This continues in pond after pond, each pond assuming a different hue because of the amount of salt contained. Finally, the water is evaporated. Machines come in and break up the salt deposit, then pile it in high hills to await shipment. Flocks of pink flamingos feed in these multicolored ponds; they love the briny water and the algae. At two points along the way, the government has restored groups of slave huts where the salt workers slept during the week. On weekends they walked to their homes in Rincón. The tiny, whitewashed, thatch-roofed huts are popular camera subjects.

The drive now leads past an old lighthouse and in due course to Sorobon, a point of land where you'll see a modern ruin — the steel framework of a hotel started years ago and abandoned when the company went bankrupt. The road along this part of the island is bordered by mangrove swamps, unique to this part of Bonaire.

If you've brought a bathing suit or picnic lunch, take a 4-mile drive off the main road to Cai, a little settlement on Lac Bay. The swimming and snorkeling here are delightful, and there are shelters to provide shade for a picnic. The drive back passes through two villages with the exotic names of Tera Cora and Nikiboko. Then you're back in Kralendijk.

SOURCES AND RESOURCES

TOURIST INFORMATION: The Bonaire Government Tourist Office, 275 7th Ave., New York, NY 10001 (212 242-7707), can provide information (including hotel rates, divers' package plans, etc.) and free literature.

On Bonaire, the Bonaire Government Tourist Bureau, at 1 Breedestraat, a couple of blocks from Cruise Ship Pier North (phones: 8322, 8649), has information, maps, and literature. The official island guide is white-uniformed Cai-Cai (pronounced kie-kie) Cecilia, a one-man bon bini committee, who's always about and may have already bade you welcome at the airport. He'll tell you where everything's at, how to get there, and fill you in on Bonaire lore. If you're lucky, you'll hear Cai-Cai and his well-known band play a gig during your stay.

Local Coverage – *Bonaire Holiday* has up-to-date information on events, shopping, and sightseeing. It's available free at the airport, tourist office, and hotels. Five daily newspapers printed in Curaçao and Aruba, in combinations of English, Papiamento, and Dutch, contain special sections for Bonaire and are distributed in Bonaire daily.

For background reading, Dr. J. Hartog's *History of Bonaire* is available in paperback; so is the *Field Guide* to Washington/Slagbaai Park, the *Antillean Fish Guide,* and the colorful, very informative *Guide to the Bonaire Marine Park* by Tom van't Hof.

Telephone – Dial direct to Bonaire by adding the international access code 011 and the prefix 599-7 to the numbers given below.

ENTRY REQUIREMENTS: Proof of citizenship (passport, birth certificate or affidavit of birth; voter's registration card) and a through ticket are all that US and Canadian citizens need to show.

CLIMATE AND CLOTHES: Constant cloudless days (rainfall totals only about 22 inches for the entire year) keep the sun shining down at a medium-well 82°F (31°C). That's the year-round average, and the thermometer stays fairly close to it, rarely reaching as high as 90°F (33°C), which can happen in September, or as low as 74°F (23°C), possible in January. The island's heat and humidity are well tempered by trade winds blowing from the northeast at an average 16 mph. Casual resortwear is the general rule, with cottons and drip-dry blends predominating for both men and women. You'll need some type of long-sleeved cover-up to slip on when you've had enough sun. Remember, you're quite near the equator. Shorts or slacks are okay for women in town, but bikinis should be confined to the beach or pool. Women may want something slightly dressy for an evening at the casino, and men may want to wear jackets there, but it's certainly not obligatory. Short-sleeved sport shirts are always permissible. *Note:* Salt water and the constant Antillean breeze make simple hairdos nearly essential for women; ditto head scarves for the beach and sightseeing drives.

MONEY: NAf (Netherlands Antilles florin, or guilder) is the official monetary unit, with a rate of exchange of approximately 1.79 NAf to the US dollar and about 25 percent less to the Canadian dollar. US dollars and traveler's checks are acceptable everywhere; Canadian dollars are somewhat less negotiable, so they should be changed to NAf for shopping, restaurants, etc. Banking hours are 9:30 AM to noon and 2 to 4 PM, Monday through Friday. Stores offer no discounts for payment in US dollars. Major credit cards are honored in most shops, hotels, and restaurants.

LANGUAGE: "Bon bini" might be the first words you hear; that's "welcome" in Papiamento, the language unique to the Netherlands Antilles. But don't worry, everybody understands and speaks English. Dutch is the official language, but — since South America is so close — there's also a lot of Spanish spoken.

TIME: Bonaire is on Atlantic Standard Time, which puts its clocks an hour ahead of Eastern Standard Time (when it's noon in New York, it's 1 PM in Bonaire). During Eastern Daylight months, the hour is the same in both places.

CURRENT: With 127 volts, 50 cycles, American appliances work, though a bit slowly; photographers with rechargeable strobes should consult the hotel manager for special instructions.

GETTING THERE: Most vacationers reach the island by flying first to Curaçao or Aruba, both of which are served daily by American Airlines from New York and by ALM (Antillean Airlines) flights from Miami, New York, and Puerto Rico. Eastern Airlines schedules daily jets from Miami to Aruba and Curaçao, from both of which ALM has regularly scheduled 20-minute hops to Bonaire's Flamingo Airport (Curaçao currently offers more and better connections). Its new runway means it can now accommodate jets directly from the States. ALM flies nonstop or one-stop from Miami on weekends. Meanwhile, direct charters — in connection with very reasonably priced winter packages — are planned for the coming winter, too; check with your travel agent, who may also be able to tell you how to visit two or all three ABC islands for the price of a single round-trip fare.

CALCULATING COSTS: Bonaire hotel rates are moderate, ranging from around $65 EP (no meals included) for two in standard accommodations to $105 up deluxe. These are winter prices, in effect from December 16 through mid-April; in summer they drop 30% to 40%. MAP (breakfast and dinner) is about $30 extra per day per person year-round. There is a 5% room tax and most hotels add 10% to 15% service charge in lieu of tips.

Scuba diving packages are offered by *Bonaire Beach* hotel (operated by *Bonaire Scuba Center*), *Habitat* (operated by *Aquaventure*), *Divi Flamingo Beach* (operated by *Dive Bonaire*), *Carib Inn* (operated by Bruce Bowker), and the *Sand Dollar Condominiums and Beach Club,* through *Sand Dollar Dive and Photo.* Typical 8-day/7-night summer plan, which includes standard hotel accommodations at the hotels, breakfasts, dinners, taxes, transfers from and to the airport, and 6 half days of diving, is in the neighborhood of $500 up per person, double occupancy, plus air fare.

 GETTING AROUND: Taxi – Unmetered, government-established rates are posted in hotels and the airport, and each driver has a list. Fare from the airport to your hotel will run about $5 to $10 per cab (four persons maximum), plus a 10% tip. Rates increase 25% after 8 PM to midnight, and 50% from midnight to 6 AM. Your hotel can get you a cab in a few minutes, or you can phone the central dispatcher at 8100.

Bus – There are no public buses.

Car Rental – The roads are narrow, but kept in good to excellent condition. So, with bird watching to do, numerous beaches to visit, and many diving sites just offshore (look for yellow markers beside the road), it's nice to be able to get around on your own wheels; it's not expensive. For drivers aged 21 to 75, daily rates, with unlimited mileage, range from about $22 to $50, depending on the size of the car. US and Canadian drivers' licenses are valid for driving on the island. Avis's Bonaire representative is *Flamingo Tours* (phone: 8310), but you can reserve your car before your trip by calling the system's 800 international reservations number. For any of Bonaire's local car rental agencies — *Boncar,* a Budget affiliate (phone: 8300; ext. 25 in town, ext. 35 for airport), *Erkar* (phone: 8536), or *ABC* (phone: 8980) — you can make reservations when you book your hotel space. Budget also has a toll-free number through which you can make reservations from the US: 800-527-0700. *Happy Chappy Rentals* (phone: 8407, 8989) rents Yamahas and other big bikes; its mopeds go for about $15 a day including free pickup and delivery. The *Divi Flamingo Beach* hotel and casino rents pedal-powered bikes for about $3 a day.

Sightseeing Taxi Tours – Drivers are good guides to the island's attractions and will take a party of up to four on a half-day tour for about $17.

Sightseeing Bus Tours – Trips are operated by *Bonaire Sightseeing,* which is also *Boncar Rental* (phone: 8300, ext. 25); *Flamingo Tours,* which is also the *Avis* rep (phone: 8310); and *Achie Tours* (phone: 8630). Each offers a choice of 2-hour guided trips: a northern tour (not including Washington/Slagbaai Park) and a southern tour, at $9 each per person, or a combination of both for $16. A special 3-hour tour of Washington/Slagbaai Park can be arranged for about $15 per person (minimum two) or $10 per person (three or more). In addition, *Bonaire Safari Tours,* based at *Habitat* (phone: 8290), now offers a good look at heretofore inaccessible nature sites — including off-the-road caves, grottoes, and interest points in the rugged National Park — using air-conditioned four-wheel-drive vehicles; the $15 per-person cost includes food and drink en route.

Sea Excursions – Ebo Domacasse, based at the *Bonaire Beach* hotel (phone: 8448, ext. 200), plans both seagoing (diving, snorkeling, fishing, sailing) and land-roving nature tours; day rates, including transport, beverages, and lunch, vary according to sport and destination. The *Divi Flamingo Beach* and *Bonaire Beach* hotels offer afternoon cruises (about $14 per person includes rum punch) and two-hour sunset voyages several times a week. Glass-bottom boat trips can be arranged through *Bonaire Scuba Center* (phone: 8448); an hour tour is around $8 per person. *Habitat* (phone: 8290), *Bonaire Scuba Center,* and *Dive Bonaire* (phone: 8285) offer water taxi trips to the uninhabited island of Klein Bonaire, off Kralendijk; for about $6 per person, they'll take you over in the morning, leave you for snorkeling, beaching, and picnicking, and pick you up in the afternoon. An alternative *Bonaire Scuba Center* trip programs a picnic lunch, a naturalist's tour of Washington Park, and snorkeling for about $25 per person. Besides daytime dive, snorkel, and picnic excursions, *Vistamar Bonaire* (phone: 8308) schedules sunset wining-and-dining cruises with beach pickup at the *Divi Flamingo Beach, Habitat,* and the *Bonaire Beach.*

Now also available are live-aboard dive boats. One of them, the 110-foot M/V *Antilles Aggressor,* offers 7-day dive trips to Curaçao and Bonaire (phone: 800-DIV-XPRT). Another, the 200-foot M/S *Aquanaut Holiday,* cruises Aruba, Curaçao, and Bonaire on dive and adventure trips (phone: 800-327-8223; in Florida, 800-432-8894).

SHOPPING: Bonaire shopping — like that in Curaçao and Aruba — though technically not entirely duty-free, offers substantial savings on a long list of imported luxuries: Swiss watches, English china, French perfumes, Danish silver, Scandinavian crystal, jewelry, and more. On the whole, however, Bonaire's selections don't begin to compare with those of its sister islands in variety. Some Curaçao/Aruba stores have Bonaire branches. *Spritzer & Führmann,* at Breedestraat (Broad St.) and Kerkweg (Church Way), is the biggest and best of these with a fine collection of divers' watches in addition to elegant trade-name merchandise by Royal Copenhagen, Spode, Omega, Kosta, and more; *Littman Jewelers* (of Curaçao) and *Aries Boutique,* at 33 Kaya Grandi, offer good buys in 14K and 18K gold, watches, Delft china, semiprecious gems, and black coral. The boutique also carries Dutch specialty foods. *El Globo Cameras* (also of Curaçao) has a Kralendijk outpost, too.

These days the *Divi Flamingo's Ki Bo Ke Pakus* (the "What Do You Want" Shop) is the island's best boutique (bright bikinis, dashikis, caftans, and pareos at nice prices; don't buy any items made with black coral, as it is endangered); the *Bonaire Beach* hotel's *Boutique Bonaire* is smaller, not so stylish. In Kralendijk's Bonaire Shopping Gallery, *Natasja & Alexander* has the town's best selection of men's and women's sports clothes, bathing suits, beach-to-evening fashions (Pucci is among their labels); *Aries* concentrates on jeans and shirts. Along Breedestraat: *Sportboetick* has Adidas sneakers, Zodiac T-shirts, sport shirts, running shorts, tank tops, socks (also — inexplicably — seeds, fertilizer, and butane lanterns). *S. G. Sloiana's* even more puzzlingly combines outdoor gear (thermoses, lanterns); soccer, diving, and biking equipment; liquor; cowboy and sailor hats. *Augustin's* has toys and craft supplies; *Things Bonaire* racks up souvenir T-shirts, Amstel tote bags; *Botica Bonaire,* a very updated drugstore, handles prescriptions, vitamins, perfumes, and some imported cosmetics. *Centro's* Woolworth-like miscellany runs the gamut from chocolate bars to Kodak film to kids' clothes. Best place for indigenous Bonaire souvenirs that are reasonably priced, reasonably attractive, and *not* unblushingly emblazoned with flamingos is the nonprofit *Fundashon Arte Industria Bonariano* workshop. *Kibra Hocha* on Caracastraat stocks hand- and shell-crafts as well as T-shirts and souvenirs. Store hours are 8 AM to noon and 2 to 6 PM daily except Sundays.

TIPPING: Ten percent is the rule (15% at the *Divi Flamingo Beach*); it's added to your hotel bill to take care of service by bellboys, room maids, etc., and is added to your check in restaurants; more is not called for unless some special service has been provided. Tip taxi drivers 10% of the fare. Give airport porters 1 NAf (about 55¢) per bag.

SPECIAL EVENTS: Bonaire's biggest wingding is the *October International Sailing Regatta,* five days of racing, steel band music, dancing, and feasting not only for the crews of participating working fishing boats, yachts, sloops, Sunfish, Sailfish, and windsurfers, but for the entire island and visitors as well. There's also lots of village folk dancing and singing on *Dia de San Juan* (St. John's Day, June 24) and *Dia de San Pedro* (St. Peter's, June 29). *Carnival* time in February is observed with costumed parades and more dancing. Official holidays, when banks and shops are closed (although some shops stay open when there's a cruise ship in port), include: *New Year's Day, Good Friday, Easter, Ascension Day, Whitmonday, Kingdom Day* (December 15), *Christmas* (December 25 and 26).

SPORTS: Bonaire's major activities are scuba diving, snorkeling, and bird watching, but the island has more to offer those with less specialized wants, as long as they involve sand and sea.

Bird Watching – Bird watchers flock to Bonaire and for good reason: it has close to 135 species. The roseate flamingos are the most famous, and there are pelicans, parrots, herons, doves, cuckoos, and such exotic fauna as the groove-billed ani, the black-whiskered vireo, and the bananaquit. Birding is best on the northern part of the island in valleys, ponds, and in Washington/Slagbaai National Park. Flamingo sanctuaries are at Goto Meer on the northwest coast and at Pekel Meer. The largest colony lives at the salt flats at the southern end. The Antilles International Salt Company, in reactivating the industry, has been so careful not to disturb the flamingos that the birds seem to be grateful. Instead of laying one egg a year, as had been their habit, they now hatch twice, in June and December. For flamingo watching, take binoculars and a telephoto lens for your camera. Flamingos are shy.

A listing of most of the species of Bonaire birds is available at the tourist offices in New York and Bonaire.

Boating – If you're on Bonaire at International Regatta time in October, you're likely to be recruited by one of the skippers as crew or just ballast. A Sunfish can be rented at your hotel for about $8 an hour; use of a windsurfer with instruction is about $10 per hour. For lessons, contact Erwin Miller at the *Bonaire Scuba Center* (phone: 8448; ext. 200). The *Playa Lechi Marina,* just south of the *Bonaire Beach* hotel, has full-service berths for various types of vessels plus a shipyard and dry-dock.

Golf – In miniature only, at the *Bonaire Beach* hotel.

Snorkeling and Scuba – Bonaire is ideal for snorkeling, and scuba is the island's varsity sport. Divers come from everywhere to take part. The island is special for diving because it is a coral reef itself, and you don't have to travel offshore to find the dive spots; most are right off the beach or a very short boat ride away. The drop-off is usually about 20 yards from shore, all along the western side of the island. In no time at all you're swimming around in an underwater forest, among eerie shapes of living coral, sea fans, sponges, and schools of angelfish, butterfly fish, feathered star-fish, mutton snappers, queen triggerfish, sea horses, and dozens of other fascinating species. Visibility in these calm waters is 100 feet and more. Snorkelers will be pleased to learn that the government and the World Wildlife Fund have developed a quarter-mile underwater trail in the Marine Park. Also of interest is the *Hilma Hooker,* a 238-foot freighter wrecked off the southwest coast that swarms with fish and other creatures of the sea. It is only 50 feet from the surface and so can be viewed by snorkelers as well as divers.

Captain Don Stewart, legendary leader in the island's determined movement to preserve its reefs and marine life, runs *Habitat* (phone: 8290; US reservations, 800-223-5581 or 212-535-9530), a complete, five-star scuba training facility with multilingual instructors; it is rated one of the Caribbean's best. *Bonaire Beach* hotel, which also has a fully equipped dive shop, offers a variety of scuba and snorkeling trips and other water sports in the protected area off the beach. The newest scuba operation on Bonaire is at *Sand Dollar Condominiums and Beach Club,* near Kralendjik, which boasts scuba instruction in four languages (English, Spanish, French, and Dutch/Papiamento) as well as dive vacation packages. Local dive centers offer a choice of scuba/stay packages: 7 nights including six guided dives, unlimited air, and accommodations for about $266 up plus air fare per person depending on hotel choice; a similar setup including twelve guided dives is about $343 up per person plus air fare; a 10% service charge is also added. There's also a variety of beginner and advanced courses of instruction, including one on underwater photography. Similar scuba programs are offered by *Dive Bonaire* (with 11 dive boats and complete underwater-photography facilities) at the *Divi Flamingo Beach* resort and casino under the guidance of expert Peter Hughes (phone: 8285; in the US and Canada, 607-277-3484 or 800-367-3484); the *Bonaire Scuba Center* at the *Bonaire Beach* hotel with divemaster Eddie Statia (phone: 8978; in New Jersey, 201-566-8866; from elsewhere in the US, 800-526-2370); and Bruce Bowker of the 12-room *Carib Inn.* There are also snorkeling packages including instruction, equipment, and reef trip for about $25 to $30 per person. Or put on a mask and fins and swim out on your own (but never alone) to explore the reefs just offshore. However you do it, don't spearfish or try to collect any coral or other marine souvenirs. That's strictly against the law.

Sport Fishing – Seven local skippers are prepared to take visitors in search of dorado, yellowfin tuna, sea bass, grouper, snapper, marlin, sailfish, bonito, and pompano. And it's not expensive: a half day on a skippered boat costs about $200 to $250 for four to six people. At press time, Bonaire was planning to add an international billfish tournament to its sports calendar, but the time and place had not yet been set. Check with the Bonaire Tourist Board.

Swimming and Sunning – Most hotels have white sandy beaches, with many more around the island. The shore is lined by low coral cliffs, with paths and stairways leading down to small coves and wider beaches, a few of which have changing facilities, but many of which are too secluded to require them. No beach is ever crowded, even those in front of the hotels. In addition to the beaches just above and below Kralendijk, others worth a special visit include: Sorobon and Cai on Lac Bay on the southeast coast, where you can watch the conch fishermen and help yourself to conch shells for souvenirs (don't do any shelling underwater on the island — it's illegal); and on the northern end of the island, the coastline of Washington/Slagbaai Park, including Playa Funchi, black coral Boca Bartol, and Playa Chiquito, or Little Beach, walled on three sides by low coral cliffs.

Tennis – Not a major drawing card on Bonaire, but there are 2 courts at the *Bonaire Beach* hotel (small charge for nonguests) and 2 in town (free; reserve through your hotel).

Water Skiing – Arranged through your hotel; rates are about $8 per quarter hour.

Windsurfing – The *Mistral Windsurfing School* at the *Bonaire Beach* hotel offers windsurfing boards free to guests, but there is a $15-per-hour charge for instruction.

 NIGHTLIFE: Most is at the hotels, with local folk dancers, a steel band, or local combo. Both the casino at the *Bonaire Beach* and the *Divi Flamingo Beach*'s informal gaming room — billed as "The World's First Barefoot Casino" — also provide occasional entertainment. The island has one downtown nightclub/disco (not to worry, Regine), called *E Wowo* — "The Eye" in Papiamento, "because it stays open late" — that currently does its thing on weekend nights; it's a private club, but temporary membership can be arranged by your hotel. The *Divi Flamingo Beach* resort and casino and the *Bonaire Beach* hotel plan something a little different each evening during the winter season, with music and dancing several nights a week. "Happy hours" and special "nights" featuring a round of international buffets are also specialties, all pleasantly casual. Bonaire has two small casinos. The *Divi Flamingo Beach*'s lively little "barefoot casino" opens at 4 PM daily. The *Black Coral Casino* at the *Bonaire Beach* hotel is larger and less casual, but still lots of fun for an evening's entertainment. Open from 9 PM nightly.

BEST ON THE ISLAND

 CHECKING IN: Bonaire's 500 hotel rooms are divided among five watersports-oriented hotels and one commercial property in town. To keep hotel architecture and commercial growth in harmony with the island's simple beauties and relaxed atmosphere, expansion is being planned with firm controls to boost the economy without spoiling Bonaire for visitors or residents.

The four best — two comfortable, one homey, one spartan — are on the shore in or near Kralendijk. Hotel prices range from inexpensive (about $35 EP, without meals, a day for a single monk's cell or roomette for scuba divers) to moderate (about $105 up for a double room and about $140 for a small suite, EP, in winter, in a newer, larger hotel).

Sand Dollar Condominium and Beach Club – Offers 38 units (with 1, 2, or 3 bedrooms) on the beach. All have air conditioning, telephone, TV, and full electric kitchens. There's also tennis, a pool, and the *Sand Dollar Dive and Photo Shop* on the premises (phone: 609-298-3844). Expensive to moderate.

Bachelor Beach Apartments – A Spanish-style villa with large sun decks, a cactus garden, private pier, and good snorkeling. Offers fully furnished 1- and 2-bedroom units for up to 6 people. Dive and vacation packages available at good rates (phone: 202-338-0690). Moderate.

Bonaire Beach – Two-story low-rise with 148 rooms recently completely refurbished. Nice beach, 2 bars, dining room, coffee shop, beach pavilion for lunch and drinks; also casino, shops, mini-golf, swimming pool, tennis courts, children's playground, steel band and folkloric entertainment. Popular group destination. Full water sports program by *Bonaire Scuba Center* (phone: 8448). Moderate.

Bonaire Beach Bungalows – A small complex offering air-conditioned 2-bedroom oceanfront villas. There's good snorkeling offshore, and management has arrangements for excellent car-rental rates for guests (phone: 717-586-9230). Moderate.

Divi Flamingo Beach – Between the airport and town at the edge of the sea; with it, yet slightly away, a pleasantly informal place with a genuinely personal feeling. There are 150 air-conditioned rooms in all; some have balconies over the water from which you can watch fish without benefit of mask (the sea is that clear); the newest are deluxe studios with kitchenettes in the Club Flamingo complex, which includes 40 condo apartments and separate dive shop/pier next to the main resort. Open-air dining rooms overlook beach and sea; bar with local entertainment; boutique; casino; new freshwater pool; Jacuzzi. Scuba diving and water activities by Peter Hughes's *Dive Bonaire* (phone: 8285). Moderate.

Habitat – Simplicity itself, oriented to divers and snorkelers, this property has 11 recently renovated two-bedroom cottages with kitchenettes and covered patios; also 7 single roomettes and 4 small doubles. There is a bar with sunset patio and a store on the premises. Casual buffet breakfast, lunch, and dinner served in the *Quarter Deck* restaurant, and Italian specialties in *Dolphina's,* a new waterfront restaurant.. Monk-cell roomettes for $25 per day are reserved for divers only. Children discouraged. More-luxurious accommodations are available in 13 lovely 2-bedroom villas in Captain Don's pride, the *Hamlet,* a seaside community project first opened in 1987 (phone for both: 8290; in the US, 800-223-5581 or 212-535-9530). *Hamlet,* moderate; *Habitat,* inexpensive.

Sorobon Beach Resort – This unusual "naturalist's" resort, between the Caribbean Sea and Lac Bay, has 16 cottages with kitchenettes but no air conditioning. Very reasonable rates for studios and 1-bedroom units. The big draw: Clothing is optional (phone: 800-828-9356 or 011-599-8080). Moderate.

Sunset Villas – Very nice, well-maintained, completely furnished cottages and villas (a total of 27 air-conditioned double rooms) at a variety of locations on Bonaire. Good rates year-round, ideal for families or couples who want to share (phone: 011-599-7-8291). Moderate.

Carib Inn – Onetime private home, now the base for Bruce Bowker's scuba operation, with pool, patio, 12 tidy rooms, one sizable seaview suite, and one efficiency apartment for rent to visiting divers. It is considered one of Bonaire's friendliest roosts and one of the best buys on the island — in 1973, Bruce was Bonaire's first "imported" scuba instructor, and his hospitality is much of the inn's appeal (phone: 8819). Inexpensive.

 EATING OUT: Generally acceptable food, simply cooked, but not much variety. The *Bonaire Beach* and *Divi Flamingo Beach* hotels try for international cuisine, feature good, fresh fish plus an occasional *rijsttafel,* the traditional Indonesian rice table of many deliciously spiced dishes. Hotels also serve native island dishes, but they don't always put them on the menu; so it's a good idea to ask about unlisted specials. Worth sampling: *keshi yena,* a tasty, if hefty, mixture of chicken and beef, pickled and cooked with onions and tomatoes, then wrapped in Edam cheese; *stobà,* a casserole of lamb served with rice and banana fritters; goat stew (nicely seasoned, it tastes a lot like veal); and fish chowder — especially grouper. An expensive restaurant will charge $15 up per person for dinner, including tip, but no drinks; those considered moderate charge between $8 and $14 per person; inexpensive, below that. Our recommendations, all in or near Kralendijk, are:

Beefeater – Intimate restaurant with quiet atmosphere and superb service, offering a variety of fresh fish, steaks, and chops, all beautifully presented. Reservations required. Breedestraat (phone: 8081). Expensive.

Den Laman – Seafood spot with inviting bar, intriguing aquarium decor, boat-based salad bar; dancing and live entertainment several times a week. Shoreside between *Bonaire Beach* hotel and *Habitat* (phone: 8955). Expensive.

Bistro des Amis – Cozily French from the start (i.e., the bar serves garlic bread with aperitifs); escargots, coquilles St.-Jacques; other specialties follow. Kerkweg (phone: 8003). Expensive to moderate.

Le Chic – The island's newest French restaurant, an intimate, casual, 32-table bistro specializing in seafood. There's a "small menu" of finger foods and a full-course dinner menu. Desserts include homemade ice cream. Dinner is served from 4:30 PM to midnight, Monday through Saturday. On Kaya C.E.B. Hellmund overlooking the harbor (phone: 8617). Expensive to moderate.

Mona Lisa – Convivial atmosphere plus a very authentic Dutch menu that features fresh fish and seafood as well as other dishes prepared with an international flair for herbs and sauces. Breedestraat (phone: 8308). Moderate.

Great China and China Garden – The first is the smaller and simpler of the two, but both serve a wide variety of Chinese specialties, seafood, and Indonesian dishes. *The Great China,* Breedestraat (phone: 8666); *China Garden,* Breedestraat (phone: 8480). Moderate.

Rendezvous – Café atmosphere with bistro menu of seafood, salads, steaks, and good desserts. Espresso and pastries are served between formal lunch and dinner hours. Kerkweg (phone: 8454). Moderate.

Hilltop – Quiet, friendly, known for Dutch dishes and island cooking (fried fish, conch stew, goat stew). About 5 minutes north of town on the Tourist Rd. No credit cards (phone: 8223). Inexpensive.

Zeezicht – That's Dutch for "Sea View"; it's a popular bistro right on the waterfront — good for sampling local specialties, including conch stew, goat curry, fresh fish platters, Chinese food, snacks, or a midafternoon beer (phone: 8434). Inexpensive.

BRITISH VIRGIN ISLANDS

On most maps, the British and US Virgin Islands appear as a weltering confusion of ink marks and tiny print muddying the space between Puerto Rico and the larger islands of the Leeward chain that stretch east and then drop south of Puerto Rico. They make very frustrating map reading, but before you begin to curse and mutter, consider the cartographer's problem: Just 60 miles separate the British Virgin Islands from Puerto Rico, a mere pencil skip away on the scale of most maps, and there are something like 50 islands in the group — rocks, cays, fragments, spits of land, volcanic bubbles, and actual islands. Just west are the US Virgin Islands, another 65 or so dollops of land, only three of which are of any size. So if the map looks as if the cartographer sneezed ink over a quarter inch of parchment, at least that speckled band of spots will tell you where, in general, the British Virgin Islands are to be found.

It won't tell you a thing about the exceptional nature of the islands, however, or inform you in the least of what these dribs and drabs of volcanic island are like in the flesh. They are most familiar to sailors, who for years — indeed, for centuries — have sailed around and through them, putting in at completely empty cays for a night's rest or a day's swimming and sunning (or for darker purposes centuries ago, when the cays were favorite lurking places of pirates awaiting richly laden galleons on the way to Europe). Only 16 of the islands are inhabited; the entire country has a population of approximately 12,000 people, most of whom live on Tortola, and a total area of only 59 square miles.

The major inhabited islands in the chain are Tortola, with the islands' capital, Road Town; Virgin Gorda; Beef Island (now connected to Tortola by a bridge); Anegada; and Jost Van Dyke.

Christopher Columbus discovered the entire Virgin Islands chain in 1493, although he and almost everyone else forgot them almost immediately. In 1595 Sir Francis Drake sailed into the channel that now bears his name, the waters that flow between Tortola to the north and Norman Island, Peter Island, Salt Island, Cooper Island, Ginger Island, and Virgin Gorda, which swing in an arc around Tortola from south to east. Within 30 years the English had established a legal claim on at least some of the islands, although they were under continual dispute — with the Spanish and the Dutch primarily — until 1672, when Tortola was annexed by the English government.

In the meantime, pirates discovered the islands. The numerous isolated and empty cays, deserted beaches, and hidden coves of the Virgin Islands were a gift to the buccaneers who raided trade ships passing between the Caribbean and Europe. Tortola became a pirates' haven for a while, and there was much

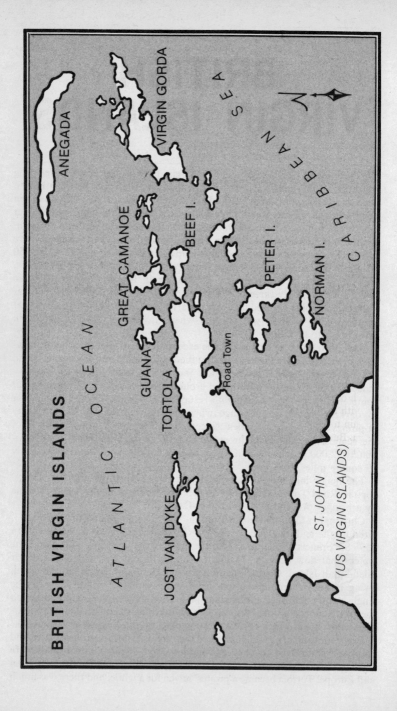

coming and going from many of the smaller cays. (Robert Louis Stevenson's *Treasure Island* is popularly believed to be BVI's Norman Island, but some think it's actually a tiny cay called Dead Man's Chest of Peter Island, because of the book's famed ditty "Fifteen men on the dead man's chest, yo-ho-ho and a bottle of rum!")

However, by the end of the seventeenth century, Tortola had begun to attract English planters, who firmly established the British right to the island.

By the middle of the eighteenth century a Quaker colony had been established, the planters far outnumbered the privateers, and hand in hand they attempted to form their own constitutional government. Meanwhile, two native sons gained fame in the wider world: Dr. William Thornton, a Quaker, designed the Capitol in Washington, DC, and Dr. John Lettsom, who was born on Jost Van Dyke, founded the Medical Society of London.

Occasional talk of independence through the years notwithstanding, the British Virgin Islands remain distinctly linked to the British Commonwealth. The governor is appointed by the Queen, but laws are made and administered by a locally elected chief minister and Legislative Council. Queen Elizabeth II visited Tortola in 1966 to open the Sir Francis Drake's highway between West End, where she landed, and Road Town, and to open and dedicate the bridge that now links Tortola with Beef Island. Much to the delight of the islanders, she returned in 1977 to open the Legislative Council as a part of her Silver Jubilee celebration. You'll find a portrait of the queen in most hotels and shops and fine manners and British courtesy everywhere. But, oddly enough, you'll find only US currency in the British Virgin Islands.

Even more than their sister islands in the US Virgin Islands, the British Virgins are a destination for tourists who want sun, sea, and nature. Development for tourism proceeds with great caution, for the very valid reason that much of the intense pleasure that these cays and islands give tourists has to do with their isolation, their tiny size, their privacy. It is likely that they will remain to a great extent the province of those lucky people who sail around them. But for anyone whose idea of leisure is the pursuit of nature itself, they are a compelling attraction.

BRITISH VIRGIN ISLANDS AT-A-GLANCE

FROM THE AIR: The British Virgin Islands are made up of more than 50 islands, rocks, and cays, many of which are clustered around the Sir Francis Drake Channel, a historic waterway that flows through many of them for 20 miles in length and 5 miles in width. The chain lies 60 miles east of Puerto Rico and directly northeast of St. John in the US Virgin Islands. Spread out as they are, they command an impressive area and run from 18°15' to 18°40' N latitude and from 64°50' to 64°10' W longitude. Over 200 ships have run aground here over the centuries and tales of sunken treasure abound, especially off the Anegada Reefs.

Fewer than ten of the islands have accommodations for tourists, although yachtsmen and day sailors "in the know" often drop anchor off several of the others. They find their own havens in the uninhabited coves of Fallen Jerusalem, Great Dog, Ginger,

Norman, and little Prickly Pear. These islands are especially beckoning to the carefree and barefoot bareboat visitor, while the seven relatively "built-up" British Virgin Islands (i.e., those with five or more guestrooms) are ready and waiting for those who yearn for tranquil cottage resorts at the edge of the sea.

For tourists, the British Virgin Islands offer a quiet retreat, without hotel chains, fancy restaurants, or casinos for entertainment. Instead, there is magnificent scenery, perfect sailing conditions, personalized hotels, secluded beaches, and welcoming, friendly islanders, many of them hotel and land owners.

 SPECIAL PLACES: Tortola – Road Town, the capital of the BVI and home of about half of its residents, is where most activity begins and ends on Tortola. There are dozens of shops to browse through all along the main street, a colorful market at the edge of town, and any number of sailing craft to take you away for the day. Several of the old buildings have been preserved, even though a new shopping plaza has gone up in the city center.

To explore the island, head west from Road Town toward Mt. Sage, the island's highest point at 1,780 feet. On its slopes, what was once a primeval rain forest makes the ideal spot for a picnic overlooking the neighboring islands and cays.

The coast road continues west past Dutch-built Fort Recovery (1660). Just beyond the anchorage at Soper's Hole (if you're thirsty, refresh at *The Pusser's Landing*) is West End town, the takeoff point for St. Thomas–bound ferries. Just around the island's western tip lie the north shore's series of splendidly unspoiled white beaches: Smuggler's Cove, with its garden of snorkeling reefs; sweeping Long Bay; Apple Bay; Carrot Bay; Cane Garden Bay (where *Stanley's Beach Bar* sets up drinks and snacks); beautifully protected Brewer's Bay (rum distillery remnants, new campgrounds); and Josiah's Bay near Tortola's eastern end. Turn south and cross the Queen Elizabeth Bridge (dedicated by Her Majesty in 1966) to Beef Island, site of Beef International Airport, launch departures for Marina and Bellamy Cays, and untrammeled shelling and sunning beaches. Then head back to Road Town for sundowners at *The Cloud Room, Skyworld,* or *The Pub.*

Virgin Gorda – The highlight of a visit to this island (third largest in the chain, with a population of about 1,000) is a trip to the Baths, where gigantic rocks and boulders, shaped by volcanic pressures millions of years ago, have come to rest, forming strange entrances to water grottoes and shaded pools. You'll crawl through one formation to find yourself ankle deep in cool water, then through another to find a long stretch of sand and sunlight. Each set of boulders offers a totally different vista. Virgin Gorda boasts some 20 beaches; favorites include Spring, Trunk, and Devil's Bays. There is also an abandoned copper mine on the southeast tip, and a 1,370-foot mountain peak in the north.

Anegada – The only coral island of the group (the rest are volcanic), its highest point is just 28 feet above sea level; it claims a population of only 250. Dozens of shipwrecks off the reefs here tempt divers. One of the sunken ships, the *Paramatta,* has been at rest 30 feet down for more than 100 years; another, the British frigate HMS *Astrea,* was built 200 years ago. There is also a Greek freighter, sunk some 50 years ago. Each wreck promises a chance at hidden treasure.

SOURCES AND RESOURCES

 TOURIST INFORMATION: The US centers for BVI data are the British Virgin Islands Tourist Board, Suite 511, 370 Lexington Ave., New York, NY 10017 (phone: 212-696-0400 or 800-835-8530) and the BVI Information Office, 1686 Union St., San Francisco, CA 94123 (phone: 415-775-0344). In

Canada, write or call BVI Information Service, 801 York Mill Rd., Suite 201, Don Mills, Ont. M3B 1X7 (phone: 416-443-1859). The British Virgin Islands Tourist Board is on Waterfront Drive in Road Town (phone: 4-3134, 4-3864, 4-3489, or 4-3865).

Local Coverage – The *Welcome* is a most informative free bimonthly guide. The *Island Sun* and *BVI Beacon* are the weekly BVI newspapers. Florence Lewisohn's *Tales of Tortola and the British Virgin Islands* ($2.50 in island shops) is readable history.

Telephone – Dial direct to the BVI by adding the area code 809 and the prefix 49 to the numbers given below.

ENTRY REQUIREMENTS: A valid passport is the "preferred" entry document, but proof of citizenship (i.e., birth certificate or voter's registration card) is also acceptable. An ongoing ticket is also required. There is a departure tax of $5 per person leaving by air; $4 per person leaving by sea.

CLIMATE AND CLOTHES: The British Virgin Islands enjoy temperatures that range from 77°F to 90°F all year. Warm days are cooled by trade winds, especially at night, when temperatures drop as much as 10°. Comfortable and casual are the bywords here. And unless you're staying at *Little Dix Bay* you can forget to pack a jacket or a tie.

MONEY: The US dollar is used throughout the islands.

LANGUAGE: The Queen's English, often with a West Indian lilt.

TIME: Atlantic Standard Time all year. In winter when it's noon in the BVI, it's 11 AM in the US Eastern time zone; when Daylight Saving is in effect, the hour is the same both places.

CURRENT: At 110 volts, 60 cycles, American appliances need no converter.

GETTING THERE: There is limited jet service to the BVI, so most visitors make connections via San Juan, Puerto Rico; St. Thomas in the US Virgin Islands; or Antigua.

Several major US and Canadian airlines serve one or more of those destinations. Air BVI provides service from San Juan, St. Thomas, and Antigua to Tortola and from San Juan to Virgin Gorda. Crownair, Eastern Express, and American Eagle fly from San Juan to Tortola and Virgin Gorda. Crownair flies from St. Thomas to Tortola. LIAT flies to Tortola from San Juan and Antigua. Virgin Islands Seaplane Shuttle flies from St. Thomas and St. Croix to Tortola.

There are also a number of ferry boats connecting Road Town and West End on Tortola and Virgin Gorda (and even Anegada and Jost Van Dyke), with various locations in St. Thomas, St. Croix, and St. John in the USVI. Some run as often as twice daily; others as infrequently as once a week. The most heavily traveled route is Charlotte Amalie in St. Thomas to Tortola, a trip that takes an hour and costs from $25 to $35. Major carriers are *Bomba Charger, Native Son/Oriole, Marie Elise,* and *Speedy's Fantasy.*

CALCULATING COSTS: Accommodations in the British Virgin Islands run the gamut — from about $16 per day for a tent and prepared site (a bare site runs about $5 a day) to more than $670 (when you add in service and tax) per day for an ultradeluxe suite for two with all meals at *Biras Creek.* A 7% accommodation tax is added to hotel bills; service charges vary from 10% to 15%.

GETTING AROUND: Taxi – Readily available only on Tortola, Virgin Gorda, and Anegada. Rates are fixed (see the *Welcome* guide).

Car Rental – Only the coolest and surest should take on the roller-coaster hills and hairpin turns of the roads in the British Virgin Islands. Vehicles range from Land Rovers, Jeeps, and Mini-Mokes to 6- and 8-passenger Suzukis and air-conditioned automatic sedans. Contact *Avis* opposite police headquarters in Road Town (phone: 4-3322 or 4-2193); *National* at Duffs Bottom (phone: 4-3197); *Caribbean Car Rental* at *Maria's Inn* or *Anytime Car Rental* at *Wayside Inn; Dennis Alphonso* in Fish Bay (phone: 4-3137), *Budget* (phone: 4-2639), *Island Suzuki* (4-3666), and *International Car Rentals* (phone: 4-2516, 4-2517) in Road Town. On Virgin Gorda, try *Speedy's* (phone: 5-5240), or *Bomba* at the Yacht Harbour (no phone). Rates begin at about $27 a day or about $162 a week, including unlimited mileage. You'll need a valid US driver's license, of course, and you must buy a temporary BVI driving license for $5 at police headquarters or the rental agency, good for 30 days. Driving is on the left.

Sightseeing Tours and Travel Services – Offered by *Travel Plan* (phone: 4-2347), *Tortola Travel Services* (phone: 4-2215 or 4-2672), and *Air B.V.I.* (phone: 5-2346) on Tortola; and *Speedy's* on Virgin Gorda (phone: 5-5235). Rates run about $35 for 1 to 3 persons for a 2-hour tour of Tortola; $8 for each additional passenger..

Inter-Island Transport – Travel between Tortola and Virgin Gorda is by plane (only 5 minutes for $8) or by local ferry service (half an hour, $8) from Tortola to Virgin Gorda's yacht harbor. Individual arrangements can be made for separate trips.

Sea Excursions – The motor-sailer *White Squall* out of Road Harbour and the catamaran *Shadowfax* out of Treasure Isle marina do picnic day trips; about $65 per person covers rum punch, lunch, open bar, snorkel gear. Rentals for longer terms, ranging from bareboating to the all-inclusive *Windjammer Flying Cloud,* are found just east of Road Town.

SHOPPING: Selections pale beside those in the neighboring USVI. Still, although Road Town is not a duty-free port — since there's no duty on British imports — some English china, fabrics, and foods are bargain-priced. Per-bottle prices on liquor are sometimes lower than those on St. Thomas or St. Croix, but because of the one-liter limit (as opposed to the one-gallon USVI allowance), most US citizens buy their Scotch in Charlotte Amalie or Christiansted. Locally handcrafted items include carved woods; hand-screened and batik fabrics; and jewelry made of black coral, conch, and tortoise shell (the last can't be imported to the US because of endangered species status).

Most shops are on Road Town's Main Street, with a few more in shopping arcades built into new marina developments. Hours are usually 9 AM to 4 PM. Best for buying, browsing: *Zenaida* on the main plaza (exotic batiks, bags, jewelry from Africa, South America, India, and the Middle East); *Little Denmark* (Scandinavian imports, gold and silver jewelry); the *Shipwreck Shop* (sometimes-better-than-others stocks of island craftwares); *Cockle Shop* (West Indian coins, watercolors, stamps, books, plus Cuban cigars and French perfumes); *Past and Presents* (good selection of books, some local crafts, old English silver, aged bits and pieces); *Sunny Caribbee Herb & Spice Company* (exotic spices, jellies, mustards, vinegars, herbs, teas, coffees, and hot sauces from all over the Caribbean); *Bonker's Gallery* (Balinese fashions by Samson, batik sarongs by Java Wraps, and hand-dyed fashions by owner Sara); *Flaxcrafts* (handcrafted jewelry by BVI designer Keith Flax); *H & B Handicrafts* (straw handicrafts from BVI and Dominica's Carib Indians); *J. R. O'Neal* (Spode china, Villeroy & Boch, and other quality housewares from all over the world); and the *Ample Hamper* at Village Cay (all sorts of edible and potable temptations, including Fortnum & Mason teas, honeys, Mrs. Thomas's mango chutney, and British Virgin Islands Native Seasoning (sea salt flavored with local herbs and spices). *Pusser's Rum Shop* features this unique BVI rum — served aboard British navy vessels for over 300 years until World War II and only recently made available to the public — in containers ranging from bottles to crocks to decorative decanters, plus fashions with the store's insignia.

In Virgin Gorda, *Island Woman* has Java Wraps and other Indonesian crafts. *Kaunda's* and the *Virgin Gorda Craft Shop* feature Caribbean crafts.

TIPPING: All hotels add a 10% to 12% service charge to bills; anything additional is up to you. The standard 10% to 15% is expected in restaurants and by service people (cabbies, etc.).

SPECIAL EVENTS: The *Spring Regatta* in April on Tortola draws sailing yachts and hordes of spectators from all the Caribbean islands as well as the US; Virgin Gorda stages a three-day *Easter Festival.* The last week in July and the first week in August, everything stops for *Festival,* to commemorate 1834's emancipation with singing, dancing, parades. Banks and offices also close for *New Year's Day, Easter Monday, Commonwealth Day* (May 24), *Whitmonday,* the *Queen's Official Birthday* (early June), *Territory Day* (July 1), *St. Ursula's Day* (October 21), the *Prince of Wales' Birthday* (November 14), *Christmas,* and *Boxing Day* (December 26).

SPORTS: Swimming and Sunning – On Tortola, Smuggler's Cove with its snorkeling reefs, the mile-long sands of Long Bay, and Cane Garden Bay are among the islands' handsomest (all with beachside restaurants, changing facilities); but the lazing is also lovely and the swimming fine on a dozen lesser-known strands. Virgin Gorda is ringed with a score of glorious beaches like Devil's Bay, Spring Bay, Trunk Bay. And dozens more — only occasionally visited — are there for you to discover on the BVI's small cays and uninhabited isles.

Snorkeling and Scuba – There's excellent snorkeling at Virgin Gorda around The Baths and at a dive site called The Indians near Peter and Norman islands. Marina Cay and Cooper Island have good snorkeling from their beaches. Anegada Island, just off the Anegada Reef, which has seen over 300 shipwrecks over the years, has excellent scuba diving and snorkeling sites; an amazing variety of fish can be seen in the decaying wreck of the *Rocus.* Other wrecks to look for are the *Paramatta* and the *Astrea.* The most popular dive site in the British Virgin Islands is the wreckage of the RMS *Rhone,* close to the western point of Salt Island almost in the middle of the islands, a little over 5 miles from Road Town. A victim of a hurricane in 1867 that sank 75 ships and killed at least 500 people, the *Rhone* is one of the Caribbean's most intriguing wrecks. It is broken in half, both parts adorned with fans, corals, sponges, and gorgonians. Schools of exceptionally tame spadefish, horse-eye jack, queen triggerfish, grunts, snappers, two-tone coneys, and small moray eels cruise in and out of the ship's interior and upright wreckage — a floating rainbow moving through an interior covered with brilliantly colored sponges. It can be reached by commercial dive boat or private charter. Other popular dive sites (there are well over 60) include Blonde Rock, between Dead Man's Chest and Salt Island; Painted Walls (shallow); the wreck of the *Chikuzen* north of Beef Island; and Brenners Bay near Norman. Among the larger dive outfits are *Baskin in the Sun,* at the *Prospect Reef* and *Treasure Isle* hotels, Road Town, Tortola (phone: 4-2858 or 4-2859; in the US, 800-233-7938); *Underwater Safaris* at the Moorings also in Road Town (phone: 4-3235; in the US, 800-535-7289); *Blue Water Divers* at Nanny Cay (phone: 4-2847); *Island Diver Ltd.* at *Village Cay Marina* (phone: 4-3878); *Kilbride's Underwater Tours* at North Sound, Virgin Gorda (phone: 4-2746), and *Dive BVI,* Virgin Gorda Yacht Harbour (phone: 5-5513). Most do snorkeling excursions as well, as does *Caribbean Images,* which also runs a glass-bottom boat from the *Prospect Reef* hotel (phone: 5-2563 or 4-3311). *Aquanaut Watersports* offers 7- and 14-day scuba and snorkeling vacation cruises aboard its two luxury ships; for information, contact Aquanaut Cruise Line Ltd., 241 E Commercial Blvd., Ft. Lauderdale, FL 33334 (phone: 800-327-8223; in Florida, 800-432-8894).

Boating – Everywhere people agree that the British Virgins are among the world's best sailing areas. More than 300 bareboats, almost 100 charter yachts, and the most developed marinas and shore facilities in the Caribbean make sailing in the British Virgin Islands what diving is to the Cayman Islands. Close to 70% of visitors to the BVI are on sailing vacations. Among the dozen yacht charter firms in Road Town are *Tortola Yacht Charters* (phone: 4-2221), *West Indies Yacht Charters* (phone: 5-2363 or 800-327-2290), and *Trimarine Boat Company* (phone: 4-2490), trimaran specialists. But tops in our book, both in quality of boats and expertise of personnel, is Ginny and Charlie Cary's *The Moorings* (phone: 4-2332; or 1305 US 19S, Suite 402, Clearwater, FL 33546; phone: 800-535-7289), the largest yacht operation in the Caribbean. Also recommended are *North South Yacht Charters* out of Virgin Gorda (phone: 5-5421; in the US, 800-387-4964) and *Tropic Island Yacht Management* out of Tortola (phone: 4-2450). In the States, *Copeland Cutler,* 183 Madison Ave., New York, NY 10016 (phone: 212-683-0400 or 800-223-1682), arranges private yacht charter packages for groups of four or more, including air fares and transfers. Yachts are based in Tortola. *Steve Colgate's Offshore Sailing School* offers courses year-round out of the *Treasure Isle* hotel (phone: 800-221-4326).

Tennis – On Virgin Gorda, *Little Dix Bay* has 7 courts for guests only; *Bitter End* has 2; and *Biras Creek* has 4. On Tortola, *Prospect Reef* has 6; *Long Bay* and *Frenchman's Cay* have 1 each; and *Treasure Isle,* 4. The *Peter Island* hotel has 3.

Camping – *Brewer's Bay Campsite,* Tortola, is on a beautiful beach. Rates are $16 a night for two, including tent and basic equipment; $2.50 per additional person; $5 for a bare site. There's a bar, restaurant, and commissary; snorkeling gear, tours, and baby-sitters available (phone: 4-3463). On Jost Van Dyke, *Tula's N&N Campgrounds* charges $25 and up per couple, $5 a night for an additional person, and $15 for a bare site; there's also a restaurant, snack bar, and live entertainment.

Horse Racing – At the Tortola track; *Festival* and other holidays are occasions for betting, music, food, and fun.

 NIGHTLIFE: Although some hotels have local music and dancing at least once a week, there is very little in the way of nightlife in the British Virgin Islands. But for those who have an excess of energy left after a full day of sun and sea and a leisurely dinner, native pubs like Virgin Gorda's *Bath and Turtle* and *Pusser's Landing* in West End offer music and dancing (often to a BVI fungi band) till early AM,. *The Pub* in Road Town has a band on Fridays and Saturdays, the *Downstairs* restaurant on Mondays, *Treasure Isle* on Wednesdays, *Virgin Queen* on Fridays. At Cane Garden Bay, there is reggae at *Rhymer's* Sunday nights and a steel band at *Stanley's* every other night. Quito Rhymer sings folk music at his *Gazebo* three times a week after dinner. *Bobby's Fast Food, Fun and Disco* on Wickham's Cay I is the only disco on Tortola. Check the *Welcome* guide for any new listings.

BEST ON THE ISLANDS

CHECKING IN: Oddly enough, with just some 40 hotels and guesthouses throughout the British Virgin Islands, the price differential is enormous. Those that operate on the European Plan (EP, no meals) range from about $40 to about $150 double during the winter; 30% less off-season. Hotels offering MAP (Modified American Plan, breakfast and dinner) run from about $60 to $220 double in spring, summer, and fall; about $80 to $325 in season; American Plan hotels (AP, all meals) command anywhere from about $120 to $350 during the winter.

Although a few of the larger hotels offer special packages which can cut costs considerably, most do not. Expect to pay from about $200 to $400 for a double room with all meals included in winter at the hotels we've listed as expensive; half that in summer with no meals. Our moderate selections will cost $100 to $150 in winter for a double, but as little as $60 to $80 in the summer. Expect to pay anywhere from $60 to $100 for a double without meals in an inexpensive hotel in winter; about $40 in summer.

TORTOLA

Frenchman's Cay – A lovely new property on a 12-acre island of its own at West End, connected to Tortola by a bridge. Its 1- and 2-bedroom villas — each with fully equipped kitchen, dining and sitting room, and terrace — accommodate a maximum of 46 guests. Quiet, friendly atmosphere, with small pool, tennis, good snorkeling, open-air restaurant and bar (phone: 5-4844). Moderate.

Long Bay – This low-rise hotel complex sits on a hillside overlooking a truly beautiful mile-long beach, the sea, and nearby islands. On the north shore, Long Bay has 88 beds in suites, beach cabanas, and cottages (some air conditioning available) as well as pitch-and-putt golf, a tennis court, swimming pool, and 2 restaurants. The beach bar is built on and around the remains of a former rum distillery. Best rooms: 12 beach cabanas with kitchenettes, patios, decks (phone: 5-4252). Moderate.

Moorings-Mariner Inn – Originally designed for pre- and post-charter overnights for Moorings' bareboaters, but so pleasant that vacationers like to squeeze in when they can. It has 40 rooms in all, with tennis court, swimming pool, dive shop, yacht charters, full-service marina, specialty food shop, good restaurant, lively bar scene (phone: 4-2332). Moderate.

Prospect Reef – This largest resort in the British Virgin Islands boasts a freshwater pool and dive tank, a stone-wall-enclosed seawater pool, 2 restaurants, 2 bars, a sizable shopping arcade, 6 tennis courts (with lessons, pro shop), even pitch-and-putt golf; scuba, snorkeling, windsurfing, water skiing, sailing, and deep-sea fishing trips can be arranged at its marina. Choice of studios, cottages, and 1- and 2-bedroom villas with kitchen facilities, all comfortably attractive. Tiny manmade beach; but transportation is provided to other island sands. And there's frequent evening entertainment in season (phone: 4-3311). Moderate.

Sugar Mill Estate – One honeymoon cottage, 4 suites, and 16 studio apartments on five acres at Little Apple Bay. Built on a 300-year-old sugar mill ruin, the estate has a circular freshwater pool, a bar and commendable restaurant, kitchenettes, and its own small beach with shaded beach bar (phone: 5-4355; in New York, 212-840-6636; elsewhere, 800-223-9815). Moderate.

Sebastian's on the Beach – One of Tortola's older properties, recently refurbished, on a lovely north shore beach with friendly beach bar and restaurant. Beach rooms all have queen-size or twin beds; courtyard rooms are a bargain. Lots of island flavor, with no pretensions (phone: 5-4212). Moderate to inexpensive.

Treasure Isle – One of Tortola's first hotels, English-owned *Treasure Isle* is a 5-minute drive from Road Town. The 15-acre complex has 40 units built around a freshwater swimming pool on a hillside overlooking Road Town Harbour. Bedrooms are air conditioned, with cool terra cotta–tiled floors and rattan furnishings. With tennis, its own marina headquarters and private dock for day sailing (sailing lessons available), snorkeling trips, and transport to the island's best beaches as well as to its own *Cooper Island Beach Club* (phone: 4-2501). Moderate to inexpensive.

Fort Burt – A small hotel overlooking the rebuilt 17th-century fort and all of Road Harbour. Its 7 very pleasant rooms have baths and terraces, and the bar is one of the island's favorite meeting spots. Charming restaurant, small pool, marine facilities, cordial English management, and historic atmosphere — all in all, a true find. Road Town (phone: 4-2587). Inexpensive.

Village Cay Marina – A terrific value in the heart of the action in Road Town. Its *Upstairs* and *Downstairs* restaurants, dive shop, and marina attract a nautical crowd. Rooms don't have great views, but do have cable TV (phone: 4-2661). Inexpensive.

GUANA

Guana Island Club – This remote and "very private" resort occupies the entire 850-acre island of Guana, a nature preserve just 2 miles and a 10-minute cruise from Tortola. Guests (a maximum of 30) stay in whitewashed stone cottages, dine in the main house, and may choose from a wide array of unprogrammed, nature-oriented activities, including fishing, sailing, snorkeling, bird-watching, and tennis (phone: 4-2354). Expensive.

NECKER ISLAND

Necker Island – Advertised simply as "The Island," this 74-acre hideaway may indeed be the ultimate in luxury retreats. British owner Richard Branson, the multimillionaire whiz kid of Virgin Records and Virgin Atlantic Airways, originally bought this island for his family and friends but then decided to lease it out — the entire island with 10-bedroom villa — when he's not there. Necker is surrounded by its own unspoiled coral reef and flanked by three white sand beaches. The villa, a remarkable Balinese-style structure, was built from rock blasted from the top of Devil's Hill, where it perches, entirely surrounded by terraces with breathtaking views. The sun filters through a lush tropical garden in the center of the spectacular open space that comprises living, dining, and bar area, above which is a gallery library bulging with books, games, and tapes for all tastes. The young British managers, Beverley and Shaun Matthews, formerly of Marina Cay, are both professionally trained chefs, and they turn out first-class meals to be consumed on the breezy deck, under the retractable roof in the dining room, or at poolside. Other amenities include an exercise room, Jacuzzis, tennis, windsurfing, sailing dinghies, water skiing, aquascooters, fishing equipment, full-size snooker table, facilities for small meetings and conferences, and an open bar and wine cellar. The daily rate of $6,500 includes all of the above plus all meals for 16 to 20 people ($4,750 for 10 or fewer). Guests are met at Beef Island International Airport on Tortola or on Virgin Gorda and are ferried over in less than 30 minutes (phone: in the US, 212-696-4566 or 800-225-4255; in London, 01-731-7515). Very expensive.

PETER ISLAND

Peter Island – Situated in an elegant cove, this clublike resort is 20 minutes by boat south of Road Town, Tortola. Its main building and cottages were the prefabricated dream of Peter Smedvig, a Norwegian shipowner, who modeled them after Norway's traditional boathouses. But best by far are the new two-story stone-and-cedar villas tucked among the sea grapes at the far end of magnificent Dead Man's Bay Beach. There are also 4 luxury villas. In addition to a full roster of water activities, there are 4 new tennis courts, horseback riding, sailing, windsurfing, and 7 stunning beaches to explore. The *Peter Island* restaurant is one of the few requiring men to wear jackets, but there is an alternative, the resort's casual *Beach Boy* (phone: 4-2561/2; 800-346-4451). Expensive.

VIRGIN GORDA

Biras Creek – Secluded resort encompassing 15 attractively modern cottages, each with 2 suites, plus 2 very private luxury suites with sunken tubs, spectacular views. The hilltop clubhouse boasts a really fine restaurant, bar, and stunning sea vista. With its own marina, a peacefully beautiful white sand beach (with honor bar), 2 tennis courts, beachside pool. The management gives careful attention to personal service (phone: 4-3555 or 5-3556). Expensive.

Bitter End Yacht Club – This hideaway, at the east end of North Sound, is primarily a sailor's haven. In 1987, it merged with the former *Tradewinds,* bringing the total number of units to 90, with 10 more planned; for the energetic, the breezy hillside chalets are good choices. The former *Tradewinds* restaurant has become the *English Carvery,* featuring roasts and grilled meats; the popular *Clubhouse* below draws the boating crowd. Unlimited use of over 80 sailboats, sailboards, skiffs, outboards, and windsurfers on full American Plan. There are also 8 live-aboard yachts. Scuba gear, snorkeling trips, and sailing instructions are available; all meals included in daily rates (phone: 4-2746; 312-944-5855, collect). Expensive.

Little Dix Bay – Tropical living is at its most relaxed in this elegant Rockresort complex. There are 102 quietly luxurious rooms, thoughtfully appointed and furnished; also Peter Burwash International tennis, horses, bikes, and extensive water sports. Fine dining, some evening entertainment (phone: 5-5555; in New York State, 800-442-8198; elsewhere, 800-223-7637). Expensive.

Leverick Bay – A new 59-acre development offering a mix of nicely styled villas and 13 private homes. There's a free-form freshwater pool, full marina services (free moorings), and dive shop that offers sailboarding and Sunfish instruction. A pleasant poolside restaurant is open for breakfast to late supper; or use the convenient launch pickup for dinner at nearby *Drake's Anchorage* on Mosquito Cay. Overlooking North Sound (phone: 5-5450). Expensive to moderate.

Mango Bay – Virgin Gorda's newest property, on its own reef-protected beach lined with palms and mahogany, midway between Little Dix and North Sound. Its seven 2-unit villas, each different from the others, are strung along the golden sand and tucked into lush vegetation. One- and two-bedroom units all have living rooms, full kitchens, and large outdoor porticos with barbecue facilities. There's a boat jetty, good snorkeling off the reef, and tennis to come. Closed September and October. Mango Bay (phone: 5-5672/3/4/5). Expensive to moderate.

Fischer's Cove Beach – Friendly islanders' favorite with 20 rooms, some housekeeping units, tasty home-cooked food, and good snorkeling. Open-air restaurant and bar are the scene of a popular weekly "jump-up"; nearby cottages are not for light sleepers. The Valley (phone: 5-5252; in Illinois, 312-296-2271; elsewhere, 800-621-1270). Moderate.

Guavaberry Spring Bay – Intriguingly clustered around, between, and atop giant boulders, these small, attractive, hexagonal cottages offer a choice of one or two bedrooms; with living areas, sundecks, and fully equipped kitchens. Commissary, but no restaurant. Set on a hillside, about 5 minutes' walk to beach (phone: 5-5227). Moderate.

Olde Yarde Inn – A personable hideaway with a breezy gazebo, a library, and classical music among its unique assets. Offering 11 small, neat, double rooms filled with familiar, well-worn furniture, it's more retreat than resort; Carol Kaufman will be happy to help you find the sites, sands, and/or seclusion you seek. A 20-minute walk from Savannah Beach. The Baths are 2 miles away. Good food and wines to come home to (phone: 5-5544). Moderate.

Ocean View – Small, simple, 12-room family-run place. Private baths and ceiling fans. There's an island-style restaurant, and beaches are within a 5-minute walk (phone: 5-5230). Inexpensive.

MOSQUITO ISLAND

Drake's Anchorage – The only resort on this mite-size island named for its size, not its animal life. Accessible only by boat, it has 10 recently refurbished cottages, 2 luxurious housekeeping setups, and a great restaurant, plus lots of anchorage, several hideaway beaches. Under savvy new management (phone: 4-2254; in Massachusetts, 617-661-4745; elsewhere, 800-624-6657). Expensive.

JOST VAN DYKE

Sandcastle White Bay – In this small, secluded colony, modern octagonal cottages are surrounded by hibiscus and bougainvillea. There's a pleasant outdoor restaurant and bar plus 200 feet of fine sandy beach (windsurfer available). This remote place seems designed for those who *really* want to get away from it all. The owner picks guests up at Red Hook, St. Thomas, US Virgin Islands (phone: 4-3502, ext. 0496, or VHF Ch. 16). Expensive.

Sandy Ground Estates – An octet of small, understatedly stylish homes for rent when their owners are away. Idyllic setting full of peace and considerable beauty on a hill overlooking a beach. Fully furnished, but since the nearest supermarket is in Road Town, provisioning — through resident management, bring-alongs (especially meats), or both — is key (phone: 4-3391). Moderate.

ANEGADA

Anegada Reefs – It looks motelish, and its beach isn't great. But, says one guest, "the hosts make it such supremely casual fun that you can't help coming back." There's spectacular sunning, swimming, snorkeling, on a miles-long coral sand beach minutes away; fine bonefishing and deep-sea fishing; fishing and diving packages. Honor bar, good island meals, Saturday fungi band parties. Favorite yacht stop (phone: 4-3111 rough marine operator). Expensive to moderate.

 EATING OUT: As in most of the British islands, the best food is simply prepared and straightfoward, with seafood a major attraction. Luxury resorts such as *Little Dix* and *Biras Creek* on Virgin Gorda dish out elaborate spreads, but several smaller inns are worth a detour for their high-quality, innovative cuisine. Necker Island is in a class of its own, the sea goddess of landlubbers. The following are our top choices. Expect to spend $50 and up for a meal for two, not including wine, tip, or drinks, in those listed as expensive; $25 to $50 in those classified as moderate; and under $25, inexpensive.

TORTOLA

Brandywine Bay – Elegant dining on the garden patio of a charming old house at the water's edge. Visiting yachtsmen are also attracted by its 15-foot anchorage and free overnight moorings. The menu includes cracked conch, caviar crêpes, linguine with scampi, and a dessert aptly called Chocolate Decadence. Dinner only; reservations necessary. Brandywine Bay (phone: 5-2301). Expensive.

Captain's Table – A French chef with much experience in the Caribbean (St. Maarten) has brought his skills and considerable flair to Tortola. The dinner menu features escargots in puff pastry, fettucine in spinach cream with garlic, and a perfectly pink rack of lamb. Lunch is less elaborate, but all meals are enjoyed al fresco on a terrace overlooking the inner harbor at Wickham's Cay. Reservations are a must (phone: 4-3885). Expensive.

Fort Burt – Delightful al fresco dining with a spectacular view on the foundations of a 17th-century fort. Friendly maître d' Dennis Selkridge advises diners on the catch of the day. Try smoked salmon with fresh asparagus, or fresh snapper in lime butter; there's also a traditional mixed grill of meats. Road Town (phone: 4-2587). Expensive.

Upstairs – Candlelit dining overlooking Village Cay Marina. Local seafood as well as ginger lemon chops and steak Diane for landlubbers. Lunch is served weekdays only. Reservations suggested. Wickham's Cay (phone: 4-2228). Expensive.

Cloud Room – Outdoor dining with a panoramic view of paradise. Pickup and delivery back to your hotel is included in the price of a full-course dinner. Reservations only. Ridge Road (phone: 4-2821). Expensive to moderate.

Moorings-Mariner Inn – A pleasant open-air bar and restaurant overlooking the busy Moorings Marina and Drake's Channel. Casual, nautical ambience from breakfast through Happy Hour; dinners candlelit and more elegant. Wickham's Cay II (phone: 4-2332). Expensive to moderate.

Sugar Mill – California food writers Jinx and Jeff Morgan have found the perfect vehicle for their culinary expertise at this 340-year-old sugar mill on Tortola's northwest shore. Their imaginative cuisine, considered by many to be the best on the island, features ingredients grown in their own gardens. Starters might include a Creole peanut soup or red pepper pasta with Caribbean black beans; and steak is always one of the alternatives to the day's main dish, which might be a Caribbean bouillabaisse, grilled quail with papaya and mango sauce, or lamb curry, followed by Amaretto soufflé or Grand Marnier cheesecake. Reservations necessary. At Apple Bay (phone: 5-4355). Expensive to moderate.

The Apple – Another happy find on Tortola's northwest coast is tucked into a little West Indian house on pretty Little Apple Bay. The house drink, "Virgin Souppy," is a must: It consists of soursop juice, cocoa lopez, and local Cruzan rum topped with a sprinkle of nutmeg — a perfect introduction to the delicious West Indian fare that follows. Try the pumpkin soup, conch fritters, whelks, or fish steamed in lime butter and served in a Creole sauce of onion, pepper, and tomato. Reservations suggested. Little Apple Bay (phone: 5-4437). Moderate.

Elena – In a lovely old house with small terrace and extended patio, this welcome newcomer to the Road Town scene offers a truly original alternative to island fare. Guyana-born Elena, with her exotic multinational background, offers a fascinating menu: Oriental specialties such as chicken wings with honey and garlic, egg rolls, potato balls, and lettuce rolls; English savories; and American favorites — chili, spinach salads. Charming ambience, great service, reasonable prices. Road Town (phone: 4-2790). Moderate.

Mrs. Scatliffe's – This is definitely a family affair, with Mrs. Scatliffe's daughter waiting tables, son-in-law mixing drinks, another daughter assisting in the kitchen, and Mr. Scatliffe strumming the guitar. After dinner the whole family jams away on ukulele, merengue box, or a handy gourd. Dinner is obviously home cooking, West Indian–style, using fresh vegetables from the garden and fish from the sea beneath the terrace restaurant. Favorite dishes also include chicken in a coconut shell and curried goat. Reservations suggested. Carrot Bay (phone: 5-4556). Moderate.

Skyworld – It's quite a drive up, but offers a spectacular view over all the Virgin Islands and fabulous sunsets. Bring a camera (and a wrap if the wind is blowing). Lunches are fairly simple; dinners are à la carte or six-course affairs. Ridge Road (phone: 4-3567). Moderate.

Mr. Fish – Air-conditioned comfort next to its sister restaurant *The Wharf* and serving similar seafood fare. Wickham's Cay (Columbus Center) behind Village Cay Marina (phone: 4-3626). Moderate to inexpensive.

Wharf Seafood – Consistently good seafood and West Indian dishes on a candlelit patio surrounded by bougainvillea. Try the conch fritters, salt fish cakes, or the weekly barbecue, which features thick, fresh swordfish steaks cooked to perfection. Wickham's Cay behind Village Cay Marina (phone: 4-3626). Moderate to inexpensive.

Carib Casseroles – New owners but the same staff and menu, specializing in West Indian and some international dishes; their frozen take-out meals have long been popular with yachtsmen. In a quaint old house near the post office in Road Town (phone: 4-3271). Inexpensive.

The Pub – A typical English pub, very informal and long popular with the yachting crowd. Open 10:30 AM to midnight, with a daily dinner special and twice-weekly entertainment. At Fort Burt Marina, next to the B.V.I. yacht Club, in Road Town (phone: 4-2608). Inexpensive.

Other inexpensive and unpretentious eateries on Tortola include Rhymer's Beach Bar and Quito's Gazebo on beautiful Cane Garden Bay; Pusser's Landing at West End; Peg Leg Landing at Nanny Cay; Maria's, Downstairs, and Bobby's Fast Food in Road Town.

VIRGIN GORDA

Dinner at the exclusive resorts of Little Dix, Biras Creek, or Bitter End Yacht Club is a pricey venture. The first two offer fine food, although nothing extaordinary. Bitter End has taken over the Tradewinds, now called the Carvery, doubling the dining possibilities there. But the popular Bitter End Clubhouse draws masses of boaters as well as hotel guests, and personalized service is gone forever. Our best luck was at the following special inns.

Drake's Anchorage – Not actually in Virgin Gorda, but close enough, and the inn sends a boat over to pick up dinner guests. Located on an island in North Sound with the unfortunate name of Mosquito, this is a small, relaxed resort with a delightful pavilion restaurant caressed by sea breezes, decorated with driftwood, illuminated by moonlight and candles, and fragrant with frangipani (mixed with a hint of garlic and maybe roast suckling pig). Savvy new managers Peter and Jamy Faust see that everything goes smoothly, while chef de cuisine Brutus (alias Martin Belmar) creates admirable delicacies in the kitchen. Call ahead and order from a tantalizing menu featuring all the sea has to offer, some local dishes, and others with a French flair. Mosquito Island (phone: 4-2254 or VHF Ch. 16). Moderate.

Olde Yard Inn – Small and special, the kind of cozy inn one dreams of coming home to after a long day of sailing, snorkeling, swimming, or just lazing in the sun. Exquisite meals are served al fresco under a thatched roof to the soft strains of classical music amid fragrant gardens. Carol Kaufman's hospitality and Charles Williams's international cuisine are worth writing home about. Seafood in puff pastry or homemade fettucine are terrific starters; vegetables are homegrown; fresh local fish or veal with shrimp, herbs, and cheese are perfect. There's also a small, well-chosen wine list. Near Spanish Town (phone: 5-5544). Moderate.

Other Virgin Gorda eateries include Michelle's for continental cuisine (though a little short on ambience); Fischer's Cove, the Bath & Turtle, and the Crab Hole for local food, local atmosphere, and often a live local band.

BEEF ISLAND

Conch Shell Point – Bargain lobster dinners as well as conch, steaks, and snacks on a breezy terrace overlooking Trellis Bay. Reservations required. Near the airport (phone: 5-2285 or VHF Ch. 16). Moderate.

The Last Resort – On its own little islet, Bellamy Cay, in the middle of a circular bay, with great anchorage for yachtsmen. This popular port of call features a fairly routine British-style buffet (from 7 PM till it's gone), followed by a rather bawdy show by owner/entertainer Tony Snell, an amazing one-man band with an often hilarious repertoire. Come over by dinghy, or call and they'll send one for you (phone: 5-2520). Moderate.

NORMAN ISLAND

William Thornton Floating Bar & Restaurant – The *William Thornton* is a converted 1910 Baltic trader that formerly plied the trade routes and is now anchored off the bight at Norman Island. The BVI's only offshore restaurant, it's open for drinks and food from 11 AM to 11 PM, and there's a launch departing daily at 5:15 PM from Fort Burt Marina to bring guests from Road Town. It's no culinary heaven, but boaters love it (phone: 4-2564 or VHF Ch. 16). Moderate.

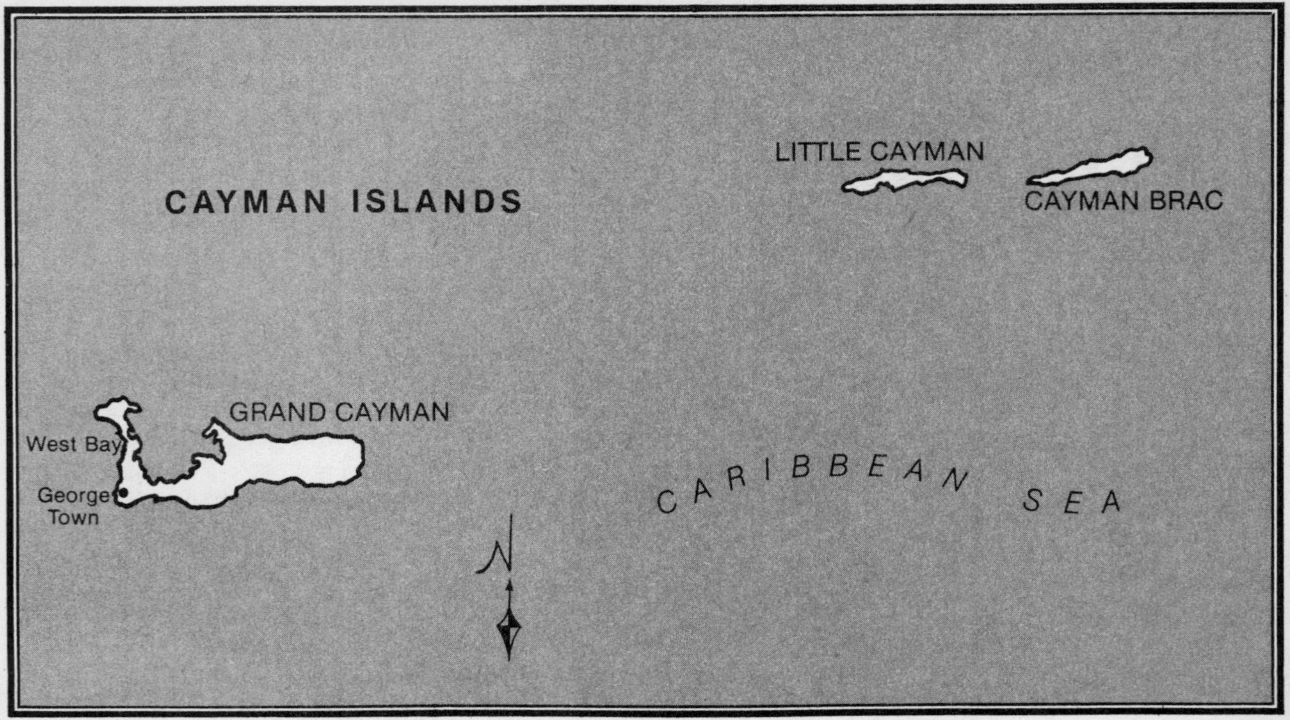
CAYMAN ISLANDS
LITTLE CAYMAN
CAYMAN BRAC
GRAND CAYMAN
West Bay
George Town
CARIBBEAN SEA
N

CAYMAN ISLANDS

It used to be, not so long ago, that if you mentioned the Cayman Islands at a cocktail party in Winnetka or a brunch on New York City's West Side, the response was likely to be "Cayman Who?" closely followed by "Where?" and "Why?" Today Grand Cayman is considered the Caribbean's condominium and the offshore financial industry's capital, as well as one of the fastest-growing Caribbean beach spots and most popular scuba-diving destinations. Its small sister isles are also being discovered by scuba enthusiasts and anglers who enjoy not only superlative sporting opportunities but also the islands' peaceful isolation.

The Cayman Islands are a trio of tiny coral dots poking out of the western Caribbean 180 miles north-northwest of Jamaica. Called Grand Cayman, Little Cayman, and Cayman Brac (Brac means "bluff" in Gaelic), they are outcroppings of the Cayman Ridge, a range of submarine mountains extending from the Sierra Maestra Range of Cuba to the Misteriosa and Rosario banks that point their underwater way southwest toward Belize. Grand Cayman, largest and most developed of the three, lies 80 miles west of its smaller sister islands, whose combined population is just over 1,700. Grand Cayman and Little Cayman, are mostly flat — the highest point on Grand Cayman rises 60 feet above sea level. "Mountainous" by comparison, mile-wide Cayman Brac has a bluff running up its spine that starts from sea level on the west end and rises 140 feet to a cliff at its easternmost point. Each Cayman is formed entirely of calcareous rock so porous that there are no streams. There are, however, freshwater wells throughout the islands and, on Grand Cayman, a large modern desalination plant which supplies the bulk of that island's water supply. As a precaution, many islanders still maintain cisterns that catch and store rainwater from their roofs.

Columbus found the Cayman Islands by accident when, en route from Panama to Hispaniola on his fourth voyage in 1503, he was blown off course "in sight of two very small islands," as his son Fernando wrote in his diary, "full of tortoise, as was the sea about, insomuch that they looked like little rocks." This profusion of turtles led Columbus to call the islands Las Tortugas, a label that didn't stick, although turtles keep cropping up in Caymanian life. Ultimately, the *tortugas* lost the name race to the *caymanas* (the Spanish-Carib word for "crocodiles"), although the *caymanas* referred to probably weren't crocodiles at all, but mistakenly identified iguanas, which are native to Caymanian shores.

In the sixteenth and seventeenth centuries, ships plying the Caribbean called at the islands for lifesaving supplies of fresh turtle meat and fresh water, but there was no rush to settle them. It was not until 1655 that the first colonists — deserters from Oliver Cromwell's army who, according to legend, sneaked off from Jamaica when England took it from the Spanish — arrived on Little Cayman and Cayman Brac. Names like Bodden and Watler, Caymanian family and place names to this day, date from those original settlers. Fifteen years later, by virtue of the Treaty of Madrid (1670), the Cayman Islands officially became a British possession, a status that has been a source of pride to loyal islanders for three centuries now, and one they endorsed again in 1962 when Jamaica, to which they'd been annexed, became independent and Caymanians elected to remain a Crown Colony.

For a relatively quiet destination, these islands have had a fairly rowdy history. Pirate tales abound, as do stories of buried treasure and sunken fortunes. Sir Henry Morgan watered his ships here; Edward Teach, the notorious Blackbeard, seized a small turtler in Grand Cayman. But the sea story Caymanians love best (and support most vigorously, though historians can find no basis for it) is the tale of the "Wreck of the Ten Sails." The story goes that on a dark November night in 1788, a convoy of merchant ships was passing east of Grand Cayman when the lead ship, *Cordelia,* struck the reef. Her signal warning the others off was misunderstood, and nine more vessels piled up with her. Residents of East End purportedly rescued many, including a royal personage, from the stricken ships. And King George III was so grateful that he granted the Cayman Islands freedom from taxation or, according to other sources, freedom from wartime conscription — both of which the islands now enjoy. How these benefits really came about doesn't much matter; Caymanians love the story either way.

On the other hand, their reaction was mixed when the first tourists — lured by stories of great sport fishing and beautiful beaches — drifted through in the early 1950s. A request for travel information in those days brought a slow, boat-mailed reply mimeographed slightly off-center on a single legal-size sheet. While admitting certain tax advantages, it pointed out the disadvantages of potholed roads, disintegrating cars, and uncertain electrical supply. It also mentioned insects. Its tone wasn't "Yankee, go home," some islanders recall, but, more candidly, "Don't say we didn't warn you."

But fishermen and beach nuts continued to arrive in increasing numbers. In the early 1960s, divers discovered the islands' spectacular underwater sites. In 1966, the Legislative Assembly passed a series of laws creating a variety of tax-haven investment opportunities on Grand Cayman favoring offshore banking, trust-company formation, and the registration of companies. These enticements spurred considerable outside interest, and there are now more than 500 banks on Grand Cayman. The Caymanian economy has been improving dramatically ever since, and tourism has come to stay.

Also in 1966, a Tourist Board was established to encourage and control the industry. It set up a system of hotel inspections that have raised standards — though there is still room for improvement. It has ridden herd on tour operators and the quality of their offerings. And, to its credit, the Tourist Board has never said the Cayman Islands have everything. Clearly, they do not. Especially in season, visitors pay top dollar for accommodations that may be attractive, clean, and well maintained, but only a few resorts — such as the *Hyatt Regency Grand Cayman, the Grand Pavilion,* and *Treasure Island* — could honestly be labeled "luxurious." Restaurants aren't inexpensive either — although food is fair to good and, occasionally, first rate. There are a few interesting historic sights, no casinos, and only a handful of nightlife and dancing options on Grand Cayman. And land vistas are not spectacular.

But there are patches of loveliness — rows of royal palms, tall pines moving in soft breezes, splashes of floral color. (More than 100 avian migratory species and 11 varieties of small, wild orchids can be found on Cayman Brac.) Cayman beaches, found primarily on Grand Cayman's west and north coasts, rank among the most beautiful in the Caribbean. Seven Mile Beach (in reality, 5.6 miles long), the island's gold coast for tourism, and the lovely, quiet, and unspoiled area of the Cayman Kai Retreat section of the North Side satisfy every traveler's expectation of pure white-sand playgrounds.

But the coral gardens, dramatic sheer walls, and sloping drop-offs of Cayman's undersea world are undoubtedly this country's most famous natural attraction. The incredible variety of marine life, ideal diving conditions (calm seas, little current, superb visibility), and the largest number of professional dive services in the Caribbean combine to create an underwater Nirvana.

Other water sports, from parasailing and boardsailing to glass-bottom boat rides and jet skis, beckon the nonamphibious vacationer. Would-be Jules Vernes can voyage to the bottom of the sea aboard one of the island's two submersibles: the *Atlantis,* and a three-passenger Perry vessel, operated by *Research Submersibles, Ltd.* Last, but certainly not least, the islands offer superb sport fishing with year-round action from bonefish (particularly good on Cayman Brac, outstanding on Little Cayman), small tarpon, and further offshore, blue marlin, wahoo, yellowfin tuna, dolphin, and other gamefish. Each June, Grand Cayman sponsors Million Dollar Month, an international saltwater competition. Indeed, when it comes to things aquatic, these islands lack nothing except an underwater hotel.

Topside, there are no spectacular sights to see in these coral isles, but they are clean, and the Caymanians take pride in their homes: even the smallest, humblest house is tidy and often brightened with flowers. The islands have little obvious poverty, one of the highest standards of living in the entire Caribbean, and residents are hospitable and courteous. There is only the rare instance of panhandling, and that's usually from ambitious young men peddling their real or imagined charms on the beach. The squadrons of souvenir salesmen who stalk visitors on other shores are absent — a fact that makes Grand Cayman one of the top cruise ship ports in the Caribbean.

The Caymans, even if not one of the most visually exciting or adventurous destinations (although divers would disagree), remain a safe, comfortable spot with a very North American atmosphere. Its pleasant people, stable government, and crime-free atmosphere are assets that keep many visitors returning each year. For those who require only sun, sand, and sea — in a non-exotic wrapper — the Caymans might be paradise — at any price.

CAYMAN ISLANDS AT-A-GLANCE

FROM THE AIR: The three Cayman Islands together have a total land area of 96 square miles. Grand Cayman, looking vaguely like a sperm whale from the air, is 76 square miles, about 22 miles long and 8 miles wide at its broadest point. Some 80 miles east-northeast of Grand Cayman is Little Cayman, resembling a sea slug 8 miles long and less than 2 miles wide, with 10 square miles of land, surrounded by crystal white beaches. Eel-shaped Cayman Brac, just 5 miles due east of Little Cayman, has a total of 14 square miles — it's 10 miles long but only 1 mile wide.

The hallmark of Grand Cayman from the air is West Bay Beach (that's the official name; everybody calls it Seven Mile Beach), which runs in a gentle curve along the island's west shore, and where virtually all the resort hotels are located. The west half of the island is sculpted by huge North Sound, whose entrance is entirely protected by a giant coral reef. North Sound digs into the body of the island and deprives it of what would be another 40 square miles of land. Grand Cayman, site of the islands' capital, George Town, has the bulk of the population, about 17,000 of the 18,750 total. Of the rest, about 1,700 live on Cayman Brac. Little Cayman is home for only a few dozen permanent residents.

Lying between 19°16' and 19°24' N latitude and 81°5' and 81°25' W longitude, Grand Cayman is almost precisely due south of Miami, some 480 miles away and about an hour by air. Jamaica lies 180 miles east-southeast. Your jet will land at Owen Roberts International Airport, just outside George Town, in the southwest corner of the island, a few miles from the hotels along Seven Mile Beach up the coast.

SPECIAL PLACES: There are no dazzlers on the Cayman Islands, but you might like to take a day away from the beach to do some wandering.

George Town – The small, clean, unpretentious capital, where building heights are limited to five stories, keeps the blue sky in sight at all times. There seem to be sea views from everywhere. Caymanian houses have a certain sameness about them, but George Town, settlements on Grand Cayman, and both sister islands are unique in one respect: There are no slums to speak of. Caymanians take special pride in the neat appearance of their homes. George Town sites to see: a clock monument to King George V; the Legislative Assembly on Fort Street; the Courts Building opposite; the Government Administration Building on Elgin Avenue, called the Glass House by locals; the General Post Office on Edward Street, near the town center, where you can buy popular stamps at cost in the Philatelic Bureau. There are also two interesting new museums, both on North Church Street. The *Cayman Islands Maritime and Treasure Museum* exhibits artifacts from sunken ships (open 9 to 5, Monday through Saturday, admission $5 US). *McKee's Museum* displays treasures recovered by the late veteran treasure diver Art McKee, including relics from the Spanish Main and colonial wrecks, and authentic coins are for sale (open 9 to 4:30, Monday through Saturday, admission $5 US).

ELSEWHERE ON THE ISLAND

To see more than what George Town offers on Grand Cayman, it's necessary to hire a cab or rent a car, motorbike, or bicycle. Some of the island's sights can be seen by driving out along Seven Mile Beach, past the beachside residence of His Excellency the Governor to the vicinity of the settlement of West Bay.

Hell – Supposedly named by a former commissioner who said, after seeing its weird coral rock formation for the first time, "This is what Hell must look like." To capitalize on the name, there is a post office nearby where the postmistress stamps all cards and letters "Hell, Grand Cayman." There is a ramp leading to a photo vantage point above the limestone fields and a gift shop where visitors can buy Hell memorabilia and refreshments.

Batabano – On North Sound, this is where local fishermen bring their catches. You can buy fresh fish, lobster in season, conch, and turtle meat. North Sound's reef is an outstanding attraction for divers and sport fishermen.

Cayman Turtle Farm – Established in 1968 by private enterprise and now owned by the Cayman government, this is the only commercial green sea turtle farm in the world. The reptiles are hatched and raised through young adulthood on the premises. There are educational exhibits and a gift shop full of items with a turtle motif, souvenirs, and turtleshell crafts. *Warning:* Until the US Government's endangered species ban is lifted, "look but don't buy" are the watchwords for Americans where tortoiseshell jewelry and other turtle souvenirs are concerned. Admission charge: $5 US.

For the sights in the other direction, head east out of George Town to:

South Sound Road – On this pine-lined street, one of the most attractive on the island, are quaint old wooden Caymanian houses, with the sea on your right. Look for one on the seaward side painted with colorful abstract designs by the owner, a Caymanian lady who prefers to remain an obscure artist in residence and not a tourist attraction. Look, enjoy, and pass on, please.

Bat Cave – Cave buffs who don't mind exploring on their hands and knees can take the dirt road off the main road (to Bodden Town, heading east) on the seaside just beyond the speed restriction sign to its end. Proceed on foot toward the sea, turn left, and walk along the cliff edge for about 30 yards until you're standing above a sandy beach. Climb down the ten-foot cliff, look away from the sea, and you'll see the low mouth of Bat Cave directly in front of you. It's formed of a central domed cavity with a few side passages. The bats are not dangerous, but they squeak a lot when you enter. Watch for falling "deposits"!

Pedro's Castle – Now a rustic bar and restaurant in the settlement of Savannah, it's a restoration of the oldest building in the Cayman Islands, supposedly dating from the 1700s. It may or may not be a former pirate hangout.

Bodden Town – The islands' first capital, its chief claims to present fame are Gun Square (marked by two cannon, stuck muzzle-first into the ground, that were used to guard the reef channel in the 18th century); Pirates Caves (small admission charge); and the *Eastern Queen,* a small restaurant serving good local food.

Cayman's "Blow Holes" – This picturesque stretch of old coral formations called ironshore is where sprays of water shoot into the air when waves hit the rock.

East End – Here, sticking out of the water, you may see a fluke of an anchor said to be a relic of the "Wreck of the Ten Sails." It's not wise to wade or swim out for a closer look because the reef there is alive with sea urchins. Farther on, around a bend, on the main channel through the reef at East End is a visible wreck of modern times, the MV *Ridgefield,* a Liberty Ship that struck the reef carrying little cargo besides 100 cases of beer. Cheers for the East Enders! East End boasts two hostelries: the scuba buff's small *Ron Kipp's Cayman Diving Lodge* and the casual *Tortuga Club.*

New Queen's Road – Opened by Elizabeth II on February 16, 1983, it lines a tranquil stretch of totally undeveloped oceanfront between East End and the small settlement at Old Man Bay. From there you can continue west to Cayman Kai and the North Sound landing or south on the cross-island road to Frank Sound through the lushest part of Grand Cayman. With royal palms and orchids growing wild, it is one place you might sight the green Cayman parrot, especially during spring mango season.

SOURCES AND RESOURCES

TOURIST INFORMATION: The Cayman Islands Department of Tourism has nine offices in North America where you can get plenty of free brochures and information on accommodations and attractions. The *Rate Sheet and Fact Folder* is especially informative and complete. The offices are in the following cities:

Atlanta: PO Box 900024, Atlanta, GA 30329 (phone: 404-934-3959)

Chicago: 333 N Michigan Ave., Suite 905, Chicago, IL 60601 (phone: 312-782-5832)

Coral Gables: 250 Catalonia Ave., Suite 604, Coral Gables, FL 33134 (phone: 305-444-6551)

Dallas: 9794 Forest Ln., Suite 569, Dallas, TX 75243 (phone: 214-931-2224)

Houston: 9999 Richmond Ave., Suite 131, Houston, TX 77042 (phone: 713-977-0604)

Los Angeles: 3440 Wilshire Blvd., Suite 1202, Los Angeles, CA 90010 (phone: 213-738-1968)

New York: 420 Lexington Ave., Suite 2312, New York, NY 10017 (phone: 212-682-5582)

Tampa: PO Box 824, Tarpon Springs, FL 34286 (phone: 813-934-9078)

Toronto: 234 Eglinton Ave. E, Suite 306, Toronto, Ont. M4P IK5 (phone: 416-485-1550)

In the islands, the Caymans are trying harder. Not only does the Department of Tourism have offices in the Government Tower Building (phone: 9-7999) in George Town, staffed to answer questions, but it also has booths with similar help at the airport and at the pier where cruise passengers land.

Local Coverage – A helpful *Tourist Weekly* is published on Fridays. For additional current information, the *Caymanian Compass,* the local newspaper, is published weekdays.

Telephone – Dial direct to the Cayman Islands by adding the area code 809 and the prefix 94 to the numbers given below.

ENTRY REQUIREMENTS: For stays up to six months, visitors from the US and Canada need only proof of citizenship (passport, birth certificate, voter's registration card — but not a driver's license) and a return or ongoing ticket. The official US consular representative, Robert Cohen, has his office on Harbour Drive near the Cayman Arms (phone: 9-2742).

CLIMATE AND CLOTHES: Average winter temperature is 75°F (24°C); summer, 5° to 10° warmer. May to October is the rainy season, and showers are intense and brief. The Cayman Islands are informal and casual. Women wear bright blouses, skirts, slacks, and shorts (and, on beaches, the inevitable bikini), and men favor slacks, sport shirts, and swim trunks. Slacks, shorts, and dresses or skirts for women are best for shopping in town. Evenings, women sometimes dress up a bit in long cotton dresses (to which they might add a sweater or shawl); but jackets and ties are rarely required for men.

MONEY: The Cayman Islands have their own currency, the Cayman dollar, which is on a fixed ratio with the US dollar (CI $1 equals US $1.25). Stores and restaurants accept US dollars. Most duty-free shops also accept credit cards (check to see if prices listed are CI or US dollars). Traveler's checks can also be cashed at a local bank (open 9 AM to 3:30 PM, Mondays through Thursdays, 9 AM to 5 PM on Fridays). There's an $8 US airport departure tax (per person); it's $6 US for cruise passengers. Credit cards are now widely accepted in Cayman shops, hotels, and restaurants.

LANGUAGE: Proud of their British heritage and their status as a modern Crown Colony, Caymanians speak a lovely English, flavored with bits of West Indian, Welsh, Irish, Scottish, and American. They pronounce the name of their largest island "Grahnd Cay-*mahn.*"

TIME: The Cayman Islands are on Eastern Standard Time all year, so the hour is the same as it is in the eastern US during EST months. When Daylight Saving is in effect, there's an hour's difference; when it's noon in New York EDT, it's 11 AM in the Cayman Islands.

CURRENT: The same as the US, with standard 110-volt, 60-cycle current. No need for converters or adapters.

GETTING THERE: Cayman Airways, Eastern, and Northwest serve Grand Cayman from Miami. Cayman Airways also flies in from Houston, Texas; Tampa, Florida; Atlanta, Georga; and Kingston, Jamaica; and offers connecting flights to Little Cayman and Cayman Brac. In addition, Cayman Airways schedules nonstop "scuba divers' special" flights from Miami to Cayman Brac twice a week. A charter service, Cayman Express, operates weekly nonstop jets from Atlanta, Baltimore, Boston, Detroit, Chicago, New York, Philadelphia, and St. Louis to Grand Cayman from December to mid-April. Eastern Airlines began daily service from Miami to Grand Cayman in early 1987, with connections to all US cities it serves.

Norwegian Caribbean Lines out of Miami and a number of other cruise lines make Grand Cayman a regular port of call, arriving offshore near George Town Harbour and sending passengers ashore by tender to the pier. In season, December to April, there may be a ship in port almost every day, and sometimes two or three.

CALCULATING COSTS: Despite their gentle nature and unspoiled atmosphere, the Cayman Islands are not a notable bargain. In the winter season, double rooms range from about $80 to $300 US European Plan (without meals); add about $35 to $50 US per day per person for Modified American Plan (breakfast and dinner). Off-season rates, normally from mid-April to mid-December, start as low as $65 US EP double. There's a 6% tax on room rates. A growing number of places serve lunch, which might run $7 to $15 US per person without drinks; and dinners can easily range all the way up to over $50 US per person, including a drink or wine and tip. Most hotels assess 15% on all bills in lieu of tipping. In some cases, there's an "energy surcharge" for air-conditioner use. There's also an $8 departure tax.

GETTING AROUND: Taxi – Taxis meet all arriving flights. Rates are fixed by the Cayman Island Taxi Cab Association and are published in the Tourist Department's *Rate Sheet and Fact Folder.* Typical one-way fares from the airport in US dollars, per taxi, maximum four passengers: to George Town, about $8 US; to most hotels on Seven Mile Beach, about $8 to $14 US per taxi. The longest rides — from the airport to *Tortuga Club* on the East End or *Cayman Kai* and Rum Point on the North Shore — are about $28 plus about 10% tip. But, given advance notice, both the *Tortuga Club* and *Cayman Kai* will provide courtesy transport.

Bus – Operating roughly once an hour from George Town and West Bay along Seven Mile Beach, buses stop at all hotels; fares depend on destination.

Car Rental – Easy to arrange and a good way to get about. Cars cannot be picked up at the airport on arrival, but can be left there on departure. Prices start at about $35 US per day (without insurance, which is $5 per day extra) for a Toyota Starlet (winter season) and go up from there. *Coconut Car Rentals* (phone: 9-4037 or 9-4377) and *Cico/Avis* (phone: 9-2468 or 9-4242) include unlimited mileage in their rates, but in summer there's a mileage charge on rentals of less than three days from *Budget* (9-5605), *Hertz* (phone: 9-2280), and *National* (9-4790). Off-season rates are about 25% less than winter's. At the time of rental, the agency will issue you a driving permit for $3 US if you prove you're at least 21 and have a valid license from home, though some firms set a minimum age of 22. *Important:* This is a British world, and driving is on the left. Gasoline costs about $1.80 CI per imperial gallon, which is 25% larger than the US gallon.

Honda motorcycles are also available for about $15 to $20 US per day, unlimited mileage, at *Caribbean Motors* (phone: 9-4051); mopeds are about $13 US per day, unlimited mileage, at *Caribbean Motors* and at *Cayman Cycle Rentals* (phone: 9-5721).

Sightseeing Taxi Tours – Arranged through the *Cayman Islands Cab & Transport Association* (phone: 7-4491), they cost about $25 per hour US for up to five persons. West Bay tours (including a Turtle Farm stop) are about $20 per car; Pedro's Castle trips, about $20.

Sightseeing Bus Tours – Regularly scheduled bus tours are operated by *Tropicana Tours* (phone: 9-4599); also by *Majestic Tours,* which offers hotel pickup, air-conditioned buses, and friendly, animated guides who are half the fun (phone: 9-7773).

Sea Excursions – *Bob Soto's Diving Ltd.* (phone: 9-2022) and *Don Foster's Dive Grand Cayman* (phone: 9-5679) offer 2-hour glass-bottom-boat trips for about $15 US per person. *Surfside Water Sports* (phone: 7-4224) also does glass-bottom trips for about $12.50 US per person. All-day boat trips to the North Shore can be organized. *Surfside Water Sports,* other water sport operators, and local skippers like Capt. Gleason Ebanks (phone: 9-3954) take parties of four or so on a small craft for a day of swimming, snorkeling, sightseeing, shelling, eating, and drinking. Captain and crew (and passengers, if they're willing and able) spear and dive for lunch, which can include conch, lobster in season, or fish, freshly caught and cooked over an open fire on a beach that's all your own. *Surfside* also offers night glass-bottom boat trips. The price is $100 for four, $25 for each additional person, and includes everything. *Charter Boat Headquarters* (phone: 7-4340) also books all types of boating and water sport activities.

Grand Cayman is one of the few places in the world offering submarine trips to view the marine life of a tropical reef system. No diving experience is necessary to ride in either the 28-passenger *Atlantis* to depths of 45 to 150 feet or the 3-passenger *Research Submersible, Ltd. (RSL)* submarine, which plunges 800 to 1,000 feet over a coral wall. Both subs operate off the island's west coast. *Atlantis* is $45 to $55 for adults; children under 12, half price (phone: 9-7700). *RSL* is $200 for a 3-hour expedition (phone: 9-8296).

Local Air Services – *Cayman Airways* (phone: 9-2311) flies from Grand Cayman to Little Cayman and Cayman Brac. It offers special three-island fares plus a choice of day-long fishing excursions and longer vacation packages bound for both islands.

SHOPPING: At one time very limited, the spectrum of acquirables has recently improved a lot in George Town with the expansion of existing duty-free shops, the opening of new ones, and a general upgrading all along the line. Many famous international brand names are all imported here with no tax added. But sellers are still free to set prices, so some bargains are better than others. Here, as elsewhere, the best protection is knowing US prices — including those at discount stores, especially on cameras and electronic equipment. *Kirk Freeport* (on Cardinal Ave. downtown, on the waterfront, and at the airport) has the biggest selections of name crystal, china, and earthenware (from Wedgwood, Royal Doulton, and Lalique to Waterford, Orrefors, Baccarat, Bing & Grøndahl, and Royal Delft), plus Swiss watches, cameras, jewelry, French perfumes, cosmetics, cashmeres, and crystal paperweights. *Treasure Cove* has smaller stocks but many large names at bargain prices. Other shops and specialties: *Viking*, near the cruise passenger landing (Scandinavian things plus Caribbean fashions, paintings, crafts); *Caymandicraft* (British sport clothes, woolens, Lyle & Scott sweaters); the *Cayman Craft Market* (leather sandals, handbags, belts); *Black Coral and . . .* on Fort St. (jewelry by American sculptor Bernard Passman); *Soto's Freeport* on Harbour Dr. (gift figurines, carvings, novelties from Europe, the islands, Mexico); and *Smith's Jewelers* on Fort St. (gold, diamond, and precious stone jewelry). A must-stop for lovers of black coral is *Richard's Black Coral Jewelry and Other Fine Gems*, on S. Church St. Richard Barile is known as the "artist of the stars"; his creations have been coveted by a galaxy of celebrities, including Larry Gatlin, Jonathan Winters, Ronnie Milsap, Conway Twitty, and Muhammad Ali.

The big Caymanian craft item used to be the king-sized rope hammock, but not many are being knotted these days. More prosaic island products (hats, baskets, straw items) are to be found at the *Craft Market* and *Heritage Crafts*. In Bodden Town, the *Eastern Queen* also sells local products. *Note:* Turtle products cannot be brought into the US.

TIPPING: There is no general rule about service charges. Some hotels add 10%, some 15%. At apartment/condominium complexes, several add 5%; a couple, 10%. To avoid double-tipping, check policy at the place you're staying when you check in. If there is a service charge added, figure that it covers everything except extra special services. If not, give bar and restaurant waiters 15%; room maids, about $1 US per room per day, rounded off to the next dollar at the end of your stay; bellboys, about $1.50 US for each two to three bags. There are airport porters, but your taxi driver will generally pick up your luggage and carry it to the car, and unless you're carrying an unusually large load, it is not necessary to tip him for the luggage lift or the ride since he probably owns his own cab.

SPECIAL EVENTS: The biggest annual events are *Batabano*, an April carnival with parades, exhibits and dances; the *Queen's Birthday* celebration in June (on the Monday following the Saturday appointed as her official birthday), which is observed with a uniformed parade and the presentation of awards and honors; and the country's national festival, *Pirates Week*, an elaborate week-long celebration with costumes, parades, and swashbuckling special events in late October. On *Ash Wednesday*, there's an *Annual Agricultural Show*, and June is *Million Dollar Month*, featuring a month-long international saltwater fishing tournament with cash prizes for record catches of marlin, tuna, wahoo, and dolphin. Other holidays when banks, stores, and government offices are closed: *New Year's Day; Good Friday; Easter Monday; Discovery Day* (third Monday in May); *Constitution Day* (first Monday in July); *Remembrance Day* (Monday after Remembrance Sunday in November); *Christmas Day;* and *Boxing Day* and the day after (December 26 and 27).

SPORTS: There are few swimming pools in the Cayman Islands. Since the sea is so warm and gentle there's no need for them, and that's why almost all sport activities take place in, on, or under the water.

Boating – *Surfside Water Sports* (phone: 7-4224) rents Hobie Cats for $20 an hour. Small boats can be chartered from a number of water-sports operators at resorts on Seven Mile Beach, including *Aqua Delights* at the *Holiday Inn; Cayman Watersports* at *Treasure Island* resort; and *Nick's Aqua Sports* at the *Hyatt Beach Club*. The cost ranges from $50 to $75 US per day. Sunday sailing races are held off Seven Mile Beach; if you want to join in, contact Gerry Kirkconnell (phone: 9-2651 or 9-7477).

Deep-Sea Fishing – Game fish abundant in Caymanian waters include marlin, tuna, yellowtail, dolphin, and bonefish. Charter fishing boats are available from a number of sources; your hotel can make arrangements. Typical rates are: half-day's open-boat fishing for one to three people, about $200 up US; full day aboard a 34-foot boat with two fighting chairs, crew, bait, tackle, ice, for up to five people, about $350 up. Little Cayman's bone and tarpon fishing are tops. *Charter Boat Headquarters* (phone: 7-4340) has complete information and prices.

Golf – A prototype course especially designed by Jack Nicklaus to accommodate a revolutionary new golf ball — the "short" ball — was opened in February 1985 at the *Britannia* resort on Grand Cayman, next to the *Hyatt Regency Grand Cayman* hotel. Because of its weight (about half that of a normal golf ball) and convex dimples (which create aerodynamic drag), the new ball flies just half the distance of a standard ball, thereby requiring a much smaller course and making it a much faster game. It tends to equalize player ability, too! Superimposed on an existing regulation 9-hole course, this 3,157-yard, 18-hole, par 72 Cayman course — the world's first "tri-course" — is as challenging as it is fun (phone: 9-8020).

Snorkeling and Scuba – Aficionados rate the Cayman Islands as one of the world's top dive areas, and Grand Cayman boasts 22 full-service dive operations from which to choose. Coral reefs teeming with marine life surround each of the islands, so there's enough underwater sightseeing close enough to shore for snorkelers and novice divers to take up fish-watching easily. For experienced divers, though boats are not really a necessity, guided trips are recommended for convenience and safety's sake. Among the brilliant and friendly fish found in clear Caymanian waters (visibility up to 200 feet) are angelfish, butterfly fish, trumpetfish, grunts, squirrelfish, snapper, and grouper. There are also shipwrecks to explore, some close enough to the surface to be viewed by snorkelers. Most hotels have fins, face masks, and snorkels to rent for about $4 to $7 US a day, and can arrange scuba trips for you. Typical rates: a two-tank diving trip including equipment is about $40 US per person; a full day with three dives and lunch, about $60; night dives (one tank), $40 US per person; half-day snorkel trip, $15 US; half-day scuba instruction course, $75 US per person; complete PADI basic certification, including several dive trips, about $300 US per person. A resort course (about $75 US) offers nondivers an introduction to scuba and will have you experiencing the underwater wonders (under a divemaster's close supervision) in a single day. Many dive shops offer rental equipment (upon presentation of a national diving association certification card only), instruction, and arrange guided dive trips. *Cayman Kai* (phone: 7-9491); *Bob Soto's Diving* (phone: 9-2022 or 9-2483); *Sunset Divers* (phone: 9-5966); *Surfside Water Sports* (phone: 7-4224); Don Foster's *Dive Grand Cayman* (phone: 9-5679); *Nick's Aqua Sports* (phone: 9-1234); and *Treasure Island Divers* (phone: 9-7777) are all first-rate. On Cayman Brac are *Brac Aquatics* (phone: 8-7429) and Peter Hughes' *Dive Tiara* (phone: 8-7313). The experienced diver can book a week-long dive expedition aboard the luxury live-aboard dive yacht *Cayman Agressor I* or its sister ship, *Cayman Agressor II*. Contact *Sea and See Inc.* (phone: 800-DIV-BOAT).

Spearfishing – Not an option for visitors since spearguns can be used by licensed residents only.

Swimming and Sunning – The most magnificent site is Seven Mile Beach — which, incidentally, is a public beach all the way and along which, not incidentally, are the majority of the island's hotels and villa and apartment complexes. But hotels and condos are small enough and far enough apart so that crowding is seldom a problem. In addition, you'll find coves, bays, and expanses of coastline all around Grand Cayman (and on the other Cayman Islands) that can be all yours for an hour or a day in the sun and sea.

Tennis – No big layouts, but more than 30 courts — all except one on Grand Cayman — at the *Beach Club Colony, Caribbean Club, Cayman Kai, Grand Caymanian Holiday Inn, Le Club Cayman, Tiara Beach, Tortuga Club, Anchorage, Beach Bay, Caribbean Paradise, Christopher Columbus, Cocoplum/Grapetree, Dolphin Point, George Town Villas, Island Club, Lacovia, Limetree Bay, Moon Bay, Silver Sands, Tamarind Bay, Victoria House, Villas Pappagallo,* the new *Grand·Pavilion,* and *Hyatt Regency.* All are free for their own guests. Nonguests can play at the *Caribbean Club, Tortuga Club,* and the *Holiday Inn* for about $4 to $8 US an hour for singles, $6 to $8 US for doubles, up to $12.50 US at night. A month's temporary membership at the *Cayman Islands Tennis Club* (4 courts) is about $20.

Water Skiing, Windsurfing – Skiing is offered by several hotels at about $40 US per hour, everything included; windsurfing boards run about $12.50 an hour, and it's about $32.50 for a 2-hour lesson. Parasail rides go for about $30 each. There's a *Mistral Windsurfing School* at *Treasure Island* resort.

 NIGHTLIFE: Nobody comes to the Cayman Islands for after-dark action, but there is casual nightclubbing at the the *Cayman Islander* near the hotel of the same name off West Bay Road, with disco music nightly (except Sundays) and live bands (and occasionally special overseas performers) on Saturdays. Admission is $6 CI. The Barefoot Man, who mixes calypso with country & western and is Cayman's most popular entertainer, can be heard in the *Wreck of the Ten Sails Lounge* at the *Holiday Inn,* and there's often a live band at the *Ports of Call*'s waterfront patio. The *Royal Palms* has live evening poolside entertainment some nights. Grand Cayman's best nightspot is the 350-seat *Silver's Night Club* at *Treasure Island* resort. Live music that includes Fifties and Sixties revues and occasional concerts by top country artists keeps this place full six nights a week (admission $4 CI). All bars and nightspots close at midnight on Saturdays, and there is no music of any kind, anywhere, on Sundays.

BEST ON THE ISLANDS

 CHECKING IN: In the conventional Caribbean sense, there are only a few complete resort hotels — the kind with all the basic day and night eating and entertainment facilities and full service built in: the *Holiday Inn Grand Cayman,* the *Royal Palms of Cayman,* and the newest additions: the *Grand Pavillion, Treasure Island,* and *Hyatt Regency.* These and Grand Cayman condo, apartment, and villa complexes and guesthouses charge top dollar. On the whole, apartment and villa rentals seem to be the best deal; fully furnished with kitchenettes, and with daily maid service, they not only allow you to be pleasantly independent, but to balance your food budget so eating costs won't overpower you.

A word about that word "condo." On Grand Cayman, where no building may rise more than five stories, condominiums are not little congested boxes in a megastructure. All properties are designed to offer spacious living and privacy. The Europeans call this a "self-catering holiday" — all the comforts of home without the housework. The condo manager often knows the best places to buy groceries (Grand Cayman lacks nothing, with several delis and lots of food stores) or can arrange for a cook to take care of everything from shopping to cleanup for an extra price. The "condo vacation" has become very popular with repeat visitors who find Cayman affordable, especially if they share with friends.

In listings below, winter rates of $120 US and up for a double room or condo apartment without meals (EP) or $160 US and up with breakfast and dinners included (MAP) is expensive; from $70 to $110 US EP double in winter or $100 to $150 US MAP for two in winter is moderate; $65 US EP and below or $90 US and below for two MAP in winter is inexpensive. Summer rates run 30% to 40% lower after mid-April until mid-December.

SEVEN MILE BEACH

Anchorage – Fresh and good-looking, this Caymanian condominium resort encompasses 14 neatly laid-out 2-bedroom apartments with full kitchens; tennis, swimming pool, and Seven Mile Beach at the door (phone: 7-4088). Expensive.

Beach Club Colony – Style that enhances but never stifles the fun is its hallmark. Rooms with balconies or terraces view the garden or the sea (water vistas cost more). The whole water sports works (scuba, snorkeling, sailing), a smooth swathe of beach, congenial gathering spots are all ready when you are. The dining is fine. Notable summer packages (phone: 9-2023). Expensive.

Caribbean Club – At the beach's midpoint. With 18 stylish villas grouped around a clubhouse with lounge, good restaurant. Good tennis court. Condominium rentals when owners are away (phone: 7-4099). Expensive.

Casa Caribe – Superb tropical decor in all units and a casually elegant atmosphere which attracts an upscale clientele. Tennis, freshwater pool, fine beach, Jacuzzi, and attentive management and staff rate this resort among the best on Cayman. Its 21 two- and three-bedroom units can be shared by four to six guests (phone: 7-4287). Expensive.

Christopher Columbus – Has 25 two- and three-bedroom apartments whose sports assets include a freshwater pool and 2 tournament tennis courts. Some good package buys. On the beach (phone: 7-4354). Expensive.

Colonial Club – A pastel pink property you'd expect to find in Bermuda. Although situated in the heart of the busy Seven Mile Beach strip, this condominium complex has a charming sense of seclusion and good taste. Two- and three-bedroom units are tastefully furnished and have fully equipped kitchens; tennis, pool, Jacuzzi, and lots of beach (phone: 7-4660). Expensive.

Grand Pavilion – Just across West Bay Road from Seven Mile Beach, this 60-room property, which opened in December 1985, has brought a touch of Continental elegance to the Caymans, with accoutrements that include Louis XV-style furniture and canopied beds. Wedgwood, crystal, and sterling extend this style in *Le Diplomat,* where the specialties of European chefs can be savored; the restaurant's wine list, which boasts over 150 selections, provides stimulating reading. Guests as well as local professionals gather on the lovely terrace and in the garden patio bar/restaurant during daily happy hours (phone: 7-4666). Expensive.

Holiday Inn Grand Cayman – No surprises. With 214 recently refurbished, air-conditioned, carpeted rooms, on the beach and with all sorts of built-in beach action, sports facilities, including 4 tennis courts (nightlit), sailing, snorkeling; diving arranged. Poolside lunching, coffee shop, first-class dining room, nightclub (phone: 7-4444). Expensive.

Hyatt Regency Grand Cayman – A $41 million, 234-room luxury resort awarded the prestigious AAA Four Diamond Award in its first year of operation. Each luxurious room comes with TV, mini-serve bar, and spacious bath with bathrobes and complimentary toiletries. Regency Club suites are available in a separate wing.

Set in lushly landscaped grounds, there are 2 pools, tennis courts, 2 restaurants (including the elegant *Garden Loggia Café*), a beach club, scuba, and the world's first 3,157-yard, 18-hole course especially designed by Jack Nicklaus to accommodate the revolutionary "short" golf ball. Other features, now under construction, will include 400 condominiums and townhouses, restaurants, and full conference facilities for meetings up to 350 (phone: 809-949-7440 or 800-527-7882). Expensive.

London House – Twenty appealing apartments that have been completely and elegantly refurbished in airy rattan and bright colors. All feature patios or balconies with sea views, air conditioning and ceiling fans, full kitchens, daily maid service. Choice of 1 or 2 bedrooms. Freshwater pool; helpful, accessible management; lovely, peaceful beach at the quiet, northern end of Seven Mile Beach. Packages (phone: 7-4060). Expensive.

Tarquynn Manor – Has 20 balconied 2- and 3-bedroom apartments with a freshwater pool as well as the beach and sea (phone: 7-4038). Expensive.

Villas of the Galleon – A 74-condominium cluster between the *Holiday Inn* and *Le Club Cayman*. One-, 2-, and 3-bedroom units with big air-conditioned rooms, fully equipped kitchens, patios or balconies (phone: 7-4433). Expensive.

West Indian Club – Toward the middle end of the beach. As posh as it gets hereabouts with 9 comfortable 1- and 2-bedroom apartments, 1 efficiency, all with maid/cook in attendance from 8:30 AM to 2:30 PM. Individually decorated, all with sizable balconies on the beach. Available for minimum 7-day stays when owners away. No bar, no lobby — presumably you'll set up your own socializing. Extra charge for air conditioning (phone: 9-2494). Expensive.

Beachcomber – Has 23 two- and three-bedroom apartments, on the beach, near shopping, restaurants. With swimming pool, air conditioning, and ceiling fans (phone: 7-4470). Moderate.

Royal Palms – Cheerful, palm-gardened beach hotel nearest town, with 83 rooms plus 40 new condominium units. Excellent scuba diving, plus all water sports, pool, beach bar, shopping. Outstanding summer packages (phone: 9-2636). Moderate.

Seagull – Has 32 new, nicely decorated, carpeted 1-bedroom apartments on the beach. No packages, but fishing, scuba easily arranged (phone: 9-5756). Moderate.

Treasure Island – A consortium of country-western stars and investors took over the derelict *Paradise Manor Beach* hotel, long unfinished, to create this unusual and wonderful 290-room Best Western resort on West Bay Road. It opened in May 1987 as the island's largest hotel and remains one of Cayman's most attractive properties, with its lavish open-air lobby and lush tropical landscaping. There are pools, tennis courts, a nightclub, and top-rated dining in *L'Escargot* under the supervision of locally renowned chef Ottmar Weber (phone: 9-7955 or 800-874-0027). Moderate.

Victoria House – Attractive apartment complex at the north end of the beach (so you'll need a car). Pleasantly decorated, well managed. From one-room studios to penthouse, it's fully furnished, with kitchenettes and air conditioning. With tennis court, shuffleboard, barbecue area; snorkeling gear to rent. Fishing, scuba, and boat trips arranged (phone: 7-4233). Moderate.

Cayman Islander – Small and slightly motel-shaped, but friendly, presentable, and a great budget buy (one of the few) because it's across the road from, not right on, the beach (phone: 9-5533). Inexpensive.

ELSEWHERE ON GRAND CAYMAN

Retreat at Rum Point – Those who've known Grand Cayman for a while will remember that fabulous, albeit rustic, refuge called *Rum Point Club*. The thatched roof, barefoot fun is gone, but the lovely beach and splendid solitude of the site remain, now enhanced by one of the island's top resorts — a welcome discovery for those interested in Cayman's advantages without the Seven Mile Beach setting. Twenty-three lavishly decorated 1-, 2-, and 3-bedroom units on 1,300 feet of beach, protected by the north coast barrier reef. Pool, tennis, sauna, and small, complete gym/exercise room — all complimentary. *Surfside Watersports* handles the scuba and aquatic fun with the same flair seen at their Seven Mile Beach facility (phone: 947-4038 or 800-423-2422). Expensive.

Tortuga Club, East End – Relaxed and informal, this longtime local getaway, watering hole, and casual beachfront hotel has 14 rooms and Miss Cleo, a truly grand Caymanian cook, in the kitchen. A good bet for beach bums seeking a casual, "soon come" (laid back) island ambience. It has expanded its scuba shop, and its summer scuba and honeymoon/lovers' packages are very appealingly priced (phone: 7-7551). Expensive.

Cayman Kai, Rum Point – Big, attractive condominium and resort complex, delightfully isolated on the island's north coast. North Wall diving aided and abetted by first-class shop (rentals, lessons, photography, guided day and night trips). Also water skiing, deep-sea fishing, sailing, lighted tennis courts. Choice of 1- or 2-bedroom sea lodges, 2-bedroom townhouses, 1- to 4-bedroom beach houses — all with living-dining areas, kitchens, patios. Clubhouse with bars, indoor/outdoor dining (phone: 7-9556). Moderate.

Sunset House – Advertised as a hotel for divers by divers, this small, award-winning resort is that and more. Just south of George Town, on the ironshore (the craggy limestone shoreline with a steel gray cast), the informal but well-managed property has 43 simple, comfortable rooms and one of the Cayman's best-run dive operations. The thatch-roofed, seaside *My Bar* is a great gathering place, day and night, for anglers, divers, pilots, and politicians. If you can't stay here, at least stop in (phone: 800-854-4767). Moderate.

CAYMAN BRAC

Brac Reef Beach – Designed and built by Bracker Linton Tibbetts, a millionaire from St. Petersburg, Florida, who is considered the godfather of Cayman Brac tourism. This lovely 32-room resort has a private beach, freshwater pool, Jacuzzi, superb native and Continental cuisine, and a special, friendly, typically Bracker atmosphere that makes time seem irrelevant. A great place to relax and really get away without roughing it. All rooms are naturally air conditioned by breezes off the cool south coast. Excellent dive and vacation packages year-round. A large on-site desalination plant gave the resort fresh water in 1985, making saline showers extinct (phone: 8-7323). Moderate.

Buccaneer's Inn – Quiet, very casual, Caymanian-owned and -managed spot, originally the *Brac*'s guesthouse, now with 39 rooms and pool, transportation to its own private beach. Its location on the north coast, with excellent diving and snorkeling just offshore, has made it a popular haunt of low-key travelers and divers for a decade. It offers excellent Caymanian food in the dining room, and the *Holey Hut* beach bar attracts lots of local characters. Rates include all meals (phone: 8-7257 or 800-535-9968). Moderate.

Divi Tiara Beach – Fresh, friendly, informal 40-room hotel with white sand beach, fine diving, fishing, tennis court, pool, and complete dive shop. There are 7 luxury apartments with ocean views, Jacuzzis, king-size beds, color TV, and telephones. An 80-seat conference center was added in 1988, and the new *Divi Village* — with 18 deluxe rooms, pool, bar, and dining room — is due for completion by 1989. Good packages for divers, honeymooners, lazers. Now related to Divi Hotels of Aruba, Bonaire, and Barbados. EP rates, MAP add-on available (phone: 8-7313 or 800-367-DIVI). Moderate.

LITTLE CAYMAN

Pirate's Point – A small, very out-island 8-room lodge run by chef-hostess Gladys Howard. Scuba packages include all meals and two dives daily. Bonefishing and deep-sea fishing also available (phone: 809-948-4210). Moderate.

Southern Cross Club – A hospitable 24-guest (10 units plus a cottage) sportsperson's enclave redone from rooftree to terrace, now casually comfortable throughout. Mike and Donna Emmanuel are the hosts. Complete scuba, fishing setups with emphasis on fly fishing; guides; inclusive packages (phone: 8-3255). Stateside contact: Southern Cross Club, 1005 E Merchants Plaza, Indianapolis, IN 46204 (phone: 8-3255 or 317-636-9501). Moderate.

EATING OUT: Caymanian cuisine stars fresh fish, turtle soup and steaks, codfish and ackee (a Jamaican specialty), conch stew, and native lobster in season (August through January). In George Town and along the beach, the choice ranges from informal hamburger places (full lunch, $4 to $6 per person) to an elegant old plantation house where dinner is served by candlelight on the verandah and the tab including wine and tip runs as high as $50 plus per person.

Although the sister islands' dining opportunities are mostly limited to hotel dining rooms, Grand Cayman has an eclectic and ever-changing array of ethnic diversions for the palate. But since restaurants — even good ones — change faster than any annual guide can keep up with, we can only recommend what is good when this book goes to press. If nothing listed below entices, ask a resident what's on that month's culinary roster. A good rule of thumb: Any establishment recommended by an islander (especially an expat with a higher than average income) is worth trying. Expats eat out often and can make or break a spot.

Le Diplomat – Very formal dining in a posh setting one would expect to find in London or Manhattan. Fine china and sterling place settings complement the near-nouvelle French fare. A place to dine, not satiate a hefty appetite, it may be too pricey and formal for most beach-weary vacationers. Possibly the island's most impressive wine list with over 150 labels. Reservations a must. Jacket and tie for men. Dinner only. In the *Grand Pavilion* hotel (phone: 7-4655). Very expensive.

Grand Old House – Now run by TV personality Chef Tell Erhardt, this former plantation house has better atmosphere than cuisine for the price. Though some dishes are superior, generally the quality of the food is inconsistent. Start with a drink in the Clown Bar, then move to the verandah for your meal. Marinated conch, escargot, Cayman land crab, and crêpes impérial serve as appetizers; entrées include fresh fish, Cayman lobster, veal cordon bleu, pepper steak, and fondue bourguignonne. Open for lunch and dinner. Reservations essential. S Church St. (phone: 9-2020). Very expensive.

Caribbean Club – Partisans claim the food, atmosphere (linen and candlelight), and service make this intimate restaurant the best on the island. Clublike, relatively plush surroundings. Lunch and dinner daily; jackets suggested for men at night. W Bay Rd. (phone: 7-4099). Expensive.

L'Escargot – At *Treasure Island* resort, renowned Cayman culinary artists Ottmar Weber and Kevin Conolly have created one of Cayman's truly elegant restaurants, serving breakfast, lunch, and dinner daily and a fine brunch buffet on Sundays. Featured are French delicacies, such as steak au poivre, veal, fine seafood (including escargots in 9 incarnations), and sinfully rich pastries. Piano music nightly, in a lovely setting with a panoramic view of the resort's landscaped grounds. Reservations suggested (phone: 9-7255). Expensive.

Garden Loggia Café – A unique and elegant café in an indoor and outdoor setting. Open for breakfast, lunch, and dinner. Its lavish luncheon buffets are a must at least once, as is the superb Sunday champagne brunch. Dine and dance on Saturday evenings to a piano/string ensemble. Reservations necessary (phone: 9-1234). Expensive.

Lobster Pot – Overlooking the sea, an old favorite with visitors and residents, due to host Clemens Geutler's fine service and consistently fine seafood (lobster and very fresh local fish), and also to Yvonne's legendary rum punches. Popular publike bar with dartboard. Lunch and dinner daily, except Sundays. N Church St. (phone: 9-2736). Expensive.

Periwinkle – Cheerful spot with unique menu of island specialties (conch fritters, turtle steak medallions, lobster) and Northern Italian dishes (lasagna Morandini, pizza Periwinkle), good homemade soups, desserts. Under the talented hand of chef/owner Johann Guschelbauer, whose Cayman reputation dates back a decade, this is another place where the residents can be found. West Bay Rd. (phone: 9-2927). Expensive.

Pappagallo – One of the island's most unusual restaurants, this thatch-roofed waterfront creation shelters an elegant interior with tropical decor, including live parrots and waiters in black tie. It features a Northern Italian menu, with seafood, veal, and pasta specialties. Smart casual dress only; reservations suggested; lunch and dinner served. At *Villas Pappagallo* resort, about 15 minutes north of George Town at Barkers in West Bay (phone: 9-3479). Expensive.

Golden Pagoda – Chinese fare with West Indian overtones to some dishes. Lunch weekdays, including a good buffet on Wednesdays; dinner nightly, except Mondays. Take-out available. West Bay Rd. (phone: 9-5475). Expensive to moderate.

Hemingway's – This delightful white pavilion is the center of the *Hyatt/Britannia Beach Club* overlooking the Caribbean. The open-air restaurant is casual, though decor and service are in *Hyatt*'s polished style. Superior rum drinks are served to you by the pool or even on the beach by saronged waitresses. Inside, dine during lunch or dinner on seafood creations such as black-peppercorn fettucine in conch and clam sauce, or fresh grilled dolphin or tuna with lemon garlic sauce. Open 11 AM to 1 AM except Sundays, when it closes at midnight. *Hyatt Regency,* Seven Mile Beach (phone: 9-1234, ext. 3009). Expensive to moderate.

Almond Tree – Under its big thatch roof, dinner is served island style. First-rate tropical punches, piña coladas; good island food. N Church St. (phone: 9-2893). Moderate.

Cayman Arms – Upstairs, on the waterfront. A favorite of the foreign business community, with reasonable prices, pub atmosphere, good food and drinks. Some rank the delicious *Mushrooms, Cayman Arms* (cheese, onion, and mushroom concoction), among the world's taste treats. Great exotic rum drinks and draft beer. Harbour Dr. (phone: 9-2661). Moderate.

Cracked Conch – Conch — in chowder, fritters, stew, and even burgers — is king, but there's all sorts of seafood, freshly caught fish, island side dishes like cho cho and fried plantain; lime and coconut pies are starred desserts. Good service, cute nautical decor. Lunch and dinner daily except Sundays. West Bay Rd. (phone: 9-5717). Moderate.

DJ's – Congenial bar, good food, fast service. Check the blackboard for entrées ranging from lobster to lasagna. With expatriate camaraderie and bistro atmosphere, it is a regular haunt of an interesting local clientele, from divers to bankers. Behind the Coconut Place shopping center (phone: 7-4234). Moderate.

Coconut Place Ice Cream Parlour – For quick lunches, picnic fare, super submarine sandwiches. Plus market-to-pantry stocks of snacks, drinks, wine, cheese, fruit, and liquor. And, oh yes, Häagen-Dazs ice cream. West Bay Rd. (phone: 7-4487). Moderate.

Santiago's – Friendly atmosphere, colorful decor, and outstanding Mexican fare at very reasonable prices. Dinner only. On West Bay Rd. (phone: 9-8580). Moderate.

West Bay Polo Club – Chalkboard menu offering good bistro fare, from fresh fish to stir fries, soups, and steaks. It's a gathering place and watering hole for residents, too, so there's lots of camaraderie. In Falls Shopping Plaza on West Bay Rd. (phone: 7-4581). Moderate.

Shanghai, Crew Road – New and already a hit with the locals for its very reasonably priced fine Chinese cuisine. Informal dining or take-out. Open daily for lunch and dinner. Near the airport (phone: 9-5886). Moderate to inexpensive.

Big Daddy's Pizza & Sub – This bistro attracts a football crowd to its TV pub for draft beer, pizza (Joel's are better than you'll find Stateside), and great overstuffed sandwiches. Good food at bargain prices. In Seven Mile Shops (phone: 9-8551). Inexpensive.

Crow's Nest, South Sound – Dine inside or out, overlooking the sea, at this tiny, informal, family-style Caymanian eatery. Seafood, burgers, and West Indian specialties are served for lunch or dinner. One of the best buys on the island and worth finding. South of George Town on the seaside road (phone: 9-2616). Inexpensive.

Liberty's, West Bay – Great dollar-stretching place for those who really want to try West Indian food at its best. Menu includes such exotica as curried goat, codfish and ackee, oxtail, and seafood Cayman style. Open daily for lunch and dinner (phone: 9-3226). Inexpensive.

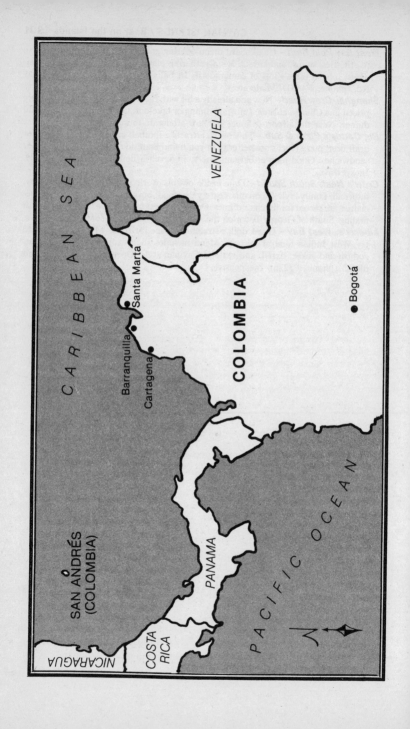

COLOMBIA'S CARIBBEAN COAST

Little of Colombia's 1,000-mile Caribbean coast has changed since European ships first landed on its shores at the beginning of the sixteenth century, when avid explorers claimed its sun-baked beaches and virgin forests for Spain in the rush to scour the entire continent for signs of El Dorado. Today the coast is still sparsely settled for a country of 28 million people. Tiny fishing villages are scattered along stretches of beach. There are large deepwater bays and hidden coves that front the jagged coastline from the desolate plains of the Guajira peninsula in the east to the dense jungles of the Gulf of Darien in the west.

Few travelers see these isolated fishing villages and almost uninhabited sections of jungle. What lures contemporary travelers are the two major resort areas on the coast — the walled city of Cartagena and historic Santa Marta; and the resorts that surround them — as well as the isolated Caribbean free-port island of San Andrés, floating almost 500 miles to the northwest in the Caribbean Sea. The gateway to Colombia's Caribbean coast is the city of Barranquilla, Colombia's largest port (population, over one million).

The first European to set eyes on Colombia's coast was the Spanish explorer Alonso de Ojeda in 1500, followed a year later by Rodrigo de Bastidas, a wealthy notary from Seville, who explored the entire coast. Almost 24 years after this expedition, Bastidas returned to set up the first permanent settlement on the American mainland in the scenic, sheltered bay of Santa Marta. He was followed in 1533 by Don Pedro de Heredia, a famous explorer who had been forced to leave Spain because of a duel. Don Pedro landed at what was then the Carib fishing village of Calamari, in a natural harbor formed by a bay and a sandspit breakwater. He promptly renamed it Cartagena de las Indias, and it soon became one of Spain's most prized New World possessions, second only to Mexico City.

The growing Spanish Empire needed gold and silver to finance further expeditions as well as to pay the military forces needed to protect these new possessions and their supply lines across the Atlantic and Caribbean. Cartagena became the principal storehouse, a formidable fortress, and the main transit point for the seemingly inexhaustible wealth that flowed to Spain from the New World; it also became a key target for devastating attacks by English, French, and Dutch pirates who preyed on shipping along the Spanish Main.

It has been sacked time and again, only to be reestablished after each attack. The breakwater became a heavily fortified island-city. Its strategic location for Spanish shipping made it irreplaceable as a Caribbean port for Spanish galleons loaded with gold, emeralds, pearls, indigo, tobacco, and coffee awaiting escort to Europe.

After the city had been captured and held for ransom by the daring sea rover Francis Drake in 1586, Spanish rulers, beginning with Philip II, spent a fortune over more than two centuries fortifying Cartagena. Philip commissioned the top military engineer in Europe, Juan Bautista Antonelli, to plan the city's defenses. The 23 forts and seven miles of walls that protect the city were completed in 1796 by a brilliant Spanish engineer, Antonio de Arevalo. A famous story relates that, upon receiving the final bill for these fortifications, the Spanish king immediately stepped out on the balcony of his palace, looked to the west, and wryly inquired, *"Dónde estan, que no las veo?"* ("Where are they — I can't see them?") meaning that at such vast cost, they should be visible from as far away as Europe.

Seven of the nine original forts still stand, much to the amazement of visitors, who marvel at the ingenious maze of underground passageways, strategic gun emplacements, cisterns for collecting rainwater, ventilation systems, dungeons, and large storage areas for ammunition and food — most of them 25 feet below the surface of the ground. As part of this remarkable defense system, tons of rock were dropped at the wide (Bocagrande) western entrance to the bay, forming an underwater barrier that still makes ship passage through this end of the bay impossible. A causeway across the strait connects mainland Cartagena with the newer sandspit section — called Bocagrande — where the city's major hotels are located.

Today, you can take a sightseeing boat cruise that gives you a pirate's-eye view of the two forts guarding this passage into the inner harbor. You can also sail the Bay of Cartagena, which is so large that at one time it was said to be big enough to hold all the world's fleets. The beaches fronting the ocean are so shallow that hostile ships could not come close enough to bombard the city with their cannon. Although ships were well protected while they were inside the bay, they would still fall prey to pirates at certain times of the year when lakes and swamps between the Magdalena River and Cartagena dried up, forcing the ships to put to sea. In order to bring their rich cargoes from the interior of the country and reach the fortress in safety, Spaniards brought thousands of black slaves from Africa to build a 65-mile canal from the Magdalena River to Cartagena that is still in use today.

Cartagena's defense proved so formidable that even the Great Liberator Simón Bolívar could not breach the city when he laid siege to the Fortress of San Felipe in 1813. He succeeded in liberating outlying areas of the city when he defeated Loyalist troops on the plains of Boyaca in 1819.

Cartagena is undoubtedly Colombia's most popular tourist destination, and is now a city of 500,000 people with a dual personality that successfully and artfully blends the colonial antiquity and easy pace of bygone days in the old city with a new city of modern, high-rise hotels, smart shops, and elegant beaches in the Bocagrande area. The crooked narrow streets, impressive fortifications, and well-preserved early churches and palatial homes of the old city recall the days when it was the mad dream of every pirate roaming the Caribbean. Though it is a standard three-day stop on most tours and a few cruise ships dock here for even shorter stays, it really deserves a week or more and, therefore, is best as part of a tour of Colombia's Caribbean coast.

The beach resort of Santa Marta and Morgan the Pirate's old hideout in San Andrés are gaining popularity, especially among foreign vacationers. In Santa Marta, the oldest European-founded city on the continent and the favored point of departure of early explorers venturing onto an unknown continent in search of gold, tourists now bask in splendor on the sparkling beaches below the towering snow-covered Sierra Nevada.

Set between two lovely beaches, Santa Marta is a notable port and commercial fishing center as well as the capital of a sizable agricultural region, where large banana and coffee plantations flourish. It was here that Simón Bolívar came to rest after his arduous battles for independence across the continent, and where he died in 1830, a sad, sick, and disillusioned man.

On the island of San Andrés, floating in the Caribbean some 500 miles northwest of the coast of Colombia, descendants of English Pilgrims and African slaves still speak English and worship in Protestant churches. And many believe that the lost treasure of the pirate Henry Morgan is still hidden here. This tropical land of lush green hills and coconut groves, from which come the island's principal product, copra, has some of the finest weather, clearest waters, and loveliest beaches in the Caribbean, plus two gambling casinos and a duty-free port. Its tiny sister island, Providencia, some 60 miles farther northeast, so far remains undiscovered except by a few snorkelers and spearfishermen; however, there is now air service between the two islands and even a delightful six-room hotel, the *Aury.*

Colombia's pride in its colonial heritage, combined with its mañana atmosphere, sometimes proves so pervasive that visitors fail to recognize its contemporary assets. Not only is the country richly endowed with natural resources and more than adequate electrical power and energy for its needs, it also boasts deep, sheltered harbors with up-to-date port facilities, good paved roads, and a modern air transport system Avianca is the second-oldest airline in the world, and the oldest (53 years) in the Western Hemisphere.

Its coastal area ranks as one of the country's major agricultural and cattle-raising regions, in addition to providing home ports for a substantial commercial fishing industry. Fortunately, reports of a high crime rate, thefts, and tourist rip-offs in Bogotá do not seem to apply to its resorts, though it's wise to use common-sense rules in Cartagena, Santa Marta, or San Andrés, as you would in any large North American city. (Don't carry large sums of money or wear extravagant jewelry; do use hotel safes to store valuables — or better still, leave them home.)

Last year close to a million people visited Colombia's Caribbean vacation lands. You can be sure that in years to come, as they begin to discover and further explore its wild and beautiful shoreline, this number will increase appreciably.

COLOMBIA AT-A-GLANCE

FROM THE AIR: Colombia's Caribbean coast stretches from Panamá to Venezuela — 1,000 miles of the northernmost edge of the South American continent — in a jagged line of deeply indented bays, protruding capes, and sandy beaches broken here and there by dense jungles and towering mountains. Only 150 miles wide at its widest point, this narrow strip of coastal lowlands occupies a delta-shaped alluvial area between the snow-capped Sierra Nevada and the central and western spurs of the Andes. When you look down from the plane as you approach Barranquilla, the gateway to Colombia's Caribbean resorts, the sparkling blue sea suddenly gives way to a lush green mat of tropical vegetation that shows scars of civilization as gray asphalt roads stretch out in long lines toward red-tiled rooftops, farmland, large estates, and the helter-skelter of low, flat warehouses, factories, streets, plazas, offices, and buildings that make up this city of one million people.

Just 2½ hours by air from Miami, Barranquilla is actually closer to Miami than is either New York or Dallas. This busy city sits at the midpoint of the Colombian coast, on the west bank of the Magdalena River, one of Colombia's principal waterways. A 1,500-meter bridge spans the river and leads to the four-lane Caribbean highway, a direct and sometimes scenic route along the coast that takes you across the now dead Ciénaga Grande (the Great Marsh, which was destroyed by the road construction) to Santa Marta, and beyond to its national parks, the Sierra Nevada, Tayrona Park, and farther to the little-known beaches, deserts, and Indian country of the Guajira peninsula on the border of Venezuela. West from Barranquilla, in the opposite direction, lies Cartagena, a charming reminder of colonial days that still preserves its Spanish heritage and romantic traditions within massive fortifications.

SPECIAL PLACES: Cartagena – The shining jewel in Colombia's Caribbean crown. Behind its languorous atmosphere is a violent history of bloody sieges and immense riches. Its once impregnable fortifications are still formidable, blocking the Bocagrande (western) entrance to the harbor (now a causeway to the island city) and guarding the Boca Chica (eastern) mouth of the bay in which the city is nestled. Walls 40 feet high and 50 to 60 feet wide encircle this "heroic city," and seven of its nine original forts remain standing. Visitors marvel at their ingeniously laid out underground passages, barracks, and storage areas.

A good way to see the city and get a full appreciation of its strategic importance is to take a boat trip around the harbor. The Old City, with its crooked narrow streets, palm-filled plazas for breathing space, and stately colonial mansions with wrought-iron gates and overhanging balconies, stands out in sharp contrast to the functional high-rise condominiums and hotels, fine restaurants, and fashionable shops in the Bocagrande strip between the bay and the Caribbean. A note on safety: Cartagena's reputation as a "dangerous" city is largely a case of mistaken identity. The city is the safest in Colombia, and tourists rarely complain of crime-related problems. In Cartagena, unlike Bogotá, it is usually safe to walk the streets at night.

Drive to the top of La Popa Hill — a $3 taxi ride — to visit a 17th-century monastery with a great view of the city and harbor. Just below here is the city's most important fortification, San Felipe de Barajas, which remains in almost perfect condition. Originally started in 1657, it was captured and destroyed in 1697 by a force of 650 French corsairs, pirates, and buccaneers, and an estimated one million pesos in gold and jewelry was taken from the city. Between 1762 and 1769 it was converted into the impressive fortress that still guards the harbor. From here you'll be able to see how the new city sprawls astride a sandspit, and why the old one could be so easily defended.

A statue of an enormous pair of shoes stands in the plaza in front of San Felipe Fortress, honoring one of Cartagena's best-loved poets, Luis Carlos Lopez. Lopez praised the city in one of his poems by claiming that it inspired as much affection and comfort as an old pair of shoes.

On the western side of Cartagena, along the Caribbean, several early buildings have been restored by public-spirited citizens who wished to preserve the town's antiquity and originality. The Church of San Pedro Claver (on San Juan de Dios) is named for the 17th-century Jesuit monk who dedicated his life to helping the African slaves imported by the Spaniards. The remains of this American saint, who was canonized in 1888, repose in a chest under the main altar. On the Plaza Bolívar is the former Palace of the Inquisition, a splendid example of colonial architecture that now houses the city's tourist office and a museum documenting the horrors of the Inquisition as well as memorabilia of the city's past. Among these is the city's receipt for the 10-million-peso ransom it paid to Sir Francis Drake for not burning the city.

The cathedral, which faces the Plaza Bolívar, was begun in a kind of Renaissance-Andalusian style in 1575 and completed in this century with a pink and white Moorish tower. Its original hand-carved altar has been restored in gold plate.

Diagonally across the Plaza Bolívar, a block north and a block west (toward the sea), is the oldest church in Cartagena, the Church of Santo Domingo, built at the end of the 16th century. You will recognize it by the tower, part of the original construction, which appears to lean slightly. Of special interest is the statue of the Virgin Mary inside, wearing a crown of gold and emeralds.

A fine colonial residence on the Calle de las Damas is the place where, according to legend, the patron saint of Cartagena appeared to Fray Alonso de la Cruz and ordered him to build the Church of La Popa on the highest hill in the area. The beautiful patio and elaborately decorated rooms are now the site of one of the finest seafood restaurants in Cartagena (*Bodegon de la Candelaria;* see *Best on the Coast*). The house of the Marques de Valdehoyos, home of a man who made a fortune trading in flour and slaves, is nearby (on Calle Factoria), only a block from the cathedral. Its vaulted Moorish ceilings, double balconies, spiral staircase, and lookout provide some outstanding examples of colonial art and architecture. On the ground floor you can see the stables and slave quarters. The house of Don Benito, a 17th-century mansion once owned by a gentleman who fell afoul of the Inquisition for preaching Judaism, is a few blocks north of here, by the Parque Madrid. It is now a popular handicraft shop.

The city's indomitable spirit and love of liberty are exemplified in the Parque Morillo opposite the Clock Tower, near the center of the Old City. On November 11, 1811, Cartagena was the first city in what are now Colombia and Venezuela to declare its independence from Spain. Freedom fighters expelled the Spanish in 1815 and held the city until Pablo Morillo retook the city-state after a three-month siege. Upon entering the city, Morillo offered the native freedom fighters "amnesty in the name of peace," and then proceeded to execute hundreds of people. Although the park bears the name of the Spanish "peacemaker," it commemorates the people he executed.

But probably the one monument that truly represents this former Carib settlement and recalls its early inhabitants is the statue of Catalina, the beautiful Indian princess who was taken prisoner by the Spanish conquistadores when she was a little girl and returned as a young maiden with Don Pedro de Heredia to help pacify her people and establish the city of Cartagena. The model for the statue was the owner of a Cartagena souvenir shop. Today, bronze replicas of her lithe, seminude form are given out as "Catalinas" — awards at the International Film Festival, which takes place here annually at the Baluarte de Santa Catalina, just off the Plaza Bovedas.

Santa Marta – South America's oldest European-founded city, Santa Marta, is also a popular resort. This 450-year-old city can be reached easily from Barranquilla, Bogotá, and other Colombian cities by plane or car; in addition, there is 22-hour train service from Bogotá — recommended only for the hardiest of travelers. Cruise ships occasionally schedule calls at its deepwater port.

Many of the visitors to Santa Marta are Colombians from other parts of the country who come here to sunbathe on its beaches and enjoy the scenic mountains, which rise 18,000 feet to their snowy crests only 30 miles from the Caribbean coastline. It is a low-key resort town, with some sightseeing and very little nightlife. Its beaches, the quiet fishing villages like Taganga (about 10 miles north) and Villa Concha (15 miles to the south), and the banana plantations surrounding the area, most accessible from the village of Sevilla (32 miles south of Santa Marta), attract visitors.

Little remains of the old forts that once protected the city from marauding pirates, but not well enough to prevent the repeated sackings of the 16th and 17th centuries. One of these forts, Castillo de San Fernando, has been restored and is well worth a visit. The hacienda of San Pedro Alejandrino, about 3 miles southeast of the city, is an interesting side trip. Simón Bolívar spent his last days here, unfortunately without his beloved mistress Manuela Saenz, who was not allowed (by government order) to accompany him into exile. Totally destitute in his final days, he accepted the hospitality of, ironically, a Spanish nobleman whose fortune had been considerably reduced by Bolívar's Wars of Independence. The Liberator remained here until his death on December 17, 1830. His few possessions are on display although his body was removed to the National Pantheon in Caracas. By special petition, the people of Santa Marta requested that his heart remain in their cathedral in a leaden casket. During a fire in 1872, the relics were removed from the church and, in the confusion, the casket was lost and has never been recovered. The stately main house is now a museum, and the entire estate is an attractive park with giant shade trees dating from Bolívar's time.

The two magnificent beaches of Santa Marta, with the snow-capped Andes and Sierra Nevada in the background, are still the principal reason 110,000 visitors come here every year. Rodadero Beach is the more modern of the two. It has the newer hotels, restaurants, and the only nightlife to speak of in town; Irotama Beach has older (but not necessarily less expensive) accommodations, is quieter, and is somewhat isolated.

San Andrés – Almost 500 miles northwest of Colombia, in the Caribbean, actually closer to the coast of Nicaragua than to the Colombian coastline, is the island of San Andrés. This tropical paradise is the largest island of a tiny archipelago that produces mainly coconuts and other fruits. Its main attraction is its luxurious sandy beaches, with excellent sun and an almost constant temperature of 80°F ten months of the year.

Unlike mainland Colombians, most San Andréans speak English. Originally discovered by the Spanish in 1527, the island was settled by English Pilgrims sailing on the *Seaflower,* sister ship to the *Mayflower,* who planted cotton and began importing African slaves to work their plantations. Later the island became a pirate refuge, and buccaneer Henry Morgan set up a base here for his raids on Spanish shipping.

Isolated from the continent, San Andrés has changed little since Morgan's time. In fact, his treasure (supposedly millions in gold and precious stones) has never been accounted for and is, according to history and rumor, still hidden in one of the many caves on this island or one of the nearby cays.

In 1822, San Andrés became part of the Colombian province of Cartagena and lay quietly in the Caribbean until it was declared a free port in the 1950s. Although regular air service was established at that time, and the free port status attracts a large number of travelers and bargain hunters (from the Colombian mainland as well as the rest of the world), the island has remained fairly primitive and underdeveloped. There are some good hotels and restaurants; however, tap water is undrinkable, hot water is often unavailable, there are occasional blackouts, and the menus depend on ship arrivals.

There are only two towns on the island: San Luis, a village, and the town of San Andrés. The airport is only a $2 US taxi ride from San Andrés, or about a 15-minute walk if you travel light. The free-port shops, for the most part, are clustered around Avenida La Playa, the main street of the resort section of San Andrés; most tourist hotels are also close by. There are several good, paved roads, and with a rental car you can drive around the island along a scenic route that meanders through several coconut groves, passes what is reputed to be Morgan's Cave and the *Hoyo Soplador,* or Blow Hole, which spouts sea water about 30 feet into the air. The small town of San Luis is home to most of the island's residents. A primitive fishing village of simple but special beauty, peace, and charm, it should not be missed when you're out exploring.

The resort area of San Andrés features the 600 or so free-port shops, but there is an older section of the town, centered around the Baptist church on La Loma Hill. Here are many old island mansions, surrounded by the oleander and banyan trees that first attracted the Pilgrims to the island. From here, also, there is an incredible seascape of the island's beaches and multihued waters. It is these beaches and warm waters that make the island the vacation spot it is today; perfect for all water sports, filled with coral reefs and colorful fish of all varieties.

There are several offshore cays, or keys; the two that attract most visitors are Johnny Key and Haines Key, accessible by launch (cost: $4 US per person) from San Andrés. There are picnic facilities on both, and beautiful waters, of course, surround everything here. Haines Key also shelters a natural aquarium within its reefs, and a scuba mask, snorkel, and fins (to protect your feet from sea urchins) are all that's necessary to explore the colorful waters.

SOURCES AND RESOURCES

TOURIST INFORMATION: The Colombia Government Tourist Office (Corporación Nacional de Turismo), 140 E 57th St., New York, NY 10022 (phone: 212-688-0151), is the best place to get information and travel brochures on what to see and do and where to stay in Colombia.

The Tourist Office also has offices in Barranquilla in the Edificio Arawak, Carrera 54, 75-45 (phone: 35-7378), and in Cartagena at the Casa de Marques de Valdehoyos on Calle Factoria (phone: 4-7012). In addition, there is Cartagena's own tourist office, in the old Palace of the Inquisition on the Plaza Bolívar; in Santa Marta at El Rodadero, Carrera 2, 16-44 (phone: 35773); and in San Andrés on Avenida Colombia 9-50 (phone: 6830). You can also obtain information on these cities, as well as tour and flight schedules, from the airlines serving Colombia.

Telephone – Dial direct to Colombia by adding the international access code 011 and the prefix 57-59 for Cartagena, 57-811 for San Andrés, and 57-501 for Santa Marta.

ENTRY REQUIREMENTS: US and Canadian citizens need valid passports and either tourist cards or visas. The cards are available free and immediately when you present two passport photos (1½ in. × 1½ in.), a passport (which you should carry with you at all times), and a round-trip ticket (or a letter from your travel agent stating reservations for your trip have been made and outlining your itinerary) at the Colombian Government Tourist Office or the office of the air or cruise line on which you'll travel. Visas, which require presentation of a passport and round-trip or ongoing tickets, are obtainable at the Colombian consulate. Smallpox vaccinations and yellow fever or cholera inoculations are required only if you're coming from an infected area. You are allowed to bring in two bottles of liquor and 200 cigarettes per person. (Try the coffee liqueur called *Coloma,* available only on

Colombia's Caribbean coast.) If you stay for more than 24 hours, you must pay a $15 airport tax when you leave the country.

 CLIMATE AND CLOTHES: The climate along the entire coast is warm and tropical all year, with average temperatures between 80°F and 84°F — ideal beach weather. It is hot and sunny during the day with cooling trade wind breezes at night to drop temperatures to the tolerable 70s. The most popular months for a visit are from January through April and from July through September, when it is relatively dry. Spring and fall tend to be rainy and humid; try to avoid Holy Week and late December, when Colombians from the cooler mountain regions flock to the beaches, making hotel reservations difficult to obtain.

Barranquilla is usually very hot and muggy, with an average temperature hovering at 85°F. Cartagena is about the same, especially in town, but the evenings and nights are cooler, as are the beaches, where fresh winds always blow. On San Andrés, the average temperature is a constant 80°F most of the year.

Dress in the cities and seaside resorts is very casual and informal, except for business. Most tourists wear slacks and sport shirts; ladies in shorts and bikinis (rarely seen a decade ago) are pretty much a part of the landscape now. Colombians like to dress in the evenings, especially for dinner at a good restaurant; men will don their fancy guayaberas or sport shirts (but seldom a jacket), and the women choose light cocktail dresses. Formal dress is not necessary in the casinos.

 MONEY: Official currency is the Colombian peso, one of South America's most stable currencies. US dollars are accepted enthusiastically in most hotels, restaurants, and shops, but at about 2% less than the official rate; so change money at the banks. Hotels and travel agencies will give you slightly less, but sometimes you can get more from shops where you buy merchandise. When you leave the country, you can only exchange a maximum of $60 worth of pesos into US currency at the airport bank, and only if you can show a receipt indicating that the original dollar/peso exchange was effected in a legal fashion. Any extra last-minute pesos usually get spent in airport shops. Shops in Colombian cities are open from 9:30 AM to 7 PM daily except Sundays; banks are open from 9 AM to 3 PM on weekdays.

 LANGUAGE: Spanish is the official language of Colombia, but you'll have little difficulty in the cities and resorts of the Caribbean coast, as most hotels, restaurants, and stores cater to English-speaking tourists. On San Andrés, everybody speaks English plus an English/Spanish dialect inscrutable to speakers of either.

 TIME: The coastal cities are on Eastern Standard Time all year. San Andrés is on the same time.

 CURRENT: At 110 volts, 60 cycles, so US appliances can be used without converters.

 GETTING THERE: You can jet to Barranquilla and Cartagena directly from Miami or New York on Avianca. Eastern Airlines also schedules daily flights from Miami to Barranquilla. Avianca has four nonstop flights each week from New York to Barranquilla and three to Cartagena. Santa Marta can be reached by connecting flights from Barranquilla and Bogotá on Avianca. The Colombian airline also flies weekly to Bogotá from Los Angeles. Cartagena can also be reached by plane from Barranquilla, Bogotá, and other Colombian cities. The Caribbean Highway links the coastal cities of Santa Marta, Barranquilla, and Cartagena with a well-paved, scenic road.

San Andrés is served by Avianca flights once a week (Wednesdays) from Miami (returning on Sundays), from Bogotá and Barranquilla; by SAM from Bogotá; and by infrequent but interesting cargo ships to and from Cartagena. Prudential Steamship Lines also serves Cartagena and Barranquilla from the West Coast of the US.

 CALCULATING COSTS: Hotel rates and food costs throughout Colombia's Caribbean coast are much lower than those at many Caribbean resort destinations. An air-conditioned double room without meals in the most expensive coast hotel is seldom more than $60, except at the *Cartagena Hilton*, which runs about $100; and the cost of dinner for two at the finest restaurants in Cartagena is about $45. In Santa Marta and San Andrés, hotel rates and restaurant meals are even less (although there are fewer air-conditioned rooms in San Andrés). Avianca package tours — including air fare, transfers, sightseeing, and hotel stay in Cartagena and Santa Marta — are priced at about $489 and up per person from Miami, about $549 and up from New York, for an 8-day/7-night trip. There is a $15 airport departure tax.

 GETTING AROUND: Taxi – Plentiful in all the coastal cities and inexpensive by US standards. You'll find taxis at the airports, docksides, hotels, and tourist offices. Rates are metered, but often that has little to do with the price. Try to get a firm price before starting out; since you do not know the town, the choice of route (and the final fare) is the driver's. San Andrés is the exception — taxi fares are based on a mileage rate. Here, also, make an agreement with the driver before the trip as to what the fare should be.

Bus – In Cartagena buses fall into two categories: large windowless types, which cost only 15¢ per person; and smaller buses with windows, which vary from 20¢ to 25¢ per person. The routes are a little complex, so check with the driver to be sure you're going where you want to end up. Santa Marta has very little in the way of local service, since there are few roads within the town. Carrera 1, which runs along the beach, is the main line, and the bus (from one end of town to the other) costs 15¢. The bus along Carrera 1 makes all stops through the shopping area. There simply is not enough business (or space) to warrant the use of buses on San Andrés.

Car Rental – Available everywhere. In Cartagena, *Autocosta* (phone: 5-3259) has four- and six-cylinder Renaults for $20 per day, plus 20¢ per kilometer. *Hertz* (phone: 5-2921), in the lobby of the *Capilla del Mar* hotel, has two- and four-door sedans available, as well as Jeeps (for traveling outside the city).

In Santa Marta, *Hertz*, which has offices at the airport and on Rodadero Beach (phone: 2-7046), has Renaults and Simcas available for about $20 a day, plus 20¢ per kilometer. San Andrés has no public transport system, so it's either taxis or rental cars. Since the rate for a Moke or a mini-jeep (Citröen) is about $18 per day, we advise that you rent your own and drive around the island. There are no mileage charges in San Andrés for rentals; after all, the island is quite small. Check at the tourist office or your hotel desk as to who has what available on any given day; there are only a few vehicles — among them, several dune buggies and motorcycles.

Sea Excursions – Most coastal resorts also have small boats for rent or charter cruisers. In Cartagena, the *Caribe* hotel rents paddleboats and canoes and other playcraft for about $3 an hour; small boats cost $10 an hour; water skiing is also $10 an hour. In Santa Marta, check with *Captain Ospina* at his beachside stand on Rodadero

Beach. Boats here rent for about $7 an hour, paddleboats and similar craft go for about $5 an hour. On San Andrés, there are very few paddleboats available; however, small boats can be chartered for anywhere from $10 an hour to $110 per day (for a fully equipped fishing cruiser with captain).

Probably the most unusual rental of all is available through *Excursiones Roberto Lemaitre El Pirata* (phone: 4-0833) in Cartagena — rent your own boat (with or without crew) and your own island in the Rosario Archipelago, just 20 miles from Cartagena. Some of these are just tiny atolls and reefs, with just enough rock or coral underneath to support a small cabin. The cost for this, including the use of an 18-foot cabin cruiser, is about $150 per day. You can also take a regularly scheduled trip to El Pirata Island for a fish or lobster lunch and swimming for $20. A few dollars more will allow you to stay overnight at one of the Lemaitre cabanas, three meals included.

A castaway tour can be arranged through *Caribe Tours* in Cartagena (phone: 4-1221). Given advance notice, they will set you adrift, on a raft equipped with whatever you request, onto your own private beach, where you will remain, abandoned, until 4 PM, when a motor launch will pick you up.

 SHOPPING: In Cartagena's Old City, keep an eye out for native handicrafts, especially in the stalls near Plaza Bolívar. There is also a chain of government shops called *Artesanías de Colombia,* which carry a wide array of goods at favorable prices. The stores in this shopping district handle all types of merchandise, from these handmade native items to fine leather goods and Colombian emeralds. The native crafts will probably be the best buy, but if you decide to purchase one of the native emeralds please do so from a reputable dealer, not from one of the many street peddlers who will approach you. Remember that the deeper the color and greater the sparkle, the more valuable the emerald. *Greenfire Emeralds* has stores in Commercial Center, Pierino Gallo, and the Bocagrande area.

On most other goods, get a good idea of prices at home before you go; after paying duty on some items, you really don't save much over US discount prices. The exception is coffee, which at 30¢ to 35¢ a pound is well worth buying in quantity if you have the space in your suitcase. Buy it at a local market, not a tourist shop. Look in the duty-free shops on San Andrés. There are some 600 stores in the shopping area, with goods from all over the world. Do not be shocked at the number of things sold here that you're used to seeing every day. This area does not cater to American buyers in particular, but rather to Colombians and Central and South American travelers in general. There are Swiss watches, French perfumes, cameras, and liquor available at, for the most part, similar prices to those in other duty-free areas. *Coloma,* a local coffee liqueur, costs about $3 for a 750mm bottle. Don't bother to shop in Santa Marta; the selection is poor and the prices are not competitive.

 TIPPING: Some hotels, restaurants, and bars add a 10% to 15% service charge to bills. If they do not, do so yourself. If it is justified, for some special service, add an extra 5% to that. Taxi drivers do not expect tips, but porters should get about 50 pesos per piece of luggage. If you leave your car under the watchful eye of an attendant, he should get 50 to 100 pesos, depending on how long it's in his care.

 SPECIAL EVENTS: Cartagena celebrates its *Independence* on November 11, and the festival is wild. Complete with masks and costumes, dancing in the streets, and fireworks, this party can get a little rough after a while. The city also hosts the annual *Caribbean Music Festival* in mid-March. The big party in Santa Marta is the pre-Lent *Carnival.* Colombia's *Independence Day* is July

20; a *Festival of the Sea* is held in late July or early August along the coast. Offices, banks, stores, and museums are also closed on *Epiphany* (January 6); *St. Joseph* (March 19); *Holy Thursday* and *Good Friday; Labor Day* (May 1); *Ascension; Corpus Christi; Sacred Heart* (June 2); *SS Peter & Paul* (June 29); *Battle of Boyacá* (August 7); *Assumption* (August 15); *Columbus* (October 12); *All Saints'* (November 1); *Immaculate Conception* (December 8); *Christmas* and *New Year's.* Banks close from December 24 to January 2. (*Note:* Religious feast days that fall on weekends are usually observed as holidays the following Monday. The same is true of *Cartagena Independence Day,* November 11.)

SPORTS: Snorkeling and Scuba – There are wrecks offshore around Cartagena that provide excellent diving. Jim Buttgen runs tours, rents equipment, and provides supplies; call him in Cartagena at 2-1221. Bill Moore, a treasure hunter, also takes divers out in his boat. Ask for him at the *Caribe Hotel. Sea Horse Inn* has San Andrés's best-equipped dive shop.

Sport Fishing – In Cartagena, the *Club de Pesca* (in the fortress of San Sebastián) can arrange charters; the Colombian Tourist Corporation owns the *Calamary Bertram 31,* which goes out for about $200 a day.

Santa Marta has excellent fishing, and Captain Ospina will be glad to charter a boat and point out the way. He operates from his stand on Rodadero Beach, and the rates vary, depending on the vessel, the weather, the time of year, and the captain's mood.

Swimming and Sunning – The Bocagrande section of Cartagena and the town of Santa Marta have good beaches, as does the island of San Andrés.

Tennis – In Cartagena, the *Cartagena Real, Hilton,* and *Caribe* hotels have courts of their own, and there are three private clubs that have arrangements with various hotels. Let the hotel desk make the reservations for you. Most of the formalities are little more than certification of your guest status by the hotel and minimal fees. The *Gaira Golf Club* and *Irotama* hotel in Santa Marta also have courts. On San Andrés, there is a 4-court Tennis Club near the *Isleno* hotel (on Avenida de la Playa), with courts available to visitors for modest fees.

NIGHTLIFE: The nightlife on the Colombian coast is found in its gambling casinos and only a few bars and discos. Although there are some live shows with local and imported talent, there are no big cabarets or lavish, spectacular floor shows. In Cartagena, the *Casino del Caribe* (Commercial Center, Pierino Gallo) has one room devoted to slot machines and another for roulette and blackjack. Minimum table bets are 200 pesos (about 80¢), so the place gets crowded. The casino remains open until 3 AM.

For discos, your best bet is the Bocagrande hotel area. Stay along Avenida San Martin to find *Moulin Rouge* (at Calle 3) or *Zorba* (about a block away). Clubs tend to come and go rapidly, but while they exist, there's plenty of dancing to US rock or good Latin-American music. Drinks are inexpensive if you stay away from imported brands, including all wines, and drink local rums. Tres Esquinas is recommended, and is often mixed with ginger ale. If there is a minimum, it will be about $4.

In Santa Marta the *Tamaca Inn* (phone: 2-7015) has a bar that offers entertainment, a disco, and a nice casino. Chips are for big bettors here, with minimums of 50¢.

San Andrés gets very quiet at night. There are small casinos at the *Royal Abacoa* and *Eldorado* hotels; both are right on the beach. They will be almost within sight of your hotel (or you'll need a cab if you don't stay on the beach). Stakes here start at 60¢, no jackets are required, and the hours are 9 PM to 3 AM at both casinos. There is a "disco" place on the island, but it is quiet compared to bars on the mainland. *Morgan's Cave* (Av. 20 de Julio) attracts small crowds — but then, it's a small island.

BEST ON THE COAST

CHECKING IN: The Colombian coastal resort cities have more than 200 hotels and guesthouses, with a total of some 4,000 rooms. Key cities such as Barranquilla, Cartagena, Santa Marta, and the island of San Andrés boast some first-class hotels. Expect to pay about $60 for a double room without meals in the places listed below as expensive (the *Hilton* is the exception; its rates start at about twice that during high season); between $50 and $60 a day in the moderate range; and less than $40 a day in an inexpensive place.

CARTAGENA

Capilla del Mar – On the beach in the Bocagrande section. With an excellent dining room, revolving bar topside (phone: 4-7140). Expensive.

Cartagena Hilton International – In the El Laguito residential neighborhood at the tip of a Bocagrande peninsula and far and away the best in town. With beach on three sides, swimming pools, lighted tennis courts, water sports. Shops, restaurants, party evenings, bar-nightclub too. All 298 rooms have balconies, air conditioning, lagoon or sea views (phone: 5-0666). Expensive.

Cartagena Real – An attractive modern resort hotel catering to Colombian, Venezuelan, and North American vacationers and businesspeople. Just across the street from the beach, with 75 air-conditioned rooms, small pool, tennis, restaurant, bar, night music (phone: 4-3765). Moderate.

Decameron – One of the newest in the city, on the Bocagrande hotel strip between the bay and the sea. It has a fine restaurant and wide beachfront (phone: 5-4400). Moderate.

Las Velas – With suites and apartments as well as hotel rooms; spectacular 18th-floor bar for sunset-watching. On the beach in the Bocagrande section (phone: 5-0000). Moderate.

Residencias Boca Grande – A family hotel on the beach with condominium apartments; they will take very good care of you (phone: 4-4435). Inexpensive.

SANTA MARTA

Tamaca Inn – On Rodadero Beach. There are 72 air-conditioned rooms, casino, bar, and good restaurant, but no hot water (phone: 2-7015). Expensive.

Santamar – A new resort/convention center complex located on a beautiful beach a mile out of town. It offers 130 air-conditioned rooms (some are bungalows), 3 pools, 2 restaurants, and 24-hour service (phone: 2-7317 or 2-7060). Expensive to moderate.

Irotama – An old-fashioned resort hotel on a fine beach, offering private, air-conditioned cottages; rates include water sports, tennis, meals (phone: 4059). Moderate.

La Sierra – Offers 74 air-conditioned rooms on El Rodadero Beach; also a seafood restaurant and a bar (phone:2-7197). Moderate.

SAN ANDRÉS

Aquarius – The island's newest, with 100 breezily contemporary Caribbean-style rooms facing the sea. Good-looking pool, water sports (phone: 6920). Expensive.

Casa Blanca – A small, friendly place (44 rooms, 14 cabanas) which caters mostly to young couples and young families from the US and Latin America. Has its own pool, water sports; just across from the beach (phone: 6315 and 6915). Moderate.

El Isleño – Considered to be on the best beach on the island, and within sight of Johnny Key. It has 42 rooms, and air conditioning isn't necessary, since the island is always cooled by the breeze (phone: 6226). Moderate.

Sea Horse Inn – A small, simple place just outside town known for its super scuba setup and congenially casual atmosphere, thanks to the cordial Canadian-Colombian couple who own and run it. Has its own small pool, bar (phone: 5529). Moderate.

 EATING OUT: The coastal resort cities are blessed with some of the finest seafood in the world. Most notable is the Caribbean lobster (a form of crayfish) and a host of other "fruits of the sea," including squid, crab, oysters, mussels, scallops, jumbo shrimp, red snapper, and even barracuda, which is specially prepared with local herbs. *Viudo de pescado* (a spicy, baked fish stew), *ceviche de camarones* (shrimp marinated in lemon juice, peppers, and onions and served cold), and *escambeche* (pickled seafood) are specialties; soups are super; ditto *canasta de coco* (coconut custard in a meringue basket). Dinner for two is about $60 at the most expensive places, between $18 and $30 at moderate establishments, and $15 or less at inexpensive restaurants. Prices do not include wine, drinks, or tips.

CARTAGENA

Bodegon de la Candelaria – Elegantly ensconced in a restored colonial mansion in the old city; one of the country's finest. Calle de las Damas (phone: 4-7251). Expensive.

Capilla del Mar – Distinct from the hotel, a fine seafood restaurant with a French accent that specializes in lobster and shrimp dishes; also boasts a fine wine cellar. Carrera 5 No. 8-59, Bocagrande (phone: 4-1001). Expensive to moderate.

Chef Julian – Very good seafood, Spanish style; Sr. Gonzalez's *triumph de cocina* involves a trio of lobster halves done three different ways (thermidor, American, grilled); try to save room for the coconut pie. Carrera 2 No. 9-161, Bocagrande (phone: 4-8220). Moderate.

Club de Pesca – Within the Fortress de San Sebastian del Pastelillo, it offers an incomparable site for dining under the stars near the ramparts of the old fort, with the lights of Cartagena shimmering on the bay. Chef Marcel, a Belgian who specializes in French cooking, is especially proud of his coquilles St.-Jacques and lobster Américaine. Fortress del Pastelillo (phone: 4-2961). Moderate.

Nautilus – Small, modern seafood spot within the old city that serves only the freshest of fish (when the catch of the day is gone, they close) done in *tipico* Cartagena style — broiled, fried, or in an herbed casserole. Calle San Pedro Martir (phone: 4-4204). Inexpensive.

SANTA MARTA

La Carabelle – Probably the best in the city, it serves both French and other European dishes as well as steaks from nearby cattle ranches and has a fine wine cellar. In the *Irotama* hotel, km 14, Carretera Santa Marta/Barranquilla (phone: 4059). Moderate.

El Galeon – Good Continental seafood specialties and beachside barbecues. In the *Puerto Galeon* hotel, Carretera Santa Marta/Barranquilla (phone: 5084). Moderate.

Pan American – A delightful stop if you're downtown, with light meals and a very informal atmosphere. Calle 18, 16-10 (phone: 2900). Inexpensive.

SAN ANDRÉS

La Fonda Antioquena – This is the place for Colombian and local specialties like *viudo de pescado* (fish stew with plaintains, yucca, in creole sauce), *lechón toli-*

mense (suckling pig), or *cabrito* (kid) with tamales and yucca. Av. Colombia, 1a-16 (phone: 6885). Moderate.

Miss Bess – Home-cooked meals, native fashion, in a very native atmosphere. The menu is mostly local specialties. La Loma (phone: 5747). Inexpensive.

El Oasis – Seafood specialties are the word here, and they're excellent. Try cazuela de mariscos en coco (seafood casserole in a coconut). The drinks, rum-based for the most part, will set you up nicely for dinner. Av. La Playa (phone: 6419). Inexpensive.

CUBA

For almost four decades, Cuba was the true glamour (and sin) spot of the Caribbean. From the 1920s through the early 1950s, it lured thousands of Americans every year — originally because they could drink in Havana during Prohibition. Later, after Repeal, they came just for the fun of it: for the sun and gorgeous beaches like Varadero, for the gambling casinos, and for the sexy nightlife (both participant and spectator).

Havana was wild and wonderful. Hemingway fell in love with it and bought a house on a hill outside town from which he would sally forth to drink at *Sloppy Joe's* (now dilapidated beyond recognition); stylish *Floridita,* self-proclaimed "Cradle of the Daiquiri"; or *La Bodeguita del Medio* — literally, "the little grocery store in the middle" — which he said made the world's best mojito, a rum mint julep still favored by visitors and the weather-beaten regulars in its back rooms.

In recent years, Cuban travel for US citizens has been a sometime thing at best. As we go to press, Cuban visits are sanctioned only for government officials on business, newspeople on assignment, people with close family in Cuba, returning Cuban residents, people specifically licensed by the US Treasury's Office of Foreign Assets Control, scholars traveling to engage in professional research (the detailed guidelines for scholars are available by calling the Office of Foreign Assets Control at 202 376-0410), and people whose trips are being paid for by persons who are not "subject to US jurisdiction." For all the above, independent and package travel can be set up through any of two tour operators and two charter companies still authorized to arrange Cuban charter flights. No other Americans are allowed to visit.

Still, lots of would-be visitors want to know what Cuba is really like. First of all, it is enormous — the Caribbean's largest island, 44,218 square miles huge, roughly 12.6 times the size of Puerto Rico and 266 times larger than the island of Barbados. In spite of efforts to diversify and bring industry into the picture, it remains basically an agricultural country, with sugar still far and away the major cash crop; tobacco, its next most famous; and citrus, pineapple, and coffee on the increase. And it is fiercely Communist, a fact that's momentarily forgettable while cruising along a country road, until a red and blue Party poster (there are no other kinds) flashes by, or you round a corner in Havana to be confronted by a portrait of Che Guevara covering most of one side of a government building.

Since Columbus discovered it in 1492, Cuba has survived a lot of history, none of it particularly peaceful. It was in 1511 that Diego de Velásquez sailed across from Hispaniola to establish the first Spanish settlement, Baracoa, at the far eastern end of the island. While Santiago de Cuba (1514, the first capital of the island) and Havana (1515) were still in their founding stages,

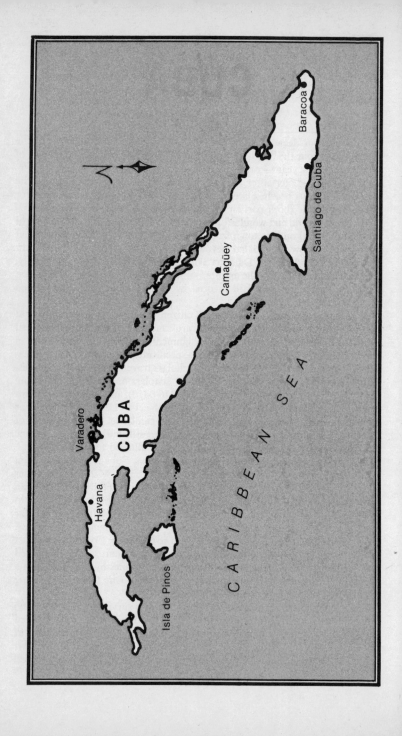

the island was already serving as a base for further Spanish explorations and as an assembly point for treasure fleets heading back to the mother country. This last made Cuba a prime target for French and British privateers in search of plunder and profit. Yet the island suffered only one successful invasion: when the British (under George Pocock and the Earl of Albemarle) came ashore east of Havana and took the capital by surprise in 1762. Except for that brief occupation, Cuba continued Spanish even through the early nineteenth century, when much of the rest of Spain's overseas empire broke away.

But Cuba was restless. Black Africans imported to replace the Arawak labor force (decimated by the Spanish early on) staged insurrections to protest the miserable conditions under which they lived and worked (Cuban slavery was not abolished until 1880). As a result, the Spanish colonies, according to Caribbean historian Eric Williams, "were kept in a state of permanent revolution, however sporadic, unorganized, and ill-timed may have been the revolts of the slaves." Revolting or not, the US South found Cuban slavery attractive and almost succeeded in compelling the US government to make Spain an offer it couldn't refuse in order to annex the island; thanks largely to the ineptness of the American ambassador, the plan was aborted. Spain continued to grant, then withdraw, rights and favors in order to keep the peace.

In 1868, Cubans fought their first war of independence, which lasted 10 years but was, in the end, unsuccessful. It was not till 1898, under the leadership of the revered poet-patriot José Martí, whose statue is the centerpiece of the Plaza de la Revolución, that the Cubans rose again. This time, thanks to the backing of the US (which declared the somewhat questionable Spanish-American War when its battleship *Maine* blew up in Havana harbor), the island — with neighboring Puerto Rico — was relinquished by Spain, only to find itself under US "protection" (Puerto Rico was annexed) and occupied pro tem. The next few years saw major American investment in Cuban plantations, factories, and railroads. The US military left in 1902, but returned in 1906 to protect its absentee nationals' interests during a revolt led by José Miguel Gómez, and again "to guarantee order in the Negro insurrection of 1912."

A decisive phase of modern Cuban history began with World War I. The island's sugar-based economy prospered while the fighting lasted and foundered when Europe recovered enough to resume sugar beet cultivation. The Depression and a lowered US sugar import quota made things worse. In the chaotic period that followed, national and local elections were rigged and there was an abundance of rebellions and bloodshed.

Franklin Roosevelt tried to bolster US-Cuban relations by setting aside the Platt Amendment (which had declared the US right to intervene in Cuban affairs), naming the distinguished Sumner Welles as his ambassador, and revising quota and tariffs in Cuba's favor. But problems caused by unemployment, lack of economic diversification, poor land use, absentee ownership, and corruption kept growing. And in 1952, before scheduled elections, the powerful (and corrupt) Fulgencio Batista seized power in a military coup. In 1953, a liberal uprising failed, and its leader, Fidel Castro, fled the country. In 1956, however, he returned, established a guerrilla base in the Sierra Maestra of Oriente Province, and began his ultimately successful revolution.

In 1958, the US withdrew its military support of the Batista government, and when Batista fled on January 1, 1959, Castro took over.

Even in the US, Fidel was something of a romantic hero until his expropriation of large American land holdings, industrial installations, and banks. When protests failed, Dwight Eisenhower canceled the US sugar quota in 1960. Then, in January of 1961, as Cuba's Communist orientation and Soviet ties became increasingly apparent and abrasive, the US broke off all diplomatic relations. The abortive Bay of Pigs invasion and the missile crisis — in which the Russians shared — came and went, leaving Cuban-American relations in an uneasy, strained state for 15 years. It was not until 1977 that what might be interpreted as an inclination toward rapprochement on both sides resulted in official permission for US citizens to travel to Cuba again. Even then, although Canadians could explore freely and independently, visitors from the near North American mainland were required to move in closely supervised groups. With time, regulations eased to the point where some individual travel was allowed. But in May 1982, the Reagan administration, angered by Cuban involvement in Angola and elsewhere in the Caribbean basin, slammed the door once more.

As a savvy friend commented, "No one I know expects the current administration to revoke these restrictions of its own accord." What's more, court challenges to the government's travel ban have been denied by the Supreme Court; the ban stands.

Those few who still visit find reminders of all Cuba's ages in Havana: sturdy sixteenth-century forts, graceful baroque churches and colonial palaces; Hemingway's house, kept just as he left it; *Floridita* still blending beautiful daiquiris and serving elegant meals; the Tropicana girls still out there kicking (if anything, there seem to be more of them); and — in contrast — the sobering Museum of the Revolution, with its relics of heroes and hardships, housed in the marble halls of what was once the Presidential Palace.

For tourism's sake, a number of big hotels have been restored to a semblance of their former luxury. The results so far are mixed. The *Havana Libre*'s new carpet and fabrics (from Canada) are good-looking and top quality, but its Hiltonesque two-story lobby seems to be missing some strategic piece of furniture, or a decorator, or both. The lobby of the *Havana Riviera,* the last hotel built in the pre-Castro era, bears an eerie resemblance to Miami Beach or Las Vegas, circa 1959. The same is true of Varadero's *International.* Newer resorts, on the other hand, with their similar, mass-produced modular furniture, remind you of each other even when their exterior design is radically different. Hotels are clean and reasonably comfortable, though maintenance (repair of towel bars, air conditioners, listing pedalboats) isn't a strong point. Food isn't sensational, but it's plentiful.

Resort staffs — particularly the maids and dining room people — are pleasant and helpful. As a matter of fact, Cuban people everywhere — but especially in Havana — are astonishingly warm and outgoing. Ask directions in wigwag English, and they'll walk you there. Or they'll take you there on the *guagua* (pronounced *wah-wah,* it means bus) and — if you are not fast with your five-centavo piece — may even pay your fare. Or sometimes they will even hail a friend in a passing car and insist that he drive you where you're going. Cuban cars are something else. You do see an occasional Brazilian-made VW, and there's been a recent infusion of Soviet Ladas (Fiats), but most automobiles are pre-1959 American numbers straight out of *Happy Days*, surviving on handmade spare parts and tender loving care — plus bailing wire, plasterboard, poster paint, and flour-sack upholstery (whatever works). Also out there running: a remarkable number of old-fashioned motorcycles with sidecars, most carrying two riders — both on the bike.

For people who seem to have nothing material of their own, Cubans are perceptibly happy and cheerful — perhaps because, as a Cubatur interpreter explained, "even if we don't achieve the goals that are set, even a little forward is progress. Right now, everything is for education of the children." And it's true there are a great number of day care centers, schools, and agricultural work-and-school projects designed to teach and develop the young. Guides point out historic spots sacred to the Revolution and worker-built housing projects, and they explain the relationship of the compañero (comrade) to his government (including the somewhat spooky-sounding functions of the Committees for the Defense of the Revolution), but considering that they are addressing a captive audience, they are remarkably unpushy about the party line.

Via wholesalers who've established working relationships with Cubatur, Canadian and authorized US travelers can reserve plane and hotel space, arrange tourist cards and/or visas when the required minimum dollars' worth of prepaid land arrangements are made. However, individual sightseeing cannot be booked ahead, but must be set up through Cubatur on location. So — especially for first-timers — an all-inclusive package covering meals, hotels, sightseeing, and special visits (to schools, housing developments, etc.) may be smarter in terms of both time and money.

In recent years, Florida has been the prime gateway for trips arranged by such Cuba-savvy US wholesalers as Marazul Tours, 250 W 57th St., New York, NY 10107 (in the forefront when it comes to handling packaged trips for authorized visitors and independent travel arrangements; phone: 212 582-9570; 800 223-5334), and Anniversary Tours, 250 W 57th St., New York, NY 10107 (phone: 212 245-7501). In Canada, Unitours, 3080 Yonge St., Toronto, Ont. M4N 3N1 (phone: 416 484-8000), is the best-known operator of Cuban trips. Prices remain reasonable: a week for about $620 up in winter, $440 up in summer, including all meals, transfers, service charges, and air fare from Miami; about $700 up in winter, $640 up in summer from Toronto. As the cliché goes, it's a nice place to visit . . .

CUBA AT-A-GLANCE

FROM THE AIR: Cuba is the Caribbean's largest island, with a landmass of 44,218 square miles and a population of 9.7 million. From its western tip (at about 85°W longitude) to easternmost Maisí Point (which almost touches 74° W longitude), it measures about 759 miles — slightly less than the distance from New York to Chicago. At its widest point, its Atlantic (northern) coast is about 115 miles from its Caribbean (southern) shore. Long and narrow, with a featherlike east-to-west curve, Cuba lies just south of the Tropic of Cancer and is surrounded by cays and islands, the largest of which is the Isle of Pines, renamed the Isle of Youth, in the Gulf of Batabanó formed by the bend of Cuba's western end.

Nearest neighbors are Jamaica (about 150 miles due south of the east Cuban province of Granma); the Bahamas, scattered across the Atlantic north of the main island's eastern end; and Florida, due north of its western midsection. The distance from Key West, the most southerly of Florida's Keys, to Varadero Beach is about 90 miles and to Havana, Cuba's capital (pop. 1.8 million), about 125.

Basically, Cuba is low, rolling, agricultural land; its chief crops are sugar, citrus, and the tobacco from which the famous cigars are made. But there are three mountain ranges: the western Organos (in Pinar del Río) are composed of porous limestone, honeycombed with caverns (in the most extensive of these, Santo Tomás, there are 18 mapped miles of caves), faced with jagged cliffs, and creased by valleys; the central Escambray hills, along the south coast around Trinidad and Sancti Spíritus, are characterized by deep valleys, waterfalls, and lakes; and the famous eastern Sierra Maestra range, including Cuba's highest peak, Pico Turquino (6,560 feet), parallels the southern coast of what was once Oriente Province. Since the redivision of the country into 14 provinces (originally there were only 6), these historic mountains lie mostly in Granma Province (named for the boat in which Fidel, Che, et al., returned to Cuba from Mexico in 1956); Oriente is the land surrounding Santiago de Cuba, the country's second city (pop. 300,000+); and Guantánamo is the far eastern section, the site of the controversial US naval base. Also characteristic are the narrow-mouthed — and therefore uniquely protective — "pouch" bays with which the island's roughly 2,560 miles of shoreline are indented; and the 137 beautiful white sand beaches that have a special appeal for visitors.

SPECIAL PLACES: Havana – Cuba's once-glamorous capital seems still to be in a state of revolutionary flux. For most North American tourists, a visit usually begins with a ride along the Malecón, the road that follows the sea wall along the ocean and harbor channel shore between the Vedado section's tourist hotels and the old colonial heart of the city. From Vedado to the channel entrance, the roadway is lined with 18th- and 19th-century houses, many of which are now in the process of restoration and have just been given their first new coats of pastel paint in decades. The Malecón makes a right-angle turn at the channel entrance guarded by the Castillo de la Punta, a 16th-century fortification now used by the Cuban navy. Facing it on the land side is a statue of Máximo Gómez, who led the Cubans to victory and independence in 1898. On the opposite shore stands Cuba's most famous castle — El Morro — built by the Spanish between 1587 and 1597; for years a prison, it is now being put to more cheerful use as a restaurant, with a nightclub addition that may be open by the time you read this. The second, larger fortification, also on the opposite shore, is the Fortaleza de la Cabaña, constructed between 1763 and 1774 and currently serving as an army barracks. To the right, at the point where the channel starts to widen, a fourth massive stone structure is the Castillo de la Fuerza (built 1538–1544), the oldest building in Cuba and the New World's second oldest fort; legend says that Hernando de Soto departed from here to explore North America and ultimately to discover the Mississippi. The golden statue of the native maiden called La Geraldilla on its weather vane (and also reproduced on Cuban swizzle sticks) is a replica of the original, which was stolen by the British in 1762; she is the city's symbol.

At this point, whether you're traveling with a tour busload or cabbing it with your own group, you should leave your wheels and begin exploring on foot. Just around the fortress and to the right is the Plaza de Armas (technically the Plaza Carlos Manuel de Céspedes, named for the independence fighter whose statue stands in its center); traditionally, this is the place where Havana, and therefore Cuba, was born. The Doric temple at the northeast corner of the square is El Templete (c. 1828); a small monument in front marks the spot where the city's first mass was said in 1519. The impressive colonial building (1780) across the plaza was once the Palace of the Captains General; now it's the Museum of the City of Havana, with a handsomely planted patio and two-section (1868–98 and 1898–1920) collection of antiques and artifacts (first-floor favorite: an ancient and splendid Cadillac, once owned by former Governor Tomás). This museum, like most others in the capital (unless otherwise noted), is open on Tuesdays through Saturdays, 2:30 till 10 PM, with an hour off for dinner between 6 and 7 PM; on Sundays it is open from 9 AM till noon (unlike others, which are open from 3 to 7 PM). Admission to all museums is free, and all are closed on Mondays.

Leaving the city museum, turn left and then left again on Calle O'Reilly; walk two short blocks, and turn right on Calle San Ignacio, which leads into the Plaza de la Cathedral. Directly across the square stands the 1704 cathedral, dedicated to both the Virgin of the Immaculate Conception and San Cristóbal; it is said to shelter some Columbian bones, but nobody quite knows whose (open weekdays, 9 to 11:30 AM; Saturday, 3:30 to 5:30 PM). Other buildings, reading clockwise around the plaza, include a gallery of graphic art (east); the Museum of Decorative Arts (south; small, intriguing collections of stained glass, china, furniture, carriage lanterns, and more); and *El Patio* restaurant and café (west) where you can pause for coffee, unless you decide to turn left at the square's northwest corner and stroll a few doors down for a mojito (a combination of rum, soda water, a dash of lemon juice, sugar, bruised mint leaves, and ice — a Cuban julep) at *La Bodeguita del Medio,* where Hemingway used to drink his.

Picking up again, follow on down Calle Empedrado to Avenida de Bélgica. Here you have a choice: a left and a quick right will take you to the lush Parque Central, across which you'll find the National Theater and the Capitol. The latter is notable for the 24-karat diamond embedded in the floor beneath its rotunda (it's ground zero for all Cuban distance measurements) and for the Museum of Natural Science that it houses. If you're pressed for time, however, skip these and turn right toward the Palacio de Bellas Artes (the National Museum) and the Presidential Palace, the enormous baroque monument which is now, somewhat incongruously, the Museo de la Revolución. From top to bottom, its displays trace the history of the revolutionary movement from Martí and his earliest struggles for independence to Castro and his campañeros of the Sierra Maestra. Texts are all in Spanish with no English translations, but there are also pictures, maps, and mementos that somehow make the walk enlightening even if you don't know the language. On a small square out back, the vehicles of the Revolution — including the bullet-riddled Fast Delivery truck used to attack the palace, and the yacht *Granma,* under glass — are on exhibition. Then, if your feet will still carry you, you can do the Bellas Artes, with its pleasant (but unremarkable) collections of paintings (many copies), sculpture, etc.

Other Havana sites generally covered by bus on Cubatur itineraries include:

Plaza de la Revolución, with its towering monument, marble Martí statue, and grandstands, surrounded by the buildings of the central government (only one, the Communist Party headquarters where Castro has offices, is off-limits to visitors) and watched over by enormous mural portraits of Communist heroes, including Marx, Lenin, and Che. It is here that Fidel speaks on national holidays.

The University of Havana, a quick sight to drive by but near enough to the *Havana Libre* and *Capri* to stroll through if you like.

The Napoleonic Museum, on Calle Ronda a block east of the university — a small, once-private collection of paintings, furniture, and relics (Tuesdays through Saturdays, noon to 2 PM; Sundays, 9 AM to 1 PM).

Colón Cemetery, a spookily impressive city of the dead; another place to drive by.

Lenin Park, a huge outdoor recreation area with sports and picnic facilities, an aquarium, a radio stadium, an al fresco movie theater, a miniature railroad, and the country's top restaurant, *Las Ruinas.*

Alamar, on the north shore between Havana and Santa María del Mar, a vast and growing apartment complex built by and for workers. Cubatur will arrange visits if groups are interested.

Optional day trips beyond the Havana area include:

Varadero Beach – A 2½-hour bus ride (each way), with stops at spectacular Bellamar's Cave en route; buffet lunch, sun, and swim on the famous sands.

Hanabanilla and Trinidad – The mountain resort, plus the charming 16th-century city the government is in the process of restoring. The resort hotel is so-so, and the bus ride is long. Antiquarians might have a better time on a trip to Trinidad only.

Guamá and Zapata National Park – Lunch at a unique "Indian village" resort (see *Checking In*), reached by a launch ride through swamp canals and across Treasure Lake. With stops at a crocodile-breeding center (full of bugs) and Girón (the Bay of Pigs), which — it turns out — doesn't look very different from other Cuban beaches.

Isle of Youth – Formerly the Isle of Pines, it was renamed in honor of the 11,000 students working to transform it into a citrus-growing center; its *Colony Hotel* still offers hunting, fishing, poolside relaxing, and nightlife. Overnight: about $45 per person with all meals.

■**EXTRA SPECIAL:** Hemingway's house, *Finca la Vigía* (literally, "Lookout Farm"), is in the suburb of San Francisco de Paula and has been preserved *exactly* as he left it — dusty rum bottles, bullfight posters, unopened *Fishing Gazettes,* and all. Most poignant is a needlepoint-covered footrest lettered "Poor Old Papa." (Daily except Sundays, 9 AM and 1 to 6 PM; Sundays, 9 AM till noon.)

SOURCES AND RESOURCES

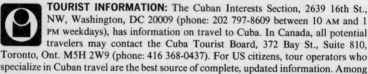

TOURIST INFORMATION: The Cuban Interests Section, 2639 16th St., NW, Washington, DC 20009 (phone: 202 797-8609 between 10 AM and 1 PM weekdays), has information on travel to Cuba. In Canada, all potential travelers may contact the Cuba Tourist Board, 372 Bay St., Suite 810, Toronto, Ont. M5H 2W9 (phone: 416 368-0437). For US citizens, tour operators who specialize in Cuban travel are the best source of complete, updated information. Among the best: Marazul Tours, 250 W 57th St., New York, NY 10107 (phone: 212 582-9570; 800 223-5334); Anniversary Tours, 250 W 57th St., New York, NY 10107 (phone: 212 245-7501); Unitours Canada, 3080 Yonge St., Toronto, Ont. M4N 3N1 (phone: 416 484-8000).

Cubatur, the official Cuban government tourist agency, handles all travel by visitors to Cuba and is the source of literature and information on sightseeing, accommodations, special events, etc. Its main office in Havana is Calle 23, #156, Vedado (phone: 32-4709). There will also be a Cubatur desk at your hotel that can provide travel advice, book optional sightseeing, and, in Havana, make restaurant reservations and arrange theater tickets (mostly for ballet and concerts; about $4 to $6 per seat).

Inside Cuba Today, by photojournalist Fred Ward (Crown, out of print; try your public library), covers life, organizations, government, the economy, agriculture, tourism, the arts, and more, in a balanced way that helps put the things you'll see on your trip in perspective. *The Complete Travel Guide to Cuba* by Paula DiPerna (St. Martin's; about $5) is also a source of practical information.

Local Coverage – Travel literature in Cuba is limited, but what there is is quite helpful: *La Habana,* Cubatur's guide to Havana, is available free in an English-language version; the map in back — though faint and difficult to read — may still be the only one available at the time of your visit; ergo, treasure it, and carry it (plus a magnifying glass) when you tour the city. *Cuba Sunshine News,* also free at hotels, contains a good deal of interesting — though rather biased — background on Cuban arts, culture, flora, fauna, and sites worth seeing, plus bare-bones specifics on hotels, restaurants, nightlife.

Granma, named for the boat that brought Fidel and his comrades to Cuba before the Revolution, is the official Communist Party paper, published daily in Spanish and weekly in English, that covers world news as the Cubans see it; it costs 5 centavos.

 ENTRY REQUIREMENTS: Both US and Canadian citizens must have valid passports and visas or tourist cards (depending on nationality, status, and reason for the trip), which tour operators arrange (the $25 fee is sometimes included in the tour package price). Visas or tourist cards are issued on arrival in Cuba. Ask your travel agent.

 CLIMATE AND CLOTHES: Quite warm in the summer months, with temperatures averaging 80°F (27°C) from May to September; the rest of the year is a bit more temperate, with an average of about 72°F (23°C). Dress is very casual. Women wear pants everywhere (shorts and bathing suits are for beaches only); men wear sport shirts, slacks, seldom jackets. In Havana, though it's not required, some tourists like to change for cocktails, dinner, nightclubs; some of the tonier cabarets (including the one at the *Habana Libre* — née Hilton) do require men to wear long-sleeved shirts or jackets. For your own convenience, concentrate on things you can wash and drip-dry yourself; laundries are scarce. Virtually none of the things you'd buy at a US drugstore are available in Cuba. So be sure to pack sun lotion, shampoo and rinse, shaving gear, cosmetics, insect repellent, sunglasses, soap (the kind supplied by the Cuban hotels doesn't lather much), cold water laundry liquid. Also worth toting: a travel umbrella, a bottle of your favorite booze if you like to imbibe (very expensive in Cuba), US cigarettes, a beach towel (hotels don't have them), a face cloth, and a magnifying glass for map reading.

 MONEY: The Cuban monetary unit is the peso, currently valued at about $1.25 US. Although the use of credit cards by American citizens is forbidden by the US government, not only are Barclays, Thomas Cook, and American Express traveler's checks now readily accepted as payment at hotels, restaurants, and tourist shops, but the US dollar itself has gained wide acceptance — in Havana and, increasingly, throughout the country as well. In most cases, it is to your advantage to pay in US dollars rather than pesos; however, since you will need pesos for small purchases, taxis, etc., it's a good idea to do some exchanging at the airport on arrival. The rate is the same at both airport and hotels, and there is no service charge. But some hotels limit currency exchange to certain hours (often 9 AM to 5 PM, with or without time out for lunch); so if you're late landing, you could get caught if you wait till you get to town. Do check your hotel cashier's schedule when you arrive.

The government maintains tight control over currency, and you are issued an exchange voucher each time you change dollars for pesos. Each voucher has spaces on the back where major purchases — mostly for food, drinks, or optional excursions — will be noted as you make them during your stay; at the end of the trip, when you turn back your remaining pesos for dollars, you are limited to the balance accounted for by your vouchers; so carry them with you at all times. As a bonus, with the voucher, you are also entitled to a 40% to 60% discount on wine and liquor at hotel and restaurant bars.

Last note on currency: Whatever you do, don't be tempted to exchange any funds with a freelance (read: black market) money changer. It's the fastest way to end up in a revolutionary jail.

 LANGUAGE: Spanish. English is studied as a second language in Cuba, and you should have little difficulty communicating in Havana hotels and restaurants and in the resort centers outside the capital. Museum guards, however, tend to speak only Spanish. So, although most Cubatur guides are fluent in English (many received part of their education in the US), a Spanish-English phrase book can be a great help.

 TIME: In fall, winter, and spring, the hour is the same in Cuba as in US East Coast cities. Cuban clocks change over to Daylight Saving Time in summer, but not always at the same time the US does; so for a week or two in spring and fall there may be a one-hour difference.

 CURRENT: At 110 volts, 60 cycles, the same as in the US, so no converters are needed.

 GETTING THERE: Three US companies — Marazul Tours, ABC charters, and Southern Tours — operate charter flights for authorized ("licensed") travelers, departing several times a week from Miami. Most readily available packages are "back-to-back" (i.e., the plane that carries one tour group down brings the previous group back), which are, therefore, generally one week (8 days/7 nights) long. Canadian citizens can fly Air Canada direct to Havana's José Martí International Airport from Toronto or Montréal; or Cubana Aviacion, from Montréal.

 CALCULATING COSTS: Figure about $86 up a day per person double occupancy in winter, about $75 up from mid-April to mid-December for a package tour that includes everything: charter air fare, rooms, ground transportation, meals, sightseeing, English-speaking guides, some evening features. Individual Cuban excursions, which must be booked through Cubatur on location, aren't expensive, but would mean additional expenditures. Rates at the most popular tourist hotels in Havana (the *Havana Libre,* the *Riviera,* the *Capri*) run from about $60 to $70 a day double EP (without meals); meals will cost at least $20 a day per person. When you add air fare, sightseeing, and other expenses, it's quite likely you'll discover you're financially better off by opting for a package.

GETTING AROUND: On a group tour, basic point-to-point travel, transfers, and Havana sightseeing are handled in modern, air-conditioned tour buses with refreshment bars in back. Taxis are readily available at Havana hotels and downtown in the city, though they don't do much cruising. Rates are reasonable: from the *Havana Libre* to the colonial part of town costs from 1 peso to 1 peso and 50 centavos; the trip from the beach resort of Santa María to Havana runs about $8 per cabload. If you can find a driver who speaks English, you can hire him for informal touring for about $8 per hour; but you ought to have a clear idea of where you'd like him to take you before you start out. There's no tipping.

Public buses, called *guaguas* (pronounced *wah-wahs*), are very cheap (5 centavos exact fare per ride) and cover most Havana points, but at rush hours they can be crowded and confusing. There are also express buses (10 centavos) that make limited stops along regular routes. Give yourself a little time to get oriented before you try them; ask for specific route information at the Cubatur desk.

Rental cars, without the formerly obligatory driver, are now available through hotel tourist desks in both Havana and Varadero. No promises on the state of maintenance, but including 100 km (60 miles) worth of gas, jeeps go for about $25 a day plus 15¢ per extra km; VWs for about $30 plus 20¢ per km. With driver, it's about $90 for up to 12 hours; about $145 per full day. But Cubatur desks offer a variety of optional sightseeing excursions ranging in price from about $5 per person for a four-hour escorted city tour to $16 per person for a night at the *Tropicana* to $20 per person for a full day's trip to Guamá and the Bay of Pigs with lunch included. Offerings vary, but one or two excursions are built into most package itineraries.

SHOPPING: There really isn't much. Rum, cigars, "Cuba Sí" T-shirts, and posters are about it. And all can be bought for US dollars at duty-free "boutiques" in tourist hotels (contrary to rumors you'll hear, there's not much difference between them). Men's guayabera shirts, sometimes called plantation shirts, with tucked fronts and long or short sleeves, can be good-looking and cool, but they're not inexpensive at about $10 to $20 each. In the handicraft department, there are some presentable straw totes and handbags (at about $6.50 to $10 US); carvings, dolls, and jewelry aren't awfully well done. Elsewhere, galleries around Cathedral Square do display some interesting paintings and graphics; and on Saturday nights from 5 to 10, the whole plaza turns into a market, selling crafts, books, records, and assorted souvenirs to the tune of spontaneous music, dance, and theatrical performances that make it all fun even if you don't buy.

CUSTOMS NOTE: US customs regulations limit returning citizens to 100 cigars per person (Cuba is currently the only country from which authorized Americans are legally permitted to bring in Cuban cigars), and one liter of rum may be brought in duty free. Pale Carta Blanca at about $3 US is most popular; dark *añejo* is aged like fine brandy and more expensive (about $7.75 US). Since the duty runs over $3 US per quart, it doesn't make sense to bring in more than one bottle. Now that José Martí's reconstruction is completed, airport duty-free shops offer good prices on rum and cigars, and you can safely wait till departure time to buy liquor and tobacco; however, recently the tourist shop at the *Havana Libre* has stocked the best rum buys. Remember, only rum with the Cuban government stamp on top can be legally exported.

TIPPING: A recent edict lifts the traditional Socialist ban on tipping in Havana and Veradero, but chances are the effect will be limited. For starts, give waiters and waitresses 10 to 15%; and leave a small tip for a maid or taxi driver who has been extra pleasant or helpful. And check with your travel agent for updated guidelines.

SPECIAL EVENTS: *Carnival time*, with dancing, parades, and lots of street partying, is celebrated on three weekends in July, climaxing on or near the big July 26 observance. Otherwise, with all religious holidays — including Christmas — deleted, pickings are pretty slim. Special days include: *New Year's* (January 1); *Labor Day* (May 1); *Moncada Anniversary* or *National Rebellion Day* (July 26, commemorating the first attack of the Revolution); and *Granma Anniversary* (December 2, celebrating Fidel's landing on Cuban soil and the founding of the National Assembly). On any or all of the above, the Maximum Leader may appear to speak in the Plaza de la Revolución.

SPORTS: Biking – On two-wheelers (about 65¢ per hour) or tandems (about $1.30 per hour), it's available at both seaside and mountain resorts.

Boating – Rowboats and canoes rent for about $1.30 an hour; so do pedalboats (called bicicletas nauticas). A half-hour's sailing with a guide is about $4; small sailboats rent for about $4 to $6.50 per hour. Motorboat rides (in a "launcha sovietica con chofer") cost about $4 per person for a half hour.

Golf – Can be played at Varadero on the 9-hole course that once belonged to the du Ponts and which the Cubans say will eventually be expanded to an 18-hole layout. Course conditions are poor to fair; greens fees run about $4 per person.

Horseback Riding – One of the star attractions at Havana's Lenin Park, where there's a Horsemanship School and a rodeo stadium. By the time you get there, it may be possible for visitors to arrange to ride. Check with the Cubatur desk at your hotel.

Snorkeling and Scuba – Trips are available through sports offices at the larger hotels. Rates run about $2.60 for a half-day's use of snorkel gear; about $8 for a 15-minute scuba lesson; about $20 for a half hour to an hour's dive with guide and all equipment included. At Santa María, a 3-hour Seafari snorkeling trip costs about $9 per person. Best areas are the Isle of Pines and the reefs off the city of Trinidad.

Spectator Sports – Cubans are embarrassingly (to some elements of the revolutionary government) fond of baseball (Fidel's favorite: the New York Yankees) and now hand-make their own high-quality bats, balls, and gloves. Basketball is coming up fast as a second favorite sport. (The first postrevolutionary Cuba-US sports competition was between home teams and a visiting team from South Dakota.) Other popular spectator sports include boxing, volleyball, water polo, track and field, and wrestling. All athletic events are free, and tourists are invited. Check with the Cubatur desk for schedules.

Sport Fishing – A Cuban passion. At lake and beach resorts, light tackle (a rod and spinning reel with bait) rents for about $3.25 a half day, about $5.20 for a full day. Treasure Lake, near the Indian village resort of Guamá, is one of the world's best bass fishing grounds. At Varadero, there's also party-boat deep-sea fishing for about $12 per person a day. Charter boats for up to six people rent for about $100 to $150 a day, including tackle and bait when available; check with the person in charge of water sports at your Varadero hotel. The annual Hemingway International Bill (Sword) Fish Tournament takes place every summer, often at Cojimár, the small seaside town that was the setting for *The Old Man and the Sea.*

Swimming and Sunning – Cuba's extraordinary white beaches and clear Caribbean waters are assets that haven't changed with the Revolution. Most tour programs include at least one or two free beach days. Both the northern and southern shorelines are dotted with small seaside resorts with simple, family-style accommodations; Guanabo, Jibacoa, Arroyo Bermejo, Bibijagua, Ancón, Santa Lucia, Guardalabarca, Siboney, Juragua, Caletón, and Mar Verde are among the best of these. Most spectacular and accessible to North American visitors are two north shore resorts: Santa María del Mar, about 20 minutes east of Havana, and famous Varadero Beach, a long skinny peninsula pointing into the sea about two hours' drive east of the capital. Beaches at both are wide, with almost unbelievably clean white sand on land and for many yards out to sea. Varadero, destination for week-long tours, seems to go on forever; many of its hotels and villa colonies date back to prerevolutionary days, but there are new ones building. On pine-lined Santa María, where a number of Havana-bound tour groups spend two or three days, there's a new government-built hotel, the *Marazul,* plus two villa colonies. At both resorts, hotels rent out boats and water sports gear, but you'll have to bring your own beach towel. And be *extremely* cautious about the sun; it can burn unprotected skin in minutes.

Tennis – Played in a *very* casual fashion. The *Nacional* in Havana does have a clay court in excellent condition. Elsewhere, courts are often concrete or black top. The sports center at the *Marazul* quotes a rate of about $1.30 per person per hour for use of a racket, ball, and net.

Water Skiing – Available at both Santa María and Varadero at about $8 US for a quarter-hour run.

NIGHTLIFE: The supershow attraction — built into many Havana packages and offered as an option on all others — is the spectacular outdoor *Tropicana* nightclub revue, a lavish, dancing, prancing relic of pre-Castro days that the government, for its own mysterious reasons, has opted to preserve. It out-Vegases Vegas with costumes that are new and incredibly elaborate (more than 150 cast members have seven changes each), and a spirit that's pure 1950s. The three-hour individual *Tropicana* package is about $20 or so per person, including transportation, two drinks, and dinner; or ask the Cubatur rep to make reservations, share a cab, and pay about $7 per person minimum (no cover). Of the Havana hotel cabaret shows, the *Riviera's Copa Room* is rated tops. There's music and a great view from the *Turquino Bar* at the top of the *Havana Libre.* In the neighborhood known as La Rampa around the *Havana Libre, Capri,* and *Nacional* hotels, a number of small boîtes offer nightly music and dancing. All have minimums, no cover charges, ask about $1 to $1.50 for beer or rum drinks; whiskey is wildly expensive.

Varadero's big night site is *The Pirate's Cave,* where music, dancing, and the show are all staged underground in what they say was once a buccaneer's hideout. A four-hour packaged evening (minimum and transportation included) is about $7 per person.

Some tour packages include nightly "happy hour" cocktail parties with hors d'oeuvres and unlimited rum drinks. And once during the trip there's a "Cuba Night," featuring a native buffet and a folkloric show with dancing and singing in ñañigo — the Afro-Cuban language.

BEST ON THE ISLAND

CHECKING IN: There's a lingering sense of the 1940s and 1950s and a strange kind of luxury about Havana hotels. PA systems waft strains of Helen O'Connell's "Green Eyes" and "Hernando's Hideaway" through elevators and lobbies. The *Riviera's* look is pure Golden Era Miami inside and out. The *Havana Libre's* rooms are large, with wall-to-wall windows and fresh carpeting, curtains, and upholstery (all handsome fabrics made in Canada); but the air conditioning has its asthmatic spells, and beds that used to be sofas by day are now perpetually made up with sheets and blankets. The *Riviera,* the *Havana Libre* (with its monogram modified from the old Hilton logo), the stately, gardened *Nacional,* and the *Capri* have all been thoroughly redone.

Outside the capital, hotels tend to be newer, with a motelish feeling about their modular plastic furniture and primary color decor. Rooms are generally small, simple, and clean (a paper strip across the toilet seat announces it has been treated for "sanitary protection" in English, Spanish, French, and Russian). Maids and dining room and desk personnel are 99% smiling and delighted both to help you and to try out their English. But nobody seems to have majored in maintenance, so the occasional loose towel bar or hookless curtain just hangs there, and the pedalboat that developed a leak yesterday is a little lower in the water today. They're not the Ritz, but if you can turn off your perfectionist streak, chances are you'll be perfectly comfortable.

Package participants won't be concerned with price, but it's worth noting that even the most luxurious city hotels fall within moderate limits. (A double at either the

Riviera or *Havana Libre* runs about $51 up a day for two; meals extra.) Rates outside the capital are inexpensive — about $35 up a day for two (meals extra) at a top resort hotel. Meals at the best hotels run about $23 per person a day. Though you may not be able to pick and choose, here's what you can expect:

HAVANA

Nacional – Havana's premier luxury hotel in the glamorous, naughty old days; it's been rescued from shabby distress by cellar-to-roof refurbishing. With a sense of real Cuban style newer places lack plus superb views of the harbor. Swimming pool, tennis court, restaurants, bars. Overlooking the malecón (phone: 7-8981). Moderate.

Riviera – Miami-esque high-rise with a still many-splendored lobby, big pool, good restaurants (including a mammoth "Swedish table" buffet — lunch or dinner — at about $10.50 per person); cabaret show reputedly the best in town. Has 400 redone medium-sized guestrooms all with spectacular views. Corner of the Paseo and malecón (phone: 30-5051). Moderate.

Havana Libre – Former Hilton with impressive two-story lobby that just misses being its handsome old self. (It looks as though they've loaned out several key pieces of furniture.) Lobby, mezzanine bar, and pool (on elevator floor 2) are popular meeting places. Ditto top-floor bar, restaurant. 568 big modern rooms with balconies, breeze that works when air conditioning doesn't. Corner Calles L and 23rd (phone: 30-5011). Moderate.

Capri – Smaller, also refurbished; rooftop swimming pool and bar with great views of city, ocean. Handy location, popular with business travelers. Has 220 large, pleasant rooms. George Raft suite in penthouse available at extra charge. Corner Calles N and 21st (phone: 32-0511). Moderate.

SANTA MARÍA DEL MAR

Marazul – Tropical indoor-outdoor design; cheerful, though mass-produced room decor. Small pool, water sports, glorious beach. Within easy reach (20 minutes by bus or taxi) from downtown Havana. Live, loud disco at night. Just across from the beach. Inexpensive.

Megano Villas – Contemporary and casual; choice of room arrangements include 2 or 4 people sharing or single occupancy; makes widely varying package rates possible. Water and land sports, open-air bar and restaurant, tourist shop, pool, night entertainment. 100 yards from beach. Inexpensive.

VARADERO BEACH

Internacional – A feeling of 1950s' elegance in lobby, bars, restaurants. Guestrooms clean, recently refurbished. Magnificent beach. On the beach toward east end of peninsula. Moderate.

Solimar – Newish neighbor of the *Internacional,* offering villa suites, beachside location, water sports, plus tennis and badminton. Moderate.

Kawama – Pleasant, Spanish-style hotel with variety of accommodations — best in two-story contemporary villa units. Casual air, good dining room. Tennis court. On the beach closer to town. Moderate to inexpensive.

MATANZAS PROVINCE

Guamá – Unique "Indian Village" resort on series of bridge-linked islands, a 20-minute launch ride from shore. Romantic thatch-hut construction, simple, comfortable rooms. Popular with Cuban honeymooners. Adjacent to Treasure Lake bass fishing, headquarters for fishing charters from US. Restaurant with music, casual nightlife on central island. Also outdoor Taino Indian museum. Destination of day tours which stop at crocodile farm near entrance (beware mosquitos). 30 miles north of Girón in Península de Zapata National Park. Inexpensive.

SANTA CLARA PROVINCE

Hanabanilla – Cool, casual mountain resort hotel on manmade lake. Overnight stop on some package tours, day-trip destination on others. Pool, sundeck, shop, boating, fishing. Picturesque countryside. Very simple, small rooms. Inexpensive.

 EATING OUT: US tourists don't do much independent restaurant hopping since most package tours include all meals. Tour food, mostly catered by hotels, is scarcely exciting but it's adequate: lots of chicken and fish; lots of ham and cheese (in sandwiches and for breakfast, yet); beautiful fresh papaya, melon, pineapple; but fresh vegetables and green salads — except for cucumbers and green tomatoes — are rare. Desserts are sweet (pastries, guava paste, and flan — caramel custard).

Restaurants, though they can be excellent, are often expensive, with dinners in Havana running $15 to $30 per person, including a drink and wine (Spanish, Portuguese, or Bulgarian). Cuisine is Continental or Cuban — with strong emphasis on seafood in either case (lobster and shrimp are only available in restaurants). Cubans occasionally rechristen basically Spanish dishes to suit their own sense of whimsy; beans and rice becomes moros y cristianos (translation: Moors and Christians); tortillas usually turn out to be omelettes. Thick chicken or black bean soup, roast suckling pig, chicken and rice (arroz con pollo), plantains (small green bananas, baked or fried), are other favorites. And Cuban ice cream is supersensational.

Cuban coffee is extra strong and good, but you can order weaker American-style brew, too. Cuban beer is served in three strengths from weak (about 3.2% strength) to *very* strong (Hatuey); which you get depends more on what the restaurant has than on what you order. Whiskey drinks are ridiculously expensive (a bottle of scotch was pegged at $250 on one restaurant menu!), but rum is good and plentiful. Favorite forms: daiquiris (always blender-whipped and served "frozen") and mojitos.

Because most Havana restaurants are some distance from tourist hotels, reservations are a good idea. Unless your Spanish is very good, you'll do better working through Cubatur or your hotel (desk or bell captain) than trying to phone yourself.

Coppelia, at Calles L and 23rd, catty-cornered from the *Havana Libre,* is the park that's really a huge outdoor ice cream parlor. Buy a ticket at the kiosk (75 centavos to 2 pesos — according to number of scoops, toppings selected), line up cafeteria-style and pick your flavors: mango, rum raisin, lemon, chocolate, and lots more — all drizzled with threads of sweet syrup. Special sundaes, splits, too. Sinful, delicious.

HAVANA

La Torre – In Vedado section, handy to tourist hotels, atop the FOCSA Building, Havana's tallest. Suave service, sophisticated atmosphere, spectacular views. First-rate steak, fish; baked Alaska for dessert. Calles M and 17th. Expensive.

Las Ruinas – Built into the ruins of an old sugar plantation house; graceful Victorian furniture, finest china, crystal, flowers. Billed as Havana's most elegant, with service to match. Continental menu complete with pâtés, tournedos, soufflés. Great style. In Lenin Park. Expensive.

Floridita – Big turn-of-the-century bar (polished wood, mirrors), which in capital letters, proclaims itself to be LA CUNA DEL DAIQUIRI — the "cradle of the daiquiri." (Hemingway thought they made the best in town.) In faded, but damask-lined, dining room, service is Old World elegant; food, delicious. Famous for lobster; shrimp and fish are excellent too. Corner Calles Obispo and Monserrate. Expensive.

El Patio – Squareside café (good for resting your feet, people-watching) and indoor restaurant with intimate family dining room atmosphere. Known for its Cuban dishes: good soups, chicken, fish. Cathedral Square. Expensive to moderate.

La Bodeguita del Medio – Tiny bar where Hemingway liked to have his mojitos (they're still *very* good), with rustic restaurant behind that serves fine roast suckling pig. After you've paid the check, you too can sign one of the walls. Off Cathedral Square. Moderate.

El Conejito – Small with Victorian English atmosphere, romantic Cuban music. Rabbit dishes are the specialty. Between *Capri* and *Havana Libre* hotels. Moderate.

VARADERO

Las Americas – The house the du Ponts built and staffed with 110 servants, now a stylish place for lunch or dinner. Continental, with Cuban seafood specialties. Ask for the house tour (cool bar below, incredible open-air ballroom on top). East end of beach beyond International hotel. Expensive.

Albacoro – Pretty terrace with tables, shell-trimmed blue and white decor. Known for its fresh fish and omelettes. Near the beach close to town. Moderate.

Castel Nuovo – With Italian ambiente, good pastas and pizzas as well as local fish and seafood. On the main road at the east edge of town. Moderate to inexpensive.

CURAÇAO

Since its earliest seismic origins as a volcanic isle — when it was nothing more than molten lava being cooled by sea water — Curaçao has followed its own, unpredictable plan of development. According to geologists, the isle was reimmersed several times, until its natural, protective coral reef finally rose permanently above the sea. The present exposed layers of lava and coral (which fringe the island) have been hewn and polished by trade winds to form an intricate filigree of caves and grottoes, interspersed with beaches of coral and volcanic sand, bleached by the Caribbean sun and sea, after being deposited here by the tides.

By the time Curaçao was discovered by European explorers (not by Columbus, incidentally, but by one of his lieutenants, Alonso de Ojeda) in 1499, it was already inhabited by the Caiquetios, a tribe closely related to the Arawaks of Venezuela and other Caribbean atolls. They were natural seafarers who probably landed on this island as a result of a voyage of discovery of their own, a journey motivated by a need to escape the fierce Carib Indians who dominated the mainland before written history. It was the Caiquetios who established the basic trade link, which still exists, with Venezuela, some 35 miles away, and the economic relationship that remains the mainstay of the island's economy today. The Caiquetios also gave the island its name, although there are several poetic tales that claim it is a corruption of the Portuguese word *coracão,* which means "heart."

The European colonizers and treasure hunters left the tiny island alone until 1527, when the Spanish returned to occupy Curaçao. They remained as a small settlement, virtually forgotten during the wars in Europe. As Spain's global power began to wane, Holland, already involved in trading with the New World (though prohibited by Spain, which claimed exclusive rights), began looking for ways to increase its commercial interests. In 1621, the Dutch West India Company was formed, both to promote trade and to encourage privateers to further hamper Spanish dominance.

Curaçao, with its fine, natural harbor, was ideally located for privateering purposes, and so (in 1634) an officer of the company, Van Walbeeck, claimed the island for the Dutch. They banished the Spanish governor, plus 400 assorted Spaniards and Indians, to Venezuela and began to use the island as the main Dutch base for trading with the rest of the Caribbean and South America.

By 1643, there were enough island inhabitants to warrant the appointment of an official governor, and the Dutch Crown dispatched young Peter Stuyvesant, 26, to the island. In an effort to increase Dutch holdings, Stuyvesant led an expedition to St. Maarten, then held by the Spanish, to inform the inhabitants that the island was a Dutch possession. In reply, the Spanish fired a shot which took off Peter's right leg. He later replaced it with a wooden one, laced

with silver, which gave rise to his nickname, "Old Silver Nails." The leg was buried in either St. Maarten or Curaçao, no one really knows for sure, and Stuyvesant was soon reassigned as governor of Nieuw Amsterdam (soon to be New York).

The islands flourished under Dutch rule and became one of the most important trading centers — especially for slaves — along the former Spanish Main (the north and eastern coasts of South America that were originally almost entirely a Spanish domain). Jews fleeing the Inquisition, from Portugal, Spain, and Mexico, as well as Brazil, found a far more tolerant atmosphere in Curaçao and established a sizable community on the island beginning in 1651. Their synagogue, Mikve Israel-Emanuel, is the oldest in the Western Hemisphere. Muslims found themselves welcome here, too, as did English Pilgrims. Simón Bolívar came to the island twice for asylum during South America's struggles for independence. So Curaçao evolved into a peaceful, thriving international community, and as such became an attractive target for greedy pirates and ambitious European nations.

It was during this initial period of development that Curaçao's capital city, Willemstad, took on the storybook air that now characterizes the entire island. Unlike most other European colonizers, the Dutch who settled this island took great pains to recreate the towns they had left behind. The carefully laid out streets trimmed with neat, well-constructed homes, even the plantation mansions, called *landhuis,* were patterned after their Dutch homeland. One of the colonial governors, however, is reported to have complained that the glaring tropical sun, reflected on the whitewashed houses, gave him severe headaches. So the obliging citizens are said to have painted the houses pink, yellow, purple — and almost every other conceivable tropical hue — in an effort to ease his eyestrain. And whether this apocryphal tale is completely true or not, Willemstad remains a uniquely colorful city even to this day.

As wars raged through Europe, Curaçao and its neighboring islands of the West Indies changed hands several times. The Dutch navy was blockaded in its home ports by the British and the French, and the British used this advantage to occupy Curaçao twice. In 1800, after several invasion attempts, they finally took the island and held it until 1803, when Curaçao-born Pedro Luis Brion, the 21-year-old chief of the island militia, defeated the occupation forces and freed the island. Then again, during the Napoleonic Wars, the British captured Curaçao (1807) and retained possession until the island was returned to the Dutch in 1816. Brion, during this time, had joined Bolívar as an admiral of the Colombian fleet to fight for the independence of Colombia and Venezuela.

The relative cessation of the European wars also signaled the end of an era for the West Indies. War, and the resultant isolation from Europe, had taken their toll on the islands' economy. Cane sugar had been replaced by beet sugar on the Continent, and by the mid-nineteenth century, the slave trade had been abolished everywhere. At this point in its history, Curaçao retired into a peaceful, isolated existence and maintained an unexciting international posture until 1914. Then, with the discovery of oil in Venezuela, Curaçao reappeared as a significant worldwide trading port.

Venezuelan oil comes to Curaçao for refining and storage, and is thereafter shipped to ports all over the world. The Royal Dutch Shell Company built one of the world's largest refineries on Curaçao, taking advantage of its stable government and the excellent deepwater port (just as the Dutch West India Company had centuries before). Shell also created the largest dry dock and bunkering facilities in the Western Hemisphere.

There is also still the same storybook air of unreality to the city of small, immaculate streets, filled with 200-year-old pastel houses. The Queen Emma Pontoon Bridge was built across the harbor in 1888, connecting the two sides of the city that were historically divided by the harbor; and ever since 1929, the island has relied upon water produced in its own desalination plants, then filtered through island coral to provide minerals and some flavor. There is also a jetport, the Curaçao International Airport, with the longest runway (11,155 feet) in the Caribbean.

The island is Dutch and part of the Kingdom of the Netherlands. In 1986, Aruba negotiated separate and autonomous status, but Bonaire, St. Maarten, Saba, St. Eustatius, and Curaçao itself are still administered through the capital island of Curaçao. This explains the city's ambience and the many fine buildings, offices, and public spaces.

A $1.5-million port expansion was completed in 1987, making Curaçao's facilities among the Caribbean's finest. Willemstad is now the seventh-largest harbor in the world, and one of the world's busiest, hosting ships of virtually every international flag. The oil-based prosperity has brought a tremendous influx of refinery and shipping workers, and, in turn, merchants and businesses from all over the world. Today, there are some 79 nationalities represented in Curaçao, ranging from Dutch and English to Spanish, Chinese, Portuguese, East Indian, Venezuelan, and Caiquetio.

Curaçao is also coming into its own as a popular tourist destination. After major expansion and renovation of many hotels in 1987–88, an aggressive tourism promotion was launched to increase the 22,000 visitor-arrival figure of previous years. At press time, the 250-room *Sonesta* hotel was scheduled for completion by late 1988, as was a $50-million convention center, which will be one of the most impressive facilities of its kind in the Caribbean.

CURAÇAO AT-A-GLANCE

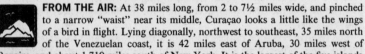

FROM THE AIR: At 38 miles long, from 2 to 7½ miles wide, and pinched to a narrow "waist" near its middle, Curaçao looks a little like the wings of a bird in flight. Lying diagonally, northwest to southeast, 35 miles north of the Venezuelan coast, it is 42 miles east of Aruba, 30 miles west of Bonaire, and about 1,710 miles south of New York. It is the largest of the five islands that make up the Netherlands Antilles, which are generally thought of as existing in two groups: the Windwards, southeast of Puerto Rico, consisting of St. Eustatius, Saba, and the Dutch segment of St. Maarten (the northern two thirds belong to France); and the Leewards, Bonaire and Curaçao. The total area of the Netherlands Antilles is about 320 square miles. Curaçao is also the most populous of the islands, with some 150,000 inhabitants; the total of *both* island groups is only about 185,000, and of that, some 165,000 live on the Leeward islands.

The initial appearance of Curaçao is similar to that of the American Southwest — fairly flat, arid, but not quite desolate. Instead of the green Caribbean palms, the island is an amalgam of browns and russet, derived from the clay soil. Willemstad, the capital of Curaçao (and of the entire Netherlands Antilles), embraces its own harbor just to the southeast of the island's narrow center, occupying the southern shore. From above it resembles a miniature gingerbread city, bright in all the colors of the rainbow. All of the houses on the island seem to cluster around the capital, and half the population of Curaçao does live in Willemstad. The rest occupy the many small villages scattered along the shores and flatlands. Outside the city, the countryside, or cunucu, takes over, with its utter flatness punctuated by cacti rising as tall as 20 feet, and the divi-divi trees forever bent before the fierce trade winds. Here and there, a mountain juts out, appearing taller than it is by contrast with its surroundings. Mt. Christoffel, at the northwestern end of the island, is the highest point in the group of Dutch islands — 1,239 feet above the sea. The coast is ringed with coves and beaches, and caves and underwater grottos of coral and lava, reminders of the island's volcanic origin.

 SPECIAL PLACES: Willemstad – Capital of Curaçao, was a natural berthing place for the Spanish and Dutch with St. Anna Bay facing the mainland (just 35 miles away) and its long, narrow channel leading into a totally sheltered harbor. Adding a couple of forts (on either side) to guard the entranceway made it a virtually impregnable trading port.

The city grew on both sides of the channel, with the eastern side becoming known as the Punda and the west as the Otrabanda, or literally "other side." Originally there were roads around the harbor and a ferry across the canal for those in a hurry (who could afford it), until the American consul, Leonard Burlington Smith, suggested a way to build a bridge that would not interfere with the shipping traffic in the canal. He advocated the use of a temporary pontoon bridge, fixed on one end only and able to swing out of the way when ships passed through the canal. The pontoon bridge was completed in 1888, and dedicated as the Koningin Emmabrug, Queen Emma Bridge. Initially, there was a toll for the use of the bridge, 2¢ for each person *wearing shoes,* thus making it perhaps the first toll based on an individual's ability to pay. But human nature (and Dutch pride) being what it is, the poorest people in town would borrow shoes just to prove their ability to pay, and the rich would take their shoes off to save the 2¢. It was later made free to all and has remained so ever since. The bridge swings open over thirty times a day, to admit the 8,000 oceangoing ships that use the harbor canal each year, and any tour of Willemstad must begin here. Spend half an hour beside the bridge, watching supertankers from all over the world come and go. The contrast between the ultra-modern ships and the 17th-century houses on either side is striking.

The Waterfort, which originally guarded the mouth of the canal on the Punda side, is now the site of the *Curaçao Plaza* hotel; its task of standing guard being left to Fort Amsterdam, just behind it and also overlooking the canal. The plaza between the two forts is dedicated to General Manuel Carlos Piar, a member of the Great Liberator's (Simón Bolívar's) staff. He was condemned to death in 1817 by a court-martial headed by Brion, supposedly because of his popularity with the people.

The far side of Fort Amsterdam is at the foot of the Queen Emma Bridge, and the yellow and white section facing the canal, along Handelskade, is now the Governor's Palace. A walk through its archway (into the courtyard beyond) puts you in an environment surrounded by the past. The entire structure dates back to the 18th century, and the old Dutch church directly opposite still has an English cannonball embedded in its walls (from 1804). The corner of the fort is at the intersection of Handelskade and Breedestraat, the beginning of Curaçao's main shopping district.

At the north end of Handelskade, just a few minutes' walk from the bridge, is an inlet of St. Anna Bay known as Waaigat, and along this channel runs Shon Sha Capriles Kade. Here is where Venezuelan schooners and sailboats still tie up to bring a true floating market to Curaçao. This last historic link with the Caiquetio Indians has been in existence since well before Ojeda claimed this land for Spain. The South Americans bring mostly tropical fruits and vegetables to Curaçao, but also haul dried meat, fish, cloth, beer, and soft drinks. It's a seller's market, and they will bring whatever people will buy. Cash is now the accepted medium, but in years past this was more a bartering and trading market, and even now haggling is the traditional practice. In 1973, a new, enclosed public market was opened for those who prefer to do business indoors, but it's just not the same.

Also on the Punda side, between Shon Sha Capriles Kade and the Fort, is the Mikve Israel-Emanuel synagogue (on the corner of Columbusstraat and Kerkstraat), the oldest extant in the Western Hemisphere. Built in 1732, it is not only a historic house of worship but also an excellent example of colonial Dutch architecture. There is a central courtyard, and the interior of the building is carpeted with a layer of white sand, symbolic of the Jews' journey through the desert to the Promised Land. The altar is set in the center, so the congregation surrounds it in much the same way as the tribes are presumed to have gathered, in a circle, in the desert. Four 24-candle chandeliers, three of which are over 250 years old, hang from the original mahogany ceiling; they are replicas of the candelabra in the Portuguese Synagogue in Amsterdam. Next door is the Jewish Historical and Cultural Museum, in a 200-year-old building that was once a rabbi's house and later a Chinese laundry, until a 300-year-old mikvah (a communal bath used for ritual purifications) was uncovered in its courtyard. Since then, the building has undergone considerable restoration. On display here are utensils for kosher butchering, beautiful silverwork, various religious articles, scales, and a torah said to date back to 1492. Open to the public from 9 to 11:45 AM and again from 2:30 to 5 PM, weekdays. The museum is closed on all Jewish and public holidays. Services are held every Sabbath and holiday evenings at 6:30 PM and 10 AM the following morning. Admission is $1 US.

On the Otrabanda (literally, other side), at the foot of the Queen Emma Bridge, is Brionplein and the statue of Curaçao's favorite son and best-known war hero, Pedro Luis Brion. Born in 1782, he was a fierce and clever fighter. He is credited with preventing several British invasion attempts, although they did finally take the island in 1800. It was Brion, then chief of militia of Curaçao, who led the island forces in their resistance against the invaders and forced the British withdrawal in 1803. In 1814, Brion became admiral of the fleet of Colombia under Simón Bolívar and fought for the independence of Colombia and Venezuela. His remains are now in the National Pantheon of Caracas, the Venezuelan government having asked (in 1881) to be allowed to honor him in this way. On the statue of Brion in Curaçao is a statement from Bolívar himself: "Colombia owes half her blessings to Brion."

The Riffort, once guardian of the canal on this side, now houses a bistro, a seafood restaurant, and the police station.

WEST OF WILLEMSTAD

It's roughly 100 miles around the island of Curaçao, and since the roads vary only between good and excellent, the route can be driven easily in a matter of hours. Although the city of Willemstad is the island's principal attraction, the countryside or "cunucu," which begins just outside the city, should not be ignored. Some of the best examples of Dutch architecture are here, the landhuizen (mansion houses) of the old plantations. These greathouses are usually set on a hill, with a commanding view of the surrounding terrain, and within sight of each other. In times of emergency, signal fires were used to communicate between neighbors, and an emergency warning could be spread from one end of the island to the other in a matter of minutes. There are still a few thatched huts in the cunucu, and natives weaving straw or pounding cornmeal, but for the most part these are things of the past.

Just beyond walking distance from the Queen Emma Bridge, on van Leeuwenhoek-straat, is the Curaçao Museum. Built in 1853 as a Seamen's Hospital (and restored in 1942), it contains relics of the Caiquetio Indians, including a funeral urn, some pottery, beautiful bits of Caribbean coral (no longer allowed to be broken off, it's now protected by law), cradles, stuffed turtles, and the cockpit of the Fokker F-XVIII trimotor (the Snipe, or Snip), which made the first commercial crossing of the southern Atlantic from Holland to Curaçao in 1934. The museum also has a replica of a colonial kitchen, painted brick red with white polka dots, either to ward off evil spirits (as a local guidebook says) or to conceal kitchen spatter and confuse the flies (as the guide also suggests). Antique wood, earthenware, and copper utensils are also on display. The museum gardens contain specimens of all the island's plants and trees. Open from 10 AM to noon and 2 to 5 PM daily except Mondays and the last Sunday of each month. Admission is $1.25 US or 2 guilders.

If you travel northwest along the highway that takes you toward the tip of the island, you'll come to the Jan Kock House. Constructed in 1650, this yellow and white landhuis may be the oldest continually inhabited building in Curaçao. The plantation here originally produced salt, but it's now a private home and sometime restaurant. Several native stories speak of the house as being haunted, and after seeing it in the daylight, you might not disagree.

Continuing west, along the north coast, you come to Ascencion Plantation, a stately 17th-century landhuis, now a rest and recreation center for the Dutch Marines. (Open to the public only on the first Sunday of each month, and then only till noon.)

As you continue along the coast, Mt. Christoffel, the highest point in the Netherlands Antilles, rises some 1,300 feet on your left. It's actually just about in the center of this end of the island, but on the flat cunucu, it's possible to see it for miles. Boca Tabla Grotto is on the coast to your right and it's a good place to stop for a short rest. It is the best known of the hundreds of grottoes that dot the coastline of Curaçao, and most representative of the island's origins. With its coral and lava — some of it polished smooth, other parts pointed, sharp, and cutting — the grotto most resembles a savage moonscape. Wear sturdy sneakers to climb down into caves and listen to the waves crashing outside. Some parts of these caves are below water, so watch your step.

NORTH AND EAST OF WILLEMSTAD

If you stand on the Queen Emma Bridge and look north, across the sheltered harbor of Willemstad, the contrast is startling: Queen Emma floats atop the waves on pontoons, mere feet above the water, and the new Queen Juliana Bridge, completed in 1974, stands almost 200 feet above the water (the tallest bridge in the Caribbean) and spans 1,625 feet. Only six ships in the world cannot sail beneath it.

Beyond the business district, on the peninsula formed by the Waaigat and an inlet of the harbor, is the US consulate, known as Roosevelt House. Situated on Ararat Hill overlooking the city and the approach to the new bridge, it was a gift from the Dutch in appreciation for the protection extended by the US during World War II.

Just northeast of the city, on this same peninsula, is Fort Nassau. Built in 1796, this fortress has an imposing view from its perch 200 feet above the inner harbor. From it you can see a good part of the Dutch dollhouse city, and the mammoth Shell refinery, one of the largest in the world, looks like a toy from this vantage point.

On Penstraat, along the coast to the southeast of town, is the odd little Octagon House. It was here that Bolívar visited his two sisters during the wars of South American independence. In the restored and furnished rooms of the mansion, now a museum, it is easy to imagine Bolívar staring across the sea at Venezuela, or recruiting young Brion or Piar to his cause.

From here swing north, traveling along the east side of the harbor, to the intersection of Fokker Weg and Rijkseenheid Boulevard, to see the very modern Autonomy Monument. Dedicated to the stable, essentially self-governing, young-old country — which was only granted its autonomous status in 1954, yet has been involved in worldwide trade since 1634 — the piece was created by native designer J. Fresco.

Continue east and north around the harbor for a treat — the original Curaçao liqueur. This famed after-dinner drink is produced, from a secret family recipe, on the 17th-century estate of Senior & Co., called "Chobolobo." Two hundred gallons of this liqueur, a by-product of a small green orange (called the laraha), are made each week in the one-room distilling facility. This special orange grows only in Curaçao and, when planted anywhere else, simply grows into a regular full-sized orange. Some sources say that three laraha skins will yield a fifth of the liqueur, while others say it takes 24 peels. Whatever the fact, there is a tasting session after each visit, and every visitor is given some free samples. The firm will not, however, tell just how many laraha skins are needed to produce a single bottle of this island favorite.

This area of the island, extending across the north end of the harbor, along Schottegatweg Noord and Schottegatweg West, is also the site of the Shell oil refinery and other Shell-created facilities, including a golf club, a yacht club, and a country club. Use of these facilities, and tours of the refinery (if you're involved in any aspect of the oil business), can be arranged by calling the Shell Public Relations Office in advance.

On Schottegatweg West, northwest of town past the Shell facilities, is the Beth Haim Cemetery, the oldest Caucasian burial ground still in use in the Western Hemisphere. It contains 2,500 graves on three acres of land, and was consecrated before 1659. The 17th- and 18th-century tombstones are very unusual, and you might like to take a rubbing of their inscriptions as a unique souvenir of the intricate stonework of three centuries ago.

The southern coast is punctuated with bays and inlets, and it is very easy to imagine that pirates preparing to raid Willemstad, or some port on the Spanish Main, might have taken shelter here to plan their attacks or just rest between lootings. Only a short distance from Westpunt is the Knip Estate, a 17th-century landhuis that still keeps watch over this section of the coastline; it is now privately owned.

To explore the island's east end, follow the coast road from Willemstad past the zoo and botanical gardens (neither is exceptional) about 2 miles to Jan Thiel Bay. Here the extraordinary Seaquarium, which opened in 1984 on 6 acres next to the *Princess Beach* hotel and the National Underwater Park, is definitely worth a stop. Over 75 huge glass tanks sunk into the coral reef actually allow you to walk beneath the clear Caribbean to view the thousands of deep-sea denizens gathered around the coral-crusted wreck of the HMS *Oranje Nassau,* which sunk in 1906. Keeping your head above water, visit the main building's collection of smaller sea creatures; dine on the terrace of the *Seaquarium* restaurant. The new manmade beach is a perfect spot to relax or to engage in some sailing, fishing, or boardsailing. Changing rooms are available. Then head east along the coast to Caracas Bay, where antique Fort Beekenberg towers above where the *QE2* and other cruise ships dock. Across the neighboring bay, four yacht clubs line the shore at Spanish Water and fleets of sail and power boats do their Sunday cruising. Farther south past Tafelberg, a unique phosphate mountain, call at Santa Barbara plantation and swim in the turquoise waters of "Boca" from Santa Barbara Beach (with changing rooms, toilet facilities, snack bar, Sunfish and windsurfer rentals; open daily until 5 PM). If you're still hungry for sights, detour north to St. Joris to admire its plantation houses and watch the bay's teal waters rush the north channel to the Atlantic.

■**EXTRA SPECIAL:** On the far western tip of the island, facing south on the coast, are *Westpunt* and *Westpunt Bay.* This area contains some of the best and most appealing small beaches on the island, all apt to be crowded with residents on weekends. During the week, however, fishermen can be seen casting their nets and gutting their catch on the beach. It's only an hour's ride from Willemstad; don't forget to bring along a swimsuit and towel. That way you can take a refreshing swim break before stopping at one of Westpunt's restaurants for a tasty lunch (see *Best on the Island* for details). There are no changing facilities (except in the solitude of the beaches themselves), though each secluded sandy spot has its own little cove, but, if things aren't too crowded, the restaurants' managements aren't averse to your using their restrooms for changing.

Nature fans may want to make a short western detour to visit Curaçao's Christoffel Park before hitting the south shore road for Willemstad. The preserve's 4,000 acres, with their centerpiece, Mt. Christoffel, are dedicated to the conservation of wildlife — flora (rare palms, cacti, and the ubiquitous bent divi-divis) and fauna (iguanas, rabbits, deer, and a number of bird species). There are two entrances near the 18th-century landhuis called Savonet, which serves as park headquarters. The eastern entrance leads to four caves embellished with Indian signs and unusual rock formations; the other, to a 45-mile network of roads that pass stately ruins and climb into the hills for stunning views of the island. Hikers can follow the winding trail 1,230 feet up to the top of the mountain. Although the park is open daily from 8 AM to 3 PM, no admissions are permitted after 2 PM as the circuit takes approximately 3½ hours to complete. Admission: $1.25 for adults; 75¢ for children between 6 and 15; children under 6 are free (phone: 6-40363).

The *Curaçao Seaquarium* is the world's only public aquarium raising and cultivating sea creatures by completely natural methods. Its 75 tanks house almost every species of marine creature found in local waters. A shark channel, glassed-in underwater restaurant, open-air bar, glass-bottom-boat rides over underwater park reefs immediately offshore, and giant water slide are other attractions. A 120-slip marina was completed in summer 1988.

SOURCES AND RESOURCES

 TOURIST INFORMATION: The Curaçao Tourist Board has an office in the US at 400 Madison Ave., Suite 311, New York, NY 10017 (phone: 212-751-8266 or 800-332-8266), and written inquiries should be directed to them at PO Box 5842, Hollywood, FL 33083 (phone: 305-374-5811 or 800-332-8266).

The Tourist Board has an office in Willemstad on the Plaza Piar, in the halls next to the *Curaçao Plaza* hotel, staffed by a team of multilingual guides. There are similar offices in the arrival and transit halls of the airport. Maps, folders, and people to answer your questions are available at all these locations. Mailing address: Curaçao Tourist Board, Plaza Piar Punda, Curaçao (phone: 61-3397 or 61-1967).

Local Coverage – An island publication, *Curaçao Holiday,* carries useful updates on special events, shopping, restaurants, nightlife; it's free at the airport, Tourist Office, and hotels.

Telephone – Dial direct to Curaçao by adding the international access code 011 and the prefix 5999 to the numbers given below.

 ENTRY REQUIREMENTS: US and Canadian citizens do not need a passport, just proof of citizenship, such as a birth certificate or voter registration card, and a return or continuing ticket to a destination outside of the Netherlands Antilles. Security between the islands is very tight; you will have to carry these things with you in order to clear customs and immigration on each Dutch island you visit. There are no special vaccinations required.

CLIMATE AND CLOTHES: Clothing is a simple matter in Curaçao; the average annual rainfall is only 22 inches, and the daytime temperatures remain constant in the high 70s to low 80s. Because of the evening trade winds, it does get cool enough at night to make a light wrap useful for women. Casual clothes are fine during the day, but beach clothes and shorts are frowned upon in town. In the evening, women may dress according to their own sense of style, and most take advantage of this freedom: you'll see everything from pants to long gowns in Curaçao. Ties are never required and men seldom wear jackets, but they do wear guayabera shirts on more formal occasions.

If you plan on exploring the beaches and grottoes of the island, wear rubber-soled walking shoes or sturdy sneakers, since many of the access trails are rough.

MONEY: The coin of the realm is the Netherlands Antilles florin or guilder (the two names are interchangeable), written NAfl ($1 US equals 1.77 NAfl). US dollars and all major credit cards are accepted virtually everywhere, so there is no need to convert any cash unless it's to your benefit. Check prices before you do. The banks are open on weekdays, 8:30 AM to noon and 1:30 to 4:30 PM, and are closed on weekends.

LANGUAGE: The official tongue is Dutch, but English and Spanish are spoken widely. The native dialect is Papiamento, a blend of Spanish, Dutch, French, English, Portuguese, plus some Caribbean and Indian dialects.

TIME: Curaçao is on Atlantic Standard time all year long. It is one hour later than Eastern Standard Time but the same as Daylight Saving Time on the East Coast.

CURRENT: With 110 to 130 volts AC, 50 cycles, US-type plugs. This is fine for razors, but a converter will be needed for hair dryers and other electrical appliances. Check at the desk of your hotel, for it will probably supply one.

GETTING THERE: American Airlines flies daily 4½-hour jet trips from New York to Curaçao. Eastern Airlines flies in from Miami, and ALM flies in from Miami, Haiti, and Puerto Rico, with connections to Aruba, Bonaire, and St. Maarten. Service is also provided by KLM, BWIA, Avianca, VIASA, Aeropostal, and Pan Am, all of which maintain offices in Curaçao. Throughout the winter season, a number of budget charters usually operate from various US cities. Check with your travel agent. Cruise ships call year-round at Willemstad. The 6-hour ferry trip to Coro (4 hours' drive from Caracas), Venezuela, costs about $30 per person one way.

CALCULATING COSTS: Remember that room rates will vary according to season. There are a 10% service charge and a 5% room tax, neither of which is reflected in the rates quoted by the hotels, and most restaurants impose a similar service charge, although it, too, may not be stated in advance. Spring, summer, and fall (approximately April 15 to December 15) comprise the summer season, and the rates will be at least 20% lower; it's a good time for travel bargains and packages. Figure anywhere from $50 to $130 a day, without meals, for two people, depending on the luxury of your hotel; add $20 to $32 per person a day for Modified American Plan (including breakfast and dinner). For 7-day stays, "Bon Bini" packages, available year-round, can mean substantial savings. When budgeting, include taxis (if your evening plans will take you away from your hotel), and add sightseeing costs, of course. Most hotels offer a daytime shuttle bus to Willemstad, but check the schedules.

 GETTING AROUND: Most of the sights and shopping in the town of Willemstad are within walking distance of one another, and again, the hotels outside the town usually provide shuttle bus service free of charge. There are also public buses available from the downtown area to indicated destinations (just check the front of the bus or ask the driver), and the fare is only 40¢. There are also limos that function as buses, called "AC" buses. They will list destinations, and show an "AC" on the vehicle. Hail one from a bus stop, check with the driver, and go. The minimum fare is about 40¢.

Taxi – Not metered. The going rate is about $8 an hour, or part thereof, and 50% higher after 10 PM. There is an official tariff sheet, which drivers must carry, and you can check the approximate fare. If you'd rather, ask the bell captain in your hotel for a copy, and you can check the fare in advance. But always come to an agreement with the driver before the journey. The run from the airport to town (or your hotel) should be about $12, but that can be split with other passengers. (It is the individual's responsibility to put a group together, since the drivers will not do so.) Be aware of whether the price is in dollars or florins (guilders), since if a florin price is quoted and you pay in dollars, you will have almost doubled the cost of the ride — and you can be sure that the driver won't complain. If you take a taxi from town to your hotel, stay on the same side of the canal as your hotel. It costs nothing to walk across Queen Emma, but your fare can double by having to cross the Queen Juliana to drive to your hotel.

Car Rental – Cars are available from the usual giants of the industry: *Avis* (phone: 61-1255), *Budget* (phone: 8-3198), *Hertz* (phone: 8-1182), and *National Car Rental* (phone: 61-3924). They all have offices at the airport and will also deliver cars to your hotel. The rates vary by company and vehicle, but range from about $28 a day plus 14¢ a kilometer for a VW Beetle to about $50 a day for a four-door sedan; unlimited mileage rates apply to rentals of three days or more and begin at about $26 a day for a Beetle. Weekly rates including unlimited mileage start at about $155. A valid US or Canadian driver's license is all that is required.

Sightseeing Bus Tours – Offered by *Taber Tours* (phone: 7-6627 or 7-6713), *Gray Line* (phone: 3-5799), *Coral Tours* (phone: 5-3615), *Daltino Tours* (phone: 61-4888). Prices vary and range from $10 for a 2½-hour tour to $16 for the full-day version. Expect to pay nearly $38 for the nightclub tour. Children's prices are lower.

Island-Hopping Tours – The scheduled carrier ALM has frequent flights to the adjacent islands or to Venezuela. Charter aircraft can be arranged through either the *Curaçao Aero Club* or *Oduber Agencies* (phone: 61-5011 or 61-5837). Day and overnight packages are available.

 SHOPPING: Willemstad's five square blocks of luxury-stocked shops testify to the fact that since the days of the first cruise ships, shopping has ranked as a leading indoor/outdoor sport in Curaçao. Facilities became even more attractive with the 1988 completion of a new shopping area in downtown Willemstad, the 32-shop *Waterfront Arches.* Local merchants upgraded their storefronts and expanded inventories during the last year as part of a $1-million "Festival Marketplace" project. The local import tax is still so low that prices are virtually duty-free, but the descending US dollar and increasing Venezuelan tourism have changed things. If you intend to make major purchases, it's essential to arrive armed with a list of US prices to help you choose the real bargains. This is especially true of French perfumes and cosmetics, cameras and electronic equipment (both of which may be less expensive in US discount stores), liquors and cigarettes (on which cruise passengers eligible for "in-bond" delivery get the best break), and imported name fashions.

But there are still excellent buys — at 20% to 25% below stateside prices — on many true luxury imports: especially fine English bone china, porcelain, crystal, Swiss watches, precious jewelry. In these categories, as a rule, the higher the price tag, the greater the percentage saving. And "close-out sale" shelves may save you as much as 50% over stateside prices. Since this is a prime cruise port, the best shopping hours are in the morning before the ship passengers debark. And though many shops close for lunch from noon till 2 PM, some stay open to accommodate the extra volume on heavy traffic days. The small plaza where Breedestraat and Heerenstraat intersect is the place to start.

Among others, these shops are tops: *Spritzer & Führmann,* with more than half a century of gilt-edged retailing to its credit, has five Breedestraat shops, plus branches at four hotels, that feature china, crystal, porcelain, limited-edition plates; watches, gold, silver, and precious-stone jewelry; small imported treasures from all over the world, including mainland China. Their greatest asset — in addition to enormous stocks — is their iron-clad guarantee backed by a New York branch that handles repairs and replacements on the spot. Prices are the same at all *S & F* branches, but in-town selections are widest. *J. L. Penha & Sons,* in the city's oldest building, the yellow and white one at the corner of Heerenstraat and Breedestraat that dates back to 1708, stocks French perfumes, European clothing, Delft and Hummel collectibles, leather goods from Italy, Spain, and South America, knits and cashmeres from the British Isles. *The Yellow House* specializes in perfumes, cosmetics, boutique accessories. *El Louvre* offers gourmet delicacies along with perfumes, cosmetics, bonded liquors, and cigarettes. *Kan* features precious jewelry, Swiss watches, Rosenthal china, crystal, flatware. *Chalet Gourmet* has Dutch cheeses, chocolates, other edible temptations; *Salas,* books, prints, reading matter; *Gallery RG,* original art.

TIPPING: Most restaurants and hotels will add a 10% (or even 15%) service charge, which covers bartenders, bellhops, chambermaids, and waiters. Taxi drivers should only be tipped for helping with bags, and porters should be tipped on a per-bag rate (50¢ each). If you feel that any of the individuals covered in the 10% deserve it, for special service, add an extra 5%.

SPECIAL EVENTS: Willemstad's monthly *Bon Topa Street Fair* is a great reason to go to town. And its pre-Lenten *Carnival* is as wild as anything anywhere. Like any typical Mardi Gras, it is characterized by costume parades, joyous spirits, dancing in the streets, and pervasive partying with little restraint. Prime Carnival activity occurs during the few days immediately preceding Ash Wednesday. *New Year's Day* (and *Eve*), *Queen Beatrix's Birthday* (January 31), *Good Friday, Easter Monday,* and *Christmas Day* are also celebrated, as are *Labor Day* (May 1), *Ascension Day* (May 19), and *Boxing Day* (December 26). Stores and banks are generally closed on these holidays.

SPORTS: Water sports are the island's mainstay, and Curaçao's public beaches — at Westpunt, Knip, Kline Knip, Daaibooi, and Santa Barbara — are among its very best. The island has a number of small cove beaches, many attached to hotels. What nature has not provided, man has, with long manmade beaches near the *Curaçao Caribbean* and the *Princess Beach* hotels. There's also swimming at most of the hotel beaches, where basic water sports equipment can also be rented. The first Open International Windsurf Championships were held off Curaçao in 1986, and it is now an annual island event attracting much local and international talent.

Boating – *Piscadera Watersports* and *Dive Curaçao and Watersports* (phone: 61-4944) are the people to see for boat rentals, unless you're a yacht club member at home, in which case the *Curaçao Yacht Club* (phone: 3-8038) may be able to make some arrangement for you with one of their members. The *Shell Yacht Club* is at Spanish Water (toward the southeast end of the island, phone: 3-8210) and welcomes visitors who give advance notice. Rentals of boats from *Piscadera Watersports* will cost between $7.50 an hour for a small sailboat on up to the $100 range for a fishing charter.

Golf – The *Curaçao Golf and Squash Club,* near the Shell refinery, welcomes visitors to a 9-hole course with oiled sand "greens" open to the public by prior arrangement (call the day before you wish to play). It's on Schottegatweg Noord (phone: 9-2664) and charges a $10 greens fee. Squash courts are available all week from 8 AM to 4:30 PM.

Horseback Riding – If you wish to ride, have your hotel contact Joe Pinedo (phone: 8-1616) at his nearby ranch. Fees are about $10 an hour, including transportation.

Scuba Diving and Snorkeling – Curaçao is becoming better known as a scuba destination and now has five well-equipped water-sports operations. Snorkels, masks, and fins, available at most hotels, can be rented from *Piscadera Watersports* (phone: 2-5000, ext. 177, at the *Curaçao Caribbean*), which has everything from scuba gear to deep-sea fishing charters. Snorkeling gear is about $1.50 to $2 an hour; scuba is usually $20 to $25 for a half day, with a guide. *Masterdive* (Fokkerweg 13, phone: 5-4312) also rents diving equipment, as do *Dive Curaçao* (phone: 1-4944 or 5-3733) and *Sun Dive* at the *Holiday Beach* hotel and casino (624-888). The island's most extensive snorkel and scuba environment, the National Underwater Park, starts at Jan Thiel Bay and stretches from the *Princess Beach* hotel along 12½ miles of shore to the island's eastern tip. Fringed by a virtually untouched coral reef that plunges to a depth of 30 feet, it boasts a 975-foot underwater trail leading to the wreck of the HMS *Oranje Nassau* (sunk in 1906) in the park's shallows. For more daring divers, 16 mooring buoys dotted along the reef's length mark deeper dive and snorkel sites. Hook and line fishing is permitted throughout the park, but no spearfishing or coral collecting. Also off Princess Beach is a unique manmade reef created in 1968, when the government deep-sixed two huge barges and 30 wrecked cars and trucks; it's now a gathering place for fish and coral in all colors of the rainbow. In nearby Caracas Bay, wreck enthusiasts can also explore a 15-foot tugboat encrusted with stag, elkhorn, head, and flowering orange tube coral. There is also a fully equipped decompression chamber on Curaçao, available 24 hours a day.

Tennis – Most of the hotels have courts; if yours doesn't, check with the activities desk to see if they have any prearranged plans for play elsewhere. If not, then call the *Netherlands Antilles Lawn Tennis Organization* (phone: 2-3110) for information.

 NIGHTLIFE: Curaçao's five casinos (in the *Curaçao Caribbean, Curaçao Plaza, Holiday Beach, Princess Beach,* and *Las Palmas Hotel and Vacation Village*) start their action at noon and remain open until 4 or 5 AM. The big hotels have nightclubs with entertainment and dancing. There are also planned entertainment nights at some of the hotels, like the *Caribbean*'s Folkloric Evenings, Thursday Night Shipwreck Party (read: Rum Party), and beachside barbecues. The *Avila* hotel has a show on Saturday night. *Infinity* at Fort Nassau and *Discoconut* at the *Bellevue* are the latest thing in discos.

BEST ON THE ISLAND

 CHECKING IN: Most of the hotels either are in Willemstad or have shuttle bus service to and from town, and most hotels have their own, albeit small, beaches. So your choice need not be based on either factor, because you can get to town easily, and there are beautiful public beaches available all around the island. Since there is considerable international commercial trade going on continuously on the island, hotels can be crowded anytime. Expensive hotels fluctuate between $80 and $125 per night, double occupancy, without meals in winter. Suites cost more, and most of the hotels are on European Plan, but have a Modified American Plan option that includes breakfasts and dinners for about $20 to $28 a day per person. Moderately priced hotels will cost between $50 and $70 a day, and the inexpensive category will include hotels in the under-$50 range. Remember that these prices can drop from 35% to 60% between April 15 and December 15, and that there is an additional 10% service charge and 5% tax.

Because of the size of the island, most of the hotels and restaurants do not bother with street names, and those that do find it necessary to name their street do not use street addresses. Admittedly, this can make things difficult if you choose to rent a car, but directions are easily obtained by calling ahead or asking any cab driver.

Curaçao Caribbean – Recently purchased by the Caribbean Investment Group, this is an exceptionally pleasant place, with a small beach, big pool, sauna, and tennis, and also one of those glass-enclosed elevators crawling up the side. A $5-million refurbishment of all 200 rooms and lobby has made it an elegant, modern resort. It's actually on Piscadera Bay and has a shuttle to downtown shopping; it also has its own shopping arcade if you'd rather do your purchasing right there. At night, it's jumping with dancing, entertainment, and the casino (phone: 2-5000 or 800-444-1010). Expensive.

Holiday Beach – The 200 balconied rooms, all with color TV connected to a satellite receiver dish, are fairly standard in decor (the hotel began life as a Holiday Inn). Big pool is center of daytime action; small manmade beach protected by manmade "reef" offers shallow swimming and water sports. Beach barbecues, steel bands, considerable evening activity — especially in the casino (phone: 2-5400). Excellent package rates available. Expensive to moderate.

Avila Beach – Right next door to the Octagon Museum, filled with memories of Bolívar the Liberator, stands the mansion built for the British military governor during the occupation of 1807-16. Its 45 rooms have been renovated and are now very pleasant. The surrounding area is residential, and the mansion is now a small, likable, well-managed hotel that overlooks the ocean and its own beach. There is an outdoor bar in the form of a ship's bow, and the restaurant serves excellent local food. Penstraat (phone: 61-4377). Moderate.

Coral Cliff – A simple, low-rise retreat with 35 air-conditioned rooms on secluded Santa Maria Bay. It has its own beach, water sports, tennis, and restaurant with entertainment several nights a week (phone: 64-16160). Moderate.

Curaçao Plaza – With 254 rooms overlooking the harbor, this is the island's largest resort. Facilities include 3 restaurants, saltwater pool, nightclub, casino, color satellite TV. Attractive packages available (phone: 612-500). Moderate.

Las Palmas – Newly refurbished and very comfortable. Includes a 100-room hotel and 90 villas — spic and span, nicely planned 2-room units with kitchenettes, which are the real buy. A mini-casino and entertainment are the newest additions. The beach is a 5-minute walk, on Piscadera Bay, and there is a program of water sports in addition to a pool, tennis courts, a convenience grocery, and a shuttle bus to town, about 10 minutes away (phone: 2-5200). Moderate.

Princess Beach – Recently renovated and expanded to 204 rooms, this fine hotel has its own beach and diving facilities, big pool, shopping arcade, excellent dining, and a lively nightspot and casino (largest in Curaçao. The *Seaquarium* is next door (phone: 61-4944). Moderate.

Trupial Inn – Visitors looking for a moderately priced base from which to explore the island by car should consider this centrally located, 74-room, informal inn. It is not on a beach, but it does have a pool, a tennis court and a restaurant with good local cuisine and entertainment (phone: 7-8200). Moderate.

EATING OUT: Dutch overtones flavor the foods of some 40 countries that are found in the kitchens of this island; even the French restaurants are proud of their Dutch-sized portions. Two of the most popular dishes are Indonesian, flavored with Dutch style: *java honden portie* (literally "a hound's portion"), which is centered around a mound of rice, served with steak, potatoes, and vegetables (here's the Dutch part) and topped with fried eggs. *Rijsttafel* is the other favorite; it's also a rice-based dish, but is served with from 6 to 24 different side dishes, and guaranteed to leave you satisfied. Créole, Swiss, Chinese, French, South American, and pure Dutch cooking are all well represented. Expect to pay $35 or more for dinner for two in an expensive restaurant, without drinks, wine, or tip; in a moderately priced place it will be between $20 and $35; and up to $20 in an inexpensive establishment. Many restaurants require jackets in the evening, and reservations are suggested. Keep an eye out for Amstel beer, brewed right on the island; it's the only beer made from distilled sea water!

Chez Susenne – A converted home that has rapidly gained a reputation for some of the finest local cooking in Curaçao. The menu is in Papiamento, but your hosts will graciously explain what's what and how it is prepared. A disco adjoins the restaurant. Plan to eat around 7 PM (reservations necessary during high season) and make a night of it (no phone at press time, check with the tourist office). Expensive.

The Penthouse – The *Curaçao Plaza*'s top (literally) restaurant runs the international gamut — deliciously — from escargots through pepper steak and duckling à l'orange to Antigua pineapple flambé on cherry ice. Fine service, fabulous night views (phone: 61-2500). Expensive.

De Taveerne – In the wine cellar of a remarkable, restored octagonal antique landhuis, once the residence of a Venezuelan president, the town's handsomest eating place features a cooked-to-order, à la carte menu that changes every five weeks. Sole meunière, filet steaks, are first-rate. Reservations essential. In Groot Davelaar residential section (phone: 7-0699). Expensive.

Willemstad Supper Club – In the *Curaçao Caribbean,* this restaurant features two seatings nightly (7 and 9 PM), music for dancing, and a show on weekends (phone: 2-5000). Expensive.

Fort Nassau – Inside the old fortress, with a commanding view of the inner harbor and the town. Serves lunch and dinner with varied menu, Dutch selections, big portions; and there is a pub as well as dining room and terrace-bar. Fort Nassau (phone: 61-3450). Expensive to moderate.

Larousse – Housed in a charming 18th-century building, it offers superb French and Curaçao dishes, seafood, fondues, excellent service, and intimate atmosphere (phone 5-5418). Expensive to moderate.

Belle Terrace – A romantic outdoor restaurant where palms and sea sounds create atmosphere. Different specialties each evening. Highly recommended. Wednesdays, sopito and keshi yena (fish stew, stuffed Edam cheese); weekends, smorgasbørd and cheese platters. At *Avila Beach Hotel* (phone: 61-4377). Moderate.

Bellevue – Family-owned, friendly, full of Antillean atmosphere. Créole and seafood specialties (red snapper, conch, squid, shrimp); try the iguana soup. Just outside Punda at Passanghran (phone: 5-4291). Moderate.

Bistro Le Clochard – The French connection on the other bank — the Otrabanda — and delicious. Considered one of Curaçao's finest restaurants, it's housed in a renovated 18th-century harbor fortress and has a unique ambience. Specialties are fresh fish platters and steaks. Riffort (phone: 62-5666). Moderate.

La Bistroelle – French provincial approach (high-backed chairs, rustic chandeliers), Continental menu (mussels in whiskey sauce, sole with salmon mousse, flambéed items) plus US prime beef. One of Curaçao's finest. Near Promenade Shopping Center outside town (phone: 7-6929). Moderate.

Golden Star – Friendly Curaçaoan atmosphere with emphasis on superior Antillean cuisine. Otrabanda on Socratesstraat (phone: 5-4795). Moderate.

Great Wall – Current wok-away winner in Curaçao's Chinese restaurant sweepstakes. Savory selections in all columns. Reserve ahead. In Centro Commercial Antilia (phone: 3-7694). Moderate.

'T Kokkeltje – A delightful Dutch bistro specializing in fresh seafood — some flown in daily from Holland by KLM. Dutch cuisine, friendly family-style atmosphere (phone: 8-1120 or 8-8014). Moderate.

Le Recif – A refreshing find tucked in under three arches at the Riffort in Otrabanda. Nautical decor to match its specialties — fresh local seafood dishes (phone: 62-3824). Moderate.

Rijsttafel Restaurant Indonesia & Holland Club Bar – One of Curaçao's not-to-be-missed dining experiences. Lavish Javanese specialties, authentic recipes, with the 20-course rijsttafel the house specialty, served buffet- style. The bar is a popular local gathering place. At 13 Mercuriusstrat (phone: 61-2606). Moderate.

Pisces – At Caracas Bay, where the big cruise ships dock, it's a casual favorite with locals. The menu features very fresh fish as well as a special catch of the day (phone: 67-2181). Moderate to inexpensive.

Fort Waakzaamheid – Friendly Dutch tavern atmosphere, Dutch and island specialties (good fish), steaks, sandwiches at lunch. On Otrabanda on Seru di Domi (phone: 2-3633). Inexpensive.

Wine Cellar – Wooden tables and candles add to the atmosphere at this intimate little restaurant, which has won top awards from European epicures. Superb wine list; simple or elaborate fare available. Only 8 tables, so reservations requested. Concordiastraat (phone: 61-2178). Inexpensive.

WESTPUNT AREA

Playa Forti – This restaurant has one of the most scenic views on the island, overlooking West Punt Bay. It is run by a former chief chef for the Holland-America Cruise Line. Have some lamb or a native conch stew or the red snapper. It's all delicious (phone: 64-0273). Inexpensive.

DOMINICA

The island of Dominica (pronounced dom-i-*nee*-ka) is still very much the primitive garden that Columbus first sighted on Sunday, November 3, 1493 — filled with tropical rain forests, plants, and animals that exist nowhere else in the world, and flowers of incredible beauty. There are also the last remnants of the fierce Carib Indian tribe whose ancestors prevented European settlements on this island for years.

The tourist trade has always been spotty here. Not everyone wants to visit an island that has so few white sand beaches, no casinos, no duty-free shops, no glittering nightlife. Still, it appeals to people who want to immerse themselves in its lush mountain jungles — botanists, serious travelers, seekers after its special and uncompromising solitude — people who have come to know and understand its very special charm. And, quietly, the island has grown to political maturity.

On November 3, 1978, the 485th anniversary of its discovery, Dominica became an independent nation within the commonwealth, with a government pledged both to encourage tourism and to protect the island's enormous natural beauty. But in 1979, unmerciful Nature dealt the new country a stunning blow: On August 29, brutal Hurricane David, followed by only slightly lesser Frederick, slammed ashore. When the 150 mph winds dropped, rain stopped, and skies cleared, 37 people were dead, an estimated 5,000 injured, and three fourths of the 75,000 population were left homeless. The Dominican economy was almost totally destroyed. Experts said, dourly, it would be three years before tourists could return.

Astoundingly, they were wrong. In less than a year, Nature healed most of its own wounds. Jungles now flourish, gardens flower, citrus thrives, and banana trees have rerooted (only the coconuts suffered lasting damage). Rebuilding, helped by Caribbean and North American neighbors, went well. Roads have been repaired (they were never very smooth), and, with a few exceptions — saddest is the congenial old *Fort Young* hotel, which has yet to be rebuilt — the island's small, friendly hotels are receiving guests again, and several new properties have been developed.

Dominica remains a land of untamed beauty. Its allure is its wild and virtually unchanged mountains, deep rain forests — some of which have never been seen by anyone but Carib Indians — and the splendor of the Emerald Pool, a grotto fed by a waterfall, lined with giant ferns, and home to darting lizards and tropical birds. The peak of Morne Diablotin, some 4,747 feet above sea level, is usually swathed in a cloudy mist caused by the moisture and density of the air. The island receives only 75 or 80 inches of rain per year on the coast, but estimates put the actual rainfall in the mountain areas at 250 to 400 inches per year. The island's profuse plant life is fed by "liquid sunshine," a native term for mist so fine it can only be seen against

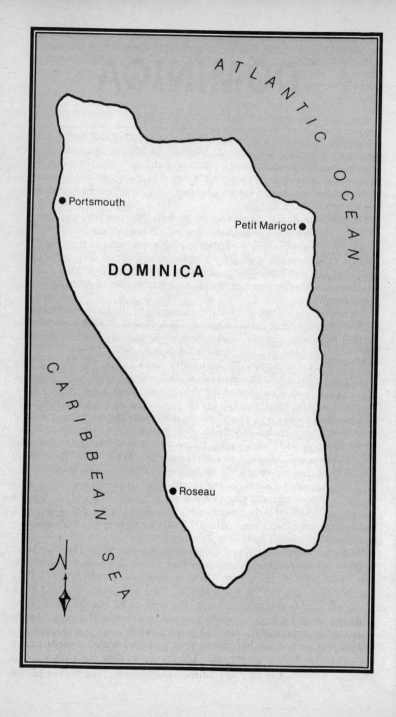

a backlight of sunshine but that inspires the island's colorful plants and flowers. Everything planted on this island grows well and quickly in the rich, volcanic soil. Even the newly planted fences of glory cedar that border the roads and plantations begin to sprout within days. Power and phone lines are interwoven with blossoming vines.

When Columbus discovered Dominica (so named to celebrate that he first glimpsed its shores on a Sunday), he found it inhabited by the fierce and determined Carib Indians. He was turned back in his search for fresh water, in fact, by the Caribs' poisoned arrows (a pity, because Dominica is filled with beautiful, deliciously clear streams).

By the time Columbus arrived, the Caribs were in possession of many of the Caribbean islands and were plundering others regularly. Although the might of the French, Spanish, and British fleets gave the Europeans control of most of the Indian lands, the Caribs could not be forced to abandon Dominica. Its rain forest interior provided them with protected bases from which to raid the European settlements as well as the villages of other Indians. Both English and French settlements were established on the island over the years, but none of these withstood the attacks of the Caribs for long.

In 1748, the French and English signed the Treaty of Aix-la-Chapelle, agreeing that neither would attempt to settle the island, leaving it to the Caribs. However, the agreement was a failure, and Dominica was awarded to the British in 1763, taken by the French in 1778, won back by the British in 1783, and finally raided by the French in 1805, after which the British paid $60,000 to be left alone by the French. Through all this, both sides were harassed by the Caribs. It wasn't until 1903 that the island was sectioned off, and the British finally managed to force the Caribs to accept fixed boundaries. About 1,000 pure-blooded Caribs still live on their reservation on the northeast coast of the island, along with another 1,500 of mixed ancestry — Carib and descendants of slaves brought from Africa.

The Carib presence prevented the island from being developed into plantations until just before the abolition of slavery, and that fortunate lack of growth during the period of European colonization throughout the rest of the Caribbean islands has resulted in Dominica's unique status. Though it is the largest of the Windward islands, its population, at 76,000, is the smallest in the group, and it remains one of the least developed.

This island is the only home of the sisserou, or imperial parrot (*Amazona imperialis*), a large, purple-breasted parrot facing extinction. The endangered jacquot, or red-necked parrot (*Amazona arausiaca*) is also a Dominican native. Both are protected. And only on Dominica will you hear the native solitaire, or siffleur, whose call sounds like the opening of Beethoven's Fifth Symphony. In its forests are gommier and châtaignier trees, some reaching 150 feet into the mountain sky, not to mention mahogany, cedar, bamboo, giant tree ferns, and palms.

Bananas have replaced lime juice as the island's major export. And the government is looking for light industries to bolster its economy. Careful control over the growth of tourism — especially hotel building — still has top priority. For, after all, it is, at least in part, the Dominican dependence on themselves rather than on a jet airstrip, super highways, and towering hotels that has enabled the island to restore itself so quickly. The lack of such "improvements" is also more than part of the reason that the rush of rivers still drowns out traffic noise on island roads, and the scent of lime is still stronger than exhaust fumes along the shore near Roseau. These things help keep this island the choice of vacationers who want to escape the "realities" of tourism a while longer.

DOMINICA AT-A-GLANCE

FROM THE AIR: Dominica lies south of Guadeloupe, just north of Martinique, and is separated from both neighbors by wide channels. It is 29 miles long and 16 miles wide at its widest point, with a total of 298 square miles of very rugged terrain culminating in the peaks of Morne Diablotin, 4,747 feet above sea level. (There are actually three mountain ranges on the island.) Small wonder that the population of Dominica is a scant 76,000.

Flying into Dominica is like arriving nowhere else in the world. Larger planes still land at Melville Hall Airfield, at the island's northeastern edge. It was carved out of a coconut plantation, and planes make their approach over thick mountain jungles, hill after tree-covered hill of palms, followed by still higher hills and more trees and whispers of mist wrapped gently around the mountaintops. Twenty feet from the airport a broad river rushes by, nearly drowning out the sound of the propellers. The opposite bank is a solid wall of green, and long looping vines hang from the tops of the trees into the river. A black and white spotted cow peers through the vegetation. The plane rolls down the sloping runway to stop just before reaching the sea.

There is a special scent in the air — lush, verdant, thick and rich, beneath a sky that is warm and blue. At first glance Dominica is like a terrarium — mists rise from the valleys and hover over palmy hillsides; giant ferns, feathery foliage — and rivers are everywhere; they splash between huge boulders and tumble-down hills. It is said that there are 365 rivers on Dominica, one for each day of the year. The 1-hour (minimum) taxi drive to Roseau takes the visitor through some of the most spectacular mountain scenery in the tropics.

Smaller aircraft (up to 19 seats) land at Canefield Airport, only five minutes from Roseau. Crosswinds here often make for an exciting landing between the mountains and the deep blue sea. Long enough for 19-seat aircraft and served regularly by LIAT, Air Martinique, Air Guadeloupe, and Air Caribe, Canefield brings the capital within day-trip range of Antigua, Guadeloupe, and other neighboring islands.

SPECIAL PLACES: Roseau – Dominica's capital city is not impressive at first glance — a few streets, a jumble of two-story buildings ringed by several blocks of one-story houses. The older buildings are wooden, and the two-story structures have balconies overhanging the sidewalk, with shutters pinned back and wooden railings set in floral designs or starburst patterns. Newer buildings are concrete block or stucco, built in the same style as the earlier ones. Many buildings are painted in bright, contrasting colors. The new market is near the river. The old market has recently been spruced up and opened as a crafts market for tourists; in front of it, the old post office will soon house the Government Tourist Board.

The peak of Morne Bruce stands behind the city and can be reached by car, threading the winding road past some of the nicer residences, or by the footpath from the nearby Botanical Gardens. There is a large cross at the top, several shade trees under which to rest, and an excellent view of the town of Roseau. From here you can see the Roseau

River as it meanders through town and watch villagers doing their wash — pounding and scrubbing the clothes on the rocks, rinsing them in the water, and drying them in the sun. The town of Roseau was named after the reeds that grow in profusion along the river. The Caribs used them to make poison-tipped arrows, and today they are used for baskets.

Most people who visit Dominica come for its fecund plant life, and a popular first stop is Roseau's Botanical Gardens, which are filled with plants from all the surrounding islands (everything grows well on Dominica), including beautiful flamboyant trees and luscious orchids, as well as Dominica's national flower, the *bwa kwaib,* or carib wood. The gardens provide a preview of what to look for in the mountains, and you will recognize the halaconia, or lobster claw, and bright red ginger plants throughout the island. The 1979 hurricane destroyed some 350 of the gardens' 500 species, but regrowth — throughout Dominica — has been remarkably fast. The huge African baobab tree, still lying upon the yellow bus it crushed, began flowering again in 1985. The *Fort Young* hotel has been rebuilt within sections of the 18th-century fortress, which for a short time withstood Carib attacks. Some of the earliest and most persistent visitors to the island were the missionaries, and the results of their work are obvious. Catholicism dominates Dominica, and the island's cathedral with its old carved wooden benches and cool stone floors is suitably impressive. The Anglican church that Hurricane David reduced to rubble has been rebuilt, and Anglicanism is still a force in the country.

Scott's Head – At the southern tip of the island, this point is accessible by motor launch or vehicle along the west coast past Pointe Michel (which was settled by refugees from Mt. Pelée in Martinique) and Soufrière, where there are sulfur springs.

The climb to the top of Scott's Head along a road mostly of stones and dirt is not difficult. The view at the crest is incredible — the Atlantic on one side, the Caribbean on the other, Martinique in the distance, and Dominica below. Before you are mountainous peaks capped with green, valleys of trees — trees dripping mangoes, almond trees with broad glossy leaves, limes, coconuts with their light green contrasted against the darker green of the tropical forest, thick seagrape leaves as large as placemats, banana leaves as large as tablecloths. The Atlantic side of the island is lined with beaches, some covered with smooth gray volcanic sands, others with smooth stones that tumble and make wonderful music as the waves pull back.

Morne Trois Pitons National Park – This is primordial rain forest, and here plants rule the earth from which they spring. Some of the trails through the park are marked and plants are identified, but even with the help, the sheer profusion of green life is staggering. No tree trunk is bare of some kind of vine or symbiotic growth; giant ferns flourish on the shady ground, and anthurium, z'ailes mouches, and bromeliads live on the limbs and trunks of trees. Liana, a variety of strangler vine, starts life growing from a host tree, and then sends out roots, attaching itself to the earth and pulling itself — and sometimes the host — to the ground. About five minutes' walk into the park is beautiful Emerald Pool, a grotto filled by a waterfall, surrounded by breathtakingly beautiful plants, flowers, and ferns. Among the park's other natural high points, literally and figuratively (bring a windbreaker up here): Fresh Water Lake — reachable by four-wheel drive — affords an expansive view of the island's eastern coast; Boeri Lake — a short hike from there — is rimmed with volcanic rock; and Boiling Lake — a rather arduous, full-day hike — is the second largest of its kind in all the world, kept bubbling by the volcanic heat of the crater in which it is cupped.

Portsmouth – Dominica's second town, facing the Caribbean on the northern end of the island. If a real harbor were built on Dominica, this is the place that could turn into a boom town. It's the best anchorage on the island, and a couple of hotels and small restaurants now line the palm-fringed, sandy beach. Portsmouth town remains three streets parallel to the bay. It's filled with colorful houses, each with its own little garden, hibiscus plants growing in tin cans, and conch shells trimming neat paths. And on the green behind the town, a cricket pitch where Saturday afternoon matches are played (Hail, Britannia!). Its most picturesque historic site is also a natural beauty spot, Cabrits National Park, a forested peninsula north of town. Once called Prince Rupert's Head, it is dominated by two steep hills covered by one of the Caribbean's few dry woodland areas. Its 18th-century Fort Shirley, one of the most impressive military sites in the West Indies, was the scene of a locally famous military mutiny in 1802. Though it was abandoned as a military post in 1854, some 50 structures survive. Restoration is currently under way, and there is a small museum. The marine section of the park, in Douglas Bay, has fascinating rock and coral formations under cliffs, great for snorkeling. To the south, emptying into Prince Rupert's Bay, is the mangrove-lined Indian River, a popular tourist attraction. Boat rides are best arranged through the local Tour Guide Service on Boroughs Square in Portsmouth, as the jetty boys tend to be a bit aggressive. Yachtspeople at anchorage off Portsmouth are also hounded by "bad boys" insistently selling their goods.

Trafalgar Falls – In the south-central section of the island, 5 miles from Roseau, the road runs high along the walls of a valley, passing through the tiny village of Trafalgar, and before reaching the falls, the car will have to be vacated. The final approach is by foot, about a 15-minute walk to the base of the falls. There are three sets of falls, all converging into a rocky pool and splashing among the huge black rocks that sprout ferns and orchids. Breadfruit trees and rare tree ferns surround the pools of flowing water, trees grow upward along the cliff face, and sunlight dapples the trees and turns green. The air is fresh and cool, scented with the richness of a greenhouse.

Sulfur Springs – Near the falls, also north and east of Roseau, are some remnants of the island's volcanic existence — sulfur springs. They are hot, bubbling pools of gray mud like a witch's cauldron, and belch smelly sulfurous fumes. There is no doubt that the island is alive and someday will probably erupt again.

■**EXTRA SPECIAL:** The *Carib Territory* consists of six villages: Salybia, where there's a church with an Indian canoe for an altar; Bataka, with the native school; Sineku, and three others. There is much discussion about how many pure-blooded Caribs are left, since women of other Indian tribes and black women have married into the tribe. Because the Caribs are such a proud and independent people, they will accept no non-Carib males into their community. Pure-blooded Caribs somewhat resemble Asians, with almond eyes, high cheekbones, and straight black hair. The reserve is now accessible — whatever the weather — thanks to a paved road that crosses a wide river and passes through a swamp and over a small mountain. A new road crosses the territory's rich agricultural area above and villages, offering spectacular view of the valleys and cliffs. The Caribs survived in Dominica only because of the dense forests, but the British did manage to push them into this reserve early in this century. They remained fairly quiet until 1930, when a "Carib War" broke out over the smuggling of tobacco and rum, and the rebellion was suppressed by a British warship, the HMS *Delhi*, which landed a contingent of marines and fired star shells over the reserve area.

The Caribs used to use two languages: Carib for the men and Arawak for the women; now they speak English and the patois of the island, French Créole like that of Haiti. Although the proud and defiant Caribs make baskets, canoes, and a few other small souvenirs for sale to tourists today, they have managed to avoid many of the ill effects of modernization. They still have a tribal chief and are still the independent race who once held their island home against the might of two of the 18th century's greatest nations. Visitors to the reserve find them friendly, hospitable, and rather shy. Their simple homes have flower gardens in front and are flanked by fruit and vegetable patches. Several small shops sell the famed Carib baskets and straw mats; fresh fruit, vegetables, and flowers are available if you ask. At present the community is focusing on a project that will offer visitors an opportunity for river bathing with changing facilities, a bar, and folklore show. The enterprising and very charming Charles Williams plans to offer tours of the territory as well as overnight accommodations and local food.

SOURCES AND RESOURCES

TOURIST INFORMATION: Dominica is represented in New York by the Caribbean Tourism Association, 20 E 46th St., New York, NY 10017 (phone: 212-682-0435).

The Dominica Tourist Board has an office in Roseau (mailing address: PO Box 73, Roseau, Dominica, WI; phone: 82351, 82186).

Local Coverage – The *Dominica Chronicle* is published weekly.

Telephone – Dial direct to Dominica by adding the area code 809 and the prefix 44 to the numbers given below.

ENTRY REQUIREMENTS: US and Canadian citizens need only proof of citizenship (passport, birth certificate, or voter's registration card) and a return or ongoing ticket.

CLIMATE AND CLOTHES: Daytime temperatures range from 70° to 90°F. However, this drops to the mid-50s in the mountains. Rainfall on the coast averages 45 inches, but the interior rain forest receives some 250 to 400 inches per year. Some days it rains a dozen times, the sun and showers creating magnificent rainbows. February through July can be considered the dry season, though in the mountains it seems to rain most of the year.

The island is very casual. In this climate, light, comfortable cotton clothes are all that are required: shorts, slacks, jeans, swimsuit, walking shoes, maybe a pair of deck shoes if you plan to do any boating. If you plan to go into the mountains (and you should), a waterproof windbreaker, long-sleeved shirt (perhaps a sweater), and good hiking shoes will be very useful. Swimsuits and shorts are not worn in the streets in town — stick to skirts and long pants. Evenings are informal, but conservative.

MONEY: The Eastern Caribbean dollar is the official currency, exchanging at about $2.68 EC to the US dollar, subject to only slight fluctuations since it is pegged to US currency. American currency is accepted throughout the island, but buying power can be increased a little by exchanging currency in a bank. Credit cards are by no means universally accepted, but a number of hotels take them; check when you make reservations.

LANGUAGE: The official language is English, but most of the natives also speak a French Créole patois, except for a small area in the north where the latter is not understood.

TIME: In the winter Dominica is one hour ahead of Eastern Standard Time; when it is 11 AM in Roseau, it is 10 AM in New York; in summer, when the US is on Daylight Saving Time, the time is the same in both places.

CURRENT: Electricity is 220-240 volts, AC, 50 cycles, often with British 3-square-pin outlets; American appliances must have a converter.

GETTING THERE: Dominica does not have a jet airport, so the island is accessible only by connecting flights from other islands. LIAT has several flights daily from Antigua, Barbados, Guadeloupe, Martinique, San Juan, and St. Lucia. Air Caribe International offers daily flights (except Sundays) from San Juan; Air Guadeloupe flies twice daily from Guadeloupe. Air Caribe offers special rates through La Robe Creole (telex: 8607 HOTELS DO). Canefield Airport near Roseau accommodates smaller planes (up to 19 seats), so only passengers on the larger LIAT aircraft have to trek across from Melville Hall, a good hourlong taxi ride. A new high-speed ferry, the *Caribbean Link,* provides daily service to Dominica from Guadeloupe, Montserrat, Antigua, and Barbuda. Carib Class (first-class) fare includes hostess service and free rum punch. The ride between Guadeloupe and Dominica takes 2 hours and 20 minutes and costs $40 US.

CALCULATING COSTS: Hotels do not really have winter and summer rates here as in the more popular Caribbean spots. Some have slightly lower rates (10% to 30%) May through November, but most do not. A stay on Dominica costs far less all around than on the glittering resort islands; the most expensive hotel only charges $70 US for a double room with full English breakfast. Dinner for two (without drinks) won't top $30 US.

GETTING AROUND: Taxi – Rates are set by law, and are about 35¢ to 50¢ per mile. The trip from Melville Hall Airport to Roseau (37 miles) is currently $35 EC, or about $13 US, per passenger, with a minimum of $120 EC ($45 US) per car. From Canefield Airport to Roseau (3 miles), the charge is a minimum $15 EC and depends on the number of passengers and their destination.

Car Rental – *Valley Rent-a-Car* (phone: 83233), *Kent Anthony* (phone: 82630), *Wilderness Adventure Tours* (phone: 82198), *STL Car Rental* (phone: 82340), and *Shillingford* (phone: 53151) have cars for rent. Costs range from about $25 to $40 US per day. Driving is officially on the left (however, local practice is the horn method — toot and then take one's half out of the middle). Many of the better roads are only wide enough for one vehicle at a time. (A note of warning: Banana and lumber trucks seem to have a running duel going on, and it is best just to stay out of their way; they don't — and sometimes can't — stop for anything.) Aside from all this, a local driver's permit can be obtained at the Traffic Department in Roseau for $12 US. Check the Tourist Board office for current availabilities.

Bus – Bus transport can be quite an adventure, considering the quality of the roads, among other things. Roseau to Portsmouth costs $7 EC. Buses don't run on Sundays.

Sightseeing Tours – There is a lot to see on the island of Dominica, and many ways to travel; tours can be arranged on land or water. Taxi sightseeing can be arranged for about $15 per car an hour, for up to four people; ask any driver at the airport. *Emerald Safari Tours* (phone: 84545), *Rainbow-Rover* (phone: 58650), and *Wilderness Adventure Tours* (phone: 82198) organize bus, car, four-wheel-drive, and hiking trips to the island's most famous beauty spots. *Dominica Tours,* at the *Anchorage* hotel in Roseau (phone: 82638), arranges hiking, scuba diving, photo safari, and other ground tours to a number of destinations including Prince Rupert Bay and the city of Portsmouth, with a transfer to a rowboat to go up the Indian River, at a cost of about $6 US per person for the river trip. All of these tour operators will arrange drivers, guides, rentals, and whatever else you need. Both *Castaways* (phone: 96244) and the *Coconut Beach* resort (phone: 55393) can set up boat charters. *Whitchurch Travel Agency* (phone: 82181) handles charters as well as air reservations. Anyone particularly interested in wildlife should contact the Forestry and Parks Service at the Botanical Gardens near Roseau (phone: 82732). Ask for director Felix Gregoire or Colmore Christian. They will set up special-interest tours for groups and provide naturalist guides; their fees go toward park conservation.

 SHOPPING: Savvy travelers will head straight to *Cee Bee*'s or *Paperbacks* bookstores for a copy of Lennox Honychurch's *History of Dominica,* a fascinating insider account of past and recent events. There is no duty-free shopping on the island; there are, however, some excellent buys on native handicrafts. *Tropicrafts,* started by the nuns of Immaculate Conception, but now a private company on Queen Mary St. and Turkey Lane in Roseau, specializes in items of vertiver grass joined with wild banana strands. They make hats, bags, placemats, square and oval rugs, and the prices are reasonable. The rugs — also sold by the one-foot square and sewn together in any dimension you might order — are acknowledged to be the strongest and best made in the Caribbean. You can watch the ladies weave them here on the premises.

The Carib Territory *Crafts Center* produces a bag made of two layers of reeds — buried in the ground to achieve a three-color effect that is incredible — with a layer of broad banana-type leaf between that makes it waterproof. A series of six little baskets that fit into one makes a nice gift at about $10 US. These Carib crafts are also available at *Caribana* on Cork St. in Roseau. *Pots 'n' Things* on Queen Mary St. also sells locally crafted Marinica Pottery, dolls, candles dipped in black volcanic sand, and other crafts. The *Dominica Handcrafts Company* markets more of the same, and at press time the *Old Market* (in the town's center, near the post office) was being converted into a crafts center with at least three shops and a "snackette."

Handmade leather bags, shoes, and sandals can be ordered from *Leathercraft,* on Lower Kennedy Ave. The tiny Woodstone Shopping Mall recently opened in town with several shops that sell clothing and other wares. Shops are open 8 AM to 1 PM and 2 to 4 PM, daily except Sundays; mornings only on Saturdays.

If you're driving near Emerald Pool, visit Brother Matthew Luke off the Imperial Highway at Pond Casse. His arts-and-crafts studio and gallery sells lovely, colorful "rain-forest creations" in Indian cotton.

 TIPPING: A 10% service charge is added by most hotels and some restaurants — but not the "native" places, so plan to add it yourself if you're satisfied with the service.

SPECIAL EVENTS: *Carnival* in Dominica is a big 10-day, pre-Lenten festival, beginning with nightly shows and culminating in a parade of floats on the Sunday afternoon before Ash Wednesday and lasting until Tuesday night. There is a band competition on Monday morning and more music and dancing in the streets (with tourists invited to join) on Monday and Tuesday. *National Day* (November 3) is preceded by a month of events celebrating Dominica's independence and culture with Creole songs, dances (both the African-influenced belaire and the French quadrille), folk narratives or *contes,* art and craft displays — graced by island women in *wob dwiyet,* the madras-and-foulard-draped national costume. *Domfesta* (the *Dominica Festival of Arts*) will be spread out over weeks or even months (to be decided) and will feature art exhibits, music and dance, literary workshops, readings, lectures, films, and street bazaars. *Korne Kon-La* festivities are held every month-end, alternating between the two fishing villages of Soufrière and Scotts Head, with street dancing and a variety of seafood. *New Year's Day, Good Friday, Easter Monday, Labor Day* (May 1), *Pentecost Monday, Emancipation Day* (first Monday in August), *Christmas,* and *Boxing Day* (December 26) are all celebrated.

SPORTS: Boating – A motorboat for six people will cost about $40 per person for a 6-hour tour, including lunch; a 2-hour snorkeling trip for a minimum of six people runs $10 per person. A sailboat trip is $25 per person for 6 hours at the *Anchorage* or *Castaways,* if they have one available, or through tour operators.

Snorkeling and Scuba – The island has its own fully equipped, NAUI-certified scuba setup, *Dive Dominica* (phone: 82188), operated — when he is on the island (make advance arrangements) — by Derek Perryman and based at *Castle Comfort Guest House.* Perryman's expeditions explore virtually virgin southern and western coastal waters; rental equipment, night dives, and snorkel trips are available, too. Prices run about $30 for a 1-tank dive, $45 for a 2-tank dive, and $50 for a resort course, which includes 2 dives. Night dives cost $25. NAUI certification courses cost $175, or $225 for open-water certification, which includes 10 dives. *Anchorage, Coconut Beach,* and *Castaways* are set up for windsurfing and snorkeling, and can arrange scuba trips, too. Also check out *James' Water World Beach Bar* at Canefield for windsurfing, surfboards, sailing, and snorkeling.

Sport Fishing – Charters can be arranged through the *Anchorage, Castaways,* or *Coconut Beach* for about $250 US per day for up to six people.

NIGHTLIFE: The best thing to say about nightlife in Dominica is that it's a beautiful island, and the rum drinks are tasty, pleasantly relaxing, and inexpensive. Some of the hotel lounges stay open until 11 PM or so, and the bar at *Reigate Hall* often jumps until later. There is music on weekends during the winter season at several of the hotels. Check out the newly reopened *Fort Young* hotel in town. For island barbecue and entertainment, reserve at *Sisserou* on Wednesday nights. In Roseau, *La Robe Créole,* a favorite gathering place, accentuates food, drink, and talk with stereo jazz nightly. Weekends there is music, mostly calypso and reggae, at the *Warehouse,* about 3 miles from Roseau; the *Good Times Bar-B-Q,* next door; the *Aquacade;* the *Bee Hive;* and the *New Grotto.*

BEST ON THE ISLAND

CHECKING IN: Dominica hotels and guesthouses offer a wide range of accommodations, none of which can be considered expensive compared to those in the rest of the Caribbean. There are some very attractive and comfortable hotels, usually built around open cocktail and dining areas (roofed to keep out the inevitable rain), with modern plumbing, sliding glass doors, individual balconies, and pools. The most expensive room on the island is probably a VIP suite at the *Reigate Hall* hotel, which goes for $110 US, including Jacuzzi and full English breakfast. The expensive hotels here cost $90 to $100 with breakfast; moderate is $50 to $90; and under $50 for inexpensive. There is a 10% tax. As they are widely spread out around the island, La Robe Creole Ltd. (phone: 84436; telex: 8607 HOTELS DO) offers 5-, 7-, and 9-night packages that allow visitors to stay at two or more hotels — for easier exploring — which include all taxi transfers, 2 meals a day, and some sightseeing. Hotels are divided into three categories: beachfront, city of Roseau, and country or mountain retreat. While prices vary little, appeal varies greatly.

Castaways – Longtime favorite (celebrating its 25th anniversary in 1988) on a gray beach 11 miles north of Roseau, with 27 seaside rooms and a popular al fresco bar and spacious dining room overlooking the beach. Water sports (manager Linda Harris is a scuba diver), tennis, tours. Nicely landscaped, clean, and friendly (phone: 96244). Expensive.

Reigate Hall – A lovingly restored estate house nestled on the mountainside a mile above Roseau, Dominica's answer to a luxury hotel. Local stonework and lovely wooden finishings and floors handsomely contrast with whitewalled interiors. The 17 rooms are tastefully appointed. Features include: swimming pool with nice view, tennis court, sauna, gym, game room, 24-hour room service, two VIP suites with private Jacuzzis. The bar is a popular meeting place. The restaurant features Continental and local cuisine (phone: 84031). Expensive.

Anchorage – On the water at Castle Comfort near Roseau, with a dock and a small black beach, the hotel — 36 simple but agreeable rooms — faces a curving bay where yachts anchor. There is a steady stream of visiting yachtsmen in the cocktail lounge and restaurant at night. This is a family business, and the kitchen has recently been given a boost with the return of a daughter who is now a US-trained chef. The hotel also runs both marine and land tours (phone: 82638). Moderate.

Coconut Beach – Five cottages and 6 rooms, with an additional 5 simple units planned on Dominica's best beach — at the end of Prince Rupert's Bay near Portsmouth, a stone's throw from Indian River. Safe anchorage for yachts, water sports, beachside restaurant. One advantage of staying by the sea is that there is much less rain than up above. Good jumping-off point for touring in the north. At Picard Beach, formerly part of Picard Estate Banana Company (phone: 55393, 55415). Moderate.

Fort Young – Destroyed by the hurricane of 1979, this charming and historic hotel, built into the stone walls of the original 1770 fort, has been carefully restored. Its 33 bedrooms, some split-level with sitting areas, all have air conditioning, ceiling fans, hardwood decks, and private baths. There's also a swimming pool; disco/entertainment center; restaurant; bar; and boutique (phone: 88501, 83908). Moderate.

Layou Valley Inn – This nature-oriented retreat in the cool Morne Trois Pitons foothills has a 180° view of the valley below. The daily program features scenic safaris, rain forest hikes, leeward side tours, waterfall bathing; there's also a 2-day, 1-night safari package. Some of the 6 simply but tastefully furnished rooms have private baths. Bar and dining room offer island and Continental drinks and dishes (phone: 96203). Moderate.

Papillote Wilderness Retreat – At the foothills of Morne Macaque, this is a very special place for nature lovers, dreamers, and children (who are both). Anne and Cuthbert Jno-Baptiste take a personal interest in the well-being of their guests, starting with a good orientation to the island's many offerings. Anne loves to show guests her exotic gardens. Kids love the hotel's pets, jungle setting, birds, river bathing, hot mineral pools, 10-minute nature trail up to Trafalgar Falls. Delightful garden restaurant popular with weekend day-trippers. Masseuse trained in shiatsu, reflexology, and acupressure conducts 3-week wave-massage sessions in hot mineral water twice yearly. Seven comfortable rooms (phone: 82287). Moderate.

Sans Souci Manor – Three tastefully appointed luxury apartments on a hillside 2 miles from Roseau, with kitchens (meal service also available), pool, color TV, and daily transportation to town (phone: 82306). Moderate.

Sisserou – A simple, oceanfront spot with 20 air-conditioned rooms and a pool, about a half mile outside Roseau (phone: 83111). Moderate.

Springfield Plantation – Picturesque Victorian plantation house and outbuildings with 5 or so rooms plus 3 apartments and cottages, furnished mostly with antiques; rooms 11 and 15 are best. Stunning views, river-fed natural pool, small swimming pool, trail maps for hikers. High in the hills, 2 miles from National Park entrance. Often cool enough for a nighttime fire (phone: 91401 or 91224). Moderate.

Castle Comfort Guest House – Only 5 rooms, all with bath and air conditioning but otherwise pleasantly old-fashioned West Indian style, on the rocky shore of Castle Comfort next to the anchorage just south of Roseau. Mrs. Perryman runs a "family home," and you're soon a part of it. Water sports and dive operation run by Mrs. Perryman's son, Derek (phone: 82188). Moderate to inexpensive.

Evergreen – Newly constructed on the shores of Castle Comfort one mile south of Roseau, with very attractive rooms of stone and brick with modern baths. Of the 10 rooms, the 2 on the seaside are somewhat larger, while 4 on the street in back also have porches with mountain views. The dining room serves good food but could use cozier lighting. Diving facilities shared with next-door *Castle Comfort Guest House.* Friendly, family-style management (phone: 82168 or 83288). Moderate to inexpensive.

Excelsior – Not nearly as grand as its name, but a welcome addition to the island's offerings; just next to Canefield Airport, so its especially suited to business travelers. Ten clean, cheerful rooms, each with bath and balcony, facing either the airstrip or parking lot; conference room for 70. Pool and pool bar planned (phone: 91501/2). Moderate to inexpensive.

Cherry Lodge Guest House – A delightful old house with 8 clean rooms, some with private bath. Family atmosphere in the heart of Roseau. Breakfast only (phone: 82366). Inexpensive.

Continental Inn – This hotel has 10 rooms, half with private bath, in the center of Roseau. Good for bargain-hunting businesspeople (phone: 82215). Inexpensive.

Emerald Pool – This Swiss-run property at 1,000 feet is a mile from the Emerald Pool, not far from Castle Bruce Lagoon and the Carib Indian Territory. Surrounded by a small tropical plantation and flower garden in the middle of the forest. The 6 A-frame Carib-style cabins have no facilities and provide a real feeling of camping in the woods. The 2-room bungalow is closer to civilization. On Castle Bruce Rd. in Fond Melle (no phone; for bookings, try 88095; better yet, Telex 8631 or cable POOL well in advance). Inexpensive.

Sunshine Village and Marina – German-run inn with 16 rooms, some with kitchen facilities. *The Umbrella* restaurant serves mostly German food, fresh fish when available. Easy access to historic Cabrits fortifications and Portsmouth; some water sports. On Purple Turtle Beach at the north end of Prince Rupert Bay (phone: 55066). Inexpensive.

Carib Territory Rural Guesthouse – For culture and nature enthusiasts unconcerned with modern frills, Charles and Margaret Williams offer 8 simple rooms in a Garden of Eden setting within the Territory. Meals and tours available (phone: 57256). Very inexpensive.

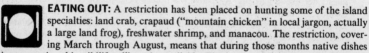 **EATING OUT:** A restriction has been placed on hunting some of the island specialties: land crab, crapaud ("mountain chicken" in local jargon, actually a large land frog), freshwater shrimp, and manacou. The restriction, covering March through August, means that during those months native dishes incorporating this wildlife will not be available. There are no restrictions, however, on the abundant seafood available year-round. In general, it is wise to order the specialty of the house, or of the day, to be sure of freshness, as food supplies can vary greatly (depending on whether the fish are biting that day and what has been delivered). The best food is often served in the plainest places.

Island cooking styles include Créole, Continental, and American, but the native dishes tend toward Créole foods like fried tee-tee-ree (tiny freshly spawned fish), lambi (conch), callaloo or pumpkin soup, and crabbacks (the backs of red and black land crabs stuffed with crab meat seasoned Créole style). Most of the hotels prepare meals for their guests and will accept nonguests if notified in advance. Bello Hot Pepper Sauce, made on Dominica, is served everywhere, with almost everything. The island fruit juices — pineapple, paw paw, guava, and lots more — are out of this world, as are the rum punches ("A day without rum punch is no day at all," is the saying on Dominica). Bartenders also blend a terrific coconut rum punch, not aged, but made fresh from coconut milk, sugar, rum, and bitters. Liquor, and local rum especially, is inexpensive; wine, although most of the island stocks some, is not. All sorts of beers and fresh fruit juices are available.

Food prices on Dominica are consistently reasonable. Expect to spend $30 to $50 for a meal for two in hotel restaurants. Restaurants listed as inexpensive charge under $20 for two. Prices do not include drinks, wine, or tips.

Reigate Hall – More Continental than Créole; European versions of local dishes — such as "mountain chicken" in champagne sauce — are often interesting. Service is smooth and sweet, and the ambience, with candles and splashing paddle-wheel, is romantic. Popular bar. Dinner until 11 PM (phone: 84031). Expensive to moderate.

La Robe Créole – Noted for its decor, ambience, and excellent Créole cuisine. Popular with visitors and businessmen for lunch as well as for dinner until 11 PM. The menu features Créole lobster, freshwater shrimp and crayfish, "mountain chicken," lambi (conch), grilled meats and fish, good soups (pumpkin, callaloo, crab), fruit punches, salads, and even hamburgers. Victoria St., Roseau (phone: 82896). Expensive to moderate.

Castaways – Pleasant service, fine sea view, good Créole food — known for its "mountain chicken," seafood, and Sunday beach barbecue with live music. A half-hour drive north of Roseau (phone: 96244). Moderate.

Coconut Beach – Large portions of the usual Dominican fare, with daily and Sunday lunch specials. Its location at Picard in Portsmouth makes it the place for lunch on a northern day tour; otherwise, it's a bit of a project to reach unless you're staying at the resort of the same name. The candlelit dinners are served al fresco (phone: 55393). Moderate.

Papillote – Very popular outdoor hotel restaurant near Trafalgar Falls, a sort of oasis in the rain forest. After lunching on tiny river shrimp (*bookh*) or crayfish with delicate homegrown salads, get Anne to take you around her tropical gardens; then take the short hike to the falls, a swim in the cool mountain river, and a hot bath in the natural mineral pools. This is a place to spend the day. Open to nonguests from 10 AM to 6 PM; dinner by reservation only (phone: 82287). Moderate.

Continental – Tasty local cookery featuring lobster, mountain chicken, crayfish, turtle, conch, freshwater shrimp — the best of what's available. Queen Mary St., Roseau (phone: 82216). Inexpensive.

Guiyave – Specializes in island dishes such as curried beef, highly seasoned "baked chicken," and octopus or crayfish when available. Congenial atmosphere, popular for business lunches, verandah dinners. Cork St., Roseau (phone: 82930). Inexpensive.

World of Food – In *Vena's* hotel. Dominican specialties, including roti, conch, crabbacks. Lunch and dinner in the old house and courtyard of famed Dominican novelist Jean Rhys. 48 Cork St., Roseau (phone: 83286). Inexpensive.

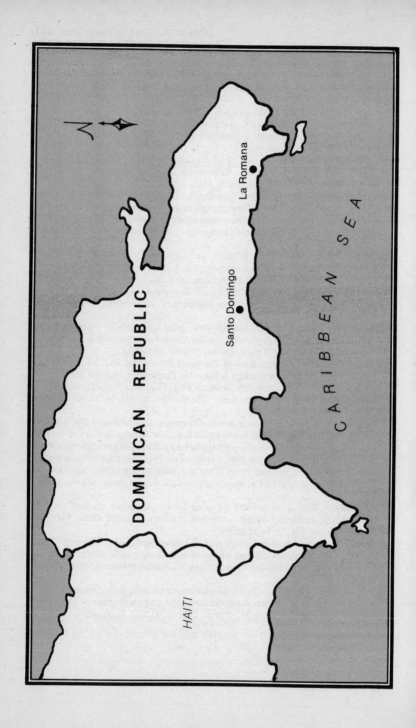

DOMINICAN REPUBLIC

The Dominican Republic, sprawled over the eastern two thirds of the big island of Hispaniola in the Greater Antilles, can claim more "oldests" than any other place in the Caribbean — indeed, the Western Hemisphere: Its capital, Santo Domingo, is the New World's oldest city, with the New World's oldest street, oldest house, oldest cathedral, the site of its oldest university, and the ruins of its oldest hospital.

The Columbus family was in on all this from the start. It was Christopher who found the island on his first voyage in 1492, and whose mortal remains may lie in the impressive marble sarcophagus in the nave of the Cathedral of Santa María la Menor ("may" is the operative word since several other locations also claim to be his last resting place). His brother Bartholomeo founded the capital city of Santo Domingo. And it was Christopher's son, Diego, who became the colony's governor in 1509 and ruled as its viceroy during the glorious days when it served as provisioning port and launching place for Spain's greatest expeditions into the Americas. Velásquez sailed from Santo Domingo to settle Cuba; Juan Ponce de León, to colonize Puerto Rico (he later died in the city of Havana on his way home from his futile fountain-hunting trip to Florida); and Cortés, to conquer Mexico. Britain's Sir Francis Drake — pirate, corsair, hero, depending on whose history you're reading — broke the charm in 1586 when he attacked, sacked, and set fire to the capital. It was centuries before Santo Domingo came to life again.

In the interim, the colony became a pawn in the Caribbean island possession game, claimed in succession by France, Spain, and itself (during the "Ephemeral Independence" proclaimed by José Nuñez de Caceres in 1821), and, shortly thereafter, by Haiti, whose president, Pierre Boyer, declared it part of his country. It was not until February 27, 1844, that Juan Pablo Duarte's La Trinitaria movement obtained his country's final freedom. Except for a brief Spanish episode in 1861, the Dominican Republic has been independent ever since.

Why, then, is the Dominican Republic's appeal so relatively new to this generation of American island lovers? The answer is traced to the influence of the strong man once known as El Benefactor, Generalissimo Rafael Leonidas Trujillo, who took power in 1930 and held fast until his assassination in 1961. Although he helped establish a degree of economic order, he siphoned off enormous sums of money for himself and his friends during his increasingly oppressive dictatorship. When the populace objected, he simply tightened his grip. The word spread: In spite of the capital's deluxe hotels and gambling casinos, Trujillo and tourism were incompatible. What had been a steady stream of business and pleasure traffic slowed to a trickle and, in the late 1950s, almost stopped.

It has taken all the years since to bring the Dominican Republic back into the Caribbean travel picture. Tourism got strong backing from President Joaquin Balaguer, whose government started things off by investing many millions of dollars in the resort infrastructure and aid to hotel development. It also received sizable support from the Gulf & Western conglomerate, which began by buying a sugar mill at La Romana, then got into tourism in a big way: first, with the super sport/land development complex *Casa de Campo* on the south coast (no longer owned by G&W), and then with two hotels in the capital itself. In the late 1970s President Antonio Guzman appointed the first cabinet-level minister of tourism; and since then, the government has remained steady in its commitment to promote tourism.

From a meager 87,000 visitors in 1967, the volume of Dominican tourism climbed to approximately 800,000 in 1988. In Santo Domingo, construction of luxury hotels has kept up with the increase in tourism; notable additions are the *Santo Domingo* hotel, the *Sheraton,* and — the newest — the *Jaragua.* The 221-room *Gran Hotel Lina* reopened with 221 rooms in 1984, and refurbishing programs are constantly under way at other big hotels. Outside the capital, the trend is toward a more casual, clubby kind of resort life. At Puerto Plata, served by La Unión International Airport, the *Dorado Naco* opened in 1982; the *Playa Dorada* in 1984. *Jack Tar Village* caters to guests buying packages; and some modest, pleasant rustic retreats have sprung up in neighboring Sosua and Samaná. The largest is the 1,000-room *Barbaro Beach* hotel at Punta Cana, on the island's far eastern tip.

Meanwhile, the restoration of the Alcázar and a number of neighboring antique buildings that miraculously escaped Drake's onslaught has been accomplished with care and understanding. Hotels and resorts function more smoothly each season, and the people of the Dominican Republic not only seem eager to please, but genuinely delighted to have American tourists.

DOMINICAN REPUBLIC AT-A-GLANCE

FROM THE AIR: The Dominican Republic is almost a primer in basic geography, illustrating many kinds of topography. Rugged peaks, rolling hills, rich valleys, lush sugarcane plantations, and fine white beaches are all part of this country where Columbus first landed in 1492. The Dominican Republic occupies the eastern two thirds of the island of Hispaniola (the western third is Haiti), the second largest of the Greater Antilles (Cuba is bigger). In the upper arch of the Caribbean archipelago, it is washed by the Caribbean on the south, the Atlantic on the north, and on the east by the 75-mile-wide Mona Passage, which separates it from Puerto Rico. At approximately 18°48′ N latitude, 71°14′ W longitude, it is also a neighbor of Jamaica (300 miles west) and Cuba (150 miles northwest).

The Dominican Republic is large compared to other Caribbean countries — 19,120 square miles with a population of almost 6½ million. Its principal mountain range — the Cordillera Central — boasts the highest peak in the West Indies, Pico Duarte, rising 10,382 feet above sea level. Three other ranges run almost parallel, west to east, across the country, and four major rivers — of which the longest is the 125-mile Rio Yaque del Norte — flow from the mountains to the ocean and the sea.

Santo Domingo, the capital, which was known as Ciudad Trujillo when the dictator Trujillo was alive, is at the mouth of the Ozama River in the center of the south coast. A wide, new, landscaped highway leads to Las Americas International Airport, about 20 miles west of the city on the edge of the Caribbean. It's about 3½ jet hours from New York, about 2 hours from Miami, and about 40 minutes from Puerto Rico.

Almost one third of the Dominican Republic's coastline is edged with beaches. For tourists, the most appealing north coast seaside towns are Puerto Plata, around which a new resort area is developing; Sosua, founded by Jewish refugees from Europe in the 1940s, and Samaná, a fishing village populated by the descendants of escaped American slaves who still speak English though they've been loyal Dominicans for generations. The *Club Med* at Punta Cana also boasts a spectacular beach; Punta Cana's 20-mile stretch of sand is the longest in the Caribbean. The best southeastern beaches are near Boca Chica and La Romana. The towns of Jarabacoa, Constanza, and Santiago (the Dominican Republic's second city), nestled in the central mountains, are a cool change from the tropical sea scene.

SPECIAL PLACES: When it comes to sightseeing, the Dominican Republic is really two places: Santo Domingo and everywhere else. In Santo Domingo, a combination of foot and taxi is probably the best way to get around. In the colonial area, parking can be a problem, but everything there is within walking distance of everywhere else. Outside that somewhat compact section, however, driving is a breeze, and Dominicans are helpful should you get lost.

Colonial Santo Domingo – Seeing the sights — modern and antique — in Santo Domingo can fill several days, especially if you take time to trace all the historic roots. But you can cover the major points in a day if you move fast. Start at the city's most symbolic point: Columbus Square, where a large bronze statue of the discoverer stands watch. On December 5, 1492, Columbus landed at La Isabela, but no matter — he looks just as at home and appropriate here.

On the south side of the square is the Cathedral of Santa María la Menor, a classic example of Spanish renaissance architecture. Collection of funds for the building began in 1514, but construction wasn't completed until 1523. It is the oldest cathedral in the Western Hemisphere, and it is here in the 450-year-old nave that the mortal remains of Christopher Columbus are said to lie in a marble and bronze sarcophagus (at least two other countries also claim to be his final resting place). Expert guides, speaking English and Spanish, will show you around (tip about $1 per person for the half-hour go-round); otherwise you might miss some fine points — the gold and silver treasures, delicate carvings, elaborate altars and shrines — that make the church as intriguing as it is antique.

Other square landmarks: Old Santo Domingo City Hall (now a bank) to the west; on the east, the Palace of Borgella, headquarters of the Haitian governor from 1822 to 1844 during the Haitian occupation. Nearby, at the corner of Calles Padre Billini and Arzobispo Merino, the Museum of the Dominican Family (Tostado House) exhibits mementos of a well-to-do Dominican family of the Victorian era.

Turning left on Calle Padre Billini, then left again on Calle Las Damas, you'll see the restored walls of the Ozama Fortress and the 1503 Tower of Homage, a massive structure where guards watched the city and condemned prisoners awaited their fate.

The oldest and one of the most beautiful streets in the New World, Calle Las Damas (named for the ladies of the viceregal court who once lived there and promenaded in the evenings), offers a number of excellent examples of 16th-century colonial architecture. One is the Bastidas House, encompassing a tropical patio, national museum workshops, and small exhibits. Another is the house of Governor Nicolás de Ovando, who planned and presided over the building of the city in the late 16th century; it is now restored as the *Hostal Nicolás de Ovando,* a small, charming hotel.

The National Pantheon, just across the street, is a must for buffs of both history and art. Once a Jesuit monastery (1714), its austere lines and massive size contrast with the graceful, smaller-scale colonial houses that surround it. Inside note the commemorative ceiling mural above the altar and the massive chandelier, gift of Spain's Franco. Many heroes — including the martyrs of June 14, 1959 — are buried within its walls.

Also along Calle las Damas: the Chapel of Our Lady of Remedies, where the first colonists attended mass; an antique sun clock; and the Museum of the Royal Houses (Museo de las Casas Reales) opened during the state visit of King Juan Carlos of Spain in 1976, with handsomely done displays and antique artifacts that tell the story of life and government in Santo Domingo's glory days. If you pick one museum to see, make it this one.

The Alcázar of Christopher's son, Don Diego Columbus, who ruled as first Spanish viceroy from 1509 to 1516, is another sightseeing must (it is also called the Columbus Palace). Built in 1510, it was so painstakingly and authentically restored in 1957 that Don Diego would probably feel completely at home today. Admission fee includes a tour with English-speaking guide. The statue on its plaza is of Columbus' queen, Isabel.

Directly across the street are the gleaming white walls of La Atarazana, once a colonial arsenal that housed the city's first customs office. It dates from 1507 and has been restored to house shops, restaurants, and galleries. (See *Shopping* below.)

Nearby, at the corner of the Calles Emiliano Tejera and Isabel la Católica, is the Casa del Cordon, where Don Diego Columbus and his wife, María de Toledo, lived while they waited for the Alcázar to be completed. Somehow it has survived hurricanes, earthquakes, and the ravages of Sir Francis Drake to remain standing as the oldest house in the New World. It is now the office of the Banco Popular, which offers free guided tours during business hours.

Two blocks west on Calle Emiliano Tejera, old stone paving leads to the ruins of the monastery of San Francisco. Built early in the 16th century, it was plagued by earthquake, pillaged by Sir Francis Drake, and bombarded by French artillery. Amazingly, much of the structure still stands.

On Calle Hostos (at Luperon) are the ruins of St. Nicolás de Bari Hospital, the first hospital in the New World, founded by Governor Nicolás de Ovando in 1503.

Santo Domingo – If you haven't worn your hiking boots, this might be the point at which to pick up a cab and head home for a rum punch — or for some of the attractions outside the colonial area. But if you're a hardy sightseeing type, point your driver toward the El Conde Gate at Independence Park. This large city square, where independence was proclaimed in 1844, marks the beginning of modern Santo Domingo. An altar-shrine to the three fathers of the country (Duarte, Sánchez, and Mella) dominates the square.

North of the Avenida Bolívar, on Avenida Maximo Gomez, the modern buildings of the Plaza de la Cultura, on the site of Trujillo's mansion, now house the Gallery of Modern Art, the National Library, the Museum of Natural History and Science, and the large and impressive National Theater. The anthropological Museum of the Dominican Man boasts a notable collection of pre-Columbian pieces and other interesting exhibits, but is a bit inscrutable without an English-speaking guide or knowledge of the local language since all the signs are in Spanish.

The new National Zoo in Arroyo Hondo, on the Avenida de los Próceres, also deserves some time. It's a free-space zoological park where animals roam around natural landscapes surrounded by a moat. The Botanical Gardens are nearby.

Los Tres Ojos (The Three Eyes), 10 minutes from Santo Domingo on Las Americas Highway, is a triplex beauty spot: three subterranean lagoons of sweet, salt, and sulfur waters fed by an underground river and surrounded by rock formations and lush vegetation. Cool, beautiful, and worth a trip.

ELSEWHERE ON THE ISLAND

Outside Santo Domingo, driving is the best way to get around. Most roads are adequate to good, and filling stations are reasonably spaced. Dominicans are more than happy to help with directions, but if you don't speak Spanish, it's a good idea to carry a Spanish phrase book; and by all means pick up a road map from the Tourist Office or a gas station.

La Romana – One of the most enjoyable day trips (or a several days' excursion, if you can arrange it) is the drive out the southeast coast to the *Casa de Campo* complex at La Romana. The resort facilities and the beauty of the spot are worth the trip. On the way, stop and sample the beaches at Boca Chica or the rum at the Pedro Justo Carrion distillery in San Pedro de Macoris. From downtown Santo Domingo, driving time is about two hours.

■**EXTRA SPECIAL:** Altos de Chavón, the evocation of a 15th-century village created by an Italian set designer near Casa de Campo. Designed to be part living museum, part artisans' colony, part tourist diversion, it now encompasses a small, ornate stone church (St. Stanislaus), a Grecian-style amphitheater, a Taino museum, workshops, studios, and galleries where visitors can not only buy but learn macramé, jewelry making, print making, and more. In addition there are four restaurants (Italian, Continental, Mexican, and Polynesian), a terrace café, and a cozy inn. The scenic site, overlooking the winding green Chavón River, plus all the above, make it worth a trip for its own sake.

North Coast – The country's newest tourist developments are here on the north coast where the mountains of the Cordillera Septentrional come down to meet the Atlantic Ocean. Because the nearby hills hold large deposits of amber, it is also called the Amber Coast. This is where you'll find the uncluttered, white sand beaches you may have missed in the south.

Puerto Plata (Port of Silver) – This town is 130 miles northwest of Santo Domingo on a crescent-shaped bay. There's a new international airport receiving an increasing number of international flights, and predicted resort development is finally becoming a reality. Take the funicular to the top of Isabel de Torres peak for a spectacular view of the countryside and the ocean. In town there are shops, restaurants, and simple, somewhat rustic places to stay. Outside town, new tourist resorts have materialized. At Playa Dorada, a number of resort hotels have opened near the Robert Trent Jones, Sr., golf course. A more ambitious development is being built farther east at Playa Grande is still on the drawing board. At the moment nearly deserted Playa Grande beach is one of the most beautiful stretches of sand in the Caribbean. Cabarete also has resort hotels and a lovely beach.

Sosua – Ten miles east of Puerto Plata, with more beautiful and almost untouched beaches. Many new small resort hotels, restaurants, and clubs have opened here in recent years, offering a nice contrast to Puerto Plata. It's popular with Canadian and European package groups, but Americans have yet to discover this bargain destination. Small cafés line the main street, the atmosphere is fun and friendly, and there's a good variety of hotels to choose from.

Cabarete – This windsurfing spot past Sosua resembles Malibu before it was built up. Its 3 miles of beach are currently being developed — hotels are popping up, houses are available for rent, and there are local restaurants here and there. The *Punta Goleta* resort is popular with French Canadians. Two new hotels scheduled to open in 1989 are *Pelican Beach* and *Camino del Sol.*

Samaná – A fishing village on a peninsula jutting out of the northeast coast that is another projected area for tourist development, inaugurated with the opening of the 60-room *Bahia Beach* resort and the 95-cabin *El Portillo Beach Club.*

SOURCES AND RESOURCES

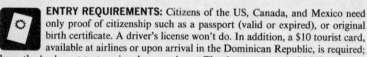

TOURIST INFORMATION: In New York, free information on accommodations, attractions, and tourist activities in the Dominican Republic is available from Dominican Tourist Information Center, 485 Madison Ave., New York, NY 10022 (212-826-0750). In Miami, consult the Dominican Republic Tourist Office, 2355 Salcedo St., Coral Gables, FL 33134 (phone: 305-444-4592). Both the private sector and government tourist organizations have centrally located offices in Santo Domingo. The Dominican Tourist Information Center (Centro Dominicano de Información Turistica) is at Arzobispo Merino 156 right across from the cathedral (phone: 687-8038 or 800-752-1151), and the government office is on George Washington Blvd. (phone: 682-8181).

Local Coverage – The *Santo Domingo News,* distributed free at hotels and shops, carries a current entertainment section that is directed more toward English-speaking residents than to tourists. *Bohío,* a free tourist magazine, is obviously ad-oriented but helpful.

The small *Official Guide to the Dominican Republic,* the most complete and available guidebook, is $2 to $3 at hotel newsstands and sundry shops, or can be obtained free from the Tourist Office. It offers, in addition to a comprehensive view of the whole country, valuable addresses and phone numbers. *Viejo Santo Domingo* is an excellent free guide with a map and a little history published by the Dominican-American Cultural Institute.

Listin Diario, El Caribe, and *Ultima Hora* are the daily local Spanish-language newspapers. Day-old Miami and New York papers are available in hotels.

Telephone – Dial direct to the Dominican Republic by adding the area code 809 to the numbers given below.

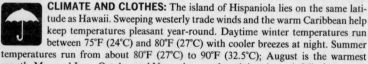

ENTRY REQUIREMENTS: Citizens of the US, Canada, and Mexico need only proof of citizenship such as a passport (valid or expired), or original birth certificate. A driver's license won't do. In addition, a $10 tourist card, available at airlines or upon arrival in the Dominican Republic, is required; keep the back part to turn in when you leave. The departure tax is $6 US.

CLIMATE AND CLOTHES: The island of Hispaniola lies on the same latitude as Hawaii. Sweeping westerly trade winds and the warm Caribbean help keep temperatures pleasant year-round. Daytime winter temperatures run between 75°F (24°C) and 80°F (27°C) with cooler breezes at night. Summer temperatures run from about 80°F (27°C) to 90°F (32.5°C); August is the warmest month. May and June, October and November are the rainiest, but rainfall often comes in short downpours followed by clear skies and a freshness in the air.

In general, daytime dress is casual and comfortable. Lightweight sportswear — slacks and shirts, skirts and dresses in natural fabrics or wash-and-wear blends — are fine for sightseeing; active sports clothes (for beach, tennis, golf, etc.) are right for resorts and the pools and courts of hotels in town. Pack summer weekend clothes with perhaps a light sweater or jacket for cooler winter evenings, air-conditioned restaurants and clubs. Evenings tend to be a touch dressier with jackets (but not necessarily ties) suggested at better restaurants and hotels. If you like to dress up, Santo Domingo has the spots: At places like the *Alcázar* dining room of the *Santo Domingo* hotel or *Mesón de la Cava,* the chic of Dominican women makes it obvious that they haven't let their *Vogue* subscriptions lapse.

 MONEY: At banks and exchange houses, $1 US buys about 5 Dominican pesos; the exchange rate at shops and restaurants may be somewhat lower. Try not to have a surplus of pesos at departure time; it's difficult and time-consuming to exchange them.

Shops and hotels accept US dollars happily but won't take Canadian money. Many larger stores accept American Express, Diners Club, MasterCard, and Visa, as do most hotels and restaurants. Ask before you buy, however, if you see no signs. Traveler's checks are welcome everywhere, but no special discounts are given for payment in either cash dollars or dollar-denomination traveler's checks.

 LANGUAGE: Spanish is the Dominican Republic's official language, but most Dominicans in tourist-related businesses speak some English. Outside of the prime tourist areas, there may be some language problem, but don't despair; Dominicans are friendly, helpful people and will find a way to communicate, even if it's via sign language.

 TIME: The Dominican Republic runs on Atlantic Standard Time. In late fall, winter, and early spring, noon in New York is 1 PM in Santo Domingo; when Daylight Saving Time is in effect in the US, noon in New York is noon in Santo Domingo.

 CURRENT: Same as that in the US and Canada — 110 volts, 60 cycles.

 GETTING THERE: Eastern, American, Pan Am, and Dominicana fly direct to Las Americas International Airport nonstop from New York; Eastern, Pan Am, and Dominicana direct from Miami. Dominicana connects with additional flights from San Juan. Puerto Plata and the North Coast are served by American, Pan Am, and Dominicana from New York, and Pan Am and Dominicana out of Miami. There are also frequent charter arrivals in Puerto Plata. Executive Air Services now provides connections between San Juan and Punta Cana (serving, primarily, Club Med). ALM and VIASA link the Dominican Republic with other Caribbean islands and South America. Direct service to Casa de Campo via San Juan is available on American Eagle, or via private plane.

 CALCULATING COSTS: The Dominican Republic has 15,000 hotel rooms priced mostly in the moderate-to-expensive range. A double room in an acceptable Santo Domingo hotel can go for as little as $27 to $29 a night European Plan (EP, no meals), while a double in a luxury resort can command $210 and up a day with breakfasts and dinners for two (MAP) or $150 and up EP. With the exchange rate heavily in favor of the dollar, however, food and beverage costs at even the finest restaurants can be quite attractive, so it might be wise to book your room EP, and then sample some of the country's many interesting restaurants. Do remember to include the costs of transfers from the airport to your hotel, sports fees (for golf, tennis, riding, etc.), 5% tax, 10% service charge, and 6% food-and-beverage tax.

An average room in the city runs about $40 EP year-round; more luxurious capital hotels are slightly higher, and because business travel remains constant all year, these rates don't change with the seasons. Resorts are off-season bargains between mid-April and mid-December when prices drop 30% to 40%. The widest choice of attractive packages is offered then, too, and sportsmen, honeymooners, shoppers, sightseers, and just plain vacationers can buy fixed-price vacations that usually include many features for which they'd have to pay extra in season.

Opting for the Modified American Plan rate (MAP, including breakfast and dinners) adds about $15 up to $30 a day. Several hotels in town offer dine-around plans that let you visit a number of different places at the MAP rate. At La Romana resorts, the MAP option may be worth taking, since there is not much restaurant choice outside the complex.

 GETTING AROUND: Airport Limousines – Airport bus service is available into Santo Domingo at about 3.50 pesos per person, though the service is not very frequent (only six trips to and from the airport each day). You can call *Expressos Dominicanos* (682-6610) to find out when the next one is due. But we'd take a cab. Another alternative is to hop onto a moto-concho — a ricksha-type cart powered by a man and his motorcycle — or buy a lift on the back seat of a motor scooter for a few pesos.

Guests headed for the *Casa de Campo* resort at La Romana are met by a hostess with an arrival list and shown to an air-conditioned courtesy suite where they can wait comfortably until all the guests have assembled; the 1½-hour bus ride costs about $24 round-trip, which is automatically added to your hotel bill.

Taxi – You'll have no problem finding one at the airport or in town. But they aren't metered; so make sure the fare (and the number of passengers it pays for) is understood and agreed on before you ride. The fare from Las Americas Airport to Santo Domingo's central tourist hotels runs about 40 pesos. There's a minimum in-town fare of 10 pesos per ride. If you have trouble finding a cab, the *Taxi Center* will send one immediately if you phone (556-2606 or 565-1313).

Bus – In Santo Domingo they are big, sometimes crowded, but also cheap and efficient, and they cover the city. Air-conditioned bus service from Santo Domingo to other towns — Bonao, Jarabacoa, La Romana, La Vega, Puerto Plata, San Pedro de Macoris, and Santiago — is comfortable and gives you a chance to meet the Dominican people and see the country. Check the number of stops, however; some routings offer quite a bit of local color you could live without. For schedule and route information, phone *Expressos Dominicanos* (682-6610) or *Autobuses Metro* (566-6590). Cool bargain: the 3-hour air-conditioned ride to Puerto Plata for about 15 pesos.

Limousine – Share-the-ride car lines travel from the capital to towns throughout the country. There are set fares and schedules. The number to call for information varies according to the direction in which you're traveling. Check the *Official Guide* for the right number, or call the *Centro Dominicano* (685-3282).

Car Rental – Available from international and Dominican companies at the airport and from branches in several cities. Rates range from $10 to $25 a day (according to the size and type of car and terms of rental), with unlimited mileage (you buy gas). Unless you have a credit card (most firms accept them), up to a 100-peso deposit is required.

Hertz and *Avis* will make reservations through their mainland 800 phone numbers. *Hertz* (phone: 688-2277), *Budget* (phone: 562-6812), *National* (phone: 562-1444), and *Avis* (phone: 532-9295) have desks at the airports in Santo Domingo and Puerto Plata and at some hotels. *Nelly Rent-A-Car,* one of the best local firms (phone: 532-7346 or 533-0859), and other Dominican Republic companies are listed in the phone book and/or have representatives in the better hotels. All companies listed above have drop-off centers at the airport in Puerto Plata; your hotel is the best source of information on rentals there.

No need to register or get a special license to drive here; your valid license is good for 90 days.

Dominican driving is easy and pleasant, but Dominican drivers do tend to use their horns instead of their brakes. In old Santo Domingo, the streets are narrow with blind corners, so watch closely. In the countryside, try to limit your driving to daylight hours; the roads aren't lit, and a meandering mule could wipe out more than your damage deposit.

Sightseeing Taxi Tours – Cost more than bus trips, but are great, providing you can find a driver who speaks your language (or you speak his), knows his Dominican history and sights, and has good springs in his car (especially out of Santo Domingo). Consult your hotel travel desk for specific names. Otherwise, you're better off on a bus tour with an English-speaking guide.

Sightseeing Bus Tours – Air conditioned, with English-speaking guides, and offered by a number of local companies. *Metro Tours* (phone: 567-2286) and *Terrabus* (phone: 567-9715) are two good ones; *Vimenca Tours* (phone: 533-2318) and *Santo Domingo Tours* (phone: 567-6818) are others. On the south coast, *Tropical Tours* at *Casa de Campo* is a top-notch operator (phone: 682-2111, ext. 3128 or 3111). Options include beach trips, city and country sightseeing, shopping, sports packages, and visits to the mountain towns of Jarabacoa, Constanza, and Santiago. There are also nightclub and dine-around deals, but — as is the case on most islands — you can probably have more fun after dark on your own. Prices run from about 20 pesos (for a half-day city sightseeing trip) to about 60 pesos per person for a full-day, out-of-town group tour with lunch included.

 SHOPPING: The best Dominican Republic buys are in products crafted on the island. Amber jewelry and decorative pieces — made from petrified pine resin that may be as much as 60 million years old — are a national specialty. Some pieces encase insects, leaves, or dew drops, which make them more valuable. Color can range from crystal clear to almost black; a golden tone is most common. But buy amber only in established shops. That nice amber piece that street vendors offer at even nicer prices often turns out to be plastic.

Larimar, or "Dominican turquoise," is another popular stone that's milky blue and perhaps even prettier than turquoise. It's often mounted with wild boars' teeth or silver. Polished pink pieces of conch shell are also crafted into striking jewelry.

Other worthwhile take-home items include rocking chairs — very popular in the Dominican Republic, sold knocked down and boxed for easy transporting — wood carvings, macramé, baskets, and leather goods. Hand-carved pre-Columbian (in shape, not age) limestone carvings sold at roadside stands near the airport might look fine on the bookshelf back home. But haggle on the price — about half the asking price is usually fair. And don't drop the one you buy; the soft limestone smashes easily.

Some of the most attractive jewelry and gift items you'll see will be made from tortoiseshell. Unfortunately for you (and the tortoise), many species — especially the hawksbill used in many pins, combs, etc. — are on the US endangered species list; so any tortoiseshell item that a US customs officer finds in your luggage will be impounded.

Generally, shopping hours are from 8:30 or 9 AM to noon. After siesta, stores reopen from 2:30 PM till about 6:30.

La Atarazana (The Terrace), a winding street across from the Alcázar and near the river, is lined with gift shops and galleries. Savvy shoppers browse here, then move on to Calle El Conde, the oldest and most traditional shopping area in the city, to do their buying.

The *Mercado Modelo,* Santo Domingo's model native marketplace on Avenida Mella, is full of stalls that offer all kinds of craft products. The crunch of humanity is nowhere near as dense as that in Haiti's Iron Market, but if you don't speak Spanish, you may want to have your cab driver come along as interpreter, or give one of the small boys at the gate $1 to lead you through, fend off some of the more eager merchants, and help you find what you're after. With or without escort, you won't be hassled, but you should bargain before you settle on a final buying price. Also look for Dominican coffee — sold unground, it is good, strong, and less expensive than special roasts back home.

Don't shop for clothing in the Dominican Republic unless you have time to have it tailor-made. All high-fashion ready-to-wear is imported and frightfully expensive. If you really need something or feel compelled to spend money, look in and around the *Plaza Naco* shopping center, where the most fashionable shops are. The *Plaza Criolla* downtown is a center for fine jewelry shops and other boutiques. For stunning designer outfits, go to *Jenny Polanco* boutique at the *Sheraton* hotel.

Supermercado Nacional shopping center includes a *farmacia,* cosmetic shop, and a big grocery that amateur cooks like to browse through for imported sherry vinegars, olive oil, and other culinary finds (coffee here, too, of course).

Duty-free shops at the Centro de los Héroes, La Atarazana, and the *Santo Domingo, Sheraton,* and *Embajador* hotels in town carry the usual range of French perfumes, liquor, camera equipment, watches, jewelry, etc. You choose from the stocks they have on hand; duplicates of the merchandise you pick are delivered to your plane or ship. The principle is the same as at airport duty-free shops, but the selection in *La Zona Franca* is greater. You must pay in dollar-denomination traveler's checks or cash dollars.

Among the best buying and browsing shops are *Mendez* (Calle Arzobispo Nouel, corner José Reyes), offering distinctive jewelry (Sr. Mendez claims to have discovered larimar and has done some handsome things with it); *Ambar Marie* (Calle Rosa Duarte 19), with one of the best and most extensive amber collections, from tiny drop earrings to museum pieces; *Monika* (Calle El Conde), a buying spot for jewelry and assorted craft gifts; *El Conde Gift Shop* (Calle El Conde 25), the place to find rocking chairs along with other Dominican wares; and *Anacaona Creations* (Plaza Henriques Urena 117), where macramé is the specialty.

In La Romanca, visit *Equis Gallery* for Dominican art, *Joyas Criollas* and *Casa Verde* for carnival masks.

In Puerto Plata, browse through the restored turn-of-the-century artisans market (Av. 30th of March at John F. Kennedy Blvd.) for local crafts, ceramics, amber jewelry, leather goods. At the *Factory Gift Shop* (23 Duarte), you can watch amber and larimar jewelry crafted before you buy. A growing number of inviting boutiques — like *Macaluro's* (32 Duarte St.) and *El Palacio Island Gifts* (14 John F. Kennedy Blvd.) — specialize in jewelry and handwork. There is a *Jenny Polanco* designer boutique at the *Eurotel Playa Dorada.* There is also a duty-free shop at the airport.

 TIPPING: Hotel bills and restaurant checks usually include a 10% service charge, which is supposed to cover all tips. For good service, though, it's customary to add 5% to 10% more — especially in restaurants not connected with hotels. Tip hotel maids $1 per day per room, bellboys and airport porters 25¢ per bag (but never less than 50¢). Give taxi drivers 10% to 15%.

 SPECIAL EVENTS: The Dominican Republic's big festival time is *Merengue Week,* celebrated in Santo Domingo in the last part of July. Rum flows and everyone takes to the dance floor — or the street or the nearest tabletop — to do the rhythmic national dance. Tourists are more than welcome to join in, and if your merengue is a little rusty, don't worry. There'll be more than enough volunteer instructors around to help.

Carnival is celebrated on Independence Day (February 27), and preparations are already under way for a yearlong celebration in 1992 of the 500th anniversary of Christopher Columbus's discovery of America.

Legal holidays — when banks, businesses, and most government offices are closed — are *New Year's Day, Three Kings' Day* (January 6), the *Day of Our Lady of Altagracia* (January 21), *Duarte's Day* (January 26), *Independence Day* (February 27), *Good Friday* and *Easter, Labor Day* (May 1), *Corpus Christi Day* (60 days after Easter), *Restoration Day* (August 16), *Feast of Our Lady of Mercy* (September 24), *Columbus Day* (October 12), and *Christmas.* (Dominicans like to be with their families on certain festive days — even if it means flying home from New York or Miami. Christmas is one of those times, so plane seats are hard to come by; reserve well ahead.)

 SPORTS: Fine year-round weather and lots of unspoiled land and beautiful water — as yet not overpublicized — make the Dominican Republic a great place to feel the sun and sea, meet the challenge of a tough par-three hole, or fight it out with a blue marlin. The opportunities are top quality now, and — with the further development of resorts like Puerto Plata — they'll be expanding.

Baseball – The Dominican passion, and many Dominican Republic–born players have become major leaguers (Cesar Cedeño, Pedro Guerrero, and the country's first Hall of Famer, Juan Marichal, among them). American stars like LA's Steve Garvey and manager Tom LaSorda have spent winters with Dominican teams. The professional winter season runs from October to the end of January; the summer season is April to September. Check local papers for schedules, or ask any Dominican for the location of the nearest game.

Boating – Small sailboats are available through hotels in Santo Domingo and on the north coast; the *Club Med* at Punta Cana and *Casa de Campo* at La Romana have their own fleets of day sailers. Large-boat charters aren't always easy to arrange; hotels and the tourist offices may have information on boats available in the Santo Domingo area. Better still, arrange ahead by corresponding through your home yacht club or marina.

Dog Races – Greyhound races are held year-round at *Canodromo El Coco,* about 15 minutes north of the capital. There are 400 dogs, 12 races a night, starting at 7 PM (4 PM on Sundays). General admission is 1 peso; 4 pesos gets you into the clubhouse. Minimum bet: 1 peso.

Horse Races – Held year-round on Tuesdays, Thursdays, and Sundays at the *Perla Antillana* near Santo Domingo's baseball stadium.

Golf – Two of the world's finest championship courses are the Pete Dye–designed layouts at *Casa de Campo* in La Romana: "Teeth of the Dog," a heartbreaker with seven spectacular seaside holes; and "The Links," a fine inland course. These are the two best golf courses in the Caribbean, and a third course is due to open in early 1989. Greens fee is about $18 in summer, $20 in winter for a full day; the cart fee for two is about the same for 18 holes, caddy included. For a starting time, call 682-2111, ext. 3187.

There is a handsome Robert Trent Jones, Sr., course at *Playa Dorada,* near Puerto Plata, and visitors can play the *Santo Domingo Country Club* course, but only on a members-first basis — which practically rules out weekend play.

Horseback Riding – Dominicans love riding, and their country offers some of the best riding in the Caribbean. Rarely do you find an animal that even remotely resembles the stereotypical tired hack horse. To ride in Santo Domingo, call the *International Horseback Riding Club* (phone: 533-6321), *Rancho School* (phone: 682-5482), or the *National Horseback Riding School* (phone: 682-5482). The resorts at La Romana raise their own horses, and about 400 homegrown steeds are available to ride at *Casa de Campo's Rancho Centro Romana,* where you can arrange to ride with a guide (required) for up to eight hours (about 12 pesos per person per hour) on a horse suited to your skill. Or take private or group lessons in riding or polo through the Activities Office at Casa de Campo (phone: 682-2111, ext. 2249).

Polo – The polo season runs from October through May, and there are regular games at *Sierra Prieta* in Santo Domingo and at *Casa de Campo* near La Romana. Guests may join the twice-a-week competition, provided they've brought their handicap from a home club. Mallets are appreciated, too, but they can be provided in a pinch. Call Brigadier (ret.) Arthur Douglas Nugent at *Casa de Campo* (phone: 682-2111, ext. 2249). This is the place to learn to play polo, or to improve your game if you already play, in a glorious setting with patient instructors and over 100 polo ponies from which to choose. Private lessons run $30 per hour.

Snorkeling and Scuba – The only completely equipped outfit in town, *Mundo Submarino* (phone: 566-0340) takes certified divers only on half-day and day-long trips; price of a half-day's diving is about $30 per person. Some of the most spectacular underwater scenery is at La Caleta, near the entrance to Las Americas Airport, where there are miles of coral reefs, caves, and some fissures more than 40 feet deep. Snorkel gear is loaned or rented for a small fee by resort hotels. Near La Romana, the *Dominicus Beach* resort offers a full water sports program. *Casa de Campo* guests can sail to nearby Catalina Island aboard the 52-foot schooner *Merengue* for a day's snorkeling. A guide leads you through trails of living coral, around to the island's spiny side, and out again; then there's lunch and some sun time before the sail home. Price: about $30 per person including lunch; reserve a day ahead.

Sport Fishing – Offshore waters are home to marlin, sailfish, dorado, bonito, and other game fish. Charter fishing boats are available through your hotel for about $100 for a half day for up to six people. Best spots are Cumayasa, La Romana, Boca de Yuma on the east; Palmar de Ocoa and Barahona on the south; Monte Cristi and Samaná on the north.

River Fishing – Flatboats, with guides, can be hired for about $35 a half day to fish for snook and tarpon at La Romana, Boca de Yuma, and on the north coast around Samaná.

Swimming and Sunning – At Santo Domingo the coast is craggy with no sand beaches, but residents enjoy swimming at Boca Chica and at Embassy Beach near San Pedro de Macoris, 30 minutes east of Santo Domingo. Tourists, to whom the water looks rough and the shore rocky, prefer to do their Santo Domingo swimming in hotel pools with chaises and snack and drink bars handy. The nearest sand beaches — and nice ones — are Boca Chica, just beyond the airport, and Juan Dolio, about 40 to 45 minutes east of town. About 2 hours out, guests at *Casa de Campo* swim at pretty Las Minitas. The *Club Med* is sited on a magnificent stretch of beach at Punta Cana on the island's far eastern tip.

The country's most beautiful beaches are those on the north coast, where resort development has grown up around the town of Puerto Plata, about 3 hours' drive north of Santo Domingo on a fast, new highway. Beach addicts drive up, lunch in the hills at Santiago, the Dominican Republic's second city, and settle on the shore for two or three days to sample the pleasures of the miles of sandy beach that line the calmer coast of the Atlantic. Sosua, Playa Dorada, and Playa Grande are all great for sunning, swimming, snorkeling, and uncrowded beachcombing.

Tennis – There are many courts and more being built. In Santo Domingo, the *Embajador, Concorde Dominicana, Santo Domingo, Hispaniola,* and the new *Sheraton* all have courts (some lighted), pro shops, teaching pros. The *Gran Hotel Lina, Jaragua,* and *Naco* have courts, too. At Puerto Plata, there are good courts at the *Jack Tar Village, Playa Dorada, Holiday Inn, Dorado Naco,* and *Villas Dorados;* those at the *Montemar* and *Cofresi* hotels and at *Villas del Mar* in San Pedro de Macoris are on the rustic side; the *Club Med*'s courts are first rate. *Casa de Campo* boasts a 13-court hillside tennis village, and there are 4 additional courts near the main guest complex.

The village has its own villas, a restaurant, pro shop, night lights, and a swimming pool. Fees are approximately $15 per hour.

Trap and Skeet Shooting – You can perfect your aim at *Casa de Campo.* Basic shooting orientation is free for beginners; clinics and lessons available for experienced marksmen.

 NIGHTLIFE: Take your pick — a Vegas-style review, a lounge with a cabaret singer or show-tune piano, New York–style disco dancing, a wild night of merengue, casinos where you can play until dawn (or almost), or maybe a quiet drink in a café by the ocean. Santo Domingo has them all.

Hotels offer more traditional fare. Smaller-scale shows are open most evenings. Current smart spot is *Las Palmas* in the *Santo Domingo,* designed by native Dominican Oscar de la Renta and featuring mirror walls painted with palm fronds under a high vaulted ceiling. The roof lounge atop the *Concorde Dominicana, L'Azotea,* and *El Yarey* at the *Sheraton* are catching on with the tourist crowd, while the *Embassy Club* at the *Embajador* is still a favorite with both Dominicans and visitors. *Lina's Salon La Mancha, Maunaloa, La Taverna de Maria Castoña,* and *El Castillo* in the *San Geronimo* hotel are the places for Latin music. Livelier types make for *Raffles* or the *Village Pub* downtown for sounds (disc, tapes, or live depending on the day of the week) and sociability, or *Drake's Pub* for drinks and 16th-century Dominican ambience; also the *Blues Bar* for jazz and drinks, *Le Café* and the *Golden Club* for drinks.

If you're afflicted with disco fever, you can find relief at the *Sheraton's* slick *Omni* or *Opus. La Belle Blu* on Av. George Washington is the latest see-and-be-seen scene; *Alexander's* on the Av. Pasteur draws discopating Dominican preppies. Later, move on to *El Viniedo* for wine, cheese, and a game of backgammon. *Mesón de Barri,* in the colonial district, is popular with artists and writers for drinks. Or, if you're still ready to roll, there's *Neon 2002* at the *Hispaniola.* The *Embajador, Sheraton, Dominican Concorde,* and *Naco* hotels have casinos; so does *Maunaloa* at the Centro de los Heros. The new *Jaragua Resort* hotel has a casino, nightclub, and cabaret.

At most places in town with entertainment, there's an admission charge ($2 up). Drinks are about $2 apiece.

Out of town, at *Casa de Campo,* options are limited but pleasant, with a quite remarkable choice of eight different dining spots on its own reservation and at the artisans' village of Altos de Chavón as well; Altos is also the site of the supersound disco called *Genesis.* At Puerto Plata, the *Castilla* hotel bar is the favorite gathering place in town; the *Montemar* has a small disco; and the *Playa Dorada Holiday Inn* has the hottest night spot on the beach. The discos at *Heavens* and *Eurotel* are also popular, but the disco *Casa del Sol* in Sosua is purported to have the best sound system in the Caribbean.

BEST ON THE ISLAND

CHECKING IN: There's new life on the Dominican hotel scene. Santo Domingo hotels cater to a fairly sophisticated crowd of history buffs, shoppers, nightlife lovers, businesspeople, gamblers, and some quickie divorcers. La Romana offers tops-in-class sports. What has been missing is that classic luxury beach hotel where guests can step from a room directly onto the sand and sea. But things are changing. The jetport near Puerto Plata is in full operation, and at nearby Playa Dorada, a number of new accommodations are opening. Beside the rustic in-town inn (the *Castilla* hotel) and a small resort hotel (the *Montemar*), there are new hotels and rental condominiums. Sosua, popular with Canadians and Europeans, has over 50 hotels from which to choose, and further hotel plans are on the drawing boards for neighboring coastal areas.

Meanwhile, the capital choices run from clean, neat, and inexpensive (as low as $25 a night for a double EP — without meals) to plush with matching prices ($50 and up for a deluxe oceanfront double, also EP); rates stay about the same year-round because of steady business traffic.

At resort hotels, the situation is different: Winter prices at La Romana's *Casa de Campo* are steep — about $180 up a day for a casita room for two without meals (rates are strictly EP, since guests can choose from so many restaurants). In summer, prices drop about 40%, depending on accommodations, and there are attractive packages. Hotels beyond Santo Domingo, La Romana, and Puerto Plata are considerably less expensive, whatever the season.

In the listings below, hotels classed as expensive charge $100 and up per night for a double without meals (MAP — breakfast and dinner — add $20 to $25 per person); moderate is in the $50 to $100 range for two without meals; inexpensive is under $50 for a double.

SANTO DOMINGO

Dominicana Concorde – This once deluxe hotel no longer lives up to its former rating; it has grown shabby, and furnishings are a hodgepodge. The pluses: a huge pool, 4 restaurants, a nightclub, big rooms (some outlooks better than others), and the city's best-laid-out tennis setup. Its fairly distant location makes getting to town something of a hassle. Two pools, 8 lighted tennis courts (with pro), gym, sauna, plus improved service, restaurants, and a new casino would make this an agreeable in-town resort (phone: 532-2531). Expensive.

Jaragua – Opened in 1988 on a 14-acre site, with 340 rooms in the 10-story tower and 2-story garden estates. Clay-court tennis, swimming pool, European-style spa, casino, and nightclub (phone: 682-2222). Expensive.

Santo Domingo – Facing the sea at Avenida Independencia and Abraham Lincoln, this luxurious city hotel, with interiors by Oscar de la Renta, is a top choice. The Premier Club, a concierge floor, is an oasis — rooms are beautifully decorated, and the staff most accommodating. The hotel offers a large pool and sundeck with bar and restaurant, sauna, shops, and 3 tennis courts. Excellent *El Alcázar* dining room in lavish Moorish-Indian decor. *Las Palmas* is its night spot. There's a most agreeable breeze-conditioned bar, too (phone: 532-1511). Expensive.

Santo Domingo Sheraton – Each room has a sea view, except on the third floor; suites have terraces. Basically a business hotel in a convenient location. Good-looking modern design with green-planted public space; management that's skilled and thoughtful. Restaurant, nightclub, pool, sauna, shops, 2 lighted tennis courts, Jacuzzi, beauty salon, a stylish casino, and a disco that's tops (phone: 685-5151). Expensive.

El Embajador – Recently given an extensive facelift. In the western part of town on a slight hill; south-facing rooms have sea views. There's a nice pool, tennis courts (one clay), and two very good restaurants — one luxury Continental and one Chinese, the *Jardin de Jade,* with dramatic decor and 136 Oriental dishes to choose from. Also a casino and the *Embassy* nightclub, a smart-set favorite (phone: 533-2131). Expensive to moderate.

Gran Hotel Lina – The reincarnation of a longtime Latino favorite, it reopened in June 1984, totally renovated, with 221 air-conditioned rooms, pool, tennis, and one of the capital's best Spanish restaurants (see *Eating Out*). Rooms are simple but attractively furnished (phone: 689-5185). Moderate.

Hispaniola – Well-liked but less sumptuous sister of the luxurious *Santo Domingo* hotel across the street. Actually, it's a pleasant, modest, but comfortable place, very popular with Dominicans and business travelers; the staff is most hospitable. Some rooms on south side have sea views. Guests are entitled to use of all facilities (all the play for less pay) of the neighboring *Santo Domingo* hotel. Moderate-size pool and sunning space, outdoor coffee shop, pool bar. *El Vivero* dining room; swinging *Neon 2002* disco (phone: 532-1511). Moderate.

Comodoro – Centrally located in newer section of town. Only 87 rooms, but with pool, restaurant. Clean, efficient, good value (phone: 687-7141). Inexpensive.

Continental – Central location with clean, if a bit spartan, rooms, lounge, restaurant, pool (phone: 689-1151). Inexpensive.

Hostal Nicolás de Ovando – In heart of Old Santo Domingo, overlooking Ozama River, it's called "the oldest hotel in the New World." The place to stay if you love atmosphere and history, and you don't care about sports. Restored colonial home of Nicolás de Ovanda, who supervised building of city — the king and queen of Spain stayed here. Small pool, good (and good-looking) restaurant (phone: 687-3101). Inexpensive.

San Geronimo – Neat, clean, but no place to write postcards home about. Some rooms with kitchenettes, all air-conditioned (phone: 533-8181). Inexpensive.

LA ROMANA

Casa de Campo – This super-complete, luxurious, southeast coast resort on 7,000 acres is dedicated to great sports — lots of them. Two top golf courses (and a third due to open in 1989), 13 composition clay and 4 all-weather Laykold tennis courts and a tennis village, 6 pools, horseback riding and polo (polo lessons available), trap and skeet shooting, ocean and river fishing, snorkeling, sailing. Transport to beaches at Las Minitas (10 minutes), Bayahibe (30 minutes). Direct air service now available via San Juan, Puerto Rico, to the resort's private airstrip. Spacious rooms in casitas or golf or tennis villas. Eight distinctively different restaurants, on the property or at nearby Altos de Chavón, a cultural center and replica of a 15th-century Mediterranean village. Very popular, so book well in advance (phone: 523-3333; in Florida, 305-856-5405). Expensive.

PUERTO PLATA

Dorado Naco – This first luxury component in the *Playa Dorada* complex opened in July 1982. It has 150 air-conditioned 1- and 2-bedroom and penthouse condominium apartments (each with a color TV, kitchen, wall-to-wall carpet, queen-size beds), rentable when owners are away; interiors have attractive Dominican furnishings, though some are a bit the worse for wear. With restaurant, coffee shop, cocktail lounge, laundry, and a small supermarket as well as a swimming pool, super beach, and horseback riding; golf on adjoining Robert Trent Jones course. Best Western affiliate (phone: 586-2019). Expensive.

Eurotel Puerto Plata – Playa Dorada resort, with unusual, colorful architecture and 402 rooms and suites designed as private beach cottages. Huge free-form swimming pool, whirlpool, and most water sports, including waterskiing and sailing (phone: 586-3663). Expensive.

Jack Tar Village, Puerto Plata – Clublike complex on the sands at Playa Dorada. All kinds of activities — sailing, snorkeling, horseback riding, Robert Trent Jones golf, tennis, bicycling, and more — covered in week-long packages linked to scheduled or charter air travel (phone: 586-3800). Expensive.

Playa Dorada – Promoted as "A Luxury Beach Resort," it has 253 deluxe air-conditioned rooms and suites with terraces, balconies, color TV; contemporary exteriors, island-Victorian decor in public areas. With three restaurants; pool with swim-up bar; full water-sports center; lighted tennis; free golf; riding; piano bar, disco, and night entertainment. Request an ocean-view room (phone: 586-3988). Expensive.

Puerto Plata Beach Resort – On the waterfront at the eastern edge of town, it is the country's only all-suite hotel, with 216 units, pool, tennis, casino, and Playa Long Beach. Though only a couple years old, the place has a decor that reflects the Victorian flavor of Puerto Plata's traditional buildings (phone: 586-4243). Expensive.

Heavens – An all-inclusive resort with 150 rooms, including 80 suites. This airy, up-to-date property also has a pool, a good disco, 2 restaurants, a beach bar, and gym. The five-minute walk to the beach runs along a beautiful lagoon. Rates include meals and activities (phone: 586-5052). Expensive to moderate.

Villas Doradas – A first-class resort with 207 rooms, pool, beach, tennis, water sports, restaurant, and golf (phone: 586-3000). Expensive to moderate.

Costambar Beach – On Puerto Plata Bay with 3 miles of bright, white beach, this condominium complex offers a choice of 1-, 2-, and 3-bedroom cottages and apartments, ocean and mountain views. Each unit sleeps two to six, has its own terrace, living/dining area, fully equipped kitchen. Daily rental includes maid service, linens, membership in country club, where there's tennis, a swimming pool, riding, volleyball and basketball, a playground, bar, and restaurant with dancing and night entertainment (phone: 586-3828). Moderate.

Montemar, Puerto Plata – Simple, modern, and hospitable, with 96 rooms and 5 housekeeping cottages facing the Atlantic Ocean. Hotel school staff. With restaurant, disco nightclub, pool, and tennis (phone: 586-2800). Moderate.

Village Caraibe – Condo-style apartments with a total of 120 rooms. Apartments have kitchens, but there's also a restaurant, plus pool, golf, and tennis (phone: 586-4054). Moderate.

SOSUA

Los Coralillos – Overlooking Sosua Bay, with great views and charming Spanish atmosphere. It's also the only hotel in Sosua with direct access to the beach. Individual guestrooms and 1- and 2-bedroom tile-roofed villas are set amid gardens and pathways. There's also a pool, an outdoor dining terrace, and a restaurant (phone: 571-2645). Expensive to moderate.

Sosua Caribbean Fantasy – A Grecian-inspired property in coral on the main road to Sosua. Five stories, with no elevator, but its 67 rooms have air conditioning, balconies, and marble bathrooms, and views from the penthouse terrace are worth the climb. The especially attractive lobby and bar make use of interesting local handicrafts, paintings, and sculpture. A lovely outdoor restaurant, pool, Jacuzzi, conference room, and disco complete the picture (phone: 571-2534). Expensive to moderate.

Los Alemendros – Located near town on the highway, it offers 78 simple, clean rooms, 21 with private balconies and some with shared balconies. A tunnel leads directly to the beach. There's also a pool and 2 restaurants (phone: 571-3515). Moderate.

Playa Chiquita – Situated on the outskirts of town, it has 90 attractive rooms done in tropical pastels, with another 90 rooms currently being added. There's tennis, water sports, a pool, restaurant, and conference center. Attractive sun decks have been built above the postage-stamp-size beach. Second- and third-floor rooms have small terraces; all have small kitchens (phone: 571-2470). Moderate.

Hostal de Lora – A unique and charming 32-room inn, with a hand-crafted atmosphere in a natural setting. It has stained-glass windows, and a three-story spiral staircase embedded with colored-glass mosaic leads up to two penthouse apartments with terraces. All rooms have kitchens, and there's also a restaurant, a small pool, and Jacuzzi (phone: 571-3939). Moderate to inexpensive.

CABARETE

Punta Goleta – Presently 150 rooms, with plans to grow to 1,850, this distinctive property is a complete resort across the road from the beach. Its large, attractive rooms all have terraces and are decorated with local contemporary art. Amenities include horseback riding, pool, restaurant, beach and pool bars, and even a lagoon for rowboating. Windsurfing, Cabarete's big drawing card, is available, as well as lighted tennis, 3 racquetball courts, and a disco (phone: 571-3036 or 571-3073). Moderate.

COSTAMBAR

Marlena – An apartment hotel offering 33 immaculate studios and 1- or 2-bedroom units with kitchenettes. The *Don Diego* next door shares the pool (and also has some lovely apartments). A 5-minute walk from the beach (phone: 586-3692). Expensive to moderate.

Cofesi – An all-inclusive resort in a most spectacular setting by the sea. It offers 115 rooms, 3 pools, tennis, horseback riding on the beach, a restaurant, disco, and nightly shows. Rooms are basic — go for the sports and pools or visit the property with a day or night pass; the latter costs $25 and includes dinner, drinks, show, and disco; a day pass costs $20 and covers use of the pools, Continental breakfast, lunch, and all you can drink. This place fills up in winter with Europeans and Canadians, so book early (phone: 586-2898). Moderate.

ELSEWHERE IN THE COUNTRY

Bavaro Beach, Punta Cana – An isolated resort with 800 superior rooms, pool, snorkeling, windsurfing, sailing, 3 lighted tennis courts, and restaurants. Rates include buffet breakfast, buffet dinner, tax, and service charge; 7-night packages include all water sports as well (phone: 682-2163 or 800-336-6612). Expensive.

El Portillo, Samaná – Still charmingly rustic, even though it has been renovated and converted to an all-inclusive resort on a beautiful beach called Las Terrenas. With 75 rooms, sailing, windsurfing, horseback riding, tennis, and volleyball (phone: 688-5748). Expensive.

Bahia Beach Resort & Out Island Villas, Samaná – Another club-concept, inclusive-rate resort with lots of beautiful beach and glorious sea. Minimum 4-day package covers fresh if not flashy room with balcony, meals with wine, unlimited rum drinks, cigarettes, water sports, tennis, picnics and partying, entertainment, airport transfers, tips, and taxes. The difference here is the choice of staying by the sociable beach or on a secluded offshore island. Informal, cheerful, much liked by young Dominicans (phone: 538-2142). Moderate.

Camino Real, Santiago – A sleek, not-quite-high-rise in the DR's second city; with 72 stylish rooms, 9 suites (all air conditioned), rooftop restaurant, piano bar, the usual business/pleasure accoutrements. Country club golf and swimming privileges nearby (phone: 582-8588). Moderate.

Club Med, Punta Cana – It's a 600-bed village of three-story bungalows facing long white beaches. Central dining/bar/dancing/show complex plus freshwater pool, specialty restaurant, disco. Tennis (10 courts), sailing, windsurfing, snorkeling, swimming, circus workshop (trapeze, tightrope, clowning), group games (including soccer), nightly entertainment, all meals (with wine) included in package rates. Optional local excursions cost extra. Charter departures from New York, Miami, Boston, Washington, DC, Atlanta, Chicago, Houston, LA, and San Francisco (reservations, information phone: 687-2606 or 800-CLUB MED). Moderate.

De Cameron, Juan Dolio – This all-inclusive resort next door to *Talanquera* offers rooms with kitchenettes, a good beach, and beach activities (phone: 529-8531). Moderate.

Talanquera, Juan Dolio – Pleasantly contemporary enclave of 80 rooms and 1- and 2-bedroom apartments on the sunny south coast. With tennis, horseback riding, biking, solarium, pool, water sports on private beach, bar, and restaurant. Linked in combination packages with *El Embajador* in town (phone: 533-2131). Moderate.

Punta Garza, Juan Dolio – A cluster of 24 little beachfront cottages owned by same group as *El Embajador*. Clean and pleasant, with a market and nice beach nearby (phone: 533-2131). Inexpensive.

 EATING OUT: Native Dominican cooking is appealing rather than tempting. You won't rush to the yellow pages to find the nearest Dominican restaurant when you get home, but you'll probably remember many island meals with pleasure. Beef is expensive (Dominicans raise fine cattle but export most of the meat); there's lots of very fresh fish and seafood, however. Island-grown tomatoes, lettuce, papaya, mangoes, passion fruit, and citrus are delicious, too. Roast pork and goat are big local favorites, as are chicharrones (crisp pork rind) or chicharrones de pollo (small pieces of fried chicken), fried yuca (casava) and moro de habicuelas (rice and beans). Dominicans are also fond of sopa criolla dominicana, a native soup of meat and vegetables; pastelon, a baked vegetable cake; sancocho, a stew made with anywhere from 7 to 18 ingredients, plus mero (bass) done in half a dozen delicious ways and such Latin-American standbys as arroz con pollo (chicken with rice) and pastilitos. Two desserts are stellar: cocoyuca, a yuca flan with chunks of coconut; and majarete, a delicious corn pudding. Try them at *De Armando* in Puerta Plata and Santo Domingo.

Dominican *El Presidente, Quispueya,* and *Bohemia* beers are first-rate; so are rum drinks (*Brugal* and *Bermudez* are the Dominican brand names to remember); rum añejo — dark and aged — on the rocks makes a good after-dinner drink.

El Alcázar – In the *Santo Domingo* hotel, a treat for eyes and taste, too. Designed by Oscar de la Renta in a Moorish motif sparkling with tiny mirrors, antique mother-of-pearl; yards and yards of tenting fabric overhead. International menu with especially delicious local fish dishes. Reservations suggested. Av. Independencia and Av. Abraham Lincoln (phone: 532-1511). Expensive.

Il Buco – Pucci Estorniollo's small, congenial *ristorante,* where the antipasto is fabulous, the pasta is homemade, and the seafood fresh as can be. Popular; be sure to reserve. At 152-A Arzobispo Merino (phone: 685-0884). Expensive.

Reina de España – A highly praised restaurant featuring Spanish specialties. Reservations necessary on weekends (phone: 685-2588). Expensive.

Café St. Michel – First-class French cuisine and ambience. The escargots and steak tartare are excellent (phone: 562-4141). Expensive to moderate.

De Armando – A branch of the award-winning restaurant of the same name in Puerto Plata, featuring the same delicious soups, steaks, lobster and other seafood, and its two famous desserts — cocoyuca (coconut chunks in a yuca flan) and majarete (corn pudding). Reservations recommended in high season (phone: 586-3418). Expensive to moderate.

Extremadura – In *Hostal Nicolás de Ovando.* Spanish dishes plus colonial atmosphere that makes up for the rather slow service. Reservations suggested. Calle Las Damas 53 (phone: 687-3101). Expensive to moderate.

Lina – Lina herself came from Spain, was once Trujillo's personal chef, and left to open her own place, which now includes the *Gran Hotel Lina.* International cuisine with strong Spanish accent; everyone talks about the paella. Decor is contemporary and food is great — especially shrimp dishes and mero (bass) done in several ways, including à la zarzuela in a casserole faintly flavored with Pernod. Reservations are a good idea. Av. Maximo Gómez and Av. 27 de Febrero (phone: 689-5185). Expensive to moderate.

Mesón de la Cava – A see-to-believe restaurant in a natural cave complete with stalagmites and stalactites. Chef's meat dishes are his pride. Popular hangout with good music, entertainment. Reservations are a must. Paseo de los Indios (phone: 533-2818). Expensive to moderate.

Vesuvio I – Sit outside and catch the night noises — including the crash of the Caribbean surf just across the road. Italian food, including a fine veal piccata; pizza, too. And a feast of an antipasto table. Make reservations on weekends. Av. George Washington (phone: 682-2766). Expensive to moderate.

El Bodegón – Small, cozy, near historic sites. Garlic soup with fresh egg is terrific; so is the ceviche — either one gets the meal off to an aromatic start. Spanish specialties and international cuisine; try the bass and the excellent house pâté. Good for lunch; you don't need reservations. Calle Arzobispo Merino 18 (phone: 682-6864). Moderate.

Boga Boga – Excellent Spanish food served family-style. Also a popular five o'clock meeting place for tapas and drinks (phone: 687-1539). Moderate.

Fonda de la Atarazana – In a restored colonial building just across from the Alcázar, which makes it ideal for lunch on a shopping/sightseeing day. At night, musicians perform on back terrace. Native menu (try the pork dishes). No reservations. La Atarazana (phone: 689-2900). Moderate.

La Fromageria – A popular spot for fondue and Crèole cooking, with modern atmosphere (phone: 567-9430). Moderate.

Jai-Alai – Its ancestry is both Peruvian and Dominican. Delicious seafood (try the Peruvian ceviche) in a simple setting with tables outdoors and in. Evenings, there's guitar music, sometimes with Spanish sing-along. Av. Independencia 411 (phone: 685-2404). Moderate.

El Jardín de Jade – Elegant, spacious, leisurely, and authentically Oriental. The chef woks his way expertly through five-, seven-, and ten-course menus that the staff seems proud and happy to serve. In the *Embajador* hotel (phone: 533-2131). Surprisingly moderate.

Vesuvio II – Known to its friends as Vesuvito, the little brother of Vesuvio I. With equally toothsome pasta, pizza. Popular at lunch. Tiradentes 17 (phone: 567-7330). Moderate.

Café Americas – Tiny, off-path place that looks like nothing, tastes like Spanish heaven. Since neither the Basque owner nor his wife speaks English, eating here can be a (justified) act of faith. But if you're the kind of food fan who can relax while the owner suggests, serves, and pours the wine, you'll love every minute and morsel. Arzobispo Noel and Santomé (no phone). Moderate to inexpensive.

La Bahía – It looks like a place into which you might not walk automatically. But there's no place like it for fresh seafood. Shrimp, lobster, or lambi (conch) with rice or in asapao are super-fine. No reservations. Av. George Washington 1 (phone: 682-4022). Inexpensive.

PUERTO PLATA

Los Pinos – The finest and freshest of local steaks, chops, vegetables, fruits, hot and cold lobster — given the tender, loving culinary care they deserve. Av. Hermanas Mirabal (phone: 586-3222). Expensive.

De Armando – Guests at Armando Rodriguez Pelegrin's award-winning restaurant feel as though they're dining in an elegant home. The service is top-notch, and the food is splendid. The menu features 9 soups (try the delicious pumpkin), super ceviche, paella, steaks, and heavenly lobster Atlantica in a special house sauce. Two of the desserts are themselves worth the visit: cocoyuca (a yuca flan with chunks of coconut) and majarete (a traditional corn pudding). A guitar trio serenades every night except on All Souls' Day (Nov. 1). Reservations necessary in high season (phone: 586-3418). Expensive to moderate.

Jimmy's – One of the two best restaurants in town for Continental cuisine (the other is *De Armando*). Very popular, so reserve (phone: 586-4325). Expensive to moderate.

Valter's – In a Victorian house with gingerbread trim and a wide porch overlooking a lush jungle of a garden — an altogether beautiful setting. The menu features soups, salads, pastas, seafood, and meats. Excellent service (phone: 586-2329). Expensive to moderate.

Adolfo's Wienerwald – One of several beachside cafés that are great for snacks. This one, with just a few tables and some palm-stump stools at the counter, is also the best place to have breakfast. Go for Adolfo's Austrian omelet, homemade strawberry jam, and friendly manner. Open 6 AM to 2 AM or later. Long Beach (no phone). Inexpensive.

Porto Fino – An Italian restaurant with casual indoor/outdoor dining in a fluorescent-green setting. Try the heavenly lasagna or some of the Dominican dishes. Crab Crèole with french fries is a bargain. No reservations needed. Av. Hermanas Mirabal (no phone). Inexpensive.

SOSUA

Marco Polo Club – The most scenic spot in Sosua for drinking and dining, with a fabulous view of Sosua Bay (phone: 571-3680). Moderate.

Tree Top Lounge – An airy, tropical upstairs meeting place for drinks and backgammon. Rattan decor with ceiling fans and lots of greenery. Order a pizza from the pizzeria downstairs (15 varieties from which to choose) and relax with a piña banana colada, the house specialty (phone: 571-2141). Inexpensive.

ELSEWHERE ON THE ISLAND

Casa del Río, Altos de Chavón – Perched on a cliff, with breathtaking views of river and valley, it provides a rustic setting for nicely done fresh fish and seafood dishes. Reservations through *Casa de Campo* (phone: 682-9656, ext. 2345). Expensive. *Note:* Other Altos choices include *Café del Sol* for pizzas and ice-cream extravaganzas, and *La Fonda* for Dominican dishes.

La Piazzetta, Altos de Chavón – Ensconced in the re-created 15th-century village above the winding green Chavón River, this *ristorante* supplies a romantic change of dinner (only) scene for *Casa de Campo* guests. Mood and food are elegant Italian, with excellent pasta, carpaccio, seafood, and a good wine list, plus violin music and candlelight. Reservations should be made through the hotel (phone: 682-9656, ext. 2339). Expensive.

De América, La Romana – Generous portions of fresh and beautifully prepared seafood, Crèole dishes, and international cuisine. Charming atmosphere (local art, paddle fans), great margaritas, good service. Popular with locals (phone: 556-3137). Moderate.

Mama Nena, La Romana – Local fresh foods — rice, beans, goat — in a simple setting. Open for breakfast, lunch, and dinner (no phone). Moderate.

Shish Kabab, La Romana – What's a nice Lebanese restaurant like this doing in a small eastern Caribbean sugar-mill town? It happens when a Lebanese chef marries a Dominican woman, and together they make beautiful *kebbehs* (Middle Eastern meatballs rolled in wheat and fried) and *pasteles en hojas* (Dominican spiced ground meat wrapped in plantain dough and cooked in a plantain leaf) together. They also do great shakes (banana, pineapple, papaya, orange) and a luscious concoction of orange juice, milk, sugar, and vanilla called *morir soñando* (literally, "to die dreaming"). Calle Castillo Marques 32 (no phone). Moderate.

The picturesque fishing village of Bayahibe, 25 minutes from *Casa de Campo,* has two good, simple restaurants — *Bayahibe* and *La Bahia* — that serve locally caught fish and lobster (and great french fries) — in open-air settings. Prices at both are moderate to inexpensive.

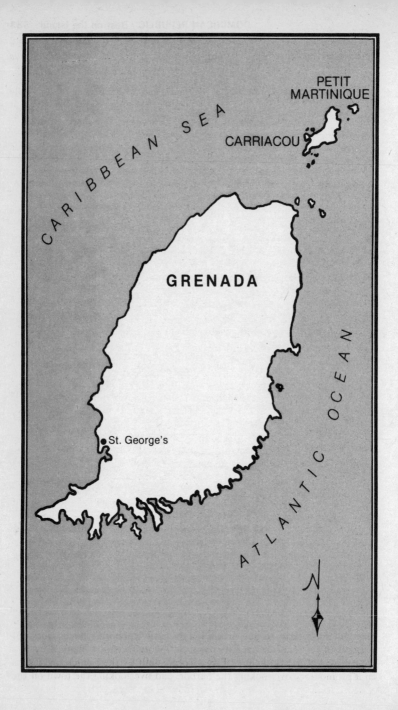

GRENADA

Grenada has been called "all the Caribbean islands in miniature" for good reason. Like so many of its neighbors, it is of volcanic origin, is endowed with lush green mountains and beautiful beaches, was discovered by Columbus, and has had its share of typically dramatic Caribbean history — during the seesawing French-English struggles of the seventeenth and eighteenth centuries and through its own twentieth-century quest for identity and independence.

Grenadians like to claim Columbus as their "first cruise visitor." His ships found Conception Bay — now called Levera Beach — at the island's northern tip during his third voyage in 1498. Though the question of whether the great man himself ever came ashore is still debated locally, it is certain that he christened the island Concepción, a name that almost immediately gave way to Granada because its hills reminded passing Spanish sailors of home. The French, in their turn, referred to it as Grenade; and the British made the final adjustment to Grenada (pronounced gren-*ay*-da), as it is known today.

It is ironic that Columbus never explored Grenada; of all the Caribbean islands he was to visit, it is the one that best approximates his original goal — to open up a source of spices to Europe by sailing west instead of east. It was his intention to find a short route to India by sailing across the Atlantic, thus eliminating the time-consuming, expensive journey around Africa's Cape Horn. That is why he named the Caribbean Islands the West Indies, and why its indigenous peoples were called Indians.

In the century and a half that followed, neither the British nor the French were able to establish settlements on the island. It was not until 1650 that a party of 200 Frenchmen, led by the capitalist-adventurers du Parquet and Le Comte, sailed from Martinique and succeeded in purchasing land from the Carib chief literally for some glass beads and a selection of metal knives and hatchets. Soon the Caribs, realizing that they had been cheated, began a futile struggle to retake the island from the French; the result was their own extinction. After a series of battles, in a final act of defiance, the last 40 Carib men threw women and children over the northern precipice (now called Morne des Sauteurs, or Carib's Leap) and followed them to death on the jagged rocks below.

But this bloody event did not give the French undisputed possession of the island. The English were already patrolling the Caribbean, and, as it had on other Windward Islands, the familiar French-British conflict began on Grenada. Amassing troops at opposite ends of the island, the two nations built substantial fortifications and proceeded to battle stubbornly for decades. As a legacy of this era, the capital city of St. George's is now flanked by two impressive historic landmarks: Fort George, built by the French in 1705, is on a promontory overlooking the harbor; and overlooking the town on the southern part of the island is Fort Frederick, begun by the French and completed by the British after the signing of the Treaty of Versailles in 1783 when they took control of the island. Grenada became a Crown Colony in 1877. After an abortive attempt to form a federation with nine other UK-associated islands, Grenada was declared a British Associated State in 1967.

It was during the 1960s that Grenada began to emerge as one of the Eastern Caribbean's first tourist destinations. With the arrival of jets and the shrinking of the time distance between North America and the islands, visitors in increasing numbers were lured by tales of its beaches and its beauties. Its capital, St. George's, with a superb natural harbor that has probably been used for more postcards than any other in the Caribbean, is perhaps the most beautiful town in the Caribbean. And of course there are the mountains, the waterfalls, and the flowers, fine white and black sands, and the sea. By the early 1970s, Grenada could boast a delightfully individual group of innlike hotels that were being added to at what seemed an ideal rate.

But the early 1970s also brought the issue of independence, and with it an identity crisis that split island politics right down the middle. So serious and consuming was the strife between the pro- and anti-independence factions that, for a time in late 1973 and early 1974, a general strike actually closed the island down. In February 1974, independence was at last proclaimed, and the island started slowly to pull itself back together. Unfortunately, Prime Minister Sir Eric Gairy proved a less than inspiring administrator, seemingly more interested in black magic and UFOs than in island economics. When his dictatorial regime was ousted in March 1979 by Maurice Bishop's New Jewel Movement, hope rose, but it soon fell once Prime Minister Bishop, a protégé of Cuban President Fidel Castro, invited Cuban military advisers to Grenada. Uneasy about the Cuban presence on the island, visitors began staying away.

The political upheaval that has put a damper on full-scale tourism development in Grenada for almost two decades has also acted as a preservative. Grenada retains an ample helping of natural charm indicative of the pre-resort, pre-homogenized Caribbean. This cuts two ways, however: Good roads, modern plumbing, and steady electricity are not by-products of natural charm, but neither is the economic well-being of an entire island population.

Yet much has happened since the "intervention" — the word used by Grenadians and much of the eastern Caribbean people to describe the events of October 25, 1983 — the day units of the US Marines and Army landed to spearhead the rout of a combined Grenadian/Cuban defense force. Along with eastern Caribbean forces from Barbados, Dominica, Jamaica, St. Lucia, and St. Vincent, the US troops deposed the former colleagues of Maurice Bishop (still the island's principal heroic figure), who had him assassinated two weeks earlier.

The lessons of its turmoil have been deeply impressed on the country, especially in a still keen sense of shock at Grenadians having killed Grenadians (many died with Bishop, their bodies allegedly disposed of at sea prior to the intervention). While Americans are still made to feel especially welcome — more than one tourist has been told "you rescued us" — much of the rosy, post-intervention outlook has been tempered by an economy still in need of rescue and by remaining seeds of political controversy.

Grenada's civil authority is now on its own; the US and most eastern Caribbean troops — supplemental police, really — have departed, and the three-year ordeal of the Bishop assassination trials has, excepting possible appeals, concluded without serious incident. But the initially popular administration of democratically elected Prime Minister Herbert Blaize is now being called nonprogressive by critics from both the Left and Right. In 1987, several of his more popular Cabinet members resigned to form their own party. Eric Gairy has resumed island residence and political activity, though he disclaims any personal intentions toward trying to regain public office. What's more, a tiny faction continues to espouse the ideals of Bishop's New Jewel movement.

Yet, bolstered by US aid, substantial improvements in basic services and infrastructure have been made, and the outlook is for steady, moderate tourism growth. Dial telephones and cable TV are no longer curiosities, and newly paved roads have halved travel times to all parts of the island. The once controversial, Cuban-constructed airport runway at Point Salines now lies next to a full-fledged, comfortable, modern international terminal building, complete with duty-free shopping. Grenada and the US signed a tax treaty in 1987, making expenses for conventions and business meetings held on the island tax-deductible under the US Internal Revenue Service code.

For visitors who have come to love the island as it was (and still mostly is), perhaps slow change is best. Grenada retains a lush, unspoiled character that any neighbor nation might covet.

GRENADA AT-A-GLANCE

FROM THE AIR: Grenada, the southernmost island of the Windward Antilles, 90 miles north of Trinidad, looks like an oval fish swimming northeast with its mouth open as though to swallow the tiny islands of the Grenadines strung between it and the island of St. Vincent 68 miles northeast. The "mouth" of the fish is Sauteurs Bay; its tail is the beach-bordered peninsula called Point Salines extending below the capital of St. George's (pop. 10,000) and forming the island's southeastern tip.

At 12°7′ N latitude, 61°45′ W longitude, Grenada is only 21 miles long and 12 miles wide at its widest point, but its 133 square miles encompass a rather astounding variety of terrain: green jungle-covered mountains, racing rivers and streams, waterfalls and lakes, and a ring of beaches of extraordinary beauty such as Grande Anse and Levera. The central mountain range, reaching heights of over 2,000 feet, divides the island diagonally in half, with stretches of desert and cactus to the southwest and banana and spice plantations in the southeastern and northwestern areas as well as canefields and coconut groves.

The highest, wettest, coolest, most densely forested areas of the island are found near the city of Grenville, halfway up the eastern coast. The route from there to the south, where most of the hotels are located, passes through the island's driest section. The drive from Point Salines International Airport to the hotel district is 15 minutes.

Some 15 miles off Grenada's northern tip lie the nation's major dependencies, Carriacou and Petit Martinique (in the island group known as the Grenadines), but only Carriacou has a small airstrip and some facilities for tourists and yachtsmen.

 SPECIAL PLACES: St. George's – Grenada's capital is one of the Caribbean's most picturesque ports. Its landlocked inner harbor, the Carenage — actually the deep crater of a dead volcano — is lined with pink, ocher, and brick-red commercial buildings and warehouses, many of which date back to the 18th century. Behind them, narrow streets climb green hills dotted with neat red- and green-roofed houses. The Esplanade (or Outer Harbour) area of the city on St. George's Bay is connected to the Carenage area by Sendall Tunnel, a one-way traffic and pedestrian passage cut through the high promontory called St. George's Point, which divides the two bodies of water.

The French built St. George's in 1732, and French architectural details — like the wrought-ironwork along the Esplanade and Market Square — survive among the British Georgian–West Indian buildings in a charming blend of European and tropical island styles. Wood has been a forbidden building material since a number of disastrous fires in the island's earliest days, so most buildings are built of brick brought over as ballast on British trading ships.

St. George's most appealing sights are vistas of the city and harbor from high points around the town. If you're sightseeing by taxi, let the driver know you'd like to stop wherever the view is especially fine. Better still, take a good hour to walk and climb around the city (it's not very big); that way you can pause and sample the view whenever you please.

Make your first stop the Grenada Tourist Board Office on the Carenage to pick up maps and sightseeing information. Then stroll a little farther east to the Botanical Gardens and Zoo; beyond its palm-lined entry you'll find not only a variety of tropical trees and flowers carefully labeled and identified, but rare Caribbean birds and animals. Then walk westward along the edge of the Carenage, where schooners, sailboats, yachts, and dinghies are tied up to concrete posts containing old spiked cannon. Call at the Grenada National Museum, on Young St., which offers both historic exhibits and a cool refuge on a sunny day. Above you, on the hill, stands the town's dominant structure, Fort George, built by the French as Fort Royal in 1705. Briefly known as Fort Rupert, in honor of Maurice Bishop's father, who was killed by Prime Minister Gairy's police during a civil protest in 1978, it ironically was the site of Maurice Bishop's death; following the US intervention, it became Fort George again, and is now the headquarters of the Grenada police force. On its ramparts, ancient cannon, still used for official salutes, are aimed out across the water; an intricate network of winding subterranean passageways, old guardrooms, and prison cells is tunneled into the solid groundworks below.

Coming down the hill again, turn right and follow Young Street to the Carenage, then go right, right again, and left through Sendall Tunnel, built by the French in the 18th century. Now you're on the west side of town, where the principal shops run along the waterfront Esplanade and up Granby Street. Follow Granby one block east to the Market Square, where on Saturday mornings Grenadian women in bright cotton dresses, aprons, and wide straw hats pile their produce — oranges, grapefruit, mangoes, bananas, coconuts, spices, tomatoes, pineapples, and papaws (papayas) — on rough cloths and flour bags for sale. Also on the square, the *Straw Mart* offers a variety of craft items made of straw, coconut, and turtle shell.

Then head east on Granby, which turns into Lucas, to Fort Frederick on Richmond Hill, where construction was started by the French in 1779 and completed by the British in 1783; its battlements command a magnificent view of the city and its harbors. Nearby is Government House, the large, impressive residence of the queen's official representative, the governor general; once occupied by the commonwealth's first woman governor general, it was originally built in the late 18th century; later additions — particularly the 1887 façade — are not all considered architectural triumphs. But the view of the port, the harbor, and the town is indisputably beautiful.

Turn back down Lucas Street. At the Church Street intersection, turn right up the hill to visit the Roman Catholic cathedral. (Inside, dark plaster saints oversee both petitioners and their prayers.) Also on Church Street, left of Lucas, the Anglican church is pink with heavy stained glass windows, frescoes, and stone memorial tablets carved in England and dedicated to British soldiers who fought against the French. Farther along, St. Andrew's Presbyterian Church, built in 1830, is crowned with the square-spired clock tower that's a trademark of the town skyline. After a call (or an admiring glance in its direction), you're entitled to head back down the hill to the Carenage for lunch or a rum punch at *Rudolf's* or the *Nutmeg* (for a Nutmeg Special).

Two lush spots not far from St. George's are worth visiting if the notion of exploring lavish landscapes appeals to you. Bay Gardens, about a 20-minute drive northeast of town, encompasses three dense acres of tropical flora and mostly feathered fauna (you may not see the island's favorite pripri birds, but you'll certainly hear them). Its walkways will introduce you to an abundance of exotic fruits and spices in their natural state. The feeling is a little like strolling through a primitive island painting.

Off in another direction, in the mountains northwest of town, Concord Falls is a wildly beautiful, yet accessible — 30–45 minutes by car — picnic destination. There you can spread out your lunch (order the night before, and your hotel will pack your favorite portable treats and potables) in a hideaway setting festooned with hanging liana vines, feathery rock plants, giant elephant ears, and other gorgeous greenery, while the misted water cascades down a 50-foot fall into a blue-green pool where you can swim.

NORTH OF ST. GEORGE'S

To explore the spice country, coastal beaches, and villages of the island's northern reaches, head north out of St. George's along the western coast. You'll travel past curving bays, small seaside settlements, and along shores where fishermen with small boats and big nets bring in their catches. As you approach, the village of Gouyave looks like an island painting, with weathered red-roofed houses along the sea wall dominated by the Anglican and Catholic churches behind them. Gouyave is a center of the nutmeg and mace industry (both are produced from a single fruit); you can visit its nutmeg processing plant, and just inland on the Dougaldston Estate you can see most of the island's spices growing naturally.

Then proceed along the coast to Sauteurs, at the north end of the island. Behind its church are the cliffs called Carib's Leap, where, in the 17th century, the last of the Carib Indians are said to have jumped to their death rather than submit to slavery under the French. East of Sauteurs is pretty, palm-edged Levera Beach, soon to become a national park, an ideal spot for a picnic and a swim (if the Atlantic is not in one of its occasionally rough moods). Not far south is the River Antoine rum distillery, an amazing establishment dating from the 18th century and one of the last agro/industrial enterprises in the hemisphere still powered by a waterwheel. It is worth a stop if one of the De Gale family members is there to provide a tour; your driver will know whether the river is low enough to ford — there's no bridge, and that's the only way in.

A note of perspective: Most of Grenada's limited wealth flows to the southwest corner of the island, where tourist interest is concentrated. Grenadians are among the friendliest, most courteous people in the Caribbean, and a vast majority favored the US–East Caribbean intervention. But in the numerous small settlements in parishes north and east of St. George's, where most people are dirt poor and have few immediate prospects for any significant advancement, they are likely to be less outgoing and to resent being photographed without permission.

■ **EXTRA SPECIAL:** Lunch at Betty Mascoll's *Morne Fendue* is an ideal stop on any island tour. This plantation house, home of three generations of her family, is worth a visit as much for Betty's stories and pleasant presence as for the food, which is island cooking, handsomely served and delicious. The menu might include callaloo soup, ginger chicken, savory pepperpot, vegetables from her garden, and homemade guava ice cream. Sunday brunch is an island event. About $12 per person. Call for reservations (phone: 433-9330).

Grenville – Then turn and travel down the east coast to Grenville, Grenada's second city, with two lively markets: the waterfront fish market doing brisk business every day except Sundays, and Saturday's bright, social fruit and vegetable market. You're welcome to visit the spice factory at the edge of town.

The Inland Road – From Grenville, turn inland toward the heart of the island along a road that passes small spice farms, girls sorting nutmegs, and — on cacao plantations — trays of chocolate brown pods spread to dry in the sun. From there, the drive winds up and up into the mountains, with each hairpin curve bringing a surprise view of lush, fern-covered hillsides, nutmeg trees brimming with yellow fruit, cacao and banana groves, and mountain streams about to start their tumble toward the sea. There is a nature-oriented interpretation center with exhibitions, snack bar, and a souvenir shop at Grand Etang Lake. The road reaches its peak here, then begins its gradual descent, offering tantalizing glimpses of blue-and-white-coved shoreline all the way to St. George's.

SOUTH OF ST. GEORGE'S

South of St. George's lie the superb beaches and rambling resorts of the Grand Anse and L'Anse aux Epines districts. To tour this end of the island, follow the Royal Drive, so named because it's the route along which Elizabeth II was escorted during her 1966 visit. Leaving St. George's, past Government House and the panoramic overlook at Richmond Hill, the drive proceeds down to Westerhall Point, a beautifully landscaped residential development on the southern coast, through the fishing village of Woburn and the canefields of Woodlands.

GRENADINES

Carriacou – One of Grenada's island dependencies, it lies 23 miles northeast of St. George's, a 13-square-mile retreat where Grenadians "get away from it all." It is a special favorite with yachtsmen. In winter, the chain of hills extending down its center is fresh and green; in summer, the land dries to pale beige, and islanders declare "leggo" season — when goats, cows, and sheep are let go to forage for themselves and gardeners guard their flowers with their lives. Whatever the season, Carriacou's attractions include excellent beaches and natural harbors (Tyrell Bay is especially beautiful), plus the prospect of relaxed living among people who seem genuinely to enjoy having visitors.

Most place names are British or French, and ruins of great houses in the hills testify to the island's once-thriving sugar industry; now it grows cotton, peanuts, and limes. Its strongest surviving heritages are African (most black islanders can trace their ancestry not just to the continent, but to a particular tribe) and Scottish. The McLarens, MacLaurences, McQuilkins, MacFarlands, and Comptons of Windward on the east side of the island still hand-build some of the Caribbean's finest sailing workboats. The sprinkling of goat's blood and holy water at launchings recognizes both cultural influences.

Excepting the annual August regatta — when 2,000 people have been known to squeeze themselves onto the island and 300 or 400 manage to dance all night at the tiny *Mermaid Inn* — launchings are Carriacou's biggest parties. Sometimes they last for days (especially when you count recovery time). Jack Iron, the white rum in which ice sinks, is generally given most of the credit/blame. Otherwise, things are pretty quiet. Visitors laze, swim, sail, snorkel, and dive (nearby Sandy Island has some interesting reef formations), search for seashells, poke and puzzle about the ruins, and gather at dusk on the terrace of the *Mermaid* in Hillsborough, the island's only town. From his Hillsborough office a senior executive officer, supervised by a parliamentary secretary, administers the affairs of both Carriacou and Petit Martinique, the island 3 miles due east.

Petit Martinique – Residents are known as master seamen (each year they carry off a lion's share of prizes from the regatta) and — some say — smugglers. Whether or not the latter is true, it has inspired some wonderful stories. Frances Kay tells one in *This — Is Carriacou:* "A very strict customs official from Grenada was sent to Petit Martinique to make a thorough check. When he arrived, he found the entire population standing mournfully around an open grave. 'Who died?' he asked. 'Nobody,' came the matter-of-fact reply. 'We dug it for you.' "

These days, the island's approximately 600 French-descended inhabitants are polite, even pleasant, to sailors who drop anchor overnight in their harbor. But there are few accommodations for visitors on this 3-square-mile island. Privacy is still an important commodity.

Grenada's other dependency islands — Île de Ronde, Kick-em-Jenny (possibly from *caye qui gene,* or "troublesome shoal"), Green Bird, and Conference, among them — are small picturesque land dots, important only as landmarks for cruising yachtsmen. Other Grenadine islands are covered under St. Vincent, by whom they are administered.

SOURCES AND RESOURCES

 TOURIST INFORMATION: The Caribbean Tourism Association, 20 E 46th St., New York, NY 10017 (phone: 212-682-0435), and the Grenada Tourist Office, 141 E 44th St., Suite 803, New York, NY 10017 (phone: 800-638-0852; for New York State only, 212-687-9554) or 143 Yonge St., Suite 102, Toronto, Ont. M5C 1W7 (phone: 416-368-1332), will supply tourist literature and answer questions about transportation, hotels, rates, and sightseeing.

The Grenada Tourist Board office on the Carenage in St. George's can supply information, maps, literature, and answers to visitors' questions. They can brief you on excursions to and lodging on Carriacou and Petit Martinique too. They're open from 9 AM until 4 PM (phone: 2001).

Local Coverage – *This — Is Grenada* by Frances Kay (Carenage Press, St. George's, about $5 US) is very informative, sensible, sensitive, and should be one of your first purchases. A shorter *This — Is Carriacou* (actually an excerpt from the Grenada book) is about $3 US. Both are available at *Grencraft* on the Esplanade (Melville St.), where you'll also find a number of other books about the island, and at *Sea 'Change* on the Carenage.

Consult the *Grenada Voice,* the island's weekly newspaper, for sports schedules and special events.

Telephone – Dial direct to Grenada by adding the area code 809 to the numbers given below.

 ENTRY REQUIREMENTS: The only documentation needed for a visit to Grenada is proof of citizenship that includes a photograph (a passport, or voter's registration card, or birth certificate) and an ongoing or return ticket.

CLIMATE AND CLOTHES: At the beach the day temperatures stay close to 80°F (27°C) the year round, with cooling trade winds to temper the sun's heat. In the mountains (around Grand Etang Lake, for example), it can be as much as 10° cooler; you may even be glad you brought a light sweater along. The dry season is from January to May, and the rainy season lasts from June to December, when there's a shower for an hour or so almost every day, and the countryside is at its greenest. Casual, lightweight resort clothes are most comfortable and appropriate for both men and women. Though bathing suits and short shorts are fine on the beach, they are frowned on in St. George's. In the evenings — especially during the winter season — people tend to dress up a bit for dinner in the better hotels and restaurants.

MONEY: Grenada's official currency is the Eastern Caribbean dollar (referred to as EC), which is worth about 40¢ US and 50¢ Canadian at this writing; it can fluctuate a bit. Prices are usually quoted in EC dollars, but sometimes shopkeepers will give them in US dollars to US citizens in an effort to be helpful. Be sure you know which dollars you're talking about before committing yourself to a purchase or a cab trip. Banking hours are 8 AM to noon Mondays through Thursdays; 8 AM to noon and 3 to 5 PM on Fridays. Traveler's checks are accepted by stores, restaurants, and hotels; most honor major credit cards as well. No shops offer discounts for cash payment in US dollars.

LANGUAGE: Grenada is a former British Crown Colony, and English is spoken everywhere with a Caribbean lilt. You may occasionally hear islanders chatting among themselves in their own patois — mostly French with some African words and rhythms mixed in.

TIME: Grenada is on Atlantic Standard Time, one hour ahead of Eastern Standard (when it's noon in New York, it's 1 PM in Grenada); when most of the US switches to Daylight Saving Time in April, Grenada and New York are on the same hour.

CURRENT: It's 220 volts, 50 cycles AC, so you need an adapter for American appliances. Most hotels supply them, but it wouldn't hurt to bring your own.

GETTING THERE: BWIA has direct service to Grenada 3 times a week from New York and daily from Miami; connections to BWIA's Grenada flights from Antigua (2 flights) or Trinidad (nonstop) can be made on BWIA, American, Eastern, Pan Am, and Air Canada. Connections to direct LIAT flights can be made in Barbados; LIAT also flies from Antigua but can make as many as 7 stops en route. Wardair of Canada provides frequent charters from Toronto to Barbados, and connects with LIAT. (British Airways began limited direct service from London in April 1987.)

Several yacht charter firms in St. Lucia and St. Vincent now offer St. George's, Grenada's capital, as a point of departure. During the winter season, cruise ships call daily at St. George's.

CALCULATING COSTS: For a small island, Grenada offers a number of deluxe and first-class hotels, most of which operate on an MAP basis (Modified American Plan, including breakfasts and dinners). There are few inexpensive guesthouses or casual inns recommendable for the average North American visitor, but several of the more luxurious places manage to stay on the reasonable side of expensive in season; in summer — between mid-April and mid-December — rates drop 30% to 40%. There's no tax on hotel rooms but a $25 EC (about $10 US) departure tax collected at the airport. There's also a new 20% VAT (valued-added tax) on food and beverages. Most restaurant meals fall within the "moderate" range (about $14 to $20 US per person for dinner, including a drink and tip); eating out at hotels is more expensive (about $20 or more per person).

GETTING AROUND: Taxi – Unmetered, so be sure to establish the price of the trip with the driver before getting into the cab. The trip from Point Salines Airport costs about $12 per cab to hotels in Lance aux Epines; about $14 to Grand Anse; about $15 to St. George's. From St. George's to most hotels at the southern end of the island, fixed rates run from $6 to $10 per cabload plus a 10% tip. Although not organized along preset lines, island taxi drivers are good guides and can tell you lots about the island. Hotels can arrange all-day, around-the-island cab tours for about $15 per hour. Usually, the cabs are shared by two or three people, depending on the size of the car and how cozy you like to be.

Bus – The older, photogenic models, painted kindergarten colors and emblazoned with names like Faith, Hope, and Gaiety, take off from the Market Square in St. George's for all parts of the island, but since seats are boards and springs are hard to come by, they aren't recommended. Many visitors have taken to the new minibuses that travel between island points and charge about 50¢ to $1 US per ride.

Car Rental – Not too expensive, and a good idea if you enjoy exploring on your own. Rates run from about $35 to $40 US a day, $200 a week with unlimited mileage in winter; they are somewhat lower in summer. Gas — at about $2.50 US per gallon — is extra. Reliable agencies include *David's* (phone: 440-2399), *Royston's* (phones: 444-4592, 444-4316), *McIntyre Bros.* (phones: 440-2044, 440-2045, or 440-2901), and *Spice Isle/Avis Rentals* (phone: 440-3936)). All will deliver cars to the airport and pick them up at the end of your stay. A US or Canadian driver's license is valid in Grenada; just *remember to drive on the left.*

Sea Excursions – The oar-powered water taxi that crosses St. George's Harbour costs 25¢ per person each way (great views for photographers). The motorized water taxi from St. George's to Grand Anse is $3 per person per ride. The glass-bottom boat *Rhum Runner* (phone: 440-4233) sails from St. George's Harbour Saturdays at 7 PM for a 2½-hour sunset cocktail cruise; the fare — about $9 per person — includes rum punches and steel band and limbo music to watch fish by. The days when cruise ships call, reef trips may be scheduled; call to check.

Twice a week a trading schooner sails from Grenada to Carriacou at noon and arrives in Hillsborough in late afternoon; fare is about $6 US per person one way. From there you can sail on to Petit Martinique — about one hour and a $2 to $3 US fare away. Check the tourist board for current details.

Tours – *Henry's Tours, Ltd.,* Woburn (phone: 443-5313), arranges custom tours for adventurous and fit tourists who wish to hike into the interior for a picnic, swim by a jungle waterfall that few Grenadians even see, or visit other lakes and natural wonders. Hiking segments range from 1 hour to a half day.

Local Air Services – The most popular is the 10-minute hop to Carriacou for a day, a night, or several days. Inter-Island Air Service, represented by LIAT (phone: 440-2796), makes the flight for about $45 US per person round-trip. Grenada Tours and Travel, St. George's, offers 30-minute sightseeing flights, in a six-person aircraft, for $29 per person.

SHOPPING: The big-tag items are luxury imports (especially British) at prices that aren't literally duty free, but close. The little-tag buys are uniquely Grenadian: woven "spice baskets" full of fresh island-grown nutmeg, mace, cinnamon, cloves, and more, roughly a thousand times more aromatic than those fading on the A&P shelves back home. So stock up for yourself and favorite cooks (*Straw Mart* and market ladies have big supplies; *Sea 'Change* has individually packed spices too). As for imported buys, though present stocks seem somewhat limited, unless you're really shopping-proof, brand names like Liberty, Pringle, Waterford, Wedgwood, Bing & Grøndahl, and Dior — at 40% to 60% below stateside prices — will tempt you to browse further.

Of the three main shopping areas, the largest is on the Esplanade side of Fort George around the Market Square and in the shops facing the harbor along Melville Street; the second is on the Carenage side along the waterfront and on Young Street; and the third, and fastest-growing, is in and near the Grande Anse shopping center, handiest to hotels.

On the Esplanade side of Fort George, *Grencraft* (Cross and Melville sts.), the retail outlet of the Grenada National Institute of Handicraft, is intriguingly stocked with baskets, coconut craft (fiber mats, etc.), coral jewelry, crochet and macramé work, wood carvings, appliquéd hangings, Spice Isle spices, preserves, sauces, and perfumes, plus kits for island-made furniture — including mahogany four-poster beds — to assemble at home.

Dinah's Originals (on the corner of Granby and Melville sts.) is a small upstairs shop that specializes in custom cutting African and Liberty prints into bikinis, shifts, tops, and patchwork skirts on the premises. If it doesn't happen to have the style you like in the fabric you like in stock, it will custom-cut it for you, and mail it home for about the same price as you'd pay for ready-to-wear. *Noah's Arkade,* near the Royal Bank of Canada, stocks an intriguing selection of island crafts. *Straw Mart* (Granby, facing Market Sq.) carries more straw mats, hats, and baskets than anyone else on the island. It has a variety of shell jewelry, carvings, and pottery. *Yellow Poui* (two galleries, one on Halifax Street and the other on the second floor near *Noah's Arkade* on Cross St.) is run by Jim Rudin, whose background with the New York Museum of Modern Art is responsible for the selections presented in both. He has picked the best artwork from Grenada and neighboring Caribbean islands as well as North American sources — be it paintings, sculpture, prints, or maps — and the prices range from $10 US to well over $100.

Just in case it's needed — *Gitten's Pharmacy* (Halifax and St. John's sts., phone: 440-2165) has prompt prescription service plus the usual cosmetics, toiletries, and film.

In the area around Young Street and the Carenage you will find *Grand Bazaar* (Young St.), a shop with one-of-a-kind, hand-painted play and party clothes. Considering that they're originals, the prices are very reasonable. *Huggins* (in the Young Street Arcade) is a slightly avant-garde dress shop that also stocks records, cameras, furniture, and appliances. The sports and jewelry items are worth browsing through. *Spice Island Perfumes,* a Carenage shop that makes and sells scents and potpourris concocted from island flowers and spices, is a treat to the nose.

Tikal (Young St.), cheerfully stocked with straw bags, hats, baskets, mats, rugs, crafted mobiles, shell jewelry, ceramics, plus some imported porcelain and glass, is easily the most browsable shop in town. *Sea 'Change* (on the Carenage) has books, records, cards and souvenirs. *Jonas Browne & Hubbard* (also on the Carenage) is strong on English china, ironstone, Danish flatwear, and home furnishings. It also carries a large stock of English cotton and linen in decorator fabrics. *Pitt's Gifts* (Carenage at the cruise pier, with a branch at the airport) is rather blatantly aimed at last-minute shoppers: gift items, some imported sportswear, assorted selections in a moderate price range; a handy stop for departing liquor buyers.

A new gift shop, *Imagine* (in the shopping center), carries both domestic and Grenadian items. *Tikal* (at the *Spice Island Inn*) features fashionable British and European imports. The shop has style, quality, real flair, and high prices. Go in anyhow; you may find something truly distinctive. *The Gift Shop* (in the shopping center) is well known for its crystal by Waterford, Tyrone, Orrefors, Baccarat, Lalique, and Daum; it also has Coalport and Wedgwood china and a selection of watches and jewelry.

TIPPING: Hotels add a 10% service charge to your bill, which takes care of bellboys, waiters and waitresses, bartenders, and maids. If you drop in for a drink or a meal, tip 10% to 15% of the check. At the airport, if there are no porters, taxi drivers will help; tip them 10% of the fare.

SPECIAL EVENTS: *Carnival* is Grenada's national festival, celebrated for two days (and nights) in mid-August with lots of steel band and calypso music, processions, pageants, and beauty contests, and climaxing in a "jump-up" parade of massed bands, floats, and street dancers on *Mardi Gras* (Tuesday); Carriacouans prefer their own smaller but equally festive "old-fashioned" Carnival partying; they really cut loose at their early August *Regatta.* Other holidays when banks and businesses are closed: *New Year's Day, Good Friday, Easter Monday and Tuesday, Labour Day* (first Monday in May), *Whitmonday* (Pentecost), *Corpus Christi, Emancipation Day* (first Monday in August), *National Day* (August 15), *Christmas,* and *Boxing Day* (December 26).

SPORTS: Not surprisingly, considering the splendid white and black sand beaches and calm blue sea that surround it, Grenada's active sports life is centered on the shoreline and in the water.

Boating – Popular as both minor and major league sport in Grenadine waters. On a small scale, there are Sunfish, Sailfish, and Hobie Cats to rent for just-offshore fun (at about $8 US up an hour) on hotel beaches. Farther out, yachtsmen rate the island cruising from Grenada north through the Grenadines to St. Vincent as some of the best in the world. Not only does St. George's have first-rate marina facilities, but Grenada is headquarters for a number of charter operations. Among them: *Grenada Yacht Services,* PO Box 183, St. George's (phone: 440-2883 or 2508); and *Spice Island Yacht Charters,* L'Anse aux Epines (phone: 444-4342). They can arrange skippered or bareboat charters for a week or longer. Prices vary enormously according to size and style of boat, provisioning, crew, etc. But, as a rule of thumb, figure $75 US or more per day per person for bareboat trips in the winter season, $100 up per person for crewed yachts. Summer rates run about 20% lower. Windsurfing boards are available at hotels for about $9 US per hour.

Cricket – This cousin of US baseball is played on pitches (fields) ranging from exquisitely manicured greens to vacant lots. Cricket is a spectator sport that is also a social event, much like Carnival. For upcoming matches, check with the tourist board of the island you plan to visit or consult the sports section of the island newspaper.

Golf – The two-way view of the Atlantic and the Caribbean is the most noteworthy thing about the 9-hole *Grenada Golf Club* course. Greens fees run about $5 to $7 US per person per day (phone: 444-4554).

Hiking – A favorite islanders' pastime, newly accessible to visitors thanks to government encouragement. The Tourist Board will brief you on location of trails, level of expertise required, and — with a day's notice — put you in touch with expert guides. Several adventures involving hiking are offered by *Henry's Tours, Ltd.* (see *Getting Around*).

Snorkeling and Scuba – Along the submerged reef that parallels most of the island's west coast, you can see and photograph a fascinating underwater world of coral formations, submarine "gardens," and friendly schools of exotic fish (blue-headed wrasse, gobies, French angelfish, etc.). Experienced divers can also explore the 594-foot-long wreck of the sunken ocean liner *Bianca C,* just offshore and 100 feet down.

Snorkeling and dive trips can be arranged through the *HMC Diving Center* (440-2508/2883) or the *Ramada Renaissance* water-sports concession (444-4371). Rates run about $10 per person US for an hour's snorkel trip, $55 US per person for a day's dive trip including lunch, drinks, air, and gear.

Sport Fishing – Best in Grenadian waters from November to March, when the catch includes sailfish, blue and white marlin, yellowfin tuna, dorado, kingfish, and wahoo. Fishing charters can be arranged through hotel water sports desks. A fully equipped high-speed Bertram charters for about $50 per hour for a party of four. Dodd Gormon (phone: 444-2508) charters his large, somewhat slower diesel yacht for deep-sea trips for about $30 per hour for a party of four, will carry up to six additional nonfishing "observers" for $10 a head. Rates include crew, bait, tackle, and drinks; charterer provides lunch for his party and crew. The annual International Game Fishing Tournament takes place in January or February, depending on the moon.

Swimming and Sunning – Grand Anse Beach is the long, beautiful, famous one; with a number of hotels and guesthouses on or just across the road from it, chances are the place you stay will have a piece of it too. (You can visit others for a small fee for the use of facilities.) The beaches at Musquetta and Horseshoe bays are other southern beauties. At the other end of the island, Levera Beach on the northeastern shore, where the Atlantic and the Caribbean meet, is palm lined, uncrowded, and a favorite picnic place. And Carriacou's most seductive sands line Paradise Beach and small Sandy Island offshore.

Tennis – Grenada doesn't have many courts. The *Ramada Renaissance* hotel, *Secret Harbour, Calabash, Coral Cove,* and *Twelve Degrees North* have facilities, and nonguests can play (if the courts are open) for a nominal fee (up to $5 US, although sometimes it's free). The *Tanteen Tennis Club, Richmond Hill Tennis Club,* and the *Carenage Club* will arrange temporary memberships (one month) for $15 US. Visiting nonmembers can play for a nominal per-person per-hour charge.

 NIGHTLIFE: For visitors, it's centered at hotels — each of which hold buffets, barbecues, island shows, and dancing (a combo one night, steel band the next) on a flexible schedule — several nights a week in season, less often in summer. (The *Ramada Renaissance* hotel and the *Spice Island Inn* are most active in this department.) You can hotel-hop, but most nights, most people are content to sit, sip, and talk on their own terraces after dinner. Islanders play late Friday and Saturday nights at *The Sugar Mill* disco (next to the Grand Anse roundabout), *Love Boat* (just off the roundabout near the drive-in movie), and the *2001,* a roistering spot on the water at Quarantine Beach. The *Bougainvillea Club,* across L'Anse aux Epines Road from the *Red Crab Pub,* has a more conventionally sophisticated atmosphere than some of the local hangouts. Insomniac visitors are welcome to join the crowd whenever they like, but not many stay awake that long. Another disco, *Panache,* is nearer to St. George's on L'Anse aux Epines Road.

BEST ON THE ISLAND

 CHECKING IN: Since 1984, Grenada has doubled its tourist accommodations to a total of more than 750 rooms — still not a lot by Caribbean standards. Expansion is expected to continue at the annual rate of 100 to 200 rooms. A central reservations number (800-255-5463; 212-840-6636 in New York State) provides rate and availability information.

Grenada's better hotels offer a more casual, understated style of elegance than many tourists may ever have experienced elsewhere. Don't look for fast-paced nightlife in the resorts; it's all low-key. And don't be surprised if a hotel advertised as "deluxe" turns out to be somewhat shy of services; take a look around — what you're paying for here are some of the most charmingly situated resort hideaways anywhere in the Caribbean, not personal bathroom TV sets or shower massages. However, the interruptions in electricity and hot water, which used to be expected vicissitudes of local hotel life, occur far less frequently now.

Maybe because of the island's almost-Iberian name, Mediterranean motifs are strong. Splendor here isn't velvet-spread beds or mirrored ceilings; it's a view of the sea and *two* four-poster beds per room (as at *Secret Harbour*). In-season rates are very reasonable compared to those on a number of neighboring islands (several hotels start at about $150 US MAP — including breakfasts and dinners for two), and deliver comparatively good value in quality of accommodations, food, and pleasantly rendered service; use of water and land sports equipment is generally included. Expect to pay about $160 up, including breakfasts and dinners, for a double room in the winter season in hotels we list below as expensive; from $65 without meals to $130 with breakfasts and dinners in those places we categorize as moderate, $90 and under in those listed as inexpensive. In the top category, rates usually include breakfasts and dinners (MAP).

GRAND ANSE BEACH

Cinnamon Hill – Villa complex landscaped into a green hillside above the beach and bay. Nice blend of Spanish architecture, West Indian atmosphere. It has 20 luxury apartments and hacienda suites plus main building with restaurant, bar, freshwater pool. Nice touches include individual terrace breakfasts, extra thick beach towels, bidets, a small health club, and its own slice of Grand Anse beach. Weekly buffets, some night entertainment (phone: 444-4301, 4302). Expensive.

Ramada Renaissance – The former *Grenada Beach* hotel, after a facelift and expansion, has emerged as a 156-room resort complete with a new lobby, 2 restaurants, and lounge bar. The 19-acre beachfront property includes lots of shady palms, 2 synthetic-surface tennis courts, and a pool. All water sports, including diving excursions via concessionaire; 4 shops; in-room, direct-dial telephone service. Dining is al fresco or indoors with air conditioning, and there's nightly entertainment (phone: 444-4371). Expensive.

Spice Island Inn – Pleasantly contemporary suites stretched along 1,200 feet of perfect white beach: 20 suites are at the edge of sand, 10 more are back a bit with their own high-walled private pools. "Spice," as it's known locally, was the premier hotel on Grand Anse 20 years ago, and has just undergone renovation. The repeat-business rate is impressive, the food and service are good, and there's usually something interesting going on in the evenings. Good summer packages (phone: 444-4258). Expensive.

Blue Horizons – Spruced up, garden-landscaped, and personably run (the Hopkins don't know how to do it any other way), its 32 cottage suites — 16 of them recently remodeled — are reasonably priced even at the height of the season. With pool, kitchenettes, cooks available. What it lacks in beach (Grand Anse is 300 yards down the road), it makes up in genuine island atmosphere, thoughtful service (phone: 444-4316). Moderate.

Coyaba – This new resort hotel occupies a lovely 2½-acre site on Grand Anse Beach. The central pavilion, which houses the reception area, bar, lounge, boutique, and open-air restaurant, is surrounded by three 2-story lodges, with a total of 30 air-conditioned rooms. All accommodations feature private verandahs with views of the beach and St. George's Harbor, color TV, and phone. Facilities include a swimming pool with swim-up bar, volleyball, tennis courts, small putting green, children's playground, and meeting room. As its name (derived from an Amerindian word meaning "heaven") implies, *Coyaba* has been designed to provide guests with a celestial vacation experience (phone: 444-4129). Moderate.

L'ANSE AUX EPINES

Calabash – With 10 cottages (22 complete suites) spread over 8 acres of beachfront land. Each has bedroom, bathroom, sitting room, kitchen (maids come in to do breakfast), and verandah just steps from the water's edge. (If money is no object, try to book the pool suite.) Other assets: pretty beach, Sunfish, lighted tennis court, billiard room, and one of the island's best restaurants. Some nighttime entertainment. Large repeat business; book early (phones: 444-4234, 4334). Expensive.

Horse Shoe Beach – The Bishop regime, which knew a good tourist location from a bad one, attempted to run this beautiful, lushly landscaped property, and for several years it was not well served. Now, however, 6 rooms have been added; the 12 elegant Mediterranean cottage suites have been spruced up (including hand-carved four-poster beds); and *Horse Shoe Beach* has emerged intact. Marvelous vistas from the dining room; small beach, but there is a pool; table tennis, billiards, and croquet (phone: 444-4410). Expensive.

Secret Harbour – The now couples-only resort features marvelous Spanish-Moorish design with tiled roofs, terraces, arches, opulent finishing touches (stained glass, sunken tubs, two big four-poster beds per room, great sense of spaciousness). About half the units have been equipped with "housekeeping" facilities — a small fridge and 2-burner stove — wedged into the dressing area; it's a draw, primarily for long-term visitors, which does nothing for the atmosphere in these otherwise charming rooms. Sandy beach, tile-framed swimming pool, putting green, tennis court, water sports — all included in rates. Quiet evenings (phone: 444-4439). Expensive.

Coral Cove – Six housekeeping apartments have been added to the 4 cottages, all of which are either 1- or 2-bedroom units overlooking a white beach suitable for some water sports (the water is very shallow in this area). A swimming pool and synthetic-surface tennis court round out the improvements. Full maid service; car rentals and charter fishing arranged (phone: 444-4422). Moderate.

Twelve Degrees North – A tastefully done arrangement of 2 two-bedroom and 6 one-bedroom cottages designed for island housekeeping the easy way. Maids, on duty from 8 AM until 3 PM, clean, launder, cook. (If you ask, they'll do dinner ahead of time for you.) Beach equipment includes a dock, float, Sunfish, Boston Whaler, plus a thatch bar and barbecue setup. There are also a pool and a tennis court. You're on your own for dinner (cook in, eat out). All very relaxing. Children at Christmas, Easter, and in summer season only. European Plan; groceries are on you (phone: 444-4580). Moderate.

CARRIACOU

Mermaid Beach – Small (12 little rooms, counting singles), simple, cheerful, and loved. Nothing much happens in the big lobby on the street side — except an occasional check-in or game of Ping-Pong. Everyone's on the terrace basking, reading, drinking, eating, swapping yarns. Boat people drop in as a matter of course — to overnight or just catch up on the news. Sailing and snorkeling available; good island food. Its charms are genuine and island-grown. But if happiness is wall-to-wall carpet and conditioned air, this is clearly *not* the place (phone: 443-7484; better yet, cable Mermaid, Carriacou, or write to Mermaid Beach Hotel, Hillsborough, Carriacou, Grenada, WI). Inexpensive.

Prospect Lodge – A newly opened refuge for writers, poets, and quiet souls. Four bedrooms, one apartment, and one cottage grace a lush hillside. Home cooking supervised by owner and writer Ann Katzenbach. Swimming at two secluded beaches (phone: 443-7380). Inexpensive.

Silver Beach – Eight simply (but fully) furnished duplex apartments, right on the white sand beach at Beausejour Bay, a bit north of Hillsborough. The Carriacou alternative; pleasant, but slightly reclusive (phone: 443-7337; cable Cayak, Carriacou, or write Silver Beach Resort, Beausejour Bay, Carriacou, Grenada, WI). Inexpensive.

 EATING OUT: Grenadian food owes its special flavor to good island cooks and very fresh ingredients: just-caught fish, lobster, crab, and conch (called lambi), just-picked garden vegetables and tropical fruits in great variety. Island dishes to try: pumpkin soup, callaloo soup (with greens and crab), conch (in conch and onion pie, or curried), turtle steaks, avocado and soursop ice cream. The national drink is rum punch, *always* with freshly grated Grenadian nutmeg on top; local Carib beer is quite good.

Food at Grenadian hotels is generally excellent. Most have Continental chefs and menus that feature Continental specialties plus a few West Indian choices. Since most dining rooms are small, with only limited space for outside guests, it is absolutely essential to call ahead for reservations if you want to sample the food at another hotel. Except for casual downtown spots (like the *Nutmeg*), dinner reservations are a good idea at local restaurants too. Expect to pay $40 to $50 US for a dinner for two at any of the places listed below as expensive; $20 to $35 in a moderate restaurant; and under $20 in any of the places we list as inexpensive. Prices don't include drinks, wine, or tips. Most hotel restaurants fall into the expensive range, which means the MAP accommodation prices make sense. For real island food, dine at *Mama's* or *La Belle Créole.*

ST. GEORGE'S

Cubby Hole – A balconied lunch and dinner spot brimming with such genuine Grenadian hospitality that you're tempted to linger and chat long after the meal. Good island food; disco later. Just off the Carenage; turn at LIAT Cargo sign (no phone). Moderate.

Mama's – Her undiluted West Indian menu and profusion of offerings (multiple courses, served family-style, are the rule for large parties) have made Mama the celebrity chef of Grenada. Always ask if she has any turtle available; try her callaloo soup and sea moss ice cream. Any cab driver can find her place on Old Lagoon Road near Grenada Yacht Services, but get reservations well in advance, or you may be edged out by a covey of food critics from the *New York Times.* Old Lagoon Rd. (phone: 440-1459). Moderate.

Rudolf's – Swiss-owned spot for lunch or dinner; pub-cozy bar. Continental with a few local specialties, potent rum punches. North corner of the Carenage (phone: 440-2241). Moderate.

Nutmeg – Overlooking the Carenage. For drinks, snacks, or a full meal, the most popular noontime drop-in spot in town. Chatty, easygoing. Forget the hamburgers; have a rum punch, callaloo soup, lobster, or lambi. The Carenage (phone: 440-2539). Moderate to inexpensive.

Pastryman – Across from the Market Square, a good spot for cool drinks, snacks, and light lunches for tired shoppers, or for tea, sandwiches, ice cream, sodas. For a substantial snack, try a beef *rôti* (spicy ground beef in pastry). Granby and Halifax sts. (no phone). Inexpensive.

ELSEWHERE

Calabash Hotel – The 1987 winner of the Golden Fork Award (Grenada's first), the restaurant offers the handiwork of chef Cecily Roberts. Fresh seafood and island-grown fruits and vegetables are prepared in Grenadian style (phone: 444-4234). Expensive.

Cinnamon Hill – On a terrace with a view of the Grand Anse shoreline, a stylishly casual place for candlelit dinners. Specialties include Swedish smorgasbørd and fresh seafood. In the villa complex of the same name (phone: 4301). Expensive.

La Belle Créole – Small and cordial balcony dining room is the scene of some really fine West Indian meals in the Hopkin family tradition. *Blue Horizons Cottage Hotel* (phone: 444-4316). Expensive to moderate.

Betty Mascoll's – Her *Morne Fendue* plantation house dining room is a must stop (see *Extra Special*), but now that the main road from St. George's to Grenville has been largely improved, a trip for the meal alone is much more feasible (lunch only). Phone in advance (phone: 443-9330). Moderate.

Red Crab Pub – English style, complete with dartboard. Favorite spot for Grenadian meeting and greeting. Good barbecued chicken, fish and chips, hamburgers, draft beer. L'Anse aux Epines Rd. (phone: 444-4424). Moderate.

GUADELOUPE

Guadeloupe and Martinique are sister islands and, like true sisters, unmistakably of the same parentage but unquestionably of different character. Each is French, Caribbean, and politically equal. Each has now been elevated to *région* status, one level above *département* (French equivalent of US state or Canadian province), and is governed as if it were physically attached to the European landmass. The people are citizens of France, vote in French national elections, are entitled to French social benefits, and are bound by France's compulsory educational requirements. (The French Antilles has one of the highest literacy rates in the Caribbean.)

Guadeloupe, immediately north of the island of Dominica, which is north of Martinique, is about midway down the Lesser (smaller) Antilles that dot the Caribbean in an east-bending arc from Puerto Rico to Trinidad and Tobago just off the Venezuelan coast of South America. Like Martinique, Guadeloupe has its own dormant (more or less) volcano, its tropically forested mountains, its impressive Parc Naturel, its cane fields, banana plantations, and pineapple stands, its surf-pounded Atlantic side and its calmer leeward bathing beaches, its Créole cuisine and beguine.

But the differences are notable. Guadeloupe (530 square miles) is larger than Martinique (425 square miles). It is actually two islands linked by a drawbridge over the Rivière-Salée. In addition, Guadeloupe has a number of dependencies: the nearby islands of La Désirade, Marie Galante, and Îles des Saintes (also called Les Saintes) — which can all be seen from Guadeloupe's shore — plus the French half of the island of St. Martin and tiny St. Barthélemy, 140 and 125 miles, respectively, northwest of their butterfly-shaped parent islands.

Guadeloupe's scenery is often stunning — especially at the wave-dashed Pointe-des-Châteaux; along the Basse-Terre coast, and in the great, green Parc Naturel. It offers not only its own two islands to explore, but day or overnight trips to intriguing, unspoiled, dependent islands as well.

In 1493, nine years before he found Martinique, Christopher Columbus happened onto Guadeloupe. Eschewing its Carib name, Karukera — Island of the Beautiful Waters — he christened it Santa María de Guadalupe de Estremadura to fulfill a promise made to the monks of the Spanish monastery of the same name. The French landed on both islands in 1635. But while Martinique flourished, Guadeloupe foundered — thanks to the ineptitude of its leaders and the lack of farming skill among its volunteer settlers, all of whom were indentured to work three years without pay in exchange for their passage from France. They managed to survive and slowly grew stronger under the administrative wing of Martinique.

The French Revolution goaded them into acting as a separate entity. Infuriated by the Declaration of the Rights of Man and the abolition of

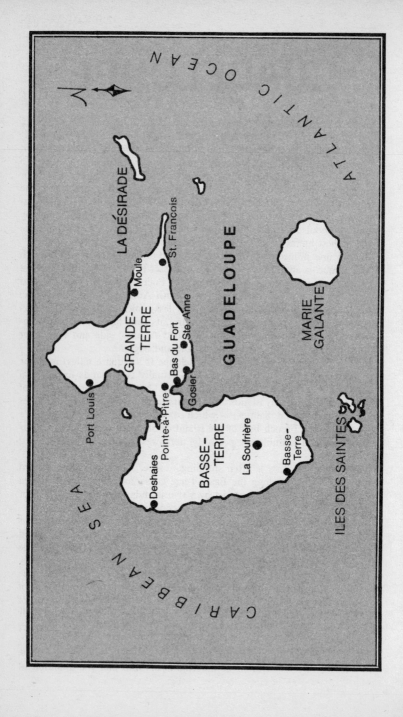

slavery (which doomed their cane fields), they declared themselves autonomous, inviting the enemy English to invade and stay awhile. Starting in April 1794, Guadeloupe seesawed for more than 20 years between France and Britain.

The Committee of Public Safety in Paris dispatched one Victor Hugues with a fleet and 1,150 men to discipline the islanders. He ousted the English from Fort Fleur d'Epée, set up guillotines in the main squares of Basse-Terre and Pointe-à-Pitre, and beheaded 4,000 Guadeloupeans before the Parisian powers-that-were removed him to Guiana. Slavery was re-established under Napoleon. The British returned and reconquered in 1810, relinquished the land to Louis XVIII during the Restoration, reoccupied it when Napoleon staged his 100-day comeback, and gave it up for good when the little emperor was permanently exiled to St. Helena in 1815.

Guadeloupe has been French ever since, but perhaps as a result of those erratic years, it has also developed its own character — a unique blend of France and the West Indies. Guadeloupe has also been the focus of a nascent (occasionally violent) independence movement that is by no means representative of overall island sentiment. For the moment, it remains on the back burner.

Still, French influence perseveres. Guadeloupe's hotels generally follow the large, luxurious, made-in-France pattern, with *tous* sports built in, or the small, French-speaking hostel-on-the-beach design, with a few inns and a *Club Med* village for variation. But unlike Martinique's capital (appropriately called Fort-de-France and looking like a miniature Cannes or Nice, very French indeed), Guadeloupe's is a small port city called Basse-Terre, which could be described as dull in comparison to its working heart, bustling Pointe-à-Pitre. Despite its new high-rise housing and burgeoning industry, it moves to a distinctly Caribbean beat. To feel it, stroll down to the waterfront, lined with chunky island boats, where blue-eyed Îles des Saintes fishermen hawk their morning catches, or pay an early morning call to market stalls piled with fruits and spices dear to the soul of its Créole cooks.

And it is Créole cuisine — vying with traditional French specialties — that fires the Guadeloupean spirit. One fistful of the tiny hot peppers vital to Créole cooking is generally considered enough to blow up an average European city. Classic French restaurants like *La Plantation* are respected and admired, but the real heroines of this island's kitchens are Prudence, Félicité, Violetta, and Trésor — and the dozen or so members of the Association of Women Chefs — who conjure up their magic blaffs, boudins, and crabes farcis in plain places in the hills and along the shores. The whole island celebrates their art with a grand parade, a cathedral blessing, music, dancing, and a five-hour feast at the annual August Fête des Cuisinières (Cooks' Festival). With the possible exception of Carnival, this is the single most colorful event of the Guadeloupe year. A celebratory lunch or dinner is an adventure and — when your eye and palate have acclimated to the spices and surprises — a special delight.

You may be drawn to Martinique first — it is more stylish, more the French-French you expect. But if you've been to Martinique, if you're looking for a place a bit more offbeat with fine beaches, and if you can say "Vive la différence" and mean it, Guadeloupe is the island you want.

GUADELOUPE AT-A-GLANCE

FROM THE AIR: Guadeloupe is a butterfly-shaped formation of two islands, Grande-Terre (218 square miles) and Basse-Terre (312 square miles), separated by a narrow strait called the Rivière-Salée (Salt River) and connected by a drawbridge. It has a total landmass of 582 square miles and a population of 330,000. Like Martinique, it is a full-fledged overseas *région* of France, and includes the three small island dependencies of Îles des Saintes, Marie Galante, and La Désirade, all just offshore, as well as the island of St. Barthélemy (also known as St. Barts) and the French part of the island of St. Martin, both of which are farther away (125 and 140 miles northwest, respectively) and are treated separately in this guide.

At 16°15′ N latitude, 61°30′ W longitude, a little less than halfway down the arc formed by the Lesser Antilles between Puerto Rico and Trinidad, Guadeloupe is one of the Leeward Islands of the Caribbean. Its nearest neighbors are Antigua (65 miles northwest), Dominica (73 miles south), and Martinique (121 miles south and slightly east). The 1,845-mile jet flight from New York to Le Raizet International Airport, just north of Pointe-à-Pitre, takes about 3½ hours; the flight from Miami (about 1,320 miles) is approximately 2½ hours; and from Montréal (about 2,138 miles), about 4½ hours.

Basse-Terre city (population just over 15,000), on the southwest edge of the island of the same name, is the capital of the *région;* but the larger city of Pointe-à-Pitre (population 100,000), on the southwest coast of Grande-Terre near the point where the Rivière-Salée separates the two islands, is its commercial center.

SPECIAL PLACES: The two wings of butterfly-shaped Guadeloupe are quite different topographically. Basse-Terre has mountain terrain inland and a rugged coastline with few (but good) beaches suited to daylong basking. On the other hand, Grande-Terre consists of flat cane fields and low, chalky hills rimmed by a number of appealing beaches. As a result, most island visitors stay on Grande-Terre at the shore hotels of Bas du Fort, Gosier, Ste. Anne, and St. François, or at any of the 20 odd small hotels and inns conforming to the high standards of service and comfort that make up the new group of Relais Créoles. They spend half a day shopping and strolling around Pointe-à-Pitre, and make a day-tour visit to Basse-Terre's Parc Naturel and its capital, also called Basse-Terre. Some rent cars to explore on their own; but since Basse-Terre's roads tend to be mountainous inland and sharply curved along the shore, most visitors sign up for organized bus tours at hotel travel desks. Athletic types who are strong of limb and lung can arrange a guided climb to the top of Soufrière, the island's once again dormant volcano. Air hops or ferry rides to the Îles des Saintes and Marie Galante combine sightseeing with a chance to laze on pleasant, secluded beaches.

Pointe-à-Pitre – Guadeloupe's port and chief city, on Grande-Terre, likes to call itself the "Paris of the Antilles," but its French look is more like a Riviera port than the city on the Seine. Apartments and condominiums form a high-rise backdrop for its 19th-century cathedral, tree-planted squares, and boat-lined harbor. It is busy, but not so bustling or big that you can't see it and get in your shopping, too, in half a day — preferably morning, when the waterfront and outdoor market are liveliest.

Start by picking up brochures and a map of Guadeloupe (including a street map of Pointe-à-Pitre) at the Office of Tourism, housed in a white colonial building across from the Place de la Victoire. The parklike Place is shaded by flamboyants and palms as well as antique sandbox trees planted by Victor Hugues, whose victory over the British in 1794 gave the Place its name. It was here that he, as Guadeloupe's first dictator, also erected the guillotine to execute enemies of the Revolution. It stood in the square for some years.

The Rue Duplessis, at the Place's southern edge, runs along La Darse, the old port where inter-island ferries leave for Marie-Galante and Les Saintes and fishing schooners tie up and where, farther out, cruise ships drop anchor. West of the harbor, the shopping district's narrow streets are crowded with shops that range from sidewalk stalls to boutiques full of French perfumes and sportwear. Chief tourist shopping streets are the Rue de Nozières and the Rue Frébault (both of which run north and south) and the Rue Achille René-Boisneuf (usually referred to by its hyphenated name alone), running east and west. At 54 Rue René-Boisneuf, a plaque marks the birthplace of Saint-John Perse, the French poet who won the Nobel Prize for Literature in 1960. A block north, bounded by Rues Schoelcher, Peynier, Frébault, and Thiers, the open-air market hums with the give-and-take of housewives and women vendors — some straw-hatted, some still in their traditional madras turbans — bargaining across stacks of fire-red pimientos, onions, carrots, pawpaws, pineapples, mangoes, bananas, and spices. A short walk north and east brings you to the peaceful Place de l'Église, where you can rest and sip a punch or a café filtre across from the yellow and white Cathédrale de St. Pierre et St. Paul, nicknamed "the Iron Cathedral" because of its skeleton of bolted iron ribs, designed to keep the church standing through hurricanes and earthquakes.

ELSEWHERE ON THE ISLAND

In Grande-Terre, most points of interest are along the shores east of Pointe-à-Pitre. As you drive east from town, they are:

Fort Fleur d'Epée – Well-preserved battlements and dungeons of an 18th-century fortress 3 miles east of Pointe-à-Pitre and commanding a view of the city, the nearby islands of Marie Galante and the Îles des Saintes, and in the distance the mountains of Basse-Terre and the island of Dominica. On the shore below, Bas du Fort is the site of three late-model resort hotels and vacation condominiums.

Gosier – Shoreside center with extensive beach 4½ miles east of Pointe-à-Pitre; site of six major resort hotels. Near the marina is the new Aquarium de la Guadeloupe, with over 150 species of fish and tropical plants housed in a glass tunnel (phone: 90-92-38)

Ste. Anne – The most quaint of Guadeloupe's villages, with pastel town hall, church, and main square dominated by a statue of emancipationist Victor Schoelcher, erected by the island's blacks to commemorate the end of slavery in 1848. *Club Med,* six small Relais Créoles inns, and extensive beaches are nearby.

St. François – A fishing village with long, white sand beaches, many good Créole and French restaurants, and an expanding resort complex (marina, casino, golf course) whose centers are the *Méridien-Guadeloupe, Hamak,* and *Golf Marine* hotels.

Pointe-des-Châteaux – The easternmost tip of Grande-Terre, where the waters of the Atlantic and the Caribbean meet; a towering castle-like rock formation, crowned by a rugged cross that has survived more than a century; crashing waves, but tranquil, coved beaches (Pointe Tarare is the *au naturel* one); fine picnic destination.

Le Moule – A small coastal fishing village and antique sugar port with a long crescent beach west of Pointe-à-Pitre. There's a small archaeological museum, and just north of town at Morel, archaeologists have unearthed a pre-Columbian Arawak village. At the Beach of Skulls and Bones, the ocean has uncovered graves and petrified remains, macabre relics of once savage warfare between the Caribs and the French and British invaders.

Or take the coastal road north from Pointe-à-Pitre to:

Port Louis and Anse Bertrand – Fishing villages with good beaches nearby.

Pointe de la Grande Vigie – At the northernmost tip of the island and named for the sweeping Atlantic view from the top of its rocky cliffs.

To see Basse-Terre, west of Pointe-à-Pitre, across the drawbridge over the Rivière-Salée — which, incidentally, is the only river anywhere that connects the Caribbean and the Atlantic — you have a choice of tour routes: west on La Traversée, the highway that crosses Basse-Terre through the lush highlands of the Parc Naturel of Guadeloupe, then south along the west coast to the capital city of Basse-Terre, and returning via the island's east coast; or you can take the coastal roads first and return traveling La Traversée west to east. Following the latter route, you visit:

Ste. Marie – The spot where Columbus landed on his second voyage in 1493 and named the island for Spain's Virgin of Guadalupe, but left hurriedly when the Caribs started peppering his crew with arrows. Today, a statue of Columbus stands in the town square, and the area is largely populated by East Indian descendants of the laborers imported to work plantations after the 1848 emancipation of black slaves. Just south of town is much-photographed Allée Dumanoir, a half-mile stretch of road lined on both sides with tall palms planted in the last century by Pinel Dumanoir, whose claim to fame is — surprisingly — his French dramatization of *Uncle Tom's Cabin.*

Les Chutes du Carbet – A trio of waterfalls that impressed Columbus' crew, who — when they sighted them from the sea — thought they were "avalanches of white stones." For a closer look, take the road inland from the coastal town of St. Sauveur past the round mountain lake called Grand Etang and up Soufrière mountain to a cleared viewing point near the three cascades. The lowest is between 60 and 70 feet high; the second and top falls are over 300 feet each. A 20-minute walk brings you to the pool at the foot of the lowest falls for an even closer inspection.

Trois-Rivières – A seaside settlement that boasts Guadeloupe's most modern town hall, but with older sights that are much more interesting: Near the harbor where ferries depart for the Îles des Saintes, rocks in a small park bear pre-Columbian inscriptions, and for a few francs one of the local boys will show you the portrait of a chieftain on the wall of a nearby grotto.

Basse-Terre – Guadeloupe's capital, a small, neat city of narrow streets and palm-filled parks set between the sea and the green heights of La Soufrière. Chief interest points: a number of nicely designed administrative buildings that make up the old Carmel quarter; the 17th-century Cathedral of Our Lady of Guadeloupe in the Saint-François section; and Fort St. Charles, which has stood guard over the city since its founding in 1643.

Vieux-Habitants – A few miles north of Basse-Terre, this small fishing village is where the first French settlers landed in 1635. The new La Maison du Café is a museum devoted to the story of local coffee production. Refreshments are available.

La Soufrière – A tenuously dormant volcano that has given Guadeloupeans some anxious moments in recent years. Although it hasn't fully erupted, it often breathes steam from its fumaroles (smoke holes) and burps sulfurous fumes from its pits and mud cauldrons. The foot of the crater can be reached by car; there, at the Savane-à-Mulets parking lot, spectators feel the heat of the subterranean lava by simply touching the ground, and enjoy a magnificent view of Basse-Terre, the sea, the Îles des Saintes, and Dominica. Adventurous types can climb one of four color-coded marked trails to the edge of the crater to view its 5-acre center of bubbling lava and eerie rock formations. The *Guide to the Natural Park,* available from the Tourist Office, grades trails by difficulty: the blue is rated 1 (easy walk); the yellow and green, 2 (some difficulty); and the red, 3 (for the experienced hiker only). The round-trip trek takes from 1 to 3 hours, depending on your stamina; guides are strongly recommended because of sudden mountain mists and shifting paths (due to fast-growing vegetation).

La Traversée – The Transcoastal Highway, an excellent road that provides a convenient way to see the Parc Naturel en route from Basse-Terre to Pointe-à-Pitre. You reach its western end by driving north along the coast past black sand beaches and the small town of Vieux-Habitants (see above); Bouillante, boiling with hot springs and geysers; and where dive trips and glass-bottom-boat rides leave for Pigeon Island and the underwater reserve developed by Jacques Cousteau. These odd names are associated with some celebrated, more familiar ones: Brigitte Bardot has lived in Bouillante; Jacques Cousteau often explores the silent depths off nearby Pigeon Island. La Traversée starts just north of Pigeon at Mahaut and travels 10½ miles east through a pass between mountains graphically referred to as Les Deux Mamelles (the Two Breasts). The road offers a broad view of the hills, valleys, and coasts of Basse-Terre and the bays called Grand and Petit Cul-de-Sac, plus closeups of the park's tropic forests, lakes, and waterfalls. On the way through, you can stop for a stroll in the *Zoological and Botanical Park* at Bouillante, or perhaps a cooling dip in the pool at the bottom of the Cascade aux Écrevisses (Crayfish Falls). The eastern end of La Traversée joins the road that crosses the Rivière-Salée drawbridge back to Pointe-à-Pitre.

■**EXTRA SPECIAL:** *Îles des Saintes* and *Marie Galante,* two unspoiled offshore island destinations for daylong getaway plane trips or ferry crossings, organized by tour operators or arranged on your own. Marie Galante offers a bit of sightseeing (sunny little town of Grand-Bourg, sugar mills, pastoral landscapes, architecturally splendid Murat Château), and fine white beaches (pack a picnic, or lunch on langouste or lambi at *Békéké* on the sand near Capesterre or some other restaurant). Most Îles des Saintes trips land breathtakingly (it's a very short runway with a mountain-pass approach) on Terre de Haut island. There are minibus "taxis de l'île," but it's a very short walk past the cemetery (white tombs, hand-carved crucifix, conch shell–framed grave sites) and over the hill to the town, which is one of the Caribbean's prettiest (tiny square, flowers, miniature houses — no two with the same painted color scheme). Lunch at Pointe Coquelet on the terrace of the *Kanaoa* hotel, the appealing restaurant *Le Foyal,* or *Le Mouillage* near the pier and bask on a beach nearby; or take the launch from the town pier or taxi out to the *Bois Joli* hotel for lunch and a choice of clothed (though often topless) or bare beaching. Other hotels recommended for overnight stays are the *PLM Azur Los Santos* and the *Anacardiers* (a Relais Créole property). Big round salako straw hats (like coolies'), unique to these islands, make super souvenirs — when you can find them.

SOURCES AND RESOURCES

TOURIST INFORMATION: The French West Indies Tourist Board, at 610 Fifth Ave., New York, NY 10020 (phone: 212-757-1125). French Government Tourist Offices are in the following North American cities:

Beverly Hills: 9401 Wilshire Blvd., Beverly Hills, CA 90212 (phone: 213-272-2661)
Chicago: 645 N Michigan Ave., Suite 430, Chicago, IL 60611 (phone: 312-337-6301)
Dallas: 103 World Trade Center, Dallas, TX 75258 (phone: 214-742-7011)
New York: 628 Fifth Ave., New York, NY 10020 (phone: 212-757-1125)
San Francisco: 1 Halladie Plaza, Suite 250, San Francisco, CA 94102 (phone: 415-986-4161)

Montréal: 1981 Ave. McGill College, Suite 490, Montréal, Que. H3A 2W9 (phone: 514-288-4264)

Toronto: 1 Dundas St. W, Suite 2405, Toronto, Ont. M5G 1Z3 (phone: 416-593-4717)

Only the New York and Beverly Hills offices will handle written inquiries.

Local Coverage – *Guadeloupe Bonjour,* the island's official tourist booklet, published periodically by the Tourist Office in both French and English, is distributed free at the Tourist Office, at the airport, and in hotels. It is full of information (including useful addresses and phone numbers) on everything from history and religious services to consulates and Carnival, plus up-to-date specifics on excursions, restaurants, and nightlife. The paperback *Guide to Guadeloupe* (Editions de la Pensée Moderne, available in English for about $4 at newsstands) — while somewhat confusingly put together and random in its selection of material — contains a good deal of chatty background and useful information on Guadeloupe.

Guadeloupe, a book of color photographs collected by Hans W. Hannau, is available at large bookstores. *A Woman Named Solitude,* a novel by André Schwarz-Bart (Atheneum, 1973), incorporates much Guadeloupean history and atmosphere, as does *Between Two Worlds* (Harper & Row, 1981) by Schwarz-Bart's wife, Simone.

In Guadeloupe, the Guadeloupe Office of Tourism, 5, Square de la Banque, near the waterfront in Pointe-à-Pitre, open from 8 AM to 5 PM on weekdays and from 8 AM to noon on Saturdays, supplies maps, information, and advice. The staff will also answer phone queries in English (phone: 82-09-30).

Telephone – Dial direct to Guadeloupe by adding the international access code 011 and the prefix 596 to the numbers given below.

 ENTRY REQUIREMENTS: For stays of up to 3 months, a valid or an expired passport (not more than 5 years old) or proof of citizenship in the form of a voter's registration card or birth certificate with raised seal accompanied by a government ID card, or similar document, *with photograph.* A return or ongoing plane ticket is also required. For a longer period, a visa is required. Entering US or Canadian citizens need no vaccination certificates. (If you plan to visit the casino, you must have some form of identification bearing your photograph.)

 CLIMATE AND CLOTHES: The weather is tropical, tempered by trade winds and with thermometer readings varying considerably between sea level and mountains. At beach resorts on the southern coast of Grande Terre, temperatures range from an average low of 72°F (24°C) to an average high of 86°F (30°C). In the higher, cooler inland regions, the averages run from 66°F to 81°F (19°C to 27°C). September and October are the wettest months; November to May, the driest. But even in the residential suburb of St. Claude, where it's said the climate is perfect — sunny, cool, and breezy year round — it showers almost every day. As a hotelier explains, "It is only to make the flowers and rainbows bloom." Most tourist accommodations are air conditioned.

On its beaches, Guadeloupe seems more casual about clothes than even Martinique. Topless sunning is taken for granted just about everywhere. On the beaches that lie a bit off the beaten track, topless walking around causes rapid eye movement only among recently arrived North Americans. And there are officially designated nude beaches on Guadeloupe proper as well as on the Îles des Saintes.

Off beach, lightweight sportswear is most comfortable. Both men and women should pack some sort of cover-up — long-sleeved shirts or beach caftans — to slip on for lunch or when you've simply had enough sun. Slacks and sport shirts for men and slacks or skirts for women are right for downtown shopping, lunching, or excursions.

For the Parc Naturel, wear sturdy, crepe-soled shoes or sneakers, and take along a light jacket (preferably waterproof) or sweater in case of a chilly spell or shower. At night, especially in the large hotels, women dress up a bit, in long-skirted cottons or evening pants with chic tops; men stay casual, in slacks and open-necked shirts with or without jackets; ties are seldom, if ever, required, but you might pack one as insurance.

 MONEY: Guadeloupe's currency is the French franc whose value in US dollars is quoted in the business sections of most major daily US metropolitan newspapers; recently it has been about 5.50 francs to $1 US. Most hotels will exchange dollars for francs in limited amounts; but French francs can be reconverted to dollars only at banks. Banks offer most favorable exchange rates, but like most Guadeloupean businesses, they are closed for lunch between noon and 2:30 PM. You'll get more for your shopping money if you pay for your purchases in dollar-denomination traveler's checks; some Pointe-à-Pitre merchants discount duty-free prices an extra 20% when paid in traveler's checks or a major credit card. Some shops accept payment in dollars but don't give the additional discount when they do.

 LANGUAGE: Guadeloupe's official language is French with the patois called Créole (African words and rhythms grafted onto French stems) as a virtual second tongue. You can count on English-speaking tour guides (if you've specified beforehand) and on some personnel in hotels and tourist-frequented shops who understand English. But if your French is rusty to nonexistent, the Office of Tourism strongly suggests you carry a dictionary or phrase book — preferably one that's situation-oriented (with useful phrases grouped under headings like "arriving," "dining," "driving," etc.) rather than in strict alphabetical order. If at first you don't succeed in making yourself understood, don't worry; patience, a smile, some hand signs, speaking slowly (loud doesn't help), and goodwill generally clarify things. The French West Indies Tourist Board's free *Helpful Hints for Visitors* includes a glossary of useful phrases.

 TIME: Guadeloupe time is 1 hour later than Eastern Standard Time (when it's noon in New York, it's 1 PM in Pointe-à-Pitre); or the same as Eastern Daylight Saving Time. Local time is also measured on a 24-hour clock, so that 1 PM is 13 *heures.*

 CURRENT: Local electricity is 220 volts AC, 50 cycles; large hotels sometimes have adapters to loan; but if your travel kit includes electric gadgets essential to your vacation well-being, better bring your own.

 GETTING THERE: American Airlines and American Eagle provide jet service from New York and other North American cities via San Juan, sometimes nonstop, sometimes on through flights via Martinique. Eastern flights from New York/Newark and other US cities make connections in Miami or San Juan. Air Canada jets in from Montréal and Toronto nonstop. Air France flies direct from Miami twice a week, nonstop from San Juan four times a week, and also schedules daily flights from Paris.

Air Guadeloupe covers the Îles des Saintes, Marie Galante, La Désirade, St. Barts, and St. Martin as well as Dominica and Antigua. LIAT provides air links between Guadeloupe and a dozen neighbor islands. Caribes Air Tourisme flies to Les Saintes twice daily.

Pointe-à-Pitre is Guadeloupe's major cruise port, and the Tourist Office provides a full range of assistance for visiting passengers, including an onboard briefing. A choice of organized sightseeing and beach excursions is available; additional taxis stationed near the wharf are available for independent touring. There is scheduled ferry service between Pointe-à-Pitre, Basse-Terre, or Trois-Rivières and the Îles des Saintes and Marie-Galante.

 CALCULATING COSTS: Winter hotel rates range from about $75 a day for a room with breakfast (CP) for two at a small hotel on the beach at Ste. Anne to $200 a day for two with full American breakfast at a four-star Gosier beach hotel. In summer, the same rooms cost about 25% to 35% less. As a rule, rates quoted in dollars are guaranteed for the whole season — winter (mid-December to mid-April) or summer (mid-April to mid-December) — against franc-dollar fluctuations.

The larger hotels offer a choice of Continental Plan (CP), with a breakfast that weighs in somewhere between a traditional Continental affair of coffee and croissants and the full American treatment (the buffet may also offer juice, fruit, cereal, bacon and eggs) and Modified American Plan (MAP), with breakfasts and lunch or dinner included. Generally, the cost difference between the two runs about $25 per person a day.

The best buys in package plans are available in the summer season (though there are all-inclusive plans — including the money-saving "Fête Française" series — available all year), with an increasing number that provide a choice of (rather than strictly stipulated) activities.

 GETTING AROUND: Taxi – Not as expensive as they used to be — slightly over $8 for the under-10-minute trip from the airport to your Gosier hotel; after 9 PM the rate jumps 40%. Since there is no airport limousine service, and buses are provided only for groups, there's no choice when it comes to transportation between airport and hotel.

Bus – The least expensive and most colorful way to go land roving — if your French and hang-loose spirit are up to it. Small, late-model jitney vans leave from two stations in downtown Pointe-à-Pitre: the Gare Routière de Bergevin for Basse-Terre destinations; the Gare Routière de la Darse for Grande-Terre hotels and resorts. They depart every 10 to 20 minutes, depending on the importance of the route.

Car Rental – Gives you maximum flexibility at reasonable rates. Major international agencies — *Avis* (phone: 82-33-47), *Budget* (phone: 82-95-58), *Hertz* (phone: 82-00-14), *InterRent* (phone: 91-42-16), and *National-Europcar* (phone: 82-50-51) — have offices in the arrival area of Le Raizet Airport. Local firms — also with airport offices — include *Car Pentier* (phone: 82-35-11); *Garage Narcisse* (phones: 82-06-54, 82-09-12); *Guadeloupe Cars* (phone: 82-10-94); *Jumbo Car* (83-60-74); and *Sol Tours* (phone: 83-39-15). *Avis, Budget, Hertz, Jumbo, National-Europcar,* and *Sol Tours* also have desks at the larger hotels.

Rates — which don't vary much from company to company — start at about $15 a day plus 8¢ a kilometer for a Citroën 2CV (very compact). An air-conditioned automatic Peugeot 505 goes for about $35 a day plus 19¢ a kilometer. Deposit (about $250 to $375, unless you're using a credit card, in which case no deposit is required), insurance, and 14% tax are additional. Some firms offer unlimited-mileage plans; and if you rent for a full week, there's a 10% discount. Automatic-transmission cars are in short supply. A valid driver's license is required; minimum renting age varies from 21 to 25 (depending on the agency), and you must have had at least one year's experience as a licensed driver.

Using government-designed self-drive tours and the Tourist Board's big clear map, it's easy to plot your own trip by tailoring a day's itinerary to your time and tastes. *One caution:* Driving on Grande-Terre, where roads are good and the land rolls gently, is easy going. On Basse-Terre's mountain roads — with their steep ascents, descents, and switchbacks — it's something else; so, if you're at all nervous about driving, it's probably wiser to go by bus.

Sightseeing Taxi Tours – Reasonable if you can put a group together to share the fare. Ask your concierge or desk clerk to get you a driver-guide and to determine the rates — standardized by the government. Samples: From Pointe-à-Pitre or Gosier to Pointe-des-Châteaux (half-day), about $50; to Soufrière Volcano (8 hours), about $70.

Sightseeing Bus Tours – Organized by local operators, these range from a half-day's Grande-Terre sightseeing with shopping in Pointe-à-Pitre to a whole day's exploration of Basse-Terre. Among the best and most personalized are the tours put together by Georges Marie-Gabrielle, a large, most accommodating man who has his headquarters at the airport (phone: 82-05-38). It is also a very good idea to check tour offerings for special features; when lunch is included, ask where before making reservations. Your concierge or hotel travel desk will have current details and rates on available tours and can make arrangements that include pickup at your hotel.

Sea Excursions – You can travel to Îlet à Caret on a choice of craft — the 50-foot sloop *Silver Heels* sailing from Baie-Mahault or the catamaran *Papyrus* departing from the marina in Pointe-à-Pitre; the daylong trip includes swimming, sun time, snorkeling, and a picnic on the white sand beach (for prices and sailing times, phone 82-87-26). If you don't mind crowds and/or choppy seas, there is also regularly scheduled ferry service from Trois-Rivières to the Îles des Saintes and from Pointe-à-Pitre to Marie-Galante and Îles des Saintes (Terre de Haut round-trip fare, about $5), but the 30-minute crossing can sometimes be rough.

Local Air Services – Flights to Guadeloupe's offshore dependencies — the Îles des Saintes, Marie Galante, and La Désirade — are arranged for groups of four by a number of local operators: *Carib Jet* (phone: 82-26-44) as well as *Georges Marie-Gabrielle* (phone: 82-05-38), *Petrelluzzi* (phone: 82-82-30), and *Poirier* (phone: 82-00-46). *Air Guadeloupe* offers scheduled service to these same islands. *Caraïbes Air Tourisme* flies to Les Saintes, and *Air Barthélemy* has charters to St. Barts. Since the out islands are popular weekend and vacation destinations for Guadeloupeans, you should book as far ahead as possible. The same operators also offer day trips to neighboring St. Barts and Dominica. Some do the same for St. Martin and Martinique. *Safari Tours* runs helicopter charters to these islands.

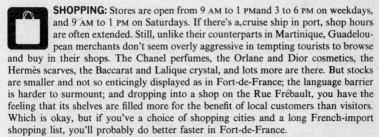 **SHOPPING:** Stores are open from 9 AM to 1 PM and 3 to 6 PM on weekdays, and 9 AM to 1 PM on Saturdays. If there's a cruise ship in port, shop hours are often extended. Still, unlike their counterparts in Martinique, Guadeloupean merchants don't seem overly aggressive in tempting tourists to browse and buy in their shops. The Chanel perfumes, the Orlane and Dior cosmetics, the Hermès scarves, the Baccarat and Lalique crystal, and lots more are there. But stocks are smaller and not so enticingly displayed as in Fort-de-France; the language barrier is harder to surmount; and dropping into a shop on the Rue Frébault, you have the feeling that its shelves are filled more for the benefit of local customers than visitors. Which is okay, but if you've a choice of shopping cities and a long French-import shopping list, you'll probably do better faster in Fort-de-France.

Local products? Guadeloupe coffee and rums that range from new and fiery white to 12-year-old and mahogany-colored — a take-home most North Americans sip and savor like a liqueur. Along with herds of stuffed iguanas and alligators and mostly unremarkable wood sculpture, indigenous souvenirs include some nicely made baskets, straw hats (both the wide-brimmed bakoua and flat coolie salako shapes), hammocks, shell things, and creole dolls in all sizes. *Au Caraïbe* (4 Rue Frébault) and *Souvenirs de la Guadeloupe* (15 Rue Nozières), both in Pointe-à-Pitre, and *La Maison de l'Ar-*

tisanat (Place Créole) in Bas du Fort are fresh, quality sources for these and more. For other imported finds, shop the Rues Frébault, Achille René-Boisneuf, de Nozières (with its galerie of shops), and Schoelcher. Here are some places to look:

Rosébleu offers largest stocks, widest choice of French cosmetics, fashion accessories, crystal. It has several quite accommodating city locations (5 Rue Frébault and 25 Rue A. René-Boisneuf, Pointe-à-Pitre; 18 Rue du Dr. Cabre, Basse-Terre) plus a duty-free shop at Le Raizet Airport. But do *not* count on the latter for any but last-minute emergency purchases; the stock is minimal and the service reluctant, at best.

Vendôme (8-10 Rue Frébault, Pointe-à-Pitre) concentrates on imported fashion (dresses, shirts, swimwear, accessories) for men and women; there are also Cardin watches, jewelry, Orlane cosmetics. And English is spoken. *Champs-Elysées* (2 Rue Frébault, Pointe-à-Pitre), under the same management as Vendôme, is big on perfumes, cosmetics, bikinis, lingerie, fashion accessories. English is spoken here, too. *Haikel* (Rue Frébault, Pointe-à-Pitre) stocks Val St. Lambert crystal, porcelains, perfumes, some ready-to-wear, and Moroccan leather things. *Phoenicia* (8 Rue Frébault, Pointe-à-Pitre) specializes in brand-name perfumes. *Le Bambou* (Rue de la Liberté, St. François) — for island-made madras clothes in both adult and children's sizes, dashikis, island souvenirs — is well worth a stop if you're in the neighborhood; the people are nice, too. *Ocean's* (25 bis Rue Lamartine, Pointe-à-Pitre) focuses on shells and shell-decorated boxes, frames, etc., plus madras dresses, dolls, other crafts. *Librairie Antillaise* (41 bis Rue Schoelcher, Pointe-à-Pitre) stocks island literature, maps and guidebooks, some English paperbacks. *Disques Celini* (53 Rue Schoelcher and 31 Boulevard Chanzy, Pointe-à-Pitre; Le Raizet Airport) has all sorts of recordings — both French and island. *Magic Store* (38 Rue Henri IV, Pointe-à-Pitre) is another music place specializing in folk recordings and "toutes les nouveautés du Hit Parade." *K-Dis* (Rue Frébault, Pointe-à-Pitre) is worth a look for French kitchen gadgets, fine food items (pâté, mustard, etc.). In the *Galerie du Port* at the foot of Rue Frébault, *La Bergerie* specializes in leather goods, and *La Casserole,* in cooking utensils. Outside Pointe-à-Pitre, two new centers — *Galerie Marina,* across from Port de Plaisance at Bas du Fort, and *La Marina* adjacent to the St. François Marina — promise chic, serener shopping closer to resort hotels. *La Véranda* (Place Créole) in Bas du Fort is an attractively sophisticated spot to shop for island-made antiques, reproductions, paintings, and decorative accessories. *Floral Antilles* (50 and 80 Rue Schoelcher) and *Casafleurs* (both in Pointe-à-Pitre and at the airport) are expert at packing island flowers (anthurium, Bird of Paradise, etc.) to go.

TIPPING: A recent French law requires that a 15% service charge be automatically added to all restaurant and bar bills. Porters should be tipped about 5 francs per bag. Most taxi drivers own their own cars and do not expect tips.

SPECIAL EVENTS: *Carnival* in Guadeloupe is more than a few days' revelry — it's a season that stretches from the first Sunday in January through Ash Wednesday, the first day of Lent, with all sorts of celebrations (masked parades, beguine contests, a beauty pageant, song competitions) scheduled each Sunday and a 5-day supergala that begins the Saturday before Mardi Gras and doesn't quit till King Vaval goes up in smoke Ash Wednesday night. On that climax weekend, everyone heads into town for nonstop partying; no islander thinks about much else for the next week. From a tourist point of view, the Sunday events can be great fun; they can also be ignored if you're so inclined. Not so, the last bash. So if crowd scenes — however good-natured and full of color and high spirits — and slightly distracted service would spoil your good time, schedule your visit with that in mind. Other special occasions: *Mi-Carême* (a mid-Lenten break with processions and the funeral of King Vaval); *La Fête des Cuisinières* (early August Cooks' Festival with a parade of Créole-costumed women, cathedral blessing, mass, and free feasting, which your hotel can arrange for you to join); *Tour de la Guadeloupe* (early-August, 10-day international cycling race); *Festival of the Sea* (celebrated August 15, along with the *Feast of the Assumption,* on Îles des Saintes); *All Saints' Day* (November 1; candle lighting in cemeteries); *St. Cecilia's Day* (November 22, musical fêtes in cities and towns); *Young Saints' Day* (December 28, special mass and children's parade). *Easter Monday, Ascension Day, Pentecost Monday, Bastille Day* (July 14), *Schoelcher Day* (July 21), *Assumption Day* (August 15), *Armistice Day* (November 11), *Christmas,* and *New Year's Day* are also public holidays.

 SPORTS: Guadeloupe's action is largely land-based on Basse-Terre (hiking in the Parc Naturel and the climb to the top of 4,813-foot La Soufrière) and sea-linked on Grande-Terre, where the best beaches are, although the beach at Deshaies is excellent. If your French isn't fluent, it's a good idea to ask your hotel travel desk or concierge for help in making sports arrangements by phone with companies outside your hotel.

Boating – Sailing, on a small scale, is as easy as walking out to the hotel beach and renting a Sail- or Sunfish. Yacht charters — both crewed and bareboat — can be arranged through *Soleil et Voile* (phone: 82-26-81), *Vacances Yachting Antilles* (phone: 90-82-95), or *Locaraïbes* (phone: 91-07-80), which offers a fleet of cruising sailboats.

Visiting yachts dock at the Carénage, in Pointe-à-Pitre. There's also the new, fully equipped, 700-berth Port de Plaisance marina at Bas du Fort and a 140-berth installation at St. François. At Gourbeyre near Basse-Terre is the 160-berth Marina de Rivière-S, good for touring Soufrière volcano. Marie Galante and the Îles des Saintes — both within easy cruising distance — offer protected anchorages too.

Cycling – An inexpensive way to get around, but not recommended for long hauls or on Basse-Terre's mountain roads. *Vélo-Vert* sponsors tours (with maps and bikes supplied) covering 270 miles (100 Rue Frébault, phone: 83-15-74). You might also try *Cyclo-Tours* in Gosier (phone: 84-11-34) or, in St. François, *Le Flamboyant* (phone: 84-45-51), *Rent-a-Bike* at *Méridien* (phone: 84-51-00), and *Loca BR* (phone: 84-47-80).

Golf – The sporty 18-hole, 6,755-yard, par-71 Robert Trent Jones course at St. François is open to guests of all the island's hotels upon payment of a greens fee of about $167 per week in high season. Electric carts rent for about $34 for two for 18 holes, pullcarts for about $7. The pro is English-speaking.

Hiking – Basse-Terre's Parc Naturel is possibly the best in the Caribbean. Well-marked trails lead through deep green rain forests to waterfalls, mountain pools, past steaming fumaroles, and finally to the edge of La Citerne crater. The excellent Parc Naturel booklet, *Walks & Hikes,* lists 18 trips with maps, times, and difficulty ratings; it's available free from the Tourist Office or the Organisation des Guides de Montagne (phone: 81-45-79) in Basse-Terre. Both can also put you in touch with guides, whose services are strongly recommended for tougher trips — including those to the top of Soufrière, which should be scheduled for early morning whenever possible.

Horseback Riding – Can be arranged at the *Relais du Moulin* (about $10 per hour or $30 for a full-day picnic; phone: 88-23-96), or at *Le Criolo* in St. Félix (about $6 per hour; phone 28-79-99).

Snorkeling and Scuba – Especially rewarding in waters off the western and southern coasts of Basse-Terre. Most hotels rent snorkeling equipment and can arrange guided snorkelers' excursions. Scuba diving gains prestige from the fact that Jacques Cousteau has spent considerable time under the local waters and described those around Pigeon Island as one of the world's ten best diving areas. US divers should be aware that most instructors and guides are certified under the French CMAS rather than PADI or NAUI, which may make a difference in the type and amount of gear you want to bring along. Complete rental outfits are available, but all components are French. The *Nautilus Club,* (phone: 98-70-34) which faces Pigeon Island across from the beach at Malendure, specializes in diving excursions to the island. But wherever you stay, lessons for beginners and excursions for experienced divers are easily arranged through the *Aqua-Fari Plongée* on Le Beethoven Beach at *La Créole Beach* hotel (phone: 84-26-26) or through *Karukera Plongée* at the *PLM Azur Callinago* in Gosier (phone: 84-25-25). In the Îles des Saintes, at Terre de Haute Denis Collin's *Centre Nautique* (phone: 99-59-49) also features some facilities, as well as *Chez Guy* (phone: 99-52-19). For any serious diving, a license and certification book, doctor's certificate, and insurance coverage are required. Single tank dives range from $20 to $55 depending on site; multiple dives and weeklong packages are available.

Spectator Sports – Cockfighting is in season from November to April; if you're interested, check with your hotel's concierge or tour desk. There are several horse racing meets a year at Bellecourt Racecourse just across the bridge from Pointe-à-Pitre, at Baie-Mahault on Basse-Terre, and at the St. Jacques Hippodrome at Anse Bertrand.

Sport Fishing – For barracuda and kingfish (January-May), tuna, dolphin, and bonito (December-March), it's best off the leeward coast of Basse-Terre. *Fishing Club Antilles* in Bouillante (phone: 86-73-77) has day and weekly charters with bungalows for rent. Your hotel water sports or travel desk can arrange half- or full-day charters for up to six people.

Swimming and Sunning – These are major preoccupations. On rugged Basse-Terre, west coast beaches are surf-combed, usually gray or black sand in the south and orange sand in the north. Grande-Terre, where, to quote the Office du Tourisme, "all serious beaching is done," has long stretches of white sand along its shores — extensive, though manmade, beaches on the southern coast between Bas du Fort and Gosier, beautifully natural from Ste. Anne and St. François to the tip of Pointe-des-Châteaux, as well as the northeastern coast at Moule and northwest at Anse Bertrand and Port Louis.

Chances are you'll spend most of your sand-and-sea time on your own hotel's beach, but if you want to visit others, most hotels will welcome you — especially if you patronize their restaurants and bars (at most, there's a small fee for changing facilities, chaises, towels). On Guadeloupe's public beaches, there's no charge or only a small parking fee per car. They're fine for picnicking, but most also have small seafood restaurants where you can pick up an inexpensive Créole lunch. Public beach names to know: Ste. Anne, Raisins Clairs at St. François, Anse Laborde and Anse Bertrand on the northeast coast, Anse du Souffleur near Port-Louis. And — only in Guadeloupe — there are officially designated nudist beaches at Pointe Tarare near the Pointe-des-Châteaux; on Ilet Gosier, a tiny offshore land dot to which several Gosier hotels provide boat transportation six days a week (it's clothed on Sundays); at the *Club Med* enclave; and at the *Bois Joli* hotel, on Îles des Saintes.

Tennis – There are floodlit courts at many island hotels; day play is free all around, but some hotels charge for night games. Hotels with courts are the *Auberge de la Vieille Tour*, the *Club Med* resort, *Méridien, PLM Azur Marissol, Relais du Moulin, Salako, Golf Marine Club, Novotel, Fleur d'Épée, Toubana, Les Marines de St. François, Arawak, Village Viva*, and *La Créole Beach*. Visitors can also arrange to play at the private *Amical Tennis Club* at Bas du Fort (monthly membership, about $19; playing fee, $5; phone: 82-13-81), *Club Tennis de Dugazon* in Abymes (phone: 82-06-81), and *Tennis Club du St. François* (phone: 84-40-01).

Water Skiing and Windsurfing – Water skiing is offered by most seaside hotels, for about $15 per half hour of boat time. Windsurfing is so good that major international events are held here. Rentals average $15 per hour, lessons about $20 per hour.

 NIGHTLIFE: No matter where the beguine began (Guadeloupeans swear it was here), they dance it with gusto from the southern tip of Basse-Terre to Grande-Terre's northernmost point. Guadeloupeans love to dance — the calypso, merengue, reggae, boogie, and zouk, the latest sensation —

just about anything that moves rhythmically. Hang a bit loose and they'll have you swinging right along in no time. The island's folk company, on stage one or two nights a week at hotels, performs the old-fashioned dances (don't miss them). Dinner dancing and hotel discos (all very intimate, Régine-moderne, favored by as many islanders as tourists) update the movements, play into the small hours. Current favorites: *PLM Azur Marissol*'s *Fou Fou, Birdy* at the *Salako,* and the European *Elysées Matignon* at Bas du Fort. The band at the *Vieille Tour* plays touch-dance music, which never went out of style here; more casual clubs include the *Jardin Brésilien, New Land, La Chaîne,* and the very popular *Mandingo* in the *Domaine Caribéen,* which also has a restaurant.

Elsewhere, *Club Med* prides itself on new shows nightly (lots of staff participation). Some hotels do once-a-week limbo shows that are all too much like those on every other island. There are also two casinos: one at St. François (admission, about $11; open 4 PM to 3 AM) and the newer *Gosier-les-Bains* (admission, about $11; open 9 AM to dawn) on the grounds of the *Arawak.* Proof of identity — with photo — is required for entry. No slots, but roulette, blackjack, craps, baccarat; at St. François there's a small discotheque.

None of this comes cheap. Count on $8 up for admission at clubs and discos (usually with one free drink), about $5 a drink for gin or whiskey, a bit less for rum or local beer.

BEST ON THE ISLAND

 CHECKING IN: Guadeloupe offers a wide range of hotels in terms of size, location, ambience, and price. The smaller ones are more intimate and service-oriented; the larger resorts attract an active, sports-minded clientele. No matter what the requirement, there's something for everyone.

However, the approach is much more Continental than Caribbean, since so many of Guadeloupe's visitors are Europeans. This has its advantages: in relatively high standards of service, in the broad range of on-site activities (Europeans on vacation don't usually just lie there — they do something), in food that's good even in coffee shops.

Where to stay? If you like hotel hopping, the answer is the Gosier strip, with its beach-to-beach lineup of one four-star and five three-star hotels, or Bas du Fort (two three-star incarnations) just down the shoreline. Farther out at Ste. Anne, and St. François on Grande-Terre, and Deshaies on Basse-Terre, there's a choice of self-contained, multi-activity resorts (it's no accident that the sports supervisor at the *Méridien* is called the *directeur d'animation*). Other choice places include more modest resort hotels and country inns, many of which now belong to an association called Relais Créoles. In the list that follows, very expensive is defined as $200 or more for two including Continental breakfast in winter; expensive is $150 to $200; moderate, $100 to $150 for two; and inexpensive — below that. Summer rates range from 25% to 35% less.

GOSIER

Azur la Vieille Tour – Now part of the PLM chain. Old (1835 sugar mill tower in front), excellent dining room with adjacent tavern and dance bar, 80 newly renovated, balconied rooms overlooking the sea. Small beach, feeling of intimacy; 3 lighted hard-surface tennis courts, pool, volleyball, seaside restaurant and formal dining room. Guests get plenty of exercise just getting from one place to another via steep stone steps (phone: 84-23-23). Expensive.

La Créole Beach – Bustling, cheerful, with 156 rooms, 8 duplex apartments, a large beach, and top water sports. Definitely one of Gosier's best. French and Swiss chefs (phone: 84-26-26). Expensive.

Arawak – Ten stories tall with 160 trim rooms, 6 penthouse junior suites. Big, bright pool, ditto beach; all sorts of on-site sports, shops, services. Popular nightclub (phone: 84-24-24). Expensive to moderate.

Cap Sud Caraibes – A very charming Relais Créole property in a tranquil setting offering 12 air-conditioned rooms with seaview balconies. near Petit-Havre Beach (phone: 88-96-02). Moderate.

Le Salako – French-speaking and modern with 120 stylish rooms, two restaurants, disco, and all water sports (phone: 84-22-22). Expensive to moderate.

Ecotel Guadeloupe – Small, relaxed, staffed by hotel school students. All 44 rooms on one garden level overlooking big, freshwater swimming pool. Free bus to beach. Friendly, with fine French restaurant, *Le Galion* (phone: 84-21-21). Moderate.

PLM Azur Callinago Village – A simple, attractive complex of apartments (93 studios, 22 duplexes) adjacent to the hotel of the same name and with full use of its facilities. All have complete kitchenettes, balconies, baths; with small supermart on premises. Good buy for families (phone: 84-25-25). Moderate.

PLM Azur Callinago Beach – Small, ultramodern, European, with 40 simply furnished rooms. Right on the beach (phone: 84-25-25). Moderate to inexpensive.

BAS DU FORT

Fleur d'Épée–Novotel – Property-wide refurbishment has done wonders for the 180 rooms (most with balconies) in three Y-angled three-story wings as well as for the newly landscaped gardens and central reception area. Lots of activity, sports options (phone: 90-81-49). Expensive.

PLM Azur Marissol – Two rambling 2- and 3-story buildings with 200 recently renovated, cheerful rooms, and bright new *réception.* There's a marina nearby, all water sports, a new beauty-and-fitness center, and a disco, *Fou Fou.* The informal staff makes guests feel welcome. Weekly folkloric shows (phone: 90-84-44). Expensive to moderate.

Le Madrépore – Attractive condominium/hotel on the lagoon. With 20 studios, 10 apartments, garden-grouped around a pretty pool. All have air conditioning, kitchenettes, balconies, or patios. Rates include maid service, breakfast. Supermarket and car rental on premises; use of *PLM Azur Marissol* beach and sports facilities just across the road (phone: 90-81-46). Moderate.

PLM Azur Sun Village – Latest link in chain with nice hilltopping studios with kitchenettes and 1-bedroom suites designed for self-catering stays. With pool, snack bar, restaurant, small market. Short drive to beach and walk to Port de Plaisance restaurants, entertainment (phone: 90-85-76). Moderate to inexpensive.

STE. ANNE

La Toubana – Cluster of 32 bungalows — each with private garden, terrace, kitchenette, super Caribbean view. Tennis, pool, small private beach, all water sports; help with car rentals, excursions. A chic, aquarium-walled dining room serves French and Créole specialties (phone: 88-25-57). Expensive to moderate.

Relais du Moulin – A country retreat comprising 40 cottages, 20 of which are new, clustered around the base of an antique sugar mill. Emphasis on peaceful, casual relaxation, water sports on beach a quarter hour's walk away. Pool, tennis, car rental, and riding stables on premises. Also very good restaurant, top-notch lounge bar (phone: 88-13-78). Expensive to moderate.

Auberge du Grand Large – Tiny (10 one-room bungalows), extremely simple, right on a beautiful beach (that's it for sports). Owner with lots of charm, no English. Good small Créole restaurant (phone: 88-20-06). Moderate.

Caravelle Club Méditerranée – Feels vast, with beach to match (nude bathing area included). Lots happening always; staff-produced show several nights a week. Three-unit hotel (300 rooms); recent property-wide renovations. Lots of singles over 30, quite a few couples. Weeklong stays only. All meals, with wine, and activities are included in price (phone: 88-21-00). Moderate.

Le Rotabas – Relaxed, cordial place, with 44 air-conditioned rooms right on the beach. Excellent water sports, good French/Créole restaurant. Management is very helpful with excursion arrangements. Rates include breakfast (phone: 88-25-60). Moderate.

TERRE DE HAUT, ÎLES DES SAINTES

Bois Joli – Tranquil hilltop setting with great view. Two pretty beaches (one for nudes); water skiing, snorkeling, sailing, boat trips available. Good Créole food. Bus and boat shuttle to town. There are 21 small, neat rooms (13 air conditioned) with various shower/bath arrangements (phone: 99-50-38). Moderate.

PLM Azur Los Santos – Three-star property at Vieille Anse, at the foot of historic Fort Napoleon. All 54 rooms, in 27 air-conditioned bungalows, have balconies with sea views; 16 rooms have kitchenettes. Restaurant on the premises. All water sports, plus underwater photography, boat trips to nearby islands (phone: 99-50-40). Moderate.

Kanaoa – On the beach at Pointe Coquelet, with 14 pleasant air-conditioned rooms (request Anse Mire cove view). All water sports, snack bar, inviting restaurant, hospitable family management. Rates include breakfast (phone: 99-51-36). Moderate.

Les Anarcadiers – In addition to good value, the attractions include charming village atmosphere, 10 comfortable, hillside rooms, a restaurant with a view of Baie des Saintes, and evening barbecues by the pool. (phone: 99-50-99). Moderate.

ST. FRANÇOIS

Hamak – An elegant, peaceful, very private retreat offering 56 stylish bungalows in tropical garden setting, each with patio and terrace. No swimming pool, but all water sports on private artificial beach; superb restaurant for open-air dining; private airstrip and Robert Trent Jones golf course next door. Very exclusive. Primarily European clientele, some Americans (phone: 88-59-99). Very expensive.

Golf Marine Club – Attractive new 74-room complex; 29 suites. Located opposite the golf course, it has a restaurant, bar, and lovely pool, and will arrange transfer to nearby beach (phone: 88-60-60). Expensive to moderate.

Méridien – Just about what you'd expect from this chain's Caribbean outposts, but well equipped for sports — especially tennis (5 courts), and water sports on a fine beach. Adjacent to Robert Trent Jones golf course; nearby marina. Offers 267 undistinguished though comfortable rooms. Fairly active nightlife. Near the casino (phone: 88-51-00). Expensive to moderate

Trois Mâts – Modern studio and duplex apartments — 36 in all — overlooking the marina. Nautical surroundings; kitchenettes, balconies. Handy to golf, water sports, snack bar, restaurant, boutiques, casino, disco. Boat and air excursions available (phone: 88-59-99). Moderate.

Les Marines de St. François – A 10-acre enclave of sleek, contemporary studios, apartments, and duplexes bordering the marina — 200 units in all — each with air conditioning, fully equipped kitchenette; maid service available. Two swimming pools and 2 tennis courts; water sports at nearby *Méridien,* sailing from adjacent marina. Golf, shops, restaurants, and a casino at doorstep. Minimum 3-day stay (phone: 88-59-55). Inexpensive.

ELSEWHERE ON THE ISLAND

Auberge de la Distillerie, Petit-Bourg – Small, tile-roofed country hotel surrounded by fields of cane and pineapple, with 12 comfortably rustic rooms and 1 bungalow named after island flowers and spices. Fine dining room by small garden pool; Continental breakfast included in rates. Route de Versailles at Tabanon (phone: 94-25-91). Moderate.

 EATING OUT: Guadeloupe's favorite cuisine is Créole — probably because its cooks are so genuinely good at it. Specialties: *crabes farcis* (stuffed crabs), *accras* (hot, puffed, cod fritters), *boudin* (blood sausage) for appetizers; lots of fresh fish and seafood — especially red snapper, lambi (conch), and langouste (Caribbean lobster); spicy fish stews and curries zinged with turmeric, mustard, and seven kinds of hot peppers; native vegetables like christophine, breadfruit, and fried plantain. For dessert: island-grown guava, pineapple, papaya, coconut, and mango ice cream. But there are restaurants where the table is classic French and excellent; dinner including a modest wine and service in any one of these will come to about $25 to $30 and up per person. In a good Créole place, the tab — including table wine and service — will be about $20 and up for dinner, maybe less for lunch.

Meals, whether Créole or *cuisine française,* are usually accompanied by French wine, which is plentiful and reasonably priced. But before and after, Guadeloupeans most often order a punch in one of several dynamite variations: 'ti-punch, a fiery rum in a small glass that packs a large wallop; plain punch, white rum with lemon; and after the meal, a vieux punch of dark rum, cane syrup, and lime. Restaurants tend to be small; some close on Sundays. Ask the hotel concierge to phone for reservations.

GOSIER

Auberge de la Vieille Tour – Hotel restaurant in best French traditional style. Guests on table d'hôte menu get credit toward such à la carte delicacies as stuffed sea urchin, red snapper pot with green-pepper sour sauce, breast of duck with avocado cream, langouste maison. Extensive wine list. Off Route de Gosier (phone: 84-23-23). Expensive.

Le Galion – Dining room of the *Ecotel* is also one of the island's best. Big-name chefs visit from metropolitan France to teach their culinary arts to student apprentices. Reservations suggested (phone: 84-15-66). Expensive to moderate.

La Chaubette – Small, friendly spot on the Ste. Anne road. Baby clam soup, langouste, and coconut ice cream are special. Reservations recommended. Route de Ste. Anne (phone: 84-14-29). Moderate.

La Créole–Chez Violetta – One of the island's best cooks. From the excellent selection of Créole specialties, try *crabes farcis* and/or *court bouillon* — not broth, but a savory fish and tomato dish (phone: 84-10-34). Moderate.

Le Baoulé – Alain Martin's Tunisian and Spanish influence spices up the traditional French and Créole menu. Choose the paella à la Valenciana or couscous royal. One of Guadeloupe's best views. Closed Sunday lunch (phone: 84-33-95). Moderate.

OTHERS ON THE ISLAND

La Plantation, Bas du Fort – One of the finest classic French restaurants in the Caribbean. Bordeaux specialties, sauces, seasonings; the crayfish (*ouassous*) is *extraordinaire*. Chic, popular; reservations required. Galerie Marina (phone: 83-17-81). Very expensive.

La Canne à Sucre, Pointe-à-Pitre – Arguably the best kitchen in the Caribbean. In a handsome colonial home, Gérard Virginius has established one of the island's finest menus. *Beignets* (fritters) of pumpkin and malanga, savory crabes farcis, sea urchin sautéed with lime and spices are *extraordinaire;* and the *coupe Canne à Sucre* (crème chantilly and coconut sherbet with banana caramel, aged rum, and a bit of cinnamon) — *c'est merveilleux!* Fine wines, but not much English spoken. Reservations essential. 17 Rue Henri IV (phone: 82-10-19). Expensive.

La Louisiane, St. François – Charming, colonial house where Daniel Hugon, formerly at the Carlton in Cannes, creates traditional French fare with Créole influence, such as pâté of sea urchin and lean duck slices with lychees flambéed in old rum. Superb food. Closed Monday (phone: 83-44-34) Expensive

Les Oiseaux, Anse des Rochers – Open-air restaurant in pastoral setting delivers first-rate Créole cuisine with a touch of French country. Fish fondue, gratinéed lobster steak, marinated conch. Friendly. Closed all day Thursday, Sunday night (phone: 88-92-56). Expensive to moderate.

Zagaya, St. François – Pretty, casual setting right on the beach, especially romantic at night. Fresh-caught, grilled lobsters, homemade desserts. Closed Monday (phone: 88-61-27). Expensive to moderate.

Chez Honoré, St. François – Homey and unpretentious, but with very good fresh fish and seafood dishes thanks to the fact that *le patron* catches his own. He and his wife are also on hand to see to everything personally (phone: 88-40-61). Moderate.

Chez Paul, Matouba – The Basse-Terre neighborhood is East Indian; the specialties are curries and Créole dishes. The set menu is changed every day; when you call for reservations, check what's on. Closed Mondays (phone: 81-41-77). Moderate.

Rosini, Bas du Fort – The Rosini family goes to great lengths to serve classic, authentic Italian dishes. Warm, friendly service. Try the mixed homemade pasta (in Italian-flag colors — red, white, and green), local river shrimps *fra diavolo*-style, and homemade desserts (phone: 90-87-81). Moderate.

Karacoli, Deshaies – One of the best for such Créole specialties as *colombos* (island curries), and *coquilles Karacoli,* served indoors or on a tree-shaded terrace at the beach's edge. Closed Thursdays. English-speaking staff (phone: 28-41-17). Moderate.

La Langouste, St. François – Casual beach spot; not surprisingly, grilled lobster is its specialty. Quality consistent with owner's other restaurant, *Chez Honoré* (phone: 88-40-61). Moderate.

La Touna, Bouillante – Always a warm welcome at this quaint, rustic, open-air spot, which is also the *Fishing Club Antilles.* The menu changes daily depending on what the boat brings in. Lunch only (phone: 98-70-10). Inexpensive.

Chez Clara, Ste. Rose – In their patio restaurant, chic Clara Lesueur and her accomplished cuisinière maman combine French dining style and authentic Créole cookery. Specialties include freshwater crayfish, curried skate, lobster, clams, classic *crabes farcis.* Homemade ice cream or sherbet (coconut, passion fruit, banana, rum raisin) is a fine finale (phone: 28-72-99). Inexpensive.

Chez LouLouse, Malendure – Cheerful rustic restaurant, a favorite drop-in spot for divers returning from Pigeon Island. Menu touristique features salad, fresh grilled fish, curried chicken, rice, wine, and fruit for about $10. No extra charge for spontaneous song accompaniment. On the beach (phone: 86-70-34). Inexpensive.

Chez Odette, Port Louis – Popular patronne, popular place for malanga or pumpkin fritters, crabes farcis, goat curry, Créole chicken with christophine gratinée. On Rue Charles Cagnet (phone: 84-92-40). Inexpensive.

L'Amour en Fleurs, Ste. Anne – Very small roadside place with very good Créole food. Try tender conch and octopus mixed with rice and beans, *boudin, blaff* (a savory fish stew), langouste, *court bouillon,* homemade ice cream (phone: 88-23-72). Inexpensive.

Le Barbaroc, Petit-Canal – The beachside bistro of Mme. Félicité Doloir, who is justifiably celebrated as a world-class chef. Uniquely inventive menu features *burgots gratinées* (sea snails), crab pâté, breaded conch, purée of breadfruit, sweet potato noodles, and aromatic *poulet de pays cuit fumé* (smoked chicken). Home-brewed *mauby* (absinthe-like flavor, mule kick) and beer are house drinks. Gastronomic/historic tours of northern Grande-Terre are a related specialty. Dinner only; closed Wednesdays (phone: 22-62-71). Inexpensive.

HAITI

In a coup, the military took control of Haiti just as we were going to press, making the question of safe travel in the country a very serious problem.

There is only one generalization true of every first visit to Haiti: It is not a neutral trip. You may be appalled, intrigued, astonished, even delighted. But you won't remain blasé or unaffected — though at first everything looks less exotic than you expect.

Haiti shares the island of Hispaniola (just 50 miles east of Cuba) with the Dominican Republic. The culture of the Dominican Republic is essentially Spanish; that of Haiti, essentially French. This cultural and political bifurcation is the result of a past as unique as any in the Caribbean, and more dramatic than most. Haiti's lurid twentieth-century history — the gunboat diplomacy of the US during and after World War I, and the rise to power of the Duvalier family under ruthless Papa Doc, succeeded by his less fearsome (though nearly as corrupt) son Jean-Claude, now in exile — has tended to obscure the country's truly heroic past. And visitors, distracted by the capital's obvious congestion and poverty (the countryside appears far less oppressed/oppressive), too often arrive and leave without understanding the island's past or the pride Haitians take in their country.

Haiti was the world's first black republic, a distinction it wrested from Napoleon's armies in 1804, after 12 years of fighting and 300 years of colonial exploitation, first by the Spanish and then the French. The island of Hispaniola was claimed for Spain by Christopher Columbus on his first voyage in 1492. Within a century the Spanish had decimated the indigenous Indian tribe which inhabited the island, and had established the beginnings of a plantation culture heavily dependent on slaves. At the same time, France was threatening Spain's dominance of the Caribbean, and French settlers, who moved onto the island's west end, mixed with slaves to sow the seeds of a Créole culture. At the end of the seventeenth century, Spain and France struck a bargain — called the Treaty of Ryswick — which, among other things, gave the west end of Hispaniola to France.

The Créole plantation culture that developed on Saint Domingue — as the planters called Haiti — was thoroughly dependent on the increasing numbers of slaves brought from Africa and ruthless in exploiting them as workhorses. In 1791 the island's slaves revolted, burning plantations and murdering plantation owners, and forcing the French governor to come quickly to terms with them because of the imminent threat of invasion by Spanish and English forces. Slavery was abolished in 1793, and one of the leaders of the black revolt, François Toussaint (known as Toussaint L'Ouverture), led a black army against the encroaching Spanish and English. Having secured Saint Domingue for the French, Toussaint was named governor

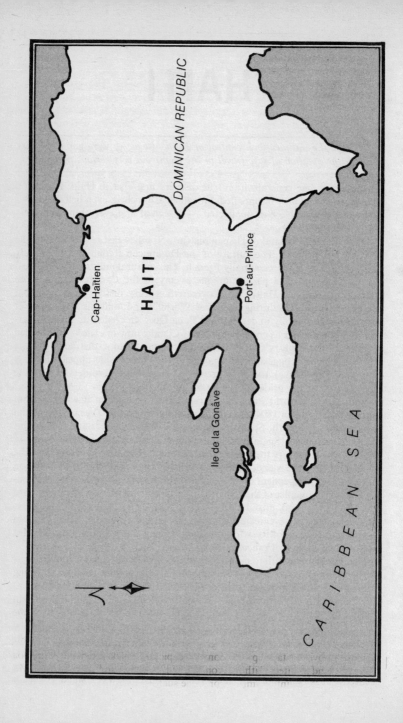

general, only to be forced to collect his army once again for a final battle against the French themselves. Napoleon, fearing France was losing control of the island, sent a large force against the islanders. The French initially defeated Toussaint (who ended his days in a French prison), but the battle was carried on by Toussaint's generals Henri Christophe, Alexandre Pétion, and Jean-Jacques Dessalines; and in 1803, the Haitians prevailed. When independence was declared, the country's name was changed to Haiti.

All was not peace. After an initial political arrangement failed, the country was divided more or less into halves, with Christophe the emperor of the north (he is the prototype of Eugene O'Neill's *Emperor Jones*) and Pétion controlling the south. Christophe spent his strange career committing his people to mammoth building projects, the culminating triumph of which was the Citadelle (see *Special Places*).

The world's first black republic was also the second country in the Americas to make a Declaration of Independence, and was an early supporter of Simón Bolívar in South America. This libertarian tradition somehow got lost in the twentieth century, thanks to the legacy of Papa Doc — and his dreaded secret police, the *tontons macoute* — and then his son, the equally despised Baby Doc, who was deposed in 1987 and driven into exile — with a significant assist from the US State Department — in the south of France. A caretaker government took charge until elections could be held. The first attempt at elections begat violence and bloodshed, and a second attempt installed a government widely believed to be puppets of the military — and, perhaps, of deposed dictator Duvalier, too. The publicity, and Haiti's increasing poverty, have done nothing to lure visitors to the country.

Haiti's tourism industry also has suffered from recent scares associated with AIDS (acquired immune deficiency syndrome). Tourists shunned the island when reports pointed to Haitians as among the groups most susceptible to the virus. Their fears were largely unfounded. Recent research indicates visitors run no risk from simply vacationing here, and in 1986 the Center for Disease Control in the US dropped Haitians from the list of groups most susceptible to AIDS. (A more relevant concern is the periodic report of malaria, found in Third World countries with poor sanitation, which can be countered by taking medical precautions before leaving home.)

Despite all the negatives, the experience of seeing Haiti firsthand can be illuminating. The airport isn't perceptibly different from any other moderately sized island terminal in the Caribbean. There are a few uniforms around, but no sinister characters or lurking *tontons macoute*. The road into Port-au-Prince offers every sort of traffic: ancient cars and pampered taxis (in one, a matched pair of silver organ pipes clearly indicates stereophonic sound) that supply the highway's only slightly prosperous sights.

Everything else moves slowly. A tall, grandmotherly woman plods up the hill majestically straight, with a galvanized tub of old shoes balanced on her head. A young girl trots barefoot down the road headed for market behind a donkey loaded with baskets of greens. At the side of the road Haiti's favorite people-mover, a tap-tap — a converted pickup truck fitted out with board seats, hand-painted with crayon-colored murals, and christened "Merci Maman," "la Sainte Famille," or some such — halts to let one more passenger squeeze aboard. A small girl tends a roadside stand (one board laid across two rocks) on which three faded, neatly pressed handkerchiefs are displayed. On a rope stretched between two trees, a patchwork rug of brown and white goatskin squares flaps slowly in a bit of afternoon breeze.

Once past the eight-year-old mahogany merchant who plants himself on the steps between you and your hotel's entrance, you're safe and insulated with a pool and all the comforts of home away from home. And, indeed, it's possible to spend the rest of your time basking and relaxing and forgetting that the world outside exists. Except that it almost never works that way in Haiti.

Even if you manage to laze about for a day, your curiosity and all the things you've heard will eventually pull you outside to explore and discover how much is really true. With a driver called Gauthier (it turns out he's the stereophonic one with a library of taped French tunes and Strauss waltzes), off you go. Circling the downtown Square of Heroes, you are regaled with tales of Toussaint L'Ouverture, the slave grandson of an African king, who managed to muster 50,000 men (3,000 of them white) to rout the British who had captured Port-au-Prince in 1793, then took on Napoleon — and was defeated; of Christophe and Pétion, who took up the struggle, downed the French, and made Haiti the world's first independent black republic, on New Year's Day in 1804; of magnificently megalomaniacal Christophe, who built the incredible Citadelle above Cap-Haïtien and ended his life with a silver bullet in his head. You pass the massive statue of the Unknown Marron (short for "cimarron," meaning wild or savage; it's a tribute to the world's fugitive slaves), and remembering tales of Papa Doc and the *tontons* again, steal a glance at the once forbidden presidential palace, which now looks on the whole rather quiet and unthreatening.

You proceed to the Iron Market and laugh at the story that explains its Moslem-looking minarets (due to a shipping error in Paris, M. Gustave Eiffel, famed for his tower, shipped to Haiti the marché he'd designed for a city in Pakistan). You've heard about crowds and poverty before, but what you see here is really staggering. And if it weren't for not wanting to admit to the apprehension you feel, you might well decline the inside tour even with protection and guidance. But follow along in spite of yourself.

The aisles are tight with people and you're sidling along when a voice inches from your ear says, "Regardez, s'il vous plaît," and you jump what feels like a foot and come down face-to-face with "Madame Sarah," who'd like you to visit her booth. Groping for your lost composure, you look at what she's holding in her hand: a small, but very bad, painting of a giraffe. You both look at it and laugh. And suddenly you're not a stranger in a strange place anymore. She asks about $4; you offer $1, and soon you own $2 worth of giraffe. Like other Haitian paintings and Haitian food — the Créole cooking that is fiery at the most surprising times — there is an innocent power about the picture. Like Haiti, it is doubly affecting — touching and exciting at the same time.

So despite the residue of turmoil of the Duvalier years, the political unrest, strikes, violent confrontations, occasional nights of terror, and the fact that Haitians still fear walking after dark, those who choose to visit Haiti will find a mysterious, complex, and beautiful country with a lot to offer any traveler. For many island fanciers, and maybe you, that makes it well worth discovering.

HAITI AT-A-GLANCE

FROM THE AIR: Haiti is a country of dramatic contrasts in appearance and feeling, with steep mountains and deep valleys tempered by the soothing blues of the seas that wash her shores. Occupying the mountainous western third of the island of Hispaniola, the country is shaped like giant jaws, with northern and southern peninsulas closing around the western Gulf of Gonâve and the big, peanut-shaped Île de la Gonâve that floats in its center. To the north is the Atlantic Ocean; to the south, the Caribbean Sea; and across the eastern border, the Dominican Republic. The eastern tip of Cuba is only 50 miles away, as is the island of Inagua in the Bahamas.

In land area, Haiti is about the size of Maryland (10,714 square miles) and has a population of more than 6 million. Although all its major cities are seaports, more than 80% of the people live in the rural interior. The capital city of Port-au-Prince lies on the west coast where the jaws meet at the deepest point of the Bay of Port-au-Prince. The mountain suburb of Pétionville, where some of the finer hotels are located, is due east of town; Port-au-Prince International Airport is a 10-minute ride to the northeast. From there, New York is 1,550 miles and 3½ hours away; Miami is 716 miles and 1¾ hours; Santo Domingo, capital of the Dominican Republic, is 161 miles and 40 minutes by air, a full day by car.

SPECIAL PLACES: In order of priority, the sites to see would be Port-au-Prince; Jacmel and/or the beaches; and Kenscoff in the mountains. Or, if you can give it the two or three days it deserves, Cap-Haïtien, in addition to or as an alternative to the Jacmel and Kenscoff trips.

A word about driving: Haiti is difficult to explore by car. Except for the roads to Jacmel, the beaches, Cap-Haïtien, and Kenscoff — all of which are in good shape and give you a pleasant look at local landscapes — country roads are rough. Driving in Port-au-Prince is confusing, tangled, noisy, and not suggested if you want to sightsee at the same time. Rather than risk wandering on your own, ask your hotel to put you in touch with a driver who's pleasant, informed, and speaks English. Hire him for a day of shopping and sightseeing in Port-au-Prince, more if you get along well. An alternative: bus tours that visit all the sites mentioned below.

Port-au-Prince – People and cars and people and street shops and people and colors and people. From villages and towns in the hills, they come to sell their wares on the sidewalk or in the market. The obvious poverty of so many people is difficult for some tourists to take. On the other hand, the hostility shown on some islands toward Americans doesn't exist here.

The Iron Market — so called because the building is wrought of the stuff, not because it sells it — is likely to be your first stop. It is huge and teeming, but the jostle is amazingly good-natured. From all sides, it's "You come my shop next," with everything from primitive paintings and hand-carved mahogany to antique hula hoops, peanuts, and ladies' underwear on sale. Browsing through the stalls inside is definitely a body-contact sport. But you can find terrific bargains. How much of it you want to take is strictly up to you. There are beggars, and they will approach you. Your best bet is to accept if your driver offers to go along with you. Or pick one of the young boys who will try to attach himself to you as a guide; with him to carry your packages and fend off the others, you'll find the going lots easier. He's well worth his 50¢ to $1 tip. Remember, too, that bargaining is part of the game — difficult for some Americans to master, but essential to the fun as far as Haitians are concerned. Listen for the seller's price, offer half, and carry on from there; getting whatever it is for two thirds to three quarters of the original asking price is considered par for the course.

Port-au-Prince's more serene sightseeing is centered around the downtown Champs de Mars (the Square of the Heroes of Independence), a landscaped park with an impressive statue of Jean-Jacques Dessalines, Haiti's first emperor in 1804. There is also the famous bronze statue of the Unknown Marron sounding a call to liberty on his conch shell. No longer in evidence are the letters that once spelled out "Duvalier — President A Vie," ripped out after Baby Doc fled.

Across the street the National Palace looks like a cross between Washington's White House and Paris' Petit Palais. Inside there's a Hall of Busts (former presidents) and, nearby, a mausoleum where Dessalines and Pétion rest; neither is a high-priority stop on tourist itineraries.

The Episcopal cathedral of Ste. Trinité, however, and the Catholic cathedral — both within walking distance of the palace — are musts: the first for its stunning murals by such Haitian masters as Obin, Bottex, and Bigaud, with a biblical perspective you may not recognize from your Sunday schooling (Judas has the white face); the second, for its handsome rose window.

Last stop in the park area is the Museum of Art, which is both a museum displaying some of the best of Haitian primitives and a shop where you can buy original works. If you're planning to shop for paintings or sculpture later, you'll find its background information helpful. It's open from 9 AM to 1 PM daily except Sundays (admission free). Special tours of Port-au-Prince's gingerbread houses depart on Thursdays from the museum. Visiting these private homes and meeting their owners is a good way to see another side of Haiti. The cost is $15 per person, with a maximum of 12 people per group (phone: 2-2510).

History buffs should also make it to the *Musée du Panthéon National,* on the Champs de Mars, which tells the story of Haiti from its discovery to the present through both historic artifacts and an impressive art collection. Among its relics: one of the six anchors of Columbus's *Santa Maria* and Toussaint L'Ouverture's pocket watch.

ELSEWHERE ON THE ISLAND

Jacmel – On the southern coast a 2-hour drive from Pétionville via a new highway, it is a pretty, old, colonial town with a choice of beaches suitable for picnics (Raymond les Bains and Ti-Mouillage are most beautiful, if somewhat primitive; Congo, with gray volcanic sand and palms, is at Jacmel's front door), and a few pleasant hotels and guesthouses of a certain age in case you decide to stay over.

Kenscoff – Many well-to-do Haitians flee the city's heat for summer homes here, high in the mountains south of Port-au-Prince. The road is winding; the views, magnificent. On Tuesdays and Fridays, you'll pass women balancing huge baskets of vegetables on their heads on their way to market. In the village, there's a fort (Jacques), an open-air market, and a Baptist Mission with a first-rate craft shop; at Furcy, a bit farther on, you can ride horseback into the hills or picnic under the pines. Going or coming, stop off at the Jane Barbancourt Distillery for a tour and free samples of rum liqueurs flavored with — among other exotica — hibiscus, mango, papaya, nougat, and spice.

■**EXTRA SPECIAL:** *Cap-Haïtien,* a 40-minute plane ride via Haiti Air Inter or a 4½-hour drive from Port-au-Prince, is headquarters for seeing the country's two most spectacular manmade sites: the ruins of the elegant Palais de Sans Souci that King Henri Christophe built to be "the most regal structure ever raised in the New World"; and his spectacular Citadelle with its 12-foot-thick walls and bristling cannon perched on a mountaintop more than 3,000 feet above the sea. Both are near the small inland town of Milot and are presently being restored. The usual procedure is to limber up your imagination by touring the skeletal palace (picture its tapestries, paneling, chandeliers, its silk-and-velvet-clad courtiers), board a jeep for the rocky trip to the parking lot halfway up, transfer to a bony horse or mule for the ride to the fort at the top of the mountain. You don't need equestrian skills for the half-hour trip up, but an iron bottom wouldn't hurt. Still, even if it means stand-up dinners for a day or so, whatever you do, don't miss this! Built by 200,000 conscripted former slaves who dragged its thousands of tons of rock and cannon and other munitions up the tortuous road, the fortress was designed to protect Henri Christophe and 9,999 companions from an attack by Napoleon, who never set foot on the island. Day tours by land or air from Port-au-Prince are available but exhausting, with hotel departures scheduled for 6:15 or 6:30 AM; prices range from about $125 per person up, including transport, sightseeing. It's a better idea to go for a night or two, rent a car, and take a Haitian guide with you; the Tourist Office in Port-au-Prince or Cap-Haïtien (phone: 2-0870) can recommend one. Other alternatives are the three- and four-hour tours originating in Cap-Haïtien, available through hotels for about $50 per vehicle, plus $6 per person for horses. Wear sturdy shoes and comfortable clothes, and bring change to buy sodas and to tip the roadside musicians as well as the two men who push-pull your mule-horse to the top and down again. Your guide should protect you from the children who will clamor around to try to sell you something or be tipped. It's important to agree on all charges before leaving. Two people will end up paying $80 to $100 for the trip, but it is spectacular and unique.

Cap-Haïtien itself is a gingerbread-trimmed colonial capital of considerable nostalgic charm. It was near here at La Navidad that Columbus is said to have landed on Christmas Day in 1492 and where his ship *Santa Maria* is the subject of a number of salvage studies that, it is hoped, will one day result in raising her from the watery grave into which she sank five centuries ago. Something of an artists' colony is collecting at Le Cap these days, and there are several comfortable hotels. La Badie village, with its beach, is a favorite destination for all-day picnics. Royal Caribbean Cruise Lines lands here several days a week; off-days, there's a $3 charge to use the beach.

SOURCES AND RESOURCES

TOURIST INFORMATION: Branches of the Haitian National Office of Tourism are located in New York City and Montréal, where information and literature are available in English and French on transportation, hotels, rates, sightseeing tours, and packages. In addition, some limited tourist information may be obtained from the Haitian embassies in Washington, DC; Ottawa, Canada; and in San Juan, Puerto Rico. The Haitian National Office of Tourism in New York City is located at Rockefeller Center, 630 Fifth Ave., Room 2109, New York, NY 10020 (phone: 212-757-3517). In Montreal: 50 Blvd. Cremazie, Suite 617, Montréal, Québec, H2P 2T3 (phone: 514-389-3517).

The Haitian National Tourist Office is near the center of Port-au-Prince on Ave. Marie-Jeanne (phone: 2-1729). There is also an information booth at Port-au-Prince International Airport and branch offices in Jacmel and Cap-Haïtien. Hotels have material on tours and entertainment.

For background reading, try *The Haitian People* by James Leyburn (Yale University Press, 1941); *Life in a Haitian Valley* by Melville J. Herskovits (Knopf, 1937); or *The Drum and the Hoe, Life and Lore of the Haitian People* by Harold Courlander (University of California Press, 1961); *Divine Horseman: The Living Gods of Haiti* by Maya Deren (Thames & Hudson, 1953), about the voodoo religion; *Haiti: The Black Republic* by Selden Rodman (Devin-Adair, 1954); *Christophe, King of Haiti* by Hubert Cole (Viking, 1967); most are available in paperback. Graham Greene's novel *The Comedians,* set in the bad, old Papa Doc days, offers more insight into Haiti's past than its present. Buy it before or after your trip — you won't find it on Haitian newsstands.

Local Coverage – The *Haiti Times,* an English-language tabloid, free at hotels and tourist spots, carries information on entertainment, shopping, and sightseeing; it's helpful, though its editorial content seems dictated strictly by advertising linage. *Le Guide* magazine details cultural events and other information of interest to tourists. *Le Nouvelliste, Le Matin,* and *Haiti Libérée* are French-language dailies. Get hold of the small but current Office of Tourism pamphlet *Haiti Hints for Visitors.*

Telephone – Dial direct to Haiti by adding the area code 509 and the city code (ask the international operator) to the numbers below.

ENTRY REQUIREMENTS: US and Canadian tourists are asked to show an onward or return ticket, plus proof of citizenship. A valid passport, voter's registration card, birth certificate, or naturalization papers will be fine. A tourist card is issued on arrival; you'll be asked to turn it in and pay a $15 departure fee when you leave. A US State Department advisory warning American tourists against visiting Haiti was issued just before we went to press, due to the military coup last summer. Before planning your trip, check the current status.

CLIMATE AND CLOTHES: Haiti's climate is consistently Caribbean: warm days, sometimes cooler evenings, showers in the late afternoons. In coastal areas, temperatures range from 70°F (22°C) to 90°F (33°C). As you climb into the mountains (where apples, peaches, and strawberries grow), the thermometer ranges anywhere from 50°F (about 10°C) to 70°F (22°C). The driest months are December through March, but even in the wetter months, rainfall rarely lasts longer than an hour or so. Most hotels are air conditioned.

For day, bring comfortable, lightweight, informal clothes. Leave your new resort clothes in the closet when you go sightseeing; a shopping stroll through the streets or a shoulder-to-shoulder session in the Iron Market kicks up some dust. While the French didn't leave a strong haute couture tradition, in the evenings the better hotels and restaurants require a well-groomed, put-together kind of dressing; very occasionally during the winter season that can mean a jacket and tie for men.

For a trip to the mountains, Cap-Haïtien, or the backcountry, you'll need heavier things: a sweater, just in case; good walking shoes; and sturdy pants, jeans, or chinos.

MONEY: One American dollar equals 5 gourdes — Haiti's official currency; since 1919 a special treaty has tied the gourde to the dollar, thus there is no market fluctuation. US dollars are accepted everywhere, as are traveler's checks in US dollar denominations. Free exchange of US and Haitian currency is an asset of the dual monetary system. But Canadian dollars are not generally accepted by shops, restaurants, and hotels, and must be converted. Banking hours are 9 AM to 1 PM on weekdays. Do not rely on the airport banking facility; it consists of one change booth that is seldom manned.

LANGUAGE: The official language is French, but natives speak a lilting Créole patois that sounds like French but has no decodable resemblance to it because of elements incorporated from the African dialect and the island's native Indian tongue. Most people in tourist-related jobs speak English.

TIME: Haiti matches its time to New York's year-round through both Eastern Standard and Daylight Saving months.

CURRENT: It's 110 volts, 60 cycles, so American appliances don't need adapters or converters.

GETTING THERE: Eastern Airlines and Pan American have daily service out of Miami; American provides daily flights from New York. A new airline, Haiti Trans Air, has direct flights from New York and Miami. Air Canada has a weekly flight from Montreal; Air Jamaica has connecting flights from San Juan. There are also connections from Santo Domingo on Pan Am and from Fort de France, Martinique, via Air France. Luggage is all too frequently lost, so keep toiletries, a bathing suit, and other essentials with you, just in case.

Royal Caribbean Cruise Lines makes regular stops at La Badie in the north.

CALCULATING COSTS: Winter hotel rates range from about $40 to $50 for two including breakfasts (BP) at a small hotel or guesthouse in downtown Port-au-Prince, Pétionville, Cap-Haïtien, or Jacmel, to about $145 plus 10% service and tax for two at *Moulin Sur Mer,* a complete resort on the beach an hour north of Port-au-Prince. Until the recent turmoil, Olivier Coquelin's chic *Relais de l'Empereur* topped the price charts at $250 a night, but current rates are less than $100 a night; they run about 25% to 35% less between mid-April and December 15. If you prefer to sample local restaurants, ask for breakfast-only (BP) rates that run $5 to $9 per person less a day. All in all, Haitian hotels are an excellent buy unless you need a beautiful beach to make you happy; with some exceptions, most tend to be long on atmosphere, short on sand. There's a 10% tax on hotel bills.

Restaurant meals may cost as little as $10 to $20 for two, including service but without drinks or wine, at a good, small, Haitian family place; $50 and up for two, including wine, at one of the tonier French establishments.

GETTING AROUND: Taxi – Plentiful at the airport and near hotels and tourist spots. It's important to check on the cost of the trip before you climb in and take off. Cabs aren't metered, but drivers are required to carry a card that spells out rates set by the government. The ride from the airport to hotels in Port-au-Prince is about $12; to Pétionville, about $14; and to beach hotels anywhere from $25 to $55. You can also rent a taxi (one to five passengers) for $7 to $8 an hour, about $30 for 4 hours, about $50 for an 8-hour day. But rates are subject to frequent review and change, so check first and/or ask your hotel to make arrangements.

Publiques – Haitian alternatives to high-priced taxis — recommended only if you are strong of heart and/or addicted to high-density, offbeat transport — include publiques, or public cars. The good news is the fare — 25¢ anywhere within Port-au-Prince, provided the driver doesn't enter your hotel grounds; the bad news is that the driver can pick up as many people as he wants, stop as often as he likes, and rarely speaks English. For about 25¢ you can also hop a minibus or small station wagon that travels between Pétionville Square and downtown Port-au-Prince. Or become part of a movable Haitian art form — the tap-tap — brightly muraled, titled pickup trucks, equipped with wooden seats and tailgate mottos. A beauty: "You love me so you will forgive me for Saturday Night." For that same 25¢, a tap-tap will take you the length of Carrefour Road to downtown Port-au-Prince, but the bad news above goes double — and their seats have no springs. Your spine will stay in better shape if you limit yourself to taking pictures of tap-taps and taking taxis for travel.

Car Rental – *Avis* (phone: 6-2460), *Budget* (phone: 6-2324), *Hertz* (phone: 6-0700), *National* (phone: 2-0611), and *Toyota Rent-A-Car* (phone: 2-3975) have representatives at the airport. Rates, quoted in US dollars, generally include insurance and unlimited mileage, but not gasoline, and a 10% tax. Rates start at about $35 per day for compacts and range up to $80 for 4-wheel-drive vehicles. Weekly rentals are also available. Since streets and houses aren't numbered, it's easy to get lost and spend lots of time going in circles. Smaller local car rental agencies in Port-au-Prince and Pétionville will take phone orders and deliver a car to the hotel. Among these are *MultiCar* (phone: 2-1600), *Secom* (phone: 7-1913), *TransAuto* (phone: 6-4359), and *Zenith* (phone 2-1986). It takes at least 36 hours to confirm an advance reservation. Most firms accept credit cards. Drivers need a valid US, Canadian, or International license.

Sightseeing Taxi Tours – The best way to see Port-au-Prince for the first time. Your hotel can arrange for an English-speaking driver who qualifies as a tour guide. He'll be more than happy to pick you up, take you where you want to go, wait, and/or reappear just when you think he's deserted you. If you like him, ask for his card or phone number so you can contact him for other expeditions. But when it comes to shopping tips, beware. Even good drivers sometimes take commissions.

Bus Tours – *Haiti Tourama* now operates a fleet of modern air-conditioned buses that handle tours for large groups. But individual sightseers usually travel by limo or minibus, and the per-person price of the tour is the charge for the vehicle divided by the number of passengers (usually one to ten). Routes are fairly standardized. Half-day trips include a morning in Kenscoff (about $40 per car) and a city sightseeing and shopping tour (about $30). All-day trips to Jacmel or the beaches are about $60 (lunches extra). Your hotel will arrange things. Or contact *Agence Citadelle* (phone: 2-5900), *Chatelain Tours* (phone: 2-4467, 2-4468, 2-4469), or *Southerland Tours* (phone: 2-1600) in Port-au-Prince; *Cap-Haïtien Travel Service* (phone: 2-0517) in Cap-Haïtien. *Southerland* also operates 3-hour cockfight tours (about $13 for each of two persons) and evening voodoo trips to *Bossou Voodoo* on Mariani Rd. ($25 per person, including hotel pickup).

Sea Excursions – The *Scuba Nautic Club* run by Jose Roy on Caçique Island offers a variety of boat excursions, including three-day trips to Gonave and Tortuga islands, fishing, snorkeling, exploring old pirate coves. His 46-foot catamaran, the *Pegasus*, can accommodate up to 40 people and costs $800 a day with drinks and food (including lobster). Deep-sea fishing charters are $500 a day. Sunday trips are $45 per person, but call first to see if he has gathered enough people. Boat trips are also offered at *Ibo Beach, Kaliko,* and *Moulin Sur Mer* beach resorts. And don't forget to take a towel, hat, long-sleeved shirt, long pants, and sun block — the sun's rays at sea can be brutal.

SHOPPING: Crafts — paintings, mahogany carvings, metal sculptures, baskets, leatherwork, printed fabrics, handmade and embroidered fashions — are Haiti's best buys. And they're sold everywhere. The moment you leave your hotel or step out of your car, some entrepreneur will be there with something to sell. (If it isn't exactly what you had in mind, say "No, merci" and keep walking. They give up eventually.) Wherever you shop — at a roadside stand, in the Iron Market, and even (though more subtly) at some of the better-known galleries — you bargain.

Paintings — wonderful and/or awful, and ranging in style from Rousseau to Dali to Walt Disney, yet still emphatically Haitian — are the island's most notable prospective buy. You'll find them hanging on country fences and stacked in Iron Market stalls, as well as on display in recognized galleries. And though prices aren't as low as they once were, you can still make excellent buys. Haitian primitives (or *naïfs*, as Madison

Avenue galleries now refer to them) are most famous, but some good surrealists, impressionists, and modernists are also at work. The most important rule, unless you're a bona fide expert, is to buy only what you like and can live with — never for speculation: the odds are too high against neophytes making a killing. If you're serious about buying, browse through the Museum of Art (see *Special Places* above) and several galleries to familiarize yourself with styles and prices before you make a decision. Avoid current best sellers (at any given time, there'll be two or three basic pictures — a particular crowd scene, animal scene, bird-in-tree design — so successful you'll find them mass-produced by the dozens) unless you fall desperately in love with one; if you do, be double-tough about the price; don't pay original prices for a knock-off. And double-check both (first and last) of the artist's names before you invest: Prefete Duffaut's works sell for several thousand each; Prego Duffaut's, though amazingly similar, may go for less.

One of the best galleries is *Issa's,* in a mountain mansion behind the reopened *Oloffson* hotel, where the atmosphere is low-key, never pushy, and selections number in the hundreds. Haitian-Lebanese Issa will charm or outrage you with his opinions, and he won't bargain. The price marked is the price charged, but his tags are fair. He has quite a few metal pieces as well as paintings. On your way out, peer through the lattice below; there's often an artist working in the studio under the gallery. Georges Nader's gallery at 92 Rue du Magasin de l'État in Port-au-Prince also has an established reputation (he has sold both Duffauts); he has been instrumental in popularizing Haitian artists with a worldwide audience. The internationally known *Galerie Monnin* has two locations: 19 Rue Lamarre in Pétionville, and 17 Rte. Laboule de Kenscoff, LaBoule. The latter location is definitely worth a visit; paintings are displayed throughout the owners' lovely and tranquil home. Other galleries worth looking into are *Rainbow Art Display,* 9 Rue Pierre Weiner, and *Le Centre d'Art,* 58 Rue Toi, in Port-au-Prince; *Galerie Mapou* and *The Red Carpet,* both on Rue Panamericaine in Pétionville; and *Galerie Marassa,* on Rue Lamarre, also in Pétionville. In the north, in Cap-Haïtien, *Galerie des 3 Visages,* Rue 5 Boulevard, is worth a look.

You'll find sculpture at many of these same spots as well as along the roadside, in the *Iron Market,* and at your hotel door. Mahogany isn't as plentiful or cheap as it once was, but it's still a bargain. *Atelier Taggart,* in a gingerbread mansion at 52 Bois Verna, houses one of the capital's widest selection of island-made items — from wind chimes to decorated pots, candle lamps, wooden masks, and ironwork — at astonishingly reasonable prices; another branch and the factory are in Cap Haïtien. Another place to purchase quality crafts is the *Mountain Maid l'Artisane Shop* of the Baptist Mission, 12 miles from Pétionville on the road to Kenscoff. In addition to good value on everything ranging from unusual hand-carved bull's horn pieces and seed bead necklaces to wooden sculptures, the site itself and the ride up into the hills are very pleasant, offering sweeping views of broad mountain valleys and glimpses of Haiti's most elegant homes. Pick up baskets or straw rugs in the market, along the street, wherever you find them.

Craft cautions: If you buy a wood carving, put it in the freezer for a few days when you get home; this will take care of any wood-craving beasties, save your souvenir — and maybe your house. Consider fumigating baskets; it takes only a minute and may save you from an invasion of little creatures. Straw rugs that dry out respond to bathtub or backyard soakings. But beware of the patched goat skin rugs sold along the roadside; the US Public Health Service will often confiscate them, since they may carry anthrax.

Gingerbread, at 52 Ave. Lamartinière, has a wide range of jewelry and objets d'art made by craftsmen and artisans under exclusive contract. Contemporary styles as well as traditional designs are available. *Gingerbread* also carries some antiques. Upstairs, there's a branch of *Atelier Taggart* with a good selection of iron art, weavings, and other crafts both wholesale and retail. *Gayra Pottery,* at 8 Ave. Delmas in Port-au-Prince, specializes in ceramics and earthenware, ranging from decorated pots and vases to candle lamps, ceiling lamps, figurines, decorative plates, and ashtrays. Specialty items include desk bells, masks, angels, and Nativity sets. Prices are reasonable, with only a few extra-large items costing more than $25. *Zin d'Art,* at 86 John Brown, carries a wonderful selection of pottery, paintings, carvings, baskets, macramé, wall hangings, and many other crafts. Haitian-made items, as well as imports from the Caribbean, Africa, and around the world, can be found at *Ambiance,* 17 Ave. M, in Port-au-Prince. A number of small shops and individual women in both Pétionville and Port-au-Prince will hand-make and embroider a dress or a shirt for as little as $18 to $20 and have it ready before you leave or mail it to your home; ask at your hotel for recommendations and shop early, to allow time for fittings.

 TIPPING: Most hotels and restaurants add a 10% service charge to your bill, which covers all but extra special service. If no service charge is added, tip waiters 10% to 15%; hotel maids, $1 per room per day; bellboys and porters 50¢ per bag. But, to quote the Office of Tourism, "Nobody — not even the Haitians — tips taxi, publique, minibus, or tap-tap drivers."

 SPECIAL EVENTS: For Haitians, the big day is January 1, or *Independence Day,* a time for parades, speeches, and fireworks that carry over to January 2, or *Forefathers' Day,* which celebrates such national heroes as Dessalines, Pétion, Christophe, and Toussaint L'Ouverture. But the tourists' favorite is *Mardi Gras,* or *Carnival,* the celebration that takes place throughout the country during the three days before *Ash Wednesday;* there's parading, with floats and costumes, dancing in the streets, and the sound of drums through the night; and hotel and airline reservations are very hard to come by.

Other national holidays observed by banks, government offices, and most businesses include *Pan American Day* (April 14), *Labor Day* (May 1), *Flag and University Day* (May 18), *Assumption Day* (August 15), *Dessalines's Death Anniversary* (October 17), *UN Day* (October 24), *All Saints' Day* (November 1), *Armed Forces Day* (November 18), *Discovery Day* (December 5), and *Christmas.* As one official says, "Haitians love a good party."

 SPORTS: Haiti is no place for you if great sport is essential to your vacation happiness. The picture on both sea and land is spotty, and likely to stay that way. Since sport isn't the reason most people come to Haiti, there's neither the money nor the impetus to install or maintain first-rate facilities. A pool and maybe a tennis court is about all you can expect from your hotel since most are inland; you'll have to rely on the person in charge of tours and sightseeing to advise you and arrange any off-premises sport expeditions. Bring your own equipment for tennis, scuba, and snorkeling — if you plan to do more than the three-hour package trip on which masks and fins are provided. But don't bother with golf clubs — the 9-hole *Pétionville Club* course isn't worth it.

Boating – *Scuba Nautic's* anchorage, at *Ibo Beach,* is a perfect water-skiing area. Parasailing is also offered (at $25 for 10 minutes), and Jose Roy will take certified divers out (phone: 7-4846). The marina at *Ibo Beach* also has sailboats and boardsailers for rent. *Kaliko Beach* has Sunfish-scale boats and a 50-foot catamaran for snorkeling and dive trips. *Ibo Beach* and *Moulin Sur Mer* also offer boat trips. Rental fees are moderate.

Horseback Riding – There is beach riding at the *Kaliko Beach* and *Ibo,* and in the hills at Furcy, near Kenscoff. Horses or mules provide the transport on day trips to Cap-Haïtien's Citadelle and to the Basin Bleu near Jacmel.

Hunting – Year-round sport with more than 50 varieties of duck sighted around lakes in the southern mountains (especially from October to April), other game birds (quail, pigeon, guinea fowl) in season from August to January. Most exotic quarry: alligators in the lake areas.

Snorkeling and Scuba – Best around Les Arcadins, La Gonave, and coastal reefs. Visibility around Les Arcadins island is 80 to 100 feet. Consult your hotel travel desk about day-trip arrangements. *Cormier Plage* and *Kaliko Beach* offer their guests diving, and *Kaliko Dive Center* (PADI Training Association) at *Kaliko Beach* has the only diving setup with gear, reef excursions, and instruction for certification (also the only air for diving tanks on the island).

Spectator Sports – Haitians are crazy about soccer; matches are held at the Sylvio Cator Stadium in Port-au-Prince (see newspapers or consult your hotel desk for schedules). Cockfights are held Saturdays and Sundays; the Gaguere cockfight arena in Exposition Grounds in Port-au-Prince is the scene of most action, but there are numerous floating matches besides. It's basically a Haitian-for-Haitians sport, but some tourists go. Ask your hotel to set it up with a driver, or contact *Southerland Tours.*

Swimming and Sunning – Mostly practiced around hotel pools. Though there are some good-looking beaches (at *Kyona* and *Ibo Beach* on Caçique Island near Port-au-Prince; *Ouanga Bay* farther out; *Raymond les Bains* near Jacmel; *Cormier Plage* and *La Badie* near Cap-Haïtien), Haitian seaside resorts, on the whole, are not up to the standards of those in the rest of the Caribbean, either in terms of comfort or built-in equipment. *Kyona* and *Kaliko Beach* north of the city come closest. *Club Med, Jolly Beach,* and *Moulin Sur Mer* also have good beaches.

Tennis – Courts are available at *El Rancho, Villa Créole, Royal Haitian, Montana, Ibo Beach, Jolly Beach,* and *Kaliko Beach* hotels. In Cap-Haïtien, there's tennis at the *Mont Joli* and *Cormier Plage.*

Water Skiing and Windsurfing – Skis and tows are available at *Ibo Beach, Jolly Beach,* and *Kyona* hotels. Charges vary, but they're not high. The *Ibo Beach, Kyona,* and *Kaliko Beach* have windsurfing boards to go.

 NIGHTLIFE: No gala revues or big names. Instead, the larger hotels take turns providing traditional folk entertainment. The major hotels in town — *Villa Créole, El Rancho, Ibo Lélé, Castelhaiti,* and *Splendid* — all have their nights to shine, usually with a mouth-watering Créole buffet and/or barbecue, followed by a folkloric show by island dancers who know all the sensuous steps and merengue moves so well they may have you doing them too. Don't worry about constant replay; the program is different each night. Dinner and entertainment run about $20 per person. Discos aren't the rage here that they are in other parts of the world, but there is enough activity to keep you from forgetting all your hustle technique. *El Rancho* has a disco, *Visage,* and you can merengue at *Club Internacional.* Cover charges run from $2 to $5 on weekends only; drinks, about $1.50 to $2. There are also casinos: at *El Rancho* and the *Chacoune* in Pétionville, and at the *Royal Haitian* in Port-au-Prince. Vegas they're not, but worth a whirl for roulette, craps, blackjack; slot machines, too.

You won't see authentic voodoo, but you can gain some understanding of it at the nightly ritual staged for patrons of a unique place called *Le Peristyle* near Mariani on the Carrefour Road. The approach is respectful and the effect sometimes stunning as the evening progresses. Go with a few other people, and stay later to talk with Max Beauvoir, the impressive *houngan* (priest) who presides. He'll do his best to explain things to you. Admission is about $10 per person, plus drinks. Shows were suspended due to security problems; call Mr. Beauvoir (phone: 4-2818) to see if any are scheduled.

BEST ON THE ISLAND

 CHECKING IN: It's no ad-copy cliché: Haitian hotels are different — from hotels in the rest of the Caribbean and from each other. No mass-produced decor, no sprawling resort complexes with something-for-everyone atmosphere (or lack of it). The hotels display an individuality as much a part of the island's ambience as the zebras and giraffes that are a part of the landscape of Haitian art.

In the Port-au-Prince area, there's a geographic choice: hotels right in town tend to be most intensely Haitian, handiest to sightseeing, but when it's hot they are very hot (air conditioning is essential to sleeping comfort here — especially in summer); hotels above town in the Pétionville hills are naturally cooler, breezier, with more resort feeling. Beach hotels are on the increase, and one of the newer *Club Med* oases is on the western coast. There are now weeklong packages that combine three-night stays at Port-au-Prince hotels with stays in Cap-Haïtien or at a choice of beach resorts.

Haitian hotel food is reliably good. But since restaurant eating is one of the island's chief pleasures, the breakfast-only option of BP seems to make most sense — especially on short stays.

Rates tend to be very reasonable — particularly when compared with winter prices elsewhere in the Caribbean. In the listings below, expensive means $100 and up for a double room, including breakfast, during the winter season (mid-December to mid-April); about $75 and up for two, BP, in summer. Moderate ranges from $55 to $95 for two, EP (without meals), in winter; about $50 to $75 double, EP, in summer. Anything below that is inexpensive. The following are special for the reasons given.

PORT-AU-PRINCE

Oloffson – Reopened in 1987 by Richard Morse and Blair Townsend, an ambitious young couple who hope to restore it to its former glory. They've put lots of time, paint, sweat, and enthusiasm into fixing ceilings, floors, and rooms. A piano has been shipped in from Connecticut and painted by Haitian artist Ra-Ra; all other furnishings were made in Haiti, some designed by the couple. The hotel's long history includes serving as a marine hospital during the American occupation (1915–24) and later as a gathering spot for famous visitors such as Graham Greene, Lillian Hellman, and Mick Jagger. Morse and Townsend hope to attract a new wave of artists, writers, and others who want to visit, or return, to Haiti (phone: 509-1-3400). Expensive to moderate.

Splendid – A Victorian mansion-turned-hotel that's a favorite of savvy sorts who visit the island regularly on business. With surrounding gardens and pool, in a pleasantly residential neighborhood, near enough to the center of town without being — strictly speaking — in it. Soothing service, relaxing atmosphere, international style, good food — all thanks to Wolfgang Wagner, whose special place it is. Rue N (phone: 5-0106). Expensive to moderate.

Castelhaiti – Reached by a steep, twisting road, this compact hotel perched on a hill overlooking Port-au-Prince offers some very lovely views of the city below and the sea beyond. Bedrooms are air-conditioned with private balconies; there's an open-air dining room and smallish pool (phone: 2-0624, 2-3777). Moderate.

Le Plaza Holiday Inn – An oasis in the middle of Port-au-Prince. A typical bedroom at this affiliate of the American chain offers such comforts as two double beds, TV, radio, and air conditioning as well as a small balcony overlooking the pool and central courtyard. Convenient downtown location across from park and Museum of Art (phone: 2-0855, 2-0821). Moderate.

Royal Haitian – Palm-tufted gardens surround Haitian-modern hotel near downtown shops, harbor. With tennis, big pool; water sports nearby. Casino makes it the choice if gambling's your game (phone: 4-0485, 4-0258). Moderate.

Villa St-Louis – Where Port-au-Prince meets Pétionville, very convenient to the airport, with 45 comfortable air-conditioned rooms and a dining room featuring wonderful Créole cuisine (phone: 5-6417, 5-6241). Moderate to inexpensive.

PÉTIONVILLE

El Rancho – A somewhat down-at-the-heels former private mansion given splashes of Haitian color and Hollywood 1930s style. It has twin swimming pools, lighted tennis court, badminton, whirlpool, gym, masseur, indoor-outdoor dining room, poolside bar with entertainment several nights a week, *Flamboyante* nightclub, and a glittering casino. With 115 rooms — from clean and simple in older building to a bit fancier in new wings (phone: 7-2080). Expensive to moderate.

Kinam – Located in town, within walking distance of restaurants, shops, and galleries, this family-run hotel has been cleverly disguised to look like a gingerbread-style house, but there's a neat and efficient operation inside the latticework and cupolas. It offers 38 rooms, 3 suites (including a lovely split-level), and even a small conference room for 20. There are rattan furnishings, tile baths with new fixtures (including shower massagers), TVs, radios, air conditioning; also a pool, a shaded terrace, and a restaurant serving Creole and French dishes (phone: 7-0462). Moderate.

Montana – In a lovely, tranquil setting with fabulous views of Port-au-Prince. The corner rooms are the best at this hotel — neatly balanced on a hillside between Pétionville and Port-au-Prince — for they have good-size balconies with mountain views in one direction, the sea in the other. Amenities include typical Haitian furnishings, air conditioning, tennis courts, super swimming pool, restaurant, boutique, and conference room. Go for lunch to enjoy the views even if you don't stay here (phone: 7-1920, 7-1921). Moderate.

Villa Créole – This restored and gracefully added-to mansion in the hills is a top choice — pretty, serene, relaxed, with 80 rooms (many freshly decorated), marble bathrooms, a large pool, restaurant, and patio dining; breakfast under the almond tree is particularly delightful. The hotel is known for its friendly atmosphere and the warm hospitality of its owner, Dr. Reindall Assad, and the staff (phone: 7-1570, 7-1571). Moderate.

Ibo Lélé – Once visited by the rich and famous, this hotel is on a spectacular site overlooking city and countryside. There's a terraced pool surrounded by sun decks plus whirlpool, game room, popular *Shango* nightclub (its big night is Friday). Standard rooms feature exceptional wood carving; superior rooms have terraces with city, mountain, and sea views. Great value (phone: 7-0845). Moderate to inexpensive.

JACMEL

La Jacmélienne – This beachfront property is big and modern for Jacmel, with 30 large rooms, all with terraces, Haitian furnishings, and ceiling fans. Swimming pool, two bars, outdoor daytime/indoor (but open-air) evening dining, very good food whenever. Jacmel Bay (phone: 07-8-3451). Moderate.

Manoir Alexandra – An unusual guesthouse that would make a great place to write your novel, but only for those unbothered by shared bathrooms, peeling paint, and slanting floors. The atmosphere is one of elegant decline, with antique furnishings, high ceilings, views of the sea, mountains, and gardens below from the verandah. Rates include breakfast (phone: 8-2711). Inexpensive.

Pension Craft – A small charmer on the town square; spartan or quaint, depending on your point of view. Tiny, spotless rooms, caring atmosphere; wonderful home-cooked Créole food (the omelets are light as soufflés). Adeline Danies is worth the trip all by herself (phone: 07-8-3331). Inexpensive.

CAP-HAÏTIEN

Mont Joli – Very pleasant, relaxed, with 40 rooms (some overlooking the sea), a large pool, tennis, and a good Haitian dining room; also a new nightclub with Haitian music, folkloric shows. Sans Souci–Citadelle tours arranged (phone: 03-2-0300). Moderate.

Roi Christophe – Built in 1724 as the residence of the French governor of Saint Domingue, this hotel has retained all its lovely arched doorways, beamed ceilings, interior courtyards, colonial wood furniture. Service is gracious and the dining room is excellent. Gardens, outdoor bar, a pool, and casino. Downtown (phone: 03-2-0414). Moderate.

Cormier Plage – Beautiful 35-unit property on a lovely beach just west of Cap-Haïtien. Perfect place to relax, enjoy a lobster lunch in the open-air restaurant; or play tennis, swim, snorkel, or scuba dive (phone: 2-1000). Moderate.

Beck – Fortresslike 30-room property, built on a hill overlooking the city. Everything here seems oversized: large terraces, two verandah swimming pools and deck area. Beautifully furnished with antiques and mahogany pieces built by staff carpenters. Delicious Continental cuisine (phone: 2-0001). Moderate to inexpensive.

ELSEWHERE ON THE ISLAND

Moulin sur Mer, Montrouis – A new hotel with a little something of everything Haiti has to offer: gorgeous beach (perfect for sunset cocktails), a water wheel fed by a 200-year-old aqueduct, a colonial sugar mill converted into a museum dedicated to Haitian independence, a great house dining room decorated in a most eclectic manner, and a salon devoted to billiards. Two suites, 26 rooms, and 8 beach cabanas. Other features include tennis, racquetball, badminton, miniature golf, and water sports, plus a saltwater swimming pool. Dinner in the greathouse is French/Continental; lunch is at *Les Boucaniers,* the beachfront barbecue restaurant. With 42 acres of ground, there is plenty of opportunity to roam the paths, which are liberally sprinkled with gardens and gazebos, plus a duck-filled pond (phone: 2-1844, 2-1918, or 2-7652). Expensive to Moderate.

Relais de l'Empereur, Petit Goave – In a small town where visitors can see how real Haitians live. Olivier Coquelin, of the now-defunct *Habitation Leclerc,* has restored "a mansion of Emperor Faustin I of Haiti" to witty (or quirky) elegance (or flamboyance). Its high-ceilinged, artifact- and antique-dazzled lounges, dining room, and 10 suites — all with hyper-opulent bathing arrangements — serve as a home and party base for guests who spend days desporting on the stunning pooled and pavilioned beach at Plantation Cocoyer, a short, exclusive boat ride away. Though the hoped-for haute monde has yet to beat a path to its door in notable numbers, M. Coquelin's posh mousetrap is ready. Once the most expensive hostelry on the island, rates are now affordable for ordinary mortals with a bit of decadence in their souls (phone: 5-0810). Expensive to moderate.

Jolly Beach – A brand-new 22-room resort in a spectacular location on the Gulf de la Gouâve, at base of Chaine de Matheux mountains. The pool seems to hang above the beach, and there's the feeling of being on a private estate, with rolling lawns and magnificent mountain views. Director Raymond Polynice is a stickler for fine points; for example, he will serve guests breakfast anywhere, anytime. Water sports, tennis courts; horseback riding and water skiing also available (phone: 3-9653). Moderate.

Ibo Beach, Cacique Island – About 35 minutes plus a short launch ride from town, this small island is big on beach life, affable atmosphere, outside activity — swimming, water skiing, sailing, snorkeling, scuba, windsurfing, tennis. The 50 A-frame bungalows are one notch above summer-camp comfort level, which serves well if you play outdoors a lot. The new Swiss owner has imported a Swiss chef and is working hard to improve the property. A breeze-conditioned dining pavilion features luscious fresh lobster, fish, chicken. All in all, it's the Swiss Family Robinson gone Haitian (phone: 7-1200). Moderate.

Kaliko Beach, La Gonave Bay – With bright-eyed new lease on life, smiling attitude, lots of action — snorkeling equipment, sailing, horseback riding, tennis, included in rates. Waterfall pool, deck, bar, disco, and *Le Triton* restaurant on premises, featuring Haitian and Continental cuisine. Ideal destination for a beach day when you're feeling very sportif (phone: 2-5773). Moderate.

Kyona Beach, Montrouis – Cottages in the palms along the shore beside a long white beach. Nothing splashy, but pleasantly done decor. No program, no rush. But should you feel like snorkeling, skin diving, water skiing, horseback riding, it's all there. Big thatch-topped outdoor dining room serves charcoal-grilled lobster, Créole specialties (phone: 2-6788). Moderate to inexpensive.

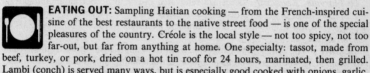 **EATING OUT:** Sampling Haitian cooking — from the French-inspired cuisine of the best restaurants to the native street food — is one of the special pleasures of the country. Créole is the local style — not too spicy, not too far-out, but far from anything at home. One specialty: tassot, made from beef, turkey, or pork, dried on a hot tin roof for 24 hours, marinated, then grilled. Lambi (conch) is served many ways, but is especially good cooked with onions, garlic, and tomato sauce and served over rice. Homard and langouste — both in the lobster family — are delicious flamed in brandy or simmered in Créole sauce; lobster ragoût is made with cooked lobster meat, cubed, sautéed in butter, flamed with rum, native vegetables, and spices. Other favorites are *griots,* pork marinated in lemon and salt, fried, and served with hot, spicy sauce; bananas *pesées,* or fried green bananas; *riz et pois rouges collés,* rice and red kidney beans; and *manba,* a spicy peanut butter.

Dining out in Haiti can be expensive, moderate, or downright cheap. At the best French dining rooms, dinner for two can run $50 or more, while at most Créole spots, $10 for two without drinks can be a realistic figure. For less than a dollar in country markets, you can try fried bananas and goat served on a piece of brown paper, which is best enjoyed while strolling the market or cruising along the highway.

PORT-AU-PRINCE

Le Récif – Remarkable seafood variety (giant shrimp, three kinds of crab, conch, kingfish, octopus, etc.), beach atmosphere, attentive service. Attractive bar. Buccaneer brochettes a specialty. Delmas Rd. (phone: 6-2605). Moderate.

Le Rond Point – Near the Exposition Grounds and newly redecorated, it's where seafood lovers go native. Freshly caught local fish are done in a variety of styles. Strange-sounding, but delectable: red snapper covered with mayonnaise, stuffed with beef and tomatoes, and poached in white wine. Av. Marie-Jeanne (phone: 2-0621). Moderate.

Le Tiffany – Tasty, downtown spot with friendly atmosphere, popular business-lunch place (phone: 2-3506). Moderate.

PÉTIONVILLE

Chez Gérard – Elegant and leisurely French dining in an old Haitian house off the square. Ask for a table on the porch and take your time (phone: 7-1949). Expensive.

Le Steak Inn – The finest charcoal-broiled steaks found on the island, served in a garden setting or in the main dining room. Live music nightly. Open for lunch weekdays, dinner nightly (phone: 7-2153). Expensive.

La Belle Époque – Old house and garden, evocative setting for very good French-Haitian lunches and dinners. 23 Rue Gregoire (phone: 7-0984). Expensive to moderate.

La Souvenance – Some of the best French food ever, in a pleasant atmosphere that mixes Provence and Haiti. Edwige and Jean Guy Barme's beautifully presented specialties include a heavenly squash pie with a light green sauce of mint, parsley, and whipping cream; caviar mousse served with toast and unbelievable avocado sorbet; lamb ribs with almonds; steak au poivre; and a great chicken curry from a recipe handed down by the owners' mother. Desserts arrive with sparklers, and coffee is served on Havilland china with antique silver (phone: 7-7688). Expensive to moderate.

Le Bolero – Super Italian food in a tropical patio. Enjoy pizzas, light-as-heaven homemade pastas, seafood, steaks, great music, and excellent service. Run by two brothers in a residential area of Pétionville (phone: 7-1929). Moderate.

Le Florville, Kenscoff – Recently renovated eatery in a cool mountain setting. Specializes in home-style dishes, particularly *griot,* the spicy island pork favorite. Open 10 AM to midnight. Entertainment weekends (phone: 5-2092 or 2-0124). Moderate.

Magritte – The owner, Luc Cosyns, is from the same Belgian town as artist René Magritte, and this is his homage to him. Garden dining, a pleasant spot for drinks or dinner if seafood and surrealism appeal. There are 10 seafood dishes, all of them grilled. Look for the Magritte sign (phone: 7-0841). Moderate.

Palmiste – A West Hollywood fantasy in black and white. One of the owners did in fact arrive via Hollywood, but his partner is from New York City, and the menu is from Mexico — nachos, tacos, tostados, and refried beans. Happy hour starts at 4 PM with margaritas (phone: 7-4775). Moderate.

BEACH AREA

Moulin Sur Mer – Meticulously restored sugar plantation set on 36 acres (six along the beach). Sophisticated restaurant set in old sugar mill, with a beachside gazebo grille perfect for lunch. Continental and Créole specialties. A must if you are in the beach area (phone: 2-1844, 2-1918, or 2-7652). Moderate.

JAMAICA

Jamaica is one of the most provocative of all Caribbean islands, tempting unsuspecting visitors with a thrilling diversity of landscapes, dramatic seascapes, more variety of flora and fauna than its Greater Antillean neighbors, and a richness of culture that has seduced even the most seasoned traveler.

"We're more than a beach — we're a country" was Jamaica's advertising theme when the island embarked on a serious campaign to recover its valuable tourism market during this decade, following several years of loss due to political problems prevalent during the late 1970s. But the media overseas couldn't convey the real meaning of that slogan: the strength of Jamaicans themselves, a multiracial blend of 2.2 million people, whose features may be African, European, Arabic, Chinese, or East Indian. And their customs comprise the essence of the national motto: "Out of many, one people."

That incredible diversity is true of Jamaica itself, the third largest of all Caribbean islands. Within its 4,411 square miles — slightly smaller than Connecticut — is a startling array of contrasts. On the south coast is the busy capital of Kingston, one of the cultural hubs of the West Indies, often overlooked by visitors. On the north coast are the fine powdery beaches of its Montego Bay and Ocho Rios vacation resorts, which originally brought the country to prominence. Negril's 7-mile expanse of sand and its much-publicized "swinging" retreat at Hedonism II added yet another dimension to the island. And the impressive selection of hotels, luxury villas, and charming small inns sprinkled throughout the island makes Jamaica one of the Caribbean's most popular destinations.

But Jamaica remains a country of mystery and adventure. It was for those very qualities that Errol Flynn — after being shipwrecked in Port Antonio Harbor on the lush, unspoiled northeast coast — adopted it as his final home. Rugged highlands and mountains dominate the landscape: More than half of Jamaica rises 1,000 feet above the sea. The highest point, Blue Mountain Peak, provides the stunning backdrop for Kingston, looming over the capital at 7,402 feet. From the plunging waterfalls and languorous Rio Grande of Port Antonio to the surrealist moonscape of Cockpit Country in the northwest, the more it is explored, the more dramatic are its contrasts.

From the hypnotic and haunting rhythms of reggae to the breeze-cooled, hidden beaches of elegant resorts like Sans Souci and Montego Bay's Round Hill, it offers stimulation and relaxation, with something to appeal to almost every vacationer, save gambling. Water sports aplenty can be pursued in and above the turquoise depths, and for those who aren't aquatically inclined, Jamaica has nine championship golf courses, hundreds of tennis courts, and a first-rate equestrian center near Ocho Rios, Chukka Cove.

Yet the Jamaican people create memories as vivid as the varied landscape of their country. Proud, resourceful, and extremely creative in many artistic

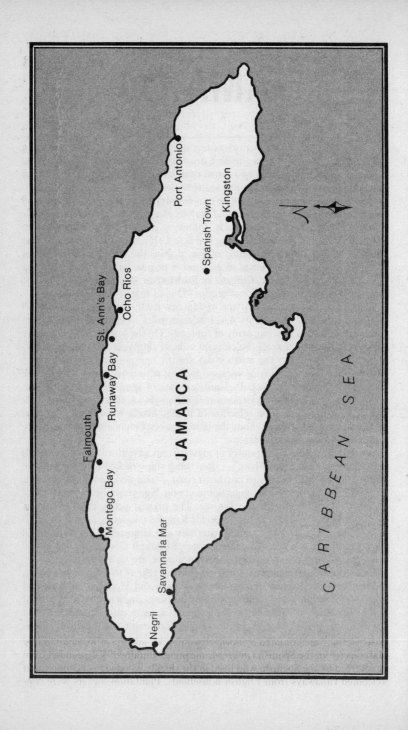

fields, from literature to music, their unrelenting good humor, ingenuity, and natural beauty make them one of the most memorable of all Caribbean cultures. And because of them, Jamaica is an island that evokes a strong reaction from those who visit. In its lilting patois, indifference is not part of the dialect.

Many have described this country as seductive, and it has cast its spell over adventurers and rogues, as well as some of the most civilized bon vivants of the last century. Noel Coward produced some of his finest works at Firefly, his hilltop retreat at Port Maria, sacred space once dear to Henry Morgan. It has inspired visitors since Christopher Columbus sighted its north coast in May 1494.

Even he found Jamaica an unusually memorable island, "the fairest island that eyes have beheld." His first visit was relatively uneventful; after sighting land in the neighborhood of Rio Bueno, he sailed west along the coast to Montego Bay and returned peacefully to Cuba. His second call in 1503 was stormier; foul weather and two crippled ships forced him to put in at St. Ann's Bay, where he and his crew were marooned for over a year until the jealous governor of Hispaniola saw fit to send a ship to rescue them.

In 1510, after his father's death, Christopher's son Diego, then governor of all the Indies and based in Santo Domingo, sent Don Juan de Esquivel to establish Spain's claim to Jamaica by founding a permanent settlement. Twenty-four years later, the town called New Seville was abandoned in favor of a new capital at what is now Spanish Town, which was originally christened Villa de la Vega, the Town on the Plain.

In 1655, having decided that Britain should have its own place on the Spanish Main, Oliver Cromwell dispatched 6,000 men to take part in a plan known as the Western Design, aimed against the Spanish monopoly of the region. Having tried and failed in Hispaniola, they succeeded against the 500 Spaniards then residing in Jamaica. Almost immediately the British, more interested in capturing Spanish gold than colonizing, set up privateering headquarters at Port Royal, which earned a seventeenth-century reputation as "the wickedest city on earth," on the tip of the long skinny arm of land called Los Palisadoes, across the harbor from what is now Kingston. The notorious buccaneer Henry Morgan, later rewarded with a lieutenant governorship, took charge and carried out a series of raids that climaxed with his sacking of the Spanish colony at Panamá and the final recognition by Spain of England's claim to Jamaica. The end of Port Royal's era of outrageous fun and profit came in 1692 with the literal fall of the city when, during a severe earthquake, more than half the town slid into the harbor.

Meanwhile, on the mainland, agriculture became the colony's chief concern. After unprofitable tries at indigo, tobacco, and cotton, the planters settled on sugar as their main crop. And sugar meant slaves. By the end of the eighteenth century, Jamaica's population consisted of roughly 300,000 African slaves and 20,000 whites. The situation was complicated by the existence of "free coloureds," born of white men and slave women, and by Maroons (from the Spanish *cimarrón,* meaning "untamed"), descended from slaves freed by the Spanish, who lived in the thickly wooded backcountry and welcomed runaways from English households. Plantation owners were constantly harassed by raids — so much so that in order to stop them, the government signed a formal treaty with the Maroons, guaranteeing them "a perfect state of freedom and liberty" within specified tax-free boundaries in return for their help against "enemies of the government" and the return of runaways when requested. Though this last provision was rarely honored, the Maroon threat was lessened. Revolts by the slaves themselves began in the mid-1700s, and in 1760 the most serious slave revolt broke out. The revolt continued until the bloodiest confrontation of all occurred in December 1831 in Montego Bay, sparked by now-hero "Daddy" Sam Sharpe, who was hanged in the square that bears his name. His actions, however, resulted in speeding the end of slavery in Jamaica, which came seven years later.

For a number of reasons — including abolition and increased competition from Cuba — sugar became a less and less profitable enterprise. In 1865, drought struck and, pushed beyond endurance, the impoverished and desperate free Negroes of Morant Bay rioted, killing a government official. The uprising was summarily put down, but in the process the Jamaican Assembly, which had previously exercised considerable control over island affairs, surrendered much of its power to the governor. As a result, in 1866, Jamaica was designated a Crown Colony, which it remained until 1944.

In that year, a royal commission "recommended measures to promote economic development and political advance," and full adult suffrage was granted. The emergence of bananas as a major crop, the very profitable discovery of bauxite, and the rise of year-round tourism shored up the economy. Eighteen years later, after a brief flirtation with the notion of joining the Federation of the West Indies, Jamaica became a fully independent nation within the British Commonwealth. With hindsight, it seems slightly prophetic that the royal presence at the independence ceremonies in the National Stadium on August 6, 1962, was vested in the Princess Margaret, a lady who has had her own ups and downs. In the recent past Jamaica has had some traumatic ups and downs, too.

To explain and document them would take several books. To oversimplify considerably, the basic problems were both economic and political. Economically, the island's balance of payments got severely out of balance during the mid-1970s. Unemployment was up, incomes were down, and people were unhappy. Further, the statements of Prime Minister Michael Manley and rumors of his government's romance with Cuba gave rise to the conviction that the island was going party-line Communist. Stories of violence — some true, all dramatically reported — surfaced and multiplied. Visitors started staying away in droves. To try to set the economy right, the government declared a massive austerity program and devalued the Jamaican dollar several times. Imports were cut *into* the bone. People hurt.

But devaluation kept Jamaican hotel and package prices low, and the island's natural beauty kept it one of the most seductive destinations on this planet. So tourism began a slow, steady recovery. With just under 600,000 arrivals in 1979, figures hit an all-time high — only to topple again in 1980 with news of pre-election strife between supporters of Manley and his more conservative Jamaica Labour Party opponent, Edward P. G. Seaga. Seaga's stunning victory inspired new hope around the world for eventual economic recovery and reassured its Caribbean neighbors — including the US. It also gave tourism an immediate and enormous emotional lift. The gradual growth of Jamaica's tourism industry reached an all-time high in 1987, with close to a million visitors. Resort projects by foreign investors now on the drawing boards could add another 3,000 rooms to the country's facilities by 1990. All of this in spite of a decision in 1986 not to introduce casino gambling on the island.

Should you grab your bathing suit and Bain de Soleil and take off for Jamaica? The answer is only a slightly equivocal "Yes." The Seaga government has made a sincere commitment to "encouraging decorum and law and order." Demonstrations are generally protests directed at government policies, not hostilities vented on tourists. In fact, reported violence has been almost entirely restricted to the area Manley himself called "ghetto Kingston," an area of West Kingston that is far from the expected paths of most visitors. Not one of the victims of such turmoil was ever a tourist. Still, new elections — Seaga vs. Manley again — are on the horizon for Jamaica, and that has recently meant disruption and loud discord. As balloting nears, we get a bit more cautious about blanket enthusiasm.

In terms of cost and comfort, however, the picture seems to be brightening by the minute. No longer must villa renters tote in cartons of staples and foodstuffs unavailable on the island, although savvy sportspersons still bring their own rackets, clubs, fishing gear, and ample supplies of tennis and golf balls, because such luxury items are scarce and/or very expensive on the island. The cost of food and gas also has sent restaurant, taxi, and car rental prices skyward. On the other hand, hotel prices remain remarkably reasonable, and the government has succeeded in provisioning resorts to keep visitors relatively unaware of what native privation still exists. Winter occupancies have climbed back to the 80% to 90% range. From Negril to Port Antonio, vacationers — including substantial new numbers of sun-worshipful Europeans — are lolling on Jamaica's beaches, splashing in its sea, seeking pleasure and finding it. Having explored Jamaica so often in past years without advance fanfare, special cosseting, or trouble, we'd probably join those lollers, splashers, sun-seekers, and fun-finders.

JAMAICA AT-A-GLANCE

 FROM THE AIR: Jamaica is a somewhat lozenge-shaped island that measures 142 miles from east to west and 52 miles from north to south at its broadest point, with a total land area of 4,411 square miles and a population of 2,030,000. A spine of dark green mountains rises from foothills in the west, stretches the length of the island, and reaches its highest point at Blue Mountain Peak (7,402 feet) in the east. The island's best-known resort areas — Montego Bay, Negril, Runaway Bay, Ocho Rios, and Port Antonio — lie along the gently curved north coast. In contrast, the long southern shoreline forms a deeper curve notched by an irregular pattern of coves, bays, and harbors. The most important of these is the peninsula-protected eastern harbor on which Kingston (pop. 700,000), Jamaica's capital and chief commercial port, is located.

Centered at 77°15′ N latitude, 18°15′ W longitude, Jamaica is about 90 miles due south of Cuba and approximately the same distance from its two other near neighbors, Haiti to the northeast and the Cayman Islands to the northwest. Its gateway airports are Norman Manley International, about 20 minutes from downtown Kingston, and Sir Donald Sangster International (where most vacationers deplane), about 10 minutes' drive east of Montego Bay; most international flights stop at both. Flight time from Miami (about 590 air miles) is about 1½ hours; from New York (about 1,450 air miles), less than 4 hours; and from Toronto (about 1,790 air miles), about 5 hours.

 SPECIAL PLACES: Jamaican sightseeing isn't an obligation; it's a delightful diversion — a perfect project when you've had enough sun, sand, and sea and don't feel like charging around the tennis court or golf course. The Tourist Board has devised some uniquely Jamaican ways (rafting, the Governor's Coach Tour) of viewing the island's cooler beauties (green mountains, waterfalls, flowers, pale stands of bamboo). There are also old Georgian towns and plantation greathouses to explore, complete with stories of swashbuckling pirates and ghosts. Each of Jamaica's vacation areas and its capital have land sites worth seeing.

Negril – Until recently, this "sleepy bohemian" side of Jamaica had only natural attractions — the beach and the sea — plus its largely counterculture citizenry. But Negril is developing rapidly, and at press time two new plantation projects were due for completion in 1988. *Spot Valley Farm* offers walking tours of a working pineapple-and-coconut farm, fruit tasting included. *Rhodes Hall,* just east of Negril, is a 500-acre plantation that includes 12 acres of ponds stocked with red tilapia and silver perch. This ambitious project will eventually offer water sports on a 2-acre lake, plus a small marina, rafting, and carriage tours.

Montego Bay – The town itself is somewhat short on picturesque spots. The city's center is the Parade (also known as Sam Sharpe Square), with its Old Courthouse (1804) and Cage (originally a jail built in 1806, now a small tour office). St. James Parish Church, at St. Claver and Church streets, is a faithful restoration (after severe damage by a 1957 earthquake) of the Georgian original (1775–82), full of fascinating monuments and surrounded by tropical gardens. Church Street itself boasts some handsomely restored Georgian homes. The Public Market on Fustic Street is also worth a visit, especially on Friday or Saturday, when it's loudest and liveliest. And the Montego Bay Craft Market on Harbour Drive is one of the cleanest, best organized, and well stocked in the entire Caribbean — a must for anyone (who likes to dicker) on the lookout for local handicrafts, woodcarvings, and assorted souvenirs.

The trip not to be missed is the Governor's Coach Tour (see *Trains,* below). Birders also flock to Rocklands Feeding Station in Anchovy (turn left on Route B8 south of town); established by artist-writer-naturalist Lisa Salmon, the sanctuary is the home of some 100 species, a number of which arrive to be fed at teatime. Card-carrying members of ornithological organizations are admitted anytime; the public, from 3:30 PM till sundown (admission $3 US for adults, $1.50 US for children, who must be at least four to be allowed in).

Falmouth – This small 18th-century port town on the north coast about 23 miles east of Montego is an interesting destination for a drive. Get an early start and drive straight through, bypassing Rose Hall for the time being. Park on or near Water Square and take half an hour or so to explore on foot: the chartreuse-roofed Albert George Market, Olivier Street (misspelled on the sign, but named for Sir Laurence's uncle), the Courthouse (a reconstruction of the 1817 building), Seaboard Street (where fishermen meet), the Customs Office, the 1796 Parish Church, and William Knibb Memorial Church (the present building at George and King streets is new, but ask about its predecessors' stories). Leaving town, turn south (away from the water); at the town of Martha Brae, the road forks.

If greathouses intrigue you, take the right, then — almost immediately, when the road divides again — the left fork to visit Good Hope, the 18th-century home of one of the wealthiest planters in Jamaican history, John Thorp (or Tharp). The main house and several outbuildings have been impeccably restored; there are stables and trails through the estate's 6,000 acres on which visitors can sometimes arrange to ride. Bearing left at Martha Brae town (following the signs), you arrive at Rafters' Village, where you can follow the 1-hour river raft ride with a dip in the pool, then with lunch in the thatched restaurant (Jamaican food at reasonable cost). Rafting the Martha Brae is such a relaxing experience, you may want to make it the point of a half-day excursion. The 1-hour trip operates daily from 9 AM to 4 PM, and a 2-person raft rents for $26 US.

Before returning to Montego Bay, drive the two miles east of Falmouth on the main road to visit the *Caribatik Island Fabrics* factory (open 10 AM to 3 PM, Tuesdays through Saturdays, closed September 16 to November 15). Established in 1970, the outlet produces fine hand-dyed batik silks and cotton fashions. Nearby, owner Muriel Chandler has an open-air studio with batiks for sale, and a gallery displaying many of her paintings. Just east of *Carabatik,* stop at *Glistening Waters Marina* for a cool drink or some seafood and a look at the beautiful Blue Lagoon. Nighttime boat rides on the lagoon depart the marina's main dock for observing the natural phenomenon of bioluminescence caused by tiny microorganisms that sparkle and glow in the water.

Heading west to Montego Bay once more, retrace your steps to Falmouth, and take the coastal road west. Just across the Trelawny–St. James Parish line, look for a greathouse with a double verandah on the hill to your left; it's Greenwood House, which belonged to members of Elizabeth Barrett Browning's family. Now open to the public (admission $1.50 US), its antiques give a truer picture of plantation life than Rose Hall, the elegantly (some say too elegantly) restored greathouse a bit farther on, once the home of the infamous White Witch. Rose Hall is Jamaica's best-known greathouse, partly due to the psychic hype about its original owner, Anne Palmer, the supposed White Witch who allegedly learned her craft from a Haitian voodoo princess and disposed of husbands and suitors accordingly during the late 18th century. Reportedly haunted, the greathouse has been restored in detail by the current owner, John Rollins, a former lieutenant governor of Delaware. Open daily from 9:30 AM to 5 PM. Admission is $3 US.

North Shore Drive – From Montego to Ocho Rios can be done as a day's excursion (to Dunn's River Falls for lunch and back) or as a link between stays in MoBay and Ocho Rios or Port Antonio. The sea is on your left as you drive, and to your right is Jamaican plantation country, some of it still in sugar cane, some now used as pasture. Detours along any one of a dozen narrow roads will show you antique greathouses and little old settlements (Wright and White's *Exploring Jamaica,* mentioned in *Sources and Resources* below, is an invaluable guide to the architecture and history involved). Going from west to east on the main road (A1), beyond Falmouth, you'll come to:

Duncans – A turn to the left here will take you to Silver Sands, where there's a pretty beach and a resort hotel.

Rio Bueno – A tiny fishing village with old stone houses, a photogenic church, a fort, and Joe James' art gallery (sample pepperpot soup and seafood in his adjoining restaurant). The historian Samuel Eliot Morison believed that Columbus did not find Discovery Bay until his fourth and final voyage but made his 1494 landing in this small horseshoe harbor.

Discovery Bay – A few miles west of Runaway Bay, this site was named before researchers found that Columbus probably first set foot on Jamaican soil in Rio Bueno. Though it is now thought unlikely that Columbus landed here before 1503, the land below these limestone cliffs probably looks much as it did when he first saw it — before imported palm trees became part of the island's landscape. The town itself is now a bauxite center (Kaiser) with a small outdoor museum and craft exhibit.

Runaway Bay – Once considered a touristic satellite of Ocho Rios, it is now a resort in its own right, with one large and several small hotels. Named for escaped slaves who hid in nearby caverns like Runaway Caves, where the tour ($3 US for adults, $1.50 US for children) includes a boat ride on eerie Green Grotto Lake, which lies at the bottom of the caves, about 120 feet beneath the earth's surface.

A mile beyond the ruined church at Priory, the Columbus Monument at the entrance of Seville Estate commemorates the explorer's year-long stay here as well as the nearby site of Sevilla la Nueva, Jamaica's first Spanish settlement. It was founded in 1509 by order of Christopher's son Diego, then the viceroy in Santo Domingo.

St. Ann's Bay – A small, cheerful town of narrow streets and old (but not very remarkable) buildings, it is the birthplace of the early black nationalist leader Marcus Garvey. (Here Route A1 turns south and the shore road becomes A3.) On the left, just east of town, the large field at Drax Hall is the site of regular polo matches.

Dunn's River Falls – The famous, oft-photographed, stair-stepped cascades splash wonderfully down the mountainside on the right, rush under the road, and join the sea by the white sand beach on the left. There are changing facilities, a snack bar, and horseback riding. (Small admission charge; 50¢ per person for the 600-foot climb to the top.) Weekly nighttime feasts are held here (see *Nightlife* below).

Ocho Rios – In spite of extensive recent building, it is still more a rambling resort area than an organized town. In addition to Dunn's River Falls, its chief sites are Fern Gully, 4 miles of shaded road winding down an old riverbed walled by giant ferns, and Shaw Park Gardens, on a hill above town from which there's a spectacular view. Other possibilities: tours of two working plantations, *Brimmer Hall* (bananas and coconuts) and *Prospect* (pimentos, citrus, and cattle); admission to either is $6 US for adults, $3 US for children. *Brimmer Hall* also serves good lunches. Ocho Rios's newest — and Jamaica's grandest — garden is *Carinosa,* a 20-acre complex that opened in 1987. It features over 200 varieties of orchids; fern, cactus, and bromeliad gardens; magnificent waterfalls; and a half-acre walk-in aviary. Open daily 9 to 5. A 1½-hour tour costs $12.50 US for adults, $6 for children.

From Ocho Rios, the North Shore Road wends east through Oracabessa, a small banana port, and Port Maria. Between the two drive slowly so you won't miss the left turn to Firefly Hill, Noel Coward's tiny home high on the hill; the once horrendous road is somewhat smoother. The simplicity of the house and its mementos (his paintings and clothes are just where he left them) is immensely touching; the view is incredible (admission, $1 US). The road briefly takes to the hills in the coconut and banana country beyond; passes Llanrumney Estate, once the property of Henry Morgan, the buccaneer who became lieutenant governor; and is joined by the railroad right of way at Albany. Nearby, you'll also see signs on the road for Marsh Farms, a new 19-acre attraction for horticulture buffs, with one acre of roses, five acres of rare anthuriums, and every kind of indigenous fruit and flower. Open daily (admission $2.50 US). There's a fabulous view of Rio Nuevo from 700 feet, too. Exactly 4 miles beyond, if you watch very closely, you'll see the left-hand turn that leads to Robin's Bay and Strawberry Fields camp resort. The main road continues on to Annotto Bay, meets the shore again, and goes through Buff Bay, Hope Bay, and St. Margaret's Bay, where it crosses the Rio Grande — Jamaica's original rafting river — then into Port Antonio.

Port Antonio – A miniature island port built around two picturebook harbors, it is 67 miles east of Ocho Rios and 134 from Montego Bay. Its quaint buildings extend onto the peninsula between the two harbors and up into the hills behind. It is famous for quiet beauty, deep-sea fishing, and river rafting, which, legend says, Errol Flynn invented as a tourist attraction when he saw the skinny bamboo craft islanders used to ferry bananas down to the port for shipping. Another Flynn landmark is *Navy Island,* in Port Antonio Harbor. Once his private hideaway, this 64-acre retreat now comprises the 15-unit *Admiralty Club* and *Lookback House and Villas,* with a good restaurant, water sports, public beach, and beach bar. It can be reached by ferry ($1.50 US each way) from the Navy Island land base in Port Antonio.

Port Antonio itself boasts two intriguing architectural sites. The first is the Folly, the crumbled ruins of a splendid concrete mansion built on an eastern headland by millionaire Connecticut Yankee Alfred Mitchell in 1906. He lived there until his death in 1912, and in 1938, when sea salt had eaten through its iron reinforcing rods, its fabled roof fell in. The second, the crenellated fantasy castle of the architect Earl Levy, commands the rockbound shoreline east of *Trident.* Neighboring natural wonders include the Blue Hole, a deep lagoon that is both a refuge for relaxation and a place of exquisite beauty. A very good restaurant and water sports concession now enhances its bank, making it a perfect place to spend an entire day. Other attractions are Somerset Falls, in the gorge of the Daniel River above Hope Bay; the Caves of Nonsuch, unique for their fossilized sealife; and the Seven Hills of Athenry, an enormous fruit-growing estate with a spectacular shore view (a tour of the two is $3.50 US for adults, $1.50 US for children). Farther east of Port Antonio lies the 2,000-acre Flynn ranch, where horseback riding can be arranged and Patrice Wymore Flynn, Errol's widow, offers tours when cruise ships are in port (ask at your hotel desk). Reach Falls, at Machioneal, offers a lovely view of what many consider Jamaica's finest waterfalls, but it's a steep climb even for hardy souls.

Kingston – Jamaica's capital is a 2- to 3-hour drive from either Ocho Rios or Port Antonio. While it's true that the city is oriented more toward commerce and government than tourism and that the past unrest has seemed to be centered here, Kingston is also undergoing something of a cultural and architectural renaissance, particularly in New Kingston and close to the harbor, where the new Convention Center and National Gallery have been built. It is the seat of government and a major port, and for the West Indies scholar, Port Royal, its educational institutions, and its museums make it more interesting than in the past. Briefly, here's what's where.

DOWNTOWN

Kingston Crafts Market – On the waterfront. Newly spruced up, with Jamaica's largest single collection of handmade straw and wood items.

National Gallery of Art – A new building near the waterfront. Collections include works (portraits, engravings, maps, etc.) that date back to the 17th century, but most interesting are the dramatic and energetic paintings and sculpture of contemporary Jamaican artists. Small admission charge.

Institute of Jamaica – 12 East St. Founded in 1870 "for the encouragement of literature, science and art," with lending and reference libraries; art, natural history, and history museums. It administers the Jamaica School of Art and museums at Spanish Town and White Marl and is a required stop for any serious research on Jamaica or the rest of the West Indies. Open from 9:30 AM to 5 PM, daily except Sundays (free).

The Parade – Where King and Queen streets meet.

National Heroes Park (formerly George VI Memorial Park) – At the north end of East Street. Once a racecourse, now 74 acres of playing fields, gardens, and memorials to Jamaica's national heroes; with government buildings on its eastern edge.

NORTH AND EAST OF NEW KINGSTON

Devon House – On Hope and Waterloo roads. This is the handsomely restored 19th-century home of George Stiebel, one of the Caribbean's first black millionaires. It boasts several elegant rooms illustrating its period through antique furniture, china, and the like. There are also a pleasant patio bar and a very good Jamaican restaurant that's a popular evening rendezvous spot for Kingstonians. The handsome horseshoe of *Things Jamaican Ltd.* shops that line its garden house the nation's best collection of island-crafted furniture and gifts (see *Shopping*). If you make only one Kingston shopping stop, it should be here.

Bob Marley Museum – Opened in 1986 to mark the fifth anniversary of the death of the reggae legend, this is the stately 19th-century home where Marley lived with his wife, Rita, and their five children. It features the most comprehensive collection of Marley memorabilia anywhere, documenting the life and work of the man whose musical influence was vast. 56 Hope Road. The $1.50 US admission fee includes a tour of the premises.

Jamaica House and Kings House – In a large park where East Kings House Road meets Hope Road, they are the official residences of the prime minister and the governor general (the queen's representative), respectively. Open by appointment only.

Hope Botanical Gardens and Zoo – On Old Hope Road. A small zoo, but the lawns and ornamental gardens are big and beautiful; don't miss the Orchid House.

University of the West Indies – North and south of Old Hope Road and east of the Botanical Gardens. The College of Arts, Science and Technology is adjacent to the gardens; University Hospital and the main campus lie to the south on the site of the old Mona sugar estate. Founded in 1948 as an affiliate of the University of London, the UWI is now independent, supported by British government grants and money from the other West Indian territories represented in its student body.

National Stadium – In Briggs Park, due east of New Kingston on Mountain Road, it was the site of independence ceremonies in August 1962.

ACROSS THE HARBOR

Port Royal – The remains of what was once Jamaica's number one city and the wickedest city on earth, at the tip of the long, skinny, natural breakwater called the Palisadoes. It was the headquarters of Henry Morgan (sometimes called pirate, sometimes — more respectably — privateer) and his Brethren of the Coast; a large chunk of it was toppled into the harbor by an earthquake and subsequent tidal wave in 1692. Surviving are St. Peter's Church, with a communion plate wishfully thought to have been the gift of Morgan; antique, slightly tipsy Fort Charles; and the old Naval Hospital, now an archaelogical museum containing some Port Royal relics recently recovered by divers (the city's submerged sector lies directly offshore). A Committee of Friends and the National Trust are working on plans for new tours, further reconstruction, and expanded attractions. All are open from 9 AM to 5 PM daily; small admission fee. There's also a small, antique pub-style restaurant as well as a full-service bar, restaurant, and small motel at *Morgan's Harbour Marina,* a popular gathering place for local boaters.

WEST OF KINGSTON

Spanish Town – Jamaica's old capital (1534–1872), 14 miles due west of Kingston on Routes A1 (confusingly, there are two leading out of the city). Its chief architectural monument is much-photographed Antique Square, which might have been designed by a Georgian wedding cake baker. The cupolaed monument celebrates Admiral Rodney and his 1782 victory over the French navy near the Îles des Saintes. Though no Spanish buildings remain, the old British House of Assembly, King's House (the governor's residence, now an archeological museum), the Old King's House stables (now the Jamaica People's Museum of Ethnic and Cultural Artifacts), the Cathedral Church of St. James, and a number of other 18th-century buildings still stand. Museums are open from 9 AM to 5 PM weekdays. Guided tours of the old town are available for a nominal fee.

At White Marl, on the way to Spanish Town, there is an Arawak Museum with displays from Jamaica's pre-Columbian past. Open from 10 AM to 5 PM daily (small fee).

■**EXTRA SPECIAL:** Jamaica's *Meet the People Program* puts visitors in touch with Jamaicans who have similar jobs, hobbies, and interests. A call to the Meet the People officer at any Tourist Board Office (in Kingston, phone: 929-9200; in Montego Bay, phone: 952-4425; in Port Antonio, phone: 993-2587/305; in Ocho Rios, phone: 974-2570 or 974-2582; in Negril, phone: 957-4243), giving your name, length of stay, and a date and time when you're available, can result in a shared excursion or a meal or drinks with a Jamaican family. There's no charge, though on an excursion you might want to pick up part of the tab. It's something to do not because you ought to, but because, judging by reports from recent years' thousands of participants, it's not only enlightening but fun.

SOURCES AND RESOURCES

TOURIST INFORMATION: The Jamaican Tourist Board's overseas offices supply brochures, maps, and information free for the asking: 866 Second Ave., New York, NY 10017 (phone: 212-688-7650); 36 S Wabash Ave., Chicago, IL 60603 (phone: 312-346-1546); 1320 S Dixie Hwy., Coral Gables, FL 33146 (phone: 305-665-0557); 3440 Wilshire Blvd., Suite 1207, Los Angeles, CA 90010 (phone: 213-384-1123); 1 Eglinton Ave. E, Suite 616, Toronto, Ont. M4P 3A1 (phone: 416-482-7850); 10 Sherbrooke St., Mezzanine, West Montréal, Qué. H3A 1G9 (phone: 514-849-6388).

The Jamaica Tourist Board's head office is at the Tourism Centre, 21 Dominica Dr., Kingston 5 (phone: 929-9200). There are regional offices in Montego Bay (at Cornwall Beach; phone: 952-4425), Ocho Rios (in the Ocean Village Shopping Centre; phone: 974-2570, 974-2589), Port Antonio (at City Centre; phone: 993-3051), and Negril (in the Plaza de Negril, No. 20; phone: 957-4243). These offices will supply you with maps and brochures and answer your questions about facilities, events, sightseeing, etc.

Local Coverage – The Visitor, published weekly to tell tourists what's going on where, is free at hotels, airports, Tourist Board offices. Also free, the widely distributed Daily Gleaner tourist guide updates shopping, dining, nightlife, every other week.

The local newspapers include the Daily Gleaner, Daily News (published in Kingston), Star, and the weekly Montego Bay Beacon. The New York Times is available at hotel newsstands on the afternoon of the day it comes out. Good locally published guidebooks are Philip Wright and Paul F. White's informative Exploring Jamaica, A Guide for Motorists (paperback, $2.50) and Clinton V. Black's Jamaica Guide.

Telephone – Jamaica now has seven-digit telephone numbers similar to those of the US and Canada. To dial direct, add 809 to the numbers below.

ENTRY REQUIREMENTS: Proof of citizenship (passport, birth certificate, or voter's registration card) and a return or ongoing ticket are the only documents required of US and Canadian citizens for stays of up to six months.

CLIMATE AND CLOTHES: In winter, daytime temperatures range from the high 70s to the mid-80s F (25° to 30°C), and in Kingston, close to 90°F (33°C); but these temperatures are moderated by the prevailing trade winds blowing from the northeast. During October and early November and again in May and early June, there are usually brief showers every day, but the sun returns quickly to dry you off. Lightweight resortwear — slacks, shorts, sport shirts — is right for daytime, plus a jacket or sweater if you're going into the cooler mountains. Short shorts and swimsuits are for beaches, not city streets. Be cautious about sunning, and even when you have a base coat, keep protection (long-sleeved shirt, pants, hat, sunscreen) handy if you're going to be exposed to the sun for a long time — sailing or rafting, for example.

Evening dress varies from barefoot-casual in Negril to quite formal in season in other resort areas, where a few hotels and restaurants still require men to wear jackets and ties at dinner. Summer is less dressed up everywhere except in Negril, where evenings stay very casual; for men, a blazer, a summer sport coat (usually without tie) and slacks or kareebas (Jamaican shirt-jack suits) are acceptable all around. But even in Negril, women often like to put on something long — skirts, pants — for cocktails and dinner.

MONEY: Jamaica's currency is the Jamaican dollar, which has been devalued twice in recent years. Check your bank or travel agent or nearest Jamaica Tourist Board office for current exchange rates before you leave. For the past two years, the Jamaican dollar (JDS) has hovered around $1 JDS to $5.20 US, and it is unlikely that rate will change drastically in either direction. (Unless otherwise noted, all prices are quoted in US dollars.)

Island currency laws now state that visitors pay all island bills in Jamaican dollars, which will require changing US or Canadian dollars to Jamaican on arrival (at the airport exchange bureaus or a bank, *not* on the street) and several times during your stay. Airport exchange bureaus are open to serve all incoming and outgoing flights (arrive early for departure; it is illegal to take Jamaican dollars out of the country). In addition, exchange bureaus offering the same rates as banks are being set up in hotels and on cruise ships. Traveler's checks are generally acceptable, and most hotels and many restaurants and shops honor major credit cards. Remember, also, that Jamaica levies a departure tax of $40 JDS, payable only in JDS, at the airport before leaving the country.

Banking hours are 9:30 AM to 3 PM Mondays through Thursdays; from 9 AM to noon and 2:30 to 5 PM on Fridays; closed weekends and holidays.

LANGUAGE: For three centuries, Jamaica was part of the British Empire, so its language is English. There is also a Jamaican patois, an intriguing British-accented mixture of English, African, and island words and rhythms — plus, some say, a bit of Welsh. The rhythms are as irresistible as the words may be incomprehensible (especially when those conversing do not care to have you comprehend).

TIME: Jamaica operates on Eastern Standard Time year-round, so in Daylight Saving months East Coast cities are 1 hour ahead. When it's noon in New York, it's 11 AM in Kingston.

CURRENT: Electricity varies from hotel to hotel; 110 volts in some, 220 in others. Where it's necessary, most hotels will supply converters or adapters for electric shavers or hair dryers; but check with your travel agent to be sure.

GETTING THERE: With the exceptions noted below, all flights land in both Montego Bay and Kingston. Air Jamaica, the island's national carrier, flies in from New York, Newark, Philadelphia, Baltimore, Atlanta, Tampa, Los Angeles, and Toronto, and during the winter season offers weekly flights from New York to Montego Bay on British Airways Concorde; American, from New York; Eastern from Miami; Air Canada, from Toronto. Eastern flies from Atlanta and Air Canada from Montréal to Montego Bay only. Suncoast Airlines offers regular DC-9 service from Orlando and Ft. Lauderdale, Florida, to Montego Bay and Kingston (phone: 800-331-3509; in Florida, 305-776-1001).

Many cruise ships sailing from Florida and Caribbean ports stop in Kingston, Port Antonio, Ocho Rios, and Montego Bay.

 CALCULATING COSTS: Hotel rates vary widely, depending on location, season, and class of accommodation. The posher Ocho Rios and Montego Bay resorts charge $150 to $200 or more per couple per day during winter, not including meals. In summer, the same resorts will charge around $90 without meals. More modest, yet comfortable, accommodations can be found for as little as $60 to $90 per day for two, European Plan (without meals), in winter and even less in summer. Many hotels that quote basic EP rates also offer MAP for an extra $30 to $40 or so a day per person. Lunch out ranges from about $5 to $10 per person at a moderately priced restaurant to $15 or so at something grander; $15 per person, including a drink and tip, is considered moderate for dinner; at name restaurants and hotels in MoBay, Ocho Rios, and Port Antonio, it runs $30 and up per person.

Ask your travel agent about package plans that include a variety of extras. Also check on the 15 different resorts offering all-inclusive rates that, with the exception of very personal expenses (laundry, phone calls, shopping), cover everything: transfers, all meals, most sports, excursions, entertainment, parties, and — in a couple of cases — even drinks and cigarettes. All of these resorts are between Negril and Oracabessa on Jamaica's north coast, and week-long packages, per person, range from $800 to $1,100 US.

Renting a villa — a Jamaican vacation house — can be economical, especially for a family or group of friends. Jamaica Association of Apartments and Villas (JAVA; 370 Lexington Ave., New York, NY 10017; phone: 212-986-4317) represents more than 265 properties of all sizes and degrees of luxury in a number of locations. Many have their own private swimming pools; most include a staff (maid, cook, gardener). Villas and Apartments Abroad (19 E 49th St., New York, NY 10017; phone: 212-759-1025) also lists a number of Jamaican properties. Prices, usually quoted on a weekly basis, vary widely depending on to size of villa and season; rates for houses with two or more bedrooms range from about $650 to $2,000 in winter, about 25% less in summer.

 GETTING AROUND: Airport Transfers – If transfers are included in your package, you'll be given a voucher with the name of the operator, and a company representative will meet you at the airport. If your arrangements are being made independently (i.e., not as part of a package plan), have your agent reserve transfer space in advance; otherwise you risk being stranded at the airport or having to pay a very high taxi fare. Fares in taxis that hold up to five people run about $5 to $10 from Sangster Airport to Montego Bay hotels; to Ocho Rios hotels, $55 to $65. From Norman Manley International to Kingston area hotels, $10 to $14, and to Port Antonio, $60 to $65 per car.

Taxi – Recommended for short trips between island points. Taxis are readily available at airports and at most resorts, but if you're going to an out-of-the-way spot, like a restaurant in the hills, arrange with the driver to return to pick you up. Some taxis are metered, others are not. The latter, called — rather loftily, the Tourist Board admits — Contract Carriages, have the legally prescribed point-to-point fares posted on the rear of the front seat. But be sure to establish the rate with the driver before you get into his cab; at your hotel, ask the doorman to make the arrangements. From midnight to 5 AM, a 25% surcharge added to the metered or posted figure is frequently negotiable.

Many Jamaican cab drivers also make good guides. Your hotel travel desk will recommend someone qualified and make the arrangements; rates run from about $12.50 to $15 an hour, which is quite economical when the tab is shared by a party of four.

Bus – Offers a good, inexpensive way to get around the Kingston and Montego Bay areas; a free map is available from Jamaica Omnibus Services, 80 King St., Kingston (phone: 922-1100); or ask Tourist Board centers for current routes, rates, and schedules. Bus service on the rest of the island is infrequent and often uncomfortably crowded, not only with people but also with chickens and produce going to market. Unscheduled, but quite frequent, minibus jitneys serving the same routes are easier on the constitution. Still, most visitors rent a car or call a cab.

Car Rental – Good roads make most Jamaican attractions accessible to visiting motorists, so renting a car is a good idea if you like driving and sightseeing at your own pace. But it has become very expensive. There are a couple of dozen agencies on the island, many of which have desks at the Montego Bay and Kingston airports as well as branches throughout the island. The major operators are: *Avis* (phone: Kingston, 926-1560; Kingston airport, 928-6013; Ocho Rios, 974-2641, 974-2057; Montego Bay, 952-4541; Montego Bay airport, 952-4543; Port Antonio, 993-2626); *Budget* (phone: Kingston, 928-4779, 928-4911; Montego Bay, 952-1189, 952-2019); *Dollar* (phone: Kingston, 926-1535; Ocho Rios, 974-2594; Montego Bay, 952-3505); *Hertz* (phone: Kingston, 926-1536; Kingston airport, 928-6028; Ocho Rios, 974-2334, 974-2666, 974-2077; Montego Bay, 952-4471; Montego Bay airport, 952-4472); *National* (phone: Kingston, 926-1620, 926-1621; Montego Bay, 952-2769). *United Car Rentals*, based in Montego Bay, offers very reasonable rates on quality cars (phone: 952-3077 or 952-1781). Major international chains accept bookings through stateside toll-free (800) numbers; be sure to request written confirmation and bring it along.

Although there are some 2,800 rental cars on the island, it's still wise to reserve well ahead because cars can unpredictably turn out to be in short supply from time to time. Depending on the make and size of car, and whether or not you want air conditioning, rates run from about $34 a day plus 30¢ a mile to about $62 plus 37¢ a mile for 1- and 2-day rentals. Unlimited or free mileage allowances apply only to rentals of 3 days or more (from about $145 to $240), in which case you pay for gas at the stiff current price of about $2 an imperial gallon (one fifth larger than the US gallon). There's also a 10% tax on time and mileage charges. Valid US and Canadian driver's licenses are good in Jamaica. Driving is on the left, which most people get used to quite quickly; there's also a dashboard sticker to remind you. *A word of warning:* some Jamaican drivers have their "cowboy" moments; mostly you won't be bothered, but the easiest way to deal with the occasional challenge — at a one-lane bridge, for example — is to yield.

Bike Rental – For the brave, *Montego Bay Bike Rentals* (phone: 952-4984) has a selection of mopeds and Honda scooters; rates begin at about $15 a day, and there is a $100 deposit.

Sightseeing Tours – Tours are run by *Martins Tours* (phone: 926-1260); *Jam Tours* (phone: 952-2887); *Blue Danube Tours* (phone: 952-0886; in New York, 212-490-1890); *Greenlight Tours* (phone: 952-2769); *Sunholiday Tours* (phone: 952-5629/5989); and in Port Antonio, *PATCO Tours* (phone: 993-2667). Prices vary with the operator and route, and can range from $15 for a few hours of around-the-town orientation and shopping to a more comprehensive $25 to $40 daylong trip with a specialty theme (history, nature, sports). The most worthwhile excursions from Montego Bay include the greathouse tour (3 hours); coast tour to Ocho Rios and Dunn's River Falls (7 hours); Negril Beach circle tour (all day). "Up, Up, & Buffet," Hilton High's day tour, includes a tethered hot-air-balloon ride as well as breakfast, a plantation tour, rum drinks and a suckling pig luncheon feast, an optional hike, and a drive home through the Cockpit Country (see your tour desk or phone: 952-3343). From Ocho Rios: plantation tour of Brimmer Hall (3½ hours); inland tour to Kingston and Spanish Town (7 hours). New "Jamaica Grande" tours from Ocho Rios to Port Antonio include several activities and are highly recommended (phone: 974-2779 or 974-2590).

Sea Excursions – Glass-bottom-boat rides are offered by most Ocho Rios hotels at about $5 per person for an hour's trip. Yacht excursions to Dunn's River Falls, with drinks and dancing on the beach, are offered by *Water Sports Enterprises* of Ocho Rios (phone: 953-2502), about $13 per person. Out of Port Antonio, the catamaran *Lady Jamaica* makes hour-long harbor cruises for about $5; 2½-hour cocktail sails for about $10 per person including snacks and drinks. At *Morgan's Harbour* hotel outside Kingston, you can arrange a boat ride to Lime Cay for swimming and/or a picnic for a nominal fee. And from Kingston you can take the ferry to Port Royal; it leaves every 2 hours from the Craft Centre, on the harbor; the 20-minute trip costs about 45¢.

Local Air Service – Air taxis save time and aggravation on long transfer runs — between Kingston or Montego and Ocho Rios or Port Antonio, for example. The surest and least expensive way to use them is to book in advance through your travel agent. Local intraisland service is provided by *Trans Jamaican Airlines,* connecting the various resort centers and providing a bit of island-seeing between points. The Kingston–Montego Bay fare is about $26. A good local charter service, *TIM-AIR,* offers tours and transportation for up to 3 people at $25 to $65 per person. Based in Montego Bay's airport (phone: 952-2516).

Train – A daily diesel still runs between Kingston and Montego Bay; the 4½-hour trip shows you a lot of the country for about $14 per person first class, about $7 coach.

Jamaica now has three sightseeing rail tours, which are popular with visitors to Montego Bay, the departure point. The *Mandeville Rail Tour* departs at 7:30 AM on Thursdays, with one stop at Balacava (where passengers can have dresses and shirts made to order at an open-air market for pickup on the return leg); one at Williamsfield, 2,000 feet above sea level; and another at Mandeville, on the south coast, for a bus tour of the "the most English town in Jamaica," where sightseers can visit private gardens and enjoy an island buffet lunch at the *Astra* hotel. The all-day excursion to the mountain countryside is $35 US per person. The *Catadupa Choo Choo & Village Tour* leaves the city at 8:30 AM on Wednesdays and returns at 2:15 PM. The highlight is a tour of Seaford Town, the island's best-known German descendant community, founded in 1835. Price is $26 US per person. The best-loved Jamaican rail tour is the *Governor's Coach Tour,* on board a train once used by the governor of Jamaica for official travel. The daylong ride chugs 40 miles into the interior for a glimpse of plantations and agricultural areas before stopping at Maggoty for a picnic lunch by the river. A short stop at Catadupa is also included. Price is $32 US per person and reservations are essential; book early — it's very popular (phone: 952-2887). The newest rail tour is the *Appleton Express,* through tiny villages to Ipswich and Cathedral Caves, starting out from Montego Bay. The price, $26 per person, includes lunch, rum punch, entertainment, and a tour of the Appleton Distillery. The activities desk at most hotels should be able to help in booking any of these tours.

River Rafting – An only-in-Jamaica experience, it's best on the Rio Grande, starting at Rafter's Rest in St. Margaret's Bay, 15 minutes west of Port Antonio; but there's a shorter trip available on the Martha Brae River in Falmouth near MoBay. A bamboo raft for two, poled by a skilled raftsman, takes you on a ride through jungles of vines and guango trees (where the blue heron live) down to the sea. Wear a bathing suit and swim from the raft. The leisurely 2½-hour Rio Grande trip is about $28 for two. The shorter Martha Brae trip is about $24 for two. Make arrangements at your hotel tour desk or one of the sightseeing firms listed above.

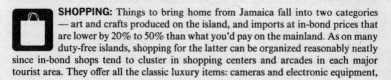 **SHOPPING:** Things to bring home from Jamaica fall into two categories — art and crafts produced on the island, and imports at in-bond prices that are lower by 20% to 50% than what you'd pay on the mainland. As on many duty-free islands, shopping for the latter can be organized reasonably neatly since in-bond shops tend to cluster in shopping centers and arcades in each major tourist area. They offer all the classic luxury items: cameras and electronic equipment,

Swiss watches, gold jewelry, French perfumes, British woolens, liquor, cigarettes, plus fine European crystal, bone china, and porcelain figurines. Stores specialize in different kinds of merchandise, and each has its exclusive brands and patterns, but prices are roughly standard. Shop hours are regular: 8:30 or 9 AM to 5 PM on weekdays, 6 PM on Saturdays.

Procedures are simple: New rules permit visitors (with proof of identity) who pay in US or Canadian dollars (cash, traveler's checks, or a wide range of credit cards) to take with them all in-bond purchases except consumables. Liquor (including Jamaican rums, coffee-flavored Tia Maria, and the unique rum liqueur Rumona), cigarettes, and those good Jamaican cigars (Royal Jamaica is the top brand) must still be picked up at the pier or the airport. But with a firm grasp of US prices to help sort out the real bargains and a shopping list thought out in advance, a morning or an afternoon should be enough to cover all the tempting in-bond buying.

Shopping for island-made things is more serendipitous. The kind and quality of goods vary from area to area, and there are always surprises. The quality of locally produced straw work, baskets, clothing, and wood items has improved tremendously in the past few years, and colorful, attractive, *and* reasonably priced goods are available. Original art by Jamaican artists in a variety of media, Jamaican fashions, and island-mined gemstone jewelry are unique. Craft outlets are everywhere. The cream of the hand-crafted crop — from four-poster beds to figurines, appliquéd quilts to antique spoons — are showcased and sold in the seven *Things Jamaican Ltd.* shops that line the garden of Kingston's Devon House; there are also branch shops at both airports, at Premier Plaza in Kingston and on Sam Sharpe Square in Montego Bay. *Harmony Hall Gallery* in Ocho Rios also offers a good selection of artwork and superior-quality crafts. Less sophisticated handmade items line the stalls in government-sponsored craft markets like those on Harbour Street near Kingston's cruise piers and in the new craft market at Montego Bay, the craft park in the center of Ocho Rios, in sections of town markets like MoBay's on St. James Street or Negril's across the bridge by the Tourist Board offices and the shiny new *Food Fair,* and in Port Antonio at the town market. At all these outdoor sources, asking prices tend to be low and bargaining (or haggling) is okay, even expected.

Straw things — hats, baskets, woven table and beach mats — run the style and workmanship gamut from terrific to tacky. The chic-est show up in boutiques at nonnegotiable fashion prices. But generally, a bit of market-stall research can unearth very similar merchandise for less. If you see something that's almost but not exactly what you want, ask; often the lady in charge will alter to suit or make just what you're looking for at no extra cost.

Carvings — statues, bookends, etc. — of lignum vitae, a rosy native hardwood, present Easter Island profiles in crafts markets and in a concentration of roadside stands along the north shore between Montego Bay and Falmouth. The government has recently backed an educational program designed to improve the breed. *The Native Shop,* in MoBay's Beachview Shopping Plaza, specializes in the works of Lester Clarke and also has hand-turned salad bowls, plates, cups and saucers, masks, and pineapple lamps.

Artwork — especially paintings by contemporary artists determined not to mass-produce wall decorations or tropical clichés — are a source of considerable, justifiable Jamaican pride. Individuality and quality are high; so are prices, but not necessarily out of sight if you find a young artist you like. The most revered names are those of the painters John Dunkley and Henry Daley, both of whom worked in the 1930s and 1940s, and Edna Manley, widow of one former prime minister and mother of another, a major sculptor and a founder of the Jamaica School of Art. More recent are Karl Parboosingh, Carl Abrahams, Eugene Hyde, Albert Huie, Barrington Watson, Ralph Campbell, Rhoda Jackson, and Gloria Escoffery. An excellent place to view some of their works as well as those of undiscovered artists is at *Harmony Hall Gallery,* near Ocho Rios (phone: 974-4222). Bar and restaurant downstairs.

The renowned primitive painter and sculptor Kapo (given name: Mallica Reynolds) lives on Gandhi Road in the Lambs Pen section of Kingston, but, because he devotes much of his time to his calling as a shepherd of the Pocomania religious sect, his works are hard to find except in museums like Kingston's National Gallery, on the waterfront. Other capital places to browse and buy include the *School of Art,* at the Cultural Training Center, Arthur Wint Dr.; and *Bolivar Gallery,* Grove Rd. off Half Way Tree Rd. More conservative, modest-budgeted types will also find old Jamaican prints and maps at the latter two galleries and good color facsimiles of antique Jamaican scenic prints at the kiosk of the *Institute of Jamaica,* 12 East St., Kingston. The *Montego Bay Gallery of West Indian Arts* displays paintings (both Jamaican and Haitian primitives), metal sculpture, prints, antique maps, and carvings.

Furniture of local mahoe wood in simple rustic designs (with woven chair seats and backs) is turned out by the *Society of Friends (Quaker) Workshop* in Highgate, just south of Route A3 between Port Maria and Annotto Bay; and it doesn't cost much to ship home.

Shopping centers and arcades, both downtown and in the hotels, are the places to look for island-designed resort fashions as well as in-bond bargains. Each of the four major tourist areas has its complement. In Montego Bay, there's the *Montego Freeport* area; the *City Centre Arcade,* not far from the Parade; the *Beachview Arcade,* across from Doctor's Cave Beach; the *Holiday Village Shopping Centre,* across from the *Holiday Inn;* and the *Half Moon Club* shopping plaza, just outside the resort. In Ocho Rios, *Pineapple Place,* on the main road about a mile east of town, is an interesting collection of duty-free shops and boutiques, with an adjacent crafts market. A little further east is *Coconut Grove Shopping Centre,* opposite *Plantation Inn; Ocean Village Shopping Centre* — the island's largest — on Ocho Rios Bay, next to *Turtle Beach Towers;* and the *Little Pub Yard,* with a few small shops adjoining the *Little Pub* restaurant. Many Kingston visitors prefer the leisurely atmosphere of the shops around the *New Kingston* hotel to the hubbub of downtown. Weekly newspapers for visitors carry information on the outstanding Kingston boutiques, which are definitely worth the time. The activities desk at most hotels can arrange shopping tours of the capital, including a few hours at the downtown crafts market.

Island fashion designers have erased all trace of loving-hands-at-home amateurishness; their present clothes are clever, stylish, and great fun to wear. Most are made up in colorful fabrics silk-screened on the island. Names to know: *Ruth Clarage,* for day and evening wear in original prints and designs that often make women's shapes look shapelier, with accessories and lighthearted jewelry, too (branches at the Freeport, *Casa Montego, Half Moon Club* shopping plaza, and Holiday Village in Montego; *Pineapple Place* and *Ocean Village* in Ocho Rios; the *New Kingston* in Kingston); *Pineapple Shop,* for island clothes in island prints, ready to wear or custom-made at quite attractive prices, also fabrics by the yard (at the Freeport, *Casa Montego,* and the *Holiday Inn* in Montego Bay); *Elizabeth Jean,* for fresh young things, lots of emphasis on shape (the clothes' and the wearer's) and bared spaces (shoulders, midriffs, necklines), mesh and crochet things too (in Beachview Arcade, Montego Bay); *Daphne Logan Hewitt,* for prize-winning sports clothes, seductive evening stuff (both clingy and loose cuts) at agreeable prices (at the *Pegasus* in Kingston and at branches in North Coast resorts). Resort accessories — hats, bags, sandals, belts, casual jewelry, plus assorted knick-knacks all made in Jamaica: the *Yellow Canary* (Coconut Grove, Ocho Rios). At the *Caribatik* works 2 miles east of Falmouth you can buy men's and women's resortwear, paintings, and wall hangings in rainbow-colored hand-dyed silks and cottons. Gemstone jewelry — coral agate from Jamaican riverbeds, black coral, and other semiprecious finds in original handwrought settings — is the specialty of *Blue Mountain Gems* (in Montego Bay's Holiday Village), where you can watch the polishing and casting.

The best menswear is at Kingston's *Lenny Harris, Lee's Fifth Avenue,* and *Farel* (with branches in Montego Bay and Port Antonio). For custom tailoring, consult *George Washington Hewitt,* 8 St. James St., Montego Bay. Resortwear for men is featured in boutiques in all the larger hotels.

In-bond shops, as noted, have branches all over the island. In alphabetical order, here are some of the best known with their specialties and locations: *Casa de Oro* specializes in perfumes, watches, and fine jewelry (Holiday Village, Montego Bay; Pineapple Place, Ocho Rios); *Chulani Ltd.* focuses on cameras, accessories, electronic equipment by Nikon, Vivitar, Panasonic (*Chulani Camera Centre,* City Centre, Montego Bay); *Caribbean Camera Centre,* Pineapple Place, Ocho Rios; the *Montego Duty Free Shop,* Montego Bay Airport); the seven shops of *L. A. Henriques* feature the best names in bone china (Wedgwood, Royal Worcester, Minton, et al.), crystal (Orrefors, Waterford, and more), figurines (Hummel, Bing & Grøndahl, among them), watches (Cartier, Longines, Pulsar, plus), gold and silver jewelry and precious stones; *Motta's* carries Sony among other electronic names (at 27 King St., the *Jamaica Pegasus* hotel, and the International Airport, Kingston); *Presita* has fine stereo names (like Sansui) and camera equipment at Freeport and City Centre, Montego Bay; and the *Swiss Stores* offer not only famous watches (Patek Philippe, Piaget, Rolex, Omega, Tissot, Juvenia, and more) but exquisitely handcrafted jewelry (at Freeport and *Casa Montego,* Montego Bay; Ocean Village, Ocho Rios; *Jamaica Pegasus* hotel, Kingston International Airport; and corner of Harbour and Church sts., Kingston).

TIPPING: Most Jamaican hotels and restaurants add a service charge of 10%; check to see if it's included in your bill. If not, tip waiters 10% to 15%; leave $1 per person per day for the chambermaid at your hotel. Airport porters and hotel bellboys should be tipped 50¢ per bag. Taxi drivers: 15% of the fare.

SPECIAL EVENTS: Twice a year, the Jamaica Tourist Board publishes a detailed calendar of events, available from their offices in the US and Jamaica. Jonkanoo is a Christmastime celebration throughout the island. Fantastically costumed and masked dancers parade and perform in streets of villages and cities, and there is much feasting and rum punch partying. *Jamaica Bruckins* is a program of events featuring free dances, cultural exhibitions, "native" feasts, and concerts, which runs from May 29 to December 1. Lots of fun for north coast resort visitors. *Jamaican Independence Day* (first Monday in August) celebrates the establishment (on August 6, 1962) of Jamaica as a sovereign country; it's also an occasion for parades, music, dancing, and an arts festival. *Reggae Sunsplash,* a week-long, mid-August music fest in Montego Bay, has been drawing reggae's top artists and huge crowds since 1981. Other holidays, when banks and most stores are closed, are *New Year's Day, Ash Wednesday, Good Friday, Easter Monday, Labour Day* (May 23), *National Heroes Day* (third Monday in October), *Christmas,* and *Boxing Day* (December 26).

SPORTS: With a lot of land and a lot of water surrounding it, Jamaica offers a wide variety of active pastimes, both wet and dry.

Boating – Most beach hotels have Sunfish, Sailfish, and/or windsurfers for rent at $10 per hour. To charter larger boats (and for details on the regattas held during the year), contact the *Royal Jamaica Yacht Club* (phone: 928-6685), the *Montego Bay Yacht Club* (phone: 952-3028), or *Morgan's Harbour Marina,* Port Royal (phone: 924-8464), which also has facilities for visiting yachts.

Cricket – This cousin of US baseball is played on pitches (fields) ranging from exquisitely manicured greens to vacant lots. Cricket is a spectator sport that is also a social event, much like Carnival. For upcoming matches, check with the tourist board of the island you plan to visit or consult the sports section of the island newspaper.

Cycling – Although Jamaican distances and the terrain are daunting except to seasoned bikers, the very active Cycling Association organizes races and tours throughout the year. Check with the local office of the Jamaican Tourist Board for details of activities during your stay. In addition, the moped craze has hit the Montego and Ocho Rios resort areas, and motor scooters are available at some rental agencies (or through your hotel) at about $15 up per day.

Fishing – Both fresh- and saltwater are very popular. Jamaica's rivers yield such freshwater game as mountain mullet, hognose mullet, drummer, and small snook. Deep-sea fishing charters can be arranged through hotels in Port Antonio (one of the outstanding deep-sea fishing centers in the Caribbean), Montego Bay, Ocho Rios, and Kingston. Rates run about $210 for a half day, $420 for a full day, including crew, bait, and tackle. The billfish run through Jamaica's north coast waters year round, although local anglers say September to April is the hottest time for blue marlin. The proximity (and proliferation) of billfish in this area has sparked international attention, and this sport may be Jamaica's next big attraction. Other gamefish include Allison tuna (March–June), wahoo (October–April), kingfish (October–April), dolphin (April–October), bonita and barracuda (September–April). Spearfishing is permitted among the reefs and yields snapper, parrotfish, grouper, mackerel, kingfish, jack, and tarpon.

Each September to October, Jamaica offers three international blue marlin and gamefish tournaments, in Montego Bay, Ocho Rios, and Port Antonio. Foreign anglers are not only welcomed but actively recruited to participate in these events and in the Ocho Rios *Big Game Angling Club*'s Blue Marlin Tournament in May and the *Falmouth Yacht Club*'s Fishing Tournament, held during the annual *Trelawny Carnival*, the third week of May. Exact dates and information are available from all Jamaica Tourist Board offices.

Golf – Over the years, Jamaica has developed some of the Caribbean's most beautiful and challenging courses, and it now offers nine championship links. Jamaica is also an official PGA golf destination, as well as the home of the annual *Mazda Champions Golf Tournament,* held at *Tryall Golf Club* in December. Montego Bay is the place for dedicated golfers to stay; there are four courses in the area, and since it's not necessary to be a guest at a hotel to play its course, you can almost always phone for a starting time that fits your schedule. MoBay courses include the 18-hole layout at *Tryall* (phone: 952-5110), plus *Half Moon* (phone: 953-2560), the *Ironshore Golf Club* (phone: 953-2800), and the *Wyndham Rose Hall Beach* hotel (phone: 953-2650). Elsewhere on the island, there are 18-hole courses at Runaway Bay (for information contact *Jamaica, Jamaica;* phone: 973-2436), where there is also a 9-hole executive course; the *Upton Country Club* above Ocho Rios (phone: 974-2528); and in Kingston, the *Constant Spring Golf Club* (phone: 924-1610) and the *Caymanas Country Club* (no phone); Mandeville has a 9-hole course (*Manchester Golf Club;* phone: 962-2403). Greens fees in winter range from $8 to $15 for 18 holes and $7 to $15 in summer. Fee at *Manchester*'s 9-hole course is about $10 per round. Caddies get about $5 for 9 holes, about $6 to $9 for 18; club rental runs $3 to $10; cart rentals, about $15 to $25 a round.

Hiking – The hills above the resort areas of the north coast are a scenic area for walking tours. An especially popular journey on foot in Ocho Rios is the climb (600 feet) to the top of Dunn's River Falls — do it in your swimsuit; it's a wonderfully damp trip. Serious mountain climbers scale the Blue Mountains in the southeastern part of the island, where the Forest Department manages mountain retreats: Chinchona, Clydesdale Forest Camp, Clydesdale Rest House, and Hollywell Recreation Centre; for information contact the Tourist Board in Kingston. The nature-oriented Jamaica Alternative Tourism, Camping & Hiking Association (JACHA), PO Box 216, Kingston 7 (phone: 927-0657), arranges hiking, climbing, and backpacking tours as well as river canoeing, biking, and low-cost camping and guesthouse accommodations. Special arrangements for the strenuous climb up 7,402-foot Blue Mountain Peak (for Land Rover pickup and a pack mule at the hill station of Whitfield Hall, 7 miles below the peak) can also be made with John Allgrove, 8 Armon Jones Crescent, Kingston 6 (phone: 927-0986 after 5 PM).

Horseback Riding – A beautiful way to explore Jamaica's backcountry of plantation lands and hills, pine forests, shaded streams, and waterfalls. Some stables are open all year; others take summer vacations on a varying schedule; it's best to ask your hotel to set things up. The top outfit is *Chukka Cove Farm* on the old Llandovery estate west of Ocho Rios. A complete equestrian operation (boarding, training, riding, jumping, dressage, and polo instruction), it offers trail, picnic, and moonlight rides at about $10 per person an hour; it also sets up 3- and 5-day Horseman's Holiday packages that include trail and picnic rides, lessons, and bus trips to thoroughbred stud farms. For reservations, write: Box 160, Ocho Rios, St. Ann, Jamaica (phone: 972-2506). Elsewhere, guided rides cost about $10 per person an hour, $15 to $20 for 2 hours. In Montego Bay, *Rocky Point Stables,* just east of the *Half Moon Club* (no phone) offers excellent instruction, as well as beach and trail rides; *White Witch Stables* (phone: 953-2746), near the Rose Hall Great House, offers daily trail rides in the hills. Also try *Good Hope Plantation* (phone: 954-2289); in Ocho Rios, *Prospect Estates* (phone: 974-2058); Negril, *Hedonism II* (phone: 957-4200) or *Horseman Riding Stables* (phone: 957-4474); and Kingston, *Saddle and Polo Club* (no phone). In Port Antonio, riding on the Flynn estate can sometimes be arranged; ask at your hotel.

Horse Racing – Races are run at *Caymanas Race Track,* Kingston, on every other Wednesday, Saturdays, and public holidays. Consult your hotel desk and the newspapers for specific times.

Sailing and Regattas – Every February, March, or April, the *Johnny Walker Cup Miami–Montego Bay Sailing Race* draws some of the sport's top teams from the US, Canada, and England to compete in the grueling contest, which ends at the Montego Bay Yacht Club. The following week is designated *Jamaica Sailing Week,* with a full roster of races, regattas, and parties on the north coast. Call 305 564-5767 or the Jamaica Tourist Board for details.

Scuba and Snorkeling – Reefs, formed of 50 varieties of coral and populated by brightly colored fish, anemones, lavender fans, and other marine flora and fauna, are accessible within 100 yards of the beach at a number of places along the north coast. Farther out — at about 200 yards — are drop-offs to depths where more seasoned divers can venture down in the clear waters to see and photograph larger fish and explore giant sponge forests, caves, and shipwrecks. There is also quite a bit of scuba activity in Kingston Harbour. Dive shops that offer rentals and guided snorkel and scuba trips include Montego Bay — *Sea World* at the *Holiday Inn* (phone: 953-2180), *Cariblue* hotel (953-2250), and *Wyndham Rose Hall Beach* (phone: 953-2650); *Poseidon Nimrod Divers Ltd.* at the *Chalet Caribe* hotel, with a branch in Montego Bay at *Marguerite's by the Sea* (phone: 952-3624); Ocho Rios — *Island Dive Shop* at *Columbus Beach Cottages* (phone: 972-2519), *Caribbean Water Sports* at Runaway Bay's *Club Caribbean* (phone: 973-3507), *Sea and Dive Jamaica* at the *Shaw Park Beach Hotel* (phone: 974-2552) and at Mammee Bay (phone: 972-2162); *Watersport Enterprise* at *Mallard's Beach* resort (phone: 973-3427); *Paul Dadd's Fantasea Divers* at *Sans Souci* (phone: 974-2353); Negril — *Hedonism II Water Sports* (phone: 957-4200), *Negril Scuba Center* at the *Negril Beach Club* (phone: 957-4220), and *Mariner's Diving Resort* (phone: 957-4348); Port Antonio — *Huntress Marine Divers* (phone: 993-3318). Scuba trips cost about $30 (one tank) to $45 (two tanks) including all equipment, $10 less if you bring your own; snorkel trips are $8 to $12. Most of these shops also offer instruction. *See and Dive Jamaica,* for instance, has a full curriculum, from a beginners' course in snorkeling (including mask, fins, snorkel; pool sessions on basic techniques; snorkeling from the beach and from a boat along offshore reefs) for $25 to a 36-hour scuba course of classwork and open-water dives, leading to an NASDS or PADI certification card.

Spectator Sports – Jamaica's British colonial past is evident today in its spectator sports. Cricket is the national pastime, and matches are played from January through August in Sabina Park, Kingston, and other locations throughout the island. The second most popular sport is football (soccer, that is), played in the fall and winter. Polo has over a century of tradition in Jamaica, and matches are played year-round in Kingston (Thursdays and Sundays, Caymanas Park, 7 miles west of the New Kingston area) and at Ocho Rios (Saturdays at Drax Hall, 5 miles west of town).

Surfing – The finest is on the north coast east of Port Antonio, where the longest and best breakers roll into Boston Bay. But it is not yet a commercial, organized activity for visitors.

Swimming and Sunning – Most of Jamaica's best beaches are on the northern coast, from secluded coves to broad stretches of white sand. Your hotel will have its own — or privileges at one nearby — and there are a number of public beaches you can visit, too. Most famous is Doctor's Cave Beach on Montego Bay, the famous 5-acre strand that helped lure the first tourists to this part of the Jamaican world; it has changing rooms and snack bars and has attracted so many people that the Tourist Board decided to expand its facilities by developing 300-yard Cornwall Beach, just east of Doctor's Cave; both charge small entry fees. For beachcombers who want more sand to themselves, Negril, at the western tip of the island, 50 miles from Montego Bay, has 7 shining white miles of it. New resorts are developing in this area, but the beach's northern segment is still far from crowded and worth a special trip. *Hedonism II,* a young, high-energy resort, has nudist beaches onshore and on a small island. The *Admiralty Club* on Navy Island, Port Antonio, has a good beach and a small nude cove; private use for day guests available on request. Jamaica's southern coast has a few good beaches, notably at Hellshire near Kingston and Treasure Beach in St. Elizabeth.

Tennis – Plenty of places to play: The last count listed 66 courts in Montego Bay, 12 in Negril, 30 in Ocho Rios, 5 at Runaway Bay, 4 at Falmouth, 6 at Port Antonio, 14 in Kingston, and 4 in Mandeville — many lighted for cooler nighttime play. Most hotels without courts have access to those of nearby properties; court use is usually free to guests; fees for nonguests run $6 to $8 per court per hour. Many resort hotels have resident pros; a number offer tennis packages that can mean considerable savings if you play a lot. The *Sans Souci* hotel has a special Tennis Week package each January, featuring tournaments, clinics, and celebrity pros. For squash fans, *Half Moon Club* in Montego Bay now also has 4 international-size courts.

Water Skiing – Part of the water sports program at most beach hotels; rates run about $12 per quarter hour. Jet skiing is also now available at Cornwall Beach in Montego Bay and on Turtle Bay in Ocho Rios; rates, about $15 for 30 minutes.

 NIGHTLIFE: At the larger resort hotels, after-dark entertainment is lots like that on most of the islands north of Trinidad. Besides small combos and occasional guitar-carrying calypso singers who provide nightly diversion, at least once a week there's a torchlit, steel-banded, y'all-come show complete with contorted limbo dancers and masochistic types who eat fire and stomp on broken bottles for a living. First-timers wouldn't — and probably shouldn't — miss it; old island hands, who've seen it a dozen times before and realize how far it's removed from authentic island beginnings, make for the nearest sound-shielded bar and wait for the commercialization to go away.

But there is a Jamaican difference. Called Boonoonoonoos — which means something special, a delight, in local patois — it's the name of and theme for a series of summer season (May-December) weekly special events and gala parties uniquely Jamaican in setting, food, and — in the case of the river nights — even transport (by dugout canoe). The drinks are rum-based and free-flowing; the entertainment, less stereotyped and with more folk feeling than most hotel productions. Each island area has its own events, which are included in the price of week-long Boonoonoonoos tour packages or available to guests on an individual basis. (To sweeten things, hotels often give MAP guests a rebate when they book Boonoonoonoos events that include dinner.) In Negril, there's a weekly Jamaica Night with Jamaican food, music, dancing, and entertainment at *Hedonism II.* In Montego Bay, Evenings on the Great River begin with a torchlit canoe ride, end with drinks, dinner, show, and dancing in a re-created Arawak Village (admission: about $25 per person); there are also Friday parties on Cornwall Beach with buffet, open bar, limbo show, and beach games (admission: about $25 per person). In Ocho Rios, there's a feast (roast chicken, suckling pig, and all the fixings) plus music, dancing, and drinks at Dunn's River Falls every Thursday (admission: adults, about $23 per person; children, about $16); and on Sundays, a Night on the White River with canoe ride, open bar, floor show, and starlit dancing (admission: adults, about $25; children, about $16).

Elsewhere, *Rick's* is the literally and figuratively way-out Negril place to be for sunset and after. MoBay's latest-playing, liveliest discos are *Evita's* at *Round Hill Estate,* the *Cave* at the *Seawind Beach, Disco Inferno* at Holiday Village, Rose Hall, *Hell Fire* at the *Wyndham Rose Hall Beach,* and *Thriller* at the *Holiday Inn; Sir Winston's Reggae Club,* on Gloucester Ave. in downtown Montego Bay, features live music several times a week and attracts a good local crowd. Ocho Rios's favorite night places are the *Little Pub* (local music, dancing, late snacks), *Silks* at Shaw Park Beach and the nightclub at the *Club Americana* for disco action; *Footprints* in the Coconut Grove Shopping Center for reggae; and *Mallard's Beach* resort nightclub. Port Antonio isn't the place for nightlife, but *Frenchman's Cove* resort holds a "Jamaica Night" beach party each Saturday. Kingston isn't the city for aimless late-night roving; but there's almost always something happening in the *Wyndham New Kingston's Jonkanoo Lounge* or the *Talk of the Town* at the *Pegasus,* primarily live reggae music and jazz. *Mingles,* at the *Courtleigh* hotel, and *Illusions* in Lane Plaza on South Ave. are other popular spots.

BEST ON THE ISLAND

 CHECKING IN: It's no secret that Jamaica's accommodations are now among the best buys in the Caribbean. Even its seven Elegant Resorts, a new association of the crème de la crème, are surprisingly reasonable for the value and ambience they offer. They include Montego Bay's *Round Hill Estate, Tryall Golf, Beach and Tennis Club,* and *Half Moon Club;* Ocho Rios's *Plantation Inn, Sans Souci Hotel, Club and Spa,* and *Jamaica Inn;* and Port Antonio's *Trident* hotel.

Jamaica's Super Clubs, and other all-inclusive resorts, are cut from *Club Med* cloth and offer outstanding value for weeklong packages — mostly for couples only, but some also for singles and families. These club-style holidays are featured at *Hedonism II, Negril Inn, Sandals, Carlyle on the Bay, Sandals Royal Caribbean* (formerly the *Royal Caribbean* hotel), *Club Paradise, Casa Montego Club,* and the *Jack Tar* villages in Montego Bay and Runaway Bay; *Trelawny Beach* in Falmouth; *Jamaica, Jamaica, Eden II, Club Americana,* and *Couples* near Ocho Rios; and *Boscobel Beach* hotel, east of Ocho Rios.

For those who prefer small, locally run inns, Jamaica's Innside Jamaica packages link major resort areas and include transfers and sightseeing or rental cars at very reasonable rates. The Jamaica Tourist Board publishes a detailed color brochure of 30 inns and small hotels, called *Inns of Jamaica,* available from any tourist board office.

Traveling friends and families benefit from Jamaica's extremely well organized vacation home and apartment rental system. Some 300 properties — most with two to six bedrooms plus a handful of one-bedroom models, with private pools or near the beach — are available for about $400 and up a week in summer, about $650 and up in winter. The price includes staff (a maid-cook, or maid and cook plus houseboy and/or gardener) who'll do grocery shopping, cook, take care of you and the place; rental cars and minibuses can also be reserved. Even paying for food, it's a scheme that cuts costs way down for a group of compatible couples or a family. Good firms to know: JAVA, 370 Lexington Ave., New York, NY 10017 (275 or more listings in all resort areas, including Negril and Port Antonio; phone: 212-986-4317); Villas and Apartments Abroad, 19 E 49th St., New York, NY 10017 (125 select Jamaican properties; phone: 212-759-1025).

Another unique outfit, Jamaica Alternative Tourism, Camping & Hiking Association (JACHA), PO Box 216, Kingston 7 (phone: 927-0657), arranges low-cost camping and informal guesthouse accommodations as well as nature- and outdoor-oriented tours of the island.

The continuing fluctuations of US and Canadian dollars vis-à-vis Jamaican dollars make it difficult to pin down hotel rates. In the listings that follow, hotels classed as expensive ask about $210 US and up for a double room, including breakfasts and dinners in season, about $100 to $120 US and up without meals (EP). Rates at moderate places run about $100 to $170 US for two MAP, about $60 to $110 US EP. They're as little as $45 for two without meals at inexpensive places. Between April 15 and December 15, prices all over the island — including those for villa rentals — drop from 25% to 50%.

NEGRIL

Negril Inn – An intimate and very special new 46-room hotel in the center of Negril's beach, offering privacy, a relaxed atmosphere, lush landscaping, and all-inclusive prices (phone: 957-4209; in the US, 800-221-4588; in New York, 212-355-6605). Expensive.

Hedonism II – Its slogan is "Pleasure comes in many forms," and it attracts pleasure-seeking singles and couples of all ages. There's plenty of action and activity — everything from scuba to horseback riding; toga parties to reggae. On 22 acres, with 280 large, recently refurbished rooms, 6 lighted tennis courts, lots of land and water sports, and a continuous fun-and-games atmosphere. One famous clothing-optional beach and another for regular sunbathing. Rates include all meals, table wine, activities, even cigarettes. On Route A1 about 4 miles north of town (phone: 957-4201, or 800-858-8009). Moderate.

Sundowner – The resort that made Negril a notable resort name. Simple, comfortable, air-conditioned rooms with refrigerators and private patio or balcony overlooking the beach. Highlights include excellent meals served at the waterside dining room. There's a casually convivial crowd. Lots of water sports for the energetic. Parties Wednesdays and Saturdays (phone: 957-4225). Moderate.

T-Water Beach – Informal complex of 60 neatly done air-conditioned rooms and suites on magnificent Long Bay Beach. Snorkeling, scuba, water skiing, boating, windsurfing, deep-sea fishing, parasailing, arranged. Children welcome. With beach bar, restaurant featuring home-style cuisine, evening cocktail bar-disco (phone: 800-654-1592; in New York, 212-519-0634). Moderate.

Charela Inn – Offers 26 neat, nicely appointed rooms with their own sunny slice of beach. Small bar, good French and Jamaican restaurant called *Le Vendome,* informal atmosphere, friendly management. On Route A1 north of town (phone: 957-4277). Moderate to inexpensive.

Negril Beach Club – Beachfront hotel with 75 rooms, including 20 air-conditioned suites with kitchens, some with beach views. Informal, friendly atmosphere, bar and good restaurant, tennis and water sports. The best feature of all: very reasonable rates year-round (phone: 957-4220). Inexpensive.

MONTEGO BAY AREA

Half Moon Club – Luxurious country-club-like 400-acre layout: It offers 18 lighted tennis courts (with resident pro); 18-hole championship golf course and club (see *Eating Out*); full beach facilities for sailing, swimming, water sports (including scuba); big freshwater pool; and 4 squash courts.There's a handsomely expanded new bar/dining/entertainment area. New suites in the main house elegantly done by Earl Levy are choice; ditto spacious, stylishly private Great House apartments, though a long hike from mainhouse doings. Some opulent villa suites have private pools. The weeklong Platinum Plan package is an affordable elegant option. On the shore 7 miles east of Montego Bay (phone: 953-2211). Expensive.

Round Hill – Where every famous name has stayed at one time or another. (The resident piano, for example, has been played by Coward, Porter, Berlin, and Rodgers, among others.) Major renovations have restored the 27 villas and 36-room Pineapple House to their legendary elegance. Its 98 acres include a near-perfect beach, every water sport, 5 tennis courts, and a new pool; riding and *Tryall* golf nearby. Evenings there's dinner dancing, occasional calypso serenades, and lively entertainment in the disco; only on Saturday nights are jacket and tie (or black tie) requested. Choice of rooms in main building or suites in hillside villas (when their owners are away). The hotel and dining room are open only for the winter season, but fully staffed villas are available — with beach facilities, etc. — for weekly rental in summer. No children or singles in February. On a peninsula 8 miles west of town (phone: 952-5150). Expensive.

Tryall Golf, Beach and Tennis Club – This exclusive 2,200-acre resort includes the 153-year-old Great House with 52 rooms, open year-round, and 50 luxury villas with 2, 3, or 4 bedrooms. On a hill overlooking a fine curve of beach, it offers quietly elegant country-estate atmosphere, with a beach club, pool, and perfect terrace for sea and sunset watching. It also has the best golfing — a 6,680-yard championship course, home of the annual Mazda Champions, senior PGA, and LPGA tournament — and 8 tennis courts, with resident pro. No greens fees and free tennis-court time during shoulder seasons. Good food; peaceful nights. Closed summers and early fall. Twelve miles west of town (phone: 800-336-4571; in New York, 212-889-0761). Expensive.

Wyndham Rose Hall – With an 18-hole championship golf course, 6 lighted tennis courts (pro, too), all kinds of beach and watersports, sea, and swimming pools. It has 500 good-looking rooms, 36 suites; appealing to groups, but individuals enjoy it, too. Choice of *Great House Verandah* or exclusive dining at *Ambrosia,* featuring excellent northern Italian cuisine; refined entertainment in the *Palmer Hall Lounge* or late-dancing *Jonkanoo* disco. Nine miles (15 minutes) east of the airport (phone: 953-2650). Expensive.

Sandals Montego Bay – One of the Caribbean's most popular couples-only, all-inclusive resorts, this lively 167-room creation of Gordon ("Butch") Stewart has become the model for other *Sandals,* including one under construction in Negril. Weeklong packages include everything except air fare, long-distance calls, laundry — all sports, meals, wine, drinks, parties (some costumed) every night. With first-rate spa, fitness club. Its huge slice of beach is the largest private stretch of sand in Montego Bay. One of the most popular all-inclusives in the Caribbean. Minimum 1-week stay. To avoid problems created by overbooking, be sure to reconfirm reservations. On the beach, minutes from the airport (phone: 800-327-1991; in Florida, 800-231-1645). Expensive to moderate.

Carlyle on the Bay – Sunny and gracious, offering 52 guest rooms with terraces facing the sea. Handy location near town, small beach across the road plus on-site pool, a clubby pub, pleasant dining room, evening entertainment. Water sports and tours arranged. All-inclusive packages for singles, couples, and families. On Kent Ave. (phone: 952-4140). Moderate.

Club Paradise – A group of Jamaican investors took the old *Chatham Beach* hotel and spent whatever necessary to restore its storybook appearance and charm. It now sports 100 comfortable, renovated rooms; elegant main building, lobby, and dining room; and superb gardens surrounding the tennis court and huge freshwater pool. One of the island's newest one-price resorts; singles, families, and couples are welcome. Within walking distance to downtown shopping and sightseeing; beach access across the road. A good choice for those who want all the amenities included without the push to take part in all activities (phone: 800-221-4588; in New York, 212-355-6605). Moderate.

Jack Tar Village – Another all-inclusive on its own beach in the heart of Montego Bay. An oasis hidden from view behind colorful grounds and freshly painted buildings, it is a good choice for those seeking all-in-one price and activities without being confined to the property — easy walking around Montego Bay from here. Very popular with families as well as couples. Pleasant, friendly staff makes the resort work. Its 128 rooms (including 5 deluxe suites) face the ocean (phone: 800-527-9299; in Dallas, 214-670-9888). Moderate.

Sandals Royal Caribbean – Big sister to the all-inclusive *Sandals,* this 165-room property caters to couples only, with the same array of activities and attractions. Garden setting, with good beach and small private island within swimming distance for nude bathing and evening theme parties — and for the more proper daily afternoon tea. One price covers it all (phone: 953-2231). Moderate.

Seawinds, Montego Freeport – West of Montego Bay, close to the Freeport shopping area, on its own protected leeward beach. High-rise with great views, pool, and tennis. Its 420 rooms are air conditioned and include 115 deluxe suites with kitchenettes. Popular *Caves* disco. Good value and lots of activities, with the beach the main draw. Across from the Montego Bay Yacht Club (phone: 800-327-5767; in New York City, 212-832-2277). Moderate.

Wexford Court – Calling itself "the inn on the park in Montego Bay," this small inn with no beach offers fine value and convenience — near Doctor's Cave Beach and Montego Bay proper. Its 24-hour restaurant ranks among the best small eateries in MoBay, with native dishes a specialty. Nothing fancy, but very affordable and safe (phone: 952-2854 or 952-3679). Moderate to inexpensive.

Richmond Hill – A former mansion with considerable style and grace, best known for top-rated restaurant (see *Eating Out*). The 23 guestrooms are small but impeccably decorated, and there's a big pool, extraordinary view of Montego Bay and the Caribbean, sociable bar. On Richmond Hill above town (phone: 952-3859). Inexpensive.

FALMOUTH

Trelawny Beach – There's a fresh look and friendly spirit about this 350-room (all air conditioned) property and an inclusive activity policy that makes up — to an appreciable extent — for its somewhat isolated location. Tennis clinics and 4 lighted Laykold courts, water sports (including a daily one-tank scuba dive), shuttle bus service to Montego Bay, nightly live entertainment, are all free. With pool, shops, disco, too. Ten minutes from Falmouth town and Martha Brae rafting (phone: 954-2450). Moderate.

RUNAWAY BAY

Jack Tar Village – The smallest of the all-inclusive couples resorts on this island, with only 52 rooms. Specializes in privacy rather than group activities on the beach. Guests are issued a VIP card — their passport to the property. Fine accommodations and superior culinary spreads. The program includes recreation, entertainment, unlimited wine, drinks, all meals, water sports, tennis, and more. For those who want this kind of vacation without the mass-market crowd (phone: 214-670-9888; 800-527-9299 in the US). Moderate.

Jamaica, Jamaica – An exuberant and recently expanded 238-room Super Clubs resort famous for its Jamaican decor and dining; its chefs have won gold medals from the Jamaican Cultural Commission for their innovative cuisine. The emphasis here is on things Jamaican, and the rates cover everything — horse-and-buggy rides, music, parties, a Kit and Caboodle (minimum shirt, shorts, and toothbrush done up in a cotton duffel), all sports (excellent scuba facilities), meals, wine with lunch and dinner, shopping shuttle, cruise, transfers, tax, tips, and entertainment. Minimum 1-week stay; adults (over 16) only (phone: 800-858-8009 or 516-868-6924). Moderate.

Silver Spray Club – Small, very casual, unprogrammed, with 19 cottage rooms right on the beach; pool, too. Continuing program of refurbishing, upgrading. Reputation for congenial company, good food. Some 20-plus miles west of Ocho Rios (phone: 973-3413). Moderate.

OCHO RIOS AREA

Jamaica Inn – Small (45 rooms), classic island inn offering all the gentle luxuries — comfortable rooms, thoughtful service, good food (with an orchestra every evening in winter), and relaxed life on a beautiful private beach. Tennis facilities are around the corner at the *Shaw Park Beach* hotel; riding and golf can be found at Upton Country Club, a short drive away. Lots of repeaters; so book early in season. About 2 miles east of Ocho Rios center (phone: 974-2514 or 800-243-9420; in Connecticut, 203-438-3793). Expensive.

Plantation Inn – One of the island's most inviting, in a lush garden setting overlooking twin crescent beaches. It offers genteel service and 80 lovely rooms with private ocean-view balconies where breakfast is served each morning. The emphasis is on tranquillity and the good resort life, with water sports and good tennis on premises; riding, golf nearby; elegant dining and quiet nightlife. Almost 2 miles east of Ocho Rios center (phone: 974-2501). Expensive.

Sans Souci Hotel, Club and Spa – An absolutely charming and truly classy enclave of 75 freshly and stylishly decorated rooms and suites terraced down a lush, gardened hillside above a small private bay. Most have wide balcony views; all have air conditioning and ceiling fans. Two pools (one freshwater, one fed by a mineral spring), 4 tennis courts, golf privileges; riding and polo arranged. *Charlie's Spa* offers a full range of beauty and body treatments, aerobics, aquacize programs, and Fitness holiday packages that include spa cuisine. Complete water-sports facilities (*Fantasea Divers*) on the beach. Very attractive and unusual *Balloon Bar;* outstanding *Casanova* restaurant (see *Eating Out*). The essence of Jamaican graciousness on the part of the staff; joie de vivre prevails. About 4 miles east of Ocho Rios center (phone: 800-237-3237). Expensive.

Couples – For the past ten years, the old *Tower Isle* hotel, handsomely facelifted and refurbished, has dedicated itself to pleasing twosomes only. Its emphasis on romance and relaxed fun draws lots of repeaters, and there have also been lots of weddings — 320 to date! Weekly rates include everything — room, airport transport, tips, taxes, all meals, all sports (water skiing, kayaking, tennis, horseback riding), entertainment, wine, bar drinks, even cigarettes. There's golf nearby, and a nude beach on a small, private island. In St. Mary, about 5 miles east of Ocho Rios (phone: 974-4271; in the US, 800-858-8009 or 516-868-6924). Expensive to moderate.

Shaw Park Beach – Appealing place with 118 rooms on a lovely slab of pure white sand with a private beach feel; active but not frantic atmosphere. Major renovations have turned this so-so hotel into an affordable upscale resort with fine beach and one of the island's best scuba diving operations. Water sports, tennis; helpful tour desk. After dark: fine dining, entertainment, *Silks* disco for night owls. About 2½ miles east of Ocho Rios center (phone: 974-2552 or 974-2554). Expensive to moderate.

Boscobel Beach – The newest Super Clubs addition is a lively 208-room, all-inclusive resort ideal for families as well as singles and couples. It offers a fine beach and also supervised activities for kids so parents can relax. About 15 minutes east of Ocho Rios, on the site of the former Playboy resort (phone: 800-858-8009 or 516-868-6924).

Club Americana – The old *Americana,* now an all-inclusive Savoy Resorts property on Ocho Rios's famous Mallard's Beach downtown. Recently refurbished, the 325-room high-rise offers good dining, plenty of water sports, tennis, and other activities (phone: 800-223-1588; in New York, 212-661-4540). Moderate.

Eden II – Jamaica's newest Savoy Resorts property, this couples-only slice of all-inclusive paradise has won enthusiastic reviews from guests. The atmosphere is more cheerfully than intimidatingly sexy (brochures notwithstanding). First-rate land and water sports, riding, golf, use of fitness center, aerobics classes, all meals, drinks, cigarettes and cigars, sightseeing, cruises, and theme parties (Champagne Sunday Brunch, Reggae Beach Party, Caribbean Carnival Night) are included in a weekly rate; so are tips, tax, and transfers. Minimum 1-week stay. Couples only (phone: 800-223-1588; in New York, 212-661-4540). Moderate.

Sheraton Mallard's Beach – Newly renovated, and the best of the downtown Ocho Rios offerings. Fine dining in the *Seagull Restaurant;* modest prices and good service in the casual *Garden Terrace.* If you want to be on the main beach strip, this is the hotel to choose: efficient, courteous staff and Sheraton standards (phone: 974-2201). Moderate.

Hibiscus Lodge – Neat little hotel (20 well-kept rooms), very personally, personably run. Limited activities (sunning, swimming, snorkeling from own reef-protected beach), golf privileges at Upton Country Club. But it's near the center of town, within walking distance of restaurants, shopping, making it good headquarters for budget-minded sightseeing holidays. Good home-style Jamaican food (phone: 974-2676). Inexpensive.

PORT ANTONIO

Trident Villas and Hotel – Built in the image of the delightful villa-style resort destroyed by Hurricane Allen, it has all the intimate English country house charm of its predecessor. Its 27 elegant, antique-furnished suites (with indoor-outdoor living room, bedroom, pantry, bath) line the dramatic, wave-dashed shore; peacocks trail across lawns; service is beautifully personal, from breakfast (served on your terrace, one course at a time) on through the day. No set plans, but instant help with any you'd like to make. Oceanfront freshwater pool; small, secluded beach; tennis. Bar and superb dining room in main house; afternoon tea a tradition. Tops in Port Antonio, but very formal after 7 PM. Its 14 acres of splendid landscaping are worth seeing even if you're not luxuriating here. About 3 miles east of town on Route A4 (phone: 993-2602 or 993-2705). Expensive.

Admiralty Club at Navy Island, Port Antonio Harbor – A private 64-acre island, once Errol Flynn's hideaway. A lovely, unspoiled setting with a small 8-slip marina and secluded, sheltered west coast beach, reached by short ferry ride from the Port Antonio marina. Newly renovated, it now has 7 studio cottages and 5 villas (cook/housekeeper optional); attractive nautical decor/native wood main building and waterfront dining rooms with magnificent views of Port Antonio and the Blue Mountains; fine swimming beach and secluded Trembly Knees cove for nude sunbathing; some water sports on premises, others can be arranged; tennis court is planned. The *Tiki Antonio* party boat offers snorkeling cruises and 7-course-dinner cruises. Casual elegance is the resort's theme, and they're working hard to establish it as a haven for frazzled but unpretentious upscale types. Host Harry Eiler is half the charm — a real raconteur who's been part of the island since 1960. A Flynn buff, he's created an Errol Flynn room with posters and memorabilia, and holds Flynn film fests each week for guests. A very unusual island holiday, Crusoe-style (phone: 993-2667, 213-312-3368, or 800-225-3614). Moderate.

Goblin Hill – To the delight of its many long-time guests, this legendary property has reclaimed its original name, after an assortment of monikers. Fresh, airy, 1- and 2-bedroom apartments in 28 townhouse-like villas, it is on the grounds of a former private home on a 700-acre hilltop estate. With tennis courts, pool; snorkeling and swimming at San San Bay; water skiing, scuba, and horseback riding arranged nearby. No dining room or bar, but each apartment has a butler and a maid who shops and cooks; there's also a commissary on the property. One of the island's most gracious and cherished refuges — the essence of the villa vacation lifestyle. Meticulous management makes this a winning buy (phone: 993-3286 or 993-3049). Moderate.

KINGSTON

Jamaica Pegasus – Favored for business stays, its 350 rooms, deluxe suites, and Knutsford Club executive floor rooms are good-sized; room and valet service are prompt and good throughout. The nouvelle cuisine restaurant is attractive, and the pool and pub are popular after-hours meeting places. There is live jazz weekly in the lobby pub and fine dining in the top-floor *Talk of the Town* restaurant. Guests have tennis privileges at the *Liguanea Club* across the road. Trusthouse Forte management. 81 Knutsford Blvd. (phone: 926-3691). Expensive to moderate.

Wyndham New Kingston – Popular with visiting businesspeople, it offers several restaurants (Jamaican, Oriental, Italian) as well as serenely spacious rooms. Amenities include an Olympic-scale pool, lighted tennis courts, health club, library, and lively *Jonkanoo* disco. Guests may choose among cabana, spacious tower, and extra-service Club Floor rooms. 85 Knutsford Blvd. (phone: 926-5430). Expensive to moderate.

Morgan's Harbour – The yacht club–like alternative to downtown Kingston. Life centers on the harborside pool complex; recreational possibilities include swimming, water skiing, scuba, and deep-sea fishing trips. Breezy open-air bar and roof-shaded restaurant have handsome view of Kingston across the bay. Neat but smallish rooms; friendly service. Ten minutes from Norman Manley Airport near Port Royal (phone: 924-8464). Moderate.

Oceana Kingston – An extensively renovated, 200-room hotel, now primarily a business and convention center, in downtown Kingston. Pool, tennis, shops, beauty salon; boating, fishing, and golf arranged. Restaurant and nightclub with live entertainment most nights. King St. on waterfront (phone: 922-0920). Moderate.

Terra Nova – What was once a graceful private home is the heart of it. There are 35 air-conditioned rooms with well-tended gardens, a pool, and a restaurant (see *Eating Out*) that's the particular favorite of government officials and capital society. Nightclub, too. On Waterloo Rd. (phone: 926-2211). Moderate.

MANDEVILLE

Astra – You can cool off at this small inn in the Mandeville hills, 2,000 feet above sea level. The *Zodiac Room* serves excellent Jamaican cuisine in a Caribbean country inn setting. Swimming pool and sauna, tennis and golf available; horseback tours of nearby plantations. Popular with Jamaicans who want to go rural for a weekend (phone: 962-3265). Moderate to inexpensive.

Mandeville – A small, 60-room resort with hints of the Victorian era in its decor, set in tropical gardens. Restaurant and bar follow this motif. Golf privileges at nearby *Manchester Club*. Another cool, country refuge much different from north coast resorts (phone: 962-2420). Inexpensive.

BLACK RIVER

Treasure Beach – A remote 16-cottage/room resort 40 miles south of Montego Bay. It appeals to naturalists — there's nude sunbathing by the pool or on a small beach. Opened in 1987 amid controversy over its outlandish brochure, which attracted lots of attention (from the government, too). Full bar and restaurant on premises; no TV or phones (phone: 305-563-0875). Inexpensive.

 EATING OUT: The trend toward EP (without meals) hotel rates is made infinitely more tempting by some very good Jamaican restaurants, most with menus featuring some island dishes, as well as Continental choices. Jamaican soups are superior — including meaty pepperpot, spicy callaloo, red pea, and pumpkin. The island's most famous concoction is saltfish and ackee — a mixture of cod and a bland local fruit that tastes something like scrambled eggs plus onions, garlic, and peppers. Another traditional dish is jerk pork or jerk chicken — barbecued/smoked, highly seasoned, over pimiento (allspice) wood (especially good at *Pork Pit* in MoBay). Most visitors prefer the spicy Jamaican patties, pastries filled with beef or vegetables; fritters, called stamp & go (codfish) or akkra (vegetable fritters); rice and peas (beans, really) served as a main or side dish, along with christophine, squash, and yams. Roast suckling pig and goat curry are also favorite main dishes; Jamaican mango chutney is fine with the latter and to take home (to keep or give to curry-fancying friends). Native fruits — mango, soursop, pawpaw (papaya), bananas, and the rest — are delicious fresh or made into tarts or ice cream. And when it comes to drinking, Jamaicans are almost as proud of their rich Blue Mountain coffee, first-rate Red Stripe beer, and liqueurs (coffee-flavored Tia Maria, pimiento dram made from allspice berries, and rummy Rumona) as they are of their famous rums.

Food prices — like those for other commodities — are in the process of sorting themselves out after recent devaluations. As closely as we can estimate, inexpensive means up to about $10 US per person for dinner, including tip or service charge and a drink; moderate runs from about $11 to $20 US per person; and expensive, from about $21 US per person and up. Generally lunch prices are lower than those for dinner. As usual, most — but not all — accept credit cards. Reading from west to east, then south, these are choice:

NEGRIL

Club Kokua – Interesting local cuisine and imaginative seafood creations — such as broiled fish in ginger. Famous for Joy's coconut pie. Open for all three meals (phone: 957-4227). Moderate.

Cosmo's – Casual waterside location at eastern end of beach. Soups, fish, lobster, Jamaican dishes, and good cracked conch (phone: 957-4330). Moderate.

Negril Tree House Club – Good island fare, especially lobster. Nice view and live reggae music at sunset. Serves all three meals (phone: 957-4287). Moderate.

Rick's Café – Very casual and all outdoors. Young types staying in nearby cottages, homes, and small hotels head for it as soon as they can get themselves, their bikinis, and paperbacks unpacked. Favorite brunch item: eggs Benedict Caribe — with filet of lobster where the ham or Canadian bacon would usually be; good soups, omelettes too. Sunset is witching (and drinking) hour. Fresh fish and lobster are dinner specialties. Toward the end of the lighthouse road (phone: 957-4335). Moderate.

Le Vendome – In the *Charela Inn,* it features à la carte and 5-course French and West Indian fare, a good wine list, nice atmosphere, and good service; all three meals served (phone: 957-4414). Moderate.

MONTEGO BAY

Diplomat – A superb view, stylish mansion setting and atmosphere account for much of this restaurant's current "in" status. Acceptable international cuisine. On the Queen's Dr. (phone: 952-3353 or 952-3354). Expensive.

Ironshore – Located at the Ironshore Country Club. Chef Bill McCabe (formerly of the *Gold Unicorn* in Mobay) applies his culinary artistry to lunches, dinners, and grand Sunday seafood buffets featuring oysters, escargots, lobster bisque, lobster and shrimp mornay, plus veal, lamb, and chicken. The desserts alone will bring you back (phone: 953-2800). Expensive.

Marguerite's – Romantic seaside setting, attentive service, and reliably fine food make this small, appealing place a repeat favorite with islanders as well as visitors. Lobster dishes, fresh local shrimp, and catch of the day are recommended; good wine list, too. Gloucester St. (phone: 952-4777). Expensive.

Richmond Hill – Romantic hilltop restaurant on terrace and around pool of mansion–turned–small hotel. Splendid view and elegant setting, especially at night under the stars. Excellent lobster, seafood, steaks. On Richmond Hill above town (phone: 952-3859). Expensive.

Calabash – Another spot with a super view and first-rate Jamaican menu; seafood too. Queen's Dr. (phone: 952-3891). Expensive to moderate.

Julia's – Covered outdoor dining area with spectacular view of the surrounding area; excellent Italian menu, with prix fixe that includes soup, pasta, main course, and dessert. Dinner only; reservations recommended. Bogue Hill (phone: 952-1772). Expensive to moderate.

Pier 1 – On the waterfront, a casual but classy gathering place for both the yachting set and businessmen. Great lobster and shrimp creations, soups, and tropical drinks, with a nice view of the marina. Lunch and dinner (phone: 952-2452). Expensive to moderate.

Siam Café – Superb, authentic Thai cuisine and an extensive menu ranging from yum woonsen and gai tom kha to spicy seafood. Diners enjoy a dramatic view of Montego Bay from a hill. A real find, and there's free transporation from hotels. Dinner only (phone: 952-5727). Expensive to moderate.

Town House – Antique colonial atmosphere in the brick-lined basement of a handsomely restored 18th-century home. Cool lunch retreat, quietly stylish at night. Very good soups (pepperpot, pumpkin), stuffed lobster, shrimp or red snapper papillote (baked in paper bag). Church St. (phone: 952-2660). Expensive to moderate.

China Gate – Quite new and already a local favorite for fine, imaginative Chinese cuisine served in huge portions at reasonable prices. Jellyfish and squid as well as more expected ingredients. Excellent wanton soup and other offerings. Good service. 18 East St. (phone: 952-5874). Moderate.

Evita's – On the sea, near Round Hill Estate, with a view of Mobay to the east. Lots of Caribbean flavor, good seafood and Jamaican fare, special dinner/nightclub entertainment packages — a pleasant way to spend the evening (phone: 952-2301). Moderate.

Pelican – For breakfast and lunch, the outside dining area is casual and inexpensive, with local soups and Jamaican dishes a specialty. The new Cascade Dining Room is more formal at night, with exotic lobster and seafood pricier but still reasonable. Gloucester Ave. (phone: 952-3171). Moderate to inexpensive.

Wexford Court Grille – Good local dishes and regular Continental fare in a clean, simple setting with good, 24-hour service. Popular with the local crowd and businessmen at lunch. Gloucester Ave. (phone: 952-2854). Moderate to inexpensive.

Pork Pit – A small open-air gazebo in the heart of Montego Bay's beach strip, off Gloucester Ave., serves the best jerk pork, chicken, and ribs we've found. Well worth finding, if you thrive on spicy local fare. Inexpensive.

Tony's Pizza – A popular newcomer with good, spicy pizza; open very late on weekends for prowlers with appetites, near *Sir Winston's Reggae Club*. In a small trailer on Gloucester Ave. (phone: 952-0346). Inexpensive.

OUTSIDE MONTEGO BAY

Half Moon Club House Grill – One of Jamaica's best, thanks to award-winning chefs trained by Hans Schenk. Gracious garden setting, good service, excellent roast beef, steaks, chops, seafood. *Half Moon Country Club,* Rte. A1 east of town (phone: 953-2228). Expensive.

Glistening Waters – Friendly, informal spot for fresh fish and seafood on the edge of Oyster Bay — brilliantly "phosphorescent" on moonless nights (ask about boat rides). Now the bailiwick of angler and raconteur Pat Hastings and his wife Patty, the kitchen wizard. Great soups, fresh fish, lobster, conch, and Jamaican dishes. Worth the trip from Mobay for a lazy day by the water. Near Falmouth (phone: 954-2338). Inexpensive.

OCHO RIOS

Casanova – Based on the quality of its food and service, this is one of Jamaica's finest restaurants. Executive Chef Deta Plunkett has won many awards in national and Caribbean culinary competitions for her innovative Jamaican cuisine, which relies heavily on seafood. *Sans Souci* hotel, east of town (phone: 974-2324). Expensive.

Moxon's – Romantic candlelit patio dining overlooking the water; small, well-thought-out menu featuring savory soups, pâté maison, fresh fish, lobsters, crisp baby chicken, homemade sweets. Top marks from the rich and famous. Excellent, attentive service under Mr. Reid and "Dixie," the elegant official greeter. A very special, quiet place for dinner only. At Boscobel Lagoon in St. Mary's, 6 miles east of Ocho Rios on Route 3 (phone: 974-3234). Expensive.

Almond Tree – Attractively set out on the *Hibiscus Lodge*'s gingerbread-trimmed back porch. Popular for Jamaican lunch dishes (pepperpot, pumpkin soup, salt fish and ackee, escovitched fish), and delectable island dinners (lobster thermidor and Almond Tree, Jamaican beef tenderloin, are choice). Reservations essential (phone: 974-2813). Expensive to moderate.

Carib Inn – Excellent, imaginative local and seafood dishes in a garden setting. Good service, almost elegant atmosphere. Worth several visits. Open for lunch and dinner. Main St. (phone: 974-2445). Moderate.

The Ruins – Diners drawn by its literally splashy setting in gardens surrounded by waterfalls have a choice of Chinese or Continental entrées (we'd opt for Oriental). The food is unremarkable, but the ambience is fun. Close to the Ocho Rios roundabout (phone: 974-2442). Moderate.

Parkway – Good, simple soups, seafood, and Jamaican dishes in a coffee-shop setting. Fast service, and a break from high prices. Off Main St. (phone: 974-2667). Moderate to inexpensive.

Little Pub – This thatch-topped, casual spot is a good choice for lunch (hamburgers or other snacks) and dinner (Jamaican dishes). It's a popular gathering place; music and dancing most nights. West of the Ocho Rios roundabout (phone: 974-2324). Inexpensive.

PORT ANTONIO

Trident – Very formal dining room (polished woods, gleaming silver, crystal, proper five-course place settings), attended by tuxedoed, white-gloved waiters who, as a matter of course, take their time to serve you. Thanks to new management, Trident once again deserves its top rating. It's a dining experience, both for casual garden luncheons and for prix-fixe formal dinners. Dinner reservations are a must year-round. Men are required to wear jackets at the bar and in the dining room after 7 PM. East of Port Antonio on Route A4 (phone: 993-2602). Very expensive.

Admiralty Club and Marina, Navy Island – A casual, relaxing restaurant overlooking Port Antonio Harbor, it offers good seafood, daily specials, and great atmosphere. Reservations necessary for lunch and dinner; ferry service provided (phone: 993-2667). Moderate.

DeMontevin Lodge – Gingerbread-trimmed family hotel that does delicious Jamaican dinners by appointment. Call a day ahead. Musgrave and George sts. (phone: 993-2604). Moderate.

Bonnie View – Small, cordial hotel with a view; it serves a traditional afternoon tea and informal Jamaican dinners. Bonnie View Rd. above town (phone: 993-2752). Inexpensive.

KINGSTON

Ristorante d'Amore – Kingston's one and only full-scale Italian restaurant perched atop the *Wyndham New Kingston*. The kitchen is quite good, but what matters most here is the atmosphere (elegant) and the nighttime view (dazzling). 85 Knutsford Blvd. (phone: 926-5430). Expensive.

Talk of the Town – Atop the *Jamaica Pegasus* hotel, with a fine view of Kingston at night. Superb Caribbean and Continental cuisines, elegant setting, outstanding lobster and beef. No jeans or tourist garb (phone: 926-3690). Expensive to moderate.

Terra Nova – Another fashionable favorite with Jamaicans as well as visitors. Classic Continental menu, dancing. Waterloo Rd. (phone: 926-2211). Expensive to moderate.

Kohinoor – Over 60 Indian main courses, described in detail on the menu. Simple setting but fine food if you like Indian fare. 11 Holborn Ave. (phone: 926-0301). Moderate.

Korea – A very popular dining spot with locals and visitors who are lucky enough to stray away from the hotels to find it. Excellent cuisine, with emphasis on tempura and ultra-fresh ingredients, especially vegetables. 73 Knutsford Rd. (phone: 926-1428). Moderate.

Orchid – Set in a delightful garden in a clean, quiet area of Kingston. The specialties here are fresh vegetables and fruits, with fresh seafood daily and imaginative vegetarian dishes a refreshing alternative to usual restaurant fare. 3 Waterloo Ave. (phone: 926-8202). Moderate.

Port Royal Grogge Shoppe – Pretty patio at government-owned showplace mansion with attractive shops and an art gallery. Jamaican dishes featured at both lunch and dinner. At *Devon House,* at Hope and Waterloo roads (phone: 926-3580). Moderate.

OUTSIDE KINGSTON

Blue Mountain Inn – With an exceptionally attractive setting in a coffee plantation greathouse on the banks of the Mammee River high in the hills overlooking Kingston, it's always cool outside, cozy in. Delightful French Provincial decor and attentive service are other pluses. *Blue Mountain Inn* features Continental and Caribbean dishes, primarily seafood, and it has an excellent wine cellar. It is well worth the special trip out of Kingston. Jackets for men and reservations are required. Complimentary shuttle service from hotels. Newcastle Road, 20 minutes from downtown (phone: 927-7400). Expensive.

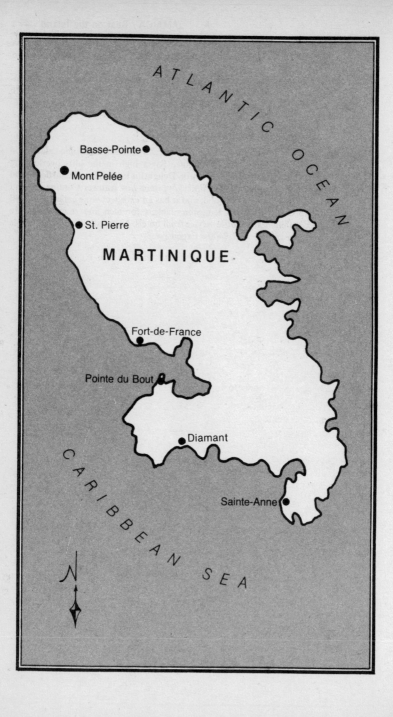

MARTINIQUE

"A bit of France in the Caribbean." As clichés often are, this one is true. Not that Martinique looks a whole lot like *la mère patrie*. Much of it is wild and tropical — a far cry from the temperate coasts of Brittany or the ordered palm gardens of the Côte d'Azur. Fort-de-France, Martinique's principal city and port, reminds some people of Nice, but it is considerably less formal and a third its size. Unlike France's snow-topped Alps, Martinique's mountains are green and jungled to their summits. One of them — Mt. Pelée — is a volcano, alive though dormant; its slumbers are monitored by a team of live-in volcanologists stationed at nearby Morne-des-Cadets. Ferns grow as big as trees in the rain forests where thick stands of pale bamboo and giant breadfruit trees thrive. Fields of shaggy sugar cane roll and shimmer in the sun. There's even a patch of desert in the south. No, Martinique doesn't look at all like France-en-Europe.

But Martinique is France. Politically, it is every bit as much a part of the mother country as if it were grafted onto the Côte d'Azur and surrounded by the Mediterranean instead of the Caribbean. It is neither colony nor possession, but a full-fledged part of France — a *région* whose citizens exercise and enjoy the same rights and privileges accorded French citizens back in Europe. In addition to having their own local government, they vote in French national elections, electing three deputies and two senators to the French parliament. They are eligible for French social security benefits, health programs, and free compulsory education. (The literacy rate in the French West Indies is over 95%.) Few people in Martinique speak of island independence; the majority can't imagine what they would have to gain.

There is a distinctly French feeling about Martinique: something in its air, or, more precisely, *air* — in French the word carries with it intimations of atmosphere, aura, ambience. It's plain to see on shop shelves full of Baccarat crystal, Chanel perfumes, and Hermès scarves. You can smell it outside a *pâtisserie*, where the croissants are only minutes out of the oven and a center counter is stacked with boxed cheeses just off the boat from Marseilles. And it's plainly heard in honking traffic full of Peugeots and buzzing *bicyclettes,* and because French is the official language of the island, in conversations everywhere. Most born Martiniquais speak both true French and Creole — a mélange of French with African words and rhythms — which, to those who speak only English, sounds so much like pure French that it might as well be. On the other hand, if your French is even passing fair, Creole is just different enough to be utterly confusing. But you don't have to be fluent in French to have a good time; in most hotels, shops, and the most popular restaurants, you'll find English-speaking staff. Islanders usually seem more willing to bridge the language gap between your French and their English than are their Parisian compatriots.

Perhaps the special thing that France (Europe) and France (Caribbean) have in common is style. Sit with a morning coffee in Fort-de-France and watch the strollers pass. At the corner, a policeman in a visored pillbox cap sorts out traffic with smartly executed hand and arm signals — very Parisian. Stroll down the block and browse through the boutique of Mouina — the styles are the same as those in the shops of St. Tropez.

But Martinique has its own personality, too. It has its sensuous climate, its lush landscapes. Its people — straight, good-looking, proud — are sometimes slow to smile (they're shy when they don't understand), but dazzling and sincere when at last they do. It has its special music — mazurkas and valses remembered from plantation days, the new, hot sounds of zouk, and the timeless, sexy beguines. (Since no one really knows whether the beguine began here or in Guadeloupe, it's a shared asset.) Its Creole cuisine laces native sea creatures and fruits — lobsterlike langoustes and the freshest fish, bananas, and breadfruit — with feisty spices — garlic, cloves, coriander, turmeric, curry powder, mustard, and fiery peppers, sometimes cooled with fresh lime juice. Its ancestry may be French, but the result is pure Caribbean.

Martinique women — like their sisters in Guadeloupe — wear fetching madras et foulard, an island costume of bright plaid shawls and skirts flounced with eyelet-embroidered petticoats. Matching head scarves are knotted to tell a girl's romantic status and/or attitude: One point means she's free; two, she's engaged ("my heart is given, but you can try"); three, she's married ("my heart is taken"); and four, married, but . . . ("my heart is taken, but I'm still interested"). Young dancers from the Grand Ballet de la Martinique wear abbreviated versions, but you will see the real thing on grandes dames in country towns and at feasts and festivals.

The most festive time of the year is Carnival. Just before Lent, it involves days of parading, masquerading, and celebrating. But before that there are weeks of dancing and gala goings-on to get everyone in condition for the main event. It comes to a wild climax on Ash Wednesday night when Vaval, the spirit of Carnival, is burned in effigy on a giant bonfire off La Savane. Devilish, black-and-white-costumed diablesses (played by both men and women) whirl in frenzied, rum-fueled dances around the pyre, then bear off his coffin for burial. After Martinique, Mardi Gras celebrations elsewhere seem routine.

Martinique's recorded history dates back to 1493, when Columbus discovered the island but for some reason didn't land. When he finally came ashore at Carbet in 1502, he was met by the resident Carib Indians firing volleys of arrows from ambush, so pointedly hostile that he took to his boats again and left the Indians to enjoy the place they called Madinina, "land of flowers."

A century later — in 1635 — a party of Frenchmen led by the nobleman adventurer Pierre Belain d'Esnambuc arrived to claim the island for France and begin permanent settlement. During the eighteenth century, the French-British struggle for the Caribbean reached its height. The ships of Nelson and Rodney ruled the waves, and many neighboring islands — Dominica and St. Lucia, for example — changed flags with confusing frequency. Martinique was more fortunate. The British conquered it in 1762, only to give it up again (along with Guadeloupe and its dependencies) a year later under the 1763 Treaty of Paris in exchange for France's relinquishing her claim to her "snowy acres" in Canada. Martinique has been French ever since.

The story is full of names: Columbus, for a start, and a remarkable Parisian-born deputy from Alsace, Victor Schoelcher, who more than any other individual was instrumental in helping to free the slaves in 1848. His father-figure status is memorialized in the statue of him with a slave child in front of the island's Palais de Justice, a Fort-de-France street, a Fort-de-France suburb, and Fort-de-France's many-splendored library — all named for him. The artist Paul Gauguin lived and painted at Carbet for a period that sounds longer, as tour guides tell it, but actually spanned only four months in 1887.

On the distaff side, there was Françoise d'Aubigné, who spent part of her girlhood at Le Prêcheur and grew up to be Mme de Maintenon, mistress of Louis XIV. Were she to return to Martinique today, Madame's nose would probably be out of joint because nobody talks about her. For most Martiniquais, the local girl who made good was Marie Josephe Rose Tascher de la Pagerie, born near Les Trois-Ilets in 1763. When she grew up, she went to France and married a famous general who became emperor and who made her an empress — just the way a local soothsayer had predicted when Marie Josephe was only eight. Through her, Martinique blood flowed into six ruling houses of Europe. Her birthplace is revered; her statue is on the Savane; her name is on the lips of every tour guide. Napoleon called her Joséphine.

At La Pagerie, where Joséphine was born, you can trace the foundation lines of the family house and sugar factory. Some of its walls and its skinny chimney still stand. In Joséphine's day and until well into the late nineteenth century, Martinique lived on its production of sugar and rum. And it lived well. Elegant plantations with generously proportioned houses, cane-processing factories, and round-towered windmills dotted the country. Except for the steepest mountainsides, the island was quilted with green fields of cane.

It was, agriculturally and intellectually, a cultivated land. In 1902, before the devastating eruption of Mt. Pelée, the city of St. Pierre — the commercial, intellectual, and cultural center of the island — boasted a splendid social life, two cathedrals, and an impressive theater copied from one in Bordeaux. Visitors compared it to Paris. Then Pelée erupted and reduced it all to cinders. Nothing on Martinique has matched its sophistication since.

Sugar — and the rum made from it — is still an important crop on Martinique. But growing it requires hard labor. For this reason and because of the gradual decline in sugar prices, crops have been diversified in recent years. More and more banana plantations and bristly fields of pineapple are appearing. Fishing and livestock remain important sources of food.

And then there's tourism. If there's any Francophile in you, the combination of Gallic culture, gentle climate, and natural beauty will be irresistible. The range of sports facilities is another big plus. They're not Best in Class in any one sport; the island's facilities are designed for enjoyment, not for Olympic training. But they are good — from biking, fishing, golf, tennis, and hiking to boardsailing, water skiing, and scuba diving.

Martinique's tourist people also have a special knack for putting together day-tour itineraries. They start with a choice of historic sites that are interestingly different — St. Pierre, La Pagerie, Diamond Rock, Fonds-St.-Jacques. They add some natural beauty — the rain forest drive along the road called La Trace, views of the rough Atlantic coast. There's always some fun and almost always a lunch to remember and perhaps a beach or a reef to explore.

Guides are attractive and speak English well. Buses are air conditioned. By joining the group and leaving the driving to a friendly tour guide, you can relax, enjoy, and learn something about the country at the same time.

Martinique offers a wide range of accommodations: tout-le-confort hotels with long lists of built-in facilities and a Continental approach; an ebullient *Club Med,* plus an association of small hotels and inns called Relais Créoles, where the atmosphere, nostalgic and personal, is unlike anything else in the Caribbean.

But style, beauty, charm, sports, and atmosphere notwithstanding, can you enjoy Martinique if you don't speak French? That really depends on how you feel about it. In small, out-of-the-way hotels and restaurants, you'd probably have difficulty making yourself understood. You won't be able to walk down the main street of a country town, striking up casual conversations with everyone in sight. One day you might find yourself in front of a shop counter giving your imitation of a waterproof watch (which is what you'd like to buy) for the benefit of a puzzled salesgirl who doesn't speak English. In Fort-de-France, as in Fort Worth, the person you want isn't always there when needed. If such things bother you, cross Martinique off your list.

On the other hand, many members of the staffs of most tourist hotels, popular shops, and restaurants speak fair-to-excellent English. Tours are guided in a choice of English or French. With the help of a good phrase book, a little patience, and a sense of humor, you'll find your room, order a meal, shop the town, see the sights, and even lose your limit at the casino. So if you don't mind asking for menu translations (quite often, they're written in) or occasionally communicating in wigwag or pantomime, and if being someplace that's really different intrigues you, you'll probably have a ball.

MARTINIQUE AT-A-GLANCE

FROM THE AIR: The island of Martinique is 50 miles long and 22 miles wide with a land area of 425 square miles and a population of 350,000. At 14°40′ N latitude, 61° W longitude, it is about halfway down the arc formed by the Windward (eastern) islands of the Lesser (smaller) Antilles. Its nearest neighbors are Dominica (51 miles north), Guadeloupe (121 miles north), and St. Lucia (50 miles south).

Seen from above, Martinique is shaped somewhat like an elongated right-hand mitten with the space between its west coast thumb-and-forefinger edge forming an admirable deepwater harbor. On the tip of the thumb sits Pointe du Bout, the island's principal resort area, with its highest concentration of medium-rise hotels and condominium apartments surrounding a handsome marina. Directly north of the point — a 20-minute ferry ride across the harbor — is Martinique's only real city, its capital and chief commercial port, Fort-de-France (pop. 100,000).

Lamentin International Airport is just inland of the harbor's eastern edge, about 20 minutes from Fort-de-France and about 30 minutes from Pointe du Bout. The 1,965-mile jet flight from New York takes about 4 hours nonstop. Flying time from Miami (about 1,470 miles away) is approximately 3 hours, sometimes nonstop, other times stopping en route, and the 400-mile flight from San Juan takes about 2 hours.

Martinique's east coast, pounded by Atlantic surf, is a combination of rugged shoreline, occasional wave-combed beaches, and a few small fishing towns: Vauclin, François, Le Robert, Tartane (on the jutting peninsula called Presqu'île de la Caravelle, which is mostly nature preserve), Ste. Marie, and Grand-Rivière. The western and southern coasts are washed by the gentler Caribbean. Lining the shore south of Pointe du Bout are some of the best bathing beaches: Anses d'Arlets, Diamant, Plage des Salines, and Ste. Anne.

Much of the northern half of the island is covered with rain forests and tall, green mountains. Most famous of these is Mt. Pelée, the dormant volcano whose 1902 eruption destroyed the city of St. Pierre on the coast of the Caribbean below. Though some of its citizens moved back, St. Pierre never really recovered. As a ghost town, it's one of the island's chief sightseeing destinations. Between it and Fort-de-France, about an hour's drive south, the first-class coast road leads through the fishing villages of Le Carbet (where Columbus landed) and Case-Pilote.

 SPECIAL PLACES: Fort-de-France – Martinique's capital is a small-scale mélange of New Orleans and Nice — with narrow streets and iron grille balconies, blue-capped *flics* (cops) marshaling traffic, and a fleet of trim-hulled yachts riding at anchor in its Baie des Flamands. As far as tourists are concerned, it's where the banks, the shops, and some of the best restaurants are, the place everybody — even the *Club Med*'s stay-at-home GMs — gets to at least once.

The heart of the city is La Savane, the big green park handsomely restored and landscaped with benches, walks, and playing fields as well as a statue of Joséphine that's a good deal kinder to its subject than her two-dimensional portraits. On the park's edge, near the harbor, a new-roofed market shades craftswomen and their stacks of baskets, straw hats, wood carvings, beads, bangles, and shells for sale. Just across the street is the ferry dock, and on the strategic hilltop to the east looms Fort St. Louis. France refuses to relinquish possession of the bastion to the island government, which would like to restore it and open it to the public as a national monument.

Walk west along the Boulevard Alfassa, which follows the harbor's edge, and you'll find the Tourist Office information center and the government-sponsored Caribbean Arts Center, where the work of selected local artisans is displayed and sold. Along the savannah's western edge runs the city's main street, the Rue de la Liberté, lined with les quick-snack vans on the park side and, on the other, with the town's chief commercial hotels — the *Lafayette* and *L'Impératrice* — the frenetic post office, the Musée Départemental, and the city's architectural chef d'oeuvre, La Bibliothèque Schoelcher, imported lock, stock, and trompe l'oeil from Paris after the Exposition of 1889. Installed in a gracefully restored and air-conditioned townhouse, the musée's collections include relics of prehistoric Arawak and Carib civilizations as well as some pretty pieces of antique furniture (small admission fee). Streets leading off Rue de la Liberté to the left (west) shelter Fort-de-France's best-stocked shops and boutiques full of perfumes, crystal, porcelains, handbags, scarves, and other elegant imports — mostly from France, but from Switzerland, Germany, Japan, and the rest of the world as well. One block west on the Rue Schoelcher and opposite its own small square stands the cathédrale — at the height of its considerable pomp during a funeral mass when a purple-plumed hearse awaits outside its doors.

ELSEWHERE ON THE ISLAND
North of Fort-de-France:

St. Pierre – Once the Paris of the West Indies and now its Pompeii, the remains of this city are Martinique's top day-tour destination. Only the ruins of the theater, the cathedral, and the broken gray walls remain of what were once homes, gardens, and stately villas before the eruption of Mt. Pelée in May 1902. A small volcanological museum named for its American founder, Dr. Franck A. Perret, displays pictures and relics — fused coins, a charred sewing machine, petrified spaghetti, a melted bottle with perfume still inside. (Small admission fee.) It's a featured stop on a number of half-day and daylong bus tours (with a lunch stop at *Leyritz Plantation*) departing from Fort-de-France and major tourist hotels. About an hour north of Fort-de-France, it's an easy drive-yourself destination, too.

Balata Church – You can see it from a distance — looking so much like Paris' Sacré-Coeur — perched in the hills above Fort-de-France. Day tours headed for St. Pierre and Leyritz give you a closer look. Or drive up and see for yourself — especially on Sunday, when families promenade in their brightest and best. And don't miss the lovely tropical *Balata Gardens,* open daily from 9 AM to 5 PM. A 15-minute drive from Fort-de-France on La Trace Road (phone: 72-58-82).

Carbet – Columbus landed here in 1502; Gauguin lived here for four months in 1887. Today it's a small fishing village with a very photogenic shoreline and Martinique's only truly Olympic-size swimming pool terraced into the hills (open to the public, small fee). There's also a little Gauguin museum (small fee).

Fonds-St.-Jacques – An antique settlement in the hills above the Atlantic where the Dominican missionary, Père Labat, established a community in 1658. (He is also the self-proclaimed hero of *Voyages to the American Islands,* a personal report of his travels which could be considered the first Caribbean guidebook.) The chapel, rebuilt in 1769, still stands, as do the partially restored buildings of the sugar estate incorporated into the complex. Most impressive: the vast purgerie — the room where sugar was dried — with its great, arched, beamed ceiling. (A stop on the all-day Leyritz tour.)

La Trace – A mountain road through Martinique's rain forest country, it scales the heights from Fort-de-France to towering Morne Rouge. Great views.

Leyritz – Family name, now place name, of the best-restored plantation on the island. Now an inn, a restaurant, a working banana concern, and doll museum housing miniatures of celebrated women, each doll made of plant materials. Open daily from 8 AM to 6 PM (small fee includes admission to Leyritz gardens and main house). Destination of some day tours; swim-and-lunch stop on others. (See *Best on the Island* for more about its rooms, food, and spa facilities.)

South and east of Fort-de-France:

La Pagerie – A ruin evoking another kind of life. Its crumbled stones outline the plantation house, the sugar factory with its tall chimney, and the grounds that Marie Josephe Rose Tascher de la Pagerie called home. The cottage that was the plantation kitchen is now a museum dedicated to the girl called Joséphine by Napoleon. Inside are paintings, a white net stocking (monogrammed and mended), and other bits of clothing, Joséphine's childhood bed, a smoldering love letter from Napoleon (with an English translation) worth the trip for itself. These and other relics were devotedly assembled by Dr. Robert Rose-Rosette, who also cleared the land, built himself a retirement home next door, and added a small museum devoted to the casava in 1983. Although he is now partly retired, consider yourself lucky if he's on hand. When he tells her story in his excellent, if reticent, French-accented English, you half expect the young Joséphine to come strolling around the corner of the cottage. Some southbound tours combine this with a beach outing and lunch at Le Diamant. If you're staying at Pointe du Bout, it's a reasonable destination for a moped picnic or stop on the way to the Trois-Ilets golf course. (Small admission fee, refreshment kiosk; closed Mondays.)

Diamond Rock – Looming out of the Caribbean off the south-coast beach at Le Diamant, it is the only rock ever commissioned as a ship in the British navy. For 18 months between 1804 and 1805, it was — officially — the HMS *Diamond Rock,* manned by the British and bombarded by the French, who were in firm possession of the rest of Martinique. The siege failed miserably until the French smuggled some rum within striking distance of the British, then landed on, and retook, the rock while its crew was still under the influence.

Savane des Petrifications – An almost-desert near Ste. Anne, it is strewn with volcanic boulders, some petrified branches, and assorted cacti. Curious, but scarcely compelling. If you're in the neighborhood, you might have a look.

Presqu'île de la Caravelle – Embellished with the antique ruins of Dubuc Castle, this peninsula juts dramatically into the Atlantic. A nature preserve with recommended campsites, it's part of the big Parc Naturel, which also encompasses the tropical mountains in the north and the highlands as far south as Les Salines.

■**EXTRA SPECIAL:** Camera angles. Bring a full supply of film with you; although shops in Fort-de-France and the sundries store in Pointe du Bout have stocks, prices are higher than they are in the US. Try to avoid shooting in the midday sun; it produces high-contrast shadows and light-bleached scenery. In general, Atlantic (east) coast sites get the best morning light; those on the Caribbean (west and south), the best afternoon sun. Exceptions: Fort-de-France's Joséphine statue, best as a morning subject because, though close to the Caribbean, she faces east with her back to the afternoon sun; also, most churches, traditionally laid out with altars east, doors west, present their best façades in afternoon light. And a note on etiquette: French West Indians pose happily only when they consider themselves properly dressed for it. Ask before you shoot. The likely answer is no when they're doing the laundry down by the river; yes when they're togged out for Sunday church or a special feast day.

Grouped by locale and/or category, here's our choice of the best subjects:

Fort-de-France: La Savane (Joséphine's statue, the open-air craft and food markets, soccer games, snack vans); La Bibliothèque Schoelcher, the cathédrale, yachts in the bay.

St. Pierre: If its top is not capped in clouds, the best place to photograph Mt. Pelée is from the road just before you reach town. In town, there is the theater, the dungeon where the prisoner Siparis survived, vine-draped ruins closer to the water. No photos in the museum.

La Pagerie: The kitchen-turned-museum with its tiled roof and festoons of bougainvillea; the chimneyed ruins of the sugar factory; two great tulip trees suitable for framing. All best lit before noon.

Seaports and Shorelines: The villages and dramatic coasts near Grand-Rivière, Le Robert, François, and Vauclin on the Atlantic. On the Caribbean, there's Le Carbet, with its beached fishing boats — called *gommiers,* they are painted in crayon-bright colors with stenciled French names — blue fishnets, and green mountain backdrops. There are also Bellefontaine, Le Diamant Beach, Diamond Rock, and the hamlet and shore near Ste. Anne.

The Rain Forest: From overlooks along La Trace, you can get close-ups and panoramas of tropical flowers, plumed bamboo, baby ferns, and deep green valleys. But the route is twisty, its curves sharp. Pick your spot carefully, and pull all the way off the road. Or stop at the beautiful *Balata Gardens,* which look out onto the Carbet Peaks and Fort-de-France Bay.

Churches: Among the most picturesque are the ones at Marin, Les Trois-Ilets, Fond-Lahaye, Schoelcher (an old Benedictine monastery), and Case-Pilote on the Caribbean side; at Balata and St. Joseph in the hills above Fort-de-France; at Macouba (with cemetery) and Fonds-St.-Jacques overlooking the Atlantic.

Other Antique Buildings: In the north, *Leyritz Plantation* with its restored main house, outbuildings, slave quarters, and gardens. Also, the 18th-century homestead at Plantation Pecoul near Basse-Pointe, and the unreconstructed Gaoule House near Le Diamant.

SOURCES AND RESOURCES

TOURIST INFORMATION: The French West Indies Tourist Board is located at 610 Fifth Ave., New York, NY 10020 (212 757-1125). There are French Government Tourist Offices located in the following North American cities:

Beverly Hills: 9401 Wilshire Blvd., Beverly Hills, CA 90212 (213-272-2661)
Chicago: 645 N Michigan Ave., Suite 430, Chicago, IL 60611 (phone: 312-337-6301
Dallas: 103 World Trade Center, Dallas, TX 75258 (phone: 214-742-7011)
Montréal: 1981 Ave. McGill College, Suite 490, Montréal, Que. H3A 2W9 (phone: 514-288-4264)
San Francisco: 1 Halladie Plaza, Suite 250, San Francisco, CA 94102 (phone: 415-986-4161)
Toronto: 1 Dundas St. W, Suite 2405, Toronto, Ont. M5G 1Z3 (phone: 416-593-4717)

In Martinique, the Tourist Office information center on Blvd. Alfassa along the waterfront in Fort-de-France is open from 7:30 AM to 12:30 PM and 2:30 to 5:30 PM Mondays through Thursdays (5:00 PM on Fridays), 8 AM to noon on Saturdays (phone: 63-79-60). The Tourist Office's airport information desk is open until after the last flight of the day arrives to answer questions and advise visitors.

For background: The deluxe picture book — one of a number for sale locally — called *Martinique* (Editions J. Delmas, about $19) is worth having for its short, readable essays by local experts on island history and culture, as well as for its dramatic photographs. *The Day the World Ended* by Gordon Thomas and Max Morgan Witts (Stein & Day; about $10) is a novel based on the eruption of Mt. Pélee in 1902.

Local Coverage – *Ici Martinique,* published seasonally by the Tourist Office and available free at the airport, hotels, and the Fort-de-France center, gives up-to-date data on hotel facilities, sightseeing, restaurants, shopping, and entertainment, and includes a map of Fort-de-France as well as briefings on culture and history. The Tourist Office also publishes monthly a helpful bilingual newspaper called *Bienvenue en Martinique.* Privately published *Choubouloute* — also free — digests much of the same material and includes a clear color map of the island.

The daily French-language newspaper, *France-Antilles,* is well written, carries easily understood (even without French) entertainment ads. Parisian papers flown in from France — including the English-language *International Herald Tribune* — arrive on the island the day after publication.

Hotel bulletin boards often carry descriptions and schedules of special tour offerings (scuba trips, cocktail sails, etc.) that depart from the hotel.

Telephone – Dial direct to Martinique by adding the international access code 011 and the prefix 596 to the numbers given below.

ENTRY REQUIREMENTS: In addition to an ongoing plane or boat ticket, proof of citizenship in the form of a valid passport, a passport expired not more than 5 years, a voter's registration certificate, or birth certificate with raised seal plus a government ID card, or similar document, *with* photograph, is required for stays of up to 3 months and a visa for visits longer than that. US and Canadian citizens need no smallpox vaccination certificates. (*Note:* Casinos require some form of identification that includes a photograph.)

CLIMATE AND CLOTHES: The average year-round temperature is 79°F (27°C). The weather is tropical and tends to be humid at sea level during the day, but can be 5° to 10°F cooler — and breezy — in the hills. Even summer days are tempered by trade winds; expect high 60s or low 70s (15° to 23°C) at night. November through April are the driest months; July to November, the wettest; but it doesn't rain every day even in the wet season, and more than a few dry days have a shower or two — especially in the rain forest areas around Morne-Rouge and La Trace. Most large tourist hotels are air conditioned, but some are not — especially smaller ones in the relais or pension category.

For daytime, it's lightweight sportsclothes, bikinis or monokinis (female) and bikini trunks (male) on the beach — if you're in shape for it. Caftans and djellabas make popular beach robes for both men and women. If you aren't already suited out, shop hotel or Fort-de-France boutiques for the latest French beach togs. For touring and town shopping, slacks and tops, cool cotton dresses or separates for women; slacks and knit or cotton-blend sport shirts for men. Nights are dressier — especially in season. For women, that could mean a long skirt or dress, fancy pants and top, or evening pajamas; for men, an open-necked shirt (long sleeves look dressier) and slacks, maybe with an ascot, if you're headed for the casino. Jacket and tie are seldom, if ever, required. Women find light sweaters, shawls, or stoles comfortable on breezy nights and in air-conditioned restaurants and discos.

MONEY: Martinique's official currency is the French franc, whose day-to-day dollar value is quoted in the business sections of major metropolitan US newspapers. But the most productive way to carry money is in dollar-denomination traveler's checks — both because they are safe and because a number of tourist-oriented shops offer an additional 20% discount when shoppers use them to pay for purchases; acceptable (to the individual store) credit cards earn the same discount, but cash dollars, while accepted at most shops, do not.

Francs are best for restaurant meals, taxi fares, and other day-to-day expenses, so convert traveler's checks in lots that will cover expenditures for two or three days at a time — always remembering to keep your traveler's check shopping fund aside. Then, when you shop, group your purchases and pay for as many as you can at one time to get maximum mileage from each check you spend, because the dollars you get in change don't earn the discount.

Banks (at the airport and in Fort-de-France) offer the best rate of exchange. Hours are 8 AM to 4:30 PM, but they close for lunch between noon and 2:30 and in the afternoon preceding a public holiday. If you miss a bank, hotels will normally cash traveler's checks at a slightly lower francs-per-dollar rate. French francs can be reconverted to dollars only at the banks (including the one at the airport) where they were originally converted or at banks in the US and Canada — not at hotels. So use the airport bank if you can, and allow enough time to reconvert leftover francs at the airport before you leave. Your home bank will charge an unconscionable amount for the reconversion service, and US banks will exchange paper bills only, so spend any leftover coins on airport candy, postcards, stamps, cigarettes, whatever. Or think of them as souvenirs.

LANGUAGE: Many employees at major tourist hotels and popular shops speak English, but country people are less likely to. The true language of the island is French, supplemented by Creole patois. If you're not fluent in French, carry a dictionary or phrase book. One organized by situation or activity (dining, shopping, sports, etc.) is handier than one arranged alphabetically. When in doubt, smile and speak slowly.

TIME: Martinique time is one hour later than Eastern Standard Time. When it's 7 PM EST in New York, it's 8 PM in Martinique. When New York is on Daylight Saving Time, the Martinique hour is the same.

 CURRENT: Local electricity is 220 volts AC, 50 cycles, so you'll need a converter and an adapter. Several large hotels lend them; but if an electric hair dryer, razor, toothbrush, or travel iron is essential to your happiness, better bring your own.

 GETTING THERE: American Airlines and American Eagle offer jet service from New York and other North American cities via San Juan, sometimes on through flights via Guadeloupe. Eastern flies in from Miami nonstop as well as via St. Croix and Guadeloupe. Air Canada jets in from Montréal and Toronto via Guadeloupe. Air France makes the flight from Miami twice a week via Guadeloupe and four times a week from San Juan via Guadeloupe, plus a number of flights from Europe.

LIAT provides air links between Martinique and a dozen neighbor islands. For *Club Med* guests, there are weekly OTC flights (one-stop tour charters) departing from US cities. A revived Air Martinique flies to and from St. Lucia, St. Vincent, Mustique, and Union Island in the Grenadines as well as to Dominica, St. Martin, Barbados, and Trinidad.

Fort-de-France is Martinique's major cruise port, and the Tourist Office provides a full range of assistance for visiting passengers.

 CALCULATING COSTS: Winter hotel rates range from about $75 a day for a double room for two (with breakfast) in a small, spotless hotel on the beach to $200 and up for two (with breakfast) at a top-of-the-line four-star (according to the French government's official rating system) resort. As a rule, hotel room rates quoted in dollars are guaranteed for the whole season — winter or summer — whatever the franc's fluctuations. The Modified American Plan rate (MAP, also called demi-pension), including Continental breakfast and dinner, runs about $25 more per person than the European Plan (EP, without meals) rate. Several hotels offer an FAP plan that includes a full American breakfast. Restaurant dinners run from about $15 per person for a three- or four-course meal, including an aperitif, at a plain but good Creole place to an average of about $20 per person for a prix fixe menu including wine or $30 per person for a 5-course menu without wine.

Between April 15 and December 15, summer hotel rates, about 25% to 35% below winter highs, are in effect. This is also the season for the best bargains in package trips which combine hotel stay, breakfasts, activities, and special features at a single price tag that is usually less than the sum of its component features bought separately. Booking a Fête Française package also entitles you to a lowered tour-basing air fare. Ask your travel agent.

 GETTING AROUND: Taxi – Travel by taxi is expensive. The fare from Lamentin Airport, where all international flights land, to Pointe du Bout hotels is about $25 during the day, about $35 at night for two people and their luggage. From Fort-de-France to Pointe du Bout, the day fare is $30; the night drive, $40.

Bus – If you feel adventurous and want to get from here to there for the lowest possible fare, investigate point-to-point buses (of which there are a few) and collective taxis, or CTs (of which there are many). The latter are eight-seat limos or vans that provide most of Martinique's public transport for rates that run from less than $1 to about $5 or so, depending on the distance. Fort-de-France departure point for most CTs is Pointe Simon on the waterfront. They operate from early morning until around 6 PM. To travel on them confidently, you should be able to speak a little French or know exactly where you want to go. Check with the Office of Tourism, a short distance from Pointe Simon on the waterfront Boulevard Alfassa, for schedules, drivers' names, approximate fare to your destination.

Car Rental – Easy to arrange, and rates aren't exorbitant: from about $20 a day plus 25¢ a kilometer for a Toyota or the smallest Renault to about $50 a day for an air-conditioned automatic-shift Peugeot. Cars average 21 to 23 miles per gallon. Renter pays for gas, insurance, and 14% local tax; unless you have a credit card, you will also have to put down a cash deposit of about $300 to $350. Most economical are weekly rentals on which there are discounts of 10%. Many companies offer a choice of day rate plus mileage or unlimited-mileage rate — whichever computes more favorably for the renter at turn-in time. Your own valid driver's license is good in Martinique for up to 20 days; if you stay longer, you'll need an international driver's permit, obtainable from a local American Automobile Association chapter for about $3 before you leave home (you don't have to be a member for the service). Minimum renter age is 21 to 25, depending on the insurance waiver of the company renting the car; and you must also have had at least one year's experience as a licensed driver. *Avis, Budget, Dollar, Europcar, Hertz,* and *InterRent* all have Martinique branches with whom you can make advance reservations, or arrange rentals at the airport or through your hotel travel desk after you arrive. Local firms include *Tropicar, Madinina, Pop's Car,* and *Safari-Car;* their rates are slightly lower than the internationals' (by about $3 to $5 a day), but sometimes they operate on a strictly cash basis; if you have a major or car-rental-company credit card, the saving is probably not worth the hassle.

The Tourist Office has outlined six self-guided tours that incorporate scenic views, historic sites, beaches, and other attractions that take a half to a full day to cover. (Driving is on the right side of the road; Martinique has more than 175 miles of well-paved but sometimes zigzagging main roads.) Following these itineraries is a good way to see the island if you really enjoy driving and feel better poking around at your own pace. But if strange, sometimes steep and curving roads make you nervous, opt for the bus.

Sightseeing Taxi Tours – Reasonable when several passengers share the ride and split the cost. Classic examples: a half-day trip from Fort-de-France to Les Trois-Îlets and Le Diamant beach (about $50) or to St. Pierre via the Caribbean coast, then on to Morne-Rouge and La Trace (about $60). Divided among four passengers, that's a good buy. Drivers speak some English, but if you want to be sure to recognize what you're seeing, take along your own good map and a sightseeing guide. And be sure the cost of the ride is agreed upon before you start.

Sightseeing Bus Tours – Neatly and efficiently organized. Local bus operators offer day and half-day tours along five key routes, each of which combines historical sites, scenery, and — often — a sample of good Creole cooking. The blends are interesting enough to tempt even avowed nonsightseers into signing on for a look around. The standard itineraries (with departures from La Savane in Fort-de-France and some tourist hotels): north to St. Pierre or *Leyritz Plantation* or a combination of the two; east to the Atlantic Coast; south to the village of Ste. Anne and the beach at Les Salines, or to La Pagerie and Le Diamant with its white sand beach and landmark rock. Among the best operators: *Carib Tours* of Pointe du Bout (phone: 66-02-56) and *Roger Albert Voyages* of Fort-de-France (phone: 71-44-44). To book a tour, ask your travel agent, hotel, or the Tourist Office.

Ferry Service – Runs from early morning until after midnight between Fort-de-France and Pointe du Bout, where a number of the best-known tourist hotels are; fare is about $1.50 one way, about $2 round-trip. Fort-de-France is linked with Anse Mitan and Anse à l'Ane from morning until late afternoon.

Sea Excursions – Gérard Voisin runs 45-minute underwater aquascope tours to

Anse Mitan to explore the coral formations and marine life. Trips leave from the Pointe du Bout and are about $12 per person. Bernard Taillefer's one-hour aquascope excursions leave from Ste. Anne between 9 AM and 4 PM (about $15 for adults, half-price for children). Full-day trips, including lunch, aboard a catamaran or a converted tuna boat from Pointe du Bout are $30. Sunset and evening cruises can also be arranged. The *Captain Cap* sails from the *Méridien* and *La Batelière* hotel casino. Ask your travel agent, your hotel, or the Tourist Office for details.

Local Air Services – For sightseeing or excursions to St. Lucia, St. Vincent, Dominica, and nearby islands, contact LIAT, Air Royal, or Air Martinique at the airport.

Through *Aero-Club de la Martinique* and Les Ailes de la Martinique at Lamentin you can rent a two- or four-seater Cessna, Beechcraft, or Cherokee, with or without pilot, by the day or the hour. To fly your own, you must obtain the French equivalent of your own back-home license by showing your valid license at the CAB at the airport.

SHOPPING: Clearly the brightest bargains around are French imports — Lalique crystal, Limoges dinnerware, fashions and fragrances from the best-known Paris houses — all at prices some 25% to 40% below US, as well as an additional 20% discount if you pay in traveler's checks (*Roger Albert* also extends the extra discount to purchases made with major credit cards). The bottom line: prices so low they not only beat those in many of the world's so-called free ports, but those in the boutiques of the French capital as well. Selections of made-in-France cosmetics — Dior, Lanvin, Orlane, etc. — are wider, better, and cheaper in Fort-de-France than any place else this side of the Faubourg-St. Honoré. Other finds include French foods (truffled pâtés, quail eggs, moutardes), kitchen gadgets (graters, food mills, crêpe pans), imported liqueurs and brandies. Martinique's own favorite rum comes in shades from *Vieux Acajou* (dark, mellow Old Mahogany) to *Jeune Acajou* (newer, paler Young Mahogany) to clear white (fiery, 100 proof). The connoisseurs' buy: deep brown, liqueurlike, 12-year-old rums bottled by two companies, *Bally* and *Clément*.

On the whole, Martinique's crafts are not remarkable. By far the most fun to take home — if you have ample wall space — are big, bright, appliquéd hangings depicting island folks and folkways. The ubiquitous Martiniquais doll, in her madras et foulard, is available in every size from Bébé Barby to Gran' Berthe. There are also some nicely woven straw hats (the pointed bakoua is the island's official topper), baskets, and place mats. Otherwise, shops are filled with unremarkable mahogany carvings, shell jewelry, bangles, beads, and bulky pink-lipped conch shells — hard to justify when it comes to budgeting suitcase space on the way home. Best for browsing: The open-air market at La Savane and the *Centre des Métiers d'Art* across from the Tourist Office in Fort-de-France, with a particularly good sampling of original patchwork tapestries priced at about $35; the *Centre* also has a branch at Ste. Anne. Notable country shopping stops: *La Paille Caraibe* in the little town of Morne-des-Esses, island-famous for its basketry (vannerie), with small shops and stands selling the best in all styles and sizes. In the village of Bézaudin near Ste. Marie, the "boutique gourmande" *Ella* purveys an intriguing assortment of homemade tropical jams, purées, preserves, liqueurs, as well as island-grown spices.

A shopping survival tip: As everywhere in the Caribbean, try to avoid cruise ship crowds. Check with your hotel desk or the Tourist Office downtown early in your stay so you can plan to shop when the fleet's not in.

Among the best places in Fort-de-France for bargain-hunting and browsing: *Roger Albert* (Rue Victor Hugo), just off the Savane, Fort-de-France's best-known and biggest specialty shop. It has been redesigned and doubled in size, now extending through to Rue Ernest Deproge. Stocks of just about everything, including a few items you never dreamed you needed (chic watches, super Step atomizers, Limoges placecard holders) — all the big names. *Au Printemps* (corner of Rues Schoelcher and Antoine Siger) and *K-Dis* (Rue Lamartine) remind you of the famous French department stores, with goods and prices that range from Woolworth to Sears — for the most part. Maybe not the kind of places you'd expect to shop away from home, but both are great for tinned, fancy foods and cuisine gadgets that would make Julia Child coo. *Santalia* (Rue Lamartine) and *Mounia* (Rue Perrinon) are very small, very up-to-date boutiques specializing in French resortwear; mostly for women (bikinis like Brigitte used to wear), some men's clothes, too. *Gisele, Gigi,* and *Mahog-Annie* are boutiques to check out. *Borsalino* (Rue Victor Hugo), *Valentino* (Rue Perrinon), *Prune* (Rue Lamartine), and *Jack* (Rue Moreau de Jonnes) are boutiques strictly for men. *Cadet-Daniel* (Rue Antoine Siger), *Montaclair* (Rue Victor Hugo), and *Thomas de Rogatis* (Rue Antoine Siger) are the places to look for gold and silver chains and other real jewelry at prices well below those back home. *La Malle des Indes* (in the suburb of Schoelcher) is full of old maps, prints, and antique pieces. *Hit Parade* (Rue Lamartine), *Georges Debs* and *Chez JoJo* (both on Rue Antoine Siger) feature the latest island discs as well as recorded folk songs, beguines, zouk, and mazurkas. The *Caribbean Arts Center,* facing the Tourist Office on the waterfront, exhibits and sells the best Martinique merchandise. Shops are open from 9 AM to 12:30 PM and 2:30 PM to 6 PM except Saturday afternoon, Sunday, and holidays.

TIPPING: A recent French law requires the automatic addition of a 15% service charge to all restaurant and bar bills. Give bellboys and porters about 5 francs per bag. Most cab drivers own their cars and do not expect tips.

SPECIAL EVENTS: Fort-de-France stages an impressive cultural festival the first 2 weeks in July and a guitar or pop music and jazz festival the first 2 weeks in December. From the weekend before Ash Wednesday is *Carnival;* in mid-March, *Mi-Car+eme,* or *mid-Lent,* is celebrated; May 1 is *Labor Day* with workers' parades; the cultural *Festival of Fort-de-France* is celebrated all through July. *All Saints' Day* (November 1), *Armistice Day* (November 11), *Easter Monday, Ascension Day* (a Thursday, 40 days after Easter), *Pentecost Monday, Bastille Day* (July 14), *Schoelcher Day* (July 21), *Assumption Day* (August 15), *Christmas,* and *New Year's Day* are also public holidays.

SPORTS: The Martiniquais attitude is that sports are to play, not to work at. So you won't find super pro golf clinics, tennis camps, or any of the popular American sweat-and-learn setups. But you will find lots of active sports and better than adequate equipment.

Boating – Sailing on your own without a skipper is practiced in one- and two-seater Sunfish, Sailfish, Hobie Cats, and other small craft rented by the hour (about $8 and up) from kiosks on most hotel beaches. Yacht charters, both bareboat and skippered, are available from *Voile et Vent Antilles* (phone: 66-00-72) and the new *Presentations Plus* (phone: 66-07-74), both at the Pointe du Bout Marina, and from *Ship-Shop,* 6 Rue Joseph-Compere, 97200 Fort-de-France (phone: 71-43-70). Motorboats are also available at the marina. But local currents are strong, and — except for Sun- and Sailfish kept close to shore — inexperienced sailors are not advised to rent without a skipper. Skippered group sailing excursions aboard larger catamarans and schooners put out from Pointe du Bout as well as *La Batelière* and the *Méridien;* trip plans usually include a stop for snorkeling, swimming, and a picnic lunch on a beach on the Caribbean side, for about $60 per person. Late afternoon cocktail sails cost somewhat less.

Cockfighting – For Martiniquais, this is the big spectator sport. Mainlanders may call it cruel or revolting, but it is far and away the Sunday favorite from December to July. There are cockpits in large and small communities all over the island, and the place and time of the action shifts from week to week. If you'd like to see what it's all about, ask at the Tourist Office or at the travel desk of your hotel; they may be getting a group together. Though you'd be perfectly safe alone, you'll probably be more comfortable sharing the experience with other people. In any case, try to find a taxi driver or guide who'll stick with you and explain the action and the betting.

Cycling – Mopeds may just be the best way to take a jaunt to La Pagerie or get yourself to the golf course at Les Trois-Îlets. Rates are about $15 a day for Vespas, on which two can ride comfortably. You should reserve a day ahead and present a credit card or leave a deposit of about $200. In Fort-de-France, *Vespa* (phone: 71-60-03), *Funny* (phone: 63-33-05), and *T. S. Autos* rent Vespas, mopeds, and bicycles.

Golf – There's an excellent Robert Trent Jones course in Les Trois-Îlets (6,640 yards, par 71); the course is rated tough but good (phone: 68-32-81). It has a well-stocked pro shop, English-speaking pro, rental clubs, carts, caddies, and *Le Country* bar/restaurant. Greens fees are about $28 per person, carts are $30 for 18 holes, hand carts about $5. Lessons cost about $14 for a half-hour. Ask your hotel to telephone for a starting time.

Hiking – It's best in the nature preserve of Presqu'île de la Caravelle, where, in addition to trails that explore the ruins of the Château Dubuc and exotic, tropical landscapes (some stamina but no special skills required), you'll find safe surf beaches (this is the Atlantic side of the island) and a fishing village called Tartane. For more serious mountaineering, contact the Parc Régional de la Martinique, Caserne Bouillé, Fort-de-France (phone: 73-19-30) to make reservations with a guide for the 2-hour Mt. Pelée climb (dense foliage, trails often overgrown, guide essential; on account of cloud cover, the view from the top can't be guaranteed) or a trek through the Gorges de la Falaise (moderate length, not too difficult) or the rain forest between Grand-Rivière and Prêcheur (choice of trails, several degrees of skill).

Horseback Riding – Along scenic hillside and banana country trails, it's available in Anses-d'Arlets at *Ranch-Jack* (phone: 68-63-97), 20 minutes from Pointe du Bout; the ranch also does group rides through nearby mountains, canefields, and around sea coves (rates from about $20 per person for a 2½-hour ride; a half-day trail ride with guide costs about $50 per person. Others are *Black Horse* at La Pagerie in Trois-Îlets (phone: 66-00-04); *La Cavale* near *Diamant-Novotel* (phone: 76-22-94); and *Leyritz Plantation* (phone: 75-53-92).

Snorkeling and Scuba – The best diving spots are the waters off Ste. Anne, Anses-d'Arlets, Îlet Ramier, Cap Saloman, and the shipwrecks at St. Pierre. *Bathy's Club* at the Méridien serves the Pointe du Bout hotels. *Diamant-Novotel*'s *Caraibe Coltri–Sun Club* has daily excursions around Diamond Rock and offers packages at sea. *La Batelière Hotel and Casino* has the *Tropicasud International Diving Center*, and at Carbet there's the *Carib Scuba Club*. All-inclusive prices range from $23 to $35 per dive; discounts for multiple dives and groups. *Club Med* has a built-in operation for guests only.

Snorkeling fins and masks are available at many hotels, including the *Bakoua Beach, Bambou, Club Med, Calalou, PLM Azur Carayou, Méridien,* and *La Batelière* hotel casino. A variety of snorkeling excursions sail from the Pointe du Bout hotels as well as *La Batelière* and *Diamant-Novotel* hotels.

Spectator Sports – There's a good deal of island soccer playing, and it draws good crowds; local papers and hotel desks can fill you in on schedules. If there's a yole regatta in town, don't miss it. It's a great thrill to see skilled seamen hanging from the rigging of huge, colorful sails while racing at daredevil speeds.

Sport Fishing – Most hotels can arrange deep-sea excursions. For example, the

Méridien's *Bathy's Club* has 3 trips daily aboard *La Mauny Plongée*. The catch is barracuda, kingfish, and tuna.

Swimming and Sunning – Fine, if not fantastic. Martinique possesses no unending miles of pure pink and white coral sand. But most hotels have their own beaches — natural, or helped along with imported sand and groin-jetties to keep it in place. As a result, Pointe du Bout beaches have never been better. The natural beach at Anse Mitan just down the shore serves small, mostly French-speaking hotels such as *Bambou, Caraïbe Auberge,* and *Auberge de l'Anse Mitan.*

Beaches north of Fort-de-France tend to be soft, volcanic gray; those to the south are whiter, and all are open to the public, though hotels charge nonguests a small fee for lockers and changing cabanas. The larger hotels provide free chaises and towels for guests, volleyball courts, beachside drink and snack bars. Usually there are also small sailboats and snorkel gear to rent. Two exceptions to the own-beach rule: *Leyritz Plantation,* which is inland and can transport its guests to the sea, and *Manoir de Beauregard,* whose guests bask on the beach at nearby Ste. Anne. The *Bakoua Beach, PLM Azur Carayou, PLM Azur La Pagerie, Diamant-Novotel, Leyritz Plantation, Martinique Cottages, Manoir de Beauregard, Caritan Beach, Club Med, Méridien,* and *La Batelière* hotel casino have swimming pools. To escape the hotel scene, plan a day's picnic trip to the pretty, palm-treed shores at Ste. Anne, Les Salines, Le Diamant, or Anses-d'Arlets. (Though Martinique has no officially designated nude beaches, topless sunbathing is okay on beaches and at poolside, but tops are de rigueur at beach bars and restaurants.)

Tennis – Courts are part of the big-hotel scene. Most are free for guests during the day and cost about $5 after dark;for nonguests, there's a charge of $10 to $15 per half hour. In either case, court time should be reserved in advance. The *Bakoua Beach, Club Med, PLM Azur Carayou, Diamant-Novotel, Leyritz Plantation, Méridien,* and *La Batelière* hotels all have tennis courts on their grounds; all except the *Plantation*'s have lights. *Club Med* and *La Batelière* have teaching pros on hand. Serious players can also arrange temporary memberships at private clubs like the *Tennis Club of Fort-de-France* or *Tennis Club du Vieux Moulin* — and through them games with local players — via hotels or the Tourist Office.

Water Skiing and Windsurfing – Available at Le Diamant, Ste. Anne, *La Batelière, Club Med,* and *Bathy's Club* at Méridien beach, within easy reach of Pointe du Bout and Anse Mitan hotels. It's about $15 for a 10- to 15-minute tow. Windsurfing costs $10 to $15 for a half-hour lesson, about $10 an hour for use of the board only.

 NIGHTLIFE: Wherever you stay, don't miss the *Grand Ballet de la Martinique* performance by a bouncy young troupe of singers, dancers, and musicians, most of them in their late teens, playing weekly at larger hotels (*Bakoua Beach, PLM Azur Carayou, Diamant-Novotel, La Batelière, Méridien,* and *Caritan Beach*) as well as on visiting cruise ships. By combining stories of plantation days with choreographed valses, beguines, and mazurkas, they give you a special feeling for island history. Best of all, they seem to have a terrific time doing it.

There are a number of cinemas in Fort-de-France that offer "original version" French films and a chance to practice one's French. *La Batelière* hotel casino shows American movies in its film room. During July, the Cultural Festival of Fort-de-France takes place, and during the first two weeks in December the bi-annual Guitar Festival and the Jazz and Popular Music Festival alternate.

Otherwise, there's enough choice of after-dark action to let you set your own pace. Small hotels have dance music one or two nights a week, sometimes more often during high season; the larger places tune up most evenings — more or less sedately during dinner (i.e., touch dancing), fairly frenetically in their discos later on. For both Martiniquais and visitors, hotel discos on the Pointe du Bout side are the place to be. The *Vesou* at the *PLM Azur Carayou* is biggest, zingiest; *Méridien's Vonvon* is small, dark, high-decibel; *Bakoua Beach* has dinner dancing, limbo shows, ballet performances, steel bands — something different every night; *PaladiumClub 21,* at *La Batelière* hotel casino, is small and chic. The sounds at all these mix some hustle, updated beguine, and a few Latin beats.

For something a bit more native, try the downtown clubs in Fort-de-France: *Hippo Club* offers dancing interspersed with song; *Le Bitaco* — weekends only, for late dancing — makes Americans feel welcome; *Le Manoir* is — and has been for years — a place to hear and dance to Martinique music. *Le Sweety,* with two dance floors, moves to both Creole tunes and disco beats; *Le Must* is a funk disco on the Blvd. Alègre. Outside Fort-de-France proper, try the *Jardin Brésilien* (an offshoot of the St. Martin original but without dancing) in the suburb of Didier, *Le Number One* in Trinité, *L'Alibi,* once a private club, but now open to all, or the *Trou Caraibe* in Carbet.

Caution: Disco drinks, especially Scotch and whiskeys, are expensive — as high as $3 to $6 each when you add taxes and service charge. Rum drinks and local *Lorraine* beer (quite good) cost less.

There are gambling casinos at both the *Méridien Trois Îslets* and *La Batelière.* Games are baccarat, craps, American roulette, blackjack, and chemin de fer. The decor is Continental, but jackets and ties are not required. What you must have is identification with your picture on it. Croupiers are European-trained islanders; minimum bet is about $3. The admission fee is about $9 at the *Méridien,* $10 at *La Batelière.* Hours are 9 PM to 3 AM nightly except Sunday, and legal gambling age is 21.

BEST ON THE ISLAND

 CHECKING IN: Martinique hotels range from a charming Relais Créole country inn or seaside cottage to a sprawling 300-room luxury resort. Grounds, though not extensive, are neatly gardened and cleverly plotted to fit a maximum number of activities into the space available. Food, even in very small places, tends to be quite good.

To our mind, Martinique hotel choices hinge on location almost as much as the specific hotel and its price range. It's Pointe du Bout if you want to be where the action — and most of the other tourists — are, make the most of sports, dine around, and avail yourself of all the nightlife tumult. For a quieter time at a self-contained resort or a country inn, pick someplace farther out (*Leyritz Plantation* or *St. Aubin,* for example). By far the best beaches are found in the southeastern part of the island. In this listing, very expensive is defined as $225 and up for two in winter, including Continental or American breakfast; expensive is $175 to $225 in winter, with breakfast; moderate, from $100 to $225 in winter, including breakfast; and inexpensive, under $100 for two without meals in winter. Prices run about 25% to 35% less in summer.

POINTE DU BOUT

Bakoua Beach – Martiniquais-owned, managed, and styled, and recently refurbished and enlarged to include 40 new luxurious oceanfront rooms, a new bar, and upgraded beach facilities. There's an informal beach restaurant and an excellent formal dining room, the *Chateaubriand.* All rooms are air conditioned, with the choicest terraced into the adjoining hillside or overlooking the beach. Recently, however, it has been reported that some rooms are uncomfortably small, and that service and maintenance are not all they should be (phone: 66-02-02). Very expensive to expensive.

Méridien Trois Îslets – Spruced up, offering 303 bright, spacious, air-conditioned rooms with small balconies and views worth seeing. Pleasant indoor-outdoor lobby, restaurant. Lots of activities — including casino and all water sports at the hotel. Good food, especially in the new *Le Cas Creole* dining room. Extremely convenient location right near the ferry dock, marina. Pleasant overall (phone: 66-00-00). Expensive to moderate.

Calalou – Very charming, small inn with 36 air-conditioned rooms on its own beach, just outside Trois-Îlets at Anse à l'Ane. A colorful carousel sits in the garden at the entrance, and there's a very good restaurant serving French and Creole cuisine (phone: 68-31-67). Moderate.

PLM Azur Carayou – Friendly, personal approach and informal atmosphere make this good for families. Has 200 air-conditioned rooms with summer cottage decor (rattan chairs, tables, striped fabrics). Pool, plus nice curve of beach, many free sports for guests (tennis, Sailfish sailing, snorkeling, pedalboating, boardsailing, archery, golf practice); average fees for scuba, fishing, boat trips; water skiing, golf, and riding nearby. Drawing card *Vesou* disco (phone: 66-04-04). Moderate.

PLM Azur La Pagerie – Studios near the marina at Pointe du Bout; clean-cut, efficient design, all with balconies. Conveniently near small new supermarket, a good choice of restaurants, beaches, and the ferry. Swimming pool, but no other sports on premises (many available within walking distance, however). Good headquarters for those who like variety, exploring, seeing, and doing different things each day. Has 100 one-room studios, all air-conditioned, 70 with kitchenettes, 30 with fridges (phone: 66-05-30). Moderate to inexpensive.

Bambou – An ever-expanding property on what was once a beach. The 60 two-unit bungalows are functional, clean, and ideally located. Mostly French clientele. Trois-Îlets (phone: 66-01-39). Inexpensive.

Madinina – Small, pin-neat modern rooms with shower baths. Cheerful Creole ambience at the edge of the Pointe du Bout marina. Creole restaurant, *Chez Sidonie*, on the premises. Beaches nearby. Has 20 rooms, all with small balconies and air conditioning (phone: 66-00-54). Inexpensive.

OTHERS ON THE ISLAND

La Batelière, north of Fort-de-France – On the west coast, very close to Fort-de-France. Popular with business travelers, but in need of some refurbishment. Its assets: 200 large, air-conditioned rooms, 6 lighted tennis courts (the island's best), *Club 21* disco, and casino (phone: 61-49-49). Expensive to moderate.

Leyritz Plantation, near Basse-Pointe – An 18th-century house and outbuildings in the center of a working banana plantation, restored with great patience and taste, in the northern part of the island. Lush garden setting for the 50 air-conditioned rooms; pretty pool but no beach; riding. Be prepared to rent a car or stay pretty much on the reservation (though there's transport to a nearby beach). With the island's only complete spa facilities, including special diet and beauty programs. Special week-long spa packages. Excellent Creole cuisine. We'd opt for the antique-furnished rooms in the main house (phone: 75-53-92). Expensive to moderate.

Buccaneer's Creek Club Med, near Ste. Anne – As Clubs Med go, this is one of the best looking, best working — possibly because it was built by Club Med, not taken over and adapted. Lots of activities, sports with leader/instructors (called GOs); French-English language lab. Long, white beach with an in-the-buff preserve. Disco, Creole restaurant. Especially popular with singles, one of the few

Club Med enclaves to retain its swinging image. Has 300 rooms (a few double beds, the rest twins) for double occupancy only, all air-conditioned. Weeklong package a must, including all activities, meals (with wine) (phone: 76-72-72). Moderate.

Diamant-Novotel, Pointe de la Chéry – A bit isolated at the southern end of the island, but with a stunning view of the sea and the great granite slab that was once the British navy's HMS Diamond Rock, surrounded by a choice of splendid white beaches (including its own). It offers 180 rooms, tennis, excellent water sports, restaurant, disco, "lobster grill," nightclub. One of the island's "Frenchest" places (phone: 76-42-42). Moderate.

Manoir de Beauregard, Ste. Anne – Informal living in an 18th-century country house a mile's stroll from the beach, about twice that from Les Salines' famous sands and the village of Ste. Anne. Small freshwater pool at manor house. Has 25 air-conditioned rooms with shower or bath; many with antiques, provincial wallpapers. With bar and delicious French, Creole food (phone: 76-73-40). Moderate.

Caritan Beach, Ste. Anne – Very casual, relaxed, ideal for families. It has 95 air-conditioned rooms with small kitchenettes, a pool, a tiny beach, water sports, and planned daily activities (phone: 76-74-12). Moderate to inexpensive.

Diamant les Bains, Le Diamant – A colonial-style relais créole on a lovely beach stretching 2½ miles and offering a great view of Diamond Rock. There are 24 air-conditioned rooms or bungalows with refrigerators; also a terraced restaurant serving seafood specialties, and a bar (phone: 76-40-14). Inexpensive.

Martinique Cottages, Le Lamentin – Martinican Jean-Marc Arnaud's new and very charming property. It's beautifully landscaped and has 14 bungalows with kitchenettes and private verandahs, plus a pool with Jacuzzi. There's tennis nearby, and a new restaurant, La Plantation, with French and Creole cuisine. M. Arnaud, who speaks Spanish, will arrange off-the-beaten-path tours (phone: 50-16-08).

St. Aubin, Trinité – A most appealing manor house converted into a small hotel, set in formal gardens overlooking the sea. It has a good-size pool and it's near some good beaches and picturesque villages. Lots of natural beauty, but not much in the way of sports. Fine place to simply be; enjoy the attentive service of its owner, award-winning former restaurateur Guy Foret (phone: 69-34-77). Inexpensive.

 EATING OUT: Two things are true of the French West Indies that aren't true anyplace else in the Caribbean: Local people eat much the same food as visitors, and the local food is exceptionally good. These are not unrelated phenomena. Restaurants range from casual to elegant, serving regional recipes, classic French fare, and everything in between. The only big restaurants on the island are in hotels. But no matter what their size, all care a great deal about their food.

Cuisines follow two persuasions — French haute and island Creole — with most restaurants serving a bit of each or a combination of the two. Steak is available, but delicious fish, seafood, and some of the more exotic sea denizens (sea urchins, octopi, conch) are basic to most menus. Most common fowl are pigeon and peacock, as well as chicken and duck à l'orange. And roast suckling pig often appears on buffets.

Favorite appetizers include *accra* (minced cod in batter — deep-fried and delicately flavored), *crabes farcis* (land-crab meat deviled with bread crumbs and mild-to-hot seasoning, served in its own shell), *soudons* (small, sweet clams often served with fresh lime and hot peppers), and *coquille de lambi* (small pieces of conch in a creamy sauce served in a shell, St. Jacques style). Entrée specialties are red snapper, *cribiches* (large river shrimp), *langouste* (clawless rock lobster), *lambi* (conch done in any one of a number of ways — from rubbery to remarkable, depending on the cook, the recipe, and the spices), *oursins* (sea urchins — again, done in many ways and surprisingly tasty), or *chatrou* (octopus) — all according to the morning's catch. *Colombo* is the Creole version of curry (usually chicken, mutton, or goat); *pâté en pot* is a thick Creole soup of Norman-French origin that's a brew of mutton, capers, vegetables, herbs, and white wine. *Blaff* is an aromatic Creole fish stew spiced with limes, garlic, cloves, thyme, parsley, and peppers, and — they say — named for the sound the poor fish makes when it's plopped into the kettle. For dessert: island fruits — pineapple, guava, mango, papaya, coconut, bananas — served fresh with imported French cheeses, or in somewhat more elaborate form, such as coconut cake or rum-fired banana flambé.

With dinner, the Martiniquais serve French wines that are good to great, and priced accordingly. Before and after, it's rum — of their own devising and in several different forms. Tourists tend to opt for les planteurs — the familiar planter's punch with a sweet fruit juice base. Islanders prefer a *décollage* — literally, a blast-off of aged, herbed rum with a fruit juice chaser — or a white punch of rum, sugar syrup, and limes. And for an after-dinner nip: liqueurlike 12-year-old rum *Bally* or *Clément.*

Reservations are always a good idea (if you have telephone trouble, ask the hotel desk to make them for you). In inexpensive places the tab will come to about $15 per person, including wine and service charge; in moderate places, about $20 to $30 per person; in expensive places, over $35.

FORT-DE-FRANCE

Le Lafayette – Overlooking La Savane and in a class by itself. Chef/manager Henri Charvet redefines nouvelle cuisine with a light approach to classic French fare flavored with a touch of Creole. The result is fresh, savory, irresistible. Impeccable service, exquisite decor (phone: 63-24-09). Very expensive.

L'Arc en Ciel – On a hillside at the *Victoria* hotel, it's chic, petit, and very Parisian. Its excellent nouvelle cuisine attracts many locals, especially businessmen and politicians for lunch; the twinkling lights of Fort-de-France below make for romantic dinners. Closed Sunday (phone: 73-61-75). Expensive.

La Biguine – A small place, simple and select, the bailiwick of Gerard Padra, skilled former maître d' of the *Bakoua* hotel. The menu blends his classic French (escargots, *filet de boeuf au poivre vert*) and Creole (*crabes farcis,* blaff) backgrounds; excellent service. 11 Route de la Folie (phone: 71-40-07). Expensive.

Le d'Esnambuc – Tiny, elegant, green and white dining room with harbor and Savane view, featuring French and Alsatian specialties. Closed for lunch Saturdays and Sundays. At the corner of Rue Ernest Deproge and Rue de la Liberté (phone: 71-46-51). Expensive.

La Fontane – Off the Route de Balata, this was once a private home. The ambience is very elegant and tranquil, and the menu imaginative, featuring French and Creole specialties. There's a tempting swimming pool that may be hard to resist between courses (phone: 64-28-70). Expensive.

Le Gargantua – As the name implies, guests enjoy gargantuan portions of Creole food on this picturesque terrace overlooking Fort-de-France and the sea. Traditional recipes with modern adaptations and presentation include a spicy conch terrine, land crab in puff pastry with crayfish sauce, seafood lasagna, and fillet of veal in papaya julienne flambéed with port (phone: 71-30-18). Expensive.

La Grand' Voile – Overlooking the water on the second floor of the town's stylish yacht club. Costly, but worth it. Seafood and classic French provincial specialties; fine cellar. Recently redecorated by new owners from Toulouse. Lots of open-air dining. Closed Sundays. Pointe Simon (phone: 70-29-29). Expensive.

La Belle Époque – With a growing reputation for fine food, this spot serves haute cuisine in a turn-of-the-century setting befitting its name. It's worth checking out. In the suburb of Didier (phone: 64-01-09). Expensive to moderate.

Le Mareyeur – Seafood specialties include all the Creole favorites — *lambis, soudons, palourdes,* and *oursins* — carefully prepared and beautifully presented. Try *blaff de poisson* (steamed fish in local spices), shark in coconut milk, shrimp fricassée, or, better yet, order the *assiette* for a taste of all the house specialties. Route Principale, Pointe des Nègres (phone: 61-74-70). Expensive to moderate.

El Raco – Authentic Spanish atmosphere, authentic Catalan dishes (especially paella, good sangria) in addition to French choices. At 23 Rue Lazare Carnot (phone: 73-29-16). Expensive to moderate.

Le Tiffany – Facing Institut Vivioz at the edge of Fort-de-France, Claude Pradine's pink-and-white gingerbread mansion is one of Martinique's most noteworthy gastronomic havens, renowned for its Creole and French haute cuisine, its intimate atmosphere, and the exuberant personality of Pradine himself (catch his magic act on Friday evenings). Special delights are filet mignon with Roquefort butter; breast of duck with mango; and fresh Guyana shrimp with pink peppercorn sauce. Diners may choose from three excellent fixed-price menus. Closed Saturday afternoons and Sundays (phone: 71-33-82). Expensive to moderate.

POINTE DU BOUT

Chateaubriand – Fine Continental and Creole cuisine. Excellent veal in white sauce, spectacular lobster maison, and memorable chocolate mousse. *Bakoua Beach* hotel (phone: 66-02-02). Expensive to moderate.

Chez Sidonie – Deliciously Creole restaurant. Fine food, deft (though primarily French-speaking) service, marina view. Closed Mondays. *Madinina* hotel (phone: 66-00-54). Expensive to moderate.

Le Matador – New setting, same savory Creole cuisine. Chef's hors d'oeuvres include *crabes farcis, calalou,* Creole-style bouillabaisse, red snapper in court bouillon, colombo of goat. Anse Mitan (phone: 66-05-36 or 66-04-05). Expensive to moderate.

L'Amphore – Guy Dawson's new spot with a slightly different flavor: Lobster is the specialty here, and you choose it right from the tank. Along with Creole starters such as *crabes farcis* and *accras,* the spiny lobster is offered in several ways, all delicious. Lovely terrace with sea view and a guitarist/vocalist for added romance. Closed Mondays. Anse Mitan (phone: 66-03-09). Moderate.

La Villa Creole – Guy Dawson's perfect combination of romantic garden ambience, soft lights, music, and excellent cuisine has made this the most popular spot in the area. Delightful, predominantly Creole dishes include blaff of sea urchins, court bouillon, conch tart, terrine of local red fish, and curried chicken, pork, and lamb. Closed Sundays. Anse Mitan (phone: 66-05-53). Moderate.

STE. ANNE

Les Filets Bleus – Open-air seafood place right on the beach. Lobster, grilled fish, clams in Creole sauce, and *crabes farcis.* Translucent floor with lobster pens beneath. Closed Sunday and Monday nights (phone: 76-73-42). Moderate.

Manoir de Beauregard – An 18th-century plantation house serving first-rate lunches and dinners. Creole/French menu (phone: 76-73-40). Moderate.

OTHERS ON THE ISLAND

Le Colibri, Morne des Esses – In the private home of Mme. Palladino in the northwestern part of the island. Sea urchin tartes, lobster omelets, stuffed pigeon, are among her specialties. Closed Sunday evenings and Monday (phone: 69-32-19). Expensive to moderate.

Leyritz Plantation, Basse-Pointe – A 1½-hour drive from town and a favored tour destination (if you're staying elsewhere on the island, avoid cruise-ship-day visits). But a truly enchanted setting in the cool of what was once the plantation's granary for very good food. French and Creole dishes. Mme. de Fossarieu is justly proud of her lambi en coquille and her special colombo recipes. Prix fixe and à la carte menus (phone: 75-53-92). Expensive to moderate.

Le Verger, Lamentin – Should your flight be delayed, this restaurant near the airport is the perfect place to go. Lunch or dinner on a pleasant terrace could be a fixed-price menu, of which there are several in various price ranges. The specialties are from Perigord — lots of foie gras, *confit de canard,* cassoulet, pheasant and other game — but there are Creole dishes as well. Closed Saturday afternoons and Sundays (phone: 51-43-02). Expensive to moderate.

La Belle Capresse, Prêcheur – A great stop for a northern tour, it features all the favorite Creole specialties, including some originals, such as fish soufflé, shrimp fritters, skewered shark, and conch gratin. There are some dishes for landlubbers, too — pork flambéed in aged rum, and chicken in coconut milk. Closed Sunday nights and Wednesdays (phone: 77-20-25). Moderate.

Mme. Edjam, Basse-Pointe – A virtuosa cook, especially skilled at seafood, does delectable Creole meals in her immaculate home at the island's northernmost tip. The long drive makes lunch preferable; reserve a day ahead (phone: 75-51-18.) Moderate.

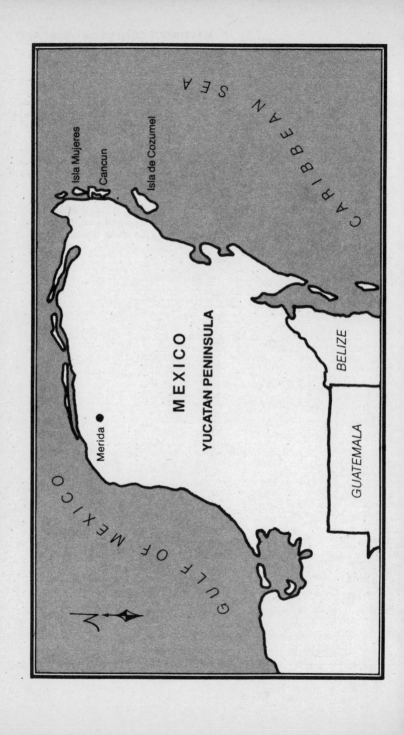

MEXICO'S CARIBBEAN COAST

CANCÚN, COZUMEL, AND ISLA MUJERES

Not very many years ago, a trip to the Yucatán — the peninsula off which lie Mexico's Caribbean islands of Cancún, Cozumel, and Isla Mujeres — meant either a cultural pilgrimage to the Maya ruins or a relaxing time in the sand and surf of a beach resort. You needed at least ten days to do both without a hassle, for there was no easy access to the major Maya sites from the sea side. Since Mérida, the Yucatán's pleasant (but relatively unexciting) capital, was the only gateway to Chichén Itzá and Uxmal, serious ruin-viewing involved staying overnight there, plus a two- or three-day expedition in the Zona Puuc, with stays at hacienda hotels beside the sites. To relax, the only realistic option was Cozumel. (Cancún was not yet developed, and reaching Isla Mujeres was just too complicated.) You touched down at Mérida's airport, then flew on to Cozumel to flop on the sand and swim.

One of the major dividends produced by the government-sponsored development of the island resort of Cancún off the Yucatán's east coast is that visitors no longer have to choose between culture and a seaside vacation. It's now easy to enjoy both, thanks to the system of roads, transport facilities, communications, etc., created as part of the Cancún Master Plan. To combine seeing the ruins with a stay on Isla Mujeres may still take a bit of arranging, but it's now at least an option. Both Cozumel and Cancún benefit from the beeline road from the sea to Chichén Itzá, along which daily tour buses now travel. And each is helped by the improvement of the route that travels south along the Yucatán coast to the snorkeling lagoon at Xel-Ha and the small (but impressive) seaside ruins at Tulum, providing an alternative to the longer, more intensive, inland trip.

This part of the Yucatecan world and its impressive ruins, most of which date back to the eleventh century AD, have intrigued travelers for centuries. One of the most amusing and articulate accounts was that by John L. Stephens, a New Englander whose Twain-like memoir, Incidents of Travel in Yucatán, first published in 1843, has been reissued by Dover in two volumes with engravings by Catherwood.

Stephens also visited Chichén Itzá, which was, even in those days, the most accessible of the major ruins, since a main travel route passed right through it. Then he saw the islands the hard way — in a native canoe with two sails, no keel, no hope of tacking to windward, and no hope of making any headway in a stiff wind. But he persevered, visiting Isla Mujeres, notorious as the resort of Lafitte the pirate.

Then, as now, turtles swam there. Stephens bought a giant shell and "had the satisfaction of learning afterward that I had paid not more than twice as much as it was worth. In the afternoon," he continued, "we steered for the mainland, passing the island of Kancune, a barren strip of land, with sand hills and stone buildings visible upon it."

Next there was Cozumel, with its "little Bay of San Miguel" where there were "several huts, built of poles, and thatched with palm leaves. The place had a sort of piratical aspect. In the hut were doors and green blinds from the cabin of some unlucky vessel, and reeving blocks, tar buckets, halliards, drinking gourds, fragments of rope, fishing nets, and two old hatches were scattered on the ground"; also a good freshwater well and a number of ruins — the shell of a Spanish church, as well as stone Mayan buildings. Ruefully, Stephens reported, "Amid all the devastations that attended the progress of the Spaniards in America none is more complete than that which was swept over Cozumel." He found it fascinating and said, "There was no place in our whole journey that we left with more regret."

One hundred and forty years or so have brought some changes. The turtles remain, but the pirates and smugglers have largely disappeared. Huts, "built of poles, and thatched with palm leaves" — now called beach palapas and designed to shade lounge chairs — still dot island beaches, but overnight accommodations are considerably grander.

"Kankune," that "barren strip of land," has become Cancún, a planner's idea of the model of a modern beach resort: perfect climate, cool sands, clear waters. And it's accessible. It has the latest in hotels, from informal family places to luxury resorts, and the greatest in sports — a Robert Trent Jones, Jr., golf course, tennis, snorkeling, diving, fishing, swimming.

On Cozumel, where rambling hotels have replaced the huts Stephens found, life is less organized, more casual than Cancún's. Although diving is a major preoccupation and excursion possibilities are available, there's not quite as much compulsion to get up and do things.

On Isla Mujeres, there's no compulsion whatever. Relaxation is total. Sunrise, sunset, and the arrival of the morning ferry are the most exciting happenings of any day.

Take your pick. Mexico's Caribbean coast is a choice place.

MEXICAN CARIBBEAN AT-A-GLANCE

FROM THE AIR: Mexico's Caribbean islands are grouped around the northeastern corner of the Yucatán, that chunky Central American peninsula that divides the Gulf of Mexico from the Caribbean Sea. They are flat, sun-baked, and sea-washed bits of land. Their centers are dense green brush and coconut palms rimmed by white limestone sand beaches. Cancún, the second largest and most recently developed, is flanked to the south by Cozumel, the largest and first to be developed, and to the north by Isla Mujeres, the smallest and sleepiest.

At approximately 21° N latitude, 87° W longitude, the islands are about 560 miles southwest of Miami (about 1½ hours by jet), about 640 miles (1½ hours) east of Mexico City, and about 185 miles (35 minutes) east of Mérida, capital of the Mexican state of Yucatán.

Cancún (pronounced can-*koon*), 14 miles long and ¼ mile wide, is shaped like an emaciated seahorse, connected by a causeway at its nose to Cancún City — the support city on the mainland where most of the resort's 190,000 residents live. (Cancún's jetport is 12 miles southwest of the city.) For most of the rest of its length, island and peninsula are separated by unruffled Nichupte Lagoon. Most of the island's resort hotels are scattered along the skinny east-west sand spit that forms the seahorse's head. And along its back, the Caribbean surf rolls in along a 12-mile length of powdery white beach, at the southern end of which is the big *Club Med* reservation.

Cozumel (ko-sue-*mehl*), an island 30 miles long and 9 miles wide, lies about 50 miles south of Cancún and about 2 miles off the Yucatán coast. Its almost straight eastern shoreline is pounded by rough, windward seas; on its leeward western side, the brilliant waters off its resort beaches are calm, the shore notched with sandy coves. The coral reefs that surround it — especially the sunken mountains of the Palancar reef chain — make it a prime skin divers' destination. Most of the island's resort hotels are just north of its only town, San Miguel (pop. 45,000), on the northwest coast. The jet airport is between the hotels and town.

Isla Mujeres (*eez*-lah moo-*hay*-rehs), 5 miles long and ½ mile wide, is 6 miles north of Cancún and 6 miles off Puerto Juárez at the tip of the Yucatán Peninsula. It has a tiny town, beautiful beaches, lagoons, reefs, and transparent waters that make it a super retreat for snorkelers, skin divers, and loafers. There's a lovely lookout point and a Maya "lighthouse" at the southern end of the island.It's not, however, the sleepy little island it once was. Most places now have phones; the few roads are paved; there's regular plane service from Cancún and Cozumel; there's a new condo-marina and even several discos and a nightclub.

 SPECIAL PLACES: There's little sightseeing on Mexico's Caribbean islands. Each has a town with restaurants and at least a few shops.

Cancún City – On the mainland, this town is sociologically interesting in that it, like the resort itself, did not evolve but was built from scratch as part of a FONATUR master plan. In 1970, it didn't exist at all; now it houses 120,000 people — many of them native Yucatecans — almost all of whom are employed on the adjoining resort island.

San Miguel – Cozumel's town square, long regarded as unique in its ugliness, has been transformed into an inviting plaza, fine for strolling, sitting, people watching. There's an esplanade on the sea side, and the Malecón, the road that follows the shore north and south, is lined with relaxed cafés and tourist shops.

Isla Mujeres – Downtown is like that of a mite-sized provincial fishing village — a place to meet the boat, have a morning cup of coffee or an afternoon glass of beer, rent a Honda, and head for the beach.

ELSEWHERE ON THE COAST

Both Cancún and Cozumel offer easy access to some of the Yucatán mainland's most famous and intriguing archaeological sites. Cobá, Tulum, Valladolid, and Chichén Itzá can all be reached via organized bus or plane trips, taxi touring, or a rented car. For anyone who wants to see more, Uxmal, Kabah, and Dzibilchaltun are also accessible. Fascinating Chichén Itzá and the ruins of the coast city of Tulum are both easy to reach. You really should see at least one of the two.

From Cancún – The daylong, air-conditioned bus trip to explore the ruins at Chichén Itzá (which date back to the early 11th century) is the best trip. All hotel travel desks book the trip, or it may be included in your basic Mexico travel package. Price, including guided tours of the site and a good Mexican lunch at a nearby resort hotel, is about $25 per person. The Tulum trip — with stops at the mainland fishing resort of Akumal and for snorkeling at the intricate, rockbound inlet called Xel-Ha — can be done in a half or full day. Take the latter — for its more leisurely pace and the beach lunch at Akumal — for about $35 per person. *Club Med* operates optional plane excursions to Chichén Itzá, Tulum, and Cobá. The last is the newest (in terms of excavation date) and potentially most intriguing of Maya archaeological sites (it includes Mexico's tallest pyramid). Cobá is easy to reach with driver or rental car: turn inland at the marked road just south of Tulum; it's 30 miles straight ahead, and there's a *Villa Arqueológica* for lunch and/or overnight. Archaeology buffs won't want to miss it. There are also first-rate full-day snorkeling cruises from Cancún to Isla Mujeres (about $50 per person).

From Cozumel – Similar day trips to Tulum and Xel-Ha (by boat and bus, about $25 per person, including lunch) are available. Are there ruins on the island? Relics do exist in the interior, but they're mostly overgrown and not worth the buggy, itchy, sweaty, dusty trip unless you're an archaeological zealot. On a day's drive around the southern end of the island, a sandy detour off the main paved road takes you to "The Tomb of the Snail." (If you're taking the Tulum or Chichén Itzá excursion, don't bother.) If you don't snorkel, do take the glass-bottom-boat ride for a 2-hour look at the reef life (about $7 per person).

■**EXTRA SPECIAL:** Cozumel's *Robinson Crusoe Cruise* to San Francisco Beach or the prettier Passion Island (the reference is religious, not romantic). En route, the crew dive for lobster, conch, and assorted fish that they cook (deliciously) on the beach while you swim and snorkel offshore. Most fun if you put together your own group of eight or ten. Arrangements can be made through most hotels.

SOURCES AND RESOURCES

TOURIST INFORMATION: The Mexican Ministry of Tourism is the best source of brochures and background material on all of Mexico. Information is yours for the asking if you contact any one of the following North American offices:

Chicago: 70 E Lake St., Suite 1413, Chicago, IL 60601 (phone: 312-565-2785)

Houston: 2707 N Loop West, Suite 1413, Houston, TX 77008 (phone: 713-880-5153)

Los Angeles: 10100 Santa Monica Blvd., Suite 224, Los Angeles, CA 90067 (phone: 213-203-8151)

Montréal: 1 Pl. Ville Marie, Suite 2409, Montréal, Qué. H3B 3M9 (phone: 514-871-1052)

New York: 405 Park Ave., Suite 1002, New York, NY 10022 (phone: 212-755-7261)

Toronto: 181 University Ave., Suite 1112, Toronto, Ont. M5H 3M7 (phone: 416-364-2455)

For background or take-along reading: *Incidents of Travel in Yucatán,* the fascinating two-volume journal of John L. Stephens, the intrepid New Englander who, with his artist friend Catherwood (whose detailed drawings illustrate the book), explored some 44 Maya sites in 1841, 85 years before the Mexican government took an interest in them (Dover; $9).

On location, the sources and quality of available information vary considerably. In Cancún, there's a thorough, modern information center on the Avenida Tulum near the Ki-Huic Market. The Tourist Office is at Av. Cobá and Nader. In Cozumel, ask your hotel activities or travel desk, the Activity and Information Centers of the *Mayan Plaza* or *El Presidente* hotel, or the desk of Cozumel Holidays (a reliable tour operator) at the *Cabañas del Caribe* hotel. The local representative of the Ministry of Tourism is upstairs in the Plaza del Sol building. On Isla Mujeres, there's a tourist office at Guerrero 8, and you can trust answers given by English-speaking personnel at *El Cañon* (north of the ferry dock on the waterfront) and/or — farther out — the person in charge of the activities desk at *El Presidente Caribe,* or Dona María Mendes at *María's* restaurant south of town.

Local Coverage – In Cancún, two free periodicals — the comprehensive *Cancún Tips,* which includes helpful information about Cozumel and Isla Mujeres as well, and *Cancún News and Events* — contain ads and some handy listings of happenings, hotels, restaurants, shops, night places, and tour possibilities. Two similar publications, *Cozumel — What to Do, Where to Go,* and *Cozumel Today,* are distributed in Cozumel. In Isla Mujeres, the *Isleño* lists current events.

Paperback *Easy Guides* — to *Mérida and Yucatán* (Comprehensive; $3), *to Isla Mujeres, Cozumel, and Cancún* ($1), and *to Tulum* ($1) — are not terribly well written, but they do give the facts about local sightseeing.

Newspapers from Mexico City arrive in Cozumel and Cancún on the day they're published, as do the *Miami Herald* and *Houston Chronicle.* Local newspapers (in Spanish) include *Quintana Roo, Novedades de Quintana Roo, El Tiempo de Cozumel,* and *Diario de Quintana Roo.* They're available on all three islands.

Telephone – *A word of warning:* Mexican phone numbers are as subject to change as a chameleon on a kilt. Those given here are as accurate as we can make them. When in doubt, try the operator, the hotel concierge, or the tour/activities desk (or all three) — and patience.

ENTRY REQUIREMENTS: US citizens need no passports, but proof of citizenship (valid passport, birth certificate, voter's registration, naturalization certificate, Armed Forces ID card); Canadian citizens need valid passports or birth certificates; both must have tourist cards obtainable free at Mexican embassies and consulates, airlines and travel agencies booking trips to Mexico, Mexican Ministry of Tourism offices, Greyhound Bus Line offices, or American Automobile Association offices. Carry both with you at all times.

CLIMATE AND CLOTHES: Year-round temperatures average in the low 80s F (about 27°C). From October through April, sunny days prevail; in July, August, and September there are brief showers, usually in the afternoons. At the resorts, most of the days you'll wear beach clothes, with cover-ups or caftans for protection from too much sun. You're requested to wear tennis clothes (though not necessarily all white), especially shoes, on the courts. For sightseeing trips, light dresses, tops and skirts, or pants are most comfortable for women; slacks and shirts for men (don't forget a bathing suit). Nights are also casual but neat (discos bar T-shirts and sneakers). Neither coats nor ties are required for men, but many women tend to dress up a bit — something like floor-length skirts or dressy pants and tops at Cancún's posher hotels. The same, on a slightly less stylish level, goes for Cancún's smaller hotels and Cozumel. On Isla Mujeres, a fresh shirt and a pair of slacks are as dressy as an evening ever gets.

MONEY: To say the Mexican government has allowed the peso to "float" is to understate the case substantially. During the latter half of 1987, the peso was officially devalued twice in relation to the US dollar and the Canadian dollar; at press time, experts still have no notion where it will finally settle. As a result, lowered hotel, restaurant, and sightseeing prices make many parts of Mexico great travel bargains. But not Cancún. So many Norte Americanos are flocking here that hotel space is hard to come by, and prices remain high, especially during the high season (December 15 to April 15). The wisest economic course seems to be to buy a package that includes transporation and accommodations at a price lower than that of these same elements if purchased individually on your own.

Relative values still apply (e.g., an expensive hotel charges more than a moderate one), so we have calculated prices at 2,500 pesos to the US dollar, which is the approximate exchange rate as we go to press. But don't fail to check current newspaper or bank quotations with your travel agent for last-minute package deals. Credit cards and traveler's checks are still widely accepted in Mexico, but cash sometimes means a saving of the 15% value added tax (IVA), at least on retail store purchases.

LANGUAGE: Spanish is official, but some English is usually understood and spoken in tourist areas of Cancún, Cozumel, and Chichén Itzá. Its use is somewhat rarer in Isla Mujeres, but with a little patience and a phrase book, you can manage fine and acquire a little Spanish in the bargain. It's more fun that way.

TIME: Mexico's Caribbean islands lie in the Central Standard Time Zone. When it's noon in Cozumel, Cancún, and Isla Mujeres, it's noon CST in Chicago and 1 PM Eastern Standard Time in New York. From spring through fall, when it's noon in these islands, it's 1 PM Central Daylight Time in Chicago and 2 PM EDT in New York.

CURRENT: Electricity in Cancún, Cozumel, and at the *El Presidente Caribe* in Isla Mujeres is 110 volts, 60 cycles, so no adapters are needed for electric appliances. But don't count on a reliable supply of electricity in other Isla Mujeres hotels.

GETTING THERE: To Cancún, Mexicana jets in from Chicago, Miami (about 1½ hours), Dallas, and Philadelphia (about 4 hours); Aeroméxico, from Atlanta, New York (about 4 hours), Houston, Miami, and Los Angeles; Continental, from Atlanta, New Orleans, Houston (about 1½ hours), San Diego, Los Angeles (about 5½ hours), and Denver (about 4¾ hours via Houston). United flies direct to Cancún from Chicago, as does American Airlines from Dallas/Fort Worth. Both Mexican airlines also jet in from Mexico City (about 1¾ hours). Lacsa flies from New Orleans. Aero Cozumel and Aero Caribe make connections between Cancún, Cozumel, and Chichén Itzá on the mainland. Increasing numbers of cruise ships are calling in winter.

To Cozumel, Mexicana also schedules daily jets from Miami. AeroMéxico provides service from Dallas, Miami, Houston (just under 2 hours) daily and from Atlanta (6½ hours) four times a week. Continental has daily flights from Houston. United flies in from Chicago three times a week. There's ferry service from Playa del Carmen on the mainland near Cancún (1 hour; one-way fare, under $1). It, too, is gaining popularity as a cruise port.

To Isla Mujeres, Aerocaribe now has two flights a day from Cancún and Cozumel. The ferry from Punta Sam on the mainland carries vehicles and people — currently for about $1 per trip per car — but the passenger boat from Puerto Juárez brings most visitors, takes an hour, and costs well under $1 per person one way.

CALCULATING COSTS: Although the Mexican peso continues to plummet, the inflation rate of well over 100% per year has caused the costs of hotel, restaurant, and other tourist services to rise precipitously. In Cancún, Cozumel, and Isla Mujeres, prepaid packages remain surprisingly economical, however, and the government has established guidelines for hotels of different categories, both for the winter and summer seasons. During the summer months, rates are often as much as 50% less than during high season. At press time, word has it that a full-scale Mexican breakfast (*huevos rancheros,* etc.) for two will usually cost about $7, and a multicourse dinner at a very nice place, from $35 to $45 for two.

Visitors must be prepared to pay a $10 airport departure tax and a 15% Value Added Tax on hotel room and meals.

GETTING AROUND: Taxi – Small green and white cabs are available at reasonable fares, according to zone, in the Cancún area (fare from the most distant hotel to the city is about $2). On Cozumel, meterless island taxis operate by arrangement; i.e., you and the driver agree on a price for the proposed trip before you get into the cab. The average ride comes to about $1.50 plus tip.

Bus – In Cancún, transfers between the airport and local hotels are handled by a fleet of minibuses that depart promptly, handle all luggage, and charge under $3 per person. From 7 AM until midnight, another bus flock covers the distance between Cancún City and the Tourist Zone's hotels and shopping area; fare is about 25¢, and it's a popular way to get around. On Cozumel, the minibus fare from the airport to island hotels runs about $1 per person.

Car Rental – On Cancún, several agencies offer rental cars from $35 to $150 a day (including mileage): *Avis* (phone: 4-2147, 3-0828); *Budget* (phone: 4-2126); *Econorent* (phone: 4-1435); *Fast,* which also rents Jeeps (phone: 3-1850); and *Holiday* (phone: 4-1061). Agencies on Cozumel include *Avis* (phone: 2-0099) and *Hertz* (phone: 2-0100); car rental runs about $50 per day (including mileage). Jeeps rent for about $65 per day (including 200 kilometers).

Mopeds – Small motorbikes, an easy way to get around, are available at many Cancún hotels. The *Casa Maya* and *Franky's* at the *Krystal* are two that rent mopeds for about $20 for an 8-hour day. On Cozumel, *Ruben's* charges the same for a 24-hour rental. On Isla Mujeres, motorbikes — available about 50 paces from the ferry dock, also for about $20 a day — are the only way to go.

Sightseeing Taxi Tours – Some taxi drivers on Cancún are guides (your hotel activities person will know several) and for about $35 for the half day will drive you to Tulum and Xel-Ha. For two or more, it's the cheapest, most pleasant way to go. Private, air-conditioned cars with English-speaking drivers are available for $100 per day (phone: 4-5255 or 4-3694).

Sightseeing Bus Tours – A number of Cancún agencies operate bus tours to sites on the mainland; chances are there is one with a desk in your hotel lobby. If not, contact *Intermar Caribe* at *El Presidente* (phone: 4-4121), *Viajes Parmarc* at the *Plaza del Sol* hotel (phone: 4-1934), or *Wagon-lits* at the *Camino Real* (phone: 3-0100).

Sea Excursions – On Cancún, take a bus or taxi (under $4 for the trip) to Puerto Juárez on the mainland north of Cancún City to catch the Isla Mujeres ferry; the voyage costs under $1 per person round trip, and you can spend the day, catch the 4:30 or 5:30 PM boat back. The *Corsario,* a 50-foot replica of an 18th-century pirate ship, sails for Isla Mujeres for snorkeling at *El Garrafón,* with a seafood lunch included. During the winter season, the *México,* billed as the world's largest water jet, makes two round trips daily from Cozumel to Playa del Carmen (phone: in Cozumel, 2-0477; in Cancún, 4-5385). The trimarans *Manta* (phone: 3-0048) and *Aqua Quinn* (phone: 3-1883) make daily sails to Isla Mujeres from Cancún for snorkeling at *El Garrafón,* with lunch, entertainment, and open bar included. Both leave at 11 AM and return around 5 PM.

Also available are the Fiesta Maya glass-bottom-boat excursion, which includes lunch, open bar, and snorkeling for $25 per person, and the Noche Pirata on the *Tropical,* an evening cruise to Isla Mujeres, with dinner and open bar, for $35 per person. Cozumel's Robinson Crusoe Cruise to Passion Island and Isla Mujeres' daylong sails to the Contoy Island bird sanctuary are good fun too. In Isla Mujeres, the yacht *Antares* can be chartered for $600 a day or about $20 per person.

Air Excursions – For a different perspective, *Aerocaribe* (phone: in Cancún, 4-1231 or 4-2562; in Cozumel, 2-0928) and *Aero Cozumel* (same phone numbers) operate daily sightseeing flights to Chichén Itzá on the Yucatecan mainland. A 4-hour trip, including guide, ground transportation, and entrance to the ruins, costs about $65 per person.

 SHOPPING: In addition to traditional Mexican crafts (silver, ceramics, papier-mâché, alabaster, leather, straw stuff), there are boutiques stocked with imported perfumes, fashions (especially accessories), crystal, china, etc. Mexican resortwear (embroidered and lace-trimmed caftans, beach cover-ups, shirts) is brightly colored, fun, and remarkably reasonable in price, considering the amount of handwork involved. But be careful about those classic Yucatecan take-homes — huipils (loose, white, native dresses embroidered at neck and hem) and guayabera shirts (dressy-casual with tucked fronts, sometimes embroidery) — they can look either terrific or very tacky. So be sure to try one on before you buy. Sisal mats, hats, rugs, and bags are another local specialty. Cancún offers the widest variety of quality shops, and Cozumel has a number of boutiques and bazaars worth looking into. On Isla Mujeres, head for the beach instead.

Cancún's tourist shops are concentrated along the Avenida Tulum, between the Avenidas Uxmal and Coba, and range from superior to so-so. In Cozumel, shop along Calle Hidalgo and the Malecón.

Pay particular attention to silver jewelry; new customs regulations make the first twelve pieces exempt from duty even when purchased for a value in excess of the $100 per person customs limit that is normally imposed. The booklet *GSP & the Traveler,* available free from the US Customs Service, PO Box 7118, Washington, DC 20044, will give you some hints about other items that may be available duty free.

La Casita (7 and 37 Av. Tulum) is stacked with super Mexican clothes — muslin caftans, batik skirts, tunics, tops, and shirts (even their guayaberas look good) — at agreeable prices. Ask if you don't see your size; they can often run one up in a day or so. Silver and coral jewelry is sold, too. *Ki Huic* (Av. Tulum near Coba) is the city-sponsored 44-stall crafts market — big and bustling with occasional finds, but not always the town's best prices. *Dominique Imports* (at Plaza Caracol and at 33 and 45 Av. Tulum) specializes in French perfumes, jewelry, fashion. *Pepe's* (Av. Tulum and in El Parian Centro Commercial) is very big in scenic T-shirts, jeans, and the usual souvenirs.

Much more elegant, overall, are the *Zona Turistica* shops in *Centro Comercial El Parian* at the Convention Center, the nearby *Plaza Caracol* and *Mauna Loa* shopping centers, *Plaza Nautilus, Costa Blanca,* and *Plaza Terramar.*

In El Parian: *L'Epoque,* a vast selection of T-shirts; *Victor,* a connoisseur's collection of Mexican jewelry, ceramics, textiles, mobiles, papier-mâché baubles, and endearing (also inexpensive) Christmas ornaments; *Ronay,* specializing in gold and black coral jewelry; *Sportif,* with all the right names in golf, tennis, fishing, diving clothes and equipment — sports excursions are offered, too; and *Anakena* for intriguing Mayan art.

In the Mauna Loa Center: *Georgia,* with lovely dresses and Mexican resortwear designed by Georgia Charujas, and *Place Vendôme,* specializing in French clothes, crystal, perfumes, and cosmetics.

In Plaza Caracol: *Galerías Colonial,* specializing in tableware with beautifully painted patterns, carved marble knickknacks, and chess sets.

In Cozumel: *Bazaar Cozumel,* in town on Av. Juárez, collects the work of 200 first-rate Mexican artisans — silver, tapestries with modern art motifs, woven work, pottery, and lots more, at fair prices; *Boutique Calypso,* at *El Presidente* hotel, is a related operation. *La Casita,* also on Raphael E. Melgar Blvd., is the parent of the Cancún store, the source of more smashing Mexican resort clothes as well as Sergio Bustamante's imaginative animals and birds. Also in downtown San Miguel: the *Plaza del Sol,* a nest of nearly a dozen art, craft, jewelry, and import boutiques including *Los Cinco Soles,* with lots of black coral, papier-mâché, carved wood, and alabaster objects; and *Casablanca,* on the Malecón, for silver and quality crafts. *Orbi,* on Rafael E. Melgar, offers clothes, jewelry, and imported specialty foods.

TIPPING: No service charge is added to hotel bills; so give the room maid the equivalent of 50¢ a night, the bellboys the equivalent of $1 for two to three bags and 50¢ for calls that require a trip to your room. Give the doorman the equivalent of 25¢ when he calls you a cab; give taxi drivers 10% of the tab, if they seem to charge a fair price. Airport porters get the same amount as bellboys. In Cancún, you don't have to leave any additional sum when a 15% service charge is added to your food or drink bill; in Cozumel and on Isla Mujeres, where there is seldom a service charge, tip 10% to 15%. Also, tip gas station attendants 100 to 200 pesos for service.

SPECIAL EVENTS: The annual *Cancún Fair* takes place in November, with cockfights, dances, and shows. In April, a sailing regatta from New Orleans ends in Cozumel. Isla Mujeres hosts regattas from St. Petersburg, Florida, and Galveston, Texas, in May and June. A unique attraction on the first day of spring or fall is the Chichén Itzá phenomenon, when light and shadow strike the Castillo pyramid in such a manner that the snake god Kukulkán appears to be crawling along the side of the monument. A recently constructed replica of "El Castillo" at the Anthropology Museum in Cancún's Convention Center reproduces this phenomenon.

Mexicans enjoy celebrating so much that they often take off the day before and the day after a holiday, as well as the big day itself. So although not all of the following are officially designated as national holidays, most banks, businesses, and government offices are closed on: January 1 (*New Year's Day*), February 5 (*Constitution Day*), March 21 (*Juárez' Birthday*), *Easter* (and often much of the preceding week), May 1 (*Labor Day*), May 5 (to commemorate the *Battle of Puebla*), September 1 (*National Day,* on which the president delivers a State of the Nation address), September 15–16 (*Independence Day*), October 12 (*Columbus Day*), November 1–2 (Days of the Dead or *All Saints' Days*), November 20 (*Anniversary of the Mexican Revolution*), December 12 (feast day of the Virgin of Guadelupe), and December 25 (*Christmas*).

SPORTS: As on most islands, water activities come first, and they're most of what it's all about on Cozumel and Isla Mujeres. But especially on Cancún, the possibilities don't end there.

Bicycling – A serpentine bike path of pink brick bordered by garden plants and the seashore is part of the Cancún Master Plan; 6 miles — with palapa-topped rest stops along it — are now open. Bicycles can be rented near the entrance to the golf club.

Boating – Boats can be rented through most hotels in Cancún and on Cozumel. Small sailboats go for about $15 an hour; outboards rent for $20 to $25. In addition to hotels, rentals are also available through *Marina Mauna Loa, Cancún Yacht Club,* and *Club de Pesca Pez Vela.* Cozumel's yacht harbor is in Caleta Inlet. Isla Mujeres has a good anchorage, and boat rentals can be arranged through *Mexico Divers;* small boats cost about $20 per hour.

Golf – Only in Cancún, where the relatively new *Pok-ta-Pok* course — complete with its own Mayan ruin — is laid out along a series of close-linked islands separating the Nichupte and Boroquez lagoons. Robert Trent Jones, Jr., devised interesting challenges in spite of the flat terrain (6,800 yards, par 72). Greens fees are about $25 per day; carts, $18 per round; club rental, about $10 per round. For starting time and free transportation, call 3-0871.

Snorkeling and Scuba – The variety of the reefs and the clarity of the water (average undersea visibility, year-round, is 100 feet, but you can often see much farther) make Mexico's Caribbean a top area for underwater exploring. Cozumel takes the diving honors. Its prime attractions are the reefs 500 yards off the island's leeward shore, along El Cantil (the Drop-Off), the edge of the shelf that borders the Yucatán Channel to the south. Famous 6-mile-long Palancar Reef has — in addition to forests of black, staghorn, and other species of live coral and friendly swarms of Day-Glo–colored fish — a number of antique wrecks in which to poke around. You can dive to look and take pictures, but removing flora or fauna is strictly forbidden.

Prices for water sports services vary considerably and can be negotiated through your hotel, various privately owned marinas, and dive shops. Several dive shops on the malecón in San Miguel — including *Aqua Safari* (phone: 2-0101), *Discover Cozumel Dive Shop* (phone: 2-0280), and *Fantasia Divers* (phone: 2-0700) — offer rental equipment, instruction, and dive trips. Most hotels also offer diving facilities at somewhat higher rates, but the on-site convenience is worth it. Scuba pool instruction (about 2 hours) costs about $50 per person. A 3-day seminar with a certified instructor (first day: pool instruction and shallow shore dive; second day: boat dive to shallow reef; third day: full boat dive to Palancar Reef) is about $290 per person. A full day's guided diving tour from Cozumel to Palancar — including equipment and lunch — is about $35. Equipment rentals run about $6 for tank and weights, under $6 for a regulator, and $6 for fins, mask, and snorkel.

For an area that offers scuba divers so much, Cozumel seems short on good snorkeling spots; best are the shallow reefs to the south, where depths range from 5 to 35 feet. Chankanab Lagoon, midway down the leeward coast, with its underwater grottoes and fairly large fish population, is a good place for beginners to get their fins wet. (However, since suntan lotion collects in the water and harms the fish, swimming and snorkeling are not always permitted.)

Cancún's best scuba diving and snorkeling are found in the reef-filled waters off its southern point. Dive trips and equipment rental can be arranged through your hotel. A 5-hour dive trip, with pool check-out and an ocean dive, costs about $50, including equipment. Snorkel gear rents for about $5 per person for the day. Guided scuba trips cost about $45 per person, including equipment rental.

Isla Mujeres is surrounded by reefs, so snorkeling is very good along its shores. Scuba divers can rent equipment from *Mexico Divers* on the waterfront or at *El Presidente Caribe* for about $45 per day. *Mexico Divers* will also arrange dive trips for about $25 per hour, including one tank of air.

Spectator Sports – Bullfights are held on Wednesdays at the Silverio Pérez ring in Cancún City, beginning at 3:30 PM. Tickets are $13 general admission and are available through hotel travel desks.

Sport Fishing – A major activity on the islands — with sailfish in season from March to mid-July, bonito and dolphin (May to early July), wahoo and kingfish (May to September), and plenty of barracuda, red snapper, bluefin, grouper, mackerel, and white marlin year-round. Out of Cozumel, fishing boats (with four fighting chairs) cost $225 to $450 a day including tackle, crew, lunch, and drinks; larger boats run from about $200 up per day. Cancún charter firms charge about $380 to $420 per day (7 AM to 3 PM) for a boat that holds up to six. At nearby Puerto Juárez, rates run about $125 to $250 a day for two to four. Groups of six to eight can be organized for approximately

$65 per person. Hotels on both islands will handle all arrangements. On Isla Mujeres, *Mexico Divers* and *El Cañon* set up deep-sea trips for about $350 ($20 per person) a day including crew, tackle, and drinks for four.

Swimming and Sunning – Cancún's beaches on both its surf-pounded Caribbean side and its more serene Bahia de Mujeres and lagoon shores are the most remarkable. The texture and whiteness of the sand is so distinctive it inspired special studies by geologists who found that many of the individual grains contain microscopic, star-shaped fossils of an organism called Discoaster, extinct for 70 million years. Through the ages, the sea has ground and polished these grains till they've become brilliant and powder-soft. What's more, their limestone composition has an air conditioning effect that makes the island's sand — even under the noonday sun — feel comfortable to bare feet or bodies in bikinis. Except right in Cancún City, chances are your hotel will have its own beach as well as a pool, but the Master Plan has provided several public strands — Playa Tortugas and Playa Chac-Mool, for just two examples, both with breezy, open-air restaurants — that you may want to visit, too.

Cozumel's beaches — mostly on the island's leeward side, north and south of San Miguel — are shaped into distinctive coves. The majority of hotels are there, too, and chances are you'll spend most of your sun and sea time on your own hotel's sands. But you can visit others, including the lengthy one at San Francisco (a bit crowded these days — particularly on weekends); the more secluded shore of Passion Island, cupped in its north coast bay; and Punta Morena, on the rough side with a sheltered lagoon nearby. Because the undertow can be tricky, it's a good idea to observe the currents before you take the plunge (plan to enter the water at one point, exit at another), and never swim alone.

On Isla Mujeres, the southern beach called El Garrafon, with its undersea gardens and intriguing formations of fish, is the target of many day trips from Cancún. Tortugas and Maria's are less crowded.

Tennis – The larger Cancún and Cozumel hotels have a tennis court or two each; and Cancún's *Club Med* has 8. Several layouts on each island are lighted for night play. Cancún's *Pok-ta-Pok Golf Club* also has 2 tennis courts where rates are about $7 per hour during the day and $9 at night. Several Cancún hotels also have squash courts.

Water Skiing and Windsurfing – Fine on the calm, leeward side of all three islands. On Cancún, ski-boat time costs about $50 an hour; Cozumel and Isla Mujeres rates run about the same or slightly lower. Windsurf boards rent for about $14 an hour.

 NIGHTLIFE: In the Mexican Caribbean, if you're looking for something more than the light of the moon and the song of the tree frog to turn things on after dark, Cancún is your place. Las Vegas it isn't, or even San Juan. But there's still plenty to do. The "happy hour" — two drinks for the price of one — is from 5 to 7 PM, but the dinner crowd doesn't start arriving until 8 or 9 PM. *Carlos 'n' Charlie's* continues to be the most popular rallying spot, a great place for meeting, eating, drinking, and dancing. For Mexican color, the must-see show is the *Ballet Folklórico,* a worthy spinoff of the famous Mexico City production, which plays the Convention Center weekly (phone: 3-0199 to find out when). The Tropical show at the *Mauna Loa* gives you the feeling it's playing the wrong ocean. Hotel bars offer "life music" (i.e., not recorded) of many *grupos* as well as fiesta nights. *Aquarius* at the *Camino Real, Tabano's* at the *Sheraton, Cristine's* at the *Krystal, LaBoom,* and *Magic* draw the sleekest disco crowds. Pirates' costumes, an open bar, a show, music, dancing, and a buffet come with the Noche Pirata cruise for about $35.

On Cozumel, *Scaramouche, Maya 2000* at the *Sol Caribe,* and *Neptune* discos appeal to a young, lively crowd. *Tropicanerías* offers Latin music. The larger hotels often feature small combos. Isla Mujeres now has *Tequila Video Disco, Bubo's, Calypso,* and *Casablanca.*

506

BEST ON THE COAST

 CHECKING IN: From our point of view, it seems a shame to travel all the way to the Mexican Caribbean and then not stay on the beach. Therefore, Cancún City hotels are not on our list, but if you must be inland, try the *Plaza del Sol* (phone: 4-3888) or *Antillano* (phone: 4-1532).

For a double room without meals in a hotel listed below, expect to pay up to $250 a day for very expensive, $125 to $140 for expensive, $75 to $100 for moderate, and under $50 for inexpensive.

CANCÚN

Camino Real – Architecturally impressive (the room wing is stair-stepped like a Mayan pyramid), magnificently sited on a point, with the Caribbean surrounding the building on three sides. Lots to do (2 beaches, pools, tennis, diving, restaurants, bars, disco, excursions). Just the right blend of style and relaxed pace (some room balconies have hammocks). A Westin hotel, with 300 rooms (phone: 3-0100). Very expensive.

Club Méditerranée – Well away from the rest of the world at the far southern end of the island. Marvelous beach; all sports. Relatively new and among the best-looking of all the Club Meds in this part of the world; with 305 rooms. All activities, meals with wine included (phone: 4-2090). Very expensive.

Exelaris Hyatt Cancún Caribe – Stylish resort with 202 terraced rooms, including 60 beachfront villas, overlooking a vast, secluded beach. Well set up in the sports department, with a large pool, 3 tennis courts; handy to golf. Friendly atmosphere (phone: 3-0044). Very expensive.

Exelaris Hyatt Regency Cancún – Beautifully housed under a glass atrium, all 300 rooms have ocean views. There is a lovely beach, pool, and 4 restaurants (phone: 3-0966). Very expensive.

Krystal – Lush and thick with greenery inside and out, and with 325 rooms, it offers one of Cancún's best beaches, tennis, and 5 fine restaurants, including a good breakfast buffet and excellent, friendly service (phone: 3-1133). Very expensive.

El Presidente – Completely remodeled, it has a Mexican-modern lobby, indoor-outdoor dining room with a vaulted roof, pool area, beach, and 2 tennis courts; adjacent to golf course; 295 stately air-conditioned rooms, suites. Fully equipped for sports; most popular beach in town (phone: 3-0200). Very expensive.

Villas Tacul – A colony of 23 Spanish-style villas with gardens, patios, and kitchens, where guests can set up luxurious housekeeping, eat out in the *Palapa Restaurant*, arrange for someone to come in — or all of the above. With 2 to 5 bedrooms per house, on a narrow (but pleasant) beach. Good for families and congenial 2- or 3-couple groups (phone: 3-0000). Very expensive.

Aristos Cancún – Friendly scale, nice sense of Mexican hospitality. Smallish but pleasant 222 rooms. Inviting pool area, beach, restaurant; popular nightly folkloric show (phone: 3-0011). Expensive.

Casa Maya – Originally built as condominiums and now a spacious hotel with sophisticated decor, it has 100 rooms and 250 suites with good kitchens, dining areas, terraces. Pool, restaurant, bar, and tennis (phone: 3-0555). Expensive.

Fiesta Americana – The grand pastel pleasure dome was planned to intensify night excitement as well as day fun. Ergo, management seems at least as proud of its high-voltage lounges, restaurants, and disco as it is of its sprawling, waterfall-fed pool, long list of water sports, and day trips. With 280 good-looking, balconied rooms overlooking the water (phone: 3-1400). Expensive.

Sheraton – Super-deluxe property with 471 rooms (some with their own Jacuzzis) on a lovely long stretch of sand at the end of the present hotel line. Somewhat "away" feeling, yet entirely accessible. Grand scale, with all the resort trimmings: multiple swimming pools, bars, theater, helpful tour desk, even aerobics classes; attractive restaurants, and popular *Tabano's* disco (phone: 3-1988). Expensive.

Cancún Viva – Fresh and pleasing, attractively informal, with 210 air-conditioned suites, rooms, huge pool, tennis, restaurant, bar, full excursion services. Especially good tennis (phone: 3-0800). Expensive.

Club Lagoon – Water-sports–oriented — casual, active, relaxed — this hotel is perched at the edge of Nichupté Lagoon, whose waters are clear and calm. It has its own marina and fleet of sailboats, windsurfers, speedboats for tows, snorkeling trips; excellent scuba, fishing connections, too. There's a multilingual staff and the clientele contains a noticeable percentage of Europeans. With 70 double rooms, 20 suites; terrace and Continental restaurants, *La Palapa* for day snacks, drinks, night fun, and dancing (phone: 3-1111). Moderate.

Maya Caribe – The 40 bright air-conditioned rooms overlook 3 pools, half with sea views, too. Intimate island atmosphere; restaurant and bar ditto (phone: 3-0602 or 800-517-7770). Moderate.

Playa Blanca – Lots of enjoyable atmosphere for not very much money. With 150 bright, attractive air-conditioned rooms, terraced suites, laid out around small gardens and patios by the sea. Little beach, pool, bar, restaurants; top water sports marina. A Best Western hotel. Midway between town and convention center (phone: 3-0344). Moderate.

COZUMEL

Cozumel Caribe – The 257 rooms are on San Juan Beach to the north. Popular and picturesque, with meals, drinks, diving, fishing, and sightseeing tours included in the price (phone: 2-0100). Expensive.

Fiesta Americana – There's been new style and life here since new management took over and refurbished this potentially handsome place built into a gardened hillside between beach and jungle. With 200 rooms, 20 suites, several bars, restaurant, and coffee shop; pool and beach with full water sports setup, 3 lighted tennis courts, a popular disco, children's playground (phone: 2-0700). Expensive.

Mayan Plaza – Run by a family that seems to care, this place has 122 rooms and 14 suites that are large and furnished with Spanish-style furniture. On the northern beach, it has the usual water sports; there's dancing in the evenings (phone: 2-0411). Expensive.

Cabañas del Caribe – It has 57 rooms, including 15 cabañas; popular with the diving crowd and deep-sea fishermen. Access to tennis facilities at the *Mayan Plaza*. Breezy dining terrace is so near the water's edge it's practically in it. Congenial. Try to get one of the new rooms (phone: 2-0072). Moderate.

Cantarell – A mile and a half north of town, it offers 15 suites and 74 sea-viewing rooms, white sand beach, 2 pools, complete dive shop, rental scooters and cars to go. The Caracol sun-and-shade bar and *Palapa* restaurant (good Mexican and international food) are popular late-day gathering spots (phone: 2-0144, 2-0127). Moderate.

La Ceiba – With 115 balconied rooms in an attractive, low-rise structure of simple lines. Wide stone terraces, pool, white sand beach; water sport boats and dock, certified scuba instruction. Most personable and pleasing. Family plan rates available (phone: 2-0379, 2-0844). Moderate.

El Cozumeleño – This property on San Juan Beach has 84 large rooms, a restaurant, and a free-form pool (phone: 2-0050). Moderate.

La Perla – Quiet, comfortable, and unpretentious, it has 22 neatly styled, nicely maintained rooms right on the shore. With a pool, private swimming cove, water sports, a dock with connections for private yachts, a dive shop, and restaurant, it can be an agreeable headquarters if independent action is your style. Continental plan rates (phone: 2-0188). Moderate.

El Presidente – Its 190 rooms and 9 suites are surrounded by palms on San Francisco Beach, south of town. Gardens, big chaise-lined pool, tennis (phone: 2-0322). Moderate.

Playa Azul – Situated on a lovely beach, this family favorite has 60 rooms and suites, restaurant, bar, tennis courts, and all water sports (phone: 2-0033). Moderate to inexpensive.

Villablanca – Small activity-oriented enclave with restaurant, beach, bar, and dive shop on one side of south shore road; 30 rooms and suites, pool, tennis courts on the other. Big on moderately priced dive packages (phone: 2-0730). Inexpensive.

ISLA MUJERES

Posada del Mar – The 42 pleasant rooms are in town; with palm-shaded grounds, pool, tennis courts, bar, and dining room. Friendly management (phone: 2-0198). Moderate.

Kan Kin – Formerly a popular restaurant called *Maria's,* now expanded to include 8 rooms and suites and 1 palapa-style bungalow. Very romantic, and El Garrafón is a short walk away (phone: 3-1420). Moderate to inexpensive.

Cabañas María del Mar – Its 35 units (including the recently remodeled original cabanas) are located in a coconut grove on the shore. There's a full-service, 20-slip marina, restaurant, and disco (phone: 2-0179). Inexpensive.

Perlas del Caribe – The old *Rocas del Caribe,* remodeled and enlarged, now has 94 rooms, 3 suites, a restaurant, and pool; telephones and TV in the lobby. At Playa Norte (phone: 2-0507). Inexpensive.

El Presidente Caribe – Redecorated and refurbished, this 6-story, 104-room hotel sits on a picturesque point with its own small beach. Full activity program, services (phone: 2-0002, 2-0122). Inexpensive.

Rocamar – Very simple, friendly 34-room hotel perched on a rocky point above the Caribbean — ergo, views are fine (each room has a balcony), but swimming not so. Still, beaches aren't far away. With informal bar, restaurant (phone: 2-0101). Inexpensive.

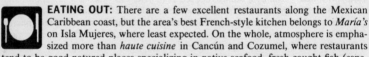 **EATING OUT:** There are a few excellent restaurants along the Mexican Caribbean coast, but the area's best French-style kitchen belongs to *María's* on Isla Mujeres, where least expected. On the whole, atmosphere is emphasized more than *haute cuisine* in Cancún and Cozumel, where restaurants tend to be good-natured places specializing in native seafood, fresh-caught fish (especially red snapper), and steaks. One or two tourist restaurants in Cancún offer Yucatecan dishes — not so pepper-hot as those of some other Mexican states. There's *sopa de lima* (chicken-based soup spiked with fresh lime juice), *pollo pibil* (chicken baked in a special sauce), and *filete de venado* (venison steak — in season). Also *panuchos, salbutes,* and *codzitos* — tortillas filled with different kinds of meat. *Muc-bil pollo* is a tamale pie filled with chicken. And desserts include *torta del cielo,* a rich almond cake, and *tejocote,* a plumlike fruit generally served stewed or candied.

Tequila, which you're most likely to meet first in a margarita cocktail made with lime juice, chilled, and served in a salt-rimmed glass, is the national drink. It is also used in martinis, punches, collinses, and sunrises mixed with grenadine and lime juice. There are also very good Mexican beers (Carta Blanca, Bohemia), rums, wines from Baja California (good and lots cheaper than imported ones), and the Yucatecan liqueur Ixtabentum, distilled from the honey of the flower of that name, which grows only in the Yucatán. And the coffee liqueur Kahlua is a native Mexican drink.

Like almost everything else Mexican, at this writing, meals cost amazingly little. Big breakfasts are about $7 per person; lunches are very little more, and dinner for two in a first-rate place seldom runs more than $45. Expect to pay $50 to $60 for two at restaurants we list as very expensive; about $35 to $40, expensive; $25, moderate; and $15, inexpensive.

CANCÚN CITY

Augustus César – Seafood and Italian dishes are served with flair in a pretty setting. Claveles 13 (phone: 4-1261). Expensive.

La Dolce Vita – Intimate dining in a European outdoor café atmosphere, where the sweet life is manifested in tasty pasta and seafood dishes. Av. Cobá 87 (phone: 4-1384). Expensive.

El Pescador – Perhaps the best seafood restaurant in Cancún, it serves up fresh lobster, shrimp, and red snapper on Mexican pottery. Don't miss the Yucatecan lime soup or the hot rolls, and try for a table outside, on the fan-cooled terrace. Calle Tulipanes 5 (phone: 4-2673). Expensive.

La Patagonia – The taste treats here are authentic Argentine beef dishes — churrasco, empanadas, chimichurri, parrilladas — plus fresh-caught Caribbean lobster and seafood. Av. Cobá 18 (phone: 4-1860). Expensive to moderate.

Soberanis – Casual offshoot of Mérida original. Seafood, regional dishes, snacks, good beer. Famous morning-after special: fiery Vuelve a la Vida (Return to Life) seafood cocktail. Av. Cobá 5 (phone: 4-1125). Moderate.

Happy Lobster – Cheerfully casual casa where the emphasis is on the freshest fish and seafood. Nothing fancy, but with a big local following. Av. Tulum 33C (phone: 4-3316). Moderate to inexpensive.

Pizza Rolandi – Famed for its wood-oven pizzas, but also recommended by local lasagna lovers, fettuccine fanciers, other pasta masters. Av. Cobá 12 (phone: 4-4047). Moderate to inexpensive.

Los Almendros – Authentic Yucatecan food is served in this branch of its famous namesake in Mérida. Av. Bonampak and Sayil (phone: 4-0807). Inexpensive.

La Parrilla – Marvelous Mexican tacos, cheese fondue, and charcoal-grilled chicken. Big local following; open till dawn. Av. Yaxchilán (no phone). Inexpensive.

CANCÚN ZONA TURÍSTICA

Mauna Loa – Like Trader Vic's in a sombrero. Dim, with an island atmosphere, snazzy rum drinks with flowers floating in them. Savory Chinese/Polynesian food. Tropical dancers appear twice nightly. Near the Convention Center (phone: 3-0092). Very expensive.

Maxime – Formerly the mayor's home, this elegant restaurant has European furniture, Oriental rugs, English china, and French crystal in its four sitting rooms, one dining room, and an upstairs piano bar. The Swiss chef recommends the *terrine de canard au poivre vert* (duck terrine with peppercorns), *feuilleté d'escargots* (puff pastry with snails), *magret de canard à l'orange* (boneless duck with orange sauce), and for dessert, *soufflé à l'orange*. Brunch is served Saturdays and Sundays. Jackets not required, but no shorts, sneakers, or bare feet. Blvd. Kukulcán 8 (phone: 3-0438). Very expensive.

Bogart's – International cuisine served with quiet elegance in exotic Moroccan surroundings. *Krystal* (phone: 3-1333). Expensive.

Chac-Mool – Cancún's most romantic setting. Outdoors, with candlelight, soft music, seafood, and Italian temptations. Continental-style service seems slow. But who's in a hurry? On the beach (phone: 3-1107). Expensive.

Compass Rose – Steaks, seafood, and salads are served in a nautical setting. In the *Mauna Loa* shopping center (phone: 3-0693). Expensive.

La Gaviota – This handsome, contemporary restaurant serves expertly prepared Mexican dishes such as *huachinango à la Veracruzano* (red snapper in a spicy sauce) as well as international fare. In the *Sheraton* (phone: 3-1988). Expensive.

Hacienda el Mortero – A copy of an authentic Mexican hacienda still standing in Súchil, Durango, the specialties are steaks and Mexican haute cuisine. Next door to the *Krystal* (phone: 3-1133). Expensive.

El Tucán – A colorful restaurant in the *Camino Real* featuring authentic Mexican food such as *Tikin Xic,* fish broiled in banana leaves and served with *adobo* (a sauce prepared with a mixture of chiles, spices, and tomatoes), and *Chichén Itzá coffee,* made with coffee, orange liqueur, and *xtabentum,* a Yucatecan nectar (phone: 3-0100). Expensive.

Carlos 'n Charlie's – Meeting, greeting, good fun, and surprisingly good food at the lagoon's edge. Blvd. Kukulcán (phone: 3-0846). Expensive to moderate.

Shima – A pleasant Japanese restaurant with teppan-yaki tables, a sushi bar, and tatami room, conveniently located in Plaza Nautilus (phone: 4-5423). Expensive to moderate.

Casa Salsa – Outdoor and indoor dining, dancing, mariachis, and even a disc jockey. Cold avocado soup, oven-baked grouper or snapper, Yucatecan tamales, and *cochinita pibil* (a pork dish with spicy sauce) are among the specialties here. On the lagoon side of the island at *Plaza Caracol* (phone: 3-1114). Moderate.

Augustus Pizza – Central garden spot that's a favorite drop-in and après-disco destination. Hamburgers and hot dogs, too. Convention Center (phone: 3-0530). Inexpensive.

COZUMEL

El Acuario – Once a real aquarium, it's now an elegant restaurant serving fine seafood. The entertainment is provided by an immense aquarium filled with exotic tropical fish in the middle of the room. On the Malecón (no phone). Expensive.

Café del Puerto – A romantic Polynesian-style restaurant located upstairs on the Malecón. Among the favorites are snails in garlic, excellent seafood and steaks, and bananas flambée (phone: 2-0316). Expensive.

Carlos 'n' Charlie's & Jimmy's Kitchen – Cozumel incarnation of ubiquitous fun-and-food chain. Malecón (phone: 2-0191). Expensive.

Morgan's – Elegant dining in a nautical atmosphere. The seafood and steaks are excellent, the desserts spectacular. On the main plaza (phone: 2-0584). Expensive.

La Laguna – Seafood and well-prepared regional cuisine served under a huge palapa at Chankanaab Lagoon (no phone). Moderate.

Pepe's – A romantic spot by the waterfront with excellent seafood and steaks. Rafael Melgar (phone: 2-0213). Moderate.

Plaza Leza – A sidewalk café serving good Mexican snacks, charcoal-broiled steaks, and seafood. On the main plaza (phone: 2-1041). Moderate.

El Portal – A favorite for breakfast or drinks. On the Malecón near the ferry dock (phone: 2-0316). Moderate.

Soberanis – Cousin of the Cancún favorite where *motuleños* (Yucatecan ham and eggs) are the big breakfast item; also fine for Mexican snacks (tortillas, tacos, beans, shellfish) and cool beer anytime. Av. Rafael Melgar 471 (phone: 2-0246). Moderate.

Las Palmeras – A great meeting place, just opposite the ferry dock, it offers a varied menu for every meal. The homemade biscuits and French toast are a treat for breakfast. On the Malecón (no phone). Moderate to inexpensive.

Playa Maya – Seafood is the specialty and it's served only a few feet from the water's edge. Open for lunch and dinner. About 10 miles from town and a quarter mile from San Francisco beach (no phone). Inexpensive.

San Francisco – Right near the *Playa Maya* restaurant, it's larger, serves seafood, and is open only for lunch. A band plays in the afternoons (no phone). Inexpensive.

ISLA MUJERES

María's – A remarkable, thatch-topped place invented and watched over by a Frenchwoman named Marie but called María by everyone on the island. She does excellent crab bouillabaisse with advance warning, and a beautiful grilled lobster anytime. Right next to El Garrafón, so it's all this and snorkeling, too. Worth planning an island day trip around; several hotel rooms available. Open from 8 AM to 9PM (phone: 3-1420). Expensive.

Ciro's Lobster House – The local lobster house, where servings are generous, seafood is delicious, and the price is right. And — *mira!* — they take credit cards. Downtown at Matamoros and Guerrero (phone: 2-0102). Moderate.

Gomar – The crowd is cheerful; the food is Mexican and very good (especially fresh fish, seafood). So if the service is slow, it's worth the wait. In the heart of town at Hidalgo 5 at Madero (phone: 2-0142). Moderate.

Buho's Paradise – The place for a late, late snack and conviviality (Buho is a night owl). Next to *Cabañas María del Mar* on Av. Carlos Lazo 1 (phone: 2-0179). Inexpensive.

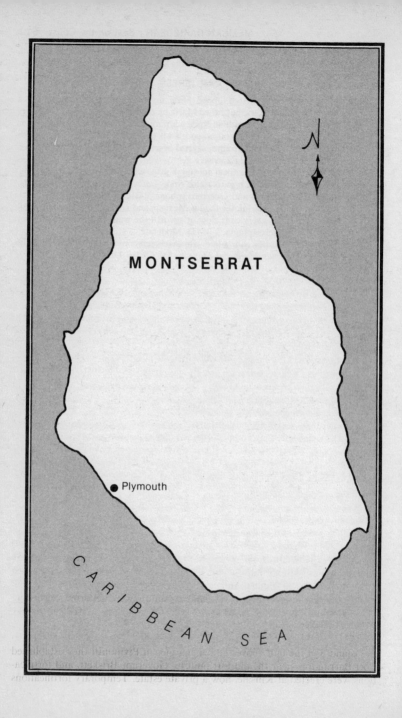

MONTSERRAT

● Plymouth

C A R I B B E A N   S E A

MONTSERRAT

The tiny volcanic island of Montserrat, a British Crown Colony floating quietly between Antigua and Guadeloupe in the Leeward Islands, was initially sighted by Columbus during his second visit to the Caribbean. It was later settled by the British, held on two occasions by the French after bitter fighting, used as a deportation colony by the British, and finally transformed into a British Crown Colony. Named by Columbus for the quiet hills surrounding the Abbey of Montserrat (where Ignatius Loyola formed the Society of Jesus), this quiet haven — the epitome of peace today — knew little tranquillity for almost 250 years.

The British decision to settle Montserrat was based more on their occupation of neighboring St. Kitts and Nevis than anything else. About 20 years after the initial English settlement, a large contingent of Irish were sent to the island; whether these people had been deported directly from Ireland as a result of their involvement in the rebellions suppressed by Oliver Cromwell, or had left the St. Kitts Colony of Sir Thomas Warner (either in search of greater autonomy, or under some pressure from the governor) is an unresolved question. There can be no doubt that a large portion of Montserrat's population was Irish at one time, and this is reflected in a number of red-haired islanders who even have a hint of brogue still left. Nevertheless, this is one of the most West Indian of all the Caribbean islands, still uncommercial and very proud of its culture and customs.

The Irish nicknamed Montserrat the Emerald Isle and justified their act of homesickness by the vibrant plant life, the forested mountains, and the incredible profusion of fruit that grew (and grows today) in the volcanic soil of the island. Beyond the skirts of gray and black volcanic beaches, Montserrat then was an island of giant ferns and tall trees climbing up the sides of its two volcanoes. It is the same today.

Shortly after the Irish made their homes on Montserrat, the French became interested in the island. The original island fortifications, which had been at Dagenham Beach, did not hold up very well (and have long since been built over). In 1664, British Governor Anthony Briskett, Jr., ordered the construction of new fortifications on a steep hill overlooking the city. The fort, never named, was considered impregnable because of the uphill approach, yet was taken by a force of French and Caribs, assisted by some Irish indentured workers, a year later. The governor and his family were deported, according to one account, "wearing only their shirts," to a British-held island, and the French remained for four years.

During the eighteenth century, the British built several new forts around the island. On the cliff above the banana pier in Plymouth they established Fort Barrington, near the old fort built by Governor Briskett, and fortifications were erected at Kinsale, now a private estate. Temporary fortifications were thrown together in 1782, in the face of another French invasion force. This fort, at St. George Hill, was overrun the following year, and the French took possession of Montserrat for the second time. It was returned to Britain by treaty shortly after the American Revolution.

Both the British and the Irish worked to make Montserrat into a farm and plantation island. Slaves were imported to develop sugar and lime plantations, and crops of potatoes, tomatoes, and other vegetables were planted. However perfect for semitropical wild growth, the terrain was simply too rugged for the kind of agriculture planned by the colonists.

The island remained an undisputed English possession for the next hundred years, but its plantations never did turn the island into the boom town and trading port for which the British had hoped. The limes and sugar produced were not sufficient to attract more than an occasional trading vessel, and the Sea Island cotton was not cheap enough, or produced in large enough quantities, to compete with other fabric sources. Traders might put into Montserrat for limes and juice, and perhaps some rum, but sailings were too infrequent for the island to be anything more than a minor port on the Caribbean. And with the abolition of slavery, agriculture was finished on the island.

Since that time, Montserrat has been more or less dependent on Britain for its economic livelihood. Though it produces enough fruit and vegetables for its own needs, and even exports bumper crops like tomatoes (vegetables grown in its water-rich volcanic soil are considered the best in the Caribbean), essentially the island remains undeveloped. Offered associate statehood by the British in 1966, Montserrat chose to remain a Crown Colony.

In recent years, the tourist trade has begun to notice Montserrat. It now boasts several first-class hotels, some pleasing restaurants, and a golf course that runs from a beach up the side of a mountain, with its clubhouse built into the ruins of a 200-year-old cotton gin. But the wild beauty that Columbus glimpsed from his ship almost 500 years ago survives: Tall ferns grow along the roads; forests stretch beyond sight into the mountain mists; and lime orchards scent the air.

The island's best-kept modern secret is hidden in a two-building compound in the northern hills. It's the home of state-of-the-art Air Studios, where the likes of Stevie Wonder, Elton John, Air Supply, and Paul McCartney have not only come to record, but returned again and again. The reason, of course, is the studio's near-perfect acoustical setup; but residents like to think the recording artists also come for the peace, privacy, and gentle welcome they find here. We'd have to agree. With accommodations for a total of 300 tourists, Montserrat, which describes itself as the island that's "the way the Caribbean used to be," should stay that way for years to come.

MONTSERRAT AT-A-GLANCE

FROM THE AIR: Montserrat is a pear-shaped island at 17° N latitude and 62° W longitude. It lies about 27 miles southwest of Antigua, and 275 miles southeast of Puerto Rico. Only about 7 miles long and 11 miles across at its widest point, almost a third of its 39 square miles is either virgin forest or unsuitable for any agricultural purpose. Half of what is left is devoted to tree crops or is otherwise cultivated. The remainder is developed or urban land. The island is of volcanic origin, with active sulfur vents from the core of the island in the mountain region. Two points are over 2,000 feet high. The approach to the island by plane stops just short of Mt. Chance, the tallest point on the island, which rises 3,000 feet above sea level.

SPECIAL PLACES: Plymouth – This colorful, charming port is marvelously West Indian in flavor but — as if still influenced by British mannerisms — tidy and well kept. It's an easy town to explore on foot, but dress properly; residents here don't appreciate bathing suits or other such skimpy dress. A small town of 2,000 people, Plymouth stretches along the Caribbean without a real harbor of its own — just a jetty to serve as a tie-up place for visiting yachtmen. The streets are quiet and clean; the entire town is very precise in its fashion — proper, neat, and serene. Touring Plymouth takes about an hour and a half, and it's best to start with Government House. This delightful Victorian structure, with its well-maintained lawns and gardens of flowering poincianas, gives the feeling that 18th-century Britain still exists; signing the visitors' book is a must. To honor the Irish who did so much to settle and cultivate this island, the building is decorated with a shamrock.

On Saturday mornings, the quiet town becomes a live-wire marketplace as rural islanders bring their produce into town and city merchants prepare for a big day of shopping. Vegetables, fruit, fresh fish, and old gossip change hands rapidly as villagers and farmers discuss island politics, weather, and argue prices in an age-old island ritual.

While in town, ask directions to the Philatelic Bureau, where there are displays of current and past stamp issues, prized by collectors and souvenir seekers alike.

From here look to St. Anthony's Church, just a few steps toward the outskirts of town. Originally constructed in 1640, the church was rebuilt in 1730, and the tamarind tree outside is said to be over 200 years old. On display inside the church are two silver chalices, which were gifts of emancipated slaves. A bit farther out on Richmond Hill, the National Trust's museum, ensconced in an antique sugar mill, displays a collection of artifacts, some of which date back to Carib times.

On another hill, about 1,200 feet above the town, is the old fort. Never really given a name, it was built in 1664 under the orders of Governor Anthony Briskett, Jr., who considered it impregnable. The French overran the fort a year later, and Governor Briskett and his family were deported.

Fort Barrington, on the cliff above the banana pier, was built in the 18th century but saw little action in the ensuing years. Fort St. George, built in the southern hills of the island, about a 15-minute drive from town, was thrown together in 1782 as a defense against an oncoming force of French and Carib invaders. The fortifications did not prevent the French from taking the island.

ELSEWHERE ON THE ISLAND

Soldiers Ghaut – The Indian word for river or ravine is *ghaut,* and in 1712 this ravine was the site of a valiant effort by an English captain and the few men in his command to prevent the invading French forces from striking while the unprepared island forces gathered themselves. It was said that the river through the ravine ran red with blood before the English let the French pass. It's in the hills near the north end of the island.

Rendezvous Beach – On the far northwest coast and reachable only by boat, it is the island's only white sand strand, a popular picnic destination.

Fox's Bay Bird Sanctuary – North of Plymouth, its mangrove swamp provides refuge for numerous sea birds and the island's "national" bird, the Montserrat oriole, found nowhere else in the world. There's also a fine black sand beach.

Galway's Estate – On the way south to Soufrière, this historic sugar plantation is the site of picturesque ruins and annual summer archaeological digs.

Galway's Soufrière – In the south-central region of Montserrat is a reminder that the volcano beneath its surface is not yet dead: a small (about 4 feet across), open crater bubbling with grayish-yellow molten sulfur. Many of the mountain guides will boil an egg in the hot sulfur, just for effect. In addition to giving off sulfur fumes, this crater also allows experts to monitor volcanic activity under the island.

Great Alps Waterfall – At the end of a healthy 1-mile hike through dense rain forest is this small waterfall, dropping 70 feet into a shallow pool of clear water — just deep enough to splash (but not swim) in. It's best to make the hike in the cool morning air. The roadway from which to start is about a 15-minute drive south of Plymouth. At noon, the overhead sun turns the mist over the pool into rainbows and reflects from the leaves of the bushes, trees, and flowers.

Chance Peak – The tallest point in Montserrat, 3,002 feet above sea level. It makes a fine viewing tower from which to plan your tour of the island, and the panorama is incredible. The climb can be difficult and hazardous without a guide, so arrange for one at any hotel before starting out. The mountain is near the airport, in the central section of the island.

SOURCES AND RESOURCES

TOURIST INFORMATION: The Montserrat Department of Tourism, 40 E 46th St., New York, NY 10017 (phone: 212-752-8660) and the Caribbean Tourism Association, 20 E 46th St., New York, NY 10017 (phone: 212-682-0435), will provide information about the island. You can write directly to the Montserrat Department of Tourism, PO Box 7, Plymouth, Montserrat, WI, with any specific questions.

On Montserrat, there is a small tourist office in Plymouth, on Church Rd. (phone: 2230). The entire downtown section runs along the waterfront. Since it's a friendly town, don't hesitate to ask questions of passersby.

Telephone – Dial direct to Montserrat by adding the area code 809 and the prefix 491 to the numbers given below.

ENTRY REQUIREMENTS: British, US, and Canadian citizens need only proof of citizenship — voter's registration card, driver's license, or passport — and a return or ongoing ticket.

CLIMATE AND CLOTHES: Temperatures in Montserrat vary between the low 70s F (20s C) and about 90°F (35°C) and the humidity is quite low. The average rainfall is about 62 inches per year, but it is irregular, and there is no wet or dry season. Dress tends to be more formal here than on other islands, so don't wear short shorts or your raggediest jeans in town. Evenings call for something slightly dressy. A sweater, light wrap, or jacket is recommended for evenings in December and January. Bring deck shoes or sneakers if you plan to go boating, sturdy, comfortable shoes if you're going to do much walking.

MONEY: Montserrat currency is the Eastern Caribbean dollar (EC) and simply called BeeWee by most people. The current exchange rate is about $1 US to $2.60 EC.

LANGUAGE: English, with the usual West Indian patois thrown in.

TIME: Montserrat is on Atlantic Standard Time. When it is 11 AM in Plymouth, it is 10 AM in New York City. During Daylight Saving months, island and US East Coast time is the same.

CURRENT: It's 220–230 volts, 60 cycles, AC; you'll need a converter for all US appliances here, although some hotels can provide one.

GETTING THERE: There is no nonstop service from North America. Most visitors fly in from Antigua, but connections can also be made through Guadeloupe and St. Kitts. The government has recently purchased two aircraft, and its own Montserrat Air Services (MAS) now controls all aspects of the 15-minute flight to and from the island. Their goals: concrete, confirmed reservations ("so nobody gets bumped"); smoother passenger and baggage handling; and maximum schedule flexibility to eliminate overnights in Antigua. Reservations are still handled through LIAT in North America and the islands. There is a $5 departure tax.

CALCULATING COSTS: Hotel rates in Montserrat vary widely depending upon the season. Winter rates run as high as $165 US for a double room with breakfasts and dinners in one of the best resorts on the island, though there are decent rooms available for less than $100 US per day, MAP. Villa rentals, an extremely popular option, range from about $400 to $1,200 and up per week in season. Off-season (mid-April to mid-December) prices drop by at least a third. Most hotels add a 10% service charge to their daily room rates, and there is a 7% tax.

GETTING AROUND: Taxi – Rates are standardized by law. The ride from the airport to Plymouth is about $9 US; from the airport to the hotels varies from about $9 to $13 US.

Bus – There are a number of private bus routes running from Plymouth to several outlying areas. The fare is nominal and based on the distance involved; it can be anything from 50¢ to $2 EC.

Car Rental – Montserrat has nearly 4,000 vehicles on the road, of which about 200 are rental cars. Contact your hotel desk or the Tourist Board to arrange a rental, or contact *Pauline's Car Rentals* on Amersham Rd. in Plymouth (phone: 2345). Standard rates are $28 to $40 US per day for a car with automatic transmission and unlimited mileage (you pay for gas). A temporary driver's license costs about $3 US from the police. Driving is on the left.

SHOPPING: Not a major preoccupation, since there are no duty-free imports to consider, but local crafts grow more interesting by the season. Worth looking into: *The Sugar Mill* on Parliament Street (lots of straw, artwork); *Montserrat Sea Island Cotton Company* on George Street (a variety of useful and wearable things, many handwoven from locally grown fiber); *Dutchers Studio* in Old Towne (intriguing decorative pieces made from salvaged bottles, tile, other usable materials). The *Red Cross Workshop for the Blind* at Dagenham sells all kinds of handcrafted straw at minimal prices. Whatever you do, don't miss the island-made rugs, wall hangings, totes, and mats displayed at Robert and Marilyn Townsend's *Tapestries of Montserrat* in the *John Bull Shop* in Wapping, just across the bridge from Plymouth; they do custom design work, too.

TIPPING: Most hotels add a 10% service charge to bills, which covers bellhops, waiters, bartenders, and maids. If not, tip from 10% to 15%, depending on the service. Many restaurants are beginning to add a service charge, but it is not yet a standard practice. Airport porters get about 30¢ to 50¢ US per bag. Taxis and other services should be tipped 10%.

SPECIAL EVENTS: *Christmas* celebrations, lasting from December 16 to January 1, are a time of parades, masquerades, parties, dinners, and dances, accompanied by singing and steel and string bands. The celebration takes place all over the island. Other holidays include *Good Friday, Easter Monday, Labor Day,* the *Queen's Birthday, Whitmonday,* and the *August Bank Holiday* (first Monday in August), and *St. Patrick's Day* (March 17).

SPORTS: Boating – The *Vue Pointe* hotel has a yacht available for day trips, the *Viking of Montserrat,* skippered by Martin Haxby. Several other yachts and some small craft may also be available for rent from individual owners. There are no formal rental facilities at this time, but check the bulletin board at the Tourist Office or at your hotel.

Climbing – Chance Peak, at 3,002 feet, affords spectacular views of nearly the entire island. A guide is necessary, but any hotel can arrange for one.

Golf – The *Montserrat Golf Club* maintains a challenging year-round 9-hole course which can be played a number of ways. Greens fees for visitors are $12.50 per day; clubs and equipment can be rented for $14.50 per day. Local members will sign to enable visitors to use the clubhouse, and visitors are welcome to enter the island's two tournaments: the *Montserrat Open,* in April, and the *British Airways Open,* in February. Other less formal local tournaments are held as well.

Horseback Riding – British equestrienne Barbara Tipsen has 11 horses at *Sanford Farms* and not only offers trail rides but organizes overnight camping trips — an unusual vacation option on this lush island. Rates per hour (with or without instruction) are $8.50 for adults, $5.50 for children (phone: 3301).

Sailing Cruises – Day cruises around Montserrat with Captain Ken Armstrong provide access to the island's 3 white sand beaches and cost $35 US per person, including open bar and snorkeling gear. Arrangements can be made through the *Vue Pointe* hotel (phone: 5210 or 5757). Captain Martin, another experienced local seaman, offers similar cruises (phone: 5738).

Snorkeling – The *Vue Pointe* hotel has equipment for guests. Otherwise, you'll need to bring your own or take one of the sailing cruises offered (above); there is no equipment for rent on the island.

Sport Fishing – The fish are out there, but special arrangements must be made. The Tourist Board or your hotel can set up something with a local fisherman. Bringing your own tackle will facilitate matters. Bruce Ferrara, Lower Dagenham, is one skipper with equipment.

Swimming and Sunning – Montserrat is well equipped for relaxed and isolated sunning on the beaches; there are volcanic sand beaches on both coasts, which are easily reached by car or are within walking distance of most hotels. Only Rendezvous Beach cannot be reached except by boat. Most of the hotels have pools and lounging areas.

Tennis – The *Vue Point* hotel has 2 lighted hard-surfaced courts on which nonguests can arrange to play for a small fee. *Montserrat Springs* also has 2 floodlit courts. Rates average $4.50 per hour for daytime play, $7.50 for night use.

NIGHTLIFE: Nights, which are on the quiet, cognac-and-conversation side at most hotels, are enlivened by island entertainment (dance bands, singers) at clubs like *Maximus,* during the season, and the *Yacht Club,* favored by residents. Popular discos include *747* and *La Cave.* Hotel parties feature steel band music, occasional crab races, and relaxed fun. *The Plantation,* in Wapping, is a popular late-night pub.

BEST ON THE ISLAND

CHECKING IN: Montserrat has five small hotels and a fine selection of rental villas and condominium vacation apartments. Air conditioning is rare but hardly necessary, since the island is naturally cooled by trade winds. Expect to pay from $125 to $165 US for a double room with breakfast and dinner in the winter season in those places we've listed as expensive; from $65 to $120 US in the moderate choices; less than that in inexpensive. Cut a third of the per-day cost for off-season visits. A 10% service charge and 7% tax are in effect year-round.

PLYMOUTH

Isles Bay Villas – Montserrat's first luxury villa complex includes 3 estate-size 3-bedroom villas, each with a private pool, fine view, large living room, well-equipped kitchen, color TV, stereo, washer-dryer, and Jacuzzi. Attractive Caribbean decor in wicker and colorful cotton, with other appointments by local artisans. Special inclusive vacation packages are available. Contact the Department of Tourism, PO Box 7, Plymouth (phone: 2230). Expensive.

Coconut Hill – A former mansion on the fringe of Plymouth, the hotel has a family feeling, 9 antique-furnished rooms with private baths, and is within easy walking distance of the beach. The dining room is pleasant, and there is a cocktail lounge (phone: 2144). Moderate.

Flora Fountain – Contemporary addition in town with 18 air-conditioned rooms. Island-basic, with no sports facilities, but a bar and a dining room featuring Caribbean, Indian, and international dishes. Church Rd. (phone: 2289). Moderate.

Wade Inn – A small hotel (10 rooms with twin beds) in the heart of Plymouth that caters to visiting businesspersons and travelers who prefer its central location. Within easy access of beaches and shopping. Dining room and lounge (phone: 2881). Inexpensive.

ELSEWHERE ON THE ISLAND

Montserrat Springs, Richmond Hill – Agreeably contemporary grouping of 17 air-conditioned rooms and 6 condominium apartments, each with phone, ceiling fan, and balcony; 100 yards from the beach. Tennis courts, large freshwater pool, and mineral water Jacuzzi. Dining room is a big island favorite (phone: 2841). Expensive.

Vue Point, Olde Towne – A charming cottage hotel on the Caribbean, with 28 separate cottages, 12 double bedrooms in connected units, a pool, lighted tennis courts, and the island's most complete water sports setup (snorkeling, scuba, windsurfing, water skiing, small-boat sailing, yacht charters). The dining room is one of the best on the island. The Michael Osborne Complex is a multipurpose conference center and venue for theater productions, as well as disco and dinner theater (phone: 5210). Expensive.

Shamrock Villas, Richmond Hill – Fifty fully furnished 1- and 2-bedroom apartments overlooking the sea, 400 yards from the beach. Freshwater pool; daily maid service at extra charge (phone: 2434). Moderate.

VILLAS

Villa rentals are an established part of tourism in Montserrat, with as many visitors — if not more — staying in villas as in hotels and guesthouses. Villa rentals are available in many price ranges, from a low of about $250 US up to $1,200 US or more per week in season, and about 30% to 50% less during summer months. Rates depend upon factors such as location, view, age, number of bedrooms, type of furnishings, whether or not there is a swimming pool, etc. Prices generally include maid service and gardening; cooks and babysitters are available on request. Cribs, rollaway beds, and rental cars are also available at daily rates. In addition to those mentioned above, several companies handle rentals: *Montserrat Estates,* PO Box 58, Plymouth (phone: 2431); *Neville Bradshaw Agencies,* PO Box 270, Plymouth (phone: 5270); and *Emerald Isle Villas and Condominiums,* PO Box 365, Plymouth (phone: 2004 or 2943).

 EATING OUT: Goat water, the favorite local stew, should be one of your objectives while you're on the island, as should mountain chicken — legs of the large frog native only to this island and to nearby Dominica. They're both considered delicacies. Rum punches are the island's real specialties — every hotel and bar on the island seems to have its own recipe. The most powerful belongs to JWR Perkins, who bottles Perk's Punch, a rum-based brew with the kick of an island mule. Island bars stock a full range of imported spirits, and the average price of a drink is about $1.50 US up. Wines vary greatly in price, but expect prices around $10 to $15 US per bottle. Expect to pay $40 US for dinner for two at a restaurant we've listed as expensive; from $20 to $35 at a moderate place; and under $20 at any of the restaurants we've listed as inexpensive. Prices do not include drinks, wine, or tips, although some restaurants do include the service charge.

PLYMOUTH AND ENVIRONS

Belham Valley – Pleasantly stylish establishment that's the bailiwick of British Chris and Barbara Crowe, who offer island drinks and Continental dishes to piano accompaniment. Reservations essential. In a former private home with a view of Old Road Bay not far from the *Vue Point* hotel (phone: 5553). Expensive.

Montserrat Springs – This is a good choice for hillside dining with sweeping views of the sunset, mountains, town, and harbor. The menu offers tempting samples of West Indian dishes (phone: 2841). Expensive.

Vue Point – A five-course table d'hôte as well as à la carte dinner menus are offered at this dining room overlooking the sea. Especially good are the West Indian curried chicken, Bessie's beautiful lime pie, and guava cheesecake. Don't miss the Wednesday night barbecue; it's a real feast (phone: 5210). Expensive.

Coconut Hill – This old plantation house dining room provides a sweeping view of the sea, as well as good home-style food. Mary's coconut pie — *not* coconut *cream* pie — is itself worth the trip (phone: 2144). Expensive to moderate.

Iguana, Wapping – American run, just across the bridge from Plymouth, featuring a full menu of exotic rum drinks, as well as a sampling of local dishes and familiar favorites like hamburgers and hot dogs (for homesick North Americans) (phone: 3637). Moderate.

The Pantry & The Attic – Near the waterfront in Plymouth, this is a popular evening spot with American and European visitors. A varied menu with some local dishes. Marine Dr. (phone: 2008). Moderate.

Wade Inn – For casual, relaxed drinking and dining, this has been an island mainstay for years, specializing in local dishes and potent rum punches. Parliament St. (phone: 2881). Moderate.

Blue Dolphin – Good local food. Fresh fish dishes are the specialty of its fisherman owner. In Parsons on the outskirts of Plymouth (phone: 3263). Moderate to inexpensive.

The Village Place, Salem – The closest thing to a soul food restaurant in Montserrat, it is a favorite with visiting musicians at Air Studios. Goat water and fried chicken are the most popular dishes (phone: 5202). Moderate to inexpensive.

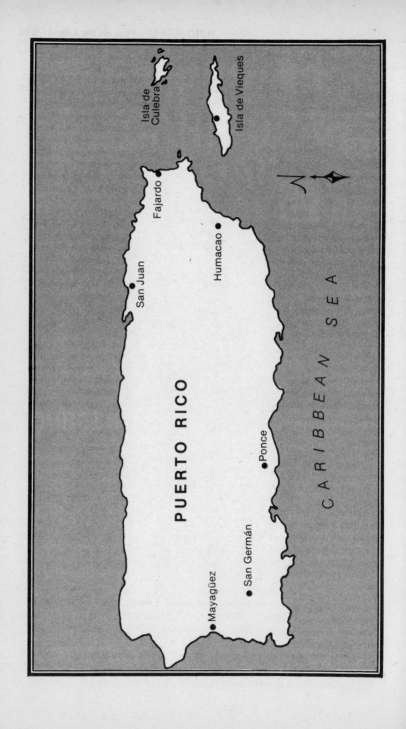

PUERTO RICO

Puerto Rico has an image problem. Ask most mainland Americans, "Quick, name three things you expect to find there." Without hesitation, they usually list: glitzy hotels, Vegas-style gambling and nightlife, and wrenching poverty. All of these exist, but they are just part of the picture. To a certain extent, they describe the city of San Juan, which is too often mistaken for the whole 3,435-square-mile commonwealth (a third of Puerto Rico's 3.2 million population lives in the metropolitan area). So the fans of big hotels and casinos frequent San Juan's beaches and tables, while less neon-oriented vacationers in search of great sports, escapist resorts, and lush island atmosphere look to other islands, even though they all can be found less than an hour's drive from Isla Verde Airport. The Puerto Rico beyond its capital offers extraordinary vacation variety, but its potential is too often ignored.

Take the hotels. San Juan does have some as tall and determined to dazzle as those along the Atlantic City boardwalk, but it also offers alternatives: a number of smaller hotels (originally geared to please business travelers) make up for what they lack in resort frills (no giant pools, sports, courts, nightclubs) with reasonable rates and the sort of personal service few bigger places ever manage. Some are only steps from the beach, and they can be ideal for vacationers looking for a home base from which to explore, rather than a hotel that's a destination in itself. Condominiums often offer all the resort facilities, plus apartments with kitchenettes that are a special find for families. In addition, there are more than a dozen small, well-run guesthouses, each with its own personality, scattered through residential neighborhoods, like Ocean Park and Punta Las Marías, as well as San Juan's Condado and Isla Verde resort sections. They line the beaches, yet their highest in-season rates are less than half the minimum charged at big-name beachfront hotels.

There are more choices outside San Juan. You won't find many better golf or tennis layouts than those at such resorts as the *Hyatt Cerromar Beach–Dorado Beach* complex and at *Palmas del Mar,* with its sports-oriented villa villages. Seaside resort towns like Rincón and Guánica and La Parguera (the fishermen's favorite) offer a casual life at low prices, as well as a chance to meet Puerto Rican families. And hotels like the *Mayagüez Hilton International* and Ponce's *Meliá* reflect the pride and Spanish heritage of cities *en la isla* (literally, "out on the island," a commonly used phrase in Puerto Rico, referring to the vast area beyond San Juan). Finally, there are Puerto Rico's unique *paradores,* inns that have been awarded government sponsorship because of their unique atmosphere, interesting sites, and high standards of food and cleanliness.

San Juan's nightlife, while not so lavish in scale, often outstrips that of Vegas in entertainment variety and local color. The big hotels split their year's billings between imported stars (Liza Minelli, Sammy Davis, et al.) and the best Puerto Rican performers; and they downplay their casinos, which are basically low key and carefully regulated. In addition to some outstanding hotel dining rooms, there are Italian, French, Swiss, Chinese, Spanish, and Puerto Rican restaurants — good ones — to try, and for a change of show scene and pace, there are San Juan's flamenco cellars and cafés, plus a number of late-playing discos.

As for poverty, Puerto Rico — like every other island in the Caribbean — has its share. But the progress that started with 1949's "Operation Bootstrap" — a program offering tax exemptions and other incentives to lure industry and new jobs to the island — has continued, though with a new orientation. More Puerto Ricans now seem to be returning from the US to live on the island than are leaving to find jobs on the mainland. The per capita income is more than thirteen times what it was in 1940, and the island has risen from an off-the-list spot to the fifth largest single overseas market for products manufactured on the mainland United States.

Bootstrap was the first in a series of self-help programs that have changed the face and future of Puerto Rico. In its early days, the seven-square-block area within the old city walls of San Juan was declared a historic zone, and ten years' tax exemption was offered to anyone who would buy and restore one of its antique buildings. The result was the salvation of what is now known as Old San Juan, the city founded by Juan Ponce de León, who was with Columbus when he discovered the island in 1493. The land that the native Taíno Indians called Borinquen — a name still used by Puerto Ricans in a mood of affection and pride — was christened San Juan by the Great Discoverer.

After he became governor, the first settlement Ponce de León established, in 1509, was at Caparra, south of San Juan Bay. Eleven years later, the Spaniards' hopes for gold had dwindled, but the island's strategic importance had increased. So in 1521, the settlement moved to the more defensible peninsula on which it now stands. Since the name of his patron saint, San Juan, already belonged to the island, Ponce had no choice but to pick another for the city. Optimistically, he called it Puerto Rico, "rich port." Later Don Juan Ponce changed his mind, and the city and island swapped names.

Building began on fortifications. A cathedral, a convent, and homes were erected. One of the prettiest of the latter, the Casa Blanca, was built to replace Ponce's original 24-square-foot house, which was destroyed by a hurricane. But Ponce de León took off on his fatal search for the fountain of youth and never lived in it. Today, it is a museum illustrating the life of sixteenth- and seventeenth-century Puerto Rico. Its restoration, along with that of numerous other irreplaceable Old San Juan landmarks, has been accomplished under the caring eye of the Institute of Puerto Rican Culture, created in 1955 as part of the subsequent Operation Serenity, dedicated to fostering the arts and an appreciation of Puerto Rico's heritage and folklore. The renowned annual Casals Music Festival is supervised by the institute, which has also had a hand in founding the Puerto Rico Symphony, a conservatory of music, and the Areyto Ballet (charged with preserving and performing the island's folk dances), whose repertory includes dances from the Taínos, the bomba dances of the African slaves, and elegant figures of the conquistadors.

After a prolonged struggle, the island achieved autonomy under Spanish rule in 1897. It had barely begun to enjoy it when, in the course of the Spanish-American War, American troops landed at Guánica on July 25, 1898. With the signing of the Treaty of Paris in April of 1899, Puerto Ricans took a giant step backward and again became subjects ruled by a foreign power — this time, the USA. It was not till 1917 that Congress granted them full American citizenship, and not till 1952 that the island, as a one-of-a-kind commonwealth under the US flag, was again given its own constitution and government. Since then, Operations Bootstrap and Serenity have helped Puerto Ricans devise creative solutions to their problems, although it will be up to the US Congress to decide if it will continue the tax incentives that have been so vital to Puerto Rican industrial development.

Maintaining Puerto Rico's share of a very volatile tourist market has taken some doing. During the 1970s, overbooking, overpricing, overbuilding, and incessant union demands sent Puerto Rico's reputation plummeting, with 1974–75 a particularly disastrous year for hotels. Some made it through; others foundered. The government's Tourism Company stepped in to try to turn things around. After a taste of the hardships caused by hotel closings, rates have steadied, and authorities have come down hard on consistent overbookers. In view of the progress that had been made at the time, a setback of the magnitude of the *Dupont Plaza* hotel's disastrous fire (New Year's Eve 1986) was regarded on the island as a national calamity, not just a tragic happening for those directly involved. Following the aftershock, there was resolve at all levels that both old and new problems would be addressed and progress resumed.

On an interpersonal basis, it is easy to see why Puerto Rico is the Caribbean's most popular tourist destination, far ahead of any other island in the region. Puerto Ricans buy (and sell) American products, crack American jokes, watch reruns on American cable TV, and like most of the same things mainlanders like; at the same time, they maintain a strong sense of traditional identity and relish being able to impress it on visitors. "I know this is a great place to live," said the owner of a Humacao Esso station recently, chatting as he pumped gas into a rental car bound for the El Yunque rain forest via a back road he'd pointed out on the map. "So . . . I guess it's a great place to visit, right?" No arguments there.

PUERTO RICO AT-A-GLANCE

FROM THE AIR: Puerto Rico is about as rectangular as an island can get. With a landmass of over 3,400 square miles (measuring 100 miles from east to west and 35 miles from north to south), it is the easternmost and the smallest (roughly three fourths the size of Jamaica) of the islands known as the Greater Antilles, which also include Cuba, Jamaica, and Hispaniola — the island shared by Haiti and the Dominican Republic. The commonwealth's nearest neighbors are the Dominican Republic, about 54 miles due west across the Mona Passage, and the US Virgin Island of St. Thomas, 40 miles to the east.

Its southern (Caribbean) coastline coincides almost exactly with the 18° parallel N latitude, as its northern (Atlantic) side does with the parallel 18°30'. Its capital, San Juan (pop. 1.5 million), is at the point where 18°30' intersects with 66° W longitude. Ponce, its second city, overlooks a bay in the center of the southern coast, and Mayagüez, the third largest metropolis, is at the middle of the western shoreline.

What it lacks in its rather unimaginative shape, Puerto Rico more than makes up for in topographical variety. Its 700-mile coastline is rimmed with beaches. But its mid-island spine of mountains — the Cordillera Central plus the northeastern Luquillo and southeastern Cayey Ranges — creates not only a lush green interior, but a green northern sector and a drier southern coastal strip, at the west end of which cactus pokes out of desert soil. Of the commonwealth's four offshore islands, Vieques and Culebra (to the east) are basically dry with some hills and uncrowded beaches; with 1,450 and 715 inhabitants respectively, both serve as getaway vacation places for islanders as well as for a few peace-seeking visitors from the north. Of the remaining two, Icacos, a sandy spit a few miles northeast of Las Croabas at Puerto Rico's northeastern corner, is uninhabited, but a favorite snorkel trip destination; and little, round Mona Island, plunked down in the western sea passage of the same name, is all barren plateau and seldom visited.

From flight height, it is difficult to spot several of the island's most distinctive geographical features: El Yunque rain forest in the northeast; La Parguera's Phosphorescent Bay in the southwest; the central island's mountain lakes, waterfalls, and teak forests; and the dramatic karst area, limestone earth pocked with deep, conical sinkholes and dotted with small haystack hills, north of the Cordillera Central. You will see evidence of farming: those vast green fields on the northern coastal plains are sugar cane; tobacco and plantains (like bananas, but bigger and mealier) are the crops greening the foothills; and the neatly lined acres that give the center of the northern plain its blue cast are producing pineapple.

Isla Verde International Airport on the eastern outskirts of San Juan is 4,000 miles (2½ hours' flying time) southeast of Miami; 1,600 miles (3½ hours) south of New York City. Flying times from Chicago and Los Angeles are 4½ and 6 hours, respectively. Over a million and a half tourists, most of them Americans, made the trip last year in planes that swoop toward a landing across the dense sprawl of the city and its suburbs, crisscrossed with traffic-clogged streets and spiked with tall buildings. Four out of every five visitors chose to stay in the high-rise hotels that line the northern beachfront between the city and the airport.

 SPECIAL PLACES: As they are in most antique cities (the island's earliest Spanish settlement moved to what is now San Juan in 1521), the capital's streets are narrow and teeming with traffic. But exploring the seven-square-block Old San Juan Historic Zone on foot is pleasant and rewarding; pick up a map at the tourist office by the docks or use the one in *Qué Pasa,* the official visitors' guide to Puerto Rico. You can hit the city's highlights in a morning, or a morning plus an afternoon — depending on the depth of your interest in Hispanic culture and the amount of boutique browsing you're tempted to do along the way. Next most popular site to see is undoubtedly El Yunque, the island's exotic rain forest (more than 100 billion gallons fall on it each year), where ferns tower high above your head and orchids grow small as a fingernail; tour companies offer dozens of guided half-day and all-day trips to it every day, and you can easily book one through your hotel travel desk. On the other hand, if you aren't all that interested in flora, you may want to substitute a day's snorkeling trip (see *Sea Excursions* below). Better still, rent a car, and combine an El Yunque visit (as long or short as you choose) with seeing a little more of the island. There's much that's surprising and pleasing — including genuine charm and beautiful countryside — about the vast area beyond San Juan that Puerto Ricans wrap up in the single phrase "out on the island." It will give you a fresh understanding of what Puerto Rico's about. Besides, it's fun. With first-rate roads circling the island and a superhighway from San Juan to Ponce, driving isn't the bumpy adventure it once was. What you will need is patience and a fairly flexible schedule, since even new roads haven't eliminated traffic jams — especially during traditional commuting hours and on weekends when all Puerto Rico climbs into cars and goes touring. Avoid Route 26 to the airport that joins Route 3 to El Yunque and Route 2 through Bayamón to Dorado between 8 and 10 AM and 4 and 6 PM. And plan to do as much of your touring as you can on weekdays. Or make the most of your time by flying to a point out on the island (like Ponce, Mayagüez, or Aguadilla), picking up a car there, and taking a slow, meandering route back to San Juan.

Whether you're staying in town, at one of the tall hotels on the Condado–Isla Verde strip, or at one of the sport resorts out on the island, you should see something of:

Old San Juan – The seven-block-square area on the tip of the peninsula that forms the westernmost part of the city, it was once completely encircled by the city wall — part of which still stands — and guarded by Forts San Cristóbal and El Morro. Administered by the US National Park Service, which provides tours of each, the forts are massively impressive, well preserved, and open to the public from 8 AM till 5 PM each day. If turrets, moats, and the history that goes with them intrigue you, set aside two mornings and do both; taxi to Fort San Cristóbal and do the rounds; stroll (or taxi) on along the Calle Norzagaray past the San Juan Cemetery (below the wall on the right-hand side). If driving a rental car and coming from the Condado–Isla Verde area on Ave. Ponce de León, bear left and look for a multi-story parking garage on Calle Recinto Sur, just after entering Old San Juan; even if it's full, you will be allowed to park if you leave the keys with the attendant. Pause at the San Juan Museum of History and Art, built as a marketplace in 1855, to view its multimedia introduction to the city. Move along to El Morro and tour; then recuperate at the nearby *Patio de Sam* (102 San Sebastián, which has the best hamburgers and low-key ambience in town). If time is short, begin at El Morro (tour or do a brief go-round on your own), and carry on with the Old San Juan walking tour outlined below.

Fort San Cristóbal, the one you see first, walls the north side of Avenida Muñoz Rivera, the route that brings you from the Condado hotel strip to the old sector. An expansion of an earlier simple redoubt, it was built from 1766 to 1772 to supplement El Morro and defend the land side of the city. The completed structure rose 150 feet above the sea, covered 27 acres, and consisted of five independent units connected by tunnels and dry moats and each defensible separately should the others fall. Admission is free. Tours are at 9:30 and 11 AM, 2 and 3:30 PM.

El Morro, though smaller than the fortress of San Cristóbal, is still big enough to accommodate a 9-hole golf course (not currently in play) within its good gray walls. The main battlements were built in 1591 on a foundation of earlier defense works that dated back to 1539. In 1595, El Morro was credited with preventing Sir Francis Drake from entering San Juan Harbor. It was attacked many times — mostly unsuccessfully. In 1598, when the Earl of Cumberland, who came overland, did manage to take it, dysentery accomplished what the Spanish defenders could not and drove him out again. Since 1783 the fort has been a single, compact unit with six levels looming 140 feet above the sea and its large land area laced with many tunnels. As at San Cristóbal, there's no admission charge; guided tours are at 9:30 and 11 AM, 2 and 3:30 PM. If you arrive by taxi, have the driver take you all the way into the fort; you'll get all the exercise you need on the long walk out.

Though standard walking and most minibus tours start at the Plaza de Colón in the center of Old San Juan, we prefer the Plaza de San José, two short blocks from El Morro's exit walk — not only because it's handy to the fort, but because from it the sightseeing route travels downhill all the way, making the walking lots easier.

The Church of San José, facing the plaza, is the church of Juan Ponce de León's descendants and the second oldest church in the Western Hemisphere. The statue on the square is that of Juan Ponce himself and was forged from British cannon melted down after Sir Ralph Abercromby's abortive attempt to conquer the city in 1797. The famous conquistador who went off to hunt fountains in Florida was wounded by Indians there. He managed to get to Cuba before he died in 1521. His body, returned to San Juan, lay buried in this church from 1559 until 1908, when it was moved to the cathedral. His coat of arms still hangs above the altar, and the vaulted Gothic ceilings are reminiscent of 16th-century Spain.

At the corner of the plaza adjacent to the church, the Pablo Casals Museum houses memorabilia — including manuscripts and the maestro's cello — left to the people of Puerto Rico. It's open from 9 AM to 5 PM, Mondays through Saturdays, and on Sundays from 1 to 5 PM.

Around the corner, on the Calle San Sebastián, stands the Casa de los Contrafuertes (House of the Buttresses), thought to be the oldest building designed as a private residence surviving on the island. Built in the early 18th century, it now houses the Pharmacy Museum, with a collection of porcelain and glass jars housed in a replica of an old apothecary's shop. Open from 9 AM to noon and 1 to 4:30 PM, Tuesdays through Saturdays; free.

The Dominican Convent, between San José Church and the Calle Norzagaray overlooking the water, is the headquarters of the Institute of Puerto Rican Culture, which maintains a Folk Arts Center and craft shop and stages exhibitions in its handsome, double-galleried patio. It was built by the Dominican friars in 1523. Open daily from 8 AM to 4:30 PM.

Next, head west toward San Juan Bay on Calle San Sebastián to the Casa Blanca, a serene white house that was built for, but never lived in by, Ponce de León. After his death, his son-in-law, Juan García Troche, had the original frame house replaced with the present masonry one, where his descendants lived for 250 years. Later a residence for both Spanish and US military commanders, it is now a museum illustrating 16th- and 17th-century Puerto Rican life. There are frequent guided tours and a small, serene, formal garden. Open from 9 AM to noon and 1 to 4:30 PM, Tuesdays through Saturdays.

Exit on Calle del Sol past "step streets" on either side, and turn right — downhill again — on Cristo. A block's walk brings you to a shaded square. Facing it, on the east side of Cristo, is San Juan Cathedral, extensively restored in 1977. The circular staircase and four nearby rooms with vaulted Gothic ceilings are all that remain of the 1540 structure; the rest is predominantly early 19th century. The body of Ponce de León now rests in a marble tomb near the transept; a relic of the Roman martyr San Pío is enshrined near it. Open daily from 6:30 AM to 5 PM.

El Convento, the imposing building with great wooden doors on your right facing the square as you leave the cathedral, was built as a Carmelite convent in the 17th century. Nowadays it's a hotel, the only one in Old San Juan, and recently refurbished, with a patio that's ideal for lunch or a refreshing drink.

Now there is a choice of directions: to find some of the city's most enticing boutiques, carry on down Calle Cristo; to explore a bit more history, follow the Caleta las Monjas (Little Street of the Nuns) from El Convento downhill to the Plazuela de la Rogativa at the city wall. The provocative statue of a bishop and three women commemorates the time (in 1797) when British soldiers mistook a religious procession (*rogativa*) for the arrival of Spanish reinforcements and decamped; the monument was erected in 1971 as part of the city's 450th anniversary celebration.

Turn left on Calle Recinto Oueste, and walk downhill past the San Juan Gate (the city's first ceremonial entrance; it has a fine bay view) to La Fortaleza, the Western Hemisphere's oldest executive mansion, home to more than 200 Puerto Rican governors. Its original single tower and patio were built in 1540 to protect the population from the cannibalistic Carib Indians; its more palatial elements were 19th-century additions. Note especially the polished reception rooms, stately mahogany staircase, the mosaic-lined chapel (once a storeroom for gold bullion), and the gardens. Free guided tours; open from 9 AM to 4:30 PM, weekdays, except holidays.

Leaving La Fortaleza, walk east (toward the city's center) on Calle Fortaleza and turn right on Cristo. At the end of the street the Parque de las Palomas, a small park named for its resident pigeons, will be on your right. Rest and admire the surrounding cluster of antique buildings: tiny Cristo Chapel, with its silver altar visible through glass doors, said to commemorate the safe landing of young Baltasar Montañez, who, in 1753, failed to make the turn and plunged over the cliff during a fiesta horse race — it also blocks the end of the street to keep others from following suit; La Casa del Libro, a scholarly book and book-making museum in an 18th-century house with special exhibitions on the first floor (open weekdays from 11 AM to 4:30 PM); and the Museum of Puerto Rican Art, with collections ranging from 18th-century to contemporary, nicely displayed in another colonial mansion (open from 9 AM to noon and 1 to 4:30 PM, except Mondays and Thursdays).

Follow the wall east one block to the Bastión de las Palmas, a defense emplacement-turned-park with a great view of the bay and the mountains beyond. Then turn north on Calle San José and walk two short blocks to the Plaza de Armas, the former heart of the city, faced on the west by the neoclassic Intendencia, which houses some Justice Department offices, and on the north by the City Hall (don't wait for tours, but stock up on tourist information at the center near the main entrance). Immediately below, on the waterfront section known as La Puntilla, is the restored 19th-century Arsenal with its handsome fountains; periodic exhibitions are held in its three galleries.

As far as seeing Old San Juan goes, this leaves only the Plaza Colón, five traffic-filled blocks east whichever *calle* you take (San Francisco and Fortaleza are both major tourist shopping streets). But you shouldn't miss the graceful Tapia Theater, now restored to its 19th-century elegance and presenting ballet, concerts, and drama to sellout audiences (on the off chance, try for tickets at the box office anyway). And, in the house on the northeast corner one block west of the plaza on Calle Fortaleza, the free Museum of Colonial Architecture has scale models of El Morro, La Fortaleza, and private houses, interesting to compare with the real things. A few steps away, *El Callejón de la Capilla* serves tasty Puerto Rican lunches and cold beer.

San Juan – There are a number of interesting sights outside the old city, but all rank below the antiquities and museums already mentioned. Still, you might call on:

Fort San Gerónimo, on the grounds of the *Caribe Hilton International* hotel, is small, with a military museum set up by the Institute of Puerto Rican Culture. Open daily, 9 AM to 4:30 PM. In name and in fact, the impressive Centro de Bellas Artes on Avenida Ponce de León is the island's fine arts center, presenting a full range of concerts, theater, opera, and dance performances spotlighting island and international performers; tickets are in demand (phone: 724-0700).

Condado Convention Center links the *Condado Beach* and *La Concha* hotels. You're bound to pass its modern façade a dozen times during your stay. One time — preferably on a weekend, when island artisans open up shop and demonstrate crafts on its plaza — stop for a look around. Inside, there is an immense and immensely handsome wall hanging on the main floor, which is the work of V'soske, the island's famous carpet-maker, who wove the abstract design, incorporating words of contemporary Puerto Rican poet Luis Llorens Torres. There's also a theater, tourist information center, and the office of the LeLoLai Festival.

The University of Puerto Rico and the Botanical Garden are both in the outlying Río Piedras section. The campus is the handsomely landscaped site of the annual Casals Festival, usually held during the first two weeks in June. Its notable archaeological and historic museum is open weekdays from 9 AM to 3 PM, except holidays. The gardens,

on the grounds of the university's Agricultural Experimental Station, encompass junglelike forests, bamboo-shaded walks, a lotus lagoon, and other exotica — over 200
species in all. Free to the public, it's open weekdays from 9 AM to 4:30 PM and on
weekends from 10 AM to 5 PM. It's sometimes closed for maintenance, so call before
you go (phone: 751-6815). The Botanical Garden is off Route 1 on Guadalcanal Street
in Barrio Venezuela.

The Museum of Conquest and Colonization, off Route 2 at Caparra, is built on the
site of the Spaniards' first settlement. In a walled park beside the foundations of a 1508
stronghold are artifacts and exhibitions related to the very early days. Not worth a
pilgrimage unless you're really into history, but a possible stop on the drive to Dorado
via Bayamón. Open weekdays from 9 AM to 5 PM, weekends and holidays from 10 AM
to 5 PM. Free.

ELSEWHERE ON THE ISLAND

Tours, tourists, and islanders (*always* on Sundays) traditionally head east from San
Juan along the north coast to take in El Yunque and/or Luquillo Beach. But with a
car, or by plane, or a combination of the two, it is also possible to visit a number of
other island points (the cities of Ponce or Mayagüez, for example) and return to a San
Juan starting point in one day-long outing. And there are dozens of other places out
on the island worth seeing for their scenic, sporting, or historic interest.

Since the island is much too large to do in a single day, the following special places
are highlights to consider whenever you have time to head out of the capital. Obviously,
the longer you can spend, the more of the island's true flavor you'll absorb. If you can
make more than a day of it, plan to stay overnight in a small hotel or one of the
government-approved *paradores* — inns chosen for native charm and interesting location, each pledged to meet firm standards of comfort, cleanliness, and cuisine.

Fantasy World Tours (phone: in New York, 212 975-9070) puts together several
week-long fly/drive packages that combine stays at *paradores* and small inns scattered
all around the island with a rental car and round-trip air fare from New York for about
$400 up per person; some plans include San Juan stopovers too.

Following the traditional route, begin by going from San Juan east to:

El Yunque – Follow Route 3 east about 25 miles, and turn right (south) onto Route
191, which climbs up into the forest surrounding El Yunque's 3,493-foot peak and that
of its taller brother, El Toro (3,532 feet). Officially called the Caribbean National
Forest, it was set aside by the Spanish Crown in 1876; later designated a forest reserve
by Theodore Roosevelt, its 28,000 acres make up the only tropical forest in the US
national system. It boasts 250 different species of trees, only 6 of which are indigenous
to the continental US; it is also a bird sanctuary, and one of the few places where you
can hear the call of Puerto Rico's national mascot — the tiny tree frog called coquí
— in the daytime. It is almost certain to shower while you're there (to meet that
100-billion-gallon yearly quota, it would have to), but don't worry: rains are brief, and
there are lots of shelters. The Sierra Palm Visitors Center on Route 191, open daily
from 9:30 AM till 5 PM, gives free nature talks and slide shows. There's also a waterfall-
fed swimming hole (picturesque, but cold) and a rustic restaurant that serves commendable Puerto Rican meals. Then make your way back to Route 3 and travel 5 miles
farther east to:

Luquillo Beach – About 30 miles east of the capital, it is certainly the most famous
(you'll recognize it from Puerto Rico's most popular postcards) of the 12 major island
beaches with government-built *balneario* facilities (lockers, showers, parking). It's
gorgeous, too — long, white, and lined with leggy palms, but apt to be crowded on
weekends. Bring your own towels and lunch (or snack on coconut milk, pionoños, and
pasteles at stands near the entrance). Fees: 25¢ per person for locker, shower, and
changing space; $1 per car for parking. Then back to Route 3 and follow the signs to:

Fajardo – A small east coast seaport, bustling but relaxed. Ferries leave from here to Vieques and Culebra islands every morning and afternoon; the fare is about $3 for the less-than-two-hour trip. At the small harbor at Las Croabas, you can hire a native sloop (capacity: six passengers) to take you out to Icacos for a swim (half-day price: $50 or so, depending on the boat and your bargaining power; bring masks and flippers if you want to snorkel). Carry on along Route 3 to:

Humacao – Not a tourist town, but with a splendid *balneario*-equipped beach (25¢ per person for locker, changing room; $1 to park your car); casual snack stands, too. Or detour south to the ambitious and beautifully set 2,700-acre sports resort called *Palmas del Mar* (see *Best en Route*). Have a swim and a rum punch (at the beach, not the pool — which tends to get overcrowded), and stay over in comfort. Or travel along Route 3 to Arroyo (another public beach — Punta Guilarte — is just east of town) and Guayama, where you turn right (north) on Route 15 to join Las Americas Expressway 52 to speed back to San Juan.

Traveling south from San Juan:

Ponce – About 75 miles south and west as the Las Americas Expressway flies (take Route 1, then 52). Founded in 1692 by Ponce de León's great-grandson, it's the island's second largest city — industrious and proud. It runs the architectural gamut from handsomely historic (see the dignified Cathedral of Our Lady of Guadalupe, dominating its central plaza) and notably modern (the small Museum of Art designed by Edward Durell Stone, famed architect of the Museum of Modern Art in New York City) to just plain kooky (the resoundingly christened Parque de Bombas — i.e., firehouse — is red and black striped with green and yellow fanlights). The marketplace at Atocha and Castillo streets is almost as colorful. The Museum of Art is purportedly the best in the Caribbean; both the Louvre and the Whitney have borrowed from its 2,000-piece collection. Its exhibitions feature the works of contemporary Latin American artists, though it is best known for its pre-Raphaelite paintings and its Baroque paintings and sculpture from Italy, Spain, and France. One of the museum's three gardens, which pay homage to Spain, the US, and the tropics, is dedicated to Abraham Lincoln. There's a fine beach called El Tuque on the shore west of the city. A *Holiday Inn* is nearby, but the *Meliá,* off the plaza has more island atmosphere. Just north of town, at the Tibes Indian Ceremonial Center, pre-Taíno ruins from AD 700 — restored to include a re-created village, museum, and remarkable total of seven intact ceremonial ball courts — are well worth a visit. The museum is open daily except Mondays.

Alternative southern destinations include:

Coamo – A mineral springs resort in the hills northeast of Ponce, it's been rediscovered and rejuvenated. The spa parador, *Baños de Coamo,* with pools, air-conditioned rooms and restaurant, makes it a pleasant detour or overnight spot.

Toro Negro State Forest – In the central mountains north of Ponce, it has woods, waterfalls, flowers, picnic tables, barbecue pits, a swimming pool, and an observation tower with sensational views. With an early start it could be a day trip from San Juan, but it's easier from Ponce.

Or take the road from San Juan west to:

Dorado – Off Route 693, which turns north off the main Route 2 a few miles west of Bayamón. There are a few interesting gift and crafts shops on the main drag and a shopping center as you exit town to the north. Nearest town to the sister resorts of *Hyatt Cerromar Beach* (younger and bigger) and *Hyatt Dorado Beach* (older and classier). Drive through the grounds, stay for lunch or a drink, and then return to Route 2 and continue west to:

Arecibo – A commercial town by the sea known for its lighthouse (picturesque), its beaches (surf-pounded), its rum distillery (Ron Rico), and its goat cheese (strong). It's also a tour turning point. To the south, Route 10 leads to a mixed bag of sites:

Río Abajo State Forest – A 5,800-acre woodland (predominantly teak) with ranger's office, sawmill, recreation area (very pretty for picnicking), and a big, blue, manmade lake called Dos Bocas on which there are launch trips (no swimming). Going and coming, Route 621 (off 10) affords good views of the karst country's haystack hills. On the whole, a pleasant, even interesting, but scarcely compelling destination.

Caguana Indian Ceremonial Park – A few miles farther south on Route 111 off Route 10 near the coffee town of Utuado, a 13-acre landscaped park with paved walks and plazas, and monoliths put there by the Taíno Indians 800 years ago. Archaeology buffs find it fascinating. Route 140 is the scenic road back to San Juan.

Arecibo Observatory – A special place for special people, with special visiting hours: between 2 and 4:30 PM on Sunday. It has the world's largest radio telescope, with a 20-acre curved reflector installed over a natural karst sinkhole 1,300 feet wide by 300 feet deep. If astronomy is one of your fascinations, it may be worth the 35-minute drive from Arecibo (via Routes 10, 651, 635, and 625).

Jayuya (pronounced ha-*ju*-ja) – West and a little south of Utuado, it's the site of a former coffee plantation house, *Hacienda Gripiñas,* that's now a most appealing *parador.* Nothing to do but enjoy the view, the peace, the good food, the pool, and the mountain air — quite enough if you're in an escapist mood.

Meanwhile, back in Arecibo, you may choose to skip the above and keep moving west along Route 2 for Quebradillas, site of the island's first parador, *Guajataca* (stop for turtle steak, smashing views of the sea, and/or an overnight); Aguadilla, where *Punta Borinquen,* a moderately priced club-type resort catering largely to charter groups, has been developed on what was once (and is still known as) Ramey Air Force Base; Rincón, the beach resort with the *Parador Montemar* and several small, casual hotels that's a favorite with island surfers (the World Championships were held here in 1968); and finally:

Mayagüez – Halfway down the west coast, Puerto Rico's third largest city. A friendly, busy port that is architecturally unremarkable, it still shines as a headquarters for exploring the western and southwestern sections of the island — largely because its unusually personable *Hilton* is such an honest-to-goodness pleasant place to come home to. Mayagüez' central plaza features a Catholic church, a city hall (no surprises so far), and 16 individually costumed bronze statues imported from Barcelona (no one seems to know why or when). This was once considered the needlework capital of Puerto Rico, and intrepid shoppers may still be able to unearth fine embroidery and drawn-thread work in the older shops downtown. The western campus of the University of Puerto Rico and the Federal Agricultural Experimental Station — the latter with the Western Hemisphere's largest collection of tropical plants — both have landscapes worth seeing. And the zoo, which is open daily except Mondays, is super. Mayagüez is also the home of *Fido's Beer Garden,* little more than a corner deli, at Berisario del Valle and Dulievre streets. Here Fido sells his locally famous, and quite potent, sangria for $5 a bottle or $10 a gallon, complete with orange-and-cherry-trimmed plastic cups. Bacardi tried to buy the secret recipe, with no success. More intriguing sites lie farther out:

Boquerón Beach – The government has installed small cottages at this west coast gem of a beach, and the prices are very low (about $15 a night), provided the application is mailed four months in advance to the Recreation and Sports Dept., Box 2923, San Juan, PR 00903 (phone: 722-1551, ext. 225). Swimming is less complicated: 25¢ per person for locker and changing space, $1 for parking.

Cabo Rojo Lighthouse – At the island's southwesternmost corner (and not to be confused with the town of the same name farther north), it's worth seeing for its own sake, but also because the drive takes you by the old salt beds and through the area called the Desert, sometimes so green it's unrecognizable. A little to the north of here are Guaniquilla Point, with a lagoon filled with spikey limestone boulders; tiny Buyé Beach; and a proliferation of seafood restaurants at Joyuda Beach.

San Germán – The island's second oldest city (pronounced san her-*mahn*) has a couple of pretty plazas, colonial atmosphere, and a winsome church that may be the New World's oldest (Porta Coeli, dating from 1606), now a museum of religious art. The charmingly restored hotel, the *Parador Oasis*, is here, along with *La Cueva de Luis Candela*, a disco that attracts the college crowd from Mayagüez.

La Parguera – This tiny fishing village on the south coast, headquarters for deep-sea charter boats, has a casual, friendly inn, the *Parador Villa Parguera*, and the famous Phosphorescent Bay that shines in the dark when the moon doesn't.

Guánica – A small beach resort, also on the south coast, it's got lots of sand, space, and an informal seaside hotel, the *Copamarina*.

■ **EXTRA SPECIAL:** The *Ruta Panorámica* meanders across the Cordillera Central and the Cayey Range from Mayagüez on the west coast to Yabucoa and Punta Tuna Lighthouse at the southeast corner of the island. Built for scenery, not speed, it offers stunning vistas all the way; it intersects with principal north-south routes so even if you can't spare 12 hours to drive from one end to the other, you can enjoy random samples. Several inns and paradores lie a few miles north or south if you want to take it really easy. Definitely not to be missed.

SOURCES AND RESOURCES

TOURIST INFORMATION: The Puerto Rico Tourism Company operates several North American offices. They offer a number of valuable brochures, free for the asking. Contact one of the following offices:

Chicago: 11 E Adams St., Suite 902, Chicago, IL 60603 (phone: 312 922-9701)
Dallas: 2995 LBJ Fwy., Suite 108, Dallas, TX 75234 (phone: 214 243-3737)
Los Angeles: 3575 W Cahuenga Blvd., Suite 248, Los Angeles, CA 90068 (phone: 213 874-5991)
Miami: 200 SE First St., Suite 903, Miami, FL 33131 (phone: 305 381-8915)
New York: 1290 Ave. of the Americas, 22nd Floor, New York, NY 10104 (phone: 212 541-6630)
Toronto: 10 King St. E, Toronto, Ont. M5C 1C3 (phone: 416 367-0190)

In addition to general material, these offices offer a seasonal list of facilities and rates at island hotels and guesthouses, details of seasonal packages and schedules of special events of interest to tourists, and a booking service for the government-sponsored *paradores.* To make reservations for *paradores* or guesthouses, call 800 223-6530 in the US.

The Puerto Rico Tourism Company maintains information centers at three key tourist points in San Juan: at the International Airport; at 301 Calle San Justo, opposite the Old San Juan piers where the cruise ships land; and at City Hall, across from the Plaza de Armas.

Out on the island, tourist information is available in the city halls of Adjuntas, Añasco, Cabo Rojo, Isla de Culebra, Dorado, Guánica, Luquillo, Maricao, Naguabo, and Rincón, as well as at Ponce's striped firehouse and its airport. There is also a tourism office on Vieques.

Local Coverage – The *San Juan Star,* Puerto Rico's English-language newspaper, is published every morning. *El Mundo* and *El Día* are Spanish-language dailies. New York City and Miami newspapers are usually available on the day of publication in hotels and at *The Book Store,* at San José 257 in Old San Juan.

Qué Pasa, the free official visitors' guide published monthly by the Tourism Company, is the best of its kind in the Caribbean, both from the point of view of the helpful, unslanted material it contains and from the way it is organized and presented, with lots of relevant times, telephone numbers, and addresses. You'll find information on special events, sports, sights, lodging, restaurants, car rentals, transportation, shopping, and crafts centers in San Juan and out on the island. There are also feature stories on island people, places, history, food, and customs. Get one at your hotel desk or at any information center. Ask at the Tourism Company for maps of historic sites and material on galleries and craft studios you can visit. A magazine/guide available only in Puerto Rico, *Walking Tours of Old San Juan* ($2.50), packs in visitors' information. It is updated twice a year, in January and July. *Puerto Rico Living,* published annually, is geared more to those who move to the island rather than to those who visit it; perhaps for that reason, it is excellent background reading and a good barometer of daily life. It's available for $2.95 in bookstores or can be ordered from Puerto Rico Living, Box 2180, Waterbury, CT 06722, for $3.50.

A Short History of Puerto Rico, by Morton J. Golding, and *The Forts of Old San Juan,* by Albert Manucy and Ricordo Torres-Reyes, are good parallel reading for history buffs. These and general English-language reading, from Garrison Keillor to Herman Hesse, are available at *Bell, Book & Candle,* at 102 Diego Ave. in Santurce, or *The Book Store* (address above) in Old San Juan.

Telephone – You can dial Puerto Rico direct by adding area code 809 to the numbers given below.

 ENTRY REQUIREMENTS: Neither passports nor visas are required of US or Canadian citizens, but Canadians must carry some form of identification (such as a birth certificate). Foreign nationals must have passports and pass through immigration before entering.

 CLIMATE AND CLOTHES: It's warm and sunny year-round on the island's resort coasts, always 5° to 10°F cooler in the mountains. Winter temperatures in San Juan range from the low 70s F (about 22°C) to the low 80s F (27° to 29°C). In summer, the spread edges up about 5°F. The wettest months are May to December; you're least likely to need an umbrella in March and April. As a general rule, however, there's more rain on the north coast than in the south. And remember: El Yunque is a rain forest. Most places a tourist is likely to stay, both in San Juan and out on the island, are air conditioned.

In San Juan, clothing needs range from daytime beach to nighttime casino; the general rule is wear what you would for a similar climate and occasion back home. But keep in mind that beyond the hotel strip, San Juan is both a city and Spanish in its heritage. That means no short shorts downtown, in churches, or in public buildings. And it means nights are dressier — especially in casinos, nightclubs, and the tonier restaurants. Until quite recently, casinos tended to be rather stuffy about the evening dress code; skirts were required for women, and jackets (preferably with ties) for men. Managements have relaxed a bit, and women now wear dressy pants. But you'll always feel more comfortable (mentally, anyway) dressing up rather than down. Women should carry light wraps to foil air-conditioning drafts.

At the larger sports resorts out on the island (*Hyatt Dorado Beach, Hyatt Cerromar Beach,* and, to a somewhat lesser extent, *Palmas del Mar*), the country-club-chic rule applies: neatness and tailoring count at all times. Days call for more or less classic sports clothes (golf clothes for golf, tennis dresses and shorts on the courts); nights go tieless but call for a certain sense of style, with blazers or jackets preferred for men, casual resort evening wear (long skirts, caftans, and the like) for women.

Both in cities and out on the island, dress is generally more casual at smaller hotels and guesthouses.

 MONEY: Only the Yankee dollar is official in Puerto Rico, though some places will — reluctantly — accept Canadian currency. It's also worth noting that major credit cards (MasterCard, Visa, American Express, Diners Club) are more widely accepted in Puerto Rican hotels, restaurants, and shops than they are perhaps anywhere else in the Caribbean (with the possible exceptions of St. Thomas and St. Croix). Banking hours are from 9 AM to 2:30 PM on weekdays, except holidays (of which the commonwealth has *lots*). The big US banks all have branches on the island.

 LANGUAGE: In cities and major tourist resorts, English is always understood, usually spoken; only in the most remote areas do you ever run into problems, and then none that can't be resolved with smiles, patience, and hand signals. With islanders, however, Spanish — though not of the pure Castilian idiom — is still *número uno.*

 TIME: Clocks keep Atlantic Standard Time — that's one hour ahead of Eastern Standard Time, the same as Eastern Daylight. So in winter, when it's noon in New York, Miami, or Boston, it's 1 PM in San Juan. From late April until late October (Daylight Saving season), noon in the eastern US is noon in Puerto Rico.

 CURRENT: It's 110 volts, 60 cycles — the same as in the continental US and Canada.

 GETTING THERE: Both American and Eastern Airlines offer frequent nonstop flights from New York's Kennedy and Newark airports; in addition, American flies in daily from Dallas and Chicago (via New York). TWA provides daily nonstop service from New York and St. Louis. Eastern also schedules nonstops out of Miami and provides direct service from Atlanta, Baltimore, Boston, and Philadelphia. Delta flies nonstop from Atlanta. Arrow Air flies daily from New York's JFK to San Juan and also offers nonstop service five days a week from Miami and Philadelphia. Numerous flights connect Puerto Rico and other Caribbean islands. St. Thomas is a short 30 minutes away, and St. Croix, 45 minutes. Eastern Metro Express (phone: 728-3131) flies to St. Thomas and St. Croix; American Eagle has daily service to St. Thomas and to La Romana in the Dominican Republic; Crown Air (phone: 728-2828) goes to the US Virgin Islands, St. Kitts, and other nearby destinations; and Virgin Islands Seaplane Shuttle offers round-trip service twice a week between San Juan and St. John. Charters are available to the Greater and Lesser Antilles (phone: 791-3295).

A great number of Caribbean cruises schedule San Juan stops. Several lines with fly/cruise connections make San Juan their home port during the winter cruise season. Among them are Chandris/Fantasy Cruises (phone: 800 423-2100), Cunard Line (phone: 800 528-6223), Ocean Cruise Lines (phone: 800 522-3414), Paquet Cruises (phone: 800 327-5620), and Sun Line (phone: 800 872-6400). The *Island Fiesta* travels back and forth to St. Thomas, five hours each way, and costs $65 round-trip; the ship, which sails daily except Fridays and Sundays, has three bands, a pool, casino, duty-free shops, bars, games, free Continental breakfast at sailing time, and reasonably priced meals otherwise. Customized charter sailing in the Virgin Islands can be arranged through Sun Island Charters (725-2817).

 CALCULATING COSTS: Most Puerto Rican hotels and guesthouses quote rates without meals (EP); only the *El San Juan* and the *Hyatt Dorado Beach* include breakfasts and dinners (MAP) as a general rule. The price range is enormous: from as little as $40 for a double at one of San Juan's better known guesthouses to a maximum of about $200 for a double without meals at the *Caribe Hilton.* In summer (from mid-April to mid-December), rates drop 25% to 50%. Out on the island, prices tend to be lower all year. Rates at government-approved *paradores* (inns) are in the $40 to $65 range all year. There is a 6% tax on all hotel rooms.

The high-city, low-country rule applies to meals, too. A full breakfast in one of San Juan's larger hotels runs $6 to $8 per person; at an average hotel out on the island, it could cost $1 less. Dinner in a medium-priced San Juan restaurant averages $12 to $25 per person, not including drinks, tips, or taxes; out on the island, a good fresh seafood dinner would run about $8 to $15. In one of San Juan's plusher places (*La Rotisserie* at the *Caribe Hilton, Los Galanes* in Old San Juan), dinners run $30 and up, plus drinks, tips, and taxes.

Especially in summer (mid-April to mid-December), package prices mean considerable savings — with week-long stays at Condado and Isla Verde hotels priced from as low as $100 per person and up, double occupancy — including LeLoLai festivities (see *Special Events*); several of the better-known hotels also offer very attractively priced weekend packages.

 GETTING AROUND: Airport Limousines – The best, least expensive way to get from Isla Verde International Airport to your hotel, although if you're staying in Condado or Old San Juan and the people who share your ride are billeted closer to the airport, you may have to sit through several stops en route. Rates are between $1 and $2 from the airport to most of San Juan's hotel areas. Unless the driver does you some very special favor — like lugging six bags around the corner to the door of *El Convento* hotel — you don't tip. (Don't count on limousine service to the airport, however; limos aren't allowed to pick up at hotels.)

Taxi – At the airport, near the cruise piers, and in lines outside major San Juan hotels. All cabs authorized by the Public Service Commission are metered (although the meter is not used on trips outside normal taxi zones; for these, you and the driver should agree on a price in advance). Basically, San Juan drivers are city boys who don't do much taxi touring. Island officials are diligent about monitoring the fleet, and their concern shows; they ask that you report any problems to 751-5050. Based on recent experience, it's a number you probably won't have to use.

The fare from the airport to an Isla Verde hotel runs about $5 including tip; it's about $7 to Condado, and about $10 to downtown San Juan plus an additional 50¢ per bag. The fare from an Isla Verde or Condado hotel to Old San Juan runs $4 to $6 plus luggage charge.

Bus – Neat, handy, and cheap, they run day and night on an exact 25¢ fare system. There are two models: a conventional bus (painted brown), and a blue and white air-conditioned model. City terminals are at the Plaza Colón and the Cataño Ferry Terminal next to Pier One; elsewhere bus stops are marked by yellow posts or metal standards reading "Parada" or "Parada de Guaguas." Routes to note: No. 1, marked "Río Piedras," which goes through the banking district in Hato Rey to the University of Puerto Rico; and Nos. T1, A7, and 2, which run from Old San Juan to Condado and Isla Verde and pass many of the hotels. Be aware that bus lanes run against traffic on main thoroughfares.

Puerto Rico Motor Coach, 327 Recinto Sur, Old San Juan (phone: 725-2460), has service between San Juan and Mayagüez every two hours from 6 AM to 6 PM.

Públicos – Cars or minibuses whose license plate numbers are followed by the letters PD or P provide point-to-point transport all over the island for reasonable rates. Basic routes run from Town A plaza to Town B plaza, with drivers stopping to pick up or drop passengers anywhere along the route. They are insured, and the Public Service Commission sets the prices. Islanders are their best customers, since most visitors touring the island would rather rent their own cars. But if your Spanish is in working order and your schedule is flexible, you might give them a whirl.

Car Rental – Easy to come by at rates that run about $43 a day, $245 a week and up (plus insurance) for a compact with automatic shift; mileage is unlimited, and the rate includes oil, maintenance, and standard insurance; you pay for gas. *Avis* (phone: 721-4499, 791-0426, 791-2500), *Budget* (phone: 791-3685, 725-1182), *Hertz* (phone: 791-0840, 791-0844), *National* (phone: 791-1805, 725-5350), and *Thrifty* (phone: 791-4241, 791-2786) are all represented in downtown San Juan, some Condado and Isla Verde hotels, Isla Verde Airport, and in Ponce and Mayagüez as well. Local firms like *Afro* (phone: 724-3720), *Atlantic* (phone: 721-3814), *L&M* (phone: 725-8416), *Rico* (phone: 723-3035), and *Target* (phone: 783-6592) offer special, low, cash deals (for weeks, long weekends, short weekends, days, and nights), but they don't take credit cards or have reassuring offices out on the island. For a day trip out of San Juan, they're okay. For longer, larger-ticket tours, the internationals are probably a wiser choice. Always opt for air conditioning.

Puerto Rican speed limits are given in miles per hour, but road signs show distances in kilometers. (A kilometer equals roughly .6 of a mile.) Also, the car horn remains a basic Puerto Rican driving device. In town it seems to be a means of personal communication, expressing emotions that range from hot-blooded midweek anger to Saturday night fever. But on twisting roads out on the island, it's imperative that you honk when approaching blind curves to warn oncoming cars to keep right. Finally, if you plan to return a rental car to the airport (Isla Verde, that is), allow plenty of time, drive slowly, and follow your car company's signs very carefully; it's confusing out there. Better still, turn in your car in town and take a cab to catch your plane.

Sightseeing Bus Tours – These are of no use downtown, and are the least imaginative way of seeing the rest of the island. If you can drive, you'll have much more fun renting a car. Still, a number of firms offer daily rain forest tours (at about $12 per person for the half-day trip to El Yunque, about $16 for the full day — including a swim at Luquillo Beach) plus assorted trips to the Bacardi rum distillery, El Comandante racetrack, and Ponce. Principal companies are *Borinquen Tours* (phone: 725-4990), Fuentes Bus Line (phone: 780-7070), *Gray Line* (phone: 727-8080), and Rico Suntours (phone: 722-2080). Offerings change, so consult *Qué Pasa* or your hotel travel desk about current best values.

Ferry Service – Boats sail every half hour from the small pier next to Pier One for the little town of Cataño across the bay; it's a neat 20¢ (round trip) way to cool off any day, but in July, when the population stages a fiesta in honor of its patron saint, it's a ticket to a party with street parades, booths, rides, dancing, and all sorts of fun in the streets. From the Cataño stop, pick up a público to the Bacardi rum distillery, the largest in the world, where free guided tours are given daily from 9:30 AM to 3 PM except Sundays and holidays. From Fajardo, at the eastern end of the island, a Port Authority launch makes daily morning and afternoon trips carrying passengers only to the islands of Vieques and Culebra (where the schedule is more sporadic). There is service between Culebra and Vieques on Mondays, weekends, and holidays. Weekdays, a ferry carrying cars makes a round trip. One-way fare: about $3 per person. If you want to take your car (not likely), call 863-0705 or 863-0852 for reservations and current schedule; it's about $10 each way.

Sea Excursions – On Sundays and holidays, the Cataño ferry makes 1½-hour trips around San Juan bay in the afternoon for $1.50. The *Clipper City,* a rebuilt 19th-century schooner, tours the harbor and ventures out into the Atlantic from January to mid-May; the cost is $20 for three hours. From Vista Marina in Isla Verde, a small, sturdy launch departs twice daily (except Mondays) to cruise along the Atlantic shoreline for an hour. Minimum number of passengers: 15 per trip. Fares: about $3 per adult; $2 per child. *Airborne,* a 35-foot sailing sloop, carries a maximum of six passengers around the bay or on open sea for morning, afternoon, or sunset sails (phone: 728-6606). The *Condado Plaza* offers two-hour sunset dinner cruises for $35; libations include champagne, rum punch, beer, and lemonade.

From Fajardo, *Capt. Jack Becker*'s catamaran sets sail at 10 AM each day for the tiny uninhabited island of Icacos, where passengers have three hours to spend sunning, snorkeling, and ingesting a buffet lunch (bring sunblock or tanning lotion, coverup, hat); the $30 per-person tab includes lunch and use of a mask and fins (phone: 863-5875 after 6:30 PM; ask your operator for Fajardo first or dial 129 for long distance). Figure on about $10 for round-trip transport from and to Condado and Isla Verde hotels. The 38-foot catamaran *Barefoot II* offers a similar trip with added coral reef stop and diving option (extra charge for gear rental) for about $40 per person, including a buffet lunch (phone: 724-6161)

The *Palmas del Mar* marina, near Humacao, arranges skippered charters for a day or longer (phone: 852-6000).

And from La Parguera (the *Villa Parguera* pier), boats depart from 7:30 PM through 12:30 AM (depending on demand) on moonless nights for a firsthand look at the luminous wonders of Phosphorescent Bay. Even on evenings when the moon is out, you can witness the sparkling phenomenon on early trips; best are the glass-bottom boats (fare, about $2 for the one-hour ride).

Local Air Services – Puerto Rico's island airlines don't provide sightseeing tours, but do offer short-hop service that can help make the most of sightseeing time out on the island. *Crown Air* (phone: 728-2828) and *Eastern Metro Express* (phone: 728-3131) fly from Isla Verde airport to Mayagüez (about $34 one way). *Crown Air*'s small planes also make transfer hops to and from the Dorado resorts (about $29 one way, $10 less for children) and to *Palmas del Mar* (about $32 each way, $10 less for children, but they may not fly unless there are 4 to 6 paid fares). It's worth considering in view of the 45-minute-plus driving time to either; for comparison, the *Dorado* limo transfer costs about $10 one way.

Vieques Air-Link (phone: 722-3736) serves the offshore islands of Vieques (about $25 one way) and Culebra (about $25 one way) from smaller Isla Grande Airport, next to the downtown area and handy to Old San Juan and close-in Condado hotels.

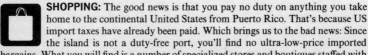

SHOPPING: The good news is that you pay no duty on anything you take home to the continental United States from Puerto Rico. That's because US import taxes have already been paid. Which brings us to the bad news: Since the island is not a duty-free port, you'll find no ultra-low-price imported bargains. What you will find is a number of specialized stores and boutiques staffed with people who obviously like being helpful and stocked with island crafts that aren't for sale at home. Quality is key. And in craft shopping, you'll get more of the best for your money if you know something about what goes into the making. Puerto Rico makes it easy because many of the learning places (government exhibitions, museums) and some of the most interesting shops exist side by side in Old San Juan.

Island crafts take lots of forms: predictable (straw work, ceramics); useful (hammocks, men's guayabera shirts); surprising (weird Loíza masks, cheery papier-mâché fruit that looks better than real); unique (guitarlike cuatros, hand-carved santos figures); and stuff you can live a whole lifetime without (much of it made out of hairy old used coconuts). Before you buy, visit the *Folk Arts Center* in the Dominican Convent (see *Special Sights*) near the Plaza San José, where exhibitions cover every kind of island handwork — lots of it for sale at reasonable prices (in the $5-or-less gift category: fringed straw hats, rag dolls, ceramic tiles, bamboo birdcages, and more). Their contemporary santos figures — carved wood statues of favorite saints and other revered persons (a best seller: the Three Kings) — are priced from about $10 to over $100. If you plan to tour the island, ask at the Folk Arts Center (phone: 724-625) about craft studios open to visitors where you can watch works in progress. Most worthwhile Old San Juan craft shop stops: *Plazoleta del Puerto* (Marina St. across from Pier Three) with the proverbial something for everyone and good workmanship overall; and *Don Roberto* (205 Calle Cristo) with authentic santos and great, gaudy baskets of papier-mâché fruits and vegetables (the mushrooms are neat) standouts in a tasteful collection. Weekends: go, watch the work, and buy at the artisans' market at the Convention Center (Saturdays and Sundays, noon to 3 PM).

Art is alive and exciting, with contemporary Puerto Ricans working in every medium — oils, sculpture, graphics, the works. Jan d'Esopo is a well-known local painter whose images of island life are sold in her shop in the *Condado Plaza.* Luis Hernandez Cruz, Myrna Baez, Francisco Rodon, Rafael Tufino, and Julio Rosado del Valle are among the island's best-known graphic artists. In sculpture, look for the names of José Buscaglia and Tomás Batista. *Galería Botello* (208 Calle Cristo in Old San Juan and at the *Caribe Hilton* and Plaza Las Américas shopping center) is among the best; it showcases the works of Botello and other island artists, and has a fine santos collection. Also visit *Galería 59* on Calle Cristo in Old San Juan and *Bocello* in the *Hyatt Cerromar Beach* in Dorado.

Cigars, made of island tobacco and hand-rolled while you watch, sell for up to $1 each at *Gillies & Woodward* (156 Calle Fortaleza), the *Caribe Cigar* factory off the Plaza de Colón on O'Donnell St., and a shop in the bus station, on Commerce St.

Rum, another Puerto Rican pride, sells for about half its stateside price, but the duty you'll have to pay on any bottles over your one-bottle-per-person allowance brings the cost close to mainland level. Ask at your hotel for a nearby shop that sells stamped bottles (the average Puerto Rican liquor store does not) where you'll have a bigger selection than at the airport shop. Most Puerto Rican rums are fine and light, but the connoisseurs' choice is aged añejo, which has the smoothness and power of a good brandy. An excellent one, Ron del Barrilito, sells for under $7 on the island, just a little more than half its typical stateside price.

For a tasty further education in the history and art of making rum, take the Cataño ferry from Old San Juan to visit the Bacardi rum distillery. The guided tours and samplings — daily until 3 PM, except Sundays and holidays — are free (see *Ferry Service,* above).

Clothes? In Old San Juan the main shopping street for apparel is Calle Cristo between Calles Fortaleza and San Francisco. *Casa Cavanagh* (202 Calle Cristo) specializes in higher-priced resort chic for both men and women. The *Ralph Lauren* shop (Cristo and San Francisco) has men's, women's, and children's clothing, including jeans, at discounts of 30% to 50%. For stunning accessories, go to *Bóveda* for original designs in jewelry. For men, *Ultra* (154 Fortaleza) has a large selection of quality guayabera shirts, the straight-hanging, no-tuck-in, pleated-front dress shirt islanders substitute for a shirt, tie, and jacket. They come in white and colors; some are embroidered and extremely elegant (check for no-iron labels). Shop and compare at *Gonzales-Padín* and the *New York Department Store* (both on the Plaza de Armas); prices run $10 to $40. *The Hathaway Outlet* (203 Calle Cristo) sells its famous men's and women's shirts at 33% to 50% below mainland prices; nearby, the *Bass Shoe Outlet* (206 Calle Cristo) also has bargains. For couture of a haute-er order, stroll along Ashford Avenue in Condado. Women should check out Fernando Pena's *Casa Bella* salon, *Level I, Elea-*

nor, and for European shoes, *La Favorita.* Trendy men, don't miss *Nono Maldonado.* If the walk along Ashford brings you as far as the *Condado Plaza,* take time to admire the beautifully restored Art Deco apartment building, called Miami, on the opposite side of the street.

Imported china, crystal, and jewelry — at what are advertised as "duty-free" prices that the sales staff claims are "as low as those in St. Thomas" — are the specialty of *Ambiance,* next to the *Condado Beach* hotel on Ashford Avenue.

Gold jewelry is the current shoppers' passion, especially among cruise passengers. *El Gallo de Oro* (200 Fortaleza) has lots and lots, with a particularly large collection of gold charms. The fine-finer-finest is at *Reinhold,* on the corner of Calles Cristo and Fortaleza. Other stores with tantalizing merchandise and prices are *Gastón Bared, Barquet,* and *Letran,* all on Calle Fortaleza. For jewelry set with fine stones, try the *Riviera* (205 Calle Cruz).

Decorative accessories and furniture — to look at even if you don't feel like going through the hassle of shipping them home — are beautiful and mostly antique at *José E. Alegría & Associates* (154 Calle Cristo); stylish and islandy at *Casa Cavanagh* (202 Calle Cristo and at the *Caribe Hilton*), where they sell tropical clothes, fabrics, and fashion accessories for both men and women.

Most major hotels have shops that are branches of downtown establishments and/or provide the necessities you left behind or used up (sunglasses, Alka-Seltzer, camera batteries). In these, as well as in downtown stores and at most places on the island, price tags mean what they say. There's no haggling. Most stores are open from 9 AM to 6 PM, Mondays through Saturdays; at Plaza las Américas they're open till 9 PM on Fridays.

 TIPPING: The commonwealth's system is like that in the continental US. Airport porters expect 50¢ per bag; and taxi drivers, 15% of the fare. Leave $1 to $2 per room per day for the hotel chambermaid; give the doorman 50¢ to $1 for calling a cab, depending on how much actual effort is required. The standard tip in hotel dining rooms and supper clubs is 15%; and, unless the package tour you bought specifically states otherwise, remember that package-trip meal coupons do not usually cover tips, so leave 15% of your estimate of the cost (not necessarily the worth) of the meal.

 SPECIAL EVENTS: In any Caribbean celebration competition, Puerto Rico would win in a walk. For starters, every town has its patron saint, and, therefore, a one- to three-day fiesta marking his or her day, and visitors are welcome — even encouraged — to join in the music, dancing, parades, and street partying. On June 24, San Juan celebrates the *Feast of St. John the Baptist,* when resort hotels often join in to sponsor beachside barbecues that culminate in the traditional mass midnight dunking — for good luck — in the surf; the three-day observance in honor of *Santiago Apostal* (St. James the Apostle), one of the island's most festive, starts on July 25 in the one-time African slave community of Loíza Aldea 15 miles east of San Juan; and there are 75 to 80 others. The last week of July, Vieques holds its Carnival, featuring calypso music and a drink called bilí, made from a small green fruit called quenebas. *Qué Pasa* carries a monthly listing on its Events page.

The *Casals Festival,* begun in 1957 by the cellist-conductor-composer Pablo Casals, takes place at the Performing Arts Center in Santurce, usually the first two weeks in June; tickets cost $4 to $12 per event and, because of the celebrity of the participants, are very hard to come by. For details, write as far in advance as possible to Corporación de las Artes Escénico-Musicales, Apto. 41227, Minillas Station, Santurce, PR 00940-1227.

Puerto Rico also seems to have more than its share of public holidays. Official national holidays are *New Year's Day, Three Kings' Day* (January 6), *Washington's Birthday, Good Friday, Memorial Day, Fourth of July, Labor Day, Thanksgiving, Veterans' Day, Christmas,* and *Election Day* (first Tuesday in November, every four years). The island also celebrates its own *Constitution Day* (July 25) and *Discovery Day* (November 19). On these days, banks, businesses, government offices, and schools are closed.

But there are also half holidays, when banks and businesses remain open but government offices and schools close: educator and patriot *Eugenio María de Hostos's Birthday* (January 11), *Emancipation Day* (March 22), writer and political leader *José de Diego's Birthday* (April 16), poet and statesman *Luís Muñoz Rivera's Birthday* (July 17), doctor and educator *José Celso Barbosa's Birthday* (July 27), and *Diá de Raza,* or Heritage Day (October 12).

LeLoLai, a musical expression borrowed from the song of the Puerto Rican *jíbaro* (freely translated "hillbilly"), is now the name of a year-round festival of weekly events, begun in 1976, that feature native dance, music, and foods. Each event takes place once a week as part of a program designed to sweeten tour packages; and all are included free in many week-long itineraries; an abbreviated version is included in shorter package stays. You can also buy tickets for individual events from information centers and hotel travel desks for about $1.50 to $28 each. They're fun if you're in the mood to mix and bounce a bit. For details, contact the LeLoLai office in the Convention Center, 1120 Ashford Ave., San Juan (phone: 723-3135).

 SPORTS: The hotels along the San Juan–Condado–Isla Verde coastline naturally concentrate on beach and water sports, plus some tennis and spectator sports. San Juan's marina is a major departure point for deep-sea fishing boats. But if you're really serious about your sporting life, you may want to head for one of the island's three extraordinary playing places out on the island: Dorado with its *Hyatt Dorado Beach* and *Hyatt Cerromar Beach* hotels, and *Palmas del Mar* near Humacao (see *Best en Route*). Baseball is as big on the island as it is on the mainland, and soccer (called *futbol*) is quite popular, too. Occasionally San Juan is the scene of title boxing bouts. Briefly, here's what's where:

Baseball – As popular on the island as on the mainland. Games are played in stadiums in San Juan, Mayagüez, Ponce, Arecibo, Caguas, and Santurce from October to mid-April.

Bicycling – The *Hyatt Dorado Beach* rents bicycles for $3.50 an hour or $12 a day. A few bucks more, and a bicycle built for two is at your disposal.

Bridge – The Puerto Rico Duplicate Bridge Club, affiliated with the American Contract Bridge League, invites visitors to sit in on their regular sessions at 1106 Ashford Ave., 2nd Floor, Condado; phone: 723-8887 for information and playing times (five days a week). There's a nominal per-session charge.

Boating – Not much on Puerto Rico except at *Palmas del Mar's Marina de Palmas Yacht Club* near Humacao (phone: 852-3450, ext. 2473), where you can rent small-to-medium-size boats for day sails; *Villa Marina Yacht Harbor* in Fajardo also rents and charters boats (phone: 863-4051). Hotels offering rentals on a very-small-boat scale (Sunfish, Sailfish) include the *Condado Plaza, Palmas del Mar* in Humacao, and the *Hyatt Dorado Beach* (paddleboats) near Dorado. Rowboats can be rented at the Condado Lagoon pier for about $3 an hour. Boating equipment is also available at La Parguera.

Cockfighting – The "sport" is as civilized as it ever gets in the Coliseo Gallistico (air conditioned, with comfortable seating, restaurant, bar, and fake-grass-carpeted pit) in Isla Verde. The feathers fly Tuesdays, Saturdays, and Sundays at 3 PM. Phone: 791-1557 to confirm.

Golf – Puerto Rico is not labeled "Scotland in the Sun" for nothing. Out on the island, nine 18-hole (and five 9-hole) courses lay waiting for the golf aficionado. Four of these — all championship Robert Trent Jones, Sr., layouts — are the joint property of Dorado's sister resorts, *Hyatt Dorado Beach* and *Hyatt Cerromar Beach.* There is another topnotch 18 at *Palmas del Mar* near Humacao. The former Ramey Air Force Base site that's now *Punta Borinquen* has an 18-hole course, and, although there are no public courses per se, tourists can arrange to play at the highly regarded *Berwind Country Club* in Río Grande (phone: 876-2230 or 876-2530) and also at *Dorado del Mar Country Club* in Dorado (phone: 724-4187). Greens fees vary widely according to course, day of the week, and season; the range is about $12 for 9 holes, $19 for 18 holes. No caddies, but golf carts rent for about $22 for 18 holes; some courses rent clubs and shoes.

The *Mayagüez Hilton International* arranges for guests to play at the private *Club Deportivo del Oeste*'s 9-hole course; there are also sporty 9-holers at *Campo Chico Golf Course* in Caguas and the *Ponce Country Club.*

Hiking – The *Hyatt Dorado Beach* holds a nature walk every Thursday at 9 AM. A little farther afield, the Caribbean National Forest has three verdant and well-maintained trails: El Yunque (an easy 15 minutes to a more difficult 2 hours), Mt. Britton (1¼ hours), and El Toro (most ambitious, at 8 hours). The Sierra Palm Visitors Center is near the park entrance.

Horseback Riding – *Palmas del Mar* has its own equestrian center and scenic paths that wind through a pine-laden nature preserve; besides trail rides, jumping and riding instruction is available. You can also arrange to ride at the *Hyatt Dorado Beach* hotel, *Ranchos Guayama* near Guayama, *Parador Hacienda Juanita,* in Maricao, and at the Ramey Air Force Base in *Punta Borinquen.*

Horse Racing – El Comandante Race Track is cheerful, colorful, fun. Year-round post time is 2:30 PM on Wednesdays, Fridays, Sundays, and holidays. There's a daily double and an exacta. Admission is $1 grandstand, $3 for the clubhouse. The 900-seat, air-conditioned restaurant opens at 12:30 PM on race days. Check with your hotel travel desk about packages including transport and entrance fee. Also ask at Tourism Information Centers about paso fino meets and rodeos.

Snorkeling and Scuba – Available through water sports desks at several major San Juan hotels. The *Caribe Hilton* (phone: 721-0303, ext. 447), the *Condado Plaza Watersports Center* (phone: 721-1000, ext. 1361 or 1592), and the *Hyatt Dorado Beach* are best equipped for instruction and equipment rental. Coral reefs, cays, and mangrove clumps along the coast make for interesting snorkeling. So do daylong picnic excursions to Icacos Island (see *Sea Excursions,* above). The best dive sites are off the *Caribe Hilton*'s beach (outside the reef there's a 33-foot drop with underwater caves) and a considerable distance out to sea. The *Caribbean School of Aquatics* in Ocean Park (phone: 723-4740) offers daily scuba trips for about $50 for six hours.

Elsewhere on the island, the *Mayagüez Hilton* runs an active underwater program in conjunction with the nearby *Yagüez Diving School* (phone: 832-9067); *Palmas del Mar Aquatics,* near Humacao, is also set up for rentals and lessons (phone: 852-6000). You can rent equipment in La Parguera, as well.

Sport Fishing – It doesn't get much publicity, but it's first rate. More than 30 world-record fish have been taken in these waters. The catch: blue marlin (April through November); white marlin (April through June, October, November); sailfish (October through June); also wahoo, allison tuna, dolphin, mackerel, tarpon, and snook, plus fighting bonefish in the shallows. Fully equipped boats with crew charter out of *San Juan Marina,* Fernández Juncos Ave., Miramar (phone: 725-0139, 723-0415). José Castillo operates half- and full-day trips aboard his 38- and 48-foot yachts at the *Palace* in Isla Verde (phone: 791-6195; 791-2020, ext. 1760). *Marina de Palmas Yacht Club* offers half-day and overnight trips (phone: 850-7921; 852-3450, ext. 2473). Rates run about $210 for a half day, about $335 for a full day for up to four people including bait, tackle, beer, and soft drinks. The biggie is Capt. Mike Benitez' island-famous 53-foot yacht *Sea Born,* which is berthed at the *Club Náutico de San Juan* (phones: 724-6265 at the *Club,* 723-2292 at home); day rate is about $350 for up to six people. More expensive is Capt. Jorge Torruella's *Gin Pole,* a 41-foot award winner available for half- or full-day excursions (phone: 725-1408).

Surfing – A north and west coast pursuit. Pine Grove Beach in Isla Verde (north) and Punta Higüero, near Rincón (west), are the most popular beaches for it. The best time to hit the waves is from December through February, at 6 AM. Punta Borinquen, near Aguadilla (west), is a good beach for body surfing.

Swimming and Sunning – On the beach or by the pool, both are only an amble away from your room at the big strip hotels. But all San Juan hotel beaches are not created equal — the *Caribe Hilton* and the *Condado Plaza* definitely have the best of them; if you prefer to do your tanning on a sandy beach instead of a sociable poolside chaise, check the hotel's setup before you make reservations. One caution: rough sea conditions can sometimes create local rip currents or undertow off the Condado–Isla Verde hotel beaches, some of which do not provide full-time lifeguards. Out on the island, *Hyatt Dorado Beach* and *Hyatt Cerromar Beach* resorts have especially fine sandy shores. By law, all Puerto Rican beaches are open to the public. But the government has installed special *balneario* facilities (lockers, showers, and changing rooms plus parking, at about 25¢ a day for a locker, $1 for parking) at a dozen of the island's most beautiful, now referred to as "public," beaches. And wherever you go, you're always near one or two of them. They're open from 9 AM to 5 PM in winter, to 6 in summer; closed Mondays. Luquillo, on the north coast about 30 miles east of San Juan, is most famous and most popular (too much so on weekends) with islanders as well as tourists. Also on the north coast, to the east of but closer to San Juan, is Isla Verde. On the east coast, there's Humacao. Along the south coast, there are 4 beaches: Punta Guilarte, near Arroyo; El Tuque, west of Ponce; Caña Gorda, near Guánica, and Rosada, near La Parguera. On the western shore: Boquerón and Añasco (not highly recommended). And along the north coast west of San Juan: Cerro Gordo, about 25 miles from the city; La Sardinera near Dorado; and Punta Salinas between Dorado and Cataño. The thirteenth one — Sombe Beach — is not on Puerto Rico but on the offshore island of Vieques. With all the public *balneario* accouterments but a special sense of faraway privacy, it is very beautiful.

Tennis – It's big stuff at two resorts out on the island: *Hyatt Dorado Beach* and *Hyatt Cerromar Beach* (where the Peter Burwash International organization oversees instruction), with 21 courts between them, and *Palmas del Mar,* with its 20-court tennis center managed by All American Sports. All have teaching pros, spiffy pro shops, spectator setups for tournament and exhibition play; and all offer tennis packages with lessons and court time built in (a good deal, since hourly rates — which live-in guests may or may not have to pay — can add up and lessons with an assistant pro run $40 up for a private hour). On account of the hot noonday sun, some hotels may offer lower midday rates; early morning and late afternoon are the best playing times.

In the San Juan area, the *Carib-Inn* (formerly the Racquet Club), *Caribe Hilton,* *Condado Plaza,* and *Condado Beach* hotels have topnotch setups. You can also play on 16 public courts in San Juan Central Park for about $1 per hour daily except Mondays. Out on the island, there are courts at *Punta Borinquen* in Aguadilla, the *Mayagüez Hilton,* the *Copamarina* hotel in Guánica, and *Parador Guajataca* in Quebradillas, in addition to the above-mentioned resorts. Visitors can also use courts at *Dorado del Mar Country Club* at Dorado (phone: 724-4187).

Water Skiing – Practiced to a limited extent on San Juan's Condado Lagoon and out on the island at Boquerón Bay. Rent equipment at the *Condado Plaza*'s water sports center.

Windsurfing – Here, as elsewhere, it's taking off. Best setups are at *Palmas del Mar,* the *Condado Plaza,* and the *Hyatt Dorado Beach,* where rentals and instruction are available. The Condado Lagoon and Boquerón Bay are popular spots for it.

NIGHTLIFE: Dining, dancing, and gaming, spiced with LeLoLai happenings, are most of what it's about. Though press releases don't shout about them, a dozen glittering casinos — where games range from baccarat to blackjack — are one of the island's big draws. By law, all are in hotels with 100 or more rooms: the *Caribe Hilton, Condado Beach, Ramada, Condado Plaza,* and *El San Juan* hotels in the San Juan area, and out on the island, *Hyatt Cerromar Beach* and *Hyatt Dorado Beach.* The government, according to *The Games of Puerto Rico Gaming Guide* (free at all casinos), is striving for a "quiet, refined atmosphere," and in spite of the jangly new rows of slot machines, it mostly succeeds. No drinking is permitted at the tables (you may order free coffee or soft drinks and sandwiches). Casinos are open from noon until 4 AM. Although rules are somewhat relaxed in the afternoon, dressy attire for women and jackets and ties for men are still firmly suggested after dark (especially at the *Caribe Hilton, Condado Plaza,* and *El San Juan*). The result is a formal but somewhat subdued atmosphere under crystal chandeliers. At press time, some of the resort areas had been closing (arbitrarily, it appears) for one or two days a week in response to a union contract clause that inordinately — say the hotels — raises the minimum number of casino employees for full-week operations compared to those that take a hiatus. If casino gambling will be a major part of your recreation, check out this situation before you check in.

Elsewhere, there's considerable eating out from 8 PM on, plus nightclub shows to contemplate. The *Chart House* remains the best spot to kick off the evening with drinks in a congenial atmosphere. All the big hotels have their "rooms"; in season, the *Hilton*'s classy *Club Caribe* imports occasional mainland names but most often spotlights the best Latin talent; the *Condado Plaza*'s *Copa Room* features a Latin revue, and its piano bar in the lobby draws a crowd. At the big hotels, a dinner-and-show evening may easily run $60 and up for two, which underscores LeLoLai's bargain-level evening prices.

Other, less expensive alternatives are hotel lounges with combos for dancing and a minimum but no cover charge. *The Patio* at *El Convento* hotel provides piano serenades; *The Place,* at 154 Calle Fortaleza in Old San Juan, has jam sessions Tuesdays and Wednesdays and folk, jazz, and popular music Fridays and Saturdays. All of the flamenco shows going are mild compared to the real, moaning Madrid thing. Of the current crop of discos, the most popular are *Juliana's* in the *Caribe Hilton, Amadeus* at the *El San Juan,* and *Isadora's* in the *Condado Plaza. Bachelor's,* a gay disco, is another favorite; *Neon's,* a video-teque, attracts the teen crowd. After dancing, snack on burgers and omelettes at *The Greenhouse* on Condado till 5 AM.

Out on the island, all's relatively quiet with the exception of the *Hyatt Cerromar Beach,* where there's *El Yunque* lounge and *El Coqui* discotheque. The *Club Cacique* at the *Mayagüez Hilton* also does its share of swinging, although Mayagüez' college crowd heads to nearby San Germán and *La Cueva de Luís Candela* disco. *The World Upside Down* is a gay disco on Route 2, just west of San Germán.

The most serene after-dark diversion out on the island is the light-trailing boat ride around La Parguera's Phosphorescent Bay, which is filled with luminescent, microscopic critters; so it's best to go on a moonless night.

BEST ON THE ISLAND

CHECKING IN: In San Juan, accommodations range from very expensive, full-service resort hotels to small, cheerful guesthouses. Their counterparts out on the island are low-slung luxury hotel and villa complexes and the island's unique network of simple country inns called *paradores* (double rooms from $30 to $76), which can be booked in the US by calling the Puerto Rico

Tourism Company (phone: 800 223-6530). With Puerto Rican tourism gaining strength, guestrooms again seem to be in fresh, up-to-date condition. More important, it's now virtually certain that the room you booked (and for which you have a confirmed reservation) will be available when you arrive, since the Tourism Company has taken a far tougher attitude toward habitual overbookers. But do reread your confirmation slip and hotel vouchers before leaving home, and do double-check with your agent or airline tour desk about operative guarantees and what to do just in case.

The most expensive San Juan area beach hotels charge $150 to $200 and up in the winter high season (mid-December to mid-April) for a double room without meals (EP), but with — in most cases — television, air conditioning, balcony, tub-shower, phone, and room service. Modified American Plan (MAP) arrangements — including breakfasts and dinners — are often available for an extra charge of about $50 per person. Rates run 25% to 50% lower during the rest of the year.

Whatever the season, check out package deals offered by airlines, tour operators, or travel agents. At the very least, they can mean free LeLoLai parties, special features (free greens fees for a round of golf, a San Juan bay cruise), and souvenirs — some of which mean real dollars-and-cents savings. And almost always packages also mean the same hotel for less money than you'd otherwise have to pay.

For families, Puerto Rico's hundreds of rental and/or resort condominiums and hotel suites equipped with kitchens not only mean substantial savings on food costs, but add scheduling flexibility. Be aware, however, that the word *motel* in Puerto Rico normally means a place primarily catering to illicit lovers, and Route 1 from San Juan to Caguas is famous for these joints.

Hotels listed here as expensive ask $150 to $200 (EP) in season; moderate, $80 to $120; inexpensive, $40 to $60. Expect to pay 30% to 50% less off-season. For the best quality for your money:

SAN JUAN–CONDADO–ISLA VERDE AREA

El San Juan – This renovated landmark (officially reopened in December 1985 after a $40-million facelift) features the Palm Court lobby — with its massive chandelier, rose marble floor, and hand-carved mahogany ceiling — where guests can enjoy high tea and chamber music. Near the airport, it has 362 rooms, including guesthouses with private patios, the largest casino in the Caribbean, a nightclub, 24-hour café, and disco. *Dar Tiffany* (the best on-premises restaurant) specializes in seafood and steaks and has one of the island's most expensive wine lists; *La Terraza* offers a choice of verandah or indoor dining. A Chinese restaurant is housed in the actual set from the Hong Kong pavilion at the 1962 Brussels World's Fair. There's also a large pool, extensive watersports facilities, and 3 tennis courts with lights (phone: 791-1000; 800 468-8588). Very expensive.

Caribe Hilton International – The high-rise that started tourism's Operation Bootstrap, and on lots of counts still the best. There are 707 well-tended rooms, suites, and the deluxe La Vista floor, plus landscaped grounds complete with antique fort. The service works more than 90% of the time — good by any island standard. Other features include a casino, beach, sports, 2 pools, children's summer and holiday day camp, dining, and popular *Juliana's* disco. The poolside bar is yacht size. Modified American plan available in winter. Old San Juan is a short cab ride away (phone: 721-0303). Very expensive to expensive.

La Concha – Upgraded and reopened in 1984, and now run by the government, it features a pleasant, large pool surrounded by fountains and heavily populated deck chairs, lovely beachfront with lanais, 2 tennis courts, water sports (including scuba), a restaurant, nightclub, casino (formerly in the *Condado Beach* hotel), and lobby and poolside bars. All 234 air-conditioned, terraced rooms have ocean views, cable TV, and direct-dial telephones (phone: 721-6090; 800 468-2822). Expensive.

Condado Beach – Hoteles HUSA International, the Spanish management firm, has done a first-rate job of restoring the Art Deco glories of the former Condado Vanderbilt, built in 1919. Pretty though not plush, it has markedly improved service, 252 rooms (half with ocean view), restaurant, casino, lounge with entertainment, pool, and use of the tennis courts at *La Concha* next door. An MAP dine-around plan is available, along with children's programs in summer and on holidays. VIP guests have a club room, honor bar, and other privileges (phone: 721-6090; 800 468-2775). Expensive.

Condado Plaza – A best seller for good reason: good looks, good service, 2 pools, lots of daytime action, and varied nightlife, with a couple of winning restaurants, disco, and big casino. The *Plaza Club* floor caters to executives, offering on-floor concierge service, key-only elevator access, a private lounge, and complimentary breakfast and snacks. The two-hotel complex includes the original 320-room beachfront property plus the 270-room Laguna section, linked by an Art Deco walkway across Ashford Ave. (phone: 721-1000; 800 468-8588). Expensive.

El Convento – A 17th-century Carmelite convent in Old San Juan, refurbished in 1986, it is now a low-key luxury hotel. The 100 air-conditioned rooms and suites with private baths and TV are smallish, but antique touches add style. Ideal base for seeing the city or for pre- and post-cruise stays. Except for small pool and sun decks, no sports at hand, but desk arranges tennis, golf, fishing. Patio is a favorite in-town lunch spot. Affiliate of Mexico's Provincial de Hoteles (phone: 723-9020; 800 468-2779). Expensive.

Pierre – A Best Western property, it has 184 rooms, a small pool, and a young, friendly staff. Rates include breakfast in the lobby. Even-numbered rooms have tubs. Somewhat removed from the beach hubbub, but not isolated; it's adjacent to the congenial *Swiss Chalet* restaurant in the Santurce section of town (phone: 721-1200). Moderate.

Ramada – Behind its modest façade, there's a surprising store of pleasant style and genuine hospitality. The 96 rooms are large, good looking, with color TV, air conditioning, all the comforts; nonsmoking rooms on each floor. Key-accessed executive floors add extra pampering. Good dining room, small pool, seaside terrace, indoor/outdoor bar popular for after-dinner drinks, dancing; casino where there is live music in the *Winners' Bar* (phone: 724-5657; 800 228-2828). Moderate.

Atlantic Beach – A small, pleasant hotel with 37 rooms, on Calle Vendig in Condado, right on the beach; it caters primarily to a gay clientele and has a disco. Reserve one of the lovely Embassy apartments with kitchen, in an annex across the street from the hotel, a month in advance (phone: 721-6900). Inexpensive.

Regency – It has 129 rooms and a good beachfront location next to the *Condado Plaza.* No frills except for a small pool, small restaurant, and cable TV. Rooms with kitchens; good buy (phone: 721-0505). Inexpensive.

SAN JUAN GUESTHOUSES

Meliá – Popular with business travelers, it is first choice for a night or two in town because of setting (facing plaza), Spanish-accented atmosphere. It has 80 rooms, swimming and golf privileges, but no pool. Continental breakfast included (phone: 842-0260). Moderate to inexpensive.

El Canario – A neat and friendly place with 25 rooms, small backyard swimming pool, and beach only steps away. Central location. Continental breakfast included in rates. Ask for a room facing the pool (phone: 724-2793). Inexpensive.

El Prado – A charming hideaway near the *Canario Inn,* it features a pool and 18 rooms. Morning coffee is served on the verandah, with breakfast and lunch optional. Run by delightful French resident Madame Petit (phone: 728-5925). Inexpensive.

Lutèce on the Beach – Also run by Madame Petit, this large two-story beachfront spot has more amenities than the *Prado,* including color TV, phone, ceiling fan, and rattan furniture in each of its 48 rooms. There is also a restaurant, patio, and pool (phone: 728-0855). Inexpensive.

DORADO

Hyatt Dorado Beach – Lushly landscaped, two-level, 287-room luxury resort with a casino, super golf (two Robert Trent Jones, Sr., layouts), top tennis (7 courts, pro clinics, lessons), a large lap pool, Jacuzzi, long sweeps of beach, snorkeling, and miles of bike paths and hiking trails. The intimate *Su Casa* restaurant, a separate building, provides evocative island dining, as well as an inviting lobby where high tea is served. Ground-floor units have patios. Hyatt's recently completed remodeling earns high marks for the refurbished rooms, which are more attractive and comfortable than ever, but low ones for the open-air (breakfast and lunch) dining area, which now has rafters that invite hordes of bold Caribbean blackbirds to perch above and prey on unattended plates. There are plans afoot for a convention center, so check before you go. Excellent summer sport packages, free summer and holiday camp for kids (phone: 796-1600; 800 228-9000). Very expensive.

Hyatt Cerromar Beach – Far less lush and far more commercial than the *Hyatt Dorado,* it's a renovated former Rockresort high-rise with 508 rooms, two more Robert Trent Jones golf courses (not nearly as good as the *Dorado*'s), 14 tennis courts (pro clinics, lessons), a health club with sauna and exercise classes, pool, a small beach, and a gigantic lawn. Extensive renovations and improvements during the summer of 1986, including the addition of what is either the world's largest swimming pool (Guinness did not agree) or a "water complex" that is longer, at about a third of a mile, than the Empire State Building is tall. It's an artificial river with currents, a waterfall, peripheral hydromassages, and other diversions for the casual swimmer — a real attraction except when rains flood the grounds. *El Coqui* disco, nightclub, casino, and movies enliven nights; summer and holiday day camp for kids. Best known as a center for meetings and conventions. Summer sport packages normally are excellent buys (phone: 796-1010; 800 228-9000). Very expensive.

PONCE

Holiday Inn – An unexceptional chain hotel, but the only choice in Ponce if you *must* have a pool as you explore the southern coast. It has 120 standard rooms, restaurant, cocktail lounge. Near El Tuque beach (phone: 844-1200). Moderate.

OTHER HOTELS ON THE ISLAND

Palmas del Mar, Humacao – A lush 2,700-acre Mediterranean-style resort comprising the luxury *Palmas Inn,* the 102-room *Candelero* hotel (group and family oriented, slightly less expensive), and 200 stylish villas grouped around a marina, a championship golf course, and a tennis complex with All American Sports clinics. Also children's programs and teen activities, nature and bike trails, an equestrian center, palm-lined beach, deep-sea fishing, water sports, casino, and 11 international restaurants. This much-ballyhooed sports center has had its share of problems (and owners) over the years but now seems to be enjoying steadier operation. Heavy emphasis on real estate development (including time-sharing villas and condos) is seen as the ultimate direction under current ownership; meanwhile, hotel accommodations, particularly at *Candelero,* have become somewhat shopworn. Dine-Around plan for MAP guests includes theme-night parties and choice of nearby island restaurants. Ask about golf packages (phone: 852-6000; 800 221-4874). Expensive.

Hilton International Mayagüez, Mayagüez – It offers personal size and service, 145 big rooms, pleasant pool, bar, restaurant, disco, 3 tennis courts, casino, and landscaped grounds with pond. A gathering place for local gentry. Ask for a renovated ground-floor room (phone: 834-7575). Expensive.

El Guajataca, Quebrabillas – Set on a dramatic sweep of beach, it has 38 basic rooms with balconies, a pool, tennis, golf nearby, restaurant, and an informal ambience; buffets on Sundays and Wednesdays. If it's full, *Parador Vistamar,* not quite as appealing, is just uphill. During your stay, visit the roadside *La Granja de Guajataca* and sample the *queso de hoja,* white layered cheese, and the *tembleque,* a white, gelatinous coconut sweet (phone: 895-3070). Moderate to inexpensive.

Baños de Coamo, Coamo – A government *parador,* modest considering that FDR and Frank Lloyd Wright once "took the waters" here; but the 48 rooms are adequate; the grounds — with giant raintree, thermal and freshwater pools — in the mountain foothills are pleasant. The old-fashioned dining room is charming but with unremarkable food. Favorite Puerto Rican weekend retreat. Pool; therapy programs, too (phone: 825-2186). Inexpensive.

Hacienda Gripiñas, Jayuya – Edgardo and Milagros Dedos's genuine pleasure in pleasing guests makes the hospitality here warm and special indeed. On the grounds of a former coffee plantation, this 200-year-old house (more manager's home than mansion) is set in lush foliage, fruit trees, flowers; its 19 rooms vary in size, but are pin neat, cheery, if sometimes small. There's a chilly mountain pool and excellent, reasonably priced Puerto Rican food. But the chance to relax in a rocker or loll in a hammock on the verandah sipping a piña colada in the green peace is what it's really about. No matter what the map says, heading south on the Ponce Speedway then north at Juana Díaz is the fastest route from San Juan (phone: 721-2884). Inexpensive.

Hacienda Juanita, Maricao – Serene 21-room inn on a coffee plantation in the cool eastern mountains that once were Taíno Indian country. Stables, scenic riding trails, tennis court, pool, pretty restaurant with terrace and excellent island food. Very picturesque, romantic (phone: 838-2550). Inexpensive.

Martorell, Luquillo – For beach nuts only, its 7 super-neat rooms are in a former private house; there is a patio but no surrounding grounds, pool, or dining room. The famous beach is only half a block away. Buffet breakfasts on the patio are included in the basic room rate. Strict management (phone: 889-2710). Inexpensive.

Montemar, Aguadilla – Invitingly relaxed hotel overlooking the Atlantic, where the good waves are. All 40 air-conditioned, balconied rooms have ocean views. Two restaurants (one great for sunset watching), pool, popular Crash Boat beach, tennis, cocktail lounge. Sunday buffets, which cost about $10 per person, are special (phone: 891-4383). Inexpensive.

Oasis, San Germán – A 200-year-old family mansion and winery, now a hospitable inn. It has 22 air-conditioned rooms and a pretty courtyard dining area and is within walking distance of the town's historic sites (phone: 892-1175). Inexpensive.

Villa Parguera, La Parguera – Classic fishermen's inn, rustic but comfortable; the dining room specializes in fresh seafood. With 51 rooms, pool. Adjacent to Phosphorescent Bay (phone: 889-3975). Inexpensive.

ON THE OFFSHORE ISLANDS

Coral Island Guest House, Isla de Culebra – A rustic, modest place that's downtown, across from the ferry dock. Its 9 rooms offer everything from bunk to twin to double beds and kitchen facilities; windsurfing, horses, scuba diving, and paddle ball. The rooftop deck offers a 360° view of the island and is the scene of convivial barbecues. Management handles all travel arrangements (phone: 742-3177; in Boston, 617 545-5120). Inexpensive.

Casa del Frances, Isla de Vieques – Small (19-room) 19th-century plantation house built around a green patio. Picturesque, but with up-and-down management. Minutes' walk from big sunny beach; home cooking, with fresh fish a specialty. Casual. No guarantees, but we'd risk it (phone: 741-3751). Inexpensive.

 EATING OUT: San Juan is a city with a predictably citified selection of Continental restaurants and steak houses — some good, some not so. In addition, there are several restaurants dedicated to doing well by the Puerto Rican way of cooking (somewhat similar to but not as olive oil based as most Spanish or as fiery as most Mexican), and they succeed. Lately, there has also been a trend toward including island dishes on more hotel menus. Worth sampling: black bean soup, very rich, often served with chopped raw onion; *bacalitos* (salt-fish fritters); *morcillas* (spicy blood sausages); *piononos* (spicy ground beef enclosed in strips of ripe plantains); *tostones* (deep-fried plantain slices, often served as a side dish); *pescado* (any fresh fish, especially good in seaside restaurants out on the island); *asopao* (a soupy but generally delicious concoction of chicken or seafood with rice); *arroz con pollo* (chicken and rice); *jueyes* (land crabs, often deviled and served in the shell); *lechón asado* (roast suckling pig); and, for dessert, Puerto Rican pineapple or guava (preserved halves or squares of "paste") served with white cheese. To drink: Puerto Rican coffee (which is the dark, strong stuff you get when you order a "small" cup), light Puerto Rican rum, and island-brewed India beer.

Lunch is generally served from noon to 2:30 PM; 8 to 10 PM is the most popular dinnertime for vacationers, though Puerto Ricans usually eat earlier, between 5:30 and 7:30 PM. Especially in the posher places, dinner reservations are a good idea since it's hard to predict which will be *the* place and, therefore, packed on any given night. Outstanding independent restaurants are often in hotels. An expensive place will charge $30 and up per person for a three-course dinner including tip, but no drinks; about $10 to $20 is considered moderate; below that, it's inexpensive. Lunches run a couple of dollars lower. These are favorites:

Back Street Hong Kong – The Chinese food is authentic, priced higher than its New York equivalent, and the decor mysterious and unique; it's the set from the Hong Kong pavilion at the 1962 World's Fair in Brussels (heaven only knows where it was before arriving in Puerto Rico). The windows reflect the lights of Hong Kong. In the *El San Juan* hotel (phone: 791-1000). Expensive.

Dar Tiffany – An elegant, very expensive, independent restaurant just off the main lobby of the *El San Juan* hotel. The dining room itself would be totally at home in New York or Miami, as would the fine servings of seafood and steaks. All credit cards are accepted; reservations well in advance are a must. At the *El San Juan,* Isla Verde (phone: 791-1000). Expensive.

Los Galanes – Handsome antique Spanish surroundings; nicely presented and prepared Spanish menu; stylishly personal service. Commendable gazpacho, seafood; excellent wine list. 65 Calle San Francisco (phone: 722-4008). Expensive.

El Gobernador – The soigné blue, white, and silver dining room has an ocean view and serves international dishes; the surroundings couldn't be handsomer. Dance floor and piano. In the *Condado Beach* hotel on Ashford Ave. (phone: 721-6090.) Expensive.

Renaissance – Perhaps the prettiest restaurant in San Juan, it is a favorite with the island's smart set. The menu fires the imagination, with sautéed shrimp in caviar, sautéed chicken marinated in Puerto Rican coconut and lime, and rainbow trout with pecan butter sauce. In the *Condado Plaza,* overlooking the lagoon (phone: 721-1000, ext. 1950). Expensive.

La Rotisserie – It specializes in shrimp and lobster with elegant trimmings, a Friday night seafood buffet, and excellent service. Bypass the beef dishes. Gents, wear jackets. In the *Caribe Hilton* (phone: 721-0303). Expensive.

La Zaragozana – Longtime favorite for Spanish–Cuban–Puerto Rican menu, dim, romantic atmosphere (ceiling stars, lantern lights, and like that). Black bean soup and the chicken Andaluz are favorites. Music, too. 356 Calle San Francisco, Old San Juan (phone: 723-5103). Expensive.

Café del Puerto – Attractively remodeled Spanish contemporary quarters upstairs in what was once a waterfront warehouse with a wide view of San Juan Bay. From 6 PM on, it's a private club serving a Continental dinner menu and welcoming reservations from visitors who call during business hours. Across from Pier 3 (phone: 725-1500). Expensive (dinner) to moderate (lunch).

La Fragua – Small, authentically Spanish find with especially fine fresh native fish dishes (try the paella and sea bass). 800 Ponce de Léon, entrance on Calle Cuevilla (phone: 722-4699). Expensive to moderate.

Amadeus – Recently opened modern restaurant, with purple and green decor, it features tapas (Spanish appetizers), sausages in sherry sauce, tenderloin roulettes in orange sauce, broiled salmon, tempura, and house dumplings. Calle San Sebastian 106, Old San Juan (phone: 722-8635). Moderate.

La Asturiana – Simple, savory Spanish seafood, featuring super bean and sausage soup, cockles in brine, other native starters; then crisply fried fish, shrimp and lobster (in garlic sauce, casseroles, salads), and a rewarding paella. House sangria goes nicely. Closed Mondays. 1654 Fernandez Juncos, Santurce (phone: 726-5719). Moderate.

El Callejón de la Capilla – Puerto Rican lunches and dinners are served on the patio of a restored 18th-century home as well as inside, where it's cooler. The bacalitos, morcillas, piononos, and pasteles are especially tasty; the India beer is cold. Closed Sundays. 317 Calle Fortaleza, Old San Juan (phone: 725-8529). Moderate.

Chart House – Ensconced in an imaginatively restored house, it is a lovely link in a chain specializing in steak, prime ribs, and seafood. Dinner only, but it's better as a meeting than an eating spot. 1214 Ashford Ave. (phone: 728-0110). Moderate.

Lotus Flower – Praised for its pepper steak and garlic shrimp, among other dishes, it's in the *Condado Plaza*. Expect to wait for a table (phone: 721-1000, ext. 1950). Moderate.

El Mesón Vasco – Basic Spanish with Basque overtones — paellas, and so on. Pretty surroundings in mellow old house, and the food is good. But the service is slow. 47 Calle Cristo, Old San Juan (phone: 725-7819). Moderate.

Palm Court Café – Quiches (try the broccoli and mushroom), sandwiches, omelettes, salads, and burgers; Sunday brunch, too. 152 Calle Fortaleza, Old San Juan (phone: 723-2432). Moderate.

El Patio de Sam – Casual, congenial oasis in Old San Juan; especially fine for lunch, with an imaginative menu (savory black bean soup, baked eggs malagueña in Créole sauce, seafood crêpes Mornay, asparagus vinaigrette, and daily specials, plus great burgers). 102 Calle San Sebastian (phone: 723-1149). Moderate.

Le Petit Chalet – Rarely found by tourists, this little gem is in a private home, where the dining room seats no more than 20 people. Reserve one or two nights in advance to sample whatever the owner has prepared for the evening's sitting. Near El Yunque, on Route 186, km 22.1 (phone: 887-5802). Moderate.

Scotch & Sirloin – Limited menu (i.e., steaks, prime ribs, lobster, with baked potato, salad bar), but long considered *the* quality steakhouse in Condado. Casual atmosphere, good Irish coffee, and a view of the lagoon. *La Roda* hotel, 1020 Ashford Ave. (phone: 722-3640). Moderate.

Swiss Chalet – Cheery decor and lively ambience combine with Swiss specialties that include veal bratwurst and St. Moritz schnitzel. There's also filet of sole and rack of lamb on the large menu; dancing at night. Next to the *Pierre* hotel. 105 De Diego (phone: 721-2233). Moderate.

Amanda's Café – The only restaurant in town with an ocean view, this tiny place specializes in drinks that are close cousins to desserts (Amanda Robles inherited her know-how from her dad, who was bar manager at *Lindy's* in New York and invented the Black Russian). Tofu salads and Mexican fish soup are among the entrées. To get here, follow the road uphill by Fort San Cristoból (phone: 722-1682). Inexpensive.

Greenhouse – What it lacks in atmosphere, it more than makes up for in good food, cordial service, and reasonable prices. Stop in for burgers, omelettes, cold plates, crêpes, daily specials, and divine desserts till 5 AM. Popular with residents. 1200 Ashford Ave., Condado (phone: 725-4036). Inexpensive.

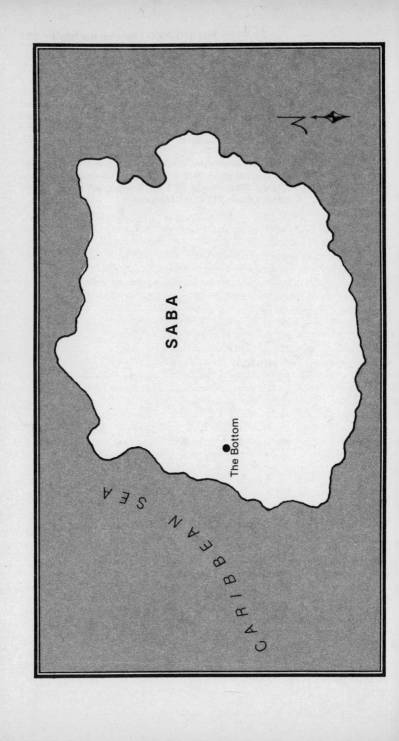

SABA

For years there was a shakily handwritten sign just outside the two-room airport at the edge of the tiny airstrip: "Welcome to Saba, the Storybook Island." Though the sign no longer touts the marvels of this round, beautiful green dot of land, Saba has lost none of its fairytale appeal.

Saba (pronounced *say*-bah) is mite-size, beachless, and mountainous. Most of the island's 5 square miles seem to go either straight up or straight down, and The Road — Saba's only thoroughfare — switches back and forth like a dragon's tail, but it never stops ascending or descending. Everything looks doll-scaled: the gingerbread-trimmed houses of Hell's Gate clinging to the mountain; English Quarter, with its picturebook church; and Windwardside, where the island's recently dedicated museum is an antique home just a bit larger than a child's playhouse. Seen from The Road above, even The Bottom, Saba's capital, looks like a Christmas-tree miniature.

Grouped with St. Maarten and St. Eustatius in the Windward Islands of the Netherlands Antilles, Saba has lived through twelve flag changes since it was discovered. Most of these were transfers that took place largely on paper, since Saba's cliffs have always provided more than adequate physical protection. In 1690, islanders repulsed a French invasion by rolling rocks down the mountainside until the attackers gave up and sailed away. It has been Dutch since 1812, but its prime spoken language is English — the legacy of the Shetland Islanders who were its first residents. ("The Dutch colonized, but they never settled," explains an island historian.)

For centuries, the steep hillsides also kept Saba isolated from the rest of the Caribbean. Its women almost never left home. Its men became expert seamen, fishermen, and special kinds of longshoremen. They learned to unload vital cargo offshore, wrestle the stuff through the surf, and haul it up the cliff no matter what the object's size or shape. Even pianos were delivered that way.

Perhaps because of its isolation, events that might seem minor anywhere else are major historical landmarks for Saba. The chronology of Dr. J. Hartog's brief history, *St. Maarten, Saba, St. Eustatius* not only lists the sighting of Statia and Saba by Columbus (1493) and Stuyvesant's attack on St. Maarten (1644), but also the opening of Windwardside's first supermarket (1963), the arrival of Saba's first cruise ship (the *Argonaut,* in 1966), and the inauguration of its first (and only) Leo A. I. Chance pier in 1972. Most Sabans would add to the list the arrival of a jeep in 1947. Lashed to two rowboats, it narrowly missed being swamped as 50 men lifted it ashore to become the island's first car.

Decades later, there are still fewer than 300 automobiles on Saba. Long the island's biggest inn, the *Captain's Quarters* — built from two century-old homes in Windwardside — has only ten rooms, a number of which have four-poster beds with down comforters for cool nights. Just up the hill, *Scout's*

Place has recently added ten new rooms to its original four, replacing *Captain's* as the island's largest "hotel."

Saba is an island scaled for individuals, and you'll meet them all, one by one: Will Johnson, a born historian who edits and publishes the monthly mimeographed *Saba Herald* (which he began in 1968), former chairman of the Saba Tourist Board and now senator of Saba; ESP-clued Pauline Paul, who gives piano lessons to young and old, and invariably arrives in her wobble-brimmed straw hat to interview visitors for her nightly Baha'i-sponsored radio show; young Glenn Holm, who heads the Tourist Bureau and spends his off-hours organizing community projects, hiking Saba's mountainsides, or exploring its surrounding waters.

Roughly one quarter of Saba's 1,042 inhabitants are named Hassell. They are descendants of Josephus Lambert Hassell, who, after every expert had said it couldn't be done, took a correspondence course in engineering and designed the impossible road which — for the next 20 years — he and his fellow Sabans proceeded to build by hand. This story reveals something important about Saba's people.

"We build our own houses and bury our own dead," says Will Johnson. And although the burial custom is fading with rising property values, it is a practical rather than a morbid tradition. Of all the world's Dutch subjects, only Sabans — because of the extreme ups and downs of their island's topography — are permitted to bury their dead in their own yards. Almost every old house has its flower garden gravesite, and the effect is more cheerfully matter-of-fact than gloomy. Sabans are self-reliant and kind, to each other and to visitors. On Saba, hitchhikers never have to lift a thumb. It's an unwritten rule of The Road that anyone with wheels who's going your way will stop and offer a ride. From The Bottom, just sit on the wall opposite the Anglican Church (from Fort Bay, on the wall opposite *Saba Deep*), if you have time to spare. Or just start walking. The first passing vehicle will give you a lift.

Driving up from the airport, Will Johnson sometimes pauses to point to a plaque in the retaining wall at the edge of The Road where a sea poem and the name Captain Charles Reuben Simmons are inscribed. Below it, the legend reads "Born, Hell's Gate, Sept. 27, 1895." The captain, who is Will's uncle, now lives nearby and likes to sit in this spot to watch the water. The plaque is the gesture of a friend who thought it would be nice to make special note of the place in his honor.

There is some development in process on Saba, but on a scale that could only be considered very modest. There is a Connecticut gentleman who has rented a school building next to the 10-bed hospital in order to open a small medical school — 20 students and 12 faculty. Another American is constructing a new building for a restaurant, while another new eatery — Sharon's Place — just debuted. And that's about it.

There is virtually no crime on the island. There have been only two murders since the turn of the century, and, you are told with a hint of pride, one was "a crime of passion." Most overnighters at The Bottom's jail are guilty of what the law describes as "visible drunkenness." To qualify, the offender must be: (1) staggering so badly he is unable to proceed under his own power, (2) incomprehensible in his speech, and (3) redolent of alcohol. If he does not qualify on all three counts, it is considered a neighborly duty just to help him home. If he does qualify, however, he is incarcerated for his own and the community's protection.

Saba's jail has three cells and a roof deck where inmates can sun during the day. It is hard to imagine why a prisoner would want to escape. But one did. They found him a few hours later enjoying the Saturday dance. As they say in Saba, when there's a party on Saturday night, everybody goes.

The Saturday night dance is as exciting as Saba ever gets. If you are not a mountain climber, botanist, or scuba diver, there's a limited amount to be seen. After you've taken the two-hour all-island tour, there are still two steproads to explore: one leads to the top of Mt. Scenery, the other down to Ladder Bay. There are also 18 marked hiking trails, mostly footpaths trod by farmers for centuries. (The tourist office in Windwardside can provide a list and/or guide.)

Otherwise there's a small pool at *Captain's Quarters,* two small dive operations, and a quasi-tennis court at The Bottom. The rest is up to you. You can read and snooze and walk around a bit. You can meet a few people and take lots of pretty pictures. If you happen on Saba on a Wednesday morning, you can join Pauline Paul for a social early breakfast at *Scout's Place:* "The purpose is just to come together and have interesting talks." You can sit in the sun a while longer. And after the day's inactivity, you can check in at *Scout's* again for some talk and some listening. It would drive some people crazy. For others, it's addictive — the perfect escape.

If you go — for a day, a week, or more — don't worry if you return feeling a little strange, as though you've been in another world. You have.

SABA AT-A-GLANCE

 FROM THE AIR: Saba is green, round, and tiny — only 5.1 square miles. Poking out of the Caribbean at 17°40' N latitude, 62°15' W longitude, about 28 miles (15 minutes' flying time) south of the Dutch/French island of St. Maarten/St. Martin and 150 miles east of Puerto Rico, it looks like a mountain up to its shoulders in sea — which is exactly what it is. Eons ago its highest peak — 2,854-foot Mt. Scenery — was an active volcano. Now its crater is dead, and a rain forest grows on its sides. Mt. Scenery and surrounding high points (variously and whimsically christened The Level, St. John's Flat, Bunker, Booby, and Old Booby Hills), which range from just over 1,000 to just under 1,700 feet, produce the extreme vertical variation of Saba's overall topography. So suddenly does the island rise out of the Caribbean that for years not a road, but instead a series of steps called The Ladder, climbing its western cliffs, provided the only access to its capital town of The Bottom. Today, visitors are dropped, suddenly but gently, via STOL (short take-off and landing) plane, onto the airstrip at Juancho E. Yrausquin Airport on northeastern Flat Point. (Landing in Saba is akin to putting down on an aircraft carrier: the 1,312-foot airstrip, one of the shortest in the world, is at 130 feet above sea level with cliffs at either end. (A new airstrip for the other side of the island, at Giles Quarter, has been promised by the Netherlands government, but its construction has been delayed by disagreement about the projected length.) Visitors are then driven by intrepid Saban taxi through

Lower Hell's Gate and Upper Hell's Gate, southwest across the island to English Quarter and Windwardside, then down again via St. John's to The Bottom. The impossible Road, which divides the island diagonally, ends at Fort Bay on the southwestern edge where there's a pier at which small boats and even tenders from larger liners can land.

It is not strictly true that Saba has no beaches. Every April, a strip of gray volcanic sand appears at the edge of Wells Bay below the old settlement at Mary Point; the trouble is that, come November, it disappears again. So there's talk of building a beach near the airport, which might help Saba's 1,042 inhabitants attract more than the 20,195 visitors they welcomed last year (up 84 from the previous year). It's not impossible.

 SPECIAL PLACES: The Road that climbs, hairpin curving back and forth, from the airport up the steep side of the island to reach Saba's interior is the island's first special sight. After experts insisted it could not be built, Josephus Lambert Hassell took his correspondence course in engineering and designed The Road which, over the next 20 years, he and his fellow Sabans proceeded to build by hand — and demonstrated something about the Saban will and spirit. The Road is now being resurfaced and widened in several places.

Hell's Gate, Upper Hell's Gate, and English Quarter – Clusters of typical houses, neatly painted in white with contrasting shutters, bright red roofs, and jigsaw-cut gingerbread trim line the way to the island's top settlement.

Windwardside – At the top of The Road, slightly east of the island's midpoint, at 1,804 feet, is Saba's second largest settlement, site of a number of tourist shops and the greater part of the island's guestrooms (10 in the two antique houses that make up *Captain's Quarters* and 4½ — soon to be 14½ — at *Scout's Place* up the hill). Windwardside is also the site of the Saba Museum (the sixth signature in its guestbook is that of Jacqueline Kennedy Onassis), dedicated to Harry L. Johnson, whose dream it was. The restored home of Esther Peterson (who died in 1970 at the age of 103) now houses a growing collection of antique Saban furnishings, a lovely "rock oven," crisp curtains of "Spanish lace," even a few pre-Columbian stone tools, and touching mementos of the severe hurricane of 1772 — see especially the letter Sabans sent to the Dutch government soliciting its help. In the grassy meadow just above the museum is a bust of Simón Bolívar, commemorating his 1816 visit to recruit help for his struggle to free South America from its colonizers. A little beyond Windwardside, a set of 1,064 hand-hewn steps scale the side of Mt. Scenery through a rain forest where some wild orchids still bloom (look, don't pick) and ferns grow taller than Saban children.

The Bottom – Saba's capital town lies in a round valley 820 feet above sea level. It takes its name from the fact that the valley is bowl-shaped (*botte* is Dutch for bowl) rather than from the fact that — as the old story ran — it sits at the bottom of a crater. Actually, its official name is not The Bottom at all. In the late 19th century, the Council voted to change it to Leverock City in honor of Moses Leverock, a patriarchal Saban who had done much for his native island. His memory is still revered, though the name never took. Among The Bottom's top sites: the governor's official residence, painted sunny yellow and white, and the small garden park adjoining it; *Heleen's Art Gallery,* with lovely watercolors and an old fireplace (open weekdays 8 AM to 2 PM or by appointment; phone: 3348); and *Cranston's Antique Inn,* once the government's guesthouse, now a private hotel and late-afternoon watering spot. Northwest of town, restoration is under way on the steps of The Ladder, a concrete and stone reminder of the way Sabans traveled and transported goods for centuries.

Fort Bay – At the end of the 9-mile cross-island Road is the island's power plant, its only gas station, offices of *Saba Deep Dive Shop,* the Saba Marine Park, and the 250-foot pier where imports and some visitors are landed. Saban children often swim off the pier.

SOURCES AND RESOURCES

 TOURIST INFORMATION: The Saba Tourist Office at 1500 Broadway, Suite 2305, New York, NY 10036 (phone: 212-840-6655) and in Canada, *New Concepts in Travel,* 410 Queen's Quay West, Suite 303, Toronto, Ontario M5V223 (phone: 416-362-7707) will send information on rates, reservation procedures, and travel to Saba. They do accept phone queries and will even make hotel or home rental reservations.

The Saba Tourist Bureau Office is in Windwardside, next to the post office. It is normally open 8 AM till noon and 1 to 5 PM (phone: 2231). Glenn Holm, the island's director of tourism, is friendly, efficient, and helpful. Two delightful books worth investigating are Will Johnson's *Saban Lore — Tales from My Grandmother's Pipe,* and *Saba — The First Guidebook,* by Natalie and Paul Pfanstiehl. In St. Maarten you might be able to find Dutch Antilles historian Dr. J. Hartog's *St. Maarten, Saba, St. Eustatius* and his *History of Saba* (currently out-of-print) in the paperback English translations, which cover a great deal of interesting history and background.

For a little island, Saba is covered with newsprint. The *Saba Herald,* edited and published by Will Johnson, is a lively, mimeographed roundup of island news and political opinion that comes out on the 24th of every month. *The Unspoiled Queen* is another local monthly. *New Age,* the *Chronicle,* the *Clarion,* and *Windward Island News Day* — all printed on St. Maarten — are delivered to Saba subscribers the day they are published. Somewhat surprisingly, the *San Juan Star* sometimes reaches Saba on the afternoon of the day of publication, and even the Sunday *New York Times* often arrives on its cover date.

Telephone – You can dial direct to Saba by adding the international access code 011 and the prefix 5994 to the numbers given below.

 ENTRY REQUIREMENTS: All that is required of US or Canadian citizens is proof of citizenship (a valid passport — or one expired less than 5 years earlier, a birth certificate with a raised seal or a notarized copy, or a voter's registration card) plus a ticket for return or ongoing transportation.

 CLIMATE AND CLOTHES: Temperatures range from a high of about 85°F (about 30°C) on a sunny day in Hell's Gate to about 65°F (around 19°C) on a cool night in Windwardside. Cottons and polyester blends can easily be laundered; there is no dry-cleaning establishment. Dress is neat but informal. Bathing suits are worn only around the pool at *Captain's Quarters.* Take rubber-soled hiking shoes and a sweater for cool evenings.

 MONEY: Official currency is the Netherlands Antilles florin, also known as guilder, and abbreviated NAf (or sometimes NA.Fl.), currently exchanged at 1.80 NAf to the US dollar, but US dollars are accepted throughout the island; Canadians should change their money for florins before departing from St. Maarten or at Banco Barclays Antilliano office in Windwardside, open from 8:30 AM to noon weekdays. (The bank may be the smallest in the world — only 10 feet wide!) Some credit cards are now accepted at *Captain's Quarters, Saba Deep,* and *Sea Saba.*

 LANGUAGE: Though most public signs are written in Dutch, the island's official language, everybody on the island speaks English, the native tongue of Saba's original Scottish-English-Irish settlers. The national greeting exchanged by Sabans passing on steps or road is "Howzzit? Howzzit?" delivered with a very slight raised-hand salute.

CURRENT: Electricity is 110 volts, 60 cycles — no problem for North American travel appliances.

TIME: Saba operates on Atlantic Standard Time, one hour ahead of Eastern Standard and the same as Eastern Daylight. In winter, when it's noon in New York, it's 1 PM on Saba; from May to October, during Daylight Saving Time, noon's the same both places.

GETTING THERE: Windward Island Airways flies STOL (Short Takeoff/ Landing Craft) from St. Maarten's Juliana Airport five times daily. This was another one of those impossible feats — like The Road — until aviation pioneer Remy de Haenen (former mayor of St. Bart's) built the amazing 950-foot airstrip, little more than half as long as the much-maligned strip on St. Bart's. (You won't forget it.) The 15-minute flight costs $40 round-trip. Flight schedules permit you to spend most of the day sightseeing and lunching on the island before catching the afternoon flight out, as well as to plan longer stays. Organized full-day tours leave St. Martin every Thursday and include air transport, sightseeing, and lunch at *Captain's Quarters* for $70. On St. Maarten, check with *Rising Sun Tours* (phone: 45334, 45282), Susan Heller at *Mystique Tours,* or *Wathey Travel* (phone: 22585, 23391).

Day trips to Saba from Great Bay Marina on St. Maarten leave at 9 AM Tuesday through Saturday, returning 5 PM, aboard the M/V *Style,* a fast open-air vessel with an open bar (phone: St. Maarten, 22167). Cost is $45 round-trip. Small cruise liners, such as Windjammer's *Polynesia, Explorer Starship,* and *Caribbean Prince,* occasionally make it a port of call.

CALCULATING COSTS: Rates at *Captain's Quarters* run about $95 a day double ($75 single) in winter; in summer, $75 double ($60 single). Elsewhere tariffs run from about $40 and up for a single, $50 to $85 for a double. Lunches are $9 to $14 per person, not including wine and service. Dinners about $20. Budget for an independent day trip for two from St. Maarten would be about $140 including air fare ($40 per person round-trip), island tour and transport, lunches, and a couple of sips at *Scout's Place.*

GETTING AROUND: Taxi – Several taxis meet every arriving flight and occasional ship; they serve both as point-to-point transport and tour vehicles. Taxi drivers are not only proficient in negotiating the zigs, zags, ups, and downs of The Road, but they will be glad to fill you in on island lore. For $6 per person, they'll do the standard two-hour tour, dropping you then at *Scout's Place* or *Captain's Quarters* for lunch. The driver will also pick you up after lunch in time to make an afternoon flight.

Car Rental – *Avis* now has a branch in Windwardside (phone: 2289). The going rate for the use of a car from the island's fleet of nine is about $30 a day from *Scout's* (phone: 3221, 2205), slightly more from *Avis* (phone: 2289), including a tank of gas and unlimited mileage; your hotel can make arrangements, but considering the precipitous Road and difficult parking, walking and/or hitchhiking are both friendlier and easier.

Hitchhiking – An approved way of getting around — especially if you're going to be on the island a few days. You don't have to use your thumb. Just start out on foot. In minutes, a Saban will stop and give you a lift as far as he's going in your direction.

Wherever he drops you, someone else is sure to pick you up. It's a great way to get to know the people and the island.

Walking – Can be a challenge — even within such a limited area as the lanes of Windwardside. Inclines are steep, and the concrete slippery. Sturdy, ground-gripping shoes are a must.

SHOPPING: It's more like stepping into someone's parlor than browsing through any boutique you've ever seen. The shops to see are in Windwardside and easy to handle in an after-lunch stroll; store hours are approximately 8 AM to noon and 2 to 6 PM. Crafts are most interesting.

For over a hundred years, Saban women have been famous for their drawn-thread work — called Spanish work here (or Saba lace) because Gertrude Johnson (who introduced it in the 1870s) learned it from nuns in her convent school in Caracas. It's a form of needlecraft that involves drawing and tying selected threads in a piece of linen to produce an ornamental pattern. Though the number of women skilled in it has dwindled, the *Island Craft Shop* still offers fairly extensive collections of Spanish-worked blouses, sheets, pillowcases, tablecloths and napkins, and handkerchiefs. The work, remarkably delicate, can be beautiful, but it does require careful laundering (it's not drip-dry) and can be expensive since the price depends on the quality of the linen as well as that of the work itself.

The new island craft is silk-screen printing on cotton, handsomely practiced and turned into resort clothes by the *Saba Artisans Foundation,* whose designs — appropriately — are adapted from Spanish-work details photographed and enlarged as well as the shapes of palm fronds, leaves, and flowers. At their main shop and workroom in The Bottom you'll find everything from silk-screened head scarves, T-shirts, and place mats to full-length dresses priced from a few dollars to the low and middle $40s. They also show leatherwork and dolls from Curaçao, black coral jewelry from Bonaire, and woodwork from Statia (St. Eustatius).

Other stopping spots: the *Captain's Store* in the *Captain's Quarters,* for a little bit of everything the island produces; *Around the Bend* for T-shirts, costume jewelry, decorative papier-mâché; *The Square Nickle Store* for clothing and souvenirs; and the new *Belle Isle Boutique* for clothing.

Special: The sign behind the bar at *Captain's Quarters* reads, "Saba Spice is nice made by Patsy Hassell of Hell's Gate." Spice — an aromatic blend of 150-proof cask rum, brown sugar, fennel seed, cinnamon, cloves, and nutmeg — home-brewed by Patsy and a number of others — is powerful and quite sweet. The traditional Saban after-meal tipple, it is also heart-warming before winter fires back home. If you enjoy that kind of spirit, you can take home a quart for about $6.

TIPPING: A 10% to 15% service charge is usually added to all restaurant, bar, or hotel bills. If not, that's the right amount to leave. Drivers, who own their own cars, don't expect tips; but if the driver is an interesting tour guide as well (as most are), you might give him a little extra. Travel light to Saba, as there are no airport porters.

SPECIAL EVENTS: *The Queen's Birthday,* April 30, honors Beatrix of Holland with sports events, parades, and fireworks. A long weekend in late July is dedicated to *Saba Carnival,* and on *Saba Days* in early December, there are greased-pole and spearfishing contests, swimming and donkey races, games of all sorts, maypole dances, and lots of partying. Legal holidays include *New Year's Day, Good Friday, Easter* and *Easter Monday, Labor Day* (May 1), *Ascension Day* (40 days after Easter), *Saba Day* (the first Friday in December), *Christmas,* and *Boxing Day* (December 26).

SPORTS: Climbing Mt. Scenery, hiking, and diving are the big attractions. Allow a half day for the trek up the 3,000-foot extinct volcano, but if a cloud hovers at the peak, wait until the morning mist burns off or go another day. Wear good walking shoes and a sunscreen; bring a camera and a canteen. Start the climb either from Windwardside at the road sign "Mt. Scenery" or midway up at the end of Mountain Road, where a concrete stairway leads to the top. (This can be slippery, but is well worth any scrambling). A tropical paradise of giant elephant ears and ferns, palms with epiphytes, bananas and mango trees, heliconias, and 17 species of wild orchids prepare you for the view from the summit. If you're uneasy going it alone, Glenn Holm at the Tourist Bureau may be able to provide a guide or to accompany you himself. He has catalogued a list of 17 other trails, complete with instructions, trail hazards, and a description of the sights en route. The trails generally coincide with the footpaths used for centuries by Saban farmers; they offer a unique opportunity to explore very different natural regions. Markers are white slashes painted on rocks at 300-foot intervals, closer together where difficult. Mt. Scenery, with its 1,064 concrete steps, is not marked, but most others are.

There are two diving operations on Saba, offering 4-, 5-, and 7-night packages to an incredible variety of dive sites — an experience *Skin Diver* magazine has termed "an adventure you will never forget." Since the entire island is a virtual drop-off, you can dive very close to shore. Visibility, normally in excess of 100 feet, can reach 200. There are both shallow and very deep dives: through incredible elkhorn coral forests, past a series of caverns, walls, and ledges, and over underwater mountains. The black sand bottom accents the striking colors of large purple sponges, breathtakingly huge stands of black coral, and abundant fish. Even the most seasoned diver will be stunned by the site called, appropriately Outer Limits: 90 feet from the surface is a large mountaintop shooting up from 2,800 feet of water — an incredible blue-water dive with excellent visibility and a plethora of marine life, including huge groupers, jacks, turtles, sharks, and rays.

Saba Deep is now owned by *Maho Watersports* and *Surfside Watersports,* with their center at Fort Bay (phone: 3347), and *Sea Saba* by Louis and Joan Bourque, both PADI instructors (phone: 2246). Special arrangements can be made for marine ecology seminars, slide presentations, underwater photography instruction, and fishing excursions to Saba Bank. In 1987, Saba formally established Saba Marine Park, an underwater national park, to protect its still undisturbed marine life. The park encircles the island and includes the waters and seabed from the high-water mark down to a depth of 200 feet, as well as 2 offshore seamounts. The *SMP* maintains a system of permanent mooring buoys to facilitate diving and to prevent anchor damage to coral. An information office is located at Fort Bay, and slide shows are offered free of charge to all visiting dive groups. Other islands would be well advised to follow Saba's excellent program for safeguarding easily destroyed resources. A 1-day package from St. Maarten, including 2 dives, all transport, lunch, and sightseeing, is available for about $155. Contact *Rising Sun Tours* on St. Maarten (phone: 45334 or 45282). Several other dive packages are now available; inquire about a proposed 1-week Saba/Statia (St. Eustatius) combination. Arrangements can also be made on St. Maarten through *Maho Watersports* (phone: 44387).

Seasonal swimming is done at Well's Bay at the beach that appears during hurricane season, but it's a 6-hour hike down the mountain to get there. Otherwise, there is a lovely pool clinging to the top of the mountain at *Captain's Quarters,* and another is being planned for *Scout's Place.* Few people take advantage of the cement tennis court at The Bottom (free, open to all); if the net isn't up, ask around. For sport fishing, contact Robbie Hassell, who will motor you in his 32-foot vessel to Saba Bank, 3 miles offshore, known for its excellent catches. Saba Bank is 32 miles long and 20 miles wide, mostly 6 to 20 fathoms deep, and in some areas the bottom can be seen clearly.

Unfortunately, it is currently under discussion as a disposal site for US garbage. Pray the Sabans will refuse this $3-million offer and save their most precious commodity.

 NIGHTLIFE: The weekly Saturday night dance — to which everyone is invited and just about everyone goes — is held at *Guido's* in Windwardside. Other action can be found at *Lime Time,* in The Bottom. That's it — although people have been known to sit up late and swap yarns and philosophical observations around the bar at *Scout's Place* or the *Captain's Quarters.*

BEST ON THE ISLAND

 CHECKING IN: A toss-up between *Captain's Quarters, Scout's Place,* and *Juliana's Apartments* in Windwardside. If hiding out on Saba is your sort of thing, you'll probably be happy at any one of the three.

Captain's Quarters – Long on antique charm (its two houses are 100 and 175 years old, with much furniture to match), its 10 rooms are big, airy, island-stylish without being cute (fresh colors, sisal rugs, antique touches). The view, the terrace, dining room, bar, and swimming pool are mighty attractive. Rates are $95 for a double in high season, $75 in summer, no meals, plus 5% tax and 10% service. Dinner runs about $20 (phone: 2201).

Scout's Place – It describes itself as "Bed 'n' Board, Cheap 'n' Cheerful" — and it's all that. Ten sparkling new rooms in the New Place, all with 4-poster beds, private baths, and balconies, go for $85 (double), $55 (single) in season; $55 and $35 for one of the original 4 rooms (only 2 of which have private bath). Rates include breakfast, but not a 5% tax and 15% service charge. A pool is being planned. The view is great, but its special thing is the feeling it has of being right at the heart of it — everybody stops by late in the day to drink a cold Heineken and talk life over. Though Scout has "retired" and turned over the business to Dianna and Harold Medero, his former cook and barman, he takes all his meals there ("For life, part of the deal") and still holds court (phone: 2205, 3321).

Cranston's Antique Inn, The Bottom – Once the government's guesthouse (Queen Juliana slept here), it has 6 rooms (1 with a bath) neatly done up with fresh paint, bright fabrics, and four-poster beds, but lacks the view and the spark of the other two hostelries and has been garnering bad word of mouth lately. Indeed, the lovely garden restaurant seems only half open most of the time. Check current conditions carefully before booking here. Doubles run about $60 a night including breakfast (phone: 3203, 3218).

Home and Apartment Rentals – Less expensive still is a selection of apartments and guesthouses, including some traditional Saban wooden cottages that rent daily, weekly, or monthly. Rates range from $45 a day, $200 to $250 a week, and $700 to about $1,200 a month.. Most are completely furnished and equipped and have hot and cold water. The new *Juliana's Apartments,* at Windwardside, are among the most expensive at $65 per day in high season for a double with bath ($95 with kitchen, living/dining, and large porch), plus 5% tax and 10% service charge (phone: 2269). Contact the tourist bureau for a full listing.

EATING OUT: Meals are filling and pleasantly served, but nothing to send postcards home about. Basically, guesthouses are the restaurants. For a change of scene in Windwardside, you might try the assorted Italian-American fare at *Guido's* or *Saba Chinese Bar & Restaurant,* which serves — not surprisingly — Chinese and fast food in typical Chinese-restaurant decor (but with atypical country-and-western music). The Chinese owner has now opened a new small terrace restaurant at his home with a far more charming ambience. In The Bottom are the *Serving Spoon,* for West Indian food such as chicken with peanut sauce, pumpkin fritters, fishcakes, and johnny cakes; *Earl's Snack Bar,* for fast food — hot dogs, hamburgers, beer, and ice cream; and the *Lime Time Bar and Restaurant,* for more local fare.

ST. BARTHÉLEMY

St. Barts is the sort of island people tend to be protective about — both for the island's sake and their own. It is tiny — only eight square miles — and it is beautiful, endowed with small green mountains, extraordinary coral sand coves and beaches, a dollhouse-scaled capital port, and a bright, free air. Its vacation life is unprogrammed, its sands uncrowded, and its denizens — including American Rockefellers and Biddles, as well as French Rothschilds — want it to stay that way. Still, over the past ten years or so, St. Barts has definitely been discovered. But with fewer than 500 hotel rooms spread across the island, an airstrip accommodating nothing larger than a 19-seat short take-off and landing (STOL) plane, and prices well beyond the means of the masses, most "overnight" visitors still come from among the privileged. The masses are limited to a few hours off an occasional cruise ship or a day-tripping catamaran from nearby St. Maarten/St. Martin.

Discovered by Columbus in 1493 and named for his brother Bartholomew, the island received its first French settlers in 1648. Except for a minor take-over by the British in 1758 (during which its French-speaking inhabitants were temporarily scattered over neighboring islands), it remained firmly Gallic till 1784, when St. Barts' citizens awoke to the astounding news that one of Louis XVI's ministers had traded the island — lock, stock, and citizens — to Sweden for a warehouse in Göteborg.

While the permanent population continued to eke out a living from stone-walled fields and the sea, the Swedes took over, rechristened its capital Gustavia in honor of their king, declared it a free port, and began making fortunes in trade. In 1878, when Europe's wars had subsided and St. Barts became French again, the free port status remained — along with such Viking legacies as neat-lined buildings, a few street signs, and the town name.

About 90% of St. Barts' population of 3,500 are white-skinned and look like no other Caribbean islanders, descended — pale and blue-eyed — from the first Norman, Breton, and Poitevin settlers. They're a sober-looking group, whose grand-aged dames pad about the village of Corossol barefoot, peering out from under their big, white, kiss-me-not sunbonnets, and spend their days weaving straw hats, place mats, and baskets to sell to tourists.

But St. Barts is also St. Tropez French — a world of monokinis and beach café lunches with lots of wine and laughter. And after the beach day is over, the evening is for small, fine restaurants where cuisine is spelled with a capital "C" and the wine cellars are well stocked. Late-night activity might include a leisurely stroll along the romantic waterfront, where the occasional strains of a visiting jazz group can be heard, or lingering over a cognac on a *Castelets* terrace, basking in the moonlight and picking out running lights on the yachts anchored in the sea below. Determined night owls flock to the *Autour du Rocher* disco in the hills above Lorient, where it is not unusual to find the

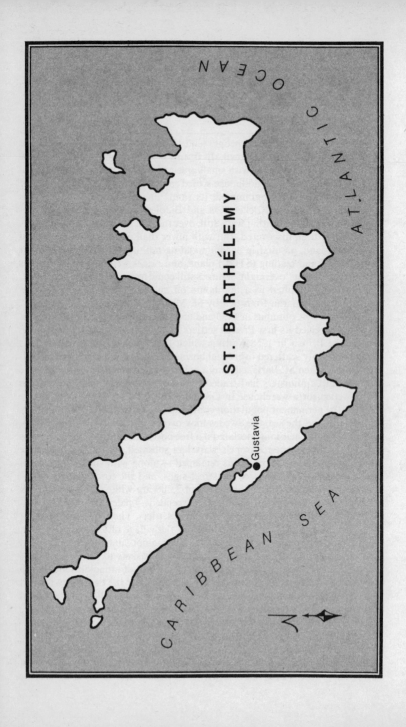

likes of Jimmy Buffet or Mick Jagger hanging out at the bar. No rush, just unwound atmosphere and small-gem perfection. You'll either be bored to tears or you'll love it. If the latter, a couple of days of such leisured existence will leave you feeling protective about St. Barts, too.

ST. BARTS AT-A-GLANCE

FROM THE AIR: Tiny St. Barts (8 square miles) is vaguely V-shaped. Its bottom point aims south, and the northwest arm is slightly narrower than the northeastern one. At 17°55′ N latitude, 62°50′ W longitude, it lies 125 miles northwest of the French island of Guadeloupe, of which it is a dependency, but only 15 miles (a 10-minute flight) southeast of the French/Dutch island of St. Martin/St. Maarten. Notable geographic features include steep, green, once actively volcanic hills, deep valleys, and beautiful beaches — white-gold and gleaming — cupped in bays scooped into its shoreline on every side. Its capital, Gustavia, is built around Port de Plaisance harbor, which cuts deep into the island's southwest coast. The town — founded by the French, ceded to the Swedish, then returned to France — is home to less than 15% of St. Bart's population. Gustav III Airport, at La Tourmente — which might have been named for the emotion first-timers feel when they contemplate its short runway — is capable of receiving 19-seat Twin Otter STOL planes. It lies north of town on the road to St. Jean. The beach at Baie de St. Jean, a great crescent of sunny sand, is the most famous beach on the island, with a number of small hotels, restaurants, bistros, and a shopping plaza nearby. It is washed with gentle waves, as are most north-facing shores. The surf is sometimes quite strong along the Anse du Gouverneur, Anse de Grande Saline, Anse du Grand Fond, and Anse à Toiny on the southern coast. Roads are, for the most part, well paved and easy to cope with in the lowlands and valleys, but often they scale hills at an angle only a chamois could love.

SPECIAL PLACES: Gustavia – St. Barts' appropriately toy-scaled capital lines the three protective sides of Port de Plaisance harbor. Too small for most cruise ships, it's a favorite layover for sailing yachts cruising the Caribbean. When a liner or large windjammer does anchor offshore, tenders ferry passengers to the principal quai on the east edge of the port. Focal point of a good deal of town activity, it is surrounded by tourist-oriented boutiques offering French imports (especially sports clothes, perfumes, cosmetics) at duty-free prices. The town, with its antique-housed cafés and restaurants and mixture of Swedish colonial (see the Town Hall, the former yacht club, the old Clock Tower at the foot of Morne Lurin) and French Créole (see almost everything else), is quaint, pretty, and pin neat. There are only a few historic monuments, and although pirates hid out here in the 18th century, they left no souvenirs. The old Wall House, which survived the fire of 1852, may become a cultural center if funds are raised. Otherwise, there is an old 10-ton English anchor (marked "Liverpool Wood–London" — it is a type that was used by 18th-century warships), inadvertently towed here from St. Thomas by a tug in 1981, perched photogenically over the harbor opposite the Anglican church. The whole stroll around town takes only an hour or two, depending on your café resistance threshold. Park at the quai, then browse down the Rue de la République and/or the Rue Général de Gaulle; turn right and follow Rue Sadi Carnot along the harborside past the Club de Voile (Sailing Club); then, if you still feel like walking, turn right and take Rue Jeanne d'Arc along the harbor's third side to the balconied *Presqu'île* hotel, the terrace of *La Marine Café*, an ideal spot for a Byrrh or a bière du pays (Heineken, here), or on to the popular new *L'Escale* restaurant next door. Then reverse, making café or snack stops at *Chez Joe, Le Sélect Bar,* or the *L'Oubli Café* back in the center of town.

ELSEWHERE ON THE ISLAND

After doing the town, there are two scenic country routes worth exploring:

Grand Fond Route – Drive east past the Baie de St. Jean and a succession of stunning north shore beaches (Anse de Lorient, Anse de Marigot, Anse du Grand Cul de Sac, and Petit Cul de Sac). Picnic or stop for lunch at *Chez Francine* or the terrace of *Le Pelican* — both right on the sand at lovely St. Jean Beach, so you can swim, too, or at the peaceful *Marigot Bay Club,* where even the snorkeling is fine between fresh fish courses. Then turn south and swing along the surf-pounded shore of the pastoral Grand Fond district, a miniature otherworld of stone-fenced farms and small, tile-roofed houses with hills for backdrop and waves breaking at their feet. Finally, continue back through the mountains to rejoin the north shore road. The circuit takes more than an hour and a half, depending on lunch and swim time.

Corossol Route – This second, somewhat shorter drive explores the northwest end. Take a sharp left (rather than going straight up the hill or turning right) at the crossroads between town and the airport, and drive parallel to the Anse de Public past the cemetery to the "straw village" of Corossol. Here live the descendants of the earliest French settlers, old ladies with bare feet and lean, weathered faces. Wearing starched, white, Breton poke bonnets, they sell fine straw hats, placemats, and similar items made in small home-parlor shops. (They are shy about being photographed — so ask before you snap.) Colorful fishing boats line the beach at the end of the road. The small *Inter-Oceans Museum* houses an exhibit of shells from the world over, the private collection of Ingenu Magras. Open Mondays through Saturdays 10 AM to 4 PM (phone: 276297). Retrace your tracks to the main road and turn left toward the Quartier du Colombier (Rockefeller country), where you can visit the atelier of artist Jean-Yves Froment (and where his famed block prints are for sale); then detour to the long, sandy Anse des Flamands (hotel site) or the Petite Anse beyond for a swim; then back over the hills and home.

SOURCES AND RESOURCES

TOURIST INFORMATION: The French West Indies Tourist Board is at 610 Fifth Ave., New York, NY 10020 (phone: 212-757-1125). There are French Government Tourist Offices in the following North American cities:

Beverly Hills: 9401 Wilshire Blvd., Beverly Hills, CA 90212 (phone: 213-272-2661)
Chicago: 645 N Michigan Ave., Suite 430, Chicago, IL 60611 (phone: 312-337-6301)
Dallas: 2050 Stemmons Fwy., Dallas, TX 75258 (phone: 214-742-7011)
Montréal: 1981 Av. McGill College, Suite 490, Montréal, Que. H3A 2W9 (phone: 514-288-4264)
San Francisco: 1 Halladie Plaza, Suite 2405, San Francisco, CA 94102 (phone: 415-986-4161)
Toronto: 1 Dundas St. W, Suite 240, Toronto, Ont. M5G 1Z3 (phone: 416-593-4717)

The tourist information bureau in Gustavia's *mairie* (town hall), on the Rue August-Nyman (phone: 27-60-08), is run entirely by its founder and *directrice* Elise Magras. It is open weekdays from 8:30 AM to noon and 1:30 to 5:30 PM. The information booth at the airport is open weekdays from 8:30 AM to 12:30 PM and 3:30 to 6:30 PM. Hotel people are also happy to suggest restaurants and beaches and to show you how to get where you want to go.

Local Coverage – Both *Bonjour St. Barth!*, a detailed French-English guide with attractive illustrations, good maps, charmingly narrated tales about the island's history, traditions, etc., as well as all the essential practical facts, and Georges Bourdin's more scholarly *History of St. Barthélemy* are usually available at *Charlie's Bookstore* and *Pêle Mêle* in Gustavia. *St. Barth Magazine,* published regularly during high season, is distributed all over the island on a complimentary basis. On Mondays and Thursdays at noon, there is an English-language radio program called "This Week in St. Barts."

Telephone – Dial direct to St. Barts by adding the international access code 011 and the prefix 590 to the numbers given below. To call St. Barts from the Dutch side of St. Maarten, dial 6 plus the 6-digit number in St. Barts. To make a long-distance call from a pay phone on St. Barts, callers must purchase a credit card for 92.4 francs or 30.4 francs (depending on how long they intend to speak rather than on the number of calls) at the post office beforehand.

 ENTRY REQUIREMENTS: For stays up to three months, in addition to a return or ongoing ticket, US and Canadian citizens require a valid passport or photo identification. For longer periods, a visa is required.

 CLIMATE AND CLOTHES: Year-round average daytime temperatures, 72° to 84°F (about 22° to 30°C) make the climate right for light cotton and cotton-blend sports clothes — especially with a French flair for casual chic. Currently, that means bikinis or monokinis on the beach for literally everybody (no matter what shape the body), plus T-shirts, tight jeans, shorts, pareos, or loose cotton shirts. Night dress is slightly spruced up but basically just as informal and comfortable, except possibly at *Les Castelets,* the *Manapany,* the *Guanahani,* or *La Toque Lyonnaise* at *El Sereno Beach,* which call for something a shade dressier — a long skirt, caftan, djellaba, or dressy pants for women; tailored casual clothes (ties and jackets aren't required) for men.

 MONEY: The official monetary unit is the French franc. Stores and restaurants freely accept payment in US dollars, a bit less freely in Canadian currency. Shops offer no discount for payment in dollar-denomination traveler's checks or US cash. Exchange rates are pretty standard, so there's little need to rush to the bank to change dollars to francs. Banking hours in Gustavia are 8 AM to noon and 2 to 3:30 or 4 PM weekdays, closed weekends. Credit cards are not honored everywhere, so before checking into your hotel, determine which cards (if any) they accept.

 LANGUAGE: Pervasively French — you'll feel at home faster if you can *parlez* a little. But beach nuts shouldn't let language be a barrier. In most shops, hotels, and restaurants, there's someone who speaks some English; and with a phrase book and patience, you'll be okay. St. Barts' second language — one you probably won't hear much — is the Norman-root dialect spoken by the old ladies of Corossol and the inhabitants of the northern part of the island.

 TIME: St. Barts runs all year on Atlantic Standard Time — the same as eastern North America's Daylight Saving Time in spring, summer, and early fall; an hour ahead of winter's Eastern Standard Time (i.e., when it is noon EST in New York, it is 1 PM AST in Gustavia).

CURRENT: Electricity is 220 volts, 50 cycles, but French plug adapters and a converter kit are needed to use American appliances. Best to bring your own adapters and current converters.

 GETTING THERE: There are no direct flights to St. Barts from the US or Canada. Principal gateway islands for North American visitors are St. Maarten, St. Thomas, and Guadeloupe, with direct service on weekends from San Juan, Puerto Rico. From St. Maarten's Juliana Airport (where most international flights land), Windward Islands Airways, known as Winair (phone: in St. Maarten, 44230 or 44237), as well as Air St. Barthélemy (phone: 27-71-90) make the 10-minute flight for about $26 one way. There is a $5 departure tax from Juliana Airport on the Dutch side. Air Guadeloupe makes the flight out of Esperance Airport, near Grand Case, on the French side, for about $46 round-trip (check fares, which depend on the current dollar/franc exchange rate). Air Guadeloupe also flies in from the island of Guadeloupe (1 hour; about $146 round-trip). Virgin Air (phone: 277176; 800-522-3084) makes the hop from St. Thomas (1 hour; about $140 round-trip) and from San Juan (about $250 round-trip). Besides regular shuttle service to St. Maarten (every half hour in the afternoons), Air St. Barthélemy flies twice a week to St. Thomas ($140 round-trip) and does weekend "champagne flights" to San Juan ($250 round-trip) on a Cessna 402 Executive. (*Note:* When arriving in St. Barts, be sure to reconfirm your departure flight.) Air St. Barts also runs a charter service for day-long or even overnight excursions to neighboring islands. When you first fly in, you'll understand why there are no night flights in or out of St. Barts! Special packages and charters are available from St. Croix, Nevis, and Anguilla on Coastal Air Transport (phone: in St. Croix, 773-6832).

There are several day sails out of Philipsburg, mostly on catamarans, such as the *Cheshire Cat, Eagle, Maho, Quicksilver,* and *El Tigre,* which depart St. Maarten daily, except Sundays, around 9 AM, arrive in St. Barts at 10:30 or 11, and depart for St. Maarten about 3 PM, arriving about 5 PM. The price is approximately $45 for the round trip, including an open bar, and most will take passengers on a one-way basis if there is space. From Marigot, on the French side of the island, the *Tee-Zech* powerboat makes the trip once or twice weekly to St. Barts for $40 round-trip, including drinks. For help with travel plans, contact Jean-Claude Varin at *St. Barth Montmarte Voyages* (phone: 276616).

 CALCULATING COSTS: In the winter season, a moderately priced double room for two goes for about $150 to $200 and up without meals (European Plan — EP); about $7 to $9 more per person a day for an American breakfast. Most Americans will find everything here very, very expensive, and it's hard to do St. Barts on the cheap, especially with the current disadvantageous relationship between the French franc and US dollar. From mid-April to mid-December, rates drop about one third across the board. St. Bartians care about food, so while *les snacks* are available at some Gustavia cafés, most days lunch is not to be taken lightly. At beachside cafés, a full lunch (appetizer, entrée, pommes frites, salad, coffee, and wine) runs at least $25 per person; some beachside places stay open for dinner. At a somewhat fancier place, with tablecloths and ambience, dinner tabs start at about $35 plus wine; *Castelets, La Toque Lyonnaise,* and others begin at roughly $50 per person, plus wine.

 GETTING AROUND: Taxi – At press time, negotiations were under way among the 32 taxi drivers on St. Barts and the Department of Tourism not to fix rates — which are reasonable — but to assure their accessibility. It seems all the drivers meet the morning arrival of catamarans full of day visitors from St. Martin, but none is on call in the evenings. The taxi stand phone is 276631. If you do manage to arrange for a cab after dark, note that there is a 33% surcharge at night. Check with the tourist office before you go to find out what has been decided. If the situation has not changed, you may prefer to rent a car.

Car Rental – More fun, more freedom, and easy to arrange (except during peak season, when advance reservations are strongly advised), providing you're of legal driving age and have at least one year's licensed driving experience. A Mini-Moke or a VW can be picked up minutes after landing at the airport with a minimum of red tape. Considering the hilly terrain, they're the only cars that make sense, but you must be able to operate a stick shift capably and comfortably. Rates are standard: about $38 to $45 a day in season for two to six days, on a sliding scale thereafter, with unlimited mileage, one full tank of gas (but be sure to check the tank, as they often arrive nearer to empty!) and free delivery (if you don't pick your car up at the airport). Collision damage insurance runs an extra $5 or $6 a day, $500 to $1,000 deductible. *Hertz* is now represented by *Henry Greaux* (phone: 276021, 277114), *Avis* by *St. Barth Car* (phone: 277143). *Guy Turbé Car Rentals* (phone: 276273) also has a New York and a toll-free number (212 334-9188, 800 223-1510). *Europcar (National)* is represented by *Caraibes Car Service* at the *Tropical* hotel (phone: 27-64-87). Then there's Mathew Aubin (phone: 276238, 277198), who also runs the Sodexa Supermarket; *Constant Gumbs* (phone: 27-61-93), an affable chap who'll probably be waiting at the airport when your plane touches down; French Caribbean Co. (phone: 276484); or try *Soleil Caraibes* (phone: 27-65-06), *Carlos* (phone: 27-61-90 or 27-64-44), *Maurice* (phone: 276504), or *Budget* (phone: 27-66-30, 276743). Some car rental agencies also have motorbikes at about $25 a day; check *St. Barth Moped Rental* (phone: 277095) and *Dennis Duffau* (phone: 276616).

Check the car's brakes carefully before charging off into the countryside. And when the man says to use first gear to climb Morne Lurin, the hill on which *Castelets* is perched, PAY ATTENTION! He means first gear and full throttle all the way — at least from the point where you turn off the main road. If you're lucky enough to be staying at *Castelets,* try to get a taxi to drive you from the airport and take advantage of free rental car delivery service *after* you've settled in. If you plan to have dinner there after dark, arrange for a cab to take you and call for you afterward.

There are three gas stations; the Shell station by the airport is the only one open Sundays, 9 to 11 AM.

Sightseeing Bus Tours – In VW minibuses operated by *Constant Gumbs* (phone: 27-61-93) and Hugo Cagan of *St. Barth Tours* (phone: 27-61-28), among others. One-hour island tours cost about $30 per car for 2 passengers. For 3 to 8 people, the cost is about $42. Each hour extra runs $11. A full-day tour with a 2-hour break for swimming or lunch (on you) costs $91. Other itineraries can be negotiated with the driver.

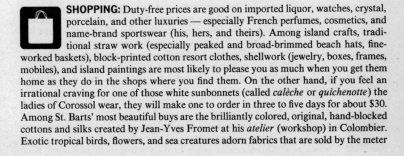

SHOPPING: Duty-free prices are good on imported liquor, watches, crystal, porcelain, and other luxuries — especially French perfumes, cosmetics, and name-brand sportswear (his, hers, and theirs). Among island crafts, traditional straw work (especially peaked and broad-brimmed beach hats, fine-worked baskets), block-printed cotton resort clothes, shellwork (jewelry, boxes, frames, mobiles), and island paintings are most likely to please you as much when you get them home as they do in the shops where you find them. On the other hand, if you feel an irrational craving for one of those white sunbonnets (called *calèche* or *quichenotte*) the ladies of Corossol wear, they will make one to order in three to five days for about $30. Among St. Barts' most beautiful buys are the brilliantly colored, original, hand-blocked cottons and silks created by Jean-Yves Fromet at his *atelier* (workshop) in Colombier. Exotic tropical birds, flowers, and sea creatures adorn fabrics that are sold by the meter and available in everything from skirts with matching shirts, bathrobes, and bedsheets, to bikinis, pareos, shorts, and jogging suits. Call ahead to arrange a visit to the workshop; he loves showing guests how it's done (phone: 27-61-72, or at lunchtime, 27-63-57). Another off-beat shop is *La Cave,* in Marigot, with an amazing collection of France's top vintages scrupulously stored in a climate-controlled building. Connoisseurs should also stop at the new wine shop in the historic stone building on Rue Jeanne d'Arc that once housed *Le Brigantin* restaurant/jazz club.

Gustavia shops worth looking into include the *Hibiscus* hotel's branch of *La Romana* for Italian and French high fashion and jewelry; Roger and Brook Lacour's *La Calèche* for fine swimwear, pareos, sandals, T-shirts, hats, and gifts; *St. Barth's Water Sports* for sports accessories (snorkeling gear, guns, etc.), film, and a handsome line of French *prêt-à-porter* fashions (Mic Mac and George Rech); *Loulou's Marine* for fishing and snorkeling gear, marine equipment, and nautical sportswear, as well as information on charter boats currently available; *Little Switzerland* for fine jewelry (18K gold chains and Les Must de Cartier at a third off US prices); *Paul et Virginie* for French beach things; *La Fonda* for exclusive Hermes beach towels and accessories; *Alma* for crocheted and embroidered linens and other elegant imports; *Boutiques Chamade St. Barth* for perfumes, watches, china, silver; *Animale* for sexy leather creations with a St. Tropez sizzle; and *Privilège* for jewelry, perfumes, and cosmetics. In the new El Sirgany Galerie are *Carat* for 18K gold jewelry, crystal, china; *Samson & Co.* for embroidered Balinese women's wear and Filipino shell jewelry; *Diva* for trendy women's sportswear (*beware:* Naf-Naf jumpsuits were recently priced at twice their cost in neighboring St. Maarten); *Uomo* for elegant menswear; and *Stephane & Bernard* for French and Italian haute couture. Down toward the pharmacy is *Vali Baba* for hand-woven fashions and some handmade jewelry.

Shoppers who begin to flag in mid-spree can take a break at the new *Taste Unlimited* deli and catering service on Rue Général de Gaulle, where Claude and Hilary Janin will fix a picnic lunch to take away or the fatigued can recharge at a table in the courtyard where breakfast, lunch, and dinner are served. Another alternative is *La Rôtisserie* (Rue Lafayette and Rue du Roi Oscar II), the long-established deli that provides hors d'oeuvres, pâtés, French sausages, roast chicken, salads, and fine wines for an elegant picnic (open daily, 9 AM to 1 PM and 4 to 6 PM; closed Sunday afternoons). There are also branches at St. Jean and Point Milou (phone: 27-63-13). Gustavia's shops are generally open from 9 AM to noon, and 2 to 5 or 6 PM.

Out at St. Jean is the new St. Jean Commercial Centre and *Villa Créole* shopping center, thankfully built in Créole style. Though a tad pricier than those in town, these shops are open later (until 7 or 8 PM), and the best boutiques have branches here (*La Romana* for more French and Italian high fashion and *Bastringue,* a bit trendier). Among other interesting shops is *La Cuisine,* with everything for the kitchen. *Avant Scène* of Paris has 3 shops (*A Touch of France, Mod' Prunelle,* and *La Maison en Fête*) selling elegant fashion, accessories, bags, porcelains, linens, bronzes, and scarves. At *Kornérupine,* gemologist–jewelry designer Dominique Elie sells his own creations and those of other top jewelers, buys and sells gems and gold, and does engraving and repairs. *Des Caraïbes* drugstore vends US newspapers and gifts. If you still haven't had your fill, there's the very attractive La Savane Commercial Centre, opposite the airport, with more chic shops, including *Thalassa* for fabulous lingerie and swimwear, *L'Igloo* for gifts, a branch of *Stephane & Bernard* for high fashion, *Optique Caribe* for chic sunglasses and prescription lenses for top European designer frames, a great food shop, a pharmacy, and a snack bar/café.

 TIPPING: A 10% to 15% service charge is normally added to both hotel bills and restaurant checks and is adequate except in the case of some extra special service. For an errand above and beyond the call of duty, tip from 5 francs or $1 (American coins are hard for islanders to exchange). If no service charge has been added, give the waiter 10% of the check total. Taxi drivers, most of whom own their own cars, don't expect a tip.

SPECIAL EVENTS: The *Festival of St. Barthélemy,* celebrated for three days in late August, is most fun — like a French country fair gone tropical. Booths line the tiny streets; there are sport competitions and goodhearted wining, dining, and partying after dark. In Corossol, the sea is blessed to ensure the safety of fishermen, and the last weekend in August, the old village of Lorient celebrates with similar activities. St. Barts also has its small *Carnival,* climaxing with *Mardi Gras* and *Ash Wednesday's* black-and-white parades and parties. In December 1989, the third *Route du Rosé Regatta* should reach St. Barts from St. Tropez, some 4,000 miles distant. The tall ships will be carrying a cargo of rosé wines from France, reviving the long-established tradition of trade between free harbors. In February 1989, St. Barts will celebrate its Fifth Annual Music Festival. Legal holidays include New Year's Day, La*or Day* (May 1), *Mi-Carême* (mid-Lent), *Easter Monday, Bastille Day* (July 14 — more fun and fireworks), *Schoelcher Day* (July 21), *Assumption Day* and *St. Barts/Pitea Day* — Pitea is the island's Swedish sister town — (August 15), *All Saints' Day* (November 1), *All Souls' Day* (November 2), *Armistice Day* (November 11), and *Christmas.*

SPORTS: Boating – Sunfish and small boats can be rented at the *Tom Beach* and *Guanahani* hotels for a nominal hourly fee. Most hotels also arrange day sails to offshore islands aboard 38-, 40-, or 42-foot sailing yachts through either *Sibarth Yacht Charter Agency* (phone: 27-62-38) or *Marine Service Boat Rental and Diving Center* (phone: 276450, 277034). Cost is per person: $65 each for up to 8 passengers for a day's swimming, snorkeling, cocktails, and buffet on an uninhabited isle, such as Île Fourchue, with a final swim stop at lovely Colombier Beach, one of St. Barts' least accessible; a sunset cruise with booze goes for $25 per person. Both itineraries are available on the *Ne Me Quitte Pas* from the *Quai de Yacht Club* (phone: 276450, 277034). Skippered charters to Anguilla, St. Maarten, Saba, and St. Kitts can also be arranged through *Sibarth* (phone: 27-62-38). In winter, a half-dozen yachts headquartered in Gustavia Harbor for the season are usually available for half-day, full-day, and longer charters; since their status changes from tide to tide, ask your hotel to investigate. Or check at *Loulou's Marine* (phone: 27-62-74), the two agencies mentioned above, or the tourism office (phone: 27-60-08).

St. Barts is a popular yachting haven midway between the Caribbean's two major sailing centers of Antigua and Virgin Gorda, in the British Virgin Islands. Still relatively uncrowded, it could accommodate 500 yachts, most at anchor. Gustavia Harbor, 13 to 16 feet deep, has mooring and docking facilities for about 40 yachts. There are also good anchorages at Public, Corossol, and Colombier.

Golf – There are 8 holes of mini-golf at *Topolino,* across from St. Jean, but there's no space for a regulation course on St. Barts.

Snorkeling and Scuba – Good off some beaches. Several of the beachside hotels have masks and fins to rent, as does the *Pelican,* on St. Jean. Otherwise bring your own equipment or buy it downtown (see *Shopping*). For snorkeling trips, see above. For scuba diving trips, gear rental, and instruction, contact Guy or Alain Blateau at *La Marine Service* (phone: 27-64-50) or *The Pelican* at St. Jean Beach (phone: 27-64-60).

Sport Fishing – Pierrot Choisy offers deep-sea fishing expeditions on his *Bertram* (phone: 276122). Other boats available for charter are posted on bulletin boards near the *Paul et Virginie* boutique and the Banque Nationale de Paris in town. *Yacht Charter Agency* (phone: 276238) will also organize deep-sea fishing. Trips with fishermen can be arranged by your hotel if you give a day's notice. It's a good idea to bring your own tackle.

Warning: For some yet-unknown reason, many fish taken around St. Barts are very

572 ST. BARTHÉLEMY / Sources and Resources

toxic and should not be eaten. Fishermen — who only fish north of the island — believe the phenomenon may be linked to the accumulation and oxidation of seaweed, especially on the large sandbanks 7 miles to the south, which in turn contaminates certain fish. If you fish, be well advised on your catch.

Swimming and Sunning – Unquestionably the reason most visitors seek out St. Barts. The island's combination of gleaming stretches of sand and its air of being relatively undiscovered make it irresistible to unwinders. Pools — where they exist — are incidental. Most beaches, with the exception, perhaps, of St. Jean, are undeveloped. No hotel really owns a beach, but some collect a small fee for the use of their facilities. People congregate in small, sociable groups here and there, and the only crowds visible will be from a visiting cruise ship. There is topless sunbathing, but — somewhat surprising on a French island — total nudism is illegal. Beauties among the beauties: spectacular St. Jean (though filled with day-trippers from St. Martin, with several hotels and seaside cafés); quiet *Marigot* and *Lorient,* favored by island families on Sundays; isolated *Colombier* (least accessible); *Shell Beach* (easiest to get to); Grand Cul de Sac (site of the chic *El Sereno Beach,* and *Le Grand Cul de Sac* and *St. Barths Beach* hotels); long, surfy, and isolated Anse de Grande Saline; Anse des Flamands, with the *Baie des Flamands* hotel and the *Taiwana Club,* but room for independents, too; and small, secluded Anse du Gouverneur, tucked behind Morne Lurin near the island's southern tip.

Tennis – The *Guanahani* hotel has 2 illuminated, artificial grass courts. There are 2 lighted courts at the *Sports Center of Colombier* (phone *Sibarth* for information: 276238); 2 courts at *Le Flamboyant* restaurant; 1 court at the *St. Barths Beach* hotel; and another, lighted at night, at the *Manapany.*

Waterskiing – Allowed only in Colombier Bay and only between 8:30 AM and 3 PM. For information on equipment and instruction, contact Michel Mantez at *ASCCO* (phone: 276107).

Windsurfing – This sport has really taken off on St. Barts. *Wind Wave Power* surf shop and school now has 3 branches, each with its own instructor: Jean Michel Marot at the *Tom Beach* hotel on St. Jean Beach, Jack Saunal at the new *Guanahani,* and Pascal Vallon at *St. Barth's Beach* hotel, the latter two on Grand Cul de Sac. Also at Grand Cul de Sac is *Atlantic Windsurfing* (ask for Calix). Board rental generally runs $14 per hour. Five-hour ($55) and 10-hour ($100) tickets can be used at any of the 3 locations. Private lessons run $46 for one person, $69 for two. Other water sports are available.

 NIGHTLIFE: Anyone who cares about food and ambience should savor a whole evening — from apéritifs through dinner — at *Castelets,* with its breathtaking view of the harbor and offshore islands; at suave *El Sereno Beach,* where *La Toque Lyonnaise* has been gathering garlands; or at the *Hibiscus* hotel's *Restaurant du Vieux Clocher,* where the piano bar draws diners and nightcappers with its grand view of Gustavia Harbor. All evening long locals and visiting crews gather at *Le Sélect* downtown for dominos, beer, and talk; or, across the road, at the slightly more yuppie *L'Oubli Café.*

The old *Autour du Rocher* disco in Lorient is still popular with the young and older night owls, while the new *La Licorne,* also at Lorient (open weekends only), seems to attract a somewhat younger crowd. Besides the piano bar at the *Pelican* and occasional live music at the *Manapany,* little else will keep visitors up much beyond midnight here.

BEST ON THE ISLAND

CHECKING IN: The largest hotel on St. Barts (80 rooms) would be small on most other islands. The very special charm of this island is still reflected in the intimate nature of its small, often luxurious hotels, many actually a string of cottages or chalets built up a hill or strung among seagrapes along a beach. The island has become so fashionable of late that prices have skyrocketed, and bargains are few and far between. Our expensive category starts at $200 for a double without meals, soaring to over $400 for a double room and to $680 for one of *Manapany*'s new Beachfront Club suites. The moderate range is $130 to $200, and anything under $130 is considered inexpensive (and you won't find a room under $50 in high season). Continental breakfasts are often included.

A number of furnished hillside and beach villas are rented by the week or month. Brook and Roger Lacour of Sibarth Rental and Real Estate, BP 55, St. Barthélemy, FWI (phone: 27-62-38; in the US, call *Wimco* at 800-932-3222 or 401-849-8012) have 170 listings of 1- to 4-bedroom houses, including all facilities and maid service. High-season rents start at about $800 a week for a 1-bedroom cottage; most 2-bedroom villas are in the $1,500-and-up range, with 4-bedroom, 4-bath villas with pool at $4,000. Summer rates generally run 25% to 40% lower. *Villa St. Barthélemy* also has a dozen or so for rent (phone: Joe Ledée, 27-64-30). Also avaiable are two well-appointed villas on a 120-acre estate at the far end of St. Jean Beach (phone: 276198). Because of the island's growing number of good restaurants, CP (Continental breakfast only) rather than MAP rates are now the norm.

ST. JEAN

Filao Beach – Forming a crescent above St. Jean Beach and the pool are 30 contemporary rooms, each with sea-viewing terrace, sitting area, refrigerator, TV, double and single beds, direct-dial telephone, radio, and bath with built-in hair dryer. Sunning, swimming, windsurfing, Sunfish sailing, water skiing, and boat charters can all be handled on site. Open for lunch only is an informal poolside restaurant popular with locals and French expatriots. Breakfast comes to your terrace or is served by the pool. Very comfortable, with good service (phone: 27-64-84, 276424). Expensive.

PLM Azur Jean Bart – The island's second largest, with 50 attractively terraced, balconied, air-conditioned rooms, 30 with kitchenettes, on a hillside overlooking Baie St. Jean. Chain identity notwithstanding, it is relatively small and comfortable, with a considerable sense of individuality and privacy. Freshwater pool, poolside bar; boat excursions, cruises can be arranged; island's most famous beach just down the road (phone: 27-63-37). Expensive to moderate.

Emeraude Plage – It has 21 bungalows, 3 suites, and 2 villas, more than half brand new, air conditioned, with kitchenettes, showers, porches, grouped around a green lawn and tropical garden right on the beach. Quiet and well managed; a good value. Restaurants nearby (phone: 27-64-78). Moderate.

Tropical – Gingerbread flounces and jigsaw trim make it look inviting. Its 20 neat twin-bedded rooms lie U-shaped around a small pool and flowered garden, each with either a verandah or a seaview balcony. On a hillside only 50 yards above the bay; with music and reading room, bar, breakfast terrace. Handy to beach, water sports, tempting restaurants (phone: 27-64-87). Moderate.

Eden Rock – Ideally placed in the center of one of the world's great beaches, this was St. Barts' first inn. It was built by former Mayor Rémy de Haenen — the first pilot ever to land here — on a great crag of quartzite jutting off into magnificent St. Jean Beach. The traditionally furnished red-roofed cottages house 6 double rooms. Breezy, but no air conditioning. Honor bar. Newly reopened restaurant (no phone; telex: 919897GL). Moderate to inexpensive.

Village St. Jean – There are lovely bay views from this 26-room "village," a Craig Claiborne favorite for years. Accommodations are in twin-bedded rooms with terraces, studios with kitchenettes (some with full kitchens next to the terrace), 1- and 2-bedroom villas, and a new deluxe Jacuzzi Suite, with the Jacuzzi on a panoramic wraparound terrace. Beach is a 5-minute downhill walk. Well-stocked commissary, a library/listening room, game room, and the attractive *Patio* restaurant for breakfast, dinner (phone: 27-61-39). Moderate to inexpensive.

Tom Beach – Small, neatly shingled place, sunworshipfully sited on St. Jean Beach next door to *Chez Francine* and now with its own beach bar/restaurant, *Bamboo*. Each of its 11 rooms has a kitchenette and bath. Price includes airport transfers and a chilled bottle of wine (phone: 27-60-43). Inexpensive.

ELSEWHERE ON THE ISLAND

Taiwana Club, Flamands – This exclusive retreat (you have to know the owner to secure — or want — a room here) boasts a quartet of winsome Créole cottages, with a total of 9 individually decorated rooms (with fine linens, tape decks, and some with four-poster beds and odd antiques). They are grouped in no-two-alike combinations to accommodate couples, families of varying sizes. With tennis court, pool. Thatch-topped club center sets up sports, al fresco meals (phone: 27-65-01). Very expensive.

Guanahani, Grand Cul de Sac – St. Barts' largest hotel, with a total of 80 rooms, includes 1- and 2-bedroom suites, junior suites, and deluxe rooms in West Indian–style cottages trimmed in gingerbread and sprawled across a spectacular beachfront site adjoining Rothschild property. All rooms have seaview patios or decks, air conditioning, ceiling fans, and radio/TV/video. Bathrooms are sparkling white, with splashes of primary colors, chrome and brass fixtures, fluffy towels, terrycloth robes, twin washbasins, and Nina Ricci toiletries. Most units have either kitchenettes or full kitchen facilities; many have their own private pools. All rooms differ in size and layout and may be interestingly combined to form family or friendly enclaves. Amenities include a freshwater pool and Jacuzzi overlooking the beach, 2 lighted tennis courts, and 2 restaurants — the intimate *Bartolomeo* and the informal poolside *L'Indigo*. Full water sports facilities and free airport transfers (phone: 27-66-60). Expensive.

Castelets, Morne Lurin – Offers 10 rooms in hilltopping chalets. What it doesn't have is a beach, and getting to even the nearest one (Anse du Gouverneur) takes some doing, so a car is essential. What it does have is quiet comfort, relaxed luxury, and privacy in some of the Caribbean's most handsome accommodations. It is as though a small, very elegant part of France had been transplanted to an island mountaintop. All — except two pleasant rooms in the main house — have antique-decorated living rooms and wide terraces with spectacular views. Small pool. Breakfast is included; other meals are expensive but superb (phone: 27-61-73). Expensive.

La Banane, Lorient – This quiet, exclusive gem near L'Orient Beach is a honeymooner's haven. Four traditional cottages hide extremely untraditional interiors: the Royal Bungalow has a fountain in the living room, antique furniture, a four-poster bed, double-headed shower, and greenery throughout; bungalows #2 and #3 can be rented together; and #4 has a very private terrace. In a tropical garden setting with many banana trees, it has a small pool, beach nearby. Breakfast included in rates (phone: 27-60-80). Expensive.

Hostellerie des Trois Forces, Vitet – Peacefully remote mountainside cluster of rustic bungalows, each designed for a different zodiac sign. The French astrologist–owner built this unusual, charming retreat himself, and he conducts early-morning yoga classes by the pool, hikes up the mountain, and astrology lessons in low season. Swim-up bar and wooden deck at the pool; the attractive poolside restaurant features grilled fish and meat done in both French and Créole style. Closed June and October (phone: 27-61-25). Expensive.

Manapany, Anse des Cayes – Posh colony of 36 luxury units in island-style red-roofed gingerbread cottages sprawled along a cove-cupped beach or tiered on the flowered hillside above. Best are the new beachfront Club Suites, each with a large marble bath, full kitchen, bar, and open-air living/dining area. The other accommodations consist of rather small double rooms and adjoining suites with bedroom, kitchenette, and large living/dining terrace, which can be rented together. Amenities include a good-sized pool (for St. Barts), lighted tennis court, 24-hour room service, closed-circuit TV, Jacuzzi, lots of water sports, and 2 excellent restaurants (phone: 27-66-55). Expensive.

El Sereno Beach, Grand Cul de Sac – A gleaming cluster of 20 invitingly private rooms, facing a patio or private garden, distinctively decorated by Marc and Christine Llepez. Each one has a refrigerator, phone, wall safe, and a TV with VCR. Top flight in every respect, with many water sports, palm-islanded pool, bar, and one of St. Barts' most acclaimed restaurants (phone: 27-64-80). Expensive.

Hibiscus, Gustavia – This intimate hillside inn (10 rooms, 1 duplex apartment) overlooking Gustavia Harbor is one of the island's prettiest, not the least of reasons being a fabulous view and the brilliant cloak of bougainvillea, oleander, and rubber plants. Great attention to decor, personal comfort. All rooms have air conditioning, ceiling fans, showers, balconies with cooking facilities. Small pool, al fresco restaurant with fine French cuisine and a piano bar, free beach transport (phone: 27-64-82). Expensive to moderate.

Baie des Flamands – Two-story motel-style inn popular with families, on the beach of the same name, facing mountainous Chevreau Island, inhabited by wild goats. One of St. Barts' older properties, it has recently been refurbished. The 24 air-conditioned rooms are good sized and have balconies. Large saltwater pool. Free airport transfers and Mini-Mokes for rent (phone: 27-64-85, 27-64-76). Moderate.

Marigot Bay Club – Marigot-Michel Ledée's charming, new seaview property, with 6 studios in all, is already in great demand. All rooms have access to the pool next door and the lovely restaurant below, as well as kitchen facilities, terrace, living room, and air conditioning (phone: 277545). Moderate.

Marigot Sea Club – This new Swiss-run property has 10 units, all with kitchen, air conditioning, and fans. Pool. Contact Marigot Bay Club. Moderate.

St. Barths Beach and Grand Cul de Sac Beach hotels, Grand Cul de Sac – Next door to each other and under the same ownership, these functional properties sport a calm stretch of beach on one side, a quiet lagoon on the other. Tour groups and families like it for the full range of water sports, tennis, and saltwater pool. There are 36 undistinguished (but perfectly comfortable) rooms, all with private bath and balcony, but the vast and minimally decorated public rooms (including the indoor dining room) are dreary. The Grand Cul de Sac has more private bungalows, 16 simple rooms with kitchenettes, and use of all St. Barths facilities. Guests are advised to rent their cars from owner Guy Turbé, or they won't be allowed to park it on the grounds (phone: 27-60-70 and 27-62-73). Both moderate.

Presqu'île, Gustavia – Right on the harborfront, with 12 simple air-conditioned rooms and a first-rate Créole restaurant (phone: 27-64-60). Inexpensive.

 EATING OUT: There's variety — snack places and town cafés, informal beachside cafés featuring charcoal-grilled steak and fresh lobster; a couple of spots for Créole-spiced island cooking; and many with truly haute cuisine. None can really be considered inexpensive by any standards, especially considering the current weakness of the dollar. St. Barts has few native dishes — except for fresh fish and lobster, which, unfortunately, are no longer inexpensive, either. Dinner reservations are recommended — especially in season. Prices range from "inexpensive" (under $25 per person per meal, not including wine), to moderate ($25 to $50 per person), and expensive ($50 to the sky!). Since dining places are small, reservations are always a good idea.

GUSTAVIA

Aux Trois Gourmands – The "Three Gourmands" of St. Martin's famed *La Vie en Rose* and *La Calanque* features the impressive creations of award-winning French chef Christophe Gasnier (who trained under Bocuse and Rocuhon), who dazzles the eye as well as the palate with dishes like fresh pasta with pâté de foie gras in a sweet-and-sour raspberry vinegar and butter sauce, and fillet of yellowtail in pink peppercorn sauce. Snippy French management. Open for lunch and dinner. La Pointe (phone: 27-71-83). Expensive.

L'Ananas – In an elegant old house with a terrace overlooking the harbor. Hallmarks are pleasing decor and a very creative menu — a product of the vast travel experiences of chef/owner Luc Blanchard, who was once a sea captain. Among the interesting offerings are appetizers such as sashimi, carpaccio, and a perfect gazpacho; entrées include spiny lobster in tarragon cream, slices of salmon and monkfish in saffron cream, and roast duck in sweet brandy sauce. Not to be missed is the famed chocolate and mocha truffle cake. Dinner only (phone: 27-63-77). Expensive.

La Crémaillère – Near the port, quiet, French (the chef trained at Maxim's). Enjoy *bisque d'homard,* yellowtail *au safran, pommes soufflées,* and a fabulous light pastry dessert of *mille feuilles chauds* in the charming garden or the rustic dining room. Closed Sundays (phone: 27-63-89). Expensive to moderate.

Au Port – One of St. Barts' oldest and most reliably good small French restaurants. Book well ahead for the popular terrace tables overlooking the harbor. Its young chef Jean Pierre Delage dispenses traditional French cuisine but with a light touch. Half the menu changes yearly, but standards include an excellent fish soup *à la provençale,* fresh pâté de foie gras, and fillet of lamb with garlic cream. This season's steamed breast of duck with orange sauce and fresh salmon with vodka and thyme were notable. Dinner only. Closed summers (phone: 27-62-36). Expensive to moderate.

Restaurant du Vieux Clocher – Besides a great view of the harbor and the old Swedish belfry, the *Hibiscus* hotel's appealing poolside restaurant/piano bar has a young French chef formerly of Anguilla's fine *Malliouhana.* Jumbo shrimp terrine, rolls of seabass in leek butter sauce, spring chicken in strawberry vinegar sauce with watercress flan, and a sensational kiwi mousse in pineapple sauce were perfect. Friendly service and delightful ambience. Dinner only (phone: 27-64-82). Expensive to moderate.

Le Casablanca – Moroccan and Créole cuisine is served in this old Swedish house that dates back more than a century. Open for lunch and dinner. Rue du Roi Oscar II (phone: 277784). Moderate.

L'Escale – On the wharf, next to *La Marine Café,* this popular newcomer features exotic salads and well-prepared traditional French cuisine with a tropical touch. Casual al fresco waterfront ambience, except when it rains and the canopy does not manage to keep diners dry. Lunch and dinner (no phone). Inexpensive.

ST. JEAN

Le Pelican – Lunch is an informal grill (langouste, fish, chicken, and salads) on the terrace, bustling with day-trippers from St. Maarten. But at dinner, talented young chef Denis Bernard presides over a very creative menu, which includes remarkable starters such as smoked salmon mousse in tomato and basil purée, a salad of pan-fried red snapper in vinaigrette (served warm), and lobster ravioli in ginger sauce. Among the other rewarding specialties are an anise-flavored stew of scallops, crayfish, and oysters, and breast of hare in pepper sauce with glazed onions and fresh noodles — to say nothing of the perfectly dreamy desserts. The lighting could be better — but not the food. Closed Sunday evenings (phone 27-64-64). Dinner: expensive; lunch: moderate.

Chez Francine – Right on the sand, this small, informal eatery is a great people-watching spot as it is often crowded with day-trippers from St. Martin. It serves steaks, fresh lobster, great pommes frites, luscious tarts for dessert (phone: 27-60-49). Expensive to moderate.

Bamboo – *Tom Beach* hotel's new beach bar/restaurant is ideal for a lunch of grilled shark *avec frites,* or for burgers and snacks (phone: 27-60-43). Inexpensive.

Beach Club – Very informal eatery on St. Jean Beach, its decor harmonizes with its setting. Salads, burgers, and straightforward dinner menu. Best at lunch. Closed Mondays (phone: 27-64-69). Inexpensive.

ELSEWHERE ON THE ISLAND

Ballahou – Young Briton Stephane Ollivier, whose impressive list of credentials includes *La Tour d'Argent,* among other stars, now presides over the *Manapany*'s elegant, candlelit restaurant. A soothing French singer/pianist keeps diners lingering over café and Cognac (phone: 276655). Expensive.

Les Castelets, Morne Lurin – Long lauded by St. Barts buffs, this special inn's restaurant is as noteworthy as the accommodations. After an apéritif in the downstairs bar (carved out of natural rock), manager Mme. Genevieve Jouany seats guests either on the terrace, with its breathtaking views, or in the elegant dining room, furnished with French provincial antiques. The seasonal menu features excellent fish soup and its "garniture traditionnelle," pink rack of lamb, or more innovative offerings such as scallops in passion fruit sauce. Desserts, wine, and service are excellent. Reservations are a must (phone: 27-61-73). Expensive.

Club Lafayette, Grand Cul de Sac – For a swim (sea or pool), a *planteur* in the palm shade, and a lunch of barbecued lobster, grilled fish, or a salad topped off with cool sherbet or an irresistible pastry. Lunch only, but reservations advisable since this place is very "in," especially in season (phone: 27-62-51). Expensive.

La Toque Lyonnaise, El Sereno Beach Hotel, Grand Cul de Sac – Marc and Christine Llepez make an outstanding contribution to an island not notably lacking in gastronomic praise. Twice a year, promising Lyonnaise chefs are invited to serve as chefs de cuisine, and the menu changes every 2 or 3 months to reflect their efforts. One extraordinary dégustation, or chef's sampler (about $55), included extremely light lobster ravioli with endive and lobster sauce, blinis with caviar and champagne butter, and fresh imported salmon marinated in lime and passion fruit served with toasted country bread and olives. Among the other enticing offerings were steamed bar (sea perch) wrapped in cabbage with cream sauce, and melt-in-your-mouth filet mignon au foie gras and truffle "juice." The foie gras is made right here, as are the excellent pastries, which are wheeled to your table despite noble protests. The wine list, like everything else, is superb. Reservations required. Closed summers (phone: 27-64-80). Expensive.

Le Rendez-vous, Anse des Lezards – A breezy new find, perched above a remote sea site. Jean-Marc Faucheux, formerly of *La Toque Lyonnaise,* offers lobster mousse wrapped in cabbage leaves, *le blanc de vivanneau au ragoût de poireaux,* and *jambonnette de volaille farcie à la langouste,* among other interesting dishes. Dinner only. Reservations through the *Normandie* hotel (phone: 27-61-66). Expensive to moderate.

Marigot Bay Club, Marigot – Extremely popular seaside spot swathed in greenery and palm trees atwitter with bananaquits. Swim or snorkel between courses of *christophine farcis* with lobster, fresh fish brochette, or grilled fish with excellent sauces (aïoli, curry, and Créole — ask for a taste of all three). The filet mignon, which is imported, is also tops. Smiling service under the supervision of friendly, well-travelled St. Bartian Michel Ledée. Special at lunch or dinner (phone: 277545). Moderate.

Maya's, Public – French Créole cuisine at its most adventurous, prepared by owner-chef Maya Beuzelin-Gurley, a Frenchwoman from Martinique. Savor whatever is going that day, which might include a savory lentil soup, conch stew or brochette, salmon or beef teriyaki, fillet of pork with an excellent *sauce chien* (hot!), an exotic salad, or shrimp in coconut milk. Dinner only. Closed June through October (phone: 276399, or sign the board at the entrance). Moderate.

Le Tamarin, Grande Saline – Dartboards under the tamarind tree, a dozen tables on the deck, and a tiny porch set the casual tone of this countryside favorite. Good salads, steak tartare, and marinated and cooked fish are featured daily at lunch and on Fridays and Saturdays at dinner during high season (phone: 27-72-12). Moderate.

Le Flamboyant, Grand Cul de Sac – Perched on a hilltop with a pretty terrace and good French and Créole cuisine at very reasonable prices. Try *cassoulet de langouste* or Tahitian lime fish. Best call in the morning for dinner. Closed Sundays (phone: 27-64-09). Inexpensive.

Au Bon Coin, L'Orient – A little house with a little terrace on a hill, with traditionally excellent Créole cuisine at bargain prices. Choices include stuffed crab, stuffed christophine, and grilled or skewered fresh fish. Dinner only. Closed Wednesdays (no phone). Inexpensive.

Chez Pompi, Cul de Sac – Bargain-priced lunch spot for island food and flavor. Closed Sundays (phone: 277567). Inexpensive.

Ginette, near Anse des Cayes – Snack bar and food shop open "24 hours, 8 days a week" near the *Manapany* (phone: 276611). Inexpensive.

Sante Fé, Lurin – Best hamburgers — and sunsets — on the island (phone: 27-61-04). Inexpensive.

ST. EUSTATIUS

Today, St. Eustatius, the small Dutch island everybody calls Statia, is very quiet. But it wasn't always that way. There was a time around 1650 when Oranjestad harbor was lined with a double row of warehouses a mile long — some so chock full of goods that their doors were jammed shut and merchandise had to be stored or removed through holes cut in their roofs. Some 75 to 80 merchant ships anchored offshore each night; at times, the number reached 200.

Then as now, Oranjestad was a split-level town. The Upper Town was a residential suburb; the Lower Town bustled with mercantile action. Its single street was "very narrow and most disagreeable, as everyone smokes tobacco, and the whiffs are constantly blown in your face," a visiting Scottish "Lady of Quality" reported. She saw not only Dutch but French and Spanish merchants selling everything from sailors' pants and iron pots to "exquisite silver plate, the most beautiful I ever saw," painted silks, French hats, and Portuguese wines. What's more, she added in a gleeful tone reminiscent of today's tourists triumphing in their duty-free bargains, she also found "English thread-stockings cheaper than I could buy them at home."

In 1768, nine million pounds of sugar were shipped from Statian stores; yet the island itself produced a mere 600,000 pounds. Unlike its neighbor islands, Statia's fortunes were tied not to agriculture, but trade. Its prosperity was, in fact, due to its importance as a transshipment point for sugar, cotton, and other commodities smuggled out of their nearby home islands by the British and French in protest against monopolies and taxes imposed by their own governments. It also specialized in selling arms — at a goodly profit — to the North American rebels for use in their revolt against the British. In the 1770s the island was known throughout the Caribbean as the Golden Rock.

What happened? Several things — one of which was Admiral George Bridges Rodney's conquest and vindictive looting of the island early in 1781. Chances are that when the Dutch commander Johannes de Graaf ordered Fort Oranje's cannon to return the salute of the US brig *Andrew Doria* on November 16, 1776, he did it routinely — not as a grand gesture of recognition of the just-born nation and certainly not to provoke war with England. But it was one incident in a string of many that finally resulted in England's declaring war on the Dutch on December 20, 1780. Less than two months later, Rodney descended, confiscated everything on the island, and began selling off goods at considerable profit. Not satisfied with found riches, he kept the Dutch flag flying from Fort Oranje for a month, thereby entrapping numerous other merchant ships and their cargos. Altogether, he captured 150 ships, about half of them North American, and amassed a fortune of three to four million pounds sterling — which was, ironically, captured by the

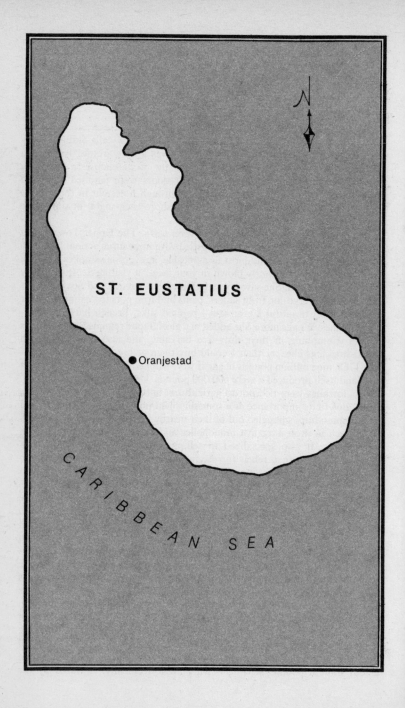

ST. EUSTATIUS

● Oranjestad

C A R I B B E A N   S E A

Dutch and French off the port of Brest during its shipment to Britain. Although his was a reign of terror — especially for Statia's sizable Jewish population — Rodney destroyed only one or two warehouses, taking timbers off the roofs to build barracks for his men. Six months later, in August of 1781, he left the island considerably poorer but virtually undamaged. In November, the French, under the Marquis de Bouillé, governor of Martinique, drove the British out. In 1784, they, too, left, returning the island peacefully to the Dutch. And by 1786, things were as bustling and prosperous as ever.

In 1792, life was elegant. A visitor described the interiors of Upper Town homes: "Fashionable people have decorated the inside walls with English wallpaper, and most of the chairs are wooden, from England and North America. Moreover, there are large mirrors, and, under these, mahogany tables laden with the finest crystal glass that I have ever seen."

But wealth had made Statia's merchants corrupt and lazy. So eager were they to make money for themselves that there was little left for the Dutch West Indies Company, which had bankrolled the island's original settlement and which had headquarters there. It foundered and, in 1791, wound up its Statian affairs and decamped. Even as the traveler quoted above enthused over the community's wealth and sophistication, things were heading steadily downhill.

Statia's fortifications — talk of its ring of "fortlets" to the contrary — had never amounted to much. In 1780, a Dutch ship's officer reported that Fort de Windt's four cannons were manned by a constable, a small boy, and a black maid. Fort Oranje's big guns could not be used because chunks of the supporting cliff dropped away every time the cannon fired. But people were too busy making money to pay attention. So the French had no trouble reconquering the island in 1795. When the British took over from them in April 1801, all trade stopped. And though Statia was finally returned to Dutch hands in 1816, by then both slavery and the sugar industry were on the wane, and the island never recovered.

Plantations had long since been allowed to go to seed in favor of the island's more profitable, less troublesome trade. Now empty warehouses crumbled into ruins. Hurricanes pushed others over, and when storms ruptured the seawall, built — in Dutch fashion — to reclaim land from the sea, no one bothered to repair it. So the water returned and foundations disappeared under it. On a calm day, you can look down from Fort Oranje on the cliffs and trace the outlines of foundations on the bottom of the bay. And you'll find dozens more on an afternoon's browse along the Lower Town's shore. On land, the old Customs House (now serving as the island's electrical station), two brick warehouses, and a network of ruined walls survive. A number of other antique buildings and substantial ruins are clustered near Fort Oranje in the Upper Town, and the Historical Foundation is doing its best to shore them up and save them.

The island's population — officially counted at 7,830 in 1790 — has dwindled to some 1,800. About 25 of those are retired North Americans who've built villas in the hills overlooking the sea. Two unretiring fellows from the United States — onetime J. Walter Thompson ad agency man Marty Scofield and Connecticut schoolteacher John May — have provided Statia with its first real spark of tourist life. Their first contribution was to build a small inn called the *Old Gin House* (that's "gin" as in "cotton"), on the foundations of an old building in the Lower Town overlooking what is sometimes a beach (hurricanes have consumed much of it, and it very nearly disappears at high tide). Its sea-viewing rooms are airy, decorated with a blend of antiques collected from their many travels and contemporary furniture. And its patio is the sooner-or-later gathering place for islanders and visitors. Across the road they've opened a companion guesthouse as well as their more formal (still, by most standards, informal) restaurant, the *Mooshay Bay Dining Room,* where Marty presides in the kitchen.

Meanwhile, tourists are trickling through at the rate of about 17,000 a year, which is an increase of 30%. Many are attracted by the unique diving possibilities recently opened up with the arrival of a full-service dive operation, *Dive Statia,* located next to the *Old Gin House.* Others do the standard sightseeing tour — which holds few thrills or surprises — then lunch, and leave wondering why they bothered. A few, determined to "really get away," move into one inn or the other, and become so addicted to the relaxed, unstructured life and the easy friendliness that they come back again and again, join the Historical Foundation, and — no matter where they happen to be between visits — become a part of the island.

Statia is still very quiet — maybe too quiet for you. But it may be just the retreat you've spent a lifetime seeking.

ST. EUSTATIUS AT-A-GLANCE

 FROM THE AIR: Little 11.8-square-mile St. Eustatius looks like a lozenge-shaped table, slightly raised above sea level, with a sawed-off volcano at its southern end and a pile of lower hills pointing northwest at its other tip. At approximately 17°32′ N latitude and 62°56′ W longitude, it is about 35 miles south of St. Maarten, about 17 miles southeast of its sister island of Saba, and about 11 miles northwest of the British Leeward Island of St. Kitts. The volcano, known as the Quill (a corruption of the Dutch word *kuil,* meaning pit, presumably referring to its crater), is almost symmetrical. You can climb up the mountain and look down into a dense green rain forest cupped in its burnt-out top. But what strikes you first is the utter flatness of Statia's central plain, De Cultuurvlakte, near the middle of which is the 1,900-foot Franklin D. Roosevelt airstrip. Lying diagonally southeast to northwest on the surface of the sea, Statia forms a 2½-by-5-mile barrier between the Atlantic Ocean and the Caribbean.

At first you see only a few houses dotted over the plain and a few skinny roads cutting across it. Then about a mile south of the airport, you notice the island's capital, the split-level (Upper and Lower) town occupying land on top of and under the pink-gray coastal cliffs. It is called Oranjestad, but Statians warn you to leave the name out of postal addresses to avoid having your letter detoured to the other Oranjestad, capital of the better known island of Aruba, hundreds of miles to the south. Soft gray volcanic beaches dot the leeward (Caribbean) side of the island from just south of Gallows Bay below Oranjestad to the base of Fort Royal hill northwest of town. Unfortunately, hurricanes have claimed some of them over the last few years. Others line the shore of Tumble Down Dick Bay a bit farther north, where an oil storage facility has been installed that will, it is hoped, provide a boost to the island economy, as well as the northeast-facing windward side, where surf from the deep blue Atlantic rolls in along the island's most picturesque gold sand beaches at Zeelandia, Concordia, Barging, and Great bays — good for experienced surfers, but swimming is not advisable because of the fierce undertow.

 SPECIAL PLACES: A list of Statia's monuments has a way of sounding more impressive than when the collection actually is viewed first hand. Before booking an extended stay, it's important to remember that when the type spells out the word *ruins,* it means just that. The island calls for all the historic imagination you can muster. True history buffs, fascinated by its mysteries, return again and again to pore over its stones and try to fill in the missing links.

Oranjestad is, in a sense, a ghost town, only now coming out of the coma into which it fell in the early 19th century. Your first stop should be Fort Oranje, where, at the tourist office, you can pick up a free Historical Foundation *Walking Tour Guide* or pay 55¢ for the booklet *Get to Know St. Eustatius,* and admire the view of the Lower Town. It is impossible to believe that the skeletal stone walls below are the vestiges of what was once the immensely rich port known as the Golden Rock.

Fort Oranje, with its three bastions, is in the best shape of any Statian landmark, having been extensively restored in honor of the US Bicentennial celebration of 1976. Now its ramparts bristle with shiny patent-black cannon; the postal service and several other government offices are housed within its walls, and further rebuilding, including museum space, is in progress. A plaque commemorates the return of the salute fired by the US brig *Andrew Doria* on November 16, 1776, by which the "sovereignty of the United States of America was first formally acknowledged." Since this act helped to bring on war with the British, it is one that — given hindsight — later islanders might well wish had been left undone.

Leaving the fort, turn right on Fort Oranjestraat and, following the *Walking Tour Guide* map, visit the Upper Town's other sights: the Gertrude Judson Memorial Library; the barracks-like Government Guesthouse (not in service at present), near which remains of four old buildings were recently found; the gingerbread-frilled house at Fort Oranjestraat 4, a 20th-century building following the old traditions, and behind it, the remains of the 18th-century house called Three Widows Corner with its restored cookhouse, patio, and herb garden. The beautifully restored Simon Doncker House, which for many years was erroneously believed to have been Johannes de Graaff's house and which served as Admiral Rodney's headquarters after he captured the island in 1781, has recently become the St. Eustatius Historical Foundation Museum. Housing relics from the golden era of the island, as well as pre-Columbian artifacts and an Amerindian skeleton or two, it is open 9 AM to 5 PM weekdays; check locally for weekend openings (entrance fee). The aforementioned booklets, a few souvenirs, and postcards are on sale here (at Wilhelminaweg in the center of Oranjestad). The Town House on the corner of the continuation of Fort Oranjestraat and Bredeweg is at the point of tumbling down entirely but still provides intimations of classic Statian stone and wood construction. Just behind it, on Synagogpad, stand the ruins of the Honen Dalim ("Charity to the Poor"), the second oldest synagogue in the Western Hemisphere. A two-story building begun around 1740, it must have been most impressive in its 18th- and 19th-century prime. There is also the tiny, lovingly tended, old Jewish cemetery on the outskirts of town, next to what is believed to be a *mikvah* (Jewish ritual bath), which was recently unearthed. There is some speculation that this could instead be part of an old rum factory.

If you're taxi touring or driving a rental car, make the stately ruins of the Dutch Reformed Church a stop on your way out of town on the way to Fort de Windt. The church's tower and choir loft have been restored by the Historical Foundation (concerts are planned), and the churchyard is full of fascinating stones — a find if stone rubbing is your hobby. Other places to pause along the way are the ruins of the old sisal factory and sugar mill just beyond the church; Fort Nassau, and tiny Fort de Windt, with newly rebuilt walls, part of a 16-emplacement chain of defenses spotted around the island's periphery.

At this point, unless you've brought a picnic, head back for the terrace of the *Old Gin House* and lunch. Then to get the real feel of the island, get into bathing things and a pair of expendable sneakers and go exploring among the ruins and along the shore in either direction. Shards of pottery and glass, coins, buttons and bones, and other remnants of Statia's rich past are still found all over the island, above *and* below the water. Or just sit in the sun and absorb the peace of it all.

SOURCES AND RESOURCES

TOURIST INFORMATION: The St. Maarten–Saba–St. Eustatius Tourist Information Office at 275 Seventh Ave., 19th Floor, New York, NY 10001-6708 (phone: 212-989-0000), and 243 Ellerslie Ave., Willowdale, Toronto, Ont. M2N 1Y5 (phone: 416-223-3501), will supply information on current rates, travel arrangements, and places to stay. They'll also accept phone inquiries.

If you're flying in from St. Maarten (which you probably will be) and have a chance to visit Philipsburg before taking off for Statia, check the tourist office at the head of the Little Pier for recently arrived supplementary reading matter. And check out a St. Maarten bookstore for Dr. J. Hartog's *St. Maarten, Saba, St. Eustatius.* It's a good idea to get all the information you can in advance because the tourist offices and museum on the island may not be stocked with literature on the day you arrive.

The St. Eustatius Tourist Office in Fort Oranje (phone: 2433) and its branch at the airport keep a small stock of literature (chiefly the Historical Foundation's *Walking Tour Guide* and the informative booklet *Get to Know St. Eustatius*). The museum and the Historical Foundation's information booth in the Lower Town opposite Roro Pier (short pier) stock similar material. The people at the Gertrude Judson Library just up the street and at the Historical Foundation's headquarters on Prinsestraat are friendly and will do all they can to help.

Local Coverage – The *San Juan Star* and an occasional copy of the *New York Times* turn up when you least expect them, and the *Chronicle,* an English daily published in St. Maarten, arrives late each morning.

St. Maarten Holiday gives only a few squibs of information about Statia. Best background sources are Dr. J. Hartog's *St. Maarten, Saba, St. Eustatius and Ypie Attema's St. Eustatius, A Short History,* sometimes found at the tourist office and almost always at the Historical Foundation, the museum, and the Mazinga Gift Shop.

Telephone – Dial direct to St. Eustatius by adding the international access code 011 and the prefix 5993 to the numbers given below.

ENTRY REQUIREMENTS: US and Canadian citizens need only proof of citizenship (a valid passport or one that is expired less than 5 years, birth certificate with raised seal or a notarized copy, or voter's registration card will do) plus a ticket for return or ongoing transportation.

CLIMATE AND CLOTHES: The climate is comparatively dry (only 45 inches of rain a year) with daytime temperatures in the mid-80s F (29° to 30°C) and nights in the 70s all year. Casual is a shade overstated for the island's mode of dress. Mostly people are neat, but style couldn't matter less.

Cottons are most comfortable, with knits and no-iron blends especially easy to deal with. You might put on a fresh shirt and pants or a cool caftan for dinner, but whether or not you do is up to you. There are no real dress-up occasions on Statia.

 MONEY: Official currency is the Netherlands Antilles florin (abbreviated NAf), also called the guilder, valued at about 1.80 to the US dollar. US dollars are as acceptable for all tourist purposes as local currency. But Canadians should change their money for florins before departing from St. Maarten or at the Banco Barclays Antilliano on Statia which is open from 8:30 AM to 1 PM on weekdays and also from 4 to 5 PM on Friday afternoons; it's closed weekends and holidays. Credit cards are not generally accepted.

 LANGUAGE: Most public signs are written in Dutch, the island's official language, but everybody speaks English. The common greeting is "awright," "ok-a-a-y."

 TIME: Statia, like Saba and St. Maarten, runs on Atlantic Standard Time year-round. In winter, when it's noon in New York and the Eastern Time Zone, it's 1 PM on Statia; in summer, when Daylight Saving Time is in effect in the US, noon is the same both places.

 CURRENT: Electricity is 110 volts, 60 cycles AC — which means no trouble for American travel appliances.

 GETTING THERE: Windward Island Airways flies STOL (short take-off and landing) Twin Otters from St. Maarten's Juliana Airport several times daily, and both Windward and LIAT serve Statia from St. Kitts and Nevis. Air transport between St. Maarten and Statia runs about $40 round-trip; from St. Kitts, $56; from Nevis, $70. Private charters can be arranged from St. Croix or St. Thomas. There are also day tours from St. Martin, Mondays through Saturdays; cost is $75, including air fare and lunch (phone: in St. Maarten, 22700, ext. 82). The cruise ship *Carib Vacationer* calls weekly each Monday year-round, and the windjammers *Polynesia* and *Phantome* come every two weeks in season. Otherwise, it is mostly sailing yachts that drop anchor in the harbor from time to time.

 CALCULATING COSTS: Rates at the *Old Gin House* run about $130 a day EP for a double in winter; in summer, about $100 and up (EP). Check your hotel's extra charges: they usually add up to another 20% to 25% more for service, utilities, and government tax. Hotel meals could run up another $50 per person (The *Old Gin House,* however, is the *only* one of the three hotels that warrants such prices.) See *Getting There* (above) for air fares.

 GETTING AROUND: Taxis – Meet incoming flights, will take you to your hotel in town for $3, and offer a whole day's touring (including lunch and swim stops) for about $30 per carload. That price also covers cassette-taped commentary, available in some (but not all) taxis, produced by the Historical Foundation, in your choice of any one of five languages: English, French, Dutch, Spanish, and German. A couple of hours' touring will cover the Upper and Lower Towns, plus a ride out the southwestern coast road to Fort de Windt, below the side of the Quill they call White Wall, where there's a spectacular view of St. Kitts. When you get back to the Upper Town, ask to be dropped at the tourist office or the museum, where you can pick up a guidebook with a map and carry on your own. But if you're not overnighting, before you let the driver go, make a date with him to pick you up and get you to the airport for your flight. Taxis also meet the small cruise ships that call in, and charge about $2 fare from the pier to town.

Car Rental – Available from several sources, a list of which may be had at the Tourist Office (ask James E. Maduro, director of tourism, or his helpful assistant, Maureen). *Avis* now has offices in town and at the airport (phone: 2421). You'll be asked to show your license; other formalities are minimal, and mileage is unlimited.

 SHOPPING: There's not much. Visitors can find a few imported Dutch items, jewelry, toiletries, liquors, cigarettes, magazines, and books among the general stock at the *Mazinga Gift Shop* in Upper Town; T-shirts and women's apparel at the *Hole in the Wall* in the garage of the Catholic church near the museum; some T-shirts, postcards, cosmetics, and appliances at *L'Etoile;* craft items and diving equipment at the small dive shop at the *Old Gin House.* But as far as local crafts are concerned, there's very little worth buying. The museum has a limited selection of postcards, books, and souvenirs.

 TIPPING: A 10% service charge is added to restaurant, bar, and hotel bills, and that takes care of waiters, maids, barmen, et al. Don't worry about bellboys and porters. There aren't any.

SPECIAL EVENTS: *Statia-America Day,* on November 16 (commemorating the first salute to the American flag by a foreign government in 1776), and *Statia Carnival* in July are the year's big celebrations, with sunup to way-past-sunset parading, partying, and the like. *The Queen's Birthday* on April 30 is also a day for fireworks, sports events, music, and dancing. Other legal holidays include *New Year's Day, Good Friday, Easter* and *Easter Monday, Labor Day* (May 1), *Ascension Day* (40 days after Easter), *Whitmonday, Christmas,* and *Boxing Day* (December 26).

SPORTS: The scale is small, but the hiking and water-sports potential is considerable and unique.

Hiking – The strong of lung and limb can climb the slopes of the Quill. Since this mountain gave up smoking some centuries back, a lush rain forest has grown up inside, and the views from the trail, and the flora within, make the effort worthwhile. It's a half-day trip that takes more energy than skill, and there are rest spots along the way. Guides (not essential) go along for about $20. In all, the Tourist Office has 12 mapped-out nature trails, from the Crater Track down into the Quill, to an easy White Bird Track along Oranjestad Beach beneath Powder Hill, where "white birds," or tropicbirds rest and nest. Contact the tourist office (phone: 2433) or the *Old Gin House* (phone: 2319) to arrange for a guide.

Snorkeling and Scuba – Most fun for these is among the underwater ruins in Oranje Bay; contrary to off-island legend, you won't find a whole city intact, but there is enough submerged masonry, a few cannons, old coins and wine bottles, and coral to make it interesting. Historians believe there are more than 200 old ships sunk in this untouched bay.

Dive Statia (phone: 2348), a dive shop run by Chuck Caldwell and Mike Brown in the warehouse next to the *Old Gin House,* offers a full range of instructional programs, from resort courses to open-water completions and specialty courses (PADI), and possibly a shared 1-week plan with Saba, Statia's friendly and equally unspoiled neighbor.

Surfing – Surfing enthusiasts will need to bring their own boards because there are none on the island. To complicate matters further, Winair (Windward Island Airways) won't fly surfboards in, so transportation probably will be by boat. These obstacles aside, the best place to surf is Concordia Bay, on the Atlantic side. There is a dangerous undertow and no lifeguards, so be sure to go with another surfer or two.

Swimming and Sunning – Pleasant areas for quick dips or leisurely swims are on all the small volcanic beaches on the southwest shore. The northeast, or windward beaches, such as Zeelandia and Lynch, are beautiful for walking or sunning but very dangerous for swimming due to the strong undertow.

Tennis – The single concrete court at the Community Center on Madam Estate is rudimentary, but it's there, open daily, and lighted for night play.

 NIGHTLIFE: The biggest show is an occasional Saturday concert by the Statia Steel Band, the Killi-Killi String Band, the Re-creation Roots Patience combo, or local reggae/calypso groups such as the J-B Beat Band. Check out *The Golden Era* or *Charlie's Bar* for weekend music, or have a nightcap at the *Kool Corner Bar*, if it's still open. Otherwise it's more doing nothing and sipping brandy, talking, and going early to bed.

BEST ON THE ISLAND

 CHECKING IN: Statia's rooms, a total of about 130, are as mixed a bag as exist anywhere. Roughly half, overlooking your choice of Oranje Bay or the Atlantic, are in three proper hotels; their moderate in-season rates range from about $80 to $150 for two without meals; breakfast and dinner will add another $30 to $40 per person a day. The other guesthouses offer basic accommodations that will cost the bargain-hunter anywhere from a rock bottom of $7 to about $35 per day for a double room. A list of them is available at the Tourist Office.

The Old Gin House – Built on the foundation of an 18th-century warehouse turned cotton gin (with the red bricks used for ballast on the old Dutch sailing ships), decorated with antiques and curious objets d'art, and smothered in bougainvillea and other fragrant tropical greenery, this is the sort of place you'll loathe if you want glittery shops and strobe-lit nightlife. On the other hand, it's got the sort of genuine, island-rooted, un-self-conscious style that lots of people wander through the Caribbean seeking but don't really expect to find — certainly not on way-out little Statia. Pick of the resort's 20 rooms are the 6 seaside luxury rooms, with custom-made furnishings and antiques, right out over the water, but it's hard to go wrong in any room (to be near the pool, pick the Mooshay side of the street). All are cooled by big ceiling fans, have private baths, good beds, and tasteful touches. No planned activity, but the beach — what little of it is left — is right there; so is lots of help for making your own day plans. Dive packages are available. The seaside *Terrace Restaurant* serves three à la carte meals daily; the more formal *Mooshay Bay* dining room is open for fixed-price, prize-winning candlelit dinners (phone: 2319). Expensive to moderate.

Golden Era – This simple but comfortable hostelry overlooks Oranje Bay in Lower Town and offers 20 air-conditioned harborfront rooms, all neat and clean, with private baths and international-access telephones. Balconies face concrete walls, and the restaurant's decor will win no awards, but the food is good and reasonably priced (phone: 2345). Moderate.

La Maison sur la Plage – This French-run, 10-room inn overlooks the isolated but lovely 2-mile stretch of Golden Rock Beach at Zeeland on the dramatic Atlantic side of the island. Spruced up in the past year, but weathered by constant salt spray and not quite enough care, the simple rooms are often dusty and slightly frayed at the seams. Still, the place has a certain raffish charm (phone: 2256). Moderate.

Henríquez Airport View Apartments – Nine comfortable, new apartments next to the airport, each with a king-size or two double beds, private bath, fridge, coffeemaker, fan, and TV. Meeting room for up to 12 people. Bar/restaurant and outdoor patio with barbecue. Caren Henríquez comes over from *L'Etoile* restaurant to do the cooking, depending on where the demand is (phone: 2299). Inexpensive.

EATING OUT: For a meal for two, expect to pay about $60 in a restaurant listed as expensive, between $35 and $60 in moderate, and less than $35 in inexpensive. Prices do not include drinks or service charge.

La Maison Sur La Plage – The other-shore alternative to the very civilized dining pleasures of *Mooshay Bay,* with a spectacular view of the wild Atlantic from the dining terrace. As we go to press, a new chef is said to be on his way from France, so if you're here more than a couple of days, you might want to give it a try. Zeelandia (phone: 2256). Expensive.

The Old Gin House: Mooshay Bay Dining Room – Co-owner Marty Scofield, an untrained but extremely imaginative, talented chef, has been receiving kudos from food writers for years. His prix fixe dinners (currently $32 per person, including two wines) might start off with freshly smoked local red snapper in salad with mousseline sauce, or grapefruit soup, followed by lobster sautéed with garlic, butter, and chives, or a chateaubriand in dijonaise sauce; then super-sinful crêpes filled with pistachio ice cream and topped with almond cream. Candlelight, crystal, and pewter services in the airy, rustic dining room next to the illuminated pool contribute to a delightful dining experience that draws guests back year after year. Open for dinner only; make reservations early — preferably before lunchtime (phone: 2319). Expensive.

Golden Era – Local food (spare ribs, curried or stewed lobster) in the late Alcatraz-style concrete block dining room is nice for a change of ambience. Be sure to let management know you're coming well in advance. Lower Town, Oranjestad (phone: 2345). Expensive to moderate.

The Old Gin House Terrace – The hotel's less formal restaurant, open for breakfast, lunch, and à la carte dinners served al fresco on a seaside terrace. Offerings include a seafood platter, lobster Antillean, various salad plates, steak, sandwiches, daily pasta and crêpe specials, and homemade sherbet (phone: 2319). Moderate.

L'Étoile – A simple upstairs snack bar/restaurant where Caren Henríquez prepares West Indian dishes such as *stews wilks* (sic), salt fish, and spare ribs (when she's not cooking for guests at the new *Airport View Apartments*). You'll also find hamburgers, hot dogs, and drinks from about 8 AM to 10 PM daily. Upper Town, Oranjestad (phone: 2299). Inexpensive.

Skells Super Burgers – Skells enlarged his hot-dog stand and now offers salt fish with johnnycakes, chicken, hamburgers, and other snacks. Upper Town, Oranjestad (phone: 2412). Inexpensive.

The Stone Oven – A good place to try Myrtle Suares' local cuisine, such as her soups ("bullfoot" or "mandungo"), stewed conch or goat, and salt fish with johnnycake. A pleasant, rustic atmosphere indoors or out, under the huge almond tree and coconut palms in the patio. Live music sometimes on Friday nights. Let her know *hours* before you're coming, lest you find no one there to cook, or only a couple of the many menu items available. Upper Town, Oranjestad (phone: 2247). Inexpensive.

Talk of the Town – Definitely the best choice for local cuisine washed down with homemade *mawby* or *sarsaparilla,* refreshing fermented drinks made from the trees of the same name. New surroundings have given this place a fresh outlook, and the trimmed-down menu now beams with the best of what's available, prepared Statian-style. Be sure to book well in advance. On the airport road (phone: 2236). Inexpensive.

Statia also has two Chinese restaurants: the *Chinese Bar and Restaurant* (phone: 2389) and *Statia's Bar and Restaurant* (phone: 2218), and snacks are usually available at the *Kool Corner,* which is also a popular meeting spot in Upper Town. Wherever you go, phone hours ahead, or you're liable to find no food available and to encounter a wait of hours while they shop and cook.

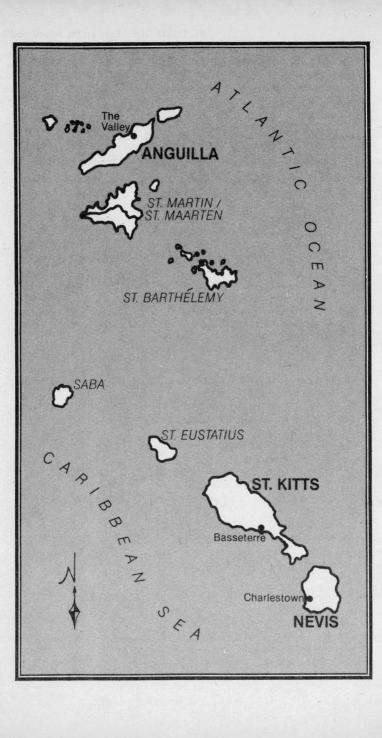

ST. KITTS AND NEVIS

They call themselves "the secret Caribbean" in tourism promotions, and to most of the world, they are. St. Kitts, with 65 square miles shaped (as Kittitians insist) like a "cricket bat," and Nevis, a round 36-square-mile "ball," are gorgeous, green, and volcanic — a photographers' playground waiting to be discovered. They offer some of the Caribbean's most dramatic panoramas — as well as one of its warmest welcomes. But their strongest attraction is their genuine "Old West Indies" charm and the small, gracious hotels and inns, many in restored plantation houses, which offer a taste of a vanishing way of life.

Despite very British roots and lingering traditions (like most of the West Indies, cricket is a national passion, driving is on the left, and English is spelled, honourably, the Queen's way), the islands are now determined, in a peaceful and stable way, to establish their own identity as the Caribbean's newest independent country. The Federation of St. Kitts–Nevis was established as a two-island nation within the British Commonwealth in September 1983, when, for a moment, the docile islands received a bit of worldwide attention.

During the past 30 years, the whimsical politics of these islands seemed to be the only thing that interested the press. Few people heard about the lush canefields and volcanic vistas, the rain forests and the black sand beaches that make St. Kitts a visual jewel; or the superb, palm-cloaked, pink sand beaches of Pinney's Bay and the secluded coves on Nevis; or the charming, centuries-old inns and rare serenity awaiting visitors to these tiny Eastern Caribbean islands.

What they did hear were bizarre tales of sibling rivalry and petty political diatribes exchanged with the distant triplet Anguilla (a charming, sandy coral isle 60 miles north with little in common, other than British rule) — part of the ongoing familial flap that got its start back in 1825, when the British made a single Crown Colony of the three. As with many other things, it was a union that just didn't work according to the Empire's divine plan in the Third World.

So when, in 1967, Anguilla declared itself independent of the St. Kitts–Nevis association, the press loved it and the reportage of the event resembled a West Indian excerpt from *The Mouse That Roared* — or Key West declaring itself the Conch Republic. Plans of an invasion of Anguilla by the hostile twins to the south and of a private kingdom set up by foreigners hit the wire services.

But Anguilla chose to remain a British Crown Colony while St. Kitts–

Nevis moved gradually away from Great Britain, and the islands again fell into relative obscurity — that is, except for occasional idle speculation that the two islands really detested each other, had a violent rivalry that made Royal Family bickerings look boring, and planned to divorce each other and ask for separate independence decrees.

Unfortunately, there was a small grain of truth in that "island scandal, but the *real* rivalry between St. Kitts and Nevis is a matter of pride and not prejudice. Kittitians, who populate "the big city," are more business-minded, tense, and anxious for development — or so the Nevisians claim (and they are, for the most part, right). Kittitians, on the other hand, refer to their neighbors as "lazy and sometimes snooty, taking too much advantage of the special laid-back atmosphere of Nevis." They are merely jealous, Nevisians insist, pointing out that every weekend and public holiday, their pristine beaches act like a magnet for weary Kittitians who make the swift two-mile crossing as quickly as they can to unwind from life in "the city." It's a very amusing story — especially to anyone who has visited both islands and knows how beautiful and slow-moving each actually is. And the "city" has a population of only 43,000 within its 65 square miles; Nevis, about 1,700.

Sugar and cotton, once sources of tremendous wealth for both islands, are no longer cash crops for Nevis, which makes tourism its primary industry. St. Kitts continues to raise cane commercially and hopes to attract more light manufacturing and industry from overseas to improve employment. Tourism is second, although during the past few years, a *Jack Tar Village* resort with a casino and a number of quality condominium vacation apartments have enhanced the island's southern Frigate Bay area.

The new country is a model of stability in the Caribbean. Anyone in search of tabloid-style intrigue had better find another tropical trouble spot. Peace and quiet and congenial, caring people are the trademarks of St. Kitts and Nevis, and that's not likely to change very soon.

Any visitor enjoying the lush tropical beauty and tranquility of these tiny Leeward islands would find it difficult to imagine their turbulent history. Columbus sighted the islands during his second voyage in 1493, and it was he who named them: St. Kitts — formally St. Christopher — for either himself or the patron saint of travelers (the story is told both ways); Nevis — originally Las Nieves, Spanish for "the snows" — because of the snow-white cloud clinging to its peak. He sailed on, leaving the islands and their resident Carib Indians undisturbed.

The British did not arrive until 1607, more than a century later. The first of them landed not on St. Kitts — which later came to pride itself on being the "Mother Colony" of the Caribbean — but on little Nevis next door. The band that came ashore did so for the express purpose of building a gallows and hanging Captain John Smith, who seems to have spent most of his historic life narrowly escaping execution. But tempers cooled, and the group left for Jamestown, Virginia, where the captain had his next brush with death and his close encounter with Pocahontas.

Led by Sir Thomas Warner, St. Kitts' first permanent residents — British — founded a settlement at Old Road Town in 1623. In 1625, they were joined by the company of a French ship seeking refuge after a skirmish with a

Spanish warship. The two groups teamed to wipe out the Caribs and then proceeded to divide the island strangely, but peaceably — with the French taking both ends and the English, the midsection. In 1629, they again joined forces to resist a Spanish attack, then turned their attention to the many islands around them. During the next decades, the British, from their St. Kitts base, fanned out to colonize Antigua, Barbuda, Tortuga, and Montserrat. The French sent landing parties to claim Martinique and Guadeloupe. St. Kitts earned its credentials as "Cradle of the Caribbean" in two languages.

Then intra-island friction sparked a seesaw struggle: By 1664, the French managed to squeeze the British off the island. The British retook it in 1689. And in 1782, the French returned to lay siege to the fort on Brimstone Hill, which had taken the British over 100 years to build. It was one of two times that this "Gibraltar of the West Indies" was ever attacked, and it fell, despite a brave defense. In 1783, the Treaty of Versailles restored both fort and island to Britain once and for all, leaving the islanders free to concentrate on sugar cane crops and business.

Nevis' history, too, has a sugar base, but with a more social flavor. In its day it was even more prosperous than St. Kitts and was nicknamed "the Queen of the Caribbees." Less than 20 years after members of Sir Thomas Warner's group established residence, more than 4,000 Europeans were recorded engaged in its sugar trade. By the late eighteenth century, the elegant *Bath* hotel that Thomas Huggins built just outside its capital, Charlestown, was attracting an equal number of tourists each year (a remarkable number for those times, although small compared to the more than 57,000 per annum who visit St. Kitts/Nevis today), who came all the way from Europe, as well as from the surrounding Caribbean, to soothe the pain of rheumatism and gout in its thermal waters.

Nevis contributed one famous son (illegitimate) and another who could be called a son-in-law. In 1755, Alexander Hamilton, the son, was born to Rachel Fawcett Lavein and James Hamilton in an estate house whose ruins are now being restored in Charlestown. The son-in-law was Horatio Nelson — later Admiral and Lord — who was a captain stationed in neighboring Antigua in the 1780s. Discovering Nevis as a source of fresh water for his good ship *Boreas,* he returned often enough to woo and eventually win the hand of the young widow Frances Herbert Nisbet, who lived on the 64-acre Montpelier estate. Their 1787 marriage is recorded in the faded register still on view in St. John's Church, Fig Tree Village.

In 1834, the abolition of slavery meant the beginning of the end of the sugar culture, and with it the eventual decline of Nevis' fortunes. St. Kitts, still deeply involved in cane production, fell into a partial slumber as the world demand for its sugar decreased.

No one — except the Anguillans — thought much about Anguilla. During the 1950s, that island became restless to break away from its southern sisters, but was unsuccessful. In 1966, Britain altered the status of the former tripartite Crown Colony to that of an Associated State within the British Empire — still without self-rule for Anguilla. On February 27, 1967, it declared itself independent of the St. Kitts–Nevis association. Islands all over the Caribbean took sides. There was even talk of invasion to bring the recalcitrant back into line. To forestall any such local moves, a British "Peacekeeping Force" parachuted out of the sky and landed on Anguilla's beaches in 1969, and in 1971, the Mother Country reassumed full responsibility for the island — much to its citizens' delight. The three have gone their two separate ways virtually ever since. And all has been relatively quiet. But nowhere near as quiet — where tourism is concerned — as it once was. St. Kitts now has an 18-hole golf course, several hotels, a casino, a deepwater port, and an airport with nonstop jet service from the US and Canada plus charter flights from Chicago, New York, and a number of other US cities. Nevis' unique, nostalgic collection of plantation homes–turned–hotels has never been more handsome or more inviting.

Today, only the impressive fortress of Brimstone Hill, overlooking the south coast of St. Kitts from an imposing perch at 700 ft., lingers as a reminder of these islands' uneasy beginning. In the distance, the peak of the dormant volcano Mt. Liamuiga, 3,792 ft., rises as proof of their explosive origins. Other than these dramatic sights, little disturbs the order and tranquility of these tiny islands northeast of Antigua in the Leewards. Rediscovery is stimulating a revival. If you want to beat it, hurry.

ST. KITTS AT-A-GLANCE

 FROM THE AIR: St. Kitts is shaped like a cricket bat (others might say a mandolin), with the narrow end pointing northwest toward the Dutch island of St. Eustatius about 5 miles away and its handle pointing toward the small, round island of Nevis, which lies to the southeast across a 2-mile channel called The Narrows. At 17°15′ N latitude, 62°40′ W longitude, it is only 5 miles across at its widest and 23 miles long from tip to handle, with an area of 65 square miles and a population of 35,000.

Basseterre, the island's capital, is tucked into a harbor on the southern shore. Golden Rock Airport is a mile from town, 45 minutes by air from San Juan, and half that from Antigua, St. Croix, and St. Maarten. The route to most of the island's resorts leads through Basseterre. Bay Road, the capital's main street, connects with the principal circle road that follows the shoreline all the way around the island. All of St. Kitts' principal settlements lie along it. The two resorts at the handle's southern tip can be reached only by boat.

At the island's northwest end, Mt. Liamuiga (3,792 feet), its highest peak, is surrounded by sugar cane fields. (On independence, the new government rechristened the mountain long known as Mt. Misery with the Carib name for St. Kitts. Pronounced lee-*a*-mwee-ga, it means "the fertile land.") Farther south, on top of 700-foot cliffs that drop straight to the Caribbean, sits Brimstone Hill's immensely impressive fortress, the landmark that made St. Kitts "the Gibraltar of the West Indies." Among other scenic assets are a crater lake — Dos d'Anse Pond — caught in the top of Verchild's Mount (2,953 feet), virgin tropical forests, tall palms, and innumerable poincianas, the flame-bloomed tree now found throughout the Caribbean but nurtured and developed here.

Kittitians will tell you that Christopher Columbus, who passed this way in 1493, was so captivated by the island's beaches and the green of its mountainous landscape that he named it St. Christopher in his own honor. It was the British who shortened it to St. Kitts, a nickname that not only stuck but put the formal name into parentheses on most Caribbean maps.

SPECIAL PLACES: St. Kitts is an island for leisurely touring, discovering bays and beaches, exploring small fishing villages, meeting people. The action, such as it is, centers around Basseterre, a quaint, friendly, and very photogenic West Indian port with a harbor that curves as a colorful harbor should and with just the proper number of low-growing palmetto trees in the background. Small craft and now, about twice a week, a large liner (occasionally including the *QE2*) lie at anchor in the waters offshore; ferryboats chug off to Nevis across the way. Among dock amenities installed to greet cruise passengers is a ride on an old sugar cane train that tours coastal plantation lands (nominal ticket price includes rum punch en route).

Basseterre – The town has looked as it does (West Indian with British overtones) for centuries, but it is punctuated with modern accents. A government-sponsored campaign for restoring and sprucing up the capital during 1988 provided a brighter look for the circus and main downtown buildings. An easy and safe place for a walking tour early in the morning or later in the afternoon (to avoid the heat), it boasts what the historian Virginia Radcliffe calls "some of the most perfect examples of West Indian architecture in the islands." The big black and white Treasury Building on the waterfront is one of them.

Basseterre's main square, called the Circus, won't remind you much of Piccadilly, but its centerpiece is the island's Big Ben, an ornate, green stone Victorian clock tower with four faces, columns, coats of arms, and a fountain in its base. In the town's other square, Independence Square (formerly Pall Mall), a park has taken the place of the old slave market. Nearby Government House is properly Georgian, as are a number of antique townhouses built in the old manner, with small, fenced gardens in front, first stories of cut stone, and second-floor overhangs dressed up with arched galleries and jigsawed trim.

Other town landmarks include the Anglican church of St. George, plagued by disasters since its first incarnation in 1670 (the earthquake of 1974 toppled its latest steeple), with its churchyard, where graves date back to the early 18th century; and the Post Office and its Philatelic Bureau, where you can buy St. Kitts and Nevis stamps, outranked in popularity only by those of the BVI in the world of Caribbean philately.

ELSEWHERE ON THE ISLAND

Taxi drivers on both islands are some of the best guides in the Eastern Caribbean. Ask your hotel to locate a loquacious driver — the best ones are well known and worth twice the established rate just for their running commentary of island life and lore. While it's safe and easy to drive yourself (a very simple road system exists), it's much more fun to sit back and listen to the amazing stories, past and present, and island gossip that only a reliable taxi driver can provide. Whether you travel with driver and taxi or in your own rental car, take the circle drive tour. You can make it all the way around the island in a little over two hours, but do it more slowly. Pack along a picnic, or call ahead to make lunch reservations at *The Golden Lemon* (phone: 7260), near Dieppe Bay. Traveling clockwise, starting north from Basseterre, you'll see:

St. Kitts Sugar Factory – At the edge of Basseterre, it provides a look into history. There are daily tours; best months: February to July, when cane is actually ground and you can see the entire process from raw cane to bulk sugar.

Fountain Estate – High on a hill north of town, it was the home of Philippe de Longvilliers de Poincy, who was for 20 years governor of the French Antilles and for whom the royal poinciana (or flamboyant) tree was named. Though a landmark, it is private property with no tours offered at present.

Bloody Point – Here the British and French massacred the Caribs in 1626.

Old Road Town – The first permanent British settlement in the West Indies and early British capital of the island. There are Carib petroglyphs on Wingfield Estate nearby.

Romney Manor – After a scenic drive through a tropical rain forest, visitors will reach the home of *Caribelle Batik,* in a 19th-century house surrounded by 5 acres of well-tended gardens, with a huge Saman tree ("rain tree") said to be over 350 years old. Visitors are invited inside the factory to watch craftsmen make the colorful cloth, which is exported throughout the Caribbean and, recently, to Florida. There is a fine selection for sale here, and shoppers can custom order clothing and wall hangings for shipment back home or, with enough notice, for island delivery. Open weekdays 8:30 AM to 4 PM. No admission charge. Just down the road is a small cluster of boulders with Carib carvings in black — a fascinating find. Ask for their location at Romny Manor.

Middle Island Village – Here Sir Thomas Warner, leader of the original British landing party, is entombed under a cracked marble slab — with a suitably weighty epitaph — in the yard of St. Thomas Church.

Half-Way Tree Village – A giant tamarind tree here marks the midpoint of Britain's holdings when the French shared the island.

Sandy Point – The first British landed here in 1623, in the shadow of Mt. Liamuiga.

Dieppe Bay – Pleasant for swimming and picnicking. Gibson's Pasture estate, which overlooks it, was once a combined sugar mill and fort; two cannons have been found on the reef below.

Black Sand Beaches – Take time to stroll along one of the unusual beaches that trim the northeast coast of St. Kitts; the sand has a unique quality (you'll find it hard to remove until it is dry). While not every beach lover's ideal, they have their own startling beauty, especially under bright sun.

Black Rocks – On the island's windward side, with eerie lava formations deposited over the years by the now dormant crater atop Mt. Liamuiga — solid evidence that this is a true volcanic island. Every November 5, Kittitians stage their Guy Fawkes Day picnic here.

Monkey Hill – A green, 1,319-foot knoll west of Basseterre, named for St. Kitts' population of black-faced vervet monkeys, originally imported by the French for reasons unknown and left behind when their masters moved on. If you're lucky, you'll sight a few in the eye of your camera; but in any case, the view from the top is worth the trip. On the way up, you'll pass the ruins of a picturesque two-story greathouse called The Glen, now tangled in green overgrowth.

Frigate Bay – Actually boasts two beaches — a surf-pounded one on the windward (Atlantic) side of the island and a calmer strand on the leeward (Caribbean) side, near the beginning of the skinny handle of land, or flank, as Kittitians call it. Designated a tourist zone by the government "in order to leave the great majority of the island exactly as it now is," Frigate Bay is the site of a number of hotel and condominium projects destined to increase St. Kitts' room count and bolster the tourist trade. Focal points of the development include the *Royal St. Kitts Jack Tar Village* hotel and casino, a golf course, and a number of smaller developments such as the *Sand and Sea* resort. There are still parts of the Frigate Bay area that are accessible only from the sea by boat. You can also arrange to tour Friar's Bay Beach and the southern tip of St. Kitts on horseback — a very enjoyable ride over the hills, with a steep decline down to the flat tip of the island. Ask at *Sun and Sand Beach Village* or your hotel for the name of the current owner of horses for rent in the Frigate Bay area.

■**EXTRA SPECIAL:** Make the most of a day visit to *Brimstone Hill Fortress* by packing a picnic to spread on a grassy hilltop spot after or midway through your explorations. (A small bar and restaurant offers supplementary drinks and snacks.) Named for the faint fume of sulfur that lingers around it, the fort commands a spectacular six-island (Nevis, Montserrat, Saba, Statia, St. Martin, and St. Barts) view, which drew "an astonished reaction" from Her Majesty, Queen Elizabeth

II, during her October 1985 visit to declare the area a national monument. Its vantage point 750 feet above the Caribbean not only made it impregnable (or so its British builders believed) but also runner-up to Henri Christophe's Haitian Citadelle in the Impossible Building Site Contest, Caribbean Division. Because of its site and size, it took 100 years to build. Its massive gray walls, 7 to 12 feet thick, link a number of bastions and enclose the remnants of extensive life-sustaining installations (hospital, storerooms, cookhouses, mental house, cemetery, and freshwater cistern system) as well as the predictable parade, barracks, officers' quarters and mess. There has been meticulous restoration of the Prince of Wales Bastion, dedicated by Prince Charles in 1973 and comprising a visitors' center, souvenir shop, and restaurant. The fortress was attacked only twice. In 1782 before it was completed, 6,000 French troops under the Marquis de Bouillé mounted a siege and bombardment that finally exhausted the British on their height. They surrendered and were permitted — as a tribute to their bravery — to march out in uniform with drums beating and colors flying. A year later, the British retook the fort and accorded the French the same honor. The data sheet available (about 40¢) from the guard at the start of the steps to the top is better than nothing. Admission fee.

Visitors can now also take escorted rain-forest adventure tours up hidden mountain trails, past waterfalls and dense vegetation, where monkeys, mongooses, and hummingbirds are often seen. All-day and half-day tours may be arranged through *Kriss Berry* (phone: 465-4042) or *Greg's Rainforest Tours* (phone: 465-4121). *Greg's* also offers boat trips to a remote beach at the *Banana Bay* resort, the sister property of *Ocean Terrace Inn.* The trips are free for *Ocean Terrace* guests.

SOURCES AND RESOURCES

TOURIST INFORMATION: The St. Kitts–Nevis Tourist Board is at 414 E 75th St., New York, NY 10021 (phone: 212-535-1234), and the Caribbean Tourism Association is at 20 E 46th St., New York NY 10017 (212-682-0435).

The St. Kitts Tourist Board has a small office (Church St., Basseterre; phone: 4040 or 2620) close to the center of things. The staff is pleasant and helpful, although sometimes short on printed information. There's also a desk at Golden Rock Airport.

Local Coverage – *A Motoring Guide to St. Kitts* (about $4) is published locally and is available at Wall's store in Basseterre. Your hotel may also have copies for sale. An excellent new detailed tourist map, indicating hotels and points of interest on both St. Kitts and Nevis, sells for about $5 US. From time to time the Tourist Board publishes a very informative *Tourist Guide,* available free at hotels and restaurants.

The Democrat is the local newspaper. Stateside papers aren't generally available, and nobody minds much.

Telephone – You can dial St. Kitts direct by adding the area code 809 and the prefix 465 to the numbers given below.

ENTRY REQUIREMENTS: Proof of citizenship — a passport, valid or expired, voter's registration card, or birth certificate (a valid driver's license is not accepted) — and a ticket for return or ongoing transportation are all that's required of citizens of the US, Canada, or the UK on short visits. A visa is necessary only for stays exceeding six months. Remember to save $5 US for departure tax, payable at the airport when you check in to leave.

CLIMATE AND CLOTHES: The temperature on St. Kitts ranges from 68° to 85°F (20° to 30°C) all year long. Dress is for casual comfort, not for chic — with cotton and cotton-blend sports clothes right for daytime and touring whatever the season. Be sure to pack sturdy walking shoes or sneakers for Brimstone Hill, et al.; plus several swimming changes. Even for May to November showers, you probably won't need a raincoat. Evenings, wear what you please. And the fact that the island lies in the path of the northeast trade winds does indeed keep it cool enough for a light wrap on winter evenings.

MONEY: Currency is the Eastern Caribbean dollar (EC) valued at about $2.68 to $1 US, and most prices in the islands are quoted in $EC. US and Canadian bills are generally accepted. Foreign coins are not welcome because they're difficult for islanders to exchange. It's a good idea to have some EC currency handy for small purchases. Banks are open from 8 AM till noon daily, except Saturdays and Sundays; on Fridays, they reopen from 3:30 to 5:30 PM. The St. Kitts–Nevis National Bank in Basseterre is also open on Saturday mornings from 8:30 till 11 AM. But generally speaking, you'll be given as good an exchange rate at hotels and shops as you will at the bank.

LANGUAGE: English has been the official language (there is a local patois, too) for more than 350 years.

TIME: St. Kitts clocks are set to Atlantic Standard Time throughout the year. So, in winter when it's noon in New York or Washington, it's 1 PM in Basseterre. When the US goes on Daylight Saving Time, at noon in New York, it's noon in Basseterre, too.

CURRENT: Here, 220 volts predominate, though a number of hotels are now wired for 110 volts (standard in the US and Canada). Check, or bring your own converter just in case.

GETTING THERE: BWIA and American Airlines are currently the only regularly scheduled airlines offering direct service from New York to St. Kitts; from Miami, BWIA flies to Antigua, with connecting flights on LIAT. Many travelers find it easier to make connecting flights via San Juan, but either the San Juan or Antigua gateways (reached by American and Eastern) are options. And many visitors arrive via connecting flights from San Juan, the US Virgin Islands, St. Maarten, and Antigua. LIAT offers daily service between St. Kitts and Antigua, Nevis, St. Croix, St. Thomas, and St. Maarten. Winair makes the run from St. Maarten several times a week. There are seasonal nonstop charters from New York, Boston, Philadelphia, Dallas, Chicago, and Toronto with land packages at local hotels required; occasionally some seats are available to nonpackage passengers.

CALCULATING COSTS: Compared to those on other Caribbean islands, the rates on St. Kitts are quite reasonable whatever the season. Accommodations at the island's top inns can run as high as $285 or so a day for two in season (from mid-December to mid-April) including breakfasts and dinners, but most run well below that. Off-season rates are in the $100 and up range (also MAP). A 10% service charge and 7% tax are added to hotel bills. Rental cottages go for about $150 and up a week, but since their plans seem to fluctuate from month to month, your best bet is to contact owners directly (the Tourist Board will supply addresses) to confirm dates and rates for your stay. So far, except for charter flight visitors, package plans haven't taken much hold. There is an airport tax of $4 per person.

Round-trip flight fares from the US to islands where connections to St. Kitts are available vary according to time of week and connecting point. The highest inter-island fare is the round trip to San Juan.

GETTING AROUND: Taxi – The mainstay. Found waiting at the airport and at the Circus in Basseterre; each hotel has its coterie of loyal drivers waiting outside in the shade or at the other end of a phone call. They are not metered, but the Taxi Association has published a list of agreed-upon point-to-point rates (ask for a copy). Even so, the price should be settled before you start off. Also, be sure you're clear about whether the rate quoted is EC or US. The ride from the airport to town generally runs about $4; it's about $7 and up to out-of-town hotels. There are no airport buses.

Bus – Between island villages, but tourists seldom use them because taxis are always handy and provide round-trip transportation (not always easy to plot using bus schedules) to exactly the place you want to go.

Car Rental – Easy to arrange, costs about $38 US and up a day, including unlimited mileage; gas is on you. You'll need a local driver's license, which you can pick up at the Police Station in Basseterre for under $8 US. The *Avis* office is on Liverpool Row in Basseterre (phone: 2631). *Sunshine* (phone: 2193), *TDC* (phone: 2511), and *Caine's* (phone: 2366) are good local firms; none accepts credit cards. Mopeds are available from *Island Mopeds,* Sprott St., Basseterre (phone: 2405), for about $20 a day. And remember: Drive on the left!

Sightseeing Taxi Tours – Popular because hotels go out of their way to team you with a driver who'll make the trip pleasant — even informative. Rates run about $8 per hour, about $25 for the 3-hour trip to Brimstone Hill and *Caribelle Batik,* about $40 for a 5-hour (including time for lunch) all-island tour for a car that holds up to four people. If you'd like extra stops or time, negotiate — or ask your hotel to — before you get in and take off. And if dates and statistics matter to you, take your guidebook along. *Delisle Walwyn & Co.* (phone: 465-2631) and *Tropical Tours* (phone: 465-4167) both offer 5-hour historic and sightseeing tours for about $40.

Sea Excursions – Trips to neighboring islands are arranged through hotels. *Ocean Terrace Inn* and *Rawlins Plantation* make a specialty of them. The ferry sails for Nevis twice daily except Thursdays and Sundays. The trip takes about 40 minutes, costs about $6 round-trip per person, and leaves you lots of lunching and exploring time. *Tropical Tours* (phone: 465-4167) also offers sightseeing boat tours, deep-sea fishing charters, and catamaran cruises.

Local Air Services – Trips to Nevis are arranged by *Four Islands Air* for about $26 per person round-trip. LIAT in Basseterre handles reservations. Interisland charters are available through *Carib Aviation* for about $240 per plane (9 seats) one way.

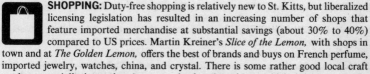

SHOPPING: Duty-free shopping is relatively new to St. Kitts, but liberalized licensing legislation has resulted in an increasing number of shops that feature imported merchandise at substantial savings (about 30% to 40%) compared to US prices. Martin Kreiner's *Slice of the Lemon,* with shops in town and at *The Golden Lemon,* offers the best of brands and buys on French perfume, imported jewelry, watches, china, and crystal. There is some rather good local craft work — especially in unglazed pottery, leather (mostly goatskin), inlaid woods (in knock-down/carry-home furniture), baskets, and embroidery. And coconut shells turn into everything from drinking cups to jewelry. Most impressive new cottage industry is ensconced in Romney Manor near Old Road. Called *Caribelle Batik,* it specializes in batiking, tie dyeing, and handpainting West Indian sea island cotton fabrics. They're strong on color, island-inspired designs (flowers, Carib petroglyphs, wildlife), and everything's guaranteed color-fast and washable. You can watch the work and buy dress lengths, wall hangings, pareos, and scarves at reasonable prices. In Basseterre, *The Craft House, The Lotus, Palm Crafts,* and *The Curio Shop* stock the best of local craft work along with some more usual souvenirs. In the Palms Arcade downtown, the *Kittitian Kitchen* and *Sunny Caribee* have a good selection of West Indian spices, teas, jams, and soaps. *Spencer Cameron Workshop* is a studio specializing in locally produced silk-screened fabrics, paintings. *Tropical Silk Screen Studios* at Bird Rock, Basseterre, offers hand-painted T-shirts, wall hangings, and souvenirs by a local artist. *Losada's Boutique* offers tasteful European imports (handsome Wedgwood, crystal, pewter, figurines) plus some good buys in island clothes from around the Caribbean. Shops in the *Palms Arcade* feature nicely styled jewelry, perfumes, curios, furniture, and resort clothes. New shopping areas downtown include Shoreline Plaza, next to the Treasury Building, with 6 boutiques offering duty-free items such as jewelry, perfume, island crafts and souvenirs; and TDC Plaza, on Fort St., with duty-free shops, fashion clothing, bar, restaurant, and banking services.

TIPPING: Hotels add 10% to 15% service charge which really covers everybody. If you're eating out and no service charge is included, tip 10% to 15%; the same goes for taxi rides. Give an airport porter 40¢ per bag, or $1 for three average-sized pieces of luggage.

SPECIAL EVENTS: *Carnival* — December 24 to January 2 — is the big party complete with parades, music, dancing; it's a great homecoming time. Legal holidays include *New Year's Day, Carnival Day, Good Friday, Easter Monday, Labour Day* (first Monday in May), *Whitmonday, Queen's Birthday* (early June), *August Monday* (first Monday in August), *Independence Day* (September 19), *Prince of Wales's Birthday* (November 14), *Christmas,* and *Boxing Day* (December 26).

SPORTS: Boating – You can arrange day sails to Nevis or one of the beaches on St. Kitts' southern peninsula, moonlight and coastal cruises through a number of outfits: *Caribbean Water Sports* at the *Royal St. Kitts Jack Tar Village* (phone: 465-8651); *Fisherman's Wharf* and *Pelican Cove Marina* at *Ocean Terrace Inn* (phone: 2754 or 2380); *Kenneth's Dive Centre* (phone: 2235); *Créole Lady* (4138); and *Gypsy Lu Water Sports* (phone: 2976 or 2876), all in Basseterre. *Banana Bay* has its own setup for sailing. A day sail, including picnic lunch, costs between $35 and $40 per person.

If you'd rather skipper your own boat, contact *Pelican Cove Marina* (phone: 2754 or 2380), which rents 16-foot Hobie Cats for $100 for 6 hours. For windsurfing lessons and board rental, contact *Caribbean Island Windsurfing* (phone: 2695).

Golf – There's a championship 18-hole course at Frigate Bay, where the greens fees are $20 per round and $15 for a cart; a caddy is paid $5 per round per bag. Six days' unlimited play runs $105 with cart; $70 without.

Horseback Riding – Especially scenic in the northern hills. With a guide, it's about $10 to $15 per person per hour. Contact *The Stable* at *Trinity Inn* (phone: 3226). *Rawlins Plantation* also has horses for experienced riders.

Mountain Climbing – Tempting for the view's sake. The *Fairview Inn* has a small mountain in its backyard. Monkey Hill is rated an easy climb. So is the day-long trip to the top of Verchild's Mount. The Mt. Liamuiga climb takes most of a day; getting to the top (you start from Belmont Estates on horseback, carry on on foot) isn't difficult, but the descent into the rain forests inside the crater and the climb back out are classed as strenuous and are considered difficult by all but those in top physical shape. Both these last trips require a hired guide for the day. *Kriss Tours* (phone: 4042) in Basseterre takes small groups of hikers into the Mt. Liamuiga crater and to Dos d'Anse Pond on Verchild's. The 8-hour trip costs about $25 per person.

Snorkeling and Scuba – Instruction, equipment, dive and snorkeling trips are offered by *Caribbean Water Sports* (phone: 8651); *Fisherman's Wharf* and *Pelican Cove Marina* (phone: 2754 or 2380); and *Kenneth's Dive Centre* (phone: 2235). A one-tank dive will cost about $30; a snorkeling trip, about $25.

Sport Fishing – You can charter boats for deep-sea fishing at *Fisherman's Wharf* and *Pelican Cove Marina* (phone: 2754 or 2380) and *Kenneth's Dive Center* (phone: 2235). A 3-hour trip will cost about $50 per person.

Swimming and Sunning – The widest and whitest sands are at the end of the island. Frigate Bay and Friars Bay have beaches on both the Atlantic and Caribbean. Banana Bay, White House Bay, and Cockleshell Bay are other good names to know. Dieppe Bay sands are volcanic gray to black. Conaree Beach on the windward (Atlantic) coast is narrow in spots and grayish, but offers surf swimming (not surfing). There's also surf on the windward side of Frigate Bay. Few hotels are directly on the beach, though most aren't far away and will arrange transportation. *Banana Bay Beach* hotel has the best beach. *Sun and Sand* is on the Atlantic side of Frigate Bay; *The Golden Lemon*, on a small black sand beach at Dieppe Bay. With the exception of *Banana Bay*, all hotels have swimming pools.

Tennis – If you're addicted, stay in or near the *Royal St. Kitts Jack Tar Village*, which has 4 lighted courts and a pro. There's only one other hotel court on the island — the grass court at *Rawlins Plantation. St. Kitts Lawn Tennis Club* (phone: 2046) will grant temporary membership to visitors.

Water Skiing – Go to *Fisherman's Wharf* at *Ocean Terrace Inn* (phone: 2754 or 2380). It's $30 for a half-hour; $50 for a full hour.

NIGHTLIFE: Low voltage. Mostly hotels have string or steel bands on regular schedules in season. *Ocean Terrace Inn* has the *Bitter End* disco, open Fridays and Saturdays in season, but call ahead to make sure (phone: 2754 or 2380). A night pass will get you into the *Royal St. Kitts Jack Tar Village* for the evening's show plus the only casino on the island, complete with slot machines, roulette, craps and blackjack tables, and a disco. Late-late night spots include *Lips* at the *Lighthouse* disco overlooking Basseterre Harbor, while *Fisherman's Wharf* at *Ocean Terrace Inn* serves food late and drinks and music as long as anyone is around to enjoy them.

BEST ON THE ISLAND

CHECKING IN: Hotels on St. Kitts tend to be small, low-profile, charming resorts with lots of personality; but except for *The Golden Lemon*, they can't be counted as luxurious. Recent development of the Frigate Bay area has added some condominium hotels to the island's supply of guest accommodations. These, too, at least so far, are small in scale.

About half the hotels listed below operate on Modified American Plan (MAP), which means that breakfast and dinner are included in the room rate. They fall into the expensive category: $195 to $250 a day for a double room with meals in winter; and about $160 and up in summer. Room only is listed as European Plan (EP). Hotels listed as moderate charge between $85 and $135 a day for double room without meals; those described as inexpensive, about $65 a day for double room without meals. Many hotels do not accept credit cards, so check ahead.

BASSETERRE

Fairview Inn – Three miles from town, on a hillside surrounded by gardens, the inn has simple, cottage-style rooms (some air conditioned, some with phones) grouped around an 18th-century greathouse. There's a freshwater swimming pool and a greenhouse bar with great view that is a popular island gathering place. Good food (phone: 2472 or 2473). Moderate.

Fort Thomas – On the old fort site, in a beautiful hillside setting overlooking the sea, there are 64 rooms, a pool, free beach shuttle, good restaurant, and excellent packages. Popular with charters (phone: 2695 or 800-221-1831). Moderate.

Ocean Terrace Inn – One of St. Kitts' best, on a hilltop at the far west hook of Basseterre harbor, with a lot of appealing qualities. The rooms have breezy terraces from which to watch the harbor life, and there are the added conveniences (especially for businesspeople) of phones and satellite TV. The grounds are charming, and the restaurant and bars (there are 4) have a lively, congenial atmosphere. Eight attractive 1- and 2-bedroom apartments have been added, as have *Fisherman's Wharf,* a water-sports center (*Pelican Cove Marina* is here), a beach pub, and an open-air restaurant that serves a great seafood buffet every Friday night. Both EP and MAP rates (phone: 2754 or 2380). Moderate.

FRIGATE BAY

Frigate Bay Beach – It isn't exactly on a beach, but rather a 5-minute stroll from the Caribbean side of the bay. The 64 1- and 2-bedroom apartments are in low-rise, vaguely Mediterranean-style buildings clustered around a big, handsome swimming pool. The good-sized apartments are pleasantly furnished in rattan and island prints, as are the terraces, which are well designed for privacy. The top units, with peaked roofs and ceiling fans, are the pick of the crop. There's a restaurant, too. Rates are EP only (phone: 8935 or 8936). Moderate.

Island Paradise Beach Village – The first condominium development in Frigate Bay, with 36 one-bedroom and 18 two-bedroom apartments, all with fully equipped kitchens. Freshwater pool and Atlantic beach; conveniences on premises include pizza and snack restaurant, food shop, liquor store, and small souvenir shop (phone: 809-465-8004). Moderate.

Leeward Cove – A new, small condominium hotel opposite the golf course, with only 6 spacious and comfortably furnished 1- and 2-bedroom units, with access to the Atlantic beach. On 5 acres; within walking distance to *Jack Tar Village* and restaurants (phone: 800-223-5695 or 809-465-8030). Moderate.

Royal St. Kitts Jack Tar Village – A 150-room resort hotel popular with charter groups, it is patterned after the other resorts of this chain, which offer reasonably priced, all-inclusive week-long packages covering everything from meals and cocktails to golf, water sports, horseback riding, and entertainment. The combination of the islands' only 18-hole golf course and a casino make this resort unusual, and for those seeking an active vacation at a typically modern resort, this is the place. Day passes are available for visitors for $65 US, all-inclusive (phone: 8652; in Dallas, 214-670-9888; elsewhere, 800-527-9299). Moderate.

Sun 'N Sand Beach Village – Eighteen cottages make up this village right on the wild Atlantic. The 2-bedroom, 2-bath cottages are simple, but pleasant, with high ceilings, fully equipped kitchens, and air-conditioned bedrooms. Cottages 2 through 5 have verandahs right on the beach. There's a small grocery and drugstore on the premises, as well as a casual beachside pub and swimming pool.

Attractive weekly rates make it a good choice for families traveling on a budget. EP rates only (phone: 8037 or 800-621-1270). Inexpensive.

ELSEWHERE ON THE ISLAND

Banana Bay Beach – Recently acquired by the owners of the *Ocean Terrace,* this once very popular resort is now back in business as an ideal hideaway for reclusive travelers who want to escape. Ten rooms sit on a secluded beach in southern St. Kitts, reached only via a scenic boat ride from Basseterre. The beach is white sand and beautiful; the sunset view of Nevis, splendid. Water sports abound, but there's no swimming pool. Atmosphere is informal, somewhat isolated, quiet. Rates include all meals, boat transfers from and to Basseterre. No summer rates (phone: in St. Kitts, 2860; in New York, 212-725-5880; elsewhere, 800-223-5695). Expensive.

The Golden Lemon, Dieppe Bay – "For the discriminating few who like to do nothing in grand style" is how the brochure puts it. And grand style it is: an old greathouse beautifully refurbished and faultlessly run by Arthur Leaman, former decorating editor of *House & Garden.* This is one of the few inns where as much attention has been lavished on sleeping rooms as public areas. You can stay in the greathouse itself or in Lemon Court, a terrifically stylish quartet of new apartments and suites at the water's edge. The inn has lovely gardens and courtyards, a freshwater pool, small black sand beach, and superb food. Rates include breakfast, dinner, afternoon tea, and laundry (phone: 7260). Expensive.

Rawlins Plantation, Mt. Pleasant – Near Dieppe Bay on the northeast coast, this family-owned estate of some 25 acres has beautiful gardens and arresting views. Accommodations are in the main house, built on the foundations of the 17-century greathouse, in a converted sugar mill, and in cottages scattered around the breezy hillside site. There's a pretty swimming pool, grass tennis court, and horseback riding. Day sails to Nevis and overnight sails to St. Barts can be arranged on the owner's 75-foot catamaran. Rates include breakfast, dinner, afternoon tea, and laundry (phone: 6221). Expensive.

EATING OUT: Local favorites include roast suckling pig, spiny lobster, turtle steak, crab back, curries. Islanders' restaurants like *Uncle T,* and *Victor's* add conch (curried, soused, or in salad), turtle stews, rice and peas, and "goat's water" (mutton stew) to the list. *The Anchorage* on Frigate Bay is a simple beach place that serves very good lobster. Christophine, yams, breadfruit, and papaya are frequently served. Choicest inns for lunch include *The Golden Lemon* (delicious food, grand service), *Fairview Inn* (friendly, especially good on island dishes), the *Ocean Terrace Inn* (in town, great view, good food), and its harborside *Fisherman's Wharf* (good barbecue, chowder, lobster, reasonably priced). Also in Basseterre, *Ballahoo,* on a breezy second-floor terrace overlooking the Circus, serves good fresh fish island-style, spicy soups, a very tasty lobster quiche, and sandwiches when you're not feeling native. *Bistro Créole* on Cayon Street in Basseterre has a way with West Indian specialties (Créole fried fish, Liamuiga, red snapper, and sweet potato pudding are especially fine). *Georgian House,* in a handsome example of the same on Independence Square, offers an elegant mix of Continental and West Indian food, with service to match. Peter Mallalieu's *Patio* at Frigate Bay is a unique and leisurely dining experience, rather like being a guest in an island home (which this was). The evening, which runs about $35 per person, features an open bar, a delicious six-course dinner, wine, liqueurs, and music. The *Lighthouse,* at Bird Rock, has good Italian and Kittitian cuisine (lobster is a specialty) and a nightclub.

NEVIS AT-A-GLANCE

FROM THE AIR: Nevis, lush, green, and ringed with beaches, lies at 17°16′ N latitude and 62°50′ W longitude, south of the Dutch islands of Saba and St. Eustatius and due west of Antigua. An almost circular island (6 miles wide by 8 miles long), it dots the exclamation point it forms with its sister island, St. Kitts, 2 miles to the north across The Narrows channel. From high up, its shape is conelike, as though it had been formed by scooping up sands from its beaches and molding them toward its 3,232-foot central peak, Mt. Nevis, its top usually capped with white clouds. This may have been the reason Columbus called it Las Nieves, Spanish for "snows." Neither Saddle Hill (1,432 feet) to the south nor Hurricane Hill (1,192 feet) to the north, which bracket Nevis' central peak, comes within 1,000 feet of equaling its height, but both are tall enough to have served as lookout posts for Nelson's fleet in the late 18th century.

Like a number of other islands settled by the British, Nevis is divided into parishes: St. George, St. John, St. Paul, St. Thomas Lowland, and St. Thomas Windward. It is the home of 9,400 Nevisians, half of whom live in the capital of Charlestown in the parish of St. Paul. Newcastle Airport, a strip just large enough to accommodate 19-seater planes, is at the water's edge 15 minutes north of town. On the island's west side, massed rows of palm trees form a coconut forest, while single palms bend in the breeze along the windward eastern coast. The one black sand beach in the northwest ranks high as a sightseeing attraction. But the white sand beaches north and west of it are more appealing for swimming. Best of them is the sandy stretch in front of Nisbet Plantation, with just enough surf for nonsurfers and more than enough fine white sand to suit sun worshipers. It is often strewn with driftwood in all sorts of exotic shapes.

SPECIAL PLACES: Charlestown is a miniature West Indian port whose life revolves around the midmorning arrival of the ferry from St. Kitts, 2 miles away. Since almost everything Nevisians want or need has to be imported, a small crowd gathers every day (except Thursdays and Sundays) at about 10 AM to wait for the boat's wares to be unloaded and transferred to the open market on the waterfront. The best way to begin exploring is by joining the waiting group on the long public pier that is crowned with a sign proudly bidding visitors "Welcome to Nevis: Birthplace of Alexander Hamilton."

Charlestown – A walking tour of the town needn't take more than an hour, but it often does. Nevisians are friendly and outgoing, so pausing to return a greeting or chat, you can lose track of time. Don't fight it. The conversations are more interesting than most local monuments. When you're ready, leave the pier, turn right at the old Cotton House and Ginnery and stroll through the marketplace. Make a left on Prince William Street and follow along to Memorial Square, a cordoned-off area dedicated to the dead of World Wars I and II. The coral stone building with the box-shaped clock tower overlooking the Square is the Court House (downstairs) and Public Library (upstairs). If you're planning to drive on the island and haven't yet gotten your local driver's license, detour right on Main Street to call at the Police Station. Otherwise, turn left for the heart of town, which is roughly three blocks long. Turn right on Happy Hill Alley and follow your nose to the Nevis Bakery for bread, warm from the oven. Then carry on down Main Street to the Customs House (handsome wall maps for sale here) and the Nevis Philatelic Bureau, where stamps are one of the island's popular souvenir buys. A block farther, the site of the Alexander Hamilton House is the town's most interesting stop for most Americans. The old gate and steps now lead up to a replica

of the original greathouse, surrounded by a peach to pink to purple range of bougainvil-
lea, hibiscus, and poinciana trees. The Alexander Hamilton Museum is downstairs; the
Nevisian House of Assembly meets upstairs. Farther down Main Street stands St.
Paul's Church, first built in the 17th century and rebuilt several times since.

At the other end of town, St. Thomas Church (c. 1640), has also been reincarnated
several times after earthquakes and hurricanes. There's also an old Jewish Cemetery
at the corner of Jews Street and Government Road.

ELSEWHERE ON THE ISLAND

Roads climbing inland up the sides of Mt. Nevis are tricky, rutted, and best left to
intrepid island drivers. The best sightseeing route is the good (relatively) main road that
circles the island. Virtually all Nevis' remaining landmarks lie along it; more important,
so do vistas and ruins that give you a sense of the days when sugar plantations and Sea
Island cotton flourished and Nevis was Queen of the Caribbees. Plan to stop for lunch
or a picnic and swim at *Pinney's Beach* or *Nisbet Plantation*. And drive defensively.
Even on the main drag you're likely to round a curve and suddenly find yourself
tailgating a flock of skittery goats, a sauntering donkey, or a slow-rolling cart —
none of which is much concerned with yielding your share of the road.

Heading north from Charlestown and proceeding clockwise, you'll come to:

Pinney's Beach – One of the island's best. The reef-protected waters are clear and
fine for swimming and snorkeling. There are 3 miles of sand for tanning and walking.
Don't leave without discovering the sleepy lagoon (very *South Pacific*) that lies through
the palms at the beach's windward edge.

Cotton Ground – A village whose chief claim to fame is Nelson's Spring, with its
lagoon, where the admiral is said to have replenished the freshwater supply of his
flagship *Boreas*.

Fort Ashby – Overlooking the site of Jamestown, a settlement that slid into the sea
when a tidal wave hit the coast in 1680.

Black Sand Beach and Hurricane Hill – The view from the top of the latter takes
in St. Kitts and Barbuda.

Newcastle – A tumbled old village near the airport.

Nisbet Plantation – A restored greathouse-hotel that serves good island lunches,
overlooks an elegant, formal sea vista lined with grass lawns and tall palms, and has
a gorgeous beach where — as at all Nevis beaches and restored greathouses — you're
welcome to stop, sup, and swim (phone: 5325).

Eden Brown Estate – Now a gaunt, gray ruin, this estate was built and elegantly
furnished by a wealthy planter for his daughter, but deserted after her fiancé and his
best man killed each other in a drunken duel on the eve of the wedding.

New River Estate – Nevis' last operating sugar mill ceased operation in 1956, but
it comes to working life again when Melford O'Flaherty tells its story. He'll be glad
to show you around.

Montpelier Estate – Now a hotel site (the original gateposts stand), this was the
scene of the marriage of "Horatio Nelson, Esquire, Captain of his Majesty's Ship, the
Boreas, to Frances Herbert Nisbet, Widow," on March 11, 1787. So reads the entry
on a tattered page of the register displayed in St. John's Church, Fig Tree Village. The
scrawled signature below is that of the Duke of Clarence — later William IV of England — who witnessed the ceremony. The sexton in attendance can be coaxed to say
a few words about the Nelson-Nisbet nuptials; but he'd rather talk about Sunday's
hymns, or the church itself, or the mossy old graveyard where stones date back to 1682.

Lord Nelson Museum – At Morning Star, a small house filled with an astonishingly
complete collection of mementos of the great admiral and his famous friends.

Bath House – The remains of a 19th-century watering place that put Nevis on the
map as "the West Indian spa" for more than 100 years. Its social life was the talk of

the islands, and its guest list included not only British gentry from all over the Caribbean but European nobility as well. Six mineral-steeped spa baths have been restored and are now open for visitors' use, and there is speculation that the massive hotel, which is still standing, may be restored as well.

■**EXTRA SPECIAL:** A visit to *Dame Eva Wilkins's Studio* at Clay Ghaut, near Montpelier in Gingerland, St. George's Parish. Dame Eva, a painter, has worked on Nevis for more than 50 years. Her studio is in the stone mill of what was the last fully functioning sugar estate on the island. Her paintings of island people, flowers, and scenes are strong, exciting, and priced like investments rather than souvenirs (from about $100 and up for a small original); the prints, produced in England, are quite reasonable (about $30 and up). And the woman herself is fascinating. Anyone on the island can direct you. It's considerate to call ahead.

SOURCES AND RESOURCES

 TOURIST INFORMATION: Contact the St. Kitts–Nevis Tourist Board, 414 E 75th St., New York, NY 10021 (phone: 212-535-1234), or the Caribbean Tourism Association, 20 E 46th St., New York, NY 10017 (phone: 212-682-0435), for brochures and current rate sheets. If they're out of literature on a place that especially interests you, write directly, air mail (39¢ US), to the hotel given in *Checking In* below (because the island is so small, the establishment, town, and island are all the address necessary); or ask your travel agent to fill you in.

Local Coverage – No newspapers or tourist periodicals are published on Nevis. Island papers are occasionally ferried over from St. Kitts, but on no regular schedule. If you're going to do any exploring, *A Motoring Guide to Nevis,* available at the Tourist Bureau (Main St., Charlestown; phone: 5494), is worth its $3.25 price. For background reading, try to get *Gorgeous Isle,* a novel by Margaret Aithurson, and Carola Oman's biography, *Nelson.*

Telephone – You can dial direct to Nevis by adding the area code 809 and the prefix 465 to the numbers given below.

 ENTRY REQUIREMENTS: Proof of citizenship (a driver's license is not acceptable) and a ticket for return or ongoing transportation are required for US, Canadian, and United Kingdom citizens. You need a visa only if you plan to stay six months or longer. Don't forget that, like St. Kitts, there is a $13 EC, or approximately $5 US, departure tax.

 CLIMATE AND CLOTHES: Nevis' temperature ranges from 70° to 90° F (about 21° to 33° C) all year. But even though the island is cooled by trade winds, it can be uncomfortably humid during the summer months. There is no rainy season as such, but when showers come, they come in torrents for an hour or two. Casual, comfortable, summer sports clothes are the daytime norm; cottons and cotton blends are coolest. Swim clothes are worn only at the beach or pool; you'll want a shirt or a coverup at lunchtime or when you've had enough sun. At night, jackets and ties are never required for men, but something about the greathouse atmosphere makes many women enjoy dressing up a bit in long (but casual) skirts, caftans, or summer evening dresses.

 MONEY: Official currency is the Eastern Caribbean dollar (EC) valued at about $2.65 to $1 US. Though most prices are quoted in $ EC, US and Canadian bills are generally accepted. Foreign coins, on the other hand, are hard for islanders to exchange. So it's a good idea to have small-denomination EC money handy for small purchases and coin tipping. Banks are open from 8 AM till noon daily, except Saturdays and Sundays, and 3:30 to 5:30 PM on Fridays only. But don't strain to get to the bank to exchange currency since you'll usually be given equally good rates by hotels and shops.

 LANGUAGE: The Queen's English — with an island lilt.

 TIME: Nevis runs on Atlantic Standard Time all year. So in winter, when it's noon in Boston or New York City, it's 1 PM in Charlestown. When the US goes on Daylight Saving Time, noon in New York is noon in Nevis, too.

 CURRENT: Electricity is 230 volts, which means that if you have American appliances, you'll need a converter. Bring it with you.

 GETTING THERE: From the North American mainland to Newcastle Airport on Nevis, you'll travel fastest via St. Kitts and the neighboring island of Antigua, or via San Juan, Puerto Rico, using LIAT or BWIA from Antigua as a connection. American Airlines flies from New York to St. Kitts with connections via LIAT (schedule according to season). Carib Aviation offers charters from Antigua. Coastal Air flies from St. Croix; Winair, from St. Maarten. Round-trip air fare from St. Kitts is about $30. It's about $3 by the ferry, which makes several trips daily except Thursdays and Sundays.

 CALCULATING COSTS: Double rates at the best former greathouses run about $150 to $200 a night for two, including breakfasts and dinners (MAP) — at the height of the season (mid-December to mid-April). During the rest of the year they're about $95 and up MAP. Since there are no full-fledged tourist restaurants, there's very little eating out, except for an occasional lunch (figure $10 to $15 per person including a drink). A few package trips are available. There is a 7% government tax on rooms and a standard 10% service charge in lieu of gratuities.

 GETTING AROUND: Taxi – There's little resemblance to the yellow honk-and-hack metropolitan cabs of the mainland. The system here is really car-and-driver, very personal and individual. Each hotel has its cadre of regulars, and most will send a driver to meet you at the airport and add the charge (about $6) to your bill.

Bus – Between villages, but schedules are sketchy, and few tourists use them. For the small amount of traveling about most visitors do, taxis are much easier.

Car Rental – Mostly Mini-Mokes, baby British jeeps admirably capable of handling rocky island roads. Easily arranged — ask your hotel to set it up. Going rate is about $25 to $40 US a day with unlimited mileage and a full tank of gas to start you off (generally you won't need a refill). You'll need a Nevis driver's license, which you can get at the Police Station in Charlestown for about $8. And remember to keep left!

Sightseeing Taxi Tours – Simple to negotiate. Your hotel will find you a driver. Rates are about $30 for a 3½-hour tour (including lunch stop) plus $8 for each additional hour for a car that holds up to four people. There are no sightseeing bus companies.

Calvin Ward, a taxi driver usually found at *Croney's Old Manor,* a charming man with a good grasp of island history, is available for island tours. He's generous with his knowledge, ditto his rates, which are negotiable according to how much you want to see and how long you want to spend. Figure about $20 for his car and services for half a day.

Sea Excursions – Strictly plan-it-yourself. The ferry sails for St. Kitts twice daily except Thursdays and Sundays. Round-trip fare runs about $6 per person; there's time for lunch and a look around the island.

Local Air Service – Trips to St. Kitts are arranged by *Four Islands Air* for about $26 US per person each way. LIAT handles reservations. *Carib Aviation,* a charter operator, charges $240 per plane (9 seats) one way.

SHOPPING: *The Arcade* has a few new shops, but, unfortunately, predictable souvenir ashtrays and Nevis T-shirts plus fairly routine island craft work (shell and straw, mostly) predominate. The *Nevis Handicraft Co-operative Society,* Lower Happy Hill Alley in Charlestown, offers the widest selection; the *Nevis Craft Studio* is another good source. *Yellow Shutters* is also worth looking into. *Shoreline Crafts* features shell and coral jewelry, crafts, paintings, plus a verandah where you can sip local drinks before, after, or while you shop. *Caribbean Confections* concocts fresh tropical fruit ice creams for immediate consumption and offers baskets of jams, jellies, and candies to take home.

Caribbee Clothes, off Main Street in Charlestown, is home base for the firm famous for its embroidered sunburst trademark on good-looking island sports things for men, women, and kids. A full range is available here, but inexplicably — at last check — prices were higher in Nevis than in the Virgin Islands.

Mrs. Jones, the last house on the right going east out of Newcastle, is the bougainvillea-garlanded home and shop of an elderly island lady who makes and sells attractive, unglazed pottery — from tiny terra cotta birds to oversized clay pots — at reasonable prices. On a larger scale, the *Newcastle Pottery,* just east of the airport, not only offers gift items and cooking pots, but invites you to watch them made and fired over the flames from burning coconut shells.

Hot item: Nevis hot pepper sauce, among the Caribbean's best, is a good souvenir for your own kitchen and fire-eating friends. It's about $1 at the *Main Street Grocery,* Charlestown. The lady in charge will gladly run 'round the corner to the lady who makes it for another bottle if the store's stock is low.

TIPPING: The 10% service charge added to your hotel bill takes care of everybody at the hotel. There are no airport porters. In restaurants, leave 10% to 15%, and tip taxi drivers 10% of the fare.

SPECIAL EVENTS: *Carnival* — December 24 to January 2 — is the Big One, with parades, pageants, and parties basically planned for home folks and homecoming relatives, which lends them a special unhokey charm. But all island visitors are genuinely and cordially welcome to party along whenever they please. Summer's *Culturama* (late July, early August) brings calypso shows, dances, parties, and special events. Legal holidays include *New Year's Day, Carnival Day, Good Friday, Easter Monday, Labour Day* (first Monday in May), *Whitmonday, the Queen's Birthday* (early June), *August Monday* (first Monday in August), *Independence Day* (September 19), *Christmas,* and *Boxing Day* (December 26).

SPORTS: Horseback Riding – English saddle is available on the premises at *Nisbet Plantation.* Other hotels arrange for guests to ride there, through Ira Dore (phone: 5528), or at the *Big "H" Stables* at Cane Gardens (phone: 5389). Charge, including a guide, is about $20 per person for a 1½-hour ride.

Horse Racing – There are races three times a year at the oval near Charlestown: Easter Monday, the first Monday in August (August Monday), and Boxing Day (December 26).

Mountain Climbing – Climbing to the top of Mt. Nevis, though not strenuous, takes the better part of a day, round-trip. Your hotel will pack a lunch and — if you like — get a guide, who'll ask about $25 for two people.

Sport Fishing – The going rate for sport fishing is about $80 for a half day and $160 for a full day. The waters are good for kingfish, bonita, snapper, and grouper.

Swimming – All beaches are public. Pinney's Beach on the Caribbean side is the longest and the best. The island's inns have private cabanas here for guests. Just up the coast is Oualie Beach at Mosquito Bay, which has a good water sports setup and casual beachside pub. Of the inns, only *Nisbet Plantation,* on the north tip of the island, is on a beach. The others have large swimming pools, usually well placed for views, and offer free beach transportation.

Tennis – There is 1 court each at *Nisbet Plantation, Golden Rock, Montpelier, Zetland Plantation, Cliffdwellers,* and *Rest Haven.*

Water Sports – *Oaulie Beach Pub* (phone: 5329) rents Sunfish, Hobie Cats, windsurfers, and surf jets (waterborne snowmobiles); and arranges water skiing, fishing, and snorkeling trips and day sails. *Golden Rock* has two small boats for guests' use; *Montpelier,* one. Scuba facilities are available through *Nisbet Plantation Inn,* with arrangements at *Ocean Terrace Inn,* St. Kitts. Snorkeling is best off reef-protected Pinney's Beach. The waters off Fort Ashby, where the settlement of Jamestown is said to have slid into the sea, are also intriguing.

 NIGHTLIFE: Hotels occasionally have steel or string bands for dancing on different nights during the season. *Pinney's Beach* and *Zetland Plantation* are where the big island parties happen (visitors welcome). Otherwise, all's quiet on the Nevisian fronts.

BEST ON THE ISLAND

 CHECKING IN: Accommodations on Nevis consist of inns that range from small to tiny (of those we recommend, the largest has exactly 30 rooms). So it's not surprising that most innkeepers would describe their places as "more of a house party, really." Guests who meet for the first time over after-dinner drinks often end up planning an outing together for the next day, and by the end of the week plans may be set to vacation together the following year. Despite that commonality, the inns have rather distinct personalities: *Zetland Plantation* and *Montpelier Plantation Inn,* for instance, are very English; *Golden Rock Estate* and *Nisbet Plantation Inn* are more American.

Much of the attraction of these inns lies in their origins as sugar plantations. A walk around the grounds with a knowledgeable owner as guide brings the plantation culture into sharp focus. (*Montpelier* and *Golden Rock* are the best preserved.) What's left of the estate buildings has been restored for use as public areas: dining rooms, bars, lounges, libraries. Except for a few accommodations in converted sugar mills, guestrooms are in bungalows of unmistakable mid-20th century design. Though comfortable, they're not especially distinctive.

Room rates that include breakfast and dinner (Modified American Plan) are the rule on Nevis. Generally, laundry, beach transportation, and sports facilities are included, too. For a double room described as expensive, expect to pay $180 and up in winter, $120 and up in summer. Those listed as moderate charge about $150 in winter, $95 in summer.

GINGERLAND

Golden Rock Estate – Old plantation buildings have been converted into 15 pleasant guest rooms that form the core of this inn. The bar, for instance, occupies the open hearth of the old kitchen. There's enough left of the old plant to get a good idea of plantation life, and the innkeeper is more than happy to fill in the gaps. The rooms, in cottages around the estate, are large and pleasant; the bamboo used to make the distinctive four-poster beds comes right off the property. The inn has a tennis court, a good-size swimming pool, and beach properties on leeward and windward sides, with free shuttle service for guests (phone: 469-5346). Expensive.

Zetland Plantation – The views from this perch 1,500 feet up the windward slope of Mt. Nevis are special, and the 21 big, attractive suites, housed in pretty pastel, white-trimmed cottages spaced around the grounds, certainly take advantage of them. There's also an inviting swimming pool and tennis court, two restaurants, and two bars. Guests use Pinney's Beach, where the *Plantation* maintains a beach club. EP rates are also available (phone: 469-5454, 800-638-4794, or 800-243-2654). Moderate.

ELSEWHERE ON THE ISLAND

Cliffdwellers – This is no fanciful appellation: The inn's 14 cottages cling to a hillside that affords spectacular views of St. Kitts, the coconut groves along the beach, and Mt. Nevis. At the top of the hill is an attractive restaurant and lounge, serving excellent seafood and Continental fare; at the foot, a gargantuan swimming pool and a small beachfront. Connecting the two is a thatch-roofed tram. The rooms, one to a building, are enormous, with canopied beds, spacious sitting areas, large dressing rooms, and long terraces. Tamarind Bay (phone: 469-5262). Expensive.

Montpelier Plantation Inn – This is the prettiest of the old estate inns, full of brick walkways through lovely gardens that dramatically demonstrate what marvels can result from marrying the English zeal for gardening with tropical fecundity. At the center is a truly elegant old greathouse with 16 rooms. The inn raises its own lamb and chicken and turns out bountiful meals. It has its own windsurfer and speedboat for water skiing, fishing, and snorkeling trips. There's an attractive pool, tennis court, and transportation to the inn's private cabana on Pinney's Beach. Montpelier (phone: 469-5462, 800-243-9420, or 203-438-3793). Expensive.

Nisbet Plantation Inn – On the site of an 18th-century plantation, with a long alley of coconut palms running from the manor house to the inn's white sand beach; on either side are the cottages, with attractive bedrooms and small screened-in sitting areas. The manor house is where everybody congregates — in the bar, the sunny, comfortable lounge, the antique-filled dining room, where excellent West Indian and Continental cuisine is served at dinner. There's a casual beachside restaurant for breakfast and lunch; horseback riding, a tennis court, lawn croquet. Newcastle (phone: 469-5325 or 218-722-5059). Expensive.

Croney's Old Manor – A restored sugar plantation with 10 spacious rooms and one of the best dining rooms on the island. The swimming pool rests among old buildings that have high ceilings and marble floors (phone: 469-5445 or 800-223-9815). Moderate.

Hermitage Plantation – One of the newest inns in one of the oldest buildings, dating back to 1740. Richard and Maureen Lupinacci have been busy adding rooms and a swimming pool, but without disturbing the mountainside views or the lush foliage. This charming inn now has 9 double rooms, including 7 with small kitchenettes, all with lovely canopy beds and antiques. Ceiling fans keep rooms cool without disturbing the ambience. Pool; elegant dining room with local cuisine worth sampling (phone: 809-465-5477). Moderate.

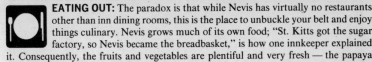

EATING OUT: The paradox is that while Nevis has virtually no restaurants other than inn dining rooms, this is the place to unbuckle your belt and enjoy things culinary. Nevis grows much of its own food; "St. Kitts got the sugar factory, so Nevis became the breadbasket," is how one innkeeper explained it. Consequently, the fruits and vegetables are plentiful and very fresh — the papaya you have for breakfast is likely to have come from a tree outside your door. Likewise, the fish is of the just-caught variety. And good raw materials inspire good cooking. Whether at an inn or a casual beachside pub, the quality of the food is unusually high.

The inns are MAP only, which means breakfast and dinner are included in the daily rate. You'll do fine if you stay put, but if you want to sample fare at other inns, join them for lunch or for special dinners, such as *Golden Rock*'s weekly lobster cookout on Pinney's Beach, when the lobster comes straight off the fishing boats. All of the inns stage such affairs — either cookouts or West Indian buffets. Call and find out when and where. Don't miss *Croney's Old Manor Estate* (phone: 5445). The fare any night is likely to be memorable — green pepper soup, light and creamy cheesecake, fruit sorbets and ice creams (cream, not available on the island, is flown in 12 quarts at a time). But the Friday night steak and lobster cookout, accompanied by a buffet of several kinds of vegetables and salads, is a real treat. So is the Sunday champagne brunch.

Outside the inns, choices are limited. *Zetland Beach Club* on Pinney's Beach is good for a light lunch; so is *Oualie Beach Pub* on Mosquito Bay. In Charlestown, try the local favorites, *The Arcade, Judy's,* or *Longstone Bar and Restaurant.*

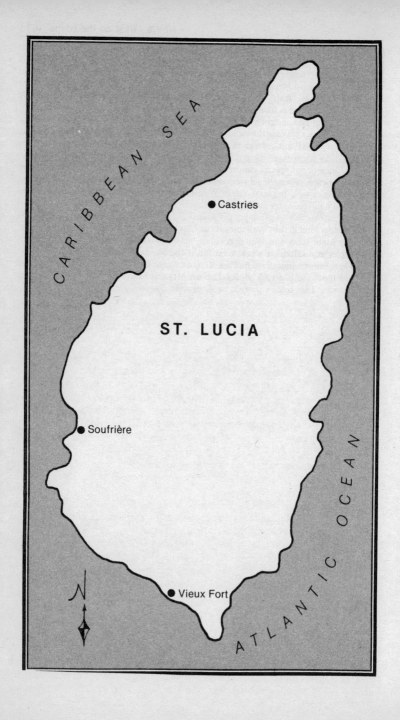

ST. LUCIA

To know where St. Lucia is located is to be able to guess a good deal about its traumatic and tempestuous past. Midway between Martinique, the French Windward Island to its north, and St. Vincent, the British Windward Island to its south (which shares St. Lucia's historic British ties), St. Lucia has spent a good part of the last 300 years bouncing between Britain and France as those two countries fought to a bloody draw over ownership and control of the entire West Indies.

What you could not know unless you'd been here is the intoxicating beauty of the island. Shaped like a fat tear sliding down the face of the Caribbean, it has some of the most magnificent shoreline in the entire island chain; remote Marigot Bay, as beautiful a sea cove as exists in the world; inland jungles with two lushly forested mountains, the Pitons, whose peaks serve as markers for any mariner headed for the island's western harbors. And it has a quiescent (but still bubbling) volcano, Mt. Soufrière, which tourists can visit and in the crater of which they can amble among smoking sulfur pits and gurgling mudholes.

The peaceful Arawak Indians apparently arrived on the island hundreds of years ago. Remains of their villages have been found on Pigeon Point, just off St. Lucia's northern tip (today joined to St. Lucia by a causeway). It is uncertain whether they actually settled on St. Lucia itself, although if they did they certainly didn't stay. They had come initially to escape the Carib Indians, whose restless expansion across the Caribbean was like a plague of locusts to indigenous Indian groups. Soon enough they arrived at St. Lucia, and it was Caribs — not Arawaks — whom the Spanish found when they discovered the island.

Just when that was is open to debate. The island celebrates December 13, 1502, as its discovery day; but the French have a counter claim based on a colony of shipwrecked French sailors who found their way to the island at about the same time. French maps of the early 1600s include the island under the name Sainte Alouise, or Sainte Alouize. However, a Vatican globe of 1520 carries the island with the name Santa Lucia, and a Spanish map from 1529 calls the island S. Luzia.

In 1605, a small group of English settlers aboard the *Olive Blossom* (or *Olive Branch* by some accounts), en route to the Guianas, was blown off course and landed on St. Lucia. They purchased huts from the Carib tribe that inhabited the Vieux Fort Bay area where they had come ashore, and the two groups settled down to a short life together. Within five weeks, only 19 of the original 67 Englishmen remained alive. These survivors procured a canoe from the neighboring Caribs and departed for Venezuela.

During the next 200 years, the island changed hands between the French and the English more than ten times. When the two countries were not strictly at war, they were conniving with the Caribs — who became free-floating agents playing both ends against the middle — to make war on one another. During the French Revolution, the British took possession of the small island, but found that French republican terrorists made the island difficult to control. The British garrison was forced to abandon the island but was later able to land a force of 12,000 troops and retake the island in May 1796. The Treaty of Amiens, in March 1802, awarded the island to the French; but by June of 1803, the two countries were at war again, and an invading English force stormed the fortifications on Morne Fortune with fixed bayonets and recaptured the island.

The island had its longest and most peaceful period of growth during the 1800s, although the abolition of slavery prevented the island's economy from developing as fully as plantation cultures had on several other islands. The early wars prevented the establishment of large, family-controlled plantations so that much of the land on St. Lucia has never been subjected to the harsh methods of the early plantation owners.

The island remained under British control until 1967, when St. Lucia became an independent state in association with Great Britain; on February 22, 1979, it was granted full sovereignty and became a full-fledged member of the British Commonwealth.

But it is not this active and colorful history that draws visitors from all over the world; it is the remarkable beauty of the island. From the elevated heights of Moule-a-Chique, below the plains of Vieux Fort, it is possible to see across the channel to St. Vincent. From the peak of Morne Fortune, near Castries, Martinique is visible, and the battlegrounds at Vigie Peninsula, Gros Islet, and Pigeon Island compose a panorama of time and space as you remember the people who fought and died to establish homes here.

And it is the lushness and beauty of the island that make so many people willing to invest their lives and energies to live here. Its bamboo forests, towering 15, 18, even 25 feet into the air, the tropical rain forests, the giant ferns and colorful parrots and hummingbirds, and the open-pit volcano of Mt. Soufrière still attract new settlers. It is the solitude of places like Marigot Bay, or Anse Chastanet on its cliffside above the Caribbean, that these new settlers are seeking. It seems that St. Lucia is finally undergoing the development and growth it was never given a chance to achieve during its violent earlier years. The growth of tourist facilities and immigration are proceeding at a controlled rate, and there has been some industrial growth to support the new economy. Yet, in spite of "progress," St. Lucia retains a unique sense of simplicity and pride that have earned it its deserved reputation as one of the "still unspoiled" islands surviving in the Caribbean today.

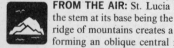

ST. LUCIA AT-A-GLANCE

FROM THE AIR: St. Lucia is almond- or palm-shaped, almost like a leaf, the stem at its base being the peninsula of Moule-a-Chique. Its Barre de l'Ile ridge of mountains creates a watershed and divides the island horizontally, forming an oblique central rib with the network of rivers carrying water down the slopes, like the veins of the leaf. The island's mountainous terrain is softened in appearance by a gentle covering of banana trees, giant ferns, bamboo, and other tropical trees and flowering plants. The highest peak is Mt. Gimie, 3,145 feet, but more prominent are the twin half-mile-tall volcanic cones called the Pitons.

The view from the sea, approaching St. Lucia's southwest coast, is what mariners and day-tripping vacationers remember most about the island. To the left, Petit Piton stands straight up from the Caribbean to the height of 2,460 feet; on the right, Gros Piton rises to 2,619 feet. In between is Jalousie Bay, or Anse de Pitons, where an elephant — left here after an unsuccessful attempt, some years back, at developing an adventure/safari park — sometimes roams the shore:

Lying between 60°53′ and 61°05′ W longitude and 13°43′ and 14°7′ N latitude, St. Lucia is 25 miles south of Martinique, separated by a channel 4,500 feet deep, and 20 miles north of St. Vincent, with a channel 2,000 feet deep between. From New York it is about 2,020 miles to St. Lucia.

 SPECIAL PLACES: Although steeped in history and crowded with historical sites, the real attraction of St. Lucia is its vivid natural beauty — black and white sand beaches, lush green foliage, rocky volcanic mountains and flowering plants that bloom in almost every color of the rainbow.

Castries – The capital city of the island, with its major port, a harbor within the flooded crater of an extinct volcano. Its architecture is basically modern, the effect of severe fires in 1948 and 1951, which swept through the older buildings in the town. Early French and British buildings have been replaced with bland low-rise concrete or steel constructions that convey nothing of the island's history or outlook. Still, it's a lively West Indian town. The morning market is still very active, especially on Saturdays. It fills up with small farmers and home industry workers, and everybody is selling — willing to trade something.

Plantain, mango, pawpaw (papaya), dasheen, breadfruit, and fresh cloves are among the foodstuffs you can expect to see being bartered and sold. The fish market is an informal cluster of boats that gather at the harborside.

Just behind the city rises Morne Fortune, from whose heights both the French and the British alternately defended the island and its port and whose slopes they alternately charged in hopes of final victory. At the crest of the hill stands Fort Charlotte, an 18th-century fortress that changed hands about a dozen times during the years of English-French colonial warfare. The stone buildings of the French occupation forces contrast with those of the British, who built their structures of brick. Constant change of ownership resulted in a hodgepodge of materials and styles, and many buildings started by one side were completed or repaired by the other. It's not so much history that lures visitors to the crest of Morne Fortune as the view from its peak — north to Pigeon Island, south to the Pitons, and a tremendous panorama of the harbor at Castries and of the Vigie peninsula. Vigie itself was the site of two major battles — both of them victories for the British.

ELSEWHERE ON THE ISLAND

Pigeon Point – North of Castries off the west coast. Formerly an island, now it is linked by a causeway to the town of Gros Islet. The ruins of Rodney's Fort are here, and it was from this island (which, by the way, gets its name from Rodney's hobby of breeding pigeons) that Rodney's fleet sailed to intercept the French in the Dominica Passage, resulting in the Battle of the Saintes. A short distance north of Pigeon Point, at its very tip, is Cap Estate, the site of a land development, as well as of the *Cariblue* hotel and a golf course. On a clear day, it is possible to see Martinique from the gentle hills of the Cap area.

Marigot Bay – On the west coast, south of Castries, is a yachtsman's haven and the scene of parts of Rex Harrison's film of Dr. Dolittle's exploits. Most of the palm-lined shore remains primitive and undeveloped, while some sections are being sold as building plots. It is still one of the most beautiful coves on the entire Caribbean. Just a few miles south along the coast is the little fishing village of Anse La Raye, where fishermen repair their nets and gut their catch on the beach and workmen still build canoes in much the same manner as Carib warriors 400 years ago. A little farther south, just below the midpoint of the island, the village of Canaries lies where one of the island's many rivers meets the sea. Here native women can be seen washing their clothing in the river, beating the fabric against the rocks to clean it, and later drying the clothes under the tropical sun.

Just inland from Marigot Bay itself are two of the three large banana plantations on the island. Cul-de-Sac is slightly north of the bay, the Roseau Estate just to the south. Both are open to visitors, who are free to wander in from the road.

Soufrière – On the west coast of the island, about a third of the way from the southern tip, is the village of Soufrière, St. Lucia's second largest city. From here, too, fishermen still put out to sea, casting homemade nets, in the same kind of narrow dugout canoes used in this area for generations. Beyond the town, past the hill of green vines and trees which helped to hide the town from attackers, lie the Pitons standing over half a mile high, stretching from the shore of the Caribbean. From the sea, they appear to rise up from the crests of the waves that crash against their bases. They are actually remains of the island's once-active volcanoes and are formed from lava and rock, coated with fertile volcanic topsoil and tropical forest.

Mt. Soufrière – A dormant volcano near the town encompasses a rocky moonscape of pits and open craters of boiling sulfur, bubbling grayish-yellow mud. A walk through the area, with its clouds of sulfur-reeking mist and intense earth-born heat, is like a visit to Dante's Inferno. Here are also some natural sulfur baths, spring-fed pools of heated waters, containing traces of sulfur and other minerals. A sample sent to King Louis XVI was found to have a mineral content similiar to the waters at the baths of Aix-la-Chapelle. The natural baths at neighboring Diamond Falls are cooler and sweeter smelling.

Moule-a-Chique – From this mountain peak you can look down upon the Caribbean's distinct blue-green waters as they mix with the Atlantic's very different blue, or look southward, slightly west, toward the nearby island of St. Vincent.

SOURCES AND RESOURCES

TOURIST INFORMATION: The St. Lucia Tourist Board, 41 E 42nd St., New York, NY 10017 (phone: 212-867-2950), supplies information, literature, and maps.

The St. Lucia Tourist Board office is on Sans Souci in Castries (phone: 2-5968). There are also visitors information centers at the Northern Wharf, where cruise ships dock, at Pointe Seraphine, and at Vigie and Hewanorra airports. All the offices dispense printed information, maps, and literature — all free. They also will provide (if any are available) a booklet on native talk, *Visitor's Guide to St. Lucia Patois,* as well as an island foods cookbook and the free, informative, official guide, *St. Lucia Visitor.*

Local Coverage – There are two local papers, *The Crusader* and *Voice of St. Lucia;* the *New York Times* is also available.

Telephone – Dial direct to St. Lucia by adding the area code 809 and the prefix 45 to the numbers below.

ENTRY REQUIREMENTS: US and Canadian citizens need only a passport or proof of citizenship, plus photo ID and a return or ongoing ticket.

CLIMATE AND CLOTHES: In winter, temperatures range between 65° and 85°; in summer, between 75° and 95°. Summers tend to be a little rainy, but winters are dry. Summer clothing is worn all year; cottons are prevalent. Women will want blouses and skirts, shorts, slacks, and long skirts, pants, tops, or caftans for evenings. Short shorts or bathing suits should not be worn into town. Men favor casual resortwear for the daytimes. Jackets and occasionally ties are required only at the larger hotels in the winter season.

MONEY: St. Lucia uses the Eastern Caribbean dollar, which exchanges at the rate of $1 US to about $2.70 EC ($2.50 in hotels and stores). Island banking hours are 8 AM to noon on weekdays and 3 to 5 PM on Fridays; closed weekends and holidays. US and Canadian dollars are accepted by stores, restaurants, and hotels, as are traveler's checks and most major credit cards (check when making reservations for meals or accommodations).

LANGUAGE: English is the official tongue of St. Lucia, and it is spoken by almost all the inhabitants. A French-Créole patois, similiar to that of Guadaloupe and Martinique, is also spoken.

TIME: St. Lucia is on Atlantic Standard Time all year: When it's noon in New York, it's 1 PM in St. Lucia. During Daylight Saving Time, it is the same time in both places.

CURRENT: Electricity is 220–230 volts, 50 cycles, AC. Most hotels have provisions for electric shavers; however, converters will be needed for hair dryers and other small appliances.

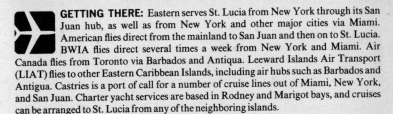

GETTING THERE: Eastern serves St. Lucia from New York through its San Juan hub, as well as from New York and other major cities via Miami. American flies direct from the mainland to San Juan and then on to St. Lucia. BWIA flies direct several times a week from New York and Miami. Air Canada flies from Toronto via Barbados and Antiqua. Leeward Islands Air Transport (LIAT) flies to other Eastern Caribbean Islands, including air hubs such as Barbados and Antigua. Castries is a port of call for a number of cruise lines out of Miami, New York, and San Juan. Charter yacht services are based in Rodney and Marigot bays, and cruises can be arranged to St. Lucia from any of the neighboring islands.

CALCULATING COSTS: St. Lucia offers a choice of luxury and first-class resorts at rates that range from $100 to over $200 per day without meals, during the winter season. Apartment units are available for about $60 to $100 without meals. Rates drop 30% to 50% during the summer season. Many hotels will add a 10% service charge to these rates, and there is an 8% tax. Dinner for two in one of the island's better restaurants could run as high as $60, without drinks, tax, or tip, but there are good, reasonably priced restaurants, too. There is an airport tax of about $7.50 US or $20 EC.

GETTING AROUND: Taxi – Unmetered, but rates are fixed by the government, and a list of point-to-point fares is available from the tourist office. Some sample fares: Vigie Airport to *La Toc* hotel, about $8; to the main shopping center, about $5. It's an hour's drive from Hewanorra Airport, the island's international airport, to the hotels in the Castries area; the cost runs about $30 to $35 per car. It is quicker and not much more expensive to make the trip by plane from Hewanorra to Vigie Airport; *Winlink* (phone: 2-2622) provides air shuttle service between the two. St. Lucia taxi drivers are very friendly and good guides and have been trained to show and tell visitors about their island. Rates per person for a party of two run $15 US to $20 for a half-day tour; $25 to $30 for a full-day tour.

Car Rental – Costs about $35 to $45 per day plus mileage charge, usually with the first 30 to 50 miles free. Agencies, which often have desks at the resorts, include *Cenac's* (phone: 2-3295), *Hertz-U-Drive* (phone: 2-4777), *National* (phone: 2-8721), and *Sun Drive*, an *Avis* agency (phone: 2-2700), as well as *St. Lucia Yacht Services* (phone: 2-5057). International licenses honored, or a St. Lucia driver's license can be obtained for about $7.50 by presenting a valid American or Canadian license to the Traffic Department on Bridge St. in Castries.

Sightseeing Bus Tours – Several tour operators in Castries offer guided half- and full-day tours. The travel desk at any hotel can help with arrangements for excursions. *Carib Touring* (phone: 2-3184) offers a 3½-hour tour of Castries, Morne Fortune, and Marigot Bay, lunch at *Rain,* and visits to a perfume factory, *Bagshaws* printed fabric shop, and a rum punch at *Hotel La Toc,* for about $17 per person. *Carib* offers a 7-hour tour to Soufrière and a tour to Pigeon Point and Cap Estate. *Fletcher's Touring Service* (phone: 2-2516), *St. Lucia Representative Services* (phone: 2-3762), and *Barnards Travel* (phone: 2-2214) offer comparable packages. For a tour designed to your own interests, call Barnard Henry (phone: 2-1251 or 2-4211). You won't find a more knowledgeable or interesting guide to the island.

Sea Excursions – Most popular is the day-long sail to the Pitons with a shore trip to Soufrière's Sulphur Springs. Lunch, drinks, swim and snorkeling stop, plus steel band music en route are included for about $30 per person. The square-rigged brig *Unicorn* sails from the *Coal Pot* several times a week (phone: 2-5643). The schooner *Buccaneer* makes similar trips (phone: 2-3762).

Local Air Services – Small-plane charters can be arranged with *St. Lucia Airways* (phones: 2-2686, 2-4944). *Island Helicopters* (phone: 2-8216) has tours of Castries and down the coast to the Pitons for $35 and $60 per person, respectively, with a minimum of four people.

SHOPPING: Duty-free shopping has come to St. Lucia at Pointe Seraphine, just outside Castries (reached by shuttle bus from town), where a number of shops and boutiques have opened for the benefit of cruise ship passengers, long-stay visitors, and residents. Castries' big department stores are *J. Q. Charles Ltd.,* on Bridge St., and *Cox's,* on Wm. Peter Blvd. — both are an experience to browse through. *Y. de Lima,* also on Wm. Peter Blvd., has stacks of imported china, crystal, porcelains, and jewelry; *Ruth Clarage* carries top-drawer resort fashion (stunning prints, smart cuts, some men's and children's wear). *Eudovics* is a must for top-quality local woodcarving, and *Tapion,* on La Toc Rd., offers good bargains on St. Lucian arts and crafts, including sculpture, paintings, pottery, leather, needlework, and jewelry. *The Island Connection Boutique* features casual and evening wear, swimwear, jewelry, and small gift items; the *Sea Island Cotton Shop,* on Bridge St., makes everything from wall hangings to beach wraps; *Caribelle Batik,* on Old Victoria Rd., has handsome island prints; and the *Bagshaws Studios* at La Toc is a must, even if you can resist buying the unique fabrics and fashions hand-screened on the spot. *Noah's Arkade* has quality West Indian gifts.

TIPPING: A 10% service charge is included on hotel bills, which covers bellhops, room maids, and dining room waiters. Extra tipping is called for only if some extraordinary service is performed. Restaurants add a 10% service charge to the check, which covers the waiter's tip. Cab drivers should be tipped about 10% of the fare. Airport porters depend on tips for a substantial portion of their income; tip 50¢ per bag.

 SPECIAL EVENTS: On *New Year's Day* and *January 2,* a festival in Castries' Columbus Square revives the old French celebration of *Le Jour de l'An,* with dances, picnics, and partying throughout the island. *Carnival,* usually in February, is the year's big festival, with the crowning of a Carnival Queen, dancing, costumed parades, steel band music, and calypso singing. Other holidays when most stores and businesses close are *Good Friday, Easter Monday, Whitsuntide, Corpus Christi, the Queen's Birthday* (in June), *Emancipation Day* (first Monday in August), *Thanksgiving Day* (first Monday in October), *St. Lucia Day* (December 13), *Christmas,* and *Boxing Day* (December 26). Usually held around Whitsuntide in May or early June is *Aqua Action,* a festival of boating and other water sports activities.

 SPORTS: Boating – St. Lucia, with excellent anchorages at Marigot Bay and Rodney Bay and in Castries Harbour, is rapidly growing in popularity with yachtsmen. Most hotels have Sunfish and windsurfers for loan or rent (rates about $7 to $10 per hour). Yachts can be chartered through *Stevens Yachts,* Rodney Bay (US address: 252 East Ave., East Norwalk, CT. 06855; phone: 800-638-7044; 2-8648 in St. Lucia); *The Moorings* at Marigot Bay (US address: 1305 US 19, Clearwater, FL 33456; phone: 800-535-7289; 3-4256 in St. Lucia); and *Trade Wind Yacht Charters,* PO Box 372, Rodney Bay, St. Lucia (phone: 2-8424). Rates depend on the craft and the season and on whether the boats are crewed or you sail them yourself.

Golf – There are two 9-hole courses, although neither is very challenging. *Cap Estate* (phone: 8523), at the northern tip of the island, charges an $11 greens fee. Toward the south, the *La Toc* hotel course (phone: 2-3081), with resident PGA pro Stuart Woodman, charges greens fees of about $5 for nonresident players and plans to expand to a full 18 holes. Both courses rent clubs for about $5 per day, pull carts are about $1.25, and caddies get $2 to $4.

Hiking – Nothing organized, but there are trails all over the island, and the Pitons are a time-honored climbers' challenge. None of the island's peaks should be attempted without a guide, because of frequent — and sudden — mists and rains..

Horseback Riding – At *Trims Stables* near Cap Estate; rides can be arranged through your hotel desk or by calling 2-8628. Rates run about $13 per hour.

Snorkeling and Scuba – The best reef is at Anse Chastanet, where there's also good diving right off the beach. For snorkeling and scuba equipment, reef and wreck trips, and instruction, contact *Scuba St. Lucia* at the *Anse Chastanet Beach* hotel (phone: 4-7355) or *Dive St. Lucia* on Vigie Beach (phone: 2-4127). Snorkeling equipment rents for about $4; the going rate for a snorkeling trip is about $18. Chances are, however, that your our hotel will provide snorkeling gear — and in some cases, instruction — gratis. A one-tank dive costs between $25 amd $35; a 3-hour introductory course including a shallow water dive, $45; a full certification course (through *Scuba St. Lucia* only), $300.

Spectator Sports – The cricket season runs from February through June. Football — we call it soccer — is played from July through January.

Sport Fishing – Gamefish in these waters include barracuda, mackerel, kingfish, tuna, wahoo, swordfish, sailfish, and cavalla. Fishing charters, fully equipped with fighting chairs, run about $150 up for a half day, and $280 up for a full day, for a party of six. If your hotel doesn't have boats of its own, it can make the arrangements for you.

Swimming – Beautiful white beaches edge the calm, leeward side of the island. These are the best swimming beaches; the eastern, windward side is rugged and often has rough surf that makes swimming unsafe and sometimes simply impossible. Outstanding beaches include Vigie Beach, just north of Castries Harbor, and Choc Bay, in the same area; Reduit Bay, well north along the coast from Castries; and Pigeon Island off the northern shore. To the south of the island are La Toc Bay, the black volcanic sand beach at Soufrière, and the reef-protected beaches of the Vieux Fort area. Most St. Lucia hotels are on the beach.

Tennis – The *La Toc* hotel has the best facilities, with 5 lighted courts and video-instruction pro John Easter. The *St. Lucian,* with 2 courts, also has a pro. Most hotels have at least one court or will arrange for guests to play at a nearby resort.

Water Skiing – Most hotels have the equipment available, or will arrange it for you, for about $10 US for 15 minutes, about $15 for a full hour.

Windsurfing – The *St. Lucian,* local affiliate of Windsurfing International, offers a certification course of three 1-hour lessons for $35. Most beach hotels will rent windsurfers to nonguests for about $9.50 US an hour.

 NIGHTLIFE: Most of the island's nightlife is confined to the hotels; they do have entertainment on a regular basis during the season and sometimes during the off-season. Friday night is jump-up (party) night and everyone at the north end of the island heads for Gros Islet. At Marigot Bay they head for *Hurricane Hole. Rain* stays open late some evenings, and there are shows and live entertainment several times a week at the *Green Parrot.* There is also *Fisherman's Wharf,* at the *Halcyon Beach Club,* with live music and disco on a covered jetty over the water; *Splash,* a popular disco and late night spot at the *St. Lucian* hotel; and *Beach Park Adventureland,* at Palm Beach, which is often open until the wee hours. Many discos are open only during high season, but check out *Graffiti,* at the *Vigie Beach* hotel, and *Sun September,* at Grand Riviere.

BEST ON THE ISLAND

 CHECKING IN: For the most part, St. Lucia offers a two-way choice of accommodations: relatively expensive luxury hotels and less costly "self-catering" setups in apartment or villa complexes. Most places offer Modified American Plan (MAP) arrangements, which add between $25 and $40 per person to the daily room rate. In winter, two people should expect to pay $200 for deluxe accommodations without meals; $150 to $200 is expensive, $100 to $150 moderate, and under $100 inexpensive.

CASTRIES AND NORTH

Couples St. Lucia – Couples only; no singles, no children, no fifth wheels. Everything is included in a single price: all meals and drinks, all sports and instruction (the list is comprehensive), 2-day excursions, nightly entertainment, even cigarettes. This 100-room resort sits on Vigie Beach, among lushly landscaped grounds. Accommodations are in beachside cottages or in the hotel section, still with plenty of water to gaze at. It feels a bit like a camp for adults, what with everyone lining up for buffets all the time, but no one seems to mind (phone: 2-4211). Expensive.

St. Lucian – Formerly the Holiday Inn, with 192 rooms in brightly colored buildings along Reduit Beach; it has a pool, tennis courts, equipment for all water sports (which, except for diving, are included in the price of your stay), and evening entertainment (phone: 2-8351). Expensive.

Steigenberger Cariblue – With 102 rooms, large terraces facing the sea on Anse du Cap Beach, at the northernmost tip of the island. European-style elegance and service; pool, tennis, horseback riding, and all water sports facilities (phone: 2-8551). Expensive.

Halcyon Beach Club – Some 140 cabana-style rooms with patios on Choc Bay; also has a pool, wharf bar and restaurant, terrace dining, and full water sports facilities. Popular wharf restaurant (phone: 2-5331). Moderate.

Harmony Apartel – Family-run, family-welcoming cluster of 21 two-bedroom apartments, each with living/dining room, one or two baths, kitchen, sizable balcony; optional air conditioning. On Rodney Bay Lagoon, with freshwater pool, small market, island/Oriental restaurant on premises (phone: 2-0336). Moderate.

Smuggler's Village – At Cap Estate, one of the few resorts with as many American as European guests. There are 77 cottages with 292 beds; self-catering — which is the Caribbean way of saying cooking facilities on the premises. A casual bar and pool are the center of social activities. Water sports (except windsurfing and water skiing) are free at hidden beach (phone: 2-0551). Moderate.

Bois d'Orange – Small colony of 8 one- and 3 two-bedroom, air-conditioned cottages with living rooms and kitchenettes — all immaculately kept — on a hilltop overlooking the island's northern tip and Reduit Bay. Spectacular view. With its own pool, once-a-day transport to Reduit Beach. Restaurant features local dishes (phone: 2-8213). Inexpensive.

East Winds Inn – The 10 beachside cottages with kitchenettes are on La Brelotte Bay; patios with thatched umbrellas; all water sports. *Very* casual, with upkeep somewhat ditto; devoted island-savvy clientele (phone: 2-8212). Inexpensive.

Green Parrot Inn – Perched on the side of Morne Fortune, with closer ties to island life than resort chic, it's best known for its popular restaurant. The 27 rooms are unremarkable except for their super views. With good dining, bar, boutiques, pool; beach is 20 minutes away (phone: 2-3399). Inexpensive.

Islander – Just across the street from Reduit Beach and the water sports center at the *St. Lucian* and near restaurants and shops, this appealing hotel has 44 contemporary rooms and suites clustered around a lively pool and restaurant area. The terraces of the suites, shaded and screened by flowering bushes, house a small living area and kitchen. A skylight keeps the bedroom bright and sunny (phone: 2-8757). Inexpensive.

SOUTH OF CASTRIES

Dasheene – On a mountain ridge high above Soufrière, with vistas so fabulous, air so fresh, that the architects of these invitingly contemporary condominiums have left their eave-sheltered western sides unwalled, open to Piton views and breezes. Stylish furnishings, pleasant dining, small but stunning pool; soothing, far from beach, but free transport provided. In all, there are 22 one-, two-, and three-bedroom units (phone: 4-7444). MAP only. Deluxe.

La Toc Suites – Formerly part of *La Toc* hotel, now a separate 54-unit, all-suite luxury resort hotel offering guests privacy, seclusion, and true VIP treatment: limovan pickup at airport; warm welcome from resident hosts Mr. and Mrs. Gerald Paul, who will also advise on sightseeing, car rental, local dining; 24-hour staff of personal chambermaids to help unpack, whisk away laundry and dry cleaning, serve breakfast in bed, and restock refreshments, reading matter, and videotaped movies. Each suite has an ocean-view balcony or patio, wet bar, refrigerator, color TV, and videotape player; some even come with a private plunge pool. Guests also have access to the golf, tennis, and complimentary water sports of *La Toc* hotel next door, which also offers instruction and equipment for sunfish sailing, windsurfing, water skiing, and snorkeling. If desired, the hotel's *Les Pitons* restaurant will serve meals *en suite*. Both *La Toc* hotel and *La Toc Suites* are operated by Cunard Hotels and Resorts (phone: 800-222-0930). Very expensive.

La Toc – With 204 rooms and 54 suites on La Toc Bay, in a lush tropical landscape, complete with 2 pools, golf course, good tennis facilities, and several dining rooms. Private villa suites available. Luxury favorite (phone: 2-3081). Expensive.

Anse Chastanet Beach – Its 24 hillside rooms in octagonal chalets are in the shadow of the Pitons, by a thatch-roofed bar and restaurant overlooking a palm-fringed beach near which 12 more units nestle. Great sense of peace and privacy. One of the Caribbean's best small inns (phone: 4-7355; in the US, 212-535-9530 or 800-223-5581). Moderate.

Marigot Bay – A yachting and water sports–oriented complex lining two sides of one of the Caribbean's most beautiful anchorages. Since the Mooring Ltd. took over in 1984, it has only improved. There are 45 spacious, airy rooms in a variety of accommodations on either side of the bay, with a courtesy water taxi to whisk guests back and forth. Water sports facilities and instruction are first-rate, and the Mooring's charter yachts are world-renowned. *Doolittle's* on the north shore and the *Rusty Anchor* on the Hurrican Hole side are both fine restaurants, with the latter doubling as a late night spot (phone: 3-4357). Moderate.

 EATING OUT: American, Chinese, and European dishes are all available on St. Lucia, but island specialties are really excellent. Try callaloo soup, stuffed breadfruit, banana bread, fried plantain, pumpkin soup, french-fried flying fish, crab backs stuffed with spiced crab and lobster meat, and baked lobster, just to get your taste buds attuned to the fresh foods of the island. The seafood was swimming this morning, and the vegetables and fruits are picked and served immediately. Those places where dinner for two, with tip and drinks, can be expected to cost $55 and over are considered expensive; restaurants that fall into the $35 to $45 range are listed as moderate; and establishments where dinner for two can be had for less than $30 are listed as inexpensive.

CASTRIES

Coal Pot – At the yacht basin, this restaurant is built on its own wharf and is a gathering place for yachtspeople and boaters. Lovely harbor view, excellent seafood, and a fine wine list. Seats about 30. Lunar Park (phone: 2-5643). Expensive.

The Green Parrot – *Claridges*-trained owner and chef Harry is an inventive interpreter of French and Créole cuisines, with a distinctly English bent. Try soup *oh-la-la,* a spicy pumpkin soup that earned its sobriquet from a French patron's instant appreciation. Chef Harry is also known for turning out especially good mixed grills and steaks. On Morne Fortune with fabulous views of Castries, this is a fun spot, very popular with visitors and locals alike. Mondays, Wednesdays, and Fridays are cabaret nights. Red Tape Lane, Morne Fortune (phone: 2-3399). Expensive.

San Antoine – Overlooking Castries harbor, fine Continental cuisine is presented in a century-old building rebuilt after a fire in 1970. Serving dinner only daily, specialties include filet mignon stuffed with crayfish, local fresh fish fillets layered with salmon, and, for an appetizer, crab and cheese soufflé (phone: 2-4660). Expensive.

Rain – A green and white building, with decor inspired by the sultry old movie *Rain,* in true Somerset Maugham–South Seas style from its tin roof on down. Powerful rum drinks, salads, local dishes done with real flair. Now with a "discreet Pizza Park" under the mango tree in the garden. Consider the Demon Rum Dinner (four courses and all the rum swizzles you can absorb) — a soused sea–island steal at

$24 per person including tip. Best "meet me at" place in town. Columbus Square (phone: 2-3022). Expensive to moderate.

Ma John's – She has a boutique downstairs and an eatery upstairs on Brazil St. in Castries. The emphasis is on native-style seafood preparations. Open Mondays through Saturdays, 8 AM until midnight (phone: 2-3939) Inexpensive.

SOUFRIÈRE

Hummingbird – Lovely for a lingering lunch on a Soufrière go-round. Glorious Piton view, pool to cool off in, delicious Créole menu with lobster, shrimp, fish lots of ways, steaks (Diane and au poivre). But The Treat is freshwater crayfish in lime or garlic butter (ask). Castries branch is planned. Reservations recommended (phone: 4-7232). Expensive.

The Still – An old rum distillery, now an excellent restaurant with much of what is served grown and produced on the owners' plantation. The Créole buffet at lunch is a real treat. Dinner is a relaxed affair, with lots of island favorites on the menu (phone: 4-7224). Moderate.

ELSEWHERE

Capone's – This restaurant at Rodney Bay features southern Italian dishes, pizza, and a complete ice cream parlor for dessert choices. The interior motif combines the Jazz Age, cops-and-mobsters 1920s with the hot pink and black, Art Deco touches of the 1930s (phone: 2-0284). Expensive to moderate.

Banana Split – Sitting right on the beach in the town of Gros Islet, this is the quintessential West Indian restaurant — open air and casual, the kind of place to linger over a long lunch. The menu offers Créole dishes, West Indian curries, plain boiled lobster, grilled steaks, sandwiches and salads for lunch. And, of course, banana splits. Go on Friday night, when the whole town is something like a carnival and the restaurant stays open until the band packs up (phone: 2-8125). Moderate.

The Charthouse – Wood paneled, full of plants, and open to the breezes from the yacht harbor it overlooks, this is a handsome steak and lobster house, which also happens to serve chicken and fish. Dinner only. Rodney Bay (phone: 2-8115). Moderate.

Dolittle's – Simple island foods, fresh seafood, vegetables, pleasanely hatly presented. Waterside setting is special; plus swimming, snorkeling, deck-sitting before and after lunch. Ferry from Marigot jetty. At Marigot des Roseaux on Marigot Bay (phone: 3-4246). Moderate.

Le Boucan – In the middle of all the activity in Castries, dine al fresco while watching the people parade by. Grilled foods and Créole specialities available at both lunch and dinner (phone 2-2415). Inexpensive.

Chak Chak – Near Vieux Fort, close to the airport, featuring West Indian Créole cooking as well as some Continental dishes. Two bars and large courtyard where there is frequent entertainment (phone: 4-6260). Inexpensive.

The Lime – A nice little place at Rodney Bay for a quick lunch, with 8 tables inside, 5 al fresco. Tough to spend $4 (US) per person, for *roti,* sandwiches, or snacks like fish lasagna and steak-and-kidney pie. Dinner runs the gamut from seafood and chicken to chops and steaks. Closed Tuesdays. No credit cards (phone: 2-0761). Inexpensive.

ST. MARTIN/ ST. MAARTEN

People have all kinds of reasons for picking a particular vacation spot in the Caribbean. Some go for super sport facilities (for learning as well as playing) or health spas. Others look for culture, historical and archaeological remains, social cachet, or nightlife.

The tiny French and Dutch island of St. Martin/St. Maarten boasts all of the above but in small quantities. Its sports facilities — including the golf course and 16 tennis courts at *Mullet Bay* — though good, are not spectacular. It hasn't a real spa to its name, although both sides now offer some fitness facilities. And culturally — in the fields of music, dance, and the graphic arts — it can't hold a candle to Puerto Rico, Jamaica, or Haiti. Archaeologically, it is, at least for now, mainly atmospheric, although recent research and restorations are turning up interesting data. Socialites and celebrities who do visit own or lease villas or take a secluded suite at *La Samanna* or *La Belle Créole,* and slip in and out very quietly. And its life after dark, though endowed with Dutch casinos for a bit of gambling, one or two "shows," and a handful of discos, is scarcely razzle-dazzle.

Yet for weeks during the winter season, and recently in July and August as well, late bookers can find no room at the inns on either side of its border. Indeed, St. Martin has boomed enormously in the past five years or so, and you're bound to run into those who say, "you should have seen it when . . ."

The secret of St. Martin's considerable success with tourists is really quite simple. It's an island on which people can relax. Its sun is dependable, and its sea and its beaches are beautiful. There is even one "clothes optional" beach — *naturellement* on the French side — and several other stretches of accessible sand secluded enough for very private relaxation and bathing. No sightseeing is requisite, but there are plenty of activities to amuse and divert anytime anyone happens to feel ambitious: golf, tennis, and all sorts of seagoing excursions (by schooner, catamaran, or motor launch to Dutch Saba, French St. Barts, British Anguilla, and uninhabited Îlet Pinel, or just across Simpson Bay Lagoon for cocktails and dinner). Visitors can scuba under the sea, ski on it, or catch the end of a spinnaker and fly over it. And whatever a traveler feels like doing on either side of the border (the island is divided into French and Dutch territories), that feeling of ease and familiarity comes in a remarkably short time, because those slogans on the billboards and in the brochures are more than just ad copy. St. Martin so far, at least, manages to remain "the Friendly Island," in spite of its ever-increasing popularity and large-scale development.

The French and the Dutch have been practicing friendship in a small space for a century and a half now. As a matter of fact, the island is the smallest piece of land shared by two sovereign powers anywhere in the world. When Columbus landed in 1493, it was Carib property, but the original French and Dutch settlements in the early 1630s signaled the end of Indian civilization. The Spanish pushed out the Dutch in the 1640s, and Peter (or Petrus) Stuyvesant, ordered by his government to retake the island, attacked the fort, which was later renamed Fort Amsterdam, in 1644 with no success. He might have saved himself one leg (which he lost in the skirmish) and a lot of trouble. Shortly thereafter, at the end of its 80-year war with the Netherlands, Spain gave up St. Martin without a struggle. The island's favorite legend — that of a Frenchman and a Dutchman (the former fueled by wine, the latter by gin) who started out back to back and walked (in opposite directions) around the periphery of the island (until they met on the other side) to determine each country's permanent share of land — is reputed to have occurred in 1648. That is also the date on the border marker by the side of the Philipsburg-Marigot road; the monument commemorates the first Dutch-French treaty of friendship, signed on Mt. Concordia in that year. Though it isn't generally emphasized, island land changed hands at least 16 times after that. But final settlement was made in 1816, and relations between the two countries have been serene ever since.

If it weren't for the monument and the sign that reads "Bienvenue Partie Française," you wouldn't realize that you were crossing the border. There is no guard, no customs. Differences between Dutch and French portions of the island are a matter of style. The island's biggest hotels had always been on the Dutch side, which, on the whole, has been more developed than the French; but building activity has been on the upswing on the French side, too. Several new hotels have opened in the past two years, including the long-awaited *La Belle Creole* and *L'Habitation* (the island's biggest), and, with the new Port La Royale complex, Marigot now claims some 200 chic shops.

Philipsburg, the Dutch capital, is a charming town three streets wide, but is bustling and commercial. In midday or late afternoon traffic, it can take almost as long to drive from one end of Front Street to the other as to cross Manhattan. Shops stocked with imported duty-free luxuries from all over the world — Tokyo, Switzerland, England, Italy, and, natch, Holland — are prosperous and full of customers, especially on a busy cruise ship day (there can be as many as eight ships in port!), when Front Street is mercifully closed to traffic and the little road and sidewalks are literally crammed with shoppers. Last year, between cruise ship passengers and overnight vacationers, the island hosted nearly 1 million visitors. Here the language is English (Dutch is seen mainly on street signs), and the mobs can be heard comparing prices in every language from Japanese to Papiamento.

The French countryside is basically bucolic; its hotels are rambling, and even on cruise ship days, there's a slightly calmer air about the French capital, Marigot. Boutique windows display the finest crystal, porcelains, and perfumes, along with the latest styles in jewelry and bikinis — and almost exclusively French and Italian designs. Shops are busy, but not overcrowded, with vacationers staying at the low-keyed French-side resorts, yachtspeople, and a smattering of cruise passengers who've bused or taxied across from the

Philipsburg pier for lunch or a day of browsing. And though there's a strong undercurrent of the French language — some pure, some patois — in shops as in hotels and restaurants, there's a lot of English spoken and understood.

The border is so invisible that visitors forget it and move about as mood and mission dictate: to the French side in search of a secluded beach; to the Dutch to catch the boat or plane for Saba or to play a round of golf; either way, or both, to shop — depending on the kind of bargain you're after. At night, Dutch-side guests cross over for a drink at one of the pleasant outdoor cafés and dinner at *Le Poisson d'Or* or one of the more reasonably priced bistros at Port La Royale. French guests reciprocate at the new *Cupecoy's, Maho's,* or one of the other casinos on the Dutch side, finishing with a disco stop on the way home.

Any hour, any day, visitors are welcomed on either the Dutch or the French side — which is not only fine for relaxing and enjoying, but adds up to being twice as nice.

ST. MARTIN/ST.MAARTEN
AT-A-GLANCE

FROM THE AIR: With a coastline of beaches notched by large and small bays, St. Martin/St. Maarten looks like an island jigsawed by a Victorian gingerbread addict. This is especially true of its southwestern section, where a curlicued framework of land surrounds a large body of blue water known as Simpson Bay Lagoon (also spelled Simson, Simpson's, and Simson's — but most often just Simpson). Juliana Airport, now the second busiest in the Caribbean (after San Juan's), occupies a slender strip of land on the south side of the lagoon. To the north is the town of Marigot, the capital of French St. Martin. Southeast, where the horseshoe of Great Bay curves into the coast, is Philipsburg, the capital of Dutch St. Maarten, occupying a narrow isthmus between the sea and Great Salt Pond.

St. Martin/St. Maarten (37 square miles; pop. about 38,000; at 18° N latitude and 63° W longitude) is the world's smallest island divided between two sovereignties. The 16-square-mile St. Maarten in the south — along with the tiny neighboring islands of Saba and St. Eustatius and the larger Curaçao and Bonaire off the northern coast of South America (formerly the ABC Islands, including Aruba, which has recently been given separate status) — is part of the Netherlands Antilles. The St. Martin half (21 square miles), with its satellite of St. Barthélemy, is a dependency of Guadeloupe, 140 miles to the southwest, and therefore is grouped with the French West Indies. St. Martin's nearest neighbors are St. Thomas in the US Virgin Islands (144 miles to the east) and Puerto Rico, a 30-minute, 144-mile jet flight away. Miami lies 1,223 miles (roughly 2½ hours' flying time) to the northeast, and the 1,460-mile flight from New York takes about 3½ hours. Its position in the midst of so many small islands and the frequency of landings at recently renovated Juliana Airport make it one of the Caribbean's crossroads islands, playing host to more and more vacationers (roughly 900,000 in 1987 each year.

SPECIAL PLACES: If you hate sightseeing but love poking around, this is your island. St. Martin's particular pleasures lie in the unexpected discoveries you make on your own: an empty beach, a seascape, antique houses, and sugar mill towers moldering away in nameless valleys. Rent a car and take off ex tempore. For visitors who really hate to drive, there are guided tours by small bus or taxi. Roads are simply laid out, though some — especially on the Dutch side — are lately in pretty bad shape. Do watch out for animals, especially at night; auto accidents have been caused by cows roaming into the middle of the road unexpectedly.

Philipsburg – Take an hour or two to stroll through Philipsburg, the Dutch capital. Its central square (recently renamed the Cyrus W. Wathey Square, but still De Ruyter-plein to most), a long, narrow rectangle laid across Front Street a few blocks east of the midpoint between its foot and head, is usually so jammed with islanders, taxis, and visitors toting shopping bags that you're likely to mistake it for an impossibly clogged intersection the first time. At its southern edge, the Little Pier, from which several excursion boats depart and where cruise passengers land, juts into the harbor. Across Front Street, opposite the tourist office and Little Pier, stands one of the town's two notable buildings: the 1793 Courthouse, restored to resemble its 1826 post-hurricane reincarnation, now the Post Office and Town Hall.

Once upon a simpler time, there were only Front and Back streets; now a third — generally called Pond Fill Road, built on land reclaimed from the Old Salt Pond (formerly an important source of island income) — has been added to relieve congestion on the first two. But Front Street is still clogged with traffic struggling east, except on major cruise ship days, when people rather than vehicles cause the congestion. Turning east from the square and creeping along with the traffic, you pass a jumble of shops, restaurants, and business places, a few in modern buildings, some in old Dutch West Indian style arcades and courtyards, still others in old, genuine porch-fronted houses recently given new coats of pastel paint. One such, once the official government guesthouse, forms the central section — lobby, bar, and dining terrace — of the *Pasanggrahan* (guesthouse) hotel. A bit farther, on the north side of the street, is another, now the *West Indian Tavern,* behind which brick ruins are reputed to be the remains of a 17th- or 18th-century synagogue (no one knows for sure). Facing the head of Front Street is the Buncamper House, a handsomely proportioned structure with a front staircase and wraparound verandah. Built by an old island family, it is one of the island's purest examples of upper-class West Indian architecture. Plans are in the works for a huge shopping mall nearby.

Marigot – The French capital is a good distance from the cruise ships and, so far, less crowded and easier to explore: a neat little harbor busy with Anguilla-bound traffic bustles with tropical sounds and colors, fragrant with West Indian spices and French criossants, especially on Saturday mornings, when the waterfront market is at its liveliest. Mellowed old West Indian buildings line the quay, many now inviting restaurants with familiar French names — *La Vie en Rose, Maison sur la Port* — and elegant air-conditioned shops with a European flair. On the main corner, opposite *La Vie en Rose,* is the tiny tourist office with a few brochures (and public washrooms). The two main shopping streets — Rue de la République and Rue de la Liberté — have been recently outclassed by the sparkling new Port La Royale complex at the southern end of town, with its impressive marina and very chic boutiques, cafés, and bistros, which come alive at sunset with live music and beautiful people.

ELSEWHERE ON THE ISLAND

A circle tour of the island might start at Philipsburg and travel clockwise past the old cemetery at the foot of Front Street, then go north of the point where of 17th-century Fort Amsterdam (currently being excavated for planned reconstruction) and pass Cay Bay, where Peter Stuyvesant — later governor of New Amsterdam — lost his leg. At a junction just over Cole Bay Hill, turn right and take the most direct route to Marigot, passing the obelisk Border Monument and Mt. Concordia, where the original Dutch-French treaty of peaceful coexistence was signed; or left to follow the road that loops around Simpson Bay Lagoon past the airport; the green, sprawling *Mullet Bay* resort complex and nearby *Maho Beach* resort; gleaming, white *La Samanna;* and Pointe du

Bluff, on which stands the recently opened brainchild of the late Claude Philippe of the *Waldorf-Astoria: La Belle Créole.* (This luxury resort ran out of money, and its empty shell stood on the bluff for nearly 20 years, until financing came from France, and Conrad International Hotels, a subsidiary of Hilton Hotels USA, took over operations and opened it in 1988.) Drive on to the town of Marigot, with its satellite, St. Tropez–style Port la Royale Marina, and to the small picturesque French settlements of Grand Case and Orleans; call at landlocked Oyster Pond Harbor; then continue on around Naked Boy Hill and along the road that skirts the Great Salt Pond and returns to Philipsburg. It's a circle route meant to be broken any time a beach or a picnic spot beckons (*Café Royal* in Philipsburg's *Royal Palm Plaza* dispenses excellent picnic baskets) or when lunch — especially at Marigot or Grand Case — feels like a good idea.

■**EXTRA SPECIAL:** A lazy day's excursion to *Oyster Pond* to swim on Dawn Beach, one of the island's most glorious, and to lunch in style at the elegant *Oyster Pond Yacht Club* next door, one of the Caribbean's unique inns (see *Eating Out*).

Children and adults alike delight in the unusual Live Eagle Show, choreographed by Jean-Pierre Bordes, who has been training birds of prey for over 20 years. Both he and his birds seem to enjoy this spectacular, which features a majestic peregrine falcon that can dive at a speed of 200 mph, 4 Griffin vultures (among the most difficult species to train), a Fisher eagle, an African owl, and frigate birds. There are daily performances at 10:30 AM, 2:30 PM, and 4 PM. Maho Bay, on the road to Point Pirouette, just past *Casino Royale*. Admission: adults, $8; children $4.

SOURCES AND RESOURCES

TOURIST INFORMATION: The St. Maarten Tourist Office is at 275 Seventh Ave., 19th Floor, New York, NY 10001-6788 (phone: 212-989-0000), and at 243 Ellercie Ave., Willowdale, Toronto, Ont. M2N 145 (phone: 416-223-3501). The French West Indies Tourist Board is at 610 Fifth Ave., New York, NY 10020 (phone: 212-757-1125). The French Government Tourist Office is in the following North American cities:

Beverly Hills: 9401 Wilshire Blvd., Beverly Hills, CA 90212 (phone: 213-271-6665)
Chicago: 645 N Michigan Ave., Suite 430, Chicago, IL 60611 (phone: 312-337-6301)
Dallas: 2050 Stemmons Fwy., Dallas, TX 75258 (phone: 214-742-7011)
Montréal: 1981 Av. McGill College, Suite 490, Montréal, Qué. H3A 2W9 (phone: 514-288-4264)
San Francisco: 1 Hallidie Plaza, Suite 250, San Francisco, CA 94102 (phone: 415-986-4161)
Toronto: 1 Dundas St. W, Suite 240, Toronto, Ont. M5G 1Z3 (phone: 416-593-4717)

Only the New York and Beverly Hills offices will handle written inquiries.

The St. Maarten Tourist Bureau (phone: 22337), where visitors can get maps of the island and literature on the Dutch side, is on Cyrus W. Wathey Square, formerly called De Ruyterplein, Philipsburg's small, crowded main square at the head of the Little Pier (where cruise passengers come ashore. The office is open weekdays 8 AM to noon and 1 to 5 PM). There is also a new tourist office on the French side in a little West Indian house at the corner of the harbor in Marigot (phone: 875326), open weekdays 8:30 AM to 12:30 PM and 2:30 to 5:30 PM, usually.

Local Coverage – *St. Maarten Holiday,* a Dutch-side newspaperlike monthly guide in English, printed on orange paper, is available free at the airport, the tourist bureau, and hotels, and contains much useful, up-to-date data on shopping, restaurants (including a few on the French side), hotels, nightlife, special events, religious services, etc.; maps of Philipsburg and the island are included. The St. Maarten Chamber of Commerce publishes a handy and informative guide, updated twice yearly, called *What to Do.* Other free publications include *St. Maarten Events; St. Maarten Nights; St. Maarten This Month; Discover; Newsday;* the daily newspaper *The Chronicle,* a good source of local, as well as some international, news; and *St. Martin's Week,* with its gossipy "Suzy Says" column. The *Flash Carson Guide,* available at the airports and bookstores, is also quite helpful — especially on the French side.

The *New York Times, New York Daily News, New York Post,* and *San Juan Star* arrive on St. Maarten newsstands the day they are published. The *International Herald Tribune* is also available.

For background, the paperback *St. Maarten, Saba, St. Eustatius* by Dr. J. Hartog, published by the Netherlands Antilles Department of Education in an English translation, provides an interesting, illustrated survey of the history and economy of the islands; it's usually available at local bookstores.

Telephone – Dial direct to the island by adding the international access code 011 and the prefix 5995 to the phone numbers given for the Dutch side and 590 to the phone numbers given for the French side. With recent improvements in the telephone system, it's now fairly straightforward to phone from one side of the island to the other: From the Dutch side to the French, add a 6 before the 6-digit number; from the French side to the Dutch, precede the 5-digit number with a 3. Be advised that when calling from St. Maarten, night rates for Chicago are the same as for neighboring Anguilla. The French side is comparable, as toll calls go through Guadeloupe.

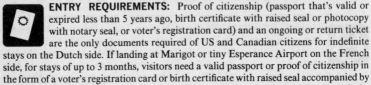

ENTRY REQUIREMENTS: Proof of citizenship (passport that's valid or expired less than 5 years ago, birth certificate with raised seal or photocopy with notary seal, or voter's registration card) and an ongoing or return ticket are the only documents required of US and Canadian citizens for indefinite stays on the Dutch side. If landing at Marigot or tiny Esperance Airport on the French side, for stays of up to 3 months, visitors need a valid passport or proof of citizenship in the form of a voter's registration card or birth certificate with raised seal accompanied by a government ID card, or similar document, *with* photo. Fortunately, French St. Maarten successfully convinced the French government of the difficulties of requiring a visa on this dual-nationality island when visas became necessary in the wake of terrorism in France. For longer periods a visa is required, plus an ongoing or return ticket.

CLIMATE AND CLOTHES: The island is sunny and warm year-round with constant trade winds that take the edge off the heat. Average daytime temperature during the winter months is about 80°F (30°C); summer's a few degrees warmer and more humid. Average annual rainfall is about 45 inches, which means more air cooling thanks to occasional showers, especially in late summer and early fall. Daytime dress for both men and women is neat but comfortably casual, with lots of cottons — woven, knit, and in no-iron blends — easy to live with and in, whatever the season. Proper tennis attire — not necessarily all white — is requested on most courts. Take two swimsuits, minimum, plus some sort of coverup to wear for lunch or when you've had enough sun but don't want to leave the beach; you'll also want to bring or buy a beach hat. Both the French and the Dutch are easygoing about beachwear (although nudism is not allowed on Dutch beaches), but that's on beaches only. Swimsuits in hotel lobbies (or on downtown streets) are definitely no go. Evenings are informal, although men may want to have a jacket (no tie) and women a shawl or sweater in the air-conditioned casinos and some of the restaurants and hotels.

MONEY: Currency in the Dutch area is the Netherlands Antilles florin, but most transactions are done in US dollars. Currency in French St. Martin is the French franc, and dollar-spending tourists will notice that some items are pricier on the French side as a result of the severe decline in recent years in the value of the dollar relative to the franc. Since US currency is accepted everywhere, there is no real reason to exchange US dollars for local money, but Canadian dollars are not as readily accepted and should, therefore, be exchanged for florins or francs. In many shops and restaurants, prices are given in both local currency (NAf or F) and US dollars, sometimes only in US dollars. A few shops offer discounts for payment in US cash, but not on transactions in traveler's checks. Banking hours on the Dutch side of the border are normally 8 AM to 1 PM Mondays through Thursdays and 4 to 5 PM on Fridays; Citco is open 9 AM to 3 PM; and Chase Manhattan is also open Saturday mornings till noon and has a window open until 5 PM. On the French side, banks are open 8:30 AM to 4 PM Mondays through Thursdays and 8:30 AM to 1 PM and 4 to 5 PM Fridays. All banks are closed on Sundays and holidays. The American Express representative is on the Dutch side: S. E. L. Maduro & Sons, Philipsburg (phone: 23407, 23408, 22678).

LANGUAGE: Dutch is the official language of St. Maarten, and French is the official language of St. Martin, but English is spoken nearly everywhere.

TIME: The island is in the Atlantic Standard time zone; in fall and winter when it's noon in Philipsburg and Marigot, it's 11 AM Eastern Standard Time in New York, the eastern US, and Canada. When the East is on Daylight Saving Time, the hour is the same as it is on the island.

CURRENT: Most hotels on the Dutch side are wired for 110 volts, as are the US and Canada; but on the French side, all run on 220-volt, 50-cycle current. So if you depend on travel appliances, bring a converter and adapter plugs.

GETTING THERE: Eastern Airlines has daily flights from Miami and a 4 times weekly flight from Philadelphia via San Juan; Pan Am, American Airlines, and ALM fly nonstop from New York, with connections available from Dallas/Fort Worth, Boston, and Atlanta, via San Juan. All land at Juliana Airport, as do Air Guadeloupe flights from San Juan and Guadeloupe; LIAT flights from St. Thomas, St. Kitts, and the southern Caribbean; ALM flights from Trinidad, San Juan, Aruba, Curaçao, and Santo Domingo; BWIA flights from Toronto (via Antigua) and Trinidad; Windward Islands Airways (Winair) flights between St. Maarten, St. Kitts, Nevis, St. Thomas, Saba, St. Eustatius, St. Barthélemy, and Anguilla; Air St. Barthélemy from St. Barthélemy; and Air BVI from St. Thomas and Tortola. Air Guadeloupe flights from St. Barts and some from Guadeloupe land at Esperance Airport near Grand Case, where French entry requirements apply. Air France has a twice weekly flight from Paris.

Passengers from California and the West can make connections at American's Dallas/Fort Worth hub; other western and midwestern passengers can connect at Miami International, Atlanta, or San Juan's Isla Verde Airport (although the San Juan airport has become notorious for losing luggage and is best avoided when possible).

Philipsburg is a very popular port of call for cruises; hundreds of liners a year (about 400,000 passengers in 1987) put into its harbor. Most send passengers ashore by launch; others dock at the Dutch pier at Pointe Blanche or at Little Pier. Nearing completion in Marigot is a new pier, which received the first cruise ship to dock on the French side in 1987.

 CALCULATING COSTS: In price and style, the variety of accommodations is wide. In winter, luxury resorts cost well over $200 a day for two without meals. And *La Belle Créole*'s rate of $490 and up can fairly be described as orbital. But there are first-class hotels and appealing guesthouses on both sides of the border that charge as little as $60 a night. Between mid-April and mid-December, hotel and package rates drop 25% to 40%. MAP (including breakfasts and dinners), when available, adds about 30% to 40% per person to basic EP (without meals) rates. Many hotels offer package rates for week-long stays that are below their advertised daily rates in winter as well as summer. A 5% tax and a 10% to 15% service and energy charge are normally added to hotel bills on the Dutch side; a minimal *tax de séjour* and 10% to 15% service charge are also added on the French side but are often included in the published rates. There is a $5 departure tax levied at Dutch side Juliana Airport; from the French side, the departure tax is included in the published air fare.

 GETTING AROUND: Taxi – Unmetered, but drivers are required to carry booklets listing rates for destinations all over the island. The trip from Juliana Airport to Philipsburg currently runs $7; to Marigot hotels, $7; to Mullet Bay, $4; to Grand Case, $14; to Oyster Pond, $15; and from Philipsburg to Grand Case, about $14 — for one or two persons, plus $1 per additional person and more again with baggage. Rates go up 25% after 10 PM and 50% from midnight to 6 AM. An extra 50¢ or $1 is an acceptable tip. For late night service, call *Around the Clock Taxi* (phone: 22359, 25012, 23196).

Taxis are ready and waiting at the airport and hotels, and since there are no limos, and rental car companies aren't allowed to garage cars on airport property, cabs provide the best transport to your hotel when you land. Though car rental agencies have airport booths, cars must be delivered to your island address.

Bus – A bargain and so popular with islanders and visitors that a calypso was written in their honor: "St. Maarten people they go a lot / Dutch Philipsburg to French Marigot. / Don't have to be rich, us ladies and gents / The bus ride costs just . . . eighty-five cents!" Buses serve main points throughout the island, in addition to making the Philipsburg-Marigot round trip. Flag them down anywhere on the road.

Car Rental – Enthusiastically recommended for those who want to sample several of the island's beaches, restaurants, and shops, rather than just stay put at a hotel. Even then — if you're staying on the 172-acre *Mullet Bay* resort preserve — your own wheels are handy for getting from cottage to beach or golf course or restaurant when you want to. Unlimited mileage rates vary from about $30 to $55 a day, depending on the size and type of car; gas — at about $1.75 per gallon — is extra; check when you take delivery; tanks aren't likely to be full. If you don't use a credit card, a deposit of $350 to $1,500 is normally required. There is an extra daily charge of $8 or so for the optional Collision Damage Waiver, which may be advisable here because you may be liable for damages even if an accident is not your fault. A US or Canadian driver's license is valid for island driving. Car rental firms in Philipsburg include: *Avis* (phone: 42322, 42316), which also has an office in Marigot at Port La Royale (phone: 875436); *Budget* (phone: 44275, 44274, 44308); *Caribbean* (phone: 45211); *Roy Rogers* (phone: 42702); *Hertz* (phone: 44314); *Lucky Car Rental/National* (phone: 44268, 42468, 44361, 42168); *Opel* (phone: 42644); *Risdon Car Rentals,* which also has an office at the airport, as well as branches at a number of hotels (phone: 23578, 44239; night, 22579); and *Sunny* (phone: 22577). On the French side, car rentals are available at *Hertz* (phone: 875081, 877301), *Paradise* (phone: 877750, 873251), *Lucky* (phone:

875124), *Caribbean* (phone: 875122, 873385, 873333), *Babi Richardson* (phone: 875111), *Dan's* (phone: 873408), *Grand Rent-A-Car* (phone: 877131, 875124), *L'Esperance* (phone: 875109), and *St. Martin Auto* (phone: 875086, 875472). All will deliver cars to the hotel, and on departure day you can drive to the airport and leave the car there.

Mopeds and motorcycles can be rented from *Carter's Cycle Center* (phone: 44251, 22621), across from Juliana Airport; *Moped Cruising* (phone: 22330 or 22520), next to the post office in Philipsburg and in Dutch Cul-de-Sac, just outside Philipsburg; and *Gar Rent-a-Scoot* in Marigot (phone: 877947). Rates run about $20 and up per day. But we would strongly discourage this mode of transport here; the roads are often pockmarked, crowded, and dangerous.

Sightseeing Taxi Tours – The way to see the island if you're set against driving yourself. Your hotel activities or travel desk will arrange for a car with a driver-guide; a 2½-hour tour around the island is about $30 for one person, with an additional charge of $7.50 for each extra passenger.

Sightseeing Bus Tours – Touring in 8- to 40-passenger buses is the third option for exploring the island. Principally designed for cruise passengers, they're operated by *St. Maarten Sightseeing Tours,* Philipsburg (phone: 22753), which offers a 2½-hour tour for $25 per car, a 4-hour tour that includes lunch for $11.50 per person; and a 6-hour trip including lunch and swimming for about $20. Others, including *St. Maarten Taxi Association,* Cole Bay (phone: 45329), *Rising Sun Tours* (phone: 45334, 45282), and *S. E. L. Maduro & Sons,* Philipsburg (phone: 23407), will arrange similar excursions.

Sea Excursions – Around St. Martin and to neighboring islands, these are as numerous and varied as exist on any Caribbean island. Several catamarans, such as the *Cheshire Cat, Eagle, Maho,* and *El Tigre,* offer breezy day sails to St. Barts daily except Sundays for about $45 round trip (phone: 22520). On Tuesdays, Thursdays, and Saturdays, the *Princess* departs Marigot's Marina Port La Royale for the 55-minute trip to St. Barts at 9 AM and returns at 4 PM for $55 round trip (phone: 877319). There are also dive boats and snorkel trips to Tintamarre or Pinel Islands and sunset cruises out of Philipsburg; check *St. Maarten Holiday* or the hotel travel desk for details and names of other craft currently afloat. Be sure to ask if the boat you choose is a member of the Charter Boat Association to insure maximum reliability and safety. Rates run about $30 for 4-hour sails, $40 to $55 for 6 to 8 hours, depending on whether lunch is included (there are almost always snacks, soft drinks, beer, and rum punch flowing). Full-day sails to St. Barts run about $45 per person with open bar; picnic sails to deserted beaches on nearby islets cost about $55 per person, including drinks and lunch; and sunset sails are about $15 per person. On Tuesdays through Saturdays at 9 AM the 73-foot M/V *Style* leaves for Saba from Great Bay and returns at 5 PM for $45 round trip (phone: 22167). As close to perfect as we have experienced was a trip aboard the 57-foot catamaran power yacht *Maison Maru,* which sails daily from Philipsburg's little pier. Her formula: a smooth coastline cruise, an hour's browsing in Marigot, super drink and food (the Bloody Marys and West Indian buffet would be worth the trip for their own sake), swimming, shelling, lazing time on a secluded French-side beach, and then home. Capacity runs about 30; tickets, about $40 each, are purchased in advance at hotel activities desks. The sleek 70-foot motor-catamaran *White Octopus* makes the crossing to St. Barts in only 90 minutes, leaving lots of time for lunch and exploring; about $35 per person round-trip includes open bar. Several, including the *Bluebeard I & II,* make day sails to precious Prickly Pear Cays off Anguilla, idyllic atolls encircled by a colorful coral reef for excellent snorkeling. On the French side, check the docks at Marigot and Anse Marcel Marina de Lonvilliers.

The *Caribe Breeze* (phone: 874019) makes twice weekly trips to St. Barts for $45 round-trip from Marigot, as does the *Tee Zech.* The latter also serves Blowing Point on Anguilla a half dozen times daily, as do five or six sturdy Anguillan-built motor-boats. The trip takes 15 to 20 minutes and costs $10 round-trip ($6 one way, except the night boat — 10:45 PM from Marigot or 10:15 PM from Anguilla — which is $10). Don't forget your swimsuit *and* your passport; there are now immigration officials on both sides and a departure tax of about $2. Some of the boats (check *Cheers*) also offer fully organized day excursions to Anguilla that include a ground tour and lunch. Check at Marigot's commerical harbor at the town's northern tip beneath the fort. There is also a weekly "night tour" to Anguilla on Fridays for $60 per person ($45 for children under 10), including all transfers, boats to and from Marigot, and dinner with live music at a beach bar/restaurant. Check with *Mystic Tours* in Marigot Harbor. The round-trip night boat, which leaves at 7 PM and returns at midnight, costs $25.

Local Air Services – Air Guadeloupe makes the 10-minute flight to St. Barts several times a day from Esperance Airport on the French side (about $38, round-trip). Air St. Barthélemy runs a shuttle between Juliana Airport and St. Barts regularly until dusk, as does Windward Island Airways (52, round-trip). Winair also schedules 2 or 3 flights daily from Dutch Juliana Airport to Saba ($40, round-trip), several times daily to St. Eustatius ($40, round-trip), and to Anguilla ($30, round-trip). In addition, Winair flies daily to St. Kitts ($82, round-trip) and St. Thomas ($112, round-trip), and several times weekly to Nevis ($100, round-trip).

SHOPPING: St. Martin/St. Maarten is that rarity — a truly duty-free island. No tax is paid on imports arriving on either side of the border. But that fact alone does not guarantee that all that glitters in either Dutch or French side shop windows is a bargain worth bringing home. For whatever they themselves have paid, individual merchants are still free to set their own prices. And certain manufacturers — especially of world-marketed items like calculators, cameras, and electronic equipment — work hard to fix prices across the international board; they are often successful enough to make savings on their products too small to bother with; you can do as well or better at your local discount store. Still, there are good buys to be had if you check prices before you leave home and then do some comparison pricing on location.

On the Dutch side, shopping hours are normally 8 or 8:30 AM to noon and 2 or 2:30 to 6 PM. Some shops remain open at lunchtime; some also open for a few hours on Sundays or holidays when cruise ships are in; and most take credit cards. Philipsburg's Front Street is lined with dozens of shops offering everything from Delftware, Swiss watches, French perfumes, and British cashmeres to Chinese embroidery, Japanese cameras and electronics, Indonesian batiks, Italian leather goods, fine jewelry, crystal, linens, porcelain, liquor, and more. The variety is enough to boggle the coolest shopping mind. It's almost impossible to resist impulse buying. But try.

If you can, shop twice — first to research and make tentative choices, and second, after a cooling-off period, to buy. And try to avoid heavy cruise ship days, particularly Tuesdays, when you are better off taking a taxi to the French side, to the New Amsterdam Mall, not far from Philipsburg, or to the shopping arcades at the major resort hotels (such as *Mullet Bay, Maho Beach,* and *Cupecoy*). On the French side, shopping is somewhat less confusing since there aren't the overwhelming cruise crowds. There are, however, dozens of new boutiques, it seems, daily, with mostly French and Italian fashions for men and women, and elegant European-designed housewares — at prices you wouldn't dream of paying back home. But you can save on French perfumes, cosmetics, fashion accessories, porcelains, and crystal.

On Philipsburg's Front Street and in its new offshoot arcades (check out the new pastel-colored Old Street in old Dutch West Indian style), shops come and go, but it's worth looking into the following:

La Romana, St. Martin's Italian fashion capital at the Royal Palm Plaza (all top designers from Fendi to Ferré, Bottega Veneta, Versace, and Armani), plus jewelry and watches at #61 (they also have branches at the airport, in Marigot, at *Mullet Bay* resort, and on St. Barts and Anguilla); *Little Switzerland,* a branch of the Virgin Island store, is full of luxury merchandise: British bone china, French crystal, and, of course, Swiss clocks and watches. *Hint:* Resist seemingly sensational buys in waterproof, shockproof, what-have-you-proof watches with unfamiliar names, no matter how glowing the guarantees that come with them, unless the salesperson can give you the name of a stateside organization that will make good. *H. Stern,* the very reputable firm, will, as will *Colombian Emeralds,* all of whose designer jewelry comes with guarantees honored by their Miami service office. *Jewel Box* has more 14K and 18K chains and bracelets, plus silver and gemstone jewelry and what the management describes as "Colombian emeralds at practical prices" — about $500 and up. *Sasha's* for gifts and, in the same arcade, the *Lil Shoppe,* next to the *Pinocchio* restaurant, for good prices on Diva and Gottex swimwear, eelskin accessories, perfumes, and other resort fashions. *Emile's Place,* on De Ruyterplein near the Little Pier, sells wines, cigars, chocolates, imported snacks, and Edams and Goudas — a good pre-picnic stop. *New Amsterdam* for jewelry, linens, Naf-Naf sportswear, and wonderful buys on fun watches like Swatch, with prices starting at $5 or so; and *The Yellow House* for perfume and cosmetics. *Penha* has imports from just about everywhere: French cosmetics and perfumes; British knits; Scottish cashmeres; big selections of women's handbags; and name European menswear, tropical shirts, and *Ralph Lauren. Shipwreck Shop* carries an eclectic stock of Caribbean and Latin American crafts, and souvenirs of every sort, as well as daily newspapers and a good selection of books and magazines on the Caribbean. *Boolchands* for more jewels and linens and *Kohinoor* for cameras and electronics. Smaller boutiques include *Gucci, Maurella Senesi,* and *Leda of Venice* for Valentino and Missoni; *Around the Bend* for stylish swimwear, dolls, pareos, and other fun gifts and decorative accessories; *Desmo* for designer leather goods, with bags and shoes from Italy.

Promenade Arcade shops include *Maximoflorence* (wonder-worked Italian leather shoes and bags, and some elegant sportswear); *Mille Fleurs* for exquisite crystal, china, jewelry, and unset, cut, and polished stones; *Printemps* for perfume and French etceteras; *The Shell Shop* for shell jewelry; *The Sandal Shop* for sandals and other shoes, bags, and luggage. Or for less costly but exceptional island originals, check the one-of-a-kind fashions and wall hangings at *Carib Batik.* The new *Old Street Marketplace,* with entrances on both Front and Back streets, has exotic batiks at *Java Wraps* and *Meli-Melo;* pricey, elegant French fashions at *Animale;* Polo sportswear at *Ralph Lauren;* fine jewelry at *Colomiban Emeralds* and *Goldfinger;* and a good place to weather a shopping slump at *Divi Divi*'s new outdoor café, *Beaujolais.* At *Mullet Bay,* you'll find *Java Wraps; Benetton; The Naf-Naf Shop,* which has the island's best prices for that French line of popular *prêt-à-porter;* a branch of *Ton Sur Ton* for that exclusive French unisex line; and a big *Bastringue.*

On the French side, most shops are open from 9 AM to noon or 12:30 PM and 2 to 6 PM, but many keep later hours at the new chic Port La Royale arcades (10 AM to 1 PM and 3 to 7 PM). Marigot concentrates on duty-free chic dispensed by shops along its rues de la Liberté and de la République, boutiques in two tempting shopping galleries (Galerie Périgourdine, Palais Caraïbe), and in the new St. Tropez–style Port La Royale Marina, a most attractive area for strolling and watching yachts or people from the many new cafés and bistros along the wharf. In a matter of months, the entire area surrounding the marina, and the streets leading to it from the center of Marigot, have been developed and are filling up with some of the most exciting fashions this side of Paris, Milan, or New York.

In Marigot, the biggest stocks of imports are found at *Oro de Sol,* in the very heart of Marigot, with luxury items such as Ebel watches; Pratesi linens; fine china and crystal by Villeroy, Boch, Christofle, Lalique, and Baccarat; as well as exquisite jewelry. (It was reported that a diamond-studded bracelet on sale for $60,000 here cost $90,000 in New York.) *Spritzer & Führmann* and *Little Switzerland* carry a similar array of merchandise. *La Romana*'s new Marigot branch, which has an attractive balcony bar to fortify customers with cappuccino and cocktails, devotes a separate section to Fendi bags and luggage (at up to 40% off US prices) and includes collections by Valentino, Gianfranco Ferré, Fila, Gianni Versace, La Perla swimwear, and Misani watches. Otherwise, the French side specializes mainly in small, elegant boutiques — a number with island exclusives on French and Italian fashion names, priced below US levels, but still very expensive. The same original, often unique, clothing may not be available back home. The new *Sportman* on Rue Félix Ebouè is *très chic* for women's wear. For wine lovers, a not-to-be-missed stop is Edmond de Rothschild's *La Cave du Savour Club*, on Rue de la Liberté, for a tasting and perhaps a vintage bottle of liqueur to take home. *Maneks* carries cameras, electronics, watches, magazines, liquors, cigarettes, sundries, and film.

In the Galerie Périgourdine (opposite the post office) are *Sandrine's* two shops for women, men, and "Plage," or beachwear), *Herbs and Spices,* Le *Jardin* snack bar, and pretty *Le Nadaillac* restaurant. And in the Palais Caraïbe (also called "Le Patio" after the once-popular restaurant in the courtyard by the *Palm Plaza* hotel) are *Elegance* for women's high fashion, *Claude* for French designer shoes and bags (Charles Jourdan, Ted Lapidus), and *Boutique Courréges.*

In the new Port La Royale arcades: *Boa,* for *Naf-Naf* sportswear; *Animale,* for very exotic, pricey women's fashions, including leather and furs, with a men's shop next door; *Deviation,* for Naf-Naf and other original sportswear, hand-painted cotton knits, and some leather clothes for women; *Dalila* for Balinese-fashioned batiks and embroidered dresses and outfits (there is a *Samson,* with similar Balinese fashions, on Rue Charles de Gaulle); *Raisonnable, Jules,* and *Ibiza* for more French fashion; *Italmania* and *Aventura* for men's and women's Italian designer fashions; *Havane* for men; *Elle,* for handicrafts and gifts; *Creations St. Martin,* for tropic-print fabrics by the yard (for pareos, home decor); *Bastringue,* with *prêt-à-porter* by Emmanuelle Khan, Kenzo, Dorothée Bis; *Crazy,* for flashy evening fashions; *Lipstick,* which has a new branch in the center of Marigot, for all sorts of salon treatments, massage, French cosmetics; *Sea Life* for original clunky jewelry, mostly shells and coral; *Maggy's* for perfumes; *Paradis Latin* for Lancel, Delsey, Lucas luggage and bags, Pollini shoes.

In case of a mid-shopping sinking spell, pause for a breezy drink on the harborside terrace of *L'Aventure* or at the bar of *La Vie en Rose* in Marigot, or try the *Café de Paris* or *Les Cocotiers* in the Port La Royale, where the island's best ice cream is found at the Italian *Etna per Dolce Vita. K-Dis,* on Rue General de Gaulle, has a vast selection of French foods and wines.

In Grand Case, *Pierre Lapin* (Dee Forbes' collection of paintings, pottery, handblocked fabrics, clothes, delightful gifts) and *L'Atelier* (intriguing original handcrafts — especially ceramics, small-scale cane furniture) are special. *Under the Waves* at *Grand Case Beach Club* has beachwear and accessories. At booming new Anse Marcel, look for Jill Walker's watercolors on gift items at the *So Much* shop, and check out *Donna Uomo* and *Deviation* for clothing. In Orleans, visit artist Roland Richardson at his lovely home. His watercolors, etchings, woodcut prints, and charcoal and oil paintings of island life and architecture make beautiful gifts. He receives on Thursdays from 10 AM to 6 PM, or by appointment (phone: 873224).

 TIPPING: Hotels add a 10% to 15% service charge to bills, which is supposed to take care of waiters and room maids. In some establishments, however, personnel see little, if any, of this charge, so leaving a small gratuity for good service is always appreciated. Most restaurants on the French side include at least a 10% service charge on the check; on the Dutch side some do, some don't; always make sure, so you won't double-tip (or zero-tip). The customary tip to taxi drivers is 50¢ or $1 above the fare, unless you've had a tour by taxi, in which case, the driver will expect more. For airport porters, $1 US or 2 gilders is about right.

SPECIAL EVENTS: One Dutch national holiday, *Coronation Day* (April 30), and a French one, *Bastille Day* (July 14), are celebrated on both sides of the island with fireworks, dancing, and sports events. The annual St. Maarten's Trade Winds Regatta takes place in the early spring. On *St. Martin's* or *Concordia Day* (November 11), Dutch-French friendship is celebrated with parades and joint ceremonies at the border. On *Schoelcher Day* (July 21), the French of St. Martin celebrate the end of slavery in the French West Indies with music, African dances, and feasting. Other holidays when banks and stores are closed (although some shops are open a few hours when cruise ships are in port) include *New Year's, Carnival* (pre-Lent on the French side, the last two weeks in April on the Dutch), *Good Friday, Easter* and *Easter Monday, Labor Day* (May 1), *Ascension Thursday* (40 days after Easter), *All Saints' Day* (French side, November 1), *Christmas,* and — on the Dutch side — *Boxing Day* (December 26).

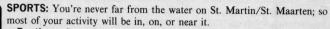

SPORTS: You're never far from the water on St. Martin/St. Maarten; so most of your activity will be in, on, or near it.

Boating – Several day sails are available from *Bobby's Marina* (phone: 22366), *Great Bay Marina* (phone: 22167), Little Pier in Philipsburg, or through your hotel activities desk, including the Antillean-owned *Orotava,* the 61-foot schooner *Gandalf* (to "Flat Island"), the 45-foot ketch *Gabrielle,* or the 41-foot ketch *Pretty Penny.* A full-day trip with lunch runs about $55. Check Port La Royale and the marina at Anse Marcel for day trips to neighboring cays. Most hotels have Sunfish or Sailfish for loan or rent, and there are larger boats available for charter; ask your hotel travel desk. Sailing instruction and sailboat rental are available from *Caribbean Watersports* at Mullet Bay Marina, where enthusiasts will also be able to arrange for waterskiing, jet skiing, parasailing, sport fishing, or a mistral board (phone: 42801, ext. 337; 44363). Big regatta of the year is the St. Maarten Trade Winds Race, which takes place every year around February or March.

Cycling – The terrain is hilly enough to make biking a strenuous way to get about and find some beaches for picnics. Bike rentals are available at *Mullet Bay* resort (phone: 42801) or at *Carter's Cycle Center,* on Bush Road, Cul-de-Sac (phone: 22621), or on the airport road (phone: 44251, 22621), for about $10 and up per day.

Golf – The windy, Joseph Lee–designed layout at *Mullet Bay* is a bit too gimmicky but has great views of the water at 14 of its 18 holes; it extends along the palm-lined shores of the bay on one side and the lagoon on the other. Nonguests can play when tee times are available (phone: 42015). Greens fee: $90 for 18 holes ($45 for hotel guests), $55 for 9 holes ($30 for hotel guests), cart included; rental clubs ($10) are also available. *Caravanserai* hotel guests share *Mullet Bay* playing privileges.

Horseback Riding – *Crazy Acres Riding Center* offers 2-hour beach rides on weekdays (for 8 persons maximum) at 9 AM for $40 (book 2 days in advance), and private beach picnics can also be arranged. Riding instruction and lessons in horse care are available. On the Wathey Estate in Cole Bay (phone: 42503, ext. 201; 44309, ext. 201).

Jogging – Several hotels have jogging on the beach, as does *Le Privilège* at Anse Marcel (phone: 873737). The *Road Runners* club meets Wednesdays at 5:15 PM and Sundays at 7 AM in the main parking lot of the *Pelican Resort* for 5- or 10-kilometer runs. Races are usually held once a month. Visitors are welcome. For information, contact Dr. Fritz Bus of the Back Street Clinic or Malcolm Maidwell of *El Tigre.*

Snorkeling and Scuba – Island water sports centers completely set up for equipment rental, programs of instruction, and dive and snorkel trips include: *Maho Watersports* (which also offers dive packages to Saba), based at *Mullet Bay* (phone: 44387, ext. 379); *Ocean Explorers* at Simpson Bay (phone: 4-5252); *Red Ensign Watersports* at Dawn Beach (phone: 22929); *Little Bay Watersports* at *Little Bay Beach* hotel (phone: 22333/4); *Watersports Unlimited* at *Holland House* in Philipsburg (phone: 23434); *St. Maarten Divers & Watersports* at Great Bay (phone: 22446); *La Samanna* (phone: 875122), *Grand Case Beach Club* (phone: 875187), and *Le Galion Beach* (phone: 875177) on the French side. The new *La Belle Créole* and *L'Habitation* also have dive operations. Dive trips run about $25 to $50 per person. *St. Maarten Watersports and Waterski Club* on Simpson Bay Lagoon offers snorkeling trips to Anguilla as well as windsurfing, water skiing, sport fishing, and parasailing. Open daily from 10 AM to 5 PM with pool and bar (phone: 44387). The waters around the island are clear (75- to 125-foot visibility), and there is a fair amount of reef life to explore. Pinel Island, just offshore, also offers good snorkeling and shallow diving, and just 1 mile off the coast there's a sunken (1801) British man-of-war, the *Proselyte,* replete with cannons and anchors, as well as good coral and fish. Other sites include "The Maze," "The Alleys," "Lois Lane," "French Reef," "Hens & Chick," and "Cable Reef." To see the aquatic world without getting your hair wet or taking off your glasses, call *Underwater Adventures,* c/o *Maho Watersports,* at *Mullet Bay* (phone: 44387), for an underwater walk wearing specially constructed bronze diving helmets. *Glass-Bottom Boat* also does lagoon cruises (phone: 42115, ext. 4240). There is parasailing on the lagoon with *Lagoon Cruises & Watersports N.V.* (phone: 42801, ext. 227) for about $25 per ride.

Spas – *L'Aqualigne,* the new health spa–beauty clinic at the Dutch side's *Pelican Resort and Casino,* offers treatments for men and women, including Weider muscle and fitness machines; sauna, steamrooms, and whirlpool; dance, aerobics, exercise, and yoga classes; health bar; Swedish and Shiatzu massages; cellulitis treatments, waxings, and facials. "Body sculpting," Gerovital therapy, weight loss, and even cosmetic surgery are available, with weekly, monthly, and daily programs; cosmetics and health foods for sale (phone: 42426). Sports facilities at *Le Privilège* (phone: 873737), the French side's chic new complex at booming Anse Marcel, include a pool, tennis, squash, jogging, weightlifting, yoga, archery, a gymnasium, racquetball, shooting, and French petanque. There is a 24-hour restaurant and a swinging disco very popular on weekends. Apartments on premises, near marina, but the best bet is a stay at pretty *L'Habitation* below.

Sport Fishing – Marlin, barracuda, tuna, wahoo, and dolphin are the best catches in the fishing grounds close by. Plenty of boats are available for hire, a number based at Simpson Bay, *Bobby's Marina* (phone: 22366), or at *Great Bay Marina* (phone: 22167) in Philipsburg; arrangements can be made through your hotel. On the French side, check the *Marina de Lonvilliers* at Anse Marcel (phone: 873737) or *Mullet Bay* resort; on the Dutch side, *Blue Water Charters* (phone: 42801, 44363). Tuna is fished year-round; dolphin, kingfish, and barracuda from December to April. Charters usually include tackle, bait, food, and drink, and average $600 for a full day.

Squash – There are 2 courts at *Le Privilège* (phone: 873737).

Swimming and Sunning – Top attractions, with 36 beaches around the island. Your hotel will likely have its own stretch of sand, and you'll want to get out to see some of the others, for there is a great variety of wide, white expanses and secluded, shady coves to enjoy. Nonguests can use changing facilities at most hotels for a small fee, but there are many beaches where you won't need any facilities because nobody else will be there. You'll find very few people on the hideaway sands of Long Bay, north of *La Samanna,* and at Plum and Rouge bays on the French side, north of Long Bay. These secluded spots also occasionally attract the unscrupulous, so it's not a good idea to leave belongings unattended. There is one designated nudist beach, on — *naturellement*

— the French side, at Orient Bay, where there's also a simple nudist resort. But even on other French side beaches, the general attitude toward bikinis, monokinis, and no kinis at all is pretty relaxed.

Tennis – Very popular. At last count there were 49 courts on the island, 14 of them at the *Mullet Bay* resort (3 lighted). Most of the larger hotels have at least 1 court: *Oyster Pond, Dawn Beach* hotel, and *Caravanserai* have 2 each; the *Maho Beach* has 4; *Little Bay Beach* has 3 (1 lighted); *La Belle Créole* has 4 courts (all lighted); *Le Privilège* has 6 courts (4 lighted) and a practice wall; *La Samanna* has 3; *Le Galion* has 2 hard courts; and the *Grand Case Beach Club, PLM Azur St. Tropez, Coralita, Great Bay,* and *Summit* have 1 each. Fees for nonguests run about $5 per hour. Courts have various features, including lessons, clinics, and pro shops.

Water Skiing – Available at most beachside hotels and on calm Simpson Bay Lagoon. Contact *St. Maarten Watersports & Waterski Club* on Simpson Bay (phone: 44387) or *Caribbean Watersports* at *Mullet Bay* (phone: 42801, 44363).

Windsurfing – Available at many beachside hotels, including *Mullet Bay* resort, *Divi Little Bay, Dawn Beach* (serving *Oyster Pond*), and *St. Maarten Beach Club,* and on Simpson Bay Lagoon. Most French-side beach hotels are also equipped or will make arrangements. Lessons average about $20 per hour.

 NIGHTLIFE: With some 300 restaurants on the island, dining out is the most popular pastime. On the Dutch side, the evening usually begins with "sundowners" on the porch of the *West Indian Tavern* or among the nautical types at *Chesterfield's* or *The Greenhouse,* and, on the French side, it starts off with an *apéritif* at one of the lively café-bars or bistros of the new Port La Royale Marina, where live music often fills the air as the temperature cools down. Later, many of the hotels have "West Indian nights" or dancing under the stars, and several have discos — currently popular are *Maho Beach*'s *Studio 7* and *Mullet Bay*'s *Le Club,* which often swing through the wee hours. French-side nocturnal types are found at *L'Atmosphere,* the very chic new disco at Port La Royale Marina, or at *Le Privilège,* at Anse Marcel, where restaurants serve resuscitation all night long. A more local flavor is to be savored at the *Night Fever* near Colombier (take the road from Marigot toward Grand Case, turn right where marked). *Le Flirt Disco,* off Philipsburg's Front Street, draws young locals, while tourists and some residents gather at the *St. Maarten Beach Club*'s *Fandango Restaurant/Heartbreak Bar, The Greenhouse,* or *Sam's Place* for pre- or post-dinner drinks and music. Hotel casinos (all on the Dutch side) include: *Cupecoy, Maho Beach, Pelican, St. Maarten Beach Club, Mullet Bay* resort, *Great Bay, Divi Little Bay,* and the *Seaview* in town. Some also have nightclubs that feature live entertainment. Several French-side hotels provide free casino transport for their guests. Minimum playing age is 18. Most are Vegas-style: craps, roulette, blackjack, slot machines. Before playing, check the house rules, for they vary slightly from one casino to another. All serve complimentary drinks, and most open at lunchtime.

BEST ON THE ISLAND

 CHECKING IN: The Dutch side has over 2,300 hotel rooms and several hundred efficiency apartments with kitchenettes. Prices vary widely — from modest (about $45, not including meals, for a minimal guesthouse room in Philipsburg in winter) to expensive (from $220 up for a double without meals at some luxury resorts and *starting* at $480 for accommodations at very luxurious resorts). And lifestyles vary wildly — from Borscht Circuit with Beach to

Smart Set by the Sea. A couple of hotels rely heavily on back-to-back charter bookings. Rates drop as much as 60% in summer. There's a 5% tax on hotel rooms and usually a 15% service charge (or 10% service and 5% "energy").

On the French side: fewer rooms (though there are well over 1,300, with more opening soon) priced from inexpensive (about $300 and up a week without meals in season for a self-sufficient apartment in the small seaside settlement of Grand Case) to stunning (about $535 and up a night in season for a suite, without meals, at *La Belle Créole*). French rates run about a third lower in summer. Here there is always a 15% service charge, and a 2 to 7 FF government tax per person per night, which is sometimes incorporated into the room rate.

A number of fully staffed private homes are rented by the week or month on each side of the border. Prices start at about $700 a week in winter, range *way* up from there. Best contacts: Ms. Judy Shepherd at *St. Maarten Rentals* (Pelican House, Beacon Hill, St. Maarten, NA; phone: 44330), *Ambria International Realty* (180 Front St., St. Maarten, NA; phone: 22711), *Carimo* (Rue Général de Gaulle, PO Box 220, Marigot 97150, St. Martin, FWI; phone: 875758); or *International Immobilier* (Marigot, 97150, St. Martin, FWI; phone: 877900 or 875814).

Best reservations advice: shop carefully to make sure what you want is what you get (especially in the atmosphere department). And book early because, when the winter gets really rotten up north, there are many weeks when the island is completely sold out. Among our recommendations below, expensive translates as $200 and up for a double without meals in winter; moderate, from $120 to $200 for two (EP) in season; inexpensive, $120 and under in winter for a double (EP).

THE DUTCH SIDE/NEAR THE AIRPORT

Mullet Bay – A recent multimillion-dollar refurbishment has restored some lost luster to this sprawling 172-acre condominium-cum-resort hotel, with 600 spacious, stylish, air-conditioned rooms and suites, and just about everything in the way of facilities: water sports center, 18 holes of golf, 14 tennis courts, 2 saltwater pools, casino, disco, grocery store, pharmacy, clinic, shopping plaza, a branch of Chase Manhattan Bank, and regular shuttle service around the vast property, although a car helps a lot. With 10 restaurants (the best of which is *Le Gourmet*) as well as extensive meeting and convention facilities, this resort is remarkably self-contained (phone: 42801). Expensive.

Cupecoy Beach Club – This attractive Mediterranean-style collection of oceanfront and hillside condominiums features spacious, tastefully decorated double rooms; 1-, 2-, and 3-bedroom suites; and villas. A new "piazza" area houses a shopping arcade, casino (with 17th-century pirate theme), and the new French restaurant *Le Vaudeville,* which has been gathering rave reviews despite occasionally brusque service. Amenities include a cliff-backed beach (when it exists; it tends to disappear, mostly during low season, July to November), 3 large freshwater pools, and a water sports center. Baby sitters available (phone: 42500). Expensive.

Caravanserai – One of St. Maarten's older, established hotels, with a devoted clientele and a sparkling new facelift. There are 85 redecorated rooms, all with air conditioning and balconies or patios facing the sea or the quiet courtyard. Facilities include 2 pools, tennis courts, watersports and activities desk. In addition, guests also have access to big sister *Mullet Bay* facilities. There is a charming gazebo bar-restaurant surrounded by water on three sides, and tea is served in the elegant *Palm Court.* This gem is small and special, offering quiet, leisurely luxury. Airport Road (phone: 44214). Expensive.

Maho Beach – Recently expanded, renovated, and reopened with 247 guestrooms and suites, including a wing of 57 rooms with color TV (cable), Italian tiles, and new furnishings, this attractive resort offers all the desirable amenities (beach, pool, 4 improved tennis courts, full water sports), as well as 3 restaurants, meeting rooms for up to 500, a casino, a medical clinic, one of the island's most popular discos, *Studio 7,* and the new *Club Caribe* nightclub, which features live entertainment. Lively day and night (phone: 42115, 42119). Expensive.

Royal Islander Club/La Plage – Maho's attractive time-sharing complex now offers 1- and 2-bedroom apartments, each with full kitchen, color TV, direct-dial phone, and air conditioning, as well as access to Maho Beach facilities next door (phone: 42505). Expensive to moderate.

Horny Toad – Onetime governor's house on Simpson Bay beach now holds 8 bright apartments — each with a big balcony or porch overlooking the sea, kitchenette, generous bath, special charms (#1 has a step-down bedroom; studio #3 has a hanging basket chair). Caring management (phone: 4-4323). Moderate.

Mary's Boon – With 12 rooms, each with bath, kitchenette, and seaside patio, and excellent service; personally operated and owned by Rush Little, a longtime adoptive St. Maarten innkeeper. Next to the Juliana airport runway, but nobody seems bothered by it. Great beach, unregimented life, honor bar. Decorated with a blend of antiques and tropical wicker, sisal, bamboo. Breeze, but no air conditioning. Pets welcome; children under 16 not. Delicious French cuisine with an American accent (phone: 44235). Moderate to inexpensive.

Summit – One of St. Maarten's older properties, with a faithful following, now under new management and with a new Italian restaurant (under a French chef). The pleasant 1- and 2-story chalets have porches (often looking onto the neighboring chalet). Large pool; shuttle service to beaches and casinos. Informal (phone: 42150, 44227). Moderate to inexpensive.

THE DUTCH SIDE/PHILIPSBURG

Great Bay – One of Philipsburg's oldest hotels, at the western end of Great Bay Beach, this 225-room property has been redecorated (although some of the older rooms still seem a bit frayed — best to book in the new Miramar wing, where all rooms face the sea and are quieter and more functional). All the rooms are spacious and come with 2 double beds, full tub, and shower. Amenities include a casino, small shopping arcade, beach, pool, tennis, water sports, and seemingly endless activities for the clientele, who are mostly there on package tours. Saturday night barbecue wih steel band (phone: 22446, 2-3008, 2-2447). Moderate.

The Jetty – At the head of Great Bay Beach in downtown Philipsburg, within walking distance of all shopping and restaurants but quietly off the main drag, next to *Bobby's Marina.* This member of the Netherlands' reputable Golden Tulip chain offers 15 spacious and breezy 1- and 2-bedroom apartments, tastefully furnished and with balconies. Friendly management. Kanaalsteeg (phone: 22922). Moderate.

St. Maarten Beach Club – In-town condo-hotel with two sections bracketing Front Street and 75 small-scale suites equipped with kitchenettes and color cable TV, direct-dial phones, and hideaway sofa beds. Some have balconies overlooking the beach; others face Front Street. Facilities include a restaurant, casino, and beach bar. Very handy to shopping (phone: 23434). Moderate.

Town House Villas – With 12 extremely attractive townhouses (each with 2 air-conditioned bedrooms, 1½ baths, 2 patios, complete kitchen, and living and dining area) on Great Bay Beach at the edge of Philipsburg (phone: 22898). Moderate.

Holland House – Dutch-style rooms and suites with kitchenettes and terraces overlooking Front Street or town beach; joint water sports with next-door *Beach Club.* TV, video. Breakfast patio and beach bar; Dutch–West Indian lunches, dinners. Scarcely palmy, but a good buy — especially in winter (phone: 22572). Moderate to inexpensive.

Pasanggrahan Royal Guesthouse – Formerly the Government Guest House, this historic West Indian building is St. Maarten's oldest inn and an old favorite of many regular visitors from statesmen to salesmen. Central Philipsburg location on the beach, with 21 charming rooms, plenty of greenery, afternoon tea, and pleasant seaside bar and restaurant (phone: 23588). Inexpensive.

ALSO ON THE DUTCH SIDE

Oyster Pond Yacht Club – Very private, romantic, and elegant inn between restless sea and placid lagoon. This long-esteemed property, with Moorish white walls, arched portals, red tile floors, hardwood balustrades, white wicker furniture, and exotic plants, glistens as never before. The 20 guestrooms, including 4 tower suites, each have a secluded terrace and are naturally air conditioned by screened louvers and Casablanca-style ceiling fans. Guests who want to leave the grounds — many don't — will need a car. French cuisine is served in the candelit dining room or, at lunch, informally, under umbrellas in the pretty courtyard. Two tennis courts, water sports, an attractive wood-decked pool, and (shared) reef-protected beach; efficient, friendly management. Very special (phone: 22206, 23206). Expensive.

Dawn Beach – With 155 spacious, air-conditioned rooms, each with full kitchenette, color TV, radio, and terrace on one of the island's most beautiful reef-protected beaches (which can be choppy on windy days). The units on the beach are by far the most desirable. Airy central building was totally redecorated following an April 1987 fire. Attractive open-air dining room, bar, raised to catch the view and sea breezes. Freshwater pool with waterfall, 2 lighted tennis courts, water sports, and popular Sunday brunch (phone: 22944, 22929). Expensive.

Belair Beach – Its long white beach — a wider extension of Little Bay's — is its great asset. The 72 condo suites, each with 2 bedrooms, 2 baths, full kitchen, dining/living room, private terrace, color TV, radio, and 2 phones, have recently been refurbished. Facilities include 2 restaurants, 2 bars, full watersports, and shops, including groceries and liquor (phone: 23362, 23366). Expensive.

Divi Divi Little Bay Beach – One of the island's oldest properties has recently joined the Divi group, the Caribbean's largest hotel operator, and has undergone vast renovations — as well as the addition of 100 new time-share units. Rooms overlook beach or garden. Other features include beach, pool, watersports, lighted tennis courts, restaurant, cocktail lounge with live entertainment, casino, and shops. Children welcome (phone: 22333). Expensive.

La Vista – Pretty new European-owned and -operated resort on the Pelican Key Estates, with 24 units ranging from studios and deluxe junior suites to luxury penthouses and modern adaptations of West Indian cottages. All have full kitchenettes, living/dining areas cheerfully decorated, and private terraces with lovely sea views. TV, tennis, pool, poolside lunch/snack bar, small beach, horseback riding. Friendly, family-run personal service (phone: 43005/8/10). Expensive.

Pelican Resort – On a hillside surrounded by 1,400 feet of sea frontage and its own manmade beach, this time-sharing resort now totals 342 well-appointed 1- and 2-bedroom suites and studios, with building still going on. Nine separate areas, each with its own pool; also a marina, Swiss/French restaurant with entertainment, casino, tennis, horseback riding, jogging paths, water sports, Jacuzzis, children's playground, video gameroom, and health spa (*L'Aqualigne*), including sauna, weight training room, whirlpools, massage rooms, medical clinic, steam baths, and yoga classes. Baby sitters available. Rates drop 60% in summer (phone: 44309, 42503). Expensive to moderate.

THE FRENCH SIDE/MARIGOT

Club Le Grand – What was formerly the *Grand St. Martin* hotel is now St. Martin's first and only all-inclusive resort, with 70 units, including 25 hillside studios, 20 well-appointed rooms in the main complex, and fully equipped 1-, 2-, and 3-bedroom apartments. Interesting split-level architecture, with some wooden beams; terraces, air conditioning, phones, and TV. Other features include the island's largest freshwater pool, tennis, fine beach, water sports, and 2 restaurants. There is a full program of activities, from Sunfish and windsurfing lessons to water polo, aerobics, hiking, and French lessons. All drinks, activities, entertainment, meals, and wine included in rate. The perfect spot for those seeking nonstop activity (phone: 875791). Moderate.

Pirate – A brand-new gleaming replacement for the former tiny property of the same name which occupied a beachfront plot within walking distance of Marigot. There are now 100 units, including 80 large studios with kitchenettes and terraces, and 20 duplexes. Other features include a small pool and a beach within strolling distance. An informal waterfront snack bar and restaurant are planned (phone: 877837). Moderate.

PLM Azur St. Tropez – After recent major renovation and expansion, this long-established property is now under capable new management. There are 116 rooms facing either the road or the beach. (The older beachfront rooms are a good bargain off-season, when they are the same price as the back rooms.) Breakfast is served on a breezy waterfront terrace, but there is no proper restaurant. Other features include a pool and tennis. Active day and night (phone: 875472). Moderate to inexpensive.

La Résidence – Charming hotel in the heart of Marigot, between the town center and the booming Port La Royale marina. The 21 rooms, studios, and apartments, each with phone, fridge, and TV, ring the quaint courtyard bar and restaurant (phone: 877037). Moderate to inexpensive.

Le Royal Louisiana – Another new "city" hotel attractively built around a central patio where breakfasts, light lunches, and ice cream are served. The 75 rooms, including 14 duplexes, are cheery and have air conditioning and TV. Good value (phone: 878651). Inexpensive.

Palm Plaza – Very good value in the "old" heart of Marigot in a lovely old West Indian building, with 21 renovated rooms and suites. Popular bar, restaurant, and shops in the patio (phone: 875196). Inexpensive.

THE FRENCH SIDE/GRAND CASE

Grand Case Beach Club – Fresh, airy, attractive studios, 1- and 2-bedroom apartments (76 in all) with full baths, kitchens, and private terraces, on one of St. Martin's most splendid beaches. Swimming, sailing, water sports, tennis, bocce, bar, panoramic restaurant; friendly and gracious American management. Very good buy in summer. On Grand Case Bay (phone: 875187). Expensive to moderate.

Hévéa – The restaurant called *Hoa Mai,* under new ownership, has moved down the road a piece. The original Hoa Mai, with her French husband, now owns this pretty 8-room guesthouse and its more renowned restaurant (phone: 875685). Expensive to moderate.

Petite Plage – Half a dozen comfortably contemporary suites plus 12 motelish (but pleasant) units just outside Grand Case. Popular with families in high season (phone: 875065). Moderate.

Bertines – On a lush green hillside in La Savane, 1½ miles from Marigot, is this simple, 5-room guesthouse of considerable island charm, featuring informal dinners on a breezy terrace overlooking Grand Case and Anguilla (phone: 877783). Inexpensive.

ALSO ON THE FRENCH SIDE

La Belle Créole – At last, after a nearly 20-year pause, the brainchild of the late Claude Philippe (once of New York's *Waldorf-Astoria*) was completed and opened in 1988. Operated by Conrad International Hotels, the 156-room resort was originally modeled after a typical fishing village on the French Riviera and is said to have been completed according to the original blueprints. There are 27 one- to three-story villas, linked by cobblestone streets, sidewalks, and courtyards, all surrounding a village square. Most units have private terraces overlooking Marigot Bay or the lagoon, and there are 42 connecting rooms, as well as 5 equipped for the handicapped. All are decorated in a provençal motif, some with beamed ceilings, and all have air conditioning, mini-bars, TV sets, and phones. Amenities include 3 beaches; freshwater pool; 4 tennis courts and pro shop; full range of watersports, including windsurfing and water skiing; deep-sea fishing and scuba diving can also be arranged. There are boutiques, secretarial services, a drugstore, car rental agency, and concierge on the premises, as well as a restaurant featuring international and Créole cuisine, a café-bar at poolside serving light meals and snacks, a beach bar and a main bar that will feature regular entertainment. Regardless of age, children stay with their parents free of charge (phone: 875866 or 800-445-8667). Very expensive.

La Samanna – Once the French side's only luxury property, the 16-year-old sleek hideaway still boasts a devoted clientele who return year after year, attracted, no doubt, by the elegant Moorish villas, Casablanca-style bar, and restaurant featuring chef Jean-Pierre Jury's exquisite tropics-inspired French cuisine. A total of 85 units includes terraced rooms, one- and two-bedroom suites and apartments, and 6 three-bedroom villas spread along the beach or hillside. Other features include a good beach for snorkeling, a large pool, 3 tennis courts, water sports, and fitness programs. In July, there is a very special 2-week spa program, supervised by experts from Arizona's *Canyon Ranch*. (Book well in advance.) This place reeks with chic, and visitors who don't are likely to feel uncomfortable. So, too, are those who don't prize pricey pretension. Closed September and October. Baie Longue (phone: 875122). Very expensive.

L'Habitation – Nestled under Pigeon Pea Hill on spectacular Anse Marcel (Marcel Cove), one of St. Martin's most beautiful beaches, this romantic retreat is spread over 150 acres. It is largely self-sufficient, with a large freshwater pool, 2 restaurants of its own (as well as several more above at *Le Privilège*), nightly entertainment, watersports, marina, and *Le Privilège* sports complex, which is connected by 24-hour shuttle service. Designed in traditional West Indian style, it consists of 5 two-story buildings overlooking a lagoon and 3 three-story structures making up the U-shaped main building that houses the deluxe rooms, suites, and dining and entertainment facilities. Each of the 189 rooms and 12 junior suites contains spacious, well-appointed baths. All rooms are air conditioned, with private balcony, direct-dial phone, TV, VCR, safe, mini-fridge, and Pullman kitchen. Each of the 1-bedroom marina suites includes a private patio (with a hammock, table, and chairs) and a fully equipped kitchen. Although large and rambling (for St. Martin), this pretty new property has a lot of charm and a professional, efficient management. Closed September. Marcel Cove (phone: 873333, 877800). Expensive.

Village Captain Olivier – Straddling the Dutch/French border is this new French luxury complex. Each of the 25 air-conditioned bungalows (18 of which overlook the sea) comes with kitchenette, terrace, direct-dial phone, radio, TV, and room service from the waterfront restaurant of the same name. Oyster Pond (phone: 873000). Expensive.

Club Orient – A "clothing optional" naturist resort on a sometimes choppy 1½-mile-long beach. Accommodations are in 61 rooms in prefabricated wooden chalets brought in from Finland. Twenty-five have kitchen and living room; others have kitchenette. Some accommodate up to 4 people. Beach bar/restaurant, water sports, boutique, and basic grocery store. No frills — but this is getting back to nature! Baie Orientale (phone: 875385 or 873385). Moderate.

Le Galion – There are 54 air-conditioned rooms, suites, and bungalows (many with kitchens), dive school, tennis, and lots of water sports, a 2-mile-long beach, with nudist beach nearby. French restaurant; spirited, informal nightlife (phone: 875177). Moderate.

EATING OUT: French cuisine is prepared very well on St. Martin/St. Maarten, in both its classic version (escargots, frogs' legs, langouste flambée) and its Créole variations (the savory fish stew called blaff, crabes farcis, curried conch, and chicken colombos). But if you're smitten with a sudden craving for bagels and lox, prime ribs, or a chocolate soda, those exist, too. For lobster lovers, this island comes close to heaven (although most of the restaurant supply now comes from nearby Anguilla). Broiled, boiled, stuffed, hot with drawn butter, cold with mayonnaise, or in a salad, the meat is sweet and tender, and the price — compared to stateside levels — is okay. There's also lots of good fish, but beware; sometimes it is "fresh frozen" before you see it on your plate. Above all, there is plenty of good French wine (served by the carafe or bottle) and lots of tasty Dutch beer.

At lunch, nobody bothers much about reservations. For dinner, they're usually a good idea.

Some restaurants without phones leave a pad and pen at the entrance (when they're closed) for prospective customers to book tables. Many, but not all, now accept some credit cards; it's a good idea to check before arriving. Most restaurants add a 10% to 15% service charge in lieu of tip, but neither government taxes meals. In the listings that follow, an inexpensive restaurant is one where dinner and service costs $25 or less per person; moderate prices range from about $25 to $50 per person; anything above that is expensive. However, there are several, such as *Le Santal* and *The Ritz,* that start at more than $75 per person — before drinks or wine. With some 300 restaurants in operation, St. Martin/St. Maarten offers a wealth of options for the hungry.

THE DUTCH SIDE/PHILIPSBURG

Le Bec Fin/La Coupole – This gastronomic duo, in a lovely 18th-century courtyard off Front Street, opens early in the morning with warm croissants at *La Coupole.* Upstairs, the elegant, long-established *Le Bec Fin* restaurant has a new French chef who offers a fairly traditonal menu, albeit with some tempting deviations, such as chilled tomato soufflé and lobster salad with mangos. Definitely worth checking out. Front St. (phone: 22976). Expensive.

Da Livio – This very attractive seafront restaurant features a standard Italian menu for lovely al fresco lunches on the terrace or for elegant candlelit dinners. *Prosciutto e melone,* manicotti with spinach and ricotta cheese, skewered scampi in garlic butter, *saltimbocca* (veal in wine sauce with ham and sage), and ricotta cheesecake with pine nuts are some of the house specialties. Soft classical music or, perhaps, Neapolitan love songs, along with the soothing lap of the waves on the shore beneath your table, contribute to the overall romantic experience. When Livio is present, the food seems to be better. Closed Sundays. Front St. (phone: 22690). Expensive to moderate.

L'Escargot – In an old townhouse, this is one of the island's oldest restaurants, but it's never really risen much above its snails. Best stick to them — *à la provençale, de Bourgogne,* in puff pastry, or in fresh mushroom caps. Seconds include crisp duck, quail in raisin sauce, and lobster thermidor. Open daily for lunch, dinner, and late suppers. A downstairs disco, *The Last Dance,* goes from 10:30 PM to the wee hours. Front St. (phone: 22483). Expensive to moderate.

West Indian Tavern – Known for its ambience more than its food, this popular tavern/restaurant is housed in a 180-year-old hand-built cedar townhouse on the site of St. Maarten's first and only synagogue. Open daily from 4 to 6 PM for "happy hour." Dinner, served from 5 PM to midnight, includes a lot of seafood, a "famous" onion soup, and New York steaks, as well as some unusual offerings: smoked blue marlin with tomato and red basil sorbet, shrimp kebab with Nigerian peanut and pepper sauce. Crowded when cruise ships are in (almost always in winter). Irish coffee, darts, chess, backgammon, and 4 romantic, tropical verandahs open until 1 AM. Evenings only. Front St. (phone: 22965). Expensive to moderate.

La Rosa – The newest arrival of merit on the Dutch side, by any other name, is a jewel. The traditional Italian menu features several of Giuseppe La Rosa's own Sicilian recipes, such as *Rigatoni La Rosa* and *Pasta alla Norma,* with fried eggplant and plenty of Parmesan, as well as classics like the fresh and moist grilled swordfish with *salmoriglio* sauce. Desserts include a sinful *tartufo* and *zuccotto alla cioccolatta.* Live piano music complements the romantic setting. Front St. (phone: 23832). Moderate.

Café Royal – A perfect stopover on a busy shopping day in the Royal Palm Plaza. Cool, shaded garden where American (and Dutch) breakfasts, light lunches (including great salads), and dinners (during high-season) are served. Try the traditional Dutch seafood: smoked eel, salmon, trout, or herring. The deli in the back prepares fancy *pique-niques* of French bread, cheese, and wine or, for the more demanding palate, lobster salad, paté, pastries — even caviar, shrimp-stuffed tomatoes, or duck à l'orange. Presiding over all this mad activity is the ever-gracious Rene Florijn, who has provided feasts for visiting Dutch and British royal families. You, too, can try the Royal Picnic Basket, but be sure to order it well ahead. You can even get a map, insect repellant, suntan lotion, or rent an ice bucket and beach umbrella here. Royal Palm Plaza, Front St. (phone: 23443). Moderate.

Greenhouse – Modeled after the popular *Greenhouse* in St. Thomas and under the same ownership, this thoroughly refurbished palm-lined green and coral version at Bobby's Marina features light lunches (soups, salads, burgers, omelettes, and fish) and dinners, which include some West Indian standards (conch acras or chowder, curried chicken, local lobster and fish, Jamaican pepper steak), as well as a few more creative dishes such as a delicious coconut scampi and a toasted brie on salad. There's a very lively happy hour from 4:30 to 6:30 PM and live music and entertainment nightly from 10 PM. Delightful waterside atmosphere on Kanaalsteeg (phone: 22941). Moderate.

Seafood Galley and Raw Bar – Fresh oysters, mussels, clams, and other seafood landed locally or imported from New England and served *au naturelle* (unless unavailable, when guests are advised of "fresh frozen" backups). Pleasant breezy bar and boat-watching site right on the dock at Bobby's Marina. Good for lunch or dinner (chicken and steaks available for landlubbers), with a happy hour from 5 to 6 PM (phone: 23253). Moderate.

Callaloo Bar and Restaurant – A popular gathering place for locals and tuned-in tourists, with gazebo bar, snacks, as well as menu featuring hamburgers, steaks, salads, pizza — just about everything (including satellite TV) except, inexplicably, callaloo. Open until 2 AM. Closed Sundays. Promenade Arcade (no phone). New branch at Juliana Airport called *Café Juliana* serves great steak sandwiches. Moderate to inexpensive.

Wajang Doll – Popular spot for authentic Indonesian feasting on *rijsttafel* of either 14 or 19 different exotic dishes. Highly acclaimed by Dutch expatriates who know their *rijsttafel* well. Front St. (phone: 22687). Moderate to inexpensive.

Fandango – A tropical garden, with blooming island greenery, right in the heart of Philipsburg at the *St. Martin Beach Club.* Open from 7:30 AM to 10:30 PM for eggs Benedict, omelettes, soups, hot and cold sandwiches, and potato skins; four versions of fettuccine, fish, coconut shrimp, chicken, and beef for dinner. At the big bamboo *Heartbreak Bar,* Poco the parrot and Coco the cockatoo attract weary shoppers. Front St. (phone: 23434 or 22906, ext. 44). Inexpensive.

Pinocchio – A jumping hang-out with a seaside terrace, open from 11 AM to 4 PM for lunch and from 6 to 11 PM for dinner, with snacks available until 2 AM, but don't expect any gastronomic greats; a new "Louisiana Cajun" touch has been added to the Italian and Créole cuisine, but the chef is the same. Drinks are two for one during happy hour; satellite TV; good frozen daiquiris, wine by the glass, espresso, and cappuccino. Lively most of the day. Front St. (phone: 22166). Inexpensive.

Sam's Place – A favorite watering hole where you'll find residents, expats, the boating crowd, and tourists sitting around the bar at all hours. American breakfasts; burgers and salads at lunch; steaks, shrimp, lobster, ribs, and other grills, as well as a daily special, for dinner. Open from 9 AM to 2 AM, with live entertainment Tuesdays through Saturdays. Daily happy hour from 5:30 to 7 PM. Front St. near Bobby's Marina (phone: 22989). Inexpensive.

ELSEWHERE ON THE DUTCH SIDE

Oyster Pond Yacht Club – Lunch or dinner at this exclusive retreat is special. Whether dining in the elegant, breezy, candlelit dining room with fine linens, Rosenthal china, and fresh flowers everywhere, or lunching informally under the umbrellas of the quiet courtyard, the ambience alone rates 5 stars. To that add the superb cuisine of chef Paul Souchette, formerly of *La Samanna* hotel on the French side. Before feasting on minted cold cucumber soup, fresh asparagus in puff pastry with chervil butter, medallions of lobster with truffles, tomato, and basil, or sliced breast of duck in green peppercorn sauce, be sure to order the banana, chocolate, or raspberry soufflé for dessert. A memorable experience. Oyster Pond (phone: 22206, 23206). Expensive.

Le Gourmet – *Mullet Bay* resort's top choice offers traditional French cuisine carefully prepared and elegantly served. Among its favorites are escargots in creamy Riesling sauce and roast rack of lamb with mustard and herbs. Other options include a ragout of seafood and vegetables in white wine, herbs, cream, and truffles; diced veal in mushroom cream sauce (perhaps too many creamy sauces); excellent grilled meats; and a tempting trolley of pastries. Mullet Bay Resort and Casino (phone: 42323, ext. 354; or 42801). Expensive.

L'Oasis – Open to the Caribbean on three sides, the refurbished octagonal gazebo restaurant/bar of the lovely *Caravanserai* hotel is truly an oasis of calm and well-being. The French menu with a local touch includes a piquant *seviche* of fresh local conch, West Indian–style gazpacho, fresh grouper in lime and caper sauce, baked duck with pineapple and lime rum sauce, and *coupe antillaise* of mango, papaya, and lime sherbet. Charming. *Caravanserai Hotel,* Airport Rd. (phone: 44214, 44273, 44218). Expensive to moderate.

Bilboquet – On the terrace of a private house; tiny and personal. Imaginative menu features marvelous soups, grilled herbed fish, piquantly sauced meats, luscious dessert mousses. Depending on what's best at market, each night's five-course prix fixe dinner offers at least two choices under each heading, with roast prime beef as a standby. Closed Mondays in season. The management insists that reservations be made in person the first time you eat there for a very practical reason: the restaurant, in the Pointe Blanche section, is difficult to find in daylight; at night it is virtually impossible, unless you've driven out at least once before. After that, they'll give you their unlisted number, so you can phone. Take Front Street all the way east; cross the bridge; turn right; drive until you reach the Pott Rum factory and ask for directions. Expensive.

Spartaco – Since its smashing debut 3 years ago, St. Martin's top Italian restaurant just seems to get better and better. Tuscan owner Spartaco Sargentoni, maitre d'hôtel at *La Samanna* for 7 years, set Italian designer Carmelo Raneri loose in an early-19th-century West Indian plantation house, where the late afternoon sun shines through a louvered verandah onto black Alessi *sottopiatti* and sparkling crystal, and mock Roman statuary lines the long stairs leading through the gardens to a flowered pool area with a view of Simpson Bay Lagoon. The talented Italian chef, formerly of the posh *Cala di Volpe* on Sardinia's Costa Smeralda, turns out imaginative dishes such as homemade tagliolini black with cuttlefish ink, fresh fettuccine with lobster sauce and chives, grilled radicchio in onion and caper vinaigrette, lobster medallions with mushrooms and fish sauce, and that irresistible northern Italian dessert *tirami su* — literally, "pick me up" (and well it might, laced with rum as it is). Service is superb, the ambience quietly romantic, the cuisine excellent, and the decor sleek yet warm. Rich in snob appeal, yet friendly — *viva l'Italia!* Dinner only. Closed Mondays in low season. Almond Grove, Cole Bay (phone: 45379). Expensive to moderate.

Le Perroquet – Named after Chicago's bastion of French cuisine, this tropical version overlooking the quiet waters of Simpson Bay Lagoon, not far from the airport, is another Dutch side favorite. The West Indian–style house offers breezy dining on a lush garden porch populated with dozens of colorful imitation parrots, gifts of well-wishing friends. French chef Pierre Castagne's menu features such unusual fare as breast of ostrich and fresh salmon, which is lightly smoked in herbs at your table (a truly memorable dish). Also good are fresh mussels with leeks in Muscadet sauce and *filet de boeuf au trois poivres.* Charming ambience and smiling service. Good wine list. Airport Rd. (phone: 44339). Expensive to moderate.

De Hollandia – Despite its name and location (*De Hollandia* is the original name of the Dutch barge built in 1915 and recently sailed across the Atlantic, restructured in Venezuela, and moored on Simpson Bay Lagoon), this recent addition to the St. Maarten night scene is run by two amiable Frenchmen from Rouen. L'apéritif is in the cozy paneled bar; dinner, on the main deck under a billowing white canopy, will also be served late, if reservations are made in advance (stop by and leave a message). No elaborate menu (the galley is small), but what there is is good: the lobster is kept live in a trap in the water until it is ordered. On Simpson Bay Lagoon (enter on Philipsburg/Airport Road). Dinner only. Closed Tuesdays (no phone at press time). Expensive to moderate.

Félix – Another French spot on the Dutch scene, convenient to the *Pelican Resort* and right on the beach — good for a swim between courses. Both owners and chef hail from Cannes, lending this Caribbean corner a delightfully provençale/Créole flavor. Lobster is live from their pond, and meat is flown in from the US. Ambience and food are trendy; service with a lot of smiles. Pelican Key (phone: 45237). Expensive to moderate.

Le Pavillon – Max Petit's small beachside restaurant with a large reputation for intimate atmosphere and excellent French and island specialties cooked to order. All the seafood is fresh and prepared to perfection; *canard à l'ananas* or *assiette tricolore* (snapper, shrimp, and lobster in three different sauces) are special. Unpretentious, friendly, and very good value. Simpson Bay Village (phone: 44254). Moderate.

Lady Mariner – Across the street from the airport is the newest floating bar/restaurant. Orginally built in the US for NATO, the 145-foot, 320-ton minesweeper of wood, brass, and bronze has been in the service of the Dutch Royal Navy, has done research on the Amazon, and has been a private yacht and party boat. She's worth a visit. Food is simple American fare. Open from 11 AM to 1 AM (phone: 42884). Moderate.

Captain Oliver's – Straddling the French/Dutch border at the Oyster Pond, this charming seaside terrace touts a French owner (Captain Oliver) and a French chef who dispenses seafood lunches and dinners at reasonable prices. Among the favorites are fish terrine in crayfish cream, tuna steak tartare, lobsters, and steak. Oyster Pond (phone: 873000). Closed Mondays. Moderate.

Calypso – Authentic, carefully prepared St. Martin Créole cuisine includes stuffed crab backs, conch fritters, saltfish cakes, christophine, lobster, fresh fish, potato pudding, coconut, guava tarts, and "Johnny cakes" served in lieu of bread. Five-course prix fixe dinner as well as à la carte salads, sandwiches, and pizzas. In Simpson Bay on Airport Rd. (phone: 44233). Inexpensive.

Paradise Café – If you get a hankering for Mexican or Tex-Mex, this is the place for such traditional fare as burritos, tacos, and nachos, along with beef, chicken, and seafood specialties grilled over glowing mesquite coals at the outdoor barbecue. Informal al fresco dining at tables overlooking a swimming pool, which guests are encouraged to use. Open for lunch and dinner daily, except Sundays and Mondays. Happy hour is 5 to 7 PM and 11 PM to midnight (pre-disco). Across from Maho Beach resort (phone: 42842). Inexpensive.

Zachary's Ribs and Spirits – Good value for hungry Americans craving baby back ribs, roast prime ribs of beef, or barbecued chicken or pork chops. The reasonably priced menu also includes deep-fried shrimp, conch, or scallops, and combinations of the three. Open for lunch daily except Mondays, noon to 2:30 PM, and for dinner, 6:30 to 10:30 PM. The big saloon-style bar is a popular place for happy hour from 4 to 6:30 PM. Castle Cove Inn, Point Blanche (phone: 22260). Inexpensive.

THE FRENCH SIDE/IN AND NEAR MARIGOT

Le Santal – Housed in a splendid seaside villa just outside Marigot, this is one of the island's most refined dining rooms. Spectacular views are reflected everywhere in cleverly placed mirrors, the blue-and-white decor of the scalloped terrace appropriately matching the reflections of the natural elements. Villeroy & Boch china, Christofle flatware, and bright fresh flowers adorn every table. The enticing menu, in French and English, is pricey, but diners will not be disappointed by either the food or the service. Very special are the lobster soufflé with spinach and eggplant and the lacquered young duck, which is marinated in a sauce of five fragrances, honey, and rice wine and served with pineapple. Dinner only. Just over the Marigot Bridge (phone: 875348). Very expensive.

La Vie En Rose – Overlooking Marigot's picturesque waterfront, this popular restaurant is as gastronomical as it is astronomical in price and, unfortunately, seems to be slipping lately. Nonetheless, if you would like one of the tables on the small seaside balcony, you'll need to say so when you reserve. There are young geniuses in the kitchen, preparing a rather modified nouvelle cuisine (nobody likes the term anymore), with menus that change daily with the rapidly fluctuating availability of ingredients on the market. Generally, the seafood is fresh and local and most meat imported, as are many vegetables and fruits. Certain seafood much loved by the French (scallops, shrimp, and fish such as lotte or salmon) are also imported — at great expense. Yet, for some reason, they cost the same or little more than local products such as spiny lobster and red snapper. Whatever you have, local or flown in fresh, you're likely to spend at least $80 per person. Enjoy — if you can — and catch your breath in the pleasant café-bar downstairs. Open daily, except Sundays, for lunch in high season, and daily for dinner. Closed Sundays during summer. Marigot Harbor (phone: 875442). Very expensive.

Le Poisson d'Or – Small and select, on the seaside terrace of a restored stone warehouse, and one of Marigot's best. Start with the house apéritif — passion fruit, Armagnac, and champagne — before you choose from an exciting menu, which might include a fresh lobster bisque, scallop ravioli with leeks, marinated fresh salmon, or home-smoked spiny lobster served in Champagne butter. If you can spare the calories, try the chocolate cake, which is the next step to paradise. For pleasant browsing, there is also a charming art gallery inside the historic building. Open daily, except Sundays, for lunch and daily for dinner. A short walk from the port off Rue d'Anguille (phone: 875033). Very expensive.

La Samanna – The justifiably well-regarded restaurant is part of the hotel of the same name. Elegant and formal, it has an airy arched terrace overlooking Baie Longue and is fragrant with tropical flowers and West Indian spices. Try for a table at the outer edge, under the thatch roof. The excellent food is prepared by Lyonnaise chef Jean-Pierre Jury, and the menu changes regularly according to the availability of the best and freshest ingredients. The ambience is romantic, the service faultless, and there's also a very respectable wine list (all French). Baie Longue (phone: 875122). Very expensive.

L'Aventure – On a lovely verandah especially pink at sunset, just across from *La Vie en Rose* and *Messalina* and sharing the same harbor and ownership. A picture-postcard view from the terrace, imaginative French cuisine, and soft guitar from the pretty café-bar downstairs make for a romantic dining experience. Good wine list. Closed Mondays during summer. Marigot Harbor (phone: 875358). Expensive.

La Calanque – Marigot's landmark harborside restaurant celebrated its 22nd anniversary in 1987 by hiring one of the island's most renowned chefs, young Frenchman Dominique Dutoya, who has introduced his own innovative *nouvelle* recipes to traditional provençale favorites such as fish soup and duck in banana sauce with "crazy" pineapple. Upstairs, overlooking the marketplace, on Blvd. de France (phone: 875082). Expensive.

Le Nadaillac – Another pricey Marigot terrace, this one with a Périgord touch, open for lunch and dinner. House specialty is a brilliant bouillabaisse, but there are also rich meat dishes, plenty of foie gras, and truffles. Try the baked goose or filet of red snapper with spinach and champagne sauce. Reliably good, pleasant, and pretty. Galerie Périgourdine, Rue d'Anguille (phone: 875377 or 875616). Expensive.

Messalina – The newest and only Italian member of the famed waterside *La Vie en Rose–Poisson d'Or–l'Aventure* group, it is less pricey, but in every way as meritorious. Lunches feature light *antipasti* of *carpaccio,* salads, and pastas; dinners combine traditional Italian fare — pasta *al pesto, al alfredo, alla bolognese, alle vongole* (with clams), or in creamy lobster and mushroom sauce, or fresh poached snapper — with exciting innovations such as chilled ginger soup with fresh beets, veal with eggplant and crab meat, or veal in a sweet and sour sauce with dates. Reserve well ahead for a table on the tiny terrace. Closed Sunday lunch. Margot Harbor (phone: 878039). Expensive to moderate.

L'Atmosphère – The sleek decor of this breezy terrace restaurant, overlooking the marina, reflects all the sophistication and imagination of its menu, which touts exotic salads (such as warm endive with duck gizzard and walnuts), fresh pasta and crab meat, an omelet with goose liver and truffles, goose neck stuffed with goose liver pâté in sorrel sauce, and medallions of monkfish in *cêpes* cream. After fortifying themselves, guests can slip into the air-conditioned disco — the current rage (and the only one in Marigot). Port La Royale (temporary phone: 878727). Moderate.

Bistrot Nu – A great local favorite — cordial, casual, and considerably priced. Menu ranges from escargots and langouste thermidor to lasagne Popeye, pizza royale, and a fabulous fish soup with Gruyère and croutons. What's more, it stays open till 2 AM every morning. On Rue de Hollande (no phone). Moderate.

Le Boucanier – Charming terraced dining room freshly done up in yellow and greenery at the harbor's edge. Lunch and dinner concentrate on French dishes and seafood; filet of duck, rack of lamb, sweetbreads sautéed in Calvados are specialties. Garden bar, sitting room for after-dinner drinks, chess, backgammon. Down the alley across from the post office on Rue d'Anguille (phone: 875983). Moderate.

Cas' Anny – Colombos, *crabes farcis, boudin,* accras, fish soup, and some French dishes, all served under the trees in a bamboo-fenced garden. Not what it was. "Lolotte" has gone to *La Rhumerie* at Colombier. Rue de la Liberté (phone: 875338). Moderate.

Davids – The spinnaker in the rafters signals that two yachtsmen, both Englishmen named David, own this plain and very pleasant place that serves conch fritters and beef Wellington as well as good, hearty steak, poultry, and fish. A "courtyard" at the back puts you under the stars. Two bars popular with jolly expats. Rue de la Liberté (phone: 875158). Moderate.

Jean Dupont – Born last season at the marina of bustling Port La Royale, *Le Santal*'s baby brother (named after the owner of both) has been a smashing success. Less formal than its elder sibling, but elegant nonetheless, it serves food of the same top caliber — but at about one-third the price. Here, the lobster soufflé comes with red and black caviar and the five-fragrance duck, with peaches rather than pineapple. Vive la différence! Port La Royale (phone: 877113). Moderate.

Maison sur le Port – With a charming setting on the terrace of one of Marigot's oldest West Indian houses, facing the port, Cristian Verdeau's friendly maison specializes in inventive salads at lunch and well-prepared dinner dishes, such as poached lobster in pink pepper sauce or *les trois filets.* Prices are reasonable (compared to most everything else around here), and the fixed-price menu is an excellent alternative for diners watching their budgets rather than their waistlines. Good for lunch, l'apéritif at sunset, or dinner with a view. Marigot Harbor (phone: 875638). Moderate.

Le Mini Club – One of Marigot's oldest terrace restaurants, still under the original ownership of Claude and Pierre Plessis. Known especially for big French/Créole buffet (more than 35 dishes and "endless carafes of French wine"), usually offered Wednesday and Saturday evenings. The *court bouillon* (fish soup, Créole style), stuffed land crab, and dessert soufflés are all excellent. Closed May to September. Rue de la Liberté (phone: 875069). Moderate.

Le Ponton – Excellent French and Créole cuisine as well as very fresh lobster chosen by you from their pool. Friendly, informal atmosphere; very good value. Over the Marigot bridge at Sandy Ground (phone: 877478). Moderate to inexpensive.

Note: In the Port la Royale complex, there are a dozen or so small, attractive places for lunch, dinner, and *le snack.* Briefly, the newest are the aforementioned *Jean Dupont* and *L'Atmosphère,* as well as *La Régence* (just below *L'Atmosphère*). The others are somewhat simpler and often good value, especially if your main goal is a good spot for people watching rather than an elaborate meal. Choices include: *Café de Paris,* for a basic French menu at reasonable prices (phone: 87-56-32); *Les Cocotiers,* for fresh seafood, French pastries, and a lively happy hour, often with live music; *Hippo Grill* for more French fare (phone: 87-58-70); *Café San Martino* for pizza, etc., 9 AM to midnight (phone: 878271); *La Fondue* for cheese, beef, seafood and dessert fondues (phone: 875606); *La Fromagerie, La Croissanterie* for snacks from 7 AM to 7 PM; *Don Camillo* for Italian (phone: 875288 or 875920); and *Etna,* the rage of St. Martin for fresh sorbets and ice cream (especially maracuja or passion fruit). The foregoing have no phones unless otherwise noted.

THE FRENCH SIDE/GRAND CASE

Le Ritz Café – Newest addition to Restaurant Row (Grand Case has over 20 restaurants now) and the talk of the town — mostly for its outrageous prices and the few celebrities who seem not to mind paying them. Others do. Pretty art deco dining room and breezy seaside terrace, 1930s-style bar, and music (recorded). Lunch and dinner daily, Sunday brunch. Frightfully French management (phone: 878158). Very expensive.

Auberge Gourmande – Homey-chic country inn setting (lanterns, crystal, brown-checked cloths, beams) for the fine Burgundian fare of owner-chef Daniel Passeri, whose cookbook is available locally. Dinner only. Stop by to make reservations or phone *Le Tastevin* (phone: 875545). Expensive.

Hévéa – Tiny (10 tables), elegant dining room enhanced with graceful china, island antiques, soft music. French cuisine with Vietnamese accent features an incredibly beautiful vegetable appetizer (*tentation de jolie Candice*), liquor-laced duck, tournedos. In *Hévéa* guesthouse. Reservations essential (phone: 875685). Expensive.

La Nacelle – Charles Chevillot's *Petite Ferme*–away–from–home, ensconced in the prettied-up gendarmerie, is now in the capable hands of his nephew, Pascal, former chef at the New York base. Features include interesting cocktails and a shorter menu, with creative yet satisfying dishes such as an elegantly presented court boullion de coquilles St. Jacques. Lovely ambience in one of Grand Case's most charming old buildings. Dinner only. Closed Sundays. Reservations essential (phone: 875363). Expensive.

Rainbow – Very pretty, very exclusive terraced restaurant overlooking the beginning of Grand Case beach. Chef John Jackson creates what he calls a "New American" cuisine of "freestyle" cooking. Sautéed sweetbread and shiitake mushroom salad with raspberry vinaigrette is excellent. Other dishes include a New Orleans–inspired spicy blackened grouper, Norwegian salmon with arrugula and ginger-soy butter, and a rich chocolate praline tarte. No pets, cigars, pipes, or children under 16! Closed Sundays and late June through October (phone: 875580). Expensive.

Le Tastevin – Prettier version of *Auberge Gourmande,* with same owner, similar traditional French fare, but a bit pricier, perhaps because of its much more attractive seaside terrace. The seafood salad appetizer and the salmon steak with leeks are excellent choices. Good wine list. Open daily, except Wednesdays, for lunch and dinner (phone: 875545). Expensive.

Chez Martine – Jean-Claude Durant's intimate guesthouse dining room in warm pink, with a gingerbread terrace overlooking the beach. The menu includes winners like a delicious mousseline of frog's legs in puff pastry, asparagus tips stewed in citrus and champagne, fillet of duck breast in passion fruit, and lobster with wild rice and coconut (phone: 875159). Expensive to moderate.

Le Fish Pot – Once the only restaurant in Grand Case, with 8 terrace tables, it has been enlarged and reopened for lunch and dinner. Among the best choices are seafood pasta, salmon in puff pastry, monkfish fillet in lobster sauce, and profiterolles for dessert. All reasonably priced. Main St. (phone: 875088). Moderate.

Sebastiano's – An old-fashioned Italian welcome, homemade pasta, and northern specialties like veal *piccatina* and *ossobuco* keep regulars coming back for more. In a modern, terraced dining room at the edge of town (phone: 875886). Moderate.

Daisy's – Another newcomer to the ever-less-affordable Grand Case "Restaurant Row." Traditional French fare with a bargain dinner "menu for two" that includes Caesar salad, escargots, rack of lamb, and a memorable *marquise au chocolat* at about $40 (for two!). In a pretty old house facing, unfortunately, the wrong way: The roadside terrace can be quite noisy from the traffic, but inside is most agreeable, with walls lined with a permanent exhibition of Roland Richardson's etchings of handsome local houses. Dinner only. After the bridge (phone: 877662). Moderate to inexpensive.

Le Neptune – Joel Richard's friendly dockside terrace restaurant and piano bar, with its affordable prices, is a most welcome addition to the Grand Case dining scene. A special lunch menu includes salads, pastas, burgers, fish, and a tasty *poulet a l'estragon* (breast of chicken in tarragon sauce), which is a bargan at $10. Dinners are truly romantic, yet also a good value. Among the favorites are the seafood crêpe and Venezuelan shrimp in garlic butter. Other choices include half a dozen pasta possibilities and veal dishes with an Italian touch, fresh fish and steaks, and a good selection of sinful desserts. Live piano music from 7 AM; jam session Wednesday nights. Open daily for lunch and dinner (phone: 877607). Moderate to inexpensive.

THE FRENCH SIDE/ELSEWHERE

La Belle France – Breezy West Indian–style restaurant at the new *L'Habitation* resort, where young French chef Patrick Labarrière displays his light, refined touch with appetizers such as *trois petites salades gourmands* (lobster, avocado, and fresh *pâté de foie gras*), Petrossian-selected Sevruga, and Caribbean lobster pâté; and entrées like monkfish sautéed in green leek sauce, steamed shrimps in butter with cucumber and lemon grass, braised Cornish hen in fresh mango, filet of duck, or veal mignon. Soft music wafts in from the poolside. Elegant experience; dinner only. Anse Marcel (phone: 873333). Expensive.

Le Privilège – The *Le Privilège* complex (with its marina/shopping plaza behind *L'Habitation* and sports complex/disco on the cliff above) boasts four restaurants, including an all-night spot catering to the disco crowd. With spectacular views of Anse Marcel and Anguilla, as well as live entertainment, *The Gourmet* offers sophisticated dining. Although more casual, *La Louisiane* also boasts an excellent menu. *Le Crêperie* is the place for lighter fare, such as crêpes, omelets, salads, etc. Prices also descend in the order of listing. Anse Marcel (phone: 873737). Expensive to moderate.

La Rhumerie – If it's authentic Créole cooking you're after, Le Moines, from Martinique, won't disappoint. Specialties include *poulet boucanne Créole* (home-smoked chicken with baked green papayas and steamed, buttered cabbage hearts), herbed conch, curried goat, salad of *poisson coffre* (a local fish), and flavorfully spiced vegetables. There's also French fare, such as escargôts, frog's legs, and duck a l'orange. Open daily, except Mondays, for lunch and dinner. Off the Marigot–Grand Case road near Colombier (phone: 875698). Moderate.

Bertines – Hillside guesthouse restaurant with a homey atmosphere and a grand view of Grand Case and neighboring Anguilla. Chicagoan Bernie Poticha prepares conch Créole, "Chicago" barbecued ribs, fresh fish, and veal dishes. Indulge in chocolate mousse pie for dessert. Dinner only. At La Savanne, between Marigot and Grand Case (phone: 875839). Moderate.

Le Grill'On – Another easy alternative for informal dining near *L'Habitation* (take the shuttle bus to the entrance, then walk for about 5 minutes). Haitian Créole and some French dishes are well prepared and a good value. French Cul de Sac (phone: 877405). Inexpensive.

Mark's Place – Rather out of the way (unless you're staying at the new *L'Habitation*

654 ST. MARTIN/ST. MAARTEN / Best on the Island

or planning to hit the *Privilège* disco at Anse Marcel) in a country setting, this extremely popular and informal restaurant specializes in very fresh lobster and seafood, plus good Créole dishes, prepared by Mark's Guadeloupienne wife, Ninotte. Daily specials are listed on a blackboard and might include octopus or goat colombo (curried), while the *assiette Créole* (acras, boudin, crab and christophine *farci*) is an interesting menu staple. Huge portions of very good food at very reasonable prices, and the rustic atmosphere, with open sides looking over the surrounding countryside and bay, has contributed to the restaurant's overwhelming success. Lunch and dinner (until 9:30 PM). Closed Mondays. French Cul-de-Sac (only regulars have their phone number, to avoid too many "no shows"). Inexpensive.

ST. VINCENT AND THE GRENADINES

St. Vincent and the Grenadine chain of more than 32 islands and cays anchored in the East Caribbean between St. Lucia and Grenada have long been known to sailors and yachtsmen for their great wealth of quiet bays and beautiful beaches, pristine water, and coral reefs. The island of St. Vincent, known locally as "the mainland," has a largely unexplored interior alive with rushing rivers and waterfalls. The Grenadines offer tourists all the luxury and charm of the Caribbean with none of the neon commercial clamor of its "glamour" destinations.

Kingstown, the major port and capital of St. Vincent, is a pleasantly bustling center of interisland sea traffic and trade. The island's uncluttered volcanic beaches and tropically forested, mountainous landscapes make it a joy to explore — both for the hundreds of yachtsmen who make it a regular stop on their annual voyages around the Caribbean and for land-based visitors who fly in from Barbados and the surrounding small islands to relax in its verdant hills or along its unspoiled shores. A steady breeze provided by the northeast trade winds tempers the Caribbean's tropical warmth and creates a climate that stays within a shade of 78°F all year. This, plus its healthy supply of rain and fertile terrain, has made St. Vincent one of the most cultivated of the West Indies, producing an abundance of fruit, vegetables, and arrowroot. It is known as the Tahiti of the Caribbean — in part because of this fecundity, in part because it was here that Captain Bligh planted the first Tahitian breadfruit tree he brought from the Pacific in 1793.

St. Vincent was one of the last strongholds of the Carib Indians; they managed to retard European colonization for almost two centuries after Columbus discovered the island and claimed it for Spain. Retard, but not stop; by the eighteenth century the French and the English were engaged in a bitter struggle for control of the Caribbean, and St. Vincent and the Grenadines were as much a part of the ongoing hostilities as any other islands. St. Vincent changed hands three times in the course of the eighteenth century: from the British to the French back to the British. In 1789 St. Vincent became a British Crown Colony, but that did not discourage the French and the Caribs from joining forces in 1795 to try to overthrow British rule on the island. They failed, and St. Vincent remained a Crown Colony until 1969, when it became a British Associated State. On October 27, 1979, with a

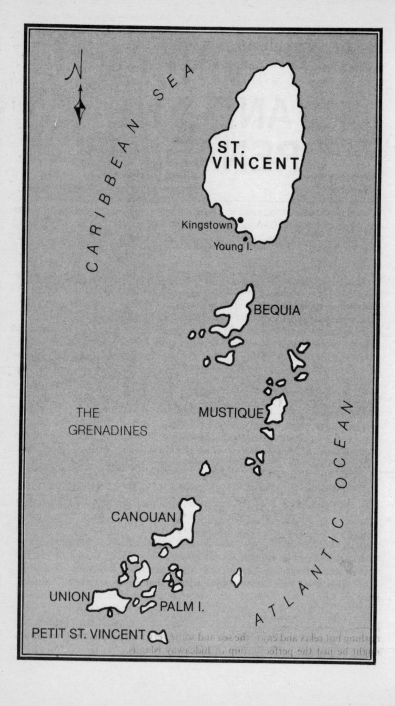

CARIBBEAN SEA

N

ST. VINCENT

Kingstown

Young I.

BEQUIA

THE
GRENADINES

MUSTIQUE

ATLANTIC OCEAN

CANOUAN

UNION

PALM I.

PETIT ST. VINCENT

representative of Her Majesty the Queen in attendance, it proclaimed its complete independence from Great Britain, but emotional and economic ties between the two remain strong, though unofficial.

Though essentially British, the islands reflect delightful traces of French cultural influences. English is the official language, but some of the islets and cays were long in French hands and have as much sense of kinship with Martinique or Guadeloupe as with nearby, steadfastly British possessions. Nor do the influences stop with Europe. During the eighteenth century, while the Caribs were fighting off shiploads of Europeans, they were welcoming stranded black slaves from a ship wrecked off the coast. As a result of their hospitality, a new race of black Caribs developed, which soon outnumbered the original tribe. Ultimately, the British settlers defeated the black Caribs and exiled them to the islands off Honduras and what is now Belize. During the mid-eighteenth century, an influx of East Indian laborers and Portuguese settlers added new strains to the multiracial population (currently about 111,000) that still exists today. But the influence of the French and the English can still be observed in both language and local architecture.

Besides outbursts of violence triggered by Carib wars and the imperialist interest of European nations, St. Vincent has suffered tragedy from the natural eruptions of its volcano, Soufrière. A major eruption killed 2,000 residents of St. Vincent in 1902, and a series of eruptions in April 1979 caused damage (though no casualties, thanks to timely warnings and speedy evacuation) in the agricultural north, but none to the island's south-based tourist plant. Now that the ash has washed away, visitors are again climbing to the crater's top for a look, but it's not a trip to be undertaken without a guide (check the Tourist Board).

The Grenadines — the principal islands of which are Bequia, Mustique, Canouan, Mayreau, Union, Palm, Petit St. Vincent — have served as safe harbors and destinations for yachts for years. Governed by St. Vincent, the islands and cays are beautiful — with exquisitely clear water and white powder beaches — but economically poor. Only eight of the islands have permanent populations, and to sustain themselves most Grenadinians turn to boat building, to work as seasonal labor on other islands, and according to legend and local lore, to smuggling.

Life in St. Vincent and on the Grenadines is slow, simple, and relaxing. Tourists are welcomed with warmth and hospitality, but Tourism — with a capital T — is not. In fact, the unobtrusive form that tourism takes on these islands probably contributes to the overwhelming friendliness that all visitors sense as soon as they arrive. As a result of this warm, unpressured atmosphere, several of the Grenadines have become the exclusive retreats of extremely well-off travelers. The rich have not taken over completely, however, and there are still many spots on the islands that are inexpensive or moderately priced and very comfortable. If you don't mind occasional interruptions in electric service, unannounced changes in inter-island boat schedules, and planes which may not arrive on time — in short, if you really want to do nothing but relax and enjoy the sea and some very nice people, the Grenadines might be just the perfect group of hideaway islands.

ST. VINCENT AND THE GRENADINES AT-A-GLANCE

FROM THE AIR: St. Vincent looks like an imperfectly shaped oval kite with the Grenadine Islands trailing behind as its tail. Although it is only 18 miles long and 11 miles wide, St. Vincent has a richly varied terrain: many sand beaches washed by calm waters on the west (Caribbean) coast; breakers rushing against steep cliffs and rocks on the east (Atlantic) coast; plantations, fertile valleys, rolling hills, winding rivers, forests, and a 4,048-foot volcanic mountain, Soufrière, inland. The island's capital, Kingstown, sits on a scenic harbor on the southwest corner of the island. Two miles from Kingstown is Arnos Vale Airfield, where flights land from Barbados and St. Lucia (the connecting point for flights from North America to St. Vincent and the Grenadines). St. Vincent lies at 13°10′ N latitude, 30°57′ W longitude, 100 miles due west of Barbados, 21 miles south of St. Lucia, and 75 miles north of Grenada; about 1,600 miles from Miami and 2,100 miles from New York.

Although there are over 100 bodies of land in the Grenadine chain, the major islands running southward from St. Vincent include Bequia, Mustique, Canouan, Mayreau, Union, Palm (officially Prune Island), Petit St. Vincent, Carriacou, and Petit Martinique. The latter two are administered by Grenada, while the others are governed by St. Vincent. All the Grenadine islands have lovely white beaches and perfectly clear blue water.

SPECIAL PLACES: Kingstown – St. Vincent's capital and commercial center, with a population of roughly 10,000, is a lively and busy port. The activity along the waterfront, where island schooners unload their cargoes and transatlantic freighters load bananas and other island produce, is fascinating to watch. On Saturday mornings, the marketplace at the south end of town bursts with color and buzzes with activity when small farmers, fishermen, and merchants from all over the island come to town to sell yams, breadfruit, eddoes, mangos, papayas, soursop, bananas, coconuts, and other produce as well as colorful fish. In the center of town, on Grenville Street, you will notice St. Mary's Catholic Church, a mishmash of architectural styles designed in the 1930s by a Flemish monk whose grasp of Romanesque, Gothic, and Moorish architecture was fanciful but flawed. On the north side of town, at the top of a winding road, on a promontory rising 636 feet above sea level, is Fort Charlotte. Named after the wife of King George III, the fort was originally built to house the soldiers and cannon used by the English to defend the island against the French. Three of the original cannons remain in place, and the living quarters of the military personnel have been turned into a museum containing a series of murals that depict black Carib history. The biggest attraction of Fort Charlotte, however, is the magnificent view of St. Vincent and the Grenadine Islands beyond. Access routes have recently been repaired, reinforced, and refurbished. East of the fort, on the north side of Kingstown, are the Botanical Gardens, the oldest of their kind in the Western Hemisphere (founded by Governor George Melville in 1765). The gardens cover an area of 20 acres and encompass a formidable display of tropical plants, blossoms, and trees (including a breadfruit tree grown from the original plant brought to St. Vincent from Tahiti by Captain Bligh in 1793 and, more recently, the *spachea perforata,* known only to St. Vincent). It is also the site of the small, artifact-filled National Museum (open Wednesday mornings, Saturday afternoons, and on the occasional cruise ship days; small admission charge).

ELSEWHERE ON THE ISLAND

Leeward Highway – North from St. Vincent, the road climbs a series of steep hills with magnificent views all along the way before dropping close to the sea. After passing the scenic *Aquaduct Golf Course,* you enter the village of Layou. Here, if you ask any one of the villagers to show you the picture rock, you will be taken to one of the several petroglyphs carved by Carib Indians over 13 centuries ago. Farther north is the whaling village of Barrouallie, where fishermen still set out with harpoons in small, brightly painted boats to hunt pilot whales, just as they did in the 18th century. Barrouallie and the nearby Grenadine island of Bequia are two of the few places left in the world where this type of whaling is still done. Off Bequia, huge humpback whales are harpooned from open boats. The Tourist Board is careful to inform tourists that "whaling here presents no danger to the extinction of the species, since so few are caught each year." (It is more probable that the whalemen here will become extinct before the whales — in recent years, catches have consisted of only one or two whales, and there have been years in which none was taken. A popular T-shirt sports a humpback whale with the slogan "Save the People!") When a whale is brought in, it is considered an occasion, and there is always a big celebration. You can continue on the Leeward Highway to Richmond Beach and take a swim before returning to Kingstown.

Windward Side Highway – Along St. Vincent's eastern Atlantic coast from Kingstown, you will see the coastal surf pounding against rocky shores. You will also see banana and coconut plantations, arrowroot fields, and gently sloping hills set in a peaceful landscape. However, things aren't always so peaceful; tropical storms and the occasional hurricane seriously damage St. Vincent's banana and coconut crops. If you want to venture past Rabacca Dry River to the northern tip of the island, you may need a four-wheel-drive vehicle, and may not be able to cross at all in the wet season. Check with the Tourist Board before setting out.

Marriaqua Valley (also called the Mesopotamia Valley) – Another area worth visiting on St. Vincent. The journey begins at the Vigie Highway, just east of the Arnos Vale Airport runway, and continues northeast, then north, to the town of Mesopotamia. You pass freshwater streams, boys on donkeys, terraced farms, winding rivers, and deep forests before heading north to Montreal Gardens (about 12 miles from Kingstown), where there are natural mineral springs, a restaurant, and a swimming pool surrounded by tropical flowers and plants. (Paved walkways run through the gardens, but there are no guides.) For romantics and/or escapists, there are a few reasonably priced cottages here for rent; contact Douglas Brisbane (phone: 458-4934).

Queen's Drive – Loops into the high hills and steep ridges east of Kingstown. The journey begins at Sion Hill, just southeast of Kingstown, halfway to the Arnos Vale Airport. After turning northeast and driving a very short distance (about a city block), you should veer sharply right and climb Dorsetshire Hill to Millers Ridge, where the road will turn south and you'll return to the airport, observing breathtaking views of the Grenadines and Kingstown along the way.

ELSEWHERE IN THE GRENADINES

Most of the 100 or more islands and islets that make up the Grenadines appear as mere dots on yachtsmen's charts. Stretching southward from St. Vincent, the major islands administered by St. Vincent are described below.

Bequia – Northernmost of the Grenadines and 9 miles south of St. Vincent, Bequia (pronounced *Beck-*wee), a picturesque island still accessible only by boat, is home to boat builders and sailors, as well as one of the last whaling stations in the world where huge humpback whales are still captured by hand-hurled harpoons. This tradition, like so many others, will soon die out, as only one old harpooner survives. A whaling and sailing museum is scheduled to open in 1989 overlooking Friendship Bay, where there was once a whaling station. Bequia's largest town, Port Elizabeth, sits at the edge of sheltered Admiralty Bay. The Bequia Tourist Bureau (phone: 458-3286), near the dock, dispenses information, sells postcards and stamps, and will recommend a driver to take you around the island (about $20 US per hour for 4 people; settle on the price in advance). Be sure to see several sites, including: the fort, which offers a sweeping view of the harbor; Industry Bay, where you can stop for a swim and a curry lunch; lovely Lower Bay with its popular *De Reef* restaurant; the beaches of Princess Margaret and Friendship Bay; Paget Farm, the last whalers' village, opposite Petit Nevis, where the catch traditionally has been sectioned; the steep vista point, where you can catch a 360° view of St. Vincent and the islands south; and Moon Hole, a remarkable American community built into the cliffs at the southern end of the island (the cave homes are private, and only special visitors are allowed; make arrangements in advance through the Tourist Bureau). In town, stop by *Mauvin's* or the *Sargent Brothers* shops, where artisans craft beautifully accurate sailboat and ship models. But save time to browse along the line of souvenir and craft shops (the *Crab Hole,* with its silkscreening studio, is a standout) and small restaurants and snack bars south of town on the beach formerly called and still often referred to as the Sunny Caribee, between the *Frangipani* and the *Plantation House.*

Mustique – Princess Margaret, David Bowie, and Mick Jagger are only the most famous of the wealthy and celebrated people who own homes on this carefully manicured private island, 15 miles south of St. Vincent. About half of these mansions can be rented when the owners are not in residence; high-season prices, which include staff and car, range from about $2,000 a week for a 2-bedroom villa to $10,000 for a 6-bedroom house (Princess Margaret's goes for a mere $6,050 in high season). Rentals are handled by *Mustique Company* (phone: 458-4621, or 800-225-4255 in the US). *Cotton House,* Mustique's one hotel, is an exquisitely restored cotton estate, designed and decorated by the late Oliver Messel of London. Cars and motorscooters are expensive to rent here, and a driver's license is required. Besides the magnificent mansions (newest and grandest is ex-Braniff king Harding Lawrence's, rumored to have cost millions), don't miss Macaroni Beach, a lovely stretch of powder-white sand flanked by clear turquoise water, or the calmer waters of Gelliceaux Bay. *Basil's Beach Bar* is where the yachting crowd gathers to drink and socialize.

Canouan – This sunny, offbeat isle, 25 miles south of St. Vincent, is visited mostly by yachtspeople. It's a little crescent-shaped haven surrounded by wide shallows and coral. Although it now has a paved airstrip and three hotels — including the *Canouan Beach* hotel, which is bringing development to the southern part of the island — it is still quiet and unspoiled. The small population of fishermen and farmers is friendly, and the white sand beaches are excellent.

Union Island – The most southern of the Grenadine Islands administered by St. Vincent, Union is a mountainous area and a well-known port of call for yachts. It has a small but busy airstrip, a few small inns, and a popular boaters' hangout with a French touch, the *Anchorage Yacht Club.* It's also a connecting point for launch access to nearby Petit St. Vincent and Palm Islands as well as the secluded islands of Mayreau and the national "water park" that surrounds the uninhabited Tobago Cays.

Tobago Cays – Four tiny islets, protected as a national park; uninhabited, but with camping and picnic sites, handsomely protected anchorages for overnighting yachts, and incredibly beautiful snorkeling reefs. A must stop on any cruise.

Mayreau – Long a favorite yacht anchorage and occasionally visited by cruise ships now, this 1½-square-mile island boasts a tropical-gardened South Seas–style hotel, *Salt Whistle Bay* resort, with villas, outdoor dining, a boutique, some yacht charter and cruising facilities; a 20-minute walk along a pleasant bush trail from the tiny village (pop. 170) at the top of the hill. The island's beaches are among the world's best.

Young Island, Petit St. Vincent, and Palm Island – These three private islands in the Grenadines are essentially resorts whose guests constitute the majority of the population. Young Island, 200 yards south of St. Vincent, is known for its South Seas atmosphere. The other two, about 40 miles south of Kingstown, are reached by flying to Union Island (20 minutes on LIAT, Mustique Airways, or Aero Services; Air Martinique flies in from Fort-de-France) and resort-launch pickup there. All major in laissez faire with beautiful beaching, swimming, sailing, snorkeling, when *you* please and as *you* like it (see *Private Islands;* DIVERSIONS).

SOURCES AND RESOURCES

 TOURIST INFORMATION: The St. Vincent and the Grenadines Permanent Mission to the UN at 41 E 42nd St., New York, NY 10017, and the Caribbean Tourism Association, 20 E 46th St., New York, NY 10017 (phone: 212-682-0435), will supply information and literature for the asking. The *St. Vincent and the Grenadines Visitor's Guide* booklet is especially helpful in providing facts, background information, and travel advice.

The St. Vincent Tourist Board Office, on Egmont St. in Kingstown (phone: 457-1502), has information on accommodations and sightseeing and also carries the *Visitor's Guide* mentioned above. There is a St. Vincent and the Grenadines information desk in the arrivals area of Grantley Adams International Airport in Barbados, open from 1 PM until the last flight to St. Vincent has gone. There is also a tourist information office on the island of Bequia (on the waterfront in Port Elizabeth) and at Clifton on Union Island.

A lovely coffee-table book now in its second printing is available in shops and some hotels: *St. Vincent and the Grenadines — A Plural Country,* by Dana Jinkins and Jill Bobrow (Concepts Publishing).

Local Coverage – Two weekly newspapers are published on St. Vincent: the *Vincentian,* which comes out on Fridays, and the *Star,* published on Saturdays. In addition to local government-owned radio and TV stations, there is cable TV and television programming beamed in from Barbados by BTS.

Telephone – Dial the islands direct by adding the area code 809 to the phone numbers given below. If dialing locally, only the final 5 digits are necessary.

 ENTRY REQUIREMENTS: Proof of identity (a passport is preferred, but a birth certificate or voter's registration card will usually do) and a return or ongoing ticket are the only documents required of US or Canadian citizens.

 CLIMATE AND CLOTHES: The thermometer hovers around 78° to 80°F (25° to 26°C) all year in St. Vincent and the Grenadines, and the northeast trade winds bring a gentle breeze that tempers the tropical heat. The mountains of St. Vincent attract more rain than the flatter atolls of the Grenadines. Summers are stiller and more humid; fall is hurricane season. Dress on the islands is very casual: Women wear bright blouses, skirts, slacks, jeans, and modest shorts; bikinis on the beach but not in town. (Topless and nude sunbathing is illegal and offends Vincentians' sense of reserve and modesty.) Men wear slacks, shorts, and sport shirts, and as evenings are informal, seldom need a jacket or tie.

 MONEY: The Eastern Caribbean dollar is the official currency of the islands. The official rate of exchange is currently $2.64 EC to one US dollar ($2.688 for traveler's checks). Always be certain when you are in stores which dollars are being quoted, EC or US. US and Canadian dollars are accepted in most restaurants, hotels, and stores, as are traveler's checks. Some hotels and restaurants honor major US credit cards. Banking hours on St. Vincent are 8 AM to noon or 1 PM on weekdays and also 2 or 3 to 5 PM on Fridays.

LANGUAGE: English is the language of this former British colony, and it is spoken with a touch of Scottish lilt, with West Indian expressions.

TIME: St. Vincent and the Grenadines are in the Atlantic Standard Time Zone: When it's noon in New York, it's 1 PM in St. Vincent. During Daylight Saving Time months, the hour is the same in both places.

CURRENT: Except for Petit St. Vincent, where there is 110 volts, 60 cycles, electricity generally operates at 220-240 volts, 50 cycles. American appliances must have converters. Some hotels can supply them, but it's more prudent to bring one along. Young Island and Mustique's *Cotton House* use British-style three-prong plugs.

GETTING THERE: There is no direct air service to St. Vincent or the Grenadines from the US. Visitors first fly to Barbados via American, Eastern, Pan Am, or BWIA direct from New York, or BWIA or Eastern direct from Miami. From Barbados you take the 35-minute flight to St. Vincent on a scheduled LIAT or chartered Mustique Airways plane. LIAT now has daily scheduled flights from Barbados to Mustique to Union Island and between St. Vincent and St. Lucia and all the way down the chain to Caracas, Venezuela.. Air Martinique operates twice daily service from Martinique, via St. Lucia, to St. Vincent and Union Island. Meanwhile, if your destination is one of the other Grenadines, you must make another short hop from St. Vincent or take a boat from Kingstown. LIAT operates scheduled small-plane service from St. Vincent to Union and Canouan. Mustique Airways has frequent and efficient charter service to Mustique. Aero Services also handles local charters, including direct Barbados-Mustique and Barbados–Union Island flights. Ask your hotel to book a connecting flight when you make your room reservations, and don't forget to confirm your return flight 72 hours before departure. An airstrip is planned for Bequia, but currently the island is reachable only by boat: the *Admiral,* which makes the trip twice daily on weekdays and once on Saturdays from Kingstown; the traditional island schooner *Friendship Rose,* which sails at 12:30 PM weekdays; the *Snapper,* which makes the circuit from St. Vincent to Bequia, Canouan, Mayreau, and Union every other weekday and from St. Vincent to Bequia on Saturdays; or the *Vicki,* which makes a weekly circuit of the islands. Check dates and times. Petit St. Vincent and Palm Island arrange launch pickups at Union Island for arriving guests.

CALCULATING COSTS: A number of the best-known resorts on these islands are worlds to themselves that offer luxury living at luxury prices, ranging from about $220 a day to over $500 US for two, American Plan (all meals). There are also less posh, but very good, hotels and guesthouses under $100 (without meals). These are winter rates; during the mid-April to mid-December period, rates can be 25% to 40% less. A tax of 5% is added to all hotel bills, and most hotels also add a 10% to 15% service charge in lieu of tipping. St. Vincent also charges an airport departure tax of $14 EC (about $5.30 US).

GETTING AROUND: Taxi – Plentiful, unmetered, with rates set by the government. A listing of fares between island points is available from the tourist office. Agree on the rate with the driver — or ask someone at your hotel to do so — before getting into any cab. The fare from the St. Vincent's Arnos Vale Airport to most hotels is about $7 US, plus a 10% tip. On Bequia, there are water taxis to the beaches from the *Frangipani* and *Plantation House* hotels.

Many of the taxi drivers provide good, well-informed guided tours. Your hotel can recommend one and negotiate the rate, about $12 US per car per hour.

Bus – Small vans set out from the market square in Kingstown and run along all the main roads. They are inexpensive, efficient, and fun. Just stick your hand out anywhere along the road and they'll stop for you. You pay when you disembark; rates run from $1 to $5 EC. Van owners display their personality with colorfully painted names like King Rat and No Time to Lose. They also love music, so be prepared to listen to some maximum-volume calypso. There are also brilliantly painted open-air buses, picturesque and cheap, but suitable only for the adventurous tourist who doesn't mind sharing a seat with a gunnysack full of garden produce.

Car Rental – *Avis* now has branches in Kingstown (phone: 458-4613) and Mustique (phone: 458-4621). Other cars are available in Kingstown from *Car Rentals* (phone: 456-1862 or 457-1614), *David's Auto Clinic* (phone: 457-1116), *Johnson's U-Drive*, Arnos Vale (phone: 458-4864), *Kim's Rentals*, Grenville St. (phone: 456-1884), and *De Freitas* (phone: 456-1862). Rates run about $35 US per day, but up to $80 per day at the *Cotton House* on Mustique ($60 from the *Mustique Company*). Shop around. The Department of Tourism's *Car Rental Services* booklet contains helpful data on these, plus other useful driver information. A temporary driver's license is required, issued upon presentation (at the airport, the police station on Bay Street, or the Licensing Authority on Halifax Street) of your US or Canadian license and the payment of a small ($10 EC) fee. International driver's licenses are also accepted. Remember St. Vincent's British heritage: You must *drive on the left.* And be very careful; there are lots of curves and sharp turns in the roads, where you should sound your horn and be certain you're still on the left after the turn.

Motorbikes – Motorbikes are available on Mustique for $20 to $30 US per day.

Sightseeing Tours – By mini-bus or taxi: best arranged through the Tourist Office (phone: 457-1502), which has a trained Tour Guide Unit, or through the Taxi Drivers Association. Tour operators in Kingstown include *Barefoot Holidays* (phone: 458-4989), *Global Travel* (phone: 456-1602), *Grenadine Tours* (phone: 458-4818), and *Campbell's Travel* (phone: 457-1067 or 457-1867).

Ferry Services – A variety of boats offer island-to-island transportation or ferry service. The mailboat runs three times a week through the Grenadines (from St. Vincent to Union Island and back), and there is regular service from Kingstown to Bequia. For information about ferry schedules and services, check with the tourist office in Kingstown or your hotel. Currently, there is service daily except Sundays on the MV *Admiral* and MV *Snapper,* the first servicing only Bequia ($5 EC), the latter going to Union ($15 EC) via Bequia, Canouan ($10 EC), and Mayreau ($12 EC) every other day. The island schooner *Friendship Rose* sails every weekday to Bequia only. All vessels take 1 to 1½ hours to travel between St. Vincent and Bequia and charge the same fare.

SHOPPING: Although St. Vincent and the Grenadines aren't shoppers' paradises, a number of stores offer batik, tie-dyed fabrics, and various handicrafts. The marketplace in Kingstown on Saturdays is the liveliest shopping "center," although the bill of fare is fresh produce and staples, not items that you can carry home, except, perhaps, a bottle of locally made hot sauce. In St. Vincent's

Kingstown, *Voyager* (Halifax St.) sells everything from cameras to handicrafts, *Norma's* (Egmont St.) and *Dan Dan* (Bay St.) are good boutiques for locally made women's clothes. *Made in the Shade, A Touch of Class,* and *Elle* (Middle St.) have some imported goods as well. *Batik Carib* (on Bay St.) stocks a fine selection of wall hangings, scarves, pareos, and clothing in original hand-painted and waxed batiks on pure cotton or silk, or visitors can buy the raw fabrics here and have custom clothes made from them. *Sprotties* also has original hand-painted silk screen designs. *The St. Vincent Craftsmen Center* and *Noah's Arkade* specialize in crafts — local and imported. *Noah's,* with a branch in Bequia at the *Frangipani* hotel, also has locally made tropical clothing, as well as herbal teas and spices. You'll find top-quality jewelry, crystal, china, and watches for reasonable prices at *Stecher's,* in the Cobblestone Arcade; *Giggles* boutique is also there; *Y. de Lima* (Bay St. at Egmont) also offers a fine selection of quality jewelry. *The Hibiscus* (James St.) sells well-made, well-designed Caribbean grass rugs, mahogany carvings, and bowls. And if you run out of some basic essential, try *E. D. Layne & Sons Department Store.* One specialty that you might consider bringing home is the hot sauce made on St. Vincent — it's pure fire if taken in heavy doses, but delicious used sparingly; you can buy bottles at any grocery store or in the market.

On Bequia, besides *Noah's,* there is the *Crab Hole* on the beach by the *Plantation House,* for unique sport clothes, hats, totes, bikinis, pareos, for men, women, and kids, all hand-sewn in original silkscreened cottons you can watch them print in the workshop out back; crafts and T's, too. In Port Elizabeth, check out *Local Color, Solana's,* and *Daphne's,* as well as *Bequia Crafts* (behind the *Port Hole* snack bar) for wooden carvings of whales, birds, etc., done by and for the local handicapped. Beautifully handcrafted model boats (including a copy of your own yacht if you so order) are done by *Mavin Hutchins* (phone: 458-3669) and at *Sargent Brothers* in Port Elizabeth. Bequia also boasts an interesting bookshop selling locally crafted scrimshaw. For a larger selection, check with Sam McDowell in Paget Farm or Ellen Schwarz on her boat, the *Piraña,* tied up by the *Frangipani* hotel in town.

On Mustique, the *Cotton House's* old sugar mill houses *Treasure,* with a fine selection of gifts including Victorian linens, antique curiosities, and fun beachwear. Also on Mustique, next to his bar, is *Basil's Boutique,* featuring Balinese batik resortwear, hand-painted T-shirts, and curiosities. *Anita's Affaer,* up at Arne Hasselqvist's spectacular *Shogun House,* carries Simon Foster's designer fashions from Barbados, Sea Island cottons from Monserrat, and lovely gifts from Bali and nearer islands.

 TIPPING: Most hotels add a 10% service charge to the bill, which takes care of bellboys, room maids, and dining room waiters. Check to make sure that the service charge is included — if not, tip bellboys 50¢ to $1 US per bag, depending on the amount of luggage; room maids $1 to $2 US per person per day; and ask the manager what is customary for waiters. Tip taxi drivers 10% of the fare if service is good. Restaurants usually include a 10% service charge in the tab; if not, that's what you should give the waiter; 15% if you're especially pleased with the service.

 SPECIAL EVENTS: The St. Vincent *Carnival,* held in late Juneearly July (moved from the traditional pre-Lenten time in February), is a week-long celebration with traditional parades, dancing, music, steel band and calypso competitions, and feasting. Other holidays, when stores and businesses close, are *New Year's Day, St. Vincent and the Grenadines* (or *Discovery*) *Day* (January 22), *Good Friday, Easter Monday, Labour Day* (May 5), *Whitmonday, Caricom Day* (first Monday in July), *Carnival Day* (Tuesday after *Caricom Day*), *Emancipation Day* (first

Monday in August), *Independence Day* (October 27), *Christmas,* and *Boxing Day* (December 26).

SPORTS: Basically it's the sea — swimming, snorkeling, skin diving, fishing, yachting, and sailing — that brings sports people to St. Vincent and the Grenadines.

Boating – Not just another sport, it's a way of life among these islands — the outstanding sailing grounds of the entire Caribbean. Various types of craft are available: Sunfish or Sailfish can be borrowed or rented from some hotels (*Young Island* and *Sunset Shores* at St. Vincent). *Basil's Beach Bum* (at *Basil's Bar*) on Mustique has Lasers and Toppers. Check *Frangipani*'s new sports facilities on Bequia, as well as the hotels at Friendship Bay. Day sails are extremely popular in the Grenadines and easily arranged; check with your hotel. *Young Island, Palm Island,* and *Petit St. Vincent* hotels do regular day sails, as do *Canouan, Cotton House,* and *Basil's* on Mustique. On Bequia, day charters on the *Apogee, So Long,* and *Secondo* run about $35 US per person. On Union Island, the *Hurricane* and *Sea Rose* charge about $40, which includes a fine lunch and open bar.

Bareboat and skippered yacht charters are also available. One of the oldest around is *CSY (Caribbean Sailing Yachts)*, Blue Lagoon, St. Vincent (phone: 458-4308); US office: PO Box 491, Tenafly, NJ 07670 (phone: 201-568-0390). Basically, it's a bareboat operation with a new fleet of 24 boats, including 44-foot Morgans, 51-foot Customs, 42- and 50-foot Gulfstars, featuring luxury amenities such as VCR and full AC power. Vincentian and Bequian skippers, men of special skill and charm, may be hired for a very reasonable per diem to sail, guide, cook, or introduce you to their islands. Charters are also available through *Mariners Watersports and Yacht Charters* (phone: 458-4228), *Young Island Resort* (phone: 458-4826), or Chris Doyle (author of *Sailors Guide to the Windward Islands* and *St. Vincent and Grenadines Visitor's Handbook*), aboard his 41-foot sloop *Helos* (phone: 458-4246). On Union Island, Captain Yannis at the *Anchorage Yacht Club* usually knows which yachts are currently offering charters in the Grenadines (phone: 458-8313 or 458-4848). There is also *Frangipani Yacht Services* on Bequia (phone: 458-3255). There's an annual Whitsun Regatta in Kingstown, and the Petit St. Vincent Yacht Race is held the week before Thanksgiving.

Golf – The 9-hole *Aquaduct Golf Course,* closed for some time, was due to reopen at press time (phone: 458-7421)..

Mountain Climbing – The Soufrière climb takes the better part of a day and should only be attempted in good weather and with a reliable guide. It's best to make arrangements through the Tourist Board. The cost of a guide and jeep runs about $28 per person. A lovely, easier tour is the Buccament Valley Nature Trail along two marked paths through tropical rain forest. There are pre-Columbian stone writings at Buccament Cave. Book through the Tourist Board.

Riding – Horseback riding can be arranged through Mustique's *Cotton House* (phone: 456-7777). Rates are $10 US per hour.

Snorkeling and Scuba – The waters around St. Vincent and the Grenadines are beautifully clear, and there's plenty of marine life to observe: coral formations, plants, brightly colored fish. Especially rewarding spots for diving are in the waters surrounding Young Island, Palm Island, Mayreau, Petit Canouan, Petit Nevis and Pigeon Island off Bequia, Pillory Rocks near Mustique, and the Tobago Cays. Off the island of Mayreau there is a sunken World War I gunboat 55 feet down. *Dive St. Vincent* at Villa opposite Young Island (phone: 457-4714) and *Mariners Watersports and Yacht Charters* (phone: 458-4228) on St. Vincent offer complete diving services, including rentals, guided dive trips, night dives, and resort courses, as well as speedboat trips along the west coast to the Falls of Baleine and Wallilabou. Full certification courses are also available now in Bequia at *Dive Bequia* (phone: 458-3504), Mustique at *Dive Mustique* (phone: 456-4777, ext. 426), and on Union Island at *Scuba Safaris* (VHF channels 16 and 68). All of them also offer "certification vacations" — learn while sailing through the Grenadines. There are dive shops and other water sports on Bequia also at the *Frangipani, Friendship Bay,* and *Bequia Beach* hotels. Snorkeling equipment is available at most major hotels, at *Basil's* on Mustique, *De Reef* at Lower Bay on Bequia, and the dive shops listed above.

Sport Fishing – Not formally organized, but most hotels and dive shops will arrange a fishing boat. Only drop lines are available, so bring your own rod and reel. Some charter yachts are equipped with deep-sea fishing gear. The catch includes sailfish, marlin, snapper, dolphin, kingfish, tuna, bonita, blue runner, mackerel, jack, grouper, and pompano. Note that spear fishing is not allowed here except by special permission.

Swimming and Sunning – There are dozens of superb beaches on the shores of these islands. Most hotels are located on beaches, and you can visit any others you want to on St. Vincent, where all are public. The sands of the volcanic island of St. Vincent vary in color from the black of the north to the golden and white coral beaches of the south (where most of the resorts are located). The waters on the leeward side and in the lagoons are best for swimming; on the windward side the sea is rough. Swimmers are warned not to go very far out and not to swim alone.

Tennis – The *Kingstown Tennis Club* has 2 lighted, hard-surfaced courts, offers temporary memberships to visitors, and charges about $6 US per court hour. Other courts are at the *Emerald Valley* hotel, *Young Island* resort, *Prospect Racquet Club,* *Grand View Beach* hotel; on Bequia at the *Plantation House, Spring on Bequia, Friendship Bay,* and *Frangipani;* at *PSV* and *Palm Island* resorts; and on Mustique at *Cotton House* and *Charlie's.* There's squash at *Cecil Cyrus Squash Complex, Grand View Beach,* and the *Prospect Racquet Club.*

Windsurfing – Available on St. Vincent at the *Windsurfing International School* (ask for Liston Phillips) at the *Mariner's Inn* (phone: 458-4287) and at *Young Island Resort* (ask for Irwyn Cumberbatch), where $20 US will buy resort guests all the lessons they need (phone: 458-4826). On Mustique, *Basil's Beach Bum* (phone: 458-4621) and the *Cotton House* hotel (phone: 456-4777) both offer instruction. Windsurfing boards are also available on Bequia at the *Frangipani, Friendship Bay,* and *Bequia Beach* hotels, and at *De Reef* restaurant at Lower Bay.

 NIGHTLIFE: The *Emerald Valley* hotel casino (with blackjack, roulette, and slot machines) is scheduled to reopen as we go to press (phone: 458-7421). *Young Island* resort has music four nights a week. Most of the action is over well before midnight. Friday nights are special: Flaming torches light the stone staircase of 18th-century Fort Duvernette on a satellite island a few yards from Young, and hotel guests are shuttled over by boat for a memorable cocktail party. Nonguests must reserve, as space on the rock is limited. *Stilly's Aquatic Club* has a live band two or three nights a week, followed by disco music until the last guest leaves; Saturday night is big action here. Once or twice a week, Stilly also puts on a nice, reasonably priced buffet or barbecue dinner, with somewhat more subdued live music. Occasionally there is some action at the *Prospect Racquet Club;* drop by the bar there and see what's happening. Otherwise, most after-dark diversion is provided by the hotels. In the Grenadines, most resort hotels have a beach barbecue or some sort of "jump-up" one night a week. On Mustique, *Basil's Beach Bar* has a jump-up every Wednesday night and whenever one of the small, posh cruise ships calls in. *Basil's* is extremely popular with yachtspeople, jet-set execs, titled homeowners, and even with the snooty celebs (looking to get away from fans and gawkers), so most of the island turns up here sooner or later.

BEST ON THE ISLANDS

CHECKING IN: The best hotels on these islands are worlds unto themselves, dreamed up and designed by island lovers for the enjoyment of guests who want casual, pampered luxury and seclusion. They can be very expensive, but in most cases are worth it, if you can afford from about $220 to over $500 for two per day in winter (with all meals). There are accommodations that offer island ambience and amenities at more moderate prices: $100 to $220 for two per day in winter, breakfast and dinner included; anything less than $60 here is a basic room without meals and qualifies as inexpensive. Prices drop by about 30% in summer.

About half of the mansions on Mustique can be rented when their owners aren't around; prices range from about $2,000 a week for a 2-bedroom villa to $10,000 for a 6-bedroom house, in high season, including staff and car. Contact *Mustique Company* (phone: 458-4621, or 800 225-4255 in the US).

ST. VINCENT AND JUST OFFSHORE

Young Island – Considered St. Vincent's prime hotel, it is actually a privately owned island resort 200 yards off the southern shore of the mother island, or "mainland." There is regular ferry service and a distinctive South Seas atmosphere. The 25-acre tropical paradise has 29 units in all — from beach-hugging havens to airy hillcrest hideaways with spacious terraces and spectacular views — king-size retreats in local stone and South American hardwood, naturally air conditioned by adjustable jalousies and louvers, entire glass-screened walls that slide away, and ceiling fans. Tiled baths lead to sexy outdoor showers secluded by ferns and luxuriant flowers. The thatch-roofed *Coconut Bar* floats in waist-high water just offshore, and another bar operates on the beach. Meals are savored under beach gazebos or in a Polynesian pavilion built into the rocks above. Amenities include full diving facilities and instruction, a free-form pool, windsurfing (and simulator) and other assorted sailing craft, and 2 sailing yachts (the *Windsong* and the *Kokoro*) that make regular day trips to Bequia and Mustique. Vincentian manager and co-owner Vidal Browne combines traditional West Indian hospitality with the luxury and comfort his well-heeled international clientele has come to expect. Reached by ferry from Villa Beach dock on St. Vincent (phone: 458-4826; in the US, 800-223-1108). Very expensive.

Grand View Beach – Caring family management, smiling efficient service, beautifully landscaped grounds, and a truly grand view from this elegant converted house. Twelve homey double rooms, each with bath, are spacious and breezy; some are also air conditioned. The photogenic swimming pool sits out on the point, and trails lead down to the beach where snorkeling is good. Tennis and squash courts; summer packages; West Indian cuisine in an uninspired dining room. Villa Point (phone: 458-4811). Expensive.

Sunset Shores – Attractive modern hotel on the beach across from Young Island, with 19 neat, air-conditioned rooms built around a well-kept lawn and pool; also deluxe rooms with private patios. Popular with families and businessmen (ticker tape with international news is posted regularly). Villa Beach (phone: 458-4411). Expensive.

Emerald Valley – If gambling, tennis, and nature walks are your thing, this is the place for you. A strange combination? The gaming room is small and sweet — not exactly Las Vegas glitter. Nestled among verdant hills, 7 miles from Kingstown, this pretty property, in new hands and undergoing major refurbishment as we go to press, should have at least 12 rooms open for 1989, in 2-unit chalets with kitchenettes and balconies. Guests will enjoy 2 freshwater pools, 2 tennis courts, horseback riding, and the adjacent 9-hole *Aquaduct Golf Course*. Penniston Valley (phone: 458-7421). Expensive to moderate.

CSY – Small, marina-based hotel, as trim, modern, and friendly as you'll find in the islands. With fancy food shop, tiered swimming pool, water sports, popular bar, breezy restaurant serving island food, and a beach bar/restaurant with a lively "happy hour." Nineteen first-class balconied rooms. Blue Lagoon (phone: 458-4031). Moderate.

Villa Lodge – Ten spacious, air-conditioned rooms (with extra beds available for children) 5 minutes from the beach, each with full tub bath and terrace, some with lovely seaview. Bar and restaurant with a Far Eastern touch. Shares a swimming pool with next-door *Breezeville Apartments*. Villa Point (phone: 458-4641). Moderate.

Cobblestone Inn – This converted 200-year-old sugar warehouse in the middle of town has 20 rooms, a popular restaurant (run by Mustique's Basil Charles), and a rooftop snack bar with a lovely view of the harbor. A favorite business travelers' stopover. Kingstown (phone: 456-1937). Inexpensive.

Heron – The second floor of this Georgian townhouse — once a plantation's warehouse — was used by the estate's owners and managers when they came to town and still serves the same purpose, providing food and 15 air-conditioned rooms on the waterfront two blocks from the Grenadines Wharf and next to the shopping district. No frills, but convenient for business travelers and vacationers heading to Bequia on the early morning boat. Kingstown (phone: 457-1631). Inexpensive.

Indian Bay Beach – Very simple, but conveniently located, self-catering 8-unit complex on the beach. The *A La Mer* al fresco restaurant is popular for its West Indian cuisine and occasional barbecues. Indian Bay Beach (phone: 458-4001). Inexpensive.

The Last Resort – Friendly, small inn on the beach with 11 air-conditioned rooms, 5 of which have been recently refurbished, in a simple but charming island style. There's also an open-air bar and restaurant serving Vincentian food and drinks, a beachside billiards table, and library. New owners and management have maintained its pleasant atmosphere. Indian Bay (phone: 458-4231). Inexpensive.

Mermaid Inn – Amiable Vincentian Bob Scott returned from Holland and opened this friendly 8-room inn on the beach. No frills, but a good bargain, with a lively bar and restaurant. Villa Beach (phone: 457-4628). Inexpensive.

Umbrella Beach – Nine simple but comfortable efficiency apartments, owned by the next-door *French Restaurant* — perfect for food-focused vacationers and businessmen who'd rather spend money on good food and wine than on posh accommodations. Front rooms have patios on the beach directly opposite Young Island. Villa Beach (phone: 458-4651). Inexpensive.

THE GRENADINES

Cotton House, Mustique – Originally a sugar plantation and later a cotton estate; the two-story main building is ringed with wide breezy verandahs witness afternoon teas and candlelit dinners, except on Saturday nights, when there is a barbecue on the beach. The decor throughout is lavish. A freshwater swimming pool sits behind the Great House in curious Romanesque ruins, flanked by a bar and a dining pergola where breakfasts and lunches are shared with shrill grackles. Accommodations are in several small houses cloaked in bougainvillea, some new (near the pool), some old and restored (near the old sugar mill–turned–boutique), and a few in a nearby house overlooking the sea — all nicely decorated and furnished. Planned for 1989 are 8 new rooms on the beach, a small disco, and special sports packages. Amenities include a lot of privacy, 2 tennis courts, water sports (full diving facilities with resident instructor, windsurfing lessons), horseback riding, and books in several languages. Free transportation by mini-jeep driven by ever-smiling Snakey, who manages all pickups with unislandlike punctuality (phone: 456-4777; in the US, 212-696-1323). Very expensive.

Petit St. Vincent Resort, Petit St. Vincent – This private island resort is about as near to perfection as you'll find anywhere. For a quiet, pampered life of understated, do-as-you-please, barefoot elegance, PSV (as it is called) offers 22 airy villas ingeniously spread over 113 acres, either high on a breezy bluff or on fairly hidden pieces of the beach, each with very private patio and sunning porch, full living room, huge bedroom, and rustic stone shower. Privacy is such that you summon room service by running up the yellow flag on the pole by your villa and — as if by magic — a Jeep arrives a half hour later. The usual water sports, including windsurfing (and simulator), health trail, tennis, badminton, croquet, table tennis, horseshoes, darts; day sails to the Tobago Cays and other Grenadines. The cuisine has been attracting a lot of favorable attention of late — meat is flown in from Julia Child's butcher in Massachusetts, lobster is really fresh, and nothing is overcooked (phone: 458-4801). Very expensive.

Anchorage Yacht Club, Union – This French-owned inn has a certain raffish charm and is popular with yachtspeople and other mostly French-speaking passersby on their way to the other Grenadines. Not nearly so grand as its name, it offers 10 rooms and bungalows, bar, and restaurant with a French chef; also yachting provisions, water sports, day charters, boutique with newspapers from everywhere. Best meeting spot around, best boating tips and gossip. Clifton (phone: 458-8244). Expensive.

Canouan Beach, Canouan – Newest of the remote island's three inns, the CBH is on a narrow isthmus in the western part, near the airstrip. On one side is a sandy beach, on the leeward side lies Charlestown Bay, anchorage for passing yachtspeople. A marina is currently being dredged. Some good snorkeling off the reefs at Friendship Point (equipment is available). There's a new dive shop and a certified instructor. Also available are windsurfing, table tennis, and volleyball as well as day sails. "Superior" bungalows are bright with spacious verandahs, while standard rooms in the main building are adequate and comfortable. All 35 units are air-conditioned, and another 140 rooms are in the planning stages. French management; so-so West Indian food in a charming restaurant/bar with friendly service. Steel band plays several evenings a week (phone: 458-4413). Expensive.

Palm Island Beach Club, Palm (Prune) Island – Not a club at all but a barefoot-informal, privately owned island resort consisting of a dozen comfortable 2-unit cottages with patios strung along the edge of a powdery white beach and loosely connected by a narrow stone path. Recent refurbishing has brightened up the rooms, patios, and dining room, enlarged the boutique, and added a health club. This spot has great appeal if it's an unsophisticated holiday you're after. The circular al fresco beach bar is popular with the bareboat yachting crowd. There are Hobie Cats, Sunfish, windsurfing, snorkeling, and scuba diving equipment (phone: 458-4804). Expensive.

Salt Whistle Bay Club, Mayreau – Another charming property on one of the world's most magnificent beaches, it is simple yet refined, romantic yet extremely informal; a total getaway — no roads, no cars. Stone bungalows are hidden among the papaya and palm trees; bathroom doors and hot water hardly seem necessary but are promised for next season. Most water sports are free to guests; also table tennis, darts, volleyball, backgammon, chess, and fishing poles. Diving and boat excursions arranged. Al fresco beach bar/restaurant, with live entertainment in season. Delightfully informal and fun (no phone; telex: 06-218309 or radio VHF Ch. 16). Expensive.

Spring on Bequia, Bequia – Secluded on a 200-year-old working plantation, cool stone cottages (purple-heart wood; natural rock showers), 12 units in all, perched on a lush hilltop above Spring Bay. With inviting Main House dining room and bar (there's a popular Sunday curry lunch buffet). Tennis, pool, and beach (good for snorkeling) a stroll away. Quiet, contemplative. Spring (phone: 458-3414). Expensive.

Friendship Bay, Bequia – Friendly new owners Eduardo and Joanne Guadagnino have reopened this handsome property after giving it a much-needed beach-to-hilltop refurbishing. There are 27 bright and cheery rooms, lovely beach with charming beach bar, a restaurant serving good American steaks and local seafood, water sports (including parasailing, windsurfing, and full diving facilities and instruction), yacht for charter and day cruising to Mustique, illuminated tennis courts for night play, and popular Saturday night barbecue with live reggae, calypso, and rock music. Friendship Bay (phone: 458-3222). Expensive to moderate.

Bequia Beach Club, Bequia – This German-run inn has 10 modern and tidy timbered chalets right out of Rhinelandia, a small pool (presumably used for testing diving equipment), and a Créole/German restaurant/bar. Water sports include full diving facilities, windsurfing, fishing, day sails, and picnic trips to neighboring islands. On Friendship Bay Beach (phone: 458-3248). Moderate.

Crystal Sands Beach, Canouan – Five 2-unit cottages with connecting doors, good for families or friends. Each room has its own bath and patio; there's also a beach bar and restaurant. Other beaches are reached by hiking or by boat excursions. Simple and gracious West Indian flavor (phone: 457-9240). Moderate.

Firefly, Mustique – "You don't have to be rich and famous to enjoy Mustique," says Billy Mitchell, who sailed the world for 19 years before building one of the island's first houses. She's now renting 4 delightful rooms with private baths and terraces overlooking Britannia Bay. Breakfast and honor bar (phone: 458-4621, ext. 414). Moderate.

Frangipani, Bequia – Friendly and fun; favorite gathering place for visiting yachtspeople and locals even before its owner, James "Son" Mitchell, became prime minister of St. Vincent and the Grenadines. Open-air bar and popular restaurant (especially for Thursday night's jump-up). The inn has 12 rooms; the newer ones have private baths and lovely terraces, the older ones — upstairs in the main building — share facilities. New tennis court, windsurfing center, dive shop and water sports, second restaurant down the beach at the club. Port Elizabeth (phone: 458-3255). Moderate.

Old Fort, Bequia – Bequia's newest and most charming hideaway is the dream-come-true of Otmar Schaedle, a well-traveled history and music professor from Germany who found the ruins of an old French fort and rebuilt it in local stone and hardwood for himself and his family. Guests share this special retreat in 4 breezy, rustic apartments, each with private bath and kitchen facilities, and a 2-bedroom gingerbread cottage with panoramic views from fragrant gardens. Perched on the lofty heights of Mt. Pleasant, this place is a world away from the bustle of the boating crowds below — on a clear day, you can see beyond the glittering lights of mundane Mustique and distant Grenada. Transportation (by 4-wheel drive) is provided regularly, breakfast and dinner available, and a small pool. A gem (phone: 458-3440). Moderate.

Plantation House, Bequia – A hospitable old plantation house with a wrap-around porch containing 8 rooms and a dining room overlooking the beach at Admiralty Bay. Seventeen recently refurbished and upgraded cottages line the back garden, each with private bath and verandah. Small pool; seaside drink and snack bar, one of Bequia's best restaurants, with hump-up to a steel band Wednesdays and Fridays; most water sports, including full diving facilities. Belmont (phone: 458-3425). Moderate.

Villa Le Bijou, Canouan – A charming 6-room guesthouse with spectacular views run by a transplanted French woman, Michelle, in love with the island and all its flavors. Built of local stone and pebbles, with a large terrace. No private baths (phone: 456-4099). Moderate to inexpensive.

Julie's and Isola's Guest House, Bequia – For the budget-minded, this 25-room property is clean and friendly, with excellent and inexpensive West Indian food. Port Elizabeth (phone: 458-3304). Inexpensive.

 EATING OUT: With very few exceptions, dining is limited to hotel restaurants. Most offer West Indian food (pumpkin and callaloo soup, local fish or lobster prepared Créole style, and local specialties) and what they believe tourists like to eat (usually overcooked steaks and imported frozen shrimp, french fries, etc.). Bartenders pride themselves on variations of rum punch — which are always stronger than they seem. Compared to most Caribbean holiday islands, St. Vincent's prices — outside the luxury hotels — are not bad. The most expensive dinner might cost $30 to $40 per person. Normally a 10% service charge and 5% government tax are added to the bill. And wine does not come cheap. For boaters, most restaurants take reservations via VHF channel 68. The following are the few recommendable additions to the hotel scene.

ST. VINCENT

The French Restaurant – The chef is Parisienne, and the cuisine an admirable marriage of Gallic savoir faire with island ingredients and the few available imports. Starters include a luscious lobster crêpe, delicate quenelles, frogs' legs, and escargots. A live lobster pool guarantees freshness, and snapper is nicely prepared. Delightful al fresco setting opposite Young Island, next to the dock. Unquestionably the island's best choice for lunch or dinner out. Villa Beach (phone: 458-4972). Expensive.

Basil's Bar 'n' Restaurant – Basil Charles, of Mustique fame, recently took over the popular ground-floor restaurant of the *Cobblestone Inn*. Renovations and refurbishing have added light to the old stone building, and the lunchtime buffet, served Monday through Friday, has proved a grand success. Other offerings include lobster salad, grilled snapper, omelets, burgers, sandwiches, escargots, and grilled lobster, with several reasonably priced French wines. The Friday night buffet is sometimes accompanied by live music. Bay St., Kingstown (phone: 457-2713). Moderate.

CSY Beach – Pleasant new waterfront restaurant of the *CSY Yacht Club* is open daily from 10 AM to 11 PM, with a lively happy hour from 5 to 7 PM. A variety of specials includes barbecued fish, ribs, chicken, and steaks on Friday nights; a seafood buffet on Saturdays; and Vincentian cuisine (souse, curry, conch fritters) for Sunday lunch. There is a live band on Wednesdays and Sundays. Blue Lagoon (phone: 458-4031). Moderate.

Juliette's – Local dishes, seafood, and — if you insist — steak. Middle St., Kingstown (phone: 457-1645). Moderate.

Stilly's Aquatic Club – Wednesday is West Indian buffet and Friday is barbecue night in the courtyard out back with a local band that would keep the neighbors awake if they weren't already here. Disco music follows — indoors. Saturday is the big jump-up, when the whole island dances into the wee hours. Good fun. Villa (phone: 458-4205). Moderate.

The Bounty – Vincentian-style fast food. Snacks, light lunches, drinks, and home-made ice cream. Business hours only (closed Sundays). Halifax St. (opposite Barclays Bank), Kingstown (phone: 456-1776). Inexpensive.

The Dolphin – Pub popular with the nautical crowd, open late if a dart game gets going. Freshly refurbished pink-and-white dining area; nice lunch buffet. The simple dinner menu includes pizzas. Villa (phone: 458-4238). Inexpensive.

Stoplight – If the light's on, stop in this friendly English pub. There is a limited menu that includes good flying fish and plenty of beer. French's Gap, Kingstown (phone: 457-2203). Inexpensive.

Other snack bars serving local food include *Black Carib,* next to *The Bounty; Pizza Party/Chicken Roost* (with seafood and lobster pizzas), next to the airport; the new *Summer Breeze* at Villa; and a locally popular *Kentucky Fried Chicken* in town.

THE GRENADINES

Basil's Beach Bar, Mustique – Even if it were not the only place to go on Mustique (besides *Cotton House*), *Basil's* would be the *only* place to go (see *Nightlife*). This appealing al fresco wicker and wood complex is open all day and stays open late. Menu ranges from full breakfasts to sandwiches, salads, seafood, lobster, and homemade ice cream. Here sailors and homeowners — viscounts and movie stars, princesses and jet-set execs — mingle when the band plays (currently Mondays and Wednesdays). Don't miss it (phone: 458-4621). Expensive to moderate.

Plantation House, Bequia – The former *Sunny Caribee,* with a new French flavor, has become Bequia's best dining spot, either on the breezy estate verandah or at *Coco's* beach bar and restaurant on Wednesdays and Fridays for buffet with steel band (phone: 458-3425). Expensive.

Mac's Pizzeria and Bakeshop, Bequia – On a lovely terrace overlooking the beach on Admiralty Bay, *Mac's* is renowned for its pizza, pita bread sandwiches, quiche, banana bread, pineapple rolls, and chocolate chip cookies — all fresh. Yachtspeople love the take-out service. On Tuesdays, there's a sit-down barbecue dinner with steel band. Near Port Elizabeth (phone: 458-3474). Moderate to inexpensive.

De Reef, Bequia – A popular beach bar and restaurant serving good local food — on island time (order, then have a swim). Special Sunday lunch. Lower Bay (phone: 458-3203). Moderate to inexpensive.

Old Fig Tree, Bequia – A guesthouse serving a set dinner menu (conch is recommended) and pizzas, local-style. Port Elizabeth (phone: 458-3201). Inexpensive.

TRINIDAD AND TOBAGO

Call them the Caribbean's Yin and Yang, the sister islands of Trinidad and Tobago are complementary opposites. What Tobago lacks in cosmopolitan sophistication, Trinidad provides; what is missing in terms of peace and quiet on Trinidad abounds on Tobago. Despite its industrialization, Trinidad has abundant wildlife, whereas Tobago is best known for its beaches. In fact, visitors to these most southerly of the Caribbean islands usually take in both, experiencing two very different vacations for the price of one.

Although they are two separate islands, Trinidad and Tobago form one nation. During the 1880s, the failure of Tobago's sugar industry forced the island to join with its larger, more economically secure neighbor to become one country. Until that time, Trinidad had been a British colony founded in 1797, when His Majesty's fleet captured the islands from the Spanish. And before, Tobago had been besieged and occasionally occupied by the Dutch, the Spanish, the British, the French — even Courlanders from Latvia.

During World War II, three US army bases and one navy base were built in Trinidad as part of the lend-lease deal with Britain, in order to protect Caribbean and Allied shipping interests from the Germans. These came under local control on August 31, 1962, when the twin-island nation became an independent member of the Commonwealth. In 1976, Trinidad and Tobago became a republic, with the president replacing the British monarch as head of state. The People's National Movement, founded by Dr. Eric Williams, was an early force in the drive for independence, and Dr. Williams served the nation as prime minister for 25 years, until his death in 1981.

Major industries in Trinidad and Tobago today include steel, natural gas, methanol, agriculture, and a growing commitment to tourism. It is oil, however, to which this tiny ridge of land has owed much of its prosperity and, more recently, its economic ups and downs, due to erratic world prices. As the third largest oil exporter in the Western Hemisphere, Trinidad has long been one of the richest and most industrialized countries in the West Indies, exceeded only by Puerto Rico. It exceeds its neighbors in natural resources, possessing — in addition to oil — the largest pitch lake in the world, which provides enough bitumen to pave the highways of the world. Every macadam street in the US contains a part of Trinidad — an awesome thought, considering that this 100-acre lake, with reserves of some 10 million tons, reproduces today what was mined yesterday.

Natural gas sources, discovered off Trinidad's east coast, promise other possibilities for industrial expansion, as do the more standard Caribbean agricultural products of sugar, cocoa, coffee, citrus, and coconuts. Trinidad

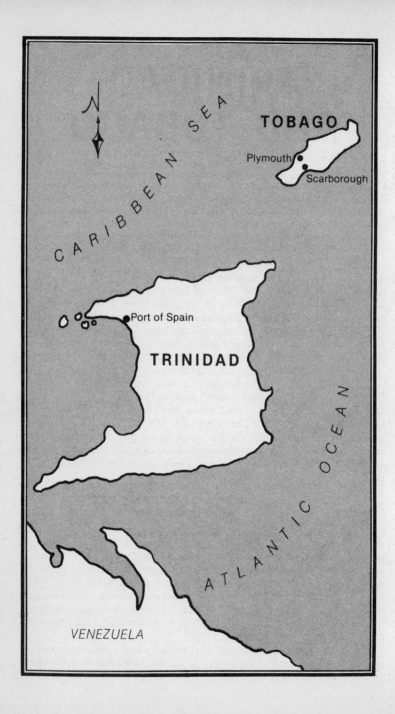

must also be credited with giving mixed drinks that added touch, as Angostura Bitters has for years been produced exclusively on the island, its magic formula scrupulously guarded.

Trinidad's mineral wealth represents a mixed blessing for tourists. Because of Trinidad's oil reserves, visitors can tour by auto to their hearts' content, using gasoline priced as low as anywhere in the Caribbean. On the other hand, the island's prosperity has, in the past, caused it to pay scant attention to visitors. Recently, however, perhaps because of the precipitous decline in oil prices, there has been a push to increase tourism by some attractive marketing packages from major hotels and airlines. Clearly, the welcome mat extends farther than ever before.

Visitors may be startled by the contrast between industry and nature on Trinidad. While the profusion of birds (over 100 species), butterflies (600-plus species), orchids (700 species), reptiles, and other fauna and flora delight and dazzle, tourists may find themselves traveling through an oil refinery to reach a bird sanctuary, or a jungle to hike through.

The expressions of welcome are as many and various as the diversity of the people in Trinidad and Tobago. In addition to the Amerindians believed to be the island's first settlers in about 5000 BC, there are strong African influences, flavored with Carib, Créole, and Portuguese. Add British, Spanish, French, German, East Indian, Chinese, Lebanese, Syrian, and North American inhabitants, and you can begin to see why Trinidad has a unique personality — one that is reflected as much in the jumble of architectural styles in the capital Port of Spain as in the mélange of spices in island food. The number and profusion of languages heard throughout the country — including Hindi, Urdu, Spanish, Chinese, a local patois, and English — is surpassed only by the spectrum of cooking styles and cuisines. It is this fortuitous blend of styles and cultures that makes a week of celebration in February unlike any other carnival in the world, the music from a set of steel drums different from any you've heard. Surprisingly, over half the population is East Indian — Hindu and Muslim. Be sure to try rôti (a large flat bread made with chick-peas and filled with curried vegetables or meats) at a roadside stand, and consider visiting during the Indian religious holidays or attending a Hindu wedding ceremony. This is as close as you'll get to visiting India without flying to Calcutta.

The varied character and hustle-bustle life on Trinidad in no way disturbs the calm of nearby Tobago; visitors find it difficult to believe they are only 22 miles apart. Tobago's present serenity, however, belies a turbulent history. It was not until 1803, when the British won a bloodless victory over the French and marched in to take their place in Scarborough, that the island found itself at peace. Before this, it had changed hands no fewer than 31 times, had been the site of three centuries of raids and counterattacks, and run a bloody gamut from the murder of 25 Swedish pioneer families to violent rebellions.

During most of the nineteenth century, Tobago enjoyed tremendous prosperity due to its monopoly of the sugar industry. Then it was a credit to a wealthy Londoner's reputation that he be deemed "as rich as a Tobago planter," and when the island was given the motto "Pulchrior evenit" ("She becomes even more beautiful"), there was a crystalline, white sparkle in her eye.

Unfortunately, disaster struck the sugar industry in 1884, when the London firm that had monopolized Tobago's financial dealings declared itself bankrupt. With the collapse of Gillespie & Company went the island's entire economy. Suddenly a poor relation, little Tobago became — somewhat reluctantly — a ward of Trinidad.

There is no sibling rivalry today between the two islands. What Trinidad offers in terms of nightlife, good restaurants, sightseeing, and a most exciting carnival scene is perfectly complemented by neighboring Tobago's dreamlike sands. It would be almost impossible to find a better combination for a Caribbean visit. Tobago, with its spectacular beaches, pastel houses, shoreline roads, and endless lanes of coconut palms, soothes where Trinidad titillates. To visit one without the other is certainly possible but not recommended. These two work like a team.

TRINIDAD AND TOBAGO AT-A-GLANCE

FROM THE AIR: The million-plus inhabitants of Trinidad occupy what is roughly a rectangle, 37 miles by 50 miles. Viewed from on high, the island looks like a jigsaw puzzle piece, ready to be moved into place next to neighboring Venezuela 8 miles away. Geologists now believe that Trinidad was, in fact, once part of the South American continent and became an island about 10,000 BC.

Trinidad's South American roots can be traced in other ways. The flora and fauna of the island closely resemble that of Venezuela, and the northern range of mountains, which stretch from east to west, is actually a continuation of the South American Cordillera. Of these peaks, the two highest are El Cerro del Aripo, 3,085 feet, and El Tucuche, 3,072. The rest of the island is fairly flat, except for the central Montserrat Hills and the Trinity Hills to the southeast.

The tiny fish-shaped island of Tobago, 26 miles long by 7 miles wide, is one-sixteenth the size of its neighbor. With mountainous terrain, except for the flat western end, Tobago differs more in topography from Trinidad than Trinidad does from Venezuela (which supports the notion that Tobago was separated from Trinidad thousands of years before Trinidad broke from Venezuela). Tobago somewhat resembles the Windward Islands to the north, with its 1,500-foot hills rolling to white, sandy beaches and clear blue water.

SPECIAL PLACES IN TRINIDAD: Port of Spain – A good starting place for a walking tour is the huge, green Queen's Park Savannah. Known simply as "the Savannah" among the citizenry, this 200-acre lawn has a racecourse, cricket fields, an abundance of joggers, amateur football and soccer players, and vendors hawking everything from coconut water to oyster cocktails.

The area was originally a sugar plantation, but when a disastrous fire swept through the capital in 1808, destroying over 400 homes, the first Trinity Church, and more, Sir Ralph Woodford, the first civil governor of the colony, surveyed the land which the City Council purchased in 1817 from the Peschier family. Today, the buildings surrounding the Savannah are some of the city's most interesting.

On the Maraval Road side of the Savannah stands the Queen's Royal College building, today a secondary school. Built in German Renaissance style, the pink and blue structure has palms in front, a lighted clock tower, and a chiming clock.

Along the same road is the Roodal Residence, called the gingerbread house and typical of the baroque architecture of the French Second Empire. In contrast to the Roodal home, the Stollmeyer Castle, built in 1904, is a copy of a German Rhinish castle. With its turrets and archways made of stone, it manages to look like a Scottish baronial mansion. Nearby, Whitehall — formerly the residence and now the office of the prime minister — is like a wedding cake baked to copy a Moorish-style home.

These homes, plus the official residence of the Anglican bishop and several other large townhouses, complete what is known as the Magnificent Seven — seven large houses in a row. They are as grand and unified as any typical group of turn-of-the-century terraced houses, yet as flamboyant and varied as the rest of Trinidadian life.

If you walk southwest from Maraval Road to Queen's Park West, you'll reach the *Queen's Park* hotel, a shabby shadow of its once-stylish self, and nearby, the National Museum and Art Gallery. In addition to an ornately carved Spanish cannon, some Amerindian relics, representative island art, and an exhibit of snakebite cures, the museum houses a colorful display of carnival costumes from past years. The care and presentation of some of the museum's collections leave a little to be desired, but admission is free and it's a pleasant detour.

Turn down Frederick Street, the narrow, bustling avenue that is the main artery of Port of Spain's shopping district. Don't be put off by the cramped quarters and somewhat disheveled appearance of many of the tiny stores lining the pavements. The jumble of merchandise and olfactory confusion of coconut oil, roasting popcorn, peppers, and sausage is part of what Trinidad is all about. Keep a lookout for local wood carvings, ivory, jewelry, and record shops selling the latest calypso discs.

Halfway down Frederick Street lies Woodford Square. Across the square on St. Vincent Street stands the Red House, a neo-Renaissance building that is the seat of the Trinidad and Tobago Parliament. Perpendicular to the Red House (so named because of its color) on Hart Street is the Holy Trinity Cathedral, worth a visit simply to admire the beautiful setting of this 1823-vintage Gothic structure. The altar carvings and choir stalls are of distinctive craftsmanship, as is a marble monument to Sir Ralph Woodford as well as other memorials to prominent citizens.

Set apart from all the activity of downtown Frederick Street, a short distance from the Savannah, is one of Port of Spain's major attractions, the Royal Botanic Gardens. Covering some 70 acres of a former sugar plantation, the gardens are brimming with tropical flowers. A guided walk will initiate you into the world of orchids, frangipani, chinettes, sapodillas, sausage trees, and lipstick plants. Keep an eye out for the raw beef tree, named because an incision in its bark resembles rare roast beef. There are also lotus lilies — sacred to the Egyptians — and the holy peepul (fig) tree under which Buddha is purported to have attained Nirvana. Perhaps you won't reach that level of spiritual enlightenment, but you'll find the excursion here a pleasant, edifying retreat. Here, too, is the Emperor Valley Zoo, 8 acres of mammals, birds, reptiles, and fish native to Trinidad, Tobago, and South America, many personally collected by curator Hans Boos and zookeeper John Seyjagat on jungle forays.

ELSEWHERE ON THE ISLAND

Asa Wright Nature Centre, Spring Hill Estate – Twenty miles from Port of Spain via car or taxi (about $35 US per car round trip), in the mountains of the northern range, the Asa Wright Nature Centre offers accommodations on acreage devoted to tufted coquettes, squirrel cuckoos, toucans, and other exotic birds. A special attraction is a breeding colony of the nocturnal oilbird or guacharo that resides in Dunston Cave at the center. This is the only easily accessible colony of the species known, and the not-so-easy trek to the Guacharo Gorge is quite an adventure; it's advisable to wear old, comfortable clothes. Ideally, it's an overnight trip (accommodations, including three meals: about $60 US per person a night, double occupancy, plus 10% service) to take advantage of both sunset and sunrise bird-watching hours; but it can also be a day expedition, with afternoon tea on the porch while enjoying the sights and sounds. Field trips on the reservation are $30 per person, and reservations should be made two days in advance.

Wild Fowl Trust – This idyllic spot, paradoxically situated on oil-refinery property, is a 60-acre oasis of flowering lotus and manmade lakes, but primarily the protected breeding grounds for endangered native species of waterfowl. There is also an educational center with Amerindian artifacts and Tobago burial group artifacts. Visitors may gain access for a one-hour guided tour by notifying Wild Fowl Trust personnel (preferably a day in advance) of arrival time, number of people, and type of transport; they will notify security guards at the oil refinery that guests are expected. Be sure to wear good hiking shoes for the forest walk and the Fairy Woods. Admission is less than $1 US, but larger donations are always welcomed by this nonprofit organization run by dedicated volunteers. Check with the tourist office in Port of Spain for the phone number of a volunteer.

Lopinot Historical Complex – In the Arouca Valley, one hour east of Port of Spain, this lushly gardened home of a 19th-century French count has been restored and converted into a plantation museum. The house has furniture, pottery, artifacts; also a cocoa-drying house, a small Anglican church, a park. The complex is also a center for parang (rustic music with Spanish roots) concerts.

Cleaver Woods Park – A mile west of Arima, an hour's drive west of Port of Spain, this 31-acre nature preserve serves as a showcase for both ethnic and natural history. Habitat for dozens of species of indigenous birds, butterflies, and flowers, it also encompasses an Amerindian museum, a pine plantation, and picnic sites.

Fort George – Built in 1804 by Governor Hislop, the fort, on a 1,500-foot peak, is only 10 miles from Port of Spain on a good hardtop road. The hour's drive affords uninterrupted vistas in all directions. The panorama of Boca Grande and the mountains of Venezuela are as much a part of this excursion as seeing the old cannon mounted on the fort's ramparts.

Pitch Lake – Touted as one of Trinidad's major attractions, 60 miles from the capital, this giant asphalt puddle (100 acres, 230 feet deep) is worth a visit only if you have an extra 3 hours. It is mined for bitumen, a source of pavement for highways throughout the world. Its top layer is strong enough to support trucks and bulldozers, and what is dug out today is fully replenished by tomorrow.

North Coast Beach – A popular excursion, this 34-mile drive begins at "the Saddle" — a pass dividing the Santa Cruz and Maraval valleys — and continues across the northern range and down to Maracas Bay. The view from 1,000 feet up — a 100-mile sweep from Tobago to Venezuela — is in itself worthy of the drive.

Enclosed by mountains, with white sand, clear water, and swaying coconut palms, Maracas Beach has changing facilities but no restaurants. Bring your own picnic and have Trinidad's best caterer of local fare, Grace Offord (phone: 628-2983), prepare it for you. Las Cuevas Beach, now with full facilities including changing rooms, a lifeguard, and snack bar is a little farther along the north coast road and farther still is Blanchisseuse Beach, another magnificent swimming spot — though unimproved — and seldom crowded.

San Fernando – Trinidad's second largest town is about 35 miles south of Port of Spain. Basically an oil-boom town, San Fernando is primarily an industrial development with little to interest tourists. It is set in a hilly countryside in the middle of oilfields, and it has a population of 50,000, with a high concentration of East Indians.

Caroni Bird Sanctuary – Trinidad's national bird, the scarlet ibis, can be seen on an excursion to the Caroni Bird Sanctuary. Actually, you will have the treat of seeing hundreds of these bright red birds swooping in to nest on the mangrove islands that fill the 450-acre sanctuary. The sight of the mangrove trees appearing to burst into blood-red flames is nothing short of exquisite, and the peaceful ride via launch through the narrow canals and open waterways is a soothing way to spend a late afternoon.

The sanctuary is about 7 miles — a half-hour drive — south of the city. Boatsmen leave the roadside dock at 4:30 AM and 4 PM; needless to say, the PM departure has more takers. Best and most reliable are Winston Nanaan's *Caroni Tours* (phone: 645-1305), priced at about $20 US per person including pickup at your hotel. Other operators charge about $50 for one or two people sharing a cab or van, covering both the boat trip and hotel transfers; it's a 4-hour excursion, with daily departures from the *Hilton* and other hotels at about 3 PM. Either way, reservations are essential. The inner sanctuary, where the birds nest, is open to the public May to October, but the rest of the sanctuary area stays open all year.

 SPECIAL PLACES IN TOBAGO: Scarborough – Tobago's capital — the tiny town of Scarborough — lays claim to few sights, although it is far from industrialized. Gossip is exchanged in the doorways of old-fashioned drapers' stores, and unintelligible Creole patois fills the square, where a lively native market can be enjoyed each morning. But life is slow moving in Tobago, and Scarborough is no exception. Plan to stop at the tourist board's small office, but otherwise, head for the beach.

For an excellent view of the island as well as a taste of Tobago's history, drive or walk up to see Fort King George, 430 feet above the town. A site for spectacular sunset-viewing, the fort testifies to the endless (and usually pointless) struggles between the French and the British that characterized Tobago's past. Much of the site has been restored, complete with old polished cannon and major buildings. Enlist a knowledgeable guide, such as Horris Job, who may be found at the fort or through the Tourist Board.

Take a look at the tombstone inscriptions in Plymouth churchyard nearby, some dating from the 1700s. For a scenic stroll, try the tiny, well-groomed Botanic Gardens beneath the fort. Bird-watching is a pleasant pastime almost anywhere, but especially among the exotic flora on the private estates.

Pigeon Point – As thin as Tobago is on sightseeing spots, it is rich in beautiful sands. Pigeon Point on the northwest coast is probably its most renowned bathing area, where the long coral beach has thatch shelters for changing and tables, benches, and lavatories. The clear, green water is unusually inviting.

Man O' War Bay – At the opposite end of the island is one of the finest natural harbors in the Caribbean. There you'll discover a long sandy beach on its south shore, and a government rest house that's perfect for picnics.

Charlotteville – Combine your visit to Man O' War with this nearby pretty little fishing village set above the bay on a hillside. Pigeon Peak, Tobago's highest mountain (1,950 feet), rises just behind it.

Speyside – Set on the crescent of Speyside Bay along the Atlantic Coast, this lovely little fishing village offers the luxury of nothing to do except admire the views, enjoy the drive along the Windward Road, and see the bay. Otherwise, swimming places are better at Mt. Irvine and Bacolet bays.

Bird of Paradise Sanctuary – Second only to sunbathing, bird-watching is the favorite Tobago activity. Actually, Little Tobago is the place to go — a 450-acre island off the coast near Speyside. There the sanctuary attracts serious ornithologists, eager to catch a glimpse of the golden-feathered namesake of the area. Since some 50 birds were brought over to the island from New Guinea in the early part of the century (when extinction threatened them), their numbers have decreased, but you can write ahead to the warden (Speyside Post Office, Tobago), and ask for the latest beak count before you go. Otherwise, don't fret, as there are many other varieties of exotic birds on Little Tobago — best seen in early morning or late afternoon.

Buccoo Reef – For a truly spectacular underwater show, complete with yellow angelfish, purple damsels, blue parrotfish, and extensive coralliferous formations, don't miss Buccoo Reef. It lies about a mile offshore from Pigeon Point, and though the tourist crowds may seem overwhelming, they don't bother the marine life and won't bother you once you've donned your mask. Departure times to the reef vary, so check at your hotel and also buy your ticket there. Pickup is at the beach, Buccoo Point, and Store Bay.

SOURCES AND RESOURCES

TOURIST INFORMATION: The Trinidad and Tobago Tourist Board has offices at 400 Madison Ave., Suite 310, New York, NY 10017 (phone: 212-838-7750 or 800-232-0082); 330 Biscayne Blvd.,, Miami, FL 33132 (phone: 305-374-2056 or 800-325-1337 — at tone, dial 700); Aetna Centre, 145 King St. and University Ave., Toronto, Ont. M5H 1J8 (phone: 416-367-0390).

In Trinidad and Tobago, the Tourist Board has offices at 122-124 Frederick Street in Port of Spain, at Trinidad's Piarco Airport, and on Tobago at the airport and in Scarborough.

Local Coverage – Trinidad's newspapers are a source of information on goings-on: the *Trinidad Guardian,* the *Trinidad Express,* and the *Evening News* are three to read.

Telephone – Dial direct to either island by adding the area code 809 to the numbers given below.

ENTRY REQUIREMENTS: Visitors are required to have a valid passport and an ongoing or return ticket from the point of embarkation. When you arrive, you'll be given an immigration card to complete and sign; keep the carbon copy, as you will be asked for it on your departure. At that time, you will also have to pay an airport tax of $20 TT (about $5.60 US) in Trinidadian currency, so don't change all your TT dollars into US.

Baggage is subject to spot checks by customs officials, but personal items are duty free, and adult visitors are allowed to bring in one carton of cigarettes (or 50 cigars or one pound of tobacco) and one quart of liquor.

Smallpox vaccinations are not required of US visitors unless you have stopped in an infected area (unlikely) en route. Yellow fever shots are up to you; again, unless you've stopped where the pest (*Aides aegypti*) resides, you won't need them.

CLIMATE: Cool trade winds tend to temper the tropical warmth of Trinidad and Tobago, where eight hours of sunshine per day is the average. The rainy season generally hits late in May and lasts until November. Average year-round temperatures are 74°F (23°C) at night; 84°F (29°C) during the day, so lightweight clothing is a must. Cocktail dresses and summer suits are often worn at night in Trinidad, while daytime Trinidad and anytime Tobago are casual.

MONEY: Local currency is the Trinidadian dollar (TT), which is exchanged at the official rate of approximately $1 US to $3.60 TT. However, US currency is universally accepted, and the single advantage of dealing in local currency is that purchases will occasionally prove less expensive. All figures in this chapter are quoted in US dollars. Most banks are open 9 AM to 2 PM Mondays through Thursdays and 9 AM to 1 PM and 3 to 5 PM Fridays.

LANGUAGE: English is spoken on both islands; Trinidad's Calypsonians have a special way with a rhyme, a song, and spur-of-the-moment lyrics.

TIME: Atlantic Standard Time all year long, 1 hour ahead of Eastern Standard Time and the same as Eastern Daylight Time.

CURRENT: Electricity is 110 or 230 volts, 60 cycles AC. At hotels, it's best to check with the management before plugging in appliances.

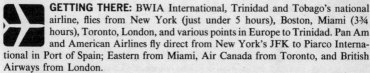

GETTING THERE: BWIA International, Trinidad and Tobago's national airline, flies from New York (just under 5 hours), Boston, Miami (3¾ hours), Toronto, London, and various points in Europe to Trinidad. Pan Am and American Airlines fly direct from New York's JFK to Piarco International in Port of Spain; Eastern from Miami, Air Canada from Toronto, and British Airways from London.

Trinidad and Tobago Airways Corporation (BWIA International) flights link the two islands with a number of daily 20-minute flights (about $25 round-trip); when booked as part of some excursion and tour-basing fares, the inter-island flights may be included at no extra charge. The luxury coastal ferry *Gelting,* with 3 restaurants, a bar, and 15 cabins, makes the trip in 5½ hours each way and charges $6 tourist class, $9 cabin class, round-trip. A new vessel, the MV *Panorama,* will accommodate 720 passengers.

CALCULATING COSTS: Most of Trinidad's top hotels begin at about $110 per night for a double; good smaller places ask about $80 and up. Modified American Plan (MAP, breakfast and dinner) will up the price another $30 to $35 per person per day. Rates at Tobago's best resort hotels range from $120 to $180 for two in season, and most are MAP. Tobago hotel rates drop substantially from mid-April to mid-December, but Trinidad's hotels don't lower rates very much, if at all, in the off-season. Special rates are in effect for *Carnival.*

GETTING AROUND: Taxi – Not a bad idea for a short stay, and many drivers will double as guides for a little extra. All cabs with an H as the first letter of their license plate tend to hover around the airport and big hotels, as well as cruise through Port of Spain. The cabs do not, however, have meters, so be sure to agree on a price — and in what currency — before heading off. The taxi ride from Piarco Airport to town usually runs about $24. From Tobago's airport to most hotels, it's $5 to $18 per car. Ask someone at your hotel for other rates if you're going sightseeing. They are all established on the basis of route distances. In general, cabs aren't expensive. The knowledge of Tobago drivers like Cecil Lyons or Adolphus James, a naturalist who works with the Audubon Society, adds a lot to a day's touring.

When it comes to touring, current wisdom has it that you're better off hiring a car and driver through a tour operator; you'll get a better car and better deal. One of the best, *Trinidad and Tobago Sightseeing Tours* (phone: 624-1984 or 625-6397), will provide a car and driver for about $75 US a day. This is the only tour company to receive the Hospitality Award from the Tourist Board.

Bus – Lines run regularly from Port of Spain, linking the various cities on the island. They cost about 15¢ to 20¢. Tobago's public buses are fairly modern and dirt cheap. They make the trip from one end of the island to the other, and while they take longer than a taxi, they do afford a good view of island life.

Car Rental – Probably the best arrangement if you don't have a problem driving on the left-hand side of the road with a right-hand mounted wheel. Gas is about $1 US per gallon. The tourist board and the hotels can make arrangements for you, or you can contact one of the following: *Bacchus Taxi & Car Rentals,* 37 Tragarete Rd. (phone: 622-5588); *Hub Travel* at the *Hilton* (phone: 624-3316); *Hertz Rent-A-Car* at Piarco Airport (phone: 624-3316); or *Tobago Rentals,* Courland Bay (phone: 639-2851). Rates start at about $50 per day with unlimited mileage. You will need an international driver's license, which you should have before you leave if you want to avoid taking the written and road tests.

 SHOPPING: Not quite up to par with some of the more sophisticated Caribbean islands, such as St. Martin/St. Maarten. Concentrate your browsing in the areas of Port of Spain's Frederick Street and Independence Square, where merchandise is sold in everything from plush shops to rickety pushcarts.

The best shopping is at *St. Ann's Village,* the shopping center in the *Normandie* hotel: jewelry, clothing, crafts, even delicious homemade ice cream, all in an attractive arcade. The island's most exciting clothing designer, Meiling, has an outpost here as well as at 16 Gray St., next door to her sister Phyllis's excellent restaurant, the *Verandah.*

Shops and pushcarts offer soft Venezuelan leather loafers for women at about $15 US per pair. They come in a wide array of styles and colors — pink, turquoise, with small pockets or designs in contrasting hues.

Don't miss Port of Spain's *Central Market* on Saturday mornings. The vendors here bring their goods — fruit, vegetables, baskets, and vetiver (a wonderful sachet for the closet) — in from the countryside.

Trinidad's most distinctive establishment, *Stecher's* (27 Frederick St.), offers a stunning collection of crystal, china, watches, jewelry, and other imported luxuries, more than any other store in town. And it carries duty-free goods, delivered, if you wish, to the airport.

The *Long Circular Mall, Esquire's* (27 Chacon St.), and *Straker's* (45 Charlotte St.) are the places to shop for the latest calypso recordings.

The *Hilton* hotel houses an attractive complex of air-conditioned shops close together for easy browsing. *Stecher's* has a branch there, and you'll find *Y. de Lima* for high-quality gold and silver jewelry, duty-free cameras, watches (other stores at 23A Frederick St. and the airport); the *Trinidad and Tobago Handicraft Cooperative; Boutique Cybèle* for batiks, women's fashion; *Meiling* for original island-designed clothes; *Kacal's* for fine art, wood carvings by local artists; *Tobiki Manshop; Begum's Indian Boutique; Fashion Focus* for cosmetics and skin-care products.

If you're looking for Indian goods, go to *Lakhan's Bazaar* (Bombay St. and Western Main Rd.) for bright saris, embroidered purses, and rugs. You'll find rattan and grass weavings — everything from furniture to fruit baskets — at the *Trinidad and Tobago Blind Welfare Association* (118 Duke St.). Colorful fabrics by the yard — both imported and local prints — are a specialty of *Aboutique,* 54 Queen St.; *Janoura's,* at the corner of Henry and Queen sts.; and *A. A. Laquis,* 30 Frederick St.

For art's sake, browse through *Art Creators & Suppliers* in Aldegonda Park at 7 St. Ann's Rd., the gallery that represents both Geoffrey and Boscoe Holder as well as other fine Trinidadian artists. *Gallery 1234,* at 10 Nook Ave., adjacent to the *Normandie* hotel, features contemporary Trinidad and Tobago artists of the highest caliber.

Good bookstores to scour are *Abercrombie Bookshop* on Abercrombie St. and *Cosmic Bookshop* in the West Mall. Interesting choices include anything by V.S. Naipal, *Some Trinidad Yesterdays* by P.E.T. O'Conner, and *Voices in the Street* by Olga Mavro Gadato.

Orchid fans will enjoy visiting Edward Moll and his sons at their *San Antonio Nursery* in upper Santa Cruz (phone: 676-8742).

On Tobago, the place is once again *Stecher's*. Both in Scarborough and at the *Crown Reef* hotel, it sports essentially the same luxury goods. *Y. de Lima* is also in Scarborough. Hotel shops also offer some local handicrafts. Liquors can be purchased at *Young's Grocery* on the corner of Main and Bacolet sts. *Khoury's* on Burnett St. and *Kawame African Arts and Crafts* on Wilson Rd. are the places to go for African goods, dolls made of shells, and native wood carvings. For Tobago art, visit the *National Fine Arts Center* (phone 639-6897), just 10 minutes from Scarborough on Orange Hill Rd. Its knowledgeable and congenial director, Wilcox Morris, an accomplished artist in his own right, exhibits some excellent local art and refers interested buyers directly to the artists.

 TIPPING: Most of the larger hotels and restaurants charge a 10% service fee that is added to your bill. Elsewhere, tips range between 10% and 15%, depending on the nature of the service provided.

 SPECIAL EVENTS: The event of the year is *Carnival* — where calypso singing and dancing are *everywhere* — the world-renowned fête that is anticipated and planned for all year long. The celebration, called jump-up in Trinidad, takes place in Port of Spain — the best place to be for it — and in San Fernando and Arima on Trinidad, and on Tobago in Scarborough.

Although the history of the Carnival dates back 200 years to the French who introduced it, it is truly a celebration of calypso and the captivating beat of steel drums. Carnival lasts from the dawn of the Monday before Ash Wednesday through midnight Tuesday. But from Sunday on, the fantastically costumed citizens of the island dance their way through the streets to the enthusiastic rhythms of steel drums and the musical lyrics of top-notch calypsonians. When the final judgments on best costumes, song, and lyrics have been announced, the soles of thousands of pairs of shoes have been worn through, and the artisans are already at work on next year's costumes.

If you plan to visit Trinidad during Carnival, make reservations at least a year in advance, and expect to pay double at some hotels.

Hosein (pronounced ho-say), another major festival on Trinidad, is a 3-day Muslim celebration in the fall. It includes parades of elaborately designed miniature mosques (called *tadjahs*), music, colorful costumes, stick fighting, chanting, tassa drumming; check with the Tourist Board.

The *Natural History Festival,* begun in 1987, runs the first two weeks of October and features Trinidad and Tobago's natural resources: the Orchid Society's annual show; bird-watching, butterfly-searching, and other field trips; lectures and slide presentations; tours; and more. Individuals may choose specific activities or join up with a group during the festival. One tour operator who knows the territory is plant explorer and tropical-fruit expert Tom Economo (Follow Nature Trail, Box 450662, Miami, FL 33145; phone: 305-285-7173), or contact the tourist office in Port of Spain for information.

The Hindu *Festival of Lights,* called *Dewali,* takes place in October or November. At that time, celebrants place lights around their homes, gardens, and temples, transforming parts of the islands into glowing spectacles. Also in October or November, a ceremony of purification, *Katik-Nannan,* is performed on Trinidad's Atlantic coast at

Manzanilla, to which hundreds of Hindus travel to bathe in the sea. Official holidays when banks and businesses are closed include: *New Year's Day, Good Friday, Easter Sunday* and *Monday, Whitmonday* (in May), *Corpus Christi* (late spring), *Labor Day* (in June), *Discovery Day* (August 1), *Independence Day* (August 31), *Republic Day* (September 24), *Christmas* (December 25), and *Boxing Day* (December 26).

Tobago's special events include the *Tobago Heritage Festival,* which takes place during the last two weeks of July and features goat and crab races, folk dancing, and other traditional activities (even a reenactment of a Tobago wedding). Goat and crab races are also held on Easter Tuesday at Buccoo Village.

 SPORTS: TRINIDAD — Cricket – This cousin of US baseball is played on pitches (fields) ranging from exquisitely manicured greens to vacant lots. Cricket is a spectator sport that is also a social event, much like Carnival. For upcoming matches, check with the tourist board of the island you plan to visit or consult the sports section of the island newspaper.

Golf – Best course on Trinidad is St. Andrews at *Moka Golf Club* in Maraval, 3 miles from Port of Spain. There is also a new 18-hole golf club course at Balandra, on the north coast, and a public course at Chaguaramas, just outside Port of Spain.

Horse Racing – A popular year-round sport with plenty of betting. The big races are the holidays — Christmas, New Year's, Carnival, Easter, and Discovery, Republic, and Independence days. At Union Park in San Fernando; Queen's Park in Port of Spain; Santa Rosa in Arima.

Hunting – Don't even think about it. A two-year ban on all hunting has been put into effect, and offenders face six months in prison or a $1,000 fine.

Soccer – Called football here, it's the national sport, played year-round. The two major leagues battle it out at the National Stadium.

Sport Fishing – For kingfish and Spanish mackerel, try the north coast, June through October. Otherwise, good catches can be had all year. Spearfishing for snapper, barracuda, and grouper takes place closer to shore, while trolling for bluefish is popular around the east and south coasts during winter months. Winston Nanan, of *Caroni Tours* (phone: 645-1305), runs fishing trips on the Caroni River and its estuaries; charge, including hotel pickup and return, is about $125 per person for a 6-hour expedition in search of grouper, tarpon, snook, yellowtail, and snapper. See your hotel tour desk for help with arrangements.

Swimming and Sunning – Visitors can choose from the beaches at Maracas and Las Cuevas in the north, Balandra and Toco to the northeast, and Manzanilla and Mayaro in the east. All beaches are accessible by car or bus. Surfing, particularly during winter months, is possible at many of the beaches.

Tennis – Best bet is to try the *Hilton* hotel, the *Trinidad Country Club,* or the *Tranquility Square Lawn Tennis Club,* where nonguests are charged an hourly rate. There are public courts in Port of Spain on the grounds of the Prince's building.

TOBAGO — Golf – The main attraction is the excellent course at the *Mount Irvine Bay* hotel, 6 miles from Scarborough. Site of many professional tournaments, this 6,800-yard course (par 72) follows the natural contours of the island, providing guests and visiting players with breathtaking views in addition to challenging fairways and greens. In fact, be sure to catch the sunset from the clubhouse even if you don't play golf.

Snorkeling and Scuba – Buccoo Reef is the place for snorkeling; best diving is at Flying Reef on the island's west side, some two dozen new dive sites (ten rated for experts only) around Man of War Bay. *Dive Tobago* (phone: 639-2385) at Store Bay is Tobago's top shop. Using the *Crown Reef, Sandy Point Beach Club,* and *Mount Irvine Bay* hotel, *Evecar Travel* and *Weekends Away* package dive trips. Winston Nanan of

Caroni Tours also conducts scuba tours for beginners through advanced (phone: 645-1305).

Sailing – Just $25 will carry you away on the *Sail with Chloe,* a 36-foot sloop skippered by Peter Abraham and accommodating up to 10 passengers. It makes four-hour trips up the coast for sightseeing and snorkeling, departing at 2 PM and returning at sunset. No alcohol served (phone: 639-2851).

Fishing and Bird-watching Excursions – David Rooks, a naturalist and past president of the Field Naturalists Society of Trinidad and Tobago, conducts half-day tours to St. Giles Island to observe frigate birds and other species, at a cost of $25 per person. He also will take up to six fisherman out in his 28-foot fiber glass boat for blue marlin, wahoo, billfish, sailfish, king mackerel, barracuda, and shark. Fishing trips cost $25 an hour.

Swimming and Sunning – Back Bay, just west of the *Mt. Irvine Bay* hotel, is picture-postcard-perfect, with palm trees, sea grapes, and usually complete privacy.

Tennis – The condition of courts at the *Mount Irvine Bay* hotel is usually good; those at *Turtle Beach* are excellent, and *Arnos Vale*'s are in good shape.

Windsurfing – Available at the *Turtle Beach* and *Mt. Irving Bay* hotels.

 NIGHTCLUBS AND NIGHTLIFE: Steel band music and shows dominate the entertainment scene, but local theater groups as well as cultural and folkloric dance and music groups perform at several sites around town and, occasionally, at hotels. There are concerts at *Queen's Hall.* For dancing, there are about a dozen established discos plus the late-night lounges at the major hotels. *The Aviary* at the *Hilton* is particularly popular Thursday, Friday, and Saturday nights, when there is a live band. Monday evening's poolside *Canboulay Fiesta* at the *Hilton* also draws a crowd. Other nightspots include *Legends* in Maraval, the *Atlantis* disco at Westmall, and *J.B.'s,* at Valpark Shopping Center, for disco and good steaks. Jazz clubs include the *Mas Camp Pub* in Port of Spain and Kalalu.

Tobago's nightlife is quiet. There are steel bands and limbo dancers at some hotels, where Saturday night fêtes usually include a barbecue and music. The *Mount Irvine Bay* hotel tends to attract the most sophisticated crowd, but the *Arnos Vale* is also a good bet. In town (Scarborough, that is), the *Old Donkey Cart House*'s al fresco slide show and conviviality attract after-dinner drop-ins. *La Tropicale* at the *Della Mira Guest House* is a favorite with islanders. Watch for billboards advertising moonlit beach barbecues. These local events, often fundraisers for churches, feature bands, plenty of chicken or fish, and rum punch, for about $10 to $15 TT, and can go on until 1 or 2 in the morning. Beyond that, there are moonlit walks and late swims.

BEST ON THE ISLANDS

 CHECKING IN: Accommodations on Trinidad run the gamut from deluxe, pool-oriented, multiroom complexes to smaller, less luxurious hostelries with a truer island flavor. There are also cottages for rent on the island — a good idea for those planning an extended stay — and for some very inexpensive rooms, there are guesthouses.

One of the most important factors to bear in mind is how much time you think you'll spend at the beach. Many of the bigger, popular hotels are near Port of Spain, an advantage for those with sightseeing, shopping, or business on their agendas, but inconvenient for the avid beachcomber, as a taxi ride to Maracas Bay, or any beach along the lovely north coast, will be costly. Check with the hotel to see if it makes special arrangements for transportation to the beach. Otherwise, you can probably hook up with fellow hotel guests and share the cost of the ride. You should also be consoled by the fact that two of Trinidad's business-oriented hotels — the *Hilton* and the *Holiday Inn* — both at least 30 minutes from the beach, have big swimming pools.

Expect to pay well over $100 up for a double room in winter at the hotels we place in the expensive category; about $80 or more in the moderate range; and less than $60 in an inexpensive hotel — all without meals. Prices are somewhat lower in the summer. Most Tobago hotels operate on the Modified American Plan (MAP, including breakfasts and dinners). Those we class as expensive charge about $170 a night up for a double in winter; moderate, about $105 to $170; inexpensive, $100 or less. A number of rental villas are also available. Summer rates on both islands drop 20% to 40%. Special rates are often in effect during *Carnival* time, and multiple-night stays may be required. Those who want to enjoy true Trinidadian hospitality, especially during *Carnival* when most hotels are full, are advised to contact Mrs. Grace Steele of the Bed and Breakfast Association. Some members offer a swimming pool and home cooking, and rates are reasonable, starting at $25 US per night.

PORT OF SPAIN, TRINIDAD

Holiday Inn – A modern, comfortable, air-conditioned hotel with 235 rooms, nightly entertainment, a large freshwater pool, and a revolving restaurant. The view from on high is superb — quite different from its location in the heart of an unattractive, commercial area of the city (phone: 625-4531). Expensive.

Trinidad Hilton International – The hilltop, upside-down *Hilton* (with the lobby at the top and resident floors below) is the top choice for businesspeople. It's a luxurious, air-conditioned hostelry with all the attendant amenities, including three premium-rate, super-service Vista Executive Floors with airport meeting service, daily newspapers, complimentary Continental breakfast, and a special lounge with a complimentary full open bar and hot hors d'oeuvres. In addition to 442 rooms, it offers the largest convention facilities of any hotel in the southern Caribbean. Two major restaurants, *La Boucan* and the *Pool Terrace,* are supplemented by pool buffets. Every Monday is Canboulay night, featuring folkloric music, dance, entertainment, and a feast of roast pig on a spit, barbecued beef and chicken, and such island favorites as callaloo, cow heel soup, souse, and coo coo. There are 2 lighted all-weather tennis courts, large swimming pool, plenty of area for sunning, renovated health club with sauna, and a two-level shopping arcade. Nightly entertainment, good service. Views are spectacular, particularly from rooms overlooking the Savannah, which seems to bustle 24 hours a day (phone: 624-3211). Expensive.

Chaconia Inn – In suburban Maraval, this 30-room inn is a popular retreat for Trinidadians as well as visitors. A freshwater pool, sun deck, restaurant, and a popular pub with dancing in the evening are among its attractions; so is its proximity to Moka golf course (phone: 628-8603). Expensive to moderate.

Kapok – In St. Clair, a quiet residential area in Port of Spain, this fairly modern establishment has passable accommodations for some 200 guests. There's a backyard pool, a good view of town from the top, a Polynesian restaurant on the roof, and the rather more elegant *Café Savanna* on the ground floor (phone: 622-6441). Moderate.

Normandie – Anna and Fred Chin Lee started remodeling and expanding here about three years ago, building on the charm of the original turn-of-the-century structure to create a distinctive property with a California/Mexico feel to it. Nestled on Nook Avenue, within easy walking distance of the Savannah and the *Hilton* hotel, it has 16 new rooms with sleeping lofts and easy access to the new conference center and gallery of shops. The 41 older rooms are clustered around the swimming pool in its garden setting. All rooms are air conditioned (phone: 624-1181). Moderate.

Monique's Guest House – In suburban Maraval, only 8 minutes from Moka golf course. Family owned, with 7 simply furnished rooms (some air conditioned) and a reputation for being so personally accommodating that guests return again and again. An engagingly informal place to experience true Trinidadian hospitality. 114 Saddle Rd. (phone: 628-3344). Inexpensive.

ELSEWHERE ON TRINIDAD

Timberline Resort and Nature Center – Converted cocoa houses in an idyllic setting on Trinidad's north coast. Nature lovers can enjoy ocean views, stroll the beach, or follow bird-watching trails. At Bella Vista Estate, Maracas (phone: 638-2263 or 676-8519). Moderate.

Asa Wright Nature Center and Lodge – Even if you're not a bird-watcher, you'll enjoy waking up to the sounds of birds outside your window at this gracious establishment. Try to reserve room 5 or 6 in the main building, both large, charming, and high-ceilinged; the other rooms are best suited to those out bird-watching all day. Rates include all meals, afternoon tea (a treat in itself), and rum punch each evening (phone: 622-7480). Moderate to inexpensive.

Mount St. Benedict Guest House – For something completely different, this 14-room hostelry is part of a monastery in the hills of Tunapuna, about 20 minutes from Port of Spain. Accommodations are neat, clean, and spartan. Go for the spectacular view and the peace and quiet as well as for the homemade bread and honey served at teatime (phone: 662-4084). Inexpensive.

TOBAGO

Tobago's hotels are more subdued than those of Trinidad. There are no high-rise buildings, and most of the hotels were built to blend in with the scenery, creating a cozy, lazy resort. Unfortunately, the flavor of Tobago will soon be changing. The harbor is being expanded to accommodate 47 cruise ships; the airstrip will be 3,500 feet longer for wide-body aircraft; and the present number of hotel rooms, 600, will be increased by 1,500.

Prices vary, but expensive hotels run about $190 and up for a double MAP in winter; and Tobago's rates are considerably lower (40% or so) in the summer season. Most hotels offer a Modified American Plan. Food at the hotels tends to be quite good, and given the dearth of restaurants, MAP rates (including breakfast and dinner) make sense.

Arnos Vale – Amid gardens of frangipani, oleander, and sprawling tropical palms, this 34-room hideaway is away from everything but the beach — a perfect sun-bathing spot with first-rate waters for snorkeling. Also has a lovely freshwater pool, underused tennis court, archery, and walking trails for naturalists. Afternoon tea, shared by colorful birds and guests, is looked forward to daily. An Italian chef is imported in the winter months (phone: 639-2881). Expensive.

Crown Reef – This large, fifties-style resort on the beach at Store Bay is better suited to groups or conventions than to honeymooners. In addition to 115 rooms and 7 suites, there is a tennis court, game room, health spa and workout gym, ocean view dining room, indoor lounge, poolside and rooftop bars. Good service; many activity options. Several boutiques on premises (phone 639-8571). Expensive.

Mount Irvine Bay – If you're a golfer, you must stay here. The course is dazzling, and guests automatically become members, entitling them to reduced greens fees ($14 per day) and use of the golf clubhouse. (Even if you don't play, you should enjoy a rum punch on the clubhouse porch.) The hotel consists of a series of 23 air-conditioned cottages, each with 2 rooms, patio, and views of the fairways or the sea; the main building has 64 rooms — all air conditioned and extremely comfortable — that wrap around a swimming pool. There are 2 floodlit tennis courts and equipment for rent. There is also a beach. The *Sugar Mill* restaurant is in a converted sugar mill where, in the evening, you can dine and dance to the band (phone: 639-8871). Expensive.

Turtle Beach – Between the *Arnos Vale* and *Mount Irvine* on a beautiful stretch of sand, this 52-room hotel overlooks the Great Courland Bay. There are 2 tennis courts and a pool, and the rooms have air conditioning and ocean views. There's water skiing and windsurfing; also a conference center for 80. The Saturday night buffet is a local attraction (phone: 639-2851). Expensive to moderate.

Cocrico Inn – Russell and Ida Jack's well-maintained motel-style property in the village of Plymouth has 16 rooms, a swimming pool, and a popular restaurant featuring good home cooking. It's a five-minute walk to the beach, and a good base from which to experience village life and Tobagan culture. Be sure to note the fine paintings by Tobagan Anthony Lewis (phone: 639-2961). Moderate.

Kariwak Village – Air-conditioned cottages (a total of 18 rooms) cluster around a pool. There's indoor and outdoor dining, first-rate island cuisine and entertainment. Minutes from the airport, a 5-minute walk from the beach (phone: 639-8545). Moderate.

Della Mira Guest House – The admittedly simple 14 rooms (all with private bath, half with air conditioning) that constitute this small inn are one of the best low-budget deals on the island. The manager, Mr. Miranda, also runs the night spot *La Tropicale,* next door, which has entertainment and dancing, and the *Della Mira*'s location (only a short pace from Scarborough) makes it popular for island residents. The hotel's bonus is Mrs. Miranda, the island's first licensed barber (phone: 639-2531). Inexpensive.

Richmond Great House – One of Tobago's oldest great houses, for those who seek peace and quiet. The 6 rooms are simple and appealing; the views are spectacular; and the main rooms are filled with African art from the collection of the owner, Dr. Hollis R. Lynch, a professor of African history at Columbia University. There's also a pool and good home cooking — all in all, a great bargain, though a bit off the beaten track (phone: 660-4467). Inexpensive.

 EATING OUT: Happily for visitors to Trinidad and Tobago, the British influence remained on the cricket fields and not in the kitchen. Everything — Chinese, Indian Créole, Spanish, French, and West Indian fare, is available in Port of Spain. There are far fewer choices in Tobago.

The islands' gustatory exotica include manicou (opossum) stew, tatou (armadillo) stew, tum-tum (mashed plantains), and fresh armadillo. Some of these delicacies are no longer served legally, due to the recent ban on hunting. But no matter, there are plenty of delicious stuffed crabs, tiny clamlike shellfish (called chip-chip), and Indian-spiced rôtis stuffed with spicy meats. Accompany all of this with a fresh rum punch — as only the island capital of Angostura Bitters can make it — or Carib or Stag beer, and you are guaranteed to limbo all night! The local rum, Old Oak, is made at the House of Angostura, along with a fairly good coffee liqueur called Mokatia.

In the listing below, two can have dinner for $35 up plus drink and service charge in a restaurant described as expensive; from about $20 to $30 in restaurants marked moderate; and for about $15 or under in inexpensive places.

PORT OF SPAIN

La Boucan – The *Hilton*'s widely known restaurant named for the smoking oven used by buccaneers to prepare meat for their voyages. The restaurant sports a replica of this cooking apparatus, and many of its dishes are characterized by a subtle, smoky taste. There are also steaks, fish, mildly flavored island dishes, like callaloo. Look for the wall painting by multitalented Trinidadian Geoffrey Holder (phone: 624-3211). Expensive.

Café Savanna – Currently favored by the capital's smart set for its heavily French-accented menu including such dishes as seafood mousse, shellfish bisque, *crabe au gratin*, filet de porc Wellington. We'd opt for those based on the freshest ingredients. In St. Clair on the ground floor of the *Kapok* hotel (phone: 622-6441). Expensive.

Mangal's – *The* Indian place to try. In a marvelous gingerbread-frilled mansion; good curries (firepower adjusted if you ask), rôtis as big as bedspreads. Queen's Park E (phone: 624-4639 or 664-1201). Expensive.

La Ronde – Try the *Holiday Inn*'s rooftop restaurant for a good meal with the best nighttime view in town. Steaks and other tourist fare are featured menu items (phone 625-3361). Expensive.

Veni Mange – A not-to-be-missed lunch spot renowned for its soups (especially callaloo, red bean, pumpkin), lobster, curried crab; some vegetarian dishes too. Also open Friday nights for drinks and snacks. 13 Lucknow St. (no phone). Expensive to moderate.

The Waterfront – In the West Mall Shopping Center rather than on the harbor, as the name might suggest. The most popular dish is "fish in a basket," the Saturday afternoon special. Westmoorings (phone: 632-0834). Expensive to moderate.

La Fantasie – A pioneer in *cuisine créole nouvelle,* which means interpreting Trinidad's diverse, traditional cooking in an updated manner. Try the *poule déshoue viande fin* (pâté of chicken with garlic and bay leaf seasoning) for starters. *Crème de croisse* is a pumpkin and bean soup, and entrées include Manzanilla Morning (fish steak or filet with herbs and sauce) and Petit Pap Bois (char-broiled filet mignon with herb bouquet and rum butter). In the *Normandie* hotel (phone: 624-1181). Moderate.

Il Giardino di Luciano – Homemade pastas and garlicky Italian-style dishes in a friendly garden setting. Don't miss the delicate caroni mussels alla marinana. Open every day but Sunday for lunch and dinner. At 6 Nook Ave. (phone: 624-1459). Moderate.

Singho – Tucked inside the Long Circular Shopping Mall, it offers the best Cantonese-style food in Port of Spain, excellent service, entertainment, and an aquarium. Try the lemon chicken, pepper shrimp, or lobster in black bean sauce. Open daily 11 AM to 11 PM for lunch and dinner (phone: 628-2077). Moderate.

Tiki Village – The Trader Vic's of Trinidad, this restaurant atop the *Kapok* hotel offers good city views and specializes in Polynesian creations with a Chinese flair. Try the Polynesian Delight, an assortment of appetizers, and/or the sweet and sour pork. Cotton Hill Rd. (phone: 622-6441). Moderate.

The Verandah – Phyllis Viera serves excellent local food in a lovely setting, a typical old-fashioned house with ceiling fans, tucked away in a residential section of Port of Spain. The menu changes daily, with such offerings as cream of watercress soup, crab backs, filet of kingfish with vermouth and herb sauce, and pumpkin risotto. Don't miss the homemade ice cream — peanut, mocha, lime, etc. — and do dine on the verandah. Open for lunch only, Monday through Friday, but drinks and snacks are served on Friday evenings after work until 9 PM. Waitresses wear the owner's sister's designs; she has two shops under the same roof. This restaurant is very popular with locals, so reservations are a must. At 16 Gray St. St. Clair (622-2987). Moderate.

Breakfast Shed – Authentic local fare in a shed frequented mainly by port workers. Breakfast of fish broth and "bacon fish" (fried flat bread with bacon on top) costs about $3 US, depending on how much you eat. Lunch costs just slightly more, and you'll need to bring your own Carib. Customers pick and choose from stalls — the cooks may even let you peek into their kettles. Hours are 5:30 AM to 3:00 PM, but if the Port Authority changes shifts, this eatery will follow suit. Referred to as the "Holiday Out" by guests of the nearby *Holiday Inn* (no phone). Inexpensive.

Seabelle – A small seafood restaurant with pleasant atmosphere on Mucurapo Rd. (phone: 622-3594). Inexpensive.

TOBAGO

On Tobago, try the restaurants at the *Mount Irvine Bay* hotel (phone: 639-8871) and the *Arnos Vale* (phone: 639-2881). The latter serves a good Sunday brunch while the *Sugar Mill* at the *Mount Irvine,* featuring local seafood and Créole cuisine, is best for dinner. *Kariwak Village* (phone: 639-8545) serves some of the best food on the island; Cynthia Clovis spins magic in the kitchen, not just with island specialties but with homemade liqueurs, ice creams, and cakes. The *Cocrico Inn* in Plymouth (phone: 639-2961) serves authentic Tobagoan dishes. Scarborough's *Old Donkey Cart House* (phone: 639-3551) serves up Continental specialties, imported cheeses, German wines, in a most convivial island setting. *The Blue Crab* in Scarborough (phone: 639-2737) offers excellent local fare, including curried goat or chicken, crab backs, conch chowder, homemade ice cream, and homemade tropical fruit wines; owners Alison Sardinha and husband/chef Kenneth are "turned on by empty plates." If red meat is your thing, try the *Steak Hut* at Sandy Point Beach Club in Crown Point (phone: 639-2531). *Hot Frost,* in Scarborough, looks like just an ice-cream parlor, but try their huge fish platter (under $5) before the banana split.

TURKS & CAICOS

"Turks and *what?*" ask friends when you tell them where you're headed. "Aren't you afraid of the Middle East these days?" "Turks and *where?*" queries the airline reservation clerk. "Are you sure we fly there?" "Turks and Caicos?" ponders an old island hand, showing obvious signs of recognition (you brighten). "Are you going there on purpose?"

It doesn't take long to learn that the rest of the world has rarely, if ever, heard of the Turks and Caicos, in spite of the fact that, anchored 575 miles southeast of Miami, they're considerably closer to the US than Puerto Rico or the Virgin Islands. With a map, a motive, and a reasonably powerful magnifying glass (you'll need all three), you too can find the cluster of tiny land dots (the Turks) and, west of them, the tiny archipelago called the Caicos, roughly 30 miles southeast of Mayaguana in the Bahamas and about 90 miles due north of Haiti. Location and landscape (like most of the Out Islands, they're cookie-flat, with shining edges of sand and some low green hills for contrast) should make them part of the Bahamas, which, in fact, they were until 1874 when, for some obscure reason, they were transferred to Jamaican jurisdiction. Since 1962, however, when Jamaica declared independence, the Turks and Caicos have been a British Commonwealth Colony with a governor appointed by the queen and their own elected ministerial government, which was ushered in by constitutional amendment in 1976.

Six of the eight major islands (Salt Cay and Grand Turk; South, Middle, and North Caicos; and Providenciales — called Provo) and a few of the 40-some mite-sized cays are inhabited. But all together they encompass only 193 square miles of land, plus an almost equal sprawl of fish-haunted tidal banks. They owe their outsized, though until recently almost totally unexploited, tourist potential to their 230 miles of beautiful beach — much of it untouched by human footprint for days at a time — and to vast surrounding rings of virtually virgin live coral reefs and spectacular drop-offs that lure a small, steady stream of divers from around the world. And to fishing so fine that the bonefishermen who've found it hardly even mention it to one another.

What has deterred other tourists? For years accommodations have been extremely limited, with styles ranging from handsomely simple to rustic. Then, in 1984, *Club Med Turkoise* opened on a 70-acre section of Provo's 12-mile beach, bringing the first major resort to this British Crown Colony. And air service, until recently, was erratic. Now Pan Am flies from Miami to Provo and Grand Turk several times each week — a milestone for these islands. Additionally, the government tourist board's small budget has meant limited promotional efforts and no glossy ads to attract the traveler's eye in overseas markets.

But that is not for want of having been historically discovered. Well over five centuries ago, Lucayan Indians arrived to set up cavekeeping on Middle

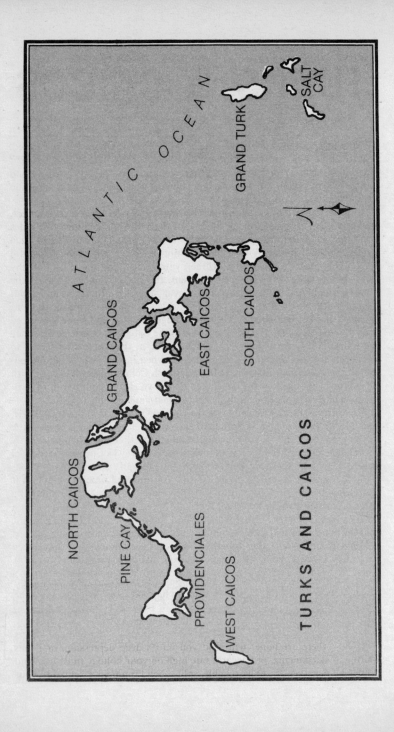

Caicos. It is possible that their name, transcribed onto Juan de la Cosa's map — dated about 1500 — as Yucayo, may have been the root from which the word *Caicos* came. Or it may simply be another version of *cayos,* the Spanish word for islands. There is, however, general agreement that the neighboring Turks isles were named for the barrel-shaped native cactus whose scarlet top looks like a Turkish fez.

Although Ponce de León's sighting during his fountain-hunting travels set 1515 as the islands' official discovery date for years, recent evidence, seconded by both University of Florida and Smithsonian Institution historians, suggests that East Caicos — rather than San Salvador in the Bahamas — was Columbus' first New World landfall in 1492. Through the next several centuries, some of the seas' most notorious pirates — including bloodthirsty Anne Bonny and marauding Mary Read — found the Caicos congenial for concealment and provisioning.

It was not until 1678 that respectable white settlers made their appearance. From Bermuda came Lightbournes, Astwoods, and Butterfields, to rake profit from the Turks' and South Caicos' wealth of sea salt. In spite of pirates, a short-lived Spanish invasion in 1710, and three French attacks in the course of the subsequent 70 years, the Bermudians kept returning, rebuilding their "pans" (shallow pools also called "salinas," from which sea water evaporates, leaving dry salt behind), and sustaining a trade that became a staple of Bermuda's economy. About this time, circa 1787, Gardiners, Williamses, Stubbses, and other Loyalists fleeing the American Revolution arrived to establish plantations on the western Caicos, and they brought slavery with them. After abolition and, ultimately, the invention of man-made fibers, the cotton and sisal industries languished. After the British nationalized salt production in 1951, many whites left the islands for good. But after three centuries of intermingling and intermarrying, the old names persist among today's Belongers — the nickname by which Turks Islanders and Caicos men and women are known.

Recently, there have been significant changes in the islands' tourist picture: Direct air service by Pan Am cuts the travel time from Miami to Grand Turk or Providenciales (Provo) to under an hour and a half; Bahamasair flies from Nassau to South Caicos in roughly the same time; Provo's airport boasts an 8,500-foot runway for wide-bodied jets; condominium construction on Provo — now the site of a full-scale 600-bed *Club Med* — is bustling; and interest in the colony's tax-free advantages as an offshore investment haven portend a rising tourist tide.

Does this mean you should immediately stuff your duffel and take flight? The answer is an unqualified yes and no. Definitely no if you're happy only in five-star hotels (not all the islands' rooms are even air conditioned) and restaurants serving haute cuisine (meals can be good, even delicious when the fish or lobster is fresh and subtly sauced, but because so much food has to be frozen to be imported, Cordon Bleu cooking is the exception, not the rule). No again, if the absence of a social director (except for *Club Med*'s organizers — GOs — there are none) will send you into a deep depression, or if bus touring, disco dancing, or baccarat rate high on your holiday must list. And double all negatives if totally reliable, split-second timing is essential to your vacation peace of mind. Waitresses, maids, guides, taxis, airplanes, you-name-it that come and go according to "island time" (always later than advertised, sometimes not at all) will make you crazy before you can say digital quartz chronometer.

On the other hand, if your natural vacation pace is a saunter, and if quiet doesn't scare you; if you genuinely enjoy miles of undeveloped beach, exploring uninhabited cays, and some sort of water sport (beachcombing, shelling, paddling, floating, fishing, snorkeling, windsurfing — and especially scuba diving); if you'd rather watch the world pass and trade talk in a waterfront bar than tromp through a museum; if you really mean it when you say you want to get away from it all and rather like beating the crowd to a place that still can be fairly described as unspoiled, the answer is an unqualified yes. However, progress is on the way; so by all means, go discover the Turks and Caicos while there's time.

TURKS AND CAICOS AT-A-GLANCE

FROM THE AIR: The Turks and Caicos Islands lie 575 miles southeast of Florida, hidden halfway between Miami and Puerto Rico, 90 miles north of Haiti. Separated from the southern end of the Bahamas by 30 miles of crystal clear water, this island group — eight large islands, only six of which are inhabited, and countless small cays, two inhabited — is an archipelago covering a land area of 193 square miles. The total population is about 8,000 — some 5,000 of whom live on the Salt Islands: Grand Turk, Salt Cay, and South Caicos.

From the air, the coral islands, only 163 feet above sea level at their highest point, look like a concentrated sprinkling of dots floating on an endless stretch of flat, bright white, sea-covered sand, encircled by a chain of continuous reefs with the aquas and purples of the deeper surrounding waters providing startling contrasts.

SPECIAL PLACES: Most of the people on these relatively remote islands live on Grand Turk, South Caicos, North Caicos, and Providenciales (Provo), with smaller settlements on Middle Caicos, Salt Cay, and Pine Cay.

Grand Turk – Once the center of the now-defunct salt industry, Grand Turk is the site of the islands' capital, Cockburn Town, reminiscent of north Bimini in the happy days, or perhaps Dunmore Town in the Bahamas' outlying islands, or Bermuda as it might have looked a hundred years ago. Donkey carts still rattle along the harbor road (which, like its Hamilton counterpart, is called Front Street). But the mahogany carriages once used to transport visitors have disappeared. So you stroll into town past tumbled antique warehouses and pastel-painted homes and gardens to have a look at the old Post Office, the ultramodern Barclays Bank, and the fresh yellow government buildings guarded by red-muzzled cannon aimed stolidly out to sea. When you're ready for a ride, an all-island taxi tour will show you the outlying sights: the lighthouse and the deserted naval station; the missile tracking station (John Glenn debriefed on Grand Turk after his 1962 space mission); near-perfect Pillory Beach; Governor's Beach, near his excellency's stately home; "Waterloo;" Hawk's Nest anchorage; old St. Thomas Church; and the South Point.

Practically speaking, Grand Turk's 9 square miles hold some 4,000 of the colony's population; it boasts a high school, a small hospital, international banks, and an airport with a 7,000-foot airstrip — the base for Turks and Caicos National (called TAC National), the inter-island airline. Of much more interest to visitors, its unique surrounding reefs form a barrier that allows more than one of its sides to be used for diving, giving divers a protected alternative site even when seas are rough. There are two good diving operations and great fishing, too.

Salt Cay – Nine miles from Grand Turk, accessible by boat and only 5 air minutes away, this 3½-square-mile island is shaped like a slice of pie pointed south. At the tip, the surf is rough, but the east side is indented with quiet bays and inlets, and the beach that stretches across its wide northern end is as white and peaceful and perfect for swimming as a shore can get. Windswept and quaint, photogenic Balfour Town boasts relics of both whaling and salt-raking days (windmills and salinas, like white skating rinks in the sun). There's no scuba, but the Talbot brothers will be glad to take you fishing.

South Caicos – Some 22 miles west of Grand Turk, across the Turks Islands Passage, South Caicos is anchored behind a sweep of coral reefs which, with the wall and the incredible drop-off, provide an enormous variety of dive sites. The little town is friendly, but not much to look at. But its Cockburn Harbour, the best natural harbor in all the islands, is not only the focus of the fishing industry that exports conch and lobster each year, but also the scene of the annual Commonwealth Regatta in late May. South Caicos' 7,500-foot runway is the touch-down point for Bahamasair flights from Nassau, a popular stopover point for private pilots too.

Middle (or Grand) Caicos – Reached by ferry from North Caicos, it is the largest of the group, but only sparsely populated (400). At present it has neither hotels nor any other form of development, except for a small government rest house for visitors. The secluded beach area near Mudjin Harbour is exceptionally beautiful. On the north coast are extraordinary limestone caves, worth a visit if only to see the reflections of the stalactites and stalagmites in the clear, still, salt pools. Since 1977, groups of US archaeologists have been coming to Middle Caicos to explore the caves and ruins near Bamberra and Lorimers for artifacts and relics of the Lucayan and Arawak Indians, the islands' earliest settlers.

North Caicos – It's best known locally for its 6-mile beach and some of the islands' best bonefishing. North Caicos's 1,200 permanent residents live in four tiny villages: Bottle Creek on its eastern edge, Kew and Whitby in the center, and Sandy Point in the northwest. *Pelican Beach* and *Prospect* hotel condominiums, at Whitby, offer real out-island hideaways for vacationers here.

Pine Cay – One of the chain of islets that links North Caicos and Providenciales, it is quietly notable for the *Meridian Club,* social center for a residential enclave of some 20 homes, that occupies the whole 800-acre island. It's exclusive, not so much in the Society sense as in the concern of its members and guests — some of whom are, indeed, listed in the *Social Register* — for the natural peace and beauty around them, their taste for uncomplicated relaxation, and their determination to preserve a place where all these can exist. Its 2-mile shimmering beach is beautiful for sunning, swimming, and strolling, and it has all the water sport assets. There are hiking trails, nature walks, Fort George Cay to explore, Water Cay and Little Water Cay for super shelling.

Providenciales – Provo marks the far western end of the colony's touristic world and also the place where a new Turks and Caicos seem to be beginning. It is the site of a modern airport, ready for wide-body 747s, *Club Med Turkoise,* and the new home for PRIDE (Society to Protect Reefs and Islands from Degradation and Exploitation) and its conch mariculture research lab, housed in a geodesic dome. Provo is also where you'll find the islands' most sophisticated land development projects (at Grace and Sapodilla bays), its center bustling and excited. Yet just over the hill beyond the bulldozers and earth-moving equipment lies the islands' greenest, coolest (Provo's average elevation is the highest among the islands) countryside, shining beaches you won't believe, trim marinas, and small, soothing shoreline inns. Fishing (both deep-sea and bone), diving, snorkeling, are all extra-commendable. With luck and care this could combine the best of all island worlds.

SOURCES AND RESOURCES

 TOURIST INFORMATION: The Turks and Caicos Islands are represented by the Caribbean Tourism Association, 20 E 46th St., New York, NY 10017 (phone: 212-682-0435), and maintain a stateside information center; write the Turks and Caicos Tourist Board, PO Box 592617, Miami, FL 33159 (phone: 305-577-0133, 800-441-4419). Also, the privately operated Turks and Caicos Information Center (4197 Braganza, Coral Gables, FL 33134) can provide current information on airlines and resorts. *Bye-Coastal Tours* (4270 Main St., Bridgeport, CT 06606; phone: 203-371-1119) is the US agent for Turks and Caicos packages.

The Ministry of Tourism (phone: 2321) has offices on the back courtyard of the Government Building on Front St. in Cockburn Town, Grand Turk.

Local Coverage – The *Turks & Caicos News,* published weekly, and the reactivated *Conch News,* published biweekly on Grand Turk, are both fun to read and full of opinions.

Telephone – Dial direct to the islands by adding the area code 809 and the prefix 946 to the numbers given below.

 ENTRY REQUIREMENTS: Some proof of citizenship. US and Canadian citizens need only a voter's registration card, birth certificate, or passport — current or expired. A driver's license is not accepted. People of other nationalities need passports.

 CLIMATE AND CLOTHES: Expect sunny, dry days and cool, clear nights year round. The average temperature is 83°F during the day and 77°F at night. Dress is informal and lightweight, with an emphasis on sports clothes and beachwear. Men wear slacks or shorts and open-neck shirts, and occasionally a necktie. Women concentrate on beachwear, occasionally wear dressy pants, caftans, or long skirts at night, and may find a light sweater useful.

 MONEY: The US dollar is legal tender. Full international banking facilities are available at Grand Turk, South Caicos, and Providenciales. Hours are weekday mornings from 8:30 AM to 1 PM, and 2 to 4:30 PM every weekday except Wednesdays. Traveler's checks are accepted at most hotels, the larger stores, and at the banks. Few places take credit cards.

 LANGUAGE: The official language of the Turks and Caicos is English.

 TIME: Turks and Caicos time is the same as Miami's during both Eastern Standard and Daylight Saving periods.

CURRENT: The electric current is 110 volts, 60 cycles, so you won't need a converter for your appliances.

GETTING THERE: Pan Am flies several times a week (depending on season) from Miami to Grand Turk and Provo. The flight takes about 1½ hours. Bahamasair departs from Nassau to South Caicos. Turks and Caicos National Airlines (locally called TAC National) makes inter-island connections.

CALCULATING COSTS: Rates for accommodations drop by about 20% from April 15 through December 15. Lowest winter rates available on the islands for two start at about $75 US EP and can climb as high as $145 without meals, $165 to $225 MAP in the best resorts. The Turks and Caicos Islands have not, as yet, become duty-free havens. They have, however, attracted recent attention as potential tax-free investment havens. There is a departure tax of $10 US.

GETTING AROUND: Taxi – One of the best ways to get an initial orientation. Most island cabbies have tours already designed (you can usually see everything of interest for about $20). Ask your hotel to make arrangements. And be sure to agree on a price before you get in and drive off. Since most drivers own their cars, negotiation is possible.

Car Rental – *Hertz* has opened up on Grand Turk at the *Island Reef* (phone: 2055) and on Provo, in BPC Plaza. Local firms also exist on Grand Turk, South Caicos, North Caicos, and Providenciales. Ask your hotel to make arrangements.

Local Air Services – *TAC National,* the inter-island plane service, makes two circle flights a day from Grand Turk to the outlying islands. Flights are fully booked with standbys waiting, so reserve ahead. Several local pilots (like Clifford Gardiner of Bottle Creek, North Caicos) as well as outfits like *Grand Turk's Flamingo Air Service* and *Provo's Blue Hills Aviation* operate charter services that can be extremely helpful. Flying time from Grand Turk to Salt Cay is all of 2 minutes; 10 minutes to South Caicos; 30 minutes to Providenciales or North Caicos.

SHOPPING: It's certainly not spectacular, except on Provo, which has some excellent boutiques for clothing, shell jewelry, ceramics, and unusual souvenirs at the resorts and in the Turtle Cove Landing shopping Center (19 stores and small restaurants) near the marina. Hand-painted clothing, unusual jewelry, locally made ceramics, and a variety of souvenirs are available. The islands' small shops have some rather nice baskets (some homemade, some Haitian), occasional rare conch pearls, shells, sponges, locally hand-screened cloth, plus the obligatory T&C T-shirts.

TIPPING: A 10% gratuity is added to the guest bill of every hotel. In restaurants, tip 10% to 15%.

SPECIAL EVENTS: On Grand Turk islanders celebrate a *Carnival* that begins the last few days in August and continues into the first week in September. The *Sailing Regatta* is the biggest event on the islands, taking place in South Caicos the last weekend in May. The *Queen's Birthday* is celebrated early in June. *Provo Days,* the islands' biggest festival, is a week-long annual celebration with races, parades, regattas, and a Miss Turks & Caicos beauty pageant at the end of July. Businesses are also closed on *New Year's Day, Good Friday, Easter Monday, Commonwealth Day* in late May, *Emancipation Day* (August 1), *Columbus Day* (early October), *Christmas,* and *Boxing Day* (December 26).

SPORTS: Bird Watching – There are bird and butterfly sanctuaries everywhere, with particularly interesting species at Penniston Cay, and at Gibb and Round Cay, a patch of small islands south and east of Grand Turk. Or observe the wildlife and beautiful scenery of the reefs, cays, and creeks around East Caicos.

Snorkeling and Scuba – Both are so spectacular that they attract underwater buffs from all over the world. The stunning Turks Passage drop-off and the virtually virgin reefs that circle Grand Turk and the Caicos are the reason. Local divers are extremely protective about their undersea fauna and flora; they take the motto of Provo-based *PRIDE* very seriously: "Take only pictures; leave only bubbles." Island dive outfits are excellent; most offer certified instruction and full equipment rental as well as dive trips. You'll find these at *Dolphin Cay Divers* on North Caicos; *Blue Water Divers* and *Omega Divers* on Grand Turk; *Provo Turtle Divers, Third Turtle Divers, Flamingo Divers, Aquatic Divers,* and *Wet Pleasures Dive and Watersports* at *Mariner Inn* on Providenciales; and a small scuba operation at PRIDE at the *Meridian Club,* on Pine Cay. Make diving arrangements through your hotel.

New — and good news for serious divers — in these islands are two luxury liveaboard dive boats: the 110-foot *Sea Dancer,* a Peter Hughes project (phone: 800-367-DIVI for rates on weeklong round-the-islands trips); and the 50-foot *Aquanaut,* operated by *Sea & Sea Travel* (phone: 800-DIV-XPRT). Both offer week-long cruises to the real virgin reefs and walls of these little-explored waters.

Another big plus for divers visiting this remote archipelago, where safety is top priority, is the opening of a recompression chamber on Provo, located at the *Erebus* hotel. Operated by trained technicians, it is also the site of regular medical training seminars conducted by former NOAA hyperbaric specialist Dick Rutkowski. For information on programs, call 305 666-4727 in Miami.

Sport Fishing – Marvelous off Grand Turk, Salt Cay, South Caicos, and Providenciales, and generally very good on all the islands. Boats can be rented for the day (rates average $250 to $300 for a half day; $450, full day) through most hotels; the *Third Turtle Inn,* Providenciales, has a trim marina with dockage for visiting sport boats. Others can rent one of 20 slips, in the Turtle Cove Marina, through the *Turtle Cove Yacht Club.* On South Caicos, a 17-foot Boston Whaler rents for about $10 per hour (minimum 4 hours; you buy gas, lunch for guide). And on Grand Turk see Capt. Sam or "Dutchie" (pronounced Doo-chie) Williams, who will take you bottom fishing for about $60 a half day, $100 a full day, including gear. On Providenciales, you can charter a small Boston Whaler for about $40 a half day, $60 a full day; an Aquasport, for about $150 a day; a day's fishing with guide in a Boston Whaler runs about $200. Deep-sea denizens include marlin, sailfish, and others of their ilk. But the big excitement is bonefishing, which, by all accounts, is incredibly good. Dolphus Arthurs (Conch Bar, Middle Caicos), Julius Jennings (South Caicos), and Provo's "Bonefish Lem" Johnson are the men to guide you.

The Turks and Caicos seem to be following the lead of the Bahamas and the Cayman Islands, which have had success drawing top sport fishers to summer tournaments. The *Turks & Caicos Islands International Billfish Tournament,* held on Provo each July, is a release-format tournament offering cash prizes. For details, write to the tournament organizers c/o PO Box 526002, Miami, FL 33152.

Swimming and Sunning – It's hard to go wrong on any of the islands' cays in the chain. With some 230 miles of beaches, the real joy of a Turks and Caicos vacation is to find one you like — and it should be an empty one if you're inclined to sunbathe nude or do a little skinny dipping — and stretch out with book, food, and nothing but time. On the larger islands, a rundown of tried and true spots is: Grand Turk, Governor's Beach; Salt Cay, the northern coast; Middle Caicos, Conch Bar; North Caicos, almost any of the island's coasts, and on Provo, Grace and Sapodilla bays.

Tennis – Courts are available at Grand Turk's *Island Reef;* on Pine Cay at the *Meridian Club* (rackets and balls are available for rental); on Provo at the *Third Turtle Inn* and *Turtle Cove Yacht Club* (a private club to which visitors can obtain passes). Provo's *Club Med* adds 8 courts, and there are so-so public courts on South Caicos.

Windsurfing – A growing sport on Provo. *Sun Glow Recreation* provides lessons, rentals. Contact through *Erebus* (phone: 4240). *Green Flash Aqua Club,* at the *Kittina* hotel on Grand Turk, offers windsurfing, water skiing, cruising, and aquascooters.

 NIGHTLIFE: Basically, some talk around the hotel bar or other watering hole and a nightcap (or several) is about as exciting as most evenings get. But when there's a dance, everybody's invited — and almost everyone comes. In addition, Grand Turk boasts two discos: *1330* and *Uprising.* The *Banana Boat* and *Disco Elite* are Provo's favorite after-dark drop-in spots. (In T&C parlance, a topless nightclub is one without a roof.)

BEST ON THE ISLANDS

 CHECKING IN: In addition to the *Club Med*'s 600, there are only about 600 additional tourist beds scattered through the islands. At present, most hotels have fewer than 20 rooms, but take pride in the personal service their size allows them to offer.

In winter, expect to budget between $110 without meals to about $225 for a double with all meals in one of the hotels we list as expensive and from $60 to $100 in a moderate hotel. Prices drop by about 20% during the summer season, but some hotels are starting to quote year-round rates. A few hotels offer full American Plan (AP, including all meals), more don't; the per-person-per-day expense total is about the same either way. Packages — especially for divers — are on the increase.

GRAND TURK

Island Reef – The island's newest and most comfortably modern hostelry, though somewhat set apart from town camaraderie. The 21 studio, 1-, and 2-bedroom condominium apartments line a secluded, reef-protected beach. With freshwater pool, tennis, restaurant, and bar (phone: 2055). Expensive to moderate.

Evans Inn – A favorite with inter-island business travelers; all 16 air-conditioned rooms have telephones and baths. With large patio, swimming pool, dining room known for its Saturday Oriental dinners, Sunday poolside buffets. A mile from town, overlooking the North Creek area (phone: 2098). Moderate.

Kittina – Grand Turk's largest (43 rooms, new suites) and very likable hotel has long been popular with residents. Remarkable, too, in that Kit Fenimore, who built it himself, even quarried the stone. Upper-story rooms, with balconies overlooking the salinas, or the sea, are big and airy (air conditioning can be added). But smaller, courtyard rooms downstairs are also pleasant. The 12 seaside, beachfront suites, some with kitchenettes, are outstanding. Good dining room, popular bar, dive shop, beach, sea only steps away (phone: 2232). Moderate.

Pillory Beach – New 16-room hotel and 8 two-bedroom condominium apartments with pool, on the beach north of Cockburn Town. Isolated but accessible; attentive local staff; dive packages available. Simple, but nice location for beach lovers (phone: 2629). Moderate.

Salt Raker Inn – A "deliberately small and informal" 150-year-old former home, with flowering garden, outdoor pub, lounge, and very good dining outdoors and in. Guest library and gallery. Scuba, snorkeling, swimming from beach across the road. Bikes, boats to rent nearby. With 9 freshly done rooms in house and garden (the 2 upstairs front, main house suites are choice) plus 2 apartments next door. A stroll from the center of town (phone: 2260). Moderate.

Turks Head Inn – Salt proprietor's house was built of pegged (no nails) Canadian pine in the late 1860s. With islands' only four-poster bedroom, 6 more plain rooms. The watering hole for a cast of local characters, it has turned seedy of late and may not appeal to visitors as a roosting place. A 220-foot beach, swimming, snorkeling; diving easily arranged. Thatched patio pub and dining room are the places to catch up with local talk at lunch, rum punch time, dinner (especially when prime ribs are served on Fridays). Also rents Driftwood Cottage next door (phone: 2466). Inexpensive.

NORTH CAICOS

Prospect of Whitby – Very out-island, as these hotel condominiums are miles from anything commercial — if such a word exists on North Caicos. Reopened in 1987 under same name. Seven miles of beautiful beach, with pool, water sports, and tennis (phone: 809-946-4250; in the US, 800-346-4295). Moderate.

Pelican Beach – An 8-room shoreside retreat with 6 miles of powder-white beach at its doorstep, it offers snorkeling and scuba (arranged with Pine Island's *PRIDE*), fishing, boat trips to nearby islands, flying excursions to the Dominican Republic (the owner's a first-rate pilot). With informal bar, dining room (radio phone only). Moderate.

PROVIDENCIALES

Nautilus Apartments – One of several small rental condominium properties, it has 18 rooms in a combination of 1-bedroom fully furnished villas and more spacious 2-bedroom units overlooking the Sapodilla Village interior of Provo (phone: 4286). Expensive.

Third Turtle Inn – Twelve bedrooms in 6 new villas have just been added to this casual, clubby haven done up in stucco, limestone, and cyprus. A find of divers and snorkeling buffs for close to 20 years, the inn is a tried-and-true outpost where wetsuits have always been in style. The offbeat, cavelike *7-Dwarfs Bar* (ask about the name!) is a famous roost of pilots, characters, and sometimes celebrities — and always good for swapping gossip. Between Turtle Cove and a rocky bank, its new managers Gale and Ann Anspach provide imaginative meals and spotless shelter. Outstanding for scuba diving, fishing, and boating. Free tennis; diving and honeymoon packages (phone: 4230). Expensive.

Admiral's Club – Twelve lovely 1- and 2-bedroom condo apartments at Turtle Cove Marina. Attractive wood/nautical style, with great bar and restaurant next door at the *Columbus Club*, overlooking the water. Reservations can be made through the Tourist Board. Moderate.

Chalk Sound Villas – Unusual, wooden, "island house"–style, these rental villas have two separate buildings, one with 2-bedrooms and bath, the other with kitchen, living and dining area. All have a beautiful view of Chalk Sound, where bonefishing is legendary. For information: 809-946-4253. Moderate.

Club Med Turkoise – This rambling 70-acre, 600-bed retreat on gorgeous Grace Bay beach claims to "welcome pressured executives (with) a seaside escape from the stresses of life in the fast track." To do the job, there are aerobics classes, a

12-station fitness center, Jacuzzis, lounges for yoga, reading, and TV/video, plus sailing, snorkeling, 8 tennis courts (4 lighted), picnic cruises, beach games. "Barefoot elegance" also calls for live classical concerts at sunset, a skillful kitchen staff, French china and crystal in the main dining room and small specialty restaurant, and, of course, dancing, shows, and disco. Rates include sports and activities, all meals (wine with lunch and dinner), superb scuba, deep-sea and bone fishing; submarine rides are extra (phone: 4491). Moderate.

Erebus – This 42-room, chalet-style resort has one of the loveliest views on Provo, overlooking Turtle Cove Marina. Also available are 4 condominium apartments. Guests have use of the *Third Turtle*'s diving and tennis facilities, and there are plans to add a spa and fitness center. Superior French cuisine in the dining room and great drinks to go with the bar's view of Turtle Cove Marina. It's worth a stop for the scenery alone (phone: 4240). Moderate.

Island Princess – Its 80 small but bright rooms have balconies or patios, gorgeous beach and sea views. Big lounge is gathering place for islanders and guests; food is good and plentiful, with lots of lobster (omelettes at breakfast, salad at lunch, whole for dinner). Great for families; it's owned and managed by the Piper family, who make all their guests feel special. All water sports (scuba is special here) easily arranged. Excellent packages (phone: 4260). Moderate.

Mariner Inn – This charming, small hotel has one of the islands' most beautiful views: the west coast "lagoon" at Sapodilla Bay. Away from the center of "civilization," it could become a favorite celebrity hideaway with a little promotion and a dash of panache. The rest is waiting. There are 25 good-size rooms and an attractive dining room; the hotel is surrounded by gardens and suffused with a pleasantly private atmosphere. *Wet Pleasures Watersports,* with diving, boardsailing, and sailing facilities, is on the premises. Sapodilla Bay (phone: 4488). Moderate.

Treasure Beach Villas – An attractive apartment alternative on Grace Bay Beach, with 20 beachfront 1- and 2-bedroom combinations that include bath, living/dining room, terrace, and kitchen completely furnished down to the knives, forks, and spoons. The Bight (phone: 4211). Moderate.

Turtle Cove – Twelve nicely appointed 1-bedroom, marina-front units are also available to non–yacht owners, who will enjoy pool, bar, restaurant, and tennis privileges (at extra cost) on 2 lighted courts when they stay here. Convenient location in the center of the Turtle Cove development, with full-service marina, tennis pro on staff, and the popular *Eagle's Nest Lounge* (phone: 4203 on Provo; or 800-351-8261). Moderate.

SOUTH CAICOS

Admiral's Arms – The stunning sea view, easy access to spectacular dive sites, and reasonably priced dive packages once lured enthusiastic scuba groups to this inn. However, it was closed at press time, and there was no news of its future. A great loss for the diving trade.

Harbour View – Simple, basic base for divers and fishermen. Friendly and helpful with local arrangements, but with no frills. With 12 rooms plus bar and island restaurant (phone: 3251). Inexpensive.

PINE CAY

Meridian Club – On privately owned island known for quiet exclusivity, but a real community of interest in relaxation, peace, and preserving the natural beauty of the land and sealife rather than social chic. Limited land development, central clubhouse (bar/lounge, dining room, pool; some Social Register members), 12 smartly comfortable adjacent suites; cottage rentals. Ecologically oriented water sports, nature walks, boat trips. Family-style meals, informal nighttimes. Fabulous unspoiled beach and protected swimming. Own airstrip, air taxi (phone: 212-696-4566; or 800-225-4255). Expensive.

EATING OUT: With rare exceptions, dining is almost exclusively in hotels, where such island specialties as whelk soup, conch chowder, turtle steak, lobster, and a number of different kinds of fresh fish are featured. On Grand Turk, the *Kittina* hotel has a good restaurant with a versatile menu that doesn't disdain to include such varied fare as hot dogs and conch chowder. The *Turks Head* draws Friday night crowds with its prime rib feast; the *Salt Raker Inn*'s special eating event is Sunday night's lobster dinner. *Papillon's Rendez-vous,* on Duke St., is not in a hotel; its French and Canadian proprietors do nightly dinners featuring such exotic fare as escargots, *pâté en croûte, poulet Louis XV,* and crêpes suzettes (simple setting, fairly expensive).

On Provo, the *Third Turtle* is an especially good find for seafood casserole, lobster, turtle steak, cherries jubilee for a finale. Favored meeting and eating places are the *Columbus Club, Alfred's,* and *Banana Boat,* at the Turtle Cove Marina; and *Henry's Road Runner* restaurant, in Blue Hills, typical of the best small places, serving very good native dishes and the freshest seafood. The restaurants at *Island Princess, Third Turtle Inn,* and *Erebus Inn* on Provo all are good, especially for seafood, but pricey. Pizza addicts: Vic Georgeff makes great all-the-way pies at B.W.I. Trading supermarket on Provo. Newcomers already popular on Provo's restaurant scene are *Fast Eddie's* and *The Office.*

THE US
VIRGIN ISLANDS

Among the most beautiful islands in the entire Caribbean are the three siblings that make up the US Virgin Islands — St. Croix, St. John, and St. Thomas. Products of a common history, set in the same sea, they are at once the same and very different — St. Thomas with steep, green mountains and lengths of shining sands; St. John with a cover of jungle and its own share of beaches, most protected from developers within the boundaries of the extraordinary Virgin Islands National Park; and St. Croix, the most undeservedly underrated of the three, with nostalgic towns, ruins of plantation houses, and rolling, breeze-combed grass hills and valleys where sugar cane once grew.

Surprisingly, despite the insistently green look of the islands, they are counted among the dry islands of the Caribbean; just why is most evident on St. Croix, where the landscape gradually browns as the dry season wears on. Prickly fingered cacti are the chief botanical feature of its Atlantic tip — which is also the easternmost tip of US territory. For tourists, the dry weather means lots of sunshine. (Days when the sun doesn't shine are few and far between.) Breezes temper the humidity so that even late summer days, with midday temperatures in the low 90s, are more comfortable than they would be elsewhere.

If the climate is good for tourists, it is perfect for flowers. Everywhere one sees showy yellow ginger Thomas (yellow trumpet, the islands' official bloom); peach, pink, scarlet, and purple bougainvillea; bushy hibiscus; orchids; sweet oleander and jasmine; Christmas poinsettias; and flamboyant trees so bright that light seems to flame out of their orange-red blossoms.

The waters around the islands — in colors of aquamarine, tourmaline, lapis lazuli, jade, and sapphire — are clean and clear thanks to the national park, which protects 5,650 acres offshore and 9,000 acres of land on the island of St. John — nearly 60% of the island. Virgin Islands National Park was established in 1956 after extensive donations of land throughout the 1950s by Laurance Rockefeller's Rockresort Foundation. It has set the pace for similar preserves in the Dominican Republic, Guadeloupe, Martinique, and Bonaire. And protected underwater parks are planned for the British Virgin Islands, Antigua, Barbados, Barbuda, the Dominican Republic, Jamaica, and St. Eustatius.

Since Columbus discovered the islands during his second voyage, in 1493, St. Croix, St. John, and St. Thomas have attracted the attention of more outside powers than any other Caribbean island. The flags of Spain, the Knights of Malta, France, England, Holland, Denmark, and the United

US VIRGIN ISLANDS

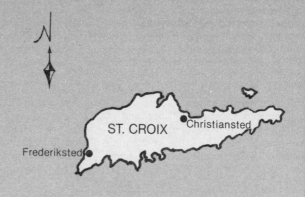

States have flown over them — in prosperity and tragedy, industry and disarray, disillusion and hope.

Columbus and his men came ashore near St. Croix's Salt River in search of water but were repulsed by Carib Indians, a party smaller than that of the Spanish crew, but ferocious. Columbus hastily named the island for the Holy Cross (Santa Cruz) and shoved off to discover and christen St. Thomas and St. John. He then named the whole group — at that time including the British Virgin Islands — for the legendary 11,000 virgin followers of St. Ursula.

Columbus sailed on to find Puerto Rico. A century later, in 1593, Sir Francis Drake put in at St. Thomas and St. John on his way to attack the Spanish at San Juan.

In 1625 — though the islands were still technically Spanish — British, Dutch, and French colonists established farms on St. Croix. By 1650, the French were gone, and Spain returned to expel the British as well. In 1653, after what seems to have been a sudden Iberian change of heart, St. Croix was willed to the crusaders' Order of St. John, better known as the Knights of Malta. The latter came, saw, and, discouraged by the rigors of island life, sold out to the French West India Company. A few years later, title was transferred to the king of France. And for the next half century or so, possession of this largest of the Virgin Islands alternated between the French and the Spanish.

The other two islands, meanwhile, had been taken over by the Danish West India and Guinea Company (St. Thomas in 1672 and St. John in 1683). The company name indicates the three cardinal points of the triangular trade in which it and others like it were involved: Denmark, where its investors lived; the West Indies, where they grew sugar cane and processed it into molasses and rum (the most easily transported forms of sugar); and Africa (then called Guinea), where they captured the slaves whose labor made the operation profitable. What glittered in the Caribbean was not the gold Columbus and the Spaniards sought, but the profits produced by the cane.

On St. Thomas, the Danes founded the town of Charlotte Amalie (pronounced ah-*mahl*-yah). By 1680, there were 50 sugar estates on the island; at the height of its sugar-producing days, St. Thomas had 170 plantations, but they dwindled almost as fast as they had grown. The terrain proved too rugged for agriculture, and St. Thomas' economic focus shifted to trade. In 1724 it became a free port where landed goods were exempt from customs duties and regulation. The laissez-faire atmosphere made it a favorite stopping place for pirates, especially the infamous Blackbeard and Captain Kidd.

While commerce — legitimate and otherwise — outstripped it on St. Thomas, cane thrived on St. John. When the Danish West India Company first took title, the island was shared by a small number of British squatters, who crossed the 5-mile strait from Tortola, and a few established Danes. A quarter of a century later, in 1717, the company sent out a contingent of settlers to set up a permanent colony and port at Coral Bay. It was expected that the town and sturdy Fort Frederiksvaern, with its fine harbor, would some day surpass Charlotte Amalie as the principal city of the Danish West Indies. Cane was planted and flourished, along with tobacco and cotton. By 1733, there were 208 whites and 1,087 slaves on the island. All seemed prosperous and serene until Sunday, November 23, 1733, when the slaves revolted, maddened by their masters' cruelty and distraught by a series of natural disasters — drought, plague, and a crop-leveling hurricane. A number of settlers and the entire white garrison at Coral Bay's Fort Berg were slaughtered. On the other side of the island, 40 planters holed up near Caneel Bay, from which many escaped to St. Thomas while others held out.

Danish expeditions, with British aid, failed at first to regain control. But by May of the following year the Danes, backed by two French warships and a company of soldiers from Martinique, retook the island and subdued the rebels. The island was devastated. Almost half of St. John's plantation houses were destroyed, and the fields were damaged. But the Danes — and the profit motive — prevailed. Homes and sugar factories were rebuilt; cane was replanted; and prosperity returned — for a while.

St. John's story might have ended differently if Denmark had not been drawn into the Napoleonic Wars on the side of the French. This was just the excuse for aggression for which the British on Tortola had been waiting. They attacked and occupied St. John in 1801 and in 1807, staying ten months the first time and seven years the second. By the time the Danes regained possession of St. John, the island's economic base had been dealt a mortal blow — not so much by the British as by time itself. Sugar beet was being grown in Europe and gradually taking over the sugar market, and in 1848 slavery was abolished on St. John. Even though the steam engine was already replacing manpower in some island sugar mill operations, the plantation lifestyle couldn't make the transition to an island of free workers. Soon after abolition, the Danish planters who hadn't already left because of failing cane markets boarded up their estates and sailed for home.

Emancipation was proclaimed at the same time in St. Croix. The Danes had bought the island from the French in 1733, and in due course, the St. Croix town of Christiansted became the capital of what was then the Crown Colony of the Danish West Indies. In 1802, Denmark led all other European-Caribbean powers in prohibiting slave trade, and in 1848, it prepared to follow Britain's example and free its slaves after a period of apprenticeship. The Danish king thought 20 years would be about right, but St. Croix slaves thought otherwise. They gathered, 8,000 strong, outside Fort Frederik in Frederiksted to protest. The angry and frightened planters huddled inside while Governor General Peter von Scholten climbed the ramparts and declared, "All unfree in the Danish West Indies are from today emancipated."

Von Scholten was a fair and a sensitive man who had taken a former slave as his mistress after his Danish wife deserted him. He was rewarded for his peacekeeping initiative by being recalled to Copenhagen and there convicted of acting without authority, even though the government stood by his decree and the slaves remained free. Nonetheless, poor von Scholten never again saw the islands nor the woman he loved there.

If it had not been for World War I, St. Croix, St. John, and St. Thomas might still be Danish. When the sugar industry began to crumble, Denmark started looking for buyers. In 1917, the United States, worried about possible unfriendly bases in the Caribbean that might threaten the Panamá Canal or the US mainland, made a successful offer of $25 million for the three islands.

Although some fine old Danish buildings remain and streets still wear Danish Gade signs, the atmosphere of the US Virgin Islands is distinctly American. St. Croix is becoming better known since the *Carambola Beach Resort and Golf Club* opened in 1986 (*Sheraton International* reportedly has plans for a 400-room hotel at Coakley Bay and *Ritz-Carlton* is planning a 500-room hotel adjacent to *Carambola*), and the condominium developers are moving in. But until the transformation is complete, it is a surprisingly lovely and livable island that combines the best of the other two US Virgins. A friendly and close-knit group of "Continentals," or statesiders (including Maureen O'Hara, Geraldine Ferraro, and Walt Fraser), has made Christiansted into a cozy and culturally active community, with enough restaurants, hotels, and nightspots to keep most visitors happy. Historical sites and water sports are plentiful, yet it is neither as developed as St. Thomas nor as rural and raw as St. John.

St. John, which pulled a blanket of jungle over its head when the Danish planters left in 1848, seems to be reawakening. This first became evident in 1956 when the national park was established and Laurance Rockefeller built his *Caneel Bay* resort, allowing visitors to enjoy the park in ultra comfort. For a couple of decades, most visitors stayed at *Caneel* or made day visits, dutifully touring the park before hurrying off to beach and buffet. A second stage of development was launched in 1976 with the new camp-in-comfort *Maho Bay* resort (preceded by the 1964 opening of *Cinnamon Bay Campground*). This attracted a new wave of more venturesome travelers genuinely intrigued with the park and the island's history. They're out exploring, discovering, and bringing new life to the island and its small, sleepy Cruz Bay town. The third stage is now under way with the opening of the *Virgin Grand* in 1986 and the inevitable condominiums.

St. Thomas takes its quickened pace from active visitors who swim, sail, windsurf, dive, and water ski off its spectacular beaches and explore its up-hill-and-down-dale roads in cars and jeeps. They gather in waterfront watering spots to seek out the evening's action from a good choice of restaurants and nightlife. Shoppers — often thousands a day — pour off cruise ships tied along the pier, determined to see everything while in port. Charlotte Amalie is a good place to avoid on days when there are more than two ships in port (Wednesdays and Fridays are generally busiest). St. Thomas' devotees are convinced that the beauty and fun of the island more than make up for the occasional inconvenience of downtown crowds, but its detractors call it "the Atlantic City of the Caribbean."

Islanders are somewhat ambivalent about the changes wrought by new development. There is controversy concerning the effects of tourism on the environment, and nowhere is that more evident than on St. John, which fears for the future of the National Park and is fighting to keep the cruise ships away. (The owners of "ecologically sensitive" *Maho* are planning a condominium complex that will follow in *Maho*'s environmental footsteps on the island's east end.) Many blacks feel they are underrepresented in management positions within the tourism industry and, as elsewhere in the Caribbean, there is an undercurrent of resentment. Lonely nighttime walks down dark streets in the big towns are not recommended; unfortunately, such warnings, sensibly and sensitively applied, have become a "given" of contemporary travel. But understanding that few places are exempt from human tensions, savvy travelers continue to return to the US Virgins, because they also recognize that few, if any, islands anywhere in the world offer so much in the way of natural beauty and potential pleasure.

US VIRGIN ISLANDS AT-A-GLANCE

FROM THE AIR: There are three major US Virgin Islands — St. Croix, St. John, and St. Thomas — plus approximately 50 smaller islets and cays, most of them uninhabited, centered at 18°21' N latitude, 64°56' W longitude, 60 miles east of Puerto Rico and just west of the smaller British Virgin Islands. Spread over some 14,000 square miles of Caribbean and Atlantic waters, they are part of the Leeward Islands in the Lesser Antilles and have a total population of over 100,000. Long, narrow St. Thomas (12 miles long and 3 miles wide) and little St. John (9 by 3 miles) are next-door neighbors, only 3 miles apart, both with northern coasts washed by the Atlantic and southern sides bathed by the Caribbean Sea. Of the three, St. Croix (pronounced *croy*) is the largest Virgin Island (23 miles long and 6 miles across at its widest point), 40 miles south of the other two and entirely surrounded by the Caribbean Sea.

St. Croix, on a map, looks like a caveman's club floating northeast (handle end) to southwest (round end) in the Caribbean. With a total area of 84 square miles, it is larger but less mountainous than its sibling islands, and its rolling land is still laid out in fields where cane used to grow. Chunky stone towers — once plantation windmills — are still dotted over its hills. It has two towns: Christiansted, tucked into a reef-protected harbor a little east of center on its north coast, and Frederiksted, its deepwater port, in the middle of its western coast. Alexander Hamilton Airport is about a 10-minute drive due east of Frederiksted. Continuing east along the south shore, you come upon St. Croix's major industrial development: the Hess Oil Refinery. The northern road out of Frederiksted leads toward the island's small rain forest (actually a microclimate) and the scenic drive that passes through it into the wild hills to the west. An unpaved road follows along the crest of these hills, overlooking Fountain Valley to the south and, to the north, Cane Bay and Davis Bay, two of St. Croix's handsome beaches.

St. John, amoeba-shaped and indented with beach-lined bays, rises to inland heights covered with tropical forest. It is hard to believe that in the days of its Danish prosperity in the early 1800s, it boasted more than a hundred sugar plantations. The end of slavery in 1848 killed St. John's sugar industry. Now ruins of the old great houses and sugar mills lie hidden in the undergrowth of the Virgin Islands National Park, which covers nearly 60% of the island's 20 square miles. The walls and foundations of one of the great houses, Annaberg, overlooking Leinster Bay, have been cleared and marked for self-guided tours.

St. Thomas has an elongated hourglass shape, its waist cinched by a deepwater harbor on the south and Magens Bay on the north. A ridge of mountains forms its spinal column. Surrounding the harbor and climbing the green hills beyond are the red-roofed houses of Charlotte Amalie, St. Thomas' only city and capital of the US Virgin Islands, with a population of over 12,000. Since it has a major cruise port and an excellent shopping center, Charlotte Amalie's population swells by thousands of visitors whenever ships come into port, which is usually every day. Beyond the town, St. Thomas is a scenic collection of hills rising up to 1,500 feet and sloping steeply down to beaches cupped in curved bays on the jagged southern coast, or down to longer sweeps of white sand on the northern shore. Cyril E. King Airport — now in the throes of being extended and modernized — is on the south shore, about a ten-minute drive west of town. About 20 minutes to the east, at the end of the island, Red Hook harbor not only has marina facilities for pleasure and deep-sea fishing boats but docks for ferries and launches that make the trip across Pillsbury Sound to St. John.

 SPECIAL PLACES: St. Croix – In the heart of Christiansted, St. Croix's largest town, is a group of handsome 18th-century buildings near the harbor. Built by the Danish West India and Guinea Company after the Danes bought St. Croix from the French, they're now a US National Historic Site. The Old Scalehouse, where Danish customs officers once weighed imports and exports, faces the waterfront; it now houses the Visitors Bureau, where, besides background brochures on the island in general, you can pick up a free *Walking Tour Guide* and map of the four-square-block historic area.

Just east of the Scalehouse, across a small park, stands Fort Christiansvaern, painted yellow and built on the foundations of a 1645 French fortress. Inside there are fine harbor views from battlements lined with cannon (never fired at an invader) and a free booklet guide to dungeons, powder magazine, barracks, officers' kitchen, and battery. (Kids like the part that shows you how to fire a cannon.) The fort's single nonmilitary exhibit tells all about Buck Island reef. Open daily from 8 AM to 5 PM. Free admission.

A block from the fort, on Company Street, the Steeple Building — originally a Lutheran church — has since served as a military bakery, a hospital, and a school. Today it's a historical museum with a small collection of Carib and Arawak artifacts, old uniforms, a diorama showing Christiansted as it was around 1800, an exhibit on black urban history during the Danish period, a new display of drawings and photos of Christiansted's historic Danish architecture, and a visitor orientation center. (Check the Visitors Bureau for hours; no admission charge.) Cater-cornered across the street, the post office does business in what was once the Danish West India and Guinea Company warehouse. Head back toward the Scalehouse, turn left, and walk one block up King Street to Government House, the impressive cream and white residence of the Danish governor general before the US bought the island in 1917. A small red Danish guardhouse still stands at the foot of the formal staircase leading from the courtyard to its grand ballroom with chandeliers, chimneyed sconces, and a dining table — copies of the originals — presented by the King and Queen of Denmark when the building was restored. Official receptions are still held there, and you can look in daily from 8 AM to 6 PM. There are government offices upstairs. Alexander Hamilton (at the age of 13) worked in Henry Kruger's hardware store, across the street, on the site now occupied by the *Little Switzerland* store.

At the outdoor market, a short stroll away on Company Street, stalls are full of island-grown vegetables and fruit — papayas, sour sops, bananas, and the pulpy green genips that are island favorites. Try one! Between Company Street and the harbor, antique buildings (or replicas thereof), arcades, patios, and walkways are full of shops; a number of them are branches of St. Thomas stores. The harbor itself with its bustling small boat traffic is fascinating to watch from sunup to dusk.

The town of Frederiksted, 17 miles from Christiansted at the west end of the island, comes to life when a cruise ship ties up at its deepwater pier (built here because Christiansted's reef made construction there impractical). At other times, it snoozes. On a summer afternoon when a number of its restaurants and shops have hung out "Closed for the season" signs, it sometimes seems to have gone to sleep entirely. Still, it's worth some browsing time because it is so different from Christiansted.

It looks different — more Victorian gingerbread than colonial Danish — though a few of its landmarks do date from the 1700s. Most buildings of that era were destroyed in a devastating fire in 1878; Frederikstedders rebuilt with wood framing rather than stone, with elaborate curlicued fretwork replacing the straightforward lines and arches of earlier Danish architecture. Try to go on a day when no cruise ship is in harbor, when you will be able to park at the north end of town near the pier. The Visitors Bureau at the end of the Frederiksted pier can provide a free *Walking Tour Guide* and map. Fort Frederik, on the other side of Lagoon Street, is the logical place to begin. Built in 1752 and recently restored and repainted (Danish-fort red and white, of course), it was the site of Danish Governor General Peter von Scholten's 1848 proclamation freeing the slaves. It also claims to have been the first foreign fort to have fired a salute to the American flag — flown by a US merchant ship — on October 25, 1776. The Dutch island of St. Eustatius files a counterclaim by virtue of its salute to the Stars and Stripes aboard the US man-of-war *Andrea Doria* on November 16, 1776. The issue seems to hinge on the ownership (private or federal) of the vessel involved. Whichever way you look at it, both the Danes and the Dutch were good guys in US eyes. At the fort, you can inspect the courtyard, the stable, the canteen, and the art exhibit in the old garrison (weekdays only, 9 AM to 4 PM; free). Two blocks south and one block east, at the corner of Prince and Queen streets, you'll find the Market Place — doing business at the same stands since the town's founding in 1751; and a block farther down Prince Street, at the corner of Market, an interesting, though unrestored, antique masonry and frame residence, beyond which is St. Patrick's Catholic Church, an 1843 version of the 18th-century cathedral. On Hospital Street (the street paralleling Prince Street, one block east) stands an 18th-century building that was originally a residence, then a school. On Strand Street, which runs along the waterfront, the Customs House (late 18th century) and Victoria House, with its elaborate gingerbread trim, are prime examples of Frederiksted's two favorite building styles. Other sites: the Old Public Library, now an arts and crafts center on the corner of Strand and Queen Cross, and the Old Apothecary Hall.

North of Frederiksted, the shore road leads past *Sprat Hall,* an old plantation home that's now a guesthouse with cottages, to the Rain Forest, the Scenic Road (see *From the Air,* above), and 150-foot-high Creque Dam (pronounced Creeky), surrounded by yellow cedar, mahogany trees, and wild lilies.

Leaving town in another direction, the Centerline Road heads northeast across what was, until very recently, St. Croix's sugar country. The land is green and rolling, still neatly divided into fields, though it has been a number of years since sugar cane was cultivated in them. (Local distilleries now make their rum from imported molasses.) Old stone mill towers (at Bodkin, Jolly Hill, Mount Eagle) give the eerie feeling that they are watching through window eyes as you drive along. And the map is scribbled with antique plantation names like Upper and Lower Love, Jealousy, Sally's Fancy, Anna's Hope, and John's Rest. The last is the site of Whim Greathouse, off Centerline Road a few minutes from Frederiksted. Distinctive in shape, it is a long graceful oval with rounded ends. Inside there are only three rooms in the main part of the house: a large living room and a large bedroom, divided by a central reception or dining room. Basically it is small — only one story high — but its 16½-foot ceiling and many tall windows give it an airy feeling. And the Landmarks Society has restored it with restraint and care (no urge to empty the attic into its rooms) that preserves that sense of spaciousness. Outside there's a watchhouse, the ruins of the sugar boiling factory, a mule mill, a steam chimney, and a windmill with its grinding machinery. On an island of now vaneless towers, it is satisfying to see all four of the mill's big sail arms restored. There's also a small museum and gift shop. Open daily from 10 AM to 5 PM. Small admission charge.

Other Country Stops – The Cruzan Rum Factory on West Airport Road (guided tours, Mondays through Fridays, 8:30 to 11:15 AM and 1 to 4:30 PM; free, as are the piña colada samples) not far from Christiansted; Judith's Fancy, impressively proportioned ruins of the onetime home of the governor of the Knights of Malta; and from the hill beyond, an overview of the mouth of the Salt River, where Columbus, who stopped only for a little fresh water, was unceremoniously driven off (he later called the place the Cape of Arrows) by resident Carib Indians in 1493; the site of their village will be a commemorative park; St. George Village Botanical Garden off Centreline Road near Frederiksted, a historically interesting combination of trees, blooms, and sugar village ruins, plus a fine, airy center building that's a site for concerts and special events and also houses a gift shop with a fine selection of Cruzan crafts and edibles — from books and wind chimes to jewelry and luscious lime marmalade.

■ **EXTRA SPECIAL:** The camera buff will love Christiansted Harbor in early morning or late afternoon, shooting from Fort Christiansvaern's battlements or the *Club Comanche*'s sundeck at sunset; also sugar mills and ruins at Judith's Fancy, Bodkin, and Whim; and Fountain Valley from the hills on its eastern side.

SPECIAL PLACES: St. John – It can take no time or forever — it all depends on how interested you are in nature. The island's town — Cruz Bay — is tiny and sleepy, with the dock, St. John's Square, a communications center, and a Chase Manhattan Bank. It also has a scattering of boutiques; *Mongoose Junction* has one of the best small island restaurants. Check the bulletin board at the dock for news of local happenings. Then have a cup of coffee at the *Back Yard,* the *Lime Inn,* or *Joe's Diner* to find out where it's at.

The real item of interest in St. John is the Virgin Islands National Park. Start explorations at the park headquarters on the dock, where there are regular briefings and slide talks about the park and its flora, fauna, and history. Rangers know all about the area's native birds (from pelicans to sandpipers), trees (including stands of mahogany and bay — from which the "bay" of bay rum comes), and flowers (tamarind, flamboyant, shower of gold). They'll also tell you about the mongooses, imported to hunt rats. Park guides lead nature walks and set up evening programs on a flexible schedule at *Maho Bay Camps, Cinnamon Bay, Caneel Bay,* and other locations. Call 776-6201 for a complete rundown of park activities.

You can rent a car or sign on a safari bus into the park. But you'll have more fun and come home with a better sense of the island if you make your first tour with one of the native drivers who gather near the dock around midmorning. The classic route takes in Trunk Bay, Annaberg Plantation with its self-guided tour, and assorted lookout points. An alternate follows the old Danish Centerline Road to the almost forgotten settlement of Coral Bay (18th-century Moravian church, Fort Berg Hill ruins), the town St. Johnians once thought would outshine Charlotte Amalie. Prices are standard — about $20 for two people for 1½ to 2 hours. (A full-day outing, including stops for swimming and snorkeling, runs about $25 for two.) But there's nothing standard or canned about the commentary of native St. John drivers. (Ask for Miss Lucy; hers is the van with the cowhorns on front.)

The park is also crisscrossed with clearly mapped hiking trails, some of which were old Danish roads and all of which — except the steep climb to see the plantation ruins and the petroglyphs above Reef Bay — are reasonably easygoing.

If you sail, you can take the sea way to Hurricane Hole, a postcard-perfect harbor surrounded by park wilderness, as well as to Coral Bay, Lameshur Bay, Reef Bay, and Chocolate Hole. Ask at the Visitors Bureau in Cruz Bay for information about local skippered or bareboat rentals. Don't forget that almost a third of the park is under water. There is a spectacular underwater trail at Trunk Bay, which the park service administers and which allows you to snorkel along coral reefs amid schools of tropical fish. Unfortunately, the sheer number of tourists has largely destroyed its appeal.

■ **EXTRA SPECIAL:** Best bets for picture taking are long shots of Trunk, Hawks- nest, and Cinnamon bays; Cruz Bay's pastel houses; and the ruins at Annaberg and Caneel Bay. If you have underwater casing for your camera, Trunk Bay's trail is a great place for underwater shots of galaxies of fantastic fish and all kinds of coral formations — especially big, round brain coral.

SPECIAL PLACES: St. Thomas – Charlotte Amalie's harbor has been a haven for ships — merchantmen, naval vessels, and buccaneer galleons — since the 1600s. The town's white and pastel buildings cover the water- front and three steep hills reading, west to east, Denmark Hill, Synagogue Hill, and Government Hill. Oldtime sailors, looking up from water level, called them Foretop, Maintop, and Mizzenmast. Along the harbor, warehouses that in another age held pirates' loot are now chock full of duty-free shops stocked with imported luxuries that lure shiploads of shoppers docked every week at the deepwater pier out toward the harbor's east end.

Start your walking tour in the narrow streets near the Charlotte Amalie waterfront at the *Grand* hotel. It's an architectural relic of the 19th century, built in 1841, that no longer takes guests but still dispenses hospitality in the Project St. Thomas ground- floor Visitors' Center. Next door is Emancipation Park, a tiny plot that commemorates the 1848 proclamation that freed the slaves. Across the street to the west of the park is the post office, embellished inside with murals by the illustrator Stephen Dohanos. Beyond the post office lies Main Street and the alleys and passages of the principal shopping district.

Southeast of the park stands Fort Christian, a venerable monument painted rust red and topped with a clock tower. Built by the Danes in 1671, it was named for King Christian V. Throughout the centuries it has served as a jail, courthouse, church, rectory, and governor's residence. Now an official national landmark, its dungeons house a small museum with a modest collection of Arawak and Carib relics and displays depicting the life of the early Danish settlement (Mondays through Saturdays, 8 AM to 5 PM; free). In the Legislative Building on the harbor side of the fort, you can sit in on a meeting when the Senate is in session.

Up Government Hill, overlooking the town and the waterfront, the white brick and wood Government House, built in 1867 as a meeting place for the Danish Colonial Council, is now the official residence of the governor of the US Virgin Islands. You can visit the first two floors, where murals portray significant moments in the history of the Virgin Islands. There's also a collection of oil paintings by St. Thomian artists, includ- ing Camille Pissarro. Pissarro, known as the father of French Impressionism, was a Spanish Jew, born Jacob Pizarro on St. Thomas in 1830. Before moving to Paris, he worked in his father's store on Main Street and lived upstairs in the building that now houses the Tropicana Perfume Shop. His parents are buried in the Jewish cemetery, Savan, on the low peninsula to the west of town. Its epitaphs date back to 1792.

On the same street (Kongens Gade, Danish for Kings Street) overlooking Emancipa- tion Park stands *Hotel 1829,* a mansion built in that year by a French sea captain named Lavalette. (His initials appear entwined in the hotel's wrought-iron balcony.) Its narrow halls open onto a cool, bougainvillea-draped courtyard. Between the hotel and Govern- ment House, the staircase known as the Street of 99 Steps (actually, there are 103) climbs to the summit of Government Hill.

Not far from this are remnants of 17th-century fortifications originally known as

Fort Skytsborg, now called Blackbeard's Castle. Historically, the name Blackbeard refers to the pirate Edward Teach, who frequented St. Thomas in the 1700s. Confusingly, there is also a Bluebeard's Castle atop another 300-foot hill at the eastern edge of town. This one — its historic origins are vague — has a honeymoon suite on its top floor and is a working part of *Bluebeard's Castle* hotel.

At the foot of Government Hill on Norre Gade, the Frederik Lutheran Church, built in 1826, is hung with impressive antique chandeliers and still uses 18th-century ecclesiastical silver brought from Denmark.

The synagogue of St. Thomas' Jewish congregation — B'racha V'Shalom U'Gemiliutha-sadim ("Blessing and Peace and Loving Deeds") — overlooks the town from neighboring Synagogue Hill. It is reached by a steep climb from Main Street up Storetvaer Gade to Krystal Gade. Built by Sephardic Jews in 1833 on the site of a 1796 structure, it is the Western Hemisphere's second oldest synagogue still standing; the oldest is in Curaçao. Benches in the traditional arrangement face inward along three sides. It also has the traditional sand-covered floor, a reminder of the time when the Jews of Spain were forced to pray secretly in unfinished basements.

Farther west, where Main Street intersects Strand Gade, is Market Square. A slave market before emancipation, it is now a roofed-over, open-air block of stalls where island farmers and gardeners sell their produce. It's open every day but Sunday. (Saturday is the biggest market day.) Action is liveliest and the light for picture taking best in the reasonably early morning. After your market rounds, follow Strand Gade to the waterfront, where you can buy a fresh coconut; ask the man who sells it to lop off its top with a machete so you can drink the sweet milk from the hull.

Having seen Charlotte Amalie on foot, get wheels (rental or taxi) to do the rest of St. Thomas. Head west out of town on Main Street, connecting with Harwood Highway. You may also want to follow Veterans Drive along the waterfront and turn off to the left at the Villa Olga sign to visit Frenchtown, also called Cha Cha Town, named from the peaked straw hats called "cha chas" made and worn then. It is an enclave of descendants of refugees who fled the Swedish invasion of St. Barthélemy in the late 18th century and who still speak a Norman-French dialect. Fishing is their business.

Farther west off Harwood Highway, turn right at Contant Hill, and climb Crown Mountain Road for super views of green hills, white beaches, and blue seas. The traditional and very worthwhile stop is at a former hotel called *Mountain Top,* where you sip a banana daiquiri while admiring the view (which really is a stunner) of the waters of Drake's Passage, which separate the British and American Virgin Islands. You get a different perspective of the same view a little farther down the road at the perch called Drake's Seat, where Sir Francis himself allegedly watched the galleons go by. From this point, there's a splendid view of the passage Drake first navigated in 1580, plus an entire panorama of almost 100 Virgin Islands — both US and British. On a clear day, it's a wide-angle shot for photographers. And more often than not, an obliging islander is standing by with a flower-decked burro, available — for a $10 fee — to provide foreground interest or pose for closeups.

Wend your way east along northern roads with fine views of Magens Bay, Mandahl Bay, and others. At the three-way intersection near the *Green Parrot* restaurant at the *Magens Point* hotel, continue east, following the signs to the intriguing manmade attraction called *Coral World* (at Coki Beach), a marine park with an underwater observatory tower planted on the sea floor. You climb down 14 feet for a wide-windowed view of reef life below the sea. The best time to visit is 11 AM, when the fish are being fed. Geodesic domes housing an aquarium, restaurant, shops, and a museum are also part of the complex (open daily; admission fee).

On your way in or out, stop off at *Jim Tillett's Art Gallery and Boutique,* built around an old sugar mill. Watch the silk screeners work; browse through the gallery (silk-screen graphics, some paintings, ceramics); shop the boutique (shirts, shifts, and similar items done in Tillett prints or skirt and dress lengths of fabric to take home and make yourself); sample tacos and refritos in its Mexican patio restaurant, *El Papagayo*.

In a clockwise direction, the road leads past Pineapple, Pelican, and Sapphire beaches, Red Hook (where the ferries leave for St. John), and — by finishing the circle — back to home base.

■**EXTRA SPECIAL:** Two favorite views of photographers are the spectacular vista from *Drake's Seat,* taking in Magens Bay and Drake's Passage, with the green British Virgin Islands scattered beyond; and the wide-angled view of Charlotte Amalie and the harbor seen from the hills above. *Mafolie,* Crown House, and *Bluebeard's Castle* are all good vantage points, especially at dusk with the lights winking on. But, like all distance shots that look great to the eye, these will go flat without foreground framing to give them depth. So find some bougainvillea, an unpotted palm, or a garden urn to shoot around.

Forget street scenes downtown, except for early morning. It's too crowded and narrow for anything but the odd shot of a sun-dappled alley or passage. Instead, concentrate on architectural details — grillework, Danish archways, antique doors — shooting from below or above to make the most of light and shade patterns and perspective. Likely places to find them: Government House, Bluebeard's Tower, *Hotel 1829* and its garden. Good morning areas are the market with its stacks of fruit, yams, and produce, and the waterfront lined with chunky island boats and fishermen and their catches.

SOURCES AND RESOURCES

TOURIST INFORMATION: The US Virgin Islands Division of Tourism, 1270 Avenue of the Americas, New York, NY 10020 (phone: 212 582-4520), supplies for the asking helpful brochures on specific island facts and background. Branch offices are in the following North American cities:

Chicago: Suite 1003, 343 S Dearborn St., Chicago, IL 60604 (phone: 312 461-0180)

Los Angeles: 3450 Wilshire Blvd., Suite 915, Los Angeles, CA 90010 (phone: 213 739-0138)

Miami: Suite 620, 7270 NW 12th St., Miami, FL 33126 (phone: 305 591-2070)

San Juan: 1300 Ashford Ave., Condado, Santurce, PR 00907 (phone: 809 724-3816)

Toronto: Suite 306, 234 Eglinton Ave. E, Toronto, Ont. M4P 1K5 (phone: 416 488-4374)

Washington, DC: 1667 K St. NW, Suite 270, Washington, DC 20006 (phone: 202 293-3707)

On the islands, the Division of Tourism maintains a number of Visitors Information Bureaus to provide on-the-spot information:

On St. Croix: Tourist bureaus at the airport, in the Scalehouse at Christiansted's harbor (phone: 773-0495), and at the end of Frederiksted's cruise ship pier (phone: 772-0357).

On St. John: Around the corner from Cruz Bay dock plus two bulletin boards — one by the Town Dock and the other out at *Cinnamon Bay* — which provide information on local happenings and special events.

On St. Thomas: Offices at the airport, on the waterfront in Charlotte Amalie, and in Havensight Mall near the cruise ship pier. As part of their Project St. Thomas, merchants maintain a Visitors Lounge in the *Grand* hotel, where visitors can pick up information, rest, even check shopping bags for a small fee.

Local Coverage – There are several sources of up-to-the-minute information: *Here's How,* with editions for each island, is a yearly 16-page guide to sightseeing, hotels, nightlife, and especially shopping (free in the islands or $4 airmail from *Here's How,* PO Box 1795, St. Thomas, Virgin Islands 00801; send check, specify edition). *WHERE, St. Thomas This Week, St. Croix This Week,* and *Today in St. Thomas* cover special events, shopping, restaurants, and nightlife. *Best Buys* is another source of shopping information, while *What to Do in St. Thomas and St. John* (published biannually) highlights activities. All are free in airports, hotels, and shops.

St. Thomas' *Daily News,* St. Croix's *Avis,* and St. John's *Tradewinds* cover local, national, and international news. The *San Juan Star* (Virgin Islands edition), *New York Times, New York Daily News, Wall Street Journal,* and *Miami Herald* are available on newsstands daily. The annual *Virgin Islands Playground* is a tourist-oriented magazine.

Island Insight, a 30-minute cable-TV program featuring information on hotels, shopping, car rentals, etc., for all three islands, runs continuously from 6 AM to 10 PM on channels 4 and 6.

The Yachtman's Guide to the Virgin Islands/Puerto Rico contains an abundance of helpful facts useful to landlubbers as well as sailors. Updated yearly, it is available for $10.95 plus $2 postage ($4 postage outside the US) from Tropic Isle Publishers, PO Box 610935, North Miami, FL 33161 (phone: 305 893-4277). A similar (but free) publication is *Virgin Cruise,* published annually by Newhart & Associates, PO Box 9999, St. Thomas, USVI 00801 (phone: 809 774-7704). *The Settler's Handbook* is an excellent resource for those considering longer stays ($4.95 from Douglas S. Burns Productions, PO Box 894, Christiansted, St. Croix, USVI 00802).

For history buffs, Florence Lewisohn's lively *The Romantic History of St. Croix* is required reading, and a new booklet, *The Undiscovered Gifts of the Caribbean,* a historical guide to the entire region, is available free from Partners for Livable Places, 1429 21st St., NW, Washington, DC 20036 (phone: 202 887-5990).

Telephone – Dial direct to the USVI by adding the area code 809 to the numbers given below.

ENTRY REQUIREMENTS: No passports or visas are required of US or Canadian citizens. For other nationalities, US Virgin Islands requirements are the same as those for entry into any other part of the US. However, bring proof of citizenship (birth certificate, passport) if you're contemplating a side trip to the neighboring British Virgin Islands.

CLIMATE AND CLOTHES: The average winter temperature is 77°F (24°C), ranging from 69°F (21°C) up to 84°F (29°C). The average summer temperature, cooled and dehumidified by the trade winds from the east, is 82°F (27°C), sometimes dropping to 75°F (24°C). Summer can bring some extremely hot days, but when the sun goes behind the mountains, there's usually a brief shower to cool off the evenings. Average annual rainfall is 40 inches, but even in the rainiest months (September through January), days with no sunshine are rare.

"Casual chic" is the phrase the Division of Tourism's literature uses. We'd say it has more to do with winter dressing than summer, and more to do with *Caneel Bay* than *Maho Bay Camp.* In practice, even the toniest hotels and restaurants rarely hold fast to the tie and jacket rule, even in season. However, *Carambola* adheres to the jacket rule, and at *Caneel Bay* wearing shorts in public places is verboten. For men and women, sports clothes — bright tops, skirts, shorts, and pants — are the daytime rule.

Cutoffs, jeans, and T-shirts are okay if you're camping or sporting, but are not generally admired around resort hotels or sit-down restaurants. Wearing an uncovered bathing suit away from the beach is against the law. For women, nights call for something pretty, with a shawl or sweater handy in winter in case it turns cool.

 MONEY: The local currency is US dollars and cents.

 LANGUAGE: Although the US Virgin Islands have lived under half a dozen different European flags, for centuries English has been their native language. But you'll still hear Norman French spoken in French Town, and islanders also speak a local patois — English Créole — that's a puzzling but musical mix of English, African, and Spanish. As there is also a large Puerto Rican population — particularly in St. Croix — Spanish can be considered the islands' second language.

 TIME: The Virgin Islands are on Atlantic Time, one hour ahead of Eastern Standard Time. When it's noon in Charlotte Amalie, it's 11 AM in New York. When the mainland is on Daylight Saving Time, Virgin Island and Eastern Daylight Time are the same.

 CURRENT: US-made electric toothbrushes, hair dryers, razors, and travel irons can be plugged in anywhere in the US Virgin Islands. Current is 110 AC, the same as on the mainland US.

 GETTING THERE: American, Eastern, and Pan Am jet nonstop from New York to both St. Thomas' Cyril E. King and St. Croix's Alexander Hamilton airports. American also flies nonstop from Dallas/Fort Worth. Midway flies from Miami to both St. Thomas and St. Croix. Eastern and American offer service from a number of US cities to both islands via flights connecting at Puerto Rico's San Juan International Airport and has direct flights from Miami. From midwestern, southern, and western cities, the handiest jet connection points are San Juan or the Miami gateway.

Passengers bound for St. John fly into St. Thomas, taxi to Red Hook (about $8.50 for one or $4.50 per person for two or more), and take the 20-minute ferry ride across Pillsbury Sound to Cruz Bay ($2 per person). With luck, the airport-to-island time runs about 1 hour. Service among other Caribbean islands is provided by Crown Air, Air Puerto Rico, Aero VI, Eastern Metro, and VI Sailplane Shuttle; charters are also available. LIAT carries passengers from and to the islands to the south.

Some 18 different cruise lines sail from New York, Norfolk, New Orleans, San Juan, Miami, and Port Everglades into Charlotte Amalie in record numbers; increasingly, Frederiksted on St. Croix is on the cruise route as well.

 CALCULATING COSTS: There's a wide range of hotels at a wide range of prices — from about $20 at an intown guesthouse off-season (spring, summer, or fall) to $380 and up for two (including all meals) at the most prestigious luxury resort in winter. Visitors pay as little as $6 a night for a bare tent site on *Cinnamon Bay*'s campgrounds. *Maho Bay*'s tent cottages — with comfortable beds, reading lights, and cooking facilities — are only $40 for two in summer. Rates at luxury resort hotels in winter generally run from about $150 up a day for two without meals. First-class hotels ask about $95 to $135 a day for two without meals. There are a number of small hotels and guesthouses with rates in the below-$40 range (also without meals). From mid-April to mid-December, summer rates about 25% to 35% below winter highs apply. In the summer, package trips are an especially good buy. For example, the Virgin Islands' Tourist Division sponsors an "American Paradise Packages" series of 1-week trips that include airfare, hotel accommodations, sightseeing, shipping discounts, souvenirs, and other special features for much less than if arranged for separately. Check with your travel agent about these and special sports packages that include court time (for tennis), greens fees (for golf), instruction, and other game-related items.

 GETTING AROUND: ST. CROIX — Taxi – Easy to find in towns and at the airport. No matter how far out your hotel may be, the desk can usually get a taxi within half an hour. Fares for most trips run about $3 to $5 per passenger, with the fare from the airport to Christiansted or Frederiksted hotels averaging about $6 per person. Unmetered; it's best to settle on a price before you get into the taxi. At the airport, a list of rates is posted by the baggage counter.

Car Rental – Ideal for exploring on your own, but hardly inexpensive. Rates run about $36 up with no mileage charge. Weekly rates average slightly less per day. *Avis* (phone: 773-4377, 778-9355 or -9365), *Budget* (phone: 773-2285, 778-4663 or -9636), *Hertz* (phone: 778-1402), and local agencies have offices in Christiansted and some also in Frederiksted. *Olympic* (phone: 773-2208) is a good local agency with somewhat lower rates. Its cars are in good shape, but not necessarily the latest models. All are listed in the yellow pages and most will deliver a car to your hotel within two hours of your call. But since demand sometimes exceeds supply, especially in high season, it makes good sense to reserve well ahead through your travel agent or the larger rental companies' toll-free reservation services. Be aware, too, that driving in the Virgin Islands is done on the left side of the road, made doubly difficult by the widespread use of left-hand-drive vehicles.

Sightseeing Taxi Tours – A good way to see the island. Drivers are usually good guides. Ask your hotel travel desk to recommend one and negotiate a price for the length of tour you have in mind.

Sightseeing Bus Tours – Mostly timed and organized with cruise ship passengers in mind, bus tours are operated by *Travelers Tours* (phone: 778-1636). A half-day island tour costs about $12 per person. *St. Croix Safari Tours* on Church St. (phone: 773-5922) offers an especially well guided 4½-hour minibus tour for about $15 per person (4-person minimum) plus a number of other interesting excursions, as does *St. Croix Sun Tours* (phone: 773-9661).

Sea Excursions – Sailing trip schedules and offerings, other than the Buck Island trip described below, depend on season and which boats are in port. Your hotel travel desk will have up-to-date data on twilight sails, cocktail cruises, and special excursions. The all-day sail to Buck Island reef — the country's only underwater national monument — is a must. The Park Service has laid down an underwater trail marked with surface floats and sea floor signs to identify coral formations and plants for passing snorkelers. The fish are fantastic. Guides aboard day trip boats help beginners get used to the gear and lead you along the reef (it's easy). Nonswimmers can ride in a glass-bottom dinghy or catch a life preserver tow. Your hotel can book you on a big boat or a small one. (You can wander down to the harbor and make your own arrangements on the spot.) Prices run about $35 per person for the full-day trip and include gear and instruction. Beer and soft drinks are provided, but bring your own picnic and an extra T-shirt for sunburn protection while you're doing the trails. Some boats offer a cookout option for an additional $7 or so per person. It's easy to lose track of time. If you're in a hurry, the glass-bottom *Reef Queen* does half-day trips for $21 per person.

Local Air Services – The way to fly from St. Croix to St. Thomas, St. John, or Tortola in the British Virgins is with *Virgin Islands Seaplane Shuttle* (phone: 773-1776,

800 524-2050), whose downtown-to-downtown flights are not only convenient but fun. *Aero VI, Eastern Metro, Crown Air,* and *American Eagle* — all based at Alexander Hamilton Airport — also offer local service and charters.

ST. JOHN — Taxi – Available, but not always where and when you want them. If you find a driver you like, take his card so you can get in touch by phone. Fares run about $4 to $10 or $12 from Cruz Bay to outlying points, depending on the number of passengers. The standard 2-hour tour is about $18 per couple, $7 per person for three or more; full-day rates are $12 per person for two people, $10 per person for three or more.

Car Rental – Can be arranged with *St. John Car Rental* (phone: 776-6103) in Cruz Bay, through the office at *Caneel Bay,* or through *Varlack Car Rental* (phone: 776-6695) at the dock and *St. John Development Corporation* (phone: 776-6343) at the gas station in Cruz Bay. Daily rates for a jeep run about $35 to $40 a day plus $3 insurance fee, with unlimited mileage (you pay for gas). Four-wheel drive is essential for exploring.

Ferry Services – Cross Pillsbury Sound to Red Hook on St. Thomas. (Check the Visitors' Bureau or dockside bulletin board for current schedule.) The trip takes about half an hour; one-way fare is $2 per adult, $1 per child. There's also launch service from the *Caneel Bay* dock to the National Park Dock at Red Hook. One-way fare is $9 per person.

ST. THOMAS — Taxi – Plentiful, unmetered, and inexpensive. Rates, based on destination rather than mileage, run $3.50 to $7 for most trips. If your hotel is in Charlotte Amalie, the fare from the airport is about $3.50 for one passenger; $3 per person for two or more riders. (It's considered okay for the driver to pick up additional people en route if they're going your way.) There's also an after-midnight surcharge of $1. *Hint:* If you're downtown shopping and want to taxi back to your hotel, head for the waterfront drive. No cab driver in his right mind would voluntarily tangle with Main Street or Back Street traffic — especially on a boat day.

Bus – Public bus service exists — just barely; it's not recommended. However, there is a Manassah Country Bus that makes one trip about every hour between town and Red Hook (fare: 75¢ per person). A safari bus also shuttles between downtown Charlotte Amalie and Red Hook hourly during the day for about $2 per person each way. Check your hotel or the Division of Tourism for schedules; ask, too, about shuttle service to *Jim Tillett's Art Gallery and Boutique* and *Coral World.*

Car Rental – Easily arranged, but relatively expensive. Rates start at about $35 a day for a compact with unlimited mileage. Weekly rentals cost somewhat less per day. *Avis* (phone: 774-1468), *Budget* (phone: 776-5774), *Hertz* (phone: 774-0841, 774-1879), *National* (phone: 774-6220), and *Thrifty* (phone: 776-3500, 776-2500) have offices at the airport. *Avis, Budget, Hertz,* and a number of local operators have downtown offices, too. *Econo-Car*'s base (phone: 775-6763) is by the marina at Red Hook. *Think Left* (phone: 774-9652) and *Sun Island Car Rentals* (774-3333) are good local firms that offer bargain rates. Major credit card holders don't have to make the usual $100 to $150 deposit. Your driver's license is good for up to 90 days on the islands. Just remember to keep left — it's a custom that dates back to plantation days, when British overseers ruled the island's roads.

Sightseeing Taxi Tours – A pleasantly effortless way to see island sights if you'd rather not drive yourself. Many St. Thomas drivers are good guides and can suggest half- and full-day itineraries, including likely lunch spots if you have nothing specific in mind. But don't rely on the luck of the taxi-stand draw. When you know when you want to go, ask your hotel tour desk to make arrangements with a driver they know. With two or more people sharing a cab, the charge for a standard 2-hour trip is about $10 per person.

Sightseeing Bus Tours – These are not a big deal on St. Thomas. Cruise passengers are their principal customers. *Tropic Tours,* with its main office in the International

Plaza (phone: 774-1855) and others in major hotels, does 2½-hour safari bus tours for about $15 per person, including a banana daiquiri at *Mountaintop* and hotel pickup and drop-off. A $19 tour (2½ hours) includes *Coral World* and *Jim Tillett's* complex; there is a $35 full-day tour of St. John, including ferry and lunch at *Cinnamon Bay*. *Greyline* (phone: 776-1515) offers a 2-hour tour for $13, a trip to *Coral World* for $20, and an outing to St. John — similar to *Tropic's* but including snorkeling gear — for $35.

Sea Excursions – Highly individualized glass-bottom boats leave from a number of docks along the waterfront. Cost is about $10 for adults, $5 for kids under 12.

It's now possible to scuba-dive here without suiting up. Aboard the *Atlantis* submarine, passengers enjoy a comfortable 90-minute cruise at a depth of 150 feet with good views. Day cruises $48 per person; night cruises $56 (phone 776-5650).

The motor ships *Bomba Charger* and *Native Son* both make the scenic run to another small world — the British Virgin Island of Tortola — in 45 minutes each way, charge about $24 per person for the round trip. Schedules leave time for a look around, lunch, a pint at the *Sir Francis Drake Pub,* and a chance to meet some nice people. The day trip to St. John offers a broad choice of boats that sail from Charlotte Amalie every morning. A park tour and a chance to do the Trunk Bay underwater trail are built into most day plans. Prices run about $60 per person, including lunch and drinks; sunset sails are $20. The catamaran *Ho-Tei,* at Coast Guard Dock, carries up to 39 passengers. Smaller yachts handle parties of six. Ask at *Sea Adventures* at Frenchman's Reef Dock or at the Visitors Bureau for current data and availability.

Local Air Services – *St. Thomas Flight Center* (phone: 776-4955) makes 30-minute small-plane sightseeing flights over St. Thomas, St. John, and the British Virgins for about $25 per person (3-person minimum). *Virgin Islands Seaplane Shuttle* offers downtown-to-downtown flights about every hour between St. Croix, St. John, St. Thomas, and Tortola that are not only fast but fun, for $29 to $60 one way (phone: 773-1776, 800 524-2050). *Aero VI, Eastern Metro, American Eagle,* and *Crown Air* also provide local service; *Virgin Air* handles small-plane charters; and there are several helicopter operators, among them *St. Thomas Air Center* (phone: 775-5000).

Ferry Services – See listings under St. John and St. Croix.

SHOPPING: If you'd rather spend most of your vacation time playing tennis, sailing, and the like, yet can't stand the idea of going home without a share of the bargains, then a little planning will help you through the maze of shops so that you end up with a few goodies and a good time. Check prices in your hometown stores before you leave so you know whether the Virgin Islands prices are worth the time and effort of such long-distance hauling. Some buys are better than others. Currently, for example, savings are minimal on photographic and electronic equipment (at best, a few dollars less than at mainland discount outlets), more worthwhile on fine china and crystal (savings from 30% to 50%). Perfume, watches, gold jewelry, and imported beauty products (makeup, bath gels) can be real bargains. Everybody buys liquor at half to two-thirds (for Scotch, liqueurs) off New York prices and almost everybody buys cigarettes at carton prices 40% or so below New York levels.

Three things have made US Virgin Islands shopping famous: (1) low, duty-free prices (on a list of 20 or so categories of most-wanted merchandise), (2) wide selections, and (3) the fact that US citizens are allowed to carry home, untaxed, double the value in goods purchased ($800 instead of the usual $400 per person); and five fifths of liquor (six, if one is locally produced) instead of the 1 quart that is permitted when returning from any other foreign place in the world (except Guam and US Samoa). Also, stateside residents may ship home from the US Virgin Islands, each day, up to $100 worth of goods as gifts, over and above the $800 exemption. US Virgin Islands products are completely tax exempt and do not count in the duty-free allowance.

The low prices are a legacy from the Danes, who stipulated as part of their 1917 treaty of sale that island retailers be forced to pay no more than 6% ad valorem duty on incoming goods. This is so much less than the tax paid elsewhere that Virgin Islands merchants can afford to sell their luxury imports for 5% to 60% less than most mainland US stores. Selections are big because volume is enormous, swelled by hundreds of thousands of cruise ship passengers' purchases, as well as those of Puerto Rican residents who often hop over for one-day buying sprees.

ST. CROIX

The following shops are in Christiansted, unless otherwise indicated, where there is a well-stocked branch of *Little Switzerland* in addition to:

Carambola Boutique – Pricey but extensive selection of sportswear, island art, books, and sundries.

Casa Carlota – Colorful, handcrafted cotton designer clothes. Caravelle Arcade.

Compass Rose – A mostly Oriental mélange of imports, from scarves and silk jackets to carvings, jade bangles, and tablecloths; some gems, some junk. Company St.

1870 Townhouse Shoppes – Attractive, reasonably priced beachwear and sportswear. King St.

Finesse Boutique – The most elegant boutique in town, full of delectable designer resortwear, handbags, shoes, costume and semiprecious jewelry, and perfumes; pricey, but definitely worth a stop. Company St. and Queen Cross.

The Gold Shop – Lots of contemporary chains, bracelets, other objets d'or, plus some stunning antique estate jewelry. King's Alley.

Grog 'N' Spirits – Portable potables — wine, liquor, beer, and mixers to go — handiest to Buck Island, yachting departures. Open Sundays. King's Wharf.

Happiness Is – Carefully selected collection of attractive handcrafted jewelry, shell things, macramé, graphics, paintings by local artists at reasonable prices. Company St.

Java Wraps – Dozens of hand-blocked pareos (sarongs), no two alike, and terrific colors, from $40 up with wrapping instructions; also shirts, sundresses, jumpsuits, and all sorts of resortwear in the same great prints. Strand St.

Jeltrup's Books – Specializing in Caribbean lore — histories, cookbooks, and tropic gardening; paperbacks too. King Cross.

Land of Oz – Children's and adult games, including backgammon and wari (an island favorite), plus jigsaw puzzles, kites, lots more. King's Alley.

Lisa's Sandals – Ideal island footwear in more variations than you can shake a thong at; belts, buckles, handbags, too. Comanche Walk.

Many Hands – Most imaginative graphics, crafts at wonderfully nonshock prices; cards, shells, enchanting Christmas ornaments, too. Pan Am Arcade.

Nancee's Leather Awl – All sorts of good-looking leather goods, some Nancee-made, some imported. Company St.

Nini of Scandinavia – Prized for bright Scandinavian sportswear, fabrics, especially Marimekko — affordable here. Church and Company sts.

Ritsu's – Creative jewelry designs, especially pearls. Caravelle Arcade.

St. Croix Leap – Native handcrafted wood gift items. Fredericksted.

Ship's Galley Liquor Locker – Small, friendly, well stocked; worthwhile specials. At the *Comanche* hotel.

Sonya Ltd. – Original hand-wrought jewelry. Company St.

Violette's Boutique – Gucci, Cartier boutiques; island's largest perfume bar; fashions, skin care products, porcelain, and watches. Strand St.

Whim Gift Shop – Antique reproductions (door knockers, hurricane globes), some period pieces (silver, paperweights, Cantonware). Good taste in a good cause — all profits go to St. Croix Landmarks Restoration. At Whim Greathouse. The small gift shop at St. George Village Botanical Gardens is also full of finds.

ST. JOHN

The Art Project – Paintings, pastels, watercolors by local artists; island-imported baskets, wall hangings, and Jean Yves Froment fabrics.

Blue Moon Boutique – Lots of cottons, batiks, island-made clothes for men, women, and kids; favored by savvy locals as well as visitors. In Lemon Tree Center.

Caneel Bay Boutique – Sportswear and a few sundries for the good casual chic life. Selection is small, prices very high. For emergency use only.

Mongoose Junction – A complex of studio shops sheltering such imaginative craftspersons as the *Pattons* (contemporary gold and silver jewelry), *Donald Schnell Studio* (original pottery and hand-blown glass), *Wicker, Wood & Shells* (gifts, decor items), *Canvas Factory* (seaworthy totes, bags, clothing, as well as sail repair), *Fabric Mill* (batiks, silk-screened prints), *The Clothing Studio* (hand-painted garments), *Marcellino's Bakery,* and *St. John Water Sports.*

Sailor's Delight – Men's clothes, nautical gifts, and hand-painted T's, plus the *Dock Shop* (more sportswear), *Stitches* and *Stitches II* (more sun and sea gear).

Sparky's – More of the same (as on St. Thomas and St. Croix), only smaller. Handy for liquor purchases, which they'll deliver to the airport or ship.

ST. THOMAS

If shopping is your favorite sport, you can spend days wandering glassy-eyed through the offerings — though true bargains are relatively scarce — in Charlotte Amalie's warehouse shops. While there are shops on St. John and St. Croix as well, the biggest stores, the largest stocks (and crowds), are on St. Thomas in Charlotte Amalie. Before heading downtown, check *Here's How, This Week,* or *Best Buys* to find out which store sells most of the brands or kinds of merchandise you want. In general, prices for similar items are the same throughout the islands, so the more items found in a single store, the fewer stops and the less time spent in cash register lines. Avoid crowded cruise ship days whenever possible, and go early — while you and the salespeople are still fresh. And do check out the shops in Bakery Square, Charlotte Amalie's newest restored shopping complex on Back Street, and Havensight Mall near the cruise ship dock.

A number of St. Thomas shops have St. Croix branches where choice may be somewhat smaller, but so are the crowds. If you're planning to island hop, you may want to shop accordingly. St. Thomas boutiques such as *Lion in the Sun, Cosmopolitan, Cuckoo's Nest,* and *Cheshire Cat* sometimes advertise high fashion at low "free port" prices. Sometimes they have it, but check prices carefully. Also, *Louis Vuitton, Guy La Roche,* and *Courrèges* all have local outlets in Palm Passage, none of which claims bargain prices. For liquor, *Bolero, A. H. Riise,* and *Sparky's,* all on Main Street, have downtown's biggest stocks and selections (ask about free delivery to airport or ship; delivery times are limited). Here are some of the best-stocked Charlotte Amalie stores with their specialties:

Benetton – High fashion in three locations.

Blue Carib Gems & Rocks – With a workshop to tour, gemstones and jewelry to buy. They'll sometimes let you design your own. In Bakery Square.

Bolero – Daum and Danish crystal, English bone china, Omega and Tissot watches, French perfumes, men's and women's fashions, liquor. Main St.

Boutique Riviera – Carries the biggest, shiniest Les Must de Cartier collection, along with Fila, Hermès, Pringle, and other luxuries. On Main St., at Havensight Mall, and at *Frenchman's Reef.*

Cardow – Long established, claims the Caribbean's biggest precious and semiprecious collection.

The Cloth Horse – Fabric and home furnishings from Haiti and Santo Domingo at 40% below US prices. In Bakery Square.

Al Cohen – Huge liqour warehouse at Havensight, across from the West India Co. dock.

Colombian Emeralds – Large selection of inset gemstones and famous-name watches. Main St. and on the waterfront.

Craft Co-op – Virgin Islands (tax-exempt) handmades. Back St.

Dockside Book Shop – In Havensight Mall, a reliable source of reading matter.

Down Island Traders – Homemade VI goods (tax exempt) like mango chutney and preserves, seagrape jelly, papaya and lime marmalades, as well as spices and teas (rum, passion fruit, mango, and coconut) and Caribbean cookbooks that make wonderful, inexpensive gifts. In Bakery Square, on the waterfront, and at *Frenchman's Reef.*

Gold Mine – Chains plus more expensive nuggets. In Drake's Passage.

Gucci – The famous. On the waterfront.

Island Newsstand – Well stocked with international magazines, newspapers, other reading material, and postcards. Main St.

Lion in the Sun – Eclectic selection of European designer labels for men and women. Riise's Alley.

Little Switzerland – As expected, a high concentration of watches, music boxes, cuckoo clocks; also elegant china, crystal, jewelry, binoculars. Main St.

A. H. Riise – Stacks of top-quality china, crystals, watches, jewelry, art objects, antiques, and decorator accessories, as well as a large stock of liquor. Nice, helpful people. Main St. and at Havensight Mall.

Sand Dollars – Gift items and Virgin Islands–made jewelry. In Bakery Square.

South American Trade – Fantastic selection of leather goods at bargain prices. Hibiscus Shopping Mall.

Sparky's – Cheerful jumble of best-selling merchandise in a number of different categories. Best known for liquor and cigarettes. Main St.

H. Stern – The prestigious South American jewelry outfit. (Advantage: worldwide locations in case anything goes wrong.)

Straw Factory – Stocks Virgin Islands–made hats, mats, purses, etc. — some woven by Frenchtown women.

Sweet Passion – If antique jewelry pieces are your weakness, don't miss the really choice collection here. In the Royal Dane Mall.

Tie Rack – All the stock is VI-made, so it's tax exempt. On Norre Gade.

Jim Tillett's – His fabrics (and sportswear cut therefrom), wall hangings, and paintings are fresh and fun. His compound at Estate Tutu on the road to *Coral World* — where they do the screen printing — is a sightseeing must even if you don't buy.

Tropicana Perfume Shop – The world's largest scents store, it has cosmetics, bath oils, and men's and women's toiletries as well. On Main St.

Zora the Sandalmaker – Custom-made sandals.

 TIPPING: When your hotel adds an automatic 10% to 15% service charge (on top of the 7½% room tax), you need not leave tips for the room maid, dining room waiter or waitress, or other hotel personnel who serve you on a regular basis. For service above and beyond the expected, give $1 to the bellboy who runs a special errand; $1 to $2 or so to the maid who presses the skirt or slacks it's too late to send to the valet; $2 to the wine steward who brings and serves your wine. When no service charge is added, give the maid $1 to $2 for each day of your stay, your dining waiter 15% of the check — or $2.50 to $3 per person a day, depending on the class of hotel and number of meals included if you're paying full or Modified American Plan rates. Bartenders and bar waiters should be tipped 10% to 15% whenever they serve you. Bellboys and porters get at least 50¢ per bag, and never less than $1 on arrival or departure. Tip taxi drivers 15% of the fare.

SPECIAL EVENTS: In addition to all the US national holidays (*New Year's Day, President's Day, Martin Luther King's Birthday, Easter, Memorial Day, Independence Day, Labor Day, Veterans' Day, Thanksgiving,* and *Christmas*), the Virgin Islands celebrate *Three Kings Day* (January 6); *Transfer Day* (March 31, the day the US flag first flew in the islands); *Holy Thursday; Good Friday; Organic Act Day* (June 16, the day in 1936 when the US Congress granted home rule and suffrage to the Virgin Islands); *Emancipation Day* (July 3, the anniversary of the 1848 day when slaves were freed in the Danish West Indies); *Supplication Day* (third Monday in July, a day of prayer for protection from hurricanes); *Columbus Day* and *Puerto Rico Friendship Day* (both celebrated on October 12); *Hurricane Thanksgiving Day* for the end of hurricane season (third Monday in October); *Liberty Day* (November 1, honoring Judge David Hamilton Jackson, who secured freedom of the press and assembly from King Christian X of Denmark). Cruzans make a two-week fiesta of *Christmas* (from December 25 to January 6, Three Kings Day); St. Thomians declare *Carnival* — "The islanders' holiday for themselves" and everyone else — the last two weeks of every April, when stilt-walking Moko Jumbis march and steel bands ping-pong all day and night; on St. John, *Independence Day* is the Big Time, celebrated with music, Moko Jumbis, a Miss St. John contest, plus the traditional fireworks.

SPORTS: ST. CROIX — Boating – *Caribbean Sea Adventures* (phone: 773-5922) handles small boat rentals and arranges charters for larger boats, bareboat and crewed. *Mile-Mark Charters'* sleek trimaran *Viti Viti* and sloop *Nau-ti-gal* do personable full- and half-day charters at reasonable rates (phone: 773-2285). Sunfish and Hobie Cats can be rented at the water sports activity centers of most beach hotels.

For those captains of their own ships, there are repair, service, and docking facilities at *St. Croix Marina* in Christiansted Harbor (phone: 773-0289) and *Green Cay Marina* on the northeast coast (phone: 773-1453).

Golf – *Carambola*'s 18-hole Robert Trent Jones course (the spruced-up former *Fountain Valley* track) is a beauty (Jones purportedly called it his prettiest) well worth playing, and open to the public (phone: 778-0747). Greens fees run about $24 per day, $20 to rent a two-rider cart in winter; about 25% less in summer. There are also special 3-, 4-, and 5-day playing packages. The new pro shop (in the new clubhouse) has rental clubs and lockers, and there's a restaurant where the steak sandwiches and the view earn it points as a recommended lunch stop even if you don't play.

The public is also invited to play the far shorter *Buccaneer* hotel's (phone: 773-2100) 18, rambling over what was once a sugar plantation. For 18 holes, greens fees run about $14, cart rental, $20 for two.

St. Croix also has a 9-hole course at the *Reef* (phone: 773-9250).

Horseback Riding – At *Sprat Hall,* a plantation homestead-turned-hotel, *Jill's Equestrian Stable* (phone: 772-2880) offers trail riding through the rain forest and over the hills beyond. The 2-hour ride ($30 per person) not only teaches you lots about local flora and fauna but a bit of horsemanship, too. After you've made a daylight excursion, you may qualify for one of their highly memorable moonlight expeditions. *Sprat Hall* has riding packages.

Horse Racing – About once a month at Flamboyant Race Track. Thoroughbred horses and informal betting, with food, drink, live music, and party atmosphere.

Snorkeling and Scuba – Waters are so clear and warm and there are so many dive sites to see that you could spend a whole vacation under water and still cover only a fraction of what's there. In addition to the underwater trails off Buck Island, St. Croix's most intriguing sites include its coral canyons and the drop-offs at Salt River, Cane Bay, and Davis Bay (site of the 12,000-foot-deep Puerto Rico Trench, the fifth deepest body of water in the world). For scuba instruction, day and night dives, and equipment rental, contact *Caribbean Sea Adventures* (Christiansted; phone: 773-5922); *Dive Experience* (Christiansted; phone: 773-3307); *Cruzan Divers* (Frederiksted; phone: 772-3701); *Sea Shadows* (Cane Bay; phone: 778-3850); or *V.I. Divers* (Christiansted; phone: 773-6045).

Snorkeling doesn't require any formal arrangements. There are plenty of good snorkeling spots right off the coast, and even the smallest hotels are likely to have equipment on hand, which they will loan gratis or rent for a small fee. However, most visitors to St. Croix — snorkelers and non-snorkelers alike — make at least one trip to see the Buck Island reef. A number of boats — catamarans, trimarans, sloops, glass-bottom boats — make half- or full-day excursions to Buck Island that include snorkeling in the underwater park and provide the equipment and, frequently, a guide. Among the charterers that do are: *Caribbean Sea Adventures* (phone: 773-5922), the *Jolly Roger* (phone: 773-0754), *Mile-Mark Charters* (phone: 773-2285), and the *Reef Queen* (phone: 773-0754). All operate out of Christiansted Harbor.

Sport Fishing – Cruzan fisherman go deep for mahimahi, wahoo, snapper, grouper, and blue dolphin (the fish, not the mammal), using light tackle for sporty jack or bonefish closer to shore. Islanders claim to hold the world billfishing record. Two-chair, two-line boats charge from about $230 for half days to almost $400 for a full day, with bait, tackle, and soft drinks included. A 3-hour light-tackle trip runs about $20 per person. *Caribbean Sea Adventures* (phone: 773-5922) arranges deep-sea trips. Since fleet members are limited, advance reservations are always a good idea; most places require a 50% deposit.

Swimming and Sunning – Beach names to know are Cane, Sugar, Pelican, and Grapetree bays, and La Grange — all pleasant, none spectacular. People staying in Christiansted tend to use the small, pretty beach on Protestant Cay or take a short shuttle out to one of the three beaches at the *Buccaneer* hotel. Cramer Park, near the island's eastern tip and, therefore, also near the easternmost land point of the US, has a beach, picnic tables, and changing rooms.

Tennis – If you're serious about the game, St. Croix's *Buccaneer* hotel has 8 near-perfect lighted courts, a first-rate pro and a pro shop, and match play facilities; it is probably the place for you. Other setups are at the *Caribbean Tennis Club* (7 lighted courts, pro, shop, swimming pool); *Hotel on the Cay* (4 courts); *Queens Quarter* (2); *Grapetree Beach* hotel (4); *La Grange Beach and Tennis Club* (2); and *The Reef* (2). There are also 7 public courts on the island.

Water Skiing – Boats, skis, and lessons are available at *Grapetree Beach* hotel and through *Caribbean Sea Adventures* (phone: 773-5922) at about $60 per hour of boat time for four to six skiers.

Windsurfing – A very popular sport in these parts — easy to learn and inexpensive (about $15 per hour) — it is available at many hotels.

ST. JOHN — Boating – *The Dock Shop* (phone: 776-6338) and *Cruz Bay Watersports* (phone: 776-6234) will arrange daily sails, as will the water sports centers at *Caneel Bay* and *Maho Bay*. St. John Water Sports (phone: 776-6256) handles both day sails and longer crewed charters.

Hiking – An extensive network of trails covers the national park. Take a four-wheeled tour first to get oriented; then ask for the free park service trail map and literature and set out on your own. Nature-walking through the park is a favorite diversion for campers at both Maho and Cinnamon bays. Two or three times a week — on a flexible schedule — a park service guide leads nature walks.

Snorkeling and Scuba – There is a fine marked underwater trail at *Trunk Bay,* with guided snorkel tours on Wednesday mornings. Other top spots are Hawksnest Bay,

Waterlemon Cay, and Salt Pond. For snorkeling and scuba trips, equipment rental, and instruction, try *St. John Water Sports* in Cruz Bay (phone: 776-6256) or *Cruz Bay Watersports* (phone: 776-6234). *The Dock Shop,* also in Cruz Bay, makes snorkeling trips and rents snorkeling equipment (phone: 776-6338). *Caneel Bay* has its own full facilities.

Sport Fishing – Book through *Caneel Bay* or check with the *Cruz Bay Watersports* (phone: 776-6234).

Swimming and Sunning – Trunk Bay, the biggest attraction, is a great white sweep of sand with the National Park Service Underwater Trail just offshore. The camps at Cinnamon and Maho bays have their own beaches, and seven more beaches edge the waters around *Caneel Bay; Caneel* also has an offshore island available for exclusive use by the day. Elsewhere around the island, swim and sun at Hawks, Reef, and Lameshur bays.

Tennis – *Caneel Bay* has 7 unlit courts, a pro shop, and a pro staff. Cinnamon Bay and Maho Bay campers can arrange to play there. There are also 2 public courts in downtown Cruz Bay.

ST. THOMAS — Boating – Virgin Islanders do the biggest charter business in the Caribbean. St. Thomas, with its sizable yacht harbor and Red Hook marina, is the heart of the business. Moving out of the Sunfish/Hobie Cat class (both of which can be rented at bathing beach centers), you can rent just about anything that floats — from a 13-foot power boat to an 80-foot schooner, and houseboats, cabin cruisers, and trimarans in between. Cruising vacations aboard a charter yacht with skipper, crew, meals, and liquor included can cost as little as $85 or as much as $325 up per person a day in winter, 10% to 20% less in summer. Or you can go bareboat and sail yourself for a per-person cost of about $45 to $65 a day in winter, roughly 20% less in summer, for the boat plus about $20 per person a day for provisioning (food and booze). (*Note:* A proficiency checkout is a standard pre-takeover requirement.)

For information on day or night sails and boat charters, ask at your hotel's travel desk, or contact *V. I. Charter Yacht League,* Homeport, St. Thomas, USVI 00802 (phone: 774-3944; 800 524-2061), who can put you in touch with any one of the abundant charter operators in the area.

Day sails, which generally include snorkeling and a picnic lunch while anchored in an out-of-the-way cove, are very popular. *Sea Adventures* at *Frenchman's Reef* hotel (phone: 774-9652, 776-8500, ext. 625, or 800 524-2096) and the *Watersports Center* at Sapphire Bay (phone: 775-6755) will charter half- or full-day sails. You can also book directly on a variety of craft, such as the schooner *True Love* (the very yacht on which Bing Crosby sang to Grace Kelly in *High Society)* (phone: 775-6547); *Nightwind,* a 50-foot yawl (phone: 775-7898); and the sloop *Tijou* (phone: 775-6135). Also ask at your hotel's activities desk.

Golf – *Mahogany Run,* on the north side of the island, charges greens fees of $29 per round and $24 for cart rental in winter, about 30% less in summer. Very scenic, though the quality of the course is less than top-notch.

Horse Racing – Now that the new track is open at Nadir, there are meets roughly once a month — usually on a holiday or a Sunday. Check the papers and go.

Snorkeling and Scuba – You can rent masks and fins for a small fee at all major hotels and on tourist beaches. Snorkel gear is standard equipment on sailing and yacht excursions, and there is no extra charge for it. Off St. Thomas there are fine beginners' dive spots (Cow and Calf, St. James Island, Stevens Cay, Coki Bay) plus any number of underwater-scapes (Congo Cay's lava archways, Thatch Cay's tunnels, Eagle Shoal's submerged mountain) fascinating for more advanced divers. From St. Thomas (or St. John) you can make the all-day dive trip to the wreck of the Royal Mail packet boat *Rhone* (now a British national park) off the British Virgin Islands.

Night dives (intermediate and advanced divers only, about $50 per person) spotlight flashing octopi, weaving basket fish, and loping lobsters in a weirdly different after-dark world.

Some firms that offer diving trips, instruction, and equipment in St. Thomas are *Aqua Action* at Secret Harbor (phone: 775-6285), *Caribbean Divers* at Red Hook (phone: 775-6384), the *Watersports Center* at Sapphire Bay (phone: 775-6100), *Virgin Island Diving Schools and Divers' Supplies* (phone: 774-8687), and *Joe Vogel Diving Company* (phone: 775-7610) on Mandahl Rd. What was once the hotel section of the Villa Olga is now the *St. Thomas Diving Club* (phone: 774-1376), a diver-oriented resort with simple quarters which sponsors daily dives from a choice of three island take-off points — its own dock or from Bolongo Bay or Pineapple beaches. Set up for instruction and certification. Its week-long packages offer the choice of seven nights' hotel stay with unlimited dives or accommodations on the custom-built live-aboard dive boat *Mohawk II,* including all meals at sea, and unlimited diving.

Sport Fishing – Big is the word for it — with 21 world-record catches (nine for blue marlin) made from Virgin Islands boats in the last dozen years. There's year-round fishing for wahoo, allison tuna, bonita, sailfish, and marlin. St. Thomians get their best blue marlin between June and August, white marlin in spring and fall, tarpon and bonefish in spring, wahoo from September to May, and sailfish and blackfin tuna in January and February.

American Yacht Harbor (phone: 775-6454) at Red Hook is prime deep-sea headquarters with boats in fine fighting trim. They can arrange in- or offshore fishing for half days, full days, overnight, or longer. *Frenchman's Reef Sea Adventures* (phone: 776-8500, ext. 625) also arranges deep-sea fishing.

Surfing – There is no real surfing to speak of since there are no really big waves. Off the beach at Hull Bay on the north coast, an occasional surfer can be seen.

Swimming and Sunning – Most resorts, hotels, condominiums, and cottage colonies are on sandy stretches of beach stocked with chaises, towels, and beach toys (snorkel gear, float boards, Sun- or Sailfish, and/or Hobie Cats, etc., for rent at small fees). Since all US Virgin Islands beaches are public, you can also take a sampler's approach: headquarter at a guesthouse with no beach to speak of, rent a car (or take advantage of your host's offer of free transportation), and visit a different sandy shoreline each day. (It's a scheme that works admirably on St. Thomas and St. John, but is slightly less successful on St. Croix, which has fewer spectacular beaches.)

Magens Bay, a wide, protected stretch of golden sand thickly edged with palms, is probably best known because it has appeared on so many lists of the World's Ten Most Beautiful Beaches. In fact, it may be a little too popular on weekends and on cruise ship arrival days, but it is gorgeous all the time. There are changing rooms and a good snack bar (small admission and parking fees). Sapphire, Morningstar, and Lindberg beaches have the same facilities, and are well known and beautiful. But for leisurely picnicking and/or putting some space between you and the crowd, you might head for Cowpet Bay or Nazareth Bay, both on the Caribbean side of St. Thomas; or, on the Atlantic side, Mandahl Bay, Hull Bay, or Stumpy Bay (clunky name, axle-fracturing road, but a good beach).

Tennis – Laykold or all-weather courts are the rule throughout the Virgin Islands. Many are lighted for night play, have pro shops and pro instruction. There are 6 free public courts on St. Thomas, available on a first come, first served basis. Otherwise, here's the private court count: *Bluebeard's Castle* (2), *Bolongo Bay* (4), *Frenchman's Reef* (4), *Limetree Beach* (2), *Mahogany Run* (2), *Stouffer Grand Beach* (4), and *Virgin Isle* (2). The courts at *Cowpet Bay, Magens Point, Sapphire Beach, Secret Harbour,* and *Watergate* are for members and hotel guests only. Some condominium complexes limit play to club members, owners, and guests.

All hotel courts require players to wear standard whites or clothes designed for the game. Guests are charged no fee (or a very small one) for court use. Nonguests pay a nominal hourly fee to play. Lessons run $8 to $10 for a half hour.

NIGHTLIFE: St. Croix – Both the *Buccaneer* hotel and *Grapetree Beach* schedule music most nights, limbo shows at least once a week. Downtown, the *King's Alley* hotel's *Marina Bar* is the place for sunset- and people-watching. Later, jazz buffs beat a path to the *Bombay Club,* or anywhere Jimmy Hamilton, who played sax with the Duke, and his band are playing. Night owls disco at *Hondo's,* tune in to piano at *Frank's,* and finally come to roost at the *Moonraker Lounge,* where there's live listening music. St. Croix's Quadrille Dancers, when you can find them, are a special treat. In bright yesterday costumes, they move to the old plantation-days calls, and before it ends, you're invited to try a few steps yourself. The amateur dancers' regular jobs make schedules erratic; but watch *This Week* for date, time, place, and go if you get a chance.

St. John – No contest. There are fish fries at *Fred's* on Fridays, and on occasional Saturdays, *Sputnik Bar* at *Coral Bay* offers native food and a live reggae/calypso band. The *Caneel* band plays regularly, but before or after the sessions there, *Ric's, The Fernhouse,* or *The Back Yard* (all in Cruz Bay) are the places to be.

St. Thomas – No star-spangled nightclub shows, no big-deal casinos. One big hotel — *Frenchman's Reef* — offers a nightly Calypso Carnival of island music and dance at its nightclub; its other entertainment room is a bar-lounge with piano music. Elsewhere, entertainment is simpler. Evenings generally progress from cocktails to dinner, a brandy, maybe a dance or two, and then bed. (All that sun and sea tends to tire folks early.) Hotels provide music — songs and a guitar or a small combo — most nights. At least one evening a week, most hotels stage outdoor barbecues with a steel band and limbo show (usually with a bit of fire-eating or broken-glass walking by way of introduction — King Voodoo, chief local punishment glutton, does both). If you've never seen a limbo show (as they say, if you've seen one . . .), it might be worth your while to pilgrimage out to the *Carib Beach* where they do it up in a proper seaside setting every Saturday night; the *Virgin Isle* stages a West Indian luau and limbo show on Fridays. *Frenchman's Reef* entertains with dance music at *La Terraza,* later dancing at the *Top of the Reef.* Around town, young after-five action starts at *Yesterday's, Rosie O'Grady's,* or on Back St., or up at *Sib's Mountain Bar* in Mafolie. The scene may or may not shift later to *Jimmy'Z,* the *Ritz* (live local sounds, weekend disco), the *Greenhouse* (on the waterfront), or the *VI*'s disco

BEST ON THE ISLANDS

CHECKING IN: The Virgin Islands have just about everything in the way of accommodations except high-rises (*Frenchman's Reef* just misses; its floors go down the hill as well as up). Among the nicest accommodations are condominiums, which, though not inexpensive, can be real money savers for families or a couple of couples sharing an apartment — especially the usually well-stocked kitchens that can be used to cut down on dining expenses. There are also modest guesthouses and small inns on all three islands. Rates range from as little as about $45 for two with breakfast at a 19th-century guesthouse in summer, to a winter high of $485 and up for two including all meals at *Virgin Grand,* and up to $450 without meals for a stylish 3-bedroom villa suite at *Mahogany Run.* In the lists that follow, very expensive is defined as $185 or more a night for a double room in winter, about $120 or more in summer — both without meals; expensive, about $130 to $185 in winter,

$80 to $130 in summer; moderate, $85 to $130 in winter, $50 to $80 in summer; and inexpensive as under $75 in winter, under $50 in summer. Modified American Plan (with breakfasts and dinners) adds about $25 to $30 per person per night.

ST. CROIX

CHRISTIANSTED AND ENVIRONS

Cormorant Beach Club – Bills itself as St. Croix's only small luxury resort (38 rooms), and locals (Cruzans) concur it's tops for both accommodations and dining. Plenty of beach, pool, tennis (phone: 778-8920; 800 372-1323). Very expensive.

Carambola Beach – Nestled on 28 acres overlooking the sea, with 156 rooms, each with private screened porch. New furniture and improved lighting have made the rooms more comfortable. Facilities include a large swimming pool, 2 Jacuzzis, 4 tennis courts and a Peter Burwash instructional operation, diving, snorkeling, deep-sea fishing off Davis Bay, horseback riding, and a fine 18-hole Robert Trent Jones championship course (formerly *Fountain Valley*), with a new clubhouse, full-service pro shop, and a luncheon terrace and bar with a breathtaking view of the surrounding valley. Also 2 restaurants that feature traditional island food and Continental dishes, a cocktail lounge, boutique, and conference center. No phones; TV in the central lounge. The newest (opened January 1987) beachfront property in St. Croix, it is the first phase of a community known as Danestad that will cover 4,000 acres. Managed by Rockresorts; full American Plan only (3 meals a day) (phone: 778-3800; 800 223-7637). Very expensive.

Buccaneer – Sprawling down a hillside outside Christiansted, with the most extensive resort facilities on the island — 3 beaches, a sporty 18-hole golf course, 8 tennis courts, a spa and fitness center, shops, plus a full roster of activities that includes two movies nightly. There's a lot happening here, but the atmosphere is easygoing, and the hotel vans shuttling around the property keep guests from getting too tuckered out. The 149 rooms, all with big private terraces, are large and nicely furnished. Favorites are the beachside rooms with fieldstone terraces right on the water, but the less expensive rooms in the flamingo-pink main building are nice, too. The view of Christiansted from the open-air *Terrace* restaurant is unequaled (phone: 773-2100; 800 223-1108). Very expensive.

Colony Cove – Large, good-looking apartments with just about anything you could need, including cable TV, washer and dryer, and dishwasher, should make this beachside newcomer a popular spot. There's a solar-tiled pool (it keeps the water warm for dips after dark) and a good water-sports center. Guests have charging privileges at the restaurant next door at *Mill Harbor*. The extra-large terraces, all facing the ocean, are especially nice. Maid service is extra. About 10 minutes from Christiansted (phone: 773-1965; 800 524-2025). Expensive.

Mill Harbour – Ten minutes from Christiansted on Sugar Beach, with large, individually decorated 1-, 2-, and 3-bedroom apartments, all with breezy terraces overlooking a saltwater lagoon. There's a pleasant poolside restaurant and bar and a good beach activities center that is shared by the property next door. Maid service is extra (phone: 773-3800; 800 524-2008). Expensive.

Hotel on the Cay – On its own island in Christiansted Harbor, with a white sand beach and lush grounds only minutes from town by ferry. It has a good water-sports center, Olympic-size pool, tennis courts on the water, and dining next to the beach or on a hill with 360° views. The 55 rooms are smallish, but comfortably contemporary, with tile floors, platform beds, and wet bars (phone: 773-2035; 800 524-2035). Expensive to moderate.

Pink Fancy – Housed in a restoration of an 18th-century Danish townhouse and its attendant buildings, this small gem is a puzzle of white-shingled, pink-shuttered buildings; walled courtyards; gardens; and terraces on different levels — all eye-pleasing and soul-soothing. The large attractive suites — all have living areas and fully stocked kitchenettes — are well-feathered nests meant for solid comfort, with comfy couches, cable TV, clock-radios, and plenty of light. There's a pretty tiled swimming pool and complimentary bar where guests help themselves to Continental breakfast and drinks. A 5-minute walk from the Christiansted wharf (phone: 773-8460; 800 524-2045). Expensive to moderate.

St. Croix by the Sea – A pretty, popular spot with 67 rooms, its own beach, huge saltwater pool, tennis, and 4 very good restaurants. Close to downtown (phone: 778-8600; 800 524-5006). Moderate.

Club Comanche – In the heart of Christiansted, it's an old-fashioned, four-story hotel with quirky, no-two-alike rooms. The new wing houses some attractive split-level suites, including a triplex with a living room, round bedroom, and sun deck right at the harbor's edge. The hotel has a breakfast porch, attractive pool deck, and a very popular restaurant (phone: 773-0210; 800 223-5695). Moderate to inexpensive.

King Christian – Its great wharfside location couldn't be more convenient. Rooms are basic but good-sized. The balconies of those facing the wharf provide a ringside seat for watching the scenic life of the harbor and town. (Rooms 201 and 301 have the best views.) It's a favorite of many repeat visitors because it's owned and run by Betty and Irwin Sperber, and much of island life goes on in and around it. Guests can use *Hotel on the Cay* sports facilities for a nominal fee (phone: 773-2285; 800 524-2012). Moderate to inexpensive.

Turquoise Bay – Though it's separated from its next-door neighbor by only a stand of trees and is just 10 minutes from Christiansted, this small hotel (3 cottages, 4 apartments) feels very private and tranquil, almost rural. (It was built 30 years ago by four Chicago couples as their private getaway and is still run by one of the original owners.) The cottages are cool and spacious with high ceilings, tiled floors, plenty of windows, and simple but well-cared-for furnishings. There's a good-sized pool, small boat dock, and a beach, though it's too rocky for serious beach pursuits. The bay, however, is most assuredly turquoise (phone: 773-0244). Moderate to inexpensive.

King's Alley – This small harborside hotel is attractively decorated and meticulously cared for. In addition to a convenient location, it has its own small swimming pool and congenial pool-deck bar that's a popular sundown meeting place (phone: 773-0103; 800 843-3574). Inexpensive.

The Lodge – Its 16 rooms, grouped around a tropical courtyard, are smallish but spic and span, and all have air conditioning, TV, refrigerators, and private baths. Though oriented to the businessperson, it's a fine town base for economy-minded vacationers. There's a swimming pool as well as a popular nightspot, *Moonraker Lounge* (phone: 773-1535). Inexpensive.

FREDERIKSTED

Sprat Hall Plantation – This folksy enclave on the west coast of the island has as its center the oldest continuously lived-in greathouse on St. Croix, endowed with a handsome dining room and lounge, guestrooms with four-poster beds, and an uncritical miscellany of antiques and memorabilia, The rooms in the old slave quarters and garden cottages are more pedestrian. Serene and bustling by turns, it is family-run and family-welcoming, with first-rate riding, fishing, scuba, and delicious island meals. The beach is just across the road (phone: 772-0305; 800 524-2026). Moderate.

King Frederik – A stroll from Frederiksted on a nice strand of beach, this hotel offers a variety of modest accccommodations, not all, unfortunately, of the same quality. It's best to request one of the 11 tidily attractive 1-bedroom apartments with a cool, ocean-facing terrace. Rates include Continental breakfast, free transportation to town, and daily maid service (phone: 772-1205; 800 524-2018). Moderate.

Royal Dane – Occupying a 225-year-old townhouse right on the harbor, it has 14 newly renovated rooms, which, while on the small side, are distinctively and attractively furnished, with nice touches like contemporary prints from the owner's collection. (The two large rooms facing the waterfront are especially nice.) There's a cosmopolitan air here: The crowd tends to be young and sophisticated. Monday night movies — ranging from classic to classic camp — are shown in the pleasant courtyard, which the rest of the week houses one of St. Croix's most promising restaurants. There's no pool, but guests have privileges at — and free transportation to — La Grange Beach and Tennis Club about ½ mile away (phone: 772-2780). Moderate to inexpensive.

Frederiksted – A compact, modern hotel, right on the waterfront, it probably gets more traffic from businesspeople than vacationers. The rooms are comfortable, each equipped with bar and refrigerator. There's a cozy courtyard bar, a pint-sized swimming pool, and free transportation to the *La Grange Beach and Tennis Club* nearby (phone: 772-0500; 800 524-2025). Inexpensive.

ELSEWHERE ON ST. CROIX

Grapetree Beach – On a great white sand beach on the calm Caribbean side of the island (the east end). The emphasis here is on water sports — snorkeling, scuba diving, windsurfing, sailing, water skiing — though the resort also has tennis and many other scheduled activities. The rooms and suites are large and attractively furnished in pastels and rattan, and all have big beachfront terraces. There's an attractive piano bar and poolside restaurant. Quiet by day, lively by night (phone: 773-9700; 800 524-0285). Expensive.

Queen's Quarter – Sitting smack in the middle of the island, these casually elegant hilltop villas have extraordinary views. The studios and 1- to 3-bedroom suites all have terraces, maid service, and laundry service. There's a shapely swimming pool and tennis courts on the property and free transportation to the beach. The restaurant here is considered one of the best on the island; the view alone is worth a sunset cocktail (phone: 778-3784). Moderate.

Tamarind Reef – The club's 16 spacious studios and 1-bedroom suites, each with a patio or screened gallery looking out to sea, sit on the Atlantic side of the island, about a 20-minute drive east of Christiansted. Interiors are clean and pleasant, if a little spartan in appointments. There's a small beach, pool, game room, poolside snack bar, free paddle boats and rowing dinghies for day trips to Green Cay, offshore. The 140-slip Green Cay Marina, with shops and restaurants, is next door. Try the *Galleon* restaurant (phone: 773-0463; 800 524-2036). Moderate.

Cane Bay – It's small, informal, and friendly, with 9 one-bedroom apartments right on the water. (The swimming beach is just down the road.) On the north shore, close to *Carambola* and midway between Christiansted and Frederiksted (phone: 778-2966). Inexpensive.

ST. JOHN

Caneel Bay – Amid the romantic ruins of an 18th-century sugar mill, this celebrated Rockresort property sprawls over rolling hills, with 7 beaches. Most of the 171 quietly luxurious rooms (no phones, no TV) are within steps of the beach. Peter Burwash International tennis; good food, good service, and peaceful nights. Exclusive, fashionable, and *very* conservative. Good buys on summer packages. Rates include all meals (phone: 776-6111; 800 223-7637). Very expensive.

Virgin Grand Beach – The first new hotel to be built on St. John in 30 years has 264 rooms, suites, and townhouses perched on a wooded hillside just outside Cruz

Bay. Enormous pool, excellent beach, tennis, water sports, private boat to St. Thomas. Rates include 3 meals a day. Lovely and modern (phone: 776-7171; 800 223-1588). Very expensive.

Cinnamon Bay – Back to the basics, for island lovers on a limited budget: tents and cottages with cooking gear, commissary, cafeteria, and bathhouses, as well as bare sites on a beachside campground owned by the National Park Service and managed by Rockresorts. Dive packages and National Park snorkeling instruction and hikes available. Inexpensive.

Maho Bay Camps – You've never seen anything quite like it. Tents are small canvas houses — with good beds, kitchen areas, refrigerators, reading lights, sun decks — dotting the hillside, with the beach below, and the national park all around. Ecologically sensitive (nonerosive boardwalks, pick-yourself herb gardens), now with expanded water sports, diving programs; simple cuisine at an open-air, island-style restaurant. A truly laid-back escape from the shoppers and cruise ship passengers thronging the other islands; its only drawbacks are the sand flies ("no-see-'ums") and the high price of food staples in the Maho commissary (phone: 776-6240; 800 392-9004). Inexpensive.

ST. THOMAS

Frenchman's Reef – This huge (520 rooms), very modern resort hotel is only 10 minutes from town. Most popular are the 96 luxurious rooms at the *Morning Star Beach Club,* each with a private entrance, tropical decor, balcony, ceiling fans, air conditioning, and many special amenities. The club occupies 5 beachfront buildings, each with its own manager. The resort also offers 6 restaurant choices (*Top of the Reef* is a supper club with entertainment nightly except Sundays; *Tavern on the Beach* is an *al fresco* favorite of island residents), 9 bars, a nightclub (live band and dancing), and 24 duty-free shops. For sports-minded guests, there are 4 lighted tennis courts and pro shop, 2 freshwater pools, and a beautiful beach. Arrangements for 10-minute and half-hour helicopter tours that depart from the grounds can be made at the desk in the hotel lobby. The panoramic ocean view is stunning; the water-sports setup is the island's most extensive. All rooms have color TV, telephone, and radio. Other services include a water taxi into Charlotte Amalie and tour and car rental desks in the lobby (phone: 776-8500; 800 524-2000). Very expensive.

Limetree Beach – The main house is above a pleasantly untrammeled stretch of sand; 84 good-looking contemporary guestrooms (some split-level) line the hill. With water sports, pool, free scuba lessons, free tennis (phone: 776-4770; 800 524-2007). Very expensive.

Mahogany Run – It bills itself as a golf and tennis resort, but golf — on its 18-hole course — is clearly preeminent at this resort condo complex on the northeast side of the island. (Tennis courts currently number only 2.) Its hill-hugging villas, studios to 3 bedrooms, are distinctly posh roosts, with large, breezy rooms, huge balconies, and extraordinary valley or ocean views, even from the shower in the nifty bathroom suite. The 325-acre enclave has 3 swimming pools. About 10 minutes from Magens Bay (no beach on the property), and though resort shuttles make several trips a day there (as well as a daily trip to Charlotte Amalie), a rental car is a good idea. The resort also lays claim to a really first-rate restaurant, the *Stone Farmhouse* (phone: 775-5000; 800-524-2129). Very expensive.

Pavilions and Pools – Unique villas, each with high-walled garden and very private pool. Lounge bar; no restaurant, but each unit has a kitchenette. Near Sapphire Beach (phone: 775-6110; 800 524-2001). Very expensive.

Point Pleasant – A small, secluded world of great charm, quiet style; villas overlooking the sea — all with balconies, many kitchenettes. Good restaurant, swimming pool, pretty beach. Free use of car, tennis court, boats, snorkel gear included in rates (phone: 775-7200; 800 645-5306). Very expensive.

Stouffer Grand Beach – An architectural departure from island-style hotels, making use of dormers, bright red awnings, and French doors, the *Grand Beach* (formerly the *Wyndham Virgin Grand*) took up residence on an inviting stretch of sand called Pineapple Beach early in 1985. When it's all finished, there will be 333 rooms and suites, 6 lighted tennis courts, dock and marina, 2 restaurants, duty-free shops, and a great beachside swimming pool. The rooms, grouped around the pool and terraced up the hillside, are very stylish, though for some reason one of the most attractive room designs does not include a terrace, nor windows that open. Still in the works is a $15-million landscape renovation that will include an iguana preserve and a lobby fountain (phone: 775-1510; 800 822-4200). Very expensive.

Hotel 1829 – This pretty pink building with the green awning and the wrought iron gate — long a landmark in historic Charlotte Amalie — houses a small, utterly charming hotel. Everything about it bespeaks a graciousness that its original owner, a French sea captain, surely intended — a wide, shady verandah for daytime reading, a sunny inner courtyard with a small swimming pool, rooms decorated with taste and imagination, and a very good (though pricey) restaurant. The harborfront rooms are simply splendid: high ceilinged, large, and cooled by sea breezes from the terrace overlooking the harbor (phone: 774-1829). Very expensive to moderate.

Magens Point – On a hill above the famous beach; trim contemporary rooms, pool, tennis courts, water sports at Magens Bay, popular *Green Parrot* restaurant. Close to championship Mahogany Run golf (phone: 775-5500; 800 524-2031). Very expensive to moderate.

Bluebeard's Castle – A historic setting with a terrific view, lush gardens, tennis courts; we're sentimentally attached to the old tower (request room 139 or 140). Near town; not for beach buffs — it has none — but it does provide a saltwater pool and beach transportation (phone: 774-1600; 800 524-6599). Expensive.

Bolongo Bay Beach – Sunny, easygoing, and right on the beach. First-rate scuba setup and extensive water-sports facilities. The management is extremely pleasant; staff is equally accomplished. Interesting evening activities. All 77 rooms have kitchenettes (phone: 775-1800; 800 524-4746). Expensive.

Ramada Yacht Haven – Excellent for sailing buffs, it offers very attractive charter yacht packages from its own private marina, the largest on St. Thomas. Built at the mouth of the cruise ship port, it has 151 rooms, a good-size pool, and evening entertainment (phone: 774-9700; 800 272-6232). Expensive.

Secret Harbour Beach – Suites with expansive sun decks and kitchenettes overlooking Nazareth Bay. Contemporary style. Right on beach with water sports, tennis, restaurant (phone: 775-6550; 800 524-2250). Expensive.

Virgin Isle – Most of the 239 rooms have private terraces; large pool overlooking the harbor, private beach club, tennis and water sports (phone: 774-1500; 800 524-2004). Expensive.

Inn at Mandahl – Tiny place with enormous charm and *Mahogany Run*'s sensational views at roughly half the price. With 8 good-sized attractive rooms, very good restaurant, pool, small beach below; golf, tennis nearby. Far out and quiet, but friendly (phone: 775-2100; 800 223-5608). Moderate.

 EATING OUT: Menus run from genuine, elegant French and Continental to casual deli — with Mexican, Italian, Chinese, American steak and seafood, and a touch of Soul sandwiched between. Original island cuisine is limited but good. Staples are delicious fish (red snapper, dolphin, wahoo, yellowtail, grouper) poached or broiled and served with a choice of sauces (we're partial to the hot lime, but Créole and spicy West Indian do nicely too), and sweet lobster with lemon butter. Fungi (pronounced *foon*-gee), deep-fried dumplings made of cornmeal, is a likely side dish. An alternative main course might be a curry (of conch or lamb or goat) or boiled chicken with vegetables. The best soup around is callaloo, thick with greens and bits of ham and crab, spiced with okra and pepper. For dessert: guava or pineapple tart or soothing soursop ice cream. And the Virgin Islands *vin du pays,* light Cruzan rum, goes along nicely.

One place to get all this together is at a fish fry, a y'all-come superpicnic with music and dancing, "invented" in 1974 by election candidates to rally political support. Election Day passed, but fries stayed on as a favorite island social event. They happen at varying intervals on the beaches of all three islands. Admission, drinks, and food come to about $15 per person, and you really are welcome.

Expect to pay $60 or more for a meal for two (including service) at a restaurant we list as expensive. Moderately priced places run about $30 to $50; inexpensive, less than $30.

ST. CROIX

Barb McConnell's – Run by an extraordinarily entertaining lady with an extraordinarily tasty and inventive repertoire of home-cooked "goodies," many of which (roast beef with sherry onion sauce, deviled crab patty, salmon mousse with horseradish and capers) may be served up on her lunch party plate. More elaborate prix fixe dinners begin with rum punch in the old (1760) vicarage garden. Noon or night, don't leave before the music. And consider yourself extra lucky if the lady has the time or inclination to sit and chat — you'll learn lots about good humor and real style. 45 Queen St., Frederiksted (phone: 772-3309). Expensive.

Queen's Quarter – Gallery overlooking the pool and cool green countryside is elegantly romantic setting for reliably beautiful dinners, thoughtfully prepared and graciously served, from savory callaloo soup and seasoned entrées (try the seafood in newburg-like sauce simmered in a coconut, luscious local lobster) to sweet-tart key lime pie, ethereal cheesecake. Many call it the island's best; it's certainly special. Pleasant lunches, bountiful Sunday brunch too. A short drive from Christiansted (phone: 778-3784). Expensive.

Top Hat – Small, delicious, and one of the best on the island. Superb Danish specialties, pâtés, cheeses, seafood, Cruzan coffee. Open in season only. In Christiansted on Company St. (phone: 773-2346). Expensive.

Club Comanche – A breezy terrace close to Christiansted Harbor. Not all Continental or all native — just some of the best of both, and reliably good. Super callaloo soup (phone: 773-0210). Expensive to moderate.

Frank's – Lovely garden, slightly loony atmosphere, nightly piano and song, make this a happy meeting, eating spot. Homemade pasta, other Italian specialties, steak, and seafood. Queen Cross St., Christiansted (phone: 773-0090). Expensive to moderate.

Royal Dane – The West Indian specialties at this stylish courtyard restaurant are drawing raves from locals, and for good reason. Here the ubiquitous conch fritter takes a light and airy form, punched up with a heady pinch of island spices. The appetizer plate alone is worth a visit: conch fritters, saltfish cakes, spinach cakes, Bajan sea cat (octopus), and breadfruit cake, served with two kinds of sauces. The sophisticated dinner menu blends West Indian curries and Créole and Continental fare, including steak au poivre and rack of lamb. Closed Mondays. Strand St., Frederiksted (phone: 772-2780). Expensive to moderate.

Tivoli Gardens – Prettiest at night when strings of lights twinkle, greenery ruffles in the harbor breeze. Owner Gary Thomson serenades while Martha Sullivan makes award-winning magic in the kitchen. Zesty soups; gazpacho pâté, escargot quiche, are commendable starters; ditto chicken Orientale, steak Diane, lobster main courses, chocolate velvet dessert. Strand St., Christiansted (phone: 773-6782). Expensive to moderate.

Le Bistro Café – The specialty at this eatery is pasta — egg and spinach, fettuccine or spaghetti — all homemade and prepared *Alfredo, marinara, al pesto, al gorgonzola, alla Bolognese,* with hot peppers and garlic, with sausage, with clams, or with a covering of scampi. The portions are generous; the prices, moderate; the staff, friendly; the atmosphere, relaxed. Caravelle Arcade, Christiansted (phone: 773-6757). Moderate.

Donn's – In the *Anchor Inn* with a back porch overlooking Christiansted Harbor. An array of omelettes and fabulous French toast (served with mounds of whipped cream and fresh fruit) make its breakfasts worth waking up for. Dinner is famed for its fresh island lobster; there's a bountiful Sunday brunch too (phone: 773-0263). Moderate.

Kendrick's – An authentic new place in an old Danish home, offering excellent service and attractive decor. Diners enjoy superb angelhair pasta, delicious fresh fish, and enticing appetizers. Queen Cross St., Christiansted (phone: 773-9199). Moderate.

King's Alley Marina Bar & Café – Good, straightforward food. But a major meeting, greeting, and people-watching point at breakfast, lunch, dinner, and especially cocktail time. In- and outdoors on King's Alley, Christiansted (phone: 773-0103). Moderate.

Sprat Hall Plantation – Old island recipes (kingfish in orange sauce, baked breadfruit, chayote) served in the island's oldest continuously lived-in plantation house. Friendly, casual atmosphere; dinner only. North of Frederiksted (phone: 772-0305). Moderate.

Bombay Club – Appetizing snack and salad spot for burgers, nachos, noshes — including addictive deep-fried potato skins, " 'shrooms," and such. Live jazz some nights. 5A King St., Christiansted (phone: 773-1838). Inexpensive.

Brady's – Well-prepared, authentic island dishes, including saltfish, callaloo, and fungi, as well as good seasoned rice. King Cross, Christiansted (phone: 773-2505). Inexpensive.

Hearts of Palm – A sandwich shop with a following, its emphasis is on vegetarian salads (tabouli, Greek, fresh fruit) and sandwiches (vegetarian sub on a whole wheat roll, hummus), but there's a wide variety of sandwiches for carnivores, too. Open weekdays for lunch and early dinner. Hospital St., Christiansted (phone: 778-8005). Inexpensive.

Nolan's Tavern – Local style in an open-air courtyard, with 10 varieties of conch and a celebrated West Indian hot sauce. 3940 Queen Cross St., Christiansted (phone: 773-7885). Inexpensive.

ST. JOHN

Fine dining on St. John is limited to the *Virgin Grand* and *Caneel Bay,* both of which demand jackets and well-endowed wallets, but they are worth it. In Cruz Bay there are a number of native restaurants — *Ric's, Meada's,* and *The Old Gallery,* among others — which offer island food at excellent prices in very informal settings. Two local safari bus drivers, Lucy and Hazel, have even been known to cook island food for visitors in their own homes; ask around at the taxi stand down by the dock. Other reliable eateries include the *Upper Deck,* about 5 minutes from town, and *Ellington's,* out at Gallows Point, both famed for their fabulous sunset views. The *Mongoose* restaurant is sociable and tasty, in the contemporary cool of Mongoose Junction; *The Lime Inn* is a pleasant outdoor spot serving 3 meals daily, with all-you-can-eat shrimp on

Wednesday nights (reservations advised); *World Headquarters,* specializing in seafood, has an open-air rock 'n' roll bar with live music; and *The Fernhouse, Raintree, The Back Yard,* and *Café Roma* are all worth trying.

ST. THOMAS

Au Bon Vivant – Ensconced in a nice old house on Government Hill. French cuisine, with specialties like pepper steak flamed in champagne, and other tours de force. Also luscious hot lemon pie. Ask for a terrace table (phone: 774-2158). Expensive.

L'Escargot – Two versions — the downtown restaurant for lunch, the sub base restaurant for dinner. One of our top choices in St. Thomas — for its excellent French food and cellar to match (phone: 774-6565, 774-8880). Expensive.

Fiddle Leaf – Stylish garden-surrounded pavilion with nouvelle-slanted menu that's refreshing rather than precious. Savory soups (cream of sorrel, carrot and orange, white bean and escarole); shrimp mandarin (with green pepper, peapods) or stuffed with scallop and salmon mousse, daily fish specialty, pecan or raspberry chicken; beautiful four-fruit tart. Even with required reservations you may have to wait; still, it's worth the 20-minute drive from town. Reservations required. At Watergate Villas above Bolongo Bay (phone: 775-2810). Expensive.

Harbour View – In an old Danish manor house high on Frenchman's Hill. Treasured as much for its atmosphere and its view as for its food. All are beautiful. After cocktails on the terrace, eat in the old brick-walled kitchen. Stay around for Irish coffee (phone: 774-2651). Expensive.

Hotel 1829 – The setting is elegant — on the verandah with a view of the harbor or inside this handsome old townhouse — and the food, excellent. Try the beef Albert — raw filet mignon marinated in green peppercorns, olive oil, and herbs, or the pasta with escargots in a white wine and cream sauce. The chef also has a delicious way with island fish and shellfish and Black Angus prime ribs. Reservations required. Dinner only (phone: 774-1829). Expensive.

Frigate at Mafolie – Small hotel terrace with large reputation for charcoal-grilled steaks, lobster, but especially for the view. Dinner only (phone: 774-2729). Expensive to moderate.

Frigate East – Spinoff of Mafolie original, similar menu, simply attractive spot across from Red Hook marina (phone: 775-6124). Expensive to moderate.

Alexander's – Delicious Austrian/German cuisine — wiener schnitzel, roast pork, strudel — in a café setting in Frenchtown (phone: 774-4349). Moderate.

Daddy's – Worth the trip to the island's east end for native food with flair — superior seafood casserole, lobster or conch with lemon and butter, homemade boiled capon. Ask for key lime pie (phone: 775-6590). Moderate.

El Papagayo – Red Hook, the parrot, presides over Mexican tacos, enchiladas, chiles rellenos, mexiburgers (if you must). At Tutu in the garden of Jim Tillett's sugar mill (phone: 775-1550). Moderate.

Piccola Marina Café – This lively open-air restaurant spills right down onto the dock of the Red Hook Marina. Dinner emphasis is on pastas, served hot wtih classic sauces (seafood marinara, pesto, Alfredo) or cold in sometimes unlikely combinations. Also good are steak, fish, and herb-marinated chicken grilled on mesquite and, for appetizers, tasty pâtés and seafood terrines. The lunch menu is nice and light — salads, fruit and cheese plates, and sandwiches (phone: 775-6350). Moderate.

Barbary Coast – Much-frequented, friendly Italian bistro in Frenchtown; prices are especially appealing. Conch parmigiana, veal marsala, minestrone, and mozzarella sticks are popular fare, and there's a special roast beef dinner on Monday nights for football fans, who come to watch the game (phone: 774-8354). Inexpensive.

Drake's Inn – Good spot for a pubby downtown lunch including burgers; hors d'oeuvres served at happy hour. Don't bother with reservations; have a pint at the bar while you wait for a table (phone: 774-9075). Inexpensive.

The Greenhouse – This shady terrace right on the Charlotte Amalie waterfront is a great place to cool off when shopping or sightseeing has taken its toll. Burgers, omelettes, salads, and tall frozen drinks are the specialties (phone: 774-7998). Inexpensive.

VENEZUELA'S CARIBBEAN COAST

If you can envision the long string of Caribbean islands known as the Lesser Antilles as the curling tail of a lizard, whipping in a great arc around the eastern curve of the Caribbean Sea to divide that body of water from the Atlantic, you will see that the tail seems to lead inexorably to Venezuela's 1,750-mile coast on the Caribbean. That's pretty much how the Spanish discovered Venezuela in the early 1500s, by following the chain of greater and lesser islands claimed by Christopher Columbus and the explorers after him. And that's still how many tourists come to Venezuela, on the lookout after repeated visits to the more popular and familiar island spots in the Caribbean.

The Spanish came for gold, but they settled for the coast itself, which in the long run proved a more valuable asset than they could have anticipated. It provided a pickup point for the great wealth that poured from Spain's other New World possessions and a vantage point from which to protect their other Caribbean holdings from the English and French. Tourists today come primarily for Caracas, Venezuela's cosmopolitan capital city nestled in a mountain valley less than an hour from the coast, and Margarita, Venezuela's most popular island possession.

It is possible that Columbus landed on the coast in 1498; the first Spanish landing of record was a year later, across from Margarita Island at what is today the town of Cumana. The coast was hardly enticing: a series of swamps, inlets, jungles, and bays dotted with tiny Indian villages filled with people ravaged by malaria and fever. The Spanish named the country Venezuela — Little Venice — because of the stilt-perched houses of the villages on the shore of Lake Maracaibo. Serious settlement of Little Venice didn't begin for almost 20 years. Initial forays were easy; the coastal Indians offered no resistance, being simply too sick to fight. However, Venezuela's inland mountain tribes put up ferocious fights, and it took years for the Spanish to exercise any kind of real control over the inland.

In 1567 Caracas was settled, acting as an anchor for continuing ventures in the Venezuela–Colombia area. From the beginning, the Spanish were obsessed with the idea of hidden stores of gold in the country. They used conquered Indian tribes — both the coastal Indians and inland peoples — as slaves in mines; and when the empire grew, they imported Africans for slave work. Yet the results were consistently disappointing. Gold flowed into Spain from the mountains of Perú and the central highlands of Mexico, but

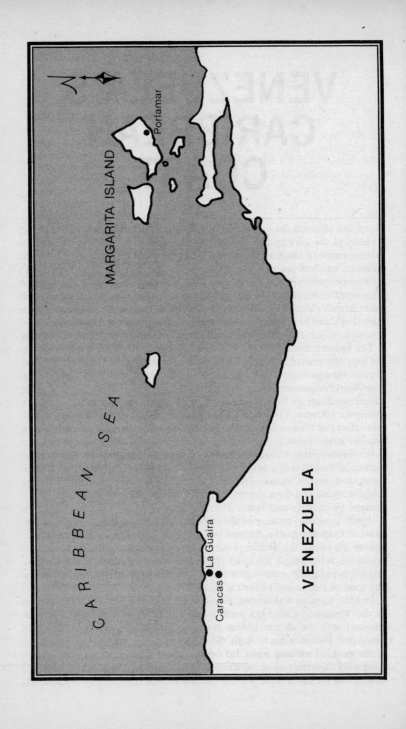

Venezuela remained unproductive. The Crown valued it primarily for the long, northern coast fronting the Caribbean.

Like all of New Spain, Venezuela participated in the wars of liberation that swept Latin America from the time of the American and French revolutions until Spain gave up its New World possessions in 1823. Violent slave rebellions had always been a part of life in the country, but by the beginning of the nineteenth century, the resentment of the dispossessed classes was fed by the frustration of the Créoles — those people of pure Spanish blood born in South America and consistently kept from full participation in the upper echelons of government by the governors of the colony. Between 1805 and 1811 a Créole named Francisco de Miranda led two attempts to take over the Spanish government of Venezuela. When he was finally captured, leadership of the revolt passed to a native Venezuelan who was to be known as the Great Liberator — Simón Bolívar.

Bolívar's wars for the liberation of South America are legendary; he is a figure whose stature equals that of George Washington. Bolívar led troops across the Andes Mountains to capture Bogotá, Colombia, and was responsible for freeing not only Venezuela, but also Bolivia, Colombia, Ecuador, Perú, and Panamá. His dream had been to create a self-governing republic, based on a democratic system, of all those nations — the Republic of Gran Colombia. On June 24, 1821, Bolívar routed the Spanish at Carabobo, and after two years of sporadic fighting, the rest of the invaders were forced to return to Spain. Their surrender was accepted by Bolívar at Puerto Cabello in 1823.

However, Bolívar's grand alliance of freed colonies never happened; the revolution succeeded, but the newly freed colonies did nothing but fight and squabble among themselves. Bolívar retired, crushed, to the estate of some friends in Colombia, and there he died, sick and heartbroken.

The next hundred years were violent and difficult in Venezuela; government changed hands by coup, and the country struggled to build itself into a self-supporting entity. Much of this struggle ended earlier this century when huge stores of oil were discovered at Lake Maracaibo; the political and economic life of the country was stabilized. Today Venezuela is one of the largest exporters of oil in the world and the richest country in South America. Caracas is a sophisticated world capital familiar to thousands of international businesspeople who carry on trade of all kinds there.

Caracas has undergone phenomenal change since the 1950s; where cattle were once driven down a dirt road on the outskirts of the town, today there are freeways and high-rises.

Gold and rumors of gold have played an important part in Venezuela's history, even though it is so noticeably lacking in real stores of the metal. The last gold rush occurred in 1935 when a bush pilot named Jimmy Angel flew a prospector named McCracken into the countryside on a gold hunt. McCracken came out of the wilds carrying $27,000 worth of gold, and the rush was on. One of the most avid hunters was Jimmy Angel, who never found gold, but in the course of his search discovered the highest waterfall in the world. Tumbling some 3,000 feet from the sides of Devil Mountain, hidden for hundreds of years, the falls now bear Jimmy Angel's name.

The real gold in Venezuela isn't gold or even oil; it is the country itself, which, as its cities and economy move toward modernization, struggles to remain a land of forests that have not been flattened and to preserve its shoreline unbesmirched. And the perfect introduction to this complex world is along its Caribbean coast, where everything began.

VENEZUELA'S CARIBBEAN COAST AT-A-GLANCE

FROM THE AIR: The contrasts along Venezuela's 1,750-mile Caribbean coast are startling: sandy beaches, tiny fishing villages, lagoons fed by mountain streams that run down the slopes of the Andes toward the sea, and, just beyond the horizon, uncounted miles of dense jungles interspersed with open plains. Caracas is a valley formed by the southern slopes of the coastal range and the northern slopes of the mountains of the central highlands. To the west, in the plains beyond a spur of the Sierra Nevada range, lies oil-rich Lake Maracaibo, the source of Venezuela's prosperity.

Inland, south of the central highlands (which are parallel to the central section of the Caribbean coast), lie the Llanos of Orinoco, the grassy plains that make up about a third of Venezuela. From here southward the country becomes increasingly mountainous, and patches of jungle begin to mingle with the forests and plains. This area has proven to be rich in gold, diamonds, oil, and many commercially valuable minerals.

Venezuela occupies a central position on South America's northern coast, bordered by Colombia to the west, Guyana and Brazil on the east and south. Its southern border stretches into the Amazon region, and its 352,150 square miles include Bolívar Peak, which rises some 16,000 feet above sea level, and Angel Falls, the tallest waterfall in the world, fifteen times as high as Niagara Falls.

There have been many changes in Venezuela since 1900, and Caracas shows all the marks of its recent and rapid jump into the 20th century. Large sections of the city have been razed to make way for modern high-rise office buildings, and a new subway — the Metro de Caracas — has been inaugurated to help alleviate traffic congestion; yet slums still line the hills above the city — complete with wooden shacks and dirt roads. Of the 20 million residents in Venezuela, roughly 4 million live in Caracas; about half of those 20 million are under the age of 30.

SPECIAL PLACES: Venezuela's Caribbean coast has missed the tourist invasion that has overtaken most of the Caribbean; in the main, its recent development has been inspired by the influx of oil money and international business. As a result, there hasn't been the same emphasis on protecting historical landmarks as in more tourist-conscious countries, nor has there been much development of tourist-oriented amusements.

Caracas – Simón Bolívar is Venezuela's greatest hero, and almost all of the city's notable landmarks pertain to the Great Liberator. In the center of the oldest section of town is the Plaza Bolívar, surrounded by government buildings. In its time, it was the center of all activity in the colony, the site of revolts against Spanish rule and of executions of revolutionaries by the Spanish governors. Today it is principally a meeting place: Under the watchful eyes of the Liberator, mounted on horseback in the 1874 statue, Caraqueños (as residents are called) gather to discuss old news and new ways — topics of interest to the older citizens who have not joined the city in its spectacular leap into the oil-fueled future. On the east side of the plaza stands the city's cathedral, a colonial structure granted cathedral status in 1637. Large sections of the building underwent reconstruction in 1876, after an earthquake.

A block south and west of Plaza Bolívar is the Capitol, easily distinguished by its gold dome. The building was constructed in 90 days in 1873. The interior is filled with paintings of the country's leaders as well as scenes of the Battle of Carabobo, and a formal garden at the rear contains a beautiful fountain. The effect of the cascading waters among the garden plants is worth the visit.

Two blocks south of the Plaza Bolívar, beyond the City Hall, is Casa Natal, the birthplace of Bolívar. The original adobe dwelling was destroyed by an earthquake, and the replacement structure was turned into a stable before being torn down. The present stone building, which houses the font in which he was baptized, his bed, and many excellent paintings by Venezuelan artists depicting the major military campaigns of the War for Independence and other events of the warrior's life, was built in the early 1920s. Directly next door is the Bolívar Museum, which contains the largest collection of the Liberator's war memorabilia ever assembled, including gifts from the Washington family (the two liberators are often thought of together in South America). Both birthplace and museum are two blocks south of Plaza Bolívar, between San Jacinto and Trasposos.

The National Pantheon, just a few blocks north of the Plaza Bolívar, at Plaza Panteón, contains the mortal remains of Bolívar as well as those of other national heroes. There is an open tomb in memory of Francisco de Miranda, whose unsuccessful attempts at freedom gave strength to Bolívar's movement. Miranda died in prison, and this final resting place awaits the body that was never recovered. (*Note:* Both men and women are advised to dress respectfully when visiting the tomb because of the almost religious attitude of Venezuelans toward this particular monument. This dress code should probably be followed when visiting most of the national monuments and historic buildings in Caracas, especially if Bolívar is the honored individual.)

It was in the Church of San Francisco, at the corner of Avenida Universidad and San Francisco, that Simón Bolívar was officially given the title of the Liberator in 1813. Most of the building dates back to 1574, although there are more recent sections, and many of the paintings and hand-carved wooden altars are from the 17th century. Many of Caracas' government buildings are renovated colonial homes that were truly magnificent in their day. To make the architecture of the 16th and 17th centuries the high point of your visit to Venezuela, make a point to see Miraflores Palace at Avenidas Urdaneta and Miraflores.

The palace was the home of Joaquin Crespo and serves as the working offices for the president of Venezuela. Information about touring the building can be obtained by phoning 81-0811; it is well worth the trouble if you have a special interest in architecture. The Museum of Colonial Art, in the former residence of the Marquis del Toro, dates from the 17th century and is also worth a visit at Quinta Anauco, Avenida Panteón, San Bernardino.

Separating Caracas proper from the Caribbean coast and its port town of La Guaira is an arm of the Andes. La Guaira is the working port familiar to any cruise passenger en route to Caracas. However, of much more interest is the beach resort of Macuto, west of La Guaira. The beach facilities of the *Macuto-Sheraton* are available for public use, and so are the public beaches. Other beaches worth visiting are within a stone's throw of Puerto La Cruz, where another hotel in the Spanish Melia chain can provide resort comforts or you can enjoy the extensive and impressive tourist complex of *Doral Beach*. To the west of the Litoral, the cays of Morrocoy National Park are idyllic for scuba diving, snorkeling, fishing, and bird watching.

Margarita Island – Floating in the Caribbean Sea, just 20 miles north of the coastal town of Cumana, is this weekend getaway spot popular with Caraqueños for its beautiful beaches (the best are on the northeast coast and the southern tip). Most activity centers around the port area of Porlamar, on the southeast coast, where duty-free shops abound — especially along the new strollers-only shopping mall.

Margarita is really two odd little islands joined Siamese-fashion by a long, narrow spit of land that forms the north side of a central lagoon, La Restinga. The curvature of the two islands forms the narrow mouth of the lagoon to the south, and pearl-bearing oysters line the bottom. It's a perfect spot for fishing or just drifting, but pearl fishing season is from December through March, and the lagoon is prime ground. The lagoon is also a refuge for the rare *ibis escarlata* — a heron with flaming red feathers.

La Asunción, the capital of this island-state, contains several colonial buildings and the Castle of Santa Rosa. On the small island of Cubagua are the ruins of the Spanish settlement Nueva Cadiz, which was destroyed by a tidal wave in the 1500s. However, its beaches, its quiet, isolated lagoons and inlets, and its fishing and other water sports are the island's real attraction.

ELSEWHERE IN VENEZUELA

Colonia Tovar – Less than 2 hours from Caracas, you will suddenly find yourself in 19th-century Bavaria in the village of Colonia Tovar, which was built by German immigrants in the 1840s. Entering the village is like walking into a different era. The town is filled with handicrafts and local history. There is a small museum (hours vary) devoted to the village's past: from the handful of settlers who decided to establish this remote community, through its early years as a totally independent, self-sufficient, and isolated village, to the building of the road (1955) that made the town accessible to travelers. Much of the German culture brought by these settlers survives today, although it is rapidly giving way, as are most of the established Venezuelan ways, to the growing trend toward an international, ultra-modern culture. For some of the older tastes, try the *Freiburg,* or *Selva Negra* for German-type beer, and maybe some sauerbraten or wurst.

■**EXTRA SPECIAL:** For those who really want to escape the cares and pains of civilization and are willing to endure a little discomfort, there is *Canaima/Angel Falls.* The area is inaccessible except by plane, and the landing strip is small. Avensa has set up an encampment on the edge of a magnificient lagoon, with its own roaring arc of falls. Cabins have electricity and running water; and there's an attractive outdoor restaurant and bar. A red sand beach, boats, and jungle walks provide diversion. The falls themselves can be viewed by air on the incoming or departing flight, weather permitting, and are a sight never to be forgotten. They are 3,212 feet high — fifteen times the height of Niagara and two and a half times as tall as the Empire State Building.

Although the civilized world did not learn of them until 1935, the Indians have known and worshipped the falls since prehistory, although religious awe and the swirling mists and strange rainbows surrounding them kept the early people at a distance.

Jimmy Angel, the pilot for whom these falls are named, was hired in 1928 to fly a prospector named McCracken into the jungle and back. On his return McCracken carried 20 pounds of gold estimated to be worth $27,000. It took Angel until 1935 to locate the area again, and although he never found the source of McCracken's gold, he did discover the falls (which had been so shrouded in mist that Angel had never seen them while in the area with McCracken).

From the base camp to the falls themselves is a three-day journey by jeep, canoe, and foot through virgin forest. The Venezuelan government has plans to develop the area, but not immediately. If you spend only 48 hours on the entire South American continent and in the Caribbean area, this is the best way to spend those few hours. There is nothing yet discovered on our earth that matches the splendor of these falls, as the river tumbles over the edge of Devil Mountain and crashes down a sheer drop of 3,000 feet past layers of multicolored rock, and then on to the seven lower falls of La Hacha, before creating the calm lagoon that washes the beaches of the encampment. This is the high plateau in the jungle, the raised savannah with rivers of gold and natural barriers to explorers, that was the model for Arthur Conan Doyle's *Lost World* locale. It is unforgettable.

SOURCES AND RESOURCES

 TOURIST INFORMATION: The Venezuelan Government Tourist and Information Center, 7 E 51st St., 2nd Floor, New York, NY 10022 (phone: 212-355-1101), will supply brochures and information on accommodations, attractions, and flights as well as answers to any questions.

The Corporation de Turismo de Venezuela, the government tourist bureau, is on the seventh floor of the Edifico Central Capriles on the Plaza Venezuela in Caracas (phone: 782-5911). There is a branch office at Simón Bolívar International Airport in Maiquetia (phone: 55-27-47, 55-10-60). Officials will answer all questions and provide literature as well as make hotel reservations.

Local Coverage – *What's Doing in Venezuela,* a quarterly magazine for visitors, gives facts on events, shopping, sightseeing, and is available at newsstands and bookstores for $1.50. There are eleven daily newspapers, only one of which, the *Caracas Daily Journal,* is published in English. Both the *New York Times* and the *Miami Herald* make their way to newsstands in the larger hotels (usually two days later).

 ENTRY REQUIREMENTS: All tourists must have a tourist card, issued by the Venezuelan consulate, or by airlines serving Venezuela, upon presentation of a valid passport. A passport, tourist card, and return or ongoing ticket are required for entry into the country. But since regulations are prone to change, it's a good idea to confirm requirements when you begin travel planning.

 CLIMATE AND CLOTHES: Although Venezuela is a tropical country, weather is almost entirely dependent upon altitude. At 3,400 feet, Caracas has one of the finest climates in the world, an eternal spring that requires light wraps in the evening. In the warm zone — from sea level to about 2,000 feet — temperatures range from the upper 70s (20s C) to the 90s (30s C). The rainy season is from May through November; regardless of the season, bring raincoats and warm sweaters, or ponchos if you're thinking of traveling into the mountains. Otherwise, summer resortwear is universally accepted all year; no-iron polyester-cotton blends are recommended. Caracas tends to be fashionable, and women dress smartly for daytime and evening, though not necessarily in long formal gowns. Jackets are usually required for men.

 MONEY: The monetary unit is the bolivar, written and called the B. The fluctuating exchange rate is about 30Bs to the US dollar or about 3¢ at press time. Traveler's checks and major credit cards are accepted by most hotels, restaurants, and stores. Banking hours are 8:30 to 11:30 AM and 2 to 4:30 PM weekdays; closed Saturdays, Sundays, and holidays.

 LANGUAGE: Spanish is the official language of the country, although English is generally understood and spoken in the hotels, restaurants, and shops of cities like Caracas, which attracts an international group of travelers. In the rural areas, English is not spoken (or understood) by most natives.

Venezuelans are friendly and helpful, and with the aid of a phrase book and some basic gestures, you should get along.

 TIME: Venezuela is on Atlantic Standard Time. While New York is on Eastern Standard Time, Caracas is 1 hour later than New York. During Daylight Saving Time in New York, the two cities are on the same time.

 CURRENT: Electricity is 110 volts, 60 cycles, AC, the same as in North America.

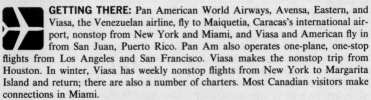 **GETTING THERE:** Pan American World Airways, Avensa, Eastern, and Viasa, the Venezuelan airline, fly to Maiquetia, Caracas's international airport, nonstop from New York and Miami, and Viasa and American fly in from San Juan, Puerto Rico. Pan Am also operates one-plane, one-stop flights from Los Angeles and San Francisco. Viasa makes the nonstop trip from Houston. In winter, Viasa has weekly nonstop flights from New York to Margarita Island and return; there are also a number of charters. Most Canadian visitors make connections in Miami.

La Guaira, Puerto Cabello, and Margarita Island are popular cruise ports for ships sailing from Miami, New York, and various West Coast departure points.

 CALCULATING COSTS: Luxury city and resort hotels in the Caracas area run from $40 to $100 for a double room. There is no off-season in Venezuela. Restaurants have a reputation for high prices, but this has changed somewhat since devaluation. Meals can be had for less than $30 (without drinks or wine), but expect to pay a minimum of $12 to $25 for a good to excellent meal for two. There is a departure tax of 17Bs (about $1) at the airport.

 GETTING AROUND: Taxi – Caracas cabs are metered. The minimum charge in Caracas is about 50¢, and 75¢ to $2 should take you any place in the city. The 12-mile trip to the city of Caracas from the airport costs between $5 and $7.50. From the airport to the Macuto resort area is about $6, and on the island of Margarita the trip into Porlamar from the airport is about $5. Taxi drivers do not expect a tip except when they carry luggage, in which case about 4 to 5Bs is standard for a couple of bags, more if the driver has been especially helpful.

Taxi sightseeing tours with English-speaking drivers are available and are best arranged through any hotel. The government has an official list of rates for this service, and you should be sure you are being charged according to its dictates. Typical rates for up to five people: full-day tour of Caracas from the *Macuto-Sheraton* hotel, about $30; a full-day tour of Margarita Island, about $20.

Metro – Operational between the west of the city and Chacaito since the early 1980s, it's by far the fastest and easiest way to get to the center of town. Fare is about 10¢.

Bus – Caracas buses come in various colors, which indicate the routes they serve, and can take you to almost any part of the city for about 5¢; however, they have been largely superseded by the Metro and minibuses. They are usually crowded, and you need a basic knowledge of the city and Spanish. From Macuto to Caracas takes 45 minutes and costs about 30¢.

Públicos – Jitneys, called por puestos, are minibuses that pick up and discharge passengers along designated routes through Caracas. Most of the city can be reached for about 8¢ to 15¢, but here, also, it is necessary to know Spanish and your way around.

Car Rental – The roads in Venezuela are very good, and the gasoline is very inexpensive. Almost every major rental company is represented here. *Hertz* has offices at Simón Bolívar Airport in Caracas, on the island of Margarita, and in a number of smaller cities. *National Car Rental* has offices at the airport, in Caracas, and at the airport on Margarita Island. *Budget Rent-A-Car* has locations in Caracas and on Margarita Island. Local agencies include *Fiesta Car Rentals,* in Caracas. Rental rates vary according to make of the car, and the source, but figure about $15 to $25 a day with limited mileage, plus gas. Insurance may be included. A credit card will be required. US and Canadian driver's licenses are valid for drivers over 18. Rush hours in and around Caracas can be devastating and should be avoided (7 to 9 AM, noon to 2 PM, and 4 to 7 PM).

Sightseeing Bus Tours – There are many tour operators in Caracas, and most offer similiar trips for about the same prices, although each has a favorite or exclusive outing. Let your hotel desk make the arrangements for you, or call 572-5041 for an excellent range of sightseeing and shopping tours. Tours in and around Caracas average about $7.50 to $20. A full-day tour to Colonia Tovar costs about $20, a two-day trip to Angel Falls and Canaima, about $9.

Ferry Services – The ferry to Margarita Island leaves from both Cumana (3 hours) and Puerto La Cruz (4 hours) twice a day, depending on the traffic. Rates are about $7.50 per person and $13 per car. The service is run by *Consolidada de Ferrys,* Av. Casanova con Las Acacias, Torre Bauoriente PB, Sabana Grande, Caracas (phone: 781-3866 or 782-8544 for current sailing information). In Porlamar, on Margarita, the firm is opposite the *Bella Vista* (phone: 61-63-97).

Local Air Services – Venezuela has some 287 airports at last count, including some small landing strips in the far reaches of the jungle and eight international airports. It's a big country, and all of it is served by the country's domestic carriers, *Avensa* and *Aeropostal.* Especially interesting among its package offerings is a two-day excursion to Angel Falls and Canaima for about $90 per person. The flight to Margarita Island is about $25 round-trip from Maiquetia's Simón Bolívar Airport. Avensa has an office in Caracas, Av. Universidad, Edf. 29-Esquina El Chorro (phone: 562-3022). *Linea Aeropostal* is in Porque Central (phone: 509-3666).

SHOPPING: The coast's selection of tipico handcrafts is wider, cheaper. Margarita Island's duty-free zone has the best buys in liquor, perfumes, and gold and silver jewelry. Still, Caracas' shopping scene is worth a go-round for the people-seeing and style-sampling in its unique collection of super-sleek centers and malls. *Centro Ciudad Comercial Tamanaco, Paseo Las Mercedes, Unicentro El Marques, Centro Comercial Concresa, Centro Comercial Chacaito,* and *Centro Plaza* not only showcase all the latest Venezuelan/international lifestyle luxuries, but shelter dozens of restaurants and night spots that serve as social meeting and greeting grounds, too. *Centro Ciudad Comercial Tamanaco* is the smartest in fashion sense and is also notably endowed with eating and entertainment possibilities.

TIPPING: Tipping is widespread in Venezuela. As a general rule, add 10% of bill. Leave more if you think your waiter has been especially attentive, and even if service has been so-so, leave a tip. Although it is not necessary, you may tip taxi drivers; the bellboy should get about 5Bs to 10Bs for his help.

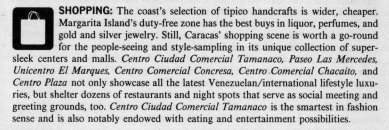

SPECIAL EVENTS: *Carnival* takes over parts of Venezuela, with dancing in the streets, costumes, and parades for the two days and nights before Ash Wednesday. And Caracas virtually closes down during *Holy Week.* All of the major Roman Catholic holidays are observed, plus the *Declaration of Independence* (April 19), *Labor Day* (May 1), *Anniversary of the Battle of Carabobo*

(June 24), *Independence Day* (July 5), *Bolívar's Birthday* (July 24), and *Columbus Day* (October 12).

SPORTS: Baseball – The Venezuelan season runs during the US off-season — October through February — and it is the same game. Games at the University City Stadium are played at night, except for afternoon games on Sundays and Mondays. Reserved seats are about $2.

Boating – Day coastal cruiser tours are available at around $50, including food and drink.

Bullfights – Traditional Sunday afternoon bullfights are held at the Plaza de Toros Nuevo Circo. Normally tickets cost about $5 for seats in the sun, $10 for shaded areas, but if there's a big-name fighter on the bill, seats can go up to $15.

Golf – Your hotel can arrange for you to use the course at the *Valle Arriba, Junko, La Lagunita,* or *Caracas Country* clubs. Greens fees start at about $15; caddies and club rental (if available) are extra. The *Macuto-Sheraton* and *Melia* have a standing arrangement regarding the 9-hole course at the *Caraballeda Golf Course,* and the *Tamanaco* has a similiar tie-in with the *Valle Arriba Golf Course* (18 holes).

Horse Racing – *La Rinconada* holds races Saturdays and Sundays; post time is 1:30 PM. Evening races, beginning at 5 PM, are held on the first Thursday of each month in Valencia. Admission is free; minimum bets are 25¢. Check the local papers for details.

Snorkeling and Scuba – The cays of Morrocoy provide the best reefs, or Cubagua Island from Margarita Island. Trips must be organized independently, however.

Sport Fishing – Chartering a cruiser for fishing, complete with crew, drinks, lunch, and all the needed gear, for up to six people, will cost between $100 and $175 a day at *Marina Mar* alongside the *Sheraton* (phone: 52-7097). Rates on Margarita are similar, but again, with the recent growth on the island, some operators find craft idle, and are willing to go out for less. Shop around the Porlamar waterfront for the best deal on any given day.

Swimming and Sunning – Venezuela's Caribbean coastline provides fine beaches for swimming and lazing in the sun. Just a short drive from Caracas, or a quick hop over the coastal mountains, will put you at the Litoral, as the entire beach area is called. The beach at Macuto, Caracas' favorite weekending place, is not remarkable. But there are appealing sands and facilities at Caraballeda, Catia La Mar, La Bahia, Playa Grande, Camuri Chico, Camuri Grande, Naiguata, and Chichiriviche. Margarita Island, just 18 miles from the coast town of Cumana, is literally surrounded with magnificent beaches.

Tennis – Arrangements can be made at the Caracas *Hilton, Macuto-Sheraton,* the *Melia Caribe,* or the *Tamanaco* for nonguests for nominal fees. Courts are on a guest-preference basis.

Windsurfing – On Margarita, the *Concorde* provides water sports facilities, but one should confirm the details beforehand, as they can be a bit hit and miss.

NIGHTLIFE: The best thing about Caracas after dark is its restaurants, which are numerous and excellent (see *Eating Out*). There are frequent plays and concerts at the new *Teresa Correño Arts Complex.* Since there is no English-speaking theater to speak of, as in most Latin countries, additional choices are limited to bars and discos that sometimes admit only couples (no singles of either sex). Though the capital's attitude toward women has been liberated somewhat in recent years, many latinos still labor under the impression that nice girls don't go out after dinner, or even for dinner, unescorted. Many restaurants don't hold with this point of view (check with the concierge) and there are ways around it (like a party of several women escorted by one male), but, unfortunately, women traveling alone will still feel more comfortable in hotel dining rooms and bars. In resorts, a jacket and tie are not often required; in Caracas, however, a suit or jacket for men is often mandatory. In the city, drinks can be expensive — so keep the running tab in mind to avoid embarrassing finales. Some of the livelier options:

Le Club and *La Eva* in Centro Chacaito; *La Mirage* and *Magic* in Las Mercedes; *New York, New York, 1900 My Way,* and the *Seasons Club* in Ciudad Tamanaco; *The Place* in Altamira; and *Rainbow* in Centro Bello Campo are all hot disco spots. Where membership is required, tourists wearing jackets and ties can usually enter by presenting a passport.

Boite-like *Montmartre,* full of French atmosphere, in the near suburb of Baruta, is an old favorite for more romantic dancing. *La Cota 880,* high up on the *Hilton*'s 15th floor, offers two orchestras, continuous dancing, and an incredible view. After dinner, *Dukes Pub,* and *Crystal Club* are worth checking out.

At the *Juan Sebastian Bar,* live jazz starts cooking at about 9:30, and from the first note, the place is crowded with singles, couples, and jazz lovers in general. *La Barra* and *Gala* in Las Mercedes do their jazz bit, too.

For female companionship, try *Club El Gato, Tiburo, Palacio Imperial,* and the Sabana Grande district. Have a drink while you decide which lady to approach. All these places will be filled, and most of the crowd will be professionals.

BEST ON THE COAST

 CHECKING IN: Hotel and resort prices in Venezuela are not subject to the seasonal fluctuations that are the rule throughout the Caribbean. However, Caracas is primarily a business center, so prices at the best hotels, though not up to those of the most luxurious Caribbean resorts, can be steep. And reservations are recommended. (There is a hotel reservation center at the airport if you should arrive without reservations; phone: 031-55-27-47, 031-55-25-99.) Expect to pay $40 to $100 or more for a double room in the hotels listed below as expensive; $20 to $35 in those listed as moderate; and under $20 in those listed as inexpensive.

CARACAS

Caracas Hilton International – A very modern hotel designed for North American visitors in luxurious fashion. Features *La Cota 880* nightclub on the 15th floor and a wide variety of other facilities. El Conde District (phone: 571-2322). Expensive.

Tamanaco – One of the finest in South America, with both resort and city hotel assets. An excellent nightclub, several bars with city views, pool, tennis, gym, sauna, every conceivable service. Av. Principal de Las Mercedes, Las Mercedes District (phone: 91-45-55). Expensive.

CCCT – Smack in the bustling Centro Ciudad Comercial Tamanaco, it offers a swimming pool, tennis, sauna, and gym, as well as restaurants and bars. Entrance Sotano 1 (phone: 92-62-22). Expensive.

Paseo – Its 197 guestrooms are pleasant, with spectacular views of mountains and valley, but its public rooms are just there. With pool, three restaurants, nightly entertainment. And it sits smack-dab on top of one of the city's best multilevel shopping centers — Paseo Las Mercedes — which is almost enough reason for checking in. Tamanaco District (phone: 91-04-44). Expensive.

Avila – Small by the standards of the *Hilton* or *Tamanaco,* but quite nice, and just far enough outside the city to have a little space of its own and a pool. Av. Jorge Washington, San Bernardino District (phone: 51-51-55). Moderate.

Crillon – Neither as classy as the *Tamanaco* nor as flashy as the *Hilton,* this is a substantial, comfortable, modern (but not too modern) establishment near the Sabana Grande shopping district. Most accommodations are two-room suites, complete with refrigerator and TV. Almost all have terraces. Av. Libertador and Av. Las Acacias (phone: 91-04-44). Moderate.

El Condor – Next to the *Metro* in Chacaito, this relatively new hotel, with restaurant and bar, has established itself rapidly. Av. las Delicias de Sabana Grande (phone: 72-99-22). Moderate to inexpensive.

Dallas – A small, new hotel with restaurant and bar. Conveniently located, close to Chacaito and Las Mercedes. Calle Guaicaipuro, El Rosal (phone: 951-3727). Inexpensive.

MACUTO

Macuto-Sheraton – The beach area of Macuto is only 20 miles from the city, and this hotel overlooks its beautiful rocky shoreline, although it does have sandy beachfront also. There is a yacht club next door and the Caribbean at its back door. Caraballeda (phone: 031-91801/17). Expensive.

Melia Caribe – A link in the famous Spanish chain, it boasts fascinating indoor architecture; much swanker and sleeker, more tropical and original than the *Sheraton* next door. Set in beautiful gardens with pool, water sports, sauna; tennis courts and golf privileges in the neighborhood (guests supply own transportation). With a wide variety of bars and restaurants; disco, too (phone: 031-92-40-11). Expensive.

Las Quince Letras – One of the older seaside hotels in the area, with an excellent seafood restaurant, near the beach. Av. La Playa, Macuto (phone: 031-45821). Moderate.

MARGARITA ISLAND

Margarita Concorde – Towering over a sweep of beach on this simple, sandy island, its 517-room bulk is overpowering. Inside, you could be anyplace in the convention-hotel world. It does promise all sports, marina, day and night tennis, "international entertainment." In winter, it offers charter-flight packages (phone: 095-61-3333). Expensive.

Bella Vista – Central and relatively modern, it has a disco as well as a bar and restaurant. Insist on a room in the new wing. Bella Vista Section (phone: 095-61-8264, 61-4831). Moderate.

Club Puerto Esmeralda – Rambling low-rise alternative to its taller Porlamar neighbors, a cluster of 105 Spanish colonial cottage suites. By the sands of Playa Moreno with assorted sports, pool, bar, pretty restaurant, disco. Near Pampatar (phone: 095-78-545). Moderate.

 EATING OUT: Excellent in Caracas, with several superior choices in every cuisine category. Expect to pay $20 to $25 for two at one of the restaurants listed below in the expensive category; from $15 to $18 in our moderate range; and under $15 for two at a restaurant listed as inexpensive. Prices don't include drinks, wine, or tips. Eating outside the capital generally costs less.

CARACAS

La Bella Epoque – Elegantly French, with particularly piquant appetizers (sopa de pesca, artichoke, asparagus), classic main courses. Closed Sundays. In Edificio Century on Av. Leonardo da Vinci (phone: 752-1342). Expensive.

Gazebo – Lutèce-away-from-home. Terribly costly, terribly chic, and absolutely delicious. Try the pargo champagne (red snapper), crêpe Gazebo. Dress the part, and reserve ahead. Closed Sundays. Av. Rio de Janeiro (phone: 92-55-68). Expensive.

Altamar – Sophisticated selection of seafood matched by international wine list. Tercera Transversal between Av. Avila and Av. San Juan Bosco (phone: 261-9765). Expensive to moderate.

La Atarraya – One of the few truly classy restaurants in the city's center; ergo a great favorite with governmental elite. Traditional *criollo* menu; *pabellon* (shredded beef, beans, rice, plantains), *cazon* (ground shark meat), natilla cheeses with *arepas* (corn cakes), house sangria are highlights. Esquina de San Jacinto (phone: 545-8235). Expensive to moderate.

La Cava del Barrilito – Small elegant restaurant specializing in Hungarian and French cuisine. Live music. Closed Sundays. Centro Plaza (phone: 283-37-42). Expensive to moderate.

Da Emore – Graceful modern setting (lots of mirrors, velvet), very good antipasto, excellent pasta pleasingly presented. Prix fixe and à la carte menus. In Centro Comercial Concresa (phone: 979-3242). Expensive to moderate.

L'Inferno – Aphrodisiac atmosphere traceable in part to Dantean decor, part to temptations of French/International menu that starts with succulent escargots and carries on from there. Reservations recommended. Calle La Trinidad, La Mercedes (phone: 92-25-02 or 92-45-02). Expensive to moderate.

Tarzilandia – Wrapped in man-planted jungle Edgar Rice Burroughs would have loved, this tropical retreat spotlights turtle specialties (soup, steak), pepper steak, banana flambée finales. Closed Mondays. At the end of Av. San Juan Bosco in Altamira (phone: 261-8419 or 261-0628). Expensive to moderate.

Chocolate – Imaginative interior modeled on a medieval castle, with extensive bar and restaurant at semi-cellar level. Spanish and international menu. Open daily. Av. Tamanaco, El Rosal (phone: 951-3434 or 951-7575). Moderate.

Hereford Grill – This steak house does prime meats to perfection. *Medallón de lomito al Oporto* (steak in port), *pollo deshuasado* Hereford (boned chicken) are special. Calle Madrid (phone: 92-51-27). Moderate.

El Hostal de la Castellana – Don Quixote and Sancho Panza stand guard at the portals of this Spanish stronghold lined with conquistador souvenirs and audible flamenco overtones (the music starts at 8:30 PM). Gazpacho, paella, *pierna cordero castellana* (leg of lamb) are all commendable. Av. Principal at Plaza Castellana (phone: 33-42-60). Moderate.

El Portón – The must on all visitors' restaurant lists: tops for criollo atmosphere and cookery. Try the pabellon, *lomito con queso* (steak with cheese), *hallacas* (leaves stuffed with a mix of cornmeal, meats, olives, and onions), *sancocho* (thick vegetable soup, Sundays only). Spanish colonial setting with tipico Venezuelan music to dine by. Av. Pichincha 18 (phone: 71-60-71). Moderate.

El Bogavante – Fishing inn decor, outstanding marine menu featuring lobster, crab, shrimp, and fresh fish. Reservations recommended. Av. Venezuela (phone: 71-86-24). Moderate.

El Café Naif – Tropical garden setting for good French cuisine and lighter snacks, served from midday to midnight daily; with separate bar. Calle Madrid, Las Mercedes (phone: 752-9298). Moderate.

Dama Antañona – Beautifully converted colonial house, its original rooms intact, it offers a genuine criollo menu. Best at midday for business lunches. Closed Saturdays. Jesuitas a Maturin No. 14 (phone: 83-72-87). Moderate.

Lee Hamilton Steak House – A very American restaurant, founded by a Marylander. Traditional steak and potatoes style; prime ribs too. Good value, agreeable setting. Av. San Felipe (phone: 32-52-27). Moderate.

El Padrino – An Italian restaurant worthwhile for its fascinating decor, full of music and festive feeling. Big, with vast menu and — especially — antipasto selections worthy of Godfatherly gusto. It's a good idea to make reservations. Plaza Sur Altamira (phone: 32-76-84). Moderate.

Shorthorn Grill – Argentine ranch decor; known for super sirloins (*churrascos*), tasty *parrillada mixta* (grilled beef, liver, sausage, kidney); swift and courteous service. Av. Libertador (phone: 71-10-52). Moderate.

Urrutia – The food served here is a blend of Spanish and seafood flavors, for example, *bacalao à la Vizcaina* (cod), *arroz à la marinara, pimientos relleños* (stuffed peppers). Las Delicias (phone: 71-04-48). Moderate.

La Cita – Simply delicious fish and seafood. In Calandria, Caracas' old Spanish section. Esquina de Peligro. Moderate to inexpensive.

ON THE COAST

Timotes – Tastefully decorated in colonial style, it is famous for fine criollo seafood; the sancocho alone is worth the cab ride from Macuto. Pleasant service as well. In the Centro Comercial Cada in Maiquetia (phone: 22-618). Expensive to moderate.

Aimara – Indoor and outdoor patio dining in a delightfully restored colonial house overlooking the sea; seafood and tipico dishes. Near both the *Melia* and *Sheraton* hotels. Av. La Playa (phone: 91-726). Moderate.

Cookery – Informal spot with international flavor — scampi, pasta, steaks, French specialties. Air-conditioned dining room, disco and bar upstairs. Short stroll from the *Sheraton*, on Av. Principal (phone: 91-866). Moderate.

El Portón de Timotes – Younger brother of *Timotes* in Maiquetia. Large, colonial-style, with criollo menu featuring seafood. Near both the *Sheraton* and *Melia*. Av. Principal (phone: 91650). Moderate.

Las Quince Letras – Simply and wonderfully romantic, the restaurant sits right at the edge of the sea, specializes in local seafood (of course) deliciously done. Have drinks upstairs on the balcony to watch the waves and the moonlight; move downstairs for dinner. In the hotel of the same name (phone: 45284). Moderate.

Welcome El Carib – A simple, clean Créole restaurant specializing in seafood and *típico* dishes, it is catching on with day visitors from Caracas to the coast. Within easy waking distance of both the *Sheraton* and *Melia.* Av La Laguna. Inexpensive.

Tomaselli – Everyone's favorite snack source: pizzas, burgers, hot dogs, ice cream, the works. Good breakfasting too. Av. Principal, Caribe (phone: 91-832). Inexpensive.

DIVERSIONS

Introduction

The urgent call of the sea is a voice that few committed sailors, swimmers, or divers can resist, and nowhere in the Western Hemisphere is it stronger than in the islands and coastal regions of the Caribbean Sea, the Bahamas, and Bermuda. Traditionally, vacations in the Caribbean are schizophrenic affairs, with periods of the most intense activity — tacking through clusters of tiny land dots in a strong wind; fighting tarpon or, in deeper water, marlin; following the twisting patterns of a coral reef into the depths — redeemed by the unabashed luxury of beachside do-nothingism, sipping cool drinks in the hot sun, enjoying the latest best-seller unharried by anything more pressing than a date with some suntan oil.

But the islands of the Caribbean are a good deal more than just beaches wrapped around volcanoes and dropped into the sea for the convenience of confessed ocean addicts. The history of the Caribbean is a weltering confusion of languages, influences, and styles and modes of government, and the profusion of cultures and peoples strewn throughout the area seems almost profligate. An embarrassment of riches, the Caribbean is as lushly endowed with manmade leisure activities as it is with those provided by generous nature and a capricious history. When the pleasures of the water begin to pale and even the most devoted sea lover has swallowed enough salt for one day, there are a multitude of other distractions — physical and cerebral — with which to pass the time.

No place could be better suited to the way people travel today. It is typical of contemporary travelers that the urge to get somewhere scratches only part of the travel itch; real satisfaction comes with being able to do something once they are there — practice a favorite sport or master a new one, pursue a familiar hobby or discover a new passion.

But where in all the islands and inlands of the Caribbean can you do it *best,* no matter what the "it" under discussion is? Even if you're content just to lie in the sun and turn brown, you might legitimately ask where among all the beaches in the Caribbean you will acquire the most even glow. DIVERSIONS is our answer to that question. What follows are our choices of the best places in the islands to pursue any of 18 different activities — from finding the best beach to enjoying the islands' best historical collections or most splendid natural wonders. Within each section is all the data needed to organize a theme-oriented trip or to pursue a favorite activity as the highlight of a visit. In each, the emphasis is firmly on the quality of experience, doing what you want to do in the best possible environment.

For the Body

Dream Beaches

Between them, the islands of Bermuda, the Bahamas, and the Caribbean have more of the world's most beautiful sand than any other area on this planet. It's true that — thanks to too many appearances on recurrent Most Beautiful lists — a few have been overdiscovered. But St. Thomas's Magens Bay remains gorgeous, Puerto Rico's Luquillo Beach is still postcard-perfect (and fun), and the Bahamas' Paradise Beach (for which Huntington Hartford renamed the island formerly known as Hog) is as Edenistic as ever — in spite of the crowds each hosts on weekends and cruise ship days.

The fact is that without climbing a soufrière or hibernating in the deep green interior of an island as big as Cuba or Jamaica, it's hard to get away from sandy shores. (The exceptions might be Dominica, which majors in river swimming, and craggy Saba.) Beaches edging settlements include the likes of Staniel Creek and Tarpum Bay, towns like Montego Bay, and capitals like Philipsburg and Oranjestad. Some of the most spectacular — Grenada's Grand Anse, Aruba's Palm Beach, Grand Cayman's Seven Mile Beach, and Veradero in Cuba — are shared by several hotels. And some of the most breathtaking — as long and stunning as *La Samanna*'s swathe of St. Martin *plage*, as naturally perfect as the circle "swimming pool" formed by the beach and reef at Tortola's tiny (4-room) *Smugglers' Cove* hotel — belong in fact or in feeling to a single hotel. Officially designated *au naturel* beaches on the French islands are deliberately secluded — far out on the Pointe des Châteaux on Guadeloupe, over the hill on the Île de Haut, around the next shoreline curve at the *Club Med* and *Club Orient*. Nudist strands at Jamaica's *Hedonism II* and *Couples* resorts are on offshore islands. Caribbean Hideaways (RD 1, Box 294, Bloomingburg, NY 12721; phone: in New York, 212-697-1225; elsewhere, 800-828-9356) arranges island-bound "clothing optional" trips.

You've got all kinds of choices. Caneel Bay has beaches for every day of the week (Honeymoon is the smallest, prettiest). And Antigua has 365, plus a couple more for leap year. In short, there are thousands. And there is no better way to pick a fight or, at the very least, get sand kicked in your face than by joining the ranks of people willing to list the Ten Most Beautiful. So we don't intend to.

The baker's dozen beaches below are not necessarily the *most* anything. They're simply thirteen of our favorites. All but two of them are a bit off the beaten track; each has its particular charms. And they happen to be the ones we dream of in the gray of mukluk season, when northern city streets (and our spirits) are full of slush and we desperately need restoring.

BACK BAY, Tobago: When you are looking for something more secluded than Pigeon Point (a destination for lots of day trips and takeoff point for the Buccoo Reef trips), walk along the cliff west of the *Mt. Irvine Bay* hotel to find a stretch of sand that is even prettier, complete with palm trees, sea grapes, and — usually — complete privacy.

CANE GARDEN BAY, Tortola, British Virgin Islands: Acknowledged to be one of the handsomest stretches (1½ miles) of fine, white beach in all the British Virgins. You have to bring your own snorkel gear, but you can buy a nice island lunch at *Stanley's* or *Rhymer's* on location. Except for a tire-and-rope swing, there is no built-in activity — just sunning, splashing, and feeling pleased you came.

PETITE ANSE, Marie Galante, French West Indies: On the cookie-shaped island a ten-minute flight from Guadeloupe's Le Raizet Airport, this beach is where the Guadeloupais — who consider it their secret — go for their weekend picnics. It's long and gold-colored, with no improvements or facilities except for a simple restaurant called *Touloulou* that serves Creole lunches and lobster in season. No excitement, but real beach buffs will find it worth the trip.

LE DIAMANT, Martinique: With 6½ miles of bright sand facing the landmark HMS *Diamond Rock,* it is a favorite swim-and-picnic destination. Bring snorkel equipment (rented from your hotel), beach towels, and a picnic — maybe langouste with white wine.

GREAT HARBOUR CAY, Great Harbour Cay, Bahamas: One of the handsomest beaches in the Bahamas. Sanibel stoopers note: When the tides are right, there is also superb shelling here.

WARWICK LONG BAY, Bermuda: It *is* long and soft and truly pink and — compared to famous Horseshoe Bay, just down the shore — utterly serene from sun-up to sunset, perfect for private picnicking, lazy sunning, sandcastle sculpture. No changing facilities or "improvements," which may account for its peace and prettiness. Bermudians love it and neighboring Jobson's Cove for late afternoon dips. Just off the South Shore Road in Warwick Parish.

NEGRIL, Jamaica: On the northwestern corner of the island, it's 7 miles of sea-edging sand that for years Jamaicans didn't talk about because they like to do their own relaxing there. Now the focal point of Jamaica's newest resort development, its southern end is dotted with hotels — all very casual. Principal occupations are diving (sites include several interesting wrecks, one antique airplane) and doing nothing. The resort called *Hedonism II* has set aside nudist strands onshore and on Booby Island just offshore. Meanwhile, up at Negril's northern end you can still pretend there isn't a hotel in sight (because there isn't), pull up under a palm, and do your own picnic thing.

PLAYA GRANDE, Dominican Republic: On the newly accessible north shore, site of the country's newest resort development, this sweep of poster-perfect sand is a great place to spend a long, lazy day (bring a picnic, playthings, and maybe a beach umbrella). Next door, Sosua offers a tranquil alternative, a semicircle of beach flanked by the town, whose cafés, shops, small hotels, and friendly atmosphere have made it popular with Canadians, Europeans, and, most recently, Americans. Notable also is the fascinating dairy and cattle-raising colony founded by German and Austrian Jewish refugees in 1940.

POINTE DES CHATEAUX, Guadeloupe: On the east-pointing tip of Guadeloupe's Grande Terre "wing," there are several idyllic sand beaches to choose from; one of them, Pointe Tarare, is dedicated to au naturel bathing, and it's a beauty. Bring a picnic along or call ahead for a lunch reservation at *Chez Jerco* (phone: 88-40-16) or the *Auberge du Grand Large* (phone: 88-20-06) on the beach in nearby St. François.

ST. JEAN, St. Barthélemy: Two adjoining curves of gold sand beach, not wide, slope into water that is beautifully clear and buoyant. In spite of its French-Swedish heritage, this is one island where nude bathing is not only discouraged, it is grounds for arrest. On the other hand, bikinis get very brief. Don't bring a picnic. Instead have lunch at *Chez Francine* right at the edge of the sand — as much for the people watching as for her good steaks and red wine. Unless you make arrangements with a nearby hotel to use its changing facilities, come wearing bathing suits and coverups; there are no dressing rooms on the beach itself.

SHOAL BAY, Anguilla: Stunning, sweeping, silvery, it is literally one of the enormous beauties of this all-but-undiscovered island. And much of the time it's enchantingly empty. The only crowds are offshore and underwater — clouds of iridescent fish that dart about the astonishing coral gardens. The drop-off and reef beyond lure experienced divers. And there are shady trees to laze under when you've had enough sun and sea. But bring *everything* with you — masks, flippers, beach towels, coverups, cool drinks, a picnic; in this paradise, so far, there are no concessionaires.

STOCKING ISLAND, off Great Exuma, Bahamas: Long and skinny and edged with gorgeous soft sand, it stretches along the far edge of George Town's harbor, a short sail or boat ride from wherever you're staying. You can nip across and settle on its faintly pink shore whenever you like. Perfect for picnicking, swimming, snorkeling, snoozing, and snail watching — should one be racing (slowly) along a nearby piece of driftwood. And it goes on. And on. And on. So if you're in an away-from-it-all mood when others arrive, alone-togetherness is a short stroll toward the far horizon.

TRUNK BAY, St. John, US Virgin Islands: Success hasn't spoiled it one iota, thanks to the diligence of the National Park Service rangers who keep watch. Its most famous asset is the underwater trail, with markers to guide you along the reef just off the beach. It's been named one of the Ten Great time and again. A favorite escape destination for *Caneel Bay* guests, it has picnic tables, changing facilities, restrooms, beverage and snack service. Part of the Virgin Islands National Park, and operated for day use only.

Best Depths: Snorkeling and Scuba

Because of the excellence of the snorkeling and diving conditions in the Atlantic and Caribbean islands — rock formations, reefs, wrecks, and the spectacular clarity of the water — most beach hotels rent snorkeling equipment, and most islands have numerous dive shops that not only rent equipment but lead diving excursions and provide day-by-day advice on local conditions.

Just about anyone can use a snorkel, mask, and flippers wherever the water is clear — and in the islands, that is almost everywhere. (If you are exploring coral reefs without fins in shallow water, you should wear sneakers or some other rubber-soled shoe.)

Scuba diving, using the sophisticated system of high-pressure cylinders full of compressed air and a "demand regulator" that balances air flow with water pressure as the diver changes depths, is something else. Handling everyday procedures and emergencies with equal aplomb takes training and practice. Therefore, though you can buy the gear you need at any dive shop, most shops will refill tanks for and rent equipment only to divers who have earned certification — in "Y" courses, which require one or two nights a week for about six weeks, or about a week of resort instruction, partly in a swimming pool and partly in open water. For information, contact: the National Association of Underwater Instructors (NAUI), PO Box 14650, 4650 Arrow Hwy., Suite F1, Montclair, CA 91763 (phone: 714-621-5801); the Professional Association of Diving Instructors (PADI), 1243 E Warner Ave., Santa Ana, CA 92705 (phone: 714-540-7234); or your YMCA. Here are some of the islands' best spots:

ANGUILLA: Sandy Island off Road Bay is reported to be a remarkable snorkeling site. *Tomarion Water Sports* (phone: 7-2461) offers PADI-certified basic and openwater as well as resort scuba classes plus dive, snorkel, and boat trips.

ANTIGUA: The wrecks off Antigua's northeast, southern, and western coasts are the preferred destinations of experienced scuba divers. Certified divers can rent equipment at several hotels including *Curtain Bluff, Half Moon Bay,* and *Halcyon Cove. Dive Antigua* (phone: 2-0256) offers one-tank day and evening diving trips for about $30, including equipment and guide. The waters off Barbuda, 32 miles north of Antigua, also provide excellent diving grounds, strewn with wrecks.

For snorkeling, most hotels have fins and masks available free or for a small fee. The special lure of the waters off Antiguan beaches is that they are rather calm, suffer no heavy breakers or dangerous undertow, but still boast an abundance of reefs. It's as close to paradise as most snorkelers ever come.

ARUBA: Divers can see a variety of coral, lacy seafans, and multicolored fish in Aruba's waters, which have a visibility of up to 100 feet. *De Palm Water Sports* (phone: 24400; 24545) and *Pelican Watersports* (phone: 2-3888) operate hotel concessions on the island, with prices ranging from $48 for a beginners course to $14 for 1-hour snorkeling trips.

BAHAMAS: The incredible clarity of the water and the amazing variety of marine life make the Bahamas superb for both snorkeling and scuba diving. Most beach hotels have snorkeling equipment available for rent or loan, and scuba equipment and instruction can be found on a number of the Bahamas' best diving bases.

Freeport/Lucaya – Probably the best instruction anywhere is offered here at the *Underwater Explorers Society* (phone: 373-1244), where scuba lessons include simulated reef dives in an 18-foot tank. They also arrange dive trips to such sites as Treasure Reef, the Wall, Black Forest Ledge, and the Caves.

Andros Island – The Andros Barrier Reef, the world's third largest, is the best diving spot; *Small Hope Bay Lodge* (near Fresh Creek, phone: 368-2015) arranges diving trips and offers both certified dive instruction and underwater photography courses. More experienced divers can explore the reef's deep outside drop-off and Blue Holes.

Nassau/Paradise – There are numerous reefs, wrecks, and coral strands off these two adjoining islands, and certified instruction and equipment can be obtained at most hotels. *Bahama Divers* (phone: 322-8431) and *Underwater Tours* (phone: 326-5644) offer certified instruction, trips, and have concessions at major hotels.

BARBADOS: The coral reefs off the west coast and the Folkestone National Marine Reserve at Holetown are popular with divers. Many island hotels offer diving and snorkeling facilities, as do *Willie's Water Sports* and *Heywood's* (phone: 425-1060) and *The Dive Shop* (phone: 426-9947 or 426-2031 at night).

BELIZE: Another area adopted relatively recently by mostly experienced divers. Off Ambergris Caye, snorkeling and scuba are splendid, but lodging and equipment are primitive; compressors and certified guides, rare. Not for first-timers; bring gear.

BERMUDA: Snorkeling is popular off most of Bermuda's best-known beaches, with equipment available from hotels, guesthouses, or rental shops. For scuba diving trips and/or instruction, check with *South Side Scuba* at the *Sonesta Beach* (phone: 238-1833; after 5 PM, 236-0394); *Dave McLeod's Skindiving Adventures* (phone: 234-1034) at Somerset Bridge; or with *Nautilus Diving* at the *Southampton Princess* (phone: 238-2332). They'll take you diving to explore the reefs that surround the island for about $60 per person for a half day. If you aren't an experienced or even an aspiring diver, try *Hartley's Under Sea Adventures* (phone: 234-2861) or *Hartley Helmet Diving Cruise* (phone: 292-4434), which will give you a helmet and take you walking on the sea floor near Flatts Inlet for about $28 per person for 3½ hours.

BONAIRE: Newly "discovered" and hailed for its wealth (c. 50) of spectacular sites within paddling distance of shore (no long boat trips). "Cap'n Don" Stewart, local diving dean, operates *Habitat* (phone: 8290; US reservations, 800-223-5581 or 212-535-9530) from his own spartan but cheerful *Habitat* dive resort. Peter Hughes's first-rate *Dive Bonaire* (phone: 8285) has its headquarters at the *Flamingo Beach* hotel. *Bonaire Scuba Center* at the *Bonaire Beach* hotel (phone: 8978) and Bruce Bowker of the *Carib Inn* (phone: 8819) are also fine. Year-round budget-priced charter packages offset the island's remote location. You can book or get additional *Dive Bonaire* information by toll-free phone (607-277-3484; in the US and Canada, 800-367-3484); for *Bonaire Scuba Center* information, call 201-566-8866 in New Jersey; 800-526-2370 elsewhere.

BRITISH VIRGIN ISLANDS: Snorkeling at Virgin Gorda around The Baths is excellent, as is the dive site called The Indians, near Peter and Norman islands. Marina Cay and Cooper Island have good snorkeling from their beaches. Anegada Island, just off the Anegada Reef, site of more than 300 shipwrecks over the years, has excellent scuba diving and snorkeling. The island is only 28 feet above sea level and is the only coral island in the Virgins chain (the rest are volcanic). An amazing variety of fish life can be seen within the decaying wreck of the *Rocus.* Other wrecks to look for include the *Paramatta* and the *Astrea.* The most spectacular dive in the islands is the wreck of the *Rhone,* which was featured in the film *The Deep;* it is now a British National Monument. The *Rhone* sank in a hurricane in 1867, in waters that range from 20 to 80 feet deep, off the western point of Salt Island, near Road Town, Tortola.

BVI firms provide diving services, organize tours, give lessons, and rent equipment. Among the best are *Baskin in the Sun* (phone: 4-2858/9) and the *Prospect Reef* (phone: 4-3311) and *Treasure Isle* (phone: 4-2501) hotels, Road Town, Tortola (information for all three: in the US, 800-233-7938). Another source is *Dive BVI,* Virgin Gorda Yacht Harbour (phone: 5-5513).

CAYMAN ISLANDS: Coral reefs, brilliantly colored marine life, and many shipwrecks quite close to the surface make the waters around all the Cayman Islands one of the world's most spectacular places for snorkeling as well as scuba diving by beginners and advanced divers alike. Snorkeling equipment is readily available at most hotels, where scuba trips are also arranged, but no diver can rent scuba gear or air unless certified. Instruction, as well as equipment, is available at *Cayman Kai* (phone: 7-9491), *Bob Soto's Diving* (phone: 9-2022 or 9-2483), *Sunset Divers* (phone: 9-5966), *Surfside Water Sports* (phone: 7-4224), *Don Foster's Dive Grand Cayman* (phone: 9-5679), *Nick's Aqua Sports* (phone: 9-1234), and *Treasure Island Divers* (phone: 9-7777).

DOMINICAN REPUBLIC: Superb underwater scenery can be found at La Caleta, where there are miles of caves, coral reefs, and fissures, some of which are more than 40 feet deep. Most of the hotels offer snorkeling equipment, and certified divers can rent scuba gear from *Mundo Submarino* (phone: 566-0340), which operates half-day and full-day trips.

GRENADA: The submerged reef that parallels most of the island's west coast is the point of attraction for snorkelers and divers here. Trips can be arranged through the *HMC Diving Centre* (phone: 440-2508/2883) or the *Ramada Renaissance* watersports concession (phone: 444-4371). *Grenada Yacht Services* (phone: 440-2883/2508) offers snorkeling day trips aboard the 40-foot *Flamingo,* at $25 per person for a party of eight.

GUADELOUPE: The snorkeling is especially good off the western and southern coasts of Basse-Terre, and most hotels rent equipment and arrange guided dives. Experienced scuba divers head for Pigeon Island, where Jacques Cousteau spends a fair amount of time. For dive trips, most operators require some evidence of experience, a doctor's certificate, and insurance coverage; they prefer that divers *not* bring their own equipment since US gear is incompatible with the French CMAS system. Lessons and dive trips are arranged by *Karukera Plongée* at the *Callinago, Aqua-Fari Plongée* on Le Beethoven Beach at *La Creole Beach* hotel, *Les Heures Saines* at the *Marissol,* the *Nautilus Club* at Malendure, and *Chez Guy,* in the Îles des Saintes.

JAMAICA: For the experienced diver, Jamaica's waters offer giant sponge forests, caves, and shipwrecks to explore. But the area is particularly good for snorkeling and learning to scuba-dive. Probably the best available instruction is that at Mike Draculich's *Sea and Dive Jamaica* in Mammee Bay (phone: 972-2162), which offers snorkeling lessons as well as a 36-hour scuba course of classwork and open-water dives, leading to an NASDS or PADI certification card (he also operates at the *Shaw Park Beach* hotel; phone: 974-2552). Other spots for lessons, dive trips, and equipment include:

Montego Bay – *Poseidon Nemrod Divers Ltd.* at the *Chalet Caribe* hotel (phone: 952-3624); *Sea World* at the *Cariblue Hotel* (953-2250) as well as the *Rose Hall Beach* (953-2650) and *Holiday Inn* (phone: 953-2180).

Negril – *Hedonism II* (phone: 957-4201; 800-858-8009); *Negril Scuba Center* at the *Negril Beach Club* (phone: 957-4220).

Ocho Rios – *Caribbean Water Sports, Club Caribbean,* Runaway Bay (phone: 973-3507).

MARTINIQUE: Scuba is relatively new, but the *Carib Scuba Club* at Grain d'Or (phone: 590-78-0227) and *Bathy's Club* at Pointe du Bout (phone: 590-66-0000), scuba centers at the *Hotel-Casino La Batelière* (phone: 590-61-4949) and the *Diamant-Novotel* (phone: 590-76-4242) all offer dive instruction, snorkel, spearfishing, trip facilities.

MEXICAN CARIBBEAN: The variety of the reefs and the incredible clarity of the western Caribbean water (average undersea visibility, all year, is 100 feet, though you can often see much deeper) make Mexico's Caribbean coast a first-class choice for underwater exploring. Prices vary and can be negotiated through hotel activities desks, private marinas, and dive shops.

Cozumel – Its prime attractions are the reefs 500 yards off the island's leeward shore, along El Cantil (the Drop-Off), the edge of the shelf that borders the Yucatán Channel to the south. Famous 6-mile-long Palancar Reef has — in addition to forests of black, staghorn, and other species of coral and friendly swarms of Day-Glo-colored fish — a number of historic wrecks to poke around.

Several dive shops cluster at the end of the San Miguel pier, including *Aqua Safari* (phone: 2-0101), *Discover Cozumel Dive Shop* (phone: 2-0280), and *Fantasia Divers* (phone: 2-0700). They offer rental equipment, instruction, and dive trips; a full day's guided dive tour from Cozumel to Palancar Reef — including equipment and lunch — runs about $35.

Isla Mujeres – Surrounded by reefs, so snorkeling is very good along its shores. Scuba divers can rent equipment from *Mexico Divers* on the waterfront or at the *El Presidente Caribe* (phone: 2-0002, 2-0122) for about $45 per day. *Mexico Divers* will also arrange dive trips for about $25 per hour including one tank of air.

SABA: *Saba Deep* (phone: 4-3347, 4-2201) takes divers on a tour of the dark volcanic sands, black coral, and pale-hued coral formations that have only recently been accessible to visitors. US representative is *Surfside* in Scranton, PA (phone: 717-346-6382; 800-468-1708).

ST. EUSTATIUS: At the bottom of Gallows Bay in Oranjestad lie the ruins of masonry walls, a few cannon, and coral formations for experienced divers to explore. Bring your own scuba gear. The dive shop next door to the *Old Gin House* hotel handles scuba and snorkeling trips.

TOBAGO: Buccoo Bay has the best snorkeling; even nonswimmers can walk along Buccoo Reef in sneakers and masks to enjoy the underwater landscape. For scuba, certification is required; most action is on the island's west coast, but all hotels arrange dive trips, as does *Dive Tobago* (phone: 639-2385).

TURKS & CAICOS: Extraordinary rings of virtually virgin coral reef and the spectacular 7,000-foot Turks Island Passage drop-off draw divers from literally all over the world to these unspoiled islands. Well-equipped dive shops include *Dolphin Cay Divers* on North Caicos; *Omega Divers* and *Blue Water Divers* on Grand Turk; *Provo Turtle Divers, Wet Pleasures Dive & Watersports, Flamingo Divers, Aquatic Divers, Third Turtle Divers,* and *PRIDE Divers* on Provo.

US VIRGIN ISLANDS: Snorkeling is terrific throughout the Virgin Islands, and most hotels rent equipment for a small fee (usually included as part of the package on yacht excursions). There are fine marked trails at St. John's Trunk Bay and St. Croix's Buck Island.

In the scuba department, the *St. Thomas Diving Club* at *Villa Olga,* a resort dedicated exclusively to divers, offers moderately priced week-long packages with daily dives by the best island outfits. Most offer both day and night dives.

St. Thomas – Has excellent beginners' diving spots at Cow and Calf, St. James Island, and Steven's Cay. More advanced divers can enjoy the lava archways at Congo Cay, tunnels off Thatch Cay, and a submerged mountain at Eagle Shoal. For diving instruction, equipment, and excursions: *St. Thomas Diving Club* at *Villa Olga* (phone: 774-1376 or 800-524-4746); *Virgin Island Diving Schools* (phone: 774-8687); *Water Sports Center* at Sapphire Bay (phone: 775-6755).

St. John – Trunk Bay's marked underwater trail is a beautiful place to start — especially on Wednesday morning's guided tour. For further submarine adventures and day and night dive trips, get in touch with *St. John Water Sports* (phone: 776-6256) or the dive shop at *Caneel Bay* resort (phone: 776-6111).

St. Croix – In addition to Buck Island's superb snorkeling, St. Croix offers fine diving in its coral canyons and drop-offs at Salt River and Davis Bay. *Caribbean Sea Adventures* (phone: 773-5922) and *V. I. Divers* (phone: 773-6045) offer full facilities, equipment rentals and sales, guided trips, instruction. *Cruzan Divers* (phone: 772-3701) also offers photographic trips.

Lots of Yachts: Sailing

Whether you charter a craft with a full crew and provisions or take out a bareboat and eat what you catch, sailing among the islands of the Atlantic and the Caribbean can be an unparalleled experience — the opportunity to explore uninhabited islets, anchor in secluded bays and inlets, and visit dozens of tropical landfalls under your own power and at your own pace.

The best islands for yachting (that is, sailing on a ship on which you can also sleep overnight) are the Bahamas, the Virgin Islands, and the Grenadines, that string of small islands that stretches from St. Vincent in the north to Grenada in the south. The waters around the Bahamas are the most protected and provide delightful day or overnight journeys. British Virgin Island waters are an excellent place to learn both sailing and navigation since they are not only well protected, but often your evening anchorage is within eyeshot of your morning starting point. (*The Moorings* and *Caribbean Sailing Yachts* in Road Town, Tortola, feature "Learn to Sail" packages; the *Offshore Sailing School* also has a BVI branch.) The Grenadines are favorites of experienced yachtspeople for their personality and hospitality as well as their steady breezes and fair weather.

Like hotel rooms, charter prices increase during the winter, decrease in the summer. The off-season is the best time to sail with children without running up astronomical bills. In peak season, charters can become scarce, and if you want a bareboat or a crewed yacht for a holiday, it should be booked at least six months in advance.

Below, some of the best sailing areas and charter operations in the islands.

ANTIGUA: Historic Nelson's Dockyard at English Harbour is not only one of the Caribbean's most picturesque and best-protected anchorages but is also the home of one of its most prestigious charter operations — *Nicholson Yacht Charters,* specializing in crewed sailing yachts, full provisioning, and maintenance facilities. Their list of available boats is so extensive that they're worth a try even for late or spur-of-the-moment bookings (US office: 9 Chauncy St., Cambridge, MA 02138; phone: 617 661-8174 or 800 662-6066; English Harbour: phone: 809-463-1530). Resorts like the *Anchorage* and *Curtain Bluff* also arrange day or overnight charters for their guests.

BAHAMAS: Every size and style of craft are available, and arrangements can be made through a travel agent, your hotel desk, or a specialist like *Nassau Yacht Haven* (phone: 322-8173) or any of half a dozen other firms. Bareboat charters can be arranged through *Bahamas Yachting Services* (phone: 367-2080) of Marsh Harbour in the Abacos. Eleuthera, the Abacos, and the Exumas offer fine anchorages.

BRITISH VIRGIN ISLANDS: There are more than 300 bareboats and almost 100 charter yachts available in the British Virgins. Start by checking with *The Moorings,* Road Town Harbour (phone: 809-49-4-2332) or 1305 US 19 S, Suite 402, Clearwater, FL 33546 (phone: 800-535-7289); *Tortola Yacht Charters,* Nanny Cay (phone: 4-2221); *West Indies Yacht Charters,* Maya Cove (phone: 809 49-5-2363) or 2190 SE 17th St., Fort Lauderdale, FL 33316 (phone: 800-327-2290); *Tropic Island Yacht Management* (phone: 4-2450) — all in Road Town, Tortola, BVI. In Virgin Gorda, *North South Yacht Charters* is recommended (phone: 5-5421; in the US, 800-387-4964). Summer rates and specials run as much as 40% below winter levels. All offer provisioning; or cater your own through the very *Ample Hamper,* Wickhams Cay (phone: 4-2784), with supplements from *Carib Casseroles,* Box 190 (phone: 4-3271), Tortola, BVI.

GRENADA: Sailors rate the sailing conditions from Grenada north through the Grenadines to St. Vincent as some of the best in the world. Not only does St. George's have first-rate marina facilities, but Grenada is headquarters for a number of charter operations. Among them: *Grenada Yacht Services,* PO Box 183, St. George's (phone: 2508 or 2883); and *Spice Island Yacht Charters,* L'Anse aux Epines (phone: 4342), or 145 King St., West Toronto, Ont. M5H 1J8 (phone: 416-365-1950). Either of these can arrange skippered or bareboat charters for a week or longer.

ST. LUCIA: With Castries Harbour, improved facilities at Marigot Bay — one of the most beautiful anchorages in the Caribbean — and continued development of marina space at Rodney Bay, St. Lucia has become an even more important takeoff point for yacht charter trips through the eastern Caribbean — north to the French West Indies and Dominica, south to St. Vincent and the Grenadines. Top outfits: *Stevens Yachts,* Rodney Bay (phone: 2-8648) or 252 East Ave., East Norwalk, CT 06855 (phone: 203-866-8989; 800-638-7044); *The Moorings,* the prestigious BVI firm with headquarters — including some overnight accommodations — at Marigot Bay (phone: 3-4256) or 1305 US 19S, Suite 402, Clearwater, FL 33546 (phone: 800-535-7289); and *Trade Wind Yacht Charters,* PO Box 372, Rodney Bay, St. Lucia (phone: 2-8424).

US VIRGIN ISLANDS: St. Thomas does most of the charter business in the US Virgin Islands, and that is considerable. The local waters are superb, and the sailing set obviously knows it. Cruising vacations aboard a charter yacht with skipper, crew, meals, and liquor included can cost as little as $85 or as much as $325 up per person a day in winter, 10% to 20% less in summer. Or you can go bareboat and sail yourself for a per-person cost of about $65 a day in winter, roughly 20% less in summer, for the boat plus about $20 per person a day for provisioning (food and drinks). (*Note:* A proficiency check is a standard requirement before you take over.)

Good boat organizations to know are *Caribbean Yacht Charters* (bareboats only), PO Box 583, Marblehead, MA 01945 (phone: in Massachusetts, 617-559-7990; elsewhere, 800-225-2520); their affiliate, *Lynn Jachney Charters,* which handles crewed yachts (phone: 617-639-0787; 800-223-2050); and *Regency International Yacht Charters* (crewed and bareboats), Long Bay Rd., St. Thomas, USVI 00802 (phone: 809-776-5950; 800-524-7676). Both the *VI Charteryacht League* (phone: 809-774-3944) and *Home Port Inc.* (phone: 774-5630) act as contacts for member crewed-charter firms (both are at Homeport, St. Thomas, USVI 00802). Crewed-charter specialists include *SailAway Yacht Charter Consultants,* PO Box 016933, Miami, FL 33101 (phone: 305-577-3355); *Whitney Yacht Charters,* 2209 N Halstead Ave., Chicago, IL 60614 (phone: 312-929-8989). *Avery's Boathouse* (phone: 776-0133) provides both crewed and bareboats.

Top Tennis

The tennis capital of the Atlantic and Caribbean islands is Bermuda, as it has been since the game was imported there from England, and where the first court was laid out in the Western Hemisphere. Today, there are thousands of courts throughout the Caribbean — some at hotels, some that are open for public play, some attached to clubs that allow nonmembers to play for a fee — that are fine for an occasional game. But serious players and those who want to get serious will find their search limited to those resorts with resident pros, ample numbers of courts, programs of lessons, and lights for night play — such as *Caneel Bay* and *Carambola Beach* in the US Virgins; *Little Dix Bay* in Virgin Gorda; *Malliouhana* and *Coccoloba Plantation* in Anguilla.

Since the dimensions of a tennis court don't usually vary and resort courts seem to alternate only between rubberized hard courts and claylike fast-drying surfaces, other factors distinguish a proper tennis facility from a casual court. For example, how many courts does a resort have in relation to its overall size? This determines how much access you will have to these courts and how much time you will really spend playing.

Similarly, are the courts lighted for nighttime play? It is often unwise to play in the tropical heat, and this means — especially if you are bent on spending considerable time on the court — that you'll want them available in the cooler evening hours.

Last, does the resort offer tennis packages? A good package will sometimes guarantee court time as well as reduce court fees where there are any. You will find few true clay courts in the islands because clay needs time to dry out after a rain, and few hotels are willing to put courts out of action after every summer shower. Barbados has a couple of public grass courts, but these are just about the last in the islands.

If you are really into rackets, these are the resorts to consider:

BUCCANEER, St. Croix, US Virgin Islands: The best tennis in the Virgin Islands. Good for watching (with several annual tournaments) as well as playing. Facilities: 8 all-weather Laykold courts, lighted for night play; private lessons with the resident pro are $18 per half hour; ball machine; pro shop; Senior Tennis Tournament usually in July, with several others during the year. (Phone: 773-2100.)

CASA DE CAMPO, La Romana, Dominican Republic: The tennis segment of this 7,000-acre complex is first class; everything works, and everything is in absolutely mint condition. Facilities: 4 all-weather Laykold courts, lighted for night play near the main administrative building; at La Terraza Tennis Village (part of Casa de Campo, a 5-minute jitney ride from the main building), there are 13 additional composition clay courts (2 are stadium courts, 6 are lighted). The resident pro is Paco Hernández; lessons are about $33.50 per hour with Hernández, $26.50 with the assistant pro, $20 with the junior assistant pro. Eight to twelve people can also set up their own daily clinic at rates that vary according to the season; ball machine; pro shop. There's a charge of $14 per court per hour of day play; $17 per hour at night in high season, except December 1 through January 31. Tennis packages year-round. A roster of terrific ballboys, including some very fine players, makes it possible to guarantee guests games at all levels of skill (phone: 809-682-2111, ext. 3165; in Florida, 305-856-5405).

HYATT CERROMAR BEACH/HYATT DORADO BEACH, Puerto Rico: Courts are scattered all around this two-resort complex; if tennis is your consuming interest, be sure your room is near some courts. Hosts tennis weeks and special packages. At *Cerromar* there are 14 Laykold courts — 1 is a stadium court; 2 are lighted. Peter Burwash International handles instruction; private lessons cost about $40 an hour, $25 a half hour; given notice, they'll arrange videotaping, clinics, tournaments for groups. Court time runs about $12 a daylight hour, $16 at night in winter, lower the rest of the year. At *Dorado,* there are 5 Laykold courts by the pro shop, 2 courts at the west end of the property, none lighted for night play. Private lessons cost $25 to $35 a half hour depending on the season and the status of the pro. Court time: about $12 an hour in season, $10 the rest of the year. Both have off-season tennis packages (phone: Cerromar, 809-796-1010; Dorado, 809-796-1600; or for both, 800-228-9000).

CLUB MED, PARADISE ISLAND, Bahamas: This Club Med enclave was specifically designed and created for tennis and is the best place in the islands for lessons. Facilities: 20 composition courts, 8 lighted; group lessons with the resident pros are free; pro shop; closed-circuit TV instruction and ball machine (phone: 809-326-2641/4; 800-528-3100).

CORAL BEACH, Bermuda: This is a very exclusive private club. With an introduction by a member (required for entrance), there is a $3 guest fee and an additional $8 per hour court charge. Facilities: 7 clay courts, one Dynaturf, 2 lighted; Derek Singleton is the director, Ann Smith-Gordon is the resident pro; lessons by the hour for an individual are $40, $20 per half hour; tennis whites are mandatory; pro shop. Every year the Bermuda Lawn Tennis Club Invitational and the Coral Beach Invitational tournaments are held here (phone: 236-2233).

CURTAIN BLUFF, Antigua: Small, select site of a well-attended annual spring tournament, it has the atmosphere of a private club. Facilities: 3 hard-surface plus 1 artificial grass court — all championship caliber; teaching alley, too; resident pro; pro shop; teaching equipment (phone: 3-1115).

GOVERNMENT TENNIS STADIUM, Bermuda: Thoroughly public facilities with a teaching pro. Facilities: 6 clay courts, 2 asphalt, 3 lighted; private lessons with teaching pro, Eugene Woods, are $13 per half hour, $26 per hour; hourly playing fees are about $4, $5 extra for night; pro shop; tennis attire mandatory; there's a ball machine. North of Hamilton (phone 292-0105).

HALF MOON CLUB, Jamaica: This island's most extensive complex with 13 tennis courts (4 lighted), 4 international squash courts occasionally co-opted by the racquetball crowd (Byron Bernard is the pro). Year-round, ex–Davis Cup/Wimbledon player Richard Russell, the head pro, sets up clinics according to guest interest, with video playback. No charge to hotel guests for day or night play; reservations necessary only in peak season (phone: 953-2211).

PALMAS DEL MAR, Puerto Rico: A complex of condominiums, where you should be sure to stay in the tennis village. Facilities are excellent; 20 courts, of which 5 are Har-Tru (more like clay), 15 Tenneflex (harder surface), 4 lighted. Private lessons with the senior pro are $45 an hour. Base for All American Sports' 3-, 4-, 5-, and 7-day packages including 2 to 4 hours of instruction per day, with maximum of four per class. The resort's own all-year packages guarantee 2 hours of court time per person, more according to availability (phone: 852-6000, ext. 51; 800-221-4874).

SANDY LANE, Barbados: Well-designed facilities, with tournaments every year. Facilities: 2 hard-surface courts and 1 grass court, all lighted; private half-hour lessons with the pro are $25 and up; fully equipped pro shop; ball machines; off-season packages (phone: 432-1311).

Golf

Teeing it up on any one of a dozen of these islands is one of life's consummate sporting joys, for all that advertising propaganda about swaying palms beside shimmering ponds is actually true on the golf courses of the Caribbean, the Bahamas, and Bermuda. And golf is probably as great a motivation for visitors to come to this part of the world as any other single activity.

The variety of the courses available for play in these islands is absolutely astounding. There are seaside layouts with holes hung over the surging ocean spray and inland courses that ramble around marvelous meadowland. There are also hillside courses that would test the climbing ability of a mountain goat and flatland layouts that somehow seem no simpler for the absence of mounds and hills. There are courses in the spare British links tradition and lush layouts that have harnessed the best of modern agronomy and watering techniques to develop fairways and manicured greens that are unequaled in the world. And among this marvelous diversity is the backdrop of tropical panoramas that can make keeping your head down a real act of will.

Within these islands are examples of the course craft of almost all of golf's premier architects. Robert Trent Jones (Sr. and Jr.), Pete Dye, Dick Wilson, Joe Lee, and other greensmakers of equal talent are represented on one island or another. Their talents, combined with weather that sometimes seems specifically designed for perfect course care, provide layouts that exist in a nearly impossible green richness.

But scenery aside, it is the superb tests of golf that prove the most powerful magnet to players who care only about challenging (and in some cases taming) the best. For most of us, just the experience of playing on one of the world's great courses is enough, and the islands offer a sufficient number of extraordinary places to set your spikes to more than satisfy any golfer.

That said, here are our choices of the best in the islands:

CASA DE CAMPO, Dominican Republic: If it was necessary to choose just one island course on which to play, it would have to be the one known — not for nothing — as "The Teeth of the Dog." Unquestionably Pete Dye's finest island work, this seaside course presents more excitement, interest, and sheer brawny challenge than any other golf course we've ever seen. Seven holes play directly along the seaside, and they are unlike any other such water holes you have heretofore experienced. Just standing on one of the championship tees can be an exercise in sheer terror, as the terrain between tee and green occasionally looks as if it might be inhabited by the Loch Ness Monster. In this instance, said monster would be a welcome relief from the rigors that Dye has wrought.

In addition to the superb seaside stretch, the other 11 holes are scarcely less challenging. Dye's unique inclination to enclose terrain within wooden retaining walls and to create traps that look like the Sahara are only part of the picture that greets each golfer from the outset. And lest you think the second course at La Romana is any real respite, "The Links" is thought by many to be even more difficult. A third course is under construction. Information: Casa de Campo, La Romana, Dominican Republic (phone: 809-682-2111, ext. 3115; in Florida, 305-856-5405).

MID OCEAN, Bermuda: One of the wonderful things about playing golf in the islands covered by this book is that you can choose the international background against which you want to play. There are Spanish islands, French islands, and Dutch islands, but for the consummate British golf atmosphere you must come to Bermuda — and nowhere is the tradition of the Empire better maintained than on the links at Mid Ocean. Technically a private club — and one that fiercely controls transient play — we include it only because there are ways in which a visitor usually can gain access to these otherwise exclusive premises. Most of the major hotels in Bermuda have at least one Mid Ocean member in their employ, and he is usually available to "introduce" hotel guests by contacting the club one day in advance. As a rule, Mondays, Wednesdays, and Fridays are the days on which such guests are made to feel at least marginally welcome, and golfers interested in challenging Bermuda's best may want to adjust their travel schedules accordingly.

The course is laid out in the best linksland tradition, although the terrain is considerably more lush than most Scottish incarnations. There are carts available, a grudging recognition of the diminution in the number of available caddies. Still, walking these rolling hills, hopefully in the company of one of the surviving bag-toters who know every knoll and roll, is best. The ultimate challenge here is the fabulous 5th hole, where a drive is forced to carry over a large lake and will find dry land only after a carry of about 200 yards. Babe Ruth himself is said to have had considerable trouble keeping out of the drink here, and chances are you will, too. And though the 5th is regularly included in the best 18 holes in the world, you may be hard pressed to distinguish it from the 17 other Mid Ocean monsters that seem equally anxious to swallow your golf ball. Information: Mid Ocean Golf Club, Tucker's Town, Bermuda (phone: 293-0330).

PORT ROYAL, Bermuda: Though lacking in Mid Ocean's exclusivity and cachet, Port Royal is still a worthy contender for the title of best on Bermuda. For some reason, public courses are generally denigrated in any links-by-links appraisal, and this is one case where such prejudice is really unfounded. Because of its rare (for Bermuda) watering system, Port Royal tends to stay in far better shape than Mid Ocean during Bermuda's hot, often arid summer, and there have been times when Port Royal has played deep and green while the other Bermuda courses presented fairways that were golden brown.

The seventh and eighth holes, a dogleg par 5 and windswept par 3 respectively, are the stars of the front nine while the 16th hole, set on the craggy cliff (that is the nightmare of any player with vertigo), sets the tone for the home 9. If you're not afraid of heights, at least walk to the far championship tee on 16, though we'd be loath to suggest that you try to hit a ball from here. Some golfers we know have all but requested a lifeline be secured to a nearby tree, lest they fall into the sea on their follow-through. It's quite a hole. Information: Port Royal Golf Club, Southampton, Bermuda (phone: 294-0974).

HYATT DORADO BEACH, Puerto Rico: Although the opulent Dorado Beach resort complex is no longer operated under the aegis of the original Rockresort management, few golfers will be able to tell the difference. The two top-flight courses that wind their way through this former grapefruit and coconut plantation are sufficiently difficult to make players regularly wish the land had been left in citrus cultivation. But that is only for those for whom their final score is everything. In fact, these are as good a pair of golfing tests as exist side by side on any island, and among the liveliest arguments heard around the 19th hole here are the discussions about which course is best (record one vote here for the East).

And if even these two fine layouts are not enough to satisfy your desire for assorted golfing venues, there is the added attraction of the two sister courses just down the road at the *Hyatt Cerromar Beach* hotel. Having all four of these to choose from permits the playing of your own private Dorado Open, and that has got to be bliss for anyone. Information: Dorado Beach Hotel, Dorado, Puerto Rico (phone: 796-1600; 800 228-9000).

TRYALL, Jamaica: About 20 miles due west of Montego Bay, the Tryall resort course is without question the finest on Jamaica. Where the other courses on this island seem somehow restricted by their flat terrain and rather repetitious hole configuration, Tryall exults in its 6,680 yards of hills and dales, and no cost seems to have been spared to create the most interesting course possible. Of some passing interest is the historic past of this golfing ground, since it was once operated as one of the island's most productive sugar plantations. All that remains of those earlier days is a rusty old waterwheel and some ruins along the course boundaries, but they do provide a context in which to survey the surrounding landscape.

Don't take too much time to reflect on history, however, for the course itself is sufficient challenge for any player. The constantly changing direction of the wind off the nearby sea restructures each hole virtually every day, so there is no paucity of fresh problems each time you set your ball on a Tryall tee. Information: Tryall Golf, Beach, and Tennis Club, Sandy Bay PO, Hanover, Jamaica (phone: 952-5110; in NY, 212-889-0761; 800-336-4571).

GOLF INTERNATIONAL DE ST. FRANÇOIS, Guadeloupe: For a long time, this course provided a source of comedy for the entire French Caribbean, as its opening took what sometimes seemed to be eons. But all that wait turned out to be worth the effort, since the 6,755-yard, par 71 course has been praised as one of the best in the Eastern Caribbean. Designed by Robert Trent Jones, Sr., its operation has been taken over by the St. François municipality. Players pay about $35 for 18 holes, about $170 for a week's play.

Maintenance has improved steadily, and there appears to be a real will to keep the course the centerpiece of the effort to lure golfers to the southeastern corner of the island. Information: Golf International, St. François, Guadeloupe (phone: 88-41-87).

CARAMBOLA BEACH AND GOLF RESORT, St. Croix, US Virgin Islands: For more than 20 years, this course was known as *Fountain Valley,* one of the most challenging golf courses in the Caribbean. Its Rockresort owners have added a fine hotel, built a new clubhouse, and refurbished the course so it is in its best condition in more than a decade. They've also changed the name of the entire complex. The course is mostly notable for its route through a deep valley, full of abundant water hazards and an inordinate number of deep ravines. From its championship tees, it plays to a length of more than 6,900 yards, which should be sufficient to exhaust even the most inveterate ball pounder. A good challenge has been made into a great one. Information: Carambola Beach and Golf Resort, PO Box 3031, Kingshill, St. Croix, US Virgin Islands 00850 (phone: 778-0747).

MAHOGANY RUN, St. Thomas, US Virgin Islands: One of the Caribbean's newer golf courses, designed by George and Tom Fazio, it runs along some of the most picturesque parts of the island through scenery well worth the few dull stretches. Relatively tight and hilly, with small greens, this is not a course for the lover of classic hole configuration. But it provides 18 good reasons for making a Virgin Islands visit. Information: Mahogany Run, Box 7517, St. Thomas, US Virgin Islands 00801 (phone: 775-5000).

DIVI BAHAMAS BEACH RESORT & COUNTRY CLUB, New Providence, Bahamas: Though this is the newest course on New Providence Island, it is by far the best. At the southwestern tip of the island usually called Nassau — though this is in fact only the name of the major metropolis on the island — it occupies high ground that provides a striking view of the area called Tongue of the Ocean.

The course, designed by Joe Lee, is highlighted by four challenging water holes, and again, the use of the unusually rolling terrain sets this layout apart from its island counterparts. It is reason enough to spend your stay on New Providence at the *Divi Bahamas,* formerly the *South Ocean Beach* hotel. Information: Divi Bahamas Beach Resort and Country Club, PO Box N8191, New Providence, Bahamas (phone: 326-4391; 800-367-3484).

MT. IRVINE, Tobago: It may seem unusual for such a small island to have such a superb golf course, but here it is, the very incarnation of the palm-shaded island links. The 18 holes run along the Caribbean coastline, where the most common hazards are falling coconuts. The best-known hole here is 9, famed for its minuscule green set at a devilishly rakish angle. The gentle terrain belies the difficulties of the taxing 6,800 yards, and it is small solace to be able to look out at the famous Buccoo Reef after an afternoon of soaring scores. Information: Mt. Irvine Golf Club, Mt. Irvine Bay Hotel, Tobago (phone: 639-8871).

Sport Fishing

The Caribbean is one of the prime sport fishing grounds in the world and attracts enthusiastic anglers from all over. Almost every variety of deep-sea game fish, and many world-record-threatening catches, have been taken in these waters. Most of the fish seem to run during the spring-summer and summer-fall seasons, although there is no off-season on most islands — just better and poorer times to go out. Some of the fish run to deep waters, others lie among the reefs and shallows; but whatever style of fishing suits you — casting, trolling, bottom or reef fishing — there is a challenge awaiting you here beneath the Atlantic and Caribbean waters. Spear fishing is illegal in many islands, so check local regulations before you dive.

Some of the game fish that abound in the Caribbean are marlin, sailfish, tuna, wahoo, mackerel, and dolphin (the dorado, not the true dolphin) — all deep-sea fish; and great barracuda, pompano, tarpon, and bonefish — all shallow-water fish.

Fish move, and local conditions change from season to season, sometimes subtly but critically. The secret of successful fishing in the best waters is your captain — his knowledge of local waters and his feeling about the prevailing conditions will lead you to the big ones. Be sure to work out all the details when you arrange a charter.

Below, our list of the best fishing around the Atlantic and Caribbean islands:

BAHAMAS: Charter a craft at Bimini, and let the captain take you where they're running. Odds are you'll end up off Walker's Cay (world-record skipjack tuna) or Cat Cay (world-record wahoo); take a boat from the town of Current to fish North Eleuthera's western coast (world-record dorado) or some special area that only the captain knows. More than 50 world-record catches have been made off the Bahamas.

BERMUDA: In 1981, the world-record amberjack was taken off the coast here, and that record still stands. There are world-class fish taken daily in these waters, and under the direction of a good captain, there's no reason one of them shouldn't be yours. The Bermuda Charter Fishing Boat Association can arrange a boat for you (phone: 292-6246), as can the Bermuda Sport Fishing Association (phone: 295-2370).

BELIZE: The barrier reef paralleling the coast harbors a huge variety of game fish, so deep-sea sport is top priority, with simple offshore fishing lodges (write *Ambergris Lodge, Paradise Hotel,* and *El Pescador,* Ambergris Caye, Belize). The *Belize River Lodge* (phone: 02-5-2002), on the Belize River, does both deep-sea and light tackle trips.

CAYMAN ISLANDS: The surrounding waters abound with marlin, tuna, yellowtail, dorado, bonefish, and others. Charters are available at *Cayman Kai,* near Rum Point, *Tortuga Club* at East End, and through *South Cove Resort, Seawise Rentals Club,* and *Quabbin Dives* as well as with several individual skippers on Grand Cayman. *Buccaneer's Inn* on Cayman Brac and *Southern Cross Club* on Little Cayman (where tarpon and bonefishing are superlative) are all dedicated to fishing and the very casual life. *Charter Boat Headquarters* (phone: 7-4340) has complete information and prices for fishing in the islands.

DOMINICAN REPUBLIC: Offshore waters are home to marlin, sailfish, dorado, bonito, and other game fish. Arrange charters in Santo Domingo, La Romana, Boca Chica, Boca de Yuma, or Samaná (though the north coast is rough); there's river fishing for snook, tarpon in Boca de Yuma, La Romana, Samaná.

JAMAICA: The best time for marlin off the north coast is from September to April, off the south coast from December to February. Port Antonio is one of the top fishing centers in these waters and holds an annual international fishing tournament in early September to October, as do Montego Bay and Ochos Rios. There's also a Big Game Angling Club Blue Marlin Tournament during May in Ochos Rios. Arrange a charter there or from Montego Bay, Ocho Rios, or Kingston.

PUERTO RICO: Over 30 world-record fish have been taken off this island. Blue marlin, white marlin, sailfish, wahoo, tuna, and other trophy-sized fighters are the targets of charter operators like Capt. Mike Benítez (*Sea Born,* at the *Club Nautico de San Juan;* phone: 724-6265 or 723-2292). Other boats can be chartered through the *San Juan Fishing Charters* on Fernandez Juncos Ave., in Miramar (phone: 725-0139 or 723-0415), *Castillo's Watersports* (phone: 791-6195; evenings, 726-5752), and at *Marina de Palmas Yacht Club* at the *Palmas del Mar* hotel in Humacao (phone: 850-7295 or 852-3450, ext. 7921 and 2473).

TURKS & CAICOS: Aficionados who've already tried it hope you won't believe the stories you hear about the incredible bonefishing in the shallows that lie off the Caicos. Privately, they say it's some of the best in the world — especially in the waters that wash the west-lying Caicos Bank. Julius Jennings is the guide to ask for on South Caicos; "Bonefish Lem" Johnson is the man on Provo.

US VIRGIN ISLANDS: Wahoo, allison tuna, bonita, sailfish, and marlin are the game; *American Yacht Harbor* (phone: 775-6454) at Red Hook, St. Thomas, is the prime charter center for serious fishermen. *Caneel Bay* (phone: 776-6111) on St. John and St. Croix's *Caribbean Sea Adventures* (phone: 773-5922) also arrange deep-sea charters.

Climbing and Hiking

 Nowhere in the islands is there the kind of mountain climbing that is likely to draw a serious mountaineer off the more challenging precipices elsewhere in the world. Many of the islands are of volcanic origin, however, and some of these are still rather threatening — dormant, but hot. And that means extremely interesting climbs are available up, into, and through volcanic craters and bubbling sulfur pits, mud pots, and steam vents to summits that, while hardly high in the eyes of the world, at least provide breathtaking views of the islands.

Less arduous but no less spectacular scenery is open to hikers who avail themselves of rain forest preserves and parks in the islands. Many islands have some kind of park system, but the rain forests of St. Lucia, Puerto Rico, and Guadeloupe offer an unparalleled sense of the island environment.

Since most of the islands are either coral formations or are of volcanic origin, there is a great disparity between their heights. Mt. Christoffel, on Curaçao, is the highest point of the six islands in the Netherlands Antilles group at only 1,300 feet above the sea; on St. Lucia, the smaller of the Pitons stands 2,460 feet tall (the larger is 2,619 feet, and the highest point on that island is Mt. Gimie, at 3,145 feet). And remember, where there are summits, there are guides. Passing through sulfur pits is a fascinating experience with a guide (a favorite trick is to boil eggs in fuming potholes); without a guide it can be dangerous.

Below, our choice of the best hiking and climbing spots in the islands and along the Caribbean coast:

BELIZE: The Maya Mountains in the southwest quarter of Belize present a challenging goal to the most avid climbers. *Victoria Peak* tops Belize's Cockscomb range, at

3,680 feet. As in all the inland areas of this country, which tend to be densely jungled, no expedition should be attempted without a guide. The Chief Forest Officer, Ministry of Natural Resources, Belmopan, Belize, will help you get in touch with a qualified expert.

DOMINICA: The central rain forests, and especially the Emerald Pool in the *Morne Trois Pitons National Park,* provide beautiful day trips; *Morne Diablotin* (4,747 feet) should not be attempted without a guide — mists the islanders call "liquid sunshine" make it impossible to judge direction near the crest.

GRENADA: Hiking is a favorite islanders' sport in which visitors are invited to join. The government is helping by grading trails, mapping, and organizing. The Tourist Board will brief you on routes, level of skill required, and — with a day's notice — put you in touch with expert guides. Several adventures involving hiking are offered by *Henry's Tours, Ltd.* (phone: 443-5313).

GUADELOUPE: The lush rain forest scenery (lakes, waterfalls, pools, steaming fumeroles) plus a system of well-marked trails make Basse-Terre's giant *Parc Naturel* exotically beautiful hiking terrain. *Walks & Hikes,* a booklet outlining 18 beckoning trails with maps and difficulty ratings, is available through the Organisation des Guides de Montagne (phone: 81-45-79) or the tourist office (phone: 82-09-30).

HAITI: The horseback trip up to the *Citadelle* is breathtaking — the old fortifications near Cap-Haïtien are set on the crest of a mountain 3,000 feet up. There are also several peaks in the Kenscoff area (*Morne La Selle* and *Chaîne-des-Mattheux* among them), south of Port-au-Prince. Have your hotel desk arrange for a guide in advance.

JAMAICA: The 7,402-foot-tall *Blue Mountain* is a rough climb, even for those in good condition. You can make arrangements with John Allgrove, 8 Armon Jones Crescent, Kingston 6 (phone: 927-0986 after 5 PM), for Land Rover pickup and mule transportation to the peak in order to see the sunrise from its crest. Or contact Jamaica Alternative Tourism, Camping & Hiking Association (JACHA), PO Box 216, Kingston 7 (phone: 927-0657), about Blue Mountain camping trips.

MARTINIQUE: For those who wish to stay closer to sea level, there's the peninsula of *Presqu'île de la Caravelle,* part of the island's Parc Naturel, with trails covering a wide range of terrain but nothing very difficult. Serious climbers should contact Parc Régional de la Martinique, Quartier Bouillé, Rue Redoute du Marouba, Fort-de-France (phone: 73-19-30), to arrange for a guide to take them to the top of *Mt. Pelée* (the dormant volcano whose 1902 eruption took a heavy toll) or through the *Gorges de la Falaise* or the rain forest between Grand-Rivière and Le Prêcheur.

MONTSERRAT: The approach to Montserrat's airport is such that every plane seems about to crash into the side of *Chance Peak,* the island's highest point (a tragedy that has occurred only once). The peak makes an excellent viewing tower from which to plan island excursions, since almost the entire island can be seen from its 3,002-foot elevation. The climb should be attempted only with a guide, which can be arranged at any hotel.

ST. LUCIA: Rising half a mile from the shore of the Caribbean, with the waves crashing upon their feet, the peaks of the *Pitons* have been a landmark for mariners since the pirate days. Climbers have been challenging these mountains for just as long. *Gros Piton* stands 2,619 feet above the sea and *Petit Piton* just 2,460 feet; but the high point of the island is *Mt. Gimie* — 3,145 feet tall. None of these peaks should be attempted without a guide, as the mists and rains which frequently and suddenly cover the island's dense rain forest areas can make visibility a problem.

ST. VINCENT: A climb to the top of St. Vincent's *Soufrière,* 4,048 feet high, takes about 3 hours' walking along the steep volcanic ridges and rocky streams, through lush rain forests, and over loose volcanic ash. Since its 1979 eruption, new trails have been blazed. This climb should not be attempted without a guide. Arrangements can be made through hotel desks or the island tourist board, which also books the easier *Buccament Valley Nature Trail*. The tour winds through tropical rain forest, and there are pre-Columbian stone writings at Buccament Cave.

Camping in Comfort

Most vacationers associate the islands with luxurious hotels, elegant casinos, frantic nightlife, and languorous days. But for those trying to escape the hustle and bustle of urban life — or simply trying to do the islands on the cheap — it is possible to camp out. Many of the islands don't have established campgrounds, simply because there is no need for them. The beaches of isles like St. John's and Grenada, for example, are excellent places to pitch a tent, and there are numerous uninhabited cays and isles throughout the Virgin Islands and Bahamas groups that make perfect hideaways.

Or you can camp in "improved" campsites, which provide platforms, tents, and in the higher flights of fancy listed below, refrigerators, bed lamps, and sun decks. You can live well under canvas, and even manage to get to nearby nightlife.

Below, our suggestions for the choicest camping places:

BRITISH VIRGIN ISLANDS: On Tortola, *Brewer's Bay Campsite* (phone: 4-3463), on a beautiful beach, asks $16 a night for two for tent and basic equipment, $2.50 per additional person, $5 per night for a bare site; with bar, restaurant, commissary, snorkeling gear, tours, and babysitters available. On Jost Van Dyke, *Tula's N&N Campgrounds* (phone: 775-3073; 774-0774) at Little Harbour charges about $25 per couple for an 8-by-10-foot tent, $35 per couple for a 9-by-11-foot tent, $5 per night for an additional person, $15 for a bare site; their assets include a restaurant and snack bar, "available" live entertainment.

JAMAICA: The best campground on the island, since *Strawberry Fields'* 1985 closing, is the *Damali Beach Village* (phone: 953-2387), near Montego Bay. To find out about other sites, contact Jamaica Alternative Tourism, Camping & Hiking Association (JATCHA), which arranges camping, climbing, hiking, and backpacking trips (PO Box 216, Kingston 7; phone: 927-2097).

PUERTO RICO: There are more camping sites on Puerto Rico than any other island — 25, with more under construction. At all areas, tenting rates vary from $5 to $12 per night, depending upon site and season (some individual sites command premium rates), with the average tent site running about $8. Many of the grounds have air-conditioned trailers available for $12 per night. Among the best sites on the island are *Mojacasabe* (with tents, trailer space, bathrooms, beach, pool) on Playa El Combate and *Villa la Mela* (tents, trailer space, cabanas, beach) on Rte. 307 — both in Cabo Rojo; *Monte del Estado* (cabanas, pool, store, camping areas) on Rte. 120 in the hills of Maricao. For information, contact the Puerto Rico Parks and Recreation Administration (phone: 809-722-1771).

US VIRGIN ISLANDS: The Virgin Islands National Park has two excellent campgrounds, both on St. John, run by private organizations. *Cinnamon Bay* (phone: 809-776-6330) is run by Rockresorts. Its fully equipped tents (with grills, stoves, cots, linens, and cooking utensils) rent for about $44 per day for two, with a charge of $6 per additional person. Cottages are available for about $56 per day for a party of two, with a $6 charge for each additional person. Bare sites, rarely used, are available for $10 per night, for two, $2 per additional person. There are 44 individual and 16 group tents, 40 cottages, and 11 bare sites, all within steps of the beach.

Maho Bay Camp Resort (phone: 776-6240; 800-392-9004) is an ecologically sensitive campsite with tents that are really small canvas houses with good beds, kitchen areas, refrigerators, sun decks, lights, with the beach below and the national park all around. Rates are $57 a day for two in winter (1-week minimum), $40 in summer; additional adults $10 each, children $7 (summer). Restaurant features health and fresh island foods.

Hunting

 There was a time when all the islands were completely open to hunters and the killing of birds and wild animals was not controlled. Today, many island species are protected, and most hunting is restricted to waterfowl and certain other species of birds on those islands where it is allowed at all. Though the days of the big bang are gone, hunting is still available on some islands.

Before planning an expedition, be aware that even in countries that still allow visitors to hunt, the paperwork involved in bringing your own guns onto certain islands can be more arduous than a five-day trek across the Sahara. After rechecking that the country you're about to visit still allows hunting (regulations often change), contact the consulate to arrange to transport your weapons into the area. The consulate will require information on the make, model, caliber (or bore), and serial number of your guns; your expected arrival and departure dates; and where, what, and with whom you intend to hunt. In addition, you will have to contact either a minister of game or forestry in the island and/or the local police. Some countries will not allow you to bring in any handguns; others limit the number of rounds of ammunition (bullets) as well as the number of weapons you can bring.

ANTIGUA/BARBUDA: Some wild ducks and deer on Barbuda. Contact the Commissioner of Police, American Rd., St. John's, Antigua, WI, for information on importing firearms.

BAHAMAS: Hunting permits are granted to non-Bahamians after a stay of 90 days. Wild boar can be hunted on Andros and the Abaco Islands, and throughout the Bahamas there is open season on most varieties of dove, pheasant, heron, and other birds from September 15 until February 28. The season on mourning doves and several varieties of duck and geese extends through March 31; boar season takes place during the winter months. For more information on hunting, including protected species, bag limits, etc., contact the Bahamas Ministry of Agriculture and Fisheries, PO Box N 3028, Nassau, New Providence, Bahamas. Check with the nearest Bahamian consulate and also the Commissioner of Police, Royal Bahamas Police Force, PO Box N 458, Nassau, New Providence, Bahamas, about a gun license and bringing guns with you. They can also help you find a guide who knows the area.

BELIZE: The jungles of Belize teem with wild pig, deer, game birds, and coastal waterfowl. It is necessary to contact the Chief Forestry Officer, Ministry of Natural Resources, Belmopan, Belize, before attempting to organize an expedition, as well as the Commissioner of Police, Police Headquarters, Belmopan, Belize, if you wish to bring guns into the country. Ask the forest officer to put you in touch with a local guide; a hunting license is also required, unless your guide holds a government concession.

COLOMBIA: For the foreseeable future, species depletion has forced the government to close hunting on all game and fowl except doves. Limited expeditions can be arranged through *Fish and Game Frontiers,* PO Box 161, Pearce Mill Rd., Wexford, PA 15090 (phone: 412-935-1577 in Pennsylvania; 800-245-1950 elsewhere), or through *Alberto Lleras,* PO Box 3444, Carrera 15, 79-51, Office 102, Bogotá, Colombia. Firearm rentals can be arranged by the same sources; if you wish to bring your own guns, contact the nearest Colombian consulate, advise them of the number of guns, including full descriptions of each with serial numbers, number of rounds of ammunition, and dates of arrival and departure (you have to submit eight copies of this information).

DOMINICAN REPUBLIC: More hunting is allowed here than on any other Caribbean island. With an abundance of birds (doves, duck, pigeons), even the two national birds — cignas and tortolas — are fair game. However, there are specific hunting seasons and restrictions on certain birds and other animals. Contact the Dominican Tourist Information Center, 485 Madison Ave., New York, NY 10022 (phone: 212-826-0750).

HAITI: Open season for ducks, wild pigeons, and guinea hens is during November. Contact the Ministry of Interior and National Defense, Palais des Ministères, Port-au-Prince. Permits can be obtained through any consulate; local guides can be arranged through the tourist board on the island.

Sunken and Buried Treasure

It doesn't take too much imagination for a Caribbean vacationer to begin dreaming about discovering sunken or buried treasure. The area is alive with tales and relics of pirates, Spanish gold, sunken ships, and yellowed parchment maps that seem to cry out for some adventurous diver or explorer to dig deeper, look further, dive farther offshore — and discover a wealth of gold and precious stones. Estimates of the number of ships sunk in the Caribbean and western Atlantic are as high as 4,000; in the Anegada Channel of the British Virgin Islands alone, some 134 ships are supposed to have gone down between 1523 and 1833.

The Spanish kept excellent records of the treasure ships transporting the wealth of the New World across the Atlantic and Caribbean. The cargo manifest of a single ship, the *Nôtre Dame de Déliverance*, shows 1,170 pounds of gold bullion (packed into 17 chests), 15,399 gold doubloons, 153 gold snuff boxes weighing six ounces each, more than one million pieces of eight, 764 ounces of silver, 31 pounds of silver ore, six pairs of diamond earrings, a diamond ring, and several chests of precious stones.

Bear in mind that most of the ships that went down during this period either ran aground or tore out their bottoms on the numerous coral reefs that lie just beneath the surface of the water. Those treasure-laden ships sent to the bottom by pirate cannonfire (or pirate ships sunk by other vessels) were a total loss to all involved. Many of the ships that were sunk by enemy fire were warships or light cargo and messenger packets, not huge treasure galleons. Tides and sifting sands can cover a ship or move the wreck miles from its original site. These same tides can cause lost treasure to rise to the surface, too, as in the case of the woman who was walking on the beach of Grand Cayman Island some years ago and happened upon an estimated $100,000 in gold and diamond jewelry, gold, silver, and platinum. The first piece of jewelry was lying on the sand, and the rest was only six inches below the surface.

What follows is a list of the best treasure-hunting spots in the Caribbean, and we ask only a modest percentage of your findings as recompense:

BAHAMAS: North of Freeport, off Gorda Cay, lies the wreck of a wooden ship. What you may find there is unknown, but it makes an excellent starting point for your treasure hunt. The wreck of the *Nuestra Señora de la Maravilla* (which went down on January 4, 1656) is thought to be lying somewhere off Little Bahama Bank. Try Morgan's Bluff, at the northern tip of Andros Island, and also look for Morgan's Cave on Cat Island (Henry Morgan was one of the most successful pirates in the Caribbean and his treasure caches have never been found). Also, try a dive near Treasure Reef, where the Lucayan treasure was found in 1964.

BELIZE: Originally a colony of shipwrecked pirates, with the world's second longest barrier reef just off its well-traveled coastline, there is every reason to believe that more than one wreck lies among these treacherous shoals. Try the area just outside the reef.

BRITISH VIRGIN ISLANDS: Robert Louis Stevenson's *Treasure Island* is based on activities rumored to have taken place on Norman Island or Dead Man's Chest, both near Tortola, which was a pirate stronghold for quite some time. Also check both Anegada and Virgin Gorda as well as the Anegada Channel between them; the channel is known to be the site of over 130 wrecks. Waters of any of the surrounding isles could hold wrecks.

CAYMAN ISLANDS: As local legend has it, during a dark night in November 1788, a convoy of British merchant ships was sailing to the east of Grand Cayman. Due to the inaccuracy of the navigating charts in those days — and the coral reefs that lie just beneath the surface — this was a particularly hazardous route in these treacherous waters. It is possible the convoy was trying to avoid pirates, for British ships were a prime target for the French and Dutch privateers as well as independent freebooters (who cared little whose ships they attacked). The lead ship, the *Cordelia,* struck a reef and raised flags of warning and distress. The other ships misunderstood the signal in the darkness, and nine more ships struck the reef before anything could be done. Many of the passengers (one rumored to be royal) were rescued by the residents of the island's East End area. The fluke of an anchor, said to be a relic of this Wreck of Ten Sails, can be seen today from land, but the reef is known to be infested with sea urchins (which effectively prevents much treasure hunting there). In addition to the jewelry found on the beach here, a platinum bar (dated 1521) was recovered from a shipwreck just off Grand Cayman.

COLOMBIA: Morgan would have had to be very successful if, indeed, he did bury treasure on all the islands that claim to be the site of one of his hidden fortunes. But because it is strategically located between the old Spanish treasure ports of Porto Bello and Cartagena, San Andrés Island is a likely possibility. The odds are better, though, on adjacent Providencia Island or on one of the others around San Andrés.

DOMINICAN REPUBLIC and HAITI: In the opening days of Spain's presence in the Americas, the city of Santo Domingo (Dominican Republic) was its Caribbean headquarters. Explorers departed from here on their quests for gold and silver, and ships put in here before journeying to Spain. Ships leaving the port city (on the southern crescent of the island) had to pass through the narrow passages at either end of the island in order to return to Spain. If they passed through the Windward Passage to the west end, they had to skirt the reefs and shallows around the Caicos Islands and pass through the Mouchoir (Silver) Bank (northeast of Hispaniola) before heading for the open sea. Once through the eastern channel (Mona Passage), they were in open waters. Île de la Tortue, off the northwest side of the island (now Haiti), made a perfect hiding place for pirates and could easily be the legendary stronghold of Tortuga. From here they watch the western passage, and if a prize should make for the sea through the eastern channel, a pirate ship could be dispatched from the island to intercept a treasure-laden galleon before it made open water. Île de la Tortue itself is a good place to look for buried treasure, and there have been reports of wrecks near Silver Bank. The wreck of the *Concepción,* discovered here late in 1978, carried about $40 million in silver and antiques.

JAMAICA: On June 7, 1692, an earthquake and tidal wave hit the island of Jamaica, and the city of Port Royal literally sank beneath the waves. Long before the city was flooded, it had often been compared with the biblical Sodom, for there was one tavern or alehouse or winery for every ten people. During the 1960s, divers brought up hundreds of pieces of silver, pewter, and ceramics, and enough ethnographic evidence to prove Port Royal's rightful claim to being the former center of sin in the West Indies. The remains of this lively city have been picked through by many divers, but something new is always being brought to the surface. There are also reports of several wrecks off Negril, and records show that six ships went down in Montego Bay (1780). The Seranilla Bank, about 250 miles southeast of Jamaica (about halfway between Jamaica and the coast of Honduras), is reputed to be where an entire Spanish treasure fleet went down during a hurricane in 1655.

ST. EUSTATIUS: The Dutch pirates were as successful at sea as the Dutch merchants were on land; with financial encouragement from the Dutch West Indies Company (which bought plundered goods for resale), Dutch pirates managed to take a goodly number of Spanish (and other) ships. The entire yield of one successful 1717 expedition, estimated at one million pieces of eight, was placed in a cave on Statia for storage; later, the mouth of the cave was sealed by an earthquake and the treasure has never been recovered. The *Zeelander,* a Dutch warship, went down off the northern tip of the island in 1792 carrying 500,000 guilders in gold and silver with it.

ST. MARTIN/ST. MAARTEN: The Portuguese galleon *Santissimo Trinidade,* carrying some 2.5 million cruzados in gold, is believed to have been lost off the eastern coast of St. Martin in 1781.

For the Mind

Best Island Museums

 It should hardly be surprising that there are so many interesting museums scattered throughout the Atlantic and Caribbean islands. For almost 500 years — first as colonies, then as independent or associated states of every ideology — they have been the beneficiaries and the victims of just about every kind of political organization of which human society is capable. In the course of this long and hardly idyllic association, first with Europe, then with North and South America, artifacts and documents have accumulated on island shores like flotsam and jetsam. And during all this time the indigenous art of the islands developed, and this, too, finds its place in the exhibits of area museums.

But the best thing about island museums is that they are easy and fun. Easy, because they are not monolithic; they can be slipped into and out of as comfortably as the sea; and they can offer an interesting hour's diversion when the rain is falling, when the beach is just a touch too crowded, or when the day's lunch is still weighing heavily. Fun, because in that hour you will assimilate more than you ever thought possible about island history and culture, and in island cultures as rich and diverse as these, that is a fine bonus to go with your suntan. Below, a survey of the best museums in the islands:

BARBADOS: The *Barbados Museum,* housed in the Old Military Barracks built by the Royal Engineers in 1820, contains an excellent collection of artifacts and relics illustrating the life, culture, history, art, and geography of Barbados. Among the items on display is a copy of George Washington's *Barbados Journal,* relics of slavery, geological and archaeological specimens, plantation furniture, china and silver, and West Indian prints dating from the 17th century. A Children's Gallery contains lovely dollhouses and historical models. One mile from Bridgetown, the museum is open Mondays through Saturdays from 9 AM to 6 PM. Small admission charge.

BERMUDA: Though rather remotely situated on Ireland Island, the *Maritime Museum* offers a formidable display of sea treasures in a unique setting. Located in an old dockyard and housed in the building where the munitions of the Royal Navy were once guarded, this museum not only offers a collection of full-scale and model ships, but also has nautical relics and equipment, charts, prints, paintings, maps, and whaling gear illustrating Bermuda's connection with the sea. It also displays Teddy Tucker's collection of underwater treasures and exhibits on the history of diving. There is also an informal restaurant. The museum is open from 10 AM to 4:30 PM daily. Admission charge.

CUBA: Havana has several fine museums. Housed in the elegant 18th-century structure that once served as the governor general's residence is the *Museo de la Ciudad de la Habana.* This museum offers an excellent display of city memorabilia and an outdoor patio filled with indigenous plants and trees. Second-story exhibitions contain documents, military relics, and artifacts from 1868 to 1898. The ground-floor exhibitions cover the period 1898–1920 (when US "protection" ended) and include a wonderful display of antique cars and carriages such as a small spit-and-polished fire engine made in London and the luxurious touring Cadillac of one of Cuba's former governors. A restoration of an elegant Victorian living room is another of the museum's highlights. The museum is across from the Plaza de Armas (technically, the Plaza Carlos Manuel Cespedes). Open daily from 3 to 6 and 7 to 9 PM. Free.

The *Museo de Artes Decorativas* primarily features furnishings and decor of prosperous Cuban homes of the late Victorian era. Of particular interest are the selection of hand-carved and polished armoires of native coama wood and the colorful examples of Cuban stained and simulated stained glass, which favors magnificent combinations of deep blues, reds, and purples. There is also a sizable display of china, mostly imported from France, England, China, and Japan. The museum is on the Plaza de la Catedral, very close to the Plaza de Armas. It is open from 1:15 to 8:30 PM Tuesdays through Saturdays, 9:15 AM to 8:30 PM on Sundays. Free.

The *Museo de la Revolución* tells the story of Cuba's revolutionary struggle from 1868 to the present. Housed in the marble-lined halls of the former Presidential Palace, the three floors of exhibitions contain an incredible collection of photographs, documents, and relics of revolutionary leaders and martyrs, including the suit of José Martí, several death masks, watches, and other personal items. All exhibits have descriptions in Spanish, but this museum is part of the New Havana tour, which has an English-speaking guide. The outdoor exhibits behind the palace include the glass-encased yacht *Granma,* which brought Fidel Castro and 81 others from Guatemala to Oriente Province; homemade tanks, small planes, and other vehicles of revolutionary significance, such as the truck, pocked with bulletholes, that was used to attack the Presidential Palace on May 13, 1957. To get to the Museum of the Revolution, follow Calle Empedrado to Avenida de Belgica and turn left until you reach the palace. It is open from 12:30 to 7:30 PM Tuesdays through Fridays; on Saturdays and Sundays from 11:30 AM to 5:30 PM. Free.

DOMINICAN REPUBLIC: The history of the Dominican Republic from 1422 to 1821 is presented in the *Museo de las Casas Reales (Museum of the Royal Houses).* Exhibits include a re-created courtroom, pharmacy, and sugar mill and an excellent display of tapestries, maps, and artifacts. The building once served as a Palace of Justice and governor's residence. On Calle Las Damas in colonial Santo Domingo, it offers tours in Spanish and English. Closed Mondays. Small admission charge.

HAITI: There are several museums of interest in Port-au-Prince. The *Musée d'Art Haïtien* features the work of modern painters such as Rigaud Benôit, Jasmin Joseph, and André Pierre, all of whom belong to the school that was once called primitive and is now referred to as *naïf.* Financial support for this museum is provided by wealthy American art patrons. Open Mondays through Saturdays from 9 AM to 1 PM. Free. On the corner of Rue Capois and Rue St. Honoré.

It is the famous primitive tempera-paint murals of the *Cathedral of the Holy Trinity (Ste. Trinité)* that first drew international attention to Haitian painting. In these murals, all the celebrated religious figures are black except Judas, who is white. The murals are open to the public from 8:30 AM to noon weekdays. The Episcopal cathedral is on the corner of Detouches and Rue S. Duvalier.

The *Musée du Panthéon National* traces the origins of Haitian man through a vast collection of national artifacts, including one of the six anchors of Columbus's flagship, the *Santa Maria,* and Toussaint L'Ouverture's pocket watch. The museum is on the Champs de Mars near the Palace. English-speaking guides are available. Hours are 9 AM to 5 PM daily (subject to change by the presiding curator). Small admission charge.

JAMAICA: The *Institute of Jamaica* in Kingston has one of the most extensive and scholarly collections of West Indian and Jamaican books, prints, and historical documents in the world. It contains both a Natural History Museum and a Historical Gallery, and its West Indian Research Library is the best outside Great Britain. Open daily except Sundays from 9:30 AM to 5 PM. Free. 12 East St.

The *National Gallery of Art,* in its own new building near the waterfront in Kingston, features Jamaican art from the 17th century to the present. Although it contains portraits of planters and their families, the gallery concentrates largely on the period from the 1920s to the present. Impressionist paintings, colorful portrayals of all aspects of Jamaican life, and abstracts are included in the impressive collection. Among the most interesting painters represented are Barrington Watson, who spent time as an artist in residence at Emory University in Atlanta, Karl Parboosingh, and Albert Huie. Sculptures and drawings by Edna Manley are also exhibited. Open daily. Small admission fee.

The *Jamaican People's Museum of Crafts and Technology* showcases crafts and techniques rooted in Africa, Europe, Asia, and Central America and the ways in which these skills and their products have been adapted to their "new" Jamaican environment. Indoors and out at Old King's House stables, Spanish Town. Open 10 AM to 5 PM Mondays through Fridays. Small admission fee.

MARTINIQUE: The birthplace of Empress Joséphine, *La Pagerie* in Trois-Ilets, has a collection of her memorabilia; and the town of St. Pierre, which suffered almost total destruction when Mt. Pelée erupted in 1902, has the *Musée Volcanologique.* La Pagerie is open daily. Small admission charge. The museum is open daily except Mondays from 9 AM to 5:30 PM. Small admission charge.

PUERTO RICO: San Juan is a city of museums. The *Pablo Casals Museum* contains a fascinating collection of memorabilia left to the people of Puerto Rico by the famous cellist. Included are manuscripts, scores, photographs, his cello, and a library of videotapes that can be played on request. Open Mondays through Saturdays, 9 AM to 5 PM, 1 to 5 PM on Sundays. Free. The museum is next door to the historic San José Church, facing the Plaza San José.

The *Museum of Puerto Rican Art* exhibits paintings and sculpture from the 18th century to the present in a lovely renovated Spanish colonial building. Open daily except Mondays and Thursdays, 9 AM to noon and 1 to 4:30 PM. Small admission charge. 253 Calle Cristo.

Two museums are housed in the renovated 18th-century Casa de Callejon. The *Museum of Colonial Architecture* is on the first floor and displays scale models of historic sites and old houses of San Juan as well as photographs and samples of woodwork, ironwork, and tiles. Open Wednesdays through Sundays from 9 AM to noon and 1 to 4 PM. Free. The *Museum of the Puerto Rican Family,* on the second floor, illustrates how a typical San Juan family lived a hundred years ago. Open Wednesdays through Sundays, 9 AM to noon and 1 to 4 PM. Small admission charge. Calle Fortaleza, corner La Capilla.

The *Museum of Conquest and Colonization* is built on the foundations of a 1508 Spanish fort. Open weekdays from 9 AM to 5 PM; weekends, 10 AM to 5 PM. Off Route 2 on the way to Dorado. Free.

One of Puerto Rico's indigenous arts, the carving of santos (figures), was brought to the island by Spanish settlers in the 16th century. Although this art form was lost for some time, there has been an effort to revitalize it in recent years. At the *Museum of Puerto Rican Santos,* in the Museum of Graphic Arts building, there is an excellent collection of the hand-carved religious figurines and statues which convey the high quality and delicacy that marked this once-flourishing craft. Open Wednesdays through Sundays from 9 AM to noon and 1 to 4 PM. Free. 101 San Sebastián (on the first floor of the Casa de los Contrafuertes) in Old San Juan.

Testaments in Stone: Historic Sites

 With the exception of the ancient Maya and Toltec ruins of Mexico and scattered Indian relics, most historic sites of the Caribbean and Atlantic islands date from the colonial period after the arrival of Columbus. These sites reflect the course of European colonialism in the New World — the presence and influence of the French, English, Dutch, and Spanish on the islands, and the struggles for control. What follows are the most compelling Caribbean sites:

ANTIGUA: *Nelson's Dockyard* was the major British naval yard in the Caribbean from 1707 until 1899, when ships simply became too large to negotiate the entrance to its harbor. It got its name (and its reputation) from the four-year period (1784–1787) when Captain Horatio Nelson was in command. The dockyard area includes the *Admiral's Inn,* a hotel and restaurant made from bricks that came to Antigua as ships' ballast; the Admiral's House (now a museum), which never actually housed Admiral Nelson; the Officers' Quarters; and the *Copper and Lumber Store,* now an inn.

BARBADOS: Some of the finest antique greathouses in the Caribbean can be found on Barbados. *Villa Nova, Porters, Mullins Mill, Drax Hall,* and *St. Nicholas Abbey* are all elegantly preserved and occasionally or regularly open to the public; check with the Board of Tourism. *Farley Hill* and the *Morgan Lewis Mill* are also relics of the old plantation days.

BERMUDA: The entire town of *St. George,* Bermuda's first capital, with its tiny, narrow lanes and 17th-century treasures, is, in a sense, a museum. Founded in 1612, its most interesting historical sites include St. Peter's Church, the oldest Anglican church in the Western Hemisphere; Fort St. Catherine, which houses historic dioramas and replicas of the crown jewels; the 1620 State House and King's Square, where the annual Peppercorn Ceremony marks the annual payment of the State House's rent; and a Confederate Museum and Carriage Museum full of assorted artifacts.

CURAÇAO: The oldest synagogue extant in the Western Hemisphere, *Mikve Israel-Emanuel* is in Willemstad on the corner of Columbusstraat and Kerkstraat. Built in 1732 in the Dutch colonial architectural tradition, the interior is carpeted with a layer of white sand, symbolizing the journey of the Jews across the desert to the Promised Land. Next door is the *Jewish Historical and Cultural Museum,* which served as a rabbinical house and, later, a Chinese laundry, until the remains of an ancient *mikvah* (ritual bath) was uncovered in its courtyard. The museum contains exhibits of centuries-old religious relics, tools, and artifacts.

CUBA: *Colonial Havana* offers one of the most comprehensive views of Spanish colonial life in all of the Caribbean. We recommend a walking tour of the area, which will take you to the Doric Temple, El Templete, the Museum of the City of Havana, and the Plaza of the Cathedral, where you will see the Museum of Decorative Arts and the Cathedral of Immaculate Conception, both in the Spanish architectural tradition.

DOMINICAN REPUBLIC: As a center of activity in the gold-hunting days, Santo Domingo became a city of elegant living. All along the Calle Las Damas in old Santo Domingo you will find buildings from these gilded days — the Bastidas House, the Chapel of Our Lady of Remedies, the Museum of the Royal Houses, and others. Also on Calle Las Damas is the National Pantheon, formerly a Jesuit monastery, built in 1714.

The oldest cathedral in the Western Hemisphere is the Cathedral of Santa María la

Menor, whose 450-year-old nave is said to house the mortal remains of Christopher Columbus. It is also in Santo Domingo, on the south side of Columbus Square.

HAITI: Perhaps the most astounding spectacle in the Caribbean is the *Citadelle,* on a remote mountaintop more than 3,000 feet above the sea. This amazing structure required the labor of 200,000 citizens, all former slaves and all conscripted by King Henry Christophe to drag thousands of tons of rocks and hundreds of cannon up the tortuous road to build a fort that would protect him and his court from an anticipated invasion. Although the journey, made partly on muleback, may take its toll in bottom-bruising, the monumental site itself is worth it. Before starting the climb, explore the ruins of King Henry's *Palais de Sans Souci,* intended to be the most regal building ever raised in the New World. The Citadelle and Palais are near the town of Milot, a short drive from Cap-Haïtien.

JAMAICA: Across the harbor from Kingston, *Port Royal* was called "the world's wickedest city" while it served as headquarters for the privateer (pirate) Henry Morgan. Although a good part of the town was toppled into the harbor by a treacherous tidal wave and earthquake in 1692, several remnants from those ribald days remain intact, including St. Peter's Church, Fort Charles, the Old Naval Hospital (now a museum of Port Royal relics), and the National Trust Tower.

MARTINIQUE: *La Pagerie,* in Trois-Ilets, was once a busy plantation and thriving sugar factory. It was also the birthplace of Marie Josephe Rose Tascher de la Pagerie, who became the Empress Joséphine, wife of Napoleon. Her childhood bed, clothes, and letters are on display in the kitchen, which occupies a separate building beside the crumbled plantation house foundations. The gentleman who assembled the collection, Dr. Robert Rose-Rosette (now semi-retired), lives next door.

Another site worth visiting is the town of *St. Pierre,* "the Pompeii of the West Indies," which was devastated by a volcano in 1902. What remains of this once-flourishing city of stately villas, mansions, and gardens are the ruins of the theater and cathedral and the broken walls of the homes.

MEXICO: *Chichén Itzá* was a flourishing Mayan and Toltec center that dominated the entire Yucatán Peninsula until 1224. Many of the ruins at this major archaeological site reflect the bellicose nature of the Toltec culture — including the ritual practice of human sacrifice. Among those buildings of particular interest are the Temple of the Warriors, the Group of a Thousand Columns, the Tzompantiti, the Temple of the Chacmool, and the ball court. Day-long bus tours from Cancún visit the site daily.

NEVIS: In Charlestown, surrounded by beautifully maintained gardens, is a replica of the estate house where Alexander Hamilton was born, in 1755, open to the public.

PUERTO RICO: The seven-square-block area of *Old San Juan,* in the westernmost part of the city, contains a myriad interesting sites dating back to Spanish colonial days, when this harbor was considered essential to Spanish supremacy in the New World. Today, you can still explore the moats, turrets, and tunnels of Fort San Cristóbal and El Morro, the two forts that were part of the wall built around the city to protect it from unfriendly visitors like Sir Francis Drake. Two blocks from El Morro's exit, at the Plaza de San José, you will find the Church of San José, the Pablo Casals Museum, and the Casa de los Contrafuertes, all interesting colonial structures. Heading west on Calle San Sebastián, you will reach Casa Blanca, the intended home of Juan Ponce de Léon, which served as the residence of his descendants and several Spanish and American military commanders before it was turned into a museum. Not far from the Casa Blanca is La Fortaleza, the Western Hemisphere's oldest executive mansion, the home of more than 200 Puerto Rican governors. Built in 1540 and given palatial additions in the 19th century, it is open to the public for guided tours.

ST. KITTS: The landmark that gave St. Kitts its reputation as "the Gibraltar of the Caribbean" is *Brimstone Hill.* On top of a 750-foot cliff, this enormously impressive fortress took the British more than 100 years to build. Although the French laid siege to Brimstone Hill and captured it in 1782 during their attempt to reconquer the island from the British, the fort returned to British hands, as did the island, under the conditions of the Treaty of Versailles in 1783.

US VIRGIN ISLANDS: In the heart of Christiansted on St. Croix stands a group of 18th-century buildings that the Danes built after buying St. Croix from the French. The US now maintains this area as a National Historic Site. At the Visitors Information Bureau in the Scale House near the harborfront, you can pick up a *Walking Tour Guide. Fort Christiansvaern,* which contains military treasures, battlements, and dungeons, is one of the site's attractions with particular appeal to children.

For the Spirit

Luxury Resorts and Special Havens

It is usually possible to generalize about US cookie-cutter hotel chains and their motel counterparts with relative safety. A room in a TraveLodge in Evansville, Indiana, closely resembles a TraveLodge room in Effingham, Illinois, or Emporia, Kansas. And on the domestic hotel scene, there are certain things you are justified in expecting. Not so in the islands, where no two big hotels — let alone small inns — are even remotely alike.

Things beyond stateside imagining regularly affect island hotel operation (if you doubt us, take a peek at Herman Wouk's *Don't Stop the Carnival*): things like hurricanes (rarely), late or nonflying planes (all too often), too much or too little rain (if it isn't one . . .). And the candle you find in the dresser drawer even at luxurious *Little Dix Bay* is there in case the electricity fails (in local parlance — "generator, he out"), which can happen anywhere — though most blackouts are momentary rather than extended events.

What you can look forward to throughout the islands, however, at large hotels and little ones, is a sort of personal attention and one-to-one thoughtfulness that has been forgotten — or has simply never existed — in other parts of the world. The manager is usually accessible — and in a small hotel or guesthouse is probably the owner. Planned activities are less often the rule than enthusiastically active help with any plans you'd personally like to make — whether they involve chartering a yacht, packing a picnic, or moving your hammock to that pair of palms nearer the beach. Other nice touches: smiles and "good mornings" that sound like they're meant, staffs that do small favors without waiting around for big tips, fresh flowers in your room as a matter of course, and (oh, most saving grace) a shelf of dog-eared paperbacks left by former guests for the very moment you finish your Agatha Christies.

The hotels and inns below are our special favorites. They are of two basic sorts: big-name resorts where a special sense of style and luxury have proved especially compatible with their island setting, and small places with an atmosphere, location, and/or service that makes them especially appealing. Most are on the expensive side (i.e., $160 and up a day for two, usually including two meals in the high season); a few, as noted, are actually reasonably priced, but each is a resort apart.

BIG NAMES

CANEEL BAY RESORT, St. John, US Virgin Islands: Perfect serenity is what it offers most. This 170-acre resort estate in one small part of the 9,700 forested acres that Laurance Rockefeller gave to the US to become the Virgin Islands National Park is still operated by the Rockresorts folk (though the company has been sold to CSX Corp.). The only thing flamboyant on the property is the tree of the same name, and only the flower colors — scarlet hibiscus, yellow trumpet vine, purple morning-glories — are loud. There are six superb beaches, and swimming, basking, snorkeling, and small-boat sailing occupy most days; tranquillity is further protected by the national park's ban on water skiing. Just next door is Trunk Bay, with its marked underwater nature trail for snorkeling; more ambitious dive trips are also available, as are ranger-led tours through the park. In the eating and drinking department, the noon buffet on the Garden Terrace is legendary, but when you've ingested one you've experienced it all; so you may want to opt for a snack at the *Sugar Mill,* a picnic at Trunk Bay, or a bite at one of Cruz Bay's native restaurants. A steel band arrives to play for dinner dancing several times a week, and there are occasional movies. Otherwise, it is happily, serenely, and early to bed. Information: Caneel Bay Resort, St. John, USVI 00830 (phone: 809-776-6111; in NY State, 212-586-4459; elsewhere, 800-223-7637).

CASA DE CAMPO, La Romana, Dominican Republic: The aim was — quite simply — to build the perfect sports resort. The result was this big complex built on 7,000 acres near the old sugar mill town of La Romana. It has just about everything: two fine Pete Dye golf courses (with a third to be added this year), a terrific 13-court tennis layout called La Terraza (there are 4 more all-weather courts elsewhere on the property), stables (both English- and Western-style riding), 2 polo fields (with coach in attendance), guides and boats for deep-sea and river fishing, trap- and skeet-shooting ranges. All this plus villa rooms that Oscar de la Renta had a hand in decorating. An improved sandy beach — Las Minitas — is the latest seaside addition; its pleasures include swaying palms, showers, changing facilities, and a snack bar where, rumor has it, the hamburgers are super (better even than the very good ones at the main club-house). The place to be at sunset is *La Caña;* an imaginative, thatched pavilion with a 360° view. There's dinner in the main dining room (grills, local lobster are special). Other appetizing options: country inn–like *La Piazzetta* (elegant Italian); *Tropicana* (seafood), *Casa del Rio* (Continental with a spectacular view), built into Altos de Chavon, the evocation of a 15th-century artisans' village atop a nearby hill, and the *Lago Grill* (breakfast and lunch). For merengue and dance-mood music, there's *La Caña;* for discoing, *Genesis* in Altos de Chavon. Information: Casa de Campo, PO Box 140, La Romana, Dominican Republic (phone: 809-682-2111; in Florida, 305-856-5405).

HYATT DORADO BEACH, Dorado Beach, Puerto Rico: The ultimate golf resort, with two of its own Robert Trent Jones courses to play (and two more down the shore at its sister *Hyatt Cerromar Beach* hotel). Opened in 1958 as one of the Caribbean's first real luxury resorts, it was not only built beautiful but *kept* beautiful by the peerless Rockresorts group. Now under the Hyatt banner, it remains quietly posh; a few luxury casita rooms (said to be the best in the house) have been added near the pool, and the tradition of quality continues. Palm-shaded, low-rise villas with stylish rooms, balconies, and patios are utterly relaxing to come home to; most are but a few bare footsteps from the beach. Off the golf course, there's first-rate tennis (with a resident pro and instruction available); swimming in two lagoons, one pool, or from one of the small scalloped beaches that line the sea. With the Hyatt's *Cerromar* next door (its guests have exchange dining privileges), you sometimes have to wait for a table at dinner, but it's worth it for the view of palms, sea, and surf, as well as the excellent food. The frankly romantic alternative is to make reservations at tiny *Su Casa,* the lantern-lit Spanish restaurant in the house that was once the home of the plantation's former owners; the menu is more Continental than Iberian, but still fine; flamenco dancing and guitars add atmosphere. Summer packages are a good buy. Information: Hyatt Dorado Beach Hotel, Dorado Beach, PR 00646 (phone: 809-796-1600; 800-228-9000).

LITTLE DIX BAY, Virgin Gorda, British Virgin Islands: There's sort of a fresh-aired exhilaration about life at Little Dix. The guests that gather on its sunny crescent of beach are younger and more active than their counterparts at Caneel Bay; they generally love sailing, sunning, swimming, and snorkeling in their own home bay and picnic trips to the island's other blissful beaches; there's also Peter Burwash tennis, horseback riding, and biking. The resort's central buildings are actually mostly terraces topped with peaked roofs that look like giant beach hats. But during the day you won't find many people under them; everybody's out and doing. At night, everyone gathers in the *Sugar Mill* bar for drinks. Sometimes there's music, dancing, or local entertainment during and after dinner. The moonrises are spectacular. Our favorite rooms are those in the shingle-topped, hexagonal stilt-houses west of the main buildings, with patios and hammocks underneath; inside, you'll find all the traditional Rockresort comforts. Its carefree, open-air life makes this a particularly great place for a family holiday. Information: Little Dix Bay Hotel, Virgin Gorda, BVI (phone: 809-495-5555; in NY State, 800-442-8198; elsewhere, 800-223-7637).

ROUND HILL, Montego Bay, Jamaica: Actually set in a quiet cove several miles west of the clamor of Montego Bay, this is the sort of traditional resort (recently renovated) that harkens back to the days of colonial Jamaica. It was once so exclusive that there was a popular impression that guest privileges were restricted to members of the peerage. Things are a little more accessible nowadays, though not much, for this is where the so-called society tends to congregate when visiting Jamaica. The protected atmosphere is accentuated by the fact that many "guests" actually own the villas in which they are staying, and the total facilities include 36 extremely stylish rooms in the very comfortable Pineapple House, plus 60 suites in the surrounding 27 villas, which are available when their owners are not in residence. The hotel operation (including the restaurants) continues to close from April 15 to December 15, but some villa suites now remain available on a weekly basis, EP (with a cook, maid, and gardener included in the rate), throughout the year. This is by far the snazziest address on Jamaica, with prices to match, and if you like to keep your upper lip stiff while sunning and swimming, this is the place for you. Information: Round Hill Hotel, PO Box 64, Montego Bay, Jamaica (phone: 809-952-5150).

LA SAMANNA, St. Martin: This spot is where the likes of Redford and Cavett come to soak up some rays as anonymously as possible. The quarter-mile crescent of white sand beach is merely perfect, and the Mediterranean-cum-Moorish design enhances the Arabian nights mystique. Air conditioning is absent in the beachside villas, but somehow the slowly rotating ceiling fans not only provide adequate ventilation but also heighten the impression that you are involved in a scene straight out of *Casablanca*. The resort is chic, sleek, more than slightly sexy, and so expensive that you're tempted to try to pay your way in 30-, 60-, and 90-day notes. And to add hunger to poverty, the room rates include no food. There are 14 air-conditioned rooms in the main building, but returning guests tend to opt for the 46 apartments in the low villas that are set beside the serene stretch of sand. The dining room offers some of the haute-est cuisine on the island, and the pervasive French flavor has a dash of Créole spice. Prices for meals can approximate the cost of a room, but lest you think these tariffs discourage visitors, there's a minimum booking of two weeks at Christmastime. In July, a special 2-week spa program is offered. The most arrogant attitude in the Caribbean, but consider that part of the "charm." Information: La Samanna, BP 159, Baie Longue 97150, St. Martin, FWI (phone: 011 590-87-51-22).

LA BELLE CRÉOLE, St. Martin: Conceived by the late Claude Philippe (of New York's *Waldorf-Astoria*) and operated by Conrad International Hotels, this 156-room luxury resort is modeled after a typical fishing village on the French Riviera. Its 27 one-to three-story villas are linked by cobblestone streets, sidewalks, and courtyards, all surrounding a village square. All units are decorated in a provençal motif and have air conditioning, minibars, TVs, and phones. Some have beamed ceilings, and most have private terraces overlooking Marigot Bay or the lagoon. There are 42 connecting rooms, five of which are equipped for the handicapped. Amenities include 3 beaches, a freshwater pool, 4 tennis courts and pro shop, and a full range of water sports. There are also boutiques, secretarial services, a drugstore, car rental agency, and concierge on the premises. The resort's restaurant features international and Créole cuisine; a café-bar at poolside serves light meals and snacks; a beach bar and a main bar offer regular entertainment. Children of any age stay with their parents free of charge. Information: La Belle Créole, BP 118, Marigot 97150, St. Martin, FWI (phone: 011 590-87-58-66 or 800-445-8667).

SMALL WONDERS

ANSE CHASTANET BEACH, Soufrière, St. Lucia: One of the great small island retreats, it's not really a hotel in the usual sense but a cluster of octagonal cottages perched on cool green hillsides above the Caribbean. Most of the 24 hillside rooms have wraparound views of St. Lucia's twin trademark mountains — the jolly green Pitons, their lush valley, and the sun-glinted sea beyond; there are also 12 beachside units. The view is beautiful and so is the privacy — ideal for reading, writing, loving, sleeping, or just watching the bougainvillea ruffle in the breeze. When you're ready, the beach is down 125 steps, a trip you aren't likely to take more than once a day. But not to worry. The fine gray sands below are equipped with a life-sustaining snack bar, chaises, Sunfish, snorkel and dive gear. At the end of the day, to reward your upward climb, the main building (another stack of octagons) offers a congenial bar, good company, food to match. And Soufrière, a truly unspoiled West Indian town, is only a short drive away. Information: Anse Chastanet Beach Hotel, Box 216, Soufrière, St. Lucia (phone: 809-454-7355).

BIRAS CREEK, Virgin Gorda, British Virgin Islands: It feels far away because it is — a 15-minute taxi ride plus a boat ride (both complimentary) from the Virgin Gorda airstrip. But what a place to soak up sun and unwind. The resort's 150 acres reach from a blue bay on one side, up and over a hill, and then down again to the sea on the other. The 30 beachside suites in 15 cottages and 2 private suites with sunken tubs are luxury in depth right down to their shaggy rugs. Nothing showy, but lots of the kind of fine contemporary decor for which the Scandinavians are famous. The whole place is that way: It's as though the Norwegian shipping magnate who founded it had sat in one of his own beach chairs musing on what might be pleasing, and voilà! (or the Norwegian equivalent). Here it is: airy bedrooms, sitting rooms (with small fridges stocked with rum and ginger ale), patios facing the sea, and discreetly walled outdoor showers that give you the feeling you're bathing in a waterfall. At the glittering beach, there's sunbathing, swimming, snorkeling, sailing, and a bar made out of a weathered boat hull to provide refreshments. There's also a small nature sanctuary and 2 tennis courts just a short stroll away. It's a 5-mile hike (or bike trip) to town (bikes are free), but day sailing trips to other beaches are more fun and often include memorable picnics. At cocktail time, everyone sleeks up and gathers in the castle-shaped clubhouse on the heights for drinks, sunset viewing, and dinner. Information: Biras Creek, PO Box 54, Virgin Gorda, BVI (phone: 809-494-3555 or 5-3556).

CAP JULUCA, Maundays Bay, Anguilla: The Caribbean's newest super-luxury resort, spread over 179 acres of southwestern coast and overlooking the smoky mountains of St. Martin. Named for the Arawak rainbow god, *Juluca* is exquisitely Moroccan, with Moorish arches, domes, and flowered courtyards. At press time, 18 rooms were ready for occupancy; 20 more are scheduled for completion by 1989. Luxury doubles and 1- and 2-bedroom suites with covered or roof terraces, and 3- and 4-bedroom villas with open patios, will be spacious and splendidly appointed. It's restaurant, *Pimms,* has already become *the* dining spot on Anguilla. There's also tennis and a full range of water sports. Information: Cap Juluca, PB 240, Maundays Bay, Anguilla, Leeward Islands, BWI (phone: 809 497-6666/6779).

CAPTAIN'S QUARTERS, Windwardside, Saba: A very small, special place on a very small island, simple and friendly and soothing. The Victorian main house was once a sea captain's home, and accommodations include 10 rooms in an adjacent 100-year-old annex, each decorated with antiques and ingenuity (some four-poster beds, lots of wicker, bright colors, and hand-painted headboards). The rooms are big and pretty and comfortable, and there's a view from the balcony outside that sweeps the surrounding hillsides and valleys all the way to the sea. Meals are served on the terrace beside the garden, and there's a small pool and deck for dips and sunning. If you feel like moving off a bit, try a hike up Mt. Scenery or ride down to the island's capital town — The Bottom — for a look around, or maybe just carry on down to the harbor where *Saba Deep* launches its scuba diving trips. In the late afternoon, stroll up to *Scout's Place* (a nearby "bed 'n' board" facility) for a cold beer and a warm conversation; Sabans are people worth meeting. This is the perfect place to get back in touch with yourself — or with someone you like a lot. Information: Captain's Quarters, Windwardside, Saba, Netherlands Antilles (phone: 011 599-4-2201).

CASTELETS, Morne Lurin, St. Barthélemy: It's as though a small, very elegant part of France had been transplanted to an island mountaintop. French provincial antiques, handsome fabrics, and chic prints decorate its 10 rooms — 6 individual and 2 two-bedroom villas — each with its own full-length balcony from which to enjoy the views of the neat little port city of Gustavia and the sea, beaches, hills, and valleys below. Meals are superb. There's a tiny pool, though no other sports facilities, and there's a nice small beach down a rugged road on the other side of the mountain. If you're a fearless driver, rent a car; otherwise, the hotel will call an island car to take you wherever you'd like to go. Breakfast is included in the rates. A beautiful retreat. Information: Castelets, Morne Lurin, 97133 St. Barthélemy, FWI (phone: 011 596-27-61-73).

COCCOLOBA PLANTATION, Barnes Bay, Anguilla: Formerly *La Santé*, this deluxe 52-villa resort reopened with new management, a new name, and a lovely new look after a $3-million refurbishment. The resort is built on a cliff overlooking the beautiful white beaches of Meads and Barnes bays, and all accommodations have unobstructed ocean views. Each of the 40 seaside cottages has a refrigerator, TV, ceiling fan, air conditioning, and patio. The main house has a lovely pool with swim-up bar, and a spa with Jacuzzi and exercise room. Standard amenities include a one-time complimentary stocked refrigerator. There's also tennis on 2 lighted courts, water sports, sunset cruises, and sightseeing and shopping excursions to neighboring islands. The resort's 2 restaurants feature Caribbean/Continental cuisine. Information: Coccoloba Plantation, PB 332, Barnes Bay, Anguilla, BWI (phone: 809 497-6871).

COTTON HOUSE, Mustique, the Grenadines: This very small isle is Princess Margaret's personal Caribbean play place (she has a house here), and the people with whom you share it are apt to be peers in stylish cutoffs or barefoot but well-heeled Americans. This hostelry was once part of a working plantation, and it has been superbly refurbished and decorated by Oliver Messell with intriguing English and Caribbean antiques — sea chests, silver, brasses, and a marvelous secretary's desk covered with cockle shells. Guest suites are in separate cottages, all very pretty and comfortable. Daytimes are apt to be casual. There are beaches to sun on and swim from, water sports (Macaroni Beach has some surf), a tennis court, and an elegant hilltop swimming pool. Nights are somewhat dressier, especially if the princess is in residence. Perhaps because the hotel has so few guests (38 at the most), the welcome seems especially pleasant and personal. Information: Cotton House Hotel, Mustique, St. Vincent (phone: 809-456-7777; in the US, 212-696-1323).

CURTAIN BLUFF, Antigua: Curtain Bluff's rooms ramble along the beach-lined edges of a breeze-catching peninsula that pokes into the Caribbean on the island's south side. Dedicated to (at most) 120 guests, who enjoy the best of island sport and don't mind being very comfortable and personally catered to while they do, this peaceful oasis offers not only pleasing rooms (the prettiest are the pastel suites), all with porches or balconies looking out on sea, surf, and sky, but impeccably maintained Sunfish sailboats, water skiing, snorkel and scuba gear (with their own compressor on the premises and rock pools and reefs just offshore), plus 3 Har-Tru and 1 artificial grass tennis court with a wintertime resident pro. Nothing flashy — just quality down to its tennis socks. Of more than passing interest, the annual spring Antigua Sailing Week, an international regatta, is cosponsored by the *Bluff*. The beach bar, shaded by plume-fronded palms, is where most daytime action is centered. Later, it all moves to the covey of buildings set among lush foliage that house the patio bar, lounge, and breeze-conditioned dining room (jackets and ties requested for dinner). Chef Ruedi Portman is well known for his imaginative island cuisine. The wine cellar is one of the best-stocked in the Caribbean. In season, a different island band (flute, steel, calypso) plays almost every night. Closed from mid-May to mid-October. Information: Curtain Bluff Hotel, PO Box 288, St. John's, Antigua (phone: 809-463-1115).

GOLDEN LEMON, Dieppe Bay, St. Kitts: This graceful, antique house was rescued from ruin by Arthur Leaman, the retired decorating editor of *House & Garden,* and is run by him with great taste and tender, loving savoir-faire. Each of the 18 rooms has its individual scheme and theme (Victorian, paisley, lemon), decorated with just the right blend of wit and charm. There's a large swimming pool plus small individual pools; a big, seal-smooth, black sand beach; scuba and riding nearby, tennis and golf about 20 miles off (few guests care enough to make the trip). Your fellow guests are often involved in the arts, theater, show biz, or all of the above; the atmosphere is sophisticated house party. And the food alone (imported meat, plus island fish, lobster, and luscious fruits given just the right spicing and saucing) is worth the trip. Now open all year. Information: Golden Lemon, Dieppe Bay, St. Kitts (phone: 809-465-7260).

GRAND CASE BEACH CLUB, Grand Case Bay, St. Martin: Fresh, airy, attractive studios and 1- and 2-bedroom apartments (76 in all) on one of St. Martin's most splendid beaches. There's swimming, sailing, water sports, tennis, and bocce, plus a restaurant, bar, and gracious American management. Information: Grand Case Beach Club, PB 339, Phillipburg, St. Martin, NA (phone: 011 590-87-51-87).

GUANAHANI, Grand Cul de Sac, St. Barthélemy: St. Barts' newest and largest hotel, with a total of 80 rooms, includes 1- and 2-bedroom suites, junior suites, and deluxe rooms in West Indian–style cottages trimmed in gingerbread and sprawled across a spectacular beachfront site adjoining Rothschild property. All rooms have seaview patios or decks, air conditioning, ceiling fans, and radio/TV/video. Most have either kitchenettes or full kitchen facilities; many have their own private pools. All rooms differ in size and layout and may be interestingly combined to form family or friendly enclaves. Amenities include a freshwater pool and Jacuzzi overlooking the beach, 2 lighted tennis courts, and 2 restaurants — the small *Bartolomeo,* serving light French cuisine with an Oriental touch, and the informal poolside *L'Indigo.* Full water sports facilities and free airport transfers. Information: Grand Cul de Sac, St Barthélemy, FWI (phone: 27-66-60).

JAMAICA INN, Ocho Rios, Jamaica: The setting is lush and green with palm trees and flowers; there is a small, perfect beach, and the rooms are not only pleasing to look at (white with cool blues, greens, yellows, for accents) but marvelously comfortable to live in. Even more exceptional is the service. It's not just that the nice lady arrives early to make up your room in the morning (though well after you've taken your own sweet time to wake up) but that mussed beds and soggy towels are plumped up and picked up (and your bed is turned down for the night) without your having to ask or hang tags on the door. On the whole, if you had dreamed up your own perfect island inn, it would probably be a lot like this one — with sailing, snorkeling, and boat rides off your own private beach, plus super swimming. Tennis is around the corner on the Shaw Park Beach Hotel courts; riding and golf (at the modest Upton Country Club) are 15 to 20 minutes away; Horseman's Holiday Packages are available through Chukka Cove. At night, some of the prettiest and tastiest meals on the island are served on the terrace here; the flavor is deliciously Continental, the setting is candlelit (jackets and ties requested during the winter season). Every evening in winter and some evenings in summer, there's a band for dancing; occasionally there's a show. Ask for one of the prime west wing rooms with a balcony over the sea. Information: Jamaica Inn, PO Box 1, Ocho Rios, Jamaica (phone: 809-974-2514; in the US, 800-243-9420; in CT, 203-438-3793).

L'HABITATION, Marcel Cove, St. Martin: Nestled under Pigeon Pea Hill on one of St. Martin's most beautiful beaches, *L'Habitation* sprawls over 150 of the island's choicest acres. Largely self-sufficient, it boasts a large freshwater pool, 2 restaurants, nightly entertainment, marina, water sports, and its own sports complex, all connected by 24-hour shuttle service. Designed in traditional West Indian style, it consists of 5 two-story buildings overlooking a lagoon and 3 three-story sections that make up the U-shaped main building, which houses the deluxe rooms, suites, and dining and entertainment facilities. Each of the 189 deluxe rooms and 12 junior suites has a spacious, well-appointed bath, air conditioning, direct-dial phone, TV, video player, safe, mini-fridge, Pullman kitchen, and private balcony; the 1-bedroom marina suites have private patios with hammocks, tables, and chairs, plus fully equipped kitchens. Closed in September. Information: L'Habitation, BP 230, Marcel Cove 97150, St. Martin FWI (phone: 011 590-87-33-33).

MALLIOUHANA, Meads Bay, Anguilla: In a soaring white Moorish structure perched on a cliff overlooking Meads Bay at the northwestern reaches of the island, this resort, which opened in 1983, is already considered one of the Caribbean's most elegant and distinguished. Here is an authentic tropical hideaway, with food and wine of high quality, and a luxurious landscape that more than makes up for an island that's otherwise rather flat and undistinguished. Owned and managed by the British magnate Leon Roydon and his wife, Annette, this Mediterranean-feeling oasis is currently undergoing some expansion, with the addition of 12 rooms to the existing 41, and a fully outfitted exercise center that should be ready by 1987. The doubles, suites, and two- and three-bedroom villas are all stunningly furnished and decorated. There are 3 swimming pools (no chlorine), 3 Laykold tennis courts, a water sports center, and a renowned restaurant created by Jo Rostang, chef-owner of the three-star *Bonne Auberge* in Antibes. It's perfect for the kind of traveler for whom escapism is an art; the price may be high, but then so is the quality of the experience. Information: Malliouhana, Meads Bay, Anguilla (phone: 497-6111).

NISBET PLANTATION INN, Newcastle, Nevis: It's the nicest kind of haunting. The land once belonged to the Widow Nisbet, who eventually married Horatio Nelson (then commander of the British fleet in nearby Antigua), and all sorts of romantic stories linger about the property. Though the house has been rebuilt, the 30 acres of surrounding coconut trees were part of the old plantation. A stay here today is like stepping back into an earlier century — with a few modern diversions and some pleasant company added. The house surveys a palm-lined vista and its own half mile of sandy beach. There's also riding, tennis, croquet, and — at least once — a drive around the island to see the sights (especially the weathered church where the Nisbet-Nelson nuptials took place). Dinners are served family-style in a dining room filled with polished antiques, some of them handed down through generations of Nisbets; the island dishes (homemade soups, lobster, fresh fruit soufflés) are especially fine. On gala evenings, a string band plays for dancing. Rooms are tucked around the landscape in cottages named for old Nevis plantations; "Gingerlands" is the special find. Information: Nisbet Plantation Inn, Newcastle, Nevis (phone: 809-469-5325; in the US, 218-722-5059).

OLD GIN HOUSE, Oranjestad, St. Eustatius: On the land side of the street, there's a restored 18th-century warehouse — *The Mooshay Bay Publick House* — now fitted out with a snug pub, a cool, high-ceilinged dining room, a terraced outdoor restaurant, and 23 guestrooms. The air is nostalgic and casual. The taste is flawless. And the road they bracket is the main street of what was once the richest port in the Caribbean. Today, much of what remains of the Lower Town lies under the water of the bay (great for scuba exploring). On land, not much happens — though the Upper Town has some ruins and an old fort. There's plenty of time for reading, swimming, and strolls down the historic ruin–lined shore. Dinner is beautifully served (Delftware and pewter, candles in tall crystal chimneys) and tastes even better. Order the snapper mousse or lobster and fish stew — a sort of Antillian bouillabaisse done with Pernod, but save room for the frozen lime soufflé or the bread nut and mango layer cake. If you ask what else there is to do, you probably shouldn't be here. On the other hand, if you have too much to do everyplace else in your world, this could be your spot to unwind. Information: Old Gin House, Oranje Bay, St. Eustatius, Netherlands Antilles (phone: 011 599-3-2319).

OYSTER POND, Oyster Pond, St. Maarten: In spite of its rustic name, it's actually a small Moorish structure on the far side of the Dutch portion of the island. Beautifully secluded on a remote point of land, it's cut off from the rest of the world by sudden hills on one side and a blue lagoon and the sea on the other. The ride down to the hotel can be slightly hair-raising, but it's still the choice of many high-powered financial types, including at least one former head of the New York Stock Exchange. Beyond the breezy lobby, furnished in white wicker with Pierre Deux fabrics and lush with tropical plants and flowers, lies a sun-dappled patio and stairs that lead up to some of the best-looking rooms in the Caribbean. All 20 — 4 are tower suites — are pastel-coordinated, naturally air conditioned by screened louvers and Casablanca-style ceiling fans, each with its own terrace, and all with smashing views of the sea. The beach (called Dawn) is perfect for swimming and picnicking, and for a quick dip there's a choice: the new, wood-decked swimming pool or the coral-protected sea beside the hotel. For sport: snorkel gear, water skis, two tennis courts. Scuba is available; so is deep-sea fishing, and a charter boat is at the ready to cruise to offshore islands. Its French restaurant is first rate, with a French chef formerly of the posh *La Samanna*. There's never a crowd: 40 guests at most, plus a few drop-in yachtsmen. Regrettably, the Dawn Beach condo and hotel crowd next door has meaningfully increased the area's population. Not for lone stays, but ideal for selective togetherness. Information: Oyster Pond Hotel, PO Box 239, Philipsburg, St. Maarten, Netherlands Antilles (phone: 011 5995-22206).

PINK BEACHES, Smith's Parish, Bermuda: Lolling on a private South Shore beach, this resort offers the kind of quiet luxury that attracts an elegant international clientele, including many celebrities. Its 82 air-conditioned rooms are in cottages rambling over a seaside estate that was the site of the romantic scenes in the film *Chapter Two.* There's a large pool, a sun terrace, fine tennis, and superb, friendly service. The toaster in your room is used by the waiter/waitress each morning after breakfast has been set on the patio. Information: Pink Beach Club, PO Box HM 1017, Hamilton, HMDX (phone: 809 293-1666).

TRIDENT VILLAS AND HOTEL, Port Antonio, Jamaica: It's impossibly romantic even in the morning, when the sun finds rainbows in the spray of the waves crashing on the rocks below your terrace and a peacock trails across the lawn to join you for breakfast. The new hotel, built in the image of its predecessor (destroyed in a 1980 hurricane), re-creates the same country house charm. Each villa and tower suite is individually decorated, full of pastels, pleasing prints, and comforting touches (a cushioned window seat, an antique desk). Service is beautifully individual too — from breakfast (brought one course at a time to your terrace or balcony) right through the day. There's a small beach, pool, tennis; the not overfamiliar pleasures of Port Antonio and green-hilled Portland (surf beaches, river rafting, plantation visits, picnics by waterfalls and blue lagoons) are invitingly accessible. Afternoon tea is a tradition; dinner is a formal, superb six-course Event, complete with white-gloved, silver-domed service in the estately dining room. Like all the rest, it's done with great style and personal attention, but utterly (and this is the special delight) without self-conscious pretension. Information: Trident, PO Box 119, Port Antonio, Jamaica (phone: 993-2602/2705).

Private Islands

At the unique Caribbean hideaways described here, the boundaries of both the resort and its island are virtually identical. Most of of these total-island resorts are mite-sized, and most consist of a central clubhouse with cottages scattered along a tradewind-cooled ridge or a perfect curve of beach. Accommodations are built along simple (though comfortably luxurious) lines, with very private patios and terraces; few break the 50-room barrier.

To Hilton habitués and Sheraton stoppers, paying $300 to $400 a night for digs that lack room telephones and color TVs is unthinkable. But to the corporate wheels that need unwinding, escaping celebrities seeking solitude, and affluent couples and families who wait eagerly to return to these private islands year after year, the absence of such "conveniences" ensures the precise peace they've left home and office to find. Even air conditioning is a sometime thing. Most guests prefer island breezes and ceiling fans, louvered shutters to plate glass windows, and bamboo-fenced outdoor showers to marble bathtubs indoors.

These islands are easy to miss on maps; even when you pinpoint them, they are not all that simple to reach. And their devoted clientele wouldn't have it any other way.

GUANA ISLAND CLUB, British Virgin Islands: Green-clad and hilly, this 850-acre island prides itself on "comfortably rustic atmosphere, lots of space and privacy." A maximum of 30 guests are lodged in whitewashed cottages that cling to the central ridge. For complete privacy, guests can rent the entire island. Seven shining beaches, a salt pond nature preserve, unusual flora and fauna, and intriguing mountain trails provide daytime diversion; the more energetic can indulge in snorkeling, sailing, fishing, windsurfing, water skiing, tennis, and croquet; scuba diving can be arranged (phone: 809-494-2354). The island is a 10-minute launch ride from Beef Island International Airport on Tortola. Information and reservations: Guana Island Club, 10 Timber Trail, Rye, NY 10580 (phone: 914-967-6050).

JUMBY BAY, Long Island, Antigua: One of the Caribbean's latest total-island resorts is a 15-minute launch ride off Antigua's northern shore. Its 77 pampered guests (max.) have the whole 300-acre islet to themselves for swimming and snorkeling off two beautiful beaches, lazing, exploring, and tennis. All food and drink, laundry service, and most sports are included in the rates; charter sailing, fishing, tennis, and scuba can be arranged. The atmosphere is sociable and totally unhurried — rather like a luxurious house party. The 200-year-old estate house boasts a library, a tree-shaded patio where tea and drinks are served, and a dining room praised for a cuisine that blends freshest island ingredients and international flair. Very pretty, private cottage suites are thoughtfully appointed (thick robes, special soaps), caringly served. There's island entertainment in season. Information: Jumby Bay, PO Box 243, St. John's, Antigua (phone: 809-463-2176).

MERIDIAN CLUB, Turks and Caicos; Barefoot-casual, it offers a gorgeous beach with an array of water sports, boat trips, nature walks, even excursions to Haiti and the Dominican Republic. The central clubhouse has a big, homey lounge, family-style dining, and a pool. Fifteen smartly comfortable double rooms and several privately owned cottages are available for rent. Pine Cay, encompassed by the club, is noted for the unspoiled beauty of its land and sea life — no spearfishing is allowed. Pan Am flies daily from Miami to Providenciales; from Provo, guests may take an air taxi to Pine Cay airport. Information: Meridian Club, c/o Resorts Managements, The Carriage House, 201½ E 29th St., New York, NY 10016 (phone: 212-696-4566; 800-225-4255).

NECKER ISLAND, British Virgin Islands: Advertised simply as "The Island," this 74-acre hideaway may indeed be the ultimate in luxurious retreats. Its owner Richard Branson, the multimillionaire whiz kid of Virgin Records and Virgin Atlantic Airways, originally bought this island for his family and friends but then decided to lease it out — the entire island with 10-bedroom villa — when he's not there. Necker is surrounded by its own unspoiled coral reef and flanked by three white sand beaches. The villa, a remarkable Balinese-style structure, was built from rock that was blasted from the top of Devil's Hill, where it perches, entirely surrounded by terraces with breathtaking views. The sun filters through a lush tropical garden in the center of the spectacular open space that comprises living, dining, and bar area, above which is a gallery library bulging with books, games, and tapes for all tastes. The young British managers, Beverley and Shaun Matthews, formerly of nearby Marina Cay, are both trained chefs, and they turn out first-class meals to be enjoyed on the breezy deck, under the retractable roof in the dining room, or at poolside. Other amenities include an exercise room, Jacuzzis, tennis, windsurfing, sailing dinghies, water skiing, aquascooters, fishing equipment, full-size snooker table, facilities for small meetings and conferences, and an open bar and wine cellar. The daily rate of $6,500 includes all of the above, plus all meals for 16 to 20 people ($4,750 for 10 or fewer). Guests are met at Beef Island International Airport on Tortola or on Virgin Gorda and are ferried over (less than 30 minutes). Information: Resorts Management, The Carriage House, 201½ E 29th St., New York, NY 10016 (phone: 212-696-4566; 800-225-4255); Ragusa & Co., 28 New Kings Rd., London SW6 4ST (phone: 01 731-7515).

PALM ISLAND BEACH CLUB, the Grenadines: John and Mary Caldwell discovered Prune Island (its legal name) when it was a bald, 110-acre islet. They planted its palms, opened its resort in 1967, and have been adding and improving ever since. Now lining stunning Casuarina Beach are 24 comfortable units in 12 cottages connected by a narrow stone path that winds among the lush palms, sea grape, casuarinas, and almond trees. A lively al fresco bar at the main beach attracts the bareboat yachting crowd; there are four other beaches, if that's not your fancy. The tennis courts are nearby, and the owners have just installed a health club. The island is reached via a 45-minute flight from Barbados to nearby Union Island and a 20-minute launch ride from there. Information: Palm Island, St. Vincent, the Grenadines, WI (809-458-4804).

PETER ISLAND HOTEL & YACHT HARBOUR, Peter Island, British Virgin Islands: It's simple but sleek and supremely first class, with Scandinavian overtones. As a matter of fact, the eight neat two-unit A-frames that house the resort's 32 original guestrooms were all prefabbed in Norway, shipped out — with all their luxurious garnishings — on the former owner's boats, then reassembled on Sprat Bay with the main clubhouse and marina. The marina and its facilities for sailing, scuba, and fishing are topnotch. The clubhouse — with its big, free-form pool, deck, bar, and rotisserie dining room — is done with that special Scandinavian flair for combining eye-pleasing looks and body-cradling comfort. But the adjacent sea and the palm trees that border it are appealingly West Indian, as are the 20 Beach House rooms on Deadman's Bay, just over the hill, one of the island's most beautiful, its bloodthirsty name notwithstanding. Sports include swimming, snorkeling (at a special beach), cruising, horseback riding (free if you don't need a guide), windsurfing, Sunfish and Squib sailing, and 4 new Laykold tennis courts with Peter Burwash International instructors. The crowd that gathers for dinner each evening is tanned and glowing; except on Tuesdays and Saturdays, jackets are requested. Less formal is the resort's new *Beach Boy* restaurant. Several nights a week a band comes over from Road Town to play for dancing.

Information: Peter Island Yacht Club, PO Box 211, Road Town, Tortola, BVI (phone: 809-494-2561/2; 800-346-4451).

PETIT ST. VINCENT RESORT, Petit St. Vincent, Grenadines: You feel like the world is yours around here — because it really is. The entire 113-acre island is a single resort, and it all belongs to you. You live in one of 22 native stone cottages that have been discreetly placed for maximum privacy (the hilltop ones have shielded terraces designed to allow total sunbathing), plus the best of all possible views. Some are set right on the beaches, others on the small breezy hills overlooking the sea. The management is nonviolently antihassle. You won't be bothered by anyone or anything until you say the word or raise the flag by the door to summon room service — which arrives by jeep. The idea is that the best of everything should be right there when you want it. And it works. For sports: swimming, sailing, snorkeling, tennis, badminton, volleyball, a health trail, croquet, and horseshoes. At night: sometime music and good talk with visiting yacht folk. Rates include all meals and all sports except those involving charter boats or scuba. Low rates from mid-April until just before Christmas. Closed in September and October. Information: Petit St. Vincent, St. Vincent, Grenadines (phone: 809-458-4801 or 513-242-1333).

YOUNG ISLAND, St. Vincent, Grenadines: If Gauguin had lingered in the Caribbean, he might have found barefoot happiness on Young Island, with its central indoor-outdoor buildings surrounded by gardens and its individual Tahitian cottages with bamboo and khuskhus decor, ceiling fans, and outdoor showers. There's a pretty beach, a small pool, water sports, tennis courts, and lots of relaxing (with lots of hammocks to do it in). Several times a week small bands of islanders ferry over to make music in the evening. Otherwise, it's sociable talk over brandy and a short stroll down the garden path to bed. Information: Young Island, Box 211, St. Vincent, Grenadines (phone: 809-458-4826; in the US, 800-223-1108).

WALKER'S CAY CLUB, Bahamas: Sport fishing was originally the island's biggest attraction (a major billfish tournament is still held here each April), but recently scuba diving has been coming on strong. Once a refuge for rumrunners, the 100-acre cay today offers a 75-slip marina, certified dive instruction, and great underwater scenery, along with all-weather tennis courts and two pools. Lunch may be a buffet at the marina; dinner is in the hotel restaurant, where the freshest seafood is a specialty. The hotel is only a 20-minute flight from Freeport, Grand Bahama Island; there is a daily flight from Fort Lauderdale. Information: Walker's Cay Club, 700 SW 34th St., Fort Lauderdale, FL 33315 (phone: 800-327-3714 or 800-432-2092 in Florida only).

Natural Wonderlands

 To most urban dwellers, the island world is one vast natural wonder — a serendipitous embrace of land, sea, and sun that is wide enough to include anyone who ventures into the area. And they aren't all that wrong. But even in paradise there are superlatives, and the spots below give a special sense of the islands' splendor.

BARBADOS: *The Andromeda Gardens,* overlooking the Atlantic coast, feature an exotic collection of hybrid orchids and other tropical plants in a mazelike, rock garden setting. Off Highway 2, *Turner's Hall Wood* is all that remains of the primeval forest that once covered the island. It is part of the Barbados National Trust, as is *Welchman Hall Gully,* a botanical ravine about 3 miles from the stalagmites and stalactites of *Harrison's Cave.*

BELIZE: *Crooked Tree Wildlife Sanctuary,* just 33 miles northwest of Belize City, is a refuge for thousands of birds and many other varieties of fauna and flora. Visitors may tour the network of lagoons, swamps, and waterways. Information: Belize Audubon Society, PO Box 1001, Belize City.

BERMUDA: The thousands of trees, shrubs, vegetables, and flowers that bloom year-round in the *Botanical Gardens of Bermuda* have been a source of education and enchantment for Bermudians and visitors since 1898. Despite severe damage from an October 1987 hurricane, every shape, color, and scent under the sun thrives in these 36 beautifully tended acres. In the Garden of the Blind, you can close your eyes and have your remaining senses feast on a myriad aromatic spices and herbs. While wandering through the Hibiscus Patch you will come across most of the 150 varieties of hibiscus that thrive on the island. By the time you have arrived in the formal gardens you may feel lost inside an Impressionist painting. And by the time you've seen the cactus collection, vegetable plot, and exotic aviary of tropical birds, your head will be buzzing with questions and a sense of contentment. Don't hesitate to inquire about the gardens from members of the staff, who know the resident plants and flowers as well as they know the palms of their own hands. The gardens are at Camden, between Berry Hill Rd. and South Shore Rd., Paget Parish.

Another of Bermuda's natural wonders is *Spittal Pond,* a seaside nature reserve that as many as 500 birds use as their winter home and all species of North American waterfowl use as a stopover during migration. Although the pond is fenced off, the undeveloped and enormously varied acreage surrounding it is open to the public. Spittal Pond is on the South Shore in Smith's Parish.

DOMINICA: Trail and plant markers have been restored in Edenesque *Morne Trois Pitons National Park,* where giant ferns and bromeliads surround trunks of trees and weave through their limbs, forming latticeworks of foliage that seem to climb to the sky. A water-filled grotto, fed by a waterfall and surrounded by beautiful plants, flowers, and ferns, lies hidden deep within the park. So do three remarkable lakes: Boeri, rimmed with volcanic rock; Fresh Water, with sweeping coastal views; and Boiling Lake, kept bubbling by the volcanic heat of the crater in which it is cupped. The park is at the southeast end of the island; the Tourist Office in Roseau will supply current information on trail conditions, tours, and guides.

Not far from Roseau, in the south-central section of Dominica, is a magnificent area where three waterfalls, surrounded by tree-covered cliffs, converge in a cluster of rocky ponds studded with ferns and orchids. Near the *Three Waterfalls* (also called Trafalgar Falls), north and east of Roseau, are the *Sulfur Springs,* hot pools of volcanic mud where the earth bubbles and steams like a huge vat of sorcerer's brew.

GUADELOUPE: A day's journey to the *Parc Naturel* in the heart of Basse-Terre is not one you are likely to forget. The tropical rain forests, lakes, waterfalls, natural mountain pools, steaming fumaroles, and the well-marked trails make this one of the loveliest hiking spots in the Caribbean. There is an excellent booklet, *Walks & Hikes,* which lists 18 trails in the park with maps and difficulty ratings. You can obtain it from the tourist office or the Organisation des Guides de Montagne in Basse-Terre (phone: 81-45-79).

JAMAICA: Off the main road from Kingston to Ocho Rios, on route A-3, a 4-mile stretch of road winds down an old riverbed surrounded by giant ferns. This stretch is called *Fern Gully,* a deep forest area that offers a taste of cool air and an opportunity to ride beneath the tall ferns — the first complex plant life to populate the island.

While driving along a 2-mile stretch of road in St. Elizabeth Parish, close to Black River, you suddenly feel surrounded by something that looks like a soft yellow-green feathery umbrella or veil. You are driving through *Bamboo Avenue,* a continuous arch of feathery bamboo that seems to appear out of nowhere. To reach this avenue you pass through Holland Estate, a former sugar factory.

PUERTO RICO: *El Yunque* is a 28,000-acre tropical rain forest and national bird sanctuary where you will see more than 250 different species of native trees, many of the primeval variety. While wandering beneath a towering pine or sierra palm you might catch a whiff of white ginger or find a wild orchid as you hear the call of the coqui, the tiny tree frog that is Puerto Rico's official mascot. Be on the alert, for there are many delicate, beautifully colored wildflowers that hide behind, beneath, and around the more conspicuous trees and shrubs. Although more than 100 billion gallons of rain fall in the forest annually, the showers are usually short, and the park provides adequate shelter for visitors caught in a downpour. On Route 191 there's the Sierra Palm Visitors Center, where you can obtain information or guides. The park is about 25 miles east of San Juan via Route 3, then south on Route 191. Open daily from 9:30 AM to 5 PM.

TRINIDAD: If you arrive at the *Caroni Bird Sanctuary* at sunset or late afternoon, you might look up and see a large cluster of bright red feathers swooping through the sky like a gigantic flame. Within moments, hundreds of scarlet ibis descend onto the 450-acre sanctuary, where they live and nest amid vast stretches of mangrove trees. The inner sanctuary of Caroni, where the birds nest, is open to the public from May to October; the rest of the sanctuary stays open all year. If you arrive during the fall, you might find a sea of red mangroves that match the feathers of the birds they house. The sanctuary is about 7 miles south of Port of Spain.

VENEZUELA: The highest waterfall (and one of the most beautiful) in the world lies deep in the Venezuelan jungle and is called *Angel Falls,* after the American pilot Jimmy Angel, who discovered it in 1935. Approximately 3,212 feet high (15 times as tall as Niagara), the falls are most often seen during a breath-catching flight en route to Avensa Airline's Canaima camp/resort in the Venezuelan interior. Steeped in swirling mists and rainbows, the falls tumble down layers of multicolored rock to the jungle floor. They can also be reached by a fairly arduous three-day foot-jeep-canoe trip from the comfortably simple cottage resort at the edge of Canaima lagoon — itself fed by a spectacular ring of seven falls. But most guests prefer shorter treks, swimming, or relaxing in the immensely beautiful jungle surroundings. Avensa offices have details.

US VIRGIN ISLANDS: The entire island of *St. John* is a natural haven. In fact, there is little to do on the island but enjoy the scenery, particularly the *Virgin Islands National Park.* Don't hesitate to ask the rangers to fill you in on the flora and fauna that abound in the park — pelicans and sandpipers, mahogany and bay, tamarind, flamboyant, and shower of gold are among the native inhabitants you are likely to run across. Park guides also lead nature walks and give nature talks several times a week.

Shopping

Shopping is always a major tourist interest and can easily become a main focus on any island vacation. Near duty-free purchases can be found in ports throughout the islands, and in-bond shops allow tourists to buy a variety of items like liquor, tobacco, perfume, and watches at low, low prices. There are also fine stores and boutiques as well as native markets for browsing. The markets are marvelous places to meet and mingle with local people, absorb atmosphere, tune your ear to the island's patois, bargain for native crafts and homemade treats (mango chutney, hot sauce, preserves), and — not incidentally — have a great time.

Remember that market dealing in the islands is done on the spot, and you should feel free to haggle a little for the price's sake and the fun of it. Local vendors enjoy a friendly negotiation, and while they will take your money for the price asked, everyone will have a better time engaging in the close, good-natured give-and-take of striking a final price. A few islands produce mostly straw and shell work, but in Jamaica, Haiti,

Puerto Rico, Barbados, the Dominican Republic, Bermuda, the Bahamas, and the Dutch islands, there is a rich choice of fine European and Asian imports and/or colorful native fashions, crafts, and art.

Customs regulations allow US citizens to bring home $400 worth of goods (including a liter of liquor and "a reasonable number" of cigarettes) duty-free — except from US territories like the US Virgin Islands, from which the limit is upped to $800, including five liters of liquor per person. An across-the-board duty fee of 10% (5% from the USVI) is levied on the next $1,000 worth of goods above that level, which should simplify inspection operations considerably. You can also mail home an unlimited number of gifts individually valued at $25 or less ($100, from the USVI), but no more than one per day to any single recipient. These must be marked "Unsolicited Gift," with value and item listed on the outside of the package.

Currently you are allowed to bring crafts and handmade goods into the US duty-free from a number of Caribbean countries and dependencies under the Generalized System of Preferences (GSP), a program established to encourage local industries in developing countries. Virtually all the islands and countries covered in this book are GSP beneficiaries, with the exception of Cuba, the French West Indies, and Venezuela. And the list of goods included under GSP is extensive (some 2,700 individual items). For more information, write for *Know Before You Go* and *GSP & the Traveler,* both yours for the asking from the US Customs Service, Information, Room 201, 6 World Trade Center, New York, NY 10048.

You should be aware that there are essentially three distinct kinds of shopping opportunities available in the Caribbean: duty-free (or almost), wherein imported goods are offered at relatively low prices because they are not taxed (or taxed at a very low rate) as imports; in-bond, where specified goods are sold to tourists as if the merchandise had never entered the vending country and where delivery is usually made to your departing plane or ship. And there are certain islands that do not tax imports from their mother countries, although goods from other countries are charged an import tax. This means that on British islands, English goods will be cheaper than the same brands in the US (which does tax British imports); French goods on French islands always represent bargains and in some cases are actually cheaper than the same goods available in France. It is crucial that you have an accurate idea of the US prices of the specific items you are after; often the so-called duty-free prices are only a tiny savings over US prices; sometimes the difference is significant.

Below, some of the best shopping areas in the Caribbean and their specialties:

BAHAMAS: Not a free port for retail goods, but nonetheless offering some excellent buys. Prices for imported china, crystal, perfumes, linens, knitwear, and cameras run 30% to 45% below those in the US. Nassau's major stores and shops are on and around Bay Street. But one should also make a point of visiting the *Straw Market,* which features native handicrafts and is on Bay Street, west of Rawson Square. On Grand Bahama Island there is Freeport's *International Bazaar,* a 10-acre, $3-million shopping complex designed by a Hollywood special effects man to showcase imports from Europe, the Far East, and the Mideast. There's also a straw market. The best buys throughout the Bahamas include British china, crystal, fabrics, liquor, Scandinavian glass and silverware, Swiss watches, and French perfume. German and Japanese cameras and electronic equipment are offered, but are not always cheaper than at US discount stores. Local offerings feature seashells (especially conch), jewelry, and straw goods like hats, mats, bags, and dolls.

BARBADOS: Though not a true free port, Barbados does have a system of in-bond shops, where a wide range of imported goods may be purchased at bargain prices. The main shopping center on the island is around Broad and Bond streets in Bridgetown. The best buys include bone china, crystal, Japanese cameras and binoculars, liquor, watches, gold and silver jewelry, French perfumes, and a wide variety of clothing, such as cashmere sweaters and ready-made worsted suits from Britain. Local handcrafts include pottery, straw work, wood carvings, and shell and coral jewelry and decorations, a specialty at the *Pelican Village* shop complex near Deep Water Harbour, outside Bridgetown. Also, Barbados rum is among the best in the Caribbean and is available at low prices.

BERMUDA: The main shopping area of the island centers around Front Street, bordering Hamilton Harbour. Although Bermuda is not a free port, it does offer an in-bond system on liquor (which is up to 50% less expensive than in the US); you must order it at least 24 hours before your departure; 48 hours is better, especially on weekends. Best buys include British and Irish woolens, Shetland and cashmere sweaters, British crystal and chinaware, Irish linen, local cedarwood products, and, as already mentioned, liquor.

BRITISH LEEWARDS — Anguilla, Antigua, Barbuda, Montserrat, Nevis, St. Kitts: Although none of this group has free port status, as a result of past and/or ongoing association with Britain, Antigua, Montserrat, Nevis, and St. Kitts still offer some bargains on goods imported from the UK. Though selections are often small, Antigua is a good place to look for British woolens and linens, cashmere sweaters, liquor (particularly Cavalier rum; liquor prices are among the best in the Caribbean), and Sea Island cottons — both by the yard and made up in resortwear. Montserrat offers its own rum-punch liqueur called Perks Punch and some locally made souvenirs (such as rugs and wall hangings) as well. In addition to limited stocks of European imports at saving prices, St. Kitts has striking island batikwork — including wall hangings and sportswear made from it — as well as pottery and inlaid wood.

BRITISH VIRGIN ISLANDS: Even though they have no free-port status, the British Virgin Islands offer tourists the chance to buy wine and liquor at prices sometimes even lower than those in the neighboring US Virgin Islands (here, however, the duty-free import limit is one liter, not the one gallon allowed from the Virgin Islands). In the shops of Road Town, Tortola, you'll find British goods at duty-free prices in limited supply — especially Liberty fabrics. At the Yacht Harbour on Virgin Gorda, you'll find watercolors by local artists and other crafts.

BRITISH WINDWARDS — Dominica, Grenada, St. Lucia, St. Vincent, the Grenadines: St. Lucia, the only island in this group with free port shops (at Pointe Seraphine, a short shuttle-bus ride from Castries), offers the tourist a limited array of bargain import shopping. The other islands — Grenada, St. Vincent, the Grenadines, and Dominica — nevertheless offer some substantial bargains. On Grenada, a popular purchase is a woven spice basket; luxury imports such as English woolens, cameras, watches, French perfume and jewelry can sometimes be found at close to duty-free prices, though stocks tend to be limited. In Kingstown's shops on St. Vincent, look for imported chinaware, crystal, and jewelry, as well as Sea Island cottons, baskets, pottery, and other handicrafts made by artisans at the *St. Vincent Craftsmen.* On Dominica, Carib Indians and others weave baskets, mats, and such, but the very best buys are the sturdy, hand-wrought grass rugs at *Tropicrafts* — they're tops in the islands.

CAYMAN ISLANDS: As a duty-free port, Grand Cayman offers a terrific array of imported bargains. China, crystal, and silver are much cheaper here than in the US, as are British woolens, Irish linen, French perfumes, and liquor. Local items for sale include coral jewelry, straw baskets and purses, and paintings by local artists, all on sale at George Town shops. US customs forbids the importation of tortoiseshell products.

COLOMBIA: In the free-port area of San Andrés, one can get good deals on items like Scotch whisky, Japanese cameras, and British tweeds. More important, Colombia is one of the emerald capitals of the world, but be sure to buy from a reputable dealer. *Greenfire Emeralds* has stores in Commercial Center, Pierino Gallo, and the Bocagrande area. Gold and silver jewelry, men's tailored clothing, warm and almost water-proof woolen ponchos, fine reproductions of pre-Columbian items and leather, alligator, and snakeskin shoes, belts, and bags are often available at meaningful savings. It is illegal to take pre-Columbian artifacts out of the country.

CUBA: There are tourist shops in all of the major hotels, but luxury items are far from a priority. Ceramics, poster art, rum, and, of course, Cuban cigars are the main items of interest. US citizens with permission to travel to Cuba can legally bring $100 worth of Cuban goods — including 100 Cuban cigars — into the US once every six months, provided the cigars were purchased in Cuba.

DOMINICAN REPUBLIC: The Dominican Republic does offer good buys in lovely amber jewelry; carvings of limestone, bone, and wood; straw goods; and embroidered fabrics. In addition, there is a free-port shopping area in Santo Domingo known as *La Zona Franca* that offers a few genuinely unusual bargains in perfume, liquor, and the like. But the *Mercado Modelo* offers lots of local crafts and is much more fun; check prices on Dominican coffee, but forget tortoiseshell items — island turtles are on the US endangered species list.

DUTCH WINDWARDS — Saba, St. Eustatius, St. Maarten: Since these islands combine free-port status with an absence of local taxes, St. Maarten's prices are among the lowest in the Caribbean. Best buys are Dutch products (Delftware, cheeses, etc.), perfumes, watches, jewelry, and liquor. Saba's specialty is drawn-work linen, locally printed cotton. Statia has only a few imported souvenirs and local items to offer.

FRENCH WEST INDIES — Guadeloupe, Martinique, St. Martin, St. Barthélemy: The French half of St. Martin, like its Dutch islandmate, is a free port with no local taxes. Imported French and Italian fashions and perfume are comparatively inexpensive. Guadeloupe and Martinique are not free ports but do offer excellent prices on anything French, as much as 40% less than the cost in the US. Some shops give an additional 20% discount on purchases paid for with traveler's checks. US dollars are accepted everywhere. French perfume is available here at the world's lowest prices; other best buys include couturier signature silk scarves and ties, crystal and porcelain, fine wines and liqueurs, watches, and French fashions. St. Barts adds its own hand block-printed cottons, silks, and finely fashioned jewelry and straw hats to the list.

HAITI: This country is world-renowned for its primitive art, supplemented by the work of a few artists who follow more contemporary trends. While prices have increased dramatically in the past few years, it is still a wonderful place to look for a yet-undiscovered genius and to see a lot of interesting, enthusiastic painting. Mahogany sculptures and straw work are still inexpensive. And resort clothes made here — skirts, tops, caftans — with hand-done appliqué and embroidery are bright and distinctive buys too. For those who enjoy bargaining, the *Iron Market* in Port-au-Prince, with scores of stalls and a bazaar atmosphere, is a must. But be prepared for a crush.

JAMAICA: Although not a free port, Jamaica does offer an in-bond system on items like Swiss watches, Japanese and German cameras, French perfumes, British woolens, silverware, crystal, jewelry, and bone china, at prices 20% to 50% lower than on the mainland. In addition, local buys feature island paintings, wood carvings, ceramics, batik fabrics, rum, Tia Maria (coffee) and Rumona (rum) liqueurs, Bay Rum cologne, and furniture (Kingston's *Devon House "Things Jamaican"* shops carry a remarkable trove of all these). The island has shopping plazas in all the major tourist areas and hotels, and native markets abound. New rules allow visitors with an ID who pay in US or Canadian dollars to take in-bond purchases, except liquor, out of the store with them.

MEXICAN CARIBBEAN: The major shopping area is in Cancún, where stores and markets offer good buys on embroidered shirts, pottery, and handicrafts from all parts of Mexico.

NETHERLANDS ANTILLES — Aruba, Bonaire, Curaçao: Although they are not technically free ports, import duties in Aruba, Bonaire, and Curaçao are so low that shopping is a very attractive activity. Indeed, Curaçao is one of the major shopping centers of the entire Caribbean, especially the well-stocked shops of the *Punda*, the oldest section of Willemstad. Swiss watches, English china and crystal, Dutch tiles, Oriental silks, Latin American handicrafts, Zulu sculptures, French perfumes, liquor, cigarettes, jewelry, Irish linen, and much more are available at very low prices. Aruba offers most of the same items in branches of the leading Curaçao stores, with a slightly smaller selection. Shops in Bonaire also offer import selections.

PUERTO RICO: Known for the quality of its native art. There is no price advantage in island shops, but you can find excellent craftwork and paintings that are available nowhere else. There are tourist shops all over the island, but the main shopping center is in Old San Juan. First-rate contemporary artists are shown in local galleries. Craft specialty items include santos, small wooden religious figures carved by local artisans who have inherited their styles from previous generations. Other finds include resort fashions; papier-mâché decorative accessories; some Spanish antiques; a large variety of rum, from light to dark and mild to heavy, making Puerto Rico the world's leading rum producer; and cigars, made in factories that can be visited by the curious tourist who wants to see how it is done.

TRINIDAD AND TOBAGO: The in-bond system functions here, especially at *Stecher's*, 27 Frederick St., Port of Spain, where you'll find good buys in English and French china and crystal, British sweaters and woolens, tailored men's clothing, East Indian fabrics and jewelry, and Caribbean rum. Local products of interest include straw, fiber, and wood work, colorful dolls, and Caribbean music. For aficionados of calypso and limbo — both of which were born here — Trinidad and Tobago have the finest steel drums and the best selection of calypso and steel-band recordings in the world.

US VIRGIN ISLANDS: A tourist shopping here is in for several special breaks. Not only are prices on imported goods 30% to 50% below mainland US levels, but a special status permits Americans to bring home twice the usual allowance of imported goods from the US Virgin Islands, including one gallon of liquor (rather than the usual liter) without paying additional duty. All island products are duty-free. Shops and warehouse stores, especially on St. Thomas, offer a smorgasbord of imports, including designer fashions, Swiss watches, French and Italian leather goods, cashmere sweaters, Danish silver, Irish and French crystal, porcelain, British bone china and stoneware, Thai cotton and silk, and liquor from around the world. There are many good buys but few great bargains.

VENEZUELA: Margarita Island's duty-free zone is quite extensive and a source of fine pearls as well as rugs, wall hangings, gold jewelry, Guajiro Indian slippers, and traditional dresses.

Horse Races

There are only four places in the whole Caribbean where a bookie stands a chance of making an honest living: Puerto Rico, the Dominican Republic, Venezuela, and Jamaica — all of which schedule flat racing on a regular basis. There's parimutuel betting at all four; the time-honored British tote-board system also operates at Jamaica's Caymanas track. On other islands where racing exists, though there's all kinds of formal and informal betting, it's a long time between meetings. And when they are off and running — once a month or four times a year — the scene is much more like a county fair and/or a big barbecue than the ritualized proceedings at Belmont or Churchill Downs: Racing fans don't just watch, they *partici-*

pate — snacking, tippling, betting, gossiping, and toe-tapping to steel bands and calypsos. And they probably have more fun than the toffs in the boxes. By all means go to the track if you get a kick out of racing, wherever you find it. But if there's island-style racing, go — even if you never follow the ponies back home. Odds are, it'll be a great party.

CONVENTIONAL RACES

DOMINICAN REPUBLIC: The *Hipodromo Perla Antillana* in Santo Domingo has races on Tuesdays, Thursdays, and Sundays, all year. The track is in town near the baseball stadium.

JAMAICA: There's racing at *Caymanas Race Track,* Kingston. Races are held every other Wednesday, Saturdays, some holidays; check newspapers for times.

PUERTO RICO: *El Comandante Race Track* is a modern track about 45 minutes from downtown San Juan on Route 3. It has 18,000 seats and an attractive restaurant. Races are held Wednesdays, Fridays, Sundays, and holidays at 2:30 PM.

VENEZUELA: *La Rinconada* in Caracas runs day races every Saturday and Sunday afternoon, and the first Thursday evening of each month there's evening racing at Valencia starting at 5 PM.

THE PARTIES

BARBADOS: The Barbados Turf Club holds race meetings on occasional Saturdays during the island's two racing seasons — from January to May and July to November — on the *Garrison Savannah* in Christ Church. Thoroughbred horses are not the only attraction — there are also steel bands, food and drink stands, and a pervasive party atmosphere. Meetings usually start at noon and end about 6:30 PM.

BRITISH VIRGIN ISLANDS: Holidays and Festival (last week of July, first week of August) meets at Tortola track. Informal betting, music, food, fun. See paper for upcoming dates, times.

ST. CROIX: On race days in Frederiksted, the activities at the *Flamboyant* racetrack promise to be flamboyant. Although the event is organized, few of the four-legged contestants bear the certified markings or demeanor of a purebred. But the races are always entertaining and amusing, especially when accompanied by lively reggae, rock, soul music, and abundant refreshments. Races are held once a month — check local papers for exact times.

ST. THOMAS: Races at the *Estate Nadir Track* are similar to those on St. Croix — amusing and lively, with down-home horses, good music, and plenty of food and drink. Check paper for monthly date, time.

Casino Countdown

Island gambling takes one of two forms: action or distraction. The presence of junkets (trips organized to deliver high rollers to the tables by the plane-load) and several casinos (rather than just one or two) usually indicates serious play. Otherwise, it's lower-case stuff — something to do with your evenings in town besides eating, dancing, or watching another island floor show.

Only a dozen island counties offer casino gambling. In these, certain generalizations apply: Basic games are roulette, craps, and 21 (or blackjack). The minimum bet is $2 (exceptions: baccarat tables, where the stakes are usually *big,* and Haiti, where $1 qualifies), but this can vary slightly (with the designation of certain $5 tables, for example) according to the night, the crowd, and who's in charge. Most islands prohibit their own nationals from gambling, but tourists aren't stopped at the door or charged admission except on the French islands, where they're very serious about rules. (There, you must have identification with a photograph that proves you are 21 — everywhere else, it's 18; also there is a 50- to 80-franc admission charge.) Once inside, there may or may not be drinks (which may or may not be free to players).

Judged by breadth of equipment, intensity of action, and the proportion of tourists who list casinos among their prime reasons for choosing a particular destination, the Bahamas, Puerto Rico, and Aruba are the islands' top gaming spots; Curaçao, St. Maarten, and St. Kitts — all of which attract some junkets — come next; then the French islands, where interest seems to be growing even though there is no junket traffic. These are the specifics:

ANTIGUA: There are three casinos: one at the *St. Charles Hotel and Casino,* another at the *Halcyon Cove Beach Resort* at Dickinson Bay, and a third at the private *St. James's Club* on Mamora Bay. There is considerable junketing. Baccarat and backgammon are played in addition to usual games. Players buy their own drinks. Hours: 9 PM to 4 or 5 AM.

ARUBA: The island's big tourist parlay is a combination of beaches and casinos at five major Palm Beach hotels: the *Golden Tulip Aruba Caribbean,* the *Aruba Palm Beach,* the *Americana Aruba,* the *Concorde,* and the *Holiday Inn,* all with adjacent cabarets in season. The *Manchebo* and other Druif Beach hotels now have their own place to play: the *Alhambra Casino,* where betting limits are low and the atmosphere, pleasantly relaxed. Frequent junkets. Drinks are free while you play; people under 18 are not admitted. Hours: midafternoon until 3 or 4 AM; slot machines are turned on earlier.

BAHAMAS: There are now four casinos in operation: the *Princess,* and the *Lucayan Beach,* which, with an assist from golf, keeps Grand Bahama tourism alive; *Paradise Island Casino* (currently undergoing expansion) on Paradise Island; and the casino at the *Cable Beach* hotel. Most junkets head for Freeport. All three feature the usual games, plus baccarat for big spenders. Paradise Island also has a small backgammon section. Hours: 1 PM to 4 AM.

BONAIRE: The island's medium-size casino, the *Black Coral Casino,* is attached to the *Bonaire Beach* hotel; and there's a "Barefoot Casino" at the *Flamingo Beach Hotel and Casino.* More casual fun than real glitter; junkets are not encouraged. Drinks are free for players; people under 18 not admitted. Hours: 9 PM and 4 PM, respectively, until 3 or 4 AM.

CURAÇAO: The most chic crowds play at the plush-lined *Curaçao Caribbean;* there are also active gaming rooms at the *Holiday Beach,* the *Princess Beach,* and the *Curaçao Plaza.* There is also a small casino at *Las Palmas Hotel and Vacation Village.* This island is one of the few Caribbean spots where you can lose your blackjack boodle to machines. Junkets are allowed. Players drink for free. Hours: noon to 4 AM.

DOMINICAN REPUBLIC: *Naco, El Embajador,* the *Sheraton,* and the *Dominican Concorde* in the capital have casinos, as does *Maunaloa,* a nightclub in the Centro de los Héroes section of Santo Domingo. All have all table games, no slot machines. US tourists seem to favor *El Embajador* and the *Sheraton.* There is little junket action. Hours: 4 PM to 4 AM.

GUADELOUPE: The *Casino de la Marina* at St. François (hours: 9 PM to 3 AM) is near both the *Méridien* and the *Hamak;* the *Gosier Les Bains Casino* (hours: 9 PM to dawn), on the grounds of the *PLM Azur Arawak,* is handy to Gosier and Bas du Fort hotels. Strict French rules apply for admission; you must present some form of identification with your picture; minimum age is 21. Admission charge is about $11. No junkets allowed. There are drinks, but they're not free.

HAITI: There are two casinos in Port-au-Prince — the waterside *International* and one attached to the *Royal Haitian* (where there's a nightclub with dancing and a sometime pseudo-voodoo show attached) — and two in Pétionville, at *El Rancho* and the *Choucoune*. All have the usual games, serve sandwiches as well as free drinks, host some junkets. Hours: 8 PM to 3 or 4 AM.

MARTINIQUE: Casinos at the *Méridien Trois-Îlets* and *La Batelière* hotels are more accessible than Guadeloupe's casinos. Same strict admission rules apply: identification with a photograph, age 21 up. Admission charge: $9 and $10, respectively. Hours: 9 PM to 3 AM nightly, except Sundays.

PUERTO RICO: The government carefully supervises the casinos at the *Caribe Hilton,* both *Holiday Inns, Condado Beach, Dupont Plaza,* and *Ramada Inn* in the Condado section, the *Palace* in Isla Verde, and the *Hyatt* duo, *Dorado Beach* and *Cerromar Beach* in Dorado. Men must wear jackets after 8 PM, and no drinking is allowed at the tables. If asked, you must be able to produce identification that proves you are at least 18. Slot machines are a recent addition. Hours: variable, but 1 PM to 4 AM is most common.

ST. KITTS: All the action is at the casino of the *Royal St. Kitts* hotel at Frigate Bay, where players drink for free. The usual games; slot machines too. Hours: 5 PM to 4 AM.

ST. MARTIN/ST. MAARTEN: The Dutch side has the gambling monopoly: at *Cupecoy, Mullet Bay Resort, Great Bay Beach, Divi Little Bay Beach, Pelican Resort,* and *Maho Reef Beach* hotels (hours: 8 PM to 3 AM). At *Seaview Casino* and *St. Maarten Beach Club* hotel in Philipsburg, gaming starts in the afternoon. Some French-side hotels provide free casino transport. There are some junkets, but they're minor in the overall tourist picture. Roulette, 21, craps, and slot machines are all there; check the rules before you play for slight differences between casinos. Since gambling is only an incidental reason for most people's trips, the atmosphere is pleasantly relaxed.

INDEX

Index

Dominica (*cont.*)
map, 350
money, 355
nightlife, 358
restaurants, 360–61
shopping, 357
sights and activities, 352–53
Roseau, 352–53
special events, 357–58
sports, 358
time, 355
tipping, 357
tourist information, 83, 355
transportation to, 356
Dominican Republic, 7, 362–83, 758
calculating costs, 369–70
climate and clothes, 368–69
current, 369
entry requirements, 67, 368
essay, 363–64
fishing, 767
hotels, 375–80, 782
hunting, 772
language, 65, 369
local transportation, 370–71
map, 362
money, 369
museums, 776
nightlife, 375
restaurants, 380–83
shopping, 371–72
sights and activities, 364–68, 758, 778–79
Santo Domingo, 366–68
special events, 372–73
sports, 373–75, 758, 767
time, 369
tipping, 372
tourist information, 26, 59, 83, 368
transportation to, 369
Dorado Beach Hotel (Puerto Rico), 531, 766, 782
Drinking, *see* Alcohol
Drugs, 71–72
Dunn's River Falls (Jamaica), 446
Dutch Windwards, *see* **Saba; St. Eustatius; St. Martin/St. Maarten**

East End (Cayman Islands), 289
Eden Brown Estate (Nevis), 605
Elbow Beach Hotel (Bermuda), 248
Electricity, 71
Eleuthera, 172

hotels, 191
See also **Bahamas**
El Yunque (Puerto Rico), 526
Entry requirements, 66–68
See also entry requirements *section under names of individual islands*
Eva Wilkins' Studio (Nevis), 606
Exumas, 172
See also **Bahamas**

Fajardo (Puerto Rico), 531
Falmouth (Jamaica), 444–45
Farley Hill (Barbados), 202
Festivals and holidays, 70
Fig Tree Drive (Antigua), 142
Fish, kinds of, 111–12
Fishing, sport, 767–68
See also under Sports
Flora and fauna, 109–13
Flower Forest (Barbados), 202
Folk tales, 114–15
Fonds-St.-Jacques (Martinique), 478
Fontein (Aruba), 156
Food and drink, island, 106–8
Foreign currency, *see* Money
Fortaleza de la Caban (Cuba), 322
Fort Ashby (Nevis), 605
Fort Bay (Saba), 556
Fort Charlotte (St. Vincent), 658
Fort-de-France (Martinique), 479
Fort de Windt (St. Eustatius), 583
Fort Fleur d'Epée (Guadeloupe), 405
Fort George (Trinidad), 678
Fort Oranje (St. Eustatius), 583
Fountain Estate (St. Kitts), 595
Fox's Bay Bird Sanctuary (Montserrat), 515
Freeport/Lucaya (Bahamas), 170–71, 179, 757
French West Indies, *see* **Guadeloupe; Martinique; St. Martin**
Frigate Bay (St. Kitts), 596

Galway's Estate (Montserrat), 516
Galway's Soufrière (Montserrat), 516
Gambling, 798–800
George Town (Bahamas), 172–73
George Town (Cayman Islands), 288
Golden Lemon (St. Kitts), 786
Golf, 76–77, 763–66
Golf International de St. François (Guadeloupe), 766
Gosier (Guadeloupe), 405

GET YOUR TRAVEL ADVICE AND GO!

Stephen Birnbaum brings you the very best travel advice in the world in his series of travel guides. Each is revised annually, to provide the most accurate information available on vacation destinations around the world.

Canada, 1989	**$12.95**
Caribbean, Bermuda, and the Bahamas, 1989	**$12.95**
Europe, 1989	**$13.95**
France, 1989	**$12.95**
Great Britain, 1989	**$12.95**
Hawaii, 1989	**$12.95**
Ireland, 1989	**$12.95**
Italy, 1989	**$12.95**
Mexico, 1989	**$12.95**
South America, 1989	**$12.95**
United States, 1989	**$12.95**

Stephen Birnbaum brings you indispensable business travel advice in two unique guides.

USA for Business Travelers, 1989	**$8.95**
Europe for Business Travelers, 1989	**$8.95**

Stephen Birnbaum brings you the best of *Disneyland* and *Walt Disney World* in the only official guides to the most famous and most popular tourist attractions in America.

Disneyland, 1989	**$6.95**
Walt Disney World, 1989	**$9.95**

Stephen Birnbaum brings you hundreds of free or low-cost attractions and activities in the Sunshine State, including where to go discount shopping.

Florida for Free	**$5.95**

Available in bookstores everywhere. Or, order directly by mail. Send your check or money order for the price listed plus $1.00 for shipping and tax (where applicable). Allow 4 weeks for delivery: Travel Guides Department GG, Houghton Mifflin Company, 2 Park Street, Boston, MA 02108.

Direct inquiries regarding discounts on bulk purchases to: Special Sales Manager, Houghton Mifflin Company, 2 Park Street, Boston, MA 02108.